THIS FILM IS DANGEROUS:
A CELEBRATION OF NITRATE FILM

Editor: Roger Smither

Associate Editor: Catherine A Surowiec

FIAF
Fédération Internationale des Archives du Film

Published with financial assistance from the Eric Anker-Petersen Charity

First edition, published in 2002 by FIAF.

ISBN: 2-9600296-0-7

Fédération Internationale des Archives du Film
Rue Defacqz 1, B-1000 Bruxelles, Belgium
Tel: (32 2) 538 3065   Fax: (32 2) 534 4774   Email: info@fiafnet.org

Graphic Design by Julia Mills.
(The front cover design is derived from photographs supplied by the Cinemateca Brasileira, the Imperial War Museum, and Roger Smither; full captions and credits are printed with these images when they are used in the text.)

Printed and bound in the United Kingdom by FiSH Books, London.

The Eric Anker-Petersen Charity is pleased to assist the publication of this book. The Charity promotes the preservation and restoration of archive film held in the UK, and the trustees are happy to consider supporting new projects in this area. Applications should be addressed to the Charity at the following address:

c/o Charles Russell Solicitors, 8 – 10 New Fetter Lane, London EC4A 1RS, UK
(Phone (44 20) 7203 5000; Fax (44 20) 7203 0200; Email enquiry@cr-law.co.uk)

Contents

Two sections of colour pictures are included in this book. Colour section 1 will be found between pages 290 and 291, and colour section 2 between pages 546 and 547.

(The opening pages of both colour sections are montages of examples of current and historic film can labels for nitrate film, which were supplied by colleagues at FIAF archives.)

Foreword

This story of nitrate is the story of the first fifty years of cinema; a brand-new art form inherently unstable and impermanent. The factors that led the first film pioneers and entrepreneurs to adopt such a volatile medium to carry their precious images is for the technical historian to explore and explain. Perhaps they were as unaware of the dubious properties of their chosen raw materials as we were when we believed that safety (acetate) film would be the permanent solution to preserving film images – before we identified the highly destructive "vinegar syndrome" that plagues so many films.

Purists and aficionados of silent cinema maintain that nitrate had luminosity and sparkle (supposed to be a result of its silver content) that is unattainable with later film stocks. They may be correct. Certainly, the silent era produced many of the cinema's great masterpieces. But it becomes increasingly difficult to know or prove this point as the last nitrate prints decay or become unprojectable. And these are just the survivors. Informed estimates suggest that the world has lost 80% of all the silent films ever made and up to a quarter of all sound films in major producing countries.

We entrust the saving of our film heritage to the world's film archives, but all of us – film-makers, industry executives, archivists, and film-lovers around the globe – need to continue to raise and sustain the level of public consciousness about the imperative of film preservation. And that is partly what this informative book on the many facets of nitrate is about. Archivists are skilled practitioners who deserve more public recognition for their perseverance and dedication. This book is their story.

We all have a responsibility to preserve the past for the future. The intentional burning of books and paintings is regarded as a cultural crime. How will future generations learn about the 20th century if, through our neglect, its greatest art form is lost?

Martin Scorsese
March 8, 2001
Rome, Italy

Introduction

CELLULOSE NITRATE (n.). Flexible transparent plastic, known also as celluloid, used almost exclusively for the manufacture of standard cinematograph film, despite its high inflammability, because of its resistance to wear and tear.

Ernest Lindgren, *The Art of the Film*
(London: Allen and Unwin, 1948), p. 201.

The person who hears the word "film" (which, by the way, comes from the Celtic "Felmen" – the cream on the milk) thinks of Lubitsch and his kind. But the idea that Lubitsch and his kind could not do their work if another type of work – at least as complicated and ingenious – was not being carried out elsewhere, that there would be no industry of art films if an industry of raw film did not work hand in hand with it and provide it with raw stock, certainly hardly ever occurs to the millions of cinemagoers in countries all over the world.

Paul Knoche, "Der Rohfilm",
in *Das Tage-Buch*, vol.3, no.14 (8 April 1922), p. 547.[1]

Sometimes I think a storm or a breath of wind would blow it away. It's a celluloid city and what's to prevent it going up in smoke?
Peter Duncan, *In Hollywood Tonight* (London: Werner Laurie, 1952), p.10, quoting an anonymous old-timer on the subject of Hollywood.

"The FIAF Nitrate Book" which you now hold in your hands has been a long time in development. The idea for such a book was one that I first suggested to my FIAF colleagues at our 1992 Congress in Montevideo. FIAF, for readers who are not familiar with it, is the International Federation of Film Archives. To borrow the wording of our current explanatory leaflet, FIAF "brings together the world's leading institutions in the field of moving picture heritage. Its affiliates are the defenders of the 20th Century's own art form. They are dedicated to the rescue, collection, preservation, and screening of moving images, which are valued both as works of art and culture and as historical documents. When it was founded in 1938, FIAF had 4 members. Today, it brings together more than 120 institutions in over 60 countries – a reflection of the extent to which preservation of moving image heritage has become a worldwide concern." Among its other activities, FIAF holds an annual Congress, which encompasses both a General Assembly and a programme of symposium/workshop sessions, and it produces publications.

At the time when I first proposed a "Nitrate Book", I envisaged it as a part of the celebrations of the centenary of cinema. It seemed, and indeed it still seems, strange and rather sad to me that, amid all the attention that was paid in the mid-1990s to the competing claims of the pioneers of the moving image and to the stars behind and in front of the camera in the hundred years that followed the work of those pioneers, so little attention was paid to the material that made the whole business and art of film possible. Film historians and film archivists looked to me like Academy Award winners who forgot to thank their mothers – in a metaphor that I was to overuse excessively over the next nine years, nitrate was the material that carried film for the first half-century of cinema, and the material that gave archivists their biggest perceived headache during the second half-century. As with many parents and their children, the history of celluloid and FIAF could be described with all the characteristics of a great love/hate relationship, with love, of course, the predominant emotion in the end. A book was surely the least such a saga deserved.

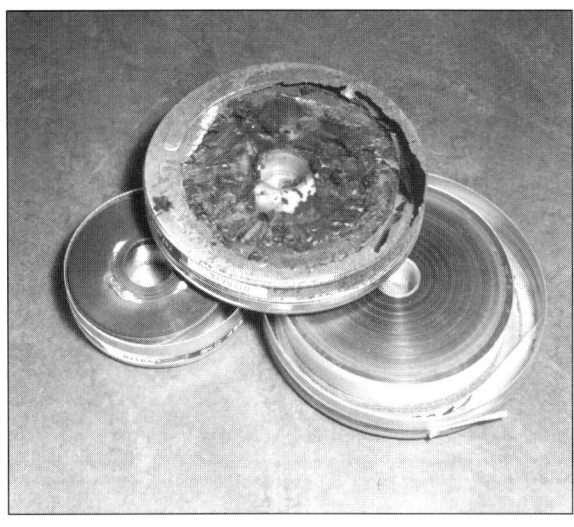

Cans of nitrate film transferred to the Imperial War Museum from a British government department ca. 1980, on arrival already showing symptoms of serious deterioration.

Imperial War Museum, London.
IWM 82/12/2.

Although the idea won some enthusiastic support from friends whose early help and encouragement it is a pleasure to recall, there was never really time to add the book to the long list of better-planned centenary projects that were already underway. After leaving it in peace for a brief period, I re-launched it as a project for the year 2000. The basic argument remained unchanged, and in some ways the end of the century offered an even better symbolic date than the mildly controversial moving target of the centenary. In the 1970s and 1980s, when archivists tended to speak of "the nitrate problem", a number of campaigns around the world cited the year 2000 as the deadline by which that "problem" would have to have been solved. Warning that "Nitrate Can't (or Won't) Wait", meaning that nitrate left unattended would destroy itself in little more than fifty years, archivists set up programmes with the goal of rounding up all nitrate film and transferring it to safety stock by the end of the century. As far as they knew, the year 2000 should have found the world saying goodbye to nitrate, while its replacements lasted into the indefinite future.[2]

The perception of nitrate, however, changed dramatically between the launch of all those "Nitrate 2000" campaigns and the arrival of the symbolic date itself. As those campaigns led to rigorous examination of nitrate film, and the weeding out and copying of the reels that showed signs of deterioration, it became apparent that the rest, including some of the very oldest nitrate film, was frequently still in remarkably good condition. Meanwhile, in archives' safety vaults, the vulnerability of acetate film to "vinegar syndrome", its own form of chemical deterioration, became increasingly widely known. Colour fading and other problems grabbed headlines too. Slogans about nitrate's ability to wait began to give place to other, more generic calls to protect old films.[3] As 2000 approached, it could be seen that "good old nitrate" still had a future as well as a past. To the familiar theoretical arguments about the archivist's duty to preserve the original for as long as possible, and to the equally familiar aesthetic arguments about the qualities of the nitrate image, we could now add a practical argument. The devil we knew was not, after all, automatically doomed to make way for newer technologies – in fact, compared to some of those technologies, it had rather the look of a safer bet. A "FIAF Nitrate Book" published in the year 2000 could truly be a celebration, and not simply an elegy.

every
minute
as we are
talking
films are
falling
to dust...

Jonas Mekas

**ANTHOLOGY FILM ARCHIVES
FILM PRESERVATION WEEK 1995**

The cover of the programme for the Anthology Film Archives' Film Preservation Week in 1995 makes effective use of the slogan coined by Jonas Mekas.

Anthology Film Archives, New York.

The decision to make "The Last Nitrate Picture Show" the theme of the two-day symposium at the FIAF Congress and the related season of screenings at the National Film Theatre in London in June 2000 provided the last and greatest impetus to try to make the book appear, and the generous agreement of Sir Paul Getty to support the publication helped finally to make sure that it would do so. The original intention was that the book should be printed before the Congress, so that those attending the symposium would have some background reading in their hands. When practical difficulties intervened to prevent the realisation of this original plan, it was decided to produce the book after the Congress instead. Disappointment at the need to abandon the original scheme was tempered by acknowledgement that the ability to use the book to reflect on the scholarship on display at the symposium could only enhance its overall value.

I just referred to "practical difficulties". There is a big gap between a good idea, however enthusiastically it might have been received, and the realisation of that idea, and I must confess that this book would not have appeared, or would at least not have appeared with me as its editor, if I had truly appreciated how big that gap was. In my naïve way, I had actually thought that it would be easy to produce or indeed that it would virtually write itself. Although I had never personally made a serious study of the history of celluloid, I carried in my own mind some nitrate stories – some apparently true, some rather more suspect – that impressed me, at least one piece of nitrate folklore that amused me, and the titles of a couple of books or films in which nitrate played a part in the plot. Whether or not I actively went looking out for them, additional nitrate references kept coming my way by happenstance – as they still do.[4] If I could so easily come up with candidate material for such a publication, surely my colleagues could do the same? The production of the book would be simply a matter of selection...

It did not quite work out like that. Although some people were instantly on my wavelength and responded with just the sort of material I expected, far more of my FIAF colleagues seemed to be bemused by the whole project and to stay that way no matter how many times I tried to explain it to them. When material failed to arrive spontaneously, I had to resort to asking for it, directly, repeatedly, and even on occasion almost rudely – an approach that sometimes worked and sometimes did not. Readers of this book may well wonder why some of the great film-producing countries and cultures and some of the great film preservation centres of the world are scarcely mentioned in it. I can only ask those readers to accept that nobody regrets these absences more than I do, but in the end people cannot be forced to make contributions when they do not want to, or do not have time.

Two unlooked-for benefits followed on from the discovery that my FIAF colleagues either do not all carry around in their own heads the same kinds of trivia as I, or prefer not to share them if they do. One was that some of the gaps were filled by people from outside FIAF – some of whom I had known previously, and others whom I have only discovered through this project – and this meant that the book has come to represent a far wider cross-section of film historians and cinema lovers than those represented only in the formal organisations that care for film heritage. The second was that the quality of the contributions moved to an appreciably higher level than I had been anticipating. I had imagined myself receiving what would essentially be a collection of photocopies and brief letters offering largely second-hand information, which it would be my job to try to assemble with some degree of coherence.[5] Instead I found I was also receiving many carefully crafted essays, the length of which varied from a single paragraph to several thousand words, but which all showed intelligence and scholarship to a level far transcending my original ambitions for the book. In several ways, I can say I did not know what I was letting myself in for, but I think the reader will appreciate the end product the more for its unexpected changes.

As a further example of my own naïveté, I must also observe that it did not occur to me until after the project was formally underway that some people would believe it was the very opposite of a good idea. These people – and I have now met quite a

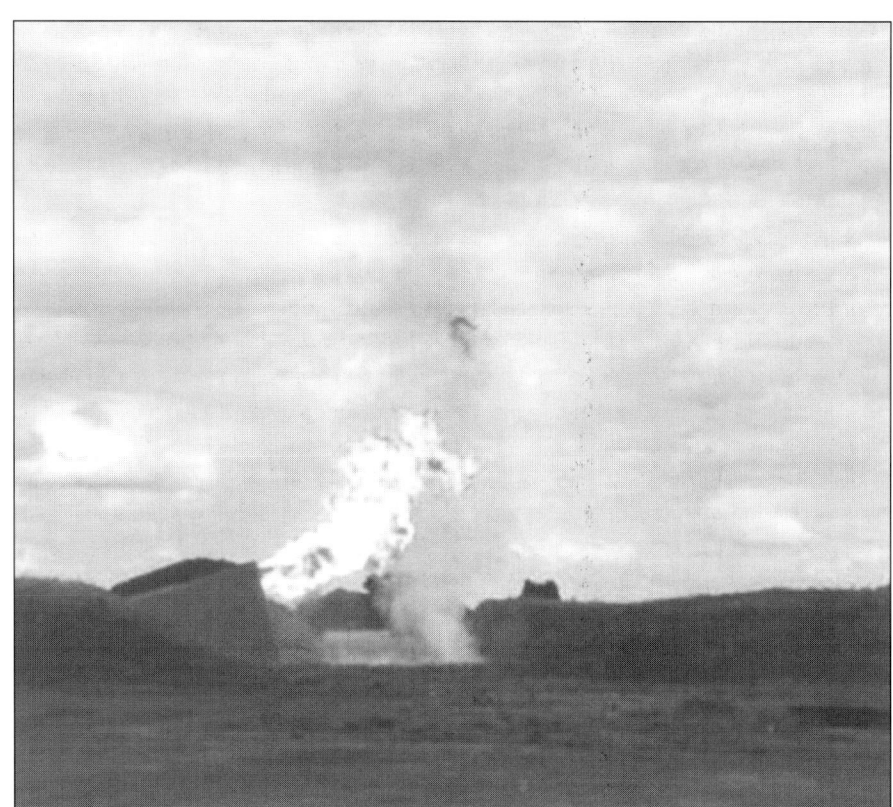

The deliberate burning of one ton of condemned nitrate film on 1 August 2000 at the Building Research Establishment, Cardington. The experiment was conducted to test the design for new vaults to be built near Duxford for the Imperial War Museum Film and Video Archive.

Imperial War Museum, London.

few of them – point out that many of the dramatic stories revolve around nitrate fires. The image of burning nitrate is the strongest impression this book is likely to make (especially once we put it on the cover as well). Was this, they asked, really the best message to be giving the public and our nervous funding agencies? Might it not backfire (pun intended) and do more harm than good to the cause of nitrate film preservation? Like the argument about the depiction of violence on screen, I treat this comment with thoughtful respect. I hope that readers will be sufficiently mature to realise that a book's most dramatic stories may not be its point, and that I will not prove to have wheeled a Trojan horse into the film archive camp. Speaking as the head of an archive which has been pursuing a major nitrate vault building programme of its own exactly in parallel with the preparation of this book (and which indeed on 1 August 2000 deliberately burned a ton of condemned nitrate to test the viability of its new vault design), I agree that bad publicity is the last thing we need.

Not only does the cover depict a fire – the book's title also alludes to the hazardous nature of nitrate. Selection of a title for "the FIAF Nitrate Book" has been another saga, like the production of the book itself, which has been enjoyable and infuriating by turns, and many of those listed as collaborators in the book have also played the title game with me. Candidate titles fell into several broad categories, and many enjoyed a brief run as chief contender, before being displaced by a new favourite. Some of those displaced live on as section or essay titles in the book itself, but I cannot resist a last roll-call of some of their rejected siblings.

In my more pompous moments, the book was nearly saddled with a portentous title derived from a quotation in one or other of the books in the bibliography – "narrow escapes" of this kind included *The Frailest of Men's Toys* and *Luminous Impressions*. A number of puns were considered more or less seriously – Count Dracula's description of wolves mutated (with echoes of the French *Nouvelle Vague's* self-characterisation as "enfants de la Cinémathèque") to suggest *Children of the Nitrate*. Memories of a certain national anthem produced *Nitrate's Last*

Gleaming, while memories from the other side of the Atlantic about a different Titanic film gave birth to *A Nitrate Remembrance*. Once the players had started to think about film titles with "night" in them, the list lengthened dramatically – *Day for Nitrate*, *In the Heat of the Nitrate*, *Nitrate on Film Street*, *Nitrate and the City*, *A Hard Day's Nitrate*, and *Nitrate Moves* were all considered.

"Night" was not the only film title theme ripe for punning – it was also possible to play with other -ight/-ite rhymes and so get to *The Nitrate Stuff*, *Love at First Nitrate*, or even *Let There Be Nitrate*. "Light" proved not to be a bad theme on its own, without benefit of puns: offerings included *Fading Light*, *Light in Darkness*, and simply *Light Years*. From "light", attention moved to silver, and another mother-lode of ideas, including the title which one of my colleagues may never forgive me for not finally selecting – *Hi ho Silver!* – and other candidates such as *Silver Blaze*. "Blaze" led into variations on burning, and although the perfect title – *Burning Passions* – had already been taken, there were other possibilities such as *Slow Burn* and *Burning Bright*, or, by simple extension, *An Old Flame*, *The Sacred Flame*, *Drawn to the Flame*, *The Flame of Life*, or, more subtly, *Freeze Flame*. From the flame/frame rhyme, we came to the wheel/reel one, which yielded *Reel of Fortune*, *Reels of Fire*, and *Danger on Reels*. From here we segued into the "danger" theme (*Laughing at Danger*, *Appointment with Danger*, *Dangerous Beauty*), and so finally to the title we selected: *This Film Is Dangerous*.

Was it the right choice? You tell me. For me it echoes a certain strand of title from the great days of nitrate film production, it quotes the actual title of a film in my own archive, and it states a salient truth about the subject matter in a way that is still, undeniably, alluring. Who but an insurance assessor would thrill to a book called *This Film Is Safe*?

After more than nine years, the project is finally completed. I hope it lives up to the promise the title now gives it. I hope that you enjoy reading it as much as I have (for most of the time) enjoyed assembling it. And if you are moved to ask: "Now why didn't he include that story?", I hope that you will feel a tiny bit guilty to think that the reason just might be because you never sent it in to begin with. Never mind – send it in now. I will forgive you (not at once, but ultimately), and there might always be a second edition...

Roger Smither
Keeper, Imperial War Museum Film and Video Archive, London, UK
Former Secretary-General, FIAF
Editor, *This Film Is Dangerous*
December 2001

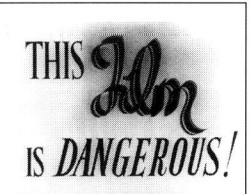
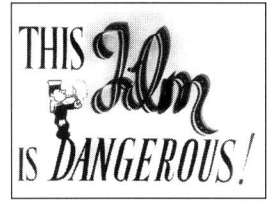
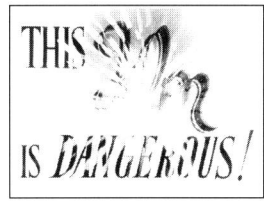

The title sequence from the 1948 British Admiralty training film from which this book has borrowed its own title.

Imperial War Museum, London. IWM FLM 3233, 3226, 3227.

Notes

1   My translation. The original reads: "Wer das Wort „Film" hört (das übrigens vom keltischen „Felmen", d. h. die Sahne auf der Milch, abgeleitet ist), denkt an Lubitsch und seine Leute. Aber daß Lubitsch und seine Leute nicht arbeiten könnten, wenn nicht eine mindestens ebenso komplizierte und ingeniöse Arbeit auf anderem Gebiet vorangegangen wäre, daß es keine Industrie des Kunstfilms gäbe, wenn nicht eine Industrie des Rohfilms Hand in Hand mit ihr arbeite und ihr den Rohstoff lieferte, – daran denken von den Millionen Kinobesuchern in aller Herren Länder sicher nur sehr wenige." I am grateful to Eva Orbanz and her colleagues at the Stiftung Deutsche Kinemathek (as it then was) for supplying this reference.

2   Consider the item under the headline "Now it's polyester heroes" in Britain's *Daily Mail* – "Rambo will go on and on – and probably outlive Sylvester Stallone. And it's all due to the material found in shirts and dresses. For the most recent Rambo film was printed on polyester, instead of cellulose triacetate, which will probably guarantee that it could still be shown in the next century – and possibly the one following." (*Daily Mail*, 23 January 1989, p. 7.)

3 A potent example, coined by Jonas Mekas, and used on the cover of the programmes for several of the Anthology Film Archives' "Film Preservation Week" events in the 1990s, appears as an illustration to this introduction. Those taking up advertising space in the programmes also echoed the theme, with American Movie Classics offering the line "Let's make sure the greatest films of all time last that long". Meanwhile, journalists had started to pick up that all was not well with safety film – see, for example, the article "At last: Acetate Won't Wait!" written as one of the series "Sam Rubin's Classic Clinic" in *Classic Images*, no.210 (December 1992), p.39.

4 Thus when, in February 2000, I finally got around to reading *Birthday Letters* (London: Faber & Faber, 1998), the justly celebrated collection of poems by Ted Hughes that explored and memorialised his relationship with Sylvia Plath, my eye was caught by the mention of "inflammable celluloid" in the poem "Visit". On the other hand, I was one of the last people I knew to have read this book, and nobody else had mentioned these lines to me. Perhaps a sensitivity to nitrate allusions is my personal form of eccentricity. In the tradition of British eccentrics, I hope at least to be considered harmless.

5 The section of the present book which most closely resembles this original conception is the collection of material with the title "Fiery Tails".

Acknowledgements

It is with great sadness that I must start by noting that this book has appeared too late to share it with two people whose names would otherwise have featured in this section, and who would, I like to think, have been appreciative readers of the finished volume. The deaths of Brigitte van der Elst, former Executive Secretary of FIAF, and of Jonathan Dennis, inspirational founder of the New Zealand Film Archive, have been deeply felt by their friends and colleagues, both within FIAF and beyond.

I am of course deeply grateful to all those who have contributed to this book, but I must nonetheless single out for special early mention a number of institutions and individuals whose involvement has been absolutely essential to its appearance.

- The costs of printing this book have been underwritten by a substantial grant from the Eric Anker-Petersen Charity.
- Sir Paul Getty's generous agreement to support the project at its original conception made the whole venture possible.
- During the summer of 2001, when the project was in financial difficulties, a number of FIAF archives agreed to provide funds to help ensure publication. Following a precedent set by a spontaneous offer from the Museum of Modern Art in New York, additional grants were offered by the Norsk Filminstitutt and the Archives du Film du Centre National de la Cinématographie in France, while other archives offered support by guaranteeing to order a number of copies of the book in advance of publication. The moral encouragement offered by these colleagues is appreciated as much as the practical help.
- Clyde Jeavons has been, from the book's conception, not only a key contributor but also an essential supporter and counsellor, even at those times when he was busiest with the work of preparing the FIAF 2000 London Congress and its Nitrate Symposium.
- Catherine Surowiec's agreement to join the project as Associate Editor brought a necessary element of focus and professionalism to what had till then been a woefully amateur undertaking, and her enthusiasm and dedication remained unbounded, even when the project grew much larger, and lasted far longer, than ever planned originally.
- Julia Mills, designer, is responsible for the book's appearance in the most literal sense, and is another person whose help and commitment to the publication have gone far beyond the scope of what was originally proposed to her.

I would also like to express particular thanks to two FIAF colleagues, whose early enthusiasm for the project from the other side of various oceans helped to convince me that it really was not such a bad idea, and to retain that conviction when I met a less enthusiastic response among others, and whose contributions to this finished book are therefore among those I value most highly: Paolo Cherchi Usai, of George Eastman House in Rochester, New York, and Ray Edmondson, of the National Film and Sound Archive in Canberra.

It has been a privilege to receive Martin Scorsese's foreword, as well as the generous statements of encouragement and endorsement from the important figures in the world of cinema whose words appear in the first pages of the book's main text – Lord Attenborough, David Brown, Fay Kanin, Richard Leacock, Leonard Maltin, Lord Puttnam, Jeremy Thomas, and Helen van Dongen. It is also a special pleasure to note among the list of contributors three of FIAF's revered honorary members: Eileen Bowser, Harold Brown, and Ib Monty.

As noted in my introduction, the book is host to important contributions from scholars, film lovers, artists, poets, and others from outside the immediate FIAF world, and from many archivists in fellow FIAF institutions. The names of these authors appear with the titles of their contributions in the table of contents, and appear again listed alphabetically in the notes on authors. To save space, I am not listing them for a third time here. I should, however, like to express my gratitude here and now to all of them collectively, not forgetting those whose contributions required, or requested, anonymity. I am grateful for their hard work, for their patience in waiting for this much delayed publication, and for their willingness to go on answering editorial questions long after they had every right to expect to be left in peace. It has been a pleasure and a privilege to serve as editor to such an array of talent.

Many individuals and institutions have provided pictorial and textual material for reproduction in this book. While every effort has been made to trace and acknowledge an appropriate source for all such material, the publishers will be glad to make suitable arrangements with any copyright holders whom it has not been possible to contact.

The staff of a number of reference libraries and record offices assisted Catherine Surowiec and myself in carrying out our own research for this book. In this context, I would like to express thanks on behalf of both of us to the staffs of the Imperial War Museum's Department of Printed Books, of the IWM's Photograph Archive, of the Public Record Office at Kew, and of the British Library Newspaper Library at Colindale. Where pictures are concerned, special thanks are also due to Kevin Brownlow; to Howard Mandelbaum of Photofest, New York; to Michelle Aubert and her colleagues at the Archives du Film du CNC, Bois d'Arcy; to the Cinémathèque Gaumont, Neuilly sur Seine; to André Chevailler of the Cinémathèque Suisse, Lausanne; to Mary Corliss of the Museum of Modern Art Department of Film and Media, New York; and to Ronald Grant and Martin Humphries of the Cinema Museum, London. Above all, we are grateful for the help and access given by the staff of the priceless reference collections of the British Film Institute, and wish in particular to thank Tom Cabot, Shirley Collier, Damon McCollin-Moore, Tessa Quinn, Markku Salmi, David Sharp, and Rob White.

In addition to those formally identified as authors, or as sources for pictures and other reproduced material, the book owes a great deal to many people who submitted anecdotes, helped find and supply illustrations, replied to enquiries, and provided many other kinds of invaluable assistance. Not forgotten in this category of helpers are those who offered material for which there was unfortunately insufficient space, and those who took the trouble to send their regrets that they had no nitrate stories to tell.

First, from outside the world of FIAF, Catherine Surowiec and I acknowledge with thanks the help given and offered by Jane Alvey, Jack Amos, Christopher Bird, Lenny Borger, Henri Bousquet, Pat Coward, Bob Curtis-Johnson, Fernando del Moral Gonzalez, Philip Dutton, Raymond Fielding, Claus Fischer, Norman Fisher, Tony Fletcher, Philip French, Christopher Galloway, Jon Gartenberg, Dennis Gaughan, Ken George, Elizabeth Heasman, Sterling Hedgpeth, Nicholas Hiley, Peter Hopkinson, Richard Huhndorf, Bernard King, Richard Koszarski, Fred Lake, Alan Lawson (of the BECTU History Project), Patrick Le Bescont, David Lemieux, Ken Locke, Martin McLean, Jean-Jacques Meusy, Richard Meyer, Hassan Muthalib, David Penn, Len Petts, Dwight Porter, Gillie Potter, Brian Pritchard,

Scott Reid, Stephan Michael Schröder, Charles Shibuk, Anthony Slide, John Straw, Ned Thanhouser, Michael Twigg, Daniel Vander Gucht, Christian Vierhaus, Lynne Wake, Andrew Ward, and Margaret Ward. We acknowledge a very special debt of gratitude to Geoff Brown.

Second, credit and thanks are owed to the following staff, former staff, and associates of archives affiliated to FIAF. It is inevitable in the case of a book that has been as long in preparation as this one has been that several members of staff are no longer with the archives where they were working when they offered their help, but as their contributions commonly represented an institutional as well as a personal one, I have taken the liberty of retaining the connection in these acknowledgements. It will also come as no surprise that some institutions have changed their names in the period while material was being collected. In such cases, I have tried to indicate both the name in which the majority of the contributions were made and the name in current use. In keeping with FIAF tradition, the list is given in alphabetical order of the cities in which affiliated archives are based:

- Amsterdam, Filmmuseum – Jan-Hein Bal, John Bosensell, Nico de Klerk, Mark-Paul Meyer
- Athinai, Tainiothiki tis Ellados – Maria Comninos
- Barcelona, Filmoteca de la Generalitat de Catalunya – Maite Rodon
- Beijing, China Film Archive – Chen Jingliang
- Berkeley, Pacific Film Archive – Nancy Goldman, Edith Kramer
- Berlin, Bundesarchiv-Filmarchiv – Barbara Heinrich-Polte
- Berlin, Stiftung Deutsche Kinemathek (now Filmmuseum Berlin – Deutsche Kinemathek) – Friedhelm Hoffmann, Eva Orbanz
- Beverly Hills, Academy Film Archive – Ed Carter, Michael Friend
- Bogotá, Fundacion Patrimonio Filmico Colombiano – Jorge Nieto
- Bois d'Arcy, Archives du Film et du Dépôt Légal du Centre National de la Cinématographie – Pierrette Lemoigne, Jim Purcell
- Bologna, Cineteca del Comune di Bologna – Enrica Serrani
- Bratislava, Slovensky Filmový Ustav – Peter Dubecky
- Bruxelles, Cinémathèque Royale/Koninklijk Filmarchief – Gabrielle Claes
- Budapest, Magyar Nemzeti Filmarchivum – Ildikó Berkes, Vera Gyürey, Blanka Szilágyi
- Cairo, Al-Archive Al-Kawmy Lil-Film – Mohamed Kamel el Kalyoubi
- Canberra, National Film and Sound Archive (now ScreenSound Australia) – Meg Labrum
- Frankfurt, Deutsches Institut für Filmkunde – Nikola Klein
- Hanoi, Vietnam Film Institute – Tran Luan Kim
- Helsinki, Suomen Elokuva-Arkisto – Timo Muinonen
- Hong Kong, Hong Kong Film Archive – Cynthia Liu
- Jerusalem, Israel Film Archive – Lia van Leer
- Lausanne, Cinémathèque Suisse – Reto Kromer
- Ljubljana, Slovenski Filmski Arhiv – Vladimir Zumer
- London, Cinema Museum – Ronald Grant, Martin Humphries
- London, Imperial War Museum Film and Video Archive – John Kerr
- London, National Film and Television Archive (now BFI Collections) – Caroline Ellis, Steve Bryant, Elaine Burrows, Michael Caldwell, Sarah Davy, Luke McKernan, Olwen Terris, Don Swift, Graham Melville, John Oliver, Tise Vahimagi
- Los Angeles, National Center for Film and Video Preservation, American Film Institute – Ken Wlaschin
- Los Angeles, UCLA Film and Television Archive – Jere Guldin, Steve Ricci, Robert Rosen

- Madrid, Filmoteca Española – Alfonso del Amo, Valeria Ciompi
- Manchester, North West Film Archive – Mark Bodner, Marion Hewitt
- Mexico, Filmoteca de la UNAM – Francisco Gaytan, Francisco Ohem, Ivan Trujillo
- Milano, Fondazione Cineteca Italiana – Luisa Comencini
- Montevideo, Cinemateca Uruguaya – Manuel Martinez Carril
- Montréal, Cinémathèque Québécoise – Robert Daudelin, Lucie Vinciarelli
- Moscow, Gosfilmofond of Russia – Oleg Botchkov, Vladimir Dmitriev
- New York, Anthology Film Archives – Robert A Haller
- New York, The Museum of Modern Art Department of Film and Media – Mary Corliss, Peter Williamson
- Ottawa, Audio-Visual Archives Section, National Archives of Canada – David Brown, Yvette Hackett, Michelle Lillie, Richard Lochead, Bill O'Farrell, Sylvie Robitaille
- Pune, National Film Archive of India – Lalit Kumar Upadhyaya
- Pyongyang, National Film Archive of the DPRK – Kim Kang Ho
- Riga, International Centre of Cinema – Augusts Sukuts
- Rochester, George Eastman House Motion Picture Department – Karen Latham Everson, Greg Linnell
- Seoul, Korean Film Archive – Bongyoung Kim
- Stockholm, Cinemateket – Svenska Filminstitutet – Henry Jones
- Taipei, Chinese Taipei Film Archive – Teresa Huang
- Tokyo, National Film Center – Hidenori Okada, Ayako Saito
- Torino, Museo Nazionale del Cinema – Stefano Boni
- Toulouse, Cinémathèque de Toulouse – Raymond Borde
- Warszawa, Filmoteka Narodowa – Waldemar Piatek
- Washington, Library of Congress, M/B/RS Division – David Francis, Madeline F Matz, Kenneth S Weissman
- Washington, National Archives and Records Administration – William T Murphy
- Wellington, New Zealand Film Archive – Frank Stark
- Wien, Filmarchiv Austria – Nikolaus Wostry
- Zagreb, Hrvatska Kinoteka – Mato Kukuljica

Thanks of course go also to Christian Dimitriu, Sonia Dermience, and the other staff at the FIAF Secretariat in Brussels, who have managed the budget for this project, and provided many other kinds of help at many stages of its development.

I offer my sincere apologies to anyone whose name should be included in the above list but is not: this has been a long project, and I am not the world's best record keeper. I have tried to include all the names of those who have helped, but I doubt I have succeeded. To my overlooked and unintentionally anonymous helpers, my penultimate expression of gratitude.

The last such expression requires a personal note: I wish to acknowledge with gratitude the tolerance and support of my wife, Linda, and my children, James and Sophie. They have all (as observant readers will find) made their own direct contributions to this book. They have also, throughout its long gestation, helped me along with such encouraging remarks as: "Well, at least I suppose it makes a change from the Somme," and "Don't tell me you're *still* working on that nitrate book." Today I can finally say: "Yes, it did," and "No, I am not."

Roger Smither

Notes on Authors

Editors' Note: Because of space constraints, authors who were at the time of writing members of the staff of a FIAF affiliate are, with apologies, identified only by their role within that institution. Guest authors are identified at slightly greater length.

Magdi Abdel Rahman: Laboratory and Archive expert, Al-Archive Al-Kawmy Lil-Film (National Film Archive), Egyptian Film Centre, Giza.

Vladimir Antropov: Deputy Head of Scientific Data Handling and Foreign Relations Department, Gosfilmofond of Russia, Moscow.

Michelle Aubert: former President of FIAF; Conservateur, Archives du Film et du Dépôt Légal du Centre National de la Cinématographie, Bois d'Arcy, France.

Sayed Badreya grew up in poverty in Port Said, movies being his only escape and his dream for the future in depressing times. He attended New York University's film school, then moved to Hollywood to pursue this dream, with acting roles in major films such as *The Insiders, Three Kings, Independence Day*, and *Stargate*. He was an assistant to actor/ director Anthony Perkins, and worked closely with James Cameron on *True Lies*. Sayed's mission is to make movies telling the Arabic story as it has yet to be told. His latest credits are as producer of the short film *After Dark*, and director of a feature called *Falafel City*. He is currently working on the documentary projects *Saving Egyptian Film Classics* and *Arabian Horse: The Real Ambassador*.

Mary Lea Bandy: former Treasurer of FIAF; Chief Curator, Department of Film and Media, The Museum of Modern Art, New York, USA.

Ann Baylis: Head of Access, ScreenSound Australia (Australian National Screen and Sound Archive), Canberra.

Tony Bicât (see text in "Nitrate Muse").

Jean-Louis Bigourdan received his diploma in the conservation of photographs from the Institut Français de Restauration des Oeuvres d'Art, in 1993. Since 1994, he has been active in research at the Image Permanence Institute (IPI), Rochester Institute of Technology, where his studies of the effect of enclosures and microenvironments on the stability of photographic film have led to the development of practical strategies for preserving acetate collections. He is currently studying the effect of cycling environmental conditions on library/archive materials, in a three-year project funded by the US National Endowment for Humanities. He lectures extensively on the preservation of photographic materials, conducts collection surveys, and consults on the implementation of cold storage. His research results have been disseminated at numerous international conferences and widely published.

Ivo Blom, formerly an archivist and restorer at the Nederlands Filmmuseum, teaches Film Studies at the University of Amsterdam and the Free University Amsterdam. He has published on early cinema in magazines such as *IRIS, KINtop, 1895*, and *Film History*, and in collections such as *A Second Life* (1996), *Cabiria e* *il suo tempo* (1998), and *The Tenth Muse* (2001). Forthcoming with Amsterdam University Press is the published English-language edition of his PhD thesis (2000) on early film distribution, cinema operation, and Jean Desmet.

Valerij Bosenko: Head of Scientific Data Handling and Foreign Relations Department, Gosfilmofond of Russia, Moscow.

Stephen Bottomore has been researching the early years of cinema since the 1980s, concentrating on the subjects of non-fiction, war and the social background of early film. He has published two books and numerous articles on film history, in such journals as the *Historical Journal of Film, Radio and Television, Archives* and *Sight and Sound*, and he is an associate editor of the journal *Film History*. He also pursues a parallel career as a documentary television producer.

Eileen Bowser: Honorary Member of FIAF; former Curator, Department of Film and Video, The Museum of Modern Art, New York, USA.

Roy Boyd (see text in "Nitrate Muse").

Harold Brown: Honorary Member of FIAF; former Head of Preservation at the British Film Institute's National Film and Television Archive.

Kevin Brownlow, film historian and film-maker, began collecting films when he was 11. He spent years with Andrew Mollo making his feature film about the supposed German occupation of England, *It Happened Here* (1964), and even more years completing his restoration of Abel Gance's *Napoléon*. Working in partnership with David Gill, he is responsible for bringing a number of silent masterpieces back to public attention via the Thames Silents and Channel 4's Live Cinema. Their work for television includes *Hollywood* (1980) and *Unknown Chaplin* (1983), as well as documentaries about Buster Keaton, Harold Lloyd, and D W Griffith. In 1990 they founded Photoplay Productions with Patrick Stanbury, which has produced the documentaries *Cinema Europe, Lon Chaney,* and *Universal Horror*. His books include *The Parade's Gone By* and *David Lean: A Biography*.

Rosa Cardona Arnau and **Jennifer Gallego Christensen** are frequent research partners with the Filmoteca Española in Madrid. In recent years, they have been specialising in the historical and technical aspects of Spanish silent film production with reference to film restoration work.

Suresh Chabria is Professor of Film Appreciation at the Film and Television Institute of India, Pune, where his courses are much in demand. An avid cinephile, he contributed to the growth of the film society movement in India. From 1992-1998 he was Director of the National Film Archive of India and was active in FIAF as member of both the Commission for Programming and Access to Collections and the Working Group on the future of FIAF. Earlier he taught Political Science and International Relations at St Xavier's College, University of Bombay. He has published several research papers and articles on Indian cinema, and edited *Light of Asia: Indian Silent Cinema, 1912–1934* which accompanied the Indian retrospective at the 13th Pordenone Silent Film Festival in 1994.

Michael Chanan has been a music critic, a documentary film-maker, and a film teacher. He has written books about the beginnings of film (*The Dream That Kicks, The Prehistory and Early Years of Cinema in Britain*) and about Cuban cinema (*The Cuban Image, Cinema and Cultural Politics in Cuba* – second edition forthcoming), as well as studies in the social history of music. He was visiting professor in the Literature Program at Duke University in 2000, and now teaches at the University of the West of England in Bristol.

Paolo Cherchi Usai: FIAF Executive Committee member; co-founder of the Pordenone Silent Film Festival, Italy; Senior Curator of the Motion Picture Department, George Eastman House, and Director of the L Jeffrey Selznick School of Film Preservation, Rochester, NY, USA.

Hong-taek Chung: Vice President of FIAF; President, Korean Film Archive, Seoul.

David Cleveland has had a lifelong interest in film, was trained by the BBC, and has been a filmmaker. He founded the East Anglian Film Archive in 1976, and has been the Director of this regional film archive, based at the University of East Anglia, Norwich, UK, ever since. He teaches on the University's MA course in Film Archiving, which he helped set up in 1990. He received AMIA's "Silver Light" award in 2001, the first person from outside the USA and Canada to be so honoured.

Carlos Roberto de Souza: Deputy Director and Curator, Cinemateca Brasileira, São Paulo.

Clive Donner started in films at Denham in 1942 at the age of 16, as an assistant editor for Fergus McDonell and David Lean. After becoming a full editor and working on *Scrooge, The Card, Genevieve, The Million Pound Note*, and *The Purple Plain*, he was given a contract to direct *The Secret Place* at Pinewood. He went on to direct the film version of Harold Pinter's *The Caretaker* (Silver Bear, Berlin Film Festival) and *Nothing But the Best*, before Hollywood beckoned. His other films as director include *Some People, What's New Pussycat?, Luv, Here We Go Round the Mulberry Bush, Alfred the Great*, and *Stealing Heaven*. His films for television include *Rogue Male, She Fell among Thieves, The Three Hostages, The Scarlet Pimpernel, Oliver Twist, A Christmas Carol*, and *Charlemagne*.

Ray Edmondson: former Deputy Director, National Film and Sound Archive, Canberra, Australia.

Leo Enticknap, after graduating from the University of Exeter in 1995, took an MA in film archiving at the University of East Anglia and a PhD in film history at the University of Exeter, writing a thesis on "The Non-Fiction Film in Britain, 1945-51". During this time he also taught undergraduates and worked as a cinema projectionist and maintenance engineer. He then worked in the cinema industry for a year after completing his research, until his appointment as Director of the Northern Region Film and Television Archive in April 2001.

Anne Fleming: former Curator and Head of Preservation at the British Film Institute's National Film and Television Archive, London and Berkhamsted.

Jennifer Gallego Christensen (see joint text with Rosa Cardona, above).

Maryann Gomes: Director, North West Film Archive, Manchester, UK.

Dr Manuel González Casanova del Valle took part in the organisation of the "Cine-Club Progreso", the first avant-garde film club in Mexico, in 1952. In 1959, he was invited to organise the official Film Section at UNAM (now the University's Direccion General de Actividades Cinematográficas); he created the Filmoteca de la

UNAM and started lecturing on Cinema in 1960, founding UNAM's Film School in 1963. He has twice been elected President of CILECT (1976, 1978), was elected to FIAF's Executive Committee in 1981, and from 1979-1984 was Vice-President of the International Committee for Film History for UNESCO. Having resigned from his various UNAM commitments by 1987, he continues to research, especially in the field of Mexican film history.

Stephen Herbert started projecting films at the age of 12. From 1970–72 he was a projectionist at the National Film Theatre in London, where he gained experience with showing nitrate film. After college training, he entered further and higher education as an AV technician, and spent ten years supervising student film productions. He returned to the NFT/Museum of the Moving Image from 1989–1996, initially as Deputy Technical Manager, then as Head of Technical Services. He is now co-director of a publishing/consultancy partnership, The Projection Box, publishing books on early film and 19th century visual media.

Frank Holland joined the British Film Institute in 1952, initially working in London as the first Associate Membership Officer at the newly-opened National Film Theatre, and then as the BFI's Distribution Manager in London, handling films from the archive's film library and material to be screened at the NFT. He worked as the BFI's Vault Manager at their Aston Clinton facilities in Buckinghamshire from 1962 until his retirement in the mid-1980s.

Jan-Christopher Horak is Curator, Hollywood Entertainment Museum. Previously, he was Director, Archives and Collections, Universal Studios; Director, Munich Filmmuseum; and Senior Curator, George Eastman House. He is an Adjunct Professor, UCLA Critical Studies, and a former Professor, Film Studies, University of Rochester; Hochschule für Film und Fernsehen, Munich; University of Salzburg. PhD, Westfälische Wilhelms-Universität, Münster, Germany. M.S. Film, Boston University. Publications include: *Making Images Move: Photographers and Avant-Garde Cinema* (1997), *Berge, Licht und Traum. Dr. Arnold Fanck und der deutsche Bergfilm* (1997), *Lovers of Cinema. The First American Film Avant-Garde* (1995), *The Dream Merchants* (1989), *Anti Nazi Filme der deutschsprachigen Emigration von Hollywood* (1984), *Fluchtpunkt Hollywood. Eine Dokumentation zur Filmemigration nach 1933* (1984).

Yoshiro Irie: Assistant Curator of Film, National Film Center, The National Museum of Modern Art, Tokyo, Japan.

Clyde Jeavons: former Treasurer of FIAF; former Curator and Consultant Curator at the British Film Institute's National Film and Television Archive, London.

Sylvia Katz is a writer, consultant and researcher on plastics and design and a founder member of the Plastics Historical Society in the United Kingdom. She qualified as a furniture designer after gaining a university degree in the arts and languages, and worked for ten years at the Design Council, London. She has written several books on the history of plastics materials and design, and curated exhibitions on various aspects of plastics. She is currently plastics research consultant for a British design group and contributes to design and consumer journals in addition to educational and trade publications.

Fereydoun Khameneipour: International Relations, Film-Khane-ye Melli-e Iran (National Film Archive of Iran), Tehran.

Ernst Kieninger: Director, Filmarchiv Austria, Vienna.

Martin Koerber: Programmer and Film Restorer, Filmmuseum Berlin – Deutsche Kinemathek, Germany.

Marilyn Koolik: Director, Steven Spielberg Jewish Film Archive, Jerusalem, Israel.

Jerome Kuehl, television producer and historian, has taught at Oxford, Stanford, and the British National Film School. He researched the BBC's *Great War* series, and was associate producer of Thames Television's *World at War* and executive producer of the special programmes derived from that series. He was responsible with Sebastian Cody for *After Dark*, an innovative discussion programme for Channel 4, and was consultant to and writer for Jeremy Isaacs' CNN production *The Cold War*. He has recently completed *La Grande Aventure de la Presse Filmée* for France 3. He is part owner of *History Today*, a member of the Executive Council of the International Association for Media and History (IAMHIST), and a trustee of the Steffin Foundation, which rewards unacknowledged creators of artistic works.

Sam Kula has been a moving image archivist for over 40 years, working at the British Film Institute, American Film Institute, and National Archives of Canada. He has taught film and media in American and Canadian universities and conducted workshops and symposia for UNESCO in Southeast Asia and Latin America. He is the author of *The Archival Appraisal of Moving Images* (UNESCO, 1983) and *Appraising Moving Images: Assessing the Archival and Monetary Value of Film and Video Records* (Scarecrow, in press). He has served on the executive committees of both FIAF and FIAT and is currently President of the Association of Moving Image Archivists, member of the executive committee of AV Preservation Trust.CA, and special advisor to the Canadian Cultural Property Export Review Board.

Márton Kurutz: film restoration and preservation projects, Hungarian National Film Archive, Budapest.

Natasha Lako: Director, Arkivi Qendror Shteteror i Filmit (the Central National Film Archives), Tirana, Albania.

Vigdis Lian: FIAF Executive Committee member; Director, Department of Archives and Museum, Norsk Filminstitutt, Oslo, Norway.

Tom Luddy was Program Director and Curator of Berkeley's Pacific Film Archive from 1972 to 1979. Active for many years on the festival scene, he is Director, with Bill Pence, of the Telluride Film Festival, which he co-founded in 1974 with Pence and James Card. Associated with Francis Ford Coppola's American Zoetrope since 1979, as its Director of Special Projects he supervised the landmark 1981–82 revival of Gance's *Napoleon*. As producer or executive producer, Luddy's film projects include *Mishima* (1985, Paul Schrader), *Tough Guys Don't Dance* (1987, Norman Mailer), *Barfly* (1987, Barbet Schroeder), *King Lear* (1987, Jean-Luc Godard), *Powaqqatsi* (1988, Godfrey Reggio), *Wind* (1992, Carroll Ballard), *The Secret Garden* (1993, Agnieszka Holland), *Mi Familia* (1995, Gregory Nava), and *Lani Loa* (1998, Sherwood Hu).

Janet McBain: Curator, Scottish Screen Archive, Glasgow, UK.

Tom McGreevey is an actor turned writer. With his wife, Joanne L Yeck, he co-wrote *Movie Westerns* (Lerner Publications, 1994) and *Our Movie Heritage* (Rutgers University Press, 1997).

Ronald S Magliozzi: former Head of the FIAF Documentation Commission;

Assistant Curator, Research and Collections, Celeste Bartos International Film Study Center, The Museum of Modern Art, New York, USA.

Jorge Martín Neira is a Spanish researcher specialising in film cataloguing and documentation. He is a collaborator of the Filmoteca Española in Madrid, and is presently working on the film collection of the Spanish electric company Iberdrola. He is completing a doctoral thesis on the History of Audiovisual Archives.

Nicola Mazzanti is the head of L'Immagine Ritrovata, the first Italian laboratory specialising in film restoration, which he founded with a group of young specialists in 1992, having previously started work on cataloguing, conservation, and collection management with the Cineteca di Bologna in 1986. A participant in several international film restoration projects, he is currently a member of FIAF's Technical Commission, and of the Gamma Group. He is on the editorial board of *Cinegrafie* and has contributed to several publications, seminars, roundtables, and workshops in the field, as well as teaching at different schools and universities in Europe and abroad. He also co-founded and still contributes to the programming of *Il Cinema Ritrovato*, the annual festival dedicated to film history and film restoration in Bologna, Italy.

Ib Monty: Honorary Member of FIAF; former Director, Danske Filmmuseum, Copenhagen, Denmark.

Mona Nagai: Collection Manager and Assistant Curator, Pacific Film Archive, Berkeley, California, USA.

P K Nair is the former Director of the National Film Archive of India. He was associated with the NFAI from its inception in the mid-1960s, and is largely responsible for pioneering film preservation in the world's largest film-producing country. As a member of FIAF's Executive Committee, he helped introduce the international community to the problems of film preservation in tropical climates. He has served as Chairman or member of several film festival juries, contributed to the important UNESCO document on "The Preservation of Moving Images", and has written extensively on Indian and world cinema. He continues to be actively involved as a freelance consultant for the spread of archivism and film literacy in the subcontinent, and the promotion of Indian films and related studies abroad.

Dinu-Ioan Nicula: Collections, Cataloguing and Documentation, Arhiva Nationala de Filme – Cinemateca Romana, Bucharest, Romania.

Sunniva O'Flynn: Archive Curator, Film Institute of Ireland/Irish Film Archive, Dublin.

Hisashi Okajima: Curator of Film, National Film Center, The National Museum of Modern Art, Tokyo, Japan.

João Socrates de Oliveira: Technical Manager at the British Film Institute's J Paul Getty Conservation Centre.

Vladimír Opela: former FIAF Executive Committee member; Director and Curator, Národni Filmový Archiv (National Film Archive), Prague, Czech Republic.

Fernando Osorio has a Master's degree in Imaging Arts and Science [MFA] from the Rochester Institute of Technology, and has twenty years in the field as a professional conservator. He was director of conservation at Mexico's Cineteca

Nacional (1998 – 2000), and has been leader of the Image Permanence Group at the National Institute of Astrophysics, Optics and Electronics since 1991. He is also a research professor at the National School of Conservation, Restoration and Museography, and was a consultant in preservation at the Mexican Film Institute in 2000. Today he is acting as Preservation Leader for the Manuel Alvarez Bravo photographic collection at the Centre for Studies in Art and Culture "Casa Lamm" in Mexico City, and as preservation consultant at Radio Educación Sound Archive.

Kurt Otzen: Conservator, New Zealand Film Archive, Wellington.

Dominique Païni: former Directeur Géneral of the Cinémathèque Française Musée du Cinéma, Paris; now Directeur du Développement Culturel at the Centre Georges Pompidou, Paris.

Jane Paul: Co-ordinator, Last Film Search, The New Zealand Film Archive, Wellington.

Mario Petrucci (see text in "Nitrate Muse").

David Pierce was, at the time of writing, an independent film historian and copyright consultant with a special interest in the feature period of the silent film. He received a Master's Degree in Business Administration from George Washington University. He has written for *American Cinematographer* on the Kodascope Libraries, *American Film* on why some films are in the public domain, and *Film Comment* on the ownership of major film libraries. His Internet site, *Silent Film Sources*, which includes *The Silent Film Bookshelf*, is located at www.cinemaweb.com/silentfilm. In 2001, he was appointed Head of Preservation at the British Film Institute (BFI Collections), London and Berkhamsted.

Diane Pivac: Collection Manager, Documentation, The New Zealand Film Archive, Wellington.

John Reed: Preservation Officer, National Screen and Sound Archive of Wales, Aberystwyth, UK.

David Robinson was successively film critic of *The Financial Times* and (for 20 years) *The Times*. More recently his work has mostly been devoted to pre-film and early film history. His books include *World Cinema* (1972, 1980), *Chaplin – His Life and Art* (1982, 2001), *From Peepshow to Palace* (1995), *Light and Image* (1996, in collaboration), and *The Cabinet of Dr Caligari* (1997). Since 1997 Director of the Giornate del Cinema Muto (The Pordenone Silent Film Festival), he has also produced and directed documentary films and devised numerous exhibitions, including the centenary exhibition "Musique et Cinéma Muet" at the Musée d'Orsay. A life-long collector, mainly of the artefacts of motion picture archaeology, he has recently formed an archive of images of pre-Revolutionary Russian Cinema.

Éric Rondepierre (see text in "Nitrate Muse").

Deac Rossell has since 1993 concentrated on his lifelong interest in the invention of moving pictures, contributing articles on the magic lantern, chronophotography, and early cinema topics to *KINtop, Griffithiana, Film History, Archivos* and other journals. He is the author of *Living Pictures. The Origins of the Movies* (1998), and *Faszination der Bewegung. Ottomar Anschütz zwischen Photographie und Kino* (2001), a book accompanying his exhibition "Die Industrialisierung des Sehens. Lebende Bilder von Ottomar Anschütz" shown at the Filmmuseum Dusseldorf and the Deutsches Filmmuseum (Frankfurt/M.). Before 1993, he worked as a film critic, programmer (Museum of Fine Arts, Boston; UCLA Film and Television Archive; National Film Theatre, London), and executive (Directors Guild of America). His history of the magic lantern will be published this year.

Sarah St Vincent Welch (see text in "Nitrate Muse").

Martin Sawyer entered professional sound recording in 1960 with Associated Rediffusion Television. In 1966, following independent television franchise changes, he joined the sound department of United Motion Pictures in London. Spells as location recordist, studio recordist, dubbing editor, and dubbing mixer preceded his becoming head of the expanding optical sound department. After ownership changes at UMP in 1982, he established Martin Sawyer Sound Services in the same premises, building a solid reputation for work in 16mm. With encouragement from Technicolor and the BFI's Jack Household, he commissioned a 35mm optical sound mono camera, and archive film sound restoration became, and remains, his core interest, with frequent consultancy and lecture commitments. MSSS relocated in 1998 to a tenancy arrangement (and close cooperation) with Hendersons Film Laboratory.

Dorin Gardner Schumacher was born in Manhattan of a handsome, Ziegfeld-chorus-boy father of Jewish-Polish-Lithuanian descent and a beautiful, never-to-grow-up, Ziegfeld-showgirl mother, descended on her father's side from thirteenth century English nobility and, on her mother's, a long line of eccentric Helens, including Helen Gardner, an early woman film pioneer. Educated in private and public schools in the USA and Switzerland, Dorin earned a PhD in French literature. The French government named her Chevalier of the Ordre des Palmes Académiques for her contributions to French culture. She lives on an island off the coast of Georgia and is currently chairman and CEO of an international biotechnology research consortium. Her tell-all book about Helen Gardner's fascinating life and groundbreaking film career is in the works.

Professor Sami Sekeroglu: Director, Sinema-TV Enstitüsü, Istanbul, Turkey.

Jan Slodowski: Assistant Director, Filmoteka Narodowa, Warsaw, Poland.

Roger Smither: Vice President and former Secretary-General of FIAF; Keeper, Imperial War Museum Film and Video Archive, London, UK.

Paul C Spehr is the former Assistant Chief of the Motion Picture, Broadcasting and Recorded Sound Division at the Library of Congress, Washington, DC, USA. He retired from the Library in 1993 after working there for more than 35 years, and is now doing research on the early years of the motion picture. He has written several articles on the invention and early development of cinema, participated in a number of symposia, and is at work on a book about the career of W K-L Dickson, Edison's assistant in the invention of the Kinetoscope and Kinetograph, the first commercially successful motion picture devices. Dickson was also an important pioneer film-maker who directed more than 500 films between 1890 and 1903.

Borislav Stanojevic (see text in "Nitrate Muse").

Catherine A Surowiec is an independent film historian, researcher, and editor. While working in the film archive of the Museum of Modern Art, New York, she contributed to the books *Rediscovering French Film* (1983), *Michael Balcon: The Pursuit of British Cinema* (1984), and *The Film Catalog* (1985). Based in London since 1985, her freelance projects for the British Film Institute include work on the Museum of the Moving Image, the London Film Festival, and the BFI's designs collection. In 1996 she edited *The LUMIERE Project: The European Film Archives at the Crossroads*. Other recent publications include *Accent on Design: Four European Art Directors* (BFI, 1992) and documentation for the Serpentine Gallery's Ken Adam exhibition catalogue (1999). In 2000 she began to edit the Giornate del Cinema Muto festival catalogue.

Francine Lastufka Taylor is executive director of the Alaska Moving Image Preservation Association (AMIPA), dedicated to the collection, preservation and public accessibility of film, video and sound on Alaska. She owns and runs Taylor Production, specialising in documentaries, in which she has won awards in regional and international competitions. She has also performed as a singer and pianist, wrote a newspaper column, and has been recognised with community, state and national awards for her work for many organisations in Alaska.

Sakari Toiviainen: Editor-in-Chief, Finnish National Filmography, Suomen Elokuva-Arkisto, Helsinki, Finland.

Angela Tong: Manager, Acquisition, Hong Kong Film Archive, China.

Dr Vanessa Toulmin is Research Director of the National Fairground Archive (University of Sheffield, UK) and is currently working on a 4-year project with the BFI to identify and document Mitchell and Kenyon films. She specialises in exhibition practices in early cinema and has published articles on early cinema and popular entertainment in *Film History*. With Simon Popple she is joint editor of *Visual Delights: Essays on the Popular and Projected Image in the 19th Century* (Flicks Books, 2000) and co-editor of *Living Pictures*.

Lojz Tršan: Head of Archive, Slovenski Filmski Arhiv / Arhiv Republike Slovenije, Ljubljana, Slovenia.

Inmaculada Trull: Curatorial Assistant, La Filmoteca, Instituto Valenciano de Cinematografia, Valencia, Spain.

Hillel Tryster: Deputy Director and Researcher, Steven Spielberg Jewish Film Archive, Jerusalem, Israel.

Nancy Turner: Head of Archives and Special Collections, University Libraries, Ball State University, Muncie, Indiana, USA.

Queenie Turner started work in the Pathé laboratories in London in 1934 and, with short breaks in 1942 (for the birth of her son) and 1948-1952 (when Pathé moved temporarily to Elstree), stayed with them until the company closed in 1967. Returning to work after the death of her husband in 1973, she became film librarian at the Imperial War Museum Department of Film. She retired in 1985.

Tedi Villalba Rodríguez: General Manager of the Spanish Academy for the Cinematographic Arts and Sciences and of the Madrid Cinema School (ECAM). (A longer introduction is given at the start of his contribution to this volume.)

Cushla Vula: Conservation Manager, New Zealand Film Archive, Wellington.

David Walsh: Head of Preservation, Imperial War Museum Film and Video Archive, London, UK.

Christine Whittaker joined the BBC to work for the World Service in Bush House on programmes to be broadcast to French speaking Canada. However, she soon moved to television, where a job as a researcher on a history programme led to a new career specialising in archive-based historical documentaries. Her credits include *All Our Working Lives, Now the War is Over, Out of the Dolls House, An Ocean Apart, Nippon,* and *Pandora's Box.* She was the Archive Producer on the 26 part series *People's Century.* She left the BBC in 1999 and now works as an archive consultant and freelance researcher.

George R Willeman: Nitrate Film Vault Leader, The Library of Congress Motion Picture Conservation Center, Dayton, Ohio, USA.

Frank Worth, at 16, filmed with his home-movie camera an air raid on Colombo, Ceylon, by the Japanese fleet that struck Pearl Harbor; later, he screened propaganda films to troops along the Burma front, then became the first Midshipman to command a combat film unit. He made seven assault landings in Burma, covered the re-taking of Rangoon, Penang, and Singapore, and went 500 miles behind Japanese lines in Malaya with colleague Russell Spurr, taking the informal surrender of its capital. He entered Sumatra and Java ten days before Allied forces, filming POW camps, Indonesian rebels, and the Japanese suicidal demolition of their huge arsenal. He was still under 21 when he filmed the aftermath of Hiroshima. Today he is an award-winning writer/director of documentaries, commercials, and feature films.

Catherine Wyler is a film producer, whose credits include both the documentary tribute to her father, *Directed by William Wyler* (1986), and the feature-film re-make of his own classic 1944 documentary, *Memphis Belle* (1990). Her most recent production is *Witness to Hope: The Life of Karol Wojtyla, Pope John Paul II.* She is Artistic Director of the new High Falls Film Festival in Rochester, New York.

Guest Editorials, Endorsements and Epigraphs

Nitrate Lives

by Eileen Bowser

Nobody could tell us about the special qualities of 35mm nitrate film stock until it began to disappear from the screen. There was no reason to speak of it since we saw little else. What would one compare it with? Nitrate was just there, the stock that all movies intended for commercial theatrical use were printed on. When it was gone, we began to think of what we might have lost.

The trajectory of film preservation was at a major turning point when I entered the profession. Triacetate film stock for printing negatives and master positives had only recently become available. The first film archivists who struggled to conserve their decomposing nitrate film stocks believed they had found the answer to their problems. They had come to fear that the repeated duplication of nitrate films onto nitrate stock over the decades, with resulting loss of image quality in each transferral, would lead to the great movies becoming mere ghosts of the originals. Now, Eastman Kodak advertisements promised archivists that just one duplication onto the new triacetate stock would guarantee survival for "400 years, or as long as the finest paper stock". Now, the only problem – a seemingly insurmountable one at the time – was to find enough money to copy all of the nitrate films onto the new stock. The curator Richard Griffith told me that he could not sleep at night for thinking that the collection he had been given the responsibility to care for was disintegrating under his eyes. He worked tirelessly to raise consciousness and funds for the copying task. Although he managed to transfer some of the most important films in the collection to triacetate, and to hold onto almost all the nitrate as well, he died before we began to receive substantial financial help for the task from the National Endowment for the Arts. As we completed copying various large and valuable parts of the collection, such as the original Biograph and Edison negatives,

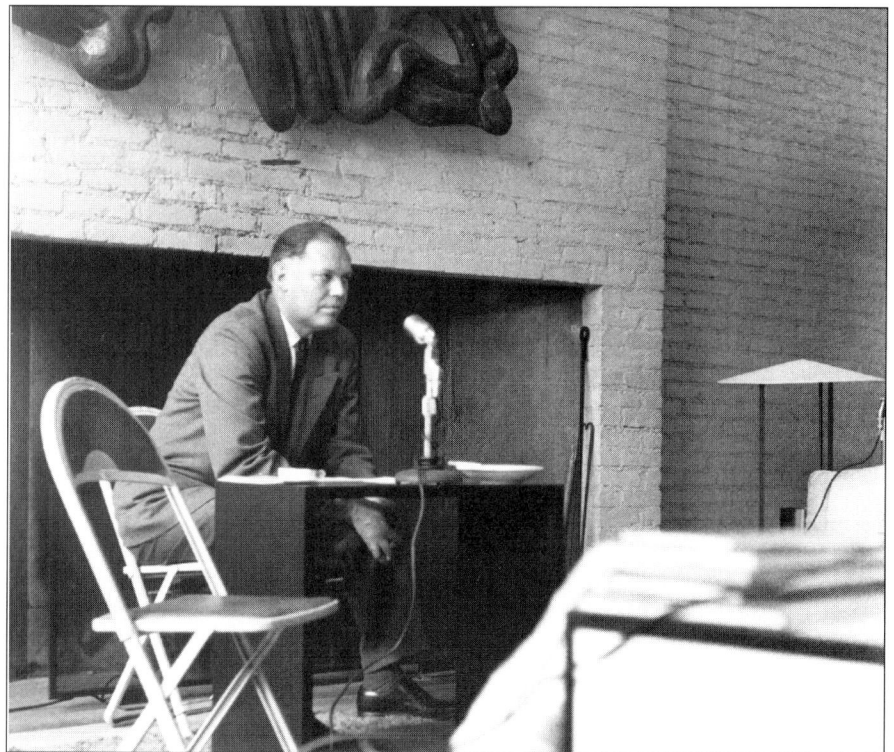

Richard Griffith at a teachers' conference, 1956.

The Museum of Modern Art/Film Stills Archive, New York.

and Eisenstein's *Que Viva Mexico* footage, I often thought of Richard Griffith. I wished he could have lived to see what had been accomplished.

Perhaps it is better that he did not discover that triacetate stock is not the perfect solution we thought it was in the 1950s and 60s. He never heard the fateful words "acetic acid", or the so-called "vinegar" syndrome. When a film that had only recently been copied on triacetate stock began to give off an acrid smell, it was blamed on a batch of defective stock. Even then we had in our collection a number of prints made on one or other of the older acetate stocks used for prints to be shown in non-theatrical venues, where one might not expect the same safety conditions as in the commercial cinemas. Most of these prints had been made for the archive by the studios' laboratories and we assumed they were nitrate, the stock that had always been used for theatrical prints. Gradually, as they were inspected and discovered to be acetate, they were separated and moved to a safety storage vault. Some of them were already shrivelled up with the smelly vinegar syndrome.

In fact, nitrate lives still, and might even live longer than acetate, perhaps. Until triacetate has been around for over a hundred years, as nitrate has, we won't know for certain. In our experience, storage conditions have turned out to be more vital than the type of stock in determining longevity, that and the care that was taken in processing the materials in the laboratory in the first place. Though delayed for decades, the Museum of Modern Art is now at last able to store its nitrate (and acetate) collection in up-to-date climate-controlled vaults, far from cities and sources of air pollution. Now I can sleep at night. I wonder what the collection would be like could the films have been stored there since the day they were first produced? Perhaps there would be no deterioration.

We kept our nitrate after it had been copied to triacetate, unless a particular reel had disintegrated to the point that one had to consider the danger to the other films in storage. If it has turned to powder, of course, there is no longer any possibility of copying it. In daily archive practice, we need to make a second inspection each time a technician advises that a nitrate reel needs to be destroyed. Frequently, it turns out that one need not destroy the whole reel, but only the leader or other small section, or sometimes it is only rust in the can, not powdering nitrate. Understandably, the vault technician is anxious to get rid of the problem. Some archives, and some production companies, destroyed their nitrate holdings after copying (or even before!) under pressure from their authorities, because of the notorious fire hazards. Why did we need to keep it? Archivists undoubtedly over-stressed the dangers of fire in the course of trying to persuade the authorities to find the resources to copy it all to triacetate. In the past, the discarded nitrate could be profitable for the silver that could be extracted from it, depending on the price of silver compared to the cost of extraction. When new environmental protection laws came into existence, it began to be expensive just to dispose of nitrate stocks, and production companies were willing at last to turn their nitrate and its problems over to film archives.

Those companies that had destroyed their nitrate holdings came to regret it. There are very practical reasons for keeping nitrate after it is copied onto triacetate. We learn by experience. In time, we learned how to achieve a higher fidelity to the original. In the 1980s and 90s we re-copied a lot of the films that were so joyously copied to triacetate in that period of the 50s through the 70s. In many cases, we were able to do the copying for the second time because the nitrate still survived. I hope the National Endowment for the Arts is not shocked by that news. In the 1970s the goal was to spread the funds as far as possible, to save as many films as we could, with the prospects of copying all our surviving nitrate before it was too late. The mantra of the 70s was "do not duplicate the work of other archives". But there are good reasons for that duplication, and for the repetition of copying films over again. Duplication of effort has insured that now, in the age of reconstruction projects, archivists working collaboratively can restore more nearly complete versions, and sometimes higher quality copies. At the Museum of Modern Art, we are very glad that we kept our nitrate.

But that was not the reason that we retained it. Not at first. We were not prescient enough to think that one day we might be re-copying some of the films. It seemed the realization of an impossible dream that we were able to copy them at all. Instead we were motivated by aesthetic concerns. We were aware that a certain warm quality could probably never be fully captured on acetate, which seems to be a colder medium. The higher amount of silver in the nitrate stock made possible a richer range of blacks and grays. The various tones and the tints of the old nitrate prints may be copied, but they cannot be precisely recaptured on the film stocks now in production, whether we copy on colour stock or resort to attempts to utilize the original processes. I recently heard a young archivist speak rather poetically of the "living qualities" of a nitrate print that trembles its way along the projection path, with occasional jumps and scratches, as opposed to the steady new acetate print. Some will consider this attitude toward the nitrate originals to be romantic. There are some times when I might not recognize a nitrate print when it is projected: the differences I see might be due to the various factors of printing quality and projection conditions. But if we compare the nitrate original with the new acetate print using side-by-side well-matched projection equipment, the differences are clearly visible.

We work with a medium that is famously reproducible. Yet we hold onto the concept of the authenticity of the original work, doubtless influenced by the circumstance that our archive exists within the framework of a museum of art. Today, even in the fine art world, that idea of the sanctity of the original is beginning to slip away. Not so long ago, there was simply no comparison between an original and a copy. If we could not keep the original print forever, we could keep it as long as possible.

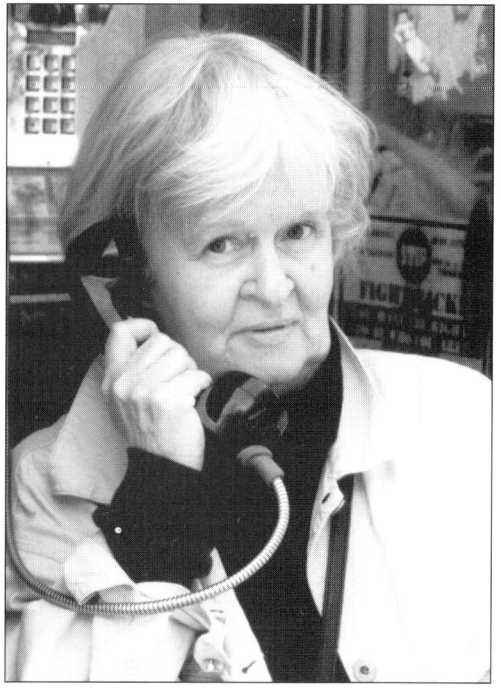

Eileen Bowser in 1995, photographed by Andrew Makowski.

Eileen Bowser.

We chose to show our nitrate projection prints as long as we could, once we had done our best work of copying them onto triacetate stock. In certain archives, original prints were never to be projected even after copying. Specialists insisted they might need to have access to them for re-copying in the future: any projection risks damage. That is true enough. We might even be able to reach a higher standard of duplication in the future. But the nitrate print may have turned to powder by then. An archive must be dedicated to the present as well as the future, or it won't have a future. Today's audiences should have an opportunity to see how films of the nitrate era looked on the screen.

At the Museum, our theatres and projection equipment meet safety standards for the projection of nitrate prints. As we know, acetate prints became the standard in the commercial film distribution business, and projectors were no longer routinely equipped with safety devices. In time, we became one of the few places of privilege where nitrate could be legally shown at all in New York and soon, in the whole country.

Today the Museum rarely shows nitrate prints, although it still does on special occasions. The prints that were shown many times became worn, sprockets weakened, and they would no longer go through the projector without breaking. Even if not worn out, the old prints became shrunken and brittle. The real culprit, though, is the modern projector, unable to tolerate much shrinkage. We reinstalled the safety gates when we replaced the old projectors, but the showing of nitrate prints became more limited. In Prague, I know, an old projector is kept in repair just for the purpose of being able to show shrunken nitrate. It is not difficult to engineer the sprocket wheels in new machines to accept shrunken film: we had a set of them made for a 35mm viewing table as well as the projectors. Of course it is a nuisance to have to change these back and forth for individual film showings.

When decomposition has set in, there is more risk of damage to the print when it is projected. Some of us have experienced the frightening moment when we see a frame of nitrate film go up in flame while in the projector, the image on the screen suddenly crumpling, although with the safety shutter working properly, it stops there. But if the print starts to catch and burn in the projector, it is probably time to retire the print from use. I am sure I am not the only archivist to have had the strange and lonely experience of watching the last projection of an original nitrate print. I imagine turning the last pages of the last real book as it crumbles into dust, leaving only electronic words alive in the world.

In the 1970s, the Executive Committee of FIAF happened to meet in a city where there were two archives, and both of them were visited by the entire committee of archivists. One was new: it had recently completed new buildings with state-of-the-art facilities, vaults, documentation centre, library, study facilities, viewing theatres. Everything was spotless and superbly equipped, and excited some envy among archivists who had to work with old makeshift facilities. Then we visited the second archive, an older one, which had shabby quarters, ancient patched-up equipment, and a long series of film vaults along a drive. As they were opened one by one, the unmistakable smell of decomposing nitrate rose to fill the nostrils. And camphor. There used to be an idea that camphor stored inside the cans would be helpful; in what way, I don't know. The archivists milled around inside the vaults, breathing in the stink of escaping nitrate gases with ecstatic smiles. "*This* is a real film archive!" they said. The other archive was a sterile place by contrast. I wonder how many of today's archivists know the delight of this indescribably awful odour? Some, no doubt, have never smelled nitrate.

Life with Nitrate

by Ib Monty

It is always tempting to express a point of view which is diverging from that of the majority. Therefore, when I was invited to contribute to this book, I may say that I was very tempted by one of the editor's suggestions: "to write a 'revisionist' view – saying perhaps that nitrate is more trouble than it is worth, or that the claims for its visual superiority are overstated".

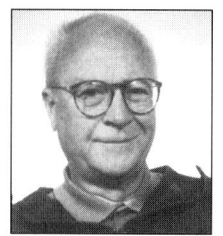

Ib Monty.

All this fuss about "Nitrate Can't Wait", for instance. Think about all the work and money, which for so many years have been invested in keeping original nitrate prints, which it gradually seems more and more difficult to show to an audience, or invested in transferring the films from the first 50 years of cinema – or rather, the surviving prints from this period – to safety material: acetate dupe negatives, masters, and projection prints, immediately second-rate compared to the originals, however meticulously the work was done.

Still, I would be dishonest if I were to claim that all the troubles we have seen with nitrate in film archives during the last half of the 20th century were needless. We knew that the nitrate films would vanish, and that future audiences would never get the opportunity to see these films the way they were seen when they were new. Only the oldest film archivists had had this experience, seeing the films in the original surroundings, in picture palaces, shown with arc-lamp projectors, accompanied by live music.

Already the second generation of film archivists, to which I belong, was debarred from these treats. We were now referred to small archive theatres with the cold light of electric lamps in their projectors to see silent films, and they really were silent.

But the visual quality of the films was obvious. And to a film-lover who, like myself, began experiencing the splendour of silent films in original prints from the end of the 1940s, the joys were never surpassed. Sitting in a small, quiet cinema among other dedicated enthusiasts, with only the faint noise of the projector in our ears, seeing not only the classics for the first time, but also discovering *True Heart Susie, Le Voyage Imaginaire*, and many others, are highlights in my film life. Restored, colorized prints with musical accompaniment cannot in my eyes and ears replace the simple joys of seeing a black-and-white silent original. And compared to what one later was exposed to in the shape of blurred third- and fourth-generation prints, lack-lustre 16mm copies, and even ugly video cassettes, I am happy that I at least saw what I saw, while nitrate was still alive. And I feel sorry for the generations of film archivists to come, who shall never see an original nitrate print on a big screen.

As for the preservation and projection of nitrate films, we were quite lucky in Denmark compared to many other countries. Of course, we lost 15–20% of our silent film production, which seems to be the rule in most countries. But almost all of the sound feature films on nitrate, which was used until 1952 in Danish laboratories, have survived.

Most Danish silent films were produced by A/S Nordisk Films Kompagni, and in the mid-1950s the company still kept many of the original negatives. The Danish Film Museum was at that time granted special funds for the making of a master and projection print from these negatives; this work ended in the mid-1960s. The Museum wanted to continue with the sound feature films on nitrate, but it took 18 years and several ministers before the Ministry of Cultural Affairs finally granted money for this work. The Museum wanted, of course, to have both masters and projection prints of the sound films, too, but the Ministry was not so generous and as concerned as the authorities had been in the 1950s. So, in order to spend the money in the best possible way, the Museum decided to make safety masters from the original negatives of all the films, and wait with the projection prints. In this manner nearly all of the 250 Danish sound films from the period 1930–1952 were secured in the mid-1990s.

In 1976 the laboratories turned over all the nitrate materials they were storing to the Danish Film Museum. The Museum did not destroy any nitrate negative or print, even if the film were already secured on safety stock. We heard rumours that some archives got rid of nitrate prints when they were transferred to acetate. I found this procedure almost a criminal act. We did not destroy our nitrate films until there were no images left – only then were they sent off to the crematorium.

Around 1990, we applied for money to start the same preservation procedure with the documentary films. The work began, and is now hopefully being carried on.

Errors were of course unavoidable. We were a small archive with a limited budget, and with a staff not trained in the intricacies of film preservation, but on the whole I have a clear conscience, and I am quite pleased that it was in my time that the surviving nitrate films were saved for posterity.

D W Griffith's *True Heart Susie* (1919).

BFI Collections – Stills, Posters & Designs, London. 103030.

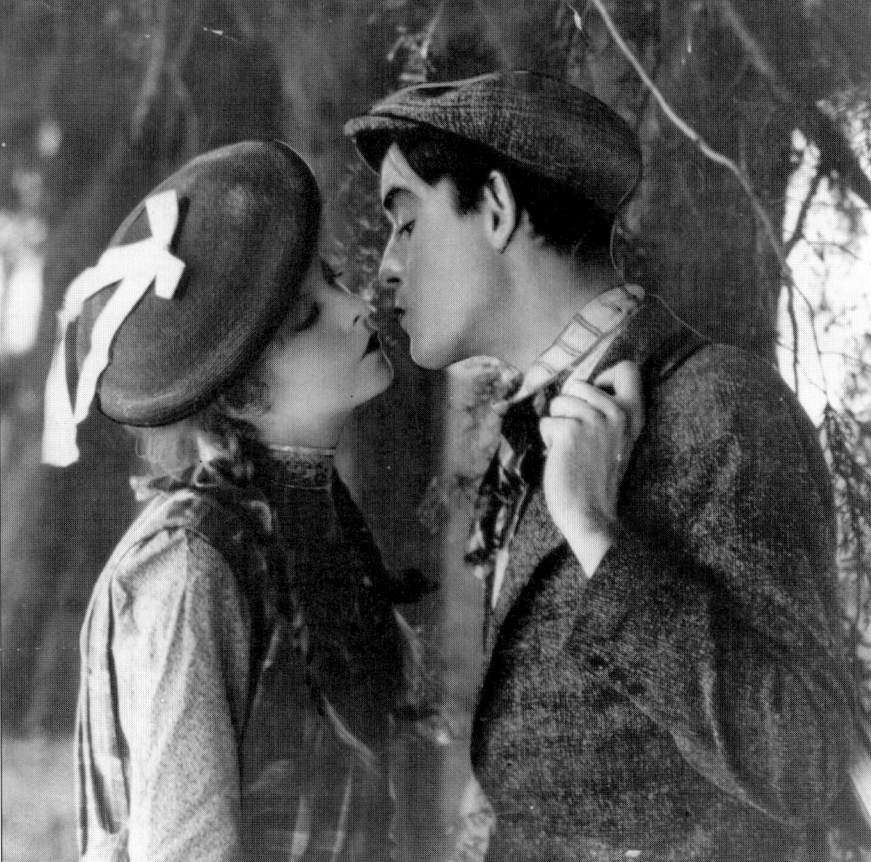

My personal experiences with nitrate started long before I became a conscious cinephile. As a boy at the end of the 1930s, I, together with friends, played at burning things with magnifying glasses. We looked for anything flammable – paper, leaves, celluloid from bicycle handlebars, etc. But best of all was nitrate film, which we could buy in small pieces at a second-hand shop in the neighbourhood. Later in life I wondered how many holes I had burned in frames from screwball comedies and Astaire-Rogers films… When I came to the Museum at the end of the 1950s, I found out that they were still dealing with the same shop-owner I had frequented in my childhood, buying old films – not, of course, in order to burn holes in them, but to save them!

Personally, I had many pleasures at the Museum when we found old nitrate films and began nursing them, preparing them for an afterlife on acetate. The largest collection we received at the Danish Film Museum came from the Nederlands Filmmuseum – more than 20 original prints of Danish silents which we did not have previously.

But my greatest pleasures at the Danish Film Museum were tied up with Carl Th. Dreyer. Films of his which were considered lost when I started my career as an archivist popped up in foreign archives in original prints, which had been stored under other titles. *Michael* came from the Staatliches Filmarchiv der DDR, where it had been lying untouched in cans marked "Unternehmen Michael". And *Die Gezeichneten* was found by a young and enthusiastic Russian Dreyer fan in Gosfilmofond, where it was catalogued under the title "Pogrom".

But the highlight was, of course, the discovery of one of the two original prints of Dreyer's *La Passion de Jeanne d'Arc*, which were in Copenhagen for the world première on 21 April 1928. The original negative was destroyed by a fire in Berlin in December 1928. In the 1960s, the Danish Film Museum decided to undertake a restoration of the film, based on prints from various sources and in foreign archives. We knew that the result was not the definitive version, but we did what we could. But then, one day during an intermission in a meeting at the FIAF Congress in Stockholm at the beginning of June 1983, Arne Petersen from the Norsk Filminstitutt came up to me and said, in a very calm way, "I think that we have found an original print of *Jeanne d'Arc* with Danish intertitles in Oslo." I was excited, and could hardly wait to see the print. It took some time – the Norwegians wanted to make their own dupe negative before they generously presented us with the print as a gift.

The print had been found in a hospital outside Oslo. A doctor interested in French medieval history had written to the distributor in Copenhagen in 1928 because he wanted to borrow the print for a screening. He got the print, and forgot to return it, and the distributor in Copenhagen forgot to get it back. And so it ended up in a cellar for 55 years.

When we received the original print we put it on a Steenbeck (it was too shrunken to be projected), and we could immediately ascertain that the visual quality was better than in any other print we had seen. You could now see the drawings on the white walls in the building where Jeanne was incarcerated. Whether it was more complete, or the camera angles were different from other prints, required a close reading and analysis by Dreyer specialists. The print was

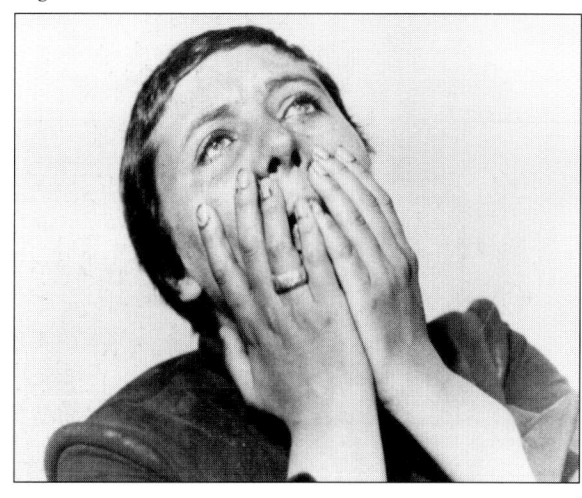

Carl Th. Dreyer's *La Passion de Jeanne d'Arc* (1928).

BFI Collections – Stills, Posters & Designs, London. 85018.

almost the same length as the known prints. But the revealing experience was to sit and realise that one was watching, with a 50% probability, the very same print that the audience saw at the world première at Palads Teatret more than half a century earlier.

It was a happy circumstance that we were allowed to work with, and even project, nitrate films in our archive cinema until the mid-1990s. This was not because the politicians and bureaucrats were especially fond of old films – rather, it was because they did not know anything about the risks of nitrate film. Denmark has been spared major fires caused by the use of nitrate. The first nitrate film fire in Denmark was in a cinema in Copenhagen in October 1907, and in the following years there were several smaller fires. The fire service accordingly intensified their demands on cinemas, and in 1917 firm rules were introduced concerning security precautions for cinemas, which were intended to make the risk of fires minimal. Nevertheless, in June 1928, a 12-year-old boy burned to death in a fire in a provincial cinema's projection booth, from where he had been watching the movie. New rules followed, and Denmark was spared bigger fires in the remaining nitrate period.

The last dramatic Danish nitrate fire was in May 1963, at the film laboratory A/S Johan Ankerstjerne in Copenhagen. A fire in a nitrate vault resulted in an explosion, which hurled the heavy metal door into the corridor; a fireman was killed. Had this accident taken place today, in an over-worried society, where accidents are not allowed to happen, the use of nitrate – in the film archive as well – would have been prohibited. After the laboratory fire, our archival work with nitrate, however, was not affected in a negative way – on the contrary: we received several nitrate prints from people in Denmark who were now afraid to have them around.

But we began to face the fact that the days of nitrate film were numbered. Until the mid-1990s, we could still present nitrate prints in our own archive cinema, but it was the only cinema in Denmark with this possibility. The training of projectionists in the handling of nitrate had long ceased, and the few remaining nitrate projectionists were approaching retirement age. More and more of the prints themselves were unprojectable, due to shrinkage and wear and tear.

The final blow came when the Danish Film Museum had to move to a larger film house in Copenhagen, together with other governmental film institutions. As always when government is involved in building activities, the budget was too small, compromises were entered into, and quantity was preferred to quality. The Museum, which was now merged with several other state-financed film bodies into a great centralised film institute, got access to three elegant cinemas, but had to sacrifice nitrate screenings. It would have been too expensive to install a cinema for nitrate in the new premises.

Well, it was a long-foreseen ending. The Museum marked the sad occasion by dedicating its last season in the old archive cinema to nitrate. Under the heading "Goodbye to Nitrate", 19 original prints from the Museum's own collections, of films from the period 1930-1947, were presented for the last time, from March to May 1996, although without much attention from press and public. The days of nitrate were over in Denmark, and very few cared. The memories live on, however, in the mind of an elderly, nostalgic ex-archivist, who still remains an ardent film-lover.

David Brown

David Brown, in partnership with Richard D Zanuck, produced some of the more memorable films of the 1970s and 1980s, including *The Sting* (1973), *The Sugarland Express* (1974), which helped establish Steven Spielberg's reputation as a director, *Jaws* (1975), *The Verdict* (1982), and *Cocoon* (1985); he also served as Executive Producer for the award-winning *Driving Miss Daisy* (1989), which Mr Zanuck and Lili Fini Zanuck produced. Mr Brown and Mr Zanuck were honoured with the Irving G Thalberg Memorial Award by the Academy of Motion Pictures Arts and Sciences in 1991, and with the David O Selznick Lifetime Achievement Award by the Producers Guild of America in 1993.

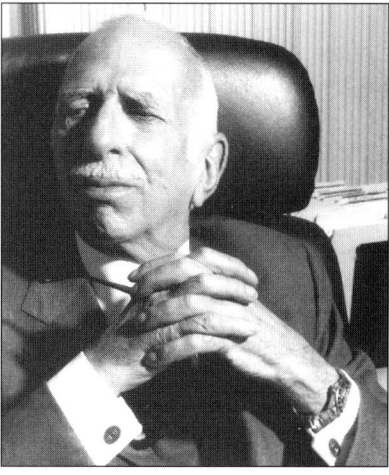

David Brown

Since 1992, David Brown has continued his run of critically acclaimed and award-winning productions through The Manhattan Project, whose successes include *A Few Good Men* and *The Player* (both 1992), *Kiss the Girls* (1997), *Deep Impact* (1998), *Angela's Ashes* (1999), and *Chocolat* (2000).

In addition, Mr Brown has produced for television and the stage, and has had a long career as a journalist, author, and magazine editor. He is a member of the Trustee Committee on Film and Media of The Museum of Modern Art and of the Board of Visitors of Columbia University's Graduate School of Journalism.

THE MANHATTAN PROJECT

Nitrate was the mother's milk of the film art and industry. For me it conveys the ultimate film experience – the great black-and-white works in the childhood, adolescence, and young adulthood of this art form. Nitrate may be dangerous and flammable, but as a canvas for movies it is unsurpassed. Flammable as it is, it inflamed our senses, our minds, and our hearts.

Warm regards,

(David Brown President, The Manhattan Project)

Helen Van Dongen

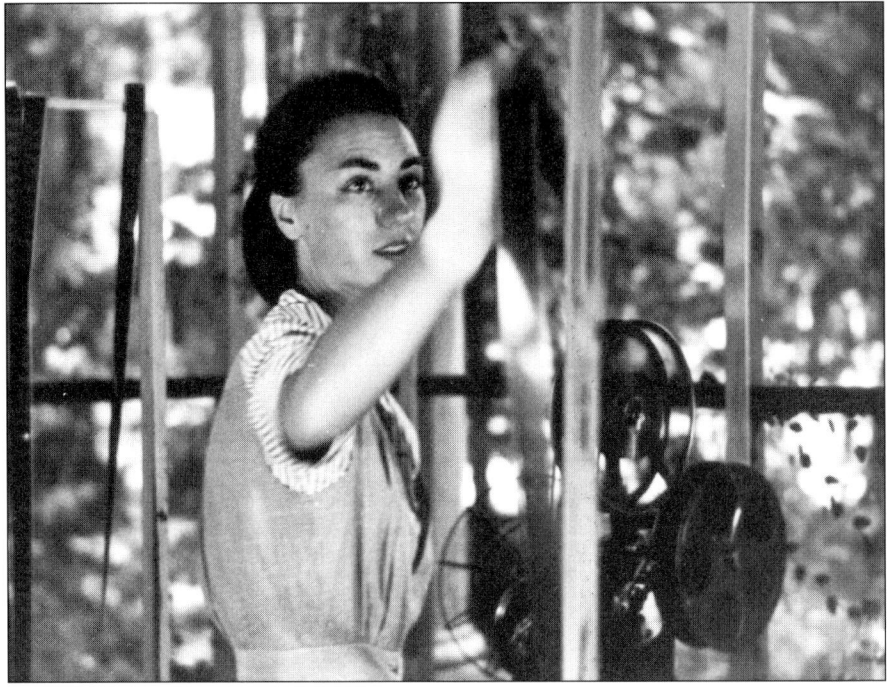

Helen van Dongen – seen here during the making of *Louisiana Story* – became interested in cinema in the 1920s when she joined Joris Ivens and others in Amsterdam in a group dedicated to the study of avant-garde films.

Her film-making career began in 1927, working in various capacities and ultimately as assistant editor with Ivens on several documentaries. In 1930-31 she travelled to Paris and Berlin to study new techniques in sound and colour, and throughout the 1930s she gained an increasing reputation for films that were both innovative and politically engaged. She worked in Moscow and visited Hollywood before settling in New York, where she continued to direct and produce her own films and worked with Joseph Losey, Ivens, and others.

During World War II, she took part in various US government programmes, and first worked with Robert Flaherty on *The Land*. She was appointed to the Film Commission for the Netherlands East Indies, but resigned in protest at Dutch resistance to Indonesian independence. She returned to America to work with Flaherty, serving as Associate Producer on *Louisiana Story*.

Helen van Dongen retired from film-making when she married in 1950. Her last film, which she produced, directed, and edited, was a United Nations project, *Of Human Rights* (1949).

Mrs. Kenneth Durant

Dear Mr. Smither:

As one who started her
film career during the
cellulose nitrate period
I send you my best wishes
for the success of the symposium
THE LAST NITRATE PICTURE
SHOW
and the publication of the
book
THIS FILM IS DANGEROUS.

Sincerely yours
Helen van Dongen.
(Mrs. Kenneth Durant)

Lord Attenborough

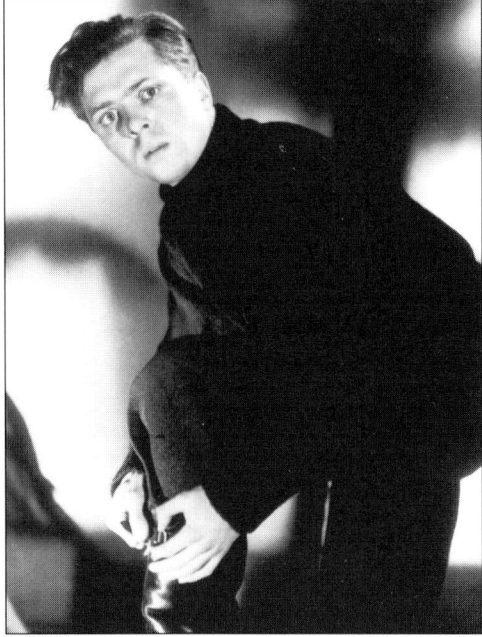

Richard Attenborough

Richard Attenborough, seen here in *Journey Together*, a 1945 Royal Air Force film production, made both his first West End stage appearance and his screen debut in 1942.

He has since starred in more than 60 films, as well as numerous theatre productions. He became an independent film producer in 1959, and made a triumphant directorial debut with *Oh! What a Lovely War* in 1969. As director, his filmography includes *A Bridge Too Far* (1977), *A Chorus Line* (1985), *Cry Freedom* (1987), *Chaplin* (1992), *Shadowlands* (1993), and *Grey Owl* (1999), although he is undoubtedly best known for the multiple award-winning *Gandhi* (1982). Now approaching 80, he is still an active film-maker and actor.

A leading figure in the creation of Capital Radio and Channel 4 Television, he is also Chancellor of Sussex University and Chairman of RADA, and a past Chairman of both the British Film Institute and the British Academy of Film and Television Arts. He continues to campaign vigorously for a viable British film industry, and remains actively involved in many different charities.

He was created a Life Peer – Lord Attenborough of Richmond-upon-Thames – in 1993 for services to cinema.

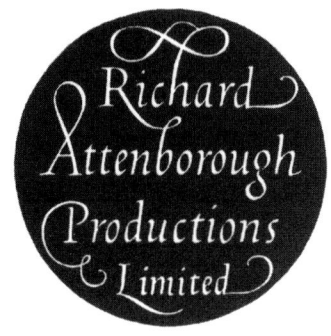

What an excellent idea to celebrate film preservation with the story of nitrate!

When I was a young actor, starting my film career in the 1940s, cinema was still less than half a century old, nitrate was universal, and film preservation was in its infancy. I don't suppose I gave a thought then to the fact that we were placing our humble immortality in the care of such a vivid but fragile medium. Pinky might have been more bothered had he known!

Since then, film has become rightly recognised as the vital recording medium of our times, in both fact and fiction, and sometimes proving a powerful tool for social and political change. The need for film archives was recognised relatively late in the day, and then they struggled for the resources necessary to achieve their remit. They still struggle – yet without archives and dedicated archivists much of the moving-image heritage of cinematography's first century would have disappeared forever. Some of them have even licked the nitrate problem (for the time being, at least) and moved on to other challenges, such as acetate decay, colour fading, and the new technologies.

But for film archivists, the history of nitrate still represents the soul, the excitement, and the real drama of conservation in action: the race against time, archaeological rescue, the tragedy of loss… And this timely book, with its fund of knowledge and personal testimony, tells us how it was, how it is, and how it will continue to be on the front line of their professional lives.

Richard Attenborough

Fay Kanin

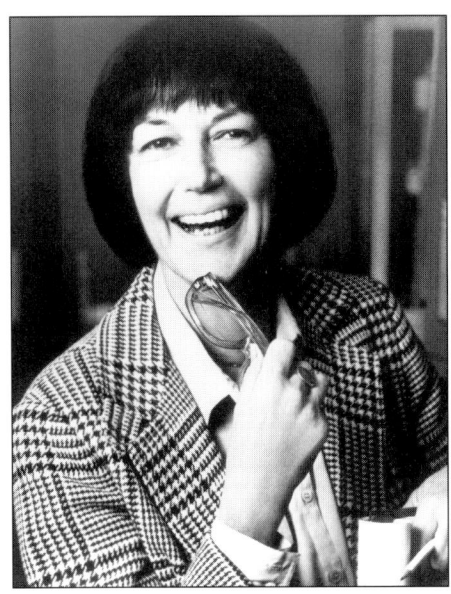

Fay Kanin

Fay Kanin, writer-producer for stage and screen, was a 4-term President of the Academy of Motion Picture Arts and Sciences – one of only two women to have occupied that position. She served as president of the Screen Branch of the Writers Guild of America, and for 10 years as Chair of the Foreign Language Film Executive Committee. She is a member of the Board of Trustees of the American Film Institute, co-chairing its Center for Film and Video Preservation; she also chairs the National Film Preservation Board.

Her script for *Teacher's Pet* (1956; co-written with her husband Michael Kanin) was nominated for an Academy Award, while her television films, including *Tell Me Where it Hurts* (1974), *Hustling* (1975), *Friendly Fire* (1979), and *Heartsounds* (1984), many of which she co-produced, have won Emmy, Peabody, Christopher, Writers Guild, and other awards. Her 1959 Broadway play *Rashomon* has been produced around the world, and her book for Harold Prince's musical *Grind* won a 1985 Tony nomination.

The Writers Guild of America has honoured her with its prestigious Valentine Davies and Morgan Cox awards. She also prizes awards from the American Civil Liberties Union, the League of Women Voters, American Women for International Understanding, and the Crystal Award of Women in Film.

Fay Kanin

April 8, 2000

In 1979, I was privileged to be elected President of the Academy of Motion Picture Arts and Sciences. It is a function of the President to make an opening statement at the Academy Awards. In view of the publication of FIAF's Nitrate Book, I thought it might be interesting to look back at my speech at the 52nd Academy Awards, when "film preservation" was not yet a household word in the industry or among the public. As I recall, in the months following the speech, I was delighted to receive letters and phone calls from a multitude of archivists thanking me for bringing the subject of film preservation to a worldwide audience.

April 14, 1980

Good evening and welcome. There's something I probably share with everyone in this theatre and with the five hundred million people in sixty countries who'll be seeing this all over the world. I love the movies. Like so many, I grew up with them. And when I got my first job in the story department of a studio and ate lunch with Ginger Rogers and Fred Astaire and Cary Grant and Irene Dunne (they happened to be at different tables, but that didn't matter) – well, I guess I thought I'd died and gone to heaven. And I'm still not sure I haven't.

We who work in motion pictures are very privileged. We are part of a medium that allows us to be creative, to be daring, to be aspiring, and sometimes even inspiring, and every once in a while, to be extraordinary. That's what this evening is about. Once a year, almost four thousand of us salute our colleagues for work beautifully and lovingly done. Every achievement recognized tonight is a labor of love, a gift of caring and commitment from someone who took a risk, who pushed the boundaries of his or her talent just a little farther.

A lot of our early great film achievements were lost, ended up moldering in basements, even dumped at the bottom of the sea. But on a trip recently to Washington and Europe I walked through film archives of our own and many other countries where I saw hundreds of thousands of films now safely stored and catalogued. In Spain, a young man at a film archive excitedly showed me a dirty tangle of celluloid, an old movie they had just discovered. I watched the way he handled the film, very gently, telling me in halting English how they were going to clean and restore it. And I realized that "movies" have become national treasures, to be preserved and esteemed as much as a nation's art or its music. At that moment, I felt a surge of appreciation for the many archivists who have labored through the years without recognition to preserve these treasures. And I felt pleased and proud to count them among all of us who are part of what is surely a glorious heritage.

Fay Kanin

Richard Leacock

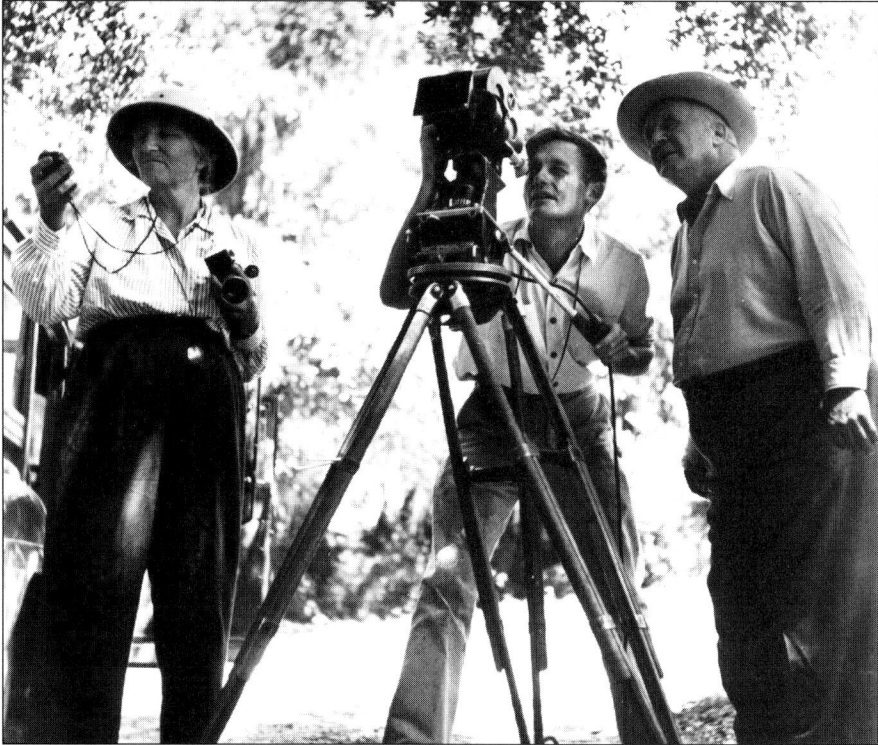

Louisiana Story

The Museum of Modern Art/Film Stills
Library, New York

Director and cinematographer Ricky Leacock – seen here with Frances and Robert
Flaherty while filming *Louisiana Story* – was born in London, and made his first
film at the age of 14. He travelled to America in 1938 to study at Harvard, then
joined Frontier Films to assist on documentaries such as *Native Land* (1942). He
served as a combat cameraman in Burma and China during World War II.

After the war, he worked with several leading documentary film-makers (Flaherty,
Willard Van Dyke, Irving Jacoby, John Ferno) before making three important
Omnibus documentaries for CBS. In 1958, he formed Drew Associates with *LIFE*
magazine editor Richard Drew, and launched the revolutionary technique known as
"direct cinema" with films such as *Primary* (1960) and *The Chair* (1961). In 1963,
Leacock formed a partnership with D A Pennebaker and went on to make a number
of influential documentaries, such as *Happy Mother's Day* (1963), and *Chiefs*
(1969). More recently, he began making works with Valérie Lalonde in Video Hi-8
format, including *Hooray! We're Fifty! 1943–1993* (1993).

Richard Leacock has taught at Hampshire College and at the Massachusetts
Institute of Technology, where he became head of the film department. His
autobiography in DVD format is in preparation.

35mm Nitrate Motion Picture Film (RIP)
In Memoriam
by Richard Leacock

Rewinding a 1000-ft roll of 35mm film for projection on the floor of Bill Hunter's room at my school in England (1935) and making sure that it was "heads out", I pulled the leader, and it went over the couch and right into an electric stove: searing flame! I ripped it off and threw it aside – and it landed on another 1000-ft roll! I leaped over and landed on the flame with my stomach... It was extinguished, but the room reeked of the nitric acid and I was shaking like a leaf, as I am right now, writing these words. One more second, and the whole place would have been ablaze. Years later, I was working as an editor in a "film" building, 1600 Broadway, just north of Times Square; it was not only illegal to smoke in that building, it was illegal to smoke within 50 ft of it!

As a combat photographer in the US Army, I walked from Myitkina to Mandalay with the British 36th Division, filming on 35mm nitrate with a hand-held Eyemo camera. The short-ends were very good for lighting fires to make tea...

Filming Robert Flaherty's *Louisiana Story* in 1946-7, we shot on nitrate but printed on safety film, so that Helen van Dongen could edit right there on location; we saw no difference in quality. When Flaherty was working on his first attempt at filming what later became *Nanook of the North*, he smoked a cigarette; his film went up in flames. He told me that his clothes were on fire so he ran out onto the street, where the local chemist knocked him down and put him out.

The last time I shot on nitrate was in Moscow, 1959: Leonard Bernstein conducting the New York Philharmonic. The Russians provided the film and camera crews. When we got back to New York, the Lab was horrified! They emptied the building that night and only the essential technicians remained as this dangerous material was developed and a safety fine-grain was made.

I know that some experienced people noted a change in quality when nitrate was replaced. I am not questioning their judgement, but think that this change was due to the reduction in the amount of silver in the emulsion – an economy that took place at about the same time.

Nitrate! May it rest in peace!

Leonard Maltin

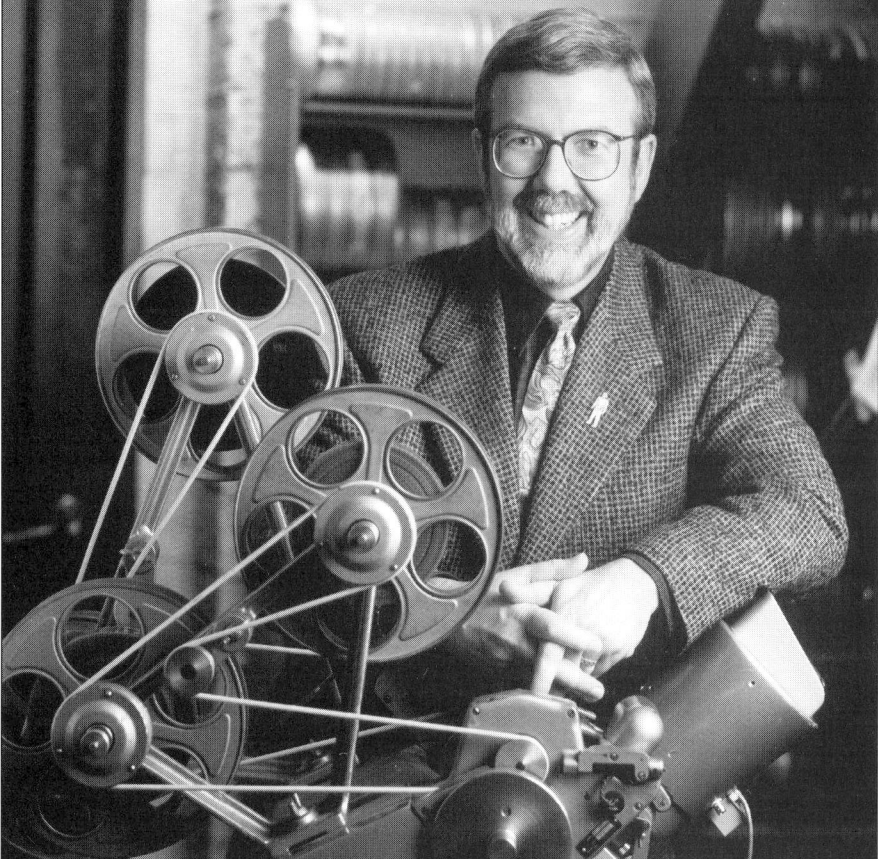

Leonard Maltin

Leonard Maltin started on a career in film scholarship while still at school, becoming a columnist for Vancouver-based *Film Fan Monthly* at 13 and its editor at 15. He was hired two years later by Signet Books in New York to write his first collection of capsule reviews, which was published in 1969 as *TV Movies* and continues to flourish today as *Leonard Maltin's Movie & Video Guide*, a widely-used paperback reference annual. He continued to write movie books while studying journalism at New York University; his titles include *The Art of the Cinematographer* (first published in 1971), *The Great Movie Shorts* (1972), *The Disney Films* (1973; Disney Press edition 2000), and *Of Mice and Magic: A History of American Animated Cartoons* (1980). His most recent book is *The Great American Broadcast: A Celebration of Radio's Golden Age* (1997). His articles have appeared in such publications as *Film Comment*, *Smithsonian*, the *New York Times*, and the *Los Angeles Times*, and he serves as film critic and columnist for *Playboy*. Since 1982 he has appeared on the popular US television programme *Entertainment Tonight*. He serves on the board of the National Film Registry, and teaches at the University of Southern California.

I will never forget the day I watched an employee at Sherman Grinberg, the venerable stock-footage company, struggle to pry open a rusted can containing the negative of a 1945 Paramount newsreel. When the lid finally came loose, a foul odor emerged, and he looked sadly at the congealing film inside. He calmly walked over to a nearby oil drum filled with water and dunked the 35mm roll. I felt my stomach knotting up, and still have a sense-memory of that moment.

But I also remember the first time I saw a 35mm nitrate film projected. It was Henri Langlois' print of the Raoul Walsh early-talkie *The Big Trail*. I'd never seen an image quite like it: the sharpness was incredible, the range of gray tones incomparable. The picture glistened on the screen.

I felt the way someone who has only eaten frozen food must feel when he tastes something fresh for the very first time. I realized that many of the vintage films I'd seen until then could not be properly judged by existing safety prints, that this quality I so admired in the print of *The Big Trail* was commonplace decades ago. (With the added enhancement of silver in many movie-palace screens, the effect must have been truly dazzling.)

It was then I realized how important it was to save what nitrate we still have, even as we struggle to make replicas for posterity. Only by showing these precious artifacts of cinema history can we truly recreate that history for viewers of today.

Lord Puttnam

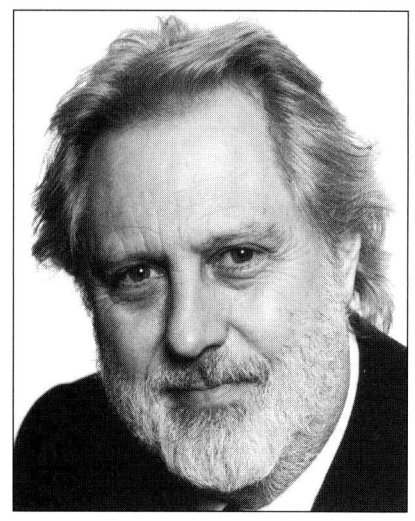

David Puttnam

Films made by David Puttnam in 30 years as an independent film producer include *Bugsy Malone* (1976), *Midnight Express* (1978), *Chariots of Fire* (1981), *Local Hero* (1983), *The Killing Fields* (1984), *The Mission* (1986), *Memphis Belle* (1990), and *My Life So Far* (1999). He was Chairman and Chief Executive Officer of Columbia Pictures 1986–1988 – the only non-American ever to have run a Hollywood studio.

He retired from film production in 1998 to focus on work in education in Britain. He is Chairman of the General Teaching Council, a member of the Education Standards Task Force, and Chairman of the Trustees of the National Teaching Awards. A former Chairman of the National Film and Television School, he is now Chancellor of the University of Sunderland, and a Governor and visiting Lecturer at the London School of Economics.

He was appointed to the House of Lords in 1997. He is Chairman of the National Endowment for Science, Technology and the Arts and of the National Museum of Photography, Film and Television, and Vice President of the British Academy of Film and Television Arts and the Royal Geographical Society. He is a Trustee of the National Museum of Science and Technology, and the Royal Academy of Arts.

The Lord Puttnam of Queensgate CBE

Robert Flaherty's *Man of Aran*, Victor Saville's *Evergreen*, Alfred Hitchcock's *The 39 Steps*, Thorold Dickinson's *The Next of Kin*, Alberto Cavalcanti's *Went the Day Well?*, Robert Hamer's *Kind Hearts and Coronets*, Charles Crichton's *The Lavender Hill Mob*... What do these British classics have in common? Firstly, they were all the inspiration of the greatest producer of truly indigenous British films, Sir Michael Balcon; secondly, they were all made in the last two decades of the nitrate era.

This is a bit like saying that Leonardo da Vinci's pictures were painted with self-combusting pigments or that Rodin sculpted in Semtex – the opportunity for tragic loss is almost exactly the same. Thank heavens, therefore, for this book, which is not only a fascinating and eye-opening science adventure story (for fifty years they made films out of WHAT?!), but also a salute – and a much-needed one – to the visionaries and archivists who took up the challenge, with scant resources, to defuse cinema's auto-booby-trap long enough to save at least a significant part of our film heritage.

As with literature or any other art form, cinema's past is every bit as important as its present. Balcon could not have produced the best British films of his era without first-hand knowledge of even earlier pioneers – Williamson and Lumière, Edison and Méliès – just as the film-makers of my generation would have been so much the poorer without Balcon. But even more strangely, perhaps none of us would have existed as film-makers at all without nitrate film, which is both the hero and the villain of this even-handed and very welcome book.

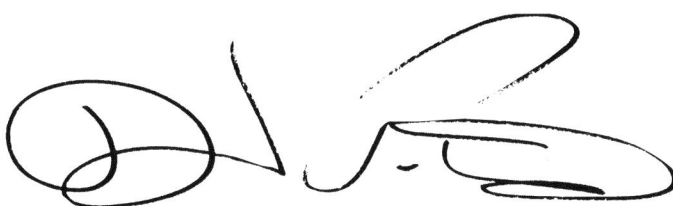

Jeremy Thomas

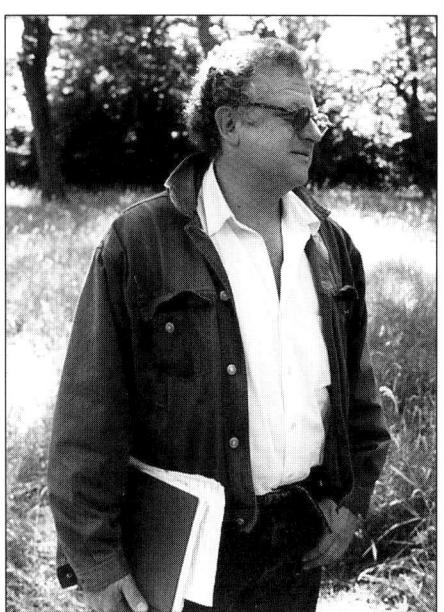

Jeremy Thomas

Son and nephew to two directors, Ralph and Gerald Thomas, Jeremy Thomas started work in the film industry straight from school, rising through minor positions to become film editor for the documentary *Brother, Can You Spare a Dime?* (1975). He produced his first film – *Mad Dog Morgan* (1976) – in Australia, then returned to England to produce Jerzy Skolimowski's *The Shout* (1977 – Grand Prix de Jury, Cannes). His extensive output of highly individual films includes Nicolas Roeg's *Bad Timing* (1980), *Eureka* (1981), and *Insignificance* (1985), Julien Temple's *The Great Rock 'n' Roll Swindle* (1978), Nagisa Oshima's *Merry Christmas Mr. Lawrence* (1982), and *The Hit* (1983), by Stephen Frears.

In 1986, he completed three years' work on the production of Bernardo Bertolucci's *The Last Emperor*, an independently financed project which swept the board at the 1987 Academy Awards. Since *The Last Emperor*, Thomas has completed many films, including Karel Reisz's *Everybody Wins* (1990), Bertolucci's *The Sheltering Sky* (1991) and *Stealing Beauty* (1995), and David Cronenberg's *Naked Lunch* (1992); he was also Executive Producer on Cronenberg's *Crash* (1995). In 1997 he directed *All The Little Animals*.

He was Chairman of the British Film Institute 1992–1997, and has been the recipient of many awards throughout the world, including the British Film Academy's Michael Balcon Lifetime Achievement Award.

You could call me a direct descendant of the nitrate era. Both my father, Ralph Thomas, and uncle, Gerald Thomas, began their careers in cinema when cellulose nitrate was the raw material of commercial film production. Perhaps I even played with the stuff in my cradle! The astonishing thing is that something so vulnerable and volatile had such a long career, and I grew up conscious of the need to respect and protect it as the carrier of much of Britain's surviving film heritage.

This became one of my priorities when I served as Chairman of the British Film Institute in the 1990s and had a hot line, as it were, to the daily work of the National Film and Television Archive and its constant task of preserving the millions of feet of threatened film in its care.

This book is therefore not only to be taken seriously, but also loudly applauded for its holistic and accessible approach to a MacGuffin (if I may steal from Hitchcock) which has materially affected half the life cycle of the art form we call cinema.

Jeremy Thomas, Film Producer and Director

"Nitrate Railways"

by Michael Chanan

The only thing that makes you look twice at this very plain photograph are the words on the side of the engine: Nitrate Railways, although then one also notices the mountains in the background. Where is this, and what does it have to do with cinema and its beginnings?

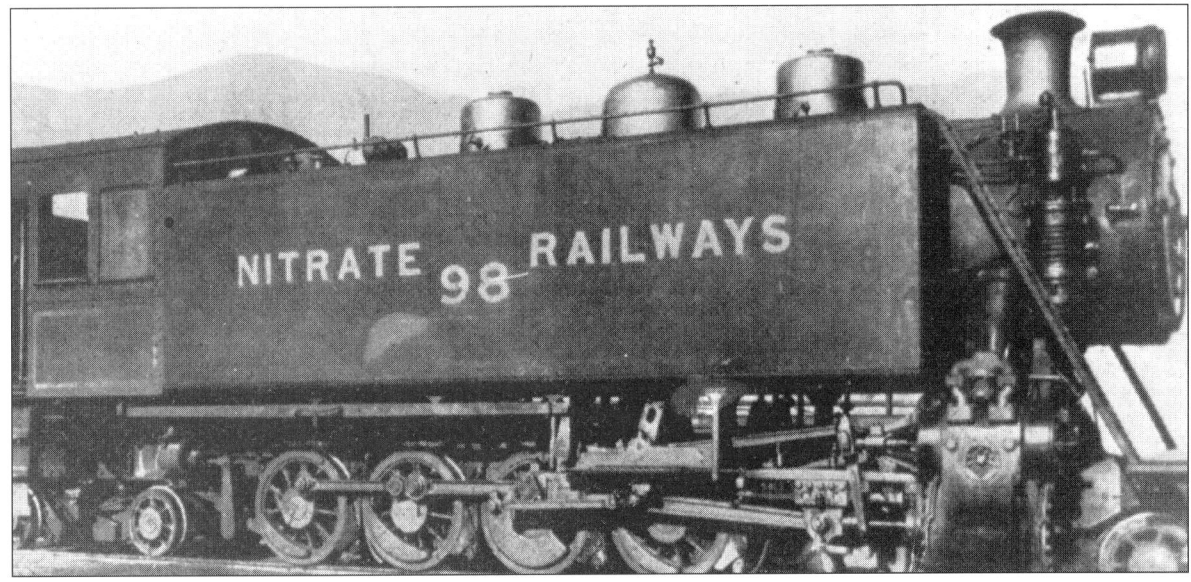

This photograph of an intriguingly labelled locomotive was found in a flea market by a friend of Edith Kramer, Director and Film Curator of the Pacific Film Archive.

Pacific Film Archive, Berkeley.

Apparently the photograph was found in a flea market in California, but I have the impression that I've seen this engine before, or another very like it, in a film. Though I can't be sure which, it would certainly have been a Chilean film. Was it *Caliche Sangriente* (Bloody Nitrate), made by Helvio Soto in 1969? Or Claudio Sapiain's documentary made a year or two later, about the massacre of striking workers in the British-owned nitrate mines of Santa Maria de Iquique early in the 20th century? Or even Miguel Littin's *Actas de Marusia* (Letters from Marusia), about another massacre in another British-owned nitrate mine in the same period?

Soto's film is about the War of the Pacific fought by Chile against Peru and Bolivia in 1879-83, of which James Blaine, US Secretary of State at the time, said, "One shouldn't speak of a Chilean/Peruvian War, but rather of an English war against Peru with Chile as an instrument." The territory over which this war was fought – by the Chileans, egged on by the British, and effectively on behalf of British capital interests – was rich in several minerals, but particularly the sodium nitrate, known as Chile nitrate, which was not only an ingredient of the new fertiliser and explosives industries which developed in the mid-19th century, but which also provided one of the raw materials in the production of celluloid, a substance invented in the 1860s which would subsequently become synonymous with cinema.

There is a poetic – or filmic – irony in the fact, given this history, and the economic role of Chile nitrates in the birth of the film industry, that the Chilean film-makers who supported Allende and Popular Unity used cinema to speak about the conditions of exploitation in the British-owned Chilean nitrate mines at the beginning of the 20th century. There is another ironic twist: at the start of the First World War the British cut off the supply of Chile nitrates to the Germans in order to impede the manufacture of explosives in Germany. The Germans, who by that time had developed a far superior chemicals industry to Britain's, responded by developing a synthetic process known as the ammonia oxidation process, which does away with the need for nitrate salts as a raw material, using nitrogen gas instead. As for nitro-cellulose film stock, Eastman had already begun to develop safety stock, that is, acetate cellulose, in the period before the First World War, partly because of the threat of competition from Germany and partly to get round the problems caused by the inflammability of nitro-cellulose, although it was still some time before celluloid was finally replaced by this new safety stock. Yet celluloid and cinema were so closely linked that the former word remained synonymous with the latter long after its use had been superseded.

Orson Welles Defines
"The Job of the Archivist"

Film has a personality, and that personality is self-destructive. The job of
the archivist is to anticipate what the film may do – and prevent it.
> – Orson Welles, quoted in *Our Movie Heritage*,
> by Tom McGreevey and Joanne L Yeck
> (Rutgers University Press, 1997), page 115.

When asked for the source of this quotation, Tom McGreevey explained:

I had the opportunity to talk to, or more accurately listen to, Orson Welles
between set-ups for a wine commercial in Los Angeles almost twenty years
ago. He answered my comment about the then-recent loss of the original
negative of *Citizen Kane* in a laboratory fire with a long statement about the
volatility and life-energy of the basic elements of a movie: the actors and the
medium itself. To my great regret, I did not have a tape recorder with me,
and these were the only pithy and coherent remarks I was able to jot down
afterwards.

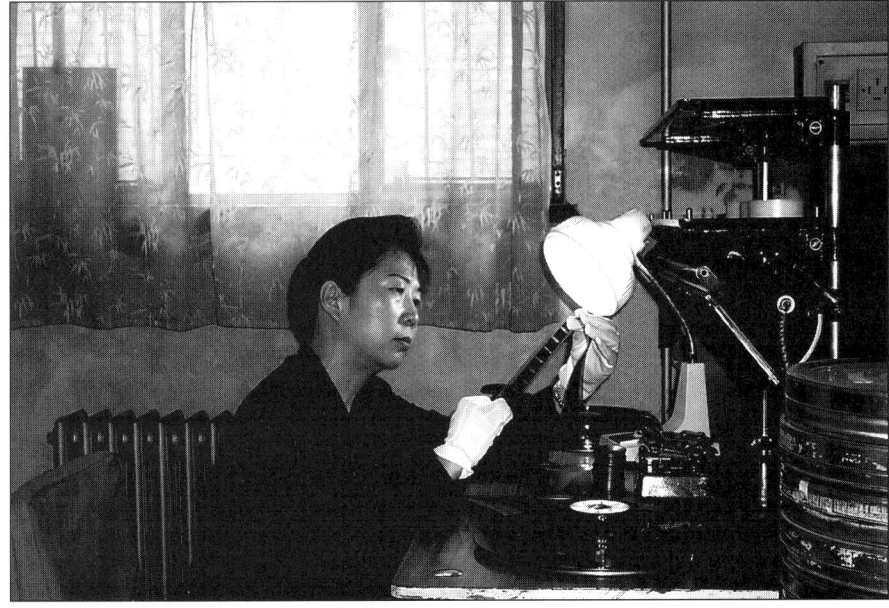

Inspecting nitrate film at the
China Film Archive.

China Film Archive, Beijing.

William Wyler Answers the Question: "How Do You Become A Director?"

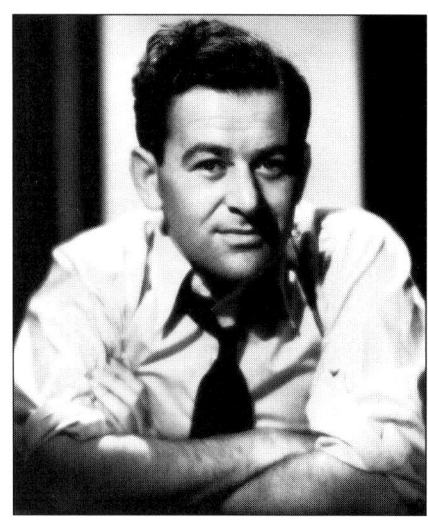

William Wyler at Universal Pictures, studio portrait by Roman Freulich.

The Wyler Family.

Catherine Wyler offers this story in memory of her father. As told here, it is quoted – with the author's kind permission – from the prologue to the biography *A Talent for Trouble: The Life of Hollywood's Most Acclaimed Director, William Wyler*, by Jan Herman (New York: G P Putnam's Sons, 1996, pp.2–4).

Wyler used to say he started his directing career as an "assistant errand boy." It was no exaggeration. In 1922, at Universal Pictures' sprawling studio in the San Fernando Valley, he began on the swing gang sweeping sets at night. A quarter of a century later, the University of Southern California invited him to give the commencement address to the graduating class of its School of Cinema-Television. Wyler, who spoke three languages but never graduated from high school, called up his friend Robert Parrish, an Oscar-winning film editor, and asked him to lunch.

"I've just been offered what I think is an honor," Wyler said, "and I need your advice"

At Musso & Frank, the Hollywood hangout, they each ordered a Bloody Mary.

"Didn't you go to USC?" Wyler wanted to know.

Parrish, who'd recently become a director, said he had.

"What'll I say?" Wyler asked. "These kids are thirty years younger than I am."

"Tell 'em what it's like to direct Bette Davis, Humphrey Bogart and Laurence Olivier. Tell 'em what it's like to win Academy Awards. Tell 'em what it's like to argue with Sam Goldwyn."

Wyler grinned and sipped his Bloody Mary.

"That's all there is to it?"

"That's just bullshit to fill in the time," Parrish said. "After that you ask if they have any questions. They'll ask you about the change from silents to sound, who's the best cameraman you ever worked with, the best cutter, the best producer, the best writer. Then one of them will ask you the key question."

"What's that?"

"How do you become a director?"

Thirty minutes after Wyler took the podium at the commencement, Parrish remembers, a newly minted graduate stood up at the back of the auditorium and asked precisely that. The audience broke into loud applause.

"I've known many directors in my day," Wyler said, "some good, some bad, and lots in between. But I don't know of any who became directors in exactly the same way. Ernst Lubitsch, John Ford, Lewis Milestone, Jean Renoir, and others are great directors. I don't think any of them became great by following the same rules."

Then he launched into a streamlined version of events surrounding his arrival in America – all of it entertaining and most of it approximate. Like many of the film colony's early immigrants, he was born in Europe. When he got to his experience on the swing gang and how he made it up the Hollywood ladder, the audience was hanging on his words.

"Part of my job," he explained, "was to sweep the street in front of the cutting department. As I was doing this one night, I saw a man standing outside leaning against the building. He was the head of the cutting department, and he had an unlit cigarette in his mouth. He said, 'Got a match?' I said yes, because I smoked too. He lit his cigarette and offered me one. I lit mine and leaned against the building with him. After a while, he said, 'We can't smoke inside because we work with nitrate film and it's highly inflammable.' He thanked me for the match. I thanked him for the cigarette. And we went our separate ways."

The next time Wyler was on the night shift, he sneaked into the head cutter's room and set up a long-distance smoking arrangement.

"I got a piece of copper tubing from the machine shop, put an ivory cigarette holder on each end and ran it from the cutting bench, through the window, to the outside. I went out and lit a cigarette and put it in the cigarette holder on the end of the copper tube. Then I ran inside to the head cutter's bench and sucked until the smoke came through. It worked. You could now smoke in the cutting room and not blow up the studio."

When the head cutter discovered the setup, he sent for Wyler and offered him a job as an apprentice in the cutting department.

"I jumped at the chance. I liked the work, I learned fast, I kept the copper tube supplied with cigarettes and I was soon promoted to assistant cutter. Before I knew it, I was invited to address the graduating class."

A Poem by Jean-Luc Godard[1]

les films sont
des marchandises
et il faut brûler les films
je l'avais dit à Langlois
mais attention
avec le feu intérieur
matière et mémoire
l'art est comme l'incendie
il naît
de ce qu'il brûle

Translation by Lenny Borger

Films are
trade goods
and they must be burned
I said as much to Langlois
but beware
with its inner flame
matter and memory
art is like a conflagration
it is born
from what it burns

Jean-Luc Godard in 1963.

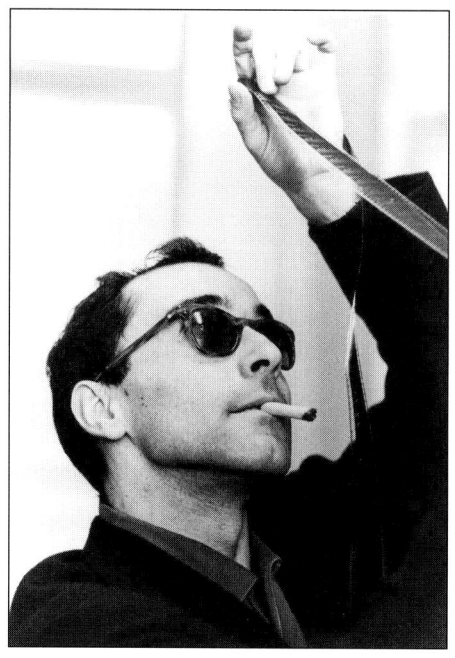

[1] Reprinted by permission of the author.

"Next to the United States Mint..."

Archivists are used to speaking of our film heritage as "priceless", but the following passage offers a startling alternative perspective on the question of value. It comes from Terry Ramsaye's monumental history, A Million and One Nights *(New York: Simon & Schuster, 1926; Touchstone paperback edition, 1986), pp.831–832. (Emphasis added.)*

The so-called raw stock or unexposed film is itself an extremely complex product, and its manufacture remains about the only important industry heavily safeguarded by secrets. Most of the secrets are George Eastman's. The film base is cellulose, nitrated and dissolved in an alcoholic solvent, coated with gelatine emulsified with photosensitive silver salts. The film's cellulose content consumes large quantities of cotton. **One thirtieth of the world's output of silver goes into Eastman products alone, making the motion picture stand next to the United States mint, the world's largest single consumer of silver.** The fine gelatine required is derived from young calves. It was formerly produced entirely in Germany but by war necessity the processes have been perfected in the United States.

I Am the Motion Picture

by Arthur James

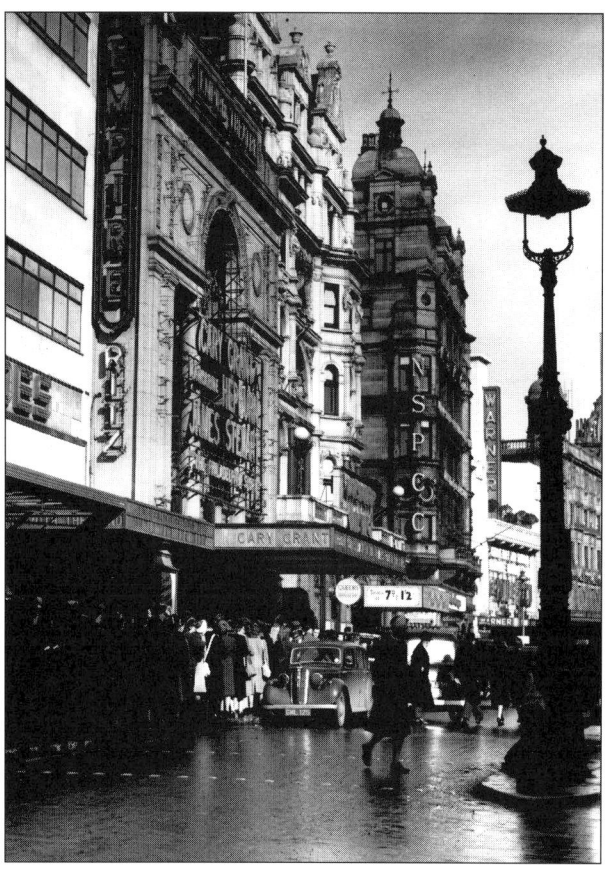

"The pleasant hour of prince and child": ignoring the war in the spring of 1941, a queue forms in Leicester Square, London, for admission to *The Philadelphia Story*, showing at the Empire cinema. Also visible in the picture are the Ritz cinema (sharing a marquee with the Empire), the Monseigneur News Theatre (with "Seats at 7d & 1/2"), and, in the distance, the Warner cinema.

Imperial War Museum, London. D 2973.

The following inspirational oration was published in Fox Photoplay News, *v.1, no.2 (Denver, Colorado, 8 July 1920), p.5. (Submitted by Ronald S Magliozzi.)*

I am the Motion Picture.

I am the child of man's genius, the triumph of man over space and time. I am a mute, but I am eloquent to millions. I travel desert sands, I climb the tallest mountain peaks. I traverse prairie, glacier, jungle, forest and sea and air and bring the vision of my journeys to the eyes of common men.

I am the pleasant hour of prince and child, of master mind and little boy. I instruct, I delight, I thrill, I entertain, I please, I shock, I cheer, I move the world to laughter and to tears.

I am the sublime story teller of all the ages. I am the drama's greater brother.

I have more friends than all the friendly men of Earth. I stir the blood, I quicken the pulses, I encourage the imagination, I stimulate the young, I comfort and I solace the old and sorrowing. I bring priceless gifts and make them yours.

I show more of travel than all the books penned by all the writers of the world. I preach sermons to congregations greater than the combined flocks of the pulpits of all lands, I make for happiness, I make for kindliness, I am the one great international friend.

I am history, written for generations to come in a tongue that every race and sect and creed can understand. I preserve heroes for posterity. I give centuries more of life to the arts and sciences. I am man's greatest and noblest invention.

I am the Motion Picture.

The Asbestos Screen and the Not-So-Flammable Nitrate.

Editor's Note: Many of the contributions to this book concentrate on or at least mention the tendency of nitrate film to burst into flames. While I was assembling those contributions, the following two items also came to my attention. They have nothing to do with each other, apart from the fact that both offer entertainingly alternative "takes" on this alarmingly constant theme of film and fire, and they have no significance beyond their curiosity value. (RS)

1. The Asbestos Screen

The British trade journal The Cinema *printed the following text – which it had itself copied from "our excellent contemporary, the* South African Pictorial" *– on page 32 of its 16 October 1919 issue, suggesting that "some of our publicity experts may like to incorporate [something similar] in their Press campaign booklets". How could I resist acting on this 80-year-old invitation in the context of* This Film Is Dangerous, *especially given the modesty of the sample text's claims, and the reminder which it provides that the nitrate era did not only mean inflammable film stock – it also offered inflamed passions…? Sadly, it has not been possible to confirm the identity of the film that originally sparked the copy-writer's enthusiasm.*

> TO-NIGHT … <u>the picture that caused all the sleepless nights in New York</u>. The most Heart-Rending, Soul-Stirring, Hair-Raising, Brain-Burning, Eyeball-Protruding, Knee-Knocking, Chest-Heaving film yet screened. Come early, and bring your smelling-salts. N.B. – We use a special asbestos screen for ALL our love scenes.

2. Not-So-Flammable Nitrate

The accompanying image is not a fake. Its finder has provided the caption.

In total defiance of its extreme combustibility, a hole burnt through the centre of a frame of an early Vitagraph print, dating from 1913. This was found in 1997 during the inspection of a newly acquired original print by George R Willeman, Nitrate Film Vault Leader for the Library of Congress Motion Picture Conservation Center.

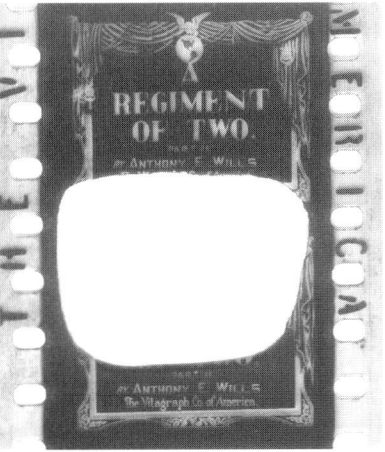

An example of the unpredictability of nitrate film. See accompanying text.

Library of Congress, Washington, DC.

"The Last Nitrate Picture Show"

This section comprises papers by the speakers at the symposium "The Last Nitrate Picture Show" which formed part of the programme of the June 2000 FIAF Congress, held at the National Film Theatre, London.

While the subjects are the same, in most cases the papers published here are expanded versions or variants of those actually given at the Symposium.

Exploding Teeth, Unbreakable Sheets, and Continuous Casting: Nitrocellulose, from Guncotton to Early Cinema

by Deac Rossell

I. The Origins of Celluloid

The origins of celluloid lie in the discovery of a method of nitrating cellulose fibres, or, in plain words, soaking cellulose fibres, usually taken from cotton or wood or one of their many products, in nitric acid and adding any one of a number of solvents. This process was first experimentally investigated in the 1830s and 1840s, and led directly to the formation of the field of organic chemistry, the combination of naturally-occurring materials with a solvent or catalyst to produce synthetic materials that do not appear in nature and which have a wide variety of different properties. Two pioneering French scientists conducted experiments in the 1830s which in themselves were only hesitant steps towards the formation of a practical discipline of organic compounds, but which bequeathed the names of their experimental materials to the later history of celluloid manufacture. Henri Bracconot combined nitric acid and potato starch into a material he called "xyloidine" in 1833, and Théophile-Jules Pelouzé used nitric acid and paper to make a material he called "pyroxyline" in 1838.[1]

The first scientist to generate a useful material by combining nitric acid and cellulose, in the form of cotton, was Christian Friedrich Schönbein, a professor at the University of Basle. Distilling sulphuric and nitric acids one day in his kitchen in 1846, his glass bottle broke on the floor, spilling the acids, and in hastily cleaning up the mess Schönbein wiped the floor with his wife's cotton apron, which he then hung over the oven to dry: instead of drying, it burned up with a smokeless flame.[2]

Schönbein wrote to his colleague Michael Faraday in England on 27 February 1846, that "I have of late also made a little chemical discovery which enables me to change very suddenly, very easily and very cheaply common paper in such a way, as to render that substance exceedingly strong and entirely waterproof".[3] In a later letter to Faraday, written on 18 March 1846, Schönbein included a sample "of a transparent substance which I have prepared out of common paper. This matter is capable of being shaped out into all sorts of things and forms and I have made from it a number of beautiful vessels".[4]

During this period of intense experimentation with the effects of nitric acid on various forms of cellulose fibres, Schönbein announced, on 11 March 1846, one of his two great discoveries: a powerful new form of explosive that he called nitrocellulose, or guncotton.[5] Quickly patenting his new material in several countries,[6] Schönbein gave exclusive rights for the manufacture of his explosive to John Hall and Sons in Britain, but their factory in Faversham blew up while experimenting with Schönbein's new material in July 1847, killing 21 workers, as did factories in France, Russia, and Germany, where experimentation with the militarily valuable new substance was quickly undertaken.[7] As others tried to exploit the explosive power of guncotton, Schönbein continued to experiment with the reaction of acids on nitrated cellulose. The key reactive solvent that emerged from these experiments was ethyl alcohol, which produced from a moderately nitrated cellulose a viscous, colourless liquid that, when dried on a flat surface, turned into a transparent sheet whose brittleness and strength could be varied according to the proportions of the ingredients in the original mixture. He sent samples of his new material to the eminent chemist J C Poggendorf in Germany, who suggested its use as a substitute for window glass, and as a tough and long-wearing replacement for paper in the making of banknotes, evidently forgetting its highly inflammable quality.

By January 1847 Schönbein's flexible, transparent material was proposed as a waterproof and flexible bandage for wounds and for use in medical surgery by the Boston physician J Parker Maynard. In its liquid form, where it was called collodion,[8] the new material found a significant and lasting use from 1851 as a vehicle for photosensitive emulsions. This was first suggested by Gustav le Gray, patented by the Boston photographer James A Cutting,[9] and then developed as a practical medium of photography by Frederick Scott Archer in England, in his wet-plate collodion process, or Archerotype.[10] The use of collodion emulsions in photography allowed much shorter exposure times for a photographic subject, an advantage which led directly to the development of "instantaneous" photography and lightweight hand cameras, liberating photography from the confines of the professional portrait studio and allowing photographers to take lifelike pictures in nature. It led as well to the instantaneous series photographs of Eadweard Muybridge, which were made on collodion wet plates.

Alexander Parkes (portrait painted by Abraham Wivell).

The Science Museum/Science & Society Picture Library, London. POR/B61000401.

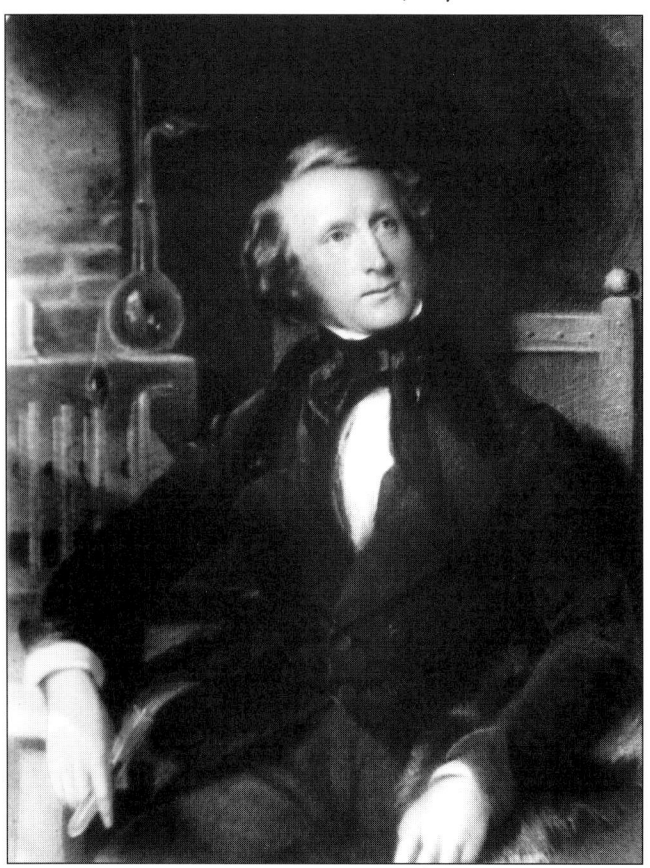

As a solid material, nitrocellulose was developed over many years of private experimentation by Alexander Parkes, the son of a brass lock manufacturer in Birmingham, England. He first exhibited his mouldable solid material at the Crystal Palace exhibition of 1862, where he won a bronze medal for the material he called Parkesine;[11] by 1865 he announced publicly that he could make nitrated cellulose into a stable, fully formable material by combining it with any of several plasticizer-solvents. His initial public discussion of Parkesine, at the Society of the Arts in London on 20 December 1865, described his success in "producing a substance partaking in a large degree of the properties of ivory, tortoise-shell, horn, hard wood, india rubber, gutta percha, &c."[12] Parkes then launched a company to mass-produce his new substance in April 1866, but it was bankrupt by 1868.[13] Again, like the initial experimenters 30 years earlier, he left a notable legacy to the subsequent history of celluloid, this time in the form of his works manager, Daniel Spill, who became obsessed with the new material and initiated a lengthy lawsuit against the successful American manufacturers of celluloid lasting from 1876 to 1884, a court action which he lost only when he died of diabetes.[14] From around 1873 Spill was associated with the British Xylonite Company, which had acquired Parkes's patents in 1868 and which ultimately became the sole major British manufacturer of celluloid at the end of the century.

The company that finally found commercial success with the new material was founded in 1870 by John Wesley Hyatt and his brother Isaiah Smith Hyatt in Albany, New York. They called their formable plastic "celluloid", and incorporated as the Albany Dental Plate Company. Hyatt used a mixture of pyroxyline and camphor in his celluloid, which he saw as a substitute for the hard rubber used by dentists in the false teeth, bridges, and other dental wares of the day.[15] The company struggled until Hyatt, trained as a printer, began to form his teeth (and billiard balls, combs, and other trinkets) under heat and pressure, which created a material that was stable and hard in nearly any shape. Hyatt's early products used no fillers, and only the "least quantity" of colouring pigments; therefore they were nearly pure guncotton, and burned rapidly if touched by a lighted cigar. Hyatt later wrote that "occasionally the violent contact of the balls would produce a mild explosion like a percussion guncap".[16]

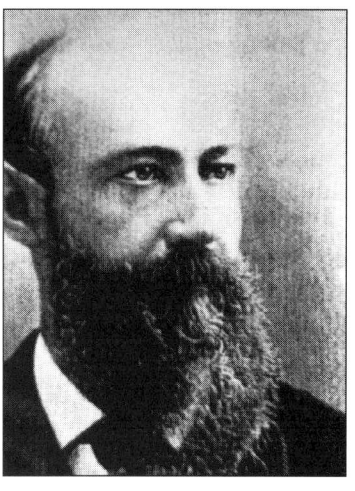

John Wesley Hyatt.
Deac Rossell.

When the Hyatt brothers tried to interest a manufacturer of hard rubber goods in their imitation material, and demonstrated their production methods using heat and pressure, the potential customer turned them down with the advice that their new process was so dangerous that they were more than likely to blow themselves up.[17] Recapitalising the business as the Celluloid Manufacturing Company and moving to Newark, New Jersey, in late 1872, the Hyatt brothers worked continuously to improve the manufacturing apparatus for volume production of celluloid, and to explore every avenue of its possible commercial exploitation.[18] John Wesley Hyatt received 61 patents between 1869 and 1891 for various celluloid-related processes,[19] and by 1880 his company had issued licenses to almost two dozen firms engaged in the manufacture of celluloid dental plates, harness trimmings, knife and cutlery handles, emery wheels, brushes, shirt cuffs and collars, shoes, piano keys, and a vast range of other items. In both Europe and America, other firms entered the new field that the Hyatts had pioneered, but the manufacture of celluloid, a slight chemical variant of guncotton with fillers added, remained a dangerous and uncertain business, as Hyatt's record attests: in its first 36 years in Newark, the factory was the site of 39 fires and explosions, which caused at least 9 deaths and 39 injuries.[20]

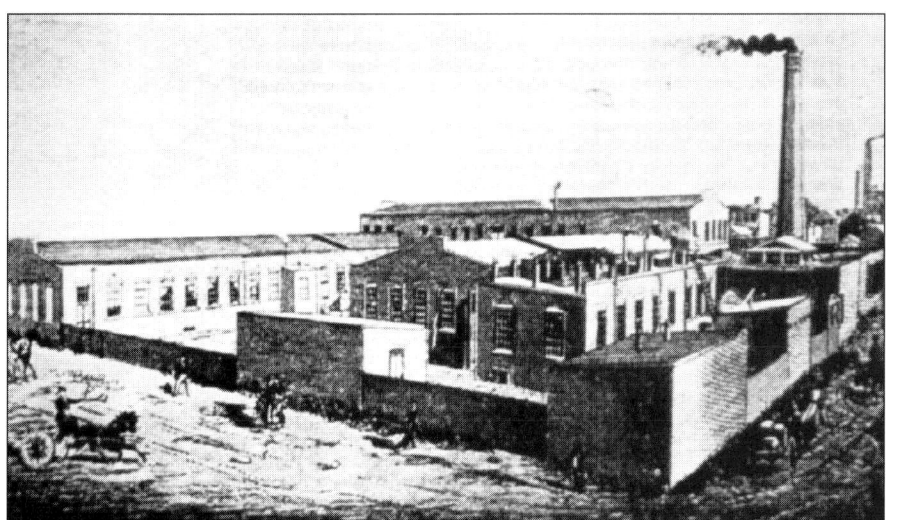

The Celluloid Company factory in New Jersey, about 1870.
Deac Rossell.

In the last quarter of the 19th century, celluloid was identified with cheap goods and imitations of the "real thing". In this respect, Parkes's failed attempts at mass production of a substance with an imperfectly understood chemistry were fully in line with the thinking of his peers: celluloid was an inferior substitute for more

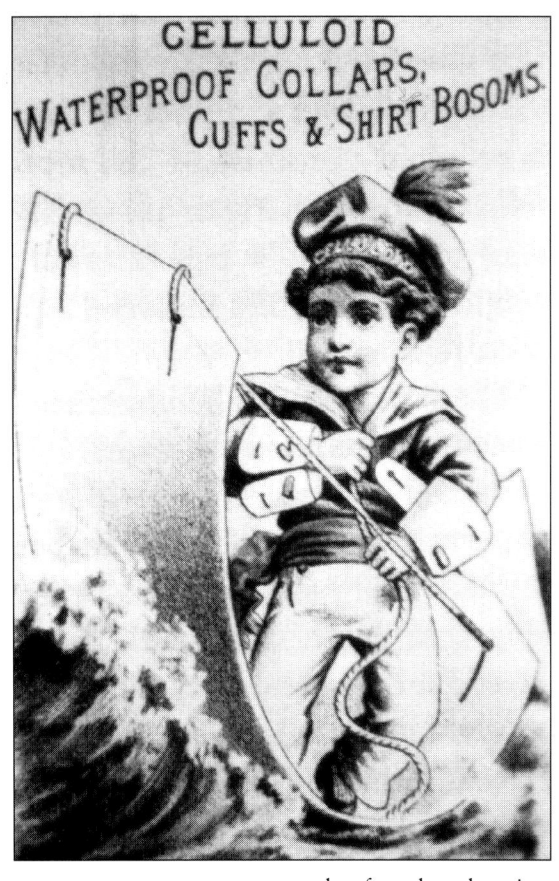

Advertising card for celluloid collars and cuffs, printed by Donaldson Brothers of Five Points, New York City, ca. 1890. Like many such advertisements, this one reflects the waterproof qualities of celluloid.

Deac Rossell.

expensive, more scarce, or more intractable natural materials. Compounding this issue of taste and style, which slowed its acceptance in many areas of manufacture, was celluloid's never-forgotten origin in Schönbein's guncotton. As early as 1875, the *New York Times* ran an editorial piece on the subject of "Explosive Teeth", referring to the propensity of celluloid dentures worn by cigar smokers to ignite.[21] In April 1892, *Scientific American* reported on the celluloid buttons on a dress bursting into flame after its wearer stood for too long near an open fireplace.[22] Yet along with some specialist items and novelties like key rings and soap dishes, two areas of growth opened the doorway to the gradual acceptance of celluloid as a material with its own advantages: its use in shirt collars and cuffs, and in inexpensive toys. With an increasingly urbanized society after 1875, detachable celluloid shirt collars and cuffs became if not quite fashionable (despite the claims of the best advertising campaigns of the era), then at least both practicable and affordable. Troy, New York, became known as "The Collar City", as more than 100 shirt collar and cuff manufacturers supplied the growing ranks of clerks and middle managers in an era of rapidly expanding business. Coated with celluloid, these collars and cuffs were waterproof and required less frequent washing. Celluloid also found a place in toy manufacture, particularly for the heads, hands, and feet of dolls, due to its easily formable qualities.

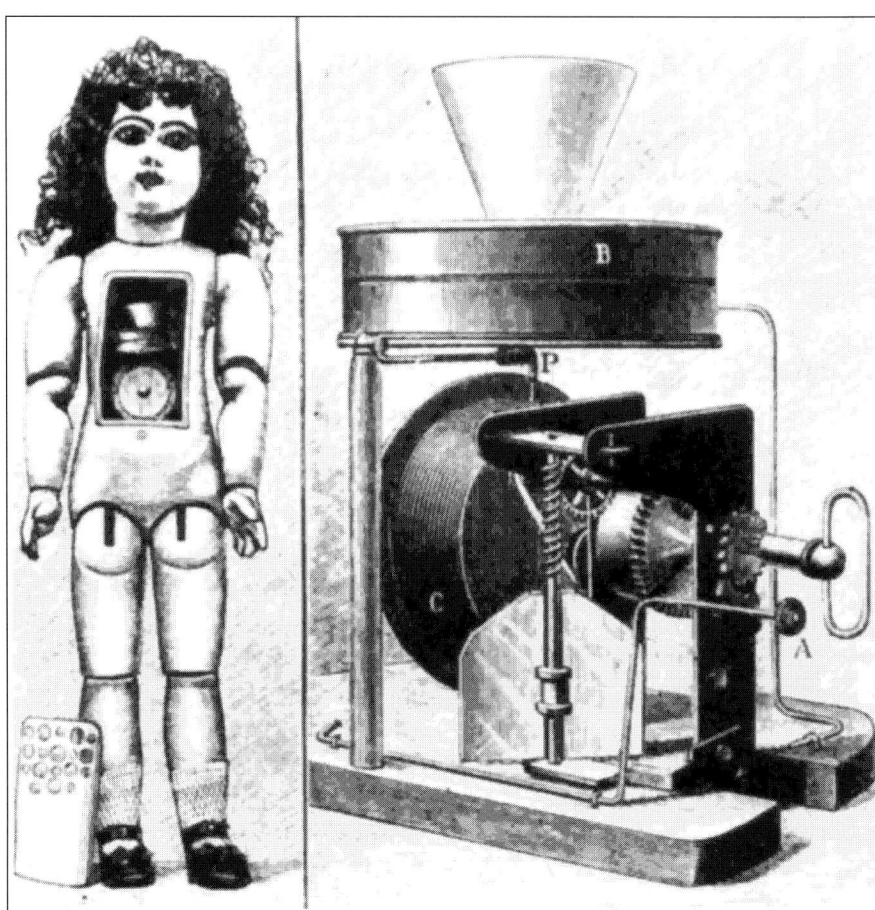

The talking doll of Henri Lioret, which used a celluloid disc recording, 1893.

Deac Rossell.

In 1893 the French inventor Henri Lioret supplied the renowned toy-maker Émile Jumeau with a small celluloid disc recording that provided the voice for a talking doll; in 1897 he used celluloid again in his loud-speaking phonograph, intended for public performances where increased volume was required. His patented process used hot water to temporarily soften the surface of the recording cylinder, which could therefore take grooves of greater amplitude than those it was possible to cut in hard wax cylinders, thereby giving his machine a greater amplification of its recorded sound.[23] His Lioretgraph was frequently used on the Continent to accompany film screenings, where the larger halls demanded greater volume.[24] The exception to these passing fancies, and the major lasting use of celluloid, was in the field of photography.

II. Celluloid in Photography and Early Moving Pictures

The emulsion-coated glass plates used by photographers since the decline of the Daguerreotype had many disadvantages. Heavy and awkward to manipulate in both the camera and the darkroom, they were problematic in the studio, but a genuine burden when travelling in the field. They were breakable, had sharp edges, and required spacious storage facilities. Magic lantern showmen also laboured with the double glass enclosures of their transparencies: several boxes of slides added noticeably to the weight and effort of an evening of entertainment at the town hall or instruction at the church hall. When Alexander Parkes took out a provisional patent in 1856 suggesting the use of his flexible, unbreakable Parkesine as a replacement for the glass plates used by photographers, his foresight was remarkable as he proposed "substituting for the sheets of glass a sheet of collodion of sufficient thickness to support the prepared film; a thick layer of collodion may be first formed on the glass, and on this layer the film of prepared collodion may be produced, and the picture taken thereon and suitably varnished or protected; afterwards the whole may be stripped from the glass together."[25] Daniel Spill also suggested the same use of celluloid at a lecture to the London Photographic Society in 1870, proposing that his xylonite could be "a flexible and structureless substitute for the glass negative supports".[26] In the following years, several photographers experimented briefly with the new material, including the Frenchmen David and Fortier, who in the 1880s formed sheets from liquid celluloid poured onto a heated glass plate and then coated with a gelatine emulsion.[27]

Advertisement for John Carbutt's flexible celluloid photographic films, from the Almanac of the British Journal of Photography, 1889.

Deac Rossell.

But it was not until November 1888 that celluloid became commercially available as a substitute for glass plates, when John Carbutt of the Keystone Dry Plate Company in Philadelphia announced that he was now making emulsion-coated sheets of celluloid for the photographic trade. Carbutt purchased his celluloid from the Hyatts' Celluloid Manufacturing Company, who formed clear celluloid blocks under pressure which they could then slice accurately to a thinness of up to ten one-thousandths of an inch thick on patented machinery.[28] Carbutt's new plates were widely noted in the photographic press, and were advertised for sale in Europe by mail with "no risk of breakage" beginning in 1889.[29]

THE STEREOSCOPIC COMPANY

Are Sole Wholesale Agents for Great Britain for

→ CARBUTT'S ←

NEW TRANSPARENT

FLEXIBLE NEGATIVE FILMS.

THESE FILMS REQUIRE EXACTLY THE SAME TREATMENT AS GLASS.

There are NO extra processes necessary!

Weight almost displaced!

NO stripping required!

NO risk of breakage!

Within a year, the British suppliers E G Wood and William England offered their own celluloid plates, as did others in France, Holland, and Germany, but the photographic profession as a whole was rather slow to adopt them, remaining by the tried-and-true methods of working on glass. In 1888 Walter Poynter Adams proposed an ingenious celluloid film band for use in the magic lantern, where "Gelatin, Algin Compounds and Celluloid are suitable for this purpose".[30] E T Potter made a similar suggestion, proposing a continuous band of celluloid lantern slides moved by a clockwork mechanism.[31] But the real breakthrough for the use of celluloid in photography came with the development of roll-film holders for lightweight and amateur cameras.

As exposure times decreased in the second half of the 19th century through new emulsion chemistry, faster lenses, and improved shutters, photographers began to widen their subjects to include pictures of people and animals in natural settings, and the advanced amateur photographer sought ever lighter and more transportable photographic equipment. From around the 1880s, there was a plethora of devices suggested or sold for "automatically" changing photographic plates inside the camera while it was being carried as a single independent instrument to the beach, the park, or a party.[32]

The lasting solution to the portability of cameras able to take multiple images before being returned to the permanent or travelling darkroom was roll film and the roll-film holder, which had been experimentally used since the 1850s but was popularised by Leon Warnerke after 1875.[33] At first, the extremely popular roll-film system, introduced by George Eastman with his Kodak camera in 1888, used paper backing, which was removed from the negative emulsion by soaking in a water or chemical bath and then stripping the negative from its opaque backing before securing it to glass for development of the image. Because of its success Eastman's developing facilities for this stripping film were overwhelmed, and he immediately began looking for a more efficiently handled substitute for his paper backing. After trying solutions of Irish moss, Japanese isinglass, and seaweed, among many other substances,[34] Eastman turned to celluloid, which because of its transparency did not need to be stripped from the emulsion during developing. Production of Eastman's new celluloid-backed roll film began in August 1889, with a viscous celluloid "dope" flowed across twelve glass tables each 3½ feet wide and 50 feet long. The celluloid was left to dry and harden overnight, and the next day was coated with photographic emulsion. When again dry, the finished film was cut into sheets of various sizes for plate cameras and into strips for roll holders.[35]

Making a suitably thin celluloid sheet, or strip, that could be tightly wound up around the spool of a roll holder required subtle changes in the chemical composition of the material to increase its flexibility. The appropriate solvent for nitrated cellulose in this case was amyl acetate, patented by the chief chemist of the Celluloid

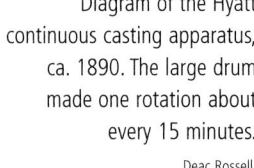

Diagram of the Hyatt continuous casting apparatus, ca. 1890. The large drum made one rotation about every 15 minutes.

Deac Rossell.

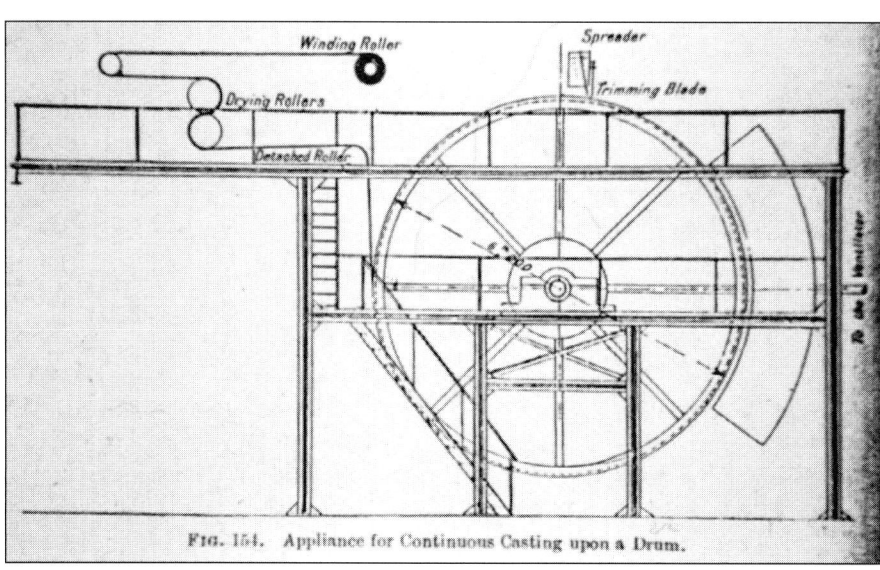

FIG. 154. Appliance for Continuous Casting upon a Drum.

Manufacturing Company, John H Stevens, in the United States in 1882.[36] The first method of producing a very thin clear sheet for roll holders, as distinct from the sliced sheet made by the Celluloid Manufacturing Company that was the basis of Carbutt's photographic celluloid plates, was to flow viscous celluloid over a long glass table, the method used by Eastman but actually first formally noted by the Reverend Hannibal Goodwin, an Episcopalian preacher in Newark, New Jersey, in May 1887.[37] A further production method was introduced by the Celluloid Manufacturing Company in 1891,[38] when they began flowing the celluloid mix over a slowly rotating heated drum about 6 feet in diameter, producing a large sheet of celluloid that they could supply either cut or uncut to many secondary manufacturers for coating with proprietary photographic emulsions.

That said, the production of a clear and flawless sheet of celluloid by any method was something akin to black magic. As one chemist wrote in a thorough study of the celluloid industry in 1894, "We still do not know today to what process the formation of celluloid is to be attributed."[39] All early photographic suppliers were "out of business" for a period in the 1890s when their key personnel (the dope mixer, principally) changed, or when new market demands (for clear instead of translucent films, for example) caused alterations in their manufacturing processes. There were a variety of problems, none easy to solve without causing another problem to spring up as a result of the altered formula. In the first instance, the cellulose mixture had to be impeccably pure, with all un-nitrated fibres removed by filtration and a consistent "mating" of the camphor and cellulose from batch to batch. The consistency of the fluid celluloid needed to be precise, just viscous enough that the material would flow evenly on the glass table but not spill off it; yet it also needed to be dilute enough so that it did not blister or crack or trap bubbles, or show any other imperfection. The photosensitive emulsion was exceedingly difficult to adhere properly to the celluloid base, while the emulsion itself needed to be consistent in its photographic sensitivity; any adjustments or improvements in the photographic qualities of the emulsion also affected its adhesion to the celluloid. In cutting and removing the finished material from the tables, it was also prone to light flares caused by static electricity and other mysterious defects. In use, roll film had a tendency to curl and twist, owing to the different coefficients of expansion between the celluloid backing and the photographic emulsion, posing yet another problem in both its manufacture and its subsequent handling.

In the early 1890s, apart from Eastman's handmade supply of specially cut strips of celluloid roll film to the Edison laboratory for experiments on the evolving Kinetoscope, all work on celluloid films was intended for the still-camera market.[40] Paul Spehr has meticulously documented the process of evolution of Edison's "35mm", or $1\frac{1}{4}$-inch film, and for the first time revealed that for W K-L Dickson and Edison's team in West Orange, as well as for Eastman, the issue of the thickness of the film (which bore on its robustness) was coexistent with the issues of its width and its perforation scheme.[41] But by the middle of 1896 there was clearly a second market for roll film in moving-picture work, and a rapidly expanding market with good returns for participating manufacturers. Now, in fact, the market was growing swiftly across Europe, and Eastman was not particularly aggressive in serving this new market until he was persuaded of its size and profitability by his British manager, George Dickman, in June 1896.[42] The British pioneer filmmaker Birt Acres, for example, complained to the *Amateur Photographer* in October 1897 that the Eastman Photographic Materials Co., Ltd, had earlier told him that it would not be worth their while to manufacture cine-film.[43] In these early days, several companies began to manufacture celluloid films for moving-picture work, although their number was still very limited due to the immense technical (and physical!) problems of dealing with nitrocellulose.

III. Early Suppliers of Moving-Picture Film to 1900

In a field torn with strife over priority, fights which hide varying and often arcane definitions of moving pictures, there can be little doubt that the Eastman Company in Rochester, New York, later the Eastman Kodak Company, was the first supplier of moving-picture negative and positive film, through their relationship with the experiments carried out in the Edison laboratory on the Kinetoscope and the Kinetograph camera.[44]

The other major American supplier of celluloid roll film for still-cameras, and therefore a significant pioneer in supplying early moving-picture customers, both at their experimental and production stages, was the Blair Camera Company of Boston, Massachusetts. This firm, a rapidly assembled agglomeration of small camera, plate, optical, and chemical companies which originated in the Blair Tourograph and Dry Plate Company, founded by Thomas Henry Blair in 1881, and which evolved into the Blair Camera Company, was "the only real competition in the American industry for the market Eastman had created" at the end of the 19th century.[45] With their Hawk-Eye roll camera, Blair thought that they had found a separate line of patents that would not infringe the Kodak patents of Eastman.

Blair bought their celluloid from the Celluloid Manufacturing Company in Newark, persuading them to make a thinner sheet on their continuous casting apparatus than had been their usual practice. Using this source of celluloid had the additional advantage of avoiding the patent fight between Eastman and Goodwin. Blair coated their purchased celluloid base with their own photographic emulsion at the factory of the Allen & Rowell Company of Boston, a manufacturer of photosensitized materials including celluloid plates, in which Blair bought a controlling interest in August 1890, specifically to obtain roll-film production facilities. Blair began commercial production in late 1891,[46] using a different production method from Eastman's glass tables, instead flowing the emulsion over a large heated drum in a continuous process that was similar to the way their celluloid sheets were made in Newark.

The nitrocellulose from the Celluloid Manufacturing Company had a different chemical composition from Eastman's celluloid, which made it slightly translucent; this made Blair film particularly suited for viewing an image by transmitted light, as in the Kinetoscope, and virtually all Kinetoscope positive prints were made on Blair stock from late 1892 through 1895.[47] The Eastman Company provided negative stock for the Kinesigraph camera, although manufacturing troubles between January 1892 and late 1893 meant that Edison had to turn to other sources. Blair's production technology was first-rate; when Eastman bought the Blair Camera Company in 1899, during a low point in their history after they had lost patent infringement lawsuits he initiated over their Hawk-Eye roll film camera, he acquired the patents on their production apparatus and converted his production facilities to continuous casting in early 1900.[48]

By that time, Thomas Henry Blair had left the company he had founded, in a reorganization initiated by his financial backers in early 1893. Blair then immediately went to Britain, where he

The European Blair emulsion coating apparatus, 1894, from French patent 236600. The celluloid band arose on the left from the casting room below, and was coated in the middle tray before being wound up on drying rollers.

Deac Rossell.

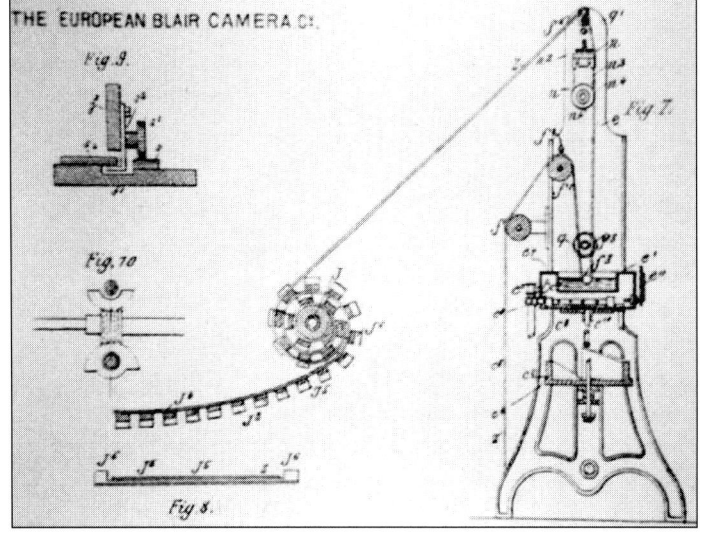

founded a new company, the European Blair Camera Company, in April 1893, partially based on his own patents and American contacts. A Memorandum of Agreement between the new company and the Blair Camera Company of Massachusetts set out the terms under which European Blair would acquire "all the right, title and interest of the Blair Camera Company in and to all letters patent in European countries relating to photography or photographic apparatus...."[49] Blair replicated most of his American firm on European soil, and promptly began the manufacture of celluloid roll film at Foot's Cray, Kent.

European Blair supplied raw nitrocellulose film stock (not always exclusively, as experimenters tried many sources in searching for the best materials) to the first experiments of the Lumière Brothers in France, to Birt Acres and Robert Paul in England, to Oskar Messter in Germany, and to most of the other pioneer inventors and filmmakers in Britain and on the Continent. During 1895, Lumière enquired about bulk orders, or even the possibility of manufacturing Blair stock under license.[50] The Blair agent in Paris, George William de Bedts, who founded the first purely cinematographic company in France, in February 1896, was himself a central figure in early cinema work in 1895–1897, in direct contact with virtually all of the French pioneering figures.[51] With the change from slightly translucent film stock useful for the Kinetoscope to perfectly clear film stock suitable for projection, European Blair changed the formulae for their materials, and again ran into serious problems of adhesion between the emulsion and the celluloid base in 1896 and 1897, but they continued to produce cine-film until they finally ceased operating in 1903.[52]

It is my contention elsewhere[53] that the Lumière experiments in moving pictures were originally intended to bring to the market a kind of inexpensive, adaptable, portable moving-picture "Kodak", based on the business model that George Eastman had found so successful in the late 1880s. If so, then the principal Lumière interest was in providing their customers, on an ongoing basis, with raw film stock and positive prints, after the manner of the Kodak system. The supply of photographic plates and materials was their core business and the source of their profits.

As the Lumière brothers experimented with the Cinématographe during 1895, they asked Victor Planchon to prepare some celluloid sheets with their own emulsion. Planchon, a photographic supplier who had established the first French photographic celluloid plate manufacturing facility in Boulogne-sur-Mer, already had the Lumière company as a customer for his photographic chemicals. Planchon, like Eastman, flowed his celluloid onto large glass sheets and then added the Lumière emulsion; the entire glass sheet, still with the completed film unstripped, was then transported to Lyon for the Lumières to test.[54]

By late 1895, the Lumières and Planchon were contending with the problems that had faced Eastman a few years earlier: difficulties of adhesion between the emulsion and the celluloid base; difficulties of achieving a constant thickness; and difficulties of achieving a consistent mixture from batch to batch. Lumière carefully analysed the Blair stock, and found that it contained about 12% acetanilid; he wrote to Planchon that "it might be an idea to adopt this ingredient, since American film is much tougher than your samples".[55] As they developed the production methods and the precise chemical formulae for moving-picture film, the Lumières launched a new company to mass-produce celluloid films, which included Jules Carpentier and others as investors. Planchon moved his business to Lyon, and by 1903 was managing the Lumières' 50-acre photochemical plant at Feyzin, just outside Lyon.[56]

Lumière was the only major producer of moving-picture celluloid film to enter the market without substantial experience in celluloid still-camera roll film. Although a number of other small suppliers were active before 1900, the specialized technology of working with celluloid was a great barrier to entry into the market, and the production of moving-picture film stock was then, as now, principally in the hands of a limited number of companies. Like the mechanical technology of the cinema, the chemistry of celluloid was also a newly emerging field in the 1890s, and there were many experiments made at the time, although the history of the supply of film stock to early cinema inventors and practitioners is very largely unresearched.

The pioneering firm of John Carbutt in Philadelphia offered cine-film from at least 1896, and by November 1897 it advertised "standard" width film perforated for either Lumière or Edison apparatus, along with "French" 60mm width and "Biograph" 2³/4-inch width, but no substantial work has been done on his moving picture activities.[57] In Germany, the major chemical company Schering produced moving-picture nitrocellulose raw stock in both negative and positive rolls in 1897–98, which had "a somewhat soft base and an irregular cut along the sides.... but the Directors of the well-known firm were at that time short-sighted, and gave up the manufacture of cine-film."[58]

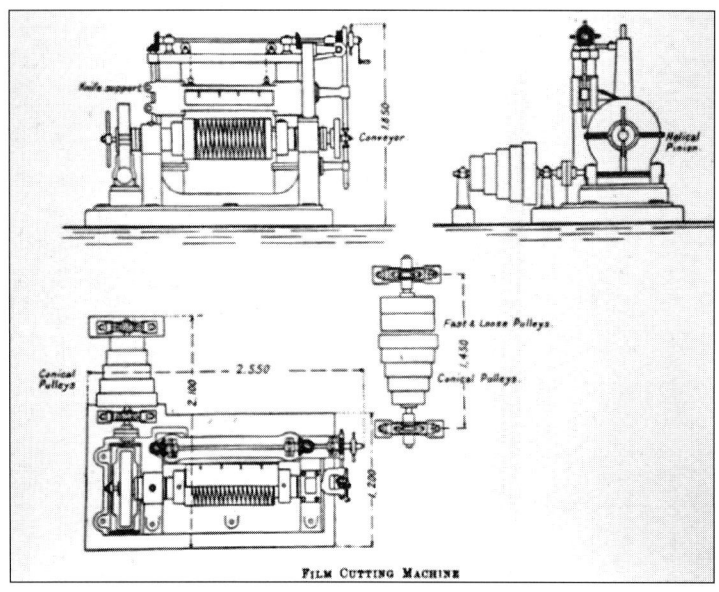

Film cutting apparatus, ca. 1909.

Deac Rossell.

Perhaps the most interesting early supplier, but also the most mysterious, since no work has been done on the firm by either photographic or cinematographic historians, is Dr J H Smith & Co. of Zürich. Smith was an Englishman who undertook part of his chemical studies in Zürich. After working for Mawson & Swan in Newcastle-upon-Tyne, he returned to Zürich to open a dry plate manufacturing company in August 1889.[59] He was offering cine-film to the market at least as early as late 1896, and advertised in March 1897: "As the demand for these films is very large, and we have a number of orders on hand, it is advisable to place all Orders without delay."[60] Smith's expertise in working with celluloid must have been outstanding, for George Eastman hired his chief chemist, William G Stuber, in late 1893, during the period when he was having great troubles in producing consistent celluloid products, and had been "out of business" for over 18 months, running through several chief chemists. Stuber brought with him to Rochester not only the expert knowledge and experience which solved Eastman's production problems, but also, by agreement, Smith's patent for an improved coating machine.[61] Smith and his Continental customers are unresearched, but the firm continued as a respected supplier, moving to Paris in 1908.[62]

Coating, cutting, and sometimes the perforation of prepared celluloid, were undertaken by any number of additional firms at this time, for while the price of raw stock fell sharply over the period 1896-1900, it had started from such astronomical levels that it was still an extremely expensive item on an exhibitor's or filmmaker's expense list, and provided good opportunities for prescient manufacturers. Before 1900 many filmmakers used multiple suppliers of raw stock, perhaps out of necessity or perhaps tracking the "good" batches that reached the market from manufacturers who always struggled to produce a consistent product. Film pioneer Guido Seeber recalled buying raw stock in 1897-98 from Oskar

Messter (who was selling Kodak stock), from Lumière in Lyon, from Philipp Wolff in Berlin (who was probably selling Lumière stock), from European Blair in London, and from Smith in Zürich, along with Schering in Berlin.[63]

The secondary market of manufacturers offering purchased celluloid coated with their own proprietary emulsions is also unresearched territory, but a few firms can be mentioned. In Britain alone, apart from European Blair and Eastman (who produced their own celluloid base), the firms of E H Fitch & Co., Marion & Co., The Reliance Roller Film & Dry Plate Company, and Birt Acres' Northern Photographic Works were supplying coated cine-film in 1897.[64]

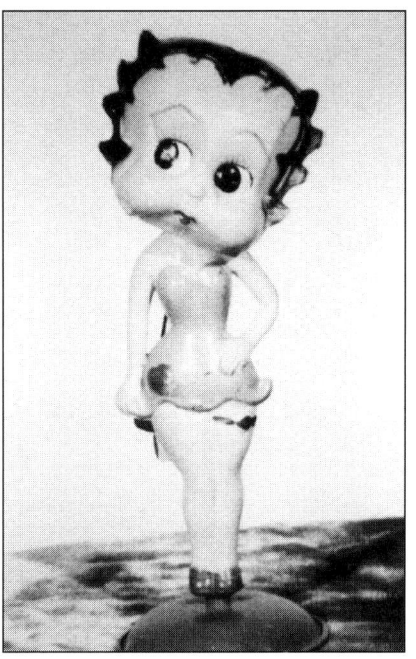

Today, celluloid is principally identified in the public mind with moving pictures, as scores of book titles attest, from *Celluloid Sacrifice* to *Celluloid Weapon* or *Celluloid Dreams*. But the physical material itself long ago lost its economic importance and technical distinctiveness. When the word "celluloid" is used today (including references to the cinema), it is only the *idea* of celluloid that survives, since the material itself is almost never present in the things to which we refer. Archivally preserved nitrate film is one of the few substantial stocks of celluloid that survives, outside a few specialist collections of antique celluloid toys, boxes, and trinkets. Celluloid was the first synthetic plastic, the first practical material from a new chemical industry, which would later develop Bakelite in the 1920s and acetate and polymer plastics in the next decades. Plastics would come to represent for many – symbolised by a young Dustin Hoffman in *The Graduate* (1967) – an all-pervasive aspect of the modern world. Not only does celluloid remain an important metaphor for the movies, conjuring up a world of imitations, hopes, and aspirations, but nitrate film also remains fixed in the public consciousness as the most dangerous aspect of the first decades of moving pictures.

Celluloid Betty Boop doll, late 1920s.

Deac Rossell.

Acknowledgements

This work is dedicated to Katharine Stone White, a member of the original staff of the Film Library at the Museum of Modern Art and the founder of film programmes at the Worcester Art Museum and the Museum of Fine Arts, Boston, where she was my predecessor and mentor for many years. For help with the content of this article I again thank generous colleagues with whom the exchange of information and opinion has been invaluable, including Stephen Bottomore, Thomas Ganz, Colin Harding, Michael Harvey, Stephen Herbert, Martin Loiperdinger, Susan Mossman, and Paul Spehr.

Notes

1 Pyroxyline came to be a synonym for crude cellulose hexa-nitrate, or guncotton. As a material, it retained the form and appearance of cotton. Xyloidine in later years lost its exact definition, but survived in altered form. Daniel Spill called his material xylonite, which was then used in the name of the major British manufacturer, the British Xylonite Company, Ltd. The name "celluloid" was first applied to pyroxyline plastics by Isaiah Smith Hyatt in the 1870s. The Hyatt brothers trademarked this name in the United States, and it was legally used only by their companies, leaving their American competitors to go back to variants of pyroxyline or xyloidine.

2 In some versions of this story, Schönbein had been prohibited by his wife from conducting experiments in her kitchen, and grabbed at the cotton apron in a panic at the thought of being discovered. In other versions, he could not find a mop, and used the nearest cloth, the cotton apron. In either case, this was not so much the case of an "accidental discovery", but rather an accident which produced an odd result – the smokelessly burning apron, a result which the good scientist then explored methodically in his laboratory.

3   Georg W A Kahlbaum and Francis V Darbishire, eds., *The Letters of Faraday and Schönbein* (Basle/London: Williams & Norgate, 1899), p. 153.

4   Ibid., p. 155.

5   Schönbein's other discovery was the allotropic form of oxygen (O_3), which he discovered again by following his curiosity: this time, of the odd smell that lingered around electrical apparatus. He named his discovery after the Greek word for smell (*ozon*), ozone.

6   John Taylor [agent for Christian Frederick Schönbein], *Improvements in the Manufacture of Explosive Compounds*. UK Patent 11,407 of 1846; filed 8 October 1846, issued 8 April 1847. Christian Frederick Schönbein, *Improvement in the Preparation of Cotton-Wool and Other Substances as Substitutes for Gun-Powder*. US Patent 4,874; issued 5 December 1846.

7   Schönbein's guncotton was finally tamed by Frederick Abel and James Dewar towards the end of the century, and was in use for many years as cordite, or Poudre B.

8   Collodion is made from weakly-nitrated cellulose (less than 10%) diluted with a 1-to-1 mixture of alcohol and ether.

9   James A Cutting, *An Improved Process of Taking Photographic Pictures upon Glass, and also of Beautifying and Preserving the Same*. UK Patent 1638 of 1854; filed 26 July 1854.

10   Frederick Scott Archer, *Certain Improvements in Photography*. UK Patent 1914 of 1855; filed 24 August 1855.

11   Parkes's 1862 exhibition materials survive, the oldest known celluloid objects, in the collections of the Science Museum, London. They include buttons, medallions, a letter opener, pill cases, and other objects that were either pressed from moulds or hand-carved.

12   Robert Friedel, *Pioneer Plastic: The Making and Selling of Celluloid* (Madison: University of Wisconsin Press, 1983), p. 8.

13   While the story of Parkes's failed attempt to exploit Parkesine is noted in several film histories, it is important to point out that Parkes was a prolific inventor, who lived entirely from the sale of rights to his more than 60 patents in metallurgy, electroplating, and organic chemistry. He invented a process of desilverizing lead that was widely used long into the 20th century, as well as methods for making seamless tubes and printing rollers. "More fortunate than many inventors," one biographer wrote, "this life of intellectual adventure never reduced him to penury" (J B Goldsmith, *Alexander Parkes, Parkesine, Xylonite and Celluloid*. 1922 manuscript, in the British Library, London; p. 36). Parkes was unsuccessful in launching his celluloid plastic as a marketable substance, as he tried to mass-produce the new material using the cheapest cotton remnants available, which contained many impurities, such as husks and pieces of wire. Due to these impurities and Parkes's imprecise understanding of the chemistry of making the new material, the quality of Parkesine varied widely from batch to batch. He failed in his attempts to make imitation ivory and pearl goods, including knife handles, earrings, piano keys, pens, buttons, combs, and all sorts of inexpensive consumer goods, as well as in his attempts to develop industrial uses such as insulating material for electrical wires and telegraph poles, gear wheels, and various components of spinning machinery. Parkes returned to the metals industry after 1868, but new research shows that he took up work on Parkesine and celluloid plastics again in 1881, after his original patents had expired, founding the London Celluloid Company with his brother Henry. This second company was also unsuccessful. See S T I Mossman, "Parkesine and Celluloid", in: S T I Mossman and P J T Morris, eds., *The Development of Plastics* (Cambridge: Royal Society of Chemistry, 1994), pp. 9–25.

14   Daniel Spill had originally come to Parkes to negotiate a contract for the use of Parkesine to improve the waterproof properties of textiles produced at his brother's factory. Spill patented many solvents for the nitric acid/cellulose reaction, including the one that turned out to be the most important solvent, camphor, and also re-patented several of Parkes's original solvents and ideas, causing Parkes, at one point in the lengthy American court proceedings, to testify against his former manager. Spill's long court battle most likely dissuaded some potential manufacturers of the new material from entering the field, at least in America, an inhibition on the rapid development of the material which was later parallelled by the long-drawn-out litigation between Hannibal S Goodwin (and his heirs) and George Eastman over the production of celluloid roll film.

15   Hyatt's original experiments were encouraged by a prize of $10,000 offered by the Phelan & Collender company in New York for patent rights in any suitable substitute for ivory in the manufacture of billiard balls, and his first celluloid-related patent was for a collodion/celluloid billiard ball (John W Hyatt, Jr., *Improved Method of Making Solid Collodion*. US Patent 91,341; issued 15 June 1869). Parkes had taken out a British patent for billiard balls made of Parkesine in 1868.

16   John Wesley Hyatt, speech on accepting the Perkin Medal; in *Journal of Industrial and Engineering Chemistry*, v.6 (1914), pp. 158–9.

17   Friedel, op. cit., p. 15.

18   There is a curious compliment to the commercial success of the Hyatts in a note made by Alexander Parkes in 1881: "I believe that the American Celluloid company [sic] have greatly extended and forced this manufacture, and by their spirit and Ability have created a large and

Profitable business in the United States," Parkes wrote, continuing, "but this manufacture only commenced long after I established the original works in London about the year 1864 or 5...." See S T I Mossman, "Parkesine and Celluloid", op. cit., (n.12), p. 21. I am indebted to Susan Mossman for referring me to this article.

19 Friedel, op. cit., pp. 56–58.

20 Ibid., p. 96. A number of other companies began to manufacture celluloid in the 1870s and 1880s, but by 1890 the only serious competitor to the Celluloid Manufacturing Company in the American market was the Arlington Manufacturing Company of Arlington, New Jersey, making a product they called "pyralin". Arlington was prominent in supplying celluloid collars and cuffs, and was taken over in 1915 by E I Du Pont de Nemours and Company. See Friedel, op. cit., pp. 68–70.

21 The *New York Times* (16 Sept 1875), p. 4. Stories of cigar smokers casually igniting celluloid must have been widespread as an urban legend at the time, for its physical possibility is hotly denied in Fr. Böckmann's 1894 *Das Celluloid, seine Rohmaterialien, Fabrikation, Eigenschaften und technische Verwendung* (Zweite, gänzlich umgearbeitete Auflage; Wien/Pest/Leipzig: A. Hartleben's Verlag, 1894), pp. 5–6.

22 *Scientific American* 66 (1892), p. 208.

23 V K Chew, *Talking Machines* (London: Her Majesty's Stationery Office [Science Museum, London], 1981), pp. 61–62.

24 Many early film showings were either accompanied by gramophone performances or were combined with them, with the gramophone playing between films while the operator changed pictures. Although patented by Thomas Alva Edison in 1877, his phonograph (and those of other inventors) only went into widespread public use in 1895–96, after the failure of attempts to rent it to business customers as a dictating machine. So recorded sound reproduced by the phonograph was a public entertainment novelty just as moving pictures were born, and the combination of the two new devices was a common entertainment presentation. Sufficient amplification of sound for these performances was always a problem, and several manufacturers introduced special models for use in public exhibitions: Edison produced a duplex phonograph in 1896 using two large horns; the Columbia Phonograph Company issued an instrument with three horns and soundboxes in 1900, and with four of each in 1904. For brief descriptions, see V K Chew, op. cit., pp. 62–66.

25 Alexander Parkes, Provisional UK Patent 1123 of 1856; not issued. Parkes abandoned the patent. Parkes's suggestion is not so far away from the famous stripping film of George Eastman that made a success of his Kodak camera system.

26 Friedel, op. cit., p. 91.

27 Colin Harding, "Celluloid and Photography: Part One – Celluloid as a Substitute for Glass", in *Photographica World*, no.75 (December 1995), p. 23.

28 John W Hyatt, Jr., *Method of and Means for Holding Celluloid and Dividing It into Sheets*. US Patent 301,995; filed 10 June 1884. The cutting process inevitably left minuscule grooves in the surface of the celluloid, which as a result was not perfectly clear and degraded slightly its photographic quality in relation to glass.

29 Advertisement, *British Journal Photographic Almanac* (1889), p. 845.

30 Walter Poynter Adams, *Improvements in Magic Lantern Slides and Apparatus in Connection Therewith*. UK Patent 16,785 of 1888; filed 19 November 1888.

31 E T Potter, Provisional UK Patent 14,171 of 1888; filed 2 October 1888. Abandoned, not issued.

32 See, for example, Arthur S Newman's bag changer of 1886, which allowed the hand-manipulation of multiple plates without removing the plate holder from the back of the camera; the falling–plate cameras of E V Swindon of 1887 and the Lumière "Automatique" camera of 1890, both of which held multiple plates vertically for exposure, which then fell to the bottom of the camera case and stacked horizontally; or Krügener's Simplex camera of 1893, where cut films interleaved by a zigzag paper band were drawn around the corner of the camera back after exposure and stacked in the top of its case. Many other types of multiple plate holders and mechanisms were brought to the market; see Brian Coe, *Cameras. From Daguerreotypes to Instant Pictures* (Gothenburg: Nordbok, 1978), Chapter 6.

33 Early roll holders were suggested by Joseph Blakey Spencer and Arthur James Melhuish in 1854, and by Humbert de Molard and J H Barr in 1855. Some used strips of calotype paper pasted together, others a silk band or black calico with the sensitive paper pasted to it. For a detailed history of both these early experiments and the introduction of mass-market roll-holder cameras by Eastman and others, see Brian Coe, op. cit., Chapters 7 and 8.

34 Reese V Jenkins, *Images and Enterprise. Technology and the American Photographic Industry, 1839–1925.* (Baltimore/London: The Johns Hopkins University Press, 1975), p. 127.

35 Demand for celluloid roll film was initially very high, and by June 1891 Eastman had a new facility making film on 12 plate glass tables, each 200 feet long. To supply European customers,

who initially got one-third of the Rochester production, a new Eastman factory was opened at Wealdstone, just outside London, which made 960 linear feet of film a day on 12 glass tables 80 feet long and 42 inches wide. Good surveys of Eastman's production are in Jenkins, op. cit., pp. 122–133. and Harding, "Celluloid and Photography. Part Two – The Development of Celluloid Rollfilm", in *Photographica World*, no.76 (March 1996), pp. 34–36.

36 John H Stevens, *Manufacture of Compounds of Pyroxyline or Nitro-cellulose*. US Patent 269,340; filed 12 June 1882.

37 When Eastman and his chief chemist Harry M Reichenbach applied for their two patents on the method and the material, the patent examiner noted that the applications by Eastman and Reichenbach interfered with each other, and that both interfered with Goodwin; the subsequent patent battle lasted from 1889 until 1914, over a decade after Goodwin's death. Goodwin's heirs won the case, aided substantially by the photographic wholesalers Anthony and Scoville (later Ansco), who bought up Goodwin's rights and his small Goodwin Film & Camera Company from his heirs. For the year and a half remaining on Goodwin's patent, Eastman paid GF&CC $5 million for a license; other smaller infringing manufacturers paid just over $300,000. Like Edison's use of his broadly written patents to harass other filmmakers in the same period, this case shaped the later history of the manufacture of celluloid roll film for both still-camera and movie use, inhibiting substantial investment in its manufacture by companies not a party to the fight. For the entire story of this case, see Jenkins, op. cit., pp. 125–30, 146–47, 156–58, 248–51, 332–35. The patents are: George Eastman, *Improvements in Flexible Photographic Film*. US Patent 306,284; filed 9 April 1889. Harry M Reichenbach, *Manufacture of Flexible Photographic Films*. US Patent 417,202; filed 9 April 1889. Hannibal Williston Goodwin, *Photographic Pellicule and Process of Producing Same*. US Patent 610,861; filed 3 May 1887, issued 13 September 1898.

38 J H Stevens and M C Lefferts, *Process of Manufacturing Pyroxyline Sheets*. US Patent 600,824; issued 15 March 1898. John H Stevens was the long-standing principal chemist in Newark, and Marshall C Lefferts was the son of the Celluloid Manufacturing Company's director and later president of the company himself. Although they applied for their patent on an improved continuous casting apparatus in 1891, the conversion of Newark production in that year is very likely the result of the Celluloid Manufacturing Company's purchase of the small American Xylonite Company of North Adams, Massachusetts, formed in 1882 to exploit Daniel Spill's patents in America; they used a continuous casting apparatus designed by Mowbray which considerably reduced the cost of manufacture. See Fr. Böckmann, op. cit., (n.21), pp. 36–43.

39 Dr. Fr. Böckmann, op. cit., (n.21), p. 47. Böckmann's book, first published in 1891, was a standard work with at least six editions through 1920, an English translation of the 3rd edition in 1907, and a later English edition in 1921.

40 The hugely increased amateur photography market that followed the introduction of the Kodak system had yet another effect on the manufacture of celluloid, since celluloid covers for photograph albums and standing celluloid photograph frames, often elaborately decorated, became a popular addition to many households. For samples of these, see Joan Van Patten and Elmer & Peggy Williams, *Celluloid Treasures of the Victorian Era* (Paducah, Kentucky: Collector Books, 1999), especially pp. 64–127.

41 See Paul Spehr, "Unaltered to Date: Developing 35mm Film", in John Fullerton and Astrid Soderbergh Widding, eds., *Moving Images: From Edison to the Webcam* (Sydney: John Libby Co., 2000). It is interesting to note that probably no pioneering cinema inventor other than the renowned Thomas Alva Edison had the standing to engage such individual attention from another outstanding and market-leading firm whose supplies, and the alterations in them, were so important to the evolution of his work. Although there were relationships between some inventors and some suppliers, the most prominent being between the Lumières and Victor Planchon, other pioneers, like William Friese Greene, Robert Paul, Max Skladanowsky, Oskar Messter, Henri Joly, Léon Gaumont, the Lathams, or Jenkins & Armat, just did not have the standing or the access to technologically leading firms to replicate the kind of remarkable collaboration that Spehr documents between the Edison laboratory and the Eastman factory.

42 I am indebted to Paul Spehr for this comment (e-mailed letter, Paul Spehr to Deac Rossell, 9 May 2000). Dickman was evidently passing up orders for moving-picture celluloid, especially from France, and pressured Eastman into focusing on this new market. In part, Spehr relates, Eastman also saw a threat that Blair could use his extensive supply of cine-film as a lever to begin competing against the Kodak in the at-the-time more profitable still-camera roll-film market.

43 Letter by Birt Acres, *The Amateur Photographer* (1 October 1897), p. 277.

44 Again, I recommend here Paul Spehr's precise account of the work between Edison and Eastman. There was some "pre-cinema" use of celluloid films or transparencies by the chronophotographers. Étienne-Jules Marey began using paper-backed roll film in October 1888, changing over to celluloid strips obtained from Georges Balagny in 1890. Ottomar Anschütz was using celluloid transparencies in his Schnellseher automat manufactured by Siemens & Halske by 1892, which drastically reduced the centrifugal forces on his spinning disc, although he probably used glass-plate picture carriers in his earlier models.

45 Jenkins, op. cit., p. 134.

46 Jenkins, op. cit., p. 138.

47 Charles Musser, *The Emergence of Cinema. The American Screen to 1907* (New York: Charles Scribner's Sons, 1990), pp. 72, 81. In the Kinetoscope, the moving film was illuminated from underneath the band, with the viewer's eyes above the band, necessitating a slight diffusion of the light across the film frame.

48 Jenkins, op. cit., p. 181.

49 Public Record Office (London), BT31/5568/38433, Ref 6406, *Agreement between Thomas Henry Blair and the European Blair Camera Company*, p. 1.

50 Letter by Louis Lumière to Fuerst Brothers, London, 19 November 1895, in Jacques Rittaud-Hutinet, ed., *Letters. Auguste and Louis Lumière* (London/Boston: Faber & Faber, 1995), pp. 47–48.

51 On the interesting career of de Bedts, see Laurent Mannoni, "George William de Bedts et la commercialisation de la chronophotographie", in Lagny, Marie, Gili, and Pinel, eds., *Les vingt premières années du cinéma français* (AFRHC,1995).

52 Charles Urban was a shareholder of the European Blair Camera Company from ca.1900, and it is likely that he used European Blair as a major source of film stock for his expanding film-making and distribution business. When European Blair closed in July 1903, the Whetstone Photographic Works of Birt Acres, his successor firm to the Northern Photographic Works, picked up some of the European Blair business, including that of Maguire & Baucus, Ltd.

53 See Deac Rossell, *Living Pictures. The Origins of the Movies* (Albany: State University of New York Press, 1998), pp. 133–39, or Deac Rossell, "Die soziale Konstruktion früher technischer Systeme der Filmprojektion", in *KINtop*, no.8 (1999), pp. 53–82, especially pp. 71–75.

54 Rittaud-Hutinet, op. cit., pp. 39–43.

55 Rittaud-Hutinet, op. cit., pp. 86–87.

56 It is my view that the very late public demonstration of the Cinématographe, on 28 December 1895, which happened, as is well known, at the urging of Antoine Lumière, is a consequence of the difficulties of achieving production of celluloid film stock: Auguste and Louis wanted to have the complete commercial system ready before they publicly demonstrated their hardware.

57 Advertisement in *The Phonogram* (November 1897), p. 9. "Standard" width film sold for 5 cents per foot unperforated, the Demenÿ "French" 60mm width for 9 cents per foot, and the Biograph for 10 cents per foot. Perforated film was 1 cent per foot more. I am indebted to Paul Spehr for this information. The inclusion of "Biograph width" stock is particularly interesting, since at this time the Biograph apparatus was not for sale but was installed under contract in leading variety theatres. It is a fair assumption that the American Mutoscope and Biograph Company was one of Carbutt's customers, and that this advertisement was just written up without really thinking through that no potential customer could order raw film for a Biograph camera other than AM&B itself. By exclusively using still-camera roll film, which was cheaper than "cine" film (and which Eastman complained about bitterly, trying to get Biograph to order their special moving picture film), Biograph ensured that its supply of raw stock could come from several manufacturers, and not be cut off as a consequence of their patent fights with Edison. See Deac Rossell, "The Biograph Large-Format Technology", in Luke Mckernan and Mark van den Tempel, eds., *Griffithiana*, special issue (Pordenone, 2001).

58 Guido Seeber, "Die ersten Jahre...", in *Filmtechnik*, Nr.18 (1927), p. 329. The firm Aktien-Gesellschaft für Anilin-Fabrikation (Agfa) only began making celluloid film for moving pictures in 1906.

59 René Perret, *Frappante Ähnlichkeit* (Brugg: BEA & Poly-Verlags Ag, 1991), p. 100. My thanks to Thomas Ganz for this reference.

60 *The Photographic Dealer* (March 1897), p.ix. My thanks to Colin Harding for this information.

61 Jenkins, op. cit., p. 154.

62 Perret, op. cit., p. 100. Smith's high reputation was particularly in the field of quality dry plates and photographic paper; he also experimented at length with colour photographic processes. In 1897 he designed and manufactured his own novel cinematographic apparatus, with which he filmed, among other subjects, Queen Victoria's Diamond Jubilee celebrations in London.

63 Guido Seeber, op. cit., p. 329.

64 John Barnes, *The Rise of the Cinema in Great Britain* (London: Bishopsgate Press, 1983), p. 25. Fitch & Co. were described in 1897 as "the well-known pioneers of celluloid films in this country", and may have been making their own celluloid. Additionally, Philipp Wolff had an office in London to supply the British market, as did Dr J H Smith, while Lumière was represented by Fuerst Brothers and had as their customers Robert Paul, Cecil Hepworth, George Cricks, and Charles Urban. See Colin Harding, "Celluloid and Photography. Part Three – The Beginnings of Cinema", in *Photographica World*, no.77 (June 1996), p. 11.

From the Nitrate Experience to New Film Preservation Strategies

By Jean-Louis Bigourdan

Introduction

It made history and then almost disappeared, but, in fact, nitrate film is still around. Historically, nitrate film is closely associated with the early cinema, and, for more than half of a century, it had a part in its development as a growing industry and art form.[1-7] The cellulose nitrate plastic made motion-picture film possible by providing a strong and transparent flexible support on which a photographic emulsion could be coated. In the late 1880s it became possible to manufacture a sufficient length of photographic film to make possible the analysis and recomposition of movement on a screen, thus inaugurating photographic moving images. In other words, the manufacturing procedure developed in 1889 by the Eastman Company launched a series of technical innovations that led to a changing film technology. This continuing evolution of film has altered not only the way motion-picture films are made but also the way our cinema heritage has been preserved and should be preserved in the future. From the beginning, film archivists have faced a variety of problems associated with film preservation. Dealing with highly flammable nitrate film base, witnessing the decomposition of nitrate, observing the spread of the so-called "vinegar syndrome" in acetate collections, and discovering faded color prints in their vaults, are all common experiences for archivists.

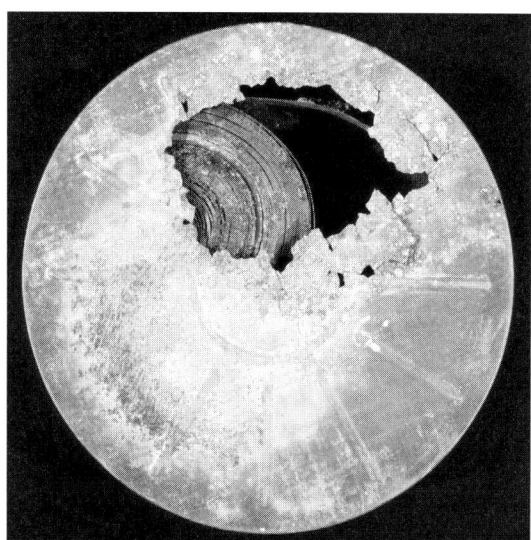

Decaying nitrate base causes further decay.

Image Permanence Institute, Rochester, NY.

Nitrate base was a predominant component of photographic film for more than fifty years, and its properties shaped an enduring idea of what film preservation should be. Until recently, nitrate represented a dreaded and impossible task for film archivists. It was looked upon as an unwanted material – one to be eradicated from the film archive world. Nitrate films were lost in fires, discarded, destroyed for silver recovery, removed from archives, and allowed to deteriorate due both to their inherent chemical instability and improper storage.[8] However, nitrate films in excellent condition constitute an invaluable portion of a number of collections, and demonstrate by their presence that nitrate film base can last for a long time. The nitrate films in archives today are older than most acetate base films. Film stability studies conducted in the 1990s confirmed the fact that, while the stability of nitrate can vary widely from one film to another, nitrate base film can achieve extended life expectancy.[9] Things have changed since the early 1950s, when motion-picture film manufacturers stopped using nitrate base and replaced it with cellulose triacetate base. Experience has been gained in collection management, large film stability studies have been conducted, and new techniques have emerged in recent years, which have led to the development of new preservation strategies. In many ways, the nitrate experience brought us to film preservation as it is today. Perhaps surprisingly, nitrate film challenges the stability of triacetate base film, which was once believed to be a more stable material than nitrate, but which today is known to be a major threat to film collections.

The main thrust of this paper is to review the properties of nitrate film base, look at the evolution of film preservation strategy, and articulate a strategy for controlling the spontaneous decay of nitrate and acetate motion-picture film collections. Today, preserving film in its original form is still a challenging task that requires prioritized strategies, and that has its undeniable costs. The nitrate experience has helped us to better define a strategy that has no other purpose than to attempt to preserve inherently unstable materials. The main steps in such a strategy are to define the key decisions to be made in controlling film decay and to suggest practical ways of extending the life expectancy of photographic film. From nitrate to polyester base, from black-and-white to today's color materials, film is subject to spontaneous chemical decay. New strategies emphasize the need for optimizing storage conditions, evaluating the state of preservation of film collections, and prioritizing duplication.

Photographic Film: Its Nature and Stability

There is an undeniable connection between a film's structure and how it should be kept for the long term. The nature of the components of a photographic film determines the intrinsic stability of that film. Film is composed of three generic components: a plastic support, an image-forming material, and a binder. Several different supports have been used over the years to manufacture motion-picture film, including nitrate, acetate, and polyester base.[6,10,11] Black-and-white images are formed by metallic silver particles, and color images are made of color dyes. Gelatin has been the undisputed binder of choice for photographic film. Although photographic film is subject to mechanical and biological decay, chemical deterioration constitutes the greatest threat to film collections: nitrate and acetate base decompose over time, color dyes fade, and silver particles corrode. While film stability depends upon intrinsic factors, such as the nature of film components, studies have demonstrated that extrinsic factors, such as the quality of the storage environment (i.e., temperature and humidity), are keys to optimizing film stability.

Film Supports: From Nitrate to Polyester

While photographic emulsion was evolving, a variety of film supports was being used in the manufacture of photographic film.[6,10,11] Only a few of these have played a significant role in the production of motion-picture stock (see Table I). These film supports can be grouped into two categories: cellulose esters (nitrate, diacetate, mixed esters, and triacetate), which are produced by chemical treatment of cellulose, and polyesters, which are obtained through the polycondensation process.

Manufacturers ultimately replaced nitrate base with triacetate, a product of the esterification of cellulose with a mixture of acetic acid, acetic anhydride, and a catalyst such as sulfuric acid. Prior to this, however, manufacturers used diacetate to produce a substandard motion-picture film for the amateur market in the early 1920s.[4] Diacetate was, in fact, partially hydrolyzed (degraded) triacetate, which had the advantage of being soluble in common solvents, a property that was essential for casting the film base. Diacetate was extremely prone to shrinkage, however, and was an unsatisfactory option for film base. The use of propionic acid or butyric acid instead of acetic acid to modify the cellulose led to the production of two mixed esters, acetate propionate and acetate butyrate, respectively. These two played a significant role in film manufacture. In the 1930s, acetate propionate was used to manufacture amateur movie film. It was only in the late 1940s that a suitable solvent for triacetate became available in commercial quantities and at a competitive price. This was the decisive step towards the industrial production of triacetate, which became an acceptable substitute for the nitrate base being used for professional motion-picture film.[12] The manufacture of nitrate film base was discontinued in the 1950s.[6,13]

In 1955, the introduction of polyester polyethylene terephthalate (PET) marked a major advance in film technology.[14] First used in a number of applications that required high dimensional stability, polyester base did not immediately gain favor as a motion-picture film support, partly because it could not be manufactured by solvent casting, as other types of film supports were. All cellulose esters were cast by adding the appropriate solvent and plasticizers to the polymer. Similar casting machines were used to produce both nitrate and triacetate base. Polyester is insoluble in common solvents, and the film base is formed by melt extrusion.[6,11,15]

As a result of the changing technology of film manufacture, motion-picture collections today are composed of films on nitrate, acetate, or polyester base. "Acetate" is a generic term that covers diacetate, acetate propionate, acetate butyrate, and triacetate base.

Table I: Film supports used to manufacture motion-picture film

Film Base	When Introduced	Major Uses
Cellulose nitrate	1889	Film base for professional motion-picture film until the 1950s.
Cellulose diacetate	1920s	Used to launch home-movies market.
Cellulose acetate propionate	1930s	Used for amateur movie film.
Cellulose acetate butyrate	1930s	Used mostly for sheet film.
Cellulose triacetate	1948	Replaced nitrate film base in the 1950s. Still used for most camera negatives.
Polyester	1955	Increasingly used for motion-picture film since the 1990s (e.g., print films, intermediate films).

Nitrate Film Base: Properties and Stability

Nitrate and Acetate Share Similarities

Nitrate, like acetate, is modified cellulose. The preparation of nitrate results in the grafting of nitrate groups onto the cellulose chain, or nitration. Acetate involves acetylation rather than nitration. Both film supports are manufactured through a similar procedure. Nitrate and acetate are prepared by chemical treatment of cotton linters. The process involved in this transformation is fundamentally the same in both cases (esterification of cellulose), although the reactants are different. The chemical transformation is obtained by the action on the cellulose chains of nitric acid for nitrate and a mixture of acetic acid and acetic anhydride for acetate, in the presence of a catalyst such as sulfuric acid. Nitrate and acetate film supports are also manufactured by the same procedure of solvent casting. After spreading the polymers mixed with adequate solvents and plasticizers on a polished surface, a transparent film is obtained after curing. Nitrate and acetate are cellulose esters. Their physical properties depend upon the polymer structure and composition of the plastic, and both materials can be expected to have similar chemical behavior.

Nitrate Properties

Nitrate film is highly flammable as compared to acetate base, which is a slow-burning material. Early investigations into replacements for nitrate base go back to the 1900s.[3,6] The first replacement, diacetate base film, was produced before the 1920s.[3,4,11] Because of nitrate's extreme flammability, the home-movie formats launched in the early 1920s and theatrical features for large audiences in Europe were put on acetate support (so-called "safety" base). Numerous disasters were caused by the use of nitrate for theatrical releases.[16] The flammability of nitrate had a direct impact on handling procedures, transportation and use regulations, vault conception, and cabinet and can design. Many of the same principles are still in place today.[17–20] Although slow-burning but unstable film bases like diacetate were replaced by mixed esters (acetate propionate and acetate butyrate) in the late 1930s, nitrate base persisted as the best choice for professional motion-picture film format until the early 1950s. Nitrate base had excellent physical properties that suited the technical requirements of the entertainment industry.[11,12,21] In terms of mechanical properties (tensile strength, toughness, flexibility, and tear strength), only the high-acetyl film base introduced in the late 1940s became a satisfactory nitrate substitute for the manufacture of standard motion-picture film.[12]

Nitrate Chemical Decay

Nitrate is modified cellulose obtained by nitration. By nature, this modified cellulose has the tendency to "unmodify" itself and return to its native form by releasing the side-groups grafted onto the side of the chain. Heat, moisture, and acid promote these chemical changes back toward unmodified cellulose. Heat accelerates chemical reactions. Moisture is the reactant that supports hydrolytic mechanisms. Acid is a catalyst of the chemical reactions involved in nitrate base decay, and, notably, acids are produced during the degradation process. As a result, nitrate chemical decay is autocatalytic. In addition to denitration, cellulose nitrate is subject to chain scission, which causes physical property changes, embrittlement, and decomposition of the film support.[22,23] Stability studies have recognized that both nitrate and acetate film base decay through similar chemical processes.[9] This can be explained by their similar nature. Both polymers are cellulose esters, i.e., their chemical structure makes them part of the same family of compounds. As a result, the chemical stability of both nitrate and acetate film is governed by the same extrinsic factors: heat and humidity. Recent stability studies have indicated that both materials also can achieve similar longevity.[9] Signs of decay, however, can manifest themselves in different ways. Nitrate decay can manifest itself by amber discoloration, image fading, softening of the emulsion, odor, and brownish powder. Five stages of decay, proposed by Calhoun, provided an empirical way to evaluate the condition of nitrate film.[13,20] They also provided clues that differentiate nitrate from acetate.

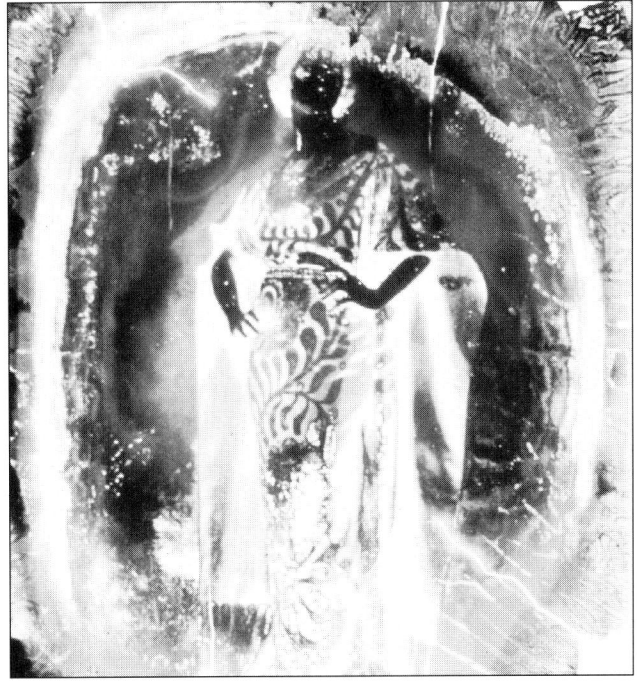

Decaying nitrate film generates oxidizing degeneration byproducts that cause silver oxidation.

Image Permanence Institute, Rochester, NY.

Silver oxidation is common in degrading nitrate, while it is unusual in acetate film. Degrading nitrate produces oxidizing compounds (nitrogen oxides) that oxidize the image-forming material of black-and-white film (metallic silver).[24] Acetate degradation byproducts are not oxidizing components and do not readily promote

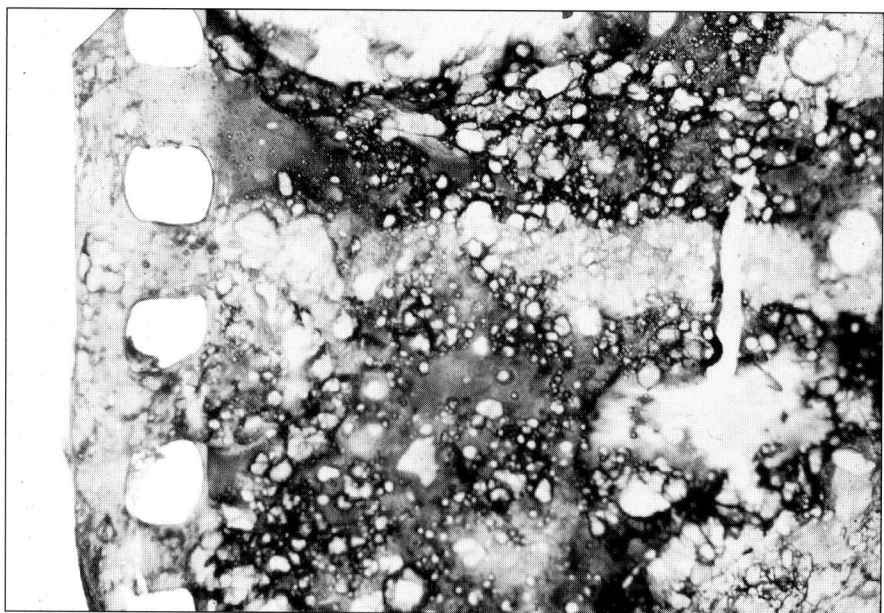

Decaying nitrate releases strong acids that decompose gelatin binder.

Image Permanence Institute, Rochester, NY.

silver attack. Combined with moisture, nitrogen oxides released by the decaying nitrate produce strong acids (e.g., nitric acid). These acids catalyze further base decay and cause hydrolysis that decomposes the gelatin binder. Once nitrate film starts to decay, further deterioration proceeds at a fast pace and the image layer can rapidly become soft and sticky. The acetate decay process generates weak acids (e.g., acetic acid) that also catalyze further decay but have a "milder" effect on the gelatin.

Preserving Nitrate Film

Film Preservation Strategy in the 1930s and 1940s

After the evolution of the entertainment industry in the 1930s, the recognition of the cultural value of motion-picture films and the increasing use of photographic film as an archival information-recording medium stimulated interest in film permanence. This interest, in turn, resulted in the development of film preservation strategies.[25–29] Because of the nature of nitrate film, attention was directed primarily at finding ways and equipment to deal with flammable materials. The literature of that time reflects progress made in vault and cabinet construction, and can design, with the ultimate goal of limiting losses in case of fire disasters. Cool storage temperatures (around 15°C) and what we would today consider high humidity levels, 60% to 70% RH, were common recommendations at that time. Periodic inspection was also recommended, so that new prints could be produced when the existing ones were found to be in poor condition. These recommendations inaugurated a strategy based on good handling practices, climate control, inspection, and reprinting as needed. The only drawback was that nothing could replace damaged original negatives, and the existing recommendations for climate control were not stringent enough to guarantee long film life. During the 1930s, a twelve-point program for preservation was articulated.[28] The plan included a number of domains to be explored, such as the effects of various parameters on film longevity (e.g., climate storage conditions, processing, can design, enclosure materials, light, and film specifications for archival purposes) and the search for more stable film materials. It was during the same period that early studies on film base stability were conducted. These studies focused on the comparison between nitrate base and the new acetate supports being developed at that time.[30] Several of these avenues of research have been and continue to be reconsidered by film archives, industry, and research initiatives. The main components for establishing an effective film preservation strategy were emerging as early as the 1930s. Storage conditions, film inspection, and duplication were all part of the approach. The definite answer, however, could not have been articulated at that time.

Preserving Nitrate Film Perceived as a Lost Cause

The introduction of cellulose triacetate film base in 1948 marked an important step in the manufacturing of photographic film. The new cellulose triacetate film support provided a slow-burning material, and also one considered to be more stable than the flammable nitrate base.[12] Triacetate film base is now known to be an inherently unstable plastic, as prone to spontaneous chemical decay as nitrate. However, this long-awaited substitute for nitrate film initiated a strategy based largely on photographic duplication techniques. In theory, any nitrate film could be duplicated onto safety film, resulting in a desirable copy that would limit the risks associated with fire and which would be more stable. This new possibility led to extensive and costly duplication programs conducted in major archives, and, to some extent, it allowed the prioritization of duplication initiatives based on the state of preservation of the originals. Film condition tests were developed to achieve this task.[31] This situation led to an approach that was unique at that time: duplication onto acetate base as the key to film preservation. In the late 1960s, such statements as "nitrate films are unstable and should be eliminated as rapidly as possible,"[32] and "since nitrate is inherently unstable, and would eventually have to be copied, effort should be concentrated on a testing and copying program, rather than on full air-conditioning to extract the maximum life out of nitrate copies,"[33] were commonplace. This indicates that the field had given up on nitrate film and that stringent storage conditions were not perceived as a possible approach to the prevention of further losses. Nitrate films, in some ways, were expected to vanish. In other words, preventing the decay of nitrate films was seen as a lost cause.

New Acetate Film Base: an Incomplete Answer for Film Preservation

Past decades have demonstrated that preserving our film heritage does not end with the copying of unstable nitrate films on triacetate film stock. Although this has been the rule for years, and many archives have spent considerable funds on copying their nitrate film collections, studies have indicated that nitrate and acetate in fact may be similarly unstable.[9] Despite the fact that triacetate film base decay was observed as early as the mid-1950s in film stored under adverse conditions, this behavior was only perceived as a major threat in the 1980s. Evidence of vinegar syndrome has been a growing issue for film archives during the past two decades. During that period, film archivists have been faced with the problem of the vulnerability of photographic film manifested as damage caused by vinegar syndrome, which is due to spontaneous chemical decay. Despite the fact that vinegar syndrome has been recognized for some time as a critical threat to film collections, film archivists may be facing an even greater preservation challenge than expected. Acetate base film represents the bulk of the film kept in collections today. The entertainment industry has produced a tremendous amount of motion-picture film on triacetate base stock since the 1950s; and it is only in recent years that polyester base has played a significant role in motion-picture film manufacture. Evidence of severe acetate deterioration in archives worldwide demonstrates that transferring nitrate onto safety film was an incomplete response to film preservation. Recent stability studies, however, have indicated that proper storage conditions can improve the stability of both nitrate and acetate film by a significant degree. During the past fifteen years, large film stability studies have been conducted that indicated ways to deal with chemically unstable materials such as photographic film. Duplicating nitrate film and providing optimum storage conditions may have been the complete response to prevent further challenges for film archivists.

Film Base Stability Studies

The importance of chemical stability prompted an early comparative study of nitrate and acetate film supports using accelerated ageing. Data reported by Hill and Weber in 1936, obtained at a high incubation temperature (100°C) and under relatively dry conditions, concluded that nitrate base had poor stability in comparison with acetate base.[30] Later studies would demonstrate that high-temperature test conditions might produce misleading results and that humidity is an important factor in the investigation of film stability. This early study, however, did pioneer a new field devoted to film stability studies. Over the years, a predictive approach was developed through further studies of the stability of cellulose acetate film base and polyester film base.[34,35] In the late 1980s and 1990s, the threat of vinegar syndrome prompted a number of investigations worldwide, and nitrate chemical stability was revisited during that same period.

Nitrate Base Film Can Last

The evidence of nitrate chemical instability is indisputable. However, quantitative data have been reported which illustrate that not all nitrate base films are inherently unstable. Using an Arrhenius prediction model, Adelstein et al. reported data that indicated that the predicted life span of a nitrate base film at 20°C, 50% RH was of the same order of magnitude as that of the acetate films that were studied.[36] This observation led to a larger stability study conducted on nitrate film samples at the Image Permanence Institute (IPI). Data developed during this research program established that the good stability determined for nitrate film in the earlier study was not an aberration.[9,36] While the predicted life of nitrate film at 20°C varies widely from one sample to another (from 50 to 600 years for two 1932 motion-picture films), nitrate film that was stable in the 1990s can be expected to have a life span many times longer than cellulose triacetate film base. This observation was fully documented in the IPI study and is important to the further preservation of nitrate film. Data reported by Adelstein et al. quantified the effect of temperature and humidity on the remaining life span of nitrate films.[9]

Figure 1 illustrates the effect of temperature on the rate of nitrate deterioration. Acidity increase over time reflects the progress of decay. Like acetate degradation, nitrate decay is autocatalytic, and the rate is strongly temperature dependent. Once started, nitrate degradation proceeds at an ever-faster pace. The rate of nitrate decay is also very dependent on humidity. Water is a reactant in the decomposition process. Figure 2 illustrates the marked benefit on nitrate stability of a humidity level lower than 50% RH. At 80°C, data showed that nitrate samples incubated at 20% and 35% RH degraded at a significantly slower rate than at 50% RH. The benefit of lower RH is reflected by the slower acidity increase in the nitrate base. Data such as those reported in Figures 1 and 2 allowed extrapolating the remaining life span of the nitrate samples tested.

Tables II and III report some of the results published by Adelstein et al.[9] Table II indicates that low initial film acidity correlates with the highest extrapolated life span determined by accelerated ageing. Although a film's original acidity may be partly a consequence of the manufacturing process, it is primarily a result of the

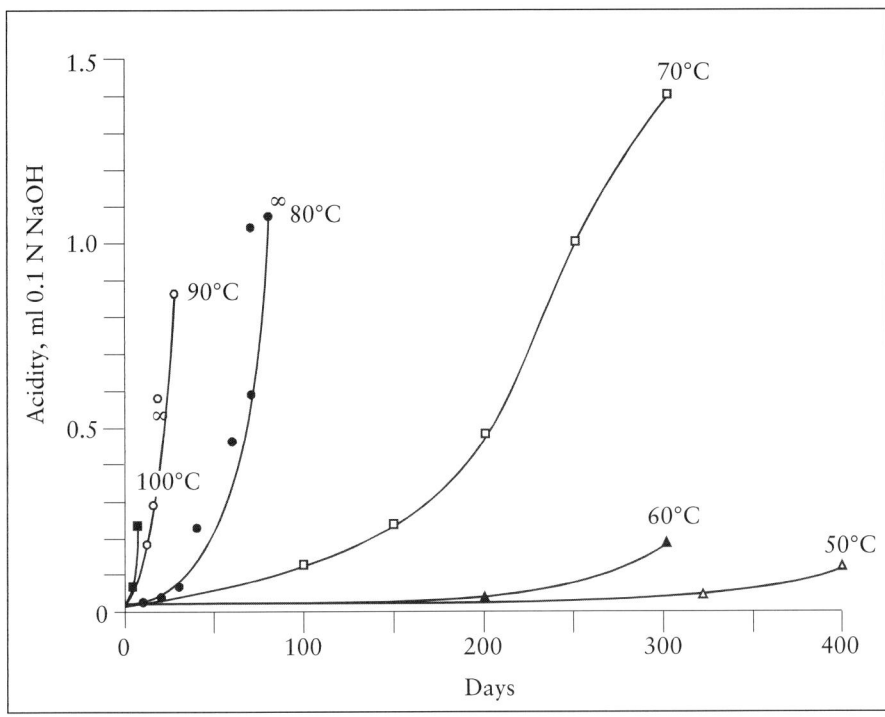

Figure 1. Effect of temperature on acidity increase of 1932 motion-picture film on DuPont cellulose nitrate base. Film preconditioned to 21°C, 50% RH and heated in sealed bags. Data from Adelstein et al.[9]

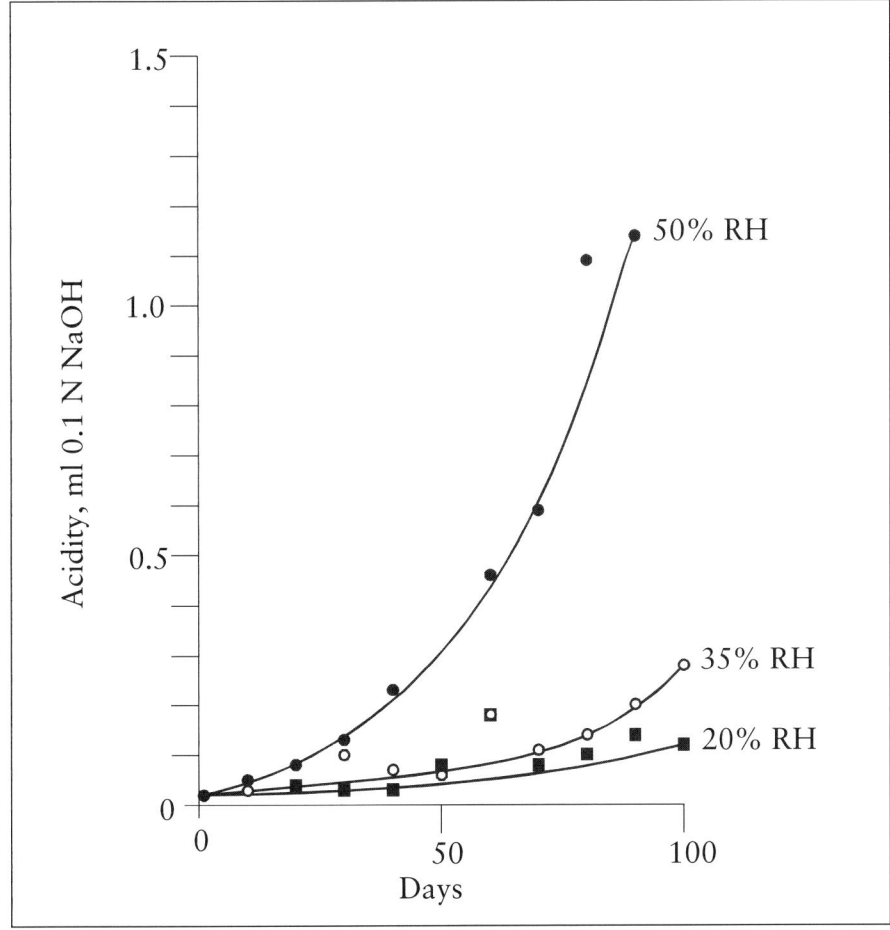

Figure 2. Effect of relative humidity on acidity increase of 1932 motion-picture film on DuPont cellulose nitrate base. Film preconditioned to 21°C and indicated RH and incubated at 80°C in sealed bags. Data from Adelstein et al.[9]

current condition of the film. Data in Table II indicate that higher original acidity (i.e., acidity prior to incubation) led to shorter extrapolated life. This is consistent with the fact that already decaying film will have a shorter useful life. Table II suggests that a direct measure of nitrate film acidity, without incubation, is a good indicator of nitrate film stability. This idea has been further explored by testing naturally aged nitrate films. IPI received 44 films from several archives to be tested for acidity and tensile properties. Results indicated that many film specimens from the 1920s and 1930s still retained good physical properties and displayed low acidity levels. Laboratory testing also indicated that nitrate films may display relatively high acidity levels while still retaining their tensile properties.[9] Table III indicates the effect of RH levels on extrapolated life span for several nitrate films. Low humidity has a marked effect on nitrate base stability.

To conclude, the data reported by Adelstein et al.[9] provides a new, positive view of nitrate stability. The study confirmed the experience of those working in the field: nitrate films can remain in good condition for an extended period of time. It recognized the relationship between current film acidity and the remaining useful life of the nitrate materials and confirmed that the measure of film acidity is the first indicator of decay for nitrate film. Finally, the data developed during the study demonstrated the impact of storage conditions on nitrate stability – information with important implications for the future of nitrate film collections.

Table II: *Stability of motion picture nitrate films. Extrapolated life based on accelerated ageing (acidity end point: 0.5). Acidity value expressed in ml 0.1M NaOH/gram of film. Data from Adelstein et al.*[9]

Film Material			Extrapolated Life (Years at 20°C, 50% RH)
Approx. Year of Manufacture	Film Manufacturer	Original Acidity Value	
1941	Kodak	0.05	100
1932	Kodak	0.09	50
1932	DuPont	0.02	600
1933	Kodak	0.02	500

Table III: *Effect of relative humidity on stability of nitrate film. Extrapolated life based on accelerated ageing (acidity end point: 0.5). Data from Adelstein et al.*[9]

Film Material		Extrapolated Life (Years at 20°C, 50% RH)		
Approximate Year of Manufacture	Film Manufacturer	20% RH	35% RH	50% RH
1930s	Kodak	350	400	–
1941	Kodak		130	100
1932	Kodak	300	–	50
1932	DuPont	>2000	–	600
1933	Kodak	>2000	>2000	500

Preserving Nitrate Film Today

The nitrate stability studies discussed above legitimate a preservation strategy based upon (1) environmental control, (2) condition assessment, and (3) a prioritized duplication program rather than item-by-item duplication of entire collections and eventual elimination of original nitrate materials.

Current guidelines for long-term storage of nitrate base film recommend cold temperature and low humidity (2°C with 20% to 30% RH).[37] Even lower (subfreezing) temperatures could be considered to stabilize already decayed nitrate film. This recommendation is key to the postponement of the chemical decay of nitrate (as well as other organic materials) and is consistent with recent studies. It differs considerably from earlier approaches, which suggested cool storage temperatures and higher humidity levels (e.g., 15°C, 60% RH). It is expected that nitrate films still in good condition today will keep for an extended period of time in cold storage, lasting longer, perhaps, than triacetate base film.

Nitrate base is subject to slow chemical changes that reduce its useful life. Since the degradation is autocatalytic, it is critical to identify the first signs of decay as early as possible. Once the process of decay has started, and under inadequate storage conditions, the condition of nitrate film can change dramatically in a short period of time. This situation represents the risk of material losses. Condition evaluation through periodic inspection has been the rule for nitrate collections. Unfortunately, non-destructive and easy-to-use survey tools for nitrate collections have not yet been developed. Standard recommendations suggest the examination of the silver image and measurement of the degree of decay using the alizarin red test method.[37] The latter requires a test film sample, as do the acidity laboratory tests used in IPI studies.[38] However, as indicated by the study results discussed above, acidity measurement has proven to be a good way to predict the remaining life of nitrate. The development of acid-detector strips for nitrate base (equivalent to A–D Strips for acetate base) would be an important step toward this end and a useful contribution to the field. Quantifying the extent of nitrate deterioration would help to set preservation priorities, among which are improving the quality of storage conditions and initiating duplication programs based on film condition. Although major archives may have already duplicated most of their nitrate holdings, this strategy would benefit many institutions by ensuring a longer life for the nitrate originals.

Beyond Nitrate Film: Today's Preservation Challenges

Fifty years after the replacement of nitrate by triacetate film base, motion-picture film archives are facing other challenges. All types of photographic film by nature undergo slow chemical changes that can greatly reduce their life span, presenting film archivists with the growing problem of ageing and degrading collections. Today it is likely that vinegar syndrome and color dye fading affect most archives.[39] Triacetate base film's inherent instability is widely recognized. To date, no technological advance in film manufacture has entirely solved the problem of film permanence. Neither has the increasing use of polyester film minimized the archivist's current challenge, because cinema collections still contain large quantities of film on triacetate base. Furthermore, polyester, which is the most stable film base,[34,35] is often associated with color dyes as the image-forming material, and while color dye stability has been improved, dyes will still fade under inappropriate storage conditions.[39,40] Film stability studies have shown us, however, that the task of extending the life span of photographic film can be addressed by focusing efforts on extrinsic factors and developing environment-based preservation strategies. Experimental data obtained under both accelerated and natural ageing conditions have demonstrated that implementing proper storage can control chemical decay and will benefit all films in a collection.

Half a century after the introduction of triacetate base most archives are confronting the problem of vinegar syndrome. This critical situation exists partly because acetate base is chemically unstable and partly because, despite tremendous efforts, an environment-based preservation strategy involving optimized climate conditions was not recommended soon enough and therefore has not been implemented on a large scale. Although photographic film is also subject to biological and mechanical decay, the control of chemical decay is recognized today as the key to future access to our film heritage.

Heat and Humidity Govern Chemical Degradation

Temperature and relative humidity (RH) are extrinsic factors that affect film stability. The chemical reactions involved in film base decay and color dye fading are hydrolytic in nature, which means that they need water as a reactant. Consequently, if more water is available, as it is in high-humidity conditions, more chemical changes will be promoted. Heat provides the energy to make the chemical changes happen. Therefore, higher temperatures induce faster chemical changes.

The impact of temperature and humidity on film stability has been consistently emphasized in the literature on this subject. Back in the 1960s, after early dye stability studies demonstrated the importance of using cold storage temperatures to prevent dye fading, low storage temperatures began to be used.[32,41,42] Color dyes and acetate base are similar in terms of instability. Both photographic components are chemically altered under inappropriate climate conditions. Recent studies have quantified the effect of temperature and RH on color dye dark stability and acetate base stability. The data have been presented in easy-to-use form in two publications written by James M Reilly: the *Storage Guide for Photographic Color Materials*,[40] and the *IPI Storage Guide for Acetate Film*.[43] These data sets are of great importance, because they provide a quantitative estimate of the impact of a wide range of temperatures, RHs, and their combinations on color dye and acetate base stability. In practice, temperature and RH determine the life span of photographic film. Proper control of these two conditions can greatly improve the chemical stability of acetate film support and color dyes. Although the effect of temperature and RH is synergistic (i.e., the benefits of lower temperatures and lower RHs are cumulative), lower temperature provides the greater benefit. These conclusions have been integrated into the revised ANSI and ISO standard recommendations for storage of photographic film.[44,45] These two documents recommend three maximum storage temperatures associated with three RH ranges for extended-term storage conditions (see Table IV). The extended-term conditions are those necessary for freshly processed photographic film to achieve a life span of 500 years.

Table IV: Temperature and RH conditions recommended for extended-term storage of black-and-white and color photographic film in ANSI/PIMA IT9.11–1998 and ISO 18911 standards.[44,45]

Image	Base	Maximum Temperature	Maximum RH Range
Black-and-white (silver)	Triacetate	2°C 5°C 7°C	20%–50% 20%–40% 20%–30%
Color (chromogenic)	Triacetate Polyester	–10°C –3°C 2°C	20%–50% 20%–40% 20%–30%

Controlling Vinegar Syndrome

One reason that acetate base decay is such a critical issue is that photographic film on triacetate base represents the major portion of motion-picture film collections.

Another is that evidence shows that vinegar syndrome is a growing problem in the film archive community. Stability studies on acetate conducted during the past fifteen years have established that acetate base stability is dependent on storage conditions, that the degradation process is autocatalytic, and that it is infectious.[46] Recent studies have helped to clarify the usefulness of the various options that are available to collection managers.[46,47] Controlled macroclimate, enclosure choice, use of sealed microenvironments, and control of infectious behavior all have a place in preserving acetate film collections. However, some of these choices are better than others in postponing film decay. While the proper choice of enclosures will provide some limited benefit to film stability, the implementation of appropriate storage conditions will provide a great benefit. The use of adsorbents (e.g., molecular sieves) in sealed microenvironments may improve the stability of already decaying acetate film by a factor of 3 to 4, depending on the quantity added, but cold temperatures would improve it by a much greater factor. The impact of these choices is summarized in Table V.

Table V: Keys to the control of vinegar syndrome

Macroclimate Control	1. Macroclimate control has much greater potential for stability improvement if low temperatures are used. Cold or subfreezing temperatures provide maximum longevity. 2. The effect of temperature and RH on film base stability has been quantified. 3. Low storage temperatures can extend the useful life of acetate base film by a factor of 100, even for film that has already started to decay.
Unsealed or Open Enclosures	1. Open film enclosures are the best housing alternative. Tight or sealed enclosures have been shown to be detrimental. 2. The use of open enclosures does not stabilize or decrease the acid content of already decaying acetate base film. 3. Enclosures do not provide a definitive method of vinegar syndrome control.
Sealed Enclosures (Microenvironments)	1. Sealed enclosures used in conjunction with moisture pre-conditioning at low RH or with moisture and acid adsorbents (e.g., molecular sieves) can extend the longevity of acetate film base by a factor of 3 to 4. 2. Improvements in film stability can be expected to be smaller from microenvironments than from macroclimate control. 3. The benefit of microenvironments is added to that of storage at low temperatures.
Control of Infectious Behavior	1. The presence of already degrading acetate base film introduces the risk of contamination and increasing rate of decay to non-degraded films in the same storage area. 2. The issue could be addressed either by segregating actively decaying film or by controlling the concentration of degradation by-products in the storage area through the use of an air filtration system.

The acidity of a film reflects its condition or state of preservation. A high acidity level indicates a film in an advanced state of decay. Figure 3 illustrates the pattern of the rate of acetate base decay. The acidity increase over time depicts the advance of chemical decay.

During the decay process, acetyl side-groups become detached from the polymer chain and, combined with water, produce acetic acid at the core of the film base. This acetic acid, in turn, further accelerates the deacetylation process of the polymer by playing the role of catalyst. Once it has started, the degradation of acetate base proceeds at an ever-increasing rate, as shown in Figure 3. The two segments of the curve characterize the change of acid content in the base. Segment 1 represents an induction period of slow change, and Segment 2 represents a period of fast change beyond the so-called "autocatalytic point". Thus, it can be said that the internal acidity of the film

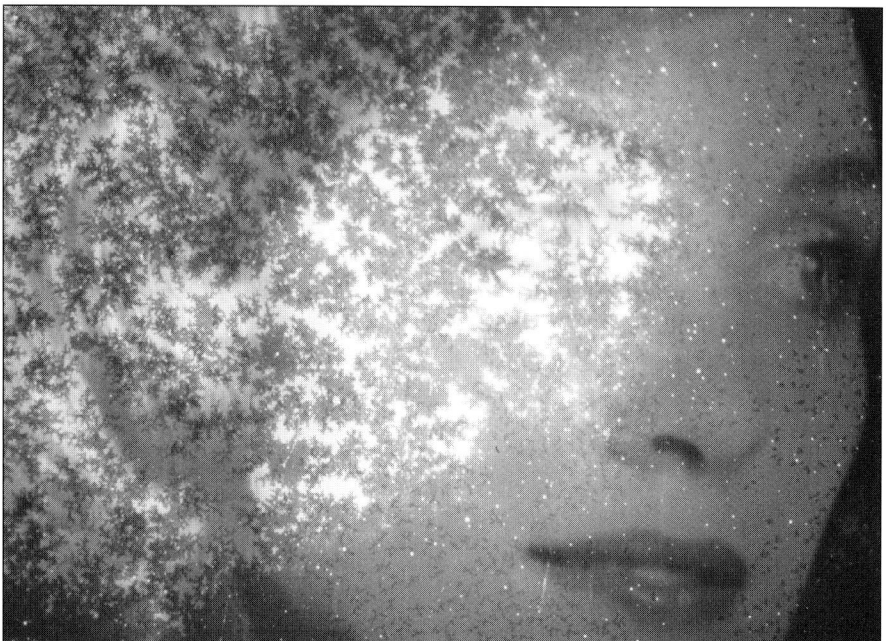

Acetate base decay. Plasticizer exudation and deposits in crystal form on 35mm motion-picture film.

Image Permanence Institute, Rochester, NY.

determines the degree of probability that the film will become unusable because of shrinkage, physical deformation, or plasticizer exudation. This also means that more stringent environmental controls will be required to slow the rate of decay for film materials that have already started to be affected by vinegar syndrome.

Figure 3:   Acidity in the film reflects the rate of acetate decay. Acidity level is expressed in ml of 0.1M NaOH/gram of film.

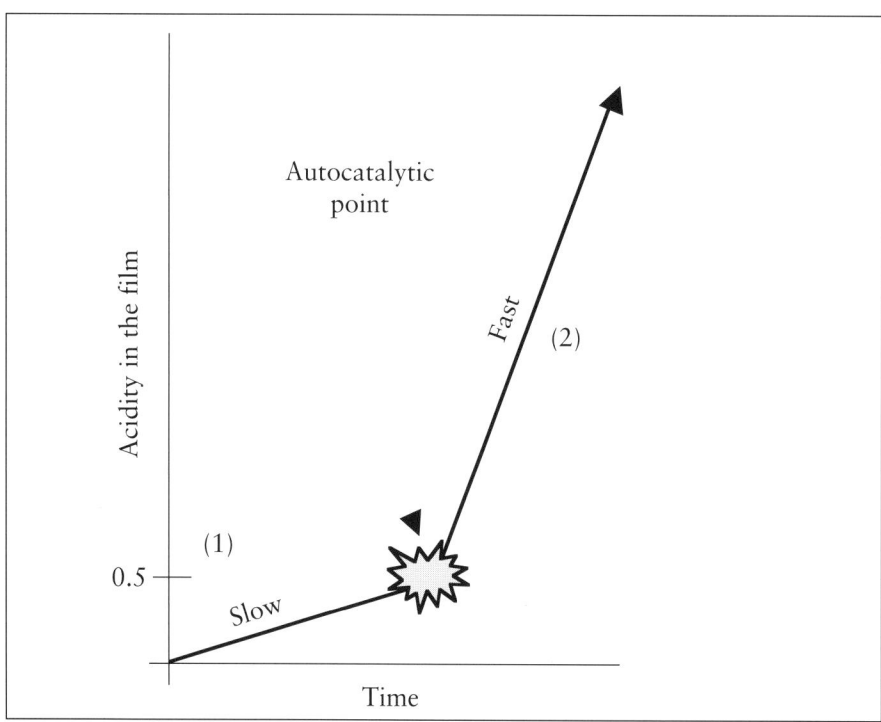

Although film acidity can be determined by laboratory testing,[38] which is a current practice in film studies, easy-to-use, non-destructive survey tools (e.g., IPI's A–D Strips) have been developed to quantify the advance of vinegar syndrome throughout collections. In the hands of collection managers, the knowledge gained and the tools developed through stability studies can help to shape film preservation strategies based on the risk assessment approach.

Controlling Vinegar Syndrome: A Risk Assessment Approach

Film stability studies have made it possible to articulate a preservation strategy based on risk evaluation. These studies have shown that both storage conditions and film condition can be used to predict a film's remaining useful life and to determine the most efficient way to extend its life expectancy.

A strategic plan can be drawn up that will achieve maximum life expectancy, or at least a reasonable life expectancy, for a given material. Maximum life expectancy can be achieved only by implementing cold storage. However, a reasonable life expectancy may be achieved by making small improvements in climate conditions. In either case, the first tasks for film archivists are to assess the *quality of the current storage environment* and to evaluate the *condition* of their acetate film collections. By thus quantifying the existing situation, they will be able to plan the required improvements and prioritize such decisions as acquiring new storage facilities or optimizing existing ones. They could also initiate a duplication program based on the condition of the films. To help archivists choose the most fitting, effective, and economical strategy from among several possible alternatives for controlling vinegar syndrome in their own real-life situations, an action plan has been proposed and a step-by-step methodology has been presented in table form in an earlier paper.[48,49] The approach focuses on controlling storage conditions and further decay.

Controlling the Storage Conditions

It is well known that preservation of photographic film is more cost-effective than restoration, and, furthermore, restoration is frequently impossible. The only way to protect film from chemical decay is to control its storage conditions. The assessment of existing storage conditions provides the basis for optimization. Maximum longevity for both film base and color dyes is obtained through storage at subfreezing temperatures. The macroenvironmental approach using low temperatures can extend the useful life of acetate base film by a factor of 100, even for film that has already started to degrade.[43,47] This is the best approach for preserving either old or new film materials. ANSI[44] and ISO[45] recommendations have been given in Table IV; planners should view these recommendations as targets for storage improvements or define the required conditions to achieve their own preservation goals. The *IPI Storage Guide for Acetate Film*[43] and IPI's *Preservation Calculator*[50] are tools that can provide a quantitative estimate of the impact of climate conditions on film life expectancy, and conversely, determine the required storage conditions to achieve the needs of the institution in terms of longevity. However, first optimizing existing storage and planning for optimum storage in the future may be the most feasible approach for many archives. In whatever way it is achieved, good storage for photographic film collections is clearly needed, the sooner the better.

Better storage can be accomplished by control of either the macroenvironment or the microenvironment. Film archivists must decide which approach is the most suitable for their institution, with respect to equipment expenditure, maintenance, accessibility, and labor cost. Table VI summarizes the impact of three basic decisions on acetate stability that archivists have to make in practice: Is macroenvironmental control the most effective alternative? How effective is the microenvironmental approach? What is the best enclosure choice? The ratings presented in Table VI are the result of acetate stability studies[43,47] and provide guidelines for selecting the best-fit option for achieving optimum longevity. In summary, enclosures play a *secondary* role in controlling vinegar syndrome. Any beneficial impact provided by a given enclosure can be cancelled by bad climate conditions or dramatically amplified by good climate conditions. Likewise, any detrimental impact can be amplified by bad conditions or minimized by good conditions. Controlling the macroenvironment and using cold temperatures provide the greatest film stability and most cost-effective storage option.

Table VI: Role of enclosures, microenvironments, and macroenvironmental control in acetate base film preservation.

Storage Options	Impact on Acetate Film Base		
	Detrimental	Limited Benefit	Great Potential Improvement
Macroenvironmental Control	Above, near or at room temperature and RH	Cool temperatures and moderate RH	Cold or freezing temperatures at moderate or low RH
Microenvironments in Sealed Enclosures	Sealed enclosures without moisture control	Moisture-controlled microenvironments using either adsorbents (e.g., molecular sieves, silica gel) or moisture pre-conditioning, stored at room temperature.	Moisture-controlled microenvironments using either adsorbents (e.g., molecular sieves) or moisture pre-conditioning, stored at cold or freezing temperatures.
Enclosures	Tight and sealed enclosures	Open enclosures (e.g., vented cans)	No enclosure provides a solution for controlling vinegar syndrome.

Controlling Further Decay

Evaluating the state of preservation of collections should immediately call attention to the urgency for improved climate control. The acetate film in any sizeable collection can usually be broken down into four categories (see Table VII). Films in the first category (those in *good* or *fair* condition) can last several centuries in proper storage. Films in the second and third categories (those that are *actively decaying* or in *critical condition*) can last long enough to be duplicated if kept in adequate storage. If the *damaged* films in the fourth category are not treated using special duplication or restoration techniques, they will be lost. The preservation options presented in Table VII reveal that proper storage is an effective option for film preservation.

Table VII: Film conditions that can be observed in collections

Film Condition Category	Characteristics	Preservation Options
Good or fair	Films are not decaying, or are just starting to decay	Films can last a century at cool temperature and several centuries if kept in cold storage.
Actively decaying	Film may decay at a fast pace depending on storage conditions.	Films can last a century in cold storage
Critical	Films are still usable. However, shrinkage and warping are imminent.	Films can be stabilized in cold storage while awaiting duplication.
Damaged	Films display various degrees of shrinkageand other extreme manifestations of decay.	Current restoration procedures may not be able to save these films. Digital techniques will extend restoration possibilities.

Figure 4: *Storage at freezing temperatures stabilizes actively decaying films. Fifteen film rolls were tested after five years of storage at room conditions (left) and subfreezing temperatures (right).*

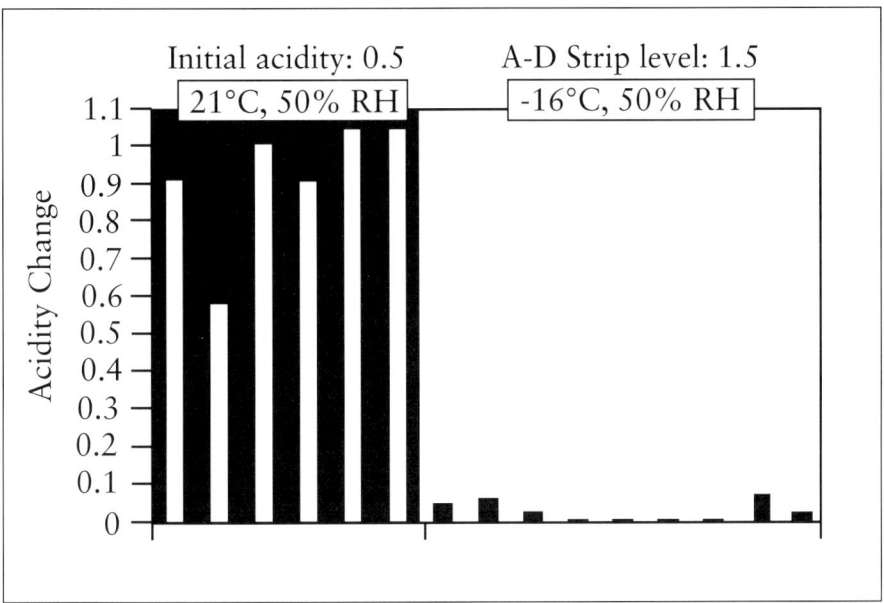

Cold storage optimizes the chemical stability of photographic film, postpones further decay, and stabilizes film in critical condition. It has been demonstrated that further acetate decay can be postponed at low temperature, while it proceeds at a fast pace at room temperature.[47] Figure 4 indicates that, after five years, the acidity of film kept at room temperature increased by a factor of 2 to 3. During the same period of time, the acidity of film kept at a subfreezing temperature (16°C) did not display any significant acidity change. This is of great practical importance because it shows that actively degrading films can be successfully stabilized while awaiting duplication. Thus, knowing the distribution of film conditions within a collection is an essential step for film archivists. A condition survey of the collection using acid-detector strips is the most efficient way to gather this type of information.

Acetate film decay. Delamination of image layer caused by severe shrinkage on 35mm motion-picture film.

Image Permanence Institute, Rochester, NY.

IPI's A–D Strips are one of the currently available acid detectors[51,52] that address the need for quantifying the degree of decay of acetate collections. These tools use a rating system that can be easily applied and interpreted by film archivists. A–D Strips are paper strips coated with bromocresol green, an acid-base indicator, in combination with sodium hydroxide. In practice, a strip is placed with the film to be tested in a confined environment (e.g., inside a film can). After exposure, the strip's color shift is evaluated against a color-reference scale printed on a pencil.

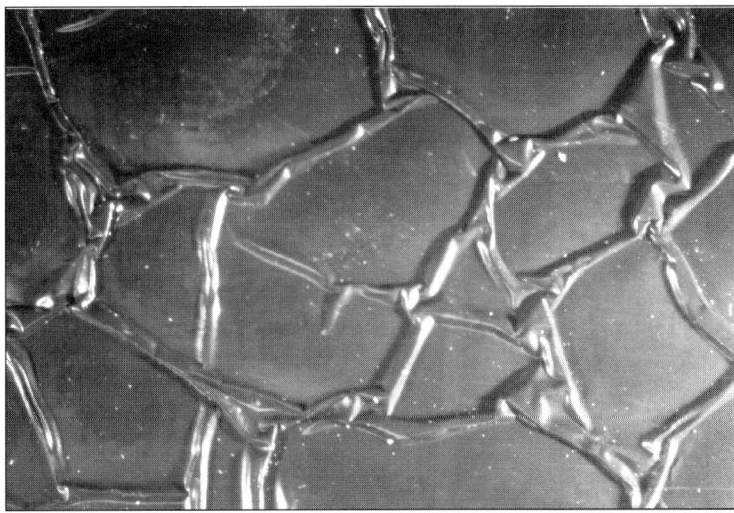

Depending on the film's condition, the color of the strip may shift from blue (its original color) to green or yellow. These color changes reflect the acid content of the film, i.e., its condition or state of preservation. The unique feature of A–D Strips is that they are calibrated to differentiate four specific levels, each level corresponding to a given amount of acidity in the film. Table VIII interprets the meaning of A–D Strip readings. The autocatalytic point (illustrated in Figure 3)

occurs between levels 1 and 2, and is therefore included in the table as noteworthy. Figure 5 illustrates the acidity range covered by A–D Strips. A–D Strips give film archivists time to act. If archivists can detect advanced decay before noticeable physical property changes (e.g., deformation, shrinkage) begin to occur, they will be able to stabilize and duplicate decaying materials before it is too late.

Figure 5. Film acidity range covered by A–D Strips. Up to level 2, A–D Strips quantify film decay before any physical property changes occur. This allows film archivists to detect early signs of decay and take action before it is too late.

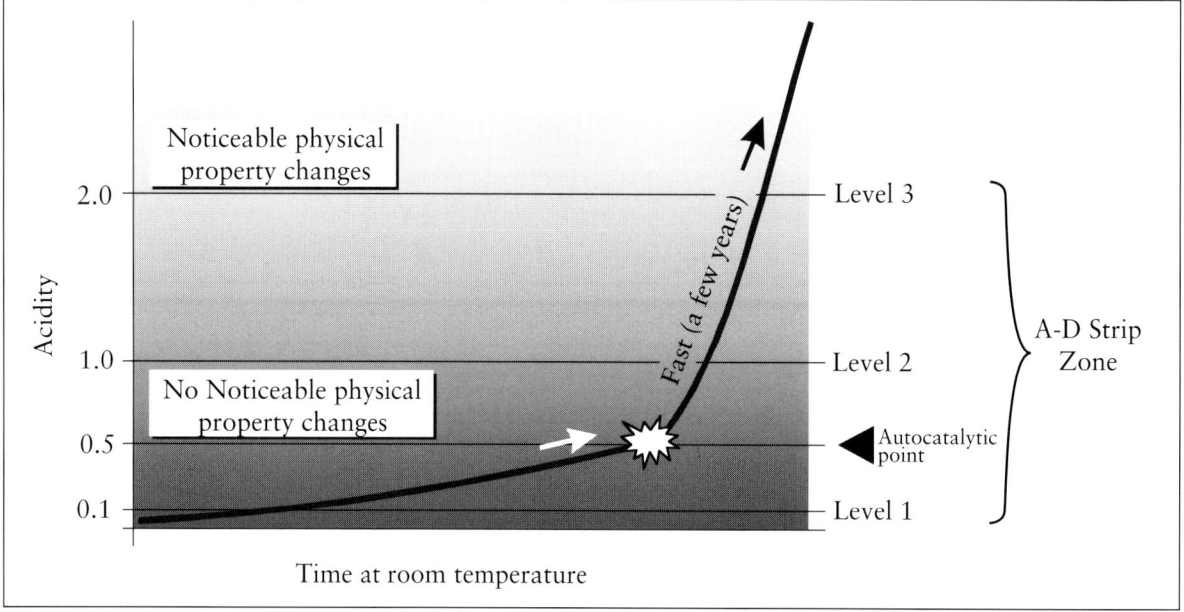

A condition survey can be conducted either by statistical sampling or by item-by-item testing. The first method identifies and evaluates affected areas in the collections. The second method evaluates individual films. Survey methods and results developed in film archives have been published.[53,54] Once archivists know the condition of their film, they can determine how much at risk their collections are and can make proactive preservation decisions. They have three basic choices of action: stabilize degrading films, duplicate decaying films if still possible, and avoid contamination of non-degraded films. Figure 6 proposes guidelines for classifying vulnerable films based on their current condition and suggests strategies for dealing with them.

Table VIII: Relationship between A–D Strip levels, film acid content, and film condition.

	A–D Strip Readings	Film Acidity	Film Condition
Blue ↓	Level 0	0 to 0.1	Good – No deterioration
	Level 1	About 0.2	Fair to good – Deterioration starting
	Midway between levels 1 and 2	0.5	Rapid degradation starting – Autocatalytic point of decay
	Level 2	About 1	Poor – Actively degrading
Yellow	Level 3	About 2 or above	Critical – Shrinkage and warping imminent; possible handling hazard

Figure 6.   Guidelines for setting priorities based on collection survey results

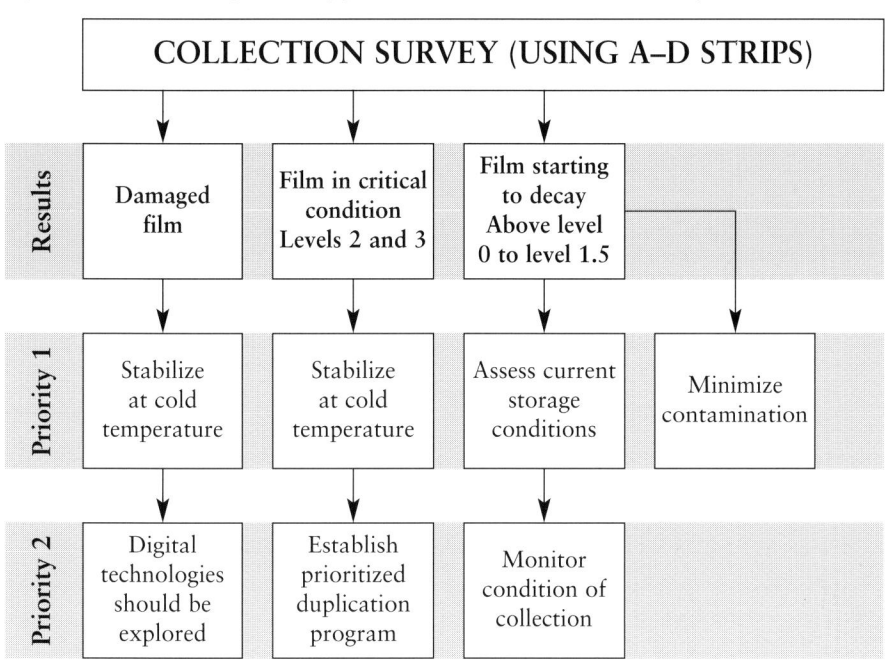

At present there is no consensus regarding an appropriate and practical laboratory treatment that will either cure or stabilize degrading acetate base film.[55] Low-temperature storage is the only widely recognized method to stabilize film in critical condition long enough to be duplicated.

The problem of contamination can be addressed in two ways. For small collections, or for portions of a larger collection, it may be practical to isolate actively degrading films by placing them in sealed cans and storing them at cold temperatures in a refrigerator, freezer, or cold vault. Including adsorbents (e.g., molecular sieves) in the sealed cans would provide added benefit.[47] Institutions with large collections may choose to provide cold temperatures and air-quality control to the entire holdings, thus improving the overall quality of the storage environment and minimizing the risk of contamination by removing degradation by-products from the air by using an air-filtration system and/or ventilation.

Any detection of decaying acetate materials calls for reassessing the quality of storage. The wheel included in the *IPI Storage Guide for Acetate Film*[43] can be used to estimate the impact of a given climate on the remaining life of already decaying acetate film. For example, an actively decaying film at A–D Strip level 1.5, stored near or at room conditions, may reach critical condition (A–D Strip level 2) within five years. The same film kept in cold storage (e.g., 2°C, 50% RH) may take 75 years to experience a similar change. This information helps to define the importance of implementing stringent storage conditions as soon as vinegar syndrome affects a film collection. Data make it evident that already decaying acetate film needs even better storage than fresh film to achieve the same useful life.

The chemical degradation of acetate base is an ongoing process which can be slowed but not stopped. For this reason, the condition of the film in a collection needs to be regularly monitored. This may sound like a daunting task, but, if cold temperatures are used, and predictions of film life expectancy have been determined, re-evaluation may be done less frequently than if storage conditions are inadequate. Film condition assessments may be required as often as every few years or as seldom as every hundred years, depending on storage conditions and the current condition of the film.[48]

Today's Situation

Film archivists are confronted by the problem of ageing and degrading film collections. Nitrate and acetate base and color dyes are the inherently chemically unstable components on which the production of moving images depends. Field experience and stability studies indicate that the loss of our film heritage is not irremediable. Nitrate and acetate film supports and color dyes can last for an extended period of time in proper storage. Cold storage for motion-picture film collections has been advocated for a long time.[42] It is still the best alternative for extending film life, and it is also a more cost-effective approach than duplication. However, many film collections may be decaying at an unacceptable rate due to improper storage and a lack of awareness of the extent of the problem. The severity of vinegar syndrome in collections is not always known or quantified, and the scale of the problem may be greater than we think. With the simple survey tools that are available today archivists can obtain this critical information and support the required initiatives to improve environmental conditions in film archives around the world. Climate control is the only way to preserve our film heritage in its original form.

A Lesson from the Nitrate Experience

The preservation of nitrate film collections set the pattern for today's overall film preservation strategy, which involves controlling storage climate, inspecting collections, and duplicating decaying materials. Each of these has been fine-tuned over time, with the establishment of more stringent storage conditions, the development of new survey tools, and the creation of comprehensive duplication programs. More importantly, our experience with nitrate has shown us that a "wait, then duplicate everything" strategy is not a good one. Duplication projects could go on forever, and costs are extremely high. Considering the amount of acetate and color film materials kept today in film collections, archivists are likely to be unable to handle the coming situation unless they act. Acting on this situation means proceeding proactively. Assessing the state of preservation of acetate film collections and the quality of current storage will allow film archivists, while there is still time, to choose the best strategy for their collections in terms of storage and prioritized duplication programs. Our experience after the transition from nitrate to triacetate base shows that new materials may not necessarily be the answer for permanence. The new technologies will potentially multiply the ways we watch moving images, renew interest in our film heritage, simplify access to film collections, and offer restoration capabilities beyond what can be done using traditional techniques. It is clear that digitization will play an increasing role in the global framework of film preservation. It will not eliminate the need for film preservation, however. What we now know about film stability indicates that nitrate can last, vinegar syndrome can be controlled, and color dye fading can be postponed in proper storage for an extended period of time. Today, film is still the best bet for the near future, and it is the only way to preserve our motion-picture heritage in its unique and original form.

Acknowledgments

This paper refers to several research projects conducted at IPI under grants from the Division of Preservation and Access of the National Endowment for the Humanities, a federal US agency. Additional support was provided by Fuji Photo

Film Co., Ltd., and Eastman Kodak Company. We also thank the Library of Congress, the British Film Institute, the National Film Board of Canada, the National Archives of Canada, the Canadian Council of Archives, and the Arizona Historical Society for their support. My personal thanks go to IPI colleagues for their invaluable contributions in the field of film preservation and their constant support.

References:

1. Deac Rossell, "A Chronology of Cinema 1889–1896", *Film History*, v.7 no. 2 (1995), pp. 115–236.

2. Earl Theisen, "The History of Nitrocellulose as a Film Base", *Journal of the SMPE*, v.20 (March 1933), pp. 259–262.

3. Kenneth Mees, "History of Professional Black-and-White Motion-Picture Film", *Journal of the SMPTE*, v.63 (October 1954), pp. 125–128.

4. Glenn E Matthews and Raife G Tarkington, "Early History of Amateur Motion-Picture Film", *Journal of the SMPTE*, v.64 (March 1955), pp. 129–140.

5. Reese V Jenkins, *Image & Enterprise: Technology and the American Photographic Industry 1839 to 1925* (Baltimore/London: The Johns Hopkins University Press, 1975).

6. Charles R Fordyce, "Motion-Picture Film Support: 1889–1976. An Historical Review", *SMPTE Journal*, v.85 (July 1976), pp. 493–495.

7. Barry Salt, *Film Style and Technology: History and Analysis* (London: Starword, 1983, 1992).

8. David Pierce, "The Legion of the Condemned – Why American Silent Films Perished", reprinted in this volume, previously published in *Film History*, v.9, no.1 (1997), pp. 5–22.

9. Peter Z Adelstein, James M Reilly, Douglas W Nishimura, and Catherine J Erbland, "Stability of Cellulose Ester Base Photographic Film: Part IV – Behavior of Nitrate Base Film", *SMPTE Journal* (June 1995), pp. 359–369.

10. John M Calhoun, "Technology of New Film Bases", *Perspective*, v.2 no.3 (1960).

11. Peter Z Adelstein, "From Metal to Polyester: History of Picture-Taking Supports", in Eugene Ostroff, ed., *Pioneers of Photography* (Springfield, VA: SPSE [The Society for Imaging Science and Technology], 1987), pp. 30–36.

12. Charles R Fordyce, "Improved Safety Motion Picture Film Support", *Journal of the SMPE*, v.51 (1948), pp. 331–350.

13. John M Calhoun, "Storage of Nitrate Amateur Still-Camera Film Negatives", *Journal of the Biological Photographic Association*, v.21 no.3 (August 1953), pp. 1–13.

14. Deane R White, Charles J Gass, Emery Meschter, and Wilton R Holm, "Polyester Photographic Film Base", *Journal of the SMPTE*, v.64 (1955), pp. 674–678.

15. Emmett K Carver, "The Manufacture of Motion Picture Film", *Journal of the SMPE*, v.29 (June 1937), pp. 594–603.

16. H Mark Gosser, "The Bazar de la Charité Fire: The Reality, the Aftermath, the Telling", *Film History*, v.10 no.1 (1998), pp. 70–89.

17. A H Nuckolls and A F Matson, "Some Hazardous Properties of Motion Picture Film", *Journal of the SMPE*, v.27 (December 1936), pp. 657–661.

18. James W Cummings, Alvin C Hutton, and Howard Silfin, "Spontaneous Ignition of Decomposing Cellulose Nitrate Film", *Journal of the SMPTE*, v.54 (March 1950), pp. 268–274.

19. Jess Daily, "The Care and Handling of Hazardous Nitrate Film at UCLA's Unique Projection Facilities", *Journal of the SMPTE*, v.99 no.6 (June 1990), pp. 453–456.

20. Eastman Kodak Company, *Safe Handling, Storage, and Destruction of Nitrate-Based Motion Picture Films* (Kodak Publication no.H–182, 1995).

21. Peter Z Adelstein, Glen G Gray, and J Mason Burnham, "Manufacture and Physical Properties of Film, Paper and Plates", in John M Sturge, ed., *Neblette's Handbook of Photography and Reprography Materials, Processes and Systems*, 1977, pp. 127–147.

22. Michele Edge, Norman S Allen, M Hayes, P N K Riley, C V Horie, and J Luc-Gardette, "Mechanisms of Deterioration in Cellulose Nitrate Base Archival Cinematograph Film", *European Polymer Journal*, v.26 no.6 (1990), pp. 623–630.

23. Alain Louvet, Bertrand Lavédrine, and Françoise Flieder, "Size Exclusion Chromatography and Mass Spectrometry of Photographic Bases in Cellulose Nitrate Degradation", *The Journal of*

Photographic Science, v.43 no.1 (1995), pp. 30–35.

24. John F Carroll and John M Calhoun, "Effect of Nitrogen Oxide Gases on Processed Acetate Film", *Journal of the SMPTE*, v.64 (September 1955), pp. 501–507.

25. John I Crabtree and Charles E Ives, "The Storage of Valuable Motion Picture Film", *Journal of the SMPE*, v.15 (September 1930), pp. 289–305.

26. E W Fowler and L B Newell, "Storage and Handling of Motion Picture Film", *Journal of the SMPE*, v.16 (June 1931), pp. 773–786.

27. W H Carson, "Report of the Committee on the Preservation of Film", *Journal of the SMPE*, v.20 (June 1933), pp. 523–530.

28. John G Bradley, "Report of the Committee on Preservation of Film", *Journal of the SMPE*, v.27 (August 1936), pp. 147–154.

29. John G Bradley, "Changing Aspects of the Film-Storage Problem", *Journal of the SMPE*, v.30 (March 1938), pp. 303–317.

30. J R Hill and C G Weber, "Stability of Motion Picture Films as Determined by Accelerated Aging", *Journal of the SMPE*, v.27 (December 1936), pp. 677–690.

31. G L Hutchison, L Ellis, and S A Ashmore, "The Surveillance of Cinematograph Record Film During Storage", *Journal of the SMPTE*, v.54 (March 1950), pp. 381–383.

32. John M Calhoun, "The Preservation of Motion-Picture Film", *The American Archivist*, v.30 no.3 (July 1967), pp. 517–525.

33. Ernest H Lindgren, "Preservation of Cinematographic Film in the National Film Archive", *Journal of the SMPTE*, v.78 (October 1969), pp. 876–879.

34. Peter Z Adelstein and James L McCrea, "Permanence of Processed Estar Polyester Base Photographic Films", *Photographic Science and Engineering*, v.9 (1965), pp. 305–313.

35. Peter Z Adelstein and James L McCrea, "Stability of Processed Polyester Base Photographic Films", *Journal of Applied Photographic Engineering*, v.7 (1981), pp. 160–167.

36. Peter Z Adelstein, James M Reilly, Douglas W Nishimura, and Catherine J Erbland, "Stability of Cellulose Ester Base Photographic Film: Part II – Practical Storage Considerations", *SMPTE Journal*, v.101 (May 1992), pp. 347–353.

37. International Standard ISO 10356, *Cinematography – Storage and Handling of Nitrate-Base Motion-Picture Films*, 1996.

38. Peter Z Adelstein, James M Reilly, Douglas W Nishimura, and Catherine J Erbland, "Stability of Cellulose Ester Base Photographic Film: Part III – Measurement of Film Degradation", *SMPTE Journal*, v.104 (May 1995), pp. 281–291.

39. Henry Wilhelm and Carol Brower, *The Permanence and Care of Color Photographs: Traditional and Digital Color Prints, Color Negatives, Slides, and Motion Pictures* (Grinnell, Iowa: Preservation Publishing Company, 1993).

40. James M Reilly, *Storage Guide for Color Photographic Materials* (Albany, NY: The University of the State of New York, New York State Education Department, New York State Library, The New York State Program for the Conservation and Preservation of Library Research Materials, 1998).

41. William Widmayer, "Cold Storage Protects Color Negatives", *American Cinematographer* (March 1961), pp. 170–173.

42. Peter Z Adelstein, C Loren Graham, and Lloyd E West, "Preservation of Motion-Picture Color Films Having Permanent Value", *Journal of the SMPTE*, v.79 (1970), pp. 1011–1018.

43. James M Reilly, IPI *Storage Guide for Acetate Film* (Rochester, NY: Image Permanence Institute, Rochester Institute of Technology, 1993).

44. *American National Standard for Imaging Materials – Processed Safety Photographic Films – Storage*, PIMA IT9.11–1997, revision and redesignation of ANSI/NAPM IT9.11–1993 (New York: American National Standard Institute, 1997).

45. International Standard ISO 18911, *Photography – Processed Safety Photographic Films – Storage Practices* (Geneva, Switz.: International Organization for Standardization, 1996); formerly ISO 5466.

46. Jean-Louis Bigourdan, "Preservation of Acetate Base Motion-Picture Film: From Stability Studies to Film Preservation in Practice", in The GAMMA Group, ed., *The Vinegar Syndrome. A Handbook: Preventions, Remedies and the Use of New Techniques* (Bologna, Italy, 2000), pp. 11–44.

47. Jean-Louis Bigourdan and James M Reilly, "Effectiveness of Storage Conditions in Controlling the Vinegar Syndrome: Preservation Strategies for Acetate Base Motion-Picture Film Collections", in Michelle Aubert and Richard Billeaud, eds., *Image and Sound Archiving and Access: The Challenges of the 3rd Millennium* (Proceedings of the Joint Technical Symposium,

Paris, 20–22 January 2000), pp. 14–34.

48. Jean-Louis Bigourdan, "Vinegar Syndrome: An Action Plan", in The GAMMA Group, ed., op. cit., pp. 45–59.

49. James M Reilly, "Assessment and Cost Management", in The GAMMA Group, ed., op. cit., pp. 61–71.

50. "Preservation Calculator": Can be downloaded from the following website: <www.rit.edu/ipi>

51. "A–D Strips and Film Preservation", <www.rit.edu/ipi> (Click "Enter", go to "Products", "A–D Strips".)

52. "Dancheck 2-Hour Acidity Tester", <www.dancan.dk/speedtest.html>

53. Bertrand Lavédrine, Renaud Duverne, Martine Leroy, Michelle Aubert, and Jean-Louis Cot, "Analyse statistique de l'état de conservation d'une collection de films sur support en triacetate de cellulose", in Michelle Aubert and Richard Billeaud, eds., op. cit., pp. 44–53.

54. Cecilia Díaz González, "Diagnóstico de acidez en acetato de celulosa en la Cineteca Nacional, México", *Journal of Film Preservation*, no.58/59 (October 1999), pp. 61–62.

55. Mark-Paul Meyer and Paul Read, "Restoration and Preservation of Vinegar Syndrome Decayed Acetate Film", in Michelle Aubert and Richard Billeaud, eds., op. cit., pp. 54–58.

Wizards of Oz: Survivals, Losses and Finds in Australian Film History

by Ray Edmondson

Among the Collectors

I do not think there is any thrill in film archiving which matches the finding of an important "lost" film. Without wanting to sound melodramatic, the comparisons which most readily come to mind are the Egyptologist stumbling across an ancient, unplundered tomb in the Valley of the Kings, or young Jim Hawkins and Long John Silver striking it rich on Treasure Island. (Visions of a cackling Robert Newton drooling over a stack of newly unearthed cans don't seem entirely incongruous. "Arrrhh now, Ray lad, what precious gems awaits us 'ere, then, eh?" he exclaims, and applies the tip of his cutlass to lever off a rusty lid....)

From the time in 1968 when I first joined the NFSA's predecessor – the embryonic film archive within the National Library of Australia – the archaeology of Australia's film history was a gradually unfolding and endlessly intriguing journey of discovery. Of the history of the Australian industry during the nitrate era, little had then been documented. But there was already a collection of several hundred titles, serious research was beginning, and many of the industry's important pioneers were still living.

As I was to discover, the network of film collectors was vibrant, active, and – of course – appropriately secretive. Many were passionate individuals whose hobbies cost them dear. Their private 35mm cinemas – perhaps a converted garage or lounge – could not be cheaply constructed. Their collections filled available space – sheds, garages, spare rooms. Because of the flammability of the films, they were understandably circumspect about advertising their enthusiasms to their neighbours or their insurance company. Where the house was shared with a wife and children (collectors were almost always male) they had often to extend a good deal of tolerance to Dad's enthusiasm!

In time, I found myself welcomed into their world. I was privileged to be so treated, because as a government-employed archivist rather than a private accumulator I represented the suspect hand of "officialdom". It needs to be remembered that any large private 35mm collection was composed, at least in part, of films that were technically "stolen property" – that is, of prints that had been officially, if not actually, junked. They had found their way into private hands by informal means, and the commercial film distributors from whom they had been sourced – who, among other things, were fearful of piracy – understandably frowned on the practice. Sometimes actively so: stories of distributor-instigated police "raids" on private collections were part of the rich apocrypha of the collector network, which abounded in yarns of finds, one-upmanship, and skulduggery at the expense of distributors or laboratory proprietors. (At the same time, I suspect the "thrill" of possessing illicit materials was actually, for some, part of the attraction of collecting.)

The stories are legion, but that of the mysterious and unnamed "Chinese Gentleman" will illustrate. In Australia at the time, 35mm prints were usually shipped to country cinemas by train – a programme would be booked for sequential playdates in a series of theatres in towns strung out along a railway line. It would "move down the line" to each of them in turn. The prints would be delivered a day or so in advance of each screening, the film trunks being plonked by the train guard on the platform to await collection by the cinema operator. There was a good deal of informality and trust involved – as I can recall from my own observation as a child, the trunks (heavy metal containers holding several reels of nitrate film) might sit on the station platform in the blazing sun for many hours, till the recipient got round to collecting them.

Enter the "Chinese Gentleman". He apparently had an arrangement with one – or more – station clerks in situations where this natural delay could work to his advantage. He would "borrow" a print for several hours, long enough to run off a dupe negative, and return it before the recipient came to claim it. The negative could then yield any number of "pirate" prints whose use – within Australia or beyond – can only be guessed at. One imagines that our Gentleman had his own private printing and processing laboratory – an entirely practical possibility in the days of black-and-white film. (I knew collectors who had their own film printers – the most important item of equipment, since the processing of film could be readily contracted out.)

Of course, the means by which collectors obtained their prints tended to fall into three categories. The first was genuine finds in unlikely places, such as old cinema projection rooms, or secondhand shops. The second was by exchange: swaps and horse-trading among fellow collectors. The third was "informal" acquisition from a distributor.

Of the latter means, I never met any collector who admitted to directly participating in this approach – but everyone knew that it happened! Hypothetically, collector Jones would know despatch clerk Smith at the Stupendous Film Company's exchange. Smith had been instructed to destroy a quantity of surplus prints and legally certify that this has been done. He casually mentioned this to Jones, who happily was able to oblige by offering to carry out this task himself. The following day, Jones arrived with his car and Smith dumped the prints in his boot. Smith could now formally write them off, while Jones – who, it transpired, was not always well organised – might sometimes forget to carry out the destruction. Variations on this theme were legion, and despite the official stances of many film companies, there was – at least some of the time – evident tolerance of the inevitable. Collectors would take the private view that, so long as no piracy was occurring and the distributor's income was not affected, the practice caused no harm, and indeed, over time, conferred benefit by contributing to the survival of films.

Over the years I got to know many collectors whose holdings, and whose vigilance, yielded unique copies of Australian nitrate films that found their way into our Archive. These included silent feature films like Franklyn Barrett's *The Breaking of the Drought* (1920), the second film version of the literary classic *Robbery Under Arms* (1920), the daring Raymond Longford feature *The Woman Suffers (while the man goes free)* (1918), Beaumont Smith's *The Adventures of Algy* (1925), and comedian Pat Hanna's *Waltzing Matilda* (1934). Just as importantly, there were countless newsreels, documentaries, and advertising films which survived solely in private collections.

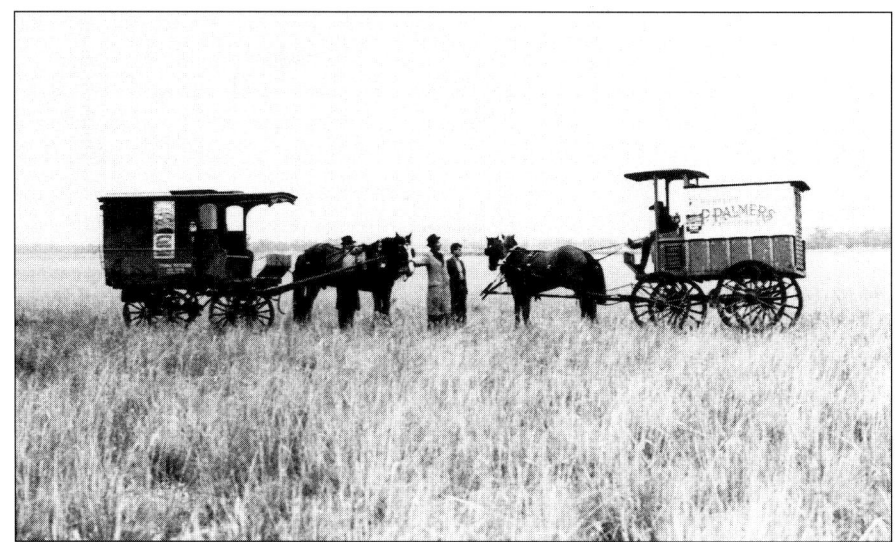

A scene from *The Picture Show Man* (1977), a film set among the travelling showmen of the 1920s.

ScreenSound Australia, Canberra.

Collectors value their privacy, but I will mention two, both now dead, who I think would be happy to be remembered in this context. John Scanes (the source of *Robbery Under Arms*) was an extraordinarily generous man who kept his collection, and his projection set-up, in his garage in an outer Sydney suburb. He alerted me whenever his activities turned up an interesting Australian title, and this usually resulted in the reels being added to the Archive's collection. He made me a welcome visitor to his home, and we would sometimes spend hours sifting through parts of his collection. Stacked in piles in his garage, each inviting can label might lead to a background story, an examination on a rewinder, or occasionally putting something up on the screen. When we had room, I offered to store some of his nitrate in our vault in Canberra: many of his unique films of European and American origin, some going back almost to the turn of the century, were progressively repatriated to archives in their country of origin.

Harry Davidson was perhaps Melbourne's best known film collector. He had two collections: the first was lost in a house fire sometime in the 1950s or 1960s (he was never precise about the date). He started over and built a second, and his home was a temple to his love of the movies: statuettes and relics from demolished theatres were sprinkled around the house, jostling for space with the film cans and memorabilia stacked in rooms and hallways, and the characteristic smell of nitrate film (and I confess that it is a smell I love) was everywhere. Harry guarded his collection jealously, but in the early 1970s he finally relented and lent me his precious print of *The Exploits of the Emden* (1928) for copying, on my assurances that it would be perfectly safe and returned to him promptly. The print was already showing signs of decomposition, and I sent it for proprietary scratch removal treatment before copying. Unexpectedly, the treatment reacted with the stock and advanced the deterioration. *I hadn't kept my promise.* It was years before Harry's trust was recovered and he again gave us access.

In about 1980, Harry died suddenly, leaving his widow Pat, and his infant daughter Theda. We were able to purchase his collection of over 2,000 reels. Many of its considerable riches – which included a tinted print of *Metropolis* and unique copies of some of Harold Lloyd's earliest work – have since been distributed to archives across the globe as part of the NFSA nitrate repatriation program of the 1990s. In every case, the accepting archives undertook to identify the material in their records as being part of the "Harry Davidson Collection". This honoured our original conditions of acquisition and also celebrated Harry's achievement – and legacy – as a collector.

While film archives often have the financial means, mostly unavailable to private individuals, to copy, properly store, and preserve nitrate film, it is more often than not the collector who has the time, contacts, and inclination to find the material in the first place. It is a partnership, though the collector's role is often unsung – and many collectors like it that way. But the partnership depends on personal relationships, involving mutual respect, a shared love of old film, and a willingness to accept the moral obligations which come from being invited into – and perhaps ultimately assuming responsibility for – a private world, the product of a lifetime of passion and persistence.

Some of the Ones That Got Away

Australia's "big three" silent film directors – Raymond Longford, Franklyn Barrett, and Beaumont Smith – were prolific, each completing over 20 feature films during their careers. Tragically, only remnants of their work now remain.

Of Longford's work, only his acknowledged masterpiece, *The Sentimental Bloke*, survives intact (see below). Substantial, though incomplete or shortened, versions of four other films exist, along with fragments of two more. Longford worked for a series of companies between 1910 and 1934, and did not always have either copyright or physical control of his films. They were held in a variety of hands, and survival has proved largely a matter of chance.

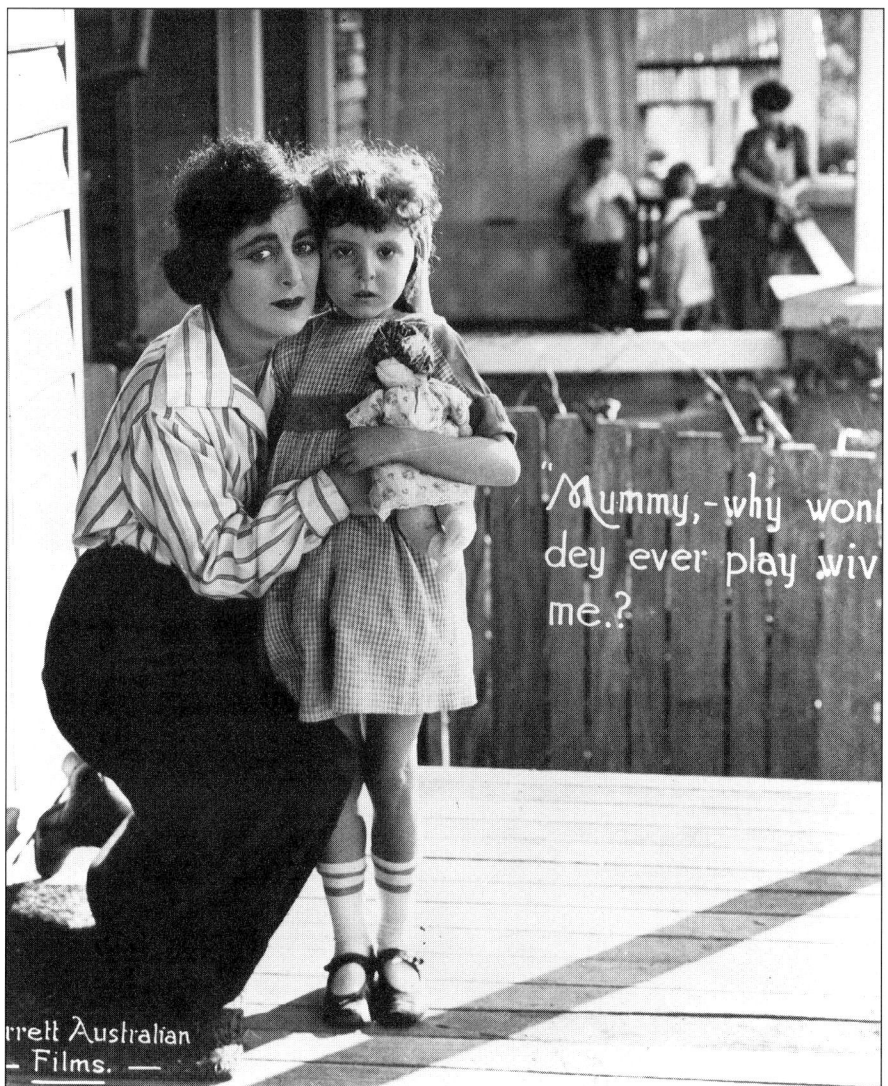

A scene from *Know Thy Child* (1921), a lost film by Franklyn Barrett.

ScreenSound Australia, Canberra.

Franklyn Barrett likewise worked for a variety of producers, later setting up his own production company, and making his last film – *A Rough Passage* – in 1922. Only two of his films – *The Breaking of the Drought* and *A Girl of the Bush*, both from 1920 – survive. For many years he appears to have kept his prints and negatives in his garage, and in the 1950s tried to awaken institutional interest in their preservation. But before any progress could be made, his garage structurally collapsed; the films, along with the rest of the contents, were carted away as debris.

From the outset, Beaumont Smith operated his own production company, making his first film in 1917 and his last in 1934. Three of his features, and a fragment of a fourth, are left to us. That we do not have his entire output is a result of timing and circumstance. Upon Smith's death in 1950, his brother inherited his surviving stock of films and retained them for many years. But a chance discussion with someone from his local fire brigade alerted him to both the practical and insurance dangers of keeping a large stock of flammable nitrate film in his home or garage. On advice, he consented to the destruction of the entire stock by the fire authorities. The National Library, then beginning a search for nitrate film by writing to every fire brigade in Australia, tracked Mr Smith down – just six months too late. Only a fragment – several minutes of the 1924 film *The Digger Earl* – had been overlooked in the purge. It was only in later years that complete copies of one of Smith's silents, and both of his talkies, were tracked down from other sources.

Four Finds

1. National Films, *Fatty Finn*, and Charlie Chaplin

National Films of New South Wales was a small independent distribution company owned by showman Gerry Tayler. For many years, until around 1960, it occupied top-storey offices in Pitt Street, the heart of Sydney's central business district. Their film vaults, containing thousands of reels of nitrate film, adjoined the offices: though they were never known to have a mishap, one can speculate that a nitrate fire would have turned the building into an interesting variation on the Roman candle!

As an independent in an industry dominated by a small number of major, overseas-owned companies, National worked in the margins, supplying city independents, country exhibitors, and specialist users. Their inventory included American product like the "Joe Palooka" series, various Australian features and short subjects, and even some silent material handed down by the majors after the advent of talkies. National regularly serviced Sydney's five newsreel theatrettes with elderly silent comic shorts – by the 1950s, the only place where one was likely to see such material on 35mm. As a schoolboy, I was a regular frequenter of the newsreel theatrettes, and among other things, over the years, they were where I first saw several of Chaplin's Mutual shorts – all of them, I later learned, part of the series reissued (with music) by the Van Beuren studio in the 1930s, and emanating from National Films.

Another 1950s frequenter of the newsreel theatrettes (whom I was to meet much later in life) was John Morris, a student at Sydney University and a keen member of its Film Group. On one occasion, he was intrigued by a silent offering which featured the antics of some Sydney children. He tracked the print to its source – National Films – and established that it was a segment of a 1927 comedy feature called *The Kid Stakes*, based on a popular comic strip called *Fatty Finn*. Morris established that National had long ago inherited three prints of the film, which they had subsequently cut up to make 20-minute fillers for the newsreel programmes. The quality of the film impressed him, and he wanted to take the matter further.

With the backing of the Film Group and the co-operation (and, one suspects, bemusement) of Gerry Tayler, Morris set about reconstructing the best complete copy of the feature he could piece together from the surviving cut-down segments. In order to make new prints, a negative had to be struck, and this was initially bankrolled by the Film Group – until the project attracted sufficient interest in the press for the National Library to be persuaded (Morris says "shamed"!) to back it. Today *The Kid Stakes* is a classic, recognised as one of Australia's best silent features, and John Morris's reconstruction has never been improved on.

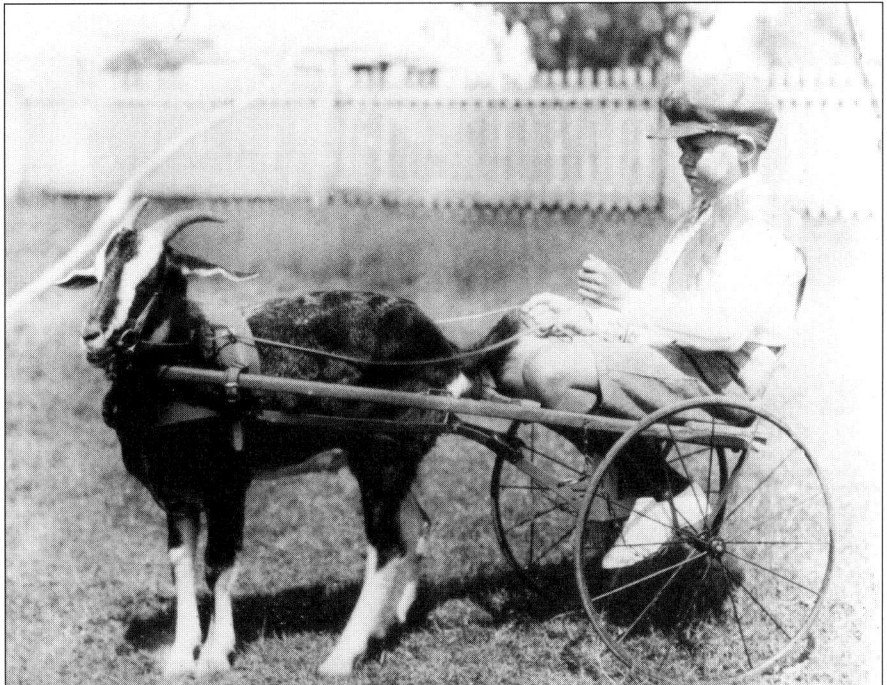

A scene from *The Kid Stakes* (1927).

ScreenSound Australia, Canberra.

Morris went on to a diverse and impressive career as a film producer and executive, running the South Australian Film Corporation in its 1970s heyday, and finally heading the Australian Film Finance Corporation until his recent retirement. In late 1999, a new cinema complex in Sydney was opened with a screening of *The Kid Stakes* supported by a live orchestral accompaniment. On that occasion, when John Morris stood up and "took a bow", his pioneering work as a film restorer was publicly recognised for the first time, nearly 50 years after the event.

The National Films story has other strands. When Gerry Tayler died and the company folded, his widow Dorothy inherited its stock in trade of nitrate film, which was relocated out of the Pitt Street premises – no doubt to the landlord's relief – to wherever it would fit in her house. Dorothy spent her twilight years carefully repairing, recanning, and disposing of this inventory. Much of it came to us at the National Library, and in the 1960s I became a regular visitor to her small weatherboard home in one of Sydney's seaside suburbs. She had constructed a rudimentary examination bench, using a few old LP records as winding plates, and she checked and identified material before putting it into newly painted cans (she did the painting herself – it lengthened the life of the can). On each visit I collected a consignment of film to take back to Canberra in my car, and the "Tayler Collection" steadily grew.

Among the inventory was a set of dupe negatives and prints of the Mutual Chaplins, mentioned above, which Dorothy offered to us. With a heavy but very rational heart, I had to reject the offer on the grounds that we did not then have the means or manpower to look after them, and that logically they should be offered to an American archive. I facilitated a contact with the American Film Institute, to whom they were ultimately sent. According to the AFI at the time, they turned out to be the best surviving negatives of the Chaplin Mutuals.

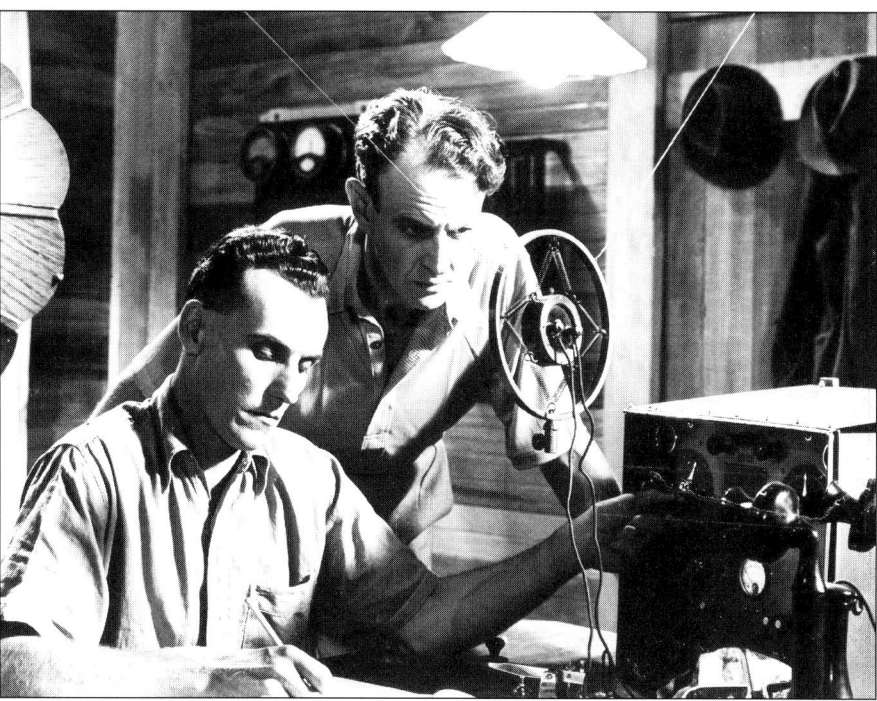

A scene from *The Flying Doctor* (1936).

ScreenSound Australia, Canberra.

2. *The Flying Doctor*

In 1936 a company called National Productions, backed by Gaumont-British and linked to the new National Studios complex in Sydney, was established to make international productions in Australia. Their first – and, as it turned out, only – film was *The Flying Doctor*, made by British director Miles Mander and starring American matinee idol Charles Farrell. The storyline was built around the famous service which provides medical care in Australia's outback, and included interesting ingredients like a cameo role for cricketer Don Bradman, then at the height of his fame. The film was released in Australia and Britain, but proved only a modest success and eventually dropped from sight. By the mid-1970s, when it figured on a list of titles for which our Archive was searching, no copies were known to exist.

One day, workmen in the Sydney suburb of Lane Cove were clearing a new building site. An early task was to demolish a small pillbox structure with steel doors, which stood in the way of the new building. Unable to open them by other means, a workman cut through the steel doors with an oxy-acetylene torch, revealing an interior stacked with hundreds of cans of what turned out to be nitrate film. Along with other site refuse, the cans were loaded onto a truck and sent off to the nearest rubbish tip.

As the truck passed the offices of the local Council, an alert staff member noticed what it was carrying, and immediately rushed out and gave chase in his car. Reaching the rubbish tip, he persuaded the driver to stack the cans in a safe place and contacted Film Australia, a government film production unit located in the nearby suburb of Lindfield. They in turn contacted the National Library, and the film was ultimately transferred into the National Film Archive collection.

Among other things, it yielded a nitrate release print of *The Flying Doctor*. Delighted and intrigued, I sat down to preview the print on an Intercine. It was good, involving stuff. But as the story neared an insoluble crisis point at the end of reel 8, it ran out. That was it. The last reel was missing!

For two years I wondered how the story ended! Then, unexpectedly, a routine search list sent to the National Film Archive in London – while drawing a blank on all the other titles – turned up a print of *The Flying Doctor* at Rank, who proved happy to donate it to us. Finally, I'd get to see the last reel! The box arrived. I unpacked it. To my dismay the Rank copy, too, was only 8 reels long. I worked through it on the Intercine. Clearly it was the same film, but it had been radically rearranged and shortened: the middle and opening sections had been swapped around, and other changes made. I worried till I got to the end of reel 7, which cut off at ... precisely the same point as reel 8 in the "Lane Cove" print! So the final reel would serve as common to both versions! Came the big moment: reel 8 unfolded, and at last I knew how the story ended!

Why were there two versions? This was actually the fate of many Australian features in the nitrate years – and beyond. Released as "A" films at home, they would often end up as "B" pictures in Britain or America – if they got a release there at all. The original negative would be sent for printing to the overseas distributor, who would often recut and/or retitle the film to enhance its marketability. (So *The Adorable Outcast* became *White Cargoes of the South Seas*, *On Our Selection* became *Down on the Farm*, *Walk into Paradise* turned into *Walk into Hell*, and *Forty Thousand Horsemen* became *Thunder over the Desert*.) The negative, and the trims, would never return to Australia – it was not worth the shipping cost – and would often, in time, be lost. Production budgets were usually too slim to allow for lavenders or other protection copies to be made for safekeeping at home: the original release prints would serve out the economic life of the film. No one anticipated future sales to something called television.

There is a postscript to this story. Years later, a travelling exhibition of stills from our collection, on show at a Sydney art gallery, brought a surprise present. As a kind donation, someone handed over the official studio stills book of *The Flying Doctor*, picked up at a suburban secondhand shop. A remarkable chain of coincidence had given us back not only both versions of the film, but a complete coverage of its stills. Truly a happy ending.

What's that? I haven't revealed what happens in the last reel? Sorry, but I don't want to spoil the film for you if you still haven't seen it. We could always sell you a video ...

3. Ned Kelly

Hanged in 1880, the iron-clad bushranger Ned Kelly had, within two decades of his death, acquired celebrity status as a symbol of courage and anti-authoritarianism. Commemorated first in stage plays, and later in works such as the paintings of Sir Sidney Nolan, he has long since become a national Australian icon. It's perhaps no surprise that he has been the subject of (to date) seven feature films, all of which survive in whole or in part. The first of these, *The Story of the Kelly Gang*, made in 1906, is of crucial importance because it arguably represents the first appearance

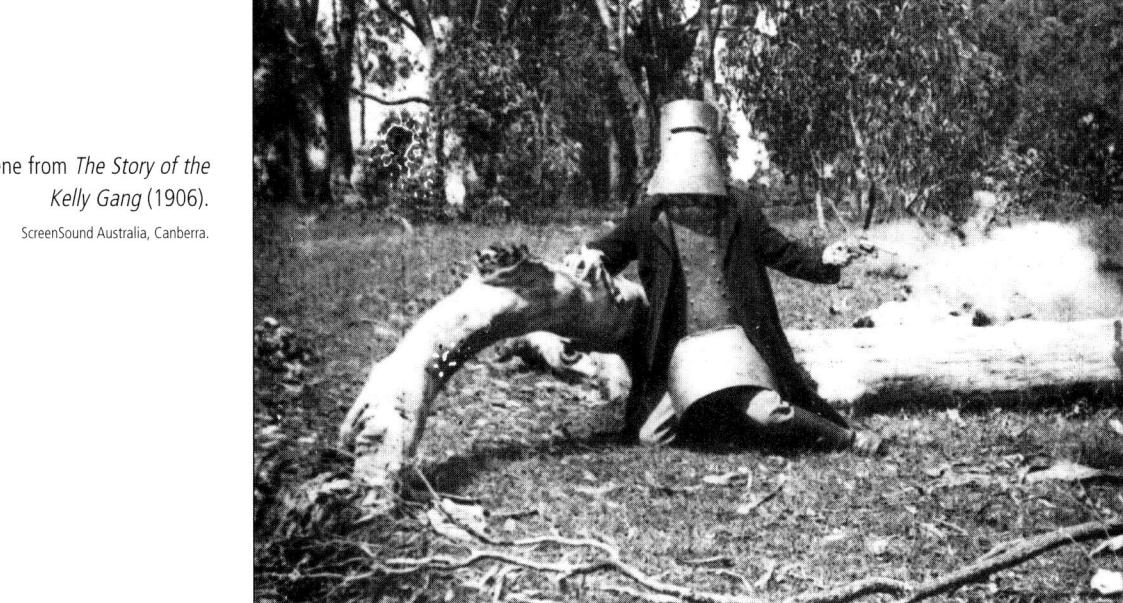

A scene from *The Story of the Kelly Gang* (1906).
ScreenSound Australia, Canberra.

in the world of the modern feature film concept. A cinematic drama running somewhere between 40 and 80 minutes (there is no exact record) and occupying the entire programme, it was a major commercial success, screening in Australia, New Zealand, and Britain. It was made in Melbourne, and to save expense the producers even persuaded the police to lend them Ned Kelly's actual armour for the actor to wear in the film.

Until the mid-1970s, however, no trace of the film was known to survive. We were fortunate to acquire a copy of the original programme booklet, which contained a detailed story synopsis and reproductions of stills from the film. But there was no actual footage....

One day I was idly sifting through a can of short nitrate film clips that had arrived as part of a small collection. My eye was caught by a clip of about ten frames with almost square perforations. It was someone dressed in Ned Kelly's characteristic armour. I looked in the can for more: there were two more similarly brief snippets. I checked them against the stills in the programme booklet. There was no doubt – I had in my hand about two feet of the original Kelly film. It was not much, but it was something at last. It was a moment I shall never forget.

We had those snippets copied – in both real time and stretched – so at last we had a tantalising glimpse of the film to show. Would we ever see any more?

In June 1979, I was contacted by a Melbourne school principal, Ken Robb. Rummaging through the effects of a deceased's estate, he had come across a can of negative film which had apparently been found under the floorboards of a house. When printed, it was possible to identify the reel as comprising two scenes from the Kelly film: possibly uncut outtakes, the scenes closely matched stills in the programme booklet. The small roll of negative was (and is) one of the most precious physical icons of Australian cinema – and just a few years short of its century, it is still in good shape! It was a profound comment on Mr Robb's public-spirited support for the Archive that he simply, and unconditionally, donated something for which he could have easily demanded a very high price.

Two years later, there was more! Some children brought into the office of the journal *Cinema Papers* a can of film which they had found on a Melbourne rubbish tip. It turned out to be about 500 feet of release print from the film – probably from its 1910 reissue version. Some of it was decomposed beyond recovery, but most could be saved. Finally we had a substantial sequence from the film, edited and with intertitles, just as original audiences would have seen it. Altogether, there was now about 5 minutes of footage – not a lot, but enough to convey the flavour and style of the film and to substantiate its historical importance.

No more has yet come to light. The chances of it doing so are slim, but not impossible – and one never gives up hope. It was appropriate that, to mark the Centenary of Cinema in 1995, we finally got Ned Kelly onto an Australian postage stamp. Legally, executed criminals can't be depicted on stamps: but a still from the 1906 film of an actor wearing Ned's actual armour – well, that's different!

4. *The Sentimental Blonde ...* er, *Bloke*

Raymond Longford's 1919 production of *The Sentimental Bloke* is generally regarded as the jewel of Australia's silent era. It is a simple love story set among the working class of suburbia, based on C J Dennis's classic narrative poem of the same name. Starring Arthur Tauchert as Bill, the "bloke", and Lottie Lyell as his girl, Doreen, the film was noted for its naturalistic performances and perceptive casting.

Dennis wrote in broad Australian slang, and the narrative titles of the film directly quote his verse. When Bill is first "intrajuiced" (introduced) to Doreen, he "dips his lid" (raises his hat), and when dressed up to meet his prospective mother-in-law, he remarks of his unaccustomed elegance:

> "Me patent leathers nearly brought the tears,
> Me stand-up collar sorin' orf me ears"

This device, of course, exploited the imaginative capacity of silent films: everyone in the audience responded to the written word by creating the characters' voices in their heads. Outside Australia, though, the device created its own language barrier. So when the film was prepared for American release, the titles were re-written in American slang! The main title became *The Sentimental Bloke: The story of a tough guy* and Dennis's verse was recast somewhat. His description of the wedding breakfast,

> "An' then we 'as a beano up at Mar's
> A slap-up feed, wiv wine an' two big geese"

became

> "Then comes the feast at Mar's: Aunt, uncle, niece,
> Done wonders with the wine an' two big geese".

With the passing of the silent era, Longford's career rapidly declined (he finished his days as a tally clerk on the Sydney waterfront) and his films slipped from sight. Most were lost: a handful have surfaced in incomplete or fragmentary form. *The Bloke* is the only one to survive more or less intact.

In 1952 a nitrate fire atop a building in downtown Melbourne saw the destruction of the film library of the former Government film production unit, the Cinema

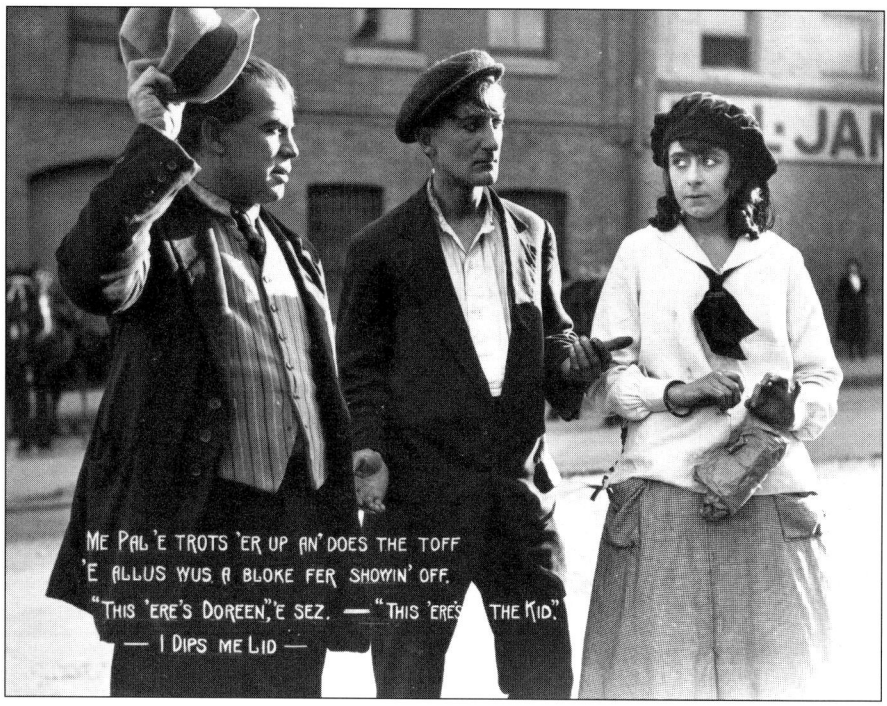

Branch of the Department of Commerce. A maker of promotional shorts and documentaries, it had effectively closed in the late 1930s. Its head, Lyn T Maplestone, was one of the earliest advocates of film preservation, and it appears that the Unit took some steps to salt away significant films, though which ones is unlikely now ever to be known. Miraculously, two boxes of film survived the fire: they were sent to the Film Division of the Commonwealth National Library in Canberra, and an examination of their contents yielded a complete nitrate release print of *The Sentimental Bloke.*

The head of the Division, Larry Lake, was quick to recognise the film's quality, and in 1954 it was sent to a Sydney laboratory for duplication. A junior technician at the lab named Anthony Buckley was given the task of remaking all the splices in the tinted print. Intrigued, he kept all of the two-frame trims: in later years, he would play a large role in re-awakening interest in Australia's film history, in the development of the National Film and Sound Archive (NFSA), and – eventually – become a major producer in his own right. (He would eventually donate the trims to the Archive and thus provide a record of the original tints and tones.)

16mm prints derived from the Library's acetate negative now began to circulate to film societies and festivals, and the *Bloke*, and Longford himself, were rediscovered. Longford has left a poignant record of his feelings in viewing the film again after so many years: by then, everyone else involved in its production was dead, and the experience was bittersweet.

Fast forward to 1973. As a young film archivist, I undertook a study tour of overseas archives which eventually led me to George Eastman House, in Rochester, New York, and its legendary film curator, James Card. I had heard rumours that George Eastman House had a nitrate copy of *The Sentimental Bloke* and I wanted to check this out, so I asked Card if the title rang a bell. He replied that he thought they had something. We trudged out through the snow to the nitrate vaults. Jim opened one of the vaults and we went inside and rummaged for a while. Eventually I came across six cans labelled *The Sentimental Blonde*. This sounded too much of a coincidence, so I opened the first can, unreeled it down to the main title, and saw the credit for Raymond Longford. It was the original negative of *The Sentimental Bloke*. I can't describe how I felt in actually holding those six cans. Every archivist treasures the moments of great finds.

How did the negative get to Eastman House? No one knew, but it is likely to have landed there with a job-lot of silent films, perhaps the stock of a defunct distributor. As noted before, when Australian producers secured an overseas release they had no choice but to send over their original negative for release printing, and often for re-editing as well: there were no satisfactory dupe negative stocks available, and even if there had been, Australian producers could not have afforded to make them. The negative was seldom returned: there were no further printing demands in the home country and the freight cost could not be justified.

Finding the negative was one thing: getting access to it quite another. Overloaded and underfunded, film archives can be notoriously slow to deal with loans or duping requests when there may be other priorities. Eventually, when Paolo Cherchi Usai took over as Senior Curator of Film at Eastman House, an exchange was arranged under which Eastman's preservation copy – a superb fine grain positive taken off the original negative – was loaned to the NFSA. Visually, it was far superior to the existing version derived from the "Cinema Branch" release print. But there were differences: it was shorter (many scenes had been trimmed and tightened), it contained a few additional shots, and all the narrative titles were in American slang!

A major reconstruction – based mainly on the Eastman visuals and utilising the original C J Dennis titles – was embarked on with a projected release date of September 2001 – a story in its own right. The tints and tones will be reinstated, utilising Anthony Buckley's "trims" as colour reference. And we can thank a chain of players – and Providence – for the survival of one of Australia's cinematic treasures.

"The sparkling surface of the sea of history" – Notes on the Origins of Film Preservation

by Stephen Bottomore

Introduction

When the cinema came onto the scene in the mid-1890s, the startling and seductive nature of this illusion captured everyone's attention, and new subjects for the camera were ever in demand. Soon hundreds of films were available, and as fast as one was released another was in production. At first this frenzy for novelty seemed to associate this new film medium with transience, impermanence. But there was another, quite contrary, quality inherent in the celluloid ribbons.

One of the more interesting features of moving photography was that for the first time one could bottle up a version of the world and then reproduce it.[1] Some people, even as early as the 1890s, suggested that these bottled-up images might be worth preserving, might indeed have a permanent value. They began to discuss the advantages, disadvantages, problems, and possibilities of preserving the film image. As so often in this early period, the discussions are full of fascinating, sometimes naïve, realisations and insights, about both the theoretical desirability of archiving film and the practical problems which might stand in the way. These discussions were not fruitless, for there were a number of efforts at preserving film which actually succeeded during this period.

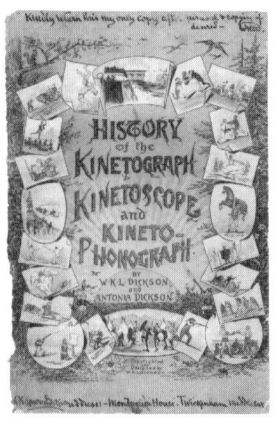

Front cover of W K-L Dickson's 1895 *History of the Kinetograph*, from the Museum of Modern Art's 2000 facsimile edition.

Suggestions for preserving non-fiction films

Possibly the earliest statement of the advantages of archiving the moving image came from the co-inventor of the Kinetoscope, W K-L Dickson, who wrote in 1894:

> Instead of dry and misleading accounts, tinged with the exaggerations of the chroniclers' minds, our archives will be enriched by the vitalized pictures of great national scenes, instinct with all the glowing personalities which characterize them.[2]

This introduces two benefits in preserving film: as a more reliable and detailed way to record historical events, and as a means of glorifying and preserving the national past. These two aspects were repeatedly referred to in discussions of the need for film archiving in the years ahead, with the theme of historical record being raised most often.

One of the first, and undoubtedly the most celebrated, statements of the desirability of preserving film as an archival resource for posterity was in the pamphlet "Une nouvelle source de l'histoire", written by Boleslaw Matuszewski (1856-?) and published in Paris on 25 March 1898.[3] This heralded the medium of film as a uniquely precise means of chronicling historical events, for it could record details more vividly than conventional, written accounts – time of day, distances, the look of things, and so on. Such an efficient recording of an event in images would thereby obviate long verbal accounts ("many lines of vague description").

Matuszewski believed that films should be accorded the same official existence in archives that other historical documents enjoyed. His appeal was well reasoned, and while similar calls for the preservation of film of historical events subsequently appeared through the early 1900s, they rarely went beyond Matuszewski in his fine analysis of the reasons for establishing film archives and the benefits of film as a historical source. In the years before the Great War, several further calls for the establishment of film archives were short on analysis, and often simply suggested that it would be pleasant to have such visual records preserved. For example, in 1906 the British journal *The Referee* predicted that at some time in the future one would be able to go to the British Museum to see "any occurrence... instead of reading about it".[4]

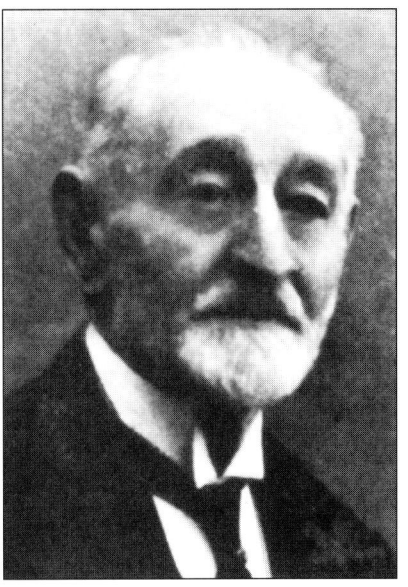

Photograph of Boleslaw Matuszewski, from the Filmoteka Narodowa's 1999 translation, *A New Source of History*.

Filmoteka Narodowa, Warsaw.

While most of us today think of film primarily as a medium for telling fictional stories, this was not so much the case in the early years, when most films were actualities, views of the real world. Non-fiction was also the central concern in most of the early discussion about, and proposals for, the archiving of film. In 1911 a writer in *Le Soir* of Brussels asserted, as almost too obvious to need further justification, that the films chosen for preservation should be *actualities*, "showing modern political, economic, and social life". The writer in question, Morgan Fredy, endorsed the film medium's claims to reliability by noting that, while an ordinary photograph could be easily retouched, "who would dare undertake the retouching of 1200 frames that make up a film?"[5] (This was a point that Matuszewski had himself made in his 1898 pamphlet.)

Also in 1911, *The Bioscope* entered a "plea for a national film museum", stressing that this was required "in order that the faces and figures of the present-day may be perpetuated for the benefit of future generations."[6] By 1914, an editorial in the same journal ("Preserving the Present") claimed that "the side of cinematography which possesses the most lasting significance and the truest human interest is represented best by what is known as the Topical Film". It added that the benefit of film for posterity was as "a record combining an accuracy greater than that of books with a realism fuller and more vivid than that of paintings!"[7]

To some commentators the benefits of preserving films for their historical value seemed almost beyond dispute. But not to all. An anonymous contributor to a trade magazine in 1913 viewed with contempt the idea that the kinematograph could help to elucidate history:

> The kinematograph camera merely gazes at the sparkling surface of the sea of history! Remembering only the pretty waves and the alluring foam. To all the vast political intrigue that goes on beneath that attractive surface it is oblivious. What advantage is derived by seeing Mr. Asquith *arrive* at the House of Commons? It is what Mr. Asquith does inside the House that matters, and this is quite beyond the camera's ken. What benefit would the student of history derive from seeing a picture of Queen Elizabeth arriving at St. James' Palace, accompanied by one of those gorgeous pagents [sic] in which her soul delighted. None at all! And yet that is the camera's entire conception of history; these are presumably the films you wish to preserve in a National repository. Worship of the past is a hindrance to progress.[8]

It is an interesting point of view, and some fifteen years earlier the visionary Matuszewski had already thought of this objection, that film can never do more than record the superficial visual surface of history. But he added that although "historical effects are always easier to seize than causes", *all* historical documents are imperfect: and oral and written documents do not offer a complete picture of historical events either. Film, he suggested, is simply another kind of historical document, with its own validity.

But though it might be acknowledged that films were worth preserving for their historical value, it was clear that such schemes would require considerable financial resources. In 1910 *The Bioscope* echoed a daily newspaper in calling for "A National Film Museum". The journal noted that for many years in Britain the National Photographic Record and Survey Association had been collecting photographs of national buildings and noteworthy scenes, which "will be of the greatest possible value to historians who have to write, a hundred years from now, of the doings of the present time". As far as films were concerned, such a scheme might have to depend on funds from philanthropic sources if the Government could not make a special grant for the purpose. Or perhaps the film companies themselves could provide resources? *The Bioscope* added:

> The film manufacturers themselves might not be unwilling to assist in such a cause in the case of topical subjects, although they could hardly be expected to give up their original negatives unless they had some assurance that they could use them at some remote date, should it be necessary.[9]

This issue of relations between private film companies and national film archives proved to be one of the most persistent stumbling blocks in plans to preserve moving images in years to come.

Suggestions for preserving acted films

All the earliest suggestions for archiving film that I have seen, from Matuszewski onwards, concentrate on the importance of preserving film as history, emphasising the non-fiction rather than the fiction film. The only exceptions are references to the possibility of immortalising great acting talent: even then it is a record of the actor more than of the film in which he or she appears that is really being talked about. When actor R Henderson Bland stepped in with his suggestions for "a National repository for Films" in 1913, he focused on its utility in preserving acting styles of the great performers of the day. Would not, he asked, the next generation "take delight in seeing the acting, however perfunctory, of Sir Henry Fielding, Forbes Robertson and Sir Herbert Tree by means of the kinematograph?"[10]

Two years later George Bernard Shaw also highlighted the capability of film to preserve performance – again mentioning Forbes-Robertson – particularly if the filmed record could be linked to a sound recording. Shaw wrote:

> When they can see and hear Forbes-Robertson's Hamlet equally well produced, it will be possible for our young people to grow up in healthy remoteness from the crowded masses and slums of big cities without growing up as savages... At all events we shall hear no more of the fugitive fame of the actor's art which perishes with himself, for Robertson's Hamlet, filmed and recorded, may delight posterity when the name of the author is forgotten.[11]

The performers too appreciated this chance to preserve their own performances for posterity. Sarah Bernhardt is reported to have said: "This is my one chance of immortality."[12] It seems that it was only after the Great War that people started to suggest that acted films as such were worth preserving. When the *Moving Picture World* asked "Why not a film museum?" in 1920, the journal also highlighted the plight of fiction films, noting that there were still some old prints to be had from the production companies. For example: "There must be a lot of that stuff in the dust-covered cans in the Vitagraph vaults, and there will never be any more like it." *Moving Picture World* also mentioned other films worth preserving, which would include a Mary Pickford film, some of the Keystone and John Bunny comedies, the old Films d'Art, *Cabiria*, and Sarah Bernhardt's *Camille*. "Such a collection would be of vast interest a quarter of a century from now," the journal claimed.[13] By the 1920s the film was increasingly being seen as having a worth in its own right, rather than as merely for its historical content. In 1929, when Foxen Cooper wrote in *The Times* of "a heritage for posterity", he stressed that his vision was not limited to non-fiction film alone:

> In contrast one notes that there has been, as yet, no general desire to preserve for posterity any one of the masterpieces of cinematography, such as *Quo Vadis?* and *Intolerance*, probably the earliest and most stupendous spectacles ever shown on the screen, or *The Four Horsemen of the Apocalypse*, possibly the finest dramatic War film ever produced. In these unique productions the critic can detect artificiality and excesses which have been employed by the producer to convey his story. Perhaps one day some international society with sufficient means at its disposal will form a library of the great films belonging to the various periods since cinematography came into being. Perhaps then these and other earlier productions will be included in such a collection if the negatives are still in existence.[14]

But not everybody was convinced of the eternal worth of film art, nor thought that the transience of film was a wholly bad thing. One writer in the mid-1930s suggested that our memory of a film performance may be a distinct improvement over the reality:

> Perhaps it is a merciful thing that the physical life of celluloid is not much more than fifty years, despite all the efforts of science to achieve some degree of permanence, for memory and romantic idealisation play a great part in maintaining the reputations of the great histrionic figures of the past. If the greatest performances of some of these shadowy figures could have been made permanent in celluloid form, then, as Hamlet says, "who shall 'scape whipping?" Recently I saw some of the earlier Chaplin comedies and I found them unbelievably tiresome. Yet there is no one, having seen and loved Chaplin's earlier successes, who when asked for his opinion does not call upon the rich store of his memory and find both enjoyment for himself and praise for that great comic genius in his recollections. Acting is an ephemeral thing always; it is best not to seek to make it permanent, but to encourage memory and imagination to maintain the reputations of the great ones in our hearts.[15]

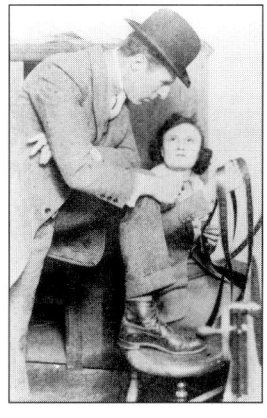

D W Griffith in conversation with a film editor (believed to be Margaret Booth).

BFI Collections – Stills, Posters & Designs, London. 85029.

Early film archives

All the opinions that I have so far quoted were no more than *theoretical* arguments for preserving films. In this section I will examine more detailed, concrete proposals for film preservation, and actual examples of archiving film in the early era.

Possibly the first films to be archived in national institutions were not deposited for preservation purposes, but to guarantee their copyright. The first such deposit was on 16 August 1893, when the Library of Congress in Washington received some "Edison Kinetoscopic Records" from W K-L Dickson, possibly including a film of the dancer Carmencita.[16] For the next few years Edison sent samples of nitrate film for copyright protection, but from 1897 paper-print copies of the complete motion picture were sent.[17] Also in 1897, pioneer film-makers deposited their films in the Cabinet d'Estampes of the Bibliothèque Nationale in Paris, including actualities such as Ernest Normandin's 1896 film of Nicholas II in Paris, and Eugène Pirou's risqué *Le Bain de la Parisienne*.[18] In November 1897 thirty Lumière films were deposited with the Conseil de Prud'hommes de Lyon, and by this action the films received copyright protection for 5 years.[19] By the mid-1890s frames from films were being sent to Britain's copyright depository, Stationer's Hall. The motivation behind all these deposits was to protect the films (or the technical process of making the films) against copying by others. For this reason, all these films were sent to their national repositories in a form not designed for projection: as a few sample frames or as paper prints.

The first concrete plan for the preservation of entire, projectable films – for viewing by future generations, for posterity – came from Robert Paul in Britain. On 21 July 1896 Paul wrote to the British Museum concerning his "Animated Photos of London Life". He proposed that several of his actuality films be preserved in the Museum, including *The Wedding of Princess Maud*, *The 'Prince's Derby'*, and *Henley Regatta*. Paul suggested that each film be placed in a sealed vessel so as to be airtight, with the title of the film engraved on the outside of the container. The British Museum showed no enthusiasm for Paul's proposal, and it seems only accepted one of Paul's films – *The 'Prince's Derby'* – and that with extreme reluctance. Nevertheless, this may be regarded as the world's first effort at actual film archiving.[20]

It is notable that this pioneer effort centred on *factual* films rather than dramatised films, and all subsequent initiatives in film archiving during the early period of cinema also focused on preserving films for their value as historical records, not as works of art in their own right. This followed the trend of the theoretical discussions which I have quoted above.

The world only had to wait a couple of years after Paul's effort before the next concrete proposal to create a film archive emerged. In 1898, possibly influenced by Matuszewski's proposal, a certain Councillor Marsoulan of the Conseil Municipal de Paris presented a plan to create a "musée d'archives cinématographiques", which would collect films to be used for educational purposes in schools. Apparently the plan was not successful, but this was the first of repeated initiatives to establish a film archive for the city of Paris. Late in 1906 plans were again afoot at the Hôtel de Ville, the seat of the city's government, to establish a municipal film archive, which was meant to preserve films of "festivals, ceremonies, and great events concerning the city of Paris". The proposal was submitted to the Conseil Municipal de Paris by a councillor, Henri Turot of the Grandes-Carrières district, who claimed that the cost would be insignificant, as all the necessary filming could be undertaken by a photographer who would be offered special facilities to film in Paris in return for giving to the city a certain number of the resulting views. A French trade journal objected to this proposed monopoly, suggesting that films could equally well be supplied by regular producers.[21] In any case the project failed: no archive was set up as a result of this proposal, nor when councillor Marsoulan again raised the matter with the Parisian authorities in 1908. Subsequent proposals by Victor Perrot in 1911 and 1921, the latter directly to the Conseil Municipal de Paris, again came to nought.[22]

But proposals for municipal film preservation elsewhere were to be more fruitful. The city of Stavanger in Norway apparently started collecting films as early as 1910.[23] In the same year the archives of the city of Brussels started a collection of films of contemporary life, and by 1911 there were some 20 films in this collection. These included the funeral of Leopold II, the arrival of King Albert, the inspection of Brussels schools in 1910, the visit of the Belgian sovereigns to Paris, the reception of the Lord Mayor and of Kaiser Wilhelm II, the inauguration of the Brussels exposition, and the opening of the Parliament.[24]

The formation of these two film collections was not the only significant event for film preservation in 1910. Also in that year, a French theorist thought up a name for this new entity of film archive: *cinématographothèque*, from the Greek words for "movement", "write", and "store". This word did not catch on, for, as the author himself noted, it was ugly; and the only slightly more mellifluous cinémagraphothèque, which had been proposed the previous year, was also abandoned.[25] But in 1913, when the French under-secretary of state for Beaux-Arts was considering the preservation of films, he proposed the more elegant term *cinémathèque*. This is a far earlier use of this word than is often realised: it is usually dated to the 1920s. "Cinémathèque" is now in the global vocabulary, though meaning an organisation specialising in film screenings and research rather than a film archive as such.[26]

The year 1910 was also significant for film preservation in Czechoslovakia, when film materials started to be kept in the graphic art department of the Museum of Technology, and from 1923 in its department of photography and cinema.[27] Other national collections of films were also underway. In 1912 a cinema museum was erected in Vienna, in which everything relating to film was to be kept, equipment and presumably films too.[28] In the same year it was announced that Italian film manufacturers had agreed to found a "National Archives of Kinematography", a film museum "where those films, which present interesting features will be collected together and preserved".[29] I have found few details about these collections, or those I mention in the following paragraphs.

A number of *specialised* film collections also started up about this time. By 1911, the Institut de Sociologie in Belgium had collected seven films showing large industry.[30] Before 1914, films of wild animal life were being preserved at the Congo Museum in Brussels, and at similar institutions in Berlin and Hamburg; in the Vatican Museum in Rome several films of religious interest were being safeguarded.[31] At about this time, the concept of a "time capsule" was becoming quite popular, and in 1911 the city of Wilkes-Barre, Pennsylvania, decided to preserve films "of importance" in "sealed packets that are not to be opened for 100 years".[32] It would be interesting to know if this initiative actually went ahead, and if a cache of films really is due to be opened in 2011.

Film processing at a studio in Brighton.

BFI Collections – Stills, Posters & Designs, London. 160236.

In reviewing progress in film preservation on the eve of the First World War, a writer in *The Bioscope* recorded a number of further moves by national governments. A cinema archive was apparently being established in the Louvre by M. Jacquiert, the Minister of Fine Arts, and the national record office in Madrid had also created a cinematograph section, where the Spanish government deposited a film of the last bullfight of the great matador Machaquito.[33] In vaults under the New York Public Library a storehouse of films was being preserved, including film of the construction of the Panama Canal, and one of "President Wilson's facial expressions".[34]

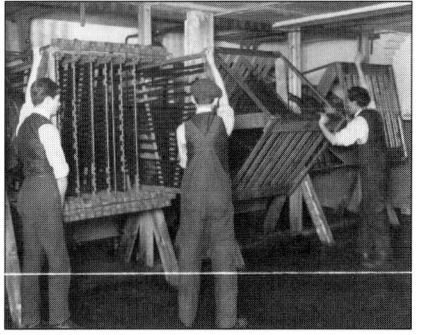

In Britain, however, by the beginning of the First World War little progress had been made in convincing the national authorities about the need for a film archive. A high official of the British Museum commented, "We hardly look upon the cinematograph as a serious proposition yet."[35] However, while there was distinct failure on a national level, in May 1910 the trade journal *The Bioscope* highlighted an initiative from a surprising place.[36] The Croydon Public Library, impressed by the success of the "Photographic Survey and Record of Surrey" which was attached to the library, had started collecting films of local interest. This was achieved through the efforts of the chief librarian, Mr L Stanley Jast, who contacted local picture palace managers, several of whom then donated prints of local films – such subjects as a prize-giving, a horse show, a funeral. Once in the library, these films would not be lent out, but were to be projected at the library on occasion. Jast also commissioned a local electrical engineer to make a device to view the films, using "an enclosed chamber" in which: "in place of the projector lens, a magnifying glass will be used. The movement will be induced by the hand…"[37]

Most of the archival initiatives that I have mentioned above were relatively minor, may not even have been successful, and probably any "archive" they gave rise to did not have a long active life. But a more impressive and lasting early archive took root in Copenhagen. This began as a result of the initiative of Anker Kirkeby, journalist at the national Danish paper *Politiken*. He contacted producer Ole Olsen, the founder of Nordisk Films, and suggested that he take several "cinematographic portraits of well-known personalities whom it would be of historical interest to have handed down to posterity." Olsen accepted, and on 10 December 1910 a contract was signed between Nordisk and *Politiken*. In 1912 a number of films were made of Danes who were prominent in the fields of the fine arts, literature, politics, science, and so on. Several old districts in Copenhagen, which were to be demolished, were also filmed, and there was an associated project to record and preserve the voices of celebrated Danish men and women.[38] At a meeting at the Royal Library on 9 April 1913 the decision was taken to establish the state Arkiv for Films og Fonogrammer. The news was made public, and Edison was among those to send his congratulations.[39]

On behalf of *Politiken*, Kirkeby donated 19 films and 178 records to the new archive. Ole Olsen presented 35 films of historical interest which had been taken by his company from 1906 to 1912, and Peter Elfelt, pioneer cinematographer and photographer to the Danish royal family, presented 20 films shot by himself in the period 1899 to 1906. The archive, based in the Royal Library, was somewhat inactive for the following 30 years, but in 1942 it was transferred to the National Museum and renamed the Statens Arkiv for historiske Film og Stemmer – i.e., the "national archive for films and voices".[40] The main purpose of the archive was (and is – it still exists) to collect films reflecting all aspects of Danish history, and primarily non-fiction material.[41]

As far as Britain was concerned, it seems that the First World War finally broke the impasse and concentrated official minds on film archiving. In 1916 *The Times* pointed out that this matter was now especially timely because of the desirability of preserving films of the war:

> Now that the greatest event in world history is transpiring, so to speak, before our cameras, the historians are offered their first extraordinary opportunity to establish archives of film records, to preserve into the indefinite future the exact replicas of today's actions. It is reported that the German government is doing just that; it is taking and filing away motion pictures of every important action of the war. The British authorities, on the other hand, in spite of earnest appeals by their own countrymen, have so far refused to consider the matter. This course has been attributed, naturally, to the well-known Anglican conservatism…[42]

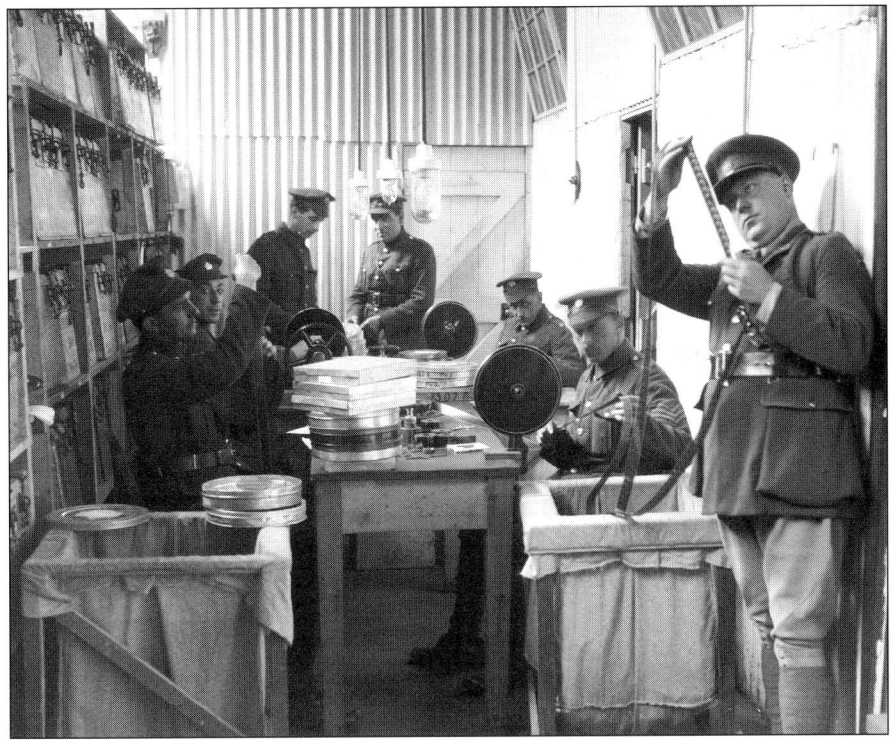

Personnel of the Army Service Corps preparing material for use in behind-the-lines cinemas for British troops in France, 1918.

Imperial War Museum, London. Q8885.

After the War, the Imperial War Museum was established, and one of its briefs was to preserve films. Edward Foxen Cooper, "Government Cinematograph Advisor", who since 1919 was responsible for preserving the Museum's film collection, said: "Future generations will probably be just as interested in seeing how we lived our everyday lives and enjoyed our sports as they will be to see how we fought our battles and heroically met death."[43]

As well as all these state and municipal archives that I have chronicled, one should also mention what was probably the first private film library for "stock-shots". This was established in the first decade of the 20th Century by Abram Stone, who set about buying up old films, especially pictures of historical events: these included the inauguration of President McKinley, many films of Theodore Roosevelt, and New York scenes and vaudeville stars. His first promotional circular in 1908 explained that he offered a film library with "Stock Scenes" such as "departing or arriving vessels, explosions, sunsets, wrecks, parades, animals, foreign cities, street and native scenes..." By using one or more of Stone's stock shots, one could create an action or effect or distant location for a film at reasonable cost without the expense of location shooting, and in this way, as Stone claimed, "a director can strengthen a weak scenario". The company slogan became "Maybe Stone has it". Abram Stone ran the business until his death just after the Great War, and it continued in the family at least until the late 1940s.[44]

Access

Before the advent of such film archives as I have mentioned, it would have been very difficult to find or to view older films. But even when films had been deposited in public institutions, the dual aims of access and preservation might sometimes be at odds. An early and fascinating contribution to this discussion comes from the pen of surrealist poet Guillaume Apollinaire (1880–1918), who visited the Bibliothèque Nationale in 1910 to try to consult some of the scripts and films which he had heard were kept there. His experiences were far from satisfactory, and he wrote a caustic newspaper article to protest the lack of access to these film materials.[45]

The Bibliothèque Nationale is France's national body for copyright deposit, and as we have seen, it had received film materials from the 1890s. It seems that by the time of Apollinaire's visit in 1910 the library was receiving large numbers of film scenarios as well as films. Apollinaire applied to see a selection of scenarios for a research project he claimed to be undertaking.[46] But he waited in vain. Finally he was brought before the librarian, who told him that he was the first person ever to ask to see film scenarios, and that while some 8,000 had been received in the library just in the past year, these were typed and unbound, and they had not yet been catalogued.

But if scripts were inaccessible, what about films? That year the library had started receiving the actual films themselves in place of scenarios, and Apollinaire went to the prints department, where he applied to see ten films, but with no better luck. The first librarian he spoke to denied they had any films there at all. A second admitted that films were held there, but insisted that they could not be consulted:

> You're being a little unreasonable. Ten films!... No Sir, we are not yet set up to make those things available... You really propose to unroll here ten of these 60-metre lengths of fragile film? No Sir, our employees are not here to roll up again what you have unrolled. At the end of the session, your place, Sir, would be a depressing sight. 600 meters of photographic film... We would have the impression, Sir, that the National Library is afflicted with a tapeworm... No, no, no; we're having none of it. We will make films available only when we have arranged a proper way to do so... Goodbye, Sir![47]

Lest one think that this was pure fantasy from the pen of this surrealist poet, the previous month an article in the leading French film journal confirmed that a certain number of films really had been deposited in the Département des Estampes of the Bibliothèque Nationale (for copyright), but that because there was no projector to view the films, one might say that they were not so much "deposited" as "interred".[48] This was an unsatisfactory situation, as Apollinaire remarks:

> ...the films and scenarios have surely not been sent to the Bibliothèque Nationale to decay in the vaults. As soon as possible they must be made available to the public, which is above all dedicated to progress.

Conclusion

The issue Apollinaire draws attention to – access – has been a pressing concern for film archivists ever since these bodies were established. His piece is a thought-provoking coda to the early history of film archives, and a suggestive pointer to how these bodies were to develop in the years after 1910. But this is not the only theme relating to film archives which is highlighted by such examples from the origins of the cinema. No doubt other issues of contemporary relevance could be revealed if further research were conducted into some of the attempts at archiving that I have referred to in this article. And I must stress that the amount of information that I have found about several of these "archives" is sketchy in the extreme, often limited to a place and a date, and not much more.

I suspect that far more details about these initiatives could be discovered by researching in written archives in the countries concerned. For example, to find out more about the sundry attempts from 1906 to establish a Paris municipal film archive, the minutes of the municipal council would be an obvious source. Similarly, local records would no doubt contain more details about the film collections started in 1910 in Stavanger and Brussels. The discussions and arguments in these sources are likely to be fascinating and illuminating. And who knows, perhaps they might reveal the whereabouts of "lost" stores of films? So I conclude this essay with a call to film archives around the world to initiate research into the early history of film preservation in their own countries and regions. Only when this further research has been undertaken will we have a truer history of the origins of film archives.

Notes

1. As a record of the world, the film medium was also a new form of evidence, and interestingly this 'witnessing' role was seen by one author as having religious implications. In an essay published in January 1897, Gabriel Aubray took the cinematograph as a metaphor for the all-seeing eye of God, with potential to record a detailed memoir of our lives and sins. Aubray's "Devant le Cinématographe" appeared in the French literary journal *La Quinzaine* on 15 January 1897, as the eighth instalment of "Lettres à ma cousine". The series started in *La Quinzaine* in November 1896, and was reprinted as a single volume later in 1897. For more information on Aubray's ideas, see my article "Reflet du cinéma dans la fiction littéraire française", *Archives* No. 61/62, avril/mai 1995, pp. 12–20.

2. Antonia and W K-L Dickson, *Edison's Invention of the Kineto-Phonograph* (Los Angeles: Pueblo Press, 1939), reprinted from the *Century Magazine*, 1894. This aspect of "national glory" was emphasised in the same year in a brochure for the Kinetoscope: "It is possible through its agency to reproduce to future ages, a living picture of any of the great leaders of the age, delivering an address..." See *Edison's Masterpiece: The Kinetoscope* (Continental Commerce Company, 1894), on reel 1, frame 9, of microfilm *Motion Picture Catalogs by American Producers and Distributors, 1884–1908*, edited by Charles Musser.

3. The date of Matuszewski's death is apparently unknown, even in Poland, although a foreword to the Filmoteka Narodowa publication listed below indicates that he was still alive and active in the early 1930s. Copies of *Une Nouvelle source de l'histoire* survive at the universities of Stanford, Yale, and Texas (Gernsheim collection), the Getty Center, and in variant versions in the Bibliothèque Nationale in Paris. Strangely, the BN does not have an original copy of Matuszewski's other work, *La Photographie animée: ce qu'elle est, ce qu'elle doit être*, but copies are held in the Getty Center, the Bernice P. Bishop Museum Library in Hawaii, and at George Eastman House in Rochester. The Filmoteka Narodowa in Poland has recently published an English translation of both works, with an introduction by Zbigniew Czeczot-Gawrack and a personal reminiscence ("I knew Boleslaw Matuszewski") by Jan Jacoby: *A New Source of History/Animated Photography – What it is, What it should be* (Warsaw: Filmoteka Narodowa, 1999). Previous English-language translations of *Une Nouvelle source...* have appeared in the UNESCO journal *Cultures* (v.2 no.1, 1974, pp. 219–222) and in *Film History* (v.7, 1995, pp. 322–324). UNESCO's translation is available through the 'Screening the Past' web-journal hosted by Latrobe University, Bundoora, Australia, and can be found (with an introduction by William D. Routt) at http://www.latrobe.edu.au/www/screeningthepast/reruns/mat.html. A German translation appears in *montage/av* (Jg.7, no.2, 1998, pp. 6–12).

4. Reprinted in "Recorders of the Future", *Optical Lantern and Cinematograph Journal* (April 1906), p. 117.

5. Morgan Fredy, "Les Archives cinématographiques", in *Courrier Cinématographique* (18 August 1911), pp. 5, 8; from *Le Soir* (Brussels), 7 July 1911.

6. "Cromwell's Head", *The Bioscope* (13 April 1911), p. 51.

7. "Preserving the Present", *The Bioscope* (23 July 1914), front page.

8. *Kinematograph and Lantern Weekly* (24 April 1913), p. 3: comment on R Henderson Bland's article, mentioned in note 10.

9. "A National Film Museum", *The Bioscope* (26 May 1910), p. 3. The next sentence must surely have been ironic: "It is, however, fairly certain that any cinematographer who wishes to have an historical subject preserved would find the authorities of the British and South Kensington Museums open to receive suggestions for the formation of a nucleus collection, to which they could have access."

10. R. Henderson Bland, "The Need of a National Repository for Films", *Kinematograph and Lantern Weekly* (17 April 1913), pp. 2489–2491. Bland had himself just achieved screen immortality through playing Christ in Kalem's *From the Manger to the Cross* (1913). Another actor, Sir Herbert Beerbohm Tree, had a more ambivalent attitude to the thought of filmed records of his performance. (Low Warren's recollections of this may be found elsewhere in the present volume.)

11. *Metropolitan Magazine* (USA), May 1915, quoted in Low Warren, *The Film Game* (London: T. Werner Laurie, 1937), pp. 86–87.

12. Quoted in Deems Taylor, et al., *A Pictorial History of the Movies* (New York: Simon and Schuster, revised and enlarged edition, 1949), p. 20.

13. "Why Not a Film Museum?", *Moving Picture World* (11 September 1920), p. 180.

14. "Historical Film Records – The Life of the Nation – A Heritage for Posterity", *The Times* (London), 19 March 1929, "Film Number", p.vii. Thanks to Roger Smither for this reference. See also: an appeal for a film archive, by Vachel Lindsay, *Moving Picture World* (9 September 1916), p. 1704; "Lest We Forget: The Motion Picture Needs a Museum", *Photoplay* (April 1923), p. 57; Tamar Lane, *What's Wrong with the Movies* (Los Angeles: Waverly Co., 1923), p. 124, which lists the 15 "greatest" films, of which only 4 survive; "Preservation of Historical Films", *Trans SMPE* (January 1927), p. 80, etc.

15. Basil Dean, "The Future of Screen and Stage", in Charles Davy, ed., *Footnotes to the Film* (London: Lovat Dickson, 1937), p. 180.

16. Gordon Hendricks, *The Kinetoscope*, reprinted in *Origins of the American Film* (New York: Arno, 1972), p. 47. The deposit took almost two months to clear, possibly due to "some doubt ... in the Copyright Office about the nature of the material being copyrighted" – see Patrick G Loughney, *A Descriptive Analysis of the Library of Congress Paper Print Collection...* (PhD diss., George Washington University, 1988) pp. 54–55.

17. Paul Spehr, "Some Still Fragments of a Moving Past", *Quarterly Journal of the Library of Congress*, v.32 no.1 (January 1975), p. 39.

18. Jacques Deslandes, *Le Boulevard du Cinéma a l'époque de Georges Méliès* (Paris: Editions du Cerf, 1963), Appendix 3, pp. 105–07; René Jeanne and Charles Ford, *Le Cinéma et la Presse* (Paris: Armand Colin, 1961), pp. 20–21, 175.

19. Jacques Rittaud-Hutinet, *Le Cinema des Origines...* (Paris?: Champ Vallon, 1985), p. 70.

20. For more on Paul's proposal and the "archiving" of his film, see my article, "'The Collection of Rubbish'. Animatographs, Archives and Arguments: London, 1896–97", in *Film History*, v. 7 no.3 (Autumn 1995), pp. 51–57. The 1896 Derby survives in the NFTVA; it is 38 feet long and, like all the rest of the NFTVA's material on this event, derives ultimately from a copy deposited in 1949 (coming from either Paul himself or the Science Museum). "This tinted print (stock date apparently 1896) was in pretty poor condition when we got it," according to Elaine Burrows.

21. "A l'Hôtel de Ville", *Phono-Ciné-Gazette* (15 November 1906), p. 433; also reported in *British Journal of Photography* (11 January 1907, p. 36, and elsewhere; René Jeanne and Charles Ford, op cit., p. 195. Information on the 1898 plan comes from the journal 1895, no.18 (1995), p. 108.

22. Victor Perrot, *A Paris il y a soixante ans naissait le cinéma* (Paris: Cinémathèque Française, 1955). Jean-Jacques Meusy kindly sent me some references to a proposed Paris film archive, including the following: In 1913 a proposal was made for a "Musée de la parole et du geste" by Emile Massard, councillor at the Conseil Municipal de Paris (*Courrier Cinématographique*, 21 June 1913). There was further news on this at the end of the Great War (*Ciné-Journal*, 25 May 1918). Finally, in 1921, after the proposal from Victor Perrot, a "cinémathèque d'enseignement municipale" was planned with funding of 25,000 francs (very little) to collect films of relevance to Paris (*Ciné-Journal*, 5 February and 12 February 1921).

23. "20 kilometer lokalhistorie", *Film og Kino* (1978), p. 53.

24. Morgan Fredy, op. cit.

25. "Une cinémagraphothèque, S.V.P.! (d'après Les Nouvelles)", *Phono-Ciné-Gazette*, no.103 (15 December 1909); "Une cinématographothèque", *Ciné-Journal* (27 February 1910), pp. 5–8.

26. Proposal of the under-secretary, Léon Bérard, in *Le Journal* (31 October 1913), p. 7. Giraud's first example of "cinémathèque' does not appear until 1921. See *Lexique français du Cinéma* (Paris, 1958).

27. Information from Narodni Filmový Archiv.

28. "Austria", *The Bioscope* (13 July 1911), p. 89; "The Cinematograph Museum", *The Bioscope* (11 July 1912), p. 93; "Ein Film-Archiv in Wien", *Licht-Bild-Bühne* (2 March 1912), p. 24.

29. "Archives of the Kinematograph", *Kinematograph and Lantern Weekly* (29 August 1912), p. 1303; *Ciné-Journal* (11 May 1912), p. 23.

30. Morgan Fredy, op cit.

31. Langford Reed, "Film Archives. What Has Been Achieved", *The Bioscope* (30 July 1914), pp. 471, 473.

32. *Popular Mechanics*, v.16 (ca. September 1911), p. 371.

33. Langford Reed, op cit. The French archive was also briefly reported in *Illustrated Films Monthly* (February 1914), p. 338.

34. Langford Reed, op cit.

35. Langford Reed, op cit. The British Museum was well set up to preserve diverse objects, and so, as one commentator noted, films would be little extra challenge: "...although there might be

certain difficulties in preserving a celluloid film for a number of years, the scientists of such a place as the British Museum, who can preserve anything, from an insect to an Egyptian mummy, would doubtless be able to solve that problem."

36. "A National Film Museum", *The Bioscope* (26 May 1910), p. 3.

37. Langford Reed, op cit.

38. The following year Kirkeby persuaded the Danish branch of His Master's Voice to record the famous Danish voices.

39. "A Cinema Record Office", *New York Times* (23 January 1914), p. 4.

40. It is now called the Nationalmuseets Audiovisuelle Samlinger, based in Lyngby.

41. Letter to the author from Ib Monty, Director of Det Danske Filmmuseum, 2 April 1981, enclosing letter from Hans Berggreen of Det Kongelige Bibliotek, 19 December 1972. Monty also sent me information including articles from *Politiken* of 27 February 1913 and 24 March 1913, and *Den danske Stats Arkiv for Film og Fotogrammer* (Copenhagen, ca.1914). See also interview with Ove Brusendorff in *Kosmorama* no. 42 (February 1959); Ole Olsen, *Filmens Eventyr og mit Eget* (Copenhagen, 1940).

42. "Historic Films – The Difficulty of Preservation", *The Times* (London), 28 November 1916.

43. "Historical Film Records – The Life of the Nation – A Heritage for Posterity", *The Times* (London), 19 March 1929, "Film Number", p.vii.

44. Dorothy T Stone, "The First Film Library", *Films in Review* (New York), v. 2 no.7 (1950), pp. 29–35.

45. Pascal Hédegat [pseudonym for Guillaume Apollinaire], "Le cinéma à la Nationale", *L'Intransigeant* (1 March 1910), pp. 1–2.

46. Apollinaire's project was about how films projected in reverse influence mores! The requested scripts were all about Rostand for some reason.

47. "Comme vous êtes peu raisonable. Dix films!... Non monsieur, nous ne sommes pas encore utillés pour communiquer ces choses-là... Songez-donc, vous voudriez dérouler ici dix fois soixante mètres de ruban fragile. Non monsieur, nos employés ne sont pas là pour enrouler ce que vous avez déroulé. Votre place, monsieur, présenterait à la fin de la séance un spectacle désolant et peu banal... 600 mètres de ruban photographique... Mais, monsieur, nous aurions l'impression que la Bibliothèque Nationale est affligée d'un ver solitaire... Non, non, non; pas de ça Lisette. On ne communiquera les films que lorsqu'on aura découvert la façon de les comminquer... Au revoir, Monsieur!"

48. "Une cinématographothèque", *Ciné-Journal* (27 February 1910), pp. 5–8. Another journal had also concluded: "...aucune installation ne permet, au Cabinet des Estampes, l'étude, c'est-à-dire la projection des photographies animées, voire le déroulement des films pour leur examen image par image. Des films n'y sont donc pas déposés. Ils y sont enterrés..." "Une cinémagraphothèque, S.V.P.!", *Phono-Ciné-Gazette*, no.103 (15 December 1909).

Trying to Save Frames

by Harold Brown

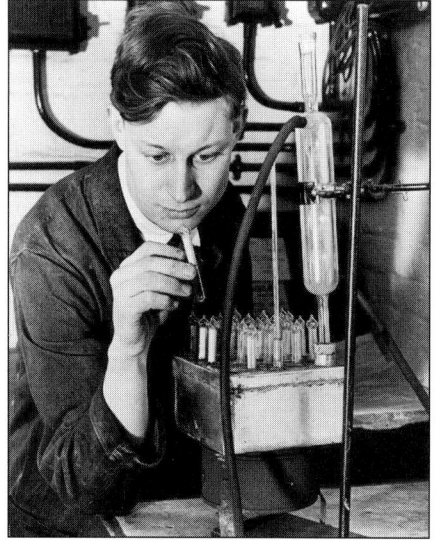

Harold Brown, with the equipment used in the chemical test for nitrate film deterioration.

BFI Collections – Stills, Posters & Designs, London. 200237.

On 15 March 1935, at the age of fifteen and a half, I started a job as an office boy in London's West End. My employer was the British Film Institute. One of the specific aims of the Institute was "To establish a repository of films of permanent value", and this was named the "National Film Library". The staff member in charge of this project was Ernest Lindgren, and two months after I started I went with him to collect the first acquisition of films. These were about forty reels of one- and two-reelers. They included a Keystone comedy, a Stan Laurel comedy, and a Bonzo cartoon. Soon I was typing fewer envelopes and film reviews in the office, and instead learning how to handle these reels. Lindgren arranged these first films into alphabetical order by title, gave them numbers in that order, and added letters indicating which reel was which and the total number of reels in the film. This is still the "Location Number" system in use in what was to become the National Film and Television Archive, now known as "bfi Collections".

I was sent by the Institute to spend some time in the projection room of the Forum Cinema, off London's Strand. There I learned the craft of film projection and was introduced by the projectionists to their method of joining film. The overlap part of the join was wetted by the tongue, and, with the blade of a pair of scissors and the film held up in the hand, the emulsion was scraped off. It was a matter of pride to remove all the emulsion with one pass of the scissor blade. The two ends of the join were then held in position between finger and thumb up in the air and the cement applied between them, first from one edge and then from the other. The cement formula which they used was two parts of acetone and one part of amyl acetate. That cement is still used in the NFTVA for nitrate film today, and I have introduced it to a number of newly-formed archives around the world since my retirement.

I will record a significant incident in my early career in the National Film Library. I encountered a film with a tear across two frames. The "correct" way to deal with this was to cut out the two damaged frames and make a normal join. What I did with it was to abut the torn ends and cement a piece of blank film over the tear. I was reprimanded, quite properly, by H D Waley, the Institute's technical man at the time; but when Lindgren saw it, he said, "You were trying to save frames, weren't you?" He clearly was thoroughly approving of that aim, whatever the quality of that first attempt of mine at film conservation. That incident epitomises the outlook which governed our work thereafter, and which I have sought to inculcate into the staff who have come into my sphere since.

The staff of the Film Institute at the beginning were not well acquainted with the physical properties of film, and were guided by a leaflet composed for us by the British Kinematograph Society. This leaflet warned against permitting projection of films which were to be permanently preserved, because of the inevitable wear of repeated projection and the risk of more serious damage. The leaflet also set out recommended conditions of temperature and humidity for long-term storage. These were 55 degrees Fahrenheit (12.8°C) and 50% Relative Humidity.

Concerning film storage: In view of the high flammability of nitrate film, the National Film Archive explored film storage. Early in its history there was built in the grounds of the Kodak establishment at Harrow, outside London, what was called "the Experimental Column". In this small experiment a series of drawers was assembled on a vertical brick column. The drawers were of asbestos, and sized to contain one reel of film. Each had an openable flap at the back which led to a flue in the brickwork. It was demonstrated that any of the reels of film could burn out completely without igniting any of the others. This was an ideally safe form of storage for nitrate film. There was just one, at that time insuperable, obstacle: the frequently occurring one of cost. The Archive finished up adopting vaults of 500 reels, and to date there has never been any incident or problem with fire in the store.

Much later in its history, in 1976, the Archive needed to establish a larger nitrate store than its site at Aston Clinton could accommodate. The NFA had moved its nitrate films from central London to Aston Clinton, a village outside London, at the outbreak of World War II. By the 1970s it was realised that a large nitrate store in a village was not ideal, and we sought a more remote location. But how remote did it need to be? In the event of any of the nitrate becoming ignited, how far would the resulting fumes have to travel before they ceased to be a hazard to people living in the vicinity? A typical storage vault for 500 reels was built on Ministry of Defence land on the remote Potton Island. The vaultful of films was burned. On the first occasion, the whole test was frustrated because the vault door which had been provided was made of soft wood and very promptly burned away, and the flame and vapour poured out through the door opening instead of through the proper channel in the roof of the vault. The test was repeated on a subsequent occasion with a secure steel door, and another 500 reels of film burned. The resulting temperature within was measured and the fumes were sampled at various distances. The conclusion was that there should be no habitation within 300 metres. A conforming site was found on a remote ex-Royal Air Force base in Warwickshire, near the village of Gaydon, which gives the site its name.

In the spring of a year in the late 1930s or early 1940s, I had occasion to wind through a First World War news item, *The Battle of Lebbeke*. This was one of the films received in that first acquisition. It was then in apparently good condition. During the following autumn I handled it again, and it had then, in the centre of the strand, some sticky patches which were also partly faded. This was our first encounter with nitrate decomposition. We were previously unaware of the possibility.

Equipment used in the chemical test for nitrate film deterioration.
Harold Brown.

The Research Department of Kodak at Harrow were consulted, and they provided us with a test which would show the approach of this state so that the film could be copied before any damage occurred. Even very frequent inspection could not do this since, when there was anything to see, what one was seeing was some image deterioration. The test consisted of taking out a punch of a quarter-of-an-inch diameter. This specimen was placed in a small test tube and the opening of the tube was closed with a plug of blue litmus paper. The tubes were cooked in a closed oven at a temperature of 134°C. The oven was opened after an hour and the litmus examined. We had to assess the degree of reddening of the litmus as "slightly red" or "fully red", and the films were re-tested after six months or a year according to the degree of redness, or copied immediately.

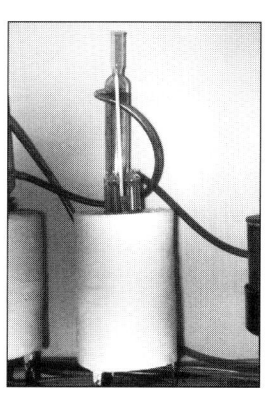

This test was used and film copied accordingly for several years, until in 1948 the Government Chemist's Department devised for us a test which used Alizarin Red as the re-agent, which bleached in contact with the acid vapour produced by heating

99

the specimen. The tubes were held in a vapour bath in such manner that the Alizarin Red papers were continuously visible. This was a more satisfactory arrangement, and the results were recorded as the time elapsed to when the paper was bleached at the bottom. Again there was a scheme of re-testing or immediate copying according to the time on the first test.

In 1937 or '38 we received from the Paisley Philosophical Institution a little collection of films made around the turn of the century. One of these was *The Highland Reel*, produced by the Warwick Trading Company. I remember it well because the emulsion was peeled from one side of about the last two feet of film. I re-attached this part to the base by softening the base with film cement and pressing the emulsion back onto it. The adhesion was good, but after a while that part of the film buckled severely! We learned to do such restorations with a solution of gelatin, and many feet of film have been so treated, mostly by Minda Horwood, who joined our staff in 1949 and only recently reached retirement age. Peeling of the emulsion from the base in these early films is widely known among the archives. The problem is that the base is non-porous and the gelatin emulsion has no firm hold, particularly as it dries out with time. The film manufacturers' solution was that when the base was cast as a viscous solution onto a smooth steel band, and while the base was still fluid, a thin layer of a solution of gelatin was cast onto it. The two fluids diffused into each other so that there was a firm bond between them. Then, when the emulsion was cast onto the base, it readily adhered to the gelatin, which was of its own kind.

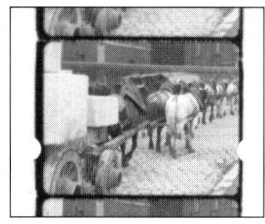

An example of Lumière film, with its characteristic perforation.

Harold Brown.

In 1954, Henri Langlois of the Cinémathèque Française was visiting Ernest Lindgren at his office at the National Film Archive in London. Langlois asked Lindgren if we could copy Lumière film, with its single pair of perforations per frame. This could not, of course, go through normal 35mm printing equipment. Lindgren asked me, "Can we copy Lumière film?" There was no suggestion of any money to get parts in order to do this; so during that year I constructed a machine using my childhood "Meccano" construction kit and various bits of wood and sheet metal, plus lengths of wire and other parts, including the now notorious "knicker elastic". Initially I had no motor to drive it, and it was turned by means of a loop of spring curtain wire connected to the take-up of a viewing machine. When I viewed my first test I found it exhibited a continuous, consistent, vertical jump. When I examined the original film I found that the pitch between alternate perforations was different. When I modified the machine to locate the Lumière film by the same perforations in relation to the frame being exposed as was used on the Lumière equipment, I obtained a steady picture.

This was shown to the Technical Advisory Committee which the Archive had at that time. Their first comment was, "It's better than we get from the laboratories." Their criticism was about the speed of printing, which then took five seconds per frame. I introduced a more powerful lamp and a mechanical shutter and raised the speed to one second per frame. Thus was born the NFA's famous "Mk IV printer". This machine could, of course, also copy film with Edison-type perforations; and for thirty years it was used for the worst shrunken or damaged film, with which normal printers could not cope. A virtue of this machine, compared with normal printers that press the two films together only at the edges (which is clearly satisfactory for normal film), is that during the exposure of each frame, that frame is pressed against the copy film by an opal glass window, which presses over the whole area of that frame with a pressure of about ten pounds per square inch. In this way, even severely buckled film is brought into good contact with the copy film, which is vital to achieving a sharp image.

This machine was also used to copy 28mm film onto 35mm, and to copy 9.5mm onto 16mm. The 28mm consisted of episodes of *The Perils of Pauline*, and the 9.5mm of scenes of Anna Pavlova in Egypt.

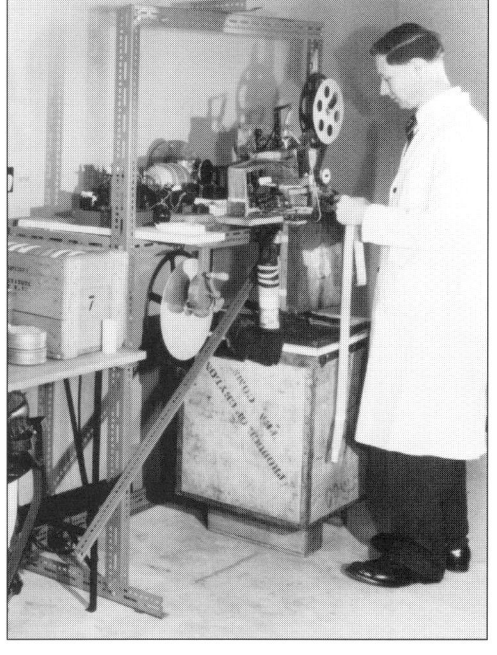

Harold Brown, with the Mark IV printer at Aston Clinton.

BFI Collections – Stills, Posters & Designs, London. 172795.

On another occasion, the Mk IV was used to copy some two-colour Technicolor film, one item of which was the colour sequence of *The Hollywood Revue of 1929*. My first take of this section proved to be faulty, because the transport pins were not correctly adjusted in their stroke to fit the degree of shrinkage of the original film. A second take produced an acceptable result.[1] The sound for *Hollywood Revue* was on disc, and was transferred to film for us by the BBC, who at that time used 16-inch 33⅓ rpm discs for some of their sound recordings. Unfortunately, in making the transfer, the speed of the discs did not exactly match that of the film, so that through each reel the sound gradually went out of synchronisation with the picture. The picture consisted of a series of individual stage acts, each of which faded in and out, so that I was able to restore synch by deleting a frame or two from the dark end of each of the fades between acts. I set synchronism in the middle of each act, so that the beginning was out in one direction and the end in the other, but the error at any time was never greater than two frames.

Subsequently we had the need to copy other non-standard gauges of film from the nitrate era. These were not 35mm and thus needed an optical set-up to copy them onto 35mm. Among the formats thus copied were Prestwich 60mm, Demeny 60mm, the 65mm Veriscope record of the Corbett-Fitzsimmons boxing match of 1897, and a 17.5mm copy of Abel Gance's *Napoléon* – part of which was subsequently incorporated into Kevin Brownlow's famous reconstruction. The projection end of the apparatus for these was in most cases constructed of "Meccano", and we used a Newman Sinclair camera which had formed part of the stereoscopic camera apparatus which was used by the Spottiswood brothers for some 1951 Festival of Britain films.

The "Mark IV" printer, now on display in the atrium of the BFI's National Film and Television Archive J Paul Getty Conservation Centre, Berkhamsted. Photographed by Harold Brown, 2001.

Harold Brown.

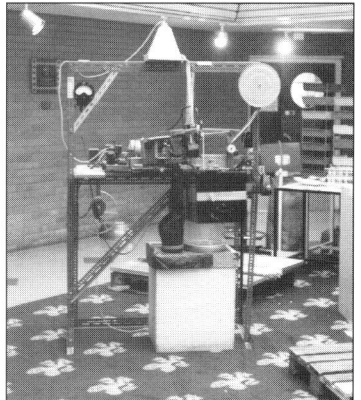

One of the features of films of the nitrate era was that there was not, through most of that period, a sufficiently inexpensive and satisfactory method of colour cinematography for it to be used for any but a few films. However, many films did have colour in the form of "tinting" and "toning". Tinting was initially achieved by passing the finished prints through a bath of dye which was absorbed by the gelatin of the film's emulsion coating. Toning was produced by a chemical action which converted the silver of the black-and-white image to an inherently coloured salt, or into a compound which would absorb certain dyes which the gelatin of the emulsion did not. It was possible first to "tone" the film with one colour, and then "tint" it with another. Thus one could typically have a romantic scene which was toned blue and tinted pink.

Many films of the nitrate era have been copied onto safety base only in black-and-white form, and the tinting/toning lost. It has been the practice in the NFA to keep a written record of the tinting scheme in those films which have it, so that it is possible to reproduce the colouring scheme in any new prints. This is easy to say; but when it comes to the technical task of actually re-creating the tinting and toning, the results which have sometimes been achieved do not look like the original colouring. The method which has often been used is to make a duplicate negative on colour stock and make a colour print from that. This does produce a "tinted"/"toned" effect, but the colours are usually not convincingly correct when compared with the original film. I believe that the most nearly accurate reproductions have been those which took a black-and-white copy and then toned and tinted it in the traditional manner. We have treated one or two films in this way, such as Alfred Hitchcock's *The Lodger* and Maurice Elvey's *At the Villa Rose*, and the results have been spectacular, but it is a slow, laborious, and messy job.

As we all know, the major film manufacturers ceased to make nitrate base for motion pictures after 1951, and introduced cellulose triacetate base, which was expected to have a useful life running to hundreds of years. Thus ended what may be called the "Nitrate Era".

I have a sequel to this.

In March 1985, the Film Archive of the Philippines, in Manila, held a "Workshop on the Development of Film Archives". During that week, we visited some stores of cellulose triacetate film, and were assailed by a most powerful odour. These films were found also to have lost the normal springiness of film and were thoroughly limp. Most of them had on both surfaces a fine grey powder, which was easily rubbed off but which soon replaced itself. Some of the worst suffered fading of the image; the fading, unlike that caused by the decomposition of nitrate film, which tends to start in the centre of the strand, occurred equally over all the surface. We were able to place the year of manufacture of some of these films, in part by reference to the Kodak code, and found that they were all within 25 years old. Of course, I reported this, and described the condition of these films in a memorandum to David Francis, who at the time was the Curator of the National Film Archive in London. Remembering the characteristic odour, I headed that memo with the words: "THE VINEGAR SYNDROME"....

Notes

1. It may be worth mentioning in connection with the copying of colour that at first I used a Kodak stock intended for copying from colour reversal film. The result was sometimes very good and at others quite hopeless. The reason was that the copy film had the sensitivities of its emulsion layers matched precisely to the transmissions of the film which it was designed to copy. They had comparatively narrow sensitivities and would not match the transmissions of many other films. When I used camera film, I regularly had reasonable results.

Projecting Nitrate

by Stephen Herbert

My own introduction to Nitrate film was in 1970, when I was a projectionist at the National Film Theatre in London – precisely the venue for "The Last Nitrate Picture Show". We were due to show a Western starring William S Hart – I think it was *The Toll Gate*. A metal trunk arrived from the United States with a 35mm print of the film. I opened the trunk, and there was a sweet, sickly smell – something that one would perhaps expect of a dead body rather than a film – or anyway, so it seemed to me in my naïveté. A small roll of the film had been separated from the rest, and on examination it was very sticky. The rest of the film seemed to be in reasonable condition. I examined it on the rewind bench. It was a beautiful print, tinted and toned, but as I lifted my arms from the bench I was rather horrified to note

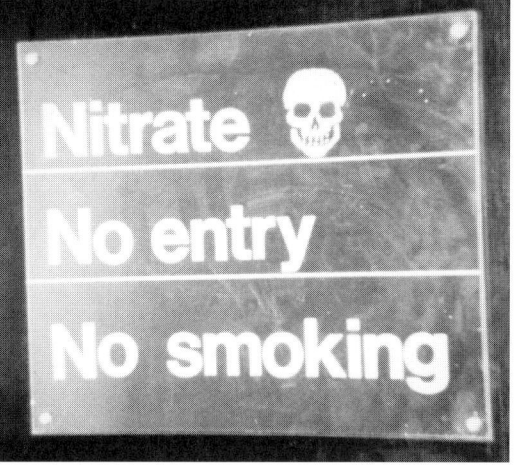

Warning sign on the door of the projection box at the National Film Theatre in London.

Stephen Herbert.

that several images had become detached from the base and were stuck on my arms like tattoos. The whole print was actually unstable. We decided to test a short section on the projector, and it rattled through – grudgingly, but it did rattle through the machine – and after some consultation with more senior staff, we were given the go-ahead to run it, which we did. We managed to coax it through the projector, for what I am fairly sure was the last time. It was later established that the film had been copied in the States before being sent over.

A film in that condition would not be projected at the NFT today. But many of the nitrate prints that we showed in those days were in fact in excellent shape, and some still are, 30 years on, for all sorts of chemical reasons that have been described by other contributors.

The most common problem for us was shrinkage, which meant that the film simply did not fit the projector sprockets properly. Clearly this is very dangerous, because if you are running a film and it does not fit the sprockets, it is going to come off them, and then it is going to find its way into or onto the very hot lamp-house, and that is *not* what you want to do with nitrate film, which is why shrinkage was our biggest worry. Sometimes the film would simply jam, sometimes it would actually feed its way into the gate only to get chopped up by the shutter into little pieces of flammable nitrate – either way, a difficult situation.

I never actually saw a nitrate fire in my days as a projectionist, though I came very close on a few occasions. Once I turned up to work to discover that there had been a fire in the projection room the previous evening. The projector mechanism had been destroyed, and there was a large hole in the ceiling where the firemen had chopped away at it to ensure there were no burning embers still alight. For weeks afterwards we would find bits of charred film around the projection room. Happily, no one was hurt on this occasion, and the machine was replaced the same day. There were one or two more fires in the National Film Theatre in the following years, but it has been many years since the last one. Things were not quite so stringent in those days, and there was perhaps a slightly more cavalier attitude of "Let's see what happens," which is certainly not the case today.

Now nitrate film is very flammable, as you know (or inflammable, and how confusing it is that in English both words mean the same thing). It will catch fire easily, and once it is burning it is very difficult, in fact close to impossible, to extinguish it, as the various training films screened during this Symposium show. In certain situations, if it is confined and burning, it will actually explode. That was the inevitable situation when cellulose nitrate was invented and first used for films.

Other participants have mentioned the Charity Bazaar fire in Paris in 1897, but I wish to stress that, as with some of the other early film fires, it was not in fact primarily caused by the film stock igniting. This fire was caused by flammable ether liquid, used in the illuminant. The ether liquid was refilled during a performance, which is always an extremely dangerous procedure, because the actual metal container for the ether liquid would almost certainly still be hot, so that it was very dangerous to try to refill it, which is what happened on this occasion. Reading the French transcriptions of the court case and investigations following the fire, it appears that the projectionist said to his assistant, "I can't see anything here," while he was refilling the ether, and that his assistant lit a match so he could see better. The fluid ignited, and the flames of course spread very quickly to the film stock, the curtains, and the temporary wooden exhibition walls, and over 100 people were killed, many of them notable members of European society. You can imagine the effect that pictures of the disaster had on European society at the time. Film shows were a new thing, and the idea that a film show had caused this destruction obviously was extremely disturbing.

Inevitably, regulations on showing film were tightened up during the following years, but I think it is important to stress again that it was often the illuminant that was the problem. In fact, these sorts of accidents preceded film: they were not uncommon at magic lantern shows, where gasbags in the early days would cause problems, perhaps explode, and later on pressurised metal gas cylinders would cause accidents as well. So it was not unknown for there to be problems at picture shows before film came along. However, the regulations were tightened in the years following these initial fires in the film business. In London and elsewhere it eventually became necessary for the projector and the projectionist to be enclosed in a metal projection booth.

1906 Gaumont advertisement for a transportable projection booth.

© Gaumont. Archives du Film du Centre National de la Cinématographie, Bois d'Arcy.

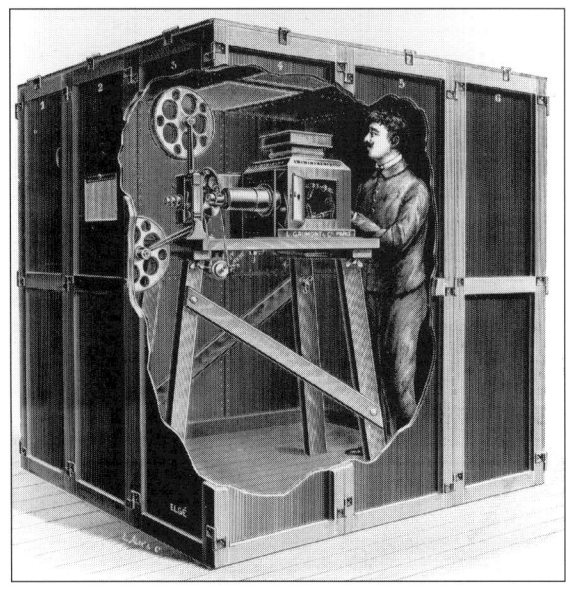

Some advertisements and other illustrations show the "ideal" self-contained metal projection booth, which was often designed to be transportable, because we are talking about the period before the establishment of purpose-built permanent cinemas. Safety regulations meant that something had to be done with the projector whether the show was to have been in a village hall, a theatre, or any other sort of location. These illustrations will often show a transportable booth with a projector using an electric arc lamp. I do not know how many of you know what happens with electric arc lamps, but they give off a rather nasty white powder, and these days, on the rare occasions when electric arcs are used, the powder is sucked out through a flue. In those days, however, the powder came out of a small chimney on top of the projector, and straight into the lungs of the projectionist. Now, some operators may have had the benefit of an electric motor to pull the film through the projector, but quite typically the projectionist would have been cranking through the reels by hand, so he was putting in some significant physical exertion, breathing in all this rather nasty stuff from the arc, as well as being enclosed with the nitrate film in a confined booth. Not exactly ideal working conditions, and if it actually did go up in flames, then obviously he was in serious trouble. Purpose-built cinemas, when they started springing up shortly afterwards, included a separate brick booth at the rear of the hall fitted with steel safety shutters.

From quite early on – in fact from around 1909 – several types of non-flammable cellulose acetate or other types of "safety" films were experimented with and marketed. There were some problems with some of those film stocks, which are again discussed by other Symposium contributors – they were perhaps not so hard-wearing, nor as translucent as cellulose nitrate. Sometimes such safety stocks were used, however, even if not in any major way until around 1950. For film shows in schools, colleges, and the home, for example, safety film was actually introduced by Pathé quite early on, with their 28mm film system in 1912. This system was designed so that it was impossible to project anything but films produced exclusively on Pathé safety stock – indeed, that was the main point of it. Similar safety stocks were later adopted for the introduction of 17.5mm, 16mm, 9.5, etc., in the 1920s.

There were, nonetheless, occasions when nitrate-based film was used in the home. From the late 1890s, in fact from 1897 until the early 1930s, toy cinematographs were made. They were popular boys' toys, a successor to the magic lantern. These machines used both specially prepared coloured film loops (usually on safety base after 1910) and clips of around 50 feet taken from scrapped cinema distribution prints, which of course were nitrate. Apart from toy projectors, another little toy that was available was a film frame viewer. Children could buy packets of film frames (which again were usually nitrate-based film) to look at in these tin viewers. These packets of nitrate-based film were sold to children in toy shops and sweet shops right up until the mid-1930s. Not surprisingly, the practice caused concern, especially after there were stories of accidents. Although the accidents were fairly few and far between, questions were eventually asked in the British Parliament.

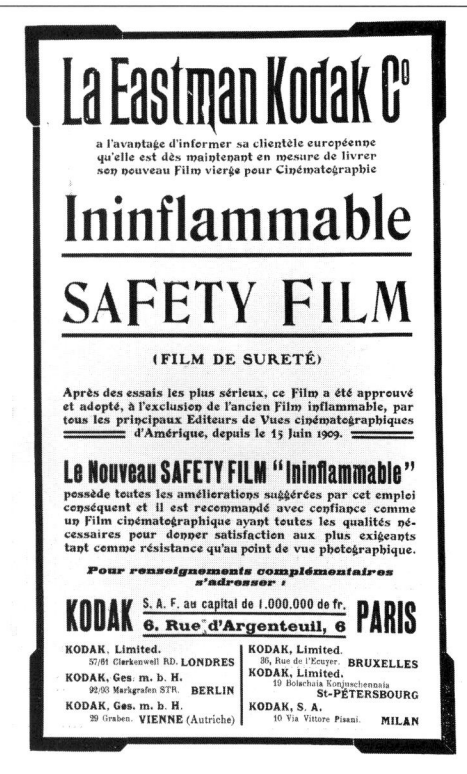

The magazine *Home Movies* started something of a campaign against the sale of these flammable films to children in the 1930s, using newspaper clippings with headlines such as this: "Five burn to death in moving picture fire in Montreal ... Private home entertainment proves tragedy. Woman and four children die. Film blaze turns party to panic." Although the disaster described took place in Canada, the magazine pointed out that this flammable film was still being sold in Britain at the time, and that a similar tragedy was bound to happen in Britain sooner or later, if inflammable 35mm film continued to be used in the home. It has recently been suggested to me that this campaign was partly a promotion by Kodak and Pathé, in association with *Home Movies* magazine, with the goal essentially of promoting the new generation of toy projectors such as the Koda Toy or the Pathé Kid – the sort of projectors using small-gauge safety film that were coming in. I do not know how true this is, but there could well be something in it.

1909 Kodak advertisement for safety film, claiming – a little prematurely – to be capable of giving satisfaction to the most demanding customers.

© Gaumont. Archives du Film du Centre National de la Cinématographie, Bois d'Arcy.

A story relating to children and inflammable film was told to me by one of the culprits. An elderly lady, who was still alive a couple of years ago, knew the film pioneer Robert Paul when she was a girl. This was in the 1920s, and Paul had left

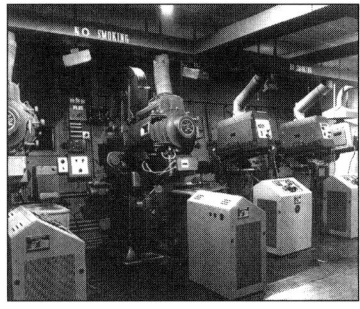

the business many years before, but he gave her and her brother a basket full of his old short films from the very early days, to show on a toy machine, which he also gave her. However, they had much more fun with this gift, by unrolling the films over the hedges in their garden and setting fire to them. So here is an instance where the flammability of the film stock led to the loss of perhaps unique prints of some early films, and there must be many more such stories. The fact that film was flammable was actually quite an attraction to children – you could do far more interesting things with it than simply project it, and this must have caused the loss of lots of movies.

The NFT projection box, ca. 1957, with Kalee 35mm projectors and arcs (left), and Bell & Howell 16mm projectors (right).

BFI Collections – Stills, Posters & Designs, London.

Many private collectors have kept and shown nitrate-based film over the years. In the 1970s I was invited to the home of an elderly collector, who showed me the special brick building in his garden that was full of film. This had been built, I believe, at the insistence of the local authorities, who were aware of his collecting activities. I was rather puzzled therefore to discover that it was full of 28mm safety film, while every nook and cranny in the house from the laundry cupboard to the attic was stacked with nitrate film. "If the house goes up," he told me, "these old Pathé reels will be OK." It did occur to me that this perhaps would have been the least of his worries if the house had gone up, because it would have taken much of the street with it.

Now we no longer have to worry about the ethics of being privy to this kind of information, since the old film collectors are mainly a thing of the past. However, as you will certainly all know, there are still odd reels in sheds and attics that turn up every year, though thankfully these tend to gravitate towards responsible, professional archives with the appropriate storage or disposal facilities.

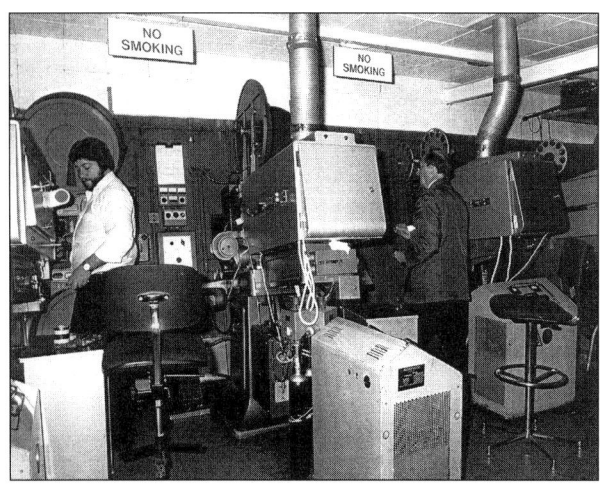

To return to film projection in the National Film Theatre in the year 2000, which may perhaps be taken as representative of any archival film theatre that is equipped to screen nitrate and which still expects to do so from time to time. When you try to enter the NFT projection room, not just when there is a nitrate programme, but all the time, you are greeted by a ferocious sign and a detailed set of instructions. The chief projectionist, Simon Allen, has produced a truly excellent guide for the guys who work on the projection of nitrate-based film. It incorporates many, many years of experience, and what is really important about it is that it includes not just the technical stuff, it also provides a procedural guide. Because it is not just knowing the chemistry or the physics of film and projectors – it is knowing the procedure to make sure that you will not have a nasty accident that is so important.

The NFT projection box, in the 1980s, now equipped with Victoria 8 35mm/70mm projectors (left – note the CO2 cylinder), and Philips 16mm projectors (right).

BFI Collections – Stills, Posters & Designs, London.

Here are some examples of what goes on back there. Firstly, all the nitrate film is kept either in boxes that have got big red labels on them saying "Nitrate" or in a special, distinctive kind of box that is used for no other purpose, so that it should be impossible to mistake which cases have got nitrate film and which have not. The projectors which are used to project nitrate are Cinemeccanica machines, which are very complicated beasts these days, as no doubt you know, incorporating all sorts of things on them, including the various digital sound systems. If you looked at those in the NFT, you would also notice that each projector has got double spool boxes, one inside the other. That second small box is a precaution, for use when showing nitrate film. Nitrate films are always shown on small 2,000-foot reels (rather than larger made-up reels), the limited capacity again being accepted, in spite of the inconvenience and extra workload, as a safety procedure. Next, you would notice that just under the lens there is a pipe that goes to the door of the projector. That pipe comes from a CO_2 extinguisher, and makes it possible to pump gas to the places where it is most likely that fire would break out, and where it can be stopped before it gets to do any serious damage.

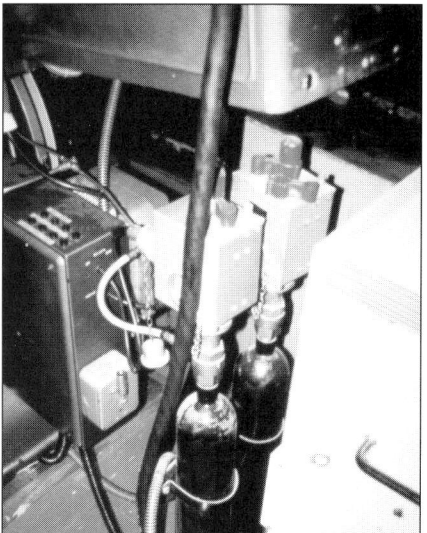

Close-up of the CO_2 system in the NFT projection box, 2000.

Stephen Herbert.

The CO_2 supply comes from behind the projector. There are two cylinders, and the red security clips are removed from around the necks of the two cylinders when a nitrate film is about to be shown. (The safety clips are there to stop the cylinders being manually activated, so they are taken off for a nitrate screening.) The pipe leads through the door, so that when the door swings closed the nozzle will be very close to the top of the gate. As it said in that little instructional film, *This Film Is Dangerous*, if the fire has not taken full hold of the reel, and is still in or near the gate, the CO_2 will hopefully actually physically blow the fire out before it catches the main part of the film reel. If the fire has already spread and the film reel is alight, then there is nothing you can do.

Further safety measures, including a safety shutter, are attached to a flammable link, so that if there is any flame the link will instantly burn away, and that will cause the whole thing to shut down, and in fact will cause the extinguishers to go off automatically. There is also a newly arranged emergency system on the projector, with an unmissably big manual plunger provided for the emergency stop. This does not only stop the machine – it actually sets off the extinguisher and everything else, just in case. So that is practically what goes on upstairs in the NFT projection box. Every foot of film – not only nitrate film, but every foot of film that goes on the screen in the NFT – is examined by hand by the projectionist; everything passes through their fingers, so they can check for damage.

Let me just cite a few extracts from the National Film Theatre regulations:

> "All films that enter the NFT should do so via the Viewing Room. All films must then be checked by the vault keeper, to see whether they are Nitrate or Safety. This is done by looking at the edge of the film, outside the sprocket holes, or between the sprocket holes, for the word 'Safety' or 'Safety Film', or just 'S'. If the film has the words 'Nitrate' and 'Safety' then it is probably Safety. If the print has no Safety mark and no Nitrate mark, then one frame must be cut out for testing."

This basically leads into a description of the flame test – the film frame is taken elsewhere and tested – which goes on for several paragraphs.

> "When prints are removed from the vaults – when the print is taken up to the rewind room – it must be kept in the can or in the Nitrate bins (which are special film bins for the Nitrate films.) It must only be on the bench when it is being checked, it must not be left on the bench when you leave the rewind room. If a lunch or tea break comes when you are half-way through, it must be spooled-off and stored. The projection room door must be locked when leaving it unattended."

It is this procedural stuff that is so very often left woolly and ignored, and that is when accidents happen. I think that this a major benefit of this kind of instruction.

Then, of course, all film must be checked for shrinkage. If film does not set onto the standard joiner, there are specially adapted joiners for nitrate-based film.

> "All prints will be checked for shrinkage by running them through the projector with the lamp switched off."

This is essential, as nitrate can shrink at different rates: checking the shrinkage at a certain point on the joiner is no guarantee that the shrinkage is not greater at another point, and that is really important to projectionists.

> "All cement joints must be taped over. If the leader of the film is Nitrate special note must be made of this on the leader. If the rack lines of the film are not very clear, white china graph rack lines must be put on the leader to make it unnecessary to open the shutter to check the racking." [And then – the original is in large bold type] **"The occasional practice of opening the shutter to see if it is in rack, must not be used when projecting Nitrate film."**

> "Nitrate Print Rehearsal. When Nitrate is being run there must be two projectionists in the box at all times. All prints must first be run through the projector with the Xenon switched off to make sure it will run through. All prints need a dry run. All Nitrate to be screened must have a full rehearsal with the lamp on, as well as the dry run with the lamp off. These rehearsals have been timetabled and will appear on the weekly schedule.... No print will be screened to the public unless it has a full rehearsal. No exceptions."

Then it goes through eight points, basically for setting up for projection:

> Step One
> "When setting up the projectors for Nitrate, one person should set it up, and the other should check it. The Nitrate boxes should be put in place on both projectors."

> Step Two
> "The four red clips should must be removed."

It then goes through the whole procedure of setting up the machine.

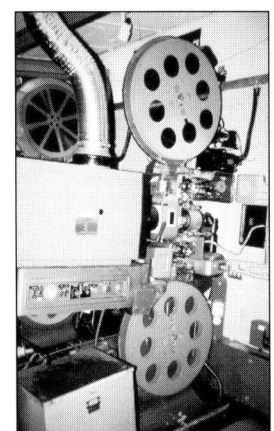

One of the Cinemeccanica projectors in the NFT projection box, 2000.

Stephen Herbert.

You often see regulations pinned on factory walls and so on, and you may think that no one has ever read them, no one has ever even looked at them. I can assure you that everything that is in the NFT regulations is adhered to, by the letter, every time. When you see a projectionist go to put a reel on the machine, he will show the leader to the other person, who has to be there to make sure that he is doing the right thing. Everything gets checked every few minutes. And there are steel safety shutters in the portholes, which can still be manually activated: simply pulling one handle will activate all the steel shutters. So if there is any danger from nitrate film in the building, you will be pleased to know that it is very much a danger to the projectionists rather than the audience.

Phantom Fires: An Evaluation of the Evidence for Nitrate Fires in Fairground Cinematograph Shows

by Dr Vanessa Toulmin

Introduction

> There remains of course, the great and all-important question of the dangers that may at any moment arise from fire.... In such cases it is, as often as not, less the actual effects of a catastrophe of the kind than the unreasoning panic springing from alarm that one has to take into account. Until the public possess the absolute certainty that the cinematographic entertainments are free from danger there must always be the possibility of such calamities taking place as that referred to.[1]

So stated the reporter from the newspaper *The World's Fair* in 1909, as the debate concerning the soon-to-be-introduced Cinematograph Act was dominating the trade press. The association between nitrate fires and early cinematograph exhibitions has entered the mythology of film history. The fatal fire of 4 May 1897 at the Bazar de la Charité in Paris, which claimed the lives of at least 120 people, has been excellently covered by Mark Gosser in *Film History*. In his article, Gosser concludes that the Paris incident, along with the fire in a fairground tent at Stafford Market, were certainly factors in the introduction of the London County Council Act of 1898.[2] However, tragedies of this kind were not necessarily unknown in such venues. Other forms of entertainment had long been the victims of fire, well before the introduction of the cinematograph. The explosive nature of early film performances may have momentarily affected their presentation in theatres, but it did not affect the promotion of cinema in a variety of other venues:

> But ordinances or not, plenty of films shows took place in small cafés and storefronts and on fairgrounds ill-equipped for safe film projection.[3]

Despite an otherwise excellent article, Gosser makes the assumption that fairgrounds were ill-equipped for safe film projections, and this belief appears to be widely held. In their book *The Travelling Cinematograph Show*, Stephen Smith and Kevin Scrivens state that the Act was introduced as a result of a fire that destroyed Ward's Pageant Pictures in Newmarket in 1908,[4] while Leslie Wood, in *The Miracle of the Movies*, shifts the blame away from the fairground showmen in the direction of the "penny gaffs", which, in his opinion:

> ...did nothing to enhance the cinema's reputation with people who considered themselves refined. They were murky little places, with vulgar bills outside, as well as a man in an ill-fitting and greasy uniform who used a military swagger cane for the dual purpose of chasing away unruly small boys and smacking the display boards to attract attention.[5]

Rachael Low agrees with Leslie Wood, stating that the period leading up to the introduction of the 1909 Cinematograph Act was "the heyday of the penny gaff",

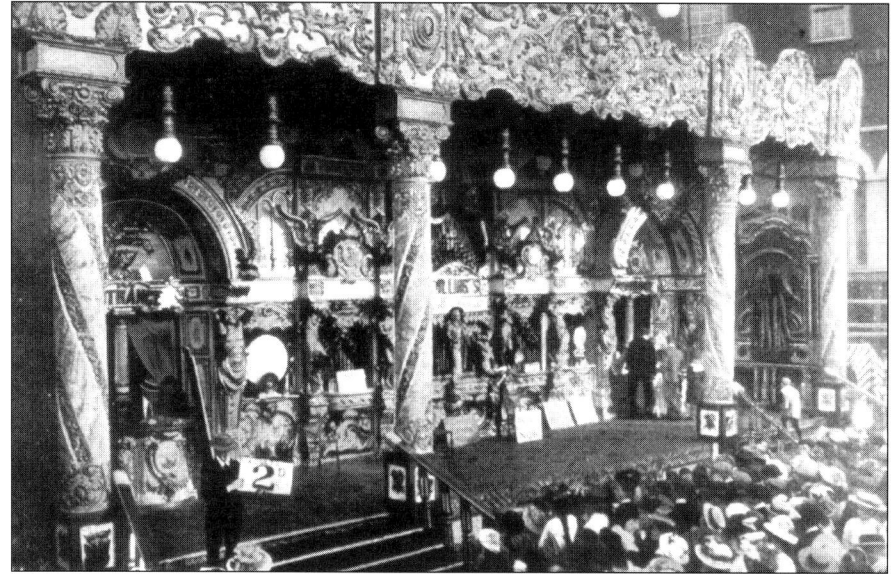

Hand-coloured close-up of Pat Collins No 2 Wonderland Show, Nottingham Goose Fair, 1908. (See also Colour Section 1.)
© National Fairground Archive, Sheffield.

with its "dirty and disreputable appearance, its bad projection and get-rich-quick policy."[6]

Therefore, the blame appears to be pointed in the direction of the itinerant exhibitor, with opinion split between the town hall or shop showman or the fairground type. The aim of this research is to discuss the relationship between travelling cinematograph presentations and nitrate fires, by examining the firsthand accounts of these events that appeared in the trade and local papers for the period immediately preceding and following the 1909 Cinematograph Act, thereby illustrating that the incidence of fire at fairgrounds was actually far lower than in other venues of the time. It will also demonstrate that instead of being "ill-equipped" amateurs, fairground showmen were actually professional exhibitors, with a long history of demonstrating pre-cinema forms of entertainment, such as ghost and magic lantern shows.

The Shows

From 1897 to 1914 there were over 150 fairground exhibitors presenting travelling cinematograph shows on fairgrounds in the United Kingdom.[7] Although the fairground season is traditionally regarded as starting at Easter and finishing in October, during the late Victorian period many venues were open during December and January for winter fairs, including the World's Fair at the Royal Agricultural Hall in Islington, which lasted six weeks, and the Glasgow Carnival, which was a Christmas holiday fair. Famous Charter fairs also took place in Sheffield, Norwich, and Bolton, and the cinematograph was a popular site at these events.[8] The introduction of animated pictures on the fairground resulted in a novelty that showmen could present and adapt for use in a variety of venues or locations at any time of the calendar year.[9]

Randall Williams is generally credited with being the first showman to present animated pictures, in his Ghost Show at the Royal Agricultural Hall in Islington on 26 December 1896.[10] His contemporaries were quick to follow suit. These shows ranged from converted ghost and marionette booths by 1900, evolving into purpose-built cinematograph exhibitions, designed and constructed solely for the showing of films, from 1905 onwards.[11] The booths were designed for quick and easy access: the easier it was to get in and out, the more rapid the turnover in the presentations of the show.[12] The showmen who operated and presented these attractions had usually been connected to the world of fairs or travelling exhibitions for many years, through magic lanterns, ghost shows, or tableaux vivants, and they were familiar with the issues involved in handling such equipment.[13] An account from Hull Fair in 1900 lists more than nine exhibitions which would have been open for ten hours a day, with the entire programme lasting an average of fifteen minutes.[14] The entrances were usually on either side of the outside stage or by the side of the booth, all of which allowed for quick and easy entrance. Blackout was achieved by the heavy canvassing of the tent, and lighting was supplied by naphtha lamps or, by 1900, electric arc lamps.

The Evidence for Nitrate Fires

The main sources of material for fairground shows are the newspapers *The World's Fair* (1904 onwards) and *The Showman* (1900–1912), both trade journals of the travelling showland fraternity. These newspapers are a marvellous resource for all aspects of the early film industry, the innovations, the types of films shown, and, for the purpose of this research, the hazards that were involved in presenting film shows. The advent of the London County Council Acts, 1898 and 1900, followed by the 1909 Cinematograph Act, resulted in legislation affecting the use of inflammable films in exhibitions.[15] The showmen were naturally suspicious of the LCC Acts, which resulted in tighter regulations, as the accompanying cartoon illustrates. However, the later 1909 Act would prove to be an even more contentious issue with the fairground fraternity, as demonstrated by the following letter, which appeared in *The World's Fair* on 25 September 1909:

> In my opinion the Act arises from the agitation of large Bioscope firms who wish to create a trade monopoly and from no other cause whatsoever. I believe their object is the extinction of small firms, private contractors, and exhibitors who work independently of the monopolists. Now to the best of my belief, the only exhibitions that have resulted in fire, panic, loss of life in this country, have been given by large firms, not travelling showmen or private exhibitors.[16]

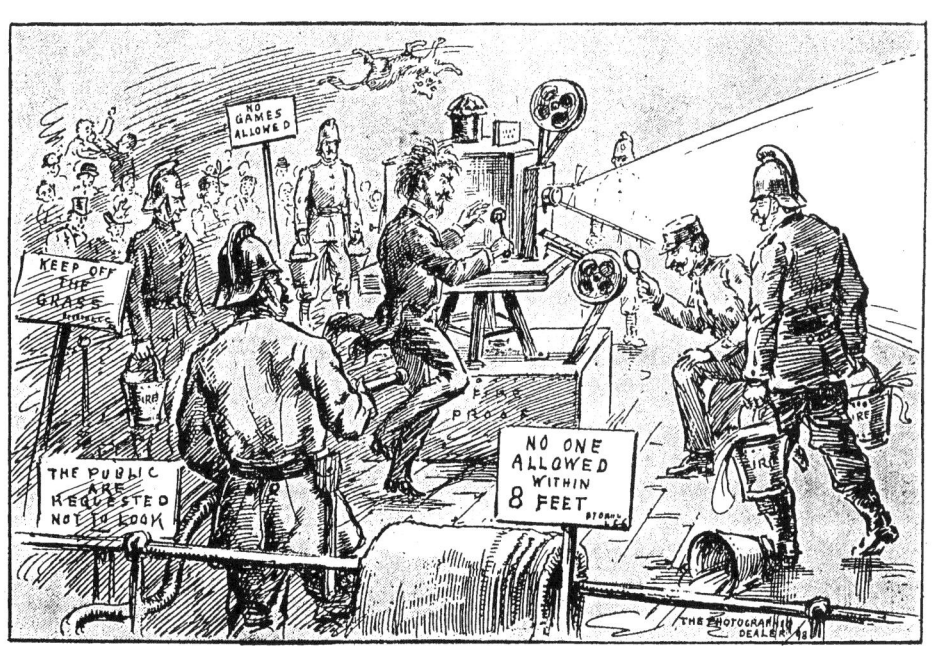

A cartoonist in *The Showman* of 8 March 1901 reacts to the latest London County Council regulations.

National Fairground Archive, Sheffield.

Cinematograph Show under the new L.C.C. Rules.

Oh! have the audience all assembled? / Have you put the barriers round? / Have you got the hydrant ready? / Laid asbestos on the ground?

Are the firemen standing steady? / Bring the blankets right up here! / Have you got the pails handy? / Is the special exit clear?

Is the fellow there who has to / Watch the films come out and in? / Have you put the fire-proof box on— / Right?—Then let the show begin! / ALPHONSE COURLANDER.

In this letter, Fred T Walker implies that fires did not occur in travelling shows either of the fairground or town hall type. The evidence from trade journals would appear to back up this argument, as very few fires are reported in fairground shows for the period 1904–1908; instead, they seem to have started in theatres or cinemas. In order to fully investigate this claim a systematic search is required, as there is no doubt that fires did occur before this date. Further research and more statistical evidence are needed in order to comprehend the seriousness of the issue. However, for the purpose of this article, a sample of the reports that appeared in the months leading up to the 1909 Act and the two years following the Act has been taken in order to see if there is a pattern.

In the months immediately preceding the 1909 Act, four incidents are recorded in *The World's Fair*. All involved the igniting of inflammable film in the cinematograph machine, resulting in considerable panic in the venues and, in the case of Southsea, one fatality. The first transpired at Stratford in London, and the following graphic description appeared in *The World's Fair*:

> In an interview with a representative, the operator who gave the alarm said: 'I was preparing to show the first film, and when I opened the shutter ready to start something went "Pouf!", and before I could close my shutter the beginning of the film caught fire. I did all I could to smother the flame with my handkerchief, but seeing I could not do any good I raised the alarm by calling out "Fire."[17]

The report from Dallington is even more vivid, describing a 20-foot flame shooting out of the operating box as the films caught fire.[18] Other incidents occurred at Southsea, where a young boy lost his life, and at Sheffield Central Hall, when the film came into contact with the outside of the lantern, resulting in "a great flash of flame".[19]

However, all of these exhibitions took place in halls or permanent structures, and not in fairground shows, with the cause in all cases being the igniting of the films. The only report that appeared in *The World's Fair* in 1909 appertaining to travelling exhibitions relates to a fire occurring in Wingate's show at Larkhall in June that year, with the cause of the outbreak being unknown and no serious damage reported.[20] An earlier report, which appeared in July 1908, tells of an exciting incident at a Leeds Picture Palace, when the cinematograph caught fire as a consequence of one of the films igniting. However, the venue was again a permanent place of public entertainment, and not a travelling exhibition.[21]

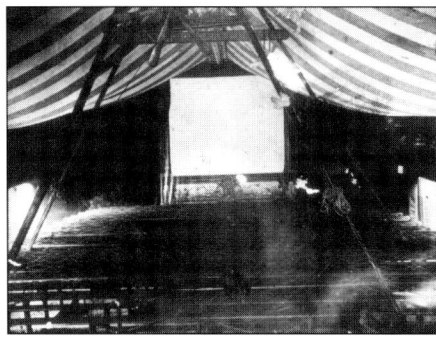

Interior of Aspland's Bioscope Show, Boston, ca. 1910.

© National Fairground Archive, Sheffield.

If we extend the search back to 1907, an account in *The World's Fair* reveals that a fire occurred in Aspland's show in August of that year. The fire started while the show was open at Shipley, when the nitrate film caught fire and over £100 of film stock was destroyed. Disaster was averted by the actions of the projectionist, who apparently grasped the films in a wet blanket and threw them out of the show.[22]

Therefore, it would appear that Mr Walker was partly right in his letter, in that very few fires took place in travelling cinematographs, and reports relating to fires in booths appear only twice after the introduction of the Cinematagraph Act. Although the evidence demonstrates that the issues of safety in travelling exhibitions does not appear to be a direct factor in the introduction of the new legislation, they were affected by the Act, and a variety of legal cases appear in the trade press involving showmen after 1910. The most common offence relates to the non-use of metal boxes for the storage of films. This appears to be a major issue, and John Wilson, a travelling showman, was prosecuted for this twice in one month at Barrow-in-Furness in Cumbria in 1911.[23] The report also contains a description of the methods used by the inspectors to test the inflammability of the film stock used at that time:

> Witness asked the accused how he knew they were non-inflammable, and the defendant said, 'I only use non-inflammable.' At the time, the operator was rewinding one of the films on the spool, which had been shown. Witness required what picture it was and he was told, 'Choosing a wife'. Sergeant Norris tore a small piece of the corner of the film, and struck a match, which instantly ignited and flamed in an instant.[24]

When called upon in court to answer the prosecution, Mr Wilson claimed in his defence that the films were known as non-inflammables by the showmen and that "all films would burn, but it was a question whether they would burn in a certain way within the meaning of the act."[25]

Other incidents in 1912 involved the Victoria Pier Syndicate in Folkstone,[26] and the New Bioscope Trading Company,[27] and, in 1913, Enoch Farrar.[28] What other prosecutions occur appear to be for building too close to permanent structures, as in the case of W H Marshall in 1910,[29] or the G. L. Syndicate in Cambridge for using 480 volts instead of the 110 voltage stated in the Act.[30] Of the six prosecutions, three are of fairground showmen. Another incident involving a travelling exhibitor took place in 1912, when James Chipperfield was fined for not having a fire extinguisher in his booth. The complexities of the new Act are demonstrated by an amusing account involving James Chipperfield that appeared in *The World's Fair* in 1912:

> *No Fire Extinguisher: Showman Who Had Read Cinematograph Regulations Until He Was 'Black in the Face'.*
>
> An interesting case under the Cinematograph Act came before the Caxton magistrates at the Petty Sessions held on Friday. James William Chipperfield, showman, was summoned for failing to have a grenade or fire extinguisher in his show at Gaminglay.

The report continues with a description of the equipment used by showmen in case of a fire, which consisted of a bucket of water, a bucket of sand, and a fire blanket 15 inches square. When asked by the magistrate if the defendant had read the Cinematograph Act, James Chipperfield responded:

> They had had licenses under the Act, ever since it came into operation, and this was the first complaint they had heard.
>
> Inspector Cheville said defendant had told him he had read the regulations 'until he was black in the face.'[31]

Despite the humorous manner in which this incident was recounted by *The World's Fair*, the introduction of the 1909 Act was seen as a serious threat by some of the exhibitors, despite the fact that the General Secretary of the Showmen's Guild had written to the Home Secretary ensuring the insertion of the clause relating to travelling exhibitions.[32] Following the incident concerning James Chipperfield, and his prosecution again under the Cinematograph Act, Alf Ball, a leading exhibitor of cinematograph shows on the fairground, wrote a letter to *The World's Fair*, in which he claimed, "Showmen are being harassed by the Cinematograph Act," despite having all the necessary safety and fire equipment available:

I have an iron operating box, outside my show, and in that I have a fire extinguisher, a bucket of sand, and a wet blanket; outside the box I have two pails of water, and another fire extinguisher hangs at the back of the organ; another extinguisher hangs on the organ front, and two pails of water at each end where the pay boxes are. Inside the booth I have two pails full and ready, also another extinguisher; three exits on each side in addition to front entrances; over each door is an emergency oil lamp lit up in case the electricity fails ... what else is wanted I really do not know.[33]

However, some showmen do not appear to have been as innocent as Mr Ball. An interesting case appears in 1911, when an unnamed showman is fined £20 for leaning over the cinematograph machine holding a cigarette! The defendant in this case denied smoking in the box but admitted holding a lighted cigarette in his hand. No fire had occurred, but the offence had been spotted by the Inspector, who saw the showman in the circumstances described.[34] Again in 1911, there is an incident at Riddings Fair in a fairground show, but it does not appear to involve a cinematograph; the outbreak was believed to have caused by the fusing of a wire in the show.[35] The most telling headline comes from the following month, when The World's Fair reports:

Exciting Incident – Comedian Overcome By Fumes.

An exciting incident occurred at a cinematograph show on the fairground at Idle belonging to James Crighton. An exhibition was being given when one of the films struck and took fire and the booth was filled with smoke .... whilst assisting in extinguishing the flames a comedian named Tom Clarke was overtaken by fumes.[36]

However, the reporter seems more interested in the fact that the comedian was overtaken by fumes rather than the fact that the films had ignited and the show set on fire.

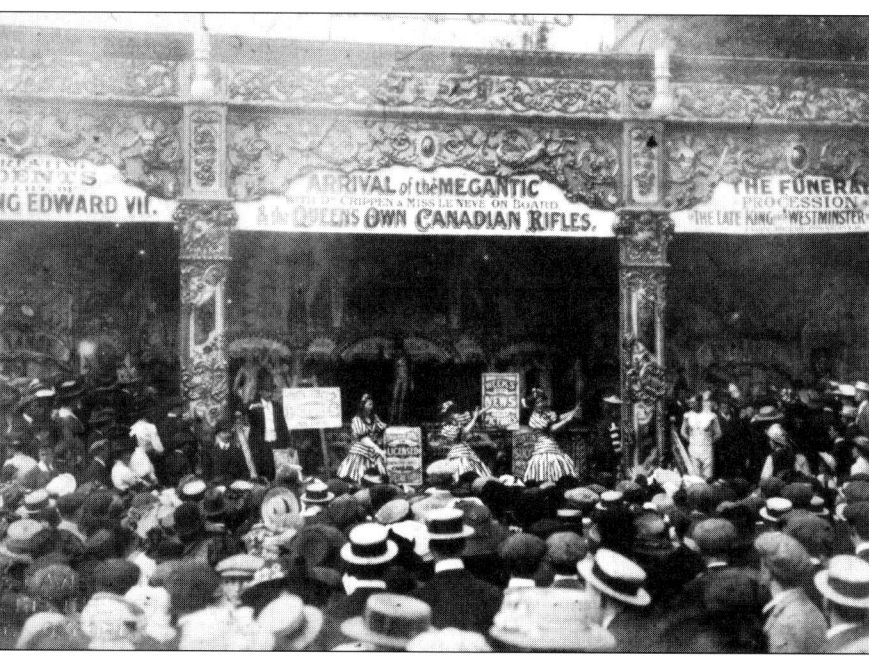

William Taylor's Cinematograph Show, Oxford St Giles Fair, 1910.

© National Fairground Archive, Sheffield.

Fires have of course affected these travelling cinematograph booths, but the evidence does not appear to point to nitrate fires. In the case of Alf Ball's exhibition in 1910, lighting appears to be the cause,[37] while Annie Holland's show was affected by a tinder from the traction engine, and the later fire in Wingate's booth in 1910 was confined to the tilt, and resulted in no loss of lives or severe damage due to the quick thinking of the showmen at the fair.[38] The famous fire at Hancock's fair in 1913 was caused by the rioting of suffragettes in Plymouth, and not through any irresponsibility on the part of the showmen. Richard Monte's show was completely destroyed by fire in 1912, but it occurred after the performance had finished, and appears to have started in the fire stoves.[39] So, although there appears to be some connection to travelling cinematograph booths and the risk of fire, with the exception of the Aspland fire in 1907 and the Wingate incident in 1908, none of these major incidents were in any way connected to the showing of films. They also occurred either when the show was on the road or closed up for the night.

Conclusion

In conclusion, the evidence appears to suggest that the fairground showmen suffered comparatively few incidents of nitrate-related fire in their travelling cinematograph shows. The sample taken is obviously reliant on the events being reported in *The World's Fair* newspaper, and should not be taken as the definitive number for the period covered. However, it does appear to suggest that showmen were professional operators who suffered relatively few fires compared to the number of shows presented on the fairgrounds at that time. Further comparative research drawing on data concerning music hall and other permanent venues is needed before we can state categorically that the Bioscopes were indeed a safe haven for the early cinema customers.

A final footnote to the story of phantom fires is an example of how the fairground operators themselves have their own mythology about this issue, which, in true showland style, was adapted to add to the attraction of the exhibition itself. A case in point is the "tale" of Mamie Paine, a fairground operator in the North of England. According to later accounts which appeared in *The World's Fair* in the 1920s, Mrs Paine heroically threw herself on top of the fire which resulted after a rocket launched from another show inadvertently landed on her films. This bravery apparently resulted in severe facial scarring, and henceforth she delivered all her lectures wearing a silver mask over her face to hide the disfigurement, while of course informing the audience of her past bravery. Interestingly, the family portraits now held in the National Fairground Archive show no evidence of any disfigurement whatsoever.[40]

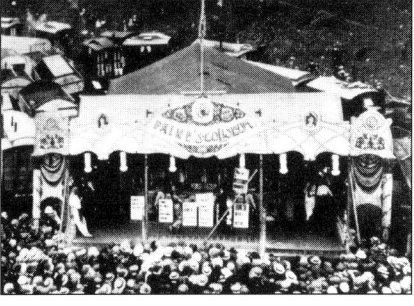

Mamie Paine's Cinematograph Show, Newcastle Town Moor Fair, ca. 1908.

© National Fairground Archive, Sheffield.

Notes

1. *The World's Fair* (9 January 1909), p. 7.

2. H Mark Gosser, "The Bazar de la Charité Fire: The Reality, the Aftermath, the Telling", *Film History*, v.10 no.1 (1998), pp. 70–89.

3. Gosser, op. cit., pp. 80–81.

4. Kevin Scrivens and Stephen Smith, *The Travelling Cinematograph Show* (Tweedale: New Era, 1999), p. 32.

5. Leslie Wood, *The Miracle of the Movies* (London: Burke Publishing Co., 1947), p. 121.

6. Rachael Low, *The History of the British Film, 1906–1914* (London: George Allen & Unwin, 1949), p. 14.

7. Kevin Scrivens and Stephen Smith provide an alphabetical listing of 158 fairground exhibitors

in their book *The Travelling Cinematograph Show* (op. cit.). However, this was taken from the trade papers, which only listed the major fairs. Local or regional papers often provide evidence for other unnamed exhibitors, so this list should not be taken as definitive; it also does not include town hall or other itinerant exhibitors from the time.

8. See the *Showmen's Guild of Great Britain Year Book*, published annually by the Showmen's Guild of Great Britain from 1900 to 1910, for a full listing of the fairs held throughout the United Kingdom.

9. See Vanessa Toulmin, "Telling the Tale: The Story of the Fairground Bioscope Show and the Showmen Who Operated Them", *Film History*, v.6 no.2 (Summer 1994), pp. 219–237.

10. *The Era* (26 December 1896), p. 18.

11. Vanessa Toulmin, "Travelling Shows and the First Static Cinemas", *Picture House*, no.21 (Summer 1996), pp. 5–12.

12. See Mervyn Heard, "'Come in please: Come out pleased': The Development of British Fairground Bioscope Presentation and Performance", in Linda Fitzsimmons and Sarah Street, eds., *Moving Performance: British Stage and Screen, 1890s–1920s* (Trowbridge: Flicks Books, 2000), pp. 101–111.

13. See Vanessa Toulmin, *Randall Williams, King of Showmen* (London: The Projection Box, 1998), for an example of a showman who presented ghost shows, tableaux vivants, and cinematograph shows.

14. *The Showman* (November 1900). See facsimile reproduction in Vanessa Toulmin, *Fun For All: An Illustrated history of Hull Fair in the 20th Century* (Oldham: World's Fair, 1999), p. 4.

15. For a full text of both Acts, see Colin Harding and Simon Popple, *In the Kingdom of Shadows: A Companion to Early Cinema* (London: Cygnus Press, 1996), pp. 46–49.

16. *The World's Fair* (25 September 1909), p. 7.

17. *The World's Fair* (2 January 1909), p. 7.

18. *The World's Fair* (20 March 1909), p. 7.

19. *The World's Fair* (28 August 1909), p. 10.

20. *The World's Fair* (3 July 1909), p. 7.

21. *The World's Fair* (11 July 1908), p. 4.

22. See *The World's Fair*, 3 and 19 August 1907, for a full account of the incident.

23. See *The World's Fair* (8 July 1911, p. 12, for the second prosecution.

24. *The World's Fair* (1 July 1911), p. 6.

25. Ibid.

26. See *The World's Fair*, 6 January 1912, p. 11, and 25 May 1912, p. 14, for a full report of the case.

27. *The World's Fair* (21 December 1912), p. 12.

28. *The World's Fair* (18 October 1913), p. 4.

29. *The World's Fair* (11 February 1910), p. 9.

30. *The World's Fair* (29 January 1910), p. 7.

31. *The World's Fair* (6 April 1912), p. 14.

32. *The Bioscope* (6 May 1909), p. 7.

33. *The World's Fair* (13 July 1912), p 10.

34. *The World's Fair* (10 June 1911), p. 8.

35. *The World's Fair* (30 September 1911), p. 11.

36. Ibid.

37. See handbill entitled "Alf Ball Subscription Fund", dated 15 July 1910, published by *The Era*; in the National Fairground Archive, Showmen's Guild of Great Britain Collection.

38. For further details of these incidents, see Scrivens and Smith, op. cit., p. 109.

39. Ibid., pp. 106, 175.

40. For further details of Mamie Paine, see Vanessa Toulmin, "Women Bioscope Proprietors: The Queens of Showland", in John Fullerton, ed., *Celebrating 1895: The Centenary of Cinema* (London: John Libby, 1998), pp. 55–65.

Rainbow Chasers – Colour in the Nitrate Era

Editors' Note: The symposium "The Last Nitrate Picture Show" contained three presentations concentrating on aspects of the technology of colour in the nitrate era. These presentations were closely dependent on the illustrative material screened, which of course cannot be replicated in book form. The following papers therefore offer a very much abridged version of the contributions which they represent.

I. Black-and-White in Colour
by João S de Oliveira

I have been working with projects involving the revival of techniques for tinting and toning to assist in the restoration of films from the nitrate era for some time now. In this presentation, I want to offer a rapid tour through a period when cellulose nitrate was practically the only base of professional film, when emulsion technology was basically black-and-white, and when tinting and toning effectively offered the only way to add colour to film stock. A certain amount of technical content is inevitable, but I will try to keep it at a level that will not put my audience to sleep.

We all know that from its earliest days cinema borrowed methods, technology, and anxieties from still photography. Such "borrowings" included cellulose nitrate itself – the flexible transparent base that was the essential foundation of cinema invention – as well as emulsion, processing, toning, etc.

It is also widely known that all the early photographic processes were sensitive only to those parts of the image that featured in the blue and ultraviolet components of the colour spectrum, and that they registered their pictures as a monochromatic image. From the earliest days of photography, an army of inventors and scientists have been hard at work to develop a system able to register natural colours. Meanwhile, the proximity between the photographer and the painter – the same person, in most cases, in the early days – made the mixing of these two techniques natural. Their characteristic product was the hand-coloured daguerreotype.

In the scientific effervescence of the 19th century, alternatives to black-and-white images were offered. As early as 1849 William Henry Fox Talbot suggested the use of sulphur (hydrogen sulphide) to modify black-and-white images to brown. Meanwhile, in 1842, John Herschel had noted the photographic application of light-sensitive organic iron salts. Many processes based upon them have since been developed, perhaps the best known being the blueprint. Another variation of the process was known as cyanotype. In 1876 Josef Maria Elder proposed the use of Prussian blue for toning, and in the same year Hauptmann Victor Toth suggested reddish toning of silver images with copper ferrocyanide.

The next 50 years were to witness an explosion of patents in this area within the photographic and film industries. In the late 19th century, when cinema made its "debut", most of the cinematographers joining this "nouveau profession" were photographers or ex-photographers, well in tune with the aesthetics of contemporary photography. Naturally, they made sure that cinema would incorporate some of these elements, especially with regard to colouring.

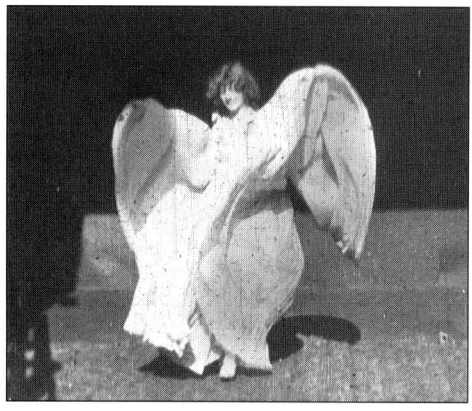

Hand colouring: a scene from
Serpentine Dance (1897).
(See also Colour Section 1.)

Kevin Brownlow Collection.

Bernard Happé has noted that films started to be coloured as early as 1896. In a direct transposition of the technique used to hand-paint daguerreotypes 50 years earlier, the pioneers of the film industry plunged into the task of adding colours by hand, frame by frame, colour by colour, onto thousands and thousands of feet of black-and-white prints, to amuse their spectators. The same transparent dye used in still photography was diluted in alcohol and transferred to the gelatine in the emulsion of the film with the help of a brush or bud. The alcohol would evaporate, leaving the dye fixed into the gelatine structure. Among the pioneers who used this technique was Méliès, who thus added further elements of magic to his celebrated trick films.

It soon became clear that the demand for this sort of finishing was much greater than could be produced entirely by hand. Although a mistake made during painting could be corrected, to do so was very laborious. To reduce the risk of human error

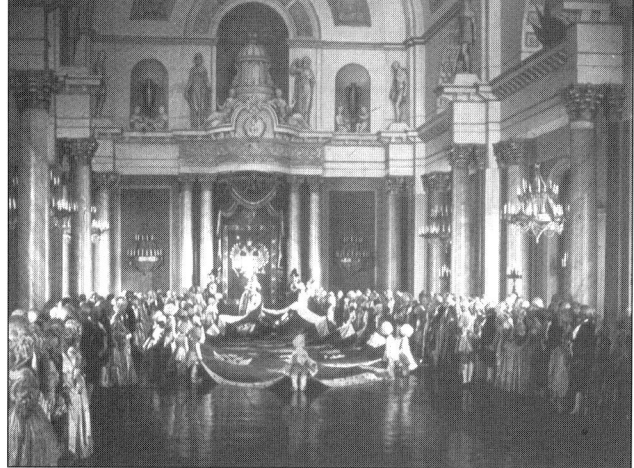

Stencil colour: a scene from
Casanova (1927).
(See also Colour Section 1.)

Kevin Brownlow Collection.

and to increase productivity, a mechanised process was devised. By means of a complicated pantograph system, a series of very precise stencils was produced for each frame and colour; subsequently, these were put in registration with a section of the black-and-white print to be coloured. Colours were sprayed or painted through the stencil onto the film emulsion with a dye solution similar to the one used for hand-colouring. The stencil-colour process developed by Pathé received the name of Pathécolor. I personally find quite amazing the levels of precision that it was possible to achieve by stencil-colour.[1]

Even with the intervention of stencils, the hand-colouring of film remained a very labour-intensive procedure. Further steps in the direction of speed and cost-efficiency were offered by the processes of tinting and toning.

As we have seen, virtually since the invention of photography, processes were being developed to change the colour of the metallic silver particles that form the black-and-white image. These processes are what we call toning. From the first early steps, as chemistry gradually developed in the 19th century and at the beginning of the 20th, toning became more and more sophisticated.

Where toning film is concerned, a printed and processed black-and-white image is required as a starting point. During the nitrate era, the period of film technology which immediately concerns us here, two different types of toning were used: *metallic ferrocyanide* toning and *mordant* toning.

In principle, toning by *metallic ferrocyanide* is based on the fact that the finely divided silver of the photographic image is an excellent reducing agent. As such, the metallic silver of the image may be converted into an image composed of silver salts (if a suitable supply of negative ions is available to form insoluble silver compounds); these silver compounds may then be converted into insoluble salts of metals other than silver. Many of the salts of heavy metals are highly coloured, so this chemical procedure serves as a method of converting a black-and-white silver image into a highly coloured non-silver image.

Examples of metals and the colours of the ferrocyanide salt produced by them include:

Cobalt	–	Violet
Copper	–	Reddish brown
Iron	–	Prussian blue
Molybdenum	–	Brown
Nickel	–	Reddish brown
Titanium	–	Yellow
Uranium	–	Reddish brown
Vanadium	–	Yellow Orange

Another family of toners are the *mordant* toners, or dye toners. Dyes are highly coloured substances, usually organic molecules, that can impart a long-lasting colour to the material to which they are applied. Dyes may be *acidic* or *basic* (alkaline). *Acidic* dyes are so called because they contain acid groups (-OH, -CO$_2$H, -SO$_3$H), which form negatively charged ions in water. *Basic* dyes contain basic groups (such as -NH$_2$), which form positively charged ions in water.

Acidic or basic dyes are usually in the form of soluble salts when added to water, but in a solution, negatively or positively charged ions exist as large agglomerated particles whose electrical condition keeps them suspended in the solution. Dye particles with the same charge repel each other, keeping them separated and suspended in the solution.

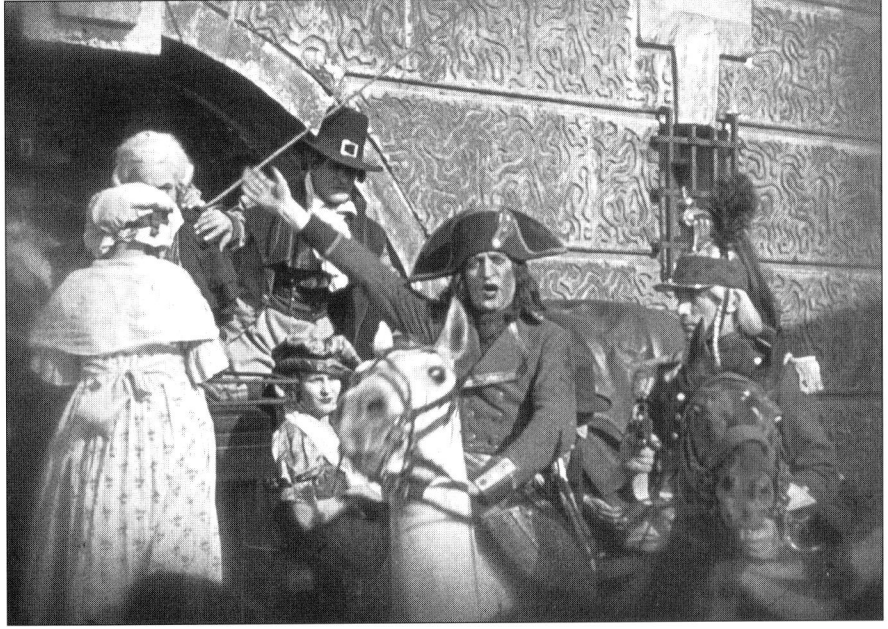

Blue chemical toning (ferric-ferrocyanide): a scene from *Napoléon* (1927). (See also Colour Section 1.)
Kevin Brownlow Collection.

The principle of dye toning is that a positively charged dye particle will be attracted by a negatively charged particle. If the electrical condition of the dye particle is sufficiently neutralised, the dye particle will be precipitated as insoluble colour matter. To colour a silver image, therefore, the silver image must acquire an electric charge opposite to that of the dye particle. Metallic silver images can be converted to a negatively charged condition such as silver iodide or indeed silver ferrocyanide; such images will then attract positively charged, i.e., basic, dyes. After the silver image has been treated to form an image that will bind basic dyes, this *mordant* image is then treated in a dye solution.

Common dyes for mordant toning are:

Safranine A	–	Red
Auramine	–	Yellow
Victoria green	–	Blue/Green
Methylene blue BB	–	Blue
Methyl violet	–	Violet

There is a third family of toning, suggested by Rudolf Fischer in 1912, known as the *dye coupling* process. This process as a form of toning was not significantly utilised in films in the nitrate era, but its importance is related to the fact that this type of dye-forming reaction is the basis of most of the present-day colour processes, such as Agfacolor, Eastmancolor, etc.

We turn now from toning to the process of *tinting* – in other words, the dyeing of the emulsion gelatine of black-and-white films. It is not possible to say with precision when tinting started to be used on film, but since the process was one of relative simplicity it was certainly very early. We have an example in BFI Collections of tinted film from 1897.

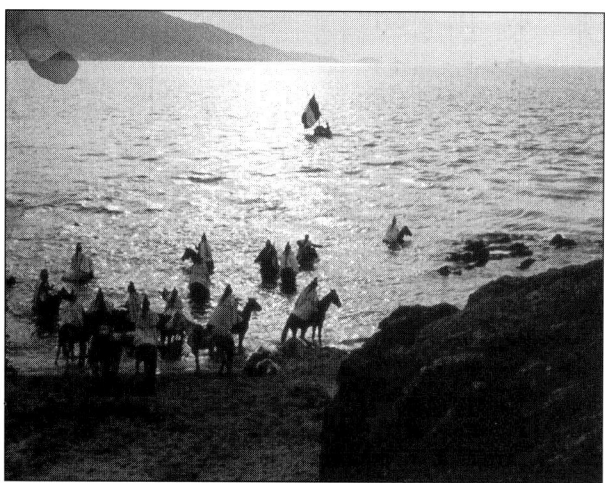

Cyan dyed film base: a scene from *Napoléon* (1927). (See also Colour Section 1.)

Kevin Brownlow Collection.

There is a strong relation between tinting and the chemistry of synthesis – producing synthetic dyes directed towards the textile market. The same dyes were used for tinting films, and in the abundant literature produced by the film manufacturers to describe this process, complete with formulas and instructions, it is possible to observe the parallel evolution of the tinting process and the dye industry. For example, in the period during and immediately after World War I, the European dye industry was perhaps more developed than the American. The Kodak tinting and toning manual for 1918 contains a reference to difficulties in obtaining certain dyes for tinting and mentions the disappointing results produced by the locally-available alternative dyes. By the next edition of this manual, in 1922, the problem had apparently been overcome – new dyes had been developed and good alternatives were available in America.

The principle of tinting is similar to dye toning, but in tinting the technician uses acid dyes instead of basic ones, because gelatine is normally positively charged. These acidic dyes will be attracted, and if the electrical condition of the dye is sufficiently neutralised the dye will precipitate as insoluble coloured matter, becoming trapped and staining the gelatine.

Common examples of dyes used in tinting are:

Croccein G	–	Amber
Amaranth	–	Pink or magenta
Xilidrine	–	Red

As a film-finishing treatment both tinting and toning could be used as individual processes. They could also be combined to produce astonishing results. Tinting and toning marked a glorious period in film history. Film developed its own aesthetic and language. It would have been impossible at the birth of cinema to predict how much difference these added colours could make.

Nevertheless, during these years the challenge to develop a satisfactory process for the recording and display of natural colours in film continued. After much time, money, and energy had been invested in development, the effort paid off. With tinting and toning such an integral part of film technology, it was natural that these early colour processes would make use of them. I propose to look briefly at some of the early colour processes that are directly related to tinting and toning.

The last twenty years of the 19th century saw a period of great experimentation in colour cinematography by inventors like William Friese-Greene. He and others tried to transpose to cinema certain principles stated by Louis Ducos du Hauron and James Clerk Maxwell in the 1860s. These were based on the additive-selective analysis of an image – the breaking down of a naturally coloured image into three black-and-white registers of the red, blue, and green components of that image. This system worked well in still photography, where the subject was stationary and film exposure could be as long as necessary to obtain a correct register, but when the image is in movement it is a completely different story.

It is well known that, because of retinal persistence (the phenomenon conventionally known as persistence of vision), the speed at which successive still images must be viewed to give a convincing impression of continuous movement needs to be at least 16 frames per second. With a colour-separated image, this must be rendered at 16 frames per second per colour, otherwise the eyes would not integrate the separations and the viewer would experience a sensation of pulsing colours. Thus, for three colours a projection speed of 48 frames per second is required.

Prior to the 1920s, however, films were not sensitive enough to shoot at these sorts of speeds, and some mechanical problems for the film and equipment would also arise when transporting film at this speed. Furthermore, the amount of light lost into filters was enormous. Another important problem related to the fact that, with the three registers (red, blue, and green) appearing in succession and therefore having a lapse of time between them, if any part of the subject or camera moved, they would be out of registration in respect to the other frames. This could create colour fringes on the outlines of parts of the image – an effect known as *time parallax*.

In spite of these restrictions, some "three-colour additive" process systems were tried. BFI Collections has one element representative of this period.

In 1899, F Marshall Lee and Edward R Turner designed a system using the three-colour additive principle. They used a 48mm black-and-white stock (and black-and-white processing), and produced successive frames with respective registers of red, blue, and green by the use of a set of filters in the camera shutter. This film was screened at 48 frames per second, using a projector equipped with a special device that would rotate an equivalent filter in front of the lens, set in such a fashion that the blue filter was there when the blue-registered image was in the projector gate, followed successively by green and red filters for the green- and red-registered images.

Friese-Greene, Lee and Turner, and others did realise that a reasonable representation of natural colours can be produced using two colours (red and green) instead of three, which would then mean that the speed could be reduced to 32 frames per second – a speed that was just viable with the stock of the time. Around 1902 this developed into a system that was the basis for Kinemacolor.[2]

Until 1917 film technology was purely black-and-white. In this period of the search for solutions to natural-colour cinematography, all the inventions were based on

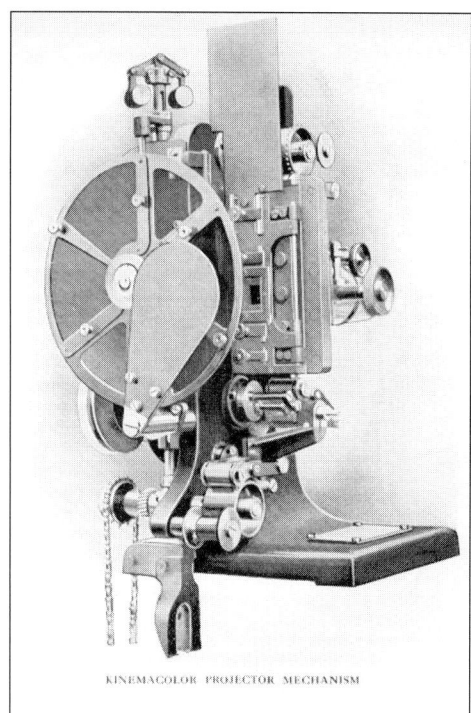

KINEMACOLOR PROJECTOR MECHANISM

A close-up of the filter mechanism for a Kinemacolor projector, reproduced from Bernard E Jones (ed.), *The Cinematograph Book* (London: Cassell, 1919 – revised edition).

Roger Smither.

changes to the camera and projector. After attending a screening of such a system, someone observed that the projectionist had to be a mixture of scientist and juggler to be able to cope with the apparatus. Moreover, each and every new colour system in this period produced its own kit that had to be added to projectors. Understandably, none of the colour systems that involved such esoteric expertise and expensive investment achieved wide acceptance in the market, but much knowledge was gained during this period.

Film emulsions became more sensitive, and chromatic sensitivity was improved. Toning techniques developed, and mordant toning was introduced. A very important invention for the colour cinema was the beam-splitter prism, which solved the time parallax problem and meant that, rather than requiring special projection equipment, film could still be projected using regular projectors.

The last use of toning in the film industry occurred in relation to the development of "two-colour subtractive" colour systems, spanning the period from the early 1920s through to the early 1950s. To make this next stage of colour cinematography possible took the development of a new stock. *Dupletised* stock was a film base with a black-and-white print emulsion applied to each one of its faces. This print stock was used in association with black-and-white separations of the red/orange and blue/green registers of the subject.

All the major film-stock makers would, in time, produce dupletised film, although the way the separations were produced would vary according with the process used. Prizma Color, for instance, originally used a complicated system of twin lenses with filters, although it later evolved into a more simple one using a beam-splitting prism. Technicolor and others had always used beam-splitters and bi-packs – systems where the image was split by a prism into the two colour components; each component was recorded on its own black-and-white negative in a double film magazine or bi-pack.

Special printing machines were used to print these separations in registration at the same time onto dupletised stock. The stock was processed in black-and-white processing solutions, and then each face was respectively toned: metallic ferrocyanide for the blue/green face, and mordant dye for the red/orange.

With the development of bi-pack, a system that could be used with normal black-and-white cameras, two-colour subtractive lens technology, dupletised film stock, and toning expertise reached their days of glory. They should not be overlooked, even if today their achievements will always be seen to be overshadowed by the riches of three-colour imbibition print Technicolor.

Notes

1. Hand-coloured films of course continued to be made outside the mass-production film industry. Animators like Len Lye and Norman McLaren are examples of this, and Len Lye's hand- and stencil-painted animation film *A Colour Box* is the subject of a separate intervention by Anne Fleming (see below).

2. The subject of a further separate intervention by Nicola Mazzanti (see below).

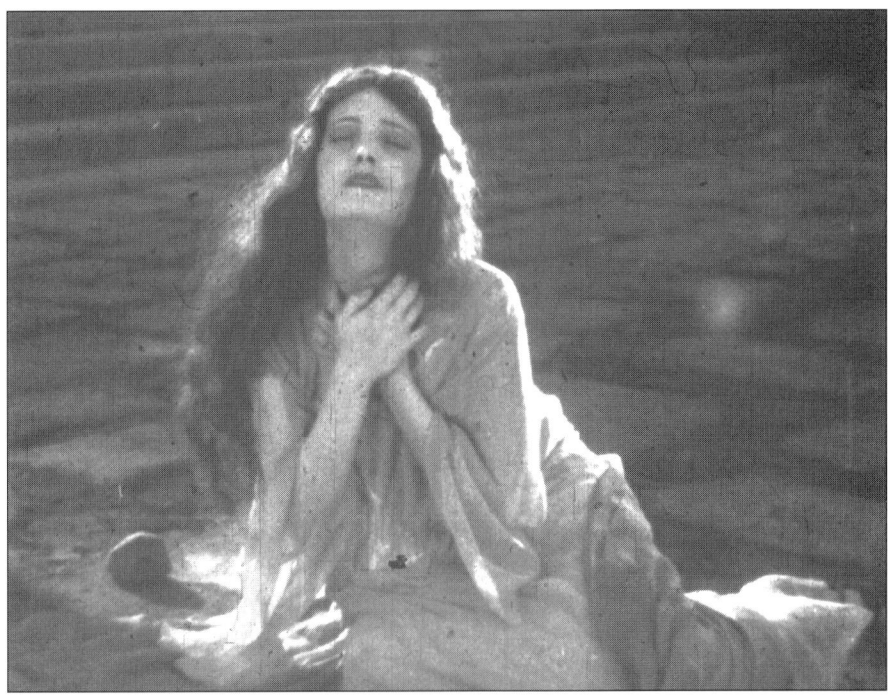

Two-colour Technicolor: a scene from *Ben-Hur* (1925). (See also Colour Section 1.)
Kevin Brownlow Collection.

II. Raising the Colours (Restoring Kinemacolor)
by Nicola Mazzanti

The reason why I think that Kinemacolor, although it is not a completely new subject, might be interesting to discuss in this context is because it raises several issues about reproduction and duplication within archives. With Kinemacolor, the physical duplication of the original nitrate film is quite easy – more complex issues arise because we have somehow to find a method to reproduce the experience in a new way, because we are simply not able to offer the system in the original form, or at least it would be extremely complicated to do so. Kinemacolor offers one example of this problem, and at that probably not the most complicated one – there are several other systems and processes which it is practically impossible to reproduce in their original form. Here the archivist confronts the problem: Where exactly is the film experience? Is it on the film, or in the projector, or on the screen? And precisely how do these many things interact with one another?

I believe that João may have left the impression that Friese-Greene was the inventor of colour cinematography, but of course George Albert Smith also claimed that honour. There were several not very conclusive lawsuits between the two men to settle the issue in the English courts. In any case, it was Smith's first patent in 1906 that marked an important step forward towards a possibly viable system of colour cinematography, because it moved from three-colour additive systems – with all the practical difficulties which João described – to two colours. Speaking of that patent in a lecture at the Royal Society of Arts on 9 December 1908, G A Smith said that "two colours give the same result as three colours," and then showed some films – harvesting scenes and a yacht race – to prove his point. The reviews of this lecture state that the greys were excellent in all of the materials.

Another of Smith's lectures was reported in the *British Journal of Photography* on 6 December 1907. It is worth quoting this review, because it tells us a few interesting things: "We were able to compare the colours in the pictures projected with some of the actual accessories used, and the rendering of the colours was strikingly accurate, particularly in the case of the reds. Only two taking and projecting filters were used, an orange-red and a blue-green, the usual third or blue-

123

violet filter being dispensed with. Naturally the whites obtained are not pure, but have a slight yellowish tinge, yet when projected on the screen with brilliant colours this defect is hardly noticeable." When I began to face the restoration of Kinemacolor a few years ago, I found these comments very striking, because all of the other restorations of early colour systems which I had seen before (such as Friese-Greene's) had the opposite tendencies. The whites are pure, and there is no yellowish hint anywhere, but they are very high-contrast.

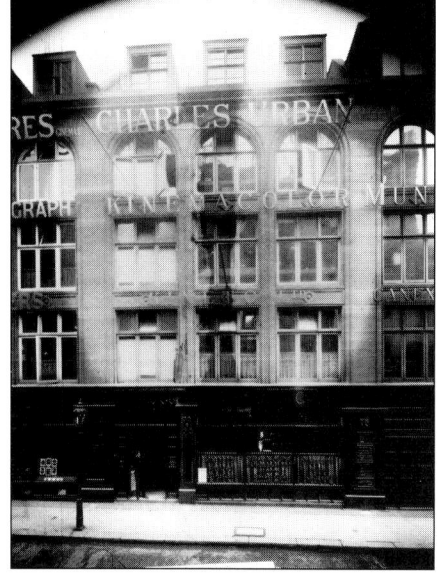

To move on with the story. In 1909 Smith's patent, which had previously had no commercial identity, acquired the trade name "Kinemacolor", and was the very first colour process to be commercialised by the Kinemacolor Company. Several films followed, including some fiction films, and the company was rather successful for a while. After that, the films more or less disappeared, or entered into a long period of complete oblivion. Many of these additive systems arrived during those years and then dropped out of film history. In our day, we are starting to know several of these systems again – Friese-Greene in the British NFTVA; Chronochrome, which has been restored at Rochester; and Kinemacolor.

A few years ago the Cineteca in Bologna received a visitor from a local regional archive, who arrived with several cans of nitrate and said, "We have some weird stuff here. I mean, these reels don't look at all conventional. Can you tell us what they are?" They turned out to be the largest collection of Kinemacolor in the world. There are 23 titles, approximately 6,000 metres of material, on 45 reels. Unfortunately, most of this material was in rather pitiful condition. Most of the reels were already decomposing, and the black-and-white image was deeply affected and was fading. Of course, if the black-and-white image fades in Kinemacolor, you just lose the colours: that's the point. The titles in the list include some that recall the 1907/1908 screenings that I mentioned earlier: there are scenes of blossoming flowers and, of course, yachts. There are lakes, scenes on the Nile, London Zoo, all sorts of parades and uniforms, and, which was particularly interesting for us, also a few things about Italy. One of the ways in which the Kinemacolor Company operated, actually, was that they sold rights, in a sort of franchising arrangement, so that licensed operators in local countries could buy the machinery, the camera and projectors, film their own films, and distribute them somehow. Some of these films are thus also quite important for Italian history, not just film history.

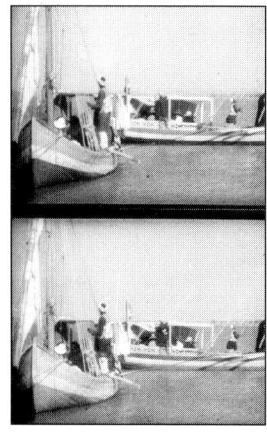

The two consecutive Kinemacolor frames representing the red and green registers of a single image.

L'Immagine Ritrovata, Bologna.

When we faced the problem of restoring this material, of course our first thought was to try to see how it looked on the screen. So a few years ago, at the Cinema Ritrovato festival in Bologna, we organised a screening of Kinemacolor by modifying a modern projector. The show worked out somehow, except that in the middle of the film there was a join which lost a frame, so that the colour just flipped the other way: the uniforms of Italian policemen changed, and even the Italian flag actually appeared in the wrong colours. Another small problem was that we burned out the motor of the projector. As you will have gathered by now, Kinemacolor is based on a two-colour additive system: a scene is recorded on film on two consecutive frames filmed alternately through a green-and-red filter, and then it is played again on a projector with the same rotating filters at 32 frames per second. Running at 32 fps just destroyed the projector. (Actually, I wanted try to do the same presentation at the National Film Theatre, but they didn't like the idea for some reason!) We also built a viewing table for Kinemacolor, which is probably the only one in existence. It may strike you as a pretty stupid thing to do, but it is very easy – just add filters to the prism of your viewing table. It also means that you can check all the splices in your films, because otherwise, as I said, you can get the colours wrong.

Thinking of methods for long-term preservation, we decided with the Cineteca that we did not much care for the idea of having colour material as a preservation master for these black-and-white originals, where we thought we might end up with acetate films which might offer much less than the original nitrate prints. Also, an early test we did, involving the production of a colour internegative, gave us slightly too high contrast, which would add to the problems of conserving this colour material. Anyway, of course, straightforward copying like that was no fun, so we decided to go another way. We copied all of the materials just as they were, in black-and-white, trying to keep a faithful record of the originals, and then we separated our copies into two black-and-white negatives, so that the subsequent shots were physically put on two different films. This meant that, if necessary, we could control density and contrast on the two separate strips of black-and-white dupe negative much more easily. These two black-and-white dupe negatives were then recombined, like conventional colour separations, to produce a positive colour print, for projection at 16 frames per second. So you could say that in a way we basically transformed this additive system into a subtractive system, but we have ensured that the two preservation masters are black-and-white.[1]

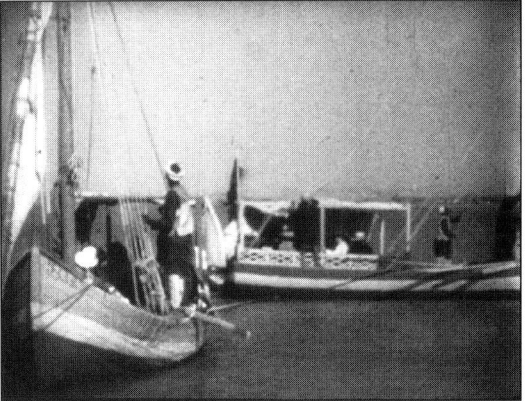

The combined colour image recreated from the pair of frames in the preceding illustration.
(See also Colour Section 1.)
L'Immagine Ritrovata, Bologna.

There remain a couple of important things to be mentioned. The literature produced by the Kinemacolor Company says that Kinemacolor cameramen had to choose different filters according to the subject. Now, they give no specific information about these different filters, but presumably various degrees of orange/red or blue/cyan/green filtering could be used, according to the subject. In practice, what we sometimes found when grading and printing these materials was that, although the first colour was always basically cyan, with the other colour, the red, we sometimes had to move more to the orange or more to the red, adding more or less of the yellow component to get the better, more natural, result that Kinemacolor wanted to achieve. Of course, the adjustment that we made at the printing stage would not have had its equivalent in the original Kinemacolor days, because even if the cameraman had the chance to vary his red/orange filter, the projection system would have been equipped with only one set of filters.

Traditionally, the major problem with Kinemacolor, as with all these additive systems, was that of time parallax, meaning that when a subject moves fast, it acquires this colour fringe that João mentioned. We also encountered another problem that we had not expected – printer parallax. We found that the films were printed in a completely unsteady way, so the image moves around all over the screen, and there is no accurate superimposition in the prints themselves.

And now we can let the restored prints speak for themselves.

Notes

1. In the meantime, an alternative approach to Kinemacolor has been developed in Amsterdam by Haghefilm, which involves dyeing, or Desmet-colourising, alternate frames in each of the two colours and then using a projector at 32 fps. The Amsterdam approach has, incidentally, resolved the big issue between Friese-Greene and Kinemacolor, because essentially it has "Friese-Greened" a Kinemacolor!

III. *A Colour Box* (Len Lye Recovered)
by Anne Fleming

João Oliveira's tour of colour processes during the nitrate period included the very earliest examples, when colour was hand-painted onto the black-and-white images recorded by the camera. Len Lye, the maker of *A Colour Box*, took this a stage further. He developed a technique whereby he painted directly onto the celluloid, bypassing the camera altogether.

As most of you will know, Len Lye was a New Zealander who came to Britain in the late 1920s and began to work on abstract experimental animation. He stayed on in Britain for the next ten years and joined the group of film-makers working with John Grierson in the public- sponsored sector, eventually leaving to move on to North America, as Grierson himself did. During this time he made a number of experimental abstract animation films, of which *A Colour Box* is one. It was eventually presented to the public through the GPO Film Unit, masquerading as an advertisement for a new cheaper parcel post service offered by the General Post Office.

The images Lye produced by hand-painting were not, of course, then copied by teams of industrious women. By 1935, when *A Colour Box* was picked up by the GPO, colour technology had developed to a point where duplication via one of a number of colour processes was the normal means for onward distribution. For Lye and for the publicly funded GPO Film Unit, the Technicolor process (in which Disney had a virtual monopoly, as far as animation was concerned) was a non-starter – it was much too expensive – so the colour process chosen was Dufaycolor.

Dufaycolor was an additive red, green and blue mosaic colour process. The colours it delivered were muted and soft. All Dufaycolor was produced on safety stock (diacetate) and as a result it has its own particular problems of instability, which there is no time to discuss in detail today. Suffice it to say that much Dufaycolor material is going acetic. The NFTVA collection holds a range of Dufaycolor safety material for *A Colour Box*, and the BFI has produced safety Eastmancolor protection material for this title from these elements. The Eastmancolor viewing copy so produced is the copy which we have made available for screening around the world. When this Eastmancolor viewing copy is compared with our only surviving Dufaycolor positive of *A Colour Box*, it is clear that simply the process of transferring Dufaycolor to Eastmancolor stock increases the colour saturation somewhat. Nevertheless, we have tried to ensure that this viewing copy reflects more or less what audiences at the time would have seen in the cinemas – despite the all-too-familiar difficulties of attempting to replicate the original colour quality when using a different colour system.

At this stage it seemed that our preservation role had been completed – at least for the moment. In October 1996, however, as a result of an access request from the Len Lye Foundation in New Zealand, we re-examined our holdings and discovered a nitrate element originating from the GPO Film Unit. On examination, it transpired that this was an original hand-painted Len Lye picture element. It was accompanied by a matching nitrate sound track, and Sarah Davy, the Access officer handling the request for the Len Lye Foundation, immediately involved the Archive's Technical Manager, João Oliveira. The nitrate picture element (from which the Dufaycolor pre-print material had been made in the 1930s) was by now in poor condition, and the questions facing us were these: How could we best preserve this element? Indeed, could it be printed at all?

One thing was immediately clear. The hand-painted colours on the nitrate reel were brighter and more saturated than anything the Dufay process had been able to reproduce. On further examination, João found that a fascinating war was going on between the different materials composing the nitrate picture element. In places the dyes or paints had interacted with the base and attacked it, making it extremely brittle and very shrunken. At other points the gases given off by the nitrate base had interacted with the dyes and discoloured them to a certain extent. The material was far from stable.

The view of the commercial labs which we consulted in the UK was that the element could not be printed. It was too fragile and too brittle. João was not to be defeated, however, and he undertook to print the reel, modifying one of our printers to cope with the shrinkage. An internegative was produced in the Conservation Centre's Research Laboratory, and the colour processing was then undertaken by our colleagues at Soho Images under João's supervision. With João supervising the grading, the new colour print was then made. The results were quite striking.

Despite the ravages of 50 years of decomposition undergone by the original nitrate, the colours on this new print are far more saturated and more intense than the Eastmancolor viewing copy produced from the Dufaycolor material. Of course, no one saw the film looking like this at the time, except perhaps when it was projected during the production process. In archival terms, it would be philosophically dangerous to argue that this is a "restoration", or that the new copy may be closer to what Len Lye would have liked to see on the screen had he had the choice. Lye isn't here to answer for himself, and none of us at the J Paul Getty Conservation Centre are in the habit of consulting mediums. All we can say is that we have tried to create from the surviving hand-painted nitrate a copy that replicates what survives of Lye's original as closely as possible. We have done this in the knowledge that it is uncertain how long the nitrate may survive even in good storage, because of the cocktail of chemical reactions that are still ongoing within the element, and because the duplication process is the only one open to us to try to protect it.

In a live presentation – though sadly not in a book – it is possible to conclude by running the Eastman print made from the Dufaycolor pre-print material side by side with the Eastman positive made via the Eastmancolor internegative from Lye's hand-painted nitrate positive, so that a viewer can see the difference in colour quality. I hope this verbal description is informative, and justifies our attempt to preserve something of the special qualities of the original hand-painted nitrate and present them on the screen.

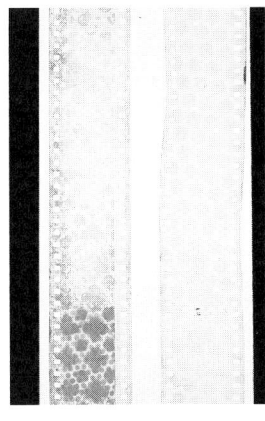

The original hand-painted picture element for *A Colour Box* (1935).
(See also Colour Section 1.)

BFI Collections (National Film and Television Archive), London.

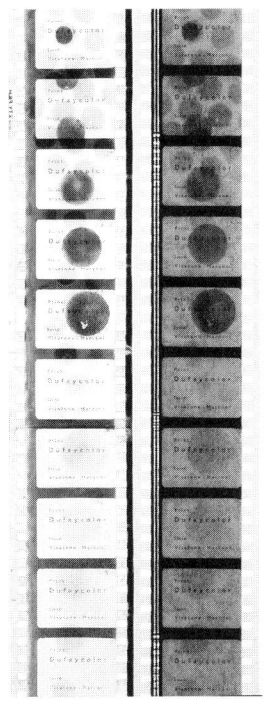

A comparison between a print replicating the original Dufaycolor appearance of *A Colour Box* (on the left) and the "far more saturated and more intense" colours of the new print generated from the nitrate element found by the BFI.
(See also Colour Section 1.)

BFI Collections (National Film and Television Archive), London.

An Epiphany of Nitrate

by Paolo Cherchi Usai

"Sex is never safe. Sex is dangerous."

– Dennis Hopper, *The Hot Spot* (1990)

My first experience of cinema in the form of nitrate motion picture film is inextricably linked to the sense of smell. It also coincides with my earliest and no less flammable experiences as an adolescent discovering the explosive pleasures of the human body. While it is certainly not my intention to impose a sexual autobiography upon the reader of a book on the moving image, I cannot answer the question of how I discovered nitrate prints without referring to one of the most multifaceted physical experiences of my life.

At the time when it happened, I was already familiar with acetate film in both its 35mm and 16mm forms. In fact, the 35mm format came quite early in my life, as the cinema theatre in the village where I was born was right across the street from my villa, and I would play with film scraps from weekly newsreels (for some reason, the owner of the theatre would not bother to return them to the distributors) as much as with the remains of the material used for carbon arc projection lamps, those odd pencils we used to trade as the mysterious remains of some radioactive experiment.

However, by the time I had come to know 16mm as a format for those prints shown in the context of discussions among cinephiles, a much more powerful cinematic experience came to my senses, determining much of the way I look at nitrate today. School was over, and my main goal for the summer was to convince a young woman to show me her breasts. She was in town for the summer – as every summer – and at age 15 she was definitely more mature than her mere age would suggest. When she eventually agreed (probably out of exasperation, as she hoped I would leave her alone after having satisfied my curiosity), the place we chose for our evening encounter was a warehouse near the theatre, close enough to home not to worry my parents, early enough to get back before the customary 10pm curfew.

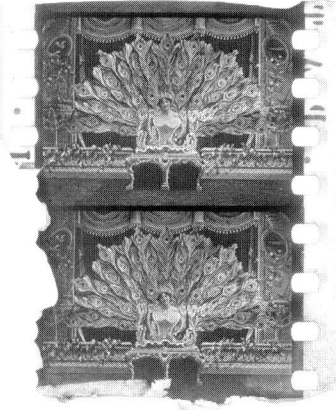

A fragment of the stencil-coloured Pathé film *Fée aux pigeons* (1906). (See also Colour Section 1.)

Paolo Cherchi Usai.

As I wanted to be romantic, I had brought candles for the event. More wisely, she came with an electric torch. My schoolmates had told me that I should enter the building through the bathroom window, but when we arrived she first tried the door, just for the heck of it. It was unlocked. I do not remember exactly what happened in the next two minutes, but I do know that soon after closing the door behind us we were inundated by an overwhelming scent, something we had never smelled before. Retrospectively, I must be grateful to the gods of good fortune that we did not light the candles. I did not see her breasts on that occasion (that happened a few days later, in the much healthier – although rather more conventional – environment of a chestnut forest), but many other things occurred in that space crammed with cobwebs, old newspapers, rat shit, pigeons, and hundreds of reels of nitrate film piled up against the walls. It was there that I clipped (yes, I did) two frames from the loose end of a reel which I had picked at random that night. Those frames, reproduced on this page, were the first nitrate images I had ever seen.

That smell never left me, and many years after the event I found myself asking an expert in perfumes how I could reconstruct the memory of that fateful scent. The perfume industry has a specialised technician – he is called "the nose", and is one of the best-paid figures in this mysterious and highly remunerative industry – and it was one of those experts whom I asked how I could recreate the perfume of nitrate film. Like all "noses", the person I contacted for this purpose was very secretive about how he managed it, but he did bring me a tiny bottle with an essence whose smell was indeed that smell, my first epiphany of nitrate.

Camphor, cinnamon, neroli, the essence derived from the pineal gland of an owl – these and many other scents were mentioned, but I was not given that ampoule, nor would I be capable of duplicating the report for the benefit of moving-image archivists. For some time, I felt ashamed at my experiment with the odours of silent cinema. If I no longer feel that way it is because I am now ready to accept the principle of correspondence at some important level between sight and the other senses. Is this fetishism? Yes indeed, insofar as fetishism – the art of establishing a physical relationship with the object of desire beyond the fulfilment of pleasure – can lead to a true form of knowledge.

One of the greatest tragedies of our profession is that we have been unable to convey the meaning of the difference between video and film to the newest generations of viewers. This defeat was supported by universities, and by the academic world's inability to endorse and stand by the methods established by art history a long time before cinema existed. This is all the more deplorable if one recalls how persistent we were in claiming that cinema has the right to stand alongside all the other forms of art. How come an original etching by Dürer (one of many "copies" derived from the master's original matrix) is perceived to have more artistic dignity than its photographic reproduction, and yet there are scholars who content themselves in writing about a film they have never seen in its proper form? If the battle for the rights of film against video or DVD has largely gone by default, then the admittedly subtler difference between a nitrate print and its ersatz in the form of an acetate or polyester print is even more likely to escape the vast majority of spectators, and we archivists need to understand the reasons for our failure in establishing ethics of film viewing. By and large, audiences accept that what they call a restored film "looks like" what they call the original. Therefore, they feel they no longer need to look at the nitrate print.

And yet we know there is a thing such as the "nitrate experience". We may even call it the "nitrate epiphany" in the sense that its unique features appeal to several senses. Can we quantify the characteristics of this "epiphany"? Maybe not, but those who have experienced it know very well that it is real. The appeal to the eye is obvious: the texture, the sharpness, the warmth of an image carried by a nitrate base. Those who have had the chance to handle a nitrate copy are also aware that its distinctive smell is accompanied by a no less remarkable tactile impression, so precise that many of us know how to recognise it simply by holding it in our hands.

Right after the original fateful experience described earlier, my own epiphany of nitrate quickly developed itself as a discipline of the senses. I was told that nitrate film decomposes and burns quickly, and I liked it even more for that. In 1984, at the former nitrate vaults of the National Film Archive in Aston Clinton, I held in my hands a hand-coloured print of Georges Méliès's *Le Royaume des fées* (1903) and a Pathé fantasy then catalogued under the title *A Trip to Davy Jones' Locker*. Since then, the impression left by their colours has never abandoned me. In 1985, the curators of the Danske Filmmuseum allowed me to handle the nitrate negative of a mysterious early film called *For en kvindes skyld* (1907), known for its unusual editing patterns. At that point, I was already well beyond the point of no return. At the retrospective on Nordic cinema at the Pordenone Silent Film Festival in 1986, the organisers of the event discovered that some prints received from Copenhagen were nitrate copies. They thought there had been a mistake. "Not at all," they were told, "all these films are well preserved, and we'd like to give you a chance to look at them in their original form." Would they do that again today? What an amazing statement of confidence in the Pordenone festival! But showing a nitrate print in a movie theatre was then, as it still is, illegal in Italy. (Like all true pleasures, nitrate is something everybody is really afraid of. Burn it! Restore it, alright, but then burn it!) The films were eventually shown in the open air, in the garden of a 15th-century cloister in the old town of Pordenone. Nobody in the audience understood why those programmes were held outside the Verdi Theatre, and we certainly didn't want to tell them, afraid as we were of the authorities, although there was nothing illegal in showing nitrate films in a garden. Nitrate film projected in a medieval cloister! What more could we ask for?

Since then, I have learned how much of this pleasure also comes from the light sources of the projectors, and come to realise that the nitrate epiphany is in fact the synthesis of nitrate cellulose, the orthochromatic emulsion, and the quality of the mirrors in the projecting machines. Those pencils I had in my hands as a child, after all, were the indicators of another epiphany of which I was completely unaware. Years later, in February 2000, the George Eastman House organised screenings in Rochester to preview nitrate films submitted by the United States archives and to select those to be included in the programme supporting the symposium at FIAF's annual congress later in the year. The epiphany was still there, alive and well, and those who witnessed it with me (David Francis from the Library of Congress, Steven Higgins from the Museum of Modern Art, Edward E. Stratmann from the George Eastman House, and the students of the L. Jeffrey Selznick School of Film Preservation) shared my view that such epiphanies can and should be repeated. In the mid-1980s, when he still was at the helm of the National Film Archive, David Francis had suggested that the two of us should put together a programme that we then planned to call "The Glory of Nitrate". We had to wait 15 years to see this happen under another title – "The Last Nitrate Picture Show" – but now we believe that this "last" show ought to be given further instalments as long as nitrate still exists and is projectable. (George Eastman House has one of the few theatres equipped for nitrate screenings, and its Century projectors can take a shrinkage ratio well over 1 percent.) We will therefore try to make the Rochester screenings a continuing event, in the hope that others are going to share with us the thrill of this renewed discovery.

I frankly do not care if the episodes I have just described are going to be mistaken for some sort of nostalgia, a remembrance of images past. I am immune from nostalgia, and I know that there is something much stronger that keeps me working with nitrate prints, something that escapes those who are unable to enjoy its unique blend of materiality and abstraction. My message to those who have never seen a nitrate film projected on a screen is twofold, and has much to do with the sense of smell. First, there is no single "nitrate look" in a motion picture film. Like smell, each combination of nitrate cellulose and silver emulsion gives the viewer a different nitrate experience – so much so that the emulsion itself may determine this "look" thanks to its interaction with the base.

The second message is a corollary of the first. Because the combination of nitrate base and orthochromatic or panchromatic emulsion determines the appearance of the moving image in its photomechanic form, we should refrain from dismissing the nitrate film (viewing) experience as the private obsession of a restricted community of acolytes of the past. It is an experience that cannot be reproduced – because no nitrate film stock is being produced today – and yet the projection of nitrate prints is the conveyor of a distinctive aesthetic visual experience. So much, then, for all our attempts at preserving the heritage of the first decades of cinema through acetate, polyester, and non-photographic media. The real experience is all there, in those odorous prints, and we are the last generation that may be able to enjoy it! Nobody else will be allowed to do that. We have the moral responsibility to absorb as much as possible of these images and these smells, and explain what they meant to a posterity who otherwise may have no idea of why we cared so much about their survival and transmission to the future.

In other words, we ought to turn what we have learned from this problem (the gradual disappearance of nitrate and the acknowledged impossibility of reproducing its "epiphany") into an opportunity. We can still show acetate and polyester prints. In other words, we can still show cinema. As Peter Kubelka has spent years describing in his enlightening and provocative lectures, we can bring to new generations of viewers what we have frequently failed to explain so far – the uniqueness of the cinematic experience. The cause of nitrate may be lost, although it is still a beautiful one to struggle for. The cause of cinema as a projected intermittent image can still be fought, and there is still a reason to fight it. Not in opposition to the electronic image, not as a reactionary answer to the digital age, but because photo-mechanical cinema has its own, specific aura. Most important of all, I repeat, it is not too late.

And it is still not yet too late to smell nitrate. If I ever have a hand in the raising of kids, I will bring them to a conservation centre as soon as they turn 14, in the hope they will understand that the art of seeing involves the willingness to take some risks. There is something depressingly safe, condom-like, in the digital image, and as much as I respect it and realise its creative potential, I cannot really feel anything when I experience it. Cinema is never safe. Cinema is dangerous. That is why I like it so much, and why I am glad I was born early enough to smell it.

The Nitrate Collections of the Archives du Film du CNC, France

by Michelle Aubert

A Curatorial Overview

The characteristics of the archival nitrate film collections of the Centre National de la Cinématographie are as follows:

There are 300,000 cans of nitrate, corresponding to 36,000 nitrate films, comprising features and shorts, fiction and documentaries, stored on the site of Bois d'Arcy, where all the activities of our archive are also centred. This affords an almost unique opportunity to work on the nitrate collections, as compared with some other colleague archives, whose nitrate sites are far away or dispersed.

The nitrate collection contains examples representing many early and unique formats, dating from 1890 to the 1920s, many originating directly from the inventors themselves, like Marey or Louis Lumière, from film companies like Eclair, Pathé and Gaumont, or from collectors like Will Day. The collection includes the two surviving original *bandes* of Emile Reynaud's Théâtre Optique, "Pauvre Pierrot" and "Autour d'une cabine". The Will Day Collection includes some rare examples of early formats and processes: some 500 continuous positive nitrate images, size 50x50mm, mounted on a cardboard mask with two rounded perforations per image; 500 original *chrono-photographies* of Jules-Etienne Marey, almost a metre in length with 20 or less images of 44mm; the original experimental film of William Friese-Greene, circa 1890, with images size 60mm x 40mm; the 1903 82mm-wide trichrome experimental film of Benjamin Jumeaux and William

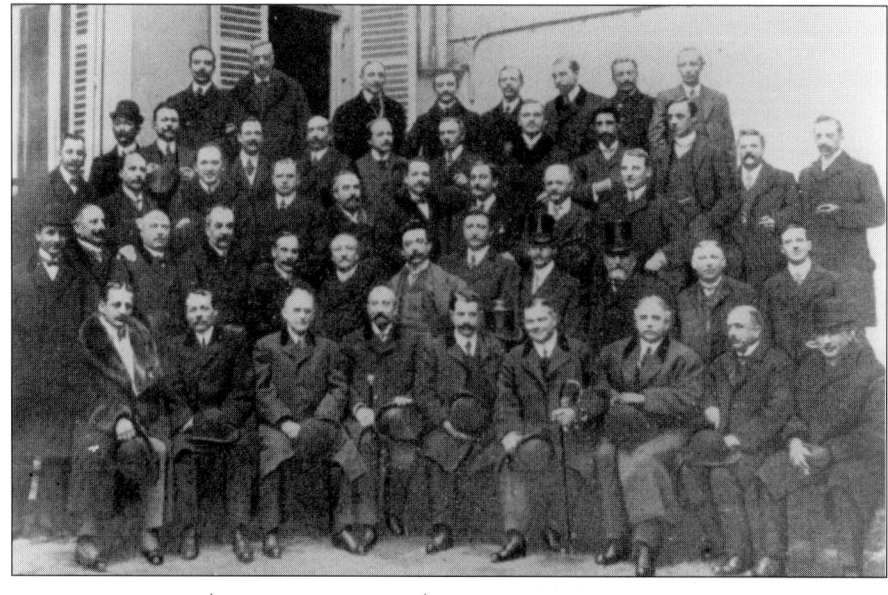

Participants in the 1909 international congress of film producers, held in Paris. The original caption misspells the name of George Eastman

BFI Collections – Stills, Posters & Designs, London. 123070.

CONGRÈS INTERNATIONAL DES ÉDITEURS DE FILMS (2–4 Février 1909)
SCIAMENGO, GANDOLFI, MAY JR, JOURJON, MÉLIÈS JR, AMBROSIO, BARKER,
ARRIBAS, ROBERT, READER, ROSSI, (…), DE BAULAINCOURT, DUSKES, PAUL, HEPWORTH,
CHENEAU, EFFING, ZEISKE, HUBCH, OTTOLENGHI, BOLARDI, AKAR, WILLIAMSON, BROMHEAD, CRICKS,
BROWN, MESSER, OLSEN, PRÉVOST, BERNHEIM, COMERIO, VANDAL, RALEIGH, MAY, WINTER,
ROGERS, CH. PATHÉ, EASTMANN, MÉLIÈS, GAUMONT, URBAN, GIFFORD, SMITH, AUSTIN.

Norman Lascelles Davidson; and another three-colour process Friese-Greene/Lascelles Davidson experimental film from 1912, on 35mm. Bois d'Arcy also houses more than 4,000 Lumière films, both positive copies (including three hand-coloured examples) and negatives with central round perforations, as well as 15 unique 75mm Lumière films shot for the 1900 Paris Exposition Universelle, recently restored in their original format. There are also original 60mm Demeny films; original nitrate positive copies of Edison films; numerous examples of hand-coloured films and *pochoir* tinted films, tinted and toned positives, and examples of more obscure colour processes. The preservation of these exceptional nitrate film formats is a responsibility which in itself requires special attention.

Deteriorated nitrate print of Louis Delluc's *Le Silence* (1920).

Archives du Film du Centre National de la Cinématographie, Bois d'Arcy.

Origins of the CNC Collections

The nitrate collections come, in the main, from former French nitrate laboratories, and as such include original negative, fine grain, and positive material. This variety of material per title requires special preparatory work prior to the launching of a restoration. Each item of composite material must be examined, compared, and analysed, not only in terms of image and sound content, but also in terms of specific physical defects.

The Archives du Film du CNC is a relatively young institution, created 30 years ago by the then-Minister of Culture, André Malraux, in the midst of the Henri Langlois Affair of 1968. All French nitrate collections are now deposited at Bois d'Arcy. They include those deposited directly to the CNC itself, those of the Cinemathèque Française, those of the Cinémathèque de Toulouse, and those of regional archives and particular companies and individuals. They started to be gathered in the early 1930s by Henri Langlois, who was actively involved in saving from destruction as many unique nitrate collections as possible: the remains of the Eclair film collection, the Pathé nitrate collection of the Vincennes laboratory, which closed in the 1930s and includes several foreign films, etc.

By the 1950s all French laboratories were ordered to stop using nitrate and storing it in large quantities. The Government then offered the former army site of Bois d'Arcy to house these collections in the tunnels of the old artillery fortifications. This type of storage later became redundant, and was replaced by special units constructed soon after the creation of the Service des Archives du Film.

The Nitrate Plan

By 1990 it became apparent that a special restoration programme was required to transfer these huge decaying nitrate collections (which nobody could use) onto safety stock.

A detailed Nitrate Plan, to last 15 years, was presented first to the CNC, then to the Minister of Culture, Jack Lang. The Plan was then presented to the Prime Minister and to the Finance Minister, so that it could receive a continuous budget throughout the 15 years. This was approved, and on 20 October 1991 the Plan was officially unveiled at Bois d'Arcy to officials, journalists, and some eminent foreign personalities like Martin Scorsese. The idea was, and still is today, to transfer and restore each year over 1 million metres of nitrate originals which have not been restored by their rights-owners or are "orphan films".

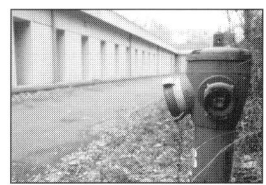

Nitrate film vaults at Bois d'Arcy.

Archives du Film du Centre National de la Cinématographie, Bois d'Arcy.

The Plan includes legal requirements whereby each film restored by the CNC must be covered by an agreement with the rights-holder which specifies such information as the costs of the restoration, the terms of reimbursement provided by the rights-owner, how and under what conditions the restored film can be shown by the CNC, the type of access provided to the rights-holder, etc.

The implementation of the Plan has given rise to many related developments. Among the most gratifying have been a renewed confidence in the future of the Archives, hitherto solely associated with the hopeless task of caring for decaying nitrate; an increased efficiency among all the staff, since the stringencies of the Plan are high, as well as the expected results; an increased knowledge of the collections as we discover unknown, rare, and forgotten films to restore; an increased use of the collections in France and abroad, as well as new releases on video and television; and increased exchanges with sister archives as we discover films thought lost, and we repatriate French films.

Thanks to the gathering of all French nitrate collections at Bois d'Arcy, and the good relationships we have established with all archives and cinematheques in France with whom we share the benefits of the Nitrate Plan, we are now able to know exactly which feature films are missing from French collections and establish a list. The statistics show an average nitrate loss of 27%, a much lower proportion than in other large film-producing countries. The loss ranges from 58% in the 1910s, to 42% in the 1920s, 21% in the 1930s, 4% in the 1940s, and 1% in the mid-1950s.

In the tenth year of the Nitrate Plan, a total of more than 9,600 titles have either been transferred or restored onto polyester safety film. The programming of the titles restored is of particular importance. Lists have been compiled, arranged chronologically, by companies, and by themes. These are continually updated and seriously monitored by all the team, as well as shared and discussed among the three national institutions, the Archives du Film du CNC, the Cinémathèque Française, and the Cinémathèque de Toulouse. In the first years of the Plan, priority was given to feature films. During the years preceding the Centenary of Cinema the rare collections of early cinema, like Emile Reynaud, Lumière, Will Day, Marey, Demenÿ, and Edison, etc., were given priority. The early shorts of Pathé and Gaumont were then given their turn, as well as serials. Nowadays, the documentary collections are being tackled by themes, authors, and periods. This gives us another opportunity to discover unknown treasures which are seldom listed in documentary catalogues, and in time we will be able to share these newly-found treasures with the public.

Foreign Collaboration

The Nitrate Plan has fostered international co-operation among foreign cinematheques, leading to unexpected results with regard to the rediscovery of old films.

Within the framework of international agreements and the expediency of negotiating help or exchanges, France has handed back to the countries in question foreign films deposited in our collections, or, inversely, has repatriated French films found abroad. In every case this has brought about a preservation or a restoration.

Among the works rediscovered in our archive, there was, to our great amazement, unknown until now, one of the three versions of the *Sortie des Usines Lumière*, deposited long ago by the National Archives of Canada. An internegative was made of this important Lumière film, which was then returned to Ottawa. We also found some Hong Kong productions, which at the request of their owner were sent to the archive in Taipei; some Tunisian films by the director Albert Samama (among them, his famous 1924 film *Ain-Ghezal, la fille de Carthage*), discovered among films deposited by the County Council of Charentes, which were returned to Tunisia; and a temporary deposit of Lumière films about Australia, which were returned to Screensound Australia (formerly the National Film and Sound Archive) in Canberra, in exchange for French primitives, including a Méliès film.

Foreign cinematheques also returned their French films: Filmarchiv Austria in Vienna returned some Pathé productions, including *Une Soif insaisissable* (1906) by Lucien Lépine; the Cinémathèque Suisse in Lausanne, who received back some of their French and German films from the 1930s and 40s, including André Cayatte's *Le Chanteur inconnu* (1947), returned some reels filmed and sequestered during the Second World War (including films by the Communist Party, about and by the Resistance).

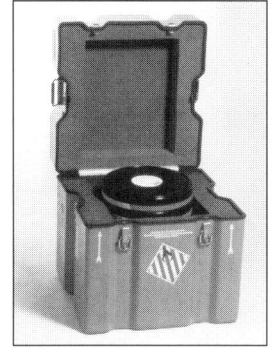

Nitrate film transport box.

Archives du Film du Centre National de la Cinématographie, Bois d'Arcy.

In each case we also contributed our technical support. We collaborated with Israel on the restoration of the Nathan Axelrod collection (covering productions filmed between 1927 and 1948), and worked with countries such as Iran to save their cinema heritage. As a matter of fact, during his visit to the 1900 Paris Exposition Universelle the Shah of Persia, Muzaffar-ed-Din, bought a Lumière Cinématographe, and between 1900 and 1906 his private photorapher filmed views in France and Persia. These were found in 1982 in Tehran, at the Palace and Museum "Le Golestan". Besides this, we were involved with the Cinémathèque Marocaine in restoring films about the Maghreb made in 9.5mm by Mohamed Osfour.

Archives often struggle in isolation, which sometimes affects restorations. Our collaborations have worked towards abolishing barriers between cinematheques, and helped to reconstruct missing films and to complete collections. In the process we have all benefitted in the common search for our patrimony.

The Sound of Nitrate

by Martin Sawyer

I would like to start by asking a question. Why do we bother to archive picture on cellulose nitrate materials, which at times can be highly dangerous? To this I'd like to add, why do we archive and restore sound on nitrate picture?

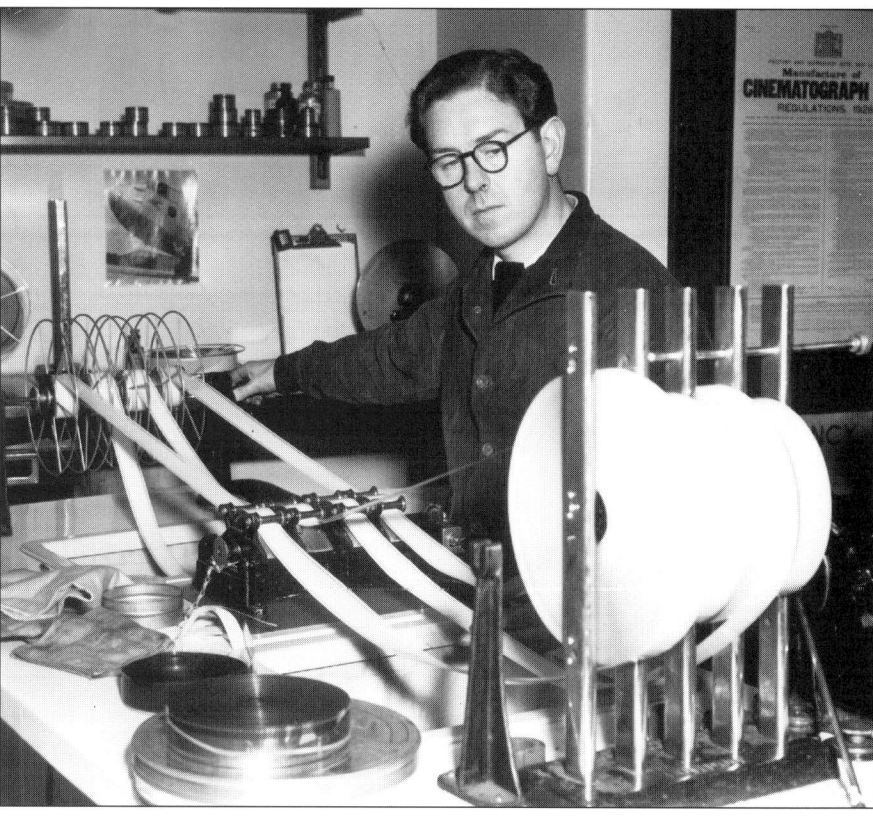

As the original caption notes: "Editing, or the assembling … of the sound and picture tracks, is a highly skilled job and can often make or mar a film." Film editor Reggie Mills at work in the cutting room on *The Red Shoes* (1948).

BFI Collections – Stills, Posters & Designs, London. 7-300-061.

Perhaps to answer my questions, and particularly the second, I might invite the reader to share a look back over my sound memories. I can remember nearly being frightened out of the cinema in my very early years, by the machine-gun sound effects on the conning tower in the Powell and Pressburger film *49th Parallel*. I can also remember being absolutely startled – like the rest of the cinema audience – when the convict Magwitch shouted on the misty Medway marshes in David Lean's *Great Expectations*. There wasn't a bottom on the seat in the cinema! How much is contributed to our film heritage and our memory of film when we hear such lines as Ingrid Bergman, in *Casablanca*, saying: "Play it once, Sam, for old times' sake. Play it, Sam." or Alastair Sim as Scrooge, muttering "Humbug!" I also remember the husky voice of Roger Livesey, in *A Matter of Life and Death*. Think of all those unique voices (which we can think of, in the present tense, just because we have recorded them for posterity): James Stewart, Herbert Lom, Felix Aylmer, Margaret Rutherford, brought to us on the various sound systems used on nitrate film. I can remember going to the cinema with my two-and-a-half-pence admission fee to see Roy Rogers, though most of us were all just waiting to cheer when we heard the raspy voice of Andy Devine – and he sang once, too, I believe!

Later, in my teenage years, my late mother, who reached 86, tried to describe to me the entertainment of her day. Later still, I also saw her doing this with my own teenage children. I never really appreciated it at the time. In giving this paper at the symposium "The Last Nitrate Picture Show" in June 2000, I screened some material from the DeForest Phonofilm Collection, entitled *Pilbeam and His Orchestra, and the Sisters Tosch*, which was produced circa 1926, and is very, very early variable-density sound-on-film. I challenged my audience, having seen the clip with the sound, could they imagine seeing it again, but without the sound? It would be flat. It would lose the spirit the director put into it. And how much information of the period that is tied into that film sound would also be lost!

So why have I made this comment? Well, my personal opinion is that archivists neglect sound. Just imagine only being able to see the *Pilbeam* film as mute.... But I've had it said to me, "Well, we've preserved the picture elements, but we can't afford or we haven't the time to do the sound." I regard that as very, very sad.

Much excellent work has already been done in the preservation of visual silent images on cellulose nitrate, not only on the 35mm gauge but also on what were once called the sub-standard gauges, in both black-and-white and colour. However, more and more nitrate sound elements are now suffering decomposition problems, be they sound negative, sound master positive, duping combined positive, combined negative, or combined prints. Importantly, too, the sound may be in variable-density format, or one of the many variable-area formats.

Having been heavily involved in archive sound restoration work for many years (in both 35mm and 16mm, though of course the latter is not nitrate), one important lesson which I have learned is that there can be no standard rules or patterns applied to sound restoration. There are, however, some depressingly standard phrases that archivists use when discussing sound preservation. Among the ones that I have heard are, "Laboratory duping is cheaper than re-recording and an adequate way of sound preservation," and "Variable-density should be re-recorded, but any form of variable-area should be duped." Add to this more recently a new dictate – "We have vinegar syndrome magnetic master sound and we wish to preserve it as a film sound negative" (whether it be 35mm or 16mm magnetic). And lastly, another comment, which concerns me most: "Our budget is so limited we can only finance our picture elements for preservation."

Before commenting further on any of these statements, it is worthwhile identifying that one fact has emerged over my years of sound preservation work: that there really are two aims or needs for archivists, although they may see it as only one. First, there is the need to preserve the sound, and second, in many cases there is also the need to preserve the element or system in which the sound was originally recorded.

The element presented for sound preservation may be shrunken, may be of low volume, may suffer from previous duping problems, may be push-pull sound, or may be a very thin light positive, all of which can be aided in re-recording to achieve a better restoration of the actual sound recorded upon the original master. Thus a dupe can be made to identify the element, *and* a re-recorded sound negative to preserve the original sound to the best obtainable quality, without too much alteration to the original. And so the sound will be in acceptable, current, variable-area twin bilateral mono format, which surely should be our aim.

Now would be the time to make perhaps not an absolute case for the re-recording of sound, but to identify its many advantages, and the advantages of prior discussions before re-recording.

It would seem, on just an initial examination of price lists, that laboratory duping is indeed more cost-effective. However, this is not always the case, as re-recording can often identify problems that may not show up until after printing laboratory dupe soundtracks, so surely the wastage costs of NG ("no good") duping of sound and the combined printing must be added to the initial duping price per foot. One might ask, what problems may be identified at the re-recording stage? A set of prints for a feature preservation can be assimilated from the best picture elements of several sets of prints. This could cause, on the sound, uneven high-frequency content reel to reel, volume differences, uneven shrinkage causing perforation ingress to the sound area on some reels, and in some cases the age differences, and source differences (donors), mean that some reels may have variable-area sound (dupes by re-recording) and others variable-density. All of these problems can be identified and adjusted in re-recording, thus resulting in fewer printing problems, wastage, and quality evenness; even differences within reels can be rectified.

Being possibly the last person on this planet to re-record using a variable-density sound camera, I can speak very highly of variable-density sound – but...

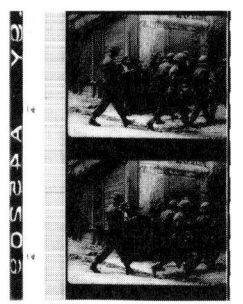

An example of variable-density optical sound, here on a combined picture-and-sound print.

Imperial War Museum Film and Video
Archive, London.

It must be stressed here that the control, or, if you wish, grading, of variable-density sound is vital to both quality and volume of duped sound materials. Signal to noise and distortion can become enormous problems if the closest of attention is not paid to sound control. One can understand why one ex-archive head insisted that all variable-density preserved sound should be turned into variable-area by re-recording.

During my years working in this field, film sound positives of all sorts have been presented for re-recording. This includes badly-shrunken material with pulsing, or dupes where this edge of perforation pulsing has been reproduced in copying. This can be removed in re-recording. Prints have also been submitted with lateral scratches running through the soundtrack area. These have been immensely reduced in re-recording, whereas mere laboratory duping would carry it through preservation.

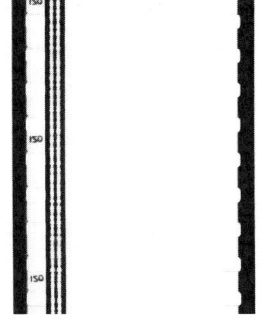

An example of variable-area optical sound, here on a separate track.

Imperial War Museum Film and Video
Archive, London.

In the past, too, with the aid of *manual* computer editing, only troublesome disturbances, such as joins, etc., could be removed without disturbing audio that did not need to be touched. This can be achieved only by re-recording. Experience tells me that re-recording is by far the best way of preserving film sound.

I confess to having had certain feelings of anger that well up when talking to people – generally younger people – in the industry. When I say, "I work on nitrate sound," they say, "Ah, nitrate – snap, crackle, and pop." Well, that might be true of some of the aged elements today, but consider the National Film and Television Archive's ambitious recent restoration of the sound of *The Third Man*. The sound for the whole film was transferred from nitrate variable-density print first onto digital audiotape, then subsequently onto a hard disc. It was then manually cleaned. It wasn't put through any algorithms or anything like that; the film sound was only touched where it needed to be touched. I'm not trying to make a comparison between density and this, but what I am trying to say is that one of the reasons why we need to preserve the sound of the period this way is that it is most suitable for certain titles that have become cinematically unique. Because I feel if we were all in the Odeon Leicester Square, in 1949, listening to a new variable-density print of *The Third Man*, we'd be listening pretty much to the quality that has come off the resulting treated prints. I know it's now variable-area, and I know it's been treated, but I have every confidence that when an audience listen to it – as they had the opportunity to do in the symposium presentation – they will get a further lesson in the value of preserving film sound by the re-recording process.

Lastly – and this is by no means the least of preservation problems, rather perhaps one of the greatest – we have vinegar syndrome in triacetate-based film, and, indeed, triacetate magnetic sound. Much has already been said on this subject, and without doubt more needs to be said. May I offer a few comments? The moment it smells, fix it, whatever the test strips show. If it is magnetic sound, leave it in magnetic – it is much more cost-effective, and you stay in the "positive" image. Remember, there will be future demand for hard disc, and so, for a while make magnetic polyester-based copies of celluloid titles, as magnetic gives the best quality and ease of transfer. This will apply much more so to 16mm gauge materials on full coat, and indeed to magnetic stripe sound.

Current 35mm optical sound negative/positive results are virtually equal to those for older 35mm vinegar-affected magnetic tracks of past times, so film can be a route for preservation. However, to pursue a preservation route that travels via sound negative recording, sound development, 35mm positive stock, 35mm sound-master positive printing and development – not to mention examination – would seem to be pretty costly in time, labour, and materials, when compared to a magnetic copy on 5mil polyester-base film.

Existing 35mm sound negatives with vinegar problems also need treating and printing, as do 16mm sound negatives.

Further action may not be necessary, but perhaps new sound negatives, or, indeed, polyester-based magnetics, may be a viable option, until needs for combined optical sound printing arise in the future.

In conclusion, I think I'd like to say, long live nitrate film! Its life has been a wonderful opportunity for us to capture talent in front of and behind the camera, in the laboratory, in the cinema. But I very much think that nitrate had to go; it wasn't safe. Kodak made an almost seamless transition. You lost the nitrate base, you went over to triacetate, the emulsion was the same. But other questions now arise. Compared with the life that we've seen in nitrate, what will happen or what has already happened to triacetate film, what will happen to the industry's current 8-track dubbing masters and digital audiotape? We've got to think *and* act, and keep not only the written record of bygone ages, but all the visual and oral experiences of more recent years. If we don't, there will be many people who will come into this business, and also those whom we seek to entertain and educate, who will never know or learn about them. So here then is our opportunity. May we continue to preserve in sight *and* sound the talents, techniques, and times cleverly placed on nitrate and triacetate film.

The coming of sound, 1928. A Movietone recording camera used by Universal under the trade name Unitone to film talking sequences for *Lonesome*. Behind the camera with the attachment which "changes sound waves to light waves", Carl Laemmle Jr (the film's producer) stands between D W Griffith and Sid Grauman.

BFI Collections – Stills, Posters & Designs, London. 158137.

The Case of the Cineteca Nacional Fire: Notes and Facts in Perspective

by Fernando Osorio

Introduction

The Cineteca Nacional was opened on 17 January 1974 on the grounds of the former Churubusco Film Studios, south of Mexico City. The National Film Archive shared the grounds, the fame, and the audience with the Churubusco Film Studios and laboratories, as well as with a film school. The film archive facilities included three film theatres, a library, a gallery, four vaults, and a film examination and conservation laboratory. A specialised bookshop and coffee shop were immediately adjacent. The National Film Bureau was located on the second floor, as well as the public film records office. Surrounding the complex was the parking lot. There was a huge lighted billboard on the main façade of the building that could be easily seen from the distance.

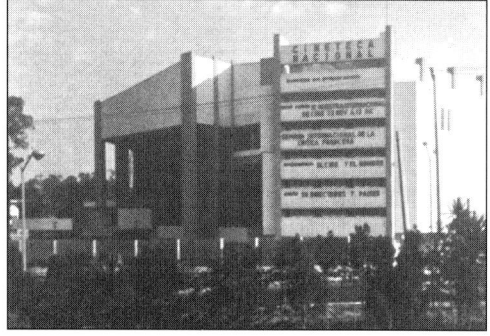

The Cineteca Nacional, Mexico DF – before the 1982 fire.
© Fernando Osorio.

The buildings were located at the intersection of two busy expressways, Calzada de Tlalpan and Rio Churubusco. It was conveniently located so that all day long students from the National University and other city colleges could attend the screenings and film programmes. The neighbourhood used to be an upper-middle-class borough where private and independent film producers and distributors settled.

The film archive soon became a centre for film culture. It was able to seat more than 700 people per screening in both theatres, the Fernando de Fuentes and the Salòn Rojo. There was a third small cinema for research screenings. Three screenings were held each day in the two main cinemas, and programmes for children were screened in the mornings at weekends. The bookshop was very successful, and many exhibitions of film posters were organised in the gallery. Over 120 people worked in the archive. For more than eight years it was the landmark institution of "cinephilia" in Mexico City.

How Things Started

24 March 1982, Mexico City. It was an extremely warm day, very dry, as was usual in the Spring. At 18:00 hours, two fire stations close to the film archive received simultaneous emergency calls. There was a possible fire at the Cineteca Nacional.

A few minutes before 6 p.m., a film examiner had noticed a smell of smoke. Having first checked his workplace, he then checked Vault No.1. As he opened the vault door he saw a cloud of white smoke. He closed the door and immediately notified his boss, who went to check the vault himself. It was impossible to get in since the heavy smoke did not let him breathe. The smell was odd, so he called the fire station.

The film studio's own fire-fighters were the first to arrive. They started to look for the source of the heat. A second group of firemen joined the first some ten minutes later, and focused their search on the vaults.

Meanwhile, the archive authorities again called the emergency services, and started to evacuate people from the theatres and all the other facilities. The Salòn Rojo film theatre was already empty at 6 p.m., but there was still a screening going on in the Fernando de Fuentes theatre.

The director of the archive led the staff in another inspection. He instructed them to bring all the fire extinguishers on the main floor close to the vaults. When the fire chief arrived on the scene, the director tried, unsuccessfully, to warn him not to use water, but to use only the extinguishers.

The Explosion

By this time there was heavy white smoke coming out of all four vaults, even though the vaults were constructed separately and had no intercommunication. This puzzled the director. But the worst thing was when he realised that the screening in the big theatre was still going on. He immediately ran to stop the screening, and so became a witness to the explosion that started the fire:

> I was asking the audience to leave at once because there was an emergency; I asked them to do it calmly. The doors were opened and everybody seemed to cooperate.... There was a group of youngsters left behind; they were claiming their money back. Then there came the eruption, and a big flame coming out of the screen reached us. I saw the ceiling falling down. I threw myself to the floor, and once the flame receded, I went to help a group of staff members who where trapped in the theatre office.... I saw how two janitors, who were standing next to me – I do not know what they were doing there – were caught by the fire... I ran down past the bookshop. Everything was in a state of great confusion.

Some of the employees were reached by the explosion while they were leaving the premises:

> I worked at the candy shop. My workmate and I closed the shop when we were asked to evacuate, and we were going to leave by the main entrance of the building when we heard a big explosion. I felt something pushing me, a sort of warm cloud behind me. When I stood up, we were 15 metres away – we had flown 15 metres! My workmate was injured by glass splinters in her arms. We reached the street, where a taxi driver took us to a nearby clinic, and while we were in the taxi I heard more explosions.

Other people had worse experiences:

> The firemen connected up the hoses to the hydrant, and asked me to turn it on when they told me to ... so I ran to the hydrant and waited. It was by the outside wall of the Fernando de Fuentes theatre. I was waiting when I heard an explosion over my head, and saw bricks starting to fall over my head. I leaped towards the street fence and hid behind a car. Part of the wall fell on my arm. I ran into the street, and a stretcher-bearer from the Red Cross told me, 'You are injured!' He led me to the helicopter that took me to the hospital. I was hurt, but there were others in worse shape than I was. Later that night I went back to the Cineteca to pick up my car.... The flames were still high.

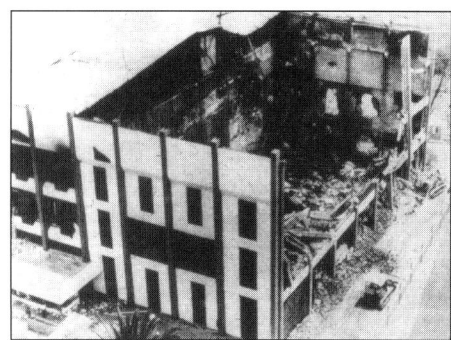

The Cineteca Nacional after the fire.

© Fernando Osorio.

The Fire

The fire lasted 14 hours. All the fire stations, including that of the National University, fought the blaze until early the next morning. The available water was rapidly used up, and the tanker-pumpers had a difficult time. Many helicopters flew over the site all night long. There was a big traffic jam on the expressways, and there was panic in the neighbourhood. If the fire was not brought under control, it could spread, and reach other parts of the district.

When the fire started there were several explosions, one of them due to the gas cylinders used in the coffee shop kitchen. Most witnesses agreed there were about three explosions. These shattered the windows of a baby day-care centre and nursing home run by the social security institute which stood (as it still stands today) across one of the expressways from the Cineteca site. Fortunately, on the afternoon of the fire, the children had been evacuated and sent to other day-care centres and hospitals.

The Aftermath

Massive media coverage of the event started immediately. Speculation spread quickly, and lasted for several days in the news headlines. The statements and declarations of high public authorities and officials did little to help the public to form a clear opinion of what really happened that day.

The fire was devastating. 99% of the film archive was destroyed. The library was lost, as well the films housed in four vaults, the public records relating to film, and the bookshop. In addition, the life of the Chief Fireman was lost – he was trapped in Vault 1 after the explosion due to the structural collapse of the building – as were those of two staff members.

TRAGEDIA

Por Jerónimo

A contemporary response to the tragedy: this cartoon by "Jerónimo" appeared in *El Heraldo de Mexico* on 26 March 1982.

El Heraldo de Mexico.

How? The Thesis and an Auxiliary Hypothesis

Once he had recovered from his injuries, the then-director of the archive asked the special investigators of the national security office to make an official report. The events were meticulously reviewed and reconstructed. The former director recalled them in a recent interview given to the current chairman of the Mexican Film Institute. The conclusion was that the fire was originally caused by the overheating of the electric wires that fed the projection systems. That was the focus of the outbreak. Then the carpets and furniture caught fire, and when the fire reached the vaults containing flammable nitrate material, the fire spread rapidly.

The informant then suggested the following additional hypothesis – that the first major explosion was produced when the water pumped by the fire-fighters into the vault came in contact with the burning nitrate films. However, this is only a hypothesis.

The Antithesis

The official report does not either directly or indirectly impute any responsibility for the fire to the lack of economic or financial resources for the maintenance of the vaults, air conditioning systems, equipment, and other facilities. The then-director of the archive had asked for a special budget in order to improve the Cineteca's facilities. According to his statement, the "money was given by the Federal Government, but it was not used for these purposes".

The Synthesis

According to the facts as described by the witnesses interviewed, and in the interests of improving archival preservation practice and strategies to prevent further disasters and respond to those that may occur, there are two aspects to the Cineteca fire where questions need to be asked:

1. The fact that smoke was seen coming from all four vaults with no automatic warning. This fact puzzled archive authorities at the time, and even now it is hard to explain. Why did the smoke detectors not respond? Were there any smoke detectors? If so, were they working properly?
2. Smoke was seen in all four vaults, but only one vault was housing nitrate – either 200 or 2000 300-metre cans, apparently not in an advanced state of decomposition, since oral history tells us that they were just about to be copied.

It appears that it was not nitrate which caused the disaster at the Cineteca Nacional, but the lack of an integral security plan. It is true that nitrate helped to spread the fire, but not only nitrate – in fact, all the material that caught fire had this effect.

The Only Conclusion

As a professional in conservation, I want to say that the lesson taught by this disaster points to the need for security planning and for the implementation of effective means to prevent disasters and to respond to a potential disaster of no matter what magnitude.

It took me over two years of research to reconstruct the fire in the Cineteca. The realisation of how vulnerable an institution's safety can be is an insight that comes continually before my mind. The daily work of a conservator must be to enhance both the physical and chemical conservation of the collection, and its interior and exterior safety as well. He or she has an important role to play in getting archive staff members to feel involved in the daily tasks relating to the security of the collection, and to realise that any omission, no matter how simple it might seem, could lead to a fatal weakness in the safety of the collection.

The Legion of the Condemned – Why American Silent Films Perished

by David Pierce

An earlier version of this article first appeared in Film History, *v.9, no.1 (1997), pp.5–22.*

Of the approximately 10,000 feature films and countless short subjects released in the United States before 1928, only a small portion survive. While some classics exist and are widely available, many silent films survive only in reviews, stills, posters and the memories of the few remaining audience members who saw them on their original release.[1]

Why did most silent films not survive the passage of time? The current widespread availability of many titles on home video, and the popularity of silent film presentations with live orchestral accompaniment might give the impression that silent films had always been held in such high regard. Instead, for many decades after the coming of sound, silent films had all the commercial appeal of last week's weather report.

This article will explore the factors that contributed to the loss of such a large number of silent films in a seemingly random fashion. There is no single villain, as an unstable storage medium and an extended period of no commercial value were contributing, but not decisive factors. The loss of most silent films resulted from shortsighted decisions by their owners, and a combination of happenstance and neglect.

Not Many Copies in Existence

Although it might seem remarkable that not a single print survives for most silent films, usually there were not many copies to begin with. While newspapers or magazines were printed and sold by the thousands, relatively few projection prints were required for even the most popular silent films. In the earliest days of the industry, producers sold prints, and measured success by the number of copies sold. By the feature period, beginning around 1914, copies were leased to subdistributors or rented to exhibitors, and the owners retained tight control. Distribution of silent features was based on a staggered release system, with filmgoers paying more to see a film early in its run. Films opened in downtown theaters, moved to neighborhood theaters, and finally to rural houses. This process was controlled by a system of clearances that dictated rentals and when a picture would be available to each class of theaters. In the 1920s, a film would normally require two years to work its way from premiere to final performance. Since the prints were in continuous use, this demand could be satisfied by a modest number of copies. In 1926, Paramount was making 150 prints for the domestic release, and an additional 50 copies for foreign use.[2]

Periodically, prints would be returned to the distributor for repair. Inspectors would fix splices and torn sprockets, sometimes cannibalizing several prints to create one showable copy. By the end of their run, pictures would be circulating to theaters that changed their program every day, in prints that were often in very poor condition. Exhibitors were constantly complaining about the poor condition of the copies they received. A small town theater running MGM's *Show People* (1928) was typical: "We were rather surprised at getting a poor print after paying the golden price we did. Parts of it were quite rainy and scratched." Theaters learned to expect well-worn prints, as with a complaint about *Our Dancing Daughters* (1928): "Naturally we would draw a slovenly inspected print for a night when we had a houseful of particular and critical people."[3]

Most Remaining Prints Were Destroyed

Regardless of the number of prints, almost all of them shared the same fate. The value of a film declined rapidly following its opening engagement. Producers wrote off the production cost of their films quickly, usually by 90 per cent in the first year. Rental for a feature might be $3,000 per week for the first run in a downtown theater, and bottom out at $10 per day by the end of its run. After theaters no longer wanted a film, the only residual value for the heavily worn prints was the silver content of the celluloid.[4]

In *Suds* (1920), Mary Pickford saves an old horse from its fate at the glue factory. In real life, Pickford and her contemporaries ensured that all excess copies of *Suds* and their other films were accounted for and sent to their cinematic doom. In 1918, Kodak established a silver recovery center in Rochester, New York, to process junk prints. Silver salvage of excess projection prints served two purposes: certifying destruction of the copies, while returning a final sliver of income to the owner. United Artists was a typical Kodak customer when they cleared out some of the older Mary Pickford releases from their distribution depots in 1925. UA sent 130 well-worn prints of *Suds*, *Little Lord Fauntleroy* (1921), *Rosita* (1923) and other older Pickford titles to Rochester. The resulting income was a modest, but undoubtedly welcome, $302.74.[5]

After a film was no longer in active distribution, the studio would retain the original negative, the original work print, and a projection print or two. Other than a copy for the studio library, these materials were usually stored outside California, because that state taxed old and new negatives on their full production cost. As a consequence, negatives were shipped to the East Coast upon completion and most release prints were manufactured by laboratories in New York and New Jersey. Storage vaults for studios, laboratories and private storage companies were located throughout Manhattan, Brooklyn, the Bronx, and Queens, and in northern New Jersey at Fort Lee, Bound Brook, Little Ferry, and Woodridge.

Destroyed For Legal Reasons

When these materials were pulled from storage, it was more likely for inspection or destruction than preservation. When a film was sold to another company for a remake, the contract often required that all copies of the original be destroyed, with the occasional exception of a reference print. Paramount sold George Melford's *The Unknown* (1915) to Universal, agreeing "to destroy the negative ... and all prints thereof in possession of the seller, except one print which the seller shall retain for library purposes." Mary Pickford's *Little Annie Rooney* (1925), remade with Shirley Temple, still exists despite such a clause. Other titles were not so lucky.[6]

Some story contracts obligated the producer to destroy the negative at the end of the license period to leave the author free to make a new agreement. The agreement with novelist Rafael Sabatini for King Vidor's *Bardelys the Magnificent* (1927) with John Gilbert required that "at final determination of contract, [MGM] must destroy all negatives and positives and render statement or proof thereof to owner."[7]

Little Perceived Value

Before the introduction of sound, some older films retained value as a small number of reissues could be offered to theaters along with new releases. Independent producers lacking new films to offer with their old found that their old films were not in demand. Thomas H Ince had been a successful independent producer before his death in 1924, and his estate was actively trying to realize as much income from his old films as possible. In 1928, a prospective reissue distributor wrote the Ince estate that

> in view of the cost of preparing a series of reissues for the market and the expenses of selling, the outright purchase of a reissue is almost out of the question. Charles Ray, Dorothy Dalton and Enid Bennett pictures do not mean much on the market, unless the pictures themselves were outstanding specials in their time.[8]

Once silent film theaters converted to sound or closed, silent films lost their audience and became worthless. *Civilization* was a big success in 1916. Anxious for income from a reissue distributor, the Ince estate sold the film outright in 1929 for $750. Reissues were rare, so the only remaining value of most pictures was their remake potential. In 1930, the Ince estate sold a group of eight Charles Ray films at $500 each, and in 1932 managed to get $1,000 for Henry King's 1919 hit *23 ½ Hours Leave* from its star Douglas MacLean. Other independents had more success, though the $40,000 price that *Tol'able David* fetched in 1930 was for the story, not the 1920 film that came with it.[9]

The assets of the failed Triangle Films Corporation included rights to as many as 2,500 films and stories. The films included productions from 1915 to 1917 supervised by D W Griffith and Thomas H Ince and Mack Sennett, with stars Douglas Fairbanks, Norma Talmadge, William S Hart and Gloria Swanson. The library sold at bankruptcy auction in 1924 for $55,000. By 1937, three owners later, the films and stories were purchased for a rock bottom $5,000.[10]

After leaving Triangle in 1917, Mack Sennett was a prolific independent producer of shorts and occasional features, but by 1933 his company was in bankruptcy. The inventory of prints and negatives was sold at auction to a speculator for $875, which was about the value of the silver salvage, while Sennett purchased the copyrights for $75. In 1939 Warner Bros. released a two reel condensation of Mack Sennett's *A Small Town Idol* (1921), and Jack L Warner weighed purchasing the Sennett material outright. A studio attorney wrote to his counterpart in New York: "I understand the picture is doing well, and thus J.L.'s desire to make this present deal."[11]

In 1940, Warner Bros. bought all rights and materials to the Sennett comedies, acquiring nine tons of nitrate negatives and prints for $10,000. The 330 properties included the original negatives to *Yankee Doodle in Berlin* (1919), *The Shriek of Araby* (1923) with Ben Turpin in a spoof of Rudolph Valentino, and three features starring Mabel Normand: *Molly O'* (1921), *Suzanna* (1922), and *The Extra Girl* (1923). This footage was used to produce a handful of additional Warner Bros. shorts.[12]

Storage Costs

An inactive film library requires a lot of storage space, but that was not usually a problem for studios that could use their own film vaults or rely on laboratories. Companies generally continued to hold their silent material until they had to pay storage fees or began to run out of room.

The situation was different for independents who kept their negatives and prints in laboratories or commercial storage facilities. Following the introduction of sound, owners began to question why they were paying storage fees on films that would probably never again provide any income. In 1930, Lloyds Film Storage in New York was charging 20 cents per reel per month for storage. The owner of a 7 reel silent feature would be paying $35 per year in storage fees for an asset with virtually no earning potential. Many owners junked their materials, or simply stopped paying storage charges.[13]

Intentional Destruction

Numerous owners evaluated the commercial value of their silent libraries and made a business decision. Producer Sol Lesser junked all of his silent productions in the 1930s when his production company needed storage space for newer films. Less verifiable, but just as credible, is the story that in the late 1940s, Columbia Pictures was presented with a significant increase in their fire insurance premiums. The decision made by Columbia executives was to reduce the material in storage by junking unneeded footage, including all of their silent films.[14]

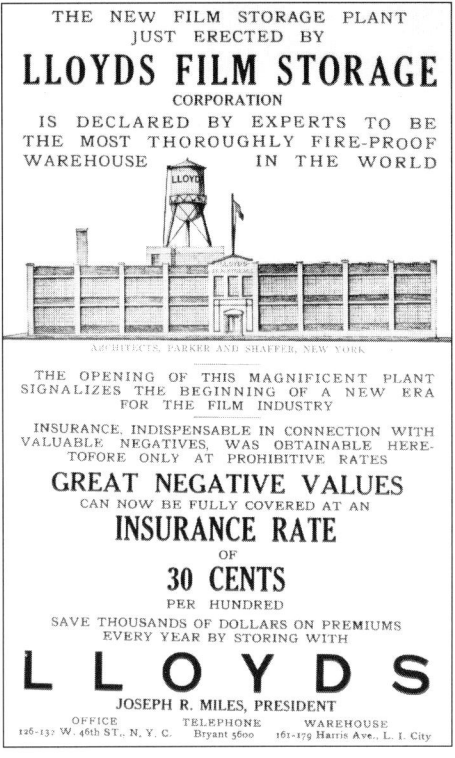

Advertisement for Lloyds Film Storage's "Thoroughly Fire-Proof new plant in New York", included in Joseph Dannenberg (ed.), *Film Year Book 1924*, (New York: The Film Daily), p.106.

David Pierce.

After becoming an independent producer in 1923, Samuel Goldwyn produced 17 silent features, including 10 starring Ronald Colman. Goldwyn's wife and business partner, Frances Howard Goldwyn, ordered the destruction of almost all of his silent films. She told historian Robert S Birchard that it was a business decision because the company needed the vault space. The only title she intentionally kept was Henry King's *The Winning of Barbara Worth* (1926) because it featured Gary Cooper and she felt it might have some commercial value.[15]

In 1954, the East Coast office of RKO asked what to do with nitrate negatives for 64 features and 74 shorts. "Not by the widest stretch of the imagination can I conceive of any possible further use for these silent picture negatives," wrote RKO's Executive Assistant to the President to his boss. "It is also my opinion that if these cans were opened we would find that the negatives have completely deteriorated. I recommend that these negatives be destroyed as they are of no further use and constitute somewhat of a fire hazard." He concluded, "You realize, of course, that the above negatives must be not less than 30 years old." Produced by RKO's predecessor companies, these 521 reels were stored at Consolidated Film Laboratories, and Bonded Film Storage vaults on 146th Street in Manhattan and in Fort Lee, New Jersey.[16]

RKO's president, J R Grainger, forwarded the query to RKO's owner, Howard Hughes, attaching a cover note: "will you please let me know your wishes on this matter as we are paying storage on this material and, while it is not a great amount, it is, nevertheless, in my opinion, a waste of money." Hughes had earlier commissioned Kodak's Research Laboratory to analyze the condition of the films he had produced. Hughes' assistant recommended that RKO do the same, noting

"I am sure that Mr. Hughes would not give a carte blanche order to destroy all this old silent film even if it seems worthless to other people, because of his attitude toward our film here."[17]

The policy changed after General Tire acquired the studio. In 1959, the question came up again, this time about the disposition of the negatives to five or six Fred Thomson westerns, accompanied by the usual comment that these films had no possible use. The response from RKO's office in New York was a handwritten annotation – "Dump Them."[18]

Nitrate Film Stock

The decision by these owners to destroy their silent films merely anticipated the inevitable disintegration of the films, because the film used a base of nitrocellulose that was not chemically stable. The 'nitrate' film base provided a luminous image, and was sufficiently flexible and resilient to withstand hundreds of projections. Eastman Kodak notes that this nitrate film stock "had excellent physical properties," but suffered from "poor chemical stability and high flammability," which meant that the film would rot if it didn't catch fire first. Nitrate film chemically deteriorates over time, and this process is accelerated by the symptoms of poor storage conditions: moisture and heat.[19]

Many silent negatives and prints were premature victims of decomposition due to poor storage conditions. Properly kept in a cool and dry environment, nitrate may outlast improperly stored safety film. While there were recommendations for ideal temperature and humidity, there were no regulations to enforce them. Since nitrate materials were often stored in far less than optimal conditions, they became more susceptible to accelerated deterioration and fire.[20]

Bureau of Explosives, *Special Bulletin No. 1* (21 December 1914).

Richard Koszarski Collection.

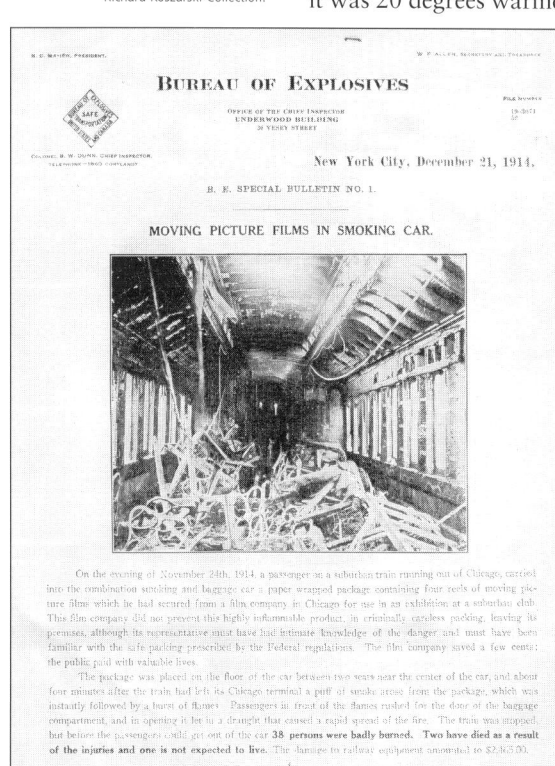

Outdoor vaults without air conditioning reach extreme temperatures in the winter and summer. A visitor to a nitrate vault in Fort Lee, New Jersey, in late October 1972 noted that although the outside temperature was 50 degrees, inside the vaults it was 20 degrees warmer, musty and damp. Most of the film stored in the vault was deteriorating. This type of storage would be damaging for safety film; for nitrate film it would rapidly accelerate decomposition that might otherwise take decades to occur.[21]

In the first stage of decomposition, the image starts to fade as the base emits gases that affect the film emulsion. The surface then becomes sticky, attaching itself to the adjacent film. Next, gas bubbles appear near the tightly wound sections of film, where the gases are unable to escape. The film softens and welds into a single mass with an overwhelming noxious odor before degenerating to a rust-colored acrid powder.[22]

The life expectancy of a reel of nitrate film depends on any number of factors including the chemical composition of that batch of film stock, how the film was developed and washed, and the type of storage. Trace amounts of chemicals remaining from when the film was originally developed play a part as the decomposition often starts in a particular portion of the negative (often the intertitles) that was insufficiently washed. Once started, the decomposition transfers throughout the roll, and storage cans often trap the gases inside, accelerating the process.

Some nitrate from the turn of the century remains in excellent condition, while other films decomposed or fell apart after only a few decades. The original negative to D W Griffith's *The Avenging Conscience* (1914) was unusable ten years after its production due to improper handling and wear. Griffith sent the negative to Europe in 1923 to make prints for release in Germany. The German lab reported that the negative was heavily deteriorated, and "the destruction and decomposition through hypo had already advanced so far that the emulsion was destroyed and came off the celluloid."[23]

Even before decomposition set in, a negative could experience shrinkage beyond the capabilities of standard laboratory equipment. MGM reported in 1954 that

> The Consolidated Laboratories have just reported to us that they cannot satisfactorily print *Sally, Irene and Mary* (1925) as the negative titles have shrunk 1.75% and the picture has shrunk 1.40%. The shrinkage that they can stand is 1.20%.[24]

When negatives were no longer able to produce prints, they became candidates for disposal. In April 1948, Universal ordered the destruction of all but a handful of their silent negatives. The comprehensive order required 18 single spaced pages to list the titles, stored in Woodridge, New Jersey, and at Pathe Labs on East 106th Street in Manhattan. The memo excluded a number of titles from immediate destruction including *The Virgin of Stamboul* (1920) and *The Goose Woman* (1925), noting that "It will be necessary for you to have the above seventeen negatives inspected. It will then be in order for you to junk what ever negatives that are not printable." As one Universal executive wrote his counterpart at Kodak in 1950, the Universal library of silent films was destroyed "due to the fact that they had all deteriorated to the point where the retention of the 'remains' was considered dangerous by the Pathe Laboratory in whose vaults they were stored." An additional incentive to destroy the films might have been Universal's ownership of the Cellofilm Corporation, a silver reclamation company.[25]

Indifference and Benign Neglect

In the most general sense, the greatest reason for the loss of such a high percentage of silent films was indifference. As there was seldom demand for older material, inspection of the materials was erratic, and they were subject to increased danger as the nitrate aged. Many films were not destroyed before their time; they simply did not last long enough for anyone to be interested in preserving them.

Owners who could afford it would continue to store their films and periodically check their condition. As soon as a print or negative displayed the symptoms of nitrate decomposition, it would be destroyed. Evidence of decomposition in any reel would be justification to junk the entire film, since a rotting film was a much greater fire hazard, and an incomplete print or negative would be of no use.

A review of various studio records shows many silent films did not survive twenty years after their production. A 1935 vault inventory of Pathe Exchange, Inc. documented that the negatives for *Mary's Lamb*, George Fitzmaurice's *At Bay* (both 1915) and *Ruler of the Road* (1918) had been "scrapped." Holdings on *Carolyn of the Corners* with Bessie Love and *Prince and Betty* (both 1919) were nonexistent beyond the story files. A 1937 inventory of films from the teens produced by the

Triangle Films Corporation showed that of 60 features with remake rights, a negative or print existed for only 20.[26]

Films held by studios still in operation fared no better. The negatives to *Broadway After Dark* (1924) with Adolphe Menjou and Norma Shearer and *Bobbed Hair* (1925) with Marie Prevost were junked on 12 November 1936. *Wolf's Clothing* (1927) with Monte Blue and Patsy Ruth Miller was destroyed on 14 September 1938. Because of decomposition in reel 5, the entire negative to Erich von Stroheim's *The Devil's Passkey* (1920) was destroyed on 8 May 1941. Four reels of the six reel negative to Mary Pickford's *Johanna Enlists* (1918) had rotted and were junked upon inspection in November 1946. Pickford's *Rosita* (1923) was already incomplete. Von Stroheim's last film for Universal, *Merry-Go-Round* (1923), was junked on 1 December 1949.[27]

The negative for von Stroheim's *The Merry Widow* (1925) was examined by MGM in November 1950, and showed so much decomposition that it was scrapped. A year later, when the negative for *He Who Gets Slapped* (1924) with Lon Chaney was pulled from dead storage, the first four reels had decomposed and were junked. Parts of the negative to Greta Garbo's first American film, *The Torrent* (1926), were "very badly decomposed" upon inspection in July 1953. Reel 3 of the negative to Merian C Cooper and Ernest B Schoedsack's *Chang* (1927) was reported as "slightly decomposed" in May 1956. The entire negative was destroyed after a visit by the Los Angeles County fire inspector. *The Lucky Devil* (1925) with Richard Dix lasted long enough to decompose in 1960, and Ernst Lubitsch's *Lady Windermere's Fan* (1925) survived to be junked on 24 January 1961. The negative to Frank Capra's *Submarine* (1928) was destroyed in the mid-1960s due to decomposition.[28]

Prints frequently outlasted the negatives that generated them, but not always long enough. "In the four years preceding Paramount's gift of about 90 feature films to [the American Film Institute], they had scrapped about 70 silent pictures," the AFI's Associate Archivist, David Shepard, said in a 1970 interview. "In November, 1968, Paramount gave the Library of Congress 90 [silent] features," he continued, but "between November and April when the films were finally shipped, 13 of them had deteriorated."[29]

In 1971 after the American Film Institute asked to borrow the last known print of James Cruze's *The City Gone Wild* (1927) from Paramount, the copy was pulled from storage and an inspection showed deterioration in one reel. The print was placed in a barrel of water and carted off by a salvage company while the AFI archivist was driving over to pick it up.[30]

Movies were not always junked, of course. Sometimes they succumbed to something closer to a natural death. In October 1969, Harold Lloyd buried 27 reels of deteriorating film in the yard adjacent to his estate's nitrate vault. The film laid to rest included odd reels of the original negatives to Lloyd's features *Why Worry* (1923), *Girl Shy* (1924), and *Hot Water* (1924), and negatives to a number of his one reel short comedies. Had Lloyd not made safety negatives for most of his features, and a single safety print for most of his shorts, the comedian would have barely outlived his life's work.[31]

Nitrate Film Fires

Films were usually junked by placing them in a barrel of water due to the risk of fire. At its best, nitrate film has a relatively low ignition temperature; decomposition lowers the flash point so rotting nitrate film can spontaneously combust at temperatures as low as 106 degrees Fahrenheit, emitting toxic fumes while burning. Once ignition begins, internal oxidizing agents accelerate the combustion, so that tightly wound film will continue burning underwater.

The flammable nature of nitrate and careless handling led to many well-publicized fires with loss of life. A fire in a Pittsburgh film exchange in January 1909 killed ten. In 1914, a courier carried four reels of film wrapped in paper into the smoking car of a Chicago commuter train. The package caught fire, killing two and badly burning 38, destroying the interior of the car. A 1919 film exchange fire injured 30.[32]

In the early teens, the Lubin Film Manufacturing Company laboratory in Philadelphia supplied release prints for the Jesse L. Lasky Feature Play Company and other producers. An explosion and fire in a storage vault on 13 June 1914, destroyed numerous negatives including *The Sea Wolf* (1913), produced by Bosworth, Inc. The Thomas Edison plant in New Jersey burned on 9 December 1914, when a fire started in a vault in the film inspecting building and quickly spread. The fire that burned the Manhattan studios of Famous Players on 11 September 1915, also destroyed the negative to *The Foundling*, an unreleased Mary Pickford film directed by Allan Dwan.[33]

These and other well-publicized disasters forced the industry to consider shifting to a safer film stock. Kodak had developed a nonflammable cellulose acetate film stock by 1909. Unfortunately, it was less durable and more expensive, with a grainier image, so a brief experiment with acetate release prints ended in 1911. Prints would warp and buckle under the high intensity open arc lights used in projectors, and distributors recognized that because of the rapid wear, the adoption of safety film would require a fourfold increase in the number of release prints. The National Fire Protection Association launched a major campaign for safety film in 1918/19, and again in 1923 with support from the International Association of Fire Engineers, but each effort was defeated by strong lobbying by film distributors and Eastman Kodak.[34]

Eastman Kodak began a rigorous fire safety program in 1919, and in 1922, the Motion Picture Producers and Distributors of America assumed administration. Because of the risk to employees, tighter building codes and stricter handling procedures were introduced for laboratories and theaters. Fireproof projection booths, storage rooms, and film vaults were equipped with sprinkler systems. Since all the prints being sent to theaters were new, the risk of fire was minimal if the reels were handled carefully. Existing or specially constructed buildings in each city were certified for storage and handling of nitrate film. MPPDA field agents reviewed the work of local film safety inspection committees. Each reel was inspected upon return from a theater, since broken sprockets or bad splices might cause film to catch in the projector and ignite. Reels of film were stored in cans placed in fireproof containers, withdrawn only as needed for projection or inspection.[35]

Proponents of safety film continued their unsuccessful crusade. A 1923 bill to allow widespread use of 35mm acetate film in schools and churches in New York state was vetoed by the governor following the vigorous opposition of the national projectionists' union. The professional standing of the projectionists was based on quality projection and safe handling of dangerous film. The wide availability of nonflammable film and portable projectors would endanger the dominant role of the projectionists within the industry.[36]

With air conditioning and automatic sprinkler systems uncommon until the 1970s, film vaults were often little more than storage sheds. MGM had better storage than most, and a higher proportion of MGM silent films survive than those produced by any other company. Roger Mayer, MGM's studio manager in the 1960s, recollected that

> None of the vaults had sprinklers. They were concrete bunk houses on what we called Lot 3, and there was a little fan in the roof. No air conditioning, no sprinklers. And that was considered good storage because [the films] couldn't be stolen.[37]

Several big fires in the early twenties destroyed many of the early Universal releases. A huge fire burned fifteen acres of the forty acre Warner Bros. Burbank studio backlot on 4 December 1934. *The Los Angeles Times* reported that "six film vaults also went up in flames, destroying hundreds of stock shots of foreign scenes and many valuable and irreplaceable films of the Vitagraph era."[38]

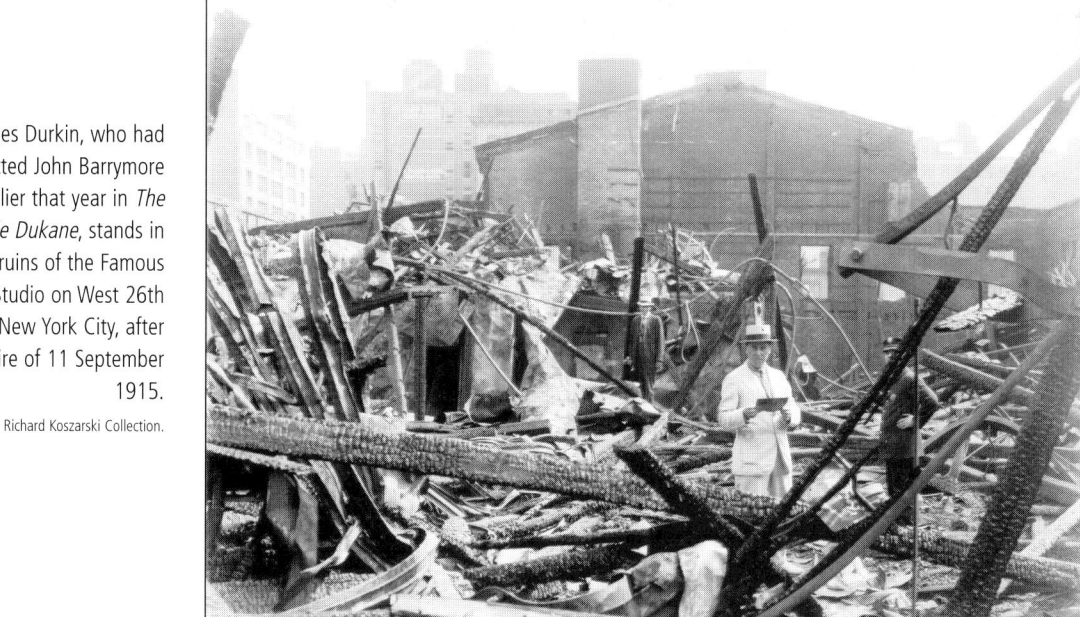

James Durkin, who had directed John Barrymore earlier that year in *The Incorrigible Dukane*, stands in the ruins of the Famous Players Studio on West 26th Street, New York City, after the fire of 11 September 1915.

Richard Koszarski Collection.

Most of the Fox Film Corp. library was destroyed in a disastrous fire in Little Ferry, New Jersey on 9 July 1937, during a period of 100 degree temperatures. The storage facility was only two years old, and although built in a residential neighborhood, the vaults were not equipped with automatic sprinklers. The building's 42 vaults held 40,000 reels of Fox and Educational prints and negatives produced from 1914 to 1932. Gases from decomposition built up due to faulty ventilation, and spontaneously ignited. The fire in the first vault led to the successive explosion of the others. One explosion emitted a sheet of flame from a vent that killed a 13 year old boy running from a nearby house. Every reel of film in the building was destroyed, and the 57 truckloads of scrap removed from the site returned $2,000 in silver salvage. Besides destroying the best and often only material on every pre-1932 Fox picture, the toll included the original negative to D W Griffith's *Way Down East* (1920), which Fox had purchased for a remake.[39]

In the late summer of 1938, a fire destroyed the foreign negative to Charlie Chaplin's *The Kid* (1920). In 1939, Harold Lloyd bought the negatives of the short films he made at the beginning of his career. Lloyd did not have them for long. He recalled that "I lost an awful lot of films, where I had control of them really. They were stored [at the Pathe Laboratory] in New Jersey, a place called Boundbrook.

Everybody stored them there, and they had a tremendous fire – Lonesome Lukes – and all of ours and all of theirs were lost. And I had a fire at the house with nitrate." On 5 August 1943, one of the film storage vaults on his estate exploded, and Lloyd lost a third of his original negatives and prints. Rushing to investigate, Lloyd collapsed in the doorway of the vault, and seven firemen and a Lloyd employee were taken to a local hospital after breathing noxious fumes.[40]

In 1965 television producer Rudy Behlmer was walking with his editor from Lot 2 to Lot 1 at MGM's Culver City studio when he "heard this loud noise – we later discovered it was one of the vaults blowing up." Roger Mayer recalled that "Someone was killed in that explosion. Somebody was working on the film at the time and as far as anybody could tell, it was an electrical short of some sort igniting the film." The explosion in vault 7 destroyed the entire contents, including the original negatives to *A Blind Bargain* (1922) with Lon Chaney and *The Divine Woman* (1928) with Greta Garbo. Mayer noted that the MGM vaults were spread out so that a fire would not reach nearby vaults, and "a sprinkler system would not have made that much difference because the amount we lost by fire was minimal."[41]

Fate Unknown

The known factors – intentional destruction, decomposition, fire – do not account for the loss of such a large proportion of the films produced during the silent era. Many mysteries remain. For example, there is uncertainty about when the Warner Bros. and First National silent features were destroyed, but there is no doubt about their fate.[42]

Figure One: Feature Films Produced by Warner Bros. and Predecessor Companies Known to be Surviving in 1958		
Year	Surviving	Lost
1918	1	0
1919	1	2
1920	2	17
1921	6	46
1922	2	29
1923	2	30
1924	4	41
1925	11	65
1926	7	58
1927	10	76
1928	11	56

In 1952 Warner-Pathe short subject producer Robert Youngson began producing a series of one reel condensations of Warner Bros. silent films. Youngson "was given the run of the vaults," recalled his friend William K Everson, "except there wasn't that much inside." Youngson was limited in the films he could abridge because Warners had "very very little left," according to Everson. "I remember I saw a list of it, and there were only about 30 silent titles."[43]

Youngson condensed Warner's surviving big budget silent features *Don Juan* (1926), *Old San Francisco* (1927) and *Noah's Ark* (1929) into ten minute short subjects. With so many films no longer in existence, Youngson turned to the Rin-Tin-Tin vehicle *Tracked by the Police* (1927), and even moved on to sound films, replacing the dialogue in *Isle of Lost Ships* (1929) with his trademark peppy narration.[44]

As detailed in Figure One, in 1958, after a thorough search, Warners could only locate 35mm material on 57 of 477 pre-1929 features that the company owned. It is not clear if the destruction was intentional, but it was certainly comprehensive, as most of Warners' 1928–1930 early sound pictures were completely missing also.[45]

No Sense of History

In retrospect, it seems remarkable that the executives of the companies that produced and still owned silent films did not invest in their survival. Many of the industry leaders during the silent era remained in charge of their companies well into the 1950s, with Harry Warner and Jack L Warner at Warner Bros., Jack Cohn and Harry Cohn at Columbia, Adolph Zukor and Barney Balaban at Paramount, and Nicholas Schenck at Loew's.

Owners showed minimal concern for the survival of older films. This active disinterest was reflected in 1928 in the authorized biography of Paramount Pictures Chairman Adolph Zukor:

> "My single chance for immortality," said Sarah Bernhardt when she consented to act for the film. Alas, all that remains to America of *Queen Elizabeth* [1912] is one disintegrating print in the storehouse of the Paramount laboratories. Frank Meyer, now laboratory superintendent, ran it off for [biographer Will Irwin] in 1927 – not for years before that had anyone unwound it from its metal reel. Many of the other early Zukor-Lasky successes have rotted or disappeared.[46]

By and large these men focused on the future. The loss of so much of the silent cinema was not all that significant to their producers, as the film industry has almost always held an unsentimental view of its history. The focus is short term, with new pictures always better than the old. Since films had a limited commercial life, and were rapidly written down as corporate assets, any expense toward better storage or preservation would reduce current profits with no future return. One industry insider noted that the studios "were in the razor business, and the films were the blades."[47]

The Museum of Modern Art's Iris Barry recognized on her initial film gathering trip to Hollywood that "no one cared a button about 'old' films, not even his own last-but-one, but was solely concerned with his new film." These very successful businessmen did not look to the past or base their business decisions on sentiment if they gave the silent films any thought at all. While these may have been "their films," it was also "their money." They did not want to watch the films, let alone preserve them. In an industry built on youth, these executives may have resented the films that reminded them and others how long they had been around.[48]

In 1947 and 1948, the Academy of Motion Picture Arts and Sciences held twentieth anniversary screenings of films from the initial Academy Awards ceremonies, given to the best films produced by the industry. With the cooperation of every company, the Academy could locate prints for only ten of fifteen titles from the first year's awards. This series offered probably the last public screenings of Lewis Milestone's comedy *Two Arabian Nights*, and two dramas starring Emil Jannings, Victor Fleming's *The Way of All Flesh* and Ernst Lubitsch's *The Patriot*. When the Museum of Modern Art inquired about *The Patriot* in 1955, that print had decomposed.[49]

Why Was This Allowed to Occur?

Industry organizations might have accomplished what individual companies would not. The Academy of Motion Picture Arts and Sciences, for example, might have ensured that each company safeguarded a few films each year. However, motion picture industry charity has always supported health care, not the arts, and nostalgia for old films would have been contrary to the focus on new pictures. During the slump in business that began in the late 1940s, and accelerated with the widespread advent of television, the industry advertised that "Movies Are Better Than Ever." If an old film was any good, it would be remade. When James Card requested *Down to the Sea in Ships* (1922) for the film collection at George Eastman House, Twentieth Century-Fox sent the 1949 remake with Richard Widmark. When Card called to explain the mix-up, the studio suggested that if he wanted a silent film, he should have the projectionist turn down the sound.[50]

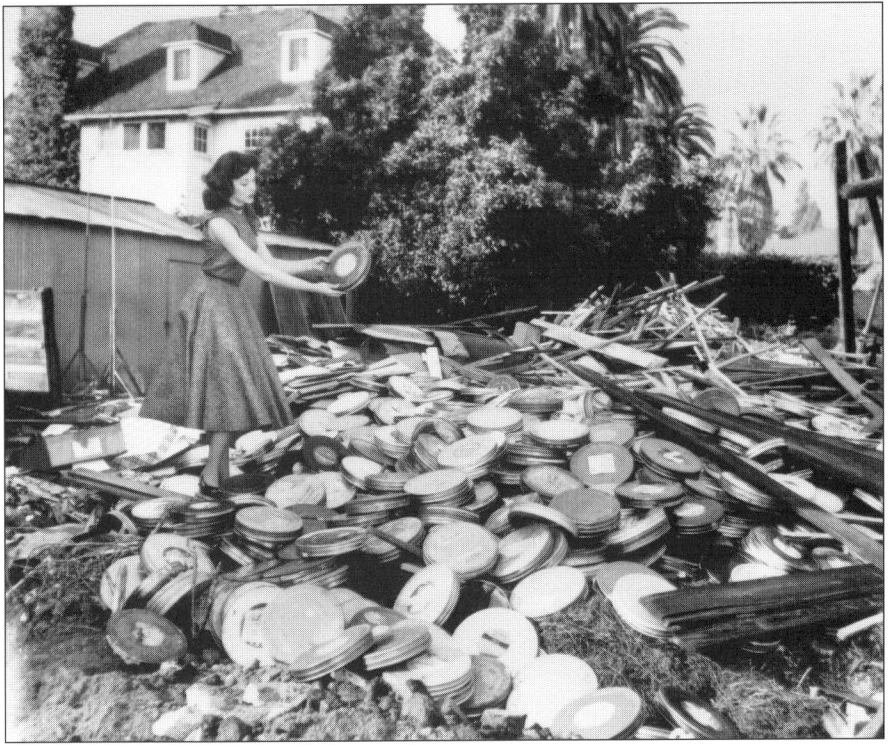

A model poses with a large collection of original Chaplin negatives, outtakes, unused sequences, home movies, etc., sold to a film salvage company in 1954 after Chaplin had been denied re-entry to the United States in 1952. A later chapter in the history of some of this material is told by Kevin Brownlow in the article "Vault Farce", elsewhere in this volume.

Scott Eyman Collection.

Studio politics probably played a role. There had been many fires, so no one expected all old films to be available. There were few requests for studio screenings of ancient titles, so their loss was not noticeable. Film storage was a cost center, not a profit center, and the dramatic benefit of cool and dry storage to the long-term stability of nitrate film was not widely recognized. After all, who in the company would want to admit that it was their fault that the old films were rotting? In 1959, during a research visit to the Paramount lot in Hollywood, William K Everson found that many Paramount silent films he hoped to see were "not available." Yet in 1967, Hazel Marshall, Paramount's film librarian since 1924, seemed sincere when she told historian Robert S Birchard, "We have everything we ever made."[51]

Any preservation effort in the thirties or forties would have copied films to nitrate stock, merely prolonging their existence, not ensuring their survival. More stable triacetate film was announced in 1948, when the industry was in a slump and profits were down. Companies focused on adapting to a rapidly changing market seldom look to the past. 3D and CinemaScope promised to make all previous sound films obsolete. Silent films had become obsolete just twenty years earlier.[52]

If there was no significant market for silent films, that was a self-fulfilling prophesy. Properly handled, a small market might have developed. None of the companies tried, and admittedly, even if they had, such a sideline could never have been very profitable. It would have been inexpensive and straightforward to make a 16mm negative or a single 35mm safety print for each film, especially as most companies had some in-house film laboratory facilities. The cost could even have been buried in the budgets of pictures in production. After all, since the old films were gradually disappearing, *not* copying the pictures was an irreversible decision. But without an emotional, historical or business justification, the owners let decomposition take its course.

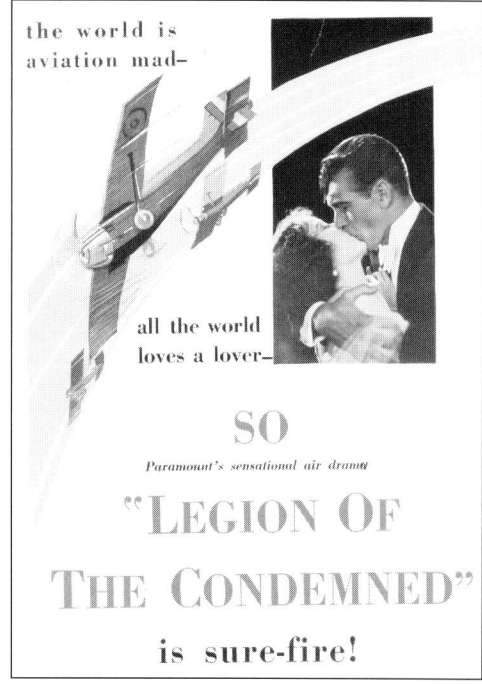

Poster for the film *Legion of the Condemned* (1928).

Frank Thompson.

Producer-stars did take some active measures. Mary Pickford, Gloria Swanson, William S Hart, Harold Lloyd, and Douglas Fairbanks donated prints and negatives to the Museum of Modern Art and George Eastman House, and Pickford was one of the few to provide any financial support. Archives offered to save the important films for posterity, at no cost to the industry. As the Museum of Modern Art's Richard Griffith noted in 1955, "Hollywood feels – and with some logic, it seems to me – that the preservation work should be carried on by some publicly supported institution." The activities of the archives may have, hypocritically, relieved the companies of any sense of obligation. Eastman House's James Card noted, "in nearly all quarters everyone felt that every film of any conceivable importance was preserved at the Museum of Modern Art."[53]

Stock footage companies and documentary producers saved films, but like their studio counterparts, they were running a business. In many cases original prints or negatives were chopped up for clips and condensations. Preservation was often only a byproduct of delivering a product to a client for a compilation film, documentary or commercial. Nitrate films were a depletable resource, much like an oil well, to be used until they ran out.[54]

Only when silent films were viewed independently of their immediate commercial value would they be saved. The publicly funded archives preserved films because their mission ignored commerce and focused on art and sociological importance. MGM saved many of their silent films due to a value-neutral policy of preserving corporate assets.[55]

In the final analysis, silent films were produced to make a profit, and many of them satisfied that short term expectation. The economic considerations that caused these films to be made in the first place also led to their demise. Unless they provided ongoing revenue, silent films did not justify their continued existence. Without the timely appearance of the archives to save many films until public interest reemerged and the comprehensive preservation policy in place at MGM, the disappearance of our silent film heritage would likely have been close to complete.

Acknowledgments:

This article is dedicated to my wife Shari, who as always has been wonderful and supportive.

I extend my appreciation to Bob Birchard, James Bouras, Kevin Brownlow, Philip Carli, Scott Eyman, Scott MacQueen, and David Shepard for reviewing drafts of this article, providing insights and making valuable comments. All errors of fact or interpretation remain mine.

For research assistance, I extend my thanks to the research facilities at my home away from home – the Library of Congress. Especially helpful were the staff of the Copyright Office, the Manuscript Division (where Anthony Slide's inventory of the Thomas H Ince papers was invaluable), and David Parker, Madeline Matz, and Rosemary Hanes of the Division of Motion Pictures, Broadcasting and Recorded Sound. Richard Koszarski was very forthcoming with his encyclopedic knowledge of Universal films. Randy Gitsch shared his knowledge freely. Paolo Cherchi Usai, Ed Stratman, Philip Carli and Kay MacRae of the George Eastman House were of great assistance. At the University of Southern California Cinema-Television Library Ned Comstock went beyond the call of duty, and Leith Adams at Warner Bros. was extremely helpful with press material on the 1934 Warner Bros. fire.

Finally, I have to thank those who came before me and saved silent films: James Card, Paul Killiam and David Shepard.

Notes

1. The American Film Institute estimated in the early 1970s that only 50% of nitrate-era (pre-1951) films survive, and less than 25% of silent-era films. The earliest appearance of a version of the AFI numbers is *The American Film Institute Report 1967/1971*, pp. 8, 11. Their veracity is discussed in Anthony Slide, *Nitrate Won't Wait*, (Jefferson, NC: McFarland, 1992), p. 5. A closer examination of American silent feature films in US and foreign archives appears in *Film Preservation 1993: A Study of the Current State of American Film Preservation*, Volume 1: Report, June 1993, Report of the Librarian of Congress, pp. 3–4. This report claims that the survival rate ranges from 7 to 12% of each year's releases for features of the teens, and from 15 to 25% during the 1920s. These numbers would be somewhat higher if studio collections (primarily the silent features preserved by MGM) and private collections were included.

2. 150 prints: Richard W Saunders, comptroller of Famous Players-Lasky, quoted in Frederick James Smith, "What Happens to Your Movie Money", *Photoplay*, March 1927, p. 45. See also: Paul V Shields, "The Movie Industry Applies Chain Store Methods", *Forbes*, 15 July 1925, p. 527, which states "as a general rule, about sixty prints of [each] film are made for foreign use and 100 for domestic use." According to a 1921 newspaper article, "the producer makes a limited number of prints for distribution. As a rule, this number is 65; it may be less, it is rarely more." See: "When a Film Grows Old", *The New York Times*, 28 August 1921.
   In the 1920s, distributors charged the cost of prints to independent producers. In those cases where the distributor was making prints at his own laboratory, a producer could find a significant portion of his potential profits spent on unneeded prints. To protect against this, distribution agreements often had a limit on the number of copies that could be manufactured. Inspiration Pictures' 19 December 1921 distribution agreement with First National allowed up to 100 prints. Three years later, Inspiration agreed to pay for up to 125 prints for domestic distribution. First National was required to have insurance on the negative until 60 prints were manufactured. Inspiration Pictures file, Warner Bros. Collection, University of Southern California Cinema-Television Library.

3. "Film Exchange Fire Prevention Results", *National Fire Protection Association Quarterly*, January 1926, pp. 224–229. Henry Anderson, "Fire Safety in the Motion Picture Industry", *National Fire Protection Association Quarterly*, July 1936, p. 21. *Show People* and *Our Dancing Daughters: The Motion Picture Almanac 1929*, (Chicago: Quigley Publishing Company), 1929, pp. 206, 204. Both reports were from the Screenland Theatre, Nevada, Ohio, "small town patronage." The exhibitor complained that the print was "rainy" because the excessive scratches caused the projected image to look like it was filmed in the rain.

4. William R Donaldson, "Valuing the Inventories of Motion-Picture Producers", *The Journal of Accountancy*, March 1927, pp. 171–179.

5. Albert F Sulzer, "The Epoch of Progress in Film Fire Prevention", *Journal of the Society of*

Motion Picture Engineers, April, 1940, p. 403. *Suds:* Letter, United Artists Corporation to Mary Pickford Company, 11 September 1925, United Artists Collection, State Historical Society of Wisconsin. See also: M Deschiens, "Recovery of Constituents of Old Motion Picture Films", *Chemical Age*, May, 1921, pp. 193–194.

6. *The Unknown:* Paramount Famous Lasky Corp. to Universal Pictures Corp., 30 September 1927. Copyright Office Assignment Records, vol. 189, pp. 80–86. Fortunately, that library print of *The Unknown* stayed with Paramount and was among the relatively few Paramount films that survived to be acquired by the American Film Institute. *Little Annie Rooney:* Assignment of Copyright, Mary Pickford Company to Edward Small Productions, Inc., 19 June 1941. Copyright Office Assignment Records, vol. 464, pp. 180–181.

7. The story rights to *Bardelys the Magnificent* were to expire in 1939. MGM memorandum, D O Decker to Paul Cohen, 9 December 1931, reproduced in Philip J Riley, *A Blind Bargain*, (Atlantic City: Magic Image Filmbooks, 1988), p. 19.

8. Letter, George D Swartz, George D. Swartz Pictures, Inc. to Mr Ingle Carpenter, 20 August 1928. Ince Collection, Manuscript Division, Library of Congress.

9. Bill of Sale, Thos. H. Ince Corporation to Warner Bros. Pictures, Inc., 30 January 1930. Ince Collection, Manuscript Division, Library of Congress. The films were *String Beans, The Hired Man* (both 1918), *Greased Lightning, Egg Crate Wallop, Red Hot Dollars, Hay Foot, Straw Foot, Crooked Straight* (all 1919), and *Paris Green* (1920). All of the films starred Charles Ray and were written by Julien Josephson. *Tol'able David:* Agreement, Joseph Hergesheimer and Inspiration Pictures, Inc., in Liquidation to Columbia Pictures Corporation, 16 June 1930. Copyright Office Assignment Records, vol. 250, pp. 42–49. *23½ Hours Leave* and *Civilization:* David Shepard, "Thomas Ince", in *The American Film Heritage*, (Washington, DC: Acropolis Books Ltd., 1972), p. 44.

10. Agreement, Albert D Levin and Triangle Liquidation Corporation to Warner Bros. Pictures, Inc., 5 October 1937. Copyright Office Assignment Records, vol. 392, pp. 92–129.

11. Films sold for $875, purchased for $10,000: Letter from Ralph Lewis, Preston & Files, to R J Obringer, Warner Bros., 26 July 1940, Sennett file, Warner Bros. Collection, University of Southern California Cinema-Television Library. Sennett purchased for $75: Order Confirming Sale of Personal Property in the Matter of Mack Sennett, Inc., Bankrupt, No. 21878-C, District Court of the United States, Southern District of California, Central Division, 31 March 1936. Copyright Office Assignment Records, vol. 1226, pp. 61–67. Sale to Warner Bros.: Bill of Sale, Paul J Guerin to Warner Bros. Pictures, Inc., 30 September 1940, Copyright Office Assignment Records, vol. 1226, pp. 76–84. Attorney: Warner Bros. memo from R J Obringer to Morris Ebenstein, 10 July 1940, Sennett file, Warner Bros. Collection, University of Southern California Cinema-Television Library.

12. Inventory of prints and negatives: Bill of Sale, Paul J Guerin to Warner Bros. Pictures, Inc., 30 September 1940. Copyright Office Assignment Records, vol. 1226. pp. 76–84. The vault inventory, probably dating from the 1936 sale by the bankruptcy court, notes that for Sennett features, there were A and F (American and Foreign) negatives for *The Shriek of Araby* (1923), *Molly O'* (1921), *Suzanna* (1922), *The Crossroads of New York* (1922), and *Down on the Farm* (1920). There were only the F negatives for *Yankee Doodle in Berlin* (1919) and *The Extra Girl* (1923). The first short released by Warners was *A Small Town Idol* (1939). The subsequent shorts using Sennett footage were two reelers *Love's Intrigue* (1940), *Happy Faces* (1941), *Wedding Yells* (1942), *Happy Times and Jolly Moments* (1943), *Once Over Lightly* (1944) and *Good Old Corn* (1945). Two one reelers, *Here We Go Again* and *Hit 'Im Again*, followed in 1953.

13. Storage fees at one facility were "at the rate of Two Dollars per month or fraction thereof per five reel unit for each of the first five such units, and at the rate of One Dollar per month or any fraction thereof for each five reel unit in addition to the first five." A 7 reel picture might include a negative and a print. Since owners were likely to have hundreds of reels, my calculation of $35 is based on the one dollar per month storage charge. Memorandum of Agreement, between Lloyds Film Storage and Mr. Ingle Carpenter, Attorney for Thos. H. Ince Corp., 5 April 1930. Thomas H. Ince Collection, Manuscript Division, Library of Congress.

14. Sol Lesser: Sol Lesser conversation with David Shepard during the restoration of Lesser's *Oliver Twist* (1922). David Shepard to author, 26 August 1995. Columbia: private source.

15. A 1956 tribute at the Museum of Modern Art showed Goldwyn's *Potash and Perlmutter* (1923) and a fragment, "all that remains", of Goldwyn's *The Eternal City* (1923). Both are now considered lost. The only other silents included in the series were Goldwyn's *Stella Dallas* (1925) and *The Winning of Barbara Worth* (1926). Destruction of Goldwyn silents: Robert S Birchard talked to Mrs Goldwyn in 1970/71 at a screening of *The Winning of Barbara Worth* (1926) at a tribute to Henry King. Robert S Birchard to author, 29 August 1996.

16. Letter, E L Walton, Executive Assistant to the President, RKO Radio Pictures, Inc. to J R Grainger, RKO Radio Pictures, Inc., 26 July 1954, private source.

17. Studio Inter-Office Correspondence, J R Grainger, RKO Radio Pictures, Inc. to Howard Hughes, 27 July 1954, private source. Letter, Nadine Henley, Secretary to Howard Hughes to J R Grainger, RKO Radio Pictures, Inc., 12 August 1954, private source.

18. Private source.

19. Excellent physical properties: *Safe Handling, Storage, and Destruction of Nitrate-Based Motion Picture Films*, (Rochester: Eastman Kodak Company, Kodak Publication No. H-182, September 1995), p. 1.

20. Storage recommendations: see Storage Standards in the section on Safe and Economical Storage in "Report of the Committee on the Preservation of Film", *Journal of the Society of Motion Picture Engineers*, vol. 35, December 1940, pp. 584–606.

21. Private source. The reels were stored in cartons which held ten cans. Storage charges were $6.00 per year per carton.

22. A H Nuckolls, "Cellulose Nitrate and Acetate Film", *National Fire Protection Association Quarterly*, January 1930, pp. 236–242. Kodak Publication No. H-182, p. 2.

23. Translation of letter from Karl Geyer Filmfabrik to Transocean Film Co., Berlin, 28 October 1926. Microfilm edition, *D.W. Griffith Papers 1897–1954*, (Frederick, M.D.: University Publications of America, 1982), reel 14, image number 1189. Griffith had the negative returned to New York and inspected by Combined Film Laboratories in New York. They reported that "the condition of this negative is very poor as it contains water marks, stains, cement marks, fog, and blank film throughout the various rolls. It appears as though the negative might have gotten wet, as the emulsion in a good many places is completely peeled off." Letter, Combined Film Laboratories to D.W. Griffith, Inc., 10 January 1927, reel 14, image number 1972. Thanks to David Shepard for directing my attention to this.

24. Letter, W D Kelly, Metro-Goldwyn-Mayer Pictures to James Card, George Eastman House, 5 March 1954. MGM file, George Eastman House International Museum of Photography and Film.

25. Destruction: Universal Film Exchanges Inc. memo from F T Murray, Mgr. Branch Operations, to Mr I Stolzer, Bound Brook, N.J., 27 April 1948. Photocopy of memo courtesy Richard Koszarski. Pathe Laboratory: Letter, John J O'Connor, Universal Pictures Company, Inc. to Edward P Curtis, Eastman Kodak Company, 20 February 1950. Universal file, George Eastman House International Museum of Photography and Film. The letter concluded "Our oldest films now start with the sound era, which means that the oldest negatives we now have in the vaults do not go back beyond 1929." It seems likely that Universal simply destroyed everything that did not have a sound track. Several silents with synchronized music scores survived to be donated to the American Film Institute in the late 1960s, suggesting that Pathe's concern over safety was an excuse, as much as a reason for destruction of the films. Cellofilm Corporation: 1927 Annual Report of Universal Pictures Company, Inc. Thanks to Richard Koszarski for directing my attention to Universal's ownership of Cellofilm.

26. Pathe Films: Schedule "A", "Negatives at Bound Brook", and "Positive Prints at Bound Brook", to Indenture between Pathe Exchange, Inc. and Columbia Pictures Corporation, 3 July 1935. Copyright Office Assignment Records, vol. 334, pp. 246–282. Triangle Films: Triangle Liquidation Corp. pp. 114–116. The survivors were mostly the higher profile films, including those starring Douglas Fairbanks.

27. Warner/First National destruction records: private source. *Johanna Enlists* and *Rosita*: Carl Louis Gregory, "Inventory of Mary Pickford's Film Collection, 14 December 1946." Mary Pickford folder, Acquisitions, Selection and Distribution, 1940–48, Records Relating to Motion Pictures 1934–54, The Archives of the Library of Congress, Manuscript Division, Library of Congress. Von Stroheim films for Universal: Richard Koszarski, *The Man You Love to Hate: Erich von Stroheim and Hollywood*, (New York: Oxford University Press, 1983), pp. 70, 111.

28. *The Merry Widow*: Letter, William LeVanway, Chief Film Editor, Metro-Goldwyn-Mayer Pictures, to James Card, George Eastman House, 14 November 1950. *He Who Gets Slapped*: Letter, W D Kelly, Metro-Goldwyn-Mayer Pictures, to James Card, George Eastman House, 30 November 1951. *The Torrent*: Letter, James Card, George Eastman House, to W D Kelly, Metro-Goldwyn-Mayer Pictures, 27 July 1953. MGM file, George Eastman House International Museum of Photography and Film. Other titles: private source.

29. David Shepard: Austin Lamont, "In Search of Lost Films", *Film Comment*, Winter 1971–72, p. 60. Some of the Paramount films that were "found at the time of assembly and packing to have disintegrated" included Clarence Badger's *Man Power* (1927) with Richard Dix, Luther Reed's *New York* (1927) with Ricardo Cortez and *The Sawdust Paradise* (1928) with Esther Ralston, Frank Tuttle's *Time to Love* (1927) with Raymond Griffith and William Powell, James Cruze's *We're All Gamblers* (1927) with Thomas Meighan, and several George Melford features: *Crystal Gazer* (1917) with Fannie Ward, *Faith Healer* (1921) with Milton Sills, and *Sunset Trail* (1917) with Vivian Martin. Private source.

30. Kevin Brownlow, *Behind the Mask of Innocence*, (New York: Alfred A. Knopf, 1990), footnote 235 on p. 529. Also Kevin Brownlow to author, 15 December 1995.

31. Undated Harold Lloyd film inventory, private source.

32. "Fire Exchange Regulations", *The American Architect*, 17 July 1918, pp. 88–94. A similar fire occurred on a Boston subway car in January, 1925, when a burlap bag containing scrap nitrate

film was placed against an electric heater. No one was killed, but 27 passengers were taken to the hospital with burns. "Film Fire in Boston Subway", *National Fire Protection Association Quarterly*, January 1925, pp. 183–184. Pittsburgh: "Film Exchange Fire Prevention Results", *National Fire Protection Association Quarterly*, January 1926, pp. 224–229. Poor vault design was occasionally a contributing factor in these conflagrations, as the exhaust from burning film entered through an adjoining vent to another vault. See: "Fire Prevention in Film Exchanges", *Safety Engineering*, November 1925, pp. 263–264.

33. Edison: "Edison Sees His Vast Plant Burn", *The New York Times*, 10 December 1914, p. 1. A more detailed account of the origin of the blaze followed the next day: "Mrs. Edison Saved Husband's Records", *The New York Times*, 11 December 1914, p. 9. Also see: "Great Edison Plant Burned: Fire Wrecks Ten Big Factory Buildings at East Orange, N.J. – Origin Not in Film Factory", *The Moving Picture World*, 19 December 1914, p. 1662. This article claims that contrary to the New York newspapers, this was not a film fire, but started in the varnishing department of the phonograph building, and that all motion picture negatives were removed before the fire reached the film building.
Lubin: "Big Fire at Lubin Plant: Explosion Wrecks Film Storage Vault Causing Damage of Between $500,000 and $1,000,000 – No Interruption in Business", *The Moving Picture World*, 27 June 1914, p. 1803. Lubin's general manager, Ira Lowry, said "some of the films which were destroyed had never been put on the market; others cannot be reproduced or duplicated. Our loss on films will be at least $500,000, and on the vault building about $5,000 more." *The Sea Wolf*: Robert S Birchard, "Jack London and the Movies", *Film History*, vol. 1, p. 32. Famous Players: *The Foundling* was quickly remade with a different director and supporting cast. Peter Bogdanovich, *Allan Dwan: The Last Pioneer*, (New York: Praeger Publishers, 1971), p. 178.

34. More expensive: In 1921, acetate positive stock cost 3 cents per foot, while the equivalent nitrate positive stock was 2 1/4 cents per foot, so users of acetate stock paid a cost premium of 33%. "Report of the Committee on Films and Emulsions", *Transactions of Society of Motion Picture Engineers*, May 1922, p. 166. "Film Exchange Fire Prevention Results", pp. 224–229. Fire Engineers: "The Inflammable Picture Film", *National Fire Protection Association Quarterly*, October 1922, pp. 109–110.

35. Nuckolls, pp. 236–242. Sulzer, pp. 405–408.

36. Discussion of W W Kincaid, "Requirements of the Educational and Non-Theatrical Entertainment Field", in *Transactions of Society of Motion Picture Engineers*, May, 1924, pp. 111–118.

37. Roger Mayer to author, 29 May 1996.

38. Universal: 9 February 1989 letter from Richard Koszarski to author. Warner fire: "Films Go On Despite Fire", *Los Angeles Times*, 6 December 1934, p. 1. The fire apparently started in a machine shop. An article in the Glendale paper states that the Vitagraph films destroyed were prints. "Films Valued as Historical Lost: Early Pictures Destroyed When Flames Rage in Library at Studio", Glendale *News-Press*, 5 December 1934, p. 6. The press accounts are uniform in stating that the destruction of sets and support buildings would not disrupt production and the loss was fully covered by insurance. In contrast, photographs of the scene show total devastation. The December 1934 edition of the *Warner Club News* observed "the boys from the publicity department staying on the job till 2:30 a.m. handling the newspapermen and the cameramen." It is possible that the studio misrepresented which films were destroyed to indicate that nothing important was lost. Nonetheless, the fire would not have destroyed the Warner Bros. and First National negatives as they were stored on the east coast. Also see: Jack L Warner, *My First Hundred Years in Hollywood*, (New York: Random House, 1965), p. 240. Thanks to Leith Adams, Warner Bros. Archivist, for providing information on this fire.

39. "Fox Film Storage Fire", *National Fire Protection Association Quarterly*, October 1937, pp. 136–142.

40. *The Kid*: David Robinson, *Chaplin: His Life and Art*, (New York: McGraw Hill, 1985), p. 225. Boundbrook: American Film Institute Seminars and Dialogues on Film, Harold Lloyd, 23 September 1969, (Microfilming Corporation of America), 1977. "Harold Lloyd Saved From Fire by Wife", *The New York Times*, 6 August 1943, p. 17. See also Adam Reilly, *Harold Lloyd: The King of Daredevil Comedy*, (New York: Macmillan, 1977), p. 7.

41. MGM eyewitness: Rudy Behlmer to author, 30 August 1996. Specific films lost: Philip J Riley, *London After Midnight*, (New York: Cornwall Books), p. 18. Cause of explosion: Roger Mayer to author, 29 May 1996.

42. There are persistent rumors that Warners junked their silent material during World War II, but I was unable to verify that story. On 4 March 1996, I interviewed Rudi Fehr, who began at the studio in the mid-1930s as an editor, and became the head of Warners' film editorial department. He had no knowledge of the fate of the company's silent films. My own check of the index to the Warner Bros. Collection at the USC Cinema-Television Library and Princeton University, and a subsequent review by USC archivist Ned Comstock found no files of interest.
The Jack L. Warner Collection at the USC Cinema-Television Library holds the surviving telegrams sent between the Burbank and New York offices. I reviewed the telegrams from 1941 through 1946, and there was no indication of destruction of any old material other than trailers. During 1944 and 1946, Jack L Warner told the east coast lab in Brooklyn to send

prints of *My Four Years in Germany* (1918), and *The Divine Lady* (1929) to the west coast. A 1944 telegram requesting a print of *Top Speed* (a 1930 sound picture) read: "If you have negative yet on *Top Speed* have lab make up black and white print whenever they not busy out of positive short ends if you have enough and send same to me via straight express. Advise." In 1958, Warners could only locate material on 49 of 76 films from 1930, so the existence of *Top Speed* could not be assumed.

In 1950, James Card at the George Eastman House ordered a print of *The Sea Beast* (1926) with John Barrymore, and it was made from the shrunken, but complete, original negative. Warner Bros. file, George Eastman House International Museum of Photography and Film. In 1952 Jack L Warner ordered a print of *Noah's Ark* (1929) to review for possible reissue, and the original negative, while deteriorating, was still in existence. Scott MacQueen, "*Noah's Ark*: Making and Restoring an Early Vitaphone Spectacle", *The Perfect Vision*, Vol. 3, No. 12, Winter 1991/92, pp. 35–45.

These actions indicate that Warner Bros. held onto its films, and could order copies on demand, while the fact that so few films survive (see footnote 45 below) suggests that at some point there was a complete housecleaning of Warners' early films. The fate of the Warner Bros. silent and early sound material is an area for further research.

43. William K Everson to author, 16 November 1984.

44. *Don Juan* (1926) became *Some of the Greatest* (1955), while *Old San Francisco* (1927) emerged as *Thrills From the Past* (1953). Other Youngson shorts include *An Adventure to Remember* (1955), adapted from *Isle of Lost Ships* (1929); *A Bit of the Best* (1955), from *Tracked by the Police* (1927); and *Magic Movie Moments* (1953) from *Noah's Ark* (1929).

45. A few additional titles were later discovered in Burbank in Jack L Warner's personal vault, along with a separate cache of silent feature and short comedies. Negatives to about 50 silent features which Warners' predecessor First National had distributed, but did not own, were deposited with George Eastman House in 1958.

Survival of Warner Films: Copyright Assignment from Warner Bros. Pictures, Inc. to P.R.M., Inc., 23 July 1958, supplementing original agreement dated 26 July 1956. Copyright Office Assignment Records, vol. 1015, pp. 168–187. This document consists of two schedules, each listing four groups of titles marked with identification numbers preceded by A, B, C or D. I matched the titles listed in each group with the films (both original negatives and projection prints) subsequently shipped by United Artists Television, Inc. (successor to P.R.M.) to the Library of Congress in 1970.

The "A" list prove to be silent titles that do not survive. "B"" are early sound titles that do not survive. "C" are silent titles with film material, and "D" are early sound films surviving, but lacking a soundtrack. The second "A" schedule includes four titles (including the 1924 Johnny Hines comedy *Conductor 1492*) footnoted as "Film Property". I have corrected the numbers in the table for these, and also deleted a few Chaplin films originally released by First National that were mistakenly included in the original assignment. The survival numbers are even more distressing when examined in detail, as 1925's eleven surviving titles include seven Lariat program westerns released by Vitagraph. The films on these lists were originally released by First National, Associated Producers, Associated First National, Vitagraph and Warner Bros. There was one surviving title from Kalem, *From the Manger to the Cross* (1912), which I did not include on the chart.

While a 13% survival rate might be understandable for such a large nitrate library in 1970, almost every title that was inventoried in 1958 was still in existence in 1970. It appears that the pictures were the victim of intentional destruction, or given the loss of so many of Warners' early sound films, there may have been some disastrous, but undocumented, fires.

46. Will Irwin, *The House That Shadows Built*, (New York: Doubleday, Doran & Company, 1928), pp. 224–225.

47. Razor business: Roddy McDowell to author, 28 August 1995.

48. Iris Barry, "The Film Library and How It Grew", *Film Quarterly*, Summer 1969, p. 22.

49. Academy screenings: Held in the fall of 1947, the complete series consisted of *Wings*, *Seventh Heaven*, *Laugh Clown Laugh*, *The Fair Coed*, *Two Arabian Nights*, *Street Angel*, *Underworld*, *The Jazz Singer*, *The Way of All Flesh* and *Telling the World*. The films that were listed as unavailable were *The Last Command*, *Sunrise*, *The Dove*, *Tempest* and *The Circus*. Of these five films, all survive in 35mm. *The Patriot* was an Oscar winner at the second ceremonies, and was shown in the continuation of the series in January, 1948. "Calendar of Screenings, Academy of Motion Picture Arts and Sciences, 1947–48." Author's collection. Museum of Modern Art inquiry: Richard W Nason, "Emergency Operation: Campaign to Save Desiccating Movie Classics Begun by Film Library", *The New York Times*, 9 October 1955.

50. James Card to author, 7 November 1987.

51. Everson was researching films for potential use in *The Love Goddesses*, which was not released until 1965. William K Everson to author, 16 November 1984. Hazel Marshall: Robert S. Birchard to author, 29 August 1996.

52. "Changes in TV (Color) and Films (Size) Up Film Interest in Video Rentals", *Variety*, 21 October 1954.

53. Richard Griffith: Nason, op. cit. James Card: Herbert Reynolds, "'What Can You Do for Us,

Barney?' Four Decades of Film Collecting: An Interview with James Card", *Image*, Vol. 20, No. 2, June 1977, p. 19.

54. As one example, silent film distributor Paul Killiam purchased Rupert Julian's *The Yankee Clipper* (1927), a Cecil B DeMille production starring William Boyd. In the 1960s, Killiam edited the original negative from eight reels to five for use as a pilot for his television series *Hour of Silents*. Killiam kept the trims, and donated all of his material on the film to the American Film Institute in 1981. Paul Killiam to author.

55. MGM: Roger Mayer to author, 29 May 1996.

Mea Culpa: How I Abused the Nitrate in My Life

by Sam Kula

Text of the paper delivered at the Symposium "The Last Nitrate Picture Show" at the London FIAF Congress, June 2000. Its spoken character has been voluntarily preserved by the author.

Like all true confessions this one starts with a little personal history. I have been a film archivist, in one capacity or another, since 1958. That was the year I started work in the Library of the National Film Archive of the British Film Institute. I ended up my brief career at the National Film Archive as Ernest Lindgren's Deputy Curator. It was Lindgren who introduced me to the first principle of film archives: to protect the "master", the copy closest to the original negative, which in our case, in those days, was almost always a 35mm nitrate print.

Lindgren also introduced me to the politics of FIAF, at which he was a master, but that would be a subject for a much longer paper, which we can thankfully save for another occasion.

The problem with the first principle, as you all know, was that if we didn't hold the original negative, the 35mm nitrate print was the "master" and it could not be projected. Lindgren was very unyielding on that principle, even after we had "protected" the print by making a duplicate negative on safety stock. The only access permitted would be through a reference safety print. Which was *the* Catch-22 in film archives. There was *never* enough money in the budget to make reference prints as well as dupe negatives. Which is why some wit claimed that NFA stood for "No Films Available".

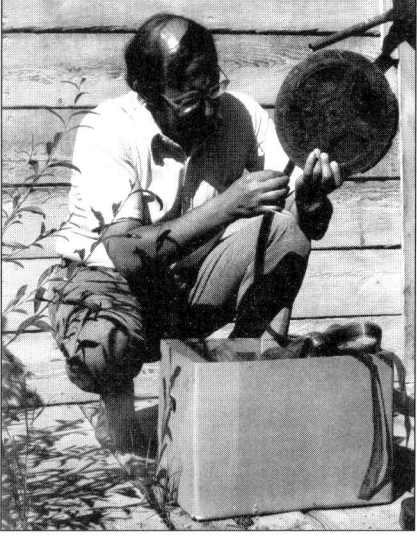

The author inspecting some of the film recovered in the Dawson City find, 1978.

National Archives of Canada/MISA, Ottawa. 15343.

Working at the National Film Archive could thus be a very frustrating experience. There we were, surrounded by all those beautiful nitrate prints, and we could never see them as they were meant to be seen.

The situation at the National Film Archive was made even more frustrating when one looked across the Channel to the Cinémathèque Française. There was Henri Langlois, projecting nitrate prints night after night to the delight of his audiences, firm in his belief that nitrate prints were like pearls or fine Persian rugs. "You keep them at their best by using them," he said, "and they will last for generations." He didn't actually say you should beat them, but he was known, on occasion, to hang them on the line.

Fortunately we had the National Film Theatre and a network of archives that were prepared to let their nitrate prints "breathe" from time to time, and to loan them out (after they had been properly protected, of course), so that we could experience the glory of nitrate on a decent screen.

It was not the true glory of nitrate, you understand, but as close an approximation as the National Film Theatre could manage. The carbon arc had given way to the Xenon lamp, an efficient and consistent but cold light source, and while the sepia-toned warmth of the nitrate print still came through, it was not the same. Or so the purists with long memories claim. Actually, many theatres were running projectors with carbon arcs well into the 1960s. It takes a long time for technological change to penetrate the distant reaches of the motion picture industry. We know that nitrate stock did not disappear overnight in 1950. A decade later it was still in use for projection prints and even for new productions in some parts of the world. No point in letting that excellent stock go to waste!

And I am not about to revive that old argument of whether we can ever duplicate the atmosphere and the film-going experience of a first-run theatre in the Thirties. For one thing, we would have to have 500 smokers in a poorly-ventilated hall to reproduce the air quality that gave the nitrate image that *je ne sais quoi* so often evoked in memoirs. Everyone seems to remember two first times in life, and one of them is going to the movies! My English colleagues used to maintain that you would also have to add the smell of 500 damp mackintoshes and the pungent aroma of fish and chips saturated in vinegar to really capture the authentic air of a cinema in the 1930s.

But this is all beside the point. My purpose here is not to persuade you that film audiences lost something wonderful when triacetate replaced nitrate as the standard stock in the industry. My purpose is to apologise for the way in which I exploited the weaknesses of nitrate film while ignoring its towering strengths as the workhorse of the industry, the dispenser of dreams, and the window to a wider world for billions of people.

Let us look at the record.

George Eastman acquired patents for flexible cellulose nitrate roll film coated with a photographic emulsion sometime between 1884 and 1892. Let us not worry about who actually invented the process. Chemists, both amateur and professional, were active on both sides of the Atlantic. We do know that flexible roll film, 35mm wide, made possible the early experiments with motion picture projection that set Edison and Lumière and a dozen lesser-known pioneers on their way.

I don't think we know exactly why it was that cellulose nitrate rather than some other chemical combination was selected. We do know that many combinations of camphor and celluloid and other wonderfully flammable substances were tried. None of them had the three characteristics needed – transparency, flexibility, and toughness – to the same degree as cellulose nitrate. Intermittent movement of the film, the key to the presentation of motion pictures, is very hard on film stock, and cellulose nitrate proved it was sufficiently stable and long-wearing so that it could be run through a projector several hundred times and still deliver an acceptable image.

Once Eastman and his rivals had improved the product, nitrate stock was able to capture and reproduce the images that created the "Kingdom of Shadows".

"Kingdom of Shadows". This is an allusion, of course, to the celebrated review that Maxim Gorky wrote after attending a Lumière show at the Nizhni-Novgorod Fair in July 1896: "Last night I was in the Kingdom of the Shadows: Suddenly there was a click, everything vanishes, and a railway train appears on the screen. It darts like an arrow straight towards you – watch out! It seems as though it is about to rush into the darkness where you are sitting and reduce you to a mangled sack of skin ... and destroy this hall and this building so full of wine, women, music, and vice, and turn it into fragments and dust...." The reference to women and vice may have had something to do with the screening room being located next door to a brothel!

Probably not that unusual a location for what passed for a theatre in those days. Even the most cursory reading of film history in every country confirms the speed at which the film-going experience spread throughout the world, and the incredible range of conditions under which films were shown before the construction of the "dream palaces". "Nickelodeons" spread like wildfire across the land. The wave of showmen, promoters, and entrepreneurs from all walks of life who entered this raw new industry used whatever was available that could conceivably be converted into a "theatre", with nothing in the way of legislation or local fire regulations to restrict them.

Here is an early description from Canada's film history. The year is 1905. The place is Hazelton, a very small village built around the Hudson Bay post at the head of navigation on the Skeena River in British Columbia, 550 miles north of Vancouver. An itinerant cinematography showman arrives, and although there are only a handful of Europeans and native people in the village, there are enough to constitute an audience. There is no suitable building in the community, but there is a cave in the side of the hill that overlooks the town. So in this cramped and unventilated space he rigs his screen and installs his projector, and on a makeshift door he nails a large piece of paper on which he scrawls "Theatre" and the programme of films "now being shown". Boxes, barrels, and logs serve as seats, and in a few hours the "vault" is packed to suffocation with every able-bodied person in town. The films – 35mm nitrate films, of course – are well past their prime in terms of condition, but they are still projectable, and still capable of amazing and enthralling the audience. Virtual "shadows in the cave". A rather touching link back to those first images created by our common ancestors.

I could go on to tell you the story about the first film-going experience even further North, in Dawson City in the Yukon Territory, following the discovery of gold in 1896. This is the story that also demonstrates the capability of nitrate film to survive in the most challenging storage conditions – in this case it was buried in the permafrost for 49 years! We pulled nearly 500 reels of film out of that hole in Dawson City, and managed to salvage close to 400 of them. I won't take the time to tell that story now. You can read about it elsewhere in this book, *This Film Is Dangerous*.

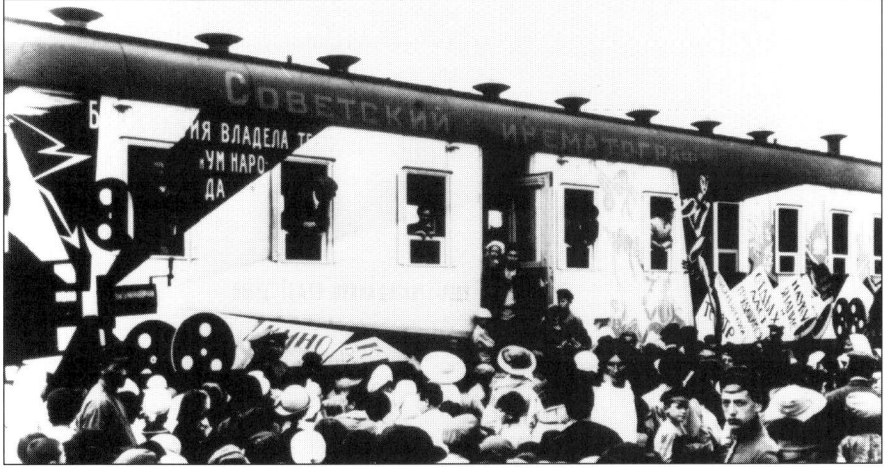

"Improbable and unsuitable venues" – an Agitprop train in the USSR in the 1920s.

BFI Collections – Stills, Posters & Designs, London. 300803.

Every country has stories of early film exhibitions in an astonishing variety of improbable and unsuitable venues. This may explain why there were fires from time to time, but it also begs the question why there were not many more fires. Yes, nitrate is flammable. Anyone who has seen the films of test burns of nitrate would have to be impressed at how successfully a nitrate film fire resists all efforts to

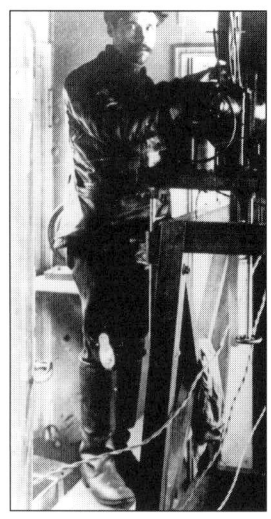

The projectionist in an Agitprop train.

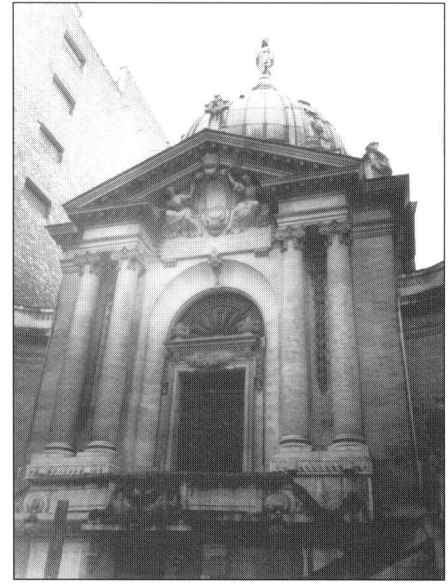

Notre Dame de Consolation – the memorial chapel in rue Jean Goujon, Paris, photographed in March 2001. A sign at the foot of the stairs reads: "Sur ces lieux, le 4 mai 1897 un terrible incendie ravagea la vente de bienfaisance organisée par l'œuvre philanthropique du Bazar de la Charité. 127 personnes périrent brûlées vives parmi lesquelles la duchesse d'Alençon et 250 grièvement blessées." (See also Colour Section 1.)

Roger Smither

extinguish it. (And we all have seen those films because we use them over and over to frighten our sponsors and our potential donors.)

But think of the conditions under which nitrate film was projected in those early years. The nitrate film didn't cause the fires. The appalling ignorance and incompetence of "theatre" owners and projectionists were responsible. Let me give you two examples.

Everyone knows about the most well-known fire in film history. It happened very early in that history, on 4 May 1897, and it established nitrate film in the public mind as a dangerous substance. Consider the circumstances. It is a charity bazaar in Paris. It is 4 o'clock in the afternoon. Some 4000 people are crowded into a long wooden building in rue Jean Goujon. The building is divided into charity stalls, divided by sheets of pasteboard. Overhead there is a false ceiling, an enormous canopy of canvas coated with tar to stiffen it. The Cinématographe is just one of the attractions, and it is being presented in a 9 x 4 projection room. There has been a problem with the lamp, and Albert Molteni, the magic lantern manufacturer, has sent over a replacement, an oxyetheric lamp – a mixture of oxygen and ether fuelling a flame which heats a small piece of lime to incandescence. The lamp is called Securitas, an ironic name under the circumstances. It is the fourth presentation of the afternoon, and while the room is in darkness the projectionist, a man named Bellac, pauses so he can refuel the lamp. Brushing aside advice that he do this outside, he returns to his canvas projection box and begins to pour the ether. His assistant, without waiting for instructions, strikes a match. Bellac stares in horror as the lamp explodes, and of course ignites the nitrate film. In seconds the fire spreads to the canopy, and in minutes the entire hall is an inferno. Burning tar falls onto the billowing gowns of the ladies and turns them into human torches. Total panic follows. Those who are not burned to death are trampled to death in the rush for the only exit. The final death toll is 121, and in a class-conscious age that number looms even larger in the press coverage as they are "the cream of French society". At the inquiry that follows the Cinématographe is blamed. In the words of one deputy "it creates danger wherever it is used", and should be banned. But in the trial that takes place that August, three men are found to be negligent. Baron Mackau, the charity bazaar organiser, is fined 500 francs; the projectionist is given a one-year prison sentence; and his assistant is sentenced to eight months.

Of course they were criminally negligent, but the damage to the reputation of nitrate film is permanent. From then on it is panic that takes more lives than the flames of burning nitrate.

Let me give you one more example, from Britain, and much more typical of fires associated with early cinema.

It is 1907. A village hall in Newmarket has been converted into a cinema. There is only one exit, a set of folding doors with one half bolted shut. The operator has set up his projector on a pile of loose boxes just inside the door. A tank of oxygen and a tank of hydrogen are propped up against the closed half of the door and are connected to the projector. The operator drops a piece of hot carbon on the floor and in his effort to stamp it out he pulls the projector off the makeshift stand and sets the film on fire. The small crowd panics and rushes towards the only exit. They knock over the oxygen and hydrogen tanks, breaking the connections. There is only one fatality, a miracle under the circumstances, and at the inquest the court decides that the oxygen and hydrogen tanks are the real cause of the fire. The real cause, of course, was an incompetent projectionist. Panic did the rest.

Panic robbed me of the cinema in my childhood. I was raised in Montréal. In 1927 a fire in the projection booth in the Laurier Palace Cinema – there was speculation in the press about smoking in the booth – triggered a panic in which several children were trampled to death. The Québec Government, enthusiastically supported by the Catholic Church, promptly banned anyone under sixteen from attending the commercial cinema. A ban that was not lifted until the 1960s!

I am not denying that nitrate film can get hung up in the projector. Is there anything more distressing than to see a frame melt before your eyes? I am also not denying that in rare cases the film ignites outside the aperture plate and sets the take-up reel on fire; but I am denying that it was a common occurrence when the equipment was well-maintained and the projectionist was experienced and competent. In fact, nitrate must have been able to accommodate a fair degree of mishandling and rough treatment when you consider the number of film presentations that took place in the first decades of the cinema, almost all by amateurs or by projectionists who were learning on the job. One report to the Home Office in Britain in 1909 stated that there were some 200 unlicensed and unsupervised exhibitions of cinematography in the London area *every day*.

All film archivists are aware of fires in archives, or in organisations pretending to be archives, which have destroyed thousands of reels of nitrate film. We are also aware that if a sufficient quantity of decomposing nitrate film is stored in an unventilated vault and allowed to heat up, the pressure of the accumulated gases can lower the flashpoint to a level where spontaneous combustion can occur. It has happened, for example, when film was stored in an unventilated metal shed on top of a building in New York City during a very hot summer. But how stupid do you have to be to store films that way?

In fact, if you examine all the other fires that have marked the history of the film archive movement, you uncover management that is breathtaking in its incompetence:

Paris, 1959, a hot summer. The Cinémathèque Française stacks some 5,000 reels of nitrate in an inner courtyard under a glass canopy that acts like a giant magnifying glass. They are waiting to be shipped. They waited a little too long.

Montréal, 1967, another hot summer. The National Film Board, the unofficial custodian of the country's film heritage, stores its nitrate films in a warehouse at Beaconsfield, on the outskirts of the city. No climate controls of any kind. The warehouse contains all sorts of other combustible material, like tanks of diesel fuel. A fire breaks out, cause unknown, and the nitrate helps make it a spectacular blaze.

Washington, 1978. It is December. Workmen are carrying out repairs at the National Archives' nitrate vaults at Suitland, Maryland. One of them is using an acetylene torch, and hot metal drops into a cardboard box, which sets the film on fire. What is a cardboard box doing in a nitrate vault? Twelve and a half million feet of Universal newsfilm outtakes make a very spectacular fire, and the world is again reminded that nitrate burns, and that it is not a good idea to carry out work with an acetylene torch in a vault filled with nitrate film. It is also a good idea to advise the fire department that opening the doors to all the vaults is not a good way to fight a nitrate fire.

Mexico City, 1982. The Cineteca Nacional loses 6,506 films, or so it is reported in the *The Guinness Book of Film Facts*. "The biggest single loss of archive film" – a dubious distinction. The actual number of titles is closer to 5,000, but many of them are unique copies, a very large segment of the surviving national film heritage. The film was being "temporarily" stored in rooms next to the auditorium in the Cineteca's main building. In retrospect, not a very suitable location for a nitrate film vault, even temporarily. Faulty wiring is believed to have caused the fire. There was also loss of life in that one, which made it even more tragic.

There are those who would argue that the loss to the Cinémathèque Française and the world film heritage when the vaults at Le Pontel burned in 1980 was even greater, although the exact number of films that were lost in that catastrophe was never revealed. What was revealed was that the storage conditions were decidedly substandard.

The point is that in all these cases, like the one here in London when the National Film and Television Archive lost 300 prints at the Henderson Laboratory (all previously copied I am assured!), the fault lay with the management of the nitrate in storage and not with the nitrate itself...

The fact is that nitrate stored in carefully controlled conditions (I will leave the ideal specifications for temperature and humidity to the experts, who like to argue whether 4° Centigrade is cold enough and whether 25% humidity is too dry) demonstrates that it can be safely stored at least as long as triacetate safety stock, and given the epidemic of vinegar syndrome we are witnessing with triacetate stock, may well last even longer. The chemists tell me that while cellulose nitrate is an inherently unstable compound – and a surprisingly large number of materials we have contrived from chemistry, like most plastics, are unstable over time – it can and has lasted for over one hundred years.

Oh yes, I know how unpredictable nitrate can be, about bad batches and improperly processed film, but we are talking about an industrial process in an era that was just beginning to discover quality control. An era in which factories manufacturing celluloid for men's collars and billiard balls exploded regularly.

So why does nitrate have the reputation as the film stock from hell?

Well, one reason is that it served our purposes as archivists to play up its weaknesses while ignoring its strengths. You cannot raise funds from governments and foundations by reminding them that nitrate was the workhorse of the industry for sixty years; that immense quantities of nitrate film were safely in circulation in every corner of the globe and under the most adverse circumstances imaginable; and that the number of people injured in fires in which nitrate was involved, and was very seldom the cause, was, statistically, totally insignificant by comparison.

It is very difficult to collect statistics on the total volume of nitrate in circulation at any one time. One estimate for the *entire* industry in 1926 was 1,250,000,000 feet, consuming in the process more silver than the United States Mint. If we take 1939 as probably the high point in nitrate film production, Kodak estimates that in the US alone some 504 million feet of nitrate stock was produced that year. Despite Hollywood's dominance of the industry, I think we can safely assume that the total for the entire world was at least five times that. Say two and a half billion feet, give or take a few. That may be conservative.

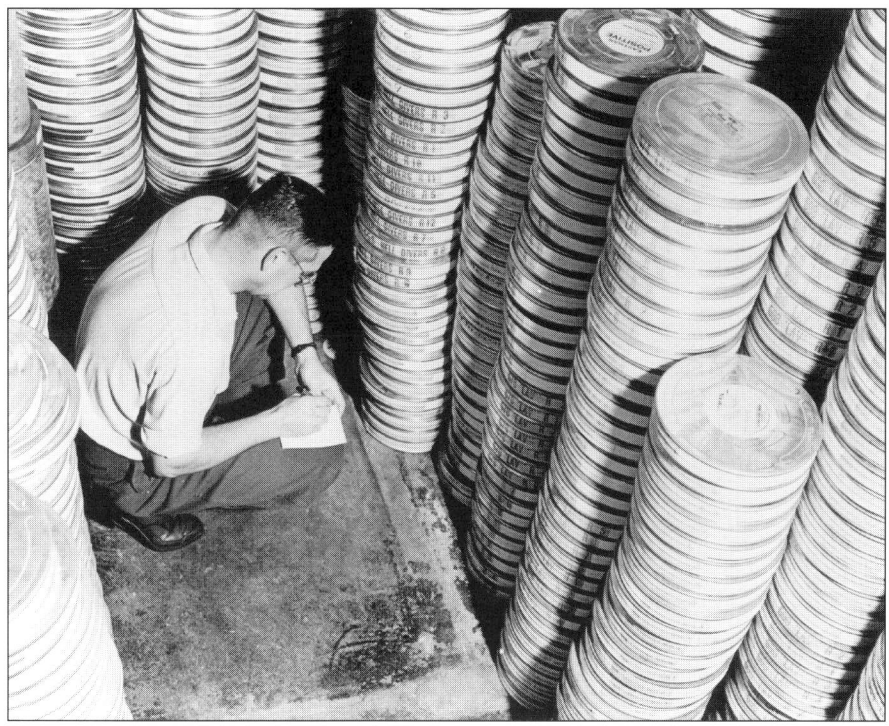

The shipping department of the MGM studio laboratories – "Hundreds of miles of film, ready to ship," states the original caption.

BFI Collections – Stills, Posters & Designs, London. 152659.

It may appear to be a lot of film, but there were a lot of theatres, over 15,000 in the US alone, and an enormous audience. The reported statistics on paid admissions for 1939 were 85 million *per week* in the US, and 23 million per week in the UK.

So many people, so much film, so much lost film, especially during the war years. And yet the sad fact is that much more nitrate was deliberately destroyed when the studios decided that silent film no longer had any revenue potential than was lost in fires or through decomposition during sixty years of production.

It is a tribute to the resilience of nitrate that so much has survived. The Nitrate Project, launched in the UK in 1988, determined that there was precisely 189,786,000 feet of pre-1953 nitrate film still in custody. The Centre Nationale de la Cinématographie, the nitrate custodian for France, currently holds 300,000 cans. That is a lot of nitrate!

The service counter at the Universal studio film library.

BFI Collections – Stills, Posters & Designs, London.

If nitrate was so dangerous, a great many people were taking risks. Consider the distribution system. These films were moved from cinema to cinema as many as three times a week, shipped by truck, by rail, by boat, by plane, or even by dog sled, to every corner of the globe, in every kind of weather, and run on equipment that ranged from state-of-the-art machines run by trained and skilled projectionists, to venerable antiques run by anyone who could be persuaded to do the work for the minimum wage.

So I am here to praise nitrate, and to apologise for all the times I have disparaged nitrate in the course of my work. I remember with shame turning up at FIAF one year with buttons saying "NITRATE CAN'T WAIT" – part of a campaign to frighten potential donors into turning their films over to the archives and to loosen the purse strings of funding sources. The nitrate, we said, was decomposing in the vaults, or it was just about to explode and destroy the entire archive, if not the entire neighbourhood! It had to be converted to safety film now! *How base* we were in thus defaming nitrate, and how little did we know how unsafe the safety stock was!

Nitrate's day is done, but I hope you now agree that it deserves a better epitaph than this one from *The Oxford Companion to Film*, a work, by the way, on which I consulted – and very typical of entries in hundreds of works on the cinema: "Nitrate film, or more correctly nitrate base, was the standard film stock base for 35mm until 1951.... It continued in use for 60 years despite considerable fire risk resulting from the film's tendency to ignite when run at speed through projectors, cameras, or editing equipment."

Amazing, isn't it, that they managed to build a multi-billion-dollar industry based entirely on such an unsuitable and dangerous product!

I have a little piece of nitrate I would like to run.

['Newsfilm' of the launch of the Ford V-8 motor car, ca.1932. 3 minutes.]

Nothing special about this little film. It was obviously a commercial designed to look like a newsreel, and released sometime after March 1932, when Ford introduced the V-8. It was distributed to Ford dealers, who would pay the local cinema to add it to their programme. It is exactly the same age as I am, and, as you can see, in considerably better shape. But the real point is that it was found in the hills of West Virginia by an antique dealer who offered it for sale on e-Bay, the Internet auction site. A friend of mine, in Ottawa, bought it for $102 Canadian dollars!

Nitrate still lives, and who knows how much more is still out there.

So I am here to say I am sorry about the way I treated the nitrate in my life, and to raise a glass in praise of nitrate, noble servant of the Seventh Art, essential medium in the diffusion of film culture throughout the world for over sixty years.

Reproduction . . . Disappearance

by Dominique Païni

Transcription of the paper delivered at the Symposium "The Last Nitrate Picture Show" at the London FIAF Congress, June 2000. Its spoken character has been voluntarily preserved by the author. Translated by Catherine A Surowiec.

When Clyde Jeavons invited me to speak about nitrate, I responded in the affirmative, but without really thinking. What would I say about this issue? It was Paolo Cherchi Usai's intervention which finally gave me my arguments. Paradoxically, they are rather contrary to his own.

Talking about how to recognize nitrate film, Paolo evoked the qualities of "perfume" and touch. I would add to this, weight. Metre for metre, a reel of nitrate film is heavier than a similar one of acetate film.

I shall screen a recently preserved film, *Paris-Londres*, directed by Jean Arroy. This film was probably commissioned to praise the combined merits of train and ship travel, showing how it saved time in the journey between France and England. Or perhaps its purpose was simply to praise the efficiency of the relevant railway and steamship companies.

This copy was made from a nitrate positive, and not from the negative, which would have been less suitable for the final result. An internegative was struck, then a positive was printed from this internegative. But in fact what you will see at first is a single image composed from two different prints projected side by side. One projector will screen the rediscovered vintage nitrate positive, while the other will show the newly preserved acetate copy. Our little guessing game will consist of being able to distinguish the two projected images. Can one recognize the nitrate by sight? Because this is fundamentally the essential thing for us archivists, determined as we are to restore to a film work a *valeur d'ancienneté* – a "value of ancientness", and it is equally important for the audience, to whom we owe the most beautiful material possible, i.e., to reconstitute a *valeur d'exposition* – a "value of exhibition".

Of course, I defy anyone to distinguish these two materials from this one screening, including those who are lovers of nitrate.

The 1920s constituted a "Golden Age", an era which could appreciate the confusion between a "publicity" film for industrial and commercial use, and an avant-garde construct/experiment. This is the case with *Paris-Londres*.

But what is it about this film that moves us, that seduces us? Is it Nitrate, and its supposed specific effects, about which we have heard so much said with trembling voices during these two days – or is it the "plasticity of the constructivism" of the framing, of the movement, of the rhythm of the editing, of this jerky image which Walter Benjamin speaks about during these same years?

Does its beauty of luminous contrasts result from the film stock which recorded them – or is it the visual taste dominating an era which constructed the representation of the world according to an ordered and dynamic conception, granting pride of place in our image of a neo-plastic architecture to the outburst of new materials (glass, steel) and the right angle, rather than the arabesque?

The quality of nitrate is not in the stock, it is in our eyes. If the constructivist taste came back today – and in a certain manner it has come back, in the citational forms of the post-modernism of the 1980s – for me there is no doubt: acetate film could restore, if one wishes, that which we love, and which fascinates us, about nitrate – its special sharpness, its shadowy light, its sfumato.

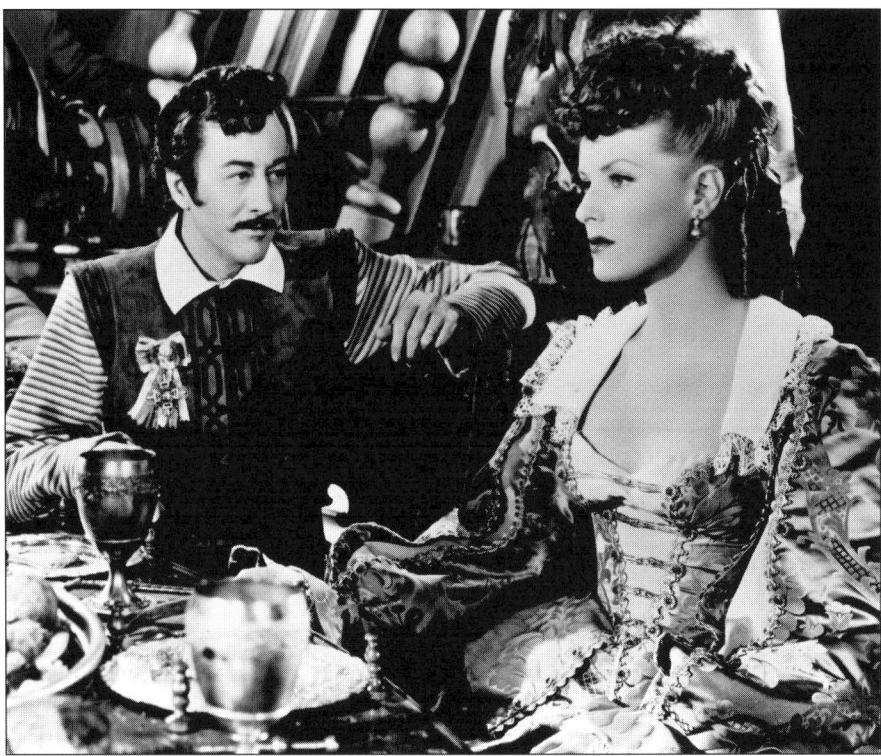

Maureen O'Hara in *The Spanish Main* (1945).

BFI Collections – Stills, Posters & Designs, London. 142719.

Moreover, it is not only film stock which has changed since Borzage's *The Spanish Main*, which we saw yesterday, and contemporary films. It is also make-up. Maureen O'Hara used powder rather than creams for her make-up foundation. There is a relation between the velvet of the actress's skin and the effect of the light and colors rendered by the projection of this image which indeed resulted from a nitrate copy. What did we see, then? The results of film stock, or of a type of make-up which is no longer used? Is it the film itself which we mourn, or the disappearance of a feminine skin which incarnated the dominant representation of women? You can guess my response.

Today, it is the grain of film which has replaced this certain type opf rosy bloom. That certain *pulverulence* – the powdering of the epidermis of actresses (and actors!) – is passé in films of high sensitivity, whose increased grain now records faces that are *painted* and not powdered.

We project many things onto nitrate for want of being able to project it! Threatened by disappearance, inflammable, dangerous? Certainly! All of this is true. But in this looking-back to nitrate there is also an imaginary realm peculiar to cinematheques, a melancholy reverie of ruins.

In effect, this imaginary realm is of two orders.

On the one hand, a medical metaphor: a domain of contamination, of contagion, contemporary with sexually transmitted diseases and computer viruses. This is the panic about the copy which will contaminate the entire collection. In the instructional and edifying film about nitrate presented by the Imperial War Museum in several episodes during the course of this symposium, one can easily spot this paradigm: to *foresee* the destruction of film and to *care for* film. The title of this film is, is it not, *This Film Is Dangerous?*

On the other hand, a social and communitarian metaphor: the image's chemical support becomes more important than its artistic expression. A consensus has finally been created, an agreement generated by... its material, almost extinct or on its way to being so; rather than a final break there is an infinite subjective diversity, varying upon accounts, revealing tastes, all too human. The scientist's "objectivity" versus the confrontation of aesthetic points of view.

Basically, we can note a "scientific" evolution – according to the acceptance of this term in the museum world – between the pioneers of the cinematheques and our generation. Three values have succeeded one another in the activities of film archivists during the past sixty years.

When the first cinematheques were being created, film's *aesthetic value* was advanced to gain the art of film a place in the bosom of the other arts. Then it was film's documentary value, its strength as testimony and its recording of life for the benefit of future generations, who would be privileged for these reasons by our preservation of film. This constituted cinema's sociological-historical virtue from the 1960s onwards. Finally, cinema's *material value* would seem to outshine the first two values today: nitrate exaggerates the importance of films, ennobles them without aesthetic distinction. The mere quality of being nitrate – fragile, dangerous, precious, threatened by technocrats and merchants – bestows value, a vaguely "antiquarian" value, a melancholy yearning for all cinema recorded on this forbidden support, which also endows it with further historical charms. In other words: the chemical dimension, in the name of which one loves the cinema, dispenses with that love in *choosing*, in *creating a hierarchy*, in advancing taste. This also poses the question of positivist retrenchment, with which the museum world has always been familar.

This positivist attitude is not a new phenomenon in the history of the arts, because this history has been marked by abandoning the supports which embody a work of art. Thus, painting was not extinguished when painters no longer ground their pigments and oxides, when wooden panels were replaced by the textile support of canvas. Men have always transferred their images from support to support. This is an important part of the reasons which led them to reproduce the images which they produced. Art is not only created from memory. It is created equally from loss, from oblivion, from the melancholy of this loss. Art, the invention of new forms, compensates and takes cares of the loss, completing the mourning for that which abandons itself, destroys itself, forgets itself. Loss creates new art.

I am therefore very perplexed by this sudden fetishisation of nitrate by certain historians and archivists, such as my friend Cherchi Usai. Because nothing allows us to think that we will not recover nitrate's lost qualities in the same manner in which video projection today is reducing the gaps in quality compared with the projected film image. The differences, and the gaps, are in the eyes of the beholder. Because if the disappointment is sometimes justified regarding a film's conservation via its transfer to acetate, this owes as much, if not more, to the taste of restorers and technicians in the laboratories than to the quality of the support.

Let's take an example in another sphere, painting. The three *Battles* of Uccello – now in London, Florence, and Paris – have been very differently restored, although they are part of the same series. Vivid and "Warholian" in London, luminously soft in Florence, sombre and nocturnal in Paris. The tastes of restorers and the value which they accord to the marks of the past are manifestly not the same in the three countries.

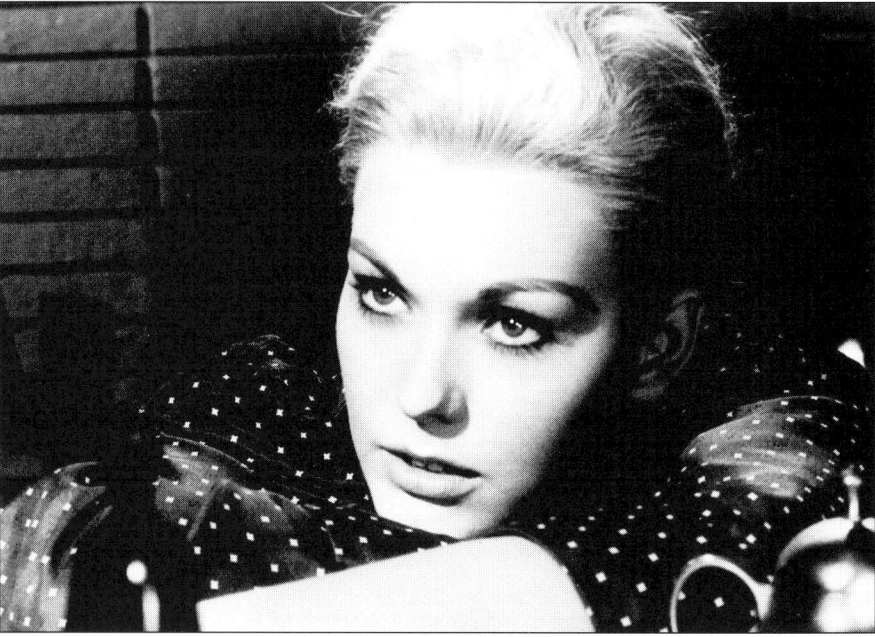

Kim Novak in *Vertigo* (1958).

BFI Collections – Stills, Posters & Designs, London. 205626.

Let's return to the cinema. Hitchcock's *Vertigo* has been reprinted and "restored", as everyone commonly says today. One can only believe that it is a question of film stock which explains the difference between copies of the period – *foxing* of the image, a very "18th century" pastel colour, the smooth face of Kim Novak – and the new copies. In these new copies, a grain seems to have covered the image. This would perhaps correspond to the taste of an era, our own, familiar with the films of John Cassavetes and Wong Kar-Waï: ultra-sensitive film stock utilised without lighting, thus with thick grain. Taste changes, what is acceptable evolves, and not only the chemical qualities of film. However, there is no doubt that it is possible to reproduce exactly the effects of the original copies.

Therefore, of course, we must keep everything, all the nitrate copies. But not in order to show them obligatorily or to worship them like relics, but in order to redo the printings, referring to them around every twenty to thirty years, when acetate loses its capacities of conservation. And this reproduction should not aim to re-view the cinema as it was in the past. This is something we will never know. Our taste today calls for a choice, assumed as a contemporary choice. Is it then necessary to reconstitute the past, including the carbon lamps of the projectors, whose light was hotter than that of xenon? Or to use the same kind of screens to intercept the light beams, and the period architecture of the auditoria?

The sweetness of the colours of Kinemacolor, the supposed "mellowness" of nitrate, translate an antiquarian, conjunctural, ephemeral taste, linked to visual styles, and are not dependent upon "scientific" necessity nor an inherited truth.

For two days, I have heard, in fact, much "moralising" ("nitrate was better"), much melancholy, and too little curiosity for the figurative innovation of past images, whatever their support. What strikes me, is not the desire to destroy nitrate. It is, rather, the strange desire to adorn it with all the virtues. Finally, does one perhaps love it more because it is a material which burns in such a spectacular manner, blazing, explosive, billowing clouds? Would nitrate be missed in the name of its *temperament* rather than in the name of its smell? In it, does one see again the "marvellous clouds" of Baudelaire?

To miss nitrate identifies itself, for me, with a desire to *remake*, to restore to life, to suppose one can abolish time, and make the past actual. This is what one might call *kitsch* taste, to which we are so sensitive unconsciously, and which attracts us at the always-unsettling moment of passing from one millennium to another.

Let us now look at the example of the Cinémathèque Française, which I know the best.

The inventory of the collections accumulated by Henri Langlois – an inventory still in progress, which is giving rise to conservations and restorations – invites us to think that the founder of the Cinémathèque Française repeated, four hundred years later, the extraordinary undertaking by Primaticcio at Fontainebleau commissioned by Francis I. In other words, *a project of preservation accomplished by the realisation of a collection*. To summarise a little: Shortly before 1540, Francis I suddenly took a lively interest in classical statuary. I will not stop here to consider the reasons which unleashed this interest, which are commented upon by the English art historians Francis Haskell and Nicholas Penny, in their work *Pour l'amour de l'Antique* (Paris: Hachette, 1988). On a grand scale, Primaticcio made casts from the originals, antique statues among the most esteemed of that time, in particular those shown in the Courtyard of the Belvedere in the Vatican. From these casts, executed in Rome and subsequently repaired in France because of damage incurred during transport, were made bronze copies. The execution of these casts, whose final decorative and social destination was the royal dwelling of Francis I, constituted *an essential stage in the diffusion and appreciation of antique statuary*.

I have never been able to abstain from comparing this exceptional enterprise in the diffusion of the knowledge of art, which formed a collection now known as the Musée d'Etat, from the enterprise of Langlois, which was the foundation of the Cinémathèque Française. Effectively, starting in 1936, Langlois and Iris Barry strove to exchange copies, and to make *contretypes*, that is, internegatives – casts – from the positives that they saved from destruction (especially of the silent cinema), and they sometimes printed from these new positives in order to start their collection, which rapidly became known as a "cinematheque" or "archive".

To choose, to make a cast, to duplicate antique sculptures, for Primaticcio, and to choose, to make a *contretype*, to duplicate films, for Langlois, were acts that are not so far apart. In both cases, the act of duplicating in order to collect, to show, and finally, to preserve, created opportunities for culture and learning previously unknown in each of these two moments in art history: love for the antique during the Renaissance, love for the cinema in the middle of the 20th century. One could even amuse oneself by noting that Primaticcio and Langlois each concentrated on limited bases, and were already setting about identifying the masterpieces of antique statuary and cinema history: for Primaticcio, it was the legendary courtyard of the Belvedere built by Bramante; for Langlois, the American studios – for which Iris Barry was the "go-between" – and German cinema – working with Frank Hensel, the head of the Reichsfilmarchiv, who as an officer in Paris during the Occupation helped Langlois to save his collections, against the orders to destroy films produced by the Allies.

Thus we return to the observation that to preserve is to *contretype*, to *duplicate*. Therefore, *it is to move away from a re(dis)covered material* (original or not), and to transfer it onto a safety support: from marble to bronze for Primaticcio, sometimes from 35mm to 16mm for Langlois (and today from nitrate to acetate. And tomorrow to digitial disc?). To preserve is thus to *add a generation* to the material which supports the image. Also, is it not rare, as a matter of fact, that a *contretype* – that is, a negative made from a positive – creates a veil, a softening of contrasts, a slight drop in sharpness of contour? But it is during this stage that the taste of a restorer intervenes: is it he who captures, or not, this softening? The *contretype* preserves the film, safeguards it, protects it, like the glass added to the frames protecting pictures: the effect of remoteness, of putting at a distance, the glazing, the nuances, the softening of contrasts, creating annoying reflections. Whatever the varnish, those who create a museum style are influencing *abusive fraternities* among painters (between Titian and Tintoretto, for example, according to Malraux); *contretypes* create a "cinematheque style", reproducing a cinematheque's taste, conscious or unconscious, thereby influencing probably equivalent "abusive fraternities" among films and *cinéastes*' styles. We must accept the remoteness of nitrate, like we accept the remoteness that the museum and the general notion of patrimony produce. But we must study the visual cultures of past cinema more closely. This is an anthropological rather than a chemical question.

Cinematheques were the first museums authorised – whose mission obliged them – to produce copies, "fakes", without the worry of disguising them as originals. For cinematheques, to conserve is to *reproduce*, to *distance ourselves from the original*, to collate "the now and the past" (to borrow once again an association from Walter Benjamin). This is what the director of a cinematheque must assume.

Enough, then, of worshipping nitrate! If the copies which we duplicate in order to preserve them from destruction do not resemble the nitrate copies, it is because *we do not really want it*. Otherwise the machines which man has invented to imitate and to reproduce would accomplish this. But we don't want it really, except perhaps a little mineral poisoning, happily momentary, which bestows a touch of the picturesque upon this FIAF Congress 2000.

Dangerous Stuff

by Kevin Brownlow

Mention the word "nitrate", and an embarrassing story comes to mind. It occurred in the early 1950s; I had just started collecting films. A kind friend presented me with a roll of 35mm silent film. What he didn't know was that I collected only films on the home movie gauge of 9.5mm. This roll was destined to remain unprojected – about 100 ft of celluloid. Adults warned me it was highly inflammable, and that bothered me. I imagined it suddenly spluttering into flame while I was at school.

Occasionally, I would unwind it and hold it up to the light; the image quality was absolutely amazing. And the subtitles gave the name of the original film: *Rupert of Hentzau*. Years later, I discovered this was the only surviving fragment of a 1915 British production, made for the old London Films at Twickenham Studios, featuring Henry Ainley and Jane Gail, directed by the outstanding American, George Loane Tucker, who had made *Traffic in Souls* and was to make *The Miracle Man*. Not a solitary frame of his highly-praised English work survives* – not even *Rupert of Hentzau*, for reasons I shall now attempt to explain.

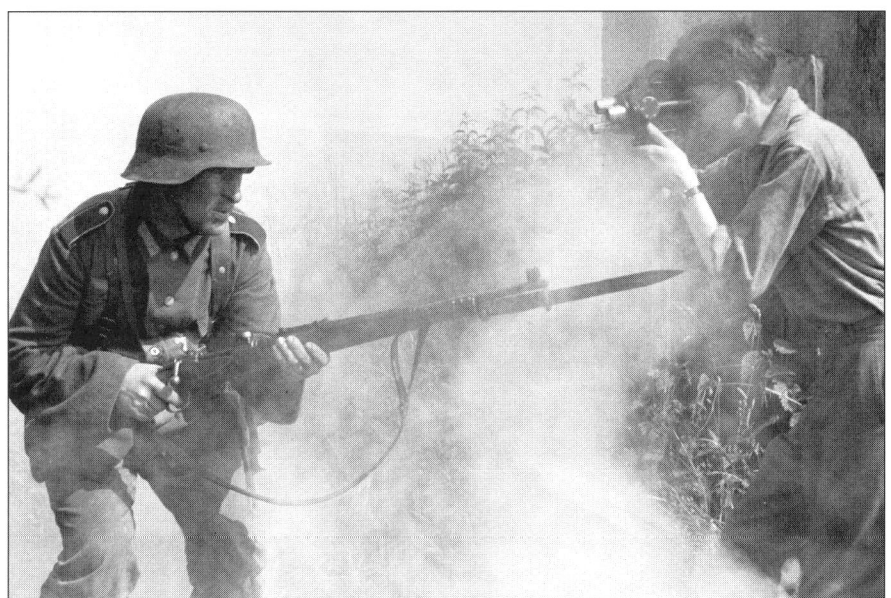

More adult war games: Kevin Brownlow filming a scene for *It Happened Here* (1964).

Kevin Brownlow Collection.

As a boy brought up during World War II, I was obsessed with the paraphernalia of warfare. I had recently moved to London from the country, and discovered that adjoining my new home were acres of bomb-sites. Many damaged buildings were still standing, surrounded by overgrown gardens, giving us the most exciting of adventure playgrounds. It was all reminiscent of *Hue and Cry* and John Boorman's wonderful film *Hope and Glory*, except that we were more organised. Convinced that my life lay with the sea, I had established a naval training unit, and we held what were euphemistically known as "exercises" on the bomb-sites. Armed with air rifles and fireworks, we spent the long evenings dressed in naval uniform, camouflaged by the thick fogs of those days, waging war on our friends. We used Aldis signalling lamps as searchlights to winkle them out, and air rifles and pistols to shoot them once we spotted them. All absurdly dangerous and great fun.

My destructive nature began to dwell upon the highly inflammable roll of nitrate. It was no use to me, I couldn't project it, it was obviously dangerous to have it around – what better fate than to be sacrificed in battle? I have this image that haunts me still. I was on top of a house, peering over the edge as my friends searched for me. I placed the nitrate in a paper bag, screwed the top into a rough sort of fuse, lit it, and dropped it. The bag flared up, and as it fell the flame became very intense; as my friends scattered the bag began to roar. The last vestiges of *Rupert of Hentzau* were destroyed on a bomb-site in Swiss Cottage by a boy who was destined to become a film historian and to regret his action again and again. The most recent occasion being the production of *Cinema Europe*, the series David Gill and I made for the BBC about the European silent film, which actually had a sequence devoted to the original London Films. The extract would have been ideal – it would have shown the exceptionally high standard of cinematography (they had the future Oscar-winner Ernest Palmer, an American, and the Danish Gustav Pauli) and art direction. The frames I remember showed a big interior court scene, with masses of extras in Ruritanian uniform. The depth of focus was astonishing...

That was the first of two films I was responsible for destroying (for details of the second, keep reading). But the wholesale destruction of nitrate continues in places like Germany, with the aid of government grants. "Copy it and destroy it" is the rule, rather like an art gallery burning canvases as soon as postcards have been produced. Apparently, German archives hand nitrate to a fire brigade, who practice fire fighting with it.

Nitrate has unique qualities which the modern black-and-white safety stock cannot duplicate. I saw a few reels of a rare French silent recently, and was very excited by the quality of the production. Apart from its setting – a film studio – the film was photographed so beautifully that the film was a pleasure to watch. The nitrate was then copied and I subsequently viewed the black-and-white dupe. I stopped after a couple of hundred feet. It had lost all interest for me. The information was there – we used some of the footage in *Cinema Europe* – but the aesthetic pleasure had gone.

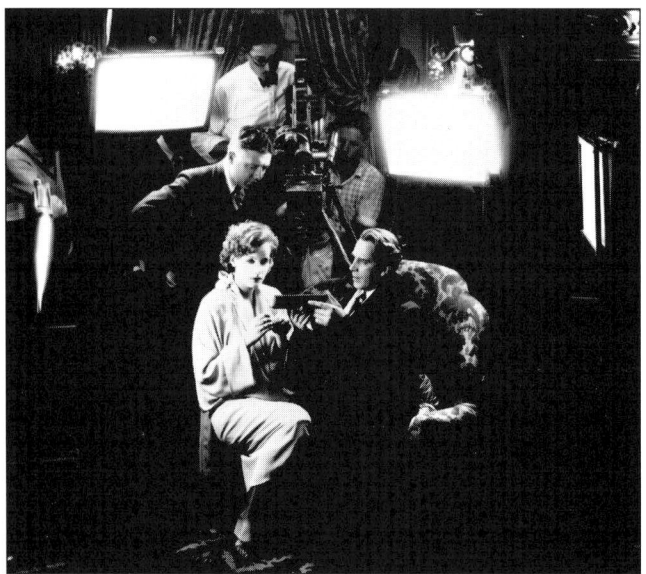

William Daniels filming Greta Garbo and Lars Hanson in *Flesh and the Devil* (1926), on the set with director Clarence Brown.

BFI Collections – Stills, Posters & Designs, London. 190192.

When I worked at the American Film Institute, in Los Angeles, I thought that Garbo's cameraman, the great William Daniels, might get a kick out of seeing the MGM studio print of his masterly *Flesh and the Devil* (1926). We were halfway through the first reel at the AFI Theatre when he leaned forward and asked, "Kevin, why are we seeing this?" Somewhat taken aback, I said, "I thought you'd enjoy seeing it again." "They don't understand the intent," he said. I have thought long and hard about that remark. What did he mean? I think he was suggesting that the people doing the grading – or timing, as it is known in America – had merely gone for the obvious, and were not aware of what he was trying to do. They did not have an original print to which to compare it.

Grading is a lost art. It was acquired instinctively when moving pictures began, and no one seemed to think anything of it. It was lost with the advent of colour; today lab technicians can cope perfectly well with colour but are lost with black-and-white. I remember when an old man at Henderson's Labs graded the 1980 restoration of *Napoléon*, and got it right the first time. This was a film with more than 200 light changes in one reel, and there were something like 25 reels. But for such veterans, grading was ingrained. How often have you seen an inaccurately-graded nitrate print? On the other hand, how often have you seen an accurately-graded monochrome print made in recent years? Most restorations suffer from grading hiccups. And now we often no longer have the nitrate to act as comparison. The recent screening of nitrate prints at the London FIAF Congress was a poignant reminder of what we have lost.

Certainly one of the most horrifying sights I have ever seen greeted me when I arrived in Culver City in 1970 to write an article on the MGM Auction. Barrels of water had been lined up inside the perimeter fence and reels of nitrate thrown into them. Alongside were piles of cans with the titles of the dying films. MGM was the one studio which had copied most of its nitrate onto safety stock – but had they kept the nitrate in the cool conditions of the salt-mine they owned in Kansas, they could have remade the prints that were botched, such as *Our Dancing Daughters*, and saved those films that never got copied at all. I took photographs of this atrocity and they were printed – much to MGM's anger – in the *Sunday Times* back in London.

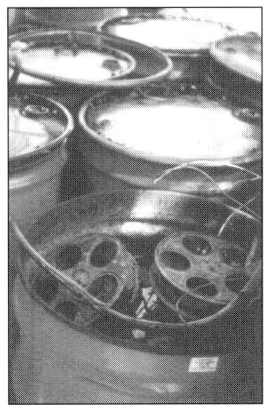

"One of the most horrifying sights…" – Lot 3 at the MGM auction, Culver City, 1970.
(See also Colour Section 1.)
Kevin Brownlow Collection.

———

Oh, where is the nitrate of yesteryear? The most exhilarating moments of my early cinema-going took place on Saturday nights, not in an Odeon or an Essoldo – but in a flat over a greengrocer's in Camden Town, where lived a veteran collector called Bert Langdon. Bert had been collecting since he was a boy, when you could buy 100 feet of nitrate from market stalls for next to nothing. These rolls had been cut from old release prints for use with toy projectors, and Bert always included a reel or two compiled of these orphan extracts. Often, like my *Rupert of Hentzau*, they were all that remained of the original feature, and Bert had amassed 80,000 feet of them. He would add to his reel of "bits" an elaborate programme including a Biograph, often with his pet Mary Pickford, a newsreel, a 2-reel featurette, and then the big film of the evening – I can remember almost every title he showed us, from *Just Another Blonde* with Louise Brooks and Dorothy Mackaill to *A Romany Lass* with Marjorie Villis. The only drawback was that Bert erred on the side of caution when it came to illumination; he used a 100-watt bulb, which wasn't nearly enough to make the nitrate glisten and gleam.

I knew what nitrate should look like because the National Film Theatre still showed nitrate as a matter of course. I remember seeing Fairbanks in *The Three Musketeers* in a tinted original print from the Museum of Modern Art. It looked almost stereoscopic. I also remember an original black-and-white nitrate print of *Don Q, Son of Zorro*, and being so exhilarated I leaped down the stairs at Waterloo underground station, and almost broke an ankle. Those were the days when the title "Museum of Modern Art" raised spirits which had been dampened endlessly by poor prints – you could be certain of the best 35mm in existence – mainly because they circulated so many original prints.

When I graduated to 16mm in 1958, I put up with the expense (£2 a reel!) because the prints came from the old Kodascope Library, had been made from fine grains taken from the original negatives, and had been given the finest possible processing. My amber print of James Cruze's 1923 epic *The Covered Wagon* was the nearest thing I had seen to nitrate – the image was as sharp as a knife and the tonal value of Karl Brown's shots of hundreds of wagons departing under cumulus clouds was simply breathtaking. People who imagine westerns began with *Stagecoach* have no idea what miracles were achieved in the silent days. But talk to people who have

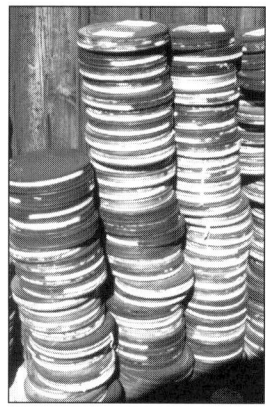

Another part of Lot 3.
(See also Colour Section 1.)

only seen *The Covered Wagon* on video and you'll get dark looks and rude responses. It's like talking to people who have only seen Ireland in a downpour. My wife (who is Irish) refers to the brilliant light that follows a storm as "nitrate weather".

The image quality of original prints can make you believe you've seen a wonderful film even when the only talent comes from the cameraman. The trouble is that as soon as you copy the nitrate, you lose the pin-sharp definition and a lot of the tonal value. I remember showing an audience at the NFT an extract from a Colleen Moore picture on 16mm and then switching over to an original nitrate print, and hearing the gasp. And the 16mm wasn't bad – as they said in the lab that produced it, "You're lucky to get anything off such an old picture." With that attitude, lab workers throughout the decades have condemned the efforts of talented technicians so that in the end not even they considered their work to have any value. I don't think any art form has been so degraded as that of the silent film.

When I first went to Hollywood in the 1960s, to interview the pioneers, I was met by blank amazement. Surely you aren't interested in silent films – those ludicrous antiques with their exaggerated acting and jerky movements and terrible prints? My greatest pleasure came in reuniting the film-makers with work they had not seen for nearly half a century – and thanks to researchers like David Shepard, then working for the American Film Institute, it was often possible to show them original tinted prints.

Louise Brooks and Thomas Meighan in *The City Gone Wild* (1927).
(See also Colour Section 1.)

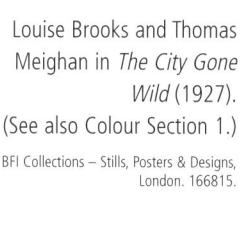

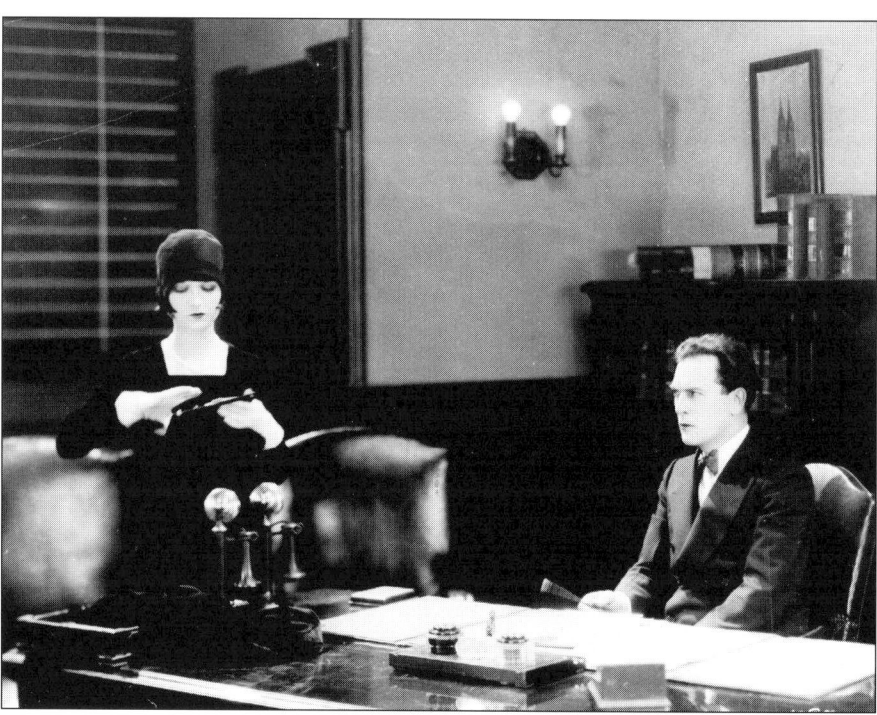

But there were tragedies, too. Paramount discovered a vault they had forgotten about, and anxious to clear it they offered it to the AFI. David Shepard showed me the list, and I was amazed. "What film would you like to see tonight?" he asked. My eye fell on a familiar title, a film I had long wanted to see, a gangster story directed by James Cruze and starring Louise Brooks, *City Gone Wild* (1927). Shepard rang the vault, and later told me what happened: the vault-keeper pulled the rusty cans from the shelf, noticed a little rust on the roll, and threw it and the other cans into a barrel of water. The barrel was then driven out even before our vehicle had arrived to pick the film up. I could have wept. If I hadn't chosen that title, it would have survived.

Equally disheartening was the time I went to the Paramount backlot and a veteran employee told me that the week before he had cleared a building and thrown out a lot of nitrate – including footage of old Hollywood shot from an airship in 1915 by Cecil B DeMille. Sometimes they tell you these stories to tease you. But I have been present at enough tragic events to know how many similar disasters must be true.

"Restoration" is the buzz-word of our age, but how often does the restored print glow with the fantastic range of quality of a nitrate print? Luckily, we older film enthusiasts have our memories. Sometimes I think the best archive we have is between our ears.

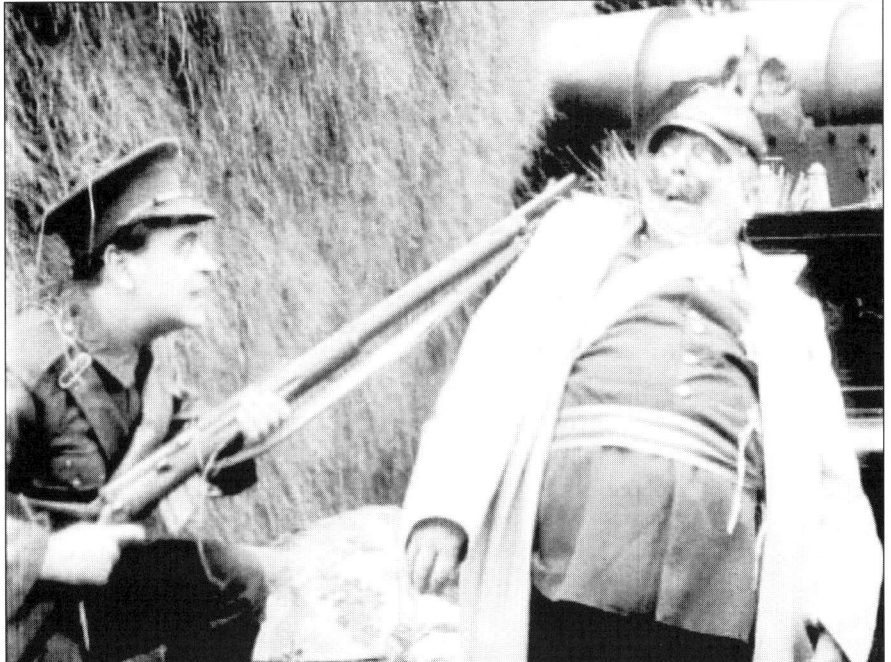

A scene from *The Revenge of Mr. Thomas Atkins* (1914).
Imperial War Museum, London.

---

* By coincidence – and such happy events occur constantly in this field – Roger Smither tells me that an incomplete nitrate print of a 1914 British propaganda comedy directed by George Loane Tucker, *The Revenge of Mr. Thomas Atkins*, has just been found in Wales and offered to the Wales Film and Televison Archive, who have generously passed it on to the Imperial War Museum. In the kind of twist characteristic of nitrate film finds, the film is said to have turned up in a boiler house. It is not, alas, one of Tucker's outstanding achievements.

The Silver Lining

A collection of original essays on nitrate-related topics, including both papers which the tight two-day schedule made it impossible to include in the programme of the symposium "The Last Nitrate Picture Show", and papers which were offered directly to this publication.

"A Fallen Star": Problems and Practices in Early Film Preservation

by Stephen Bottomore

It is a truism that a large proportion of films made in the silent era have been lost forever. While the figure is not known exactly, it is thought that only around 20% of what was originally produced in the 1920s, and around half that proportion for the 1910s, still exists.[1] Perhaps we would not be in this situation if some of the early attempts at establishing film archives, which I have mentioned in my other essay in this volume, had been more successful. But film archives could not have solved all the problems of film preservation at this time, and some of the blame for such a high rate of attrition of early films must come down to the poor keeping qualities of early film stock under the then-inadequate storage conditions, as well as from the careless behaviour of early film companies.

Storing Films

A writer in 1926 noted that "many early films are fading out and others are becoming warped and wrinkled, so that much of the best historical material of the last thirty years is in danger of perishing."[2] But even in the very early days of cinema some experts realised that films would decay over time, and suggested ways to avert it, or at least to slow it down. One of the earliest suggestions came from French photographic expert Léon Vidal in late 1901, in a letter published in the *British Journal of Photography*. Vidal recognised that celluloid would deteriorate with time, and suggested that perhaps the solution was to transfer the film images onto another more stable medium. He proposed photographic bromide paper for this task. The resulting positive print would then be treated with pure paraffin, and the roll of paper placed in a can with a label showing the subject and date. Vidal suggested that the paraffin would render the film strip translucent so that negatives could be run off in the future, though it seems doubtful that a sharp image could have been obtained in this way due to the grain of the paper.[3] Interestingly, the renowned paper print collection in the Library of Congress in Washington was made in a similar way (though apparently without the paraffin), and it has proved a major task to return the paper strips to projectable film. One suspects that Vidal's solution would not be a popular choice among today's film archivists!

Later suggestions about archiving films concentrated on preserving the celluloid originals. It was realised from relatively early on that the survival time of a film copy might depend on how the film had been developed and treated. In 1911 a British trade journal replied to an enquiry by advising that the most important factor in the "keeping quality" of a film was that it be well washed in the process of development.[4] But those who wanted to preserve films had little control over how those films had originally been developed, so the "archivers" tended to stress the conditions of storage. By 1907 various departments of the US Government were starting to use film, and their technicians had their own ideas about storing films. A system developed whereby films were placed, loosely rolled, in cans which had a space at the top and bottom into which sponges saturated with gelatine were inserted. The cans were then sealed shut with insulating tape, and it was claimed that under these conditions the films stayed in prime condition for long periods. A trade journal reported:

> Several films which had remained under Government seal for a period of five years were forwarded from Washington for use at Fort Leavenworth, and upon being removed from the cans were found to be as fresh looking, reliable, and in all other respects as good as a freshly printed positive.[5]

An expert at this time suggested that "a film placed in a hermetically sealed can and kept in a cool place should last indefinitely".[6] That phrase "cool place" was perhaps the key, and others also emphasised the importance of temperature if films were to be stored for the long term. In 1910 a British cinema-owner, Mr W M Borradaile, writing in support of preserving films of historical interest, suggested that "a special chamber, in which the air would always be at the same temperature, would probably have to be provided". He added that "the films would have to be placed in charge of a man who was something of a chemist, besides having a knowledge of the moving picture industry."[7] This need for chemical expertise in film archives to control the decay of films has proved uncannily prescient, and temperature-controlled vaults are these days, of course, standard practice.

The Fire Danger

The dire consequences of not maintaining a cool storage temperature were realised from very early on. A trade writer in 1910 explained:

> As the temperature of the store-room rises, a ripening, or seasoning process takes place in the film. A vapour is given off, which if the tin is air-tight has no means of egress. Something is going to happen, and that something will be spontaneous combustion.[8]

He suggested that many of the film fires which had taken place by that date may have been due to poor storage conditions. He added that to remedy this danger it was most important, firstly, that film cans should have a vent or hole to allow the vapour to escape, and secondly, that the cans of film should be stored in a cool, dry room, which itself was well ventilated to the outside air.

The risk of fire was what everyone feared, as the celluloid nitrate base of early film stock was indeed highly flammable. The 1897 Bazar de la Charité fire had had a profound effect on the early film industry, and several more fires had subsequently occurred in film shows. But in places where large amounts of film were stored, the potential for disaster would surely be all the greater. In the early years of the century many British film companies were based in Cecil Court in central London, and a number of film fires occurred there, culminating in one on 17 May 1911 which seriously endangered the lives of people in the neighbourhood. A representative of a local firm unconnected with the film industry wrote to the *Times* to complain. He pointed out that all the upper parts of the buildings in Cecil Court were residential, and therefore a fire in the building posed an especial danger. In his opinion precautions by the film companies were inadequate, as "from our back windows we can see people handling the films with lighted cigarettes in their mouths". Films, in his opinion, should not be stored in such a densely populated neighbourhood, but in some "isolated position".[9]

This complainant approached the London Country Council (LCC) and the British Parliament, and a few days later the matter was raised in the House of Commons, with the Home Secretary suggesting that legislation was necessary to control the problem. He proposed to the LCC that restrictions should be imposed on the storage and sale of film. The LCC concurred, and initiated plans to license premises where films were stored or sold. However, the danger of film fires had by now become a

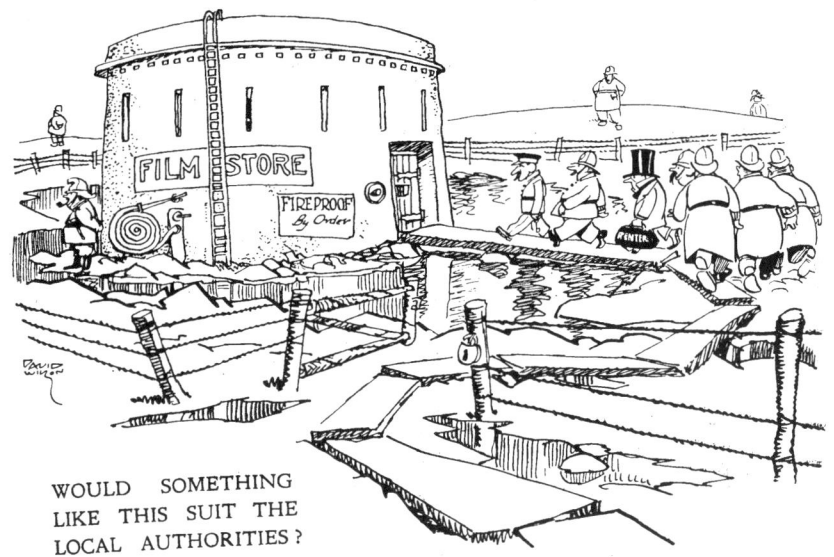

WOULD SOMETHING
LIKE THIS SUIT THE
LOCAL AUTHORITIES?

An editorial cartoon by David Wilson in the British trade journal *Kinematograph Weekly*, 9 December 1920, offers a sardonic response to the concerns of "the authorities" about fire hazards.

British Library, Colindale, London. LD94.

nagging fear in many peoples' minds, and the idea of storing films for archival or other purposes was viewed with trepidation. It seems that this fire danger remained an important reason behind official reluctance (in Britain at least) to institute archival preservation of films. When in 1916 the British Museum was (once again) called on to accept historic films for preservation – notably Herbert Ponting's film of the Scott Antarctic expedition – the Director replied that this matter of archiving films had not been overlooked "but as special risk was incidental to the storage of films" the Trustees were reluctant to agree to it.[10]

Fungal Decay

As well as being at risk of destruction from combustion, it was also realised in the early years of cinema that stored films might face another more insidious enemy. In 1914 an expert on fungi, James Scott, suggested that films could be subject to attack by these micro-organisms, leading to the surface becoming mouldy. This was especially likely if the film had been coated with glycerine, a standard method to keep the material pliable, for glycerine captured dust and "holding it continually against the film, it would thus give the spores opportunities for germination".

The illustration to an article entitled "Films versus Micro-Fungi" by James Scott, published in the British trade journal *Kinematograph and Lantern Weekly*, 24 December 1914.

Stephen Bottomore.

Scott tested some strips of film by soaking them in water and then placing them in test-tubes for several weeks. "It was noticed that they slowly lost their lustre, and the dimness was found to be due to the occurrence all over the surface of very slender, branching, interlacing threads, of the kind shown in Fig. 1.... The whole film surface was similarly covered, and appeared minutely speckled." He explained that this insidious decay took place by the fungi secreting "ferments" which soften the substance they have settled on so that they can better absorb it. In the process the substance is destroyed. If this decay were allowed to proceed on a film, Scott warned, it "would utterly spoil a picture". If one tried to screen such an affected film, "the effect would doubtless be that of a thick fogginess, entirely obliterating the picture". He issued a warning to those who planned to archive films for the long term:

> Unless every circumstance connected with the preparation of films intended for storage in museums for the edification of future

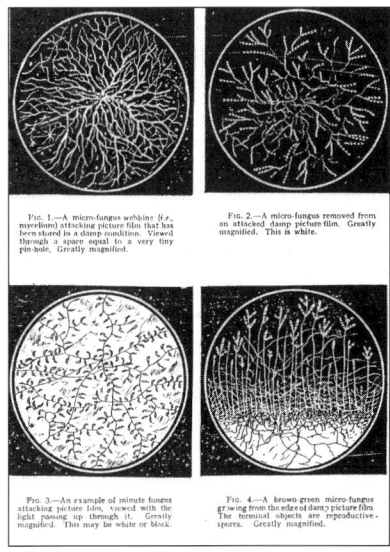

generations is exceptionally propitious, the sealing up of a picture might be analogous to the imprisonment of its enemies (spores exist in myriads in the air) in such a suitable, undisturbed environment that it would be like leaving it to be attacked instead of protecting it.[11]

Junking Films

While stored films would face the risks of fire or fungal disintegration which I have outlined above, at least they had a chance of survival. But many films in the early era were not destined to be stored at all, for most producers and renters in this period had no intention of keeping their films for a day longer than they had to. This was for purely financial reasons. The most profitable period for a film is in the few weeks after its initial release (or a few days, in the case of newsreels).[12] After the first run the film is in less demand and will spend more and more time on the distributor's shelf. In any business excess inventory, especially if it has little prospect of ever making money, is a liability. In order to turn old film prints into profit, the first strategy of early film companies was to sell them at a reduced price on the secondhand market, such prints probably ending up in small local cinemas ("fleapits") or being shown in the more remote parts of the world.

But when all exhibition demand had been exhausted for prints – and indeed negatives – they faced a bleak future. The final few pence could be extracted by recycling the chemicals in the film. (Archivists of a nervous disposition should skip this section.) There is little coverage of this in the early trade press – after all, no one delights in publicising the destruction of their own product – but it seems that it was a well established part of the early film industry. Early film stock was made from a cellulose nitrate (celluloid) base coated with an emulsion containing silver, and both components had some value. It emerged in 1911 that old films were being sold to shoe manufacturers, who treated the celluloid with chemicals, and then used the resultant "glaze" to make the shine on patent leather boots and shoes.[13] The triumphs of film art ending up as mere footwear! A London periodical appreciated the irony, and later that year published a poem on this theme:

> *A Fallen Star*
> Full oft, my boots, have I rejoiced to see
> Your patent radiance, exquisitely glossy,
> Knowing they made your humble wearer (me)
> Appear in every way distinctly dossy.
> But now when I go glittering down the street,
> I'm filled with sorrow, having gained an inkling
> That I possess a "star" upon my feet
> To cause the wondrous "twinkling."
> …[14]

But all this should be taken with a pinch of salt. Harry Rowson, later a stalwart of the British film industry, recorded in his unpublished autobiography that in this same year, 1911, he started out in the business of obtaining celluloid scrap which would be used by patent leather manufacturers. He says that, running short of celluloid from other sources, he tried moving picture film, but that this was not as suitable as other forms of celluloid. (Perhaps because it was contaminated with gelatine from the emulsion?) However, he did find that there was a big demand for waste film as "blank film" or "leader", which could be sold for $15 per reel. He started a business to exploit this product, which he called the Waste Utilisation Company, located at 500 5th Avenue (at 42nd Street) in New York City, and bought such waste from as far afield as the Lumières' business in France.[15] To judge from

Rowson's testimony, while it is possible that some old film was used for patent leather "shine", its use as "leader" would seem to be more likely. Either way, many a silent film must have been destroyed for these paltry ends.

As well as the celluloid base, the silver emulsion could also be reclaimed. The silver content of films had a small value, and this was extracted as a deposit after the films were burnt. An account from early 1914 indicates how this was accomplished in the case of 125,000 feet of negative belonging to the Selig company. A bonfire of this film took place at the premises of Eclipse at Boulogne-sur-Seine in France, and a reporter, shown around by the managing director, Mr Bates, described what he saw:

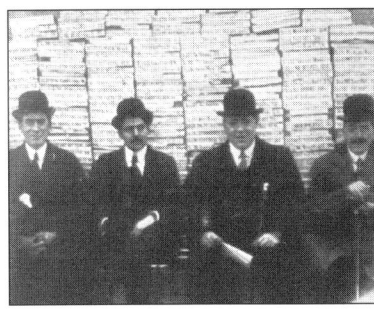

One of the illustrations to the article describing the Eclipse bonfire. The original caption reads: "Some of the Tins of Films".

Stephen Bottomore.

> A pit, properly built and cemented, is arranged near the studio, and after being plunged in water, the films are taken from their tins and thrown in one at a time. When the flames, which occasionally danced up to the height of the adjoining building, became too overpowering, pails of water were thrown in. The fire started about eleven in the morning, and when I left at one o'clock, only a quarter of the stack had been demolished. Mr. Bates told me that afterwards they would clear the ashes and find upwards of £10 worth of silver remaining from the emulsion.[16]

All those irreplaceable negatives destroyed for a mere £10! To the modern film historian and archivist this seems a tragic irony, given the numbers of eagerly-sought "lost films" from the silent period. But to the film companies of the time it made perfect sense. Old films soon became dated in style and technique, and therefore were rarely reissued.[17] Films had a certain, brief shelf-life, after which they were indeed of no more value to the company than the silver in their emulsion and the celluloid in their base. Even the once-lauded Cecil Hepworth's films were sold off to be melted down for aircraft "dope".[18] It was only when a combination of national legislation and profits from reissues became compelling that film companies changed their attitude.

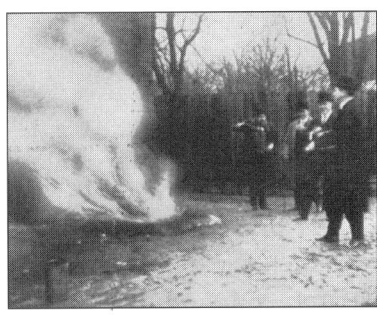

The second illustration to the article describing the Eclipse bonfire. The original caption reads: "The Burning Pit".

Stephen Bottomore.

Notes

1. For an extremely well researched and well presented article on this issue, see David Pierce, "The Legion of the Condemned – Why American Silent Films Perished", reprinted in this volume, after prior publication in *Film History*, v.9, no.1 (1997), pp. 5–22.

2. "Movie Archives To Preserve Historic Scenes", *Literary Digest* (27 November 1926), p. 22.

3. "History by the Cinematograph", *British Journal of Photography* (6 December 1901), p. 783. The letter appeared in French (surely almost inconceivable in English-language journals of today!). The writer was reacting to an article that had appeared in the journal on 22 November, pp. 737–38, under the same heading.

4. "Preserving films", *Kinematograph and Lantern Weekly* (10 August 1911), p. 743.

5. "Uncle Sam's Films – How He Preserves Them", *Views and Films Index* (16 February 1907), n.p.

6. "Uncle Sam's Films – How He Preserves Them", op. cit. In 1929 Edward Foxen Cooper stated, "We know that for 30 years, under suitable conditions of storage, it is possible to reproduce from the original negative a positive copy that can be screened successfully. A practical example of this reproduction will be seen at the public cinemas shortly, when scenes taken during the reigns of Queen Victoria and King Edward VII. will be included in a production." From "Historical Film Records – The Life of the Nation – A Heritage for Posterity", in *The Times* (London), 19 March 1929, "Film Number" section, p. vii.

7. "A National Film Museum", *The Bioscope* (26 May 1910), p. 3.

8. "How Films Should Be Stored", *Kinematograph and Lantern Weekly* (28 April 1910), p. 1380.

9. "Fire in Cecil-Court", letter from Spillman and Co., 101–102 St Martin's Lane, in *The Times*

(London), 19 May 1911, p. 7.

10. "Historic Films – The Difficulty of Preservation", *The Times* (28 November 1916). *Motography* no. 14 (3 April 1915) confirmed that "The British Museum officials decline to store film because of its inflammable nature."

11. James Scott, "Films versus micro-fungi", *Kinematograph and Lantern Weekly* (24 December 1914), pp. 33, 35. With some scepticism, *The Times* reported this suggestion that a film "left untouched for five years... becomes covered with a fungus growth". See "Historic Films – The Difficulty of Preservation", op. cit.

12. Small ads regularly appeared in film trade journals in the early 1910s for old film prints for sale. In the case of news films it is particularly clear that prices dropped with each passing week.

13. "A travers la presse", *Ciné-Journal* (17 June 1911), p. 24; ironically in the adjacent column is a call for the formation of a film archive in France, where people of the year 2000 might see again the world of 1911.

14. "A Fallen Star", *London Opinion* (23 September 1911), p. 454. There are two further verses.

15. Harry Rowson, *Ideals of Wardour Street* (manuscript in BFI Special Collections), pp. 23–26.

16. Stroller, "Paris and the Trade", *Kinematograph and Lantern Weekly* (19 February 1914), pp. 5–6. Stroller's trip was facilitated by Mr Bates, managing director of Eclipse, Radios, and other production companies.

17. Though *The Film Index*, beginning in August 1910, canvassed exhibitors for suggestions of popular films to be revived. Lists of films appeared in the following issues of *The Film Index*: 20 August 1910, p. 2; 27 August 1910, p. 2; 3 September 1910, p. 2; 10 September 1910, p. 2; 17 September 1910, p. 2; 15 October 1910, p. 2; 4 February 1911, p. 3; 8 April 1911, p. 8.

18. Information from British Hepworth historian Fred Lake.

Don't Try This at Home: Some Thoughts on Nitrate Film, with Particular Reference to Home Movie Systems

by David Cleveland

Although the 1897 Bazar de la Charité fire in Paris is the most famous, and the "Newmarket Blaze" of 7 September 1907, in which at least one woman died, is the one closest to the residents of the part of England where the East Anglian Film Archive is based today, these were just two of the many fires that occurred at cinematograph shows in the early days. Early projectors were not really designed with safety in mind. The reels of film on the projector were not enclosed in containers. Some did not have a take-up spool, and it was not uncommon for film to fall to the floor once it had been through the projector, where it lay vulnerable to any stray carbon fragment or cigarette end. Many projectors had front shutters, offering no protection from the light source, so that often when the operator was "lacing up", the hot light might fall directly on the film in the gate before he had started to turn the handle. If the film stopped for some reason in the gate during the show, again it would catch fire. Many projectors of this time did not have safety shutters that automatically cut off the light source if there were a problem. The heat of the illuminant, whether it was gas, arc, limelight, or whatever, was intense. Water in a glass container between the light and the projector was one method that was suggested to cut down the amount of heat that reached the nitrate film.

The thought of a hot light source (quite often a naked flame), the nitrate film in the machine, and a roll of possibly several hundred feet on the top spool arm, together with the audience in close proximity, seems absurd today, but then the cinematograph was the latest wonder, and all thought of danger was pushed aside. Nitro-cellulose film was certainly a hazard, but it was the only flexible support available for movie film at that time. There were those who wanted a safer film, and others who just did not want to know.

In November 1897 *The Optical Magic Lantern Journal* announced: "Those who have been scared with the absurd thought that celluloid films are dangerous to use as they are very inflammable can console themselves with the report that they can be made uninflammable as follows:– ordinary celluloid is dissolved in acetone and a solution of magnesium chloride in alcohol added". What became of this idea we do not know. In the June issue of 1899 a new film was announced that was fireproof. It was called Flexoid, but nothing seems to have come of this intended product.

Authorities were obviously trying to do something about the dangers of this highly inflammable material where they could. A report of a fire caused by nitrate film at the Hammersmith Theatre of Varieties in March 1899 noted that the fire was contained because the projector was housed in a fireproof room built to a design approved by the London County Council. The LCC had approved regulations in November 1898 regarding the exhibition of cinematograph films in premises licensed by them. Basically, the regulations stated that the projector should "stand in a fire-proof room which shall be entirely enclosed". The regulations went on to say that all films must be kept in metal cases when not being shown, that competent operators should be employed, and that "where possible the electric arc light shall be adopted as an illuminant".

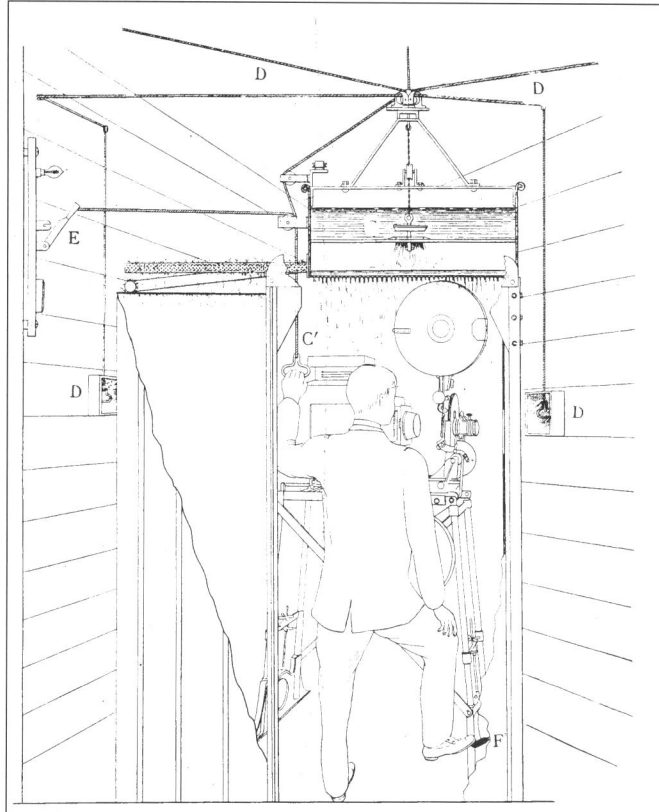

A "flushing cistern" system to douse projector fires, advertised in France as the "Cabine Extincteur P. Ruez". Stephen Bottomore, who suggested this illustration, commented: "surely one of the silliest anti-fire inventions ever for cinemas."

Laurent Mannoni Collection.

There were inventions to quench cinematograph fires, like the "flushing cistern" above the projector. *The Bioscope* reported a demonstration in December 1908: "the cistern's valve action is adjusted so that when the film was set on fire by a match the flames burned through a cotton cord attached to the valve apparatus, the valve opened, and the blaze was instantaneously drenched out by the water from the sprinkler." Critics did not like it because it was "drenching a valuable machine and destroying perhaps fifty pounds worth of films". Actually, it is surprising that the report suggests that the device succeeded in putting out the fire, because once nitrate starts to burn, nothing will stop it. Water will only extinguish a nitrate fire if it is caught in the first few seconds.

After films for the general public came the idea for moving pictures in the home. In 1898 the film pioneer Birt Acres made a narrow-gauge film camera-cum-projector for home use. This used 17.5mm film, which was basically 35mm cut in half – nitrate, of course.

In 1899 another home cinematograph projector came on the market – the Biokam. This was more successful than its predecessor. It also used 17.5mm film, but this time it was specially slit and perforated, with the sprocket hole in the middle of the film on the frameline. This meant that no one could easily buy 35mm film and adapt it to the Biokam. The Biokam film must have been treated in some way, for it is not quite nitrate and not quite safety. In chemical tests it floats between the two. (The "flotation test" is one of the standard ways of testing for nitrate film. A small piece from the side of the film is cut out and dropped into a beaker of trichloroethylene. Safety film will float, and nitrate will sink.) This ambiguous result is possibly the result of experiments to make the highly combustible celluloid film less flammable by adding "various metallic salts". Someone was thus evidently concerned about the use of highly flammable film in the home, but as there was no "safety" or non-flammable film generally available, home systems continued for the time being to use nitrate film, whatever the gauge.

In 1903 the Ernemann Kino was put on the market for the home user, again with 17.5mm specially-perforated nitrate film. In the same advertisements, the Ernemann Kino for "standard size film" was being offered to amateurs. Using 35mm for home movies must have been dangerous and expensive, but there were those who used the full-size gauge for their new hobby.

Another way for small pieces of nitrate film to find their way into the home was by way of a visit to the "pictures". Projectionists have been known not only to keep the odd frame of a favourite film as a memento for themselves, but even on occasion to provide a similar service for favoured patrons.[1] Some exhibitors turned the practice into a business venture: it was a way for them to get rid of worn out prints. "The idea is to announce a souvenir night after the film has had its life's run, cut the celluloid up into small lengths, and present each person attending on the souvenir night with a part of the famous picture." One enterprising exhibitor did this in 1900, and sold each clip for one penny per packet. "I often drew as much as 6/- or 7/- each night." Seven shillings in Britain's old pre-decimal currency (which is what "7/-" indicates) would have represented 84 one-penny packets of nitrate film carried home to unsuspecting households!

There was still a recognised need for a non-flammable film base, and there must have been a race behind the scenes to produce a "non flam" film, as it was called, for two safety film stocks came on the market within a year of one another.

"The licensed manufacturers have the non-inflammable film on the market at last," reported the *Kinematograph and Lantern Weekly* in July 1909. "Thus far no adverse criticisms regarding the new stock have been heard, nor can it be said that enthusiasm over its introduction has run to a high pitch. The explanation for this is that both renters and exhibitors are awaiting the results of practical use. Many are sceptical regarding it, but up to the present time there appears to be no justification for scepticism." This report was prompted by the fact that the Lumières' London office was advertising "Lumière Non Flam Positive – The First and Only Commercial – The Film of The Future" in *The Bioscope* in March 1909. In a further advertisement, in July 1909, the manufacturer claimed: "Lumière non-inflammable Positive Film ... Possesses all the high qualities of the Lumière Ordinary Positive, and yields prints of extraordinary brilliance and great durability." In 1910 Kodak put their first safety film on the market.

There was, however, no great rush by the industry to supply prints on the new acetate-based safety film stock. It seems it was not liked, mainly because, it has been said, it was more expensive than nitrate film. It also seems that the acetate base was not as durable as celluloid. The prints wore out quicker. The exhibitors believed the image on the screen was not as clear and sharp as that on celluloid-base films. It was more brittle, and tended to shrink. The new safety film was used by a few producers of educational and scientific films, but this was a specialised market.

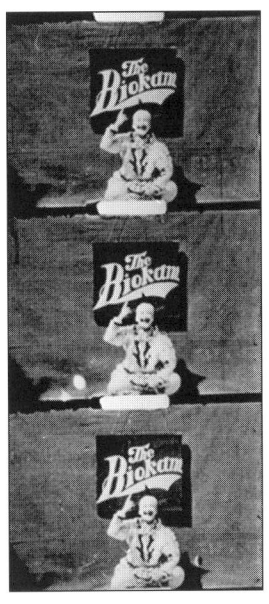

"Not quite nitrate and not quite safety" – 17.5mm Biokam film.

East Anglian Film Archive, Norwich.

Around 1912/1913 *Pathé's Animated Gazette*, a cinema newsreel issued twice a week in the United Kingdom by "Pathé Frères Cinema Ltd.", was printed on safety stock. The production company went so far as to incorporate this fact into its product – the words "safety film" appeared on the main title, and the phrase "printed on safety film" recurred on the individual intertitles that introduced each story. Whether this was a way of reassuring the audience or just an advertisement for the main (French) Pathé company is not known.

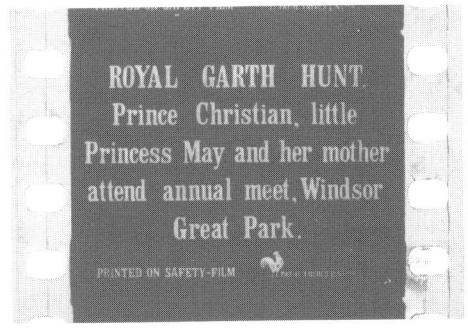

Pathé's Animated Gazette advertises its safety film credentials.
(See also Colour Section 1.)

East Anglian Film Archive, Norwich.

Despite occasional experiments such as this, the cinema industry stuck to celluloid for their projection prints. Consequently there were many fires, a fact which is confirmed by a look through the trade magazines of the time.

In Britain, the 1909 Cinematograph Act helped to safeguard audiences and to keep any fires under control. Among other things, it stated that there had to be adequate exits; there were to be no obstructions in the gangways; water and sand buckets had to be available; fire extinguishers had to be provided; projectors were to be in a fireproof room with portholes for the projection of the film; no smoking was allowed in the projection room; and projectors had to be fitted with metal spool boxes. These are just a few of the rules and orders of the Act, which came into force in 1910. The result was that "Picture Palaces" and "Electric Theatres" began to be built. The cinema began to have its own purpose-built home.

There were also improvements for those showing films in the home. In 1912 two home systems were launched that used specially slit and perforated safety film: Edison introduced his Home Kinetoscope, using film 22mm wide, with three rows of pictures running vertically down the film, and Pathé brought out their superior 28mm "Pathé-Kok" system.

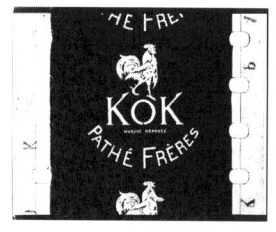

28mm film for the "Pathé-Kok" system.

East Anglian Film Archive, Norwich.

The Pathé product was the more successful of the two. The Pathé-Kok projector had a dynamo to power the light: as the handle was turned to transport the film, the light came on. The 28mm film was of excellent quality, and the system was backed with a huge library of films on safety stock that could be hired, or bought outright. The latest "cinema" films soon found their way onto the 28mm gauge. A camera was also put on the market for those who wanted to shoot their own films. The 28mm negative film used in the camera was nitrate stock. This did not matter, as the negative would not have been run on a projector. All positives were on safety stock.

Before World War I, Pathé had started work on an even smaller gauge of film, 9.5mm. Work stopped during the war, but restarted as soon as it ended, and in December 1922 Pathé launched 9.5mm as a home cinema system, under the name "Pathé-Baby". Again, there was soon a library of cinema films available, though often considerably cut down in length to make them more affordable. Next there was a camera for customers to make their own films.

All 9.5mm film was on safety stock, both camera film and projector film. Pathéscope, the company in the UK that promoted 9.5mm, always emphasised that it was safety. One of their pieces of advertising in 1935, however, suggested that not all their competitors were as trustworthy. It warned, underneath a red triangle containing the words "Safety Film": "Be sure your films are non-inflammable. Insist upon getting Pathéscope Films in the genuine package bearing a red triangle. The films giving easily the longest projection duration. Beware of celluloid imitations which are dangerous." There are two possible reasons for this last

Left to right: standard 8mm, 9.5mm, 16mm, 35mm.

East Anglian Film Archive, Norwich.

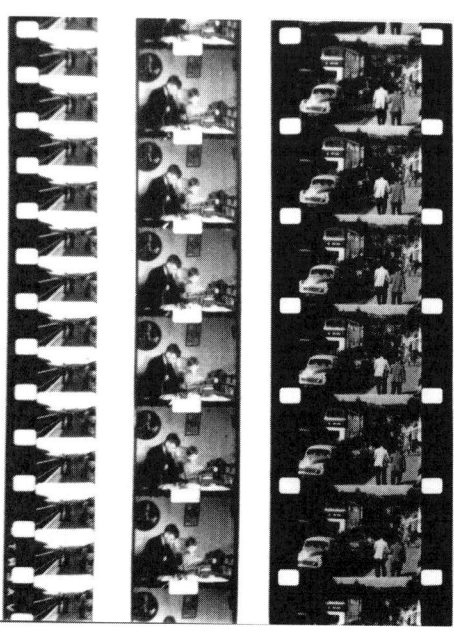

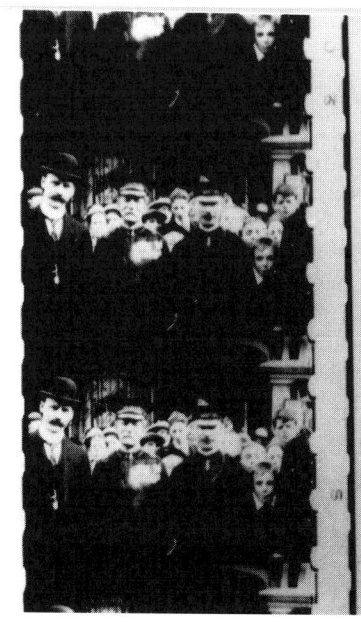

statement. The more probable is that it was an advertising ploy: that Pathéscope simply wanted to get the customer to buy their film. Another reason, however, is that perhaps there was some other manufacturer who did issue, or was thinking about making, 9.5mm film from nitrate stock. As far as this author knows, no 9.5mm nitrate stock has been found. An archivist should, however, always keep this possibility in mind when an unusual piece of 9.5mm is encountered.

In 1923, Kodak launched the 16mm gauge as a home movie-making outfit. The Cine-Kodak, as it was known, also used safety film in the camera, and in its Kodascope projector. Again, there were libraries of Kodascope films on 16mm. There are persistent stories in circulation of some 16mm nitrate being found – sometimes attributed to production in the old USSR. There are few documented encounters with 16mm nitrate film,[2] but that does not mean it could not happen again. Once again, an archivist should always just check. Most 16mm reversal film was made by Kodak, and has the words "safety film" written down the side of the film. Sometimes, though, there is nothing, particularly when it is a print from a negative. If there is any doubt, this is the time for an archivist to check and make sure.

Cine-Kodak 8, or "Standard 8mm" as we know it today, was introduced by Kodak in 1932 as a home movie-making outfit using safety film throughout.

Returning to the subject of standard-size 35mm cinema film, in 1916 controls were brought in concerning the manufacture and storage of celluloid film. Professional film remained on nitrate, despite stories that a switch to "non-flam" in one country or another, or internationally, was imminent. In the *Kinematograph Year Book* for 1928, for example, there is mention of a scheme for a factory at Liverpool to produce a non-inflammable film base. Nothing seems to have come of it, even though it was stated, "a factory has now been taken." Another section records: "In the meantime, the French Government at long last decided to put into operation on January 1st, 1928, the regulation for the compulsory use of non-flam film."

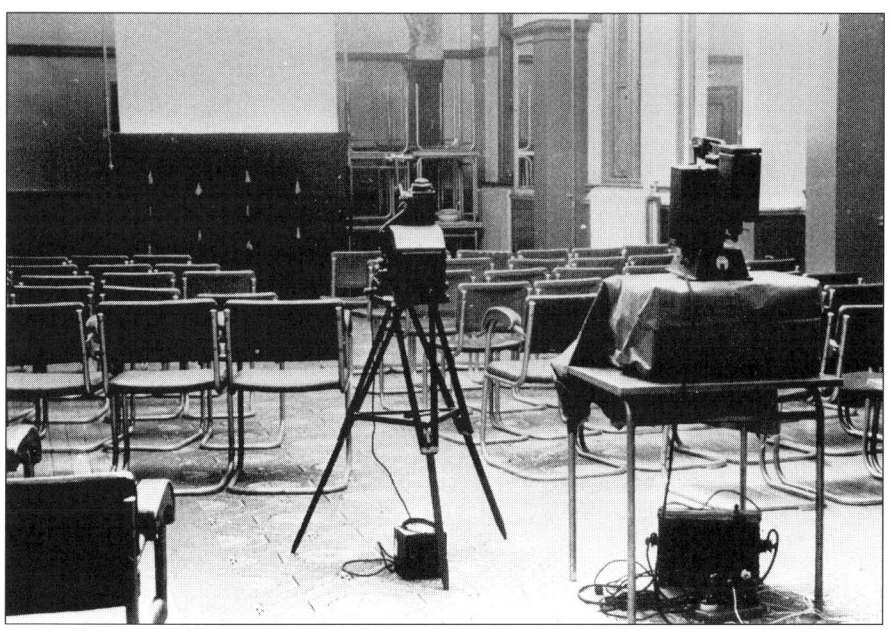

A typical film show set up in a community hall, ca. 1938, with a 16mm Kodak A projector and a 9.5mm Pathéscope projector – both using safety film.

East Anglian Film Archive, Norwich.

In the early 1930s the firm Spicers, of Sawston, in Cambridgeshire, was experimenting with a new colour process, Dufaycolor. This was basically a black-and-white system, the colour coming from microscopic lines of colour printed on the base of the film. These lines crossed one another, producing dots of colour. Though Dufaycolor was not the success the promoters had hoped for in the theatrical market, there are a few 35mm Dufaycolor films of the 1930s in existence. They are usually on safety stock, as the printing inks adhered better to safety base than nitrate stock.

The Projectionist's Handbook for 1933 states that "regulations should be hung up in every box" so that the projectionist would be reminded of the dangers of using nitrate film. "Never start a show without a quick glance round to make sure that all fire fighting equipment is in its place". Specific hints include the following:

> "It seems a wiser plan to keep an asbestos blanket unfolded, thus saving valuable seconds in the rush when it has to be gathered and flung over burning film."

> "Above all, because the indirect results of even a small fire are more serious than any question of money or damage to property, do all you can to deceive the audience into sitting still. If the show can be kept going – keep it going."

Because of entirely justified fears that a panic could be more damaging than the fire itself, if a fire did break out it was suggested that staff could pass information among themselves in whispered voices using a code phrase such as "Mr Sand has arrived", meaning there was a fire. Perhaps this was a code to use the sand buckets that were kept handy for such occasions. Cinemas would also have a recognised "fire record" which the projectionist might play over the public-address system to alert fellow staff members that a problem was being dealt with.

In 1939 an "indestructible metal film" was said to be about to arrive on the market. This metal alloy film, it was said, would have the advantage of not shrinking, would be capable of withstanding considerable heat, would give absolute permanence to the film (being completely non-corrodible and rust-proof), and would be cheaper than existing film. The "film" was said to be 1/250th of an inch thick, and capable of being coated with an emulsion in the normal way.

Whether this was to be a replacement for inflammable nitrate film was not stated by the company, the Taylor Sloane Corporation of New York. They did, however, note that, in order to project the resulting film, "Some slight modification of the apparatus is needed, since the light must fall on the face of the film and be reflected back from the bright surface of the metal (through the image in the emulsion) into the projection lens." The conversion of all cinema projectors for reflected light, a far from "slight" modification, seems improbable to say the least. One wonders how the "film" would have been joined, and what sort of noise it would have made when running through the projector. Although no more seems to have been said about the invention, there are some examples of metal film in existence.

In 1948 Kodak produced a safety stock that was no more expensive than nitrate. Kodak triacetate was given many tests, and found to be "for all practical purposes the equal of nitrate". Gevaert also produced a safety stock, acetate butyrate.

The new safety stock proved difficult to join. Where the old nitrate stock had been easy to splice using the methods described by Harold Brown elsewhere in this volume, safety film was more difficult. Robert Rigby, the film equipment maker and supplier, made special 35mm "safety" joiners for cinema operators. Projectionists complained, however, that it took longer to make a join. The emulsion was harder to scrape off. Usually, a splicer was needed to hold the film in position while the emulsion was removed with a special scraper or a razor blade, and then to hold the join under pressure for 20 or so seconds, until it was "done".

Nonetheless, the new safety stock was soon accepted, and in 1950 the production of nitrate base film in the USA ceased. In the UK, production stopped in 1951. But that was not the end of celluloid. There was still stock on the shelves to be used up. It is not uncommon to come across a cut negative of the mid-1950s with nitrate and safety spliced together. Prints on nitrate stock continued to circulate around British cinemas for another ten years. As time went on, a "nitrate film" notice was cut into the leader of the film to warn the projectionist. An archivist needs to know if films dating from this change-over period are definitely safety or nitrate. The best method of determining this is the "flotation test" (described earlier in this article).

Has nitrate film disappeared yet? No. It is surprising how much nitrate film still exists in archives, in private vaults, in laboratories, and in the homes of film collectors. The presence of nitrate sometimes can be quickly detected just by walking into a film collector's home – by its distinctive smell. The problem is that few collectors realise that storing nitrate can invalidate house insurance. The storage of nitrate has to be licensed, or at least reported to the authorities. The transport of nitrate is now becoming a difficult issue, and it will not be long before regulations require nitrate to be moved by specialists.

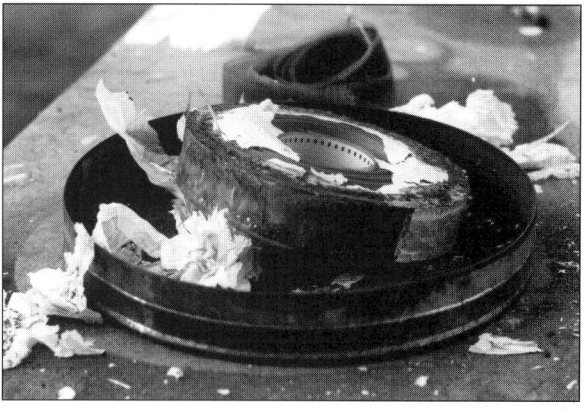

35mm nitrate film in a state of severe decomposition: this reel is beyond saving.

East Anglian Film Archive, Norwich.

The extraordinary thing is that celluloid is still being made. At Brantham, in Suffolk, England, Wardle Storeys still make celluloid, as they have done on the site since the 1880s. It is not for motion-picture film, however – it is now used solely for capsules for explosive material. The advantage is that it burns quickly, and leaves little residue. Apparently, nothing else does this job so efficiently. In 1999, a batch was made at the factory for the Ministry of Defence. The cost? Reportedly £34,000 per ton.

Notes

1. For example, I was recently shown a letter sent to the Imperial War Museum Film and Video Archive in June 1995, referring to a newsreel extract which the correspondent had just seen in a programme marking the 50th anniversary of the end of the Second World War. "The last time I saw this," he wrote, "was as a boy when I dashed to the projection room of my local cinema in 1944 and asked for a frame or two. It shows my old next door neighbour from Dundee." Roger Smither of the IWMFVA had annotated the letter: "No wonder films reach archives incomplete!"

2. *Editor's note: one such came in a letter to Roger Smither from Ken Locke, of Greenford, Middlesex, UK dated 25 October 1999 and received while this book was in preparation.* The relevant passage reads as follows: "In the early '60s, I hoped to demonstrate how 16mm safety base was of low flammability to a trainee in the cutting rooms at the BBC. I clipped a piece from a Soviet documentary which had lain in the cutting room for years unwanted, and put a match to it – Whoosh! Russian 16mm was not only uncommon, but nitrate! This was the only Russian 16mm I ever came across, so I do not know if this was an oddity – or standard in the USSR at that time."

The Degradation and Disappearance of Cellulose Nitrate Objects

by Sylvia Katz

Woody: "Tuesday night's plastic corrosion awareness meeting was, I think, a big success." *Toy Story* (USA, 1995)

Dramatic fires in cinema booths caused by inflammable cellulose nitrate film are legendary, but cellulose nitrate (celluloid) as a coating or in a more solid and mouldable form was also the material used to make a wide variety of inflammable products which found their way into our homes, such as collars and cuffs, mirrors and combs, cutlery handles and clock cases, jewellery, pens, and toys.

Cellulose nitrate is made from cellulose in the form of cotton which is treated with nitric and sulphuric acids. Cellulose nitrate with a 12–13% nitrogen content is better known as an explosive, guncotton, and 90% of the time taken in processing celluloid sheets for moulding is concerned with getting rid of the combustible nitrate solvent through evaporation. Early cine-film had a higher nitrogen level than the less-combustible sheets from which solid domestic celluloid objects were fabricated, while later film stock was made from conventional 11% nitrogen celluloid. Nevertheless, although hazardous, this did not prevent gentlemen in the 1890s who enjoyed smoking from wearing inflammable collars, nor ladies from wearing large, ornate combs in their hair while taking tea beside the fire.

Nor did it prevent somewhat inappropriate uses of this new moulding material in the 19th and early 20th century. One of the first applications developed by John Wesley Hyatt, who with his brother patented and successfully commercialised celluloid in 1869, was as a convincing substitute for ivory in the manufacture of billiard balls at a time when ivory was growing scarce due to over-demand. It is not surprising that a few problems were encountered, although the verdict on whether they were true or apocryphal must be left open. "A lighted cigar applied (to a ball) would at once result in a serious flame," Hyatt is reported to have said, adding, "occasionally the violent contact of the balls would produce a mild explosion like a percussion guncap. We had a letter from a billiard saloon proprietor in Colorado mentioning this fact, and saying that he did not care so much about it, but that instantly every man in the room pulled a gun."

Flammability proved to be the downfall of celluloid, but the exact number of fires it caused will never be known. Its production was hazardous, and fires are recorded to have completely destroyed the stock and machinery of cellulose nitrate manufacturers. Today, however, the products of this historical industry are highly collectable, provided they are still in good condition, which means free of degradation. And here lies the rub.

It was only in the 1980s that museums and collectors began to seriously heed the fact that certain plastics artefacts were showing disturbing symptoms of decomposition – warping, embrittlement, crazing, and stickiness. Beautiful exhibits in collections around the world were definitely sick, and cellulose nitrate and cellulose acetate (the two main cellulose esters), together with PVC, seemed to be the worst affected. In 1991 the Plastics Historical Society (PHS) in Britain responded by co-publishing with the Museums & Galleries Commission the first guide to tackling the problem: *Conservation of Plastics – An Introduction*, by John Morgan.

The cellulosic plastics usually emit acidic products as they degrade, and if the decomposing objects are not removed and isolated, these acid fumes can cause further reactions which can further speed up decomposition and the eventual destruction of the object itself. Worse, cellulose-based objects close by can also be infected, and even packaging can be attacked. It is a shock to touch the tissue paper wrapped around a celluloid object only to have the paper disintegrate into fragments. Although the celluloid itself may look in good condition, the destruction of the paper is a sign that the plastic is giving off fumes and is on its way out.

Different plastic materials have different conservation requirements. An ABS camera, for example, can be stained by plasticiser migrating from a PVC strap. Pity the conservator caring for a collection of objects made from a mixture of plastics. In addition, some plastics are hygroscopic and prefer a stable, higher humidity environment.

A useful tool for detecting acidic vapours has been found in old plastic silver-rimmed British Telecom phonecards. If a BT card is placed next to but not touching a celluloid object and the silver rim slowly disappears to reveal the dark plastic card below, this is a sure sign that there is acid in the air indicating decomposition. Good ventilation is always crucial for the display and storage of cellulosic plastics.

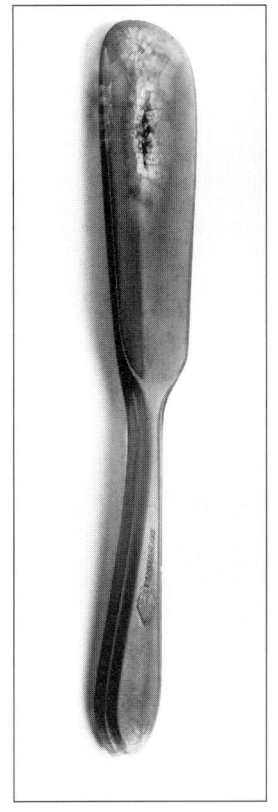

Decomposing celluloid shoehorn, USA. Photograph by Ken Kirkwood. (See also Colour Section 1.)

© Katz Collection.

The conservator responsible for a collection of plastics, and also rubber which is a member of the family of organic materials, probably faces the most serious problems affecting modern materials. Like a doctor, he is trained to look after and preserve his charges, and yet most of these objects were not made with museums in mind and were not created to last forever. However, in the plastics industry a new attitude exists towards designing either for a long and useful life or for recycling. In the arts world, certain artists have left instructions for prolonging the life of their work. The constructivist artist Naum Gabo, for example, was one of the first artists to experiment with plastics. Tragically, most of his early work in cellulose nitrate and cellulose acetate is beyond saving, and some pieces have completely "disintegrated". When polymethyl methacrylate – acrylic (Perspex) – became available in the 1930s, Gabo was able to translate his ideas into this new, more stable, transparent plastic sheet, which he strung with nylon filament to create the kinetic works he is best known for. Gabo left instructions that if his work does not look as "pristine" as he intended, the nylon filaments are to be replaced. In fact, many have yellowed and snapped, such as his sculpture entitled *Linear Construction No 1* (1942–43).

Tony Cragg is a British artist who produced works in the early 1980s composed of discarded plastics salvaged from roadsides and riverbanks, which had therefore already suffered accelerated degradation before being recycled into art. After 19 years, thanks to controlled museum conditions, the plastics pieces still look as brightly coloured as they were when found. Cragg, too, has left instructions that if any parts of his work are lost, replacements are to picked up along any river or road.

A "plastic" is not a single resin-type material, as might be supposed. It is a basic polymer (or polymers), which needs different kinds of additives incorporated in order to be processed, moulded, and usable. For example, a plasticiser may have to be added to ensure that the material flows more easily during processing and to help make the finished product softer and more flexible. Other additives help counteract the environmental effects of ozone which causes oxidation. Unfortunately, over time, plasticisers can migrate to the surface of certain plastics and pollute the atmosphere inside a display or storage case and affect surrounding objects. Other unseen forces are at work, too. When plastics, including celluloid film, are moulded, unavoidable stresses are locked into the material. Artists who work with acrylic (Perspex) must anneal their work afterwards to relieve these in-built stresses; otherwise, they can appear later as crazing and stress cracking.

All this gives the impression that a plastics conservator's work is an almost hopeless task. The bad news is that there are even more problems. A private collector may clean or repair his plastics with substances that would horrify a museum archivist, who prefers, if possible, the non-invasive approach. And the private enthusiast usually handles his collection without protective cotton gloves and may pass his prized objects round the greasy and acidic hands of friends and family.

Despite all these hazards it is astonishing how many beautiful celluloid artefacts still survive in perfect condition. But it must never be forgotten that all plastics are considered ultimately unstable. The clock is ticking, and natural ageing processes, some faster than others, are running their course. Derek Pullen, Head of Sculpture Conservation at Tate Britain and Tate Modern, acknowledges that plastics cannot be preserved forever, but his team is devising many ways of dealing with the problem. For example, a same-size hologram has been made of the warped and darkened Gabo sculpture *Construction in Space: Two Cones* (1927), before its final collapse and death. A replica can now be made from this for future educational and research purposes, and for providing a record in 3D of the artist's vision.

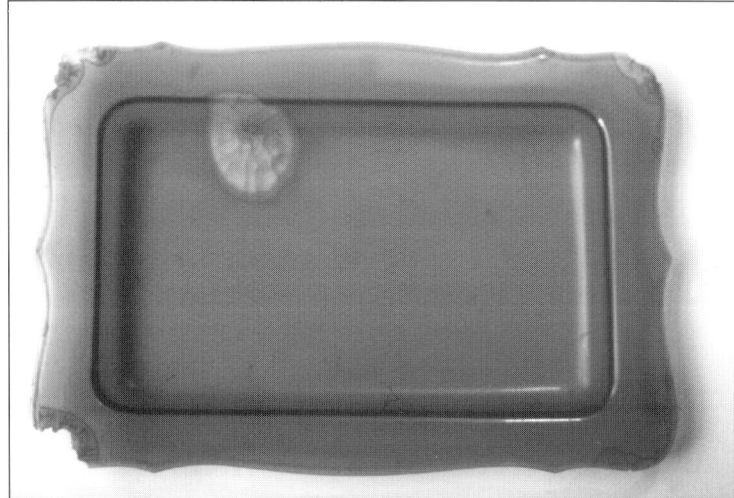

Decomposing cellulose nitrate dressing table tray, 1920s. (See also Colour Section 1.)

© Katz Collection.

In line with modern medicine and dentistry, the key word is "prevention". Preventive conservation is, as John Morgan wrote in the book mentioned above, the prime hope for the salvage of plastics. Work is being carried out on this subject around the world, and a recently published book, *Plastics Collecting and Conserving*, edited by Anita Quye and Colin Williamson, takes this research much further and provides valuable information for all collectors and conservators. In the meantime, until conservation scientists come up with better solutions, the best that can be done is to try and store our treasures in ideal conditions: cool, dark, well-ventilated, humidity-controlled underground bunkers, where relics from a bygone era are individually isolated and only handled with gloves.

One small product is still in production today as a reminder of the special place celluloid holds in our lives. The table tennis ball is still made from two heat-shaped pieces of cellulose nitrate glued together, because no modern synthetic material can match its lightness, flexibility, and the sound which gives it its popular name – ping-pong.

References

1. Morris Kaufman, *The First Century of Plastics: Celluloid and Its Sequel* (London: Plastics Institute, 1963).

2. John Morgan, *Conservation of Plastics – An Introduction* (London: Plastics Historical Society/The Conservation Unit, Museums & Galleries Commission, 1991).

3. Derek Pullen, "Managing Change. The Conservation of Plastic Sculptures", in Jackie Heuman, ed., *Material Matters. The Conservation of Modern Sculpture* (London: Tate Gallery Publishing, 1999).

4. Anita Quye and Colin Williamson, eds., *Plastics Collecting and Conserving* (Edinburgh: NMS Publishing Ltd, 1999).

The Film Industry's Conversion from Nitrate to Safety Film in the Late 1940s: A Discussion of the Reasons and Consequences

by Leo Enticknap

Introduction

The use of new technologies within the film industry has traditionally happened in two stages: the research and development of the technology itself, and its subsequent commercial exploitation. In some instances, most notably the introduction of synchronous sound, these two processes were closely connected. Indeed, as a number of historians have pointed out, the financial resources necessary for the development of the Warner Brothers' Vitaphone system to the point of entering mass-production were made available with the expressed intention of commercially exploiting it in an attempt to gain an advantage over their business rivals.[1] The Technicolor corporation, with their beam-splitting camera and dye-transfer printing technique, was another example of the development and commercial exploitation of new technologies taking place in an integrated context.

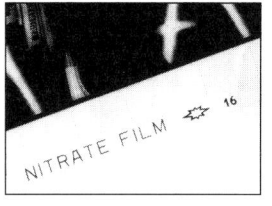

Edge marking – nitrate film.
East Anglian Film Archive, Norwich.

In other cases, however, these two phases have been separated by significant lapses of time, or were instigated by different individuals and organisations. Single-strip colour, and the technique of dye-coupling which enabled it, were originally invented by the Nazis, but were not used on a global scale until the US and Soviet film industries took over the patents in the late 1940s.[2] Despite the invention and limited use of both 70mm and anamorphic cinematography in the late 1920s, widescreen production did not begin on any significant scale until the mid-1950s, when these two methods were adopted by Todd-AO and Twentieth Century-Fox respectively.[3] Stereo optical sound-on-film, despite having been successfully demonstrated by Alan Blumlein in 1936, was not exploited commercially until Ray Dolby began marketing equipment in 1976. And digitally recorded sound, despite having been on sale to domestic consumers in the form of compact discs since 1983, was not available to film exhibitors until the near-simultaneous launch of three competing formats in 1992.

The technology which I shall consider in this paper differs significantly from the examples given above in that it does not fit into either of these categories quite as easily. The development and commercial introduction of safety film – that is, film stock which is not so highly inflammable, and potentially explosive, that special safety procedures are necessary wherever it is handled – took place gradually over the first half of the 20th century. But the exact form of this technology, which enabled it to supersede cellulose nitrate (inflammable) stock, was developed and launched in a comparatively short time scale, in the decade or so immediately following World War II. I will present a brief historical overview of the conversion process, and consider why the development and adoption of safety film has so few similarities with that of other comparable processes of technological change in the history of the film industry.

Safety Stocks before the Conversion

Although there was no safety film available which equalled the durability and mechanical tolerances of nitrate until the final stage of research and development that led to the industry's wholesale conversion, non-flammable stocks were being marketed a lot earlier. Arguably, the earliest sign of activity in this area was in 1904, when W C Parkin, a French chemist, was granted a patent for a method of inhibiting the flammability of nitrate by adding a soluble metallic salt to the base.[4] Research into inherently non-inflammable cellulose suitable for use as photographic film also took place during this period, as a technical writer noted in an article published in early 1950:

> Much of the literature on cellulose plastics published during the period 1905–1910 contains numerous references to the triacetate of cellulose [the safety base film to which the industry finally converted]. In fact, as early as 1910 the nitrates, acetates, formates, propionates, butyrates, palmitates, stearates, benzoates, acetonitrates, acetopropionates, acetobutyrates, propiono-butyrates, etc., of cellulose had been the subjects of intensive research.[5]

While cellulose acetate stocks did establish a market foothold in some applications, most notably still photography, this research had very little impact on the manufacture of moving image film stocks, which continued to be almost exclusively on nitrate. Consumers of the stock gradually evolved working practices intended to minimise the fire risk, encouraged by various combinations of legislation and industry self-regulation. In Britain, the 1909 Cinematograph Act required all premises where nitrate film was present and to which the public were admitted to be licensed by the local authority, following a number of fatal accidents earlier in the decade.[6] It was this piece of legislation which provided the basis for most aspects of Government regulation of the film industry in Britain, most importantly censorship. This was because the Act gave local authorities the right to grant or withdraw operating licences to cinemas, but did not restrict the criteria for doing so to issues of fire safety.[7] It is interesting to note that this legal situation gave rise to one of the few significant instances of safety stock being used for theatrical film exhibition before the conversion, as the 1909 Act exempted the use of "non-flam" from its provisions. The film society movement, private organisations, and some individuals were thus able to show safety prints on unlicensed premises which had not been approved by the British Board of Film Censors, as such exhibitions could not be subjected to any legal regulation. When a Home Office committee issued a report in August 1939 advising that no such regulation should be imposed, it was welcomed by the liberal press as a cultural safeguard:

> It [the report] is of permanent importance since it establishes the right of societies which may want to study foreign or other films that do not meet with the approval of the British Board of Film Censors to continue to do so if they obtain them in slow-burning form.[8]

Cinema exhibitors, however, took a different view. "Trade Safeguards Ignored" was the headline one industry publication used to describe the report, sarcastically opining that its main recommendation was "obviously based on the false assumption that all such films were educational".[9] The article detailed a number of concerns raised by cinema owners, ranging from unlicensed, unregulated operators undercutting their admission prices and driving them out of business to the unhindered distribution of pornography.

In the US, there was also industry opposition to safety film, although in this case it came from a more specific lobby – the National Projectionists' Union, who feared that their influential position within the industry would be threatened by the abolition of the special handling precautions necessitated by the use of nitrate.[10]

The use of safety film as a way of circumventing the censor was mainly due to a legal anomaly which only affected Britain. The other, more widespread application for this technology prior to the conversion began with the commercial launch of a new film format in 1923, one that was intended for use by amateurs: 16mm. While other "home movie" gauges such as 28mm, 17.5mm, and 9.5mm also went on the market at around the same time, 16mm is especially significant because (a) it was produced exclusively on safety stock (initially on a diacetate base), and (b) it eventually made the transition from an amateur to a professional medium. As I shall argue, it was this process which was partly responsible for safety film making a similar transition, and its eventual use in 35mm stocks. But it was the amateur market which necessitated the use of safety film to begin with; as Brian Winston puts it, "…there was a clear understanding that, for amateurs, nitrate was simply too dangerous."[11] Indeed, George Eastman himself expressed his belief that the use of safety film was essential to any successful amateur gauge. In a letter of June 1912 to the Edison Company, he wrote: "… in our opinion, the furnishing of cellulose nitrate for such a purpose [amateur cinematography] would be wholly indefensible and reprehensible."[12] It would seem that, at the time, his was a minority view. Of 41 amateur film systems sold to the public between 1898 and 1923, only 10 used safety stock.[13] 16mm was certainly the first major film format to be produced exclusively on safety, and aggressively marketed to consumers on that basis.

The use of this format remained primarily in the amateur domain until World War II, when the need to transport films to and show them at temporary locations which could not be equipped for the safe handling of nitrate resulted in the widening use of 16mm. The Allied armed forces decided to adopt 16mm as its standard gauge for the distribution of training and propaganda films, as well as for reduction prints of Hollywood features for entertainment purposes.[14] Other Western government agencies began to use 16mm for civilian applications. This adoption of 16mm in the semi-professional domain was made possible, in part, by further improvements to safety base technology introduced in 1937. The new cellulose acetate-propionate stock used propionic acid as the organic solvent in which the cellulose was dissolved to produce a flexible material (as opposed to acetic or butyric acid),[15] with the result that the new stock was considerably more durable than any existing safety film at the time. The Kodak scientist whose research paved the way for the industry's eventual conversion estimated that acetate-propionate stock "afforded physical qualities midway between cellulose nitrate and the former acetate".[16] Acetate-propionate enabled the widespread use of 16mm release prints that could withstand the occasional worn projector sprocket or less-than-perfect handling, which in turn encouraged the use of the format as an origination medium by field cameramen and the newsreel industry. This led to complaints that its high level of shrinkage made acetate-propionate unusable in the new generation of 16mm cameras which used registration pins in the gate to ensure picture steadiness. One such article concluded:

> But the 16mm medium is no longer confined to amateur use, and has not been for a long time. Being used by professionals for professional purposes in a professional manner, professionals have long been hampered by the shortcomings of this slow-burning base. […] There is only one solution to this problem, and that is the use of nitrate.[17]

Given the long-established reputation of 16mm as a safety-only gauge, the manufacture of 16mm nitrate was clearly out of the question. And not only did acetate-propionate prove unsatisfactory for use as a 16mm camera negative stock: once again, safety film was ignored by the 35mm market. Brian Winston advances a conspiracy theory, which argues that the systems of legislation and regulation controlling the use of nitrate stock was one of the ways in which the Hollywood film industry exercised commercial control over its output:

> … nitrate stock was not finally to disappear from the industry until the early 50s, no less than half a century or so after the first patent for the safe alternative. This can be seen as a further elegant, or perhaps extreme, example of industrial conservatism; in effect, the power of suppressive forces inhibiting the introduction of new techniques and materials. [...] The business protection that this provided was worth the odd projection booth conflagration.[18]

If we accept this argument, then it would go some way to explaining why 16mm remained in the amateur domain, despite improvements in emulsion density, until the events of World War II forced a change in policy. Certainly, the production of large numbers of Hollywood features on 16mm enabled them to be shown on a significant scale outside licensed cinemas, and some of these prints ended up in the hands of criminals. In September 1946 five men, including the chief sound engineer of British Paramount News, appeared at the Old Bailey, charged with the theft of 832 reels of 16mm features from the armed forces.[19] A month later, a British newspaper reported the existence of a "big black market in little films". A private investigator hired by the main British distributors found that the 16mm prints had "just vanished, like so many of the Forces' stores did", and claimed to have discovered a number of organised criminal gangs showing them in village halls, workers' clubs, and similar venues.[20] The fears expressed by exhibitors when the 1939 Home Office report encouraging the use of safety film was published appeared to have been realised, and given the existence of such activity it seems reasonable to speculate that the studios and distributors did not want to make 35mm vulnerable to piracy as well. Producing large numbers of 35mm prints on safety stock would certainly have had that effect. Furthermore, they could have been transported without the need for any safety precautions to any one of the hundreds of thousands of cinemas worldwide (i.e., their exhibition would not have been restricted to *ad hoc* venues using portable projectors), where they could then have been shown without the need for any technical modification to the projection and sound equipment.

But if Winston is right, and the resistance to 35mm safety stock was the result of industrial protectionism, why did nitrate cease to be manufactured less than four years after the events described above? One point to bear in mind is that the British film industry's response to the 1939 report did not express hostility to safety film *per se*, but only to the fact that, due to a quirk of the British legal system, its commercial use was unregulated. However, the immediate answer lies more in the technical domain than the political. Cellulose acetate-propionate, though a vast improvement on cellulose diacetate, early forms of cellulose triacetate, and cellulose acetate-butyrate, came nowhere near to matching the performance of nitrate in terms of flexibility, tensile strength, shrinkage, and durability. One series of tests established that an acetate propionate print failed due to perforation damage after 380 projections, whereas a nitrate print run in identical circumstances lasted for 644. In other words, a nitrate print would last almost twice as long as an acetate-propionate one in an average cinema, and therefore double the number of prints would be needed to distribute a title on safety. Moreover, acetate propionate suffered "excessive" focus drift when projected under a 175-amp high-intensity carbon arc (not an issue with the low-power tungsten lamps used for 16mm projection), and "appreciable" image embossing.[21] For the physical qualities expected of a release print, nitrate remained the state of the art – just as long as it didn't ignite.

The German Connection

It would take the launch of a new type of acetate stock to come close to matching the performance of nitrate at a comparable cost and thus trigger the conversion. A number of files at the Public Record Office in London provide evidence to suggest that, as with tri-pack colour emulsions, the process of research and development which eventually led to the announcement of this stock by Kodak in 1948 may have had its origins in Nazi Germany.

The manufacture of film base of any sort has never taken place in Britain on any significant scale (even today, the polyester base which is used in most cinema film is imported from the US and Far Eastern countries). During World War II this became a national security issue, as raw stock imports became caught in the Battle of the Atlantic, resulting in the strict rationing of stock for release printing, especially where newsreels were concerned.[22] In mid-1945, the Ministry of Aircraft Production started to investigate the possibility of removing film-base manufacturing plant from Germany in order to establish a facility in Britain. A memo from the Director-General of the Aircraft branch of the Board of Trade sets out the rationale behind this:

> As you will be aware, the production of film base has never been carried on in this country to any appreciable extent and from strategic and economic points of view, it is important that we should no longer have to rely on imports of this commodity.[23]

Attempts to import a plant directly from the US were found to be impossible due to cost:

> Demands for industrial equipment of this kind having a very obvious post-war value have been off lend-lease since November 1943. The alternative of a cash purchase would involve expenditure running into millions of dollars.[24]

The Ministry's motivation in this instance was to ensure a safe supply of film for use in aerial photography for Intelligence purposes. However, the supply of raw stock to the cinema industry was also an issue which the Board of Trade had been addressing for some time previously, and its officials were closely interested in the Ministry's project, largely for this reason. Earlier that year they had approached the Eastman Kodak company, which operated a factory in north London for coating emulsion onto imported raw stock, seeking their co-operation in establishing film-base manufacturing plant in Britain. The result was a meeting on 19 April 1945, in which Kodak representatives told the Government that "their own technical knowledge of film casting was not for sale".[25]

A memorandum prepared by the Ministry of Aircraft Production for the War Cabinet Reconstruction Committee, dated 7 April 1945, detailed two key problems that had to be overcome. One was the acquisition of cellulose-casting plant, the other was the chemical composition of the film base. For use on board aircraft, nitrate was clearly not an option, while the manufacture of safety film had thus far been extremely problematic. The memo noted that "… the greatest difficulty has been in obtaining the right type of cellulose acetate: nitrate film has given far less trouble".[26]

That summer a group of British scientists and technicians drawn mainly from Ilford (a British-owned company which operated the second-largest film emulsion coating facility after Kodak), on the advice of eight former employees of the German Agfa company who had been captured as prisoners-of-war and were being held at a converted school in Wimbledon, visited Germany in an attempt to locate film-casting plant and to learn what they could about the chemistry of base manufacture. They discovered that the Americans had got there first, and were keeping the remaining infrastructure of the Nazi film manufacture industry under very close control.

When the delegation attempted to visit the factory of Kalle & Co. in Wiesbaden, they found the premises "under especially close control, with a resident U.S. Army administrator".[27] A year later, British attempts to remove a Koebig band-casting machine (the equipment needed to mould cellulose into 35mm-wide strips) from an Agfa laboratory were systematically blocked by the US authorities. On 1 October 1946 the British Intelligence Objectives Sub-Committee reported that the US Army had decided that the Koebig machine was "obtainable only by reparations" and had refused to issue papers authorising its transport.[28] The following summer, British Rhine Army Intelligence reported that "I have now received advice from our officer in Germany that the Americans have refused to clear this item for procurement either as reparations, booty or by purchase."[29] The US authorities were not the only ones trying their hardest to ensure that no film-base manufacturing plant ever became established in Britain: two months after the British delegation set out, the British embassy in Washington reported that "Kodak do not favour the proposal to establish film base casting capacity in the UK".[30] While Kodak's reluctance to provide infrastructural support to the British government was already clear, the fact that this opposition was also being expressed in Washington raises the question of whether Kodak had anything to do with the US Army's refusal to allow British access to the captured German equipment.

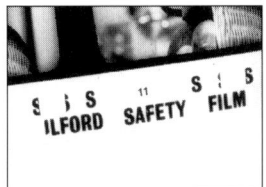

Edge marking – safety film.
East Anglian Film Archive, Norwich.

The issue of cellulose chemistry is especially significant when considering the timing of the final programme of research undertaken by Kodak immediately prior to the launch of their new safety stock in 1948. The British delegation sent samples of two cellulose bases manufactured by I G Farben for Agfa for examination by scientists at Ilford. One, known as "Cellit B", was a compound consisting of 42.5% acetic acid and 16.4% butyric acid; these proportions were similar to the cellulose acetate-butyrate used in 16mm stocks during the 1920s and 30s.[31] None of these would have represented significant improvements on the cellulose acetate-propionate sold by Kodak since 1937. The other I G Farben product, "Cellit F", is described only as "56.3% acetic acid, viscosity 2.6 ost [sic]" (the new American safety stock had an acetyl content of 42.5–44%, without the need for any other organic solvent such as butyric acid), while the British delegation found that several other plants manufacturing cellulose acetates were also still operating: for example, Dr Alexander Wacker-GmbH of Burghausen produced a "photographic cellulose acetate" compound of 55% combined acetic acid.[32] But these files do give the impression that acetate film was far more widely used in Germany than in the West, and, significantly, there is no reference anywhere in these files to the manufacture of nitrate. This could have been because the British delegation were simply interested in film for Intelligence purposes and thus were not looking for anything to do with nitrate (an undated Ministry of Aircraft Production briefing document makes the point that the cinema film industry was the only remaining significant consumer of nitrate film by that stage). However, the systematic opposition by Kodak and the US authorities to the British attempts to benefit from the technological infrastructure of the Nazi film industry, coupled with the fact that Kodak were simultaneously working on a new form of acetate stock that would become the industry standard within half a decade, seems more than coincidence. As has been shown in the case of colour, Nazi technology was considerably ahead of its time and was eventually adapted and further developed by the American film industry in general, and by Kodak in particular. If the Nazi technology in this case was essentially obsolete, why did the Americans, in the form of the US military authorities, possibly with encouragement from the government and/or the Eastman Kodak corporation, go to so much trouble to prevent the British from obtaining it?

"High-Acetyl Cellulose": The Industry Converts

In a report to shareholders issued on 5 March 1947 (three months before the US Army finally issued a blanket refusal for the British to export the Koebig machine), the Eastman Kodak company announced that it was equipping a large laboratory in Kingsport, Tennessee, "to study the special problems of cellulose esters and their applications, and the work of the company in related fields is being concentrated there",[33] and a later statement by a Kodak spokesman confirmed that the Kingsport facility was being used for the manufacture of acetate film base.[34] Just over a year later, on 17 May 1948, Charles R Fordyce, Kodak's superintendent of manufacturing experiments, told the SMPE annual convention that his company was launching a new "high-acetyl" cellulose acetate, the performance of which almost equalled that of nitrate, and which would be tested as a "possible substitute" for nitrate in the professional motion picture industry. Fordyce explained that Kodak had been working on it "since early in 1946" – a few months after the British technicians had discovered intense American interest in what remained of the Nazi film manufacturing infrastructure.[35]

The essential difference between this new stock and its predecessors was that, in Fordyce's words:

> Cellulose triacetate, the product of complete acetylation of cellulose, is soluble in only a limited number of organic solvents, and would be of doubtful success for motion picture film base because of the difficulty of splicing. Furthermore, casting procedures are difficult with this material, tending to give brittle film. By selecting an intermediate chemical composition, within the range of 42.5 to 44.0 per cent acetyl content, it has been found possible to retain the advantages of high physical strength and at the same time eliminate the problem of proper manufacturing quality and splicing behaviour.[36]

Fordyce's reference both to casting problems and to the use of partially acetylated cellulose raises the possibility of Kodak's research having involved an examination of German casting plant, and the chemical composition of the cellulose esters that were used by the Nazis. The timing of Kodak's research and the American embargo on British access to the Koebig machine would tend to support this speculation. After all, it took 14 years of ongoing research between the launch of Kodak's first mass-produced 16mm safety film in 1923 and its replacement by acetate-propionate in 1937. If Fordyce's statements are correct, the research and development of this revolutionary new base, which finally enabled the film industry to cease using nitrate, happened from start to finish in a little over two years.

His data certainly backs up the claim that the new acetate release print stock, designated by Kodak as Type 5302, was comparable to nitrate when subjected to the usage normally inflicted on motion picture film. Tensile strength was almost identical, with a more than 30% improvement over acetate-propionate, while curl and shrinkage during processing were within acceptable limits.[37] Wearing quality was not quite as good (with failure due to perforation damage after 520 projections, compared to 644 for nitrate), but laboratory projection quality was of a near-identical standard, with the new stock more resistant to frame embossing than even nitrate.[38] Field tests of trial prints used in cinema distribution showed that the new stock was slightly more susceptible to perforation damage, but that the prints had a similar useful life to their nitrate counterparts in all except the most intensive use.[39]

As Brian Winston points out, the film industry had consistently rejected 35mm safety stock for the previous half-century, which makes it all the more surprising (and also undermines his argument that the use of nitrate was deliberately continued as a restrictive practice) that the process of wholesale conversion began almost as soon as the new Kodak stock went on sale. In October 1948 Edward Peck Curtis, Kodak's vice-president, announced that the supply of stock to the Hollywood studios would undergo a "planned immediate switch" to the new acetate.[40] Interestingly, the reason given for this was "pressure put on the producers by the Los Angeles Fire Department as a fire prevention measure".[41] Campaigns against the use of nitrate on the grounds of fire safety were nothing new – for example, the National Fire Protection Association ran major campaigns in 1918–19, and again in 1923[42] – but they had thus far been resisted by the film industry, mainly because the only safety stocks available were fundamentally unsuitable for use in motion picture film transport mechanisms (i.e., cameras, printers, and projectors). The launch of Type 5302 removed this obstacle, and with it the reluctance of the industry to convert. However, the fire issue remained live: in mid-1950, for example, 17 firemen were seriously injured after they inhaled nitrate fumes while fighting a cinema fire in Dallas.[43] To make things worse, research published earlier that year showed that nitrate was even more dangerous than had been previously thought. Two US government scientists investigating a spate of nitrate fires in the New York area following the unusually hot summer of 1949 found that, if stored at temperatures exceeding 100°F for a period of several days, the stuff could spontaneously ignite![44]

DUAL MARKINGS
SAFETY AND NITRATE FILM

It has been reported that there are in circulation a number of black and white prints that are marked "nitrate" film along one edge and "safety" along the other. These films may be either of safety or nitrate base, and this can be determined by the fact that the wording correctly describing the material of which the film base is made is that printed in **black letters on a transparent base.** The white letters on a black base are printed through from the negative and therefore indicate the material of which the negative was made.

Renting organisations are taking steps to remedy the matter but there are a number of films still in circulation which bear this dual, misleading wording.

Dangerous confusion: an announcement from the UK Cinematograph Exhibitors' Association *Film Report* for 17 November 1950.

The Cinema Museum, London.

With this continuing adverse publicity, and no significant performance advantage over the new acetate, it is hardly surprising that the days of nitrate were numbered. In May 1949, Eastman announced that a sixth of all US release prints in circulation were being made on Type 5302, and forecast that the figure would rise to a quarter by September.[45] In July 1950, Kodak reported that they had ceased producing nitrate and that the conversion was 85% complete.[46] Interestingly, it was reported that newsreel producers were continuing to use nitrate (supplied by DuPont, the one other significant film-base manufacturer in the US), as the newsreel distributors felt that the comparatively short life of each release print did not justify the slightly higher costs of the new safety film.[47] With this level of momentum behind the conversion process, though, it was only a matter of time before nitrate disappeared completely from circulation. It is notable, however, that this final stage of the conversion process did not happen instantly. Projectionist manuals and training publications from the early 1950s continued to stress that, even while tiny numbers of nitrate prints remained in use, full-scale safety precautions had to be maintained in every projection room. One such British publication advises:

> Not until every last foot of nitrate film is out of circulation can the regulations be relaxed. **It may indeed be suggested that while there remains the risk that prints mainly on safety base may have leaders, run-outs or reprinted sections on nitrate, there exists an added element of danger. The projectionist will therefore be wise if, for some years to come, he regards every reel of film as potentially inflammable, and exercises the same precautions to which he has in the past been accustomed.**[48]

The US insurance industry was equally wary. The National Board of Fire Underwriters refused to classify acetate film as "slow burning" until November 1950, following extensive tests.[49] In order to convince nervous officials in New York City that acetate film was safe, Kodak, in co-operation with a group of cinema owners, invited members of the City authorities to its Rochester plant for a day of demonstrations.[50]

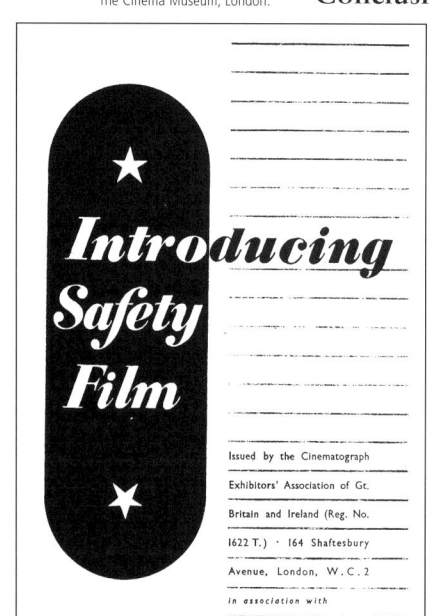

Front cover of a booklet published and circulated by the Cinematograph Exhibitors' Association at the start of 1950. Subscribers to *Film Report* were each sent three copies with the issue of 6 January, and asked "Will you please hand one copy each to your 1st, 2nd and 3rd projectionists. Further copies are available on application…".

The Cinema Museum, London.

Conclusion

The film industry's conversion from nitrate to acetate did not follow any of the established patterns of widespread technological change in the film industry. As with sound, the conversion happened as soon as a product became available which fulfilled certain technical and economic criteria. Unlike sound, however, attempts had been going on to produce such a product for decades before it finally materialised. These attempts were unsuccessful – it was not a case, as with widescreen and as argued by Brian Winston in the case of safety film, that a satisfactory product was available but was rejected by potential consumers. Acetate-propionate was a lot more expensive than nitrate, and its performance was demonstrably inferior.

If my interpretation of the German connection is correct, then the Nazis had, at the very least, made some progress in developing a more durable safety stock. The fact that (a) Kodak continually opposed the establishment of a British film-base manufacturing facility, (b) the US authorities assisted them in preventing the British from doing so, and (c) Kodak were developing their new acetate stock over an astonishingly short time scale during the same period, would strongly suggest that these events were in some way related.

The widespread use of cellulose acetate-propionate for 16mm illustrated the potential advantages of safety stock, and also the potential drawbacks, such as piracy. But at a time when the film industry was still largely vertically integrated, a 35mm safety base which came close to matching the performance of nitrate offered the possibility for reduced overheads and increased flexibility in the distribution and exhibition sectors, just as the emerging technology of digital projection today offers the possibility of eliminating print manufacture and transport costs. Although, to a certain extent, Winston is right, and the safety precautions associated with nitrate helped Hollywood to regulate the circulation of its films, the reduction in overheads offered by safety film more than offset any disadvantages in this regard.

References

1. Cricks, R Howard, "Problems of Safety Stock", *Technical Information for Projectionists* (a series of pamphlets issued by the Gaumont-British Kalee corporation, copies available in the BFI National Library), no.6 (1950).

2. Cummins, James W, et al., "Spontaneous Ignition of Decomposing Cellulose Nitrate Film", *Journal of the SMPE*, v.54 (March 1950), pp. 268–274.

3. Fordyce, Charles R, "Improved Safety Motion Picture Film Support", *Journal of the SMPE*, v.51 (October 1948), pp. 331–350.

4. Mees, C E Kenneth, "History of Professional Black-and-White Motion Picture Film", *Journal of the SMPE*, v.63 (October 1954), pp. 125–140.

5. Mitchell, Robert A, "The Film Base: Nitrate and Triacetate Stock", *International Projectionist*, v.25, no.2 (February 1950), pp. 7–9, 32, 34.

6. Pickard, R W, and D Hird, "A Test to Measure the Flammability of Kinematograph Safety Film", *British Kinematography*, v.21, no.3 (September 1952).

7. Pierce, David, "The Legion of the Condemned – Why American Silent Films Perished", reprinted in this volume, previously published in *Film History*, v.9, no.1 (1997), pp. 5–22.

8. Simmons, Norwood L, "Kodak: Innovator Behind-the-Scenes in the Motion Picture Industry", *Communications*, no.70 (April 1970), pp. 9–10.

9. Thiesen, Earl, "The History of Nitrocellulose as a Film Base", *Journal of the SMPE*, v.20 (March 1933), pp. 259–262.

10. "Questions and Answers on Safety Film", *International Projectionist*, v.24, no.8 (September 1949), p. 14.

11. Winston, Brian, *Technologies of Seeing* (London, BFI Publishing, 1998).

Notes

1. Douglas Gomery, "Warner Bros. and Sound", *Screen*, v.17, no.1 (1976), pp. 40–53; Donald Crafton, *The Talkies: America's Transition to Sound, 1926–1931* (New York: Charles Scribner's Sons, 1997) [v.4 of the series "History of the American Cinema"]; and Scott Eyman, *The Speed of Sound: Hollywood and The Talkie Revolution, 1926–1930* (New York: Simon & Schuster, 1998).

2. See Dudley Andrew, "The Post-War Struggle for Colour", in Stephen Heath and Teresa de Lauretis, eds., *The Cinematic Apparatus* (London: Macmillan, 1980), pp. 61–75.

3. See John Belton, *Widescreen Cinema* (Cambridge: Harvard University Press, 1992), passim.

4. Earl Thiesen, "The History of Nitrocellulose as a Film Base", *Journal of the SMPE*, v.20 (March 1933), p. 259.

5. Robert A Mitchell, "The 35mm Projection Positive Film", *International Projectionist*, v.25, no.5 (February 1950), p. 7.

6. Dorothy Knowles, *The Censor, The Drama and the Film* (London: Allen & Unwin, 1934), p. 169.

7. Neville March Hunnings, *Film Censors and the Law* (London: Allen & Unwin, 1967), pp. 48–54.

8. *Manchester Guardian*, 23 November 1939 (source: cutting from microfiche in BFI National Library).

9. *Kinematograph Weekly*, 10 August 1939, p. 5.

10. David Pierce, "The Legion of the Condemned – Why American Silent Films Perished", reprinted in this volume, previously published in *Film History*, v.9, no.1 (1997) pp. 5–22, passim.

11. Brian Winston, *Technologies of Seeing* (London: BFI Publishing, 1998), p. 60.

12. Quoted in Glenn E Matthews and Raife G Tarkington, "Early History of Amateur Motion-Picture Film", *Journal of the SMPTE*, v.64 (March 1955), reprinted in Raymond Fielding, ed., *A Technological History of Motion Pictures and Television* (Berkeley: University of California Press, 1967), p. 130.

13. Ibid., pp. 130–131.

14. Winston, op. cit., p. 75.

15. J M Calhoun, "The Physical Properties and Dimensional Behaviour of Motion Picture Film", *Journal of the SMPE*, v.43 (October 1944), pp. 227–267.

16. Charles R Fordyce, "Improved Safety Motion Picture Film Support", *Journal of the SMPE*, v.51 (October 1948), p. 331.

17. *International Photographer*, v.18, no.3 (April 1945), p. 22.

18. Winston, op. cit., p. 60.

19. *Evening News* (London), 17 September 1946.

20. *Daily Herald* (London), 4 October 1946.

21. Fordyce, op. cit., p. 342.

22. For more on this, see Leo Enticknap, "The Non-Fiction Film in Britain, 1945–51", unpublished PhD thesis, University of Exeter, 1999, pp. 66–70, 85–90.

23. Public Record Office (PRO), London, BT 64/4497, memo dated 18 October 1945.

24. PRO BT 64/4499, cable from the British Air Commission, Washington, DC, to the Ministry of Aircraft Production, 27 April 1945.

25. PRO BT 64/4499.

26. Ibid., Memorandum by the Ministry of Aircraft Production on the Manufacture of Film Base, 7 April 1945, p. 6.

27. Ibid., cable to the Ministry of Aircraft Production, 13 August 1945.

28. PRO BT 64/4497, cable to the Ministry of Aircraft Production, 1 October 1946.

29. Ibid., cable dated 4 June 1947.

30. Ibid., cable dated 2 October 1945.

31. Ibid., memo from the Chemical Industries Branch of the Board of Trade to the Ministry of Aircraft Production, 12 February 1946.

32. Ibid., memo dated 19 March 1946.

33. Quoted in *International Photographer*, v.19, no.4 (April 1947), p. 29.

34. *International Photographer*, v.20, no.10 (October 1948), p. 18.

35. *International Photographer*, v.20, no.6 (June 1948), p. 20.

36. Fordyce, op. cit., p. 332.

37. Ibid., p. 334.

38. Ibid., p. 342.

39. Ibid., p. 345.

40. *International Photographer*, v.20, no.10 (October 1948), p. 18.

41. Ibid.

42. Pierce, op. cit., passim.

43. Dallas Morning News, 15 June 1950, reported in *International Projectionist*, v.25, no.7 (July 1950), p. 30.

44. James W Cummings, et al., "Spontaneous Ignition of Decomposing Cellulose Nitrate Film", *Journal of the SMPTE*, v.54 (March 1950), p. 271.

45. *International Projectionist*, v.24, no.5 (May 1949), p. 18.

46. *International Projectionist*, v.25, no.7 (July 1950), p. 26.

47. Ibid.

48. R Howard Cricks, "Problems of Safety Stock", *Technical Information for Projectionists* (a series of pamphlets issued by the Gaumont-British Kalee corporation, copies available in the BFI National Library), no.6 (1950). Author's emphasis.

49. International Projectionist, v.25, no.11 (November 1950), p. 9.

50. Variety, 24 February 1954, p. 13.

Up from the Permafrost:
The Dawson City Collection

by Sam Kula

> There are strange things done in the midnight sun
> By the men who moil for gold;
> The Arctic trails have their secret tales
> That would make your blood run cold;
> The Northern Lights have seen queer sights,
> But the queerest they ever did see
> Was the time we mined the nitrate find
> From the pool behind Diamond Tooth G.[1]

Robert Service would have loved the story of the Dawson City film find. Five hundred reels of motion picture film were recovered from the permafrost after being buried for 49 years. Every reel capturing moments from historical events as recorded in newsreels, or offering fragments from the comedies and dramas that entranced millions in film theatres around the world. Enough stories to inspire a poet for a lifetime!

But how did the films get into the deep freeze of Dawson City in the Yukon Territory of Canada in 1929?

Dawson City today has a population of about 1,000, and the air of a place frozen in time. Almost the entire town is being restored by Klondike National Historic Sites, the restoration arm of Parks Canada in the region, to what it was like at the turn of the last century, when the last great gold rush of modern times turned Dawson City into a boom town.

An estimated 100,000 amateur prospectors poured into the territory after George Washington Carver, his Indian brother-in-law "Skookum Jim", and "Tagish Charlie" discovered gold on Rabbit Creek (immediately renamed Bonanza Creek!) in 1896. Dawson City, at the confluence of the Yukon and Klondike Rivers, with a floating population of 30,000, became the largest community in Canada west of Winnipeg by 1898. By the turn of the century it could boast it had telephones, electricity, and even motion pictures.

For most of the gold-seekers, getting to the Klondike was adventure enough. The rich could go all the way by water; the rest had to struggle over the White Pass or the Chilkoot Pass (3,500 feet), and brave the hazards of the trip down river from Lake Bennett to Dawson City on rafts or hastily constructed boats. The Royal Canadian Mounted Police controlled entry into the Yukon Territory, and they decreed that everyone had to have at least a ton of supplies to ensure that they could survive the winter.

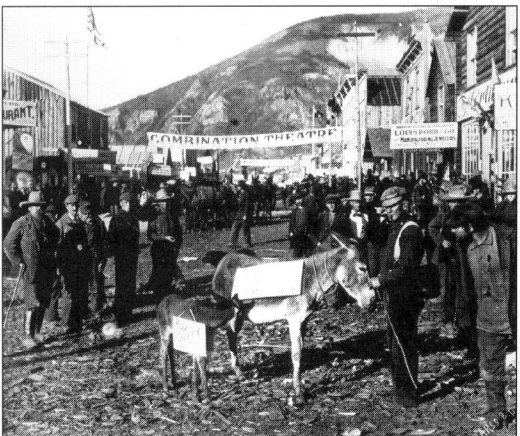

A view of Dawson City in Gold Rush times.

National Archives of Canada/MISA, Ottawa. 14608.

The most vivid image of the Yukon gold rush is a photograph of a long line of men carrying their supplies up the last four miles of the Chilkoot Pass, a 35-degree slope of ice and blowing snow. It is a photograph by Eric Hegg.

Prospecting for gold apparently fascinates photographers, or is it the faces of the remarkable men and women who become obsessed with finding that magic metal? It was the lower Fraser River gold rush of 1858, in what is now British Columbia, that brought the first two photographers to Victoria, and the Caribou "strike" of 1862 brought more of them to the region. It is, therefore, not too surprising that when news of the extent of the "find" in the Klondike spread south, Hegg, a young and obviously very fit photographer, decided to join the "rush". He must have been very fit because he not only hauled his ton of supplies and his camera and his glass plates up the Chilkoot Pass, but he did it again up the White Pass to record the tremendous effort involved in just getting to the gold fields.

Once his studio was established in Dawson City, Hegg photographed miners and would-be miners and the conditions under which they worked, and he documented the astonishing growth of a "boom" town. His photographs remain among the most vivid evocations of the "stampede" in any media. And what happened to them is the stuff of another legend that Robert Service could have easily worked into another saga of the North.

Consider the scenario. Hegg has itchy feet, and when gold is discovered in Nome, Alaska, he sells his studio to two other photographers, Larss and Duclos, and because of their sheer bulk he leaves his glass plate negatives behind. There are various accounts of what happened next. Larss either uses them as insulation, or simply hides them behind the wallboards in his cabin. In the mid-1950s the cabin is purchased by a young lady, who discovers the plates and reportedly uses some of them as window panes. Apparently, she seriously considers using the rest of them to construct a greenhouse, until she is persuaded by a store owner that they may have some value as photographs and he offers to trade plain glass for the plates. In a neat, if almost implausible, conclusion, Ethel Anderson Becker, the daughter of Hegg's first partner when he set up shop in 1897, visits Dawson City and buys the plates. Some 4,000 of them are now held by the University of Washington.

Enter the National Film Board of Canada, and the innovative team from Unit B: Colin Low, Wolf Koenig, and Tom Daly. They hear about the plates, track them down in 1957, and select 329 of them on which to base their award-winning film on the rise and fall of Dawson City, *City of Gold*.

They would have been happy to use motion pictures from the period, if any had survived. We know that cinematographers followed the prospectors as well as photographers, and that Richard Bonine from the Edison Company was filming in Dawson City as early as the summer of 1898.

We know as well that along with gambling and prostitution (But never on Sunday! The RCMP saw to that!), the cinema was one of the pleasures that gold dust could buy in Dawson City by the summer of 1898. There are advertisements for the *Animatograph* and the *Projectoscope*, but there is no evidence that these were more than limited presentations by enterprising itinerant showmen.

The Dawson Amateur Athletic Association (DAAA), which was established in 1902, began presenting films occasionally the following year. The Orpheum Theatre, which opened as a playhouse in March 1910, probably presented films from time to time as well, but there is no hard evidence that there were regular scheduled screenings before 1910. By August of that year the Arctic Brotherhood Hall was advertising screenings in the *Dawson Daily News* fairly regularly, and on 14 October 1910 the Orpheum re-opened as a functioning cinema. By 1913 the DAAA was in competition with film programmes that changed two or three times a week. The programmes usually consisted of one educational or scenic, three short fiction films, and one newsreel.

Physical access to films in distribution was obviously a severe problem. There are many references to films that had arrived "on the last steamer from the outside" before the close of navigation for the winter, or to shipments of films that were held up at Whitehorse because of inclement weather. The time gap between the release of newsreels in Western Canada and their presentation in Dawson City in the 1913–1923 period was normally six months, and for fiction films the gap was frequently more than two years. *The Birth of a Nation* and *Intolerance* finally made it to Dawson City in 1918; three years and two years, respectively, after they were first released.

Dawson City was obviously considered the end of the line for newsreels and most short fiction films such as one-reel comedies and multi-part serials. The cost of shipping and the lengthy time delays diminished the value of the physical property, and distributors adopted the practice of leaving marginal films in the care of the Canadian Bank of Commerce, which had opened in Dawson City in 1897.

For reasons that are unclear, except that it was one of the few stone buildings in Dawson City with a basement, the bank stored the film in the basement of the Carnegie Library. Those in charge were either ignorant or oblivious of the danger in storing nitro-cellulose stock in a public place! Since Dawson City lies close enough to the Arctic Circle so that the ground is permanently frozen at a depth between 10 and 15 feet, one can assume that the library basement approximated the cold storage conditions, if not the humidity control, recommended for nitrate film.

The rest of the story comes from Clifford Thomson, who worked at the bank between 1928 and 1932. He also served as Treasurer of the Hockey Association, which operated a rink next to the DAAA building. It appears that there was also a swimming pool on the site (It does get warm enough in summer to justify an outdoor pool!), roughly 20 feet by 30 feet, which was covered by boards so that the area could be flooded to set up the hockey rink. The problem was that the boards were not strong enough, and the ice used to sag over the pool area.

By 1929 the bank was running out of storage space in the library basement. Thomson contacted some of the distributors in order to return the films, but was asked to destroy them instead. Even in those days dumping that quantity of nitrate film into the Yukon River was considered unacceptable pollution, and as the pool was no longer in use Thomson decided he could solve two problems at once by stacking the film in the pool, covering the stack with boards, and then covering the boards with a layer of earth to provide a level surface for the ice.

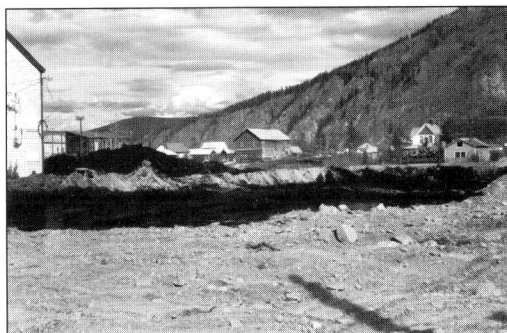

A view of the excavation site in Dawson City, 1978.

National Archives of Canada/MISA, Ottawa. 15355.

Ironically, the entire DAAA complex, which included a theatre, a boxing ring, and a gymnasium, burned to the ground in 1951. The suspected cause was the nitrate film that had accumulated in the building! More films had accumulated in the basement of the Carnegie Library, but this was cleared out in the early 1950s, and dispersed or destroyed with no record.

In 1978 the site of the DAAA was a vacant lot at the corner of Fifth Avenue and Queen Street, just behind Diamond Tooth Gertie's. In a nice example of the wheel turning full circle, the lot was selected as the site for a recreational centre by the

Dawson City Council, and in levelling the ground the workmen broke through the boards and uncovered the films.

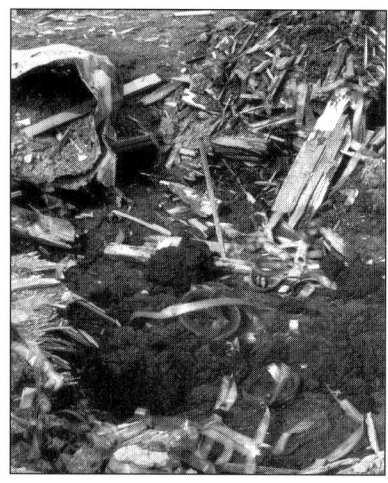

Breaking through the wooden floor of the skating rink.

Michael Gates, Curator of Collections for Klondike National Historic Sites, was called in, and recognizing the value of the "find", called me. I was then Director of the National Film, Television and Sound Archives Division at the National Archives of Canada. I visited the site, confirmed the value of the "find", and negotiated an agreement with Kathy Jones, then Director of the Dawson City Museum and Historical Society, to supervise the excavation of the site. Gates located an icehouse at Bear Creek Mining Camp, also under restoration as an historic site, which was carved out of a hillside and covered in sod. It was the ideal temporary vault for the film, as it maintains a near-freezing temperature all year round. The Bear Creek Acetylene Plant, with a stone floor and metal-lined walls, served as a film-handling room, where the worst of the debris was removed from the cans and the films were rewound and re-canned if necessary.

Early estimates were that only fragments of the films could be "saved", because, although the base was in surprisingly good shape after 49 years in the permafrost, the seepage from the spring thaws had bleached most of the image. The emulsion had also been attacked by chemicals in the soil used to cover the boards, and by the chemicals released in the decomposition of both the metal reels on which the film was mounted and the metal transfer cases in which the reels were packed – six to eight reels to a case.

Sam Kula and Mike Gates inspecting the film.

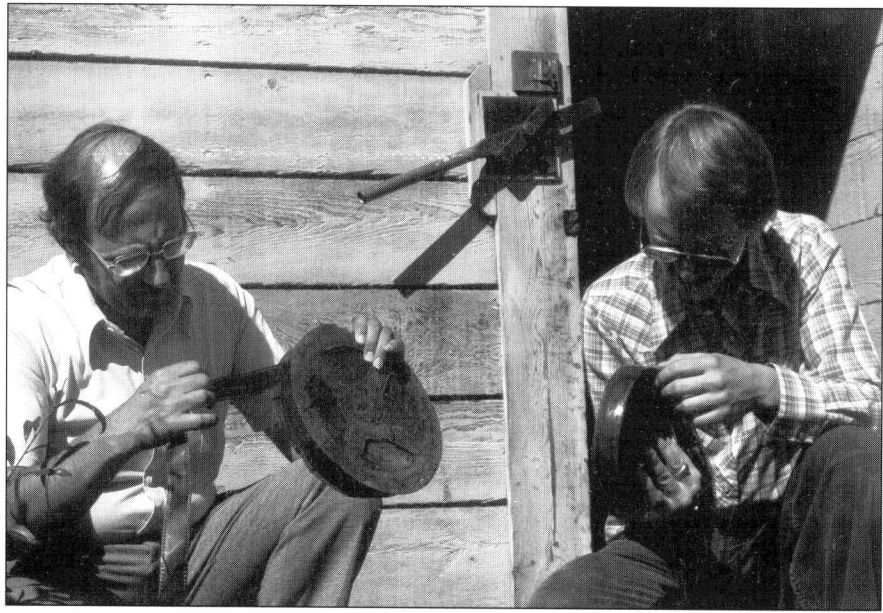

As the excavation proceeded, however, estimates on the quantity and the condition of the films began to change drastically. Films below the surface emerged in much better condition, although affected by damp and corrosion. Many of them had leaders and titles in good enough shape to allow positive identification, and some were even equipped with censor bands and shipping instructions.

When all the film was out of the ground and the initial recovery was complete, the next problem was transportation. How do you move almost one ton of nitrate film to Ottawa, where the restoration and conservation work was to take place?

After a few false starts – in Canada nitrate film is classed as a hazardous substance and cannot be shipped on any common carrier – the 4,506-km (2,800-mile) journey was begun by shipping the film 563 kms (350 miles) south to Whitehorse by refrigerated truck. In Whitehorse the film was repacked in wooden crates lined with tin – to comply with regulations! – and even then none of the commercial airlines would touch it. Only a last-ditch appeal to the Department of National Defence to provide Air Force assistance enabled the Archives to fly the film to Ottawa.

The challenge, once the film was unpacked at the National Archives film laboratory, was to clean, wash, and restabilize the film so it could be copied to safety stock. This turned out to require the development and application of several innovations in "emergency" film processing.[2]

The final inventory in November 1978 listed 507 reels. An additional 26 reels were "liberated" from the Dawson City site in 1980, recovered after being stored in an outhouse! Their condition ranged from almost perfect – practically ready to screen, aside from the inevitable shrinkage – to almost beyond salvage. There were reels in which the emulsion just slid right off the base when the reel was unwound, or reels in which the film had gelled in a solid mass that resisted all efforts to unwind it.

A stack of four of the salvaged reels of film.

National Archives of Canada/MISA, Ottawa. 15341.

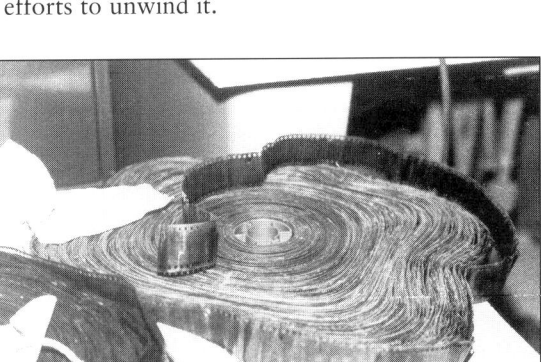

While the National Archives of Canada had the expertise and the equipment to carry out the optical step-printing required for very fragile and dimensionally abnormal film, it did not have the resources to copy the entire Dawson City Collection before the film (now subject to mould growth) deteriorated to the point where it could not be copied. In our experience, moving nitrate that has been stored in sub-standard conditions has a tendency to accelerate the rate of decomposition. As most of the short fiction films and the serials were American, it seemed only fair to share the burden and the cost of copying the film with the Library of Congress in Washington, a fellow member of FIAF, under whose regulations repatriations of this type are often carried out.

Recovered films in the cold storage building.

National Archives of Canada/MISA, Ottawa. 14598.

By May 1984, all 533 reels of the Dawson City Collection – some 500,000 feet of severely damaged film – had been converted to safety film, many of them after months of work to bring them to the stage where they could be copied in whole or in part. Collectively, they enrich the world's stock of film from the pre-1930 nitrate era, an era in which the losses are estimated at greater than 50%.

There were no earth-shattering individual discoveries among the films that emerged from their long winter's nap. Many of the studios involved – Thanhouser, 101-Bison, Selig, Essanay, and Rex – were as little known as the films they made. Although it was gratifying to add such titles as *Wild Fire* (1915), the only film in which Lillian Russell appeared, and *Bliss* (1917), a "lost" Harold Lloyd short, to the survival list, it is clear that the "big" pictures were shipped south again after exhibition in Dawson City. Ads in the *Dawson Daily News* regularly reminded patrons to see the "big" picture now, before the last steamer of the season carried it off.

The Dawson City Collection, however, is rich in serials – all the great early heroines of the genre, Pearl White, Ruth Roland, and Helen Holmes, are represented – and newsfilm, particularly for the period 1913 to 1921. It may well be that mobilization for World War I interrupted normal traffic to and from Dawson City, so that more of the films remained there. There are some hundred newsfilms in the Collection, from both American and British companies – *Universal Screen Magazine, Hearst-Selig News, Pathé Animated Gazette, Gaumont-British World Wide News, British War Office Official News*, etc. – and from one Canadian company, *British Canadian Pathé News*. This was a very important "find" for the National Archives of Canada, as not a single issue of this lonely effort to produce a newsreel in Canada prior to 1919 – by Ernest Ouimet, the pioneer exhibitor and distributor – was known to exist in any archive. By the time the restoration work on the Dawson City Collection was completed, there were 26 issues of *British Canadian Pathé News* (1919–22) available for study.

The Dawson City Collection also provides a glimpse into the distribution system that served isolated communities in North America, if one assumes that what went into the swimming pool between 1913 and 1929 is a reasonable cross-section of the films that were screened in the community. The productions are overwhelmingly American, as the Canadian distributors were all subsidiaries of American companies, and they tell American stories. When the stories are set elsewhere, they are characterized by American stereotypes of the "foreign". One serial, *The Red Ace* (1917), seems to encapsulate the Hollywood view of the Far North, and must have vastly amused the filmgoers in Dawson City. Imagine a little town called Lost Hope, described as somewhere "up there in the wilderness", in which a gang of enemy agents (this is 1917 and America has declared war) are out to control a mine vital to the war effort, and their secret weapon is a troop of trained apes!

Perhaps the most important contribution of the Dawson City "finds", the photographs and the films, bizarre as they may be, is to remind us that all the surviving early silent films or historic photographs have by no means been recovered. If the permafrost of the Klondike can yield up important collections after half a century, what treasures may still be locked away in attics and basements all over the world, and in the forgotten corners of the film industry's vaults?

Notes

1. With apologies to Robert Service. The poem is "The Cremation of Sam McGee", from *Songs of a Sourdough*. The cremation reportedly took place on the "marge of Lake Lebarge", en route to the gold fields in Dawson City. "Diamond Tooth G" refers to Diamond Tooth Gertie's, the restored dance hall and casino that is the most celebrated tourist attraction in Dawson City.

2. An account by Leonard Green of the technical challenges and how they were met by Archives staff appeared in *The Journal of the British Kinematograph, Sound and Television Society*, May 1983, and in *Perforations* (published by the National Film Board), September-October 1983.

Nitrate? Bah! Humbug!
A Personal View from an Archive Heretic

by John Reed

"A film should have certain properties to meet the exacting demands made upon it. It should be strong, supple, transparent, homogeneous, unaffected by atmospheric conditions and changes, and, last but not least, it should be non-flammable."

This statement, made in the second edition of *Hopwood's Living Pictures* in 1915, is interesting, as, with hindsight, nitro celluloid – "celluloid" or "nitrate" – just does not seem to meet many of the criteria. We know that it is affected by changes in atmospheric conditions; strong and supple it isn't, after a few years of use; and as for non-flammability, well, try telling that to any one of several laboratories, archives, and fire services around the world. A further disadvantage that we all know about is that it is not dimensionally stable. How many nitrate-based negatives or prints have you seen that have more than 1% shrinkage and, to make matters worse, exhibit uneven shrinkage over the picture area?

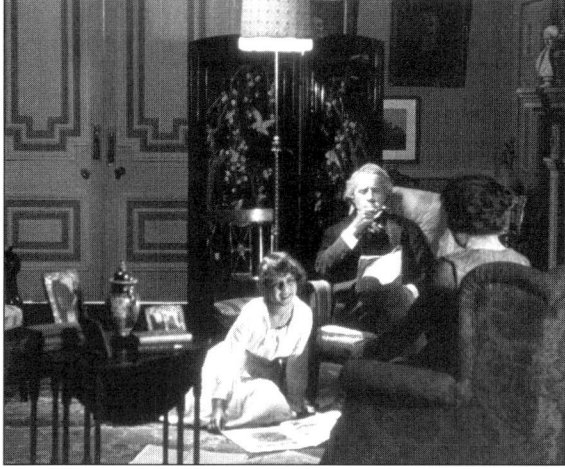

A scene from Maurice Elvey's *The Life Story of David Lloyd George* (1918), a film suppressed before its release and considered irretrievably lost until it was rediscovered three-quarters of a century later in a barn belonging to Lloyd George's grandson, Lord Tenby. After restoration by John Reed at the Wales Film and Television Archive, it was at last shown to the public in 1996. The full story is told in David Barry and Simon Horrocks (eds.), *David Lloyd George: The Movie Mystery* (Cardiff: University of Wales Press, 1998).

National Screen and Sound Archive of Wales, Aberystwyth.

Why then do we have a mythology surrounding nitrate, in particular the superiority of the image projected from a nitrate base?

Let us first look closer at the material we are talking about. There is no denying that without nitro celluloid the film industry could not have progressed so quickly beyond the stages of the "Mutoscope" or "Phasmatrope". However, the ingenuity of the pioneers of cinema would no doubt soon have found a practical alternative. After all, *di-acetate* was available from the turn of the century and *tri-acetate* shortly afterwards, and although perhaps delaying the development of the film industry by a short time the concentrated search for a viable alternative would surely not have resulted in too long a delay. Had the Hyatt brothers not discovered nitro celluloid in 1869, we might not now be in the unenviable position today of storing mountains of nitrate film, much of which is decomposing and just the thought of which turns the constitution of the most fearless safety officer to that of a quivering jelly.

An Explosive Tale – A Short Lesson in Chemistry and Manufacture...

Take a quantity of bleached cotton fibre (cellulose $C_6H_{10}O_5$), and convert it into nitro-cellulose by treating it with a strong mixture of nitric and sulphuric acids. This treated material, which forms a "pulpy" mass, is often called Pyroxylin, more commonly known as gun-cotton. Why gun-cotton? Simple. It is because, as its name implies, it was used as an explosive.

To turn raw gun-cotton into nitrate film, this pulpy mass is next bleached using a solution of *permanganated potash* or *chlorinated lime*. After bleaching, thorough washing is essential to remove all traces of the acids to avoid later contamination or, as Hopwood suggests, by-products that will produce inferior quality films or even decomposition.

The next stage is to "plasticise" the mass and make it flexible. This is accomplished by treatment with a mixture of *alcohol, ether, acetone, amyl acetate*, and *camphor*, until the mass becomes homogeneous. It may then be formed into large sheets, or, in the case of film stock, run out in a continuous form through a wedge-shaped opening onto an endless band, which creates a smooth temporary support until the solvents are evaporated and the "dry" film can be detached from the belt. At this stage, the "base" is ready for coating with the relevant adhesives (sub-coats) and emulsion or emulsions (suspensions of silver halides in gelatine). Once these are applied, the raw stock is ready for use.

Nothing in the stages of production outlined above is designed to reduce the basic flammability or – under extreme circumstances – the explosiveness of the celluloid base (although the introduction of camphor during the plasticising process is thought to reduce combustibility). The end product is still highly flammable.

The process of manufacturing acetate (CH_3CO_2) is similar, except that the treatment is with *ethanoic (acetic) acid* instead of nitric acid.

Loads of Silver

The raw photographic "emulsion" with which the film is coated is, as we all know, a suspension of silver halides in gelatine and not an emulsion in the true sense of the word. Without delving too deeply, it is perhaps worth outlining the chemistry of the manufacture of photographic emulsions. Basically, *metallic silver* (the purer the better) is dissolved in nitric acid with various halogens being added to the solution to form silver salts or *halides*. The halides are mixed into, or suspended, in gelatine, and then coated onto a base of some form and allowed to set, the result being a light-sensitive material that for our purposes we call film. Various *halogens* have been and still are used, including *bromine, chlorine*, and *iodine*. The earliest of these was bromine, which has been used in photography and cinematography since the earliest days, and is still the basic halogen in even the most modern colour materials.

Exposure to light creates a minute chemical change to the halides in the emulsion, and they start to break down into metallic silver to form a latent image. The process known as "development" – which should more correctly be called "reduction" – magnifies the effect of the light on the "exposed" halides by the order of about one thousand million times, and an image of metallic silver is formed.

Early photographic emulsions used for cinematography, although fundamentally the same as those we use today, were relatively crude in several respects. At first the emulsions available were only sensitive to blue light; thereafter, until the early 1920s, they were in general only sensitive to the blue and green parts of the spectrum, although they were optimistically called "Orthochromatic" (*correct colour*). It was only in the 1920s that the introduction of "Panchromatic" (*all colours*) emulsions extended sensitivity into the red part of the spectrum.

The speed (sensitivity to light) of these emulsions was relatively slow in comparison to those available today, but the grain structure was still noticeably coarser. We now

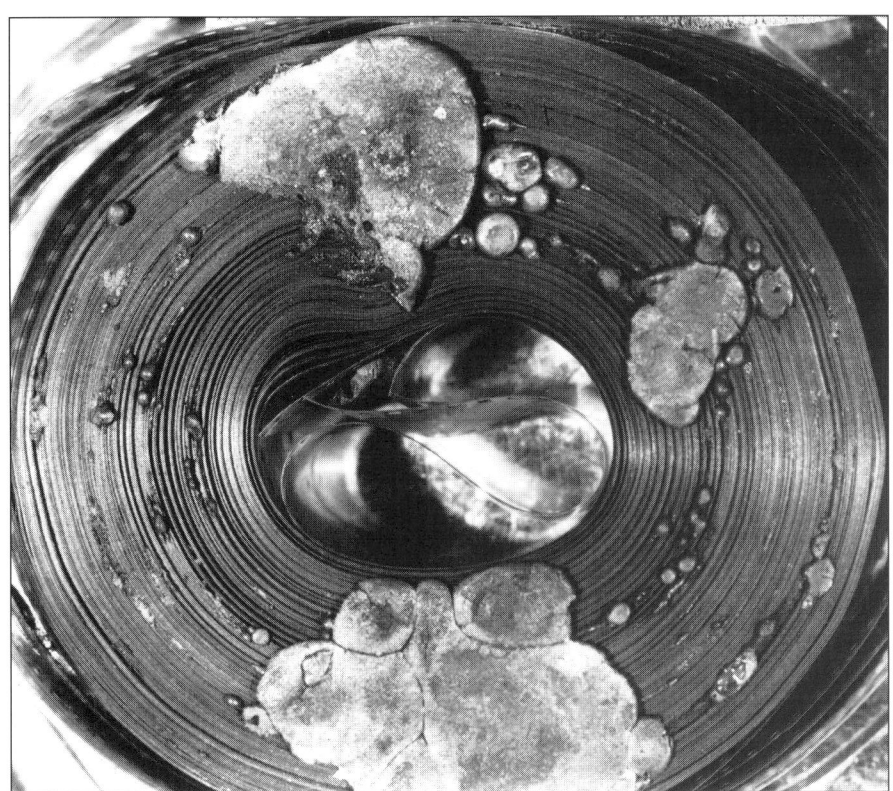

The classic image of nitrate deterioration from The Museum of Modern Art, New York. This picture featured widely in campaigns about "the nitrate problem" in the 1970s and 1980s.

The Museum of Modern Art, New York.

expect slow emulsions to have fine grain structure and fast emulsions to have a relatively coarse one. However, a major development in emulsion chemistry is the fine grain structures achieved in modern fast films compared to the slower films used in the days of nitrate bases.

The grains in an emulsion are rarely larger than about 2 microns in size, and are only visible under magnification of about 50x or higher. However, when viewed on the screen the grains may be more noticeable than would be expected, partly due to their random distribution in the emulsion and partly due to "clumping" as part of the manufacturing or processing operations. Grain tends to be most noticeable in the mid-tone regions of an image, as the highlight regions contain very little metallic silver and the shadow areas may be too dense to see this clumping of the silver.

It should perhaps be noted here that in the subtractive colour system, the metallic silver is bleached from the emulsion and only regions of the relevant dye remain, making the colour image to all intents and purposes "grain free".[1] Black-and-white materials, however, retain the metallic silver in the emulsion,[2] and in a print viewed on the screen the image is represented by differing densities of metallic silver, the highest density representing shadow or dark areas, and the lowest density, highlights. (In negatives of course the opposite is the case: highlights have the highest density of silver and shadows have very little.)

Grain is perhaps the major factor that has resulted in the description of film as a "living" medium when viewed. Many believe that the continual variation of the random grain structure creates this "living" image. Scratches and other blemishes on or in the film seen on the screen as the film rushes through the gate at 24 frames per second also probably contribute to the "life" of film.

After this brief look at how film is made and its unique characteristics, is there an argument to be made for the claim that nitrate prints look better than safety prints? Yes – there is, and they do, but I do not believe that it is anything to do with the use of nitro celluloid instead of cellulose tri-acetate: it is much more accidental than that. I will concentrate on the black-and-white image, as any attempt to compare colour images creates a far more complex set of arguments (although I think they would be equally valid). Rather than a consequence of the use of any particular base, I would contend that the apparent difference is primarily a result of the direction of emulsion research taken by the photographic manufacturers after the 1930s, and latterly of the introduction of alternative grain structures such as "T" grain, coupled with the economic and environmental advantages of using less silver in emulsion manufacture.

The high points in the quality of the black-and-white film image were, in my opinion, reached in the late 1930s and continued into the period following World War II up to about the early 1950s. This period of course runs roughly concurrently with the last fifteen years of the use of nitrate base for cinema release, but that is, I believe, a matter of coincidence, not causality.

Before the 1935 introduction of the integral tri-pack subtractive colour system by Agfa in Germany and Kodak in America, the primary research and development into photographic emulsions would have concentrated on improving the emulsion for the production of black-and-white films both for general release and for the rapidly expanding amateur/home movie market. Laboratories were devoted to the high quality processing of films, both negative/positive and reversal, which comprised black-and-white materials even if they were the basis for one of the many systems of additive colour that were devised. Quality control was good, and most of the major developments in the design of laboratory equipment had been introduced.

With the introduction of subtractive colour materials, and the obvious future growth in the demand for colour in the movies, it was natural for the emulsion manufacturers to devote increasingly greater resources to the improvement of emulsions for colour rather than for black-and-white. Although the basic emulsion in the subtractive colour system is a black-and-white emulsion, the characteristics required for this emulsion are not necessarily those which would give the optimum black-and-white image, and it is quite reasonable to assume that research and development of emulsions for solely black-and-white materials would decline as manufacturers favoured the new and more exciting colour products. It has indeed been suggested that the black-and-white duping materials used today indicate only minor technical advances over those available in the early 1950s.

Why then do we hear that images on nitrate are better? The answer is simple: it is down to "loads of silver". In the good old days, the silver content in black-and-white emulsions appears to have been considerably higher than in modern emulsions. A high density of silver in the finished print gives a "depth" of image that seems not to be achievable in any other way. Shadow and darker areas appear to have a "solidity", while even the highlights seem to have a "life" to them. If you have any doubts about the difference between contemporary emulsions and earlier emulsions, try toning a "T" grain emulsion with one of the traditional industry toners.

Can we perform an effective comparison of image quality on the screen? Side-by-side viewing of nitrate-based images and safety-based images is in general an unfair way of comparing the quality of the projected image, not because of any difference created by the nitrate but because the image on the safety film is far more likely to be formed with a modern low-silver content emulsion than the thicker silver-heavy emulsion of the days of nitrate. Of course the nitrate print will look better.

To overcome this "unfairness", an emulsion identical to that of the nitrate print should be used on the safety print, and then processed at the slower processing speeds used by the laboratories in the days of nitrate, for preference in one of the standard MQ developers of the period rather than a "Phenidone"-based developer.

Unfortunately, such an exercise is now probably impossible, as it is unlikely that any manufacturer is making such an emulsion to coat onto the safety base. Until a few years ago, an emulsion of this type was manufactured in the People's Republic of China, and it is worth viewing some of the film restorations of the China Film Archive to see the quality of image that can be achieved on safety-based film.

An unusual but possibly interesting comparison would be to project side by side a nitrate print and a *fine grain positive* (not wet-gate printed) from the same negative. Although not intended for projection, the image formed on a fine grain positive has something like the density of a silver-rich emulsion and should faithfully reproduce the grain structure of the original negative.

A further factor, I believe, is that the older emulsions were physically thicker than modern emulsions. Although this would probably only give a minor variation in projection quality, possibly because of a marginally higher internal reflection within the emulsion, it is perhaps also something to consider.

Certainly the chemical formulae of the developer used will have an effect upon the image, as will developer temperature and speed of development. Surprisingly, even the fixer used can affect the final image – a minute difference of image may be noticed between an emulsion fixed in *potassium thiosulphate* and one fixed in *ammonium thiosulphate*.

One further practical problem with side-by-side screening is that the nitrate print is invariably not pristine, and unless the comparison print exhibits a similar level of blemishes and general wear it is immediately obvious which is the nitrate. No matter how hard the viewer tries to offer an unbiased opinion, prejudices can and probably will creep into the assessment.

Viewed Through Arc-Coloured Glasses

"I remember watching [insert your preferred title here] years ago, and the quality on the screen was beautiful. You just don't get that sort of image from safety film."

How many times have you heard someone extol the quality of the image of a nitrate-based print in words of this type? Well, I remember that the summers of my childhood were always long and hot, that the trains ran on time, and we were happy with a few simple toys as Christmas presents! (Now please excuse me while I go and feed my flying pigs.) Proximity to an event is important, and we all have a capacity for "improving" our recollections of events. The further away they become the more rose-coloured the events seem to be tinted.

I would argue that the same effect can be found when recalling the "quality" of images seen on the screen, and that many who assure us that the images seen on the silver screen were better in the days when nitrate prints were the standard are discounting the passage of time in colouring their memories. Perhaps this is another and as yet unstudied effect of the persistence of vision.

This retrospective persistence of vision of course does not allow for those who are still in the fortunate position of regularly viewing nitrate prints, but I would argue that because of the difficulties of performing a fair comparative test as described earlier, other factors come into play.

When did you last see a nitrate print projected? If it was recently, what light source did the projector use? Were the optics pre-World War II or post-war? What screen was being used? Was smoking allowed in the auditorium? What make of projector was being used? All these factors should be taken into consideration if a true comparison is to be made.

The light source of the projector is of fundamental importance in the gauging of projected picture quality. Most modern projectors and projection facilities will now be using Xenon lamps, which have an approximate colour temperature of 6,500°K and a fairly flat spectral transmission. In the days of nitrate prints – and indeed up until about the mid-1970s – the standard projector light source would have been *carbon arc*, followed by *"low current high intensity"* carbon/cerium arc, with colour temperatures somewhere in the region of 5,000°K. *"Low intensity"* carbon *arcs* had a colour temperature of about 3,800°K. A third type of carbon arc is the *high intensity "white flame" arc*, which has a colour temperature in the region of 7,000°K. All arc light sources emit a spectrum in a series of bands and peaks with a continuous background. (Light quality may vary from one installation to another or from one projector make to another, and depends very much on the skill of the projectionist.)

"High intensity" carbon arcs, although fairly even in their spectral emission, are not as consistent as the modern Xenon and have a tendency to give a slightly "colder" image on the screen. Carbon arcs generate a comparatively high *Infra Red* output in comparison to Xenon lamps, and this high IR output may have an effect upon image quality. The *Ultra-Violet* emission of carbon arcs is also higher than that of Xenon lamps; they emit a blue-violet light, which if not correctly controlled may give a distinctly pinkish/lavender or even greenish/white hue. (A "white flame" arc would give a "colder" bluish image on the screen while a low intensity arc would give a comparatively yellow light.)

Pre-war optics were uncoated, and as such had higher *flare factors*, which resulted in a slightly lower-contrast image when projected than would be expected with a post-war lens with *anti-reflection* coatings. Lenses with higher flare factors have a tendency to spread the image highlights into the shadow areas, and although this does not affect the resolution of the image it does give a slightly "softer" (and, many would argue, more pleasing) overall image, with the additional effect of enhancing the "graininess" (an aspect of film which, as we have seen, many believe creates the "living" image of film compared to the "plasticity" of the electronic image).

The advent of sound in the cinema brought with it the perforated screen. Many small provincial cinemas, however, were slow to change their old "silent" screens to accommodate behind-the-screen speakers, especially when in 1947 entrance charges were just a few pence and a replacement screen was likely to cost in the region of £5 per square metre. I am sure that many of us were going to cinemas still using silent screens up to the late 1950s. The un-perforated screen was a relatively solid affair, with a fairly high reflectivity and low light absorption, often backed with a second layer of material to make it perfectly opaque. Images projected onto a good silent screen will tend to look brighter and crisper than those projected onto even the latest perforated sound screen, which, simply because of its construction, cannot compete in terms of reflectivity.

The ban on smoking in cinemas has also "changed" what we see on the screen. As with anti-reflection coatings on optics, the smoke-free atmosphere that we now enjoy when going to the movies has reduced image flare and given us another increase in image contrast. Here again we have a small but perceptible change in our viewing which will alter our perception of the image we see on the screen.

A combination of all the above factors will affect what we see on the screen and may account for some of the mythology surrounding the image quality of nitrate. These are, however, only ancillary factors, and not directly the focus of my argument – that it is the emulsion, not the base, that creates the quality of image.

Flash! Bang! Wallop!

Nitrate is more trouble than it is worth! Take a reel of highly flammable material that cannot be extinguished once it is burning, and has a flashpoint that can drop as low as 60°C; put a series of images on it, then pass it through the gate of a projector, where it will be flooded with the concentrated beam from a light source which can generate temperatures well in excess of 100°C. To cope with the potential dangers involved in such an exercise, install your projector in a box with the characteristics of a fireproof blockhouse, equipped with a multitude of safety features and governed by a barrage of regulations to protect the cinema-going public. Why bother?

Add to all the above the dangers inherent in transporting and storing this highly combustible material. Bear in mind that, when unstable, it becomes downright dangerous, and even under normal circumstances special care has to be taken to allow for its "fiery" nature. Ask a commercial laboratory to dupe it, and immediately you are faced with a massive handling surcharge. Store it, and your vault costs escalate, and your insurance premiums rocket on an almost logarithmic scale. The continual programmes of inspection and re-inspection, just to ensure that your beautiful collection of nitrate prints has not suddenly decided to decompose, soak up valuable archive resources. After all this, it seems reasonable to question the sanity of holding onto nitrate as a film base. Of course it is great to hold the original material, in much the same way as its nice to handle an old book or an antique piece of furniture, but surely it is the images that are the important thing, not the base that they are on – especially if the preceding arguments are accepted. Give me acetate or polyester any day: I'll take my chances with vinegar syndrome – at least it is easy to identify – and I'll sleep easy knowing that my vault is not going to go "wallop" in the middle of the night!

Notes

1. The process of "silver enhancement" used in colour usually relies upon a slight variation of the bleaching process, thus leaving a small quantity of metallic silver in the final image to give the colour film the effect of grain. Although technically a hybrid additive/subtractive colour system, it is perhaps worth noting that some early Technicolor prints were produced using a fourth light metallic silver matrix which enhanced shadow density and gave the image a "graininess" not normally associated with colour.

2. In the 1980s, both Ilford and Agfa marketed a range of "chromogenic" B/W materials which could be processed in either standard B/W chemistry or in colour negative chemistry. These B/W materials are more related to colour than B/W, as, like colour, no metallic silver is retained in the emulsion after processing. Primarily aimed at the photographic market, it is thought that this material was never used in the film industry.

Firetraps of Tsarist Russia

by David Robinson

The calendar of nitrate film fires in this volume records a disastrous conflagration in a cinema theatre at Bologoie, in the south of Novgorod province. Apart from this, little anecdotal evidence has come down to us about conflagrations in Russia's proliferating – and often hurriedly run-up – cinema theatres of the era before the First World War. It is not in any case a Russian habit to publicise catastrophe; and the censorship of the Tsars frowned on the spreading of alarm of any kind. Moreover, like the fairground showmen of Britain, early Russian cinema proprietors must have been very conscious of the risks of the combination of nitrate film stock and their often shacky and wood- constructed theatres, and were appropriately vigilant. By comparison, the organisers of the Bazar de la Charité were carefree and inexperienced.

The accompanying illustrations – none of which has been reproduced before – give some idea of the hazards of cinemagoing in far-flung corners of the old Empire. All images are from the author's private collection.

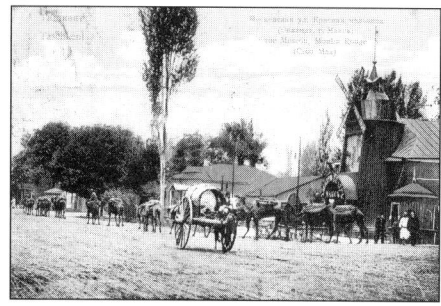

THE MOULIN-ROUGE ELECTRO-THEATRE IN TASHKENT is an unusually elaborate early cinema, seemingly purpose-built of wood. Tashkent is the capital of Uzbekhistan, annexed by the Russian Empire in the late 19th century. The Bactrian camel, of which a number are seen in the photograph, take their name from the region of Bactria, an area divided between Uzbekhistan, Tadjikistan, and Afghanistan.

(See also Colour Section 2.)

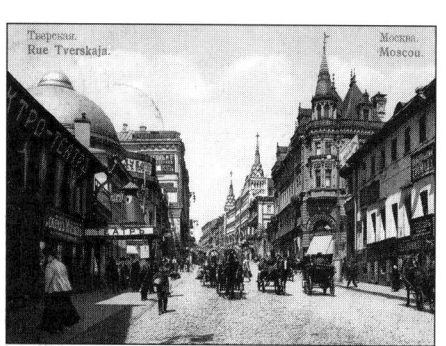

THE "MOULIN"(?) ON TVERSKAIA STREET, MOSCOW. Tverskaia Street was and is still the major thoroughfare of central Moscow. Known during Soviet times as Gorki Street, it has since reverted to its original name, though it is today unrecognisable from this evocative image of cobbled roadway and 19th century buildings. No name is visible on the "Electro-Theatre" at the left, but the large model of a mill over the canopy suggests that it might have been another "Moulin Rouge".

(See also Colour Section 2.)

THE CINEMA "TRIUMPH" IN PERM was probably photographed in the early years after the Revolution, to judge from the vigorous, but unfortunately illegible, posters and the bigger-than-life-size cut-out figure mounted on the side of the cinema. The long banner down the side reads "Chempion Mira" (Champion of the World). Perm, renamed Molotov between 1940 and 1957, is the capital of the *oblast* (province) of Perm, and stands on the West flank of the Ural Mountains on the River Kizel. Founded in 1788, the town grew rapidly after the establishment of the railway in 1890, and was made a city in 1926.

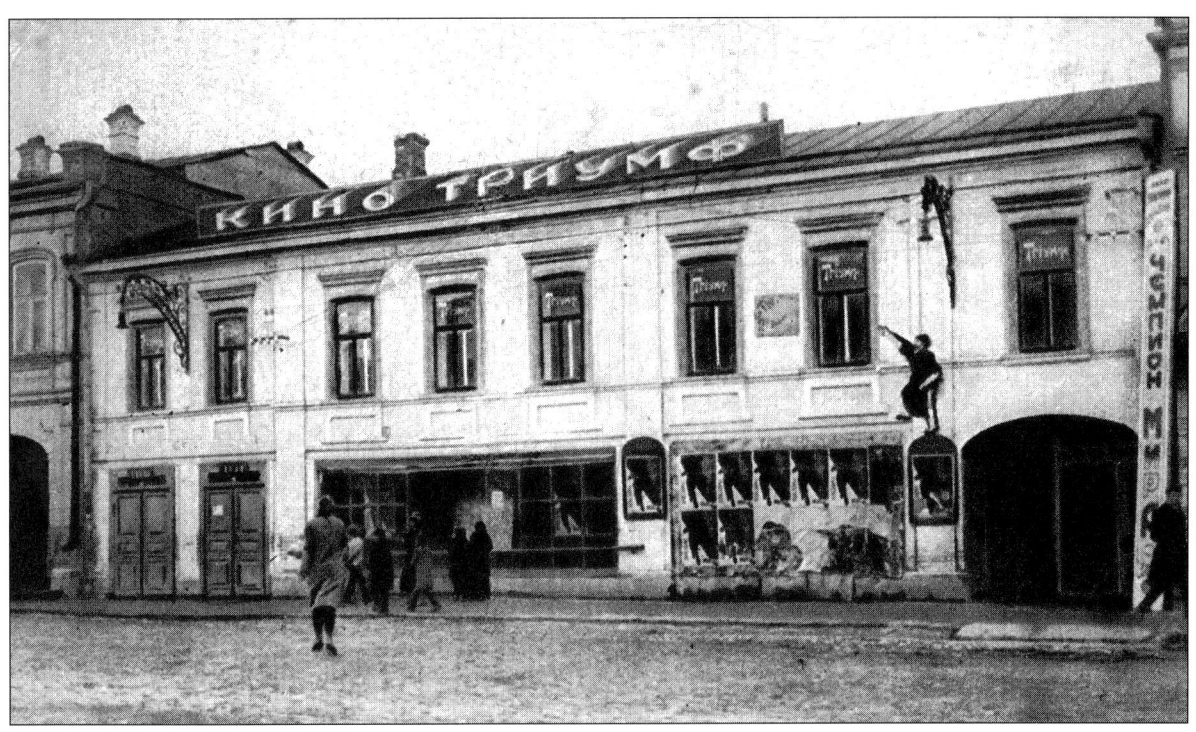

THE "ART KINEMATOGRAPH" IN SARATOV. Saratov, capital of the *oblast* of the same name and for centuries an important trade centre, became heavily industrialised after it was linked by rail to Moscow in 1870. The ambitious design of the "Art Kinematograph", on the corner of Nemetskoi and Volgodskoe Streets, reflects the city's contemporary cultural aspirations: the Art Museum had been founded in 1885, the university in 1909, and the music conservatoire in 1912.

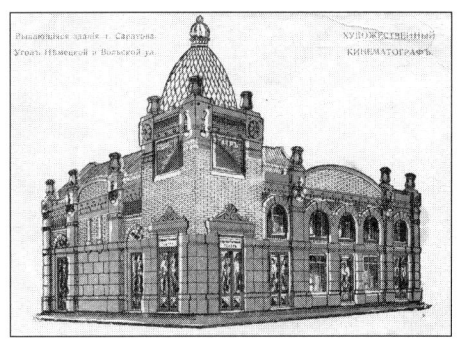

(See also Colour Section 2.)

THEATRE REKKORD-BIO IN PIATIGORSK. Piatigorsk ("Five Mountains") lies in the northern foothills of the Caucasus Mountains in south-west Russia. Built around mineral springs and favoured with a mild climate, it became a fashionable resort in the 19th century and a favourite place with artists – the poet Lermontov was killed in a duel near the town in 1841. The Kazennaya Hotel was one of the city's fashionable venues, and incorporated a cinema (perhaps in the basement like the Lumières' in the Grand Café), with an entrance in the enclosed *terrasse* at the left of the building. The name changes from one photograph to another. The earliest seems to have been "Electro-Biograph", with the proprietor identified as R Streicher. Later it is "Theatre Rekkord-Bio".

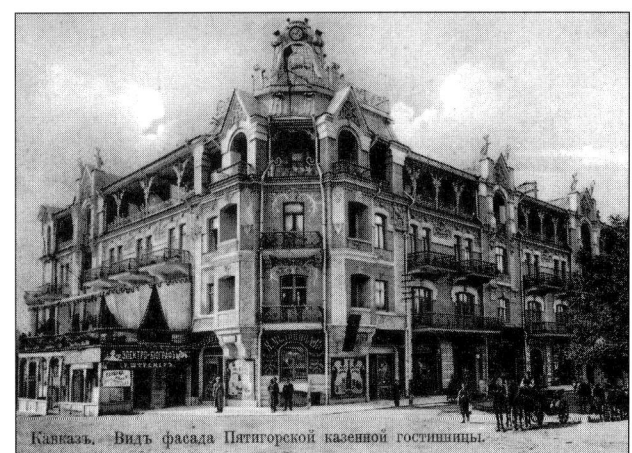

THE "MODERN" ELECTRIC THEATRE, ASTRAKHAN. An ancient Tartar city, Astrakhan acquired new importance as a port with the development of the oil industry in Baku from the 1870s. This cinema, with its eclectic mix of old and new, indigenous styles and art nouveau, seems to be an adaptation of a building or buildings designed for some earlier purpose.

(See also Colour Section 2.)

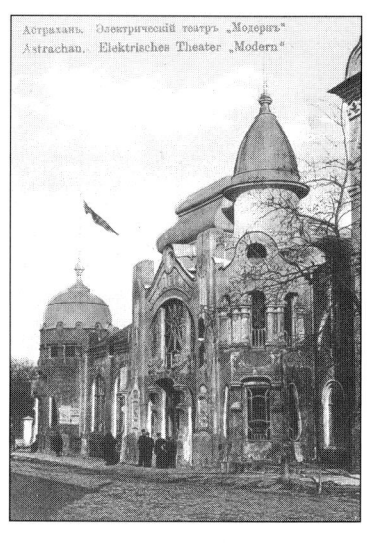

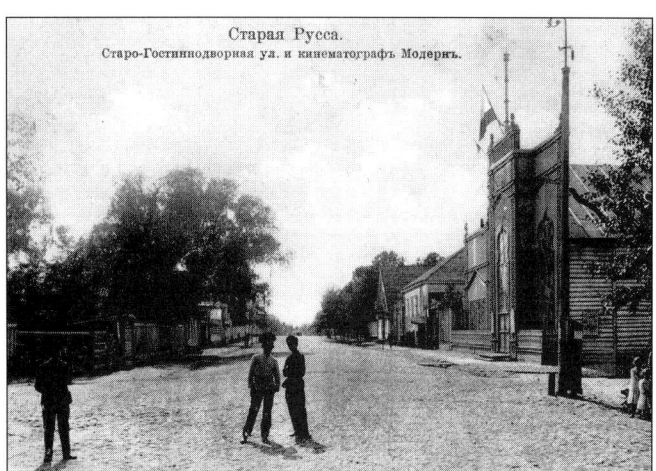

MODERN KINEMATOGRAPH IN STARAIA RUSSA. Staraia Russa is an important port in the province of Novgorod in north-western Russia, whose mineral springs made it a popular spa resort in the 19th century. The Modern Kinematograph on Staro-Gostinnodvornaia Street, photographed in 1913, is a barn-like wooden structure, disguised with an elaborate but flimsy painted façade.

THE ZELICHOW KINO, described as "the Austrian Cinema, near the town of Dubno", appears to be a small structure of logs. Dubno has not been identified, but the postcard was published in Petrograd, sometime after 1914.

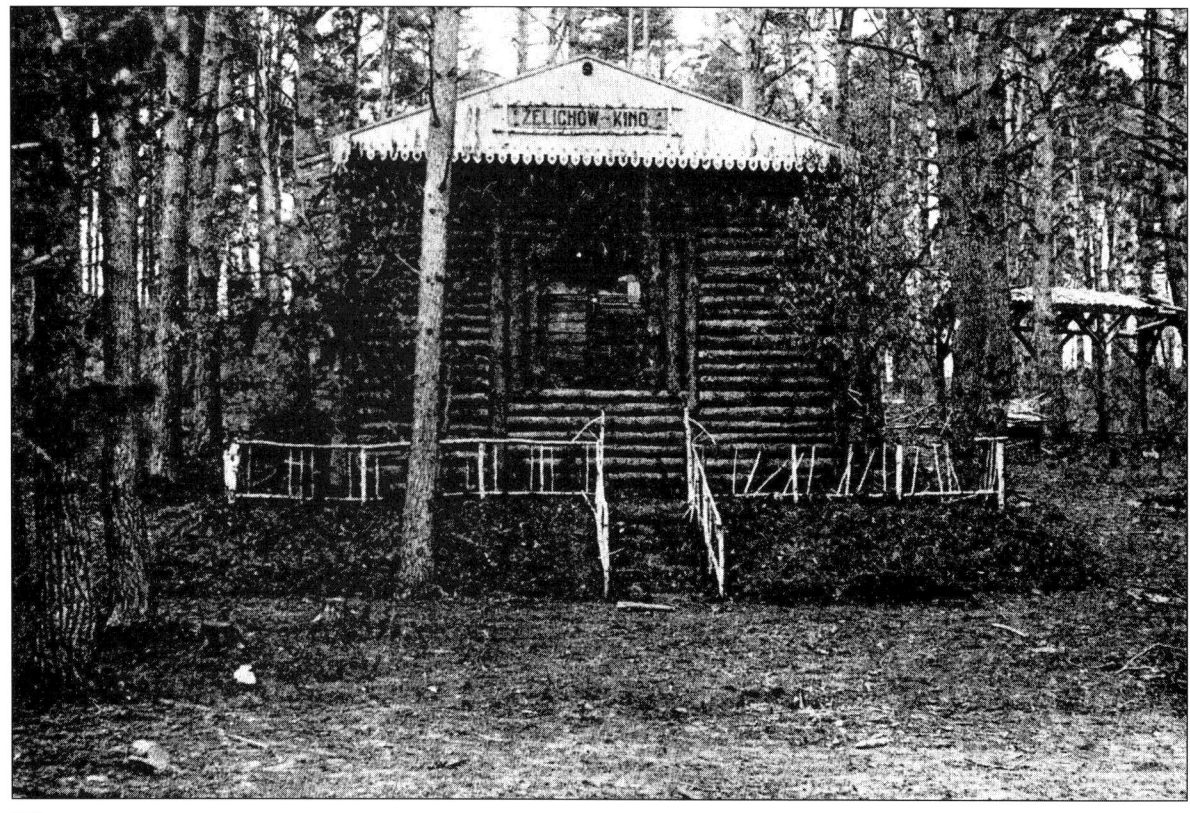

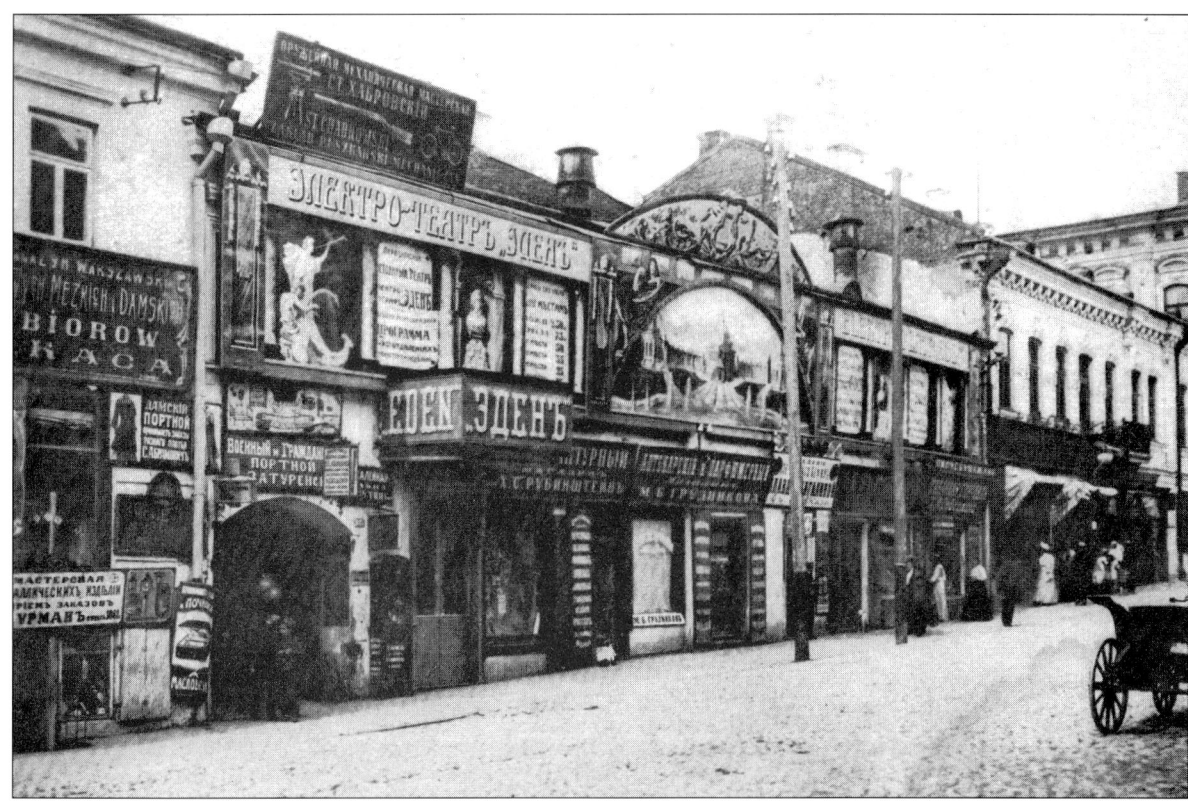

THE ELECTRO-THEATRE EDEN, MINSK, on Sakharevskaya Street, in the commercial district of the capital of Belorussia. Though the cinema's florid advertising covers a considerable extent of the first-floor exterior, the entrance, between the pavement-level shops (including a tailor, metal-worker, and hairdresser), appears very modest.

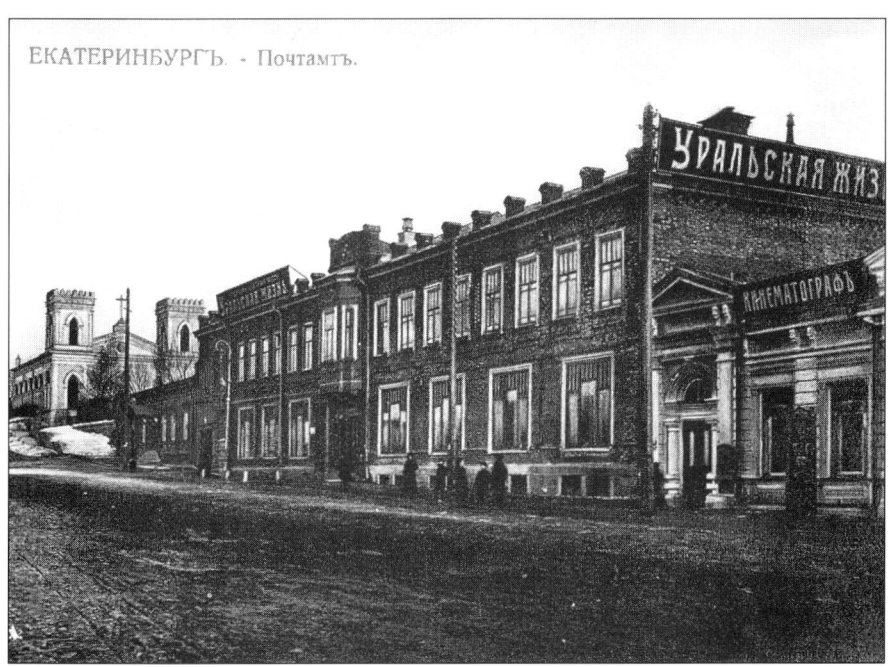

KINEMATOGRAPH, EKATERINBURG. At this modest theatre, in the city where the Royal Family was to be exterminated a few years later, the well-publicised current attraction is a film titled "Life in the Urals".

The Library of Congress and Its "Nitrate Problem"; or, It Was Necessary to Destroy the Nitrate in Order to Preserve It

by Paul C Spehr

Thinking back on some 35 years at the Library of Congress, it is difficult to single out a few experiences with nitrate film as being the most memorable. Nitrate was a dominant part of our lives – an everyday concern. It turned out to be a continual worry. Not a worry to our staff – we worked with it on a daily basis – but it worried the Library's administration, who found it difficult – almost impossible – to deal with nitrate as anything else but a problem: "the Nitrate Problem."

When I started working with the collection in 1958, the Library's management had only one answer to the "Problem" – Get rid of it! This became policy before I started, primarily because of safety considerations, but also under the influence of a concern felt by many of the professional librarians that movies did not really belong in a library. Where did Mickey Mouse, the Three Stooges, and Clark Gable fit into the world of Dickens, Shakespeare, and Walt Whitman?

The anxiety about fire was very genuine. The Library of Congress was custodian of many national, and international, cultural treasures: George Washington's papers, Thomas Jefferson's library, Lincoln's Gettysburg Address, Woodrow Wilson's library, not to mention a world-class collection of rare books, with one of the three surviving complete Gutenberg Bibles as a showpiece, and many other lesser treasures. A realistic concern about fire was neither paranoia nor bureaucratic folly, and the situation was aggravated by the Library's unique administrative position. As the library for the United States Congress, it was first and foremost responsible to the members of Congress, the members of the Senate and the House of Representatives. In effect, it had 500 highly placed and very political bosses, who expected immediate service, who lived by a credo of economy and saving money for taxpayers, and who were all too happy to leap upon and benefit from problems and scandals – if they could be used for publicity and votes. A nitrate fire destroying rare national treasures could be just such a scandal, and was therefore one to be avoided at all costs.

This kept the Library in a bind for many years. The nitrate was banished from the buildings on Capitol Hill, first to commercial vaults in the New York City area, then, in the late 1940s, to a nitrate vault constructed in Suitland, Maryland, an area that was then sparsely populated but close to Washington. Instructions were put in place to remove all nitrate received at the Capitol Hill buildings on the day of receipt and take it to the vault, a practice that was faithfully observed. But what to do about the 15,000 to 17,000 cans of nitrate that the Library had acquired, mostly during the 1940s? There were Hollywood features and shorts deposited for copyright registration, the personal collection of Mary Pickford, including her early Biograph films and many of her features, the surviving films of film pioneer George Kleine, as well as a small but rich treasury of other film donations. Most vexing of all, almost half of the nitrate films were not even American – they were films from

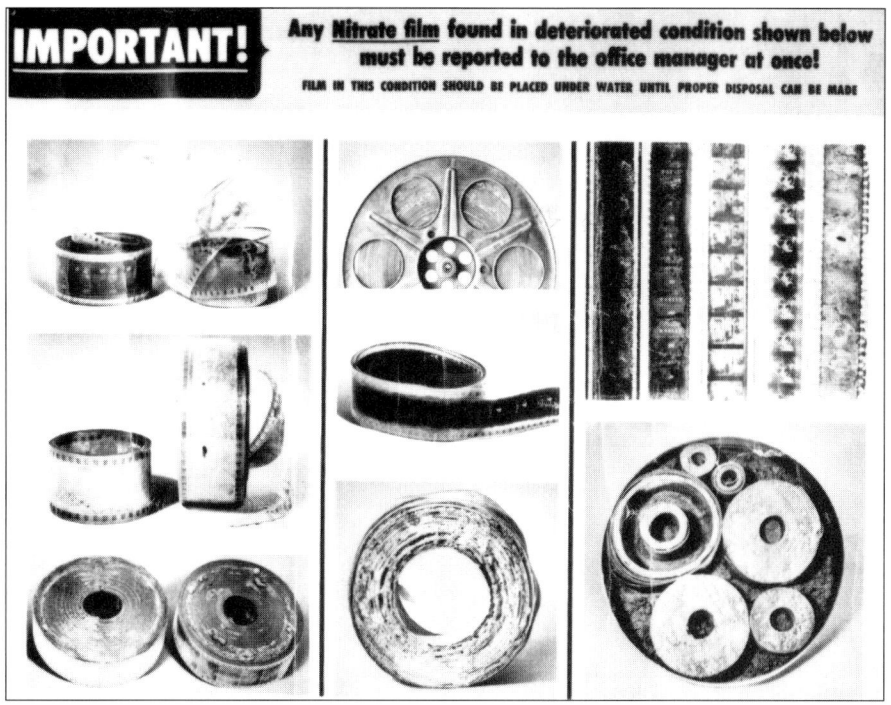

Nitrate as problem: pictured like the villain on a "Wanted" notice, and threatened with being "placed under water until proper disposal", in this poster displayed widely in film exchanges, etc., after the late 1950s.

Dennis Gaughan.

Germany, Japan, and Italy acquired during and immediately after World War II, including features, short cultural films, propaganda, newsreels, military films, etc.

One solution was to weed through and destroy unwanted films – duplicates and cultural trash. But the Library did not have staff with the time and expertise to do this, and the notion of mass destruction of cultural material – even slightly suspect cultural material – was offensive to most of the staff, even those who questioned the value of movies. The compromise solution was to make copies on safety base and throw the originals out, but during the 1950s it was difficult to approach the Congress and ask for money for this. This was the Eisenhower era, the first period when the Republicans had some political clout after the long Roosevelt/Truman years, and they were making government economy a watchword. To approach Congress and ask for money to copy Nazi films and Hollywood productions was to invite immediate rejection – Hollywood could pay for their own, the argument went, they were rich enough. And as for that Nazi stuff, don't even consider asking for money.

Paul Spehr (right) with Kemp Niver in the doorway of Niver's office/workshop in Hollywood where he copied the Library's paper prints. Photograph taken in April 1978.

Paul Spehr.

The Paper Prints came to the rescue. Since the early 1950s the Academy of Motion Picture Arts and Sciences had been paying costs for copying the collection, but after spending about $300,000 on the project they decided that they could not continue to fund it. Academy officials, led by George Seaton and Margaret Herrick, therefore persuaded Thomas Kuchel, California's Republican Senator, to sponsor a bill to appropriate funds for the Library to pay for the preservation work. The bill was to include money for some nitrate preservation as well. Kuchel had substantial respect in Congress, but the bill had opponents and it looked like it might die in

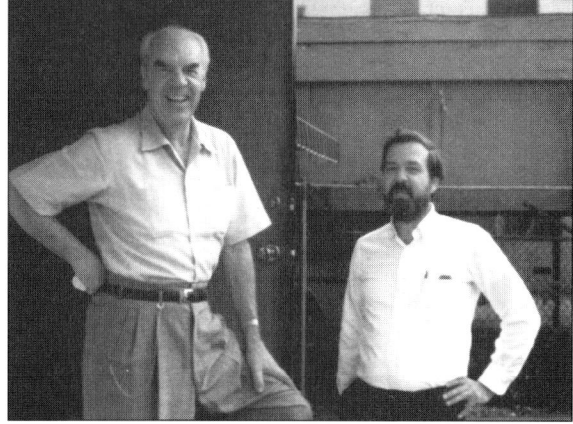

Committee. The turning point came during testimony about the film heritage that had been lost due to nitrate deterioration. The Committee seemed unimpressed by stories of silent features and other treasures destroyed by neglect and decay. This was, apparently, still Hollywood's problem. But the mood changed when the Library reported that among the films that had been lost because of deterioration was a newsreel of President Taft signing the bill making Arizona a state in 1912. One of the delegates from Arizona present at the signing was a young Arizonan, Carl Hayden. In 1957 Hayden was Congressman from Arizona and a power in the US House of Representatives – more importantly, he was a member of the Library's Appropriation Committee. He was shocked to learn that his own image was among the losses. The Library received an appropriation of $60,000 for preservation – $50,000 for Paper Prints and $10,000 for nitrate. It was the first appropriation for motion picture work that the Library had received, and it was continued each year as part of the regular budget for the Library. I benefited directly from this because I was hired to do the paperwork for the new project. Thank you, Messrs Hayden and Kuchel, and Mrs Herrick!

But all was not rosy – at least, not yet. Preservation meant "copy the original, then destroy it". The Library had told this to Congress. It was not a happy prospect, but it was one that the very inexperienced members of the small Motion Picture Section could hardly forestall. There were no motion picture specialists on the staff. I probably came the closest, with a degree in history and a general love of movies, but the movies I knew were American films from the 1940s and 1950s, plus a smattering of standard film classics. Jim Culver, who was in charge, was a collections specialist who had been raised as the son of a Baptist missionary in India, where he saw hardly any films until he was 20 years old. Jim was sincere, hard-working, and very much caught between management pressure and his personal instinct to save and conserve the collections in his charge. He had little choice but to enforce the instructions he received: to spend as little as possible on copying, and then destroy the originals of those that were copied.

The only bright spot in this otherwise bleak picture was that $10,000 did not go very far, so not too many nitrate films were "preserved". But there was enough to copy most of the George Kleine Collection, and the resulting copies sadly provide a model of how not to preserve a collection. The copies were all on 16mm – chosen because it was less expensive than 35mm. There was no experienced staff at the Library to evaluate the quality of the copies, and no specialised equipment to handle the film in inspection. Finding appropriate laboratories was a problem. We were saved by being able to use the film laboratory at the US Department of Agriculture – a government facility that charged modest rates and had a number of experienced lab people, among them Ed Janow, now manager of WRS Laboratories in Pittsburgh. When the Department of Agriculture had to close their lab in the late 1960s it caused a major crisis. During the 1970s the search for adequate, experienced laboratories would be a major factor in dealing with nitrate.

The "get rid of it" philosophy carried with it one other major problem: vaults. No matter how much nitrate there was, there was no question of building new vaults to store it. The vaults the Library occupied at Suitland, Maryland, were assigned to the National Archives, and the Library occupied one of the three buildings under an agreement between the organisations. The vaults were designed to commercial standards, but they were intended to be temporary buildings until better, more permanent ones could be constructed – which never happened. The vaults at Suitland were constructed with porous cinder blocks rather than reinforced concrete, and although there were individual air-conditioning units attached to a central master unit, there was no humidity control. There was an absolute minimum of workroom space, and no loading area for shipping and receiving of material. The design, based on a code meant for commercial vaults, assumed that the film would come and go in small shipments, of one or two shipping containers at a time, and that it would go immediately to vault storage. While there were small shipments, it was common for the Library to receive large shipments consisting of a truckload and even more. This presented logistical problems which drove the safety officers mad. If there were vacant vaults the boxes could go into them, but usually stacked on the floor because the boxes did not fit on the shelves. If there were no empty vaults, the boxes went on the floor in a vault that was already filled to the capacity approved for fire safety. If it was raining, the trucks were unloaded in the rain.

There were other problems as well. During the hot Washington summers the iron fire doors would sweat, and streams of water ran down the corridors. Each fall, as the seasons changed, a flood of crickets invaded the vault building – though only for a few days, and they were uninterested in meals of nitrate. Until the office was remodelled in the 1970s, a cold wind blew through the porous cinder blocks, making it uncomfortable to work with your back to the walls.

At the end of the 1960s, when the American Film Institute began a national program to locate unpreserved nitrate, the quantities of film being acquired quickly outran the capacity of the Washington area vaults. A solution was found at Wright-Patterson Air Force Base, located at the edge of Dayton, Ohio. There was a building with 99 vaults, which had been built in the 1940s when the base was the location of the Air Force's production center. The Air Force was happy to have the Library take them over. These vaults were more solidly constructed than those at Suitland, but had not been used for a number of years. The air-conditioning was in poor shape, and the roof of the building was deteriorating. We moved in, and began a 25-year marathon effort to get these two problems corrected – a saga too long and complicated to go into here. Suffice it to say that the problem involved having to deal with layers of bureaucracy, several of which were staffed with people convinced that their mission was to find a reason for not doing it that way.

Since old vaults had problems, why not design and build new ones? This obvious solution was never considered by the Library's management – it would have been an admission that nitrate was here to stay. Why build a building for a substance that would self-destruct in a few years? Fifty years was supposed to be an outside life-expectancy for nitrate: as the last nitrate was made before 1950, then by 2000 it would all be gone.

But it didn't go away easily. Ironically, even if you wanted to get rid of it, it was not easy to do so. In the 1950s and through most of the 1960s this was a minor problem: it could be taken into a field and burned or buried. One of the staff of the National Archives used to put scraps and nitrate dust from the work tables on the tomatoes she raised outside the vault. They looked great! But as fire safety and environmental specialists became a part of mainstream thinking, more and more obstacles appeared. To comply with government regulations, the Library had to have disposal done by a contractor appointed through open competition. During the "burn or bury" period of the 1960s we could find locals who would bid on it. They would collect the barrels of nitrate scrap, take it to an open field, string out a long strip of nitrate as a fuse, light it, and watch the pile burn. But not always safely – there was an unconfirmed rumor that an employee was killed when hit by a steel plate that had been put over the top of a large pile to control the burning but which was apparently blown some distance when the pile ignited.

By the 1980s the safety and environmental monitors put an end to burning. Nitrate had to be sent to specialists in breaking down hazardous materials. It was not only difficult to find such specialists, but the costs were prohibitive. The companies that could do chemical breakdown were located at a distance from the vaults, and they wanted contracts that guaranteed a quantity of material – impossible to comply with, because the amounts of deteriorating nitrate were declining. Fewer large shipments were being received, and most of the nitrate in storage had stabilized. If a company was found that was willing and able, it was difficult to ship the film to them because deteriorating nitrate was put under water in the containers, and to ship the container with hazardous material under water violated shipping regulations. For a while there was an impasse, but a solution was found: our landlords at Wright-Patterson, the US Air Force, agreed to take our celluloid and include it with their own hazardous materials disposal. Wright-Patterson had been a Strategic Air Command base during the Cold War, and people who dealt daily with high-test aviation fuel, napalm, and H-bombs were not phased by a few barrels of decayed nitrate film.

Wright-Patterson became available in time to help the Library accommodate two particularly memorable acquisitions.

One day in the late 1970s, we received a call from Canada. The National Film and Television Archives had found a buried treasure in a most unlikely place, a swimming pool in Dawson City, Yukon Territory – certainly one of the most unusual archival finds to date. Sam Kula has told the remarkable story of the discovery and recovery of these films in another essay in this volume. The Library became involved because there was a problem – the film had been frozen, and it thawed too rapidly, so that by the time it reached Ottawa condensation was being found in the cans. There was more film than they could handle there, and most of the feature films and theatrical shorts were American productions. Hence the call: would the Library take them – right away, like tomorrow or the day after? We agreed, but had to do some fast talking to convince the Library management, always nervous about more fire hazards, that it was both good for the Library and good for international relations to be co-operative. Before the Library's management meetings could adjourn, Bill O'Farrell and his Canadian crew arrived at Suitland with a truck filled with sopping nitrate. I am not sure how they talked their way through Customs at the border, but Bill is nothing if not resourceful.

After the truck was unloaded, we dispatched our own crew, including several of our laboratory staff, to begin inspecting the film. It was immediately decided that some drying process was essential, because the reels were so wet that the emulsion was lifting off the base with normal handling. There was no way that the rolls of film could dry without serious damage. Our lab manager, Rudy Buchel, recommended building a drying reel, like those used in labs in the nitrate era. He quickly made a sketch and took it to the Library's carpenter shop. It was built within a day or two, and set up in the workroom at Suitland, where the lab's nitrate preparation staff began a cautious process of gingerly unwinding the rolls and then winding the film onto the wooden drying reel, base down, emulsion out. The drying reel could only take about 300 feet, so the 1,000-ft-long reels had to be cut into thirds (to reduce picture loss, the cuts were made as far as possible where there were titles). It was found that film tended to dry rather quickly on the reel. Sometimes just winding onto the reel and then removing it immediately was enough. During the first couple of days, some film was also strung about in the workroom and in the vaults. This made the Library's Safety Officer, a bald-headed man whose looks and bearing were not unlike the Oscar statuette, very unhappy, but we persuaded him that we were making every effort to handle the film as safely as possible in difficult circumstances. He reluctantly let us go ahead.

Every film was dried and eventually copied, but unfortunately many reels suffered serious damage from bits of the emulsion that lifted or flaked off. The edges of the frames were most affected, and the damage was most pronounced at the head and tail of the reels. They were copied, damaged frames and all, but our older staff members can recognise a "Dawson" reel immediately by the edge damage. The wetting and drying of the film had an unexpected benefit, however: it corrected quite a lot of other damage. Dawson films are now remarkably free of projection scratches, digs, etc., and when there is no edge damage the images are remarkably good. It was worth the effort! Almost all of the films were unique, and the collection, most of it dating from the 1910s, makes it possible to see the work of many film companies, directors, and performers whose work is otherwise hard to find.

The nitrate found in Dawson is the most dramatic find in North America, but a collection discovered in a barn in rural Michigan may claim second place. In April 1987, while I was in Dayton for a supervisory visit to the film vaults and laboratory at Wright-Patterson, I received a call from Professor Jo Collier at the University of Toledo, in northern Ohio. She and an associate, Scott Nygren, had been telling their film history class about nitrate preservation and the loss of films from the silent era. One of their students remarked that his family had film in a barn on their farm in nearby southern Michigan. It was collected years ago, during the silent era. It had been shown to the family from time to time, but now it had been stored there for years, although the children were occasionally allowed to burn some as a substitute for fireworks on the Fourth of July. As a student work project in film preservation, and with the family's approval, Collier, Nygren, and some students drove to the farm, where they collected several dozen large paint cans filled with nitrate and drove it to Toledo. They took the film to a building which the University's Theater Department rented in a run-down area on the edge of downtown, and began a class project to check and inventory the collection. It did not take long to find deterioration, which they were not equipped to handle. They had no rewinds, no replacement cans, and no experience in handling nitrate. Hence the call to the Library of Congress. Could I come and advise them?

I made a couple of calls to Washington and got an OK to drive to Toledo, about three hours north of Dayton. Two days later, with George Willeman from our vaults along, I was in Toledo. Although Collier and Nygren meant well, the film could hardly have been in a worse place. It was an old building in run-down condition in an area where most of the neighbouring buildings were empty and awaiting redevelopment. The Theater Department used it to store sets, props, and costumes. The paint cans that had been used to store the film were shaped like an old-fashioned milk can, a cylinder that narrowed towards the top. Sealed with fairly tight lids, they had allowed no way for the nitrate gases to escape. The accumulated gases had apparently affected the top cans more than the rest, because when the paint cans were opened the first can often had serious deterioration. It was a fire waiting to happen. I told Collier and Nygren that the collection needed to be in a vault and inspected by experienced staff. They agreed that the Library could take it, but the family had to OK any long-term arrangement. Knowing that it might take months to get an agreement from the Library's bureaucracy, I called Susan Dalton at the American Film Institute. The Library had an agreement with the AFI allowing them to store film temporarily at the Library while they negotiated donation. Two days later Susan flew from Washington, DC to Toledo, rented a truck, loaded the film into it, and drove to Wright-Patterson with it. She arrived about 5:10 p.m., at the end of the working day. We immediately unloaded the truck, discovering as we unloaded that the bed of the truck under the paint cans filled with nitrate had become very hot during her drive. Susan was glad she didn't know about the risk of fire while travelling at high speed on the busy interstate highway.

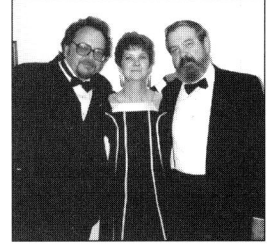

Paul Spehr (right), with Bob Rosen of the UCLA Film and Television Archive and Susan Dalton of the American Film Institute, photographed at Spehr's house before the AFI's Preservation Ball in Washington, DC on 21 May 1988.

Paul Spehr.

While we were unpacking the cans we began getting calls from the press. Professors Collier and Nygren, who recognized it was a good story, had contacted the *Toledo*

Blade, who interviewed me about the collection while I was in Toledo. The article appeared on Saturday, and it stimulated a rush of press coverage. *Variety* had an article the next Wednesday, the *Dayton Daily News* put it on the AP wire service, a Dayton television station sent a crew to film the staff working on the collection in the vaults and the laboratory, WABC radio in New York did an interview, and CNN, CBS, the *Cincinnati Enquirer*, the *Detroit News*, and National Public Radio all did stories. As a result, the Library and the American Film Institute received several calls from people with film collections, and, remarkably, the family discovered more nitrate on the farm where the original collection was found.

Ironically, nitrate did not self-destruct as predicted. The Library has nitrate that is more than 100 years old, and I have seen strips that are close to 110 years old that are in remarkably good condition. Even with vaults that are far from ideal, once the Library had done the initial inspection of new nitrate and removed already deteriorating portions, the deterioration rate was considerably reduced. The nervousness of the Library's management has also been reduced. Perhaps *that* was what deteriorated.

Playing with Fire

by Clyde Jeavons

"To find a formula for fire-proofing celluloid is a very difficult factor."
(*The Love Test*, 1935, dir Michael Powell)

Combs. Hair combs. These and other seemingly innocuous personal adornments, popularly made from celluloid, the first commercial plastic and a cheap substitute for tortoiseshell, ivory, amber, and the like, were the cause of more domestic accidents between the World Wars in Britain – some of them fatal – than fires set off in the home by the projection of nitrate film.[1]

All kinds of domestic articles and trinkets, such as hairpins, cuffs, collars, collar stiffeners, toys (especially dolls and babies' rattles), boots, buckles, toothbrushes, soap dishes, zip fasteners, spectacle frames, and knife handles might contain or be made of celluloid, and bizarre accidents could occur. In a number of incidents recorded by the London County Council (LCC) in 1937, two children were burned on separate occasions by their rattles apparently igniting while they were in their perambulators in the garden; sparks from a man's pipe fell into a pocket and set his spectacles on fire; and (supplying a full dose of irony) in the stalls of the Rio Cinema, Craigmillar, Edinburgh, a lighted match "was carelessly thrown down and came into contact with one of the shoes worn by a lady. The heel of her shoe was made of wood and encased in celluloid which burst into flames".

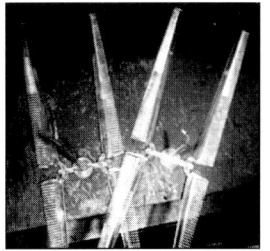

The manufacture of combs – one of the uses of recycled celluloid, according to the French film *L'Age du Plastique* (1943).

Archives du Film du Centre National de la Cinématographie, Bois d'Arcy.

Celluloid knife handles – manufactured in large quantities in Sheffield to imitate bone or ivory – were common catalysts of fire in the kitchen, as were electric irons, and in one case reported by a Mr T Breaks (honestly!) of the Home Office Fire Brigades Division, the two colluded improbably but spectacularly: an electric iron left on a table burned through the table-top and into a drawer underneath containing knives with celluloid handles, causing "a tremendous burst of flame". ("It is a common thing," commented Mr Breaks informatively, "for an electric iron to burn through the table, but it generally drops straight on to the floor." Quite.)

However, "the largest cause of fire is the comb," said Lt Col Sir Vivian Henderson, Chairman of a Home Office Departmental Committee on the Use of Celluloid in the Manufacture of Toys and Fancy Goods, Etc. (of which more in due course), taking evidence from the London County Council in March 1938 – a fact noted many years earlier by another governmental report, that of the Departmental Committee on Celluloid in 1912/13, which stated, "The articles most likely to cause accidents are those worn on the person, such as combs (and) hairpins ... [and] ... special risks attach to wearing celluloid in the hair." Half the celluloid-induced fires tabled by the LCC between 1931 and 1936 (fourteen in all) involved combs, and Henderson's Committee – meeting in December 1937 – quoted the case of a badly-injured Newcastle girl, in 1928, "wearing a celluloid comb in her hair, who put her head over a snapdragon". A snapdragon? Not the popular flower in this case, but a Christmas game of snatching raisins out of burning brandy – dangerous enough, one would have thought, without the addition of celluloid in the hair.[2]

By the earliest days of publicly projected cinema, the hazardous nature of celluloid (i.e., cellulose nitrate plasticized with camphor) was, of course, already well known – the stuff had, after all, been around since the late 1860s – though highlighted (as it were) by various serious fires in shops and factories (notably in Sheffield's cutlery workshops) and those "associated with the trade in cinematograph films". As referred to by David Cleveland (in his article "Don't Try This at Home", also in this volume), the Cinematograph Act of 1909 had led to the construction of purpose-built cinemas, which helped to reduce dramatically the incidence of film fires in public places, but enough concern remained for the Celluloid Committee (see above) to be convened in 1912, "to inquire and report as to the precautions necessary in the use of celluloid in manufacture and the handling and storage of celluloid and celluloid articles".

This Committee, having acknowledged the benefits of celluloid ("It is hard, tough and elastic … capable of being moulded into shapes"), went on to describe in vivid and familiar terms its dangerous properties: "Celluloid possesses the serious defect of being highly inflammable. It ignites very readily, and burns with great rapidity and fierceness … in certain circumstances it may ignite without the direct application of flame. The ignition of a film in a cinematograph machine is a familiar occurrence… When well alight, great jets of flame are shot out…" There is awareness of "large volumes of inflammable and poisonous gases, which will ignite or explode on contact with fire", but already the myth of liability to "spontaneous ignition at ordinary temperatures" or "that it is explosive in ordinary circumstances" is seen to lack scientific evidence. Nor does the Committee hold out much hope for the successful neutralisation of celluloid's inflammability without sacrificing the properties "on which its commercial value depends".[3]

The positive aspects of these remarks, together with cellulose nitrate's recognised special virtue of dimensional stability, perhaps go some way towards explaining why the substance – perilous and self-destructive though it may have been – lasted so long, especially as the carrier for professional motion pictures. It was widely used for many serious as well as decorative purposes – for example, in cycle and motor accessories, the printing trade, and surgical instruments and appliances – and the Celluloid Committee itself was surprised at the extent of its use, estimating that celluloid "in one form or another is to be found in between 40 to 50 percent. of the shops in certain districts of London".

Significantly, however, the general danger from celluloid was thought to be exaggerated, notwithstanding the relatively few fatal fires which had involved loss of life between 1893 and 1912. Concerning the "private use of celluloid" there was a lack of information, but serious accidents again seemed to be rare considering how much celluloid was in circulation. Nevertheless, the conveyance and storage of celluloid should, the Committee said, be strictly regulated and controlled, and shopkeepers were warned of particular hazards, such as placing celluloid articles in windows where the sun's rays might focus upon them, or using hot sealing wax on parcels containing celluloid (the cause, it was claimed, of the infamous 1912 disaster in Moor Lane which killed nine people), or soldering packages containing celluloid "without the interposition of a protective plate between the part soldered and the celluloid" (the cause, it seems, of several serious fires in Paris – obviously the Soldering Capital of Europe). The point, really, was that the manufacture and sale of celluloid to the public was a major industry and not to be restricted, but safety measures should be introduced and enforced, particularly those relating to smoking, fire hazards, and storage close to habitation.

Even more significant, though, in the present context, was the Committee's statement that "The trade in cinematograph films requires separate consideration…" Why? Because, it said, "The celluloid used in the manufacture of films is more highly nitrated than ordinary celluloid", ignites more readily, and "burns more fiercely". For this reason, vigilance should be that much greater and regulations more stringently applied, but in particular – and remember, this was said in 1912, almost 40 years before nitrate film finally ceased to be made – "The replacement of celluloid in cinematograph films by a less inflammable substitute is very much to be desired..." Indeed, some articles, including film, were already being made of non-flammable cellulose triacetate.

The 1913 Report of the Departmental Committee on Celluloid concludes quite abruptly with two curt statements. The first says: "It has come to our notice that in certain cases films are festooned in shop windows. This practice, which is repudiated by the regular trade, is inexcusable and should be absolutely prohibited." The second, more pertinent to this piece, says the following: *Toy Cinematograph Machines. —* We desire to call attention to the fact that toy machines as well as strips of disused films are being sold to children. The machine is being sold at a very low price and contains no safeguard for preventing the film (the whole length of which is exposed) from catching fire. We are of opinion that the sale of cinematograph films to children should be prohibited."

Which neatly carries the story forward. In 1915, the London County Council (Celluloid, Etc.) Act made it "an offence in the County of London to sell to another person...under the age of sixteen years ... any cinematograph (celluloid) film..." In 1916, controls were brought in to regulate the manufacture and storage of nitrate film in Britain, later strengthened by the Celluloid and Cinematograph Films Act of 1932. And in 1921, the Royal Commission on Fire Brigades and Fire Prevention reiterated the view that the sale of celluloid articles and toys should be prohibited unless they were plainly marked "inflammable". It was not until 1937 that the Home Office turned its attention to the subject once again by setting up the Departmental Committee on the Use of Celluloid in the Manufacture of Toys, Fancy Goods, Etc. (see above), with particular attention to "Accidents and Deaths from the Ignition of Cinematograph Film for Home Projectors".

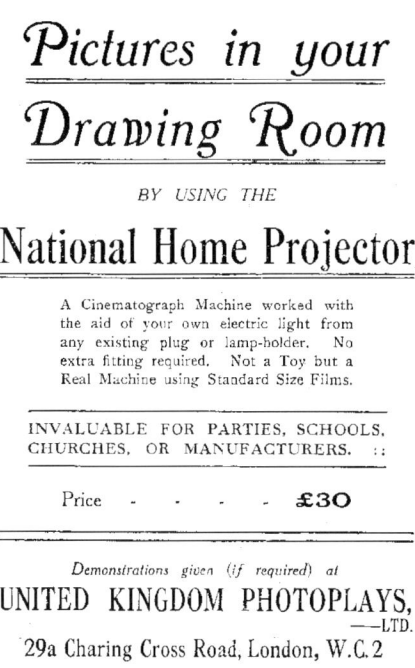

YOU CAN GIVE YOUR FRIENDS

Pictures in your

Drawing Room

BY USING THE

National Home Projector

A Cinematograph Machine worked with the aid of your own electric light from any existing plug or lamp-holder. No extra fitting required. Not a Toy but a Real Machine using Standard Size Films.

INVALUABLE FOR PARTIES, SCHOOLS, CHURCHES, OR MANUFACTURERS. ::

Price - - - - **£30**

Demonstrations given (if required) at

UNITED KINGDOM PHOTOPLAYS,
——LTD.

29a Charing Cross Road, London, W.C. 2

Telephone:
GERRARD 8742

Telegrams:
UNIKINPHOS
Phone London

An advertisement for a projector using "Standard Size" – 35mm nitrate – film, for use at home, included in Valentia Steer, *The Secrets of the Cinema* (London: C Arthur Pearson, 1920).

East Anglian Film Archive, Norwich.

As has been noted, there were a number of domestic fires in the 1930s caused or exacerbated by the presence of celluloid objects other than film, and many of these resulted in deaths, often to small children: 21 such fatal incidents are recorded in the 1937 Committee's findings. There were perhaps an equal number of reported fires involving the projection of nitrate film in the home, mostly on "toy" projectors, yet only two deaths: in Sutton Coldfield, in 1937, two boys aged 11 and 5 used a miner's acetylene lamp to illuminate the threading of a 100-ft roll of film, with lethal consequences. The Home Office Fire Brigades Division regarded celluloid fires as "so few and far between" that they did not consider them as a "category". Normally, they would put them down as "children playing with fire". Mr Breaks, the Fire Brigades representative, said that at one time "I used to have them at Christmas with the small cinema, but even that has gone".

Mr Breaks expands usefully in the Departmental Committee's report on the nature of "toy cinemas". "We should not confuse the toy cinema," he is reported as saying, "... with the small cinema of today where they use miniature non-flam film which is practically perfectly safe. The toy cinema ... is a very cheap model which was a Japanese product ... [using] the standard width film, junk film ... obtained from all sorts of places … and the illuminant was an ordinary little paraffin lamp which in itself was a definite danger." Subsequent prosecution of culpable toyshop-keepers had, he said, virtually stopped this illicit trade. A later expert witness offered a variation on Mr Breaks's description, comparing the toy cinema with amateur and professional models: "The toy cinema is a thing built as a toy. It is made of pressed tin, as German toys normally are,[4] with spool boxes quite exposed, and revolving on pieces of wire. It is very lightly built, and is purely a toy … and in every case I think it is hand-operated. With regard to the amateur machine … [it] is built quite solidly like a professional machine, but is used for hand operation. But in that case the spool box is nearly always exposed. It is more or less a skeleton projector."

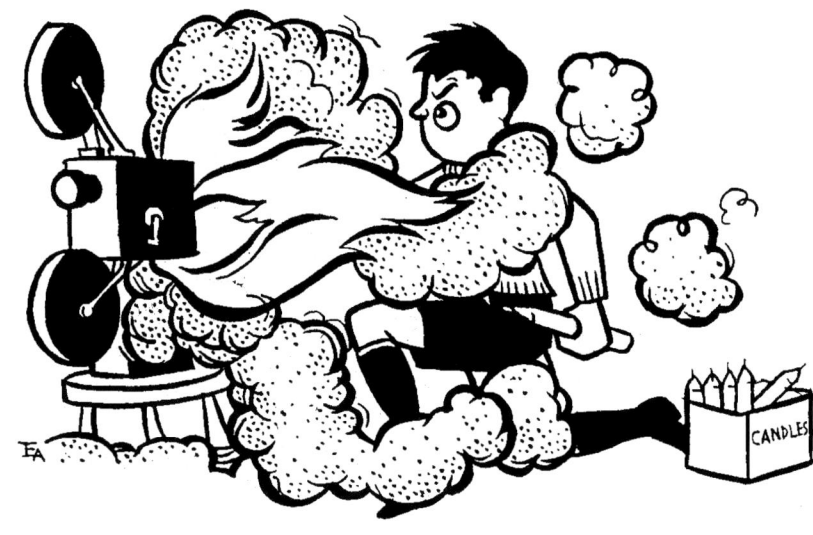

A drawing prepared by "EA" [E Andrewes?] in 1958 as an illustration for an apparently unfinished book project, "Film Presentation by T L Pilkington". The drawing post-dates the official switch to nitrate by several years, so the exact point it was seeking to illustrate remains a little obscure.

BFI Collections – Stills, Posters & Designs, London.

Another advertisement for a home projector using films "the same as the theatre uses", from *The Secrets of the Cinema*.

East Anglian Film Archive, Norwich.

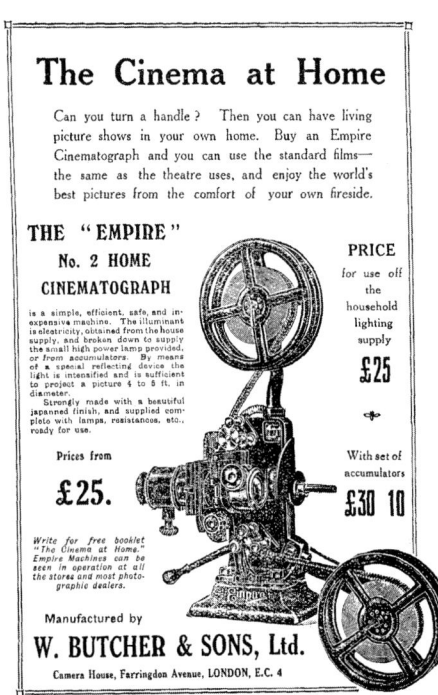

The Cinema at Home

Can you turn a handle ? Then you can have living picture shows in your own home. Buy an Empire Cinematograph and you can use the standard films— the same as the theatre uses, and enjoy the world's best pictures from the comfort of your own fireside.

THE "EMPIRE"
No. 2 HOME
CINEMATOGRAPH

is a simple, efficient, safe, and inexpensive machine. The illuminant is electricity, obtained from the house supply, and broken down to supply the small high power lamp provided, or from accumulators. By means of a special reflecting device the light is intensified and is sufficient to project a picture 4 to 5 ft. in diameter. Strongly made with a beautiful japanned finish, and supplied complete with lamps, resistances, etc., ready for use.

Prices from

£25.

Write for free booklet "The Cinema at Home." Empire Machines can be seen in operation at all the stores and most photographic dealers.

PRICE
for use off
the
household
lighting
supply

£25

With set of
accumulators

£30 10

Manufactured by
W. BUTCHER & SONS, Ltd.
Camera House, Farringdon Avenue, LONDON, E.C. 4

In any event, the Committee chose to remain concerned about the dangers of nitrate film in the home. "The celluloid industry is a definite menace," said Mr Breaks, despite his dismissal of the paltry statistics, and incidents involving the juxtaposition of inflammable film with candles, cigarettes, hot lamphouses, open fires, and (in one case) fireworks were sufficiently worrying to make them want to find a formula for prohibiting the sale of toy cinemas designed for 35mm film and to eliminate the petty traffic in small lengths of junk nitrate film, and this was its conclusion.[5] The prevention of a single death was sufficient reason. "If the toy machine could be washed out [sic]," said one expert witness, "practically all your cases would disappear." They did not, however, wish to penalise "responsible adults" using properly made standard-width machines. [Other solutions were put forward, including mutilation of cinema films "after use" by the renter, and running each film "through a very cheap printing machine [to] black it all out". Yes, this Committee had its passengers like any other: another member was under the impression that nitrate film had "entirely gone out of use so far as the big cinema [sic] is concerned", and that they now used "all this so-called non-flam stuff".]

Side issues relating to the Departmental Committee Report of 1937/38, the last of its kind on this topic until the 1970s, included a very peremptory and partial look at comparable situations overseas. Belgium and Poland, it was observed, had no regulations governing the sale of articles made of celluloid, but quoted in full was the law in the State of Kentucky, USA, where it was "not permissible for any persons, firm or corporation to sell any toy or miniature motion picture machine containing nitro-cellulose motion picture film or to sell, lease or otherwise dispose of any nitro-cellulose motion picture film to any person not properly licensed". There was also a reference to another American disaster, at the Cleveland Clinic, in Ohio, some years previously, where "over 90 or 100 people" were killed as a result of hospital X-rays on nitrate film "becoming ignited or starting to decompose owing to [the] proximity of the boilers".[6]

The Committee does not seem to have been aware of a source for other stories originating in America, in which they might perhaps have found an anecdote more relevant to their deliberations than the Cleveland Clinic fire. The *National Fire Protection Association Quarterly*, which regularly reported on fires of all kinds, had reported in its issue of July 1926 the sad story of 15-year-old Louis Lelong and his 4-year-old sister Mary, who perished following a fire in the basement of their home in South Orange, New Jersey. The Lelong children gave regular moving picture shows for their friends, the laundry room becoming, for this purpose, the "Realm Theatre – Latest Reels Every Saturday at 10 A.M.", equipped with a German-made projector called an Optica showing 35mm nitrate film. On the morning of 1 May 1926, according to the survivors, when Louis tried to rectify a film mis-feed without shutting off the lamp, a fire started which quickly spread to the spare reels of film, the paper decorations, and the fabric screens that formed the projection "booth". Louis led seven or eight guests to safety outside, but then noticed that Mary was not among them and rushed back to look for her, only to be overcome by fumes. "When later found by the firemen," noted the *Quarterly*, "his body was bent over that of Mary in an attitude of protection. The girl never regained consciousness, but the boy lived long enough to tell the story of the attempted rescue, and to 'hope that little Mary was all right.'"[7] Despite its touching conclusion, however, and the opportunity it gave to draw an obvious lesson – "The prevention of the recurrence of such a tragedy as this lies in the absolute prohibition of the sale of moving picture films of nitro-cellulose stock except when they are to be used in a standard fire-resistive booth and handled by a licensed operator." – the story was, nonetheless, worth the telling principally because such incidents were so comparatively rare.

To emphasise this point, film history offers a very celebrated case history of one young boy who never experienced a domestic celluloid fire, despite repeatedly exposing himself and his household to just the same risks as those described above. Ingmar Bergman has on several occasions explained how he longed for a cinematograph as a child.[8] At last, in December 1928, when he was 10 years old, there was one among the Christmas presents – but it was addressed to his elder brother! Bitterly disappointed, and determined to secure the machine for himself, the future director bartered half his army of lead soldiers to get it. He then retreated into a "spacious wardrobe" in the family's "big wooden house", where he proceeded to project the 3-metre loop of 35mm nitrate film that came with the hand-cranked machine by the light of its paraffin lamp. In these dangerous circumstances, an addiction was born...

Notes

1. The reports and minutes on which this article is largely based were kindly provided to the editors by David Francis in June 2000.

2. For additional information on the dangers of wearing celluloid hair combs, see "The Common Hazards of Fire Insurance", elsewhere in this volume.

3. Interestingly, in the light of future archival experience, research tests at the time concluded that

"Celluloid of good quality does not undergo appreciable deterioration when stored for some months at a tropical temperature ... [and] does not seriously deteriorate when kept from 20 to 35 years."

4. It is interesting that these two witnesses have between them implicated both Britain's future wartime enemies as the villains in this particular piece! For a comprehensive account of toy and other home projectors in the British market, see Gerald McKee, *The Home Cinema: Classic Home Movie Projectors 1922–1940* (privately published by Mr McKee in 1989, reprinted by The Ipswich Book Company, 1994).

5. *Editor's note: An example of precisely the situation that concerned the Committee was provided in a personal nitrate reminiscence sent by Ian Rintoul to Roger Smither in 1998:* "My first encounter with this combustible material came as a primary schoolboy swapping comics and bits of string to acquire a German-made tinplate hand-cranked toy projector, the light source being a household candle, along with a 'loop' of film which ran continuously and featured a cartoon dog going in and out of a kennel. A local secondhand shop ... sold 'films', small lengths of 10 to 30 feet ... openly displayed in the window... I was to find out much later that these short film lengths – 'Various Subjects' – had been randomly cut from silent 35mm cinema feature films... Some time later came the realisation that I was playing about with a highly inflammable material – 'nitrate' – in these small reels which I treasured."

6. For more information on the 1927 Cleveland Clinic disaster (and other film fires), see the "Calendar of Nitrate Fires" elsewhere in this volume.

7. "Children Die in Film Fire", in *National Fire Protection Association Quarterly*, v.20, no.1 (July 1926), pp. 49–50, supplied by David Pierce.

8. Three English-language sources for this story are: Ingmar Bergman, *The Magic Lantern: An Autobiography*, translated from Swedish by Joan Tate (London: Hamish Hamilton, 1988), pp. 13–16; "Introduction: Bergman Discusses Film-making", in *Four Screenplays of Ingmar Bergman*, translated from the Swedish by Lars Malmstrom and David Kushner (New York: Simon and Schuster, 1960), pp. xiii–xv; *Bergman on Bergman*, interviews with Ingmar Bergman by Stig Björkman, Torsten Manns and Jonas Sima, translated from the Swedish by Paul Britten Austin (London: Secker & Warburg, 1973), pp. 6–11.

Not So Dangerous:
Some Recollections

by P K Nair

The fragile and inflammable nature of cellulose nitrate cinematograph film never occurred as a serious threat to early film-makers in India. In fact, many of them treated it as casually as any other material in daily use, and the inherent danger never bothered them. The first signs of danger were noticed when accidental fires took place in projection cabins. Even fires of this kind were attributed to electrical short circuits rather than the inflammable nature of the film stock. When such projection-cabin fires became frequent, the authorities stepped in to enforce laws for the licensing of cinema buildings to protect public health and safety, and to ensure adequate precautionary measures for the prevention of fire hazards. These regulations never spelled out the dangerous aspect of nitrate film itself in clear terms, although the rules for railways put films in the "inflammable" category, prohibiting passengers from carrying any film material as personal luggage inside compartments. Ironically, these rules are still operative; the carrying of films as personal luggage inside compartments is prohibited even today. According to the railways' rule book, all film material is regarded as "explosive", whether nitrate or safety. Significantly, although there have been a number of fires in railway compartments in the last century, to the best of my knowledge none has been attributed to the transportation of nitrate films. But still the fear persists; hence the precautions.

Major Losses

Nitrate fire has not been the only cause of the loss of some of our precious film heritage. There have been several other factors, like sheer neglect on the part of film-makers, and, more importantly, the lack of realisation by society at large that film is a cultural product that needs to be preserved for posterity. Films, whether nitrate or safety, have always had a low level of priority in our national consciousness; Cinema was not considered to be respectable or on a level with the other Arts. The debate still goes on as to whether films form part of our country's culture or not. Our first major fire-related loss

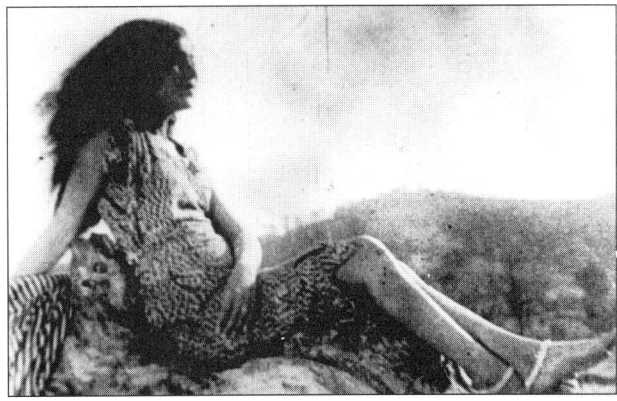

A still from the lost film Alam Ara (1931).

National Film Archive of India, Pune.

occurred with the first of D G Phalke's films, *Raja Harischandra* (1913). The only surviving print was lost in a fire a few years later, while it was being transported in a bullock cart from one tent-cinema to another. The actual cause of the accident was not known, but it was reported that the nitrate print had already had a large number of screenings and was practically worn out, and that the accident may have happened while loading or unloading. In 1917, when Phalke found out that the original negatives had also vanished, he hurriedly went ahead and re-shot the film, duplicating the original shot by shot, taking the opportunity to insert title cards asserting his claim to be "the father of the Indian film industry" and "the great Pioneer of the East". Simultaneously, he made a short film entitled *How Films Are Prepared* (1917). This showed him at work on the making of the first Indian film, *Raja Harischandra*, directing the actors, editing the film, supervising set construction, and fixing up wardrobes and costumes for the artists. [1]

More Losses

Other major losses included the first Indian talkie, *Alam Ara*, made in 1931 by Ardheshir M Irani of the Imperial Film Company of Bombay, and the country's first colour film, *Sairandhri* (1933), made by the Prabhat Film Company of Pune and directed by the veteran V Shantaram. This was one of the earliest films shot in the Agfacolor process. The film was processed in Babelsberg in Germany. The casualty list includes many more significant titles.

A Historic Nitrate fire

A major fire took place in Calcutta during World War II, in the film storage vaults of the famous New Theatres Studio at Tollygunge. The following account was narrated to me by Mr Dilip Sircar, the son of Birendranath Sircar (popularly known as B N Sircar), the founder and architect of Calcutta New Theatres, one of the major studios, which was responsible for some of the outstanding Indian films of the 1930s and 1940s.

> It was in the month of August 1940 (I do not remember the exact date), when I had been to the Mohan Bagan football ground here in Calcutta along with my father (B N Sircar), to watch Mohan Bagan play in the local League fixtures. A person came and whispered something into my father's ear. My father left immediately, telling me someone else would take me home. On reaching home, my grandfather Sir N N Sircar, told me (of course I did not realise its implications then) that I did not know the huge loss I myself had suffered that evening (being the heir-apparent of New Theatres). That "loss" was that of many prints and original negatives of some of the classic New Theatres' films, made in the 30s. A devastating fire had engulfed the laboratories. The cause of the fire was not known then.

> My father reached the Studio and silently watched the films, representing the efforts of the Company in the first decade of its existence, go up in flames. (I do not know the exact titles which were destroyed.) P C Barua (one of the creative directors of the studio), came running to enquire about the fate of his 1935 classic, *Devdas*. B N Sircar coolly mentioned, "No, Devdas is standing next to me only." (Barua played the role of Devdas in the Bengali version of the film, besides directing it.)

> With the very meagre technical facilities available at the time, "dupes" of the films whose original negatives had been destroyed were prepared from good quality positive prints which were in circulation with our distributors, Aurora Film Corporation Ltd. in Calcutta.

> The studio staff initially lent a helping hand – the fire service joined later. The cause of the fire could have been an accident, or due to the hot summer and the rising temperature outside.

Natural vs Man-made Fires

There were several such fires in the film godowns [warehouses] of Bombay and Madras in the 1930s and 1940s. Unfortunately, no authentic details of the cause and the extent of damage of these fires are available. But what really baffles me is an intriguing case of a supposedly accidental fire that sent two entire decades' worth of production of an established Bombay studio up in flames some time in the late 1940s. The studio I am referring to is Ranjit Movietone, of Chandulal Shah and

Gohar Kayoum Mamajiwala (the actress Gohar Bai). The studio, established at the very end of the silent era, made over 120 films in the 1930s and 1940s, most of which, I believe, were highly successful. The National Film Archive of India in Pune managed to get hold of only three or four of this studio's titles. It seems that Ranjit Movietone was going through a bad phase in the late 1940s, with increasing liabilities, and was on the verge of liquidation. The studio boss, Mr C J Shah, a regular racegoer, lost heavily in the Bombay Races and was heavily in debt. One of the stories that circulated about the godown fire was that it was all cleverly manipulated, with the sole intention of collecting a fat insurance claim. It is not known whether Mr Shah and his colleagues succeeded in their intentions or not, but in any case the studio soon went into liquidation, and the three or four left-over titles became entangled in a copyright dispute.

Fires and Beyond

The above incident might offer an interesting case study. The wilful destruction of nitrate films (both prints and negatives) for petty monetary considerations has always existed. To the early film-maker or distributor it was a routine affair, once a film's commercial possibilities had dried up and there was no hope of getting any further returns. It was too much of a burden to take care of the nitrate footage, so they took the easy path of writing it off as waste. No eyebrows were raised then, perhaps not even now, as it was the normal practice. If the film-maker was broke and had nowhere to turn, this was the last resort, as the silver extracted from the films could bring him some income to keep going. In addition, the waste cellulose film could also be traded to fetch extra returns. Film disposal units operating in major film production centres were thriving business enterprises, providing raw material for the manufacture of bangles, ladies' handbags, wallets, and similar utilitarian items for the daily use of the common man or woman. So it was that the box-office was not the only hope for the film entrepreneur – other options were also open to him. Terms like "cultural heritage" and "preservation for posterity" were way beyond his frame of mind and business practices. And so, fires or no fires, nitrate or otherwise, destruction and cultural loss will continue to be there, however much we archivists may struggle to prevail.

Why Blame Nitrate?

By now everyone in the film business is fully aware that it is risky to dump too many nitrate cans in a non-air-conditioned godown and not care about their upkeep. An impartial analysis of all the nitrate fires that have taken place in India or elsewhere would reveal that the large majority of them have occurred due to human error, and not because of the highly publicised self-ignition theory, or the self-destructive nature of nitrate. So why blame the stock, when we ourselves have faltered somewhere along the line? It is too idealistic to expect that some archive-friendly entrepreneur would manufacture a wonderful stock that would last forever. We all know by now that even so-called "safety" stock is not as safe as the manufacturers claim. I have come across instances where safety stock has deteriorated much faster than nitrate. The maximum damage in nitrate has been noted in stock that came to the country in the 1940s, during the war. Presumably because of war priorities, substandard stock was sent to countries like India, which had by then become established as a major film-producing country. For a manufacturer to admit this in public would be embarrassing. Perhaps they might confess it in private. Besides, there is ample proof in the extent of deterioration that has taken place in films from that period.

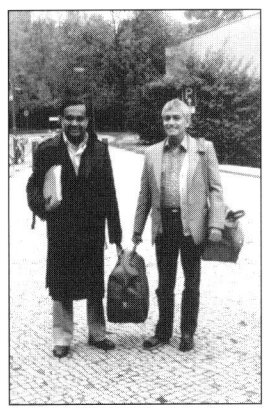

Archival solidarity: P K Nair (left) with Hector Garcia Mesa of the Cinemateca de Cuba at a meeting of the FIAF Executive Committee in Berlin, May 1987.
Paul Spehr.

I have often wondered why there were no strong protests from film-lovers and film archivists about the loss of image quality when the manufacturers switched over from nitrate to safety. Were we perhaps carried away with the euphoria of their exaggerated claims, being ourselves keen to get rid of our "inflammable" nitrate? Pity! Only after the transfer did we realise that we lost something in the process. Every new product that comes out on the market has its pluses and minuses. If we want to go all-out for the pluses, we should be prepared to put up with the minuses also. Alternatively, let us not throw away the old, however risky it may be, while availing ourselves of the benefits of the new. Whether it is a fire hazard or not, let us keep nitrate, and not destroy it.

Notes

1. The finding of this particular film was described in an article by the late Harish S. Booch published in the memorial volume *Green Leaves*, as follows:

   "In the course of my own quest for rare films, I came across a precious record in celluloid showing D G Phalke writing, photographing, directing, and supervising the production of India's very first motion picture, *Raja Harischandra*. It also contained shots from Phalke's films *Kaliya Mardan* and *Krishna Janma*, and from *Harischandra* itself.

   When I approached Phalke's eldest son Bhalchandra, who had played the role of the boy Rohit in *Harischandra*, and who had preserved this material with great care, he was reluctant to lend it, because in the past an important member of a Government-sponsored documentary unit had borrowed some material which was neither used nor returned. After considerable persuasion, Bhalchandra agreed to part with it.

   Time had ravaged the material, a "positive". My suggestion to re-process it was at once accepted by the Secretaries of the Indian Motion Picture Producers' Association and the Film Federation of India, and a negative and print were made. Bhalchandra Phalke, who died some time ago, supervised this work, and the unique record was shown to a distinguished gathering at the inaugural function of the Talkie Silver Jubilee at the Liberty Cinema, Bombay, on December 16, 1956."

Henri Langlois and Nitrate, Before and After 1959

by Roger Smither

No study on any aspect of the history of the world of film archives can long ignore the larger-than-life figure of Henri Langlois (1914–1977). Co-founder both of the Cinémathèque Française and of the Fédération Internationale des Archives du Film (FIAF) in the years before the Second World War, he also encouraged and assisted the creation and development of many other archives and cinematheques around the world in the years after the war. The screenings which he arranged in Paris at that time are credited with the education and inspiration of the film-makers of France's *Nouvelle Vague*, and the *"Affaire Langlois"* – the extraordinary sequence of mass protests that followed the French government's attempt to remove him from control of the Cinémathèque in February 1968 – is commonly portrayed as a kind of dress rehearsal for the larger-scale *"événements"* of May that year. In 1974, he became the only film archivist to be honoured with a special Oscar by the American Academy of Motion Picture Arts and Sciences. Since his death, there have been two full-length biographies with highly evocative titles – "A Passion for Films", "First Citizen of Cinema"[1]. Film archivists in the rest of the world can ruefully, and rightly, question whether their own dismissal would awaken more than a flicker of interest in the general consciousness, or their deaths merit so much as a mention in the national press. Even those who never met him can recognise that there must indeed have been something special about Langlois – as Sam Kula, who did meet him, has written, Langlois was "one of the most remarkable and controversial figures ever to grace any profession, let alone the putative one of film archivist." Jacques Ledoux, of the Cinémathèque Royale de Belgique, speaking at the first FIAF Congress after the death of Langlois, paid him the following somewhat qualified tribute:

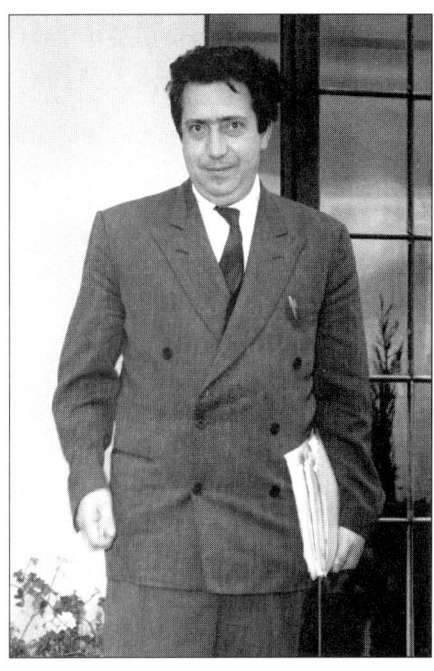

Henri Langlois at the 1953 FIAF Congress in Vence.
FIAF, Brussels.

> Those who knew him recognise that he was a man of excess in all things, but fascinating in his very excesses, an extraordinary mixture of inspiration and preconceived ideas, of generosity and jealousy.[2]

While many continue to offer Langlois a kind of canonisation (to the extent even of wishing on him an unlikely form of stigmata[3]), his image in the film archive world is not wholly without blemish. Above all, FIAF – although these days proclaiming itself as made up of his "children" – recalls the permanent rift that developed between Langlois and the Federation in 1959. Although primarily a matter of personalities and managerial style, the rift took the course it did partly because of matters relating to nitrate film, and that background, as well as an episode in Langlois's life after the breach, are therefore worth some brief exploration in this book.

In the iconography of film archivism, the opposite of Henri Langlois – negative to his positive, or vice versa – is commonly found in the figure of Ernest Lindgren (1910–1973), first curator of Britain's National Film Archive. In the words of

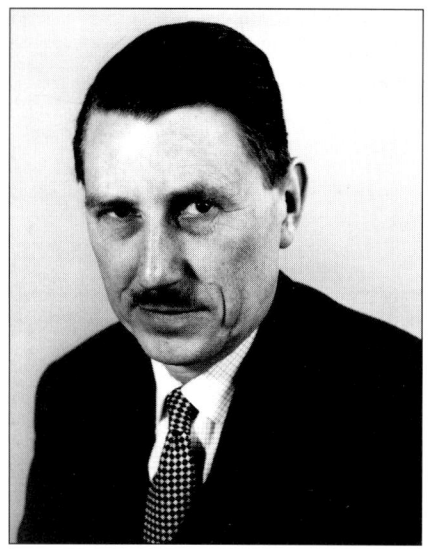

An informal portrait of Ernest Lindgren.

The Lindgren Family.

Penelope Houston's history of the film archives: "They were opposites in every possible way: in physique, in temperament, in their policies and attitudes and views about the role of the collections they built up."[4] Most famously, or notoriously, this opposition made itself manifest in their attitudes to the material acquired by their archives. Langlois believed passionately that the role of the cinematheque was to put film on the screen; Lindgren believed with equal conviction that the role of the archive was to ensure that the film was preserved.

Defenders of Lindgren point out that he started his career as a film programmer, that he was committed to the screening of material from the archive (and led the way with both classic titles and his own compilations of less obvious archive material), and that his own vision of the perfect film archive, set out in 1948 as the "Utopian ideal which I cling to", included at its heart "a small cinema of some 500 seats, attractively designed and representing the last word in comfort" for the screening of films. He had said, in the same article, "there is no reason why a film archive should be a mausoleum"[5] – an understated English paraphrase (conscious or not) of Langlois's earlier war-cry, "A cinémathèque must not be a cemetery!" Nonetheless, for Lindgren the pre-condition for projection was preservation – "It goes without saying, of course, that no preservation print ... should ever be used for projection, but only for providing prints for that purpose."[6] His determination in this matter lent itself to unkind misrepresentation: he was saving the National Film Archive's films "for posterity", but when would posterity arrive? The question led to the cruel (and never justified) taunt that the letters NFA secretly stood for "No Film Available".

The explanation for the "posterity" problem was that the NFA was pursuing a preservation policy based on making the best possible use of a limited budget in accordance with a set of logical principles. Unique material should not be put at risk by screening it before it has been copied for preservation. Because resources are tight, they are applied where there is most need – in other words, to films that are already badly in need of attention. Making a "preservation master" copy of a film does not make that film accessible, since such a copy must, by definition, itself be protected from the risks involved in projection. Ideally, one needs to generate both a preservation master and an access copy. If funds are tight, however, is it really more responsible to spend those funds on making a preserved film accessible, or to invest them in making a preservation master of another endangered film? The impeccable chain of logic of the precise Ernest Lindgren could not help looking small-minded and bureaucratic compared to the romantic aura of the flamboyant Henri Langlois's Cinémathèque screenings across the Channel, which parted company with that chain at the first link.

"Punched like a Métro ticket" – preparing samples of National Film Archive film for Alizarin Red chemical testing at Aston Clinton.

BFI Collections – Stills, Posters & Designs, London. 324884.

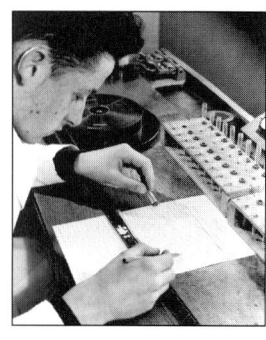

The emotional difference between their perceptions of the purpose of archives was reflected in their reaction to nitrate film. For Lindgren, the material of which the film was composed contributed added risk to the responsibility for preserving it. The important priority was to find a reliable way to assess that risk, so that preservation work could be undertaken before it was too late. Under the urgings of Lindgren, Mr S A Ashmore, the British Government Chemist (his official title), developed during the Second World War the Alizarin Red accelerated ageing test.[7] This test, which has subsequently been adopted by many other archives around the world, examines the reaction of a small sample of film to measured quantities of heat. From the reaction, the onset of nitrate deterioration can be anticipated, and preservation may be undertaken before deterioration is too far advanced. The appeal of such a procedure to the methodical Lindgren could be predicted: so, too, could the hostile reaction of the emotional Langlois. For Langlois, the material of which film was composed was part of the very film itself. To him, the removal of the samples required for the Alizarin Red test – leaving the film "punched like a Métro ticket" – constituted a gross violation.

> One day at the avenue de Messine, the Cinémathèque's employees heard an unmistakably angry outburst from Langlois's office. Each one of his collaborators knew that for Langlois to get worked up into such a state, someone somewhere must have struck a blow at the sacred integrity of his films. The *corpus delicti* was resting on his table: a film had returned from London with holes punched out from the middle of its frames. After having vented his anger through screaming, Henri was completely depressed and, head in hands, repeated, "They've gone completely crazy. We must stop this massacre!" .... He could not understand Lindgren's revulsion for old film stock when he himself felt a veritable veneration for the stuff.[8]

In Paris, the argument tended to look for metaphor to a very obvious cultural neighbour. Film historian Georges Sadoul wrote "Must [a film] now be destroyed because it's on nitrate and therefore flammable? But then, isn't that also the case for the piece of wood on which the *Mona Lisa* is painted? Must we toss it on the fire and replace it with a life-size reproduction on cement-backed asbestos?" André Malraux is also reported to have stated that if the *Mona Lisa* were painted on dynamite, he would still preserve it. Richard Roud, Langlois's other biographer, further develops the same theme:

> Since nitrate film was, for him, alive, it could die in its cans. Taking the film out of the cans and projecting it, or at least rewinding it, protected it. The state of nitrate film depends on many imponderables – how the film was developed, the actual film stock – which varied over fifty-five years; so Langlois's methods of preservation varied also. When the original tinted print of Renoir's first feature, *La Fille de l'Eau*, started to become sticky, he hung it up with clothespins, like washing on a line, and after a few days the stickiness went, and the print is still in good condition.[9]

The difference in attitudes on either side of the English Channel leads Roud to accuse Lindgren of an "almost pathological loathing of nitrate", but this is an unwarranted representation of Lindgren's real position. In the article previously quoted, Lindgren gave his own description of the ideal processes for film preservation. The modern reader will not find much that suggests anything so emotional as loathing, even if, with the added wisdom of a further half-century of hindsight, the same reader may smile at Lindgren's confidence in the durability of cellulose acetate:

> ...standard cinematograph film, employing a nitro-cellulose support, is not only highly inflammable, but within a comparatively short time (possibly between fifty and a hundred years) it is liable to become unstable and disintegrate; if kept under unsuitable conditions it will do so much sooner. The chief function of the film archive, therefore, is to acquire copies of historically valuable films and to preserve them in perpetuity by storing them under the best possible conditions....

> [Copies acquired for archival preservation] are never used for projection: for this purpose dupe prints must be made. The originals are treated as master prints, and are kept in specially constructed storage vaults erected on a country site of several acres. The temperature and humidity in the vaults are

carefully controlled, and the films are subjected to chemical tests at regular intervals to check their condition. When a print appears unstable under test, a new copy must be made, and this in its turn is preserved. This new copy is made on cellulose acetate stock, which is far more stable than celluloid and also non-inflammable. In ten or fifty years time the scientists may have found an even more durable substitute.[10]

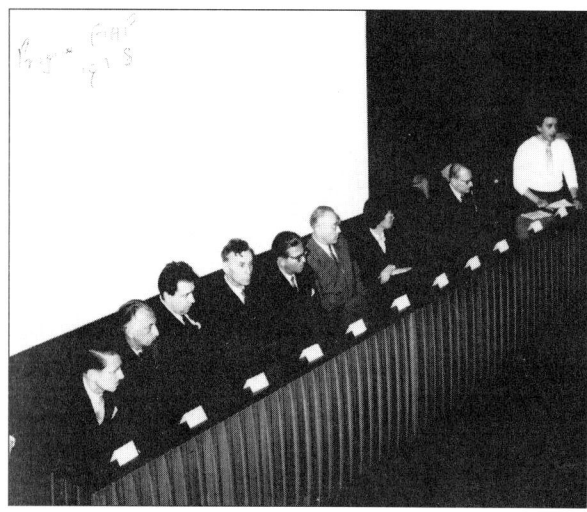

Before the breach: among other members of the FIAF Executive Committee at the Congress in Prague in 1958 are Ernest Lindgren (at the left of the picture, leaning forward), and Henri Langlois (two seats to the right).

The Lindgren Family.

There was unquestionably an element of stubborn arrogance in Lindgren's attitude – most obvious in his reported application of the Alizarin Red test without asking permission to films borrowed from other archives – just as there was a degree of stubborn romanticism in that of Langlois. Another reflection of the same disparity was to be found in Lindgren's fondness for procedures and documentation, set against Langlois's notoriously secretive and imprecise (if not actually non-existent) record-keeping. Lindgren and his institution paid the price by acquiring a dour, unfriendly reputation. Many would say that Langlois's institution paid a much more serious and tangible price for his own flamboyance in the Cinémathèque fire of 10 July 1959, and in its after-effects.

The fire broke out among films stored under a glass roof in a courtyard at the Cinémathèque's headquarters in the rue de Courcelles. The commonly-accepted explanation for the fire is that it was started by spontaneous combustion of unstable nitrate on a summer's day when the sun's heat was intensified by the glass roof,[11] although the Myrent/Langlois biography includes the comments recorded in an interview with Georges Franju, who witnessed the fire and blames an employee's careless cigarette. What is more peculiar is the amount of uncertainty that surrounded – and surrounds – the extent of the fire. Franju is also quoted as saying, "What followed was a lot of smoke and a very small fire. If the fire had been worse, as it would have been with a quantity of nitrate stock, then everything would have exploded."[12] Nonetheless, two pages later, the same book lists the quantity of film destroyed as 5,000 reels – a far from trivial quantity of nitrate, which, in burning, would have generated a fire that would have been anything but "small." The Roud biography notes that "Some archivists doubted whether the fire actually ever took place – as if it had been a fake, a plot by Langlois to pretend that some films had been burned so he could hang on to them," although Roud himself adds, "I was in Paris at the time and can testify to the fire: I read about it in the newspaper early on the morning after it happened, and went to the Cinémathèque to offer condolences. The smell was still in the air, and Langlois was half crazed."[13]

As these rather curious quotations suggest, the disaster of the fire was twofold. First, some films were beyond question lost, including both material in store at or on loan to Langlois's institution from the FIAF archive in Warsaw and elsewhere, as well as treasures of the Cinémathèque Française itself, including a unique copy of the second part of Stroheim's *The Wedding March, The Honeymoon*. Second, it appeared that Langlois could not – or, more sinisterly, perhaps would not – provide details as to which films had been lost. (The resulting speculations and allegations mean that, as some historians have pointed out, virtually every "lost" film in film history has been attributed to this mysterious tragedy at one time or another.) In the atmosphere of uncertainty about how big the fire had been, and what had actually been destroyed, Langlois, who was by all accounts himself a conspiracy theorist of the first rank, became the target of suspicion on the part of his fellow archivists.

These suspicions in turn nourished the increasing discontent that many of those fellow archivists felt at the way Langlois, as the Federation's long-standing Secretary General, had been running FIAF, and provided a focus for confrontation at the Stockholm FIAF Congress, September 1959.

The actual circumstances of the rift between FIAF and Langlois comprised a complex mixture of incompatible personalities, justified suspicions of conspiracy, and less justified paranoia, mutual accusations of participation in (or tolerance of) piracy, and legal arguments about the formal establishment of the Federation in France. As the role of nitrate was limited to the part played in generating the background tension between what might be termed the Langlois and Lindgren tendencies and the immediate occasion of the Cinémathèque fire, the details of FIAF politics need not be considered here: it needs only to be recorded that the rift remained unbridged until long after Langlois's death and a second major fire involving the Cinémathèque's films – the fire at Le Pontel in August 1980, for which many again blamed his failure to institute and follow appropriate procedures.[14]

The extreme emotions of the Langlois/Lindgren debate are now largely a matter of the past for FIAF. The preservation priorities of Lindgren and the commitment to screening of Langlois are both represented in the preamble to the *Code of Ethics* which FIAF formally adopted in 1998. The relevant text reads: "Film archives recognise that their primary commitment is to preserve the materials in their care, and – provided always that such activity will not compromise this commitment – to make them permanently available for research, study and public screening." Over the page, the concerns of Langlois's adherents are met by a clause which states: "Archives will not unnecessarily destroy materials even when they have been preserved or protected by copying. Where it is legally and administratively possible and safe to do so, they will continue to offer researchers access to nitrate viewing prints as long as the nitrate remains viable."[15] Perhaps FIAF members can now be said to be the children of both Langlois and Lindgren.

Postscript

During the period following the 1959 rift, there is one further chapter in the history of Langlois and nitrate which awaits further study. Outside FIAF, Langlois looked for another environment in which he could bring together those who shared his ideas, and seems to have toyed with the idea of creating both a specialist committee of cinema museums within ICOM, the International Council of Museums, and an independent Union Mondiale des Musées du Cinéma. The proposed organisations had other uses for Langlois, as he sought to cover his tracks from his real or imagined enemies. Following the 1980 fire at Le Pontel, press reports noted that Langlois had rented the store about fifteen years earlier in the name of the "Union Mondiale des Museées", not of the Cinémathèque, further noting that the Union "had disappeared on his death."[16]

Circumstantial evidence of his activities in the name of these organisations is provided in the correspondence between Langlois and Maria Adriana Prolo, founder of the Museo Nazionale del Cinema in Turin, published as *Le Dragon et l'Alouette*, and in a few other places, but little direct evidence of his plans or achievements in this area has so far come to light.

One exception to this general pattern has, however, emerged. Under the aegis of the Venice Biennale in 1966, Langlois apparently organised what he called a *Colloque sur la sauvegarde et la conservation des oeuvres d'art sur pellicule nitrate*. He explained the aims of the Colloquium in the following words, in a letter to Maria

Adriana Prolo dated 17 August 1966: "I remind you ... that the meeting devoted to the safeguarding of cinematographic works of art has as its goal to associate cineastes and workers in and critics of cinema with the resolution which we passed in Rio de Janeiro, to establish the position with regard to nitrate film in the various member countries with a view to opposing those measures which might impede our work, to study the different problems of restoration and conservation, not only between conservators but with scientists and experts ..."[17]

During the Biennale, the following press release was issued

XXVII MOSTRA INTERNAZIONALE D'ARTE CINEMATOGRAFICA

International Meeting on the Problems of Film Conservation

Tomorrow, on the 3rd of September in the Sala Grande at 3 p.m. before the projection of the film The Crowd *in the 'retrospective' section, there will conclude the colloquium on the problems involved in the conservation of nitrate films from the 1920s and earlier. The leaders of the discussion, who are Roberto Rossellini, James Card, Joris Ivens, and Henri Langlois, will communicate their conclusions, which are of particular interest for the history of cinema.*[18]

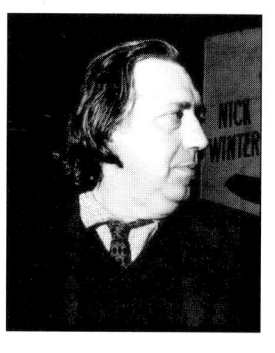

Henri Langlois in his cherished Musée du Cinéma, Paris.

BFI Collections – Stills, Posters & Designs, London.

The Colloquium is not mentioned in any of the official schedules, the daily festival newspaper, or any of the critical round-ups or pieces about the festival in the international press (including those of *Le Monde* and *Le Figaro*), and the timing for the formal "conclusion" noted in the press release would have been very tight – the screening of *The Crowd* was scheduled for 3:30. However, the people listed all had other reasons to be in Venice. Ivens was on the Festival jury, and Rossellini's *La Prise de pouvoir par Louis XIV* was the festival's closing film. The retrospective that year, of which *The Crowd* formed a part, was the highly successful "American Film in the Roaring Twenties", mounted with the collaboration of George Eastman House, MGM, and the Cinémathèque Française, which accounts for the presence of Card and Langlois. It is difficult to escape the supposition that, despite the grandiose ambitions which Langlois had outlined to Prolo, the "Colloquium" was little more than an opportunistic seizing of the convenient presence in Venice of a number of Langlois's friends.

Although there appears to be no formal record of any Colloquium proceedings, a file on the 1966 Venice Festival held by the British Film Institute's National Library does contain a French typescript text which may be assumed to be what was presented on 3 September as the formal resolution. Although unsigned, this text carries the unmistakable stamp of Henri Langlois, and voices, with characteristic passion, a number of his major and minor concerns about nitrate film. The following is an English translation of the text:

MEETING ABOUT THE CONSERVATION OF NITRATE FILM

The participants of the Venice colloquium on the safeguard and conservation of classic works of cinematic art were unanimously alarmed by reports that there is a risk in some countries that certain regulations will obstruct the work of saving and conserving our cinema heritage, and sometimes even prevent access to works in the form in which their authors originally made them and would wish them to exist.

Even more serious appears to be pressure exercised to obtain an injunction against future printing of copies from original nitrate negatives, and the transport and handling of this original material by laboratories; this would even apply to positive or negative film held by archives and cinema museums.

Such a measure would not fail, sooner or later, to lead to their destruction, the raison d'être of their conservation having become redundant.

We should all remember (1) that cinema is a photographic art, therefore one of the plastic arts, and that as such film should be regarded and protected like all other works of art; (2) that it is absolutely false to claim that a cinematic or photographic internegative is equivalent to an original negative, or that a positive printed from an internegative has the same value in these terms as one printed from an original negative.

In such a case, on the contrary, there necessarily is, by the laws of physics, some loss of light and definition.

Let everyone remember that this may be corrected but never nullified, and that under these conditions, even in the case of either works or documents previously copied or reproduced, even with the best, most state-of-the-art technology, the prohibition of printing from, and the destruction of, original prints represents for cinematic art and for historians of all disciplines a catastrophe comparable to the destruction of libraries and works of art by the barbarians.

The participants at this gathering unanimously protest, calling upon world opinion in order to ensure that cinematheques, having naturally first taken all security precautions, may continue to have access to original master material, to print it, to collect it, and to transport it, and that there be an end to the risk of destruction of these works of art and historical documents, which would have cultural consequences as grave as those imagined by Fahrenheit 451.[19]

This colloquium agrees that necessary measures also be taken in order to posit and study means of restoring and conserving indefinitely original works by scientific procedures, contrary to those methods which serve as an alibi for those who want to recover silver salt, and the colloquium wishes to place all archives especially on their guard against the use of the test which involves removing sample fragments from films.[20]

This test, if it is applied systematically, results within a few years in the destruction of works under the pretext of diagnosing them, and, even if it is applied under the guise of limited samples, has a pseudo-scientific pretext destined to justify their destruction.[21]

In other contexts, Langlois appears to have associated additional names such as those of Georges Sadoul and Robert Bresson with this document, or something very like it.[22] There is, however, no evidence that it succeeded in launching the crusade for which he had hoped.

This one episode is all that has so far come to this author's attention to show a tangible result from Langlois's attempts to create an institutional framework for the film archive movement outside FIAF. If or when more information does emerge, it should make interesting reading.

Notes

1. Richard Roud, *A Passion for Films: Henri Langlois and the Cinémathèque Française* (New York: Viking Press, 1983); Glenn Myrent and Georges P Langlois (translated from the French by Lisa Nesselson), *Henri Langlois: First Citizen of Cinema* (New York: Twayne Publishers, 1995).

2. Sam Kula, "Film Archives at the Centenary of Film", review article, *Archivaria*, no.40 (Fall 1995), p. 211; Minutes of the 33rd FIAF Congress (Varna, Bulgaria), 27–28 May 1977. ("Ceux qui l'ont connu savent que c'était un homme excessif en toutes choses mais fascinant par ses excès mêmes, un mélange extraordinaire d'inspiration et d'idées préconçues, de générosité et de jalousie.")

3. "All those who knew Henri knew that his fingers bore the indelible burn marks left by the nitrate stock he was forever handling. Like the vocation of the pioneer radiologists, Henri's passion was one that literally burned." (Myrent and Langlois, op. cit., pp. 32–33). Despite the romantic impact of such an image, it must prosaically be noted that most film professionals, who handle nitrate even more regularly than Langlois ever did, have managed to avoid such disfigurement. Concerns have from time to time been raised about possible medical side-effects of prolonged exposure to nitrate, but these tend to relate more to problems caused by inhalation (of gases or dust from decomposing celluloid, or of spores from fungal contamination) than to skin burns caused by physical contact.

4. Penelope Houston, *Keepers of the Frame: The Film Archives* (London: BFI Publishing, 1994), p. 37.

5. Ernest Lindgren, "The Importance of Film Archives", in Roger Manvell, ed., *The Penguin Film Review 5* (London: Penguin Books, 1948), pp. 47–48.

6. Ernest Lindgren, "The Permanent Preservation of Cinematograph Film", *Proceedings of the British Society for International Bibliography*, v.5, part 5 (1943), p. 99.

7. An article by Oliver Bell, Director of the British Film Institute, described this chemical testing as "a recent innovation" in October 1943. Bell went on to note: "This work is costly but valuable. It may reduce the amount which the Institute can spend on short term policy but as a long term investment the Governors feel that it is abundantly justified." Oliver Bell, "The First Ten Years", *Sight and Sound*, v.12, no.47 (October 1943), pp. 56–58.

8. Myrent and Langlois, op. cit., pp. 161–162. Sam Kula, in a letter to the author, 27 September 1999, points out that the samples needed for the Alizarin Red test were almost always taken from blank frames at the beginning or the end of a film, and never damaged an image. He also questioned whether Lindgren would test borrowed nitrate, pointing out that the NFA had more than enough to do to monitor their own collection. The complaint about borrowed prints returning from London with test samples punched out by Lindgren's staff is, however, attributed by Myrent and Langlois to James Card of George Eastman House as well as to Langlois.

9. Roud, op. cit., pp. 86–87.

10. Lindgren, "The Importance of Film Archives", (op. cit.), pp. 50–51.

11. This was the explanation offered by Langlois shortly after the fire in a letter to his friend James Card, quoted in *A Collective Endeavour: the First Fifty Years of George Eastman House* (Rochester: George Eastman House, 1999), pp. 51–52.

12. Myrent and Langlois, op. cit., p. 197.

13. Roud, op. cit., p. 76.

14. As Sam Kula has pointed out: "There is a direct link between the fire in '59, the events of '68 and the Le Pontel fire in '80. Malraux and his minions tried to dismiss Langlois in '68 because, among other things, millions of francs had been given to the Cinémathèque in the Sixties to make safety copies from nitrate originals and the money was siphoned off to support exhibitions and Langlois' dream of a film museum. Langlois' victory in '68 was decidedly Pyrrhic, as Malraux shut off most of the funding in an effort to starve the Cinémathèque into submission. As a result, even if Langlois had wanted to preserve his treasures the money was no longer there to do so. The result was that a very large quantity of nitrate – no one knows how large – sat there in those substandard vaults for another 12 years and eventually went up in smoke." (Letter to the author, 27 September 1999)

15. *Code of Ethics/Code d'éthique/Código de ética* (Brussels: FIAF, 1998), pp. 5–6.

16. Agence France Presse release 031932, August 1980.

17. (Translated from) Dr Sergio Toffetti, ed., *Le Dragon et l'Alouette* (Turin: Museo Nazionale del Cinema, 1992), p. 135.

18. Translated from the bilingual (Italian/French) Biennale press release no.80 of 1966, supplied by the Archivio Storico delle Arti Contemporanee of the Biennale di Venezia.

19. Truffaut's film was shown at that year's Venice festival. (Translator's note)

20. In other words, the alizarin red test. (Translator's note)

21. Information about the Venice Colloquium was researched in the 1966 Venice Festival File at the British Film Institute's National Library by Catherine A Surowiec, who also translated the resolution text from the French original.

22. Herman G Weinberg, "Lost Ones", in *Film Comment*, v.5, no.3 (Fall 1969), p. 7.

Everyday Nitrate

A collection of original contributions and reprinted material providing an insight into the various ways in which cinema professionals and amateurs have worked with celluloid both during the nitrate era, and after it.

"A Sight Worth Travelling a Long Way to See"

The following passage is extracted from "Behind the Scenes of the Cinema: Some Moving-Picture Secrets", by Foster Grange, published in Penny Pictorial, *17 February 1912, pp.473–475. (Submitted by Dr Nicholas Hiley.)*

The Hepworth film factory is at Walton-on-Thames, and the first thing you are invited to do on entering is to deposit your matches and smoking materials in a rack, many of the compartments of which are labelled with the names of the male members of the staff. The materials used in the preparation of moving pictures are mostly so very inflammable that the "No Smoking" rule must be enforced with the greatest strictness...

Mr. Hepworth leads the way into a room illuminated only by a faint ruby glow. "Perforating-room," he says, "where all blank negative films on their arrival are perforated, so that they may afterwards pass through the different machines. Must have holes in them for the sprocket wheels and so forth to 'engage' with, as the mechanics say. And this next room, again, with the trough in the middle, is our negative-developing room. Darker than the other? That couldn't be. Now look here at the trough, with the films moving along in it. With its attachments it develops and fixes the pictures, washes the film, dresses it with glycerine to keep it soft, and finally winds it up all wet on a spool. Look at the pictures gradually appearing as the film travels along in the liquid chemicals. See, see! Now, this way out! There!"

Through the outer door and back to the studio upstairs last visited. In the wings a coster-girl – all smiles and vivid raiment. We pass on, for the principal to take another picture. A gorgeous coster crowd now fills the stage. A donkey and cart have been brought upstairs, somehow. The ass is nibbling hay. This scene taken, we explore the positive-film dark-room downstairs. The positive perforating-room is lighted with but faint ruby glows, and the pungent but not exactly unpleasant smell of chemicals fills the air. A noisy place this room, crowded with electrically-operated contrivances, but it is the series of positive printing and developing rooms we next pass into which constitutes a sight worth travelling a long way to see.

Having passed through the various electrically-driven machines, the wet films are taken on spools up to the positive drying-rooms, of which there are four. From the ceilings hang countless hooks. With the aid of little motors, girls here unwind the films and hang them up to dry. Three miles of films can hang in each room. Of course the moment one positive film with a drama, or a comedy, or a "trick" picture on it is being "hung up," the negative film downstairs is at work printing a scene exactly like it on another length of positive film. It is almost like printing the *Penny Pictorial*. A limitless number of copies can be produced. In one of the drying rooms, by the way, is a series of hooks, from which depend a number of chamois leathers, brilliantly coloured. Blue, yellow, pink, amber, and other hues are represented. These wash-leathers are used to wipe off the surface moisture from stained films. Ordinarily, the films take twenty-four hours to dry, but in this room is a huge "drum" on which urgent work can be wound. Switch a motor on and – hey, presto! – the films are dry in a few minutes. The nine developing machines at these works, it should be stated, can turn out ten miles a day of printed pictures for the "halls."

Back upstairs to the studio to see those costers celebrate a "wedding." How they work! Leaving that confetti-strewn floor, we pass a young couple rehearsing a love scene – alas! under a stage-manager's watchful eye! We wend our way to the positive "assembling-rooms," where young ladies are fixing "titles" or descriptions on the finished picture films. The "assembly-rooms" [sic] also are very interesting. Here lengths of the prepared and dried film are sorted out and joined together into their respective "scenes" by spirit gum – got ready, in short, for the adjoining packing-room and the market...

Reckless Disorder

"Reckless Disorder 1": W G Barker gives evidence to a Government committee on the realities of working with nitrate in a busy film company in London, 1913.

The following transcript is extracted from Sessional Papers 1914, *"Minutes of Evidence and Appendices of the Departmental Committee on Celluloid," Evidence of W G Barker, 17 July 1913, pp.289–293. (Submitted by Dr Nicholas Hiley.)*

Chairman: You are managing director of the Barker Motion Photography Company, Limited?

Barker: Yes.

Chairman: And you have been engaged, I think, in that business for a considerable number of years?

Barker: Sixteen or seventeen years...

Chairman: How many persons do you employ?

Barker: About 60 at Soho Square, and of course a lot more at Ealing. That is where we handle the film.

Chairman: And you are not under the Factory Acts?

Barker: No.

Chairman: Do customers visit your premises to any extent?

Barker: Yes. I have been taking notes of them for about 18 to 19 months, and our average works out at less than 3. About 2.7 is the number of people at any one time, and I have had as big a party there as 25 friends. Yet it averages down to 2.7.

Chairman: Have you ever had suggestions made to you as to the precautions it would be desirable to take against fire?

Barker: None from either local authorities or my insurance company.

Chairman: What is your insurance rate?

Barker: 10s. per centum; and to show you what the insurance companies think of the kinematograph business, I am just at this moment building a £6,000 dark room at Ealing, and the insurance company have told me that when I go in my insurance rate will be down at 5s. I am paying for the surrounding property there.

Chairman: Do you either manufacture celluloid or put emulsion on?

Barker:	No.
Chairman:	All that you do is to take the photographs?
Barker:	Yes, and turn them into a negative, and from a negative into a positive... We hear a very great deal about storing in tin boxes, fireproof chambers, and all the rest of it. That is utterly impossible when we are so-called "manufacturing" films. I will call it "manufacturing" because it is a handy word to use, but we do not manufacture. What we really do is to print on a piece of sensitised celluloid. I have no other business than that. We have out at a time as much as 50,000 feet kicking about over the place, some in the drying-room, some in a dark room, some being perforated and some being joined together. My girls and my men make as many as 500 or 600 what you call repairs, but what we call joins, a day, and there are 8 or 10 of them at work all day long. There is no harm in it; but we are always snipping, and the place is covered with cuttings and the rest of it. Twice a day, and if we are extra busy about three times a day, there is a general gathering up. I keep a 5s. 6d. sanitary dustbin, and when it gets full it is taken down to the basement, poured out into a large box and taken off the premises as soon as ever we can get a load of it.
Chairman:	What is the proportion of film you have exposed in the process of what you call manufacturing to the amount you have stored?
Barker:	Our storage is fairly small. It would not run up to much more, except at Coronation time or something like that, when it would run up to say 250,000 feet than something like 100,000 feet ordinarily. Then, on the top of that, we should have 50,000 feet kicking about in the meantime every day. Of course we are trying to get rid of that off the premises just as fast as we can, naturally, to get our money. The business is done in rather a peculiar way; that is to say, we are packing up orders for a given negative for six weeks in advance, and on a given day we send out all those orders together. That is what is called the release date. The consequence is that if we are going to release on a Thursday or a Monday, which are our release days in the trade, we try for the Thursday release not to start printing until the Monday previously; so that the whole of that we release on the Thursday is in the course of manufacture and regulation, joining, staining, toning, etc., during those five days previously. If the order is a very large one we may start two or three weeks ahead, and that is all kicking about in the meantime.
Chairman:	How do you keep that which is not exposed?
Barker:	In very large tin canisters... it happens to come over from America in that way.
Chairman:	Is it stored in a special room?
Barker:	No, it is stored in different parts of the premises. You see, when the film comes to us, we get it in roughly about 60,000 feet lengths inside large tin canisters in a large case. That is as it comes across the Atlantic. It is taken from there and taken up to the third floor to

punch all these little tiny holes in, and they work very fast. Those holes are punched in at the rate of roughly about 200 to 250 a minute ... A manufacturer does not make stock in our business, so that he cannot keep his business running from 9 o'clock in the morning to 7 o'clock at night like a gigantic machine. What he has to do is this: he starts off with a mighty rush between 9 and 12, and perhaps then he will get no more work the rest of that day. Then he will get a very large order in, and he will have to stick at it night and day in order to get that order through ...

Mr. Ollis: There is no reckless scattering of film over the floor?

Barker: Yes, there is, in the joining department. There is a reckless disorder. As a man said to me one day, it is an ordered confusion, and must of necessity be.

Ollis: Is it necessary for the purposes of your business?

Barker: It is absolutely necessary, for the simple reason that the largest piece of film we develop at a time is roughly about that size. Then they all have to be joined together to make up a film of that size of 1,000 feet, and in between it we have the titles to put in. Then it all has to be examined and the pieces cut out where there is some bad photography, or blotches, or flaws ... We turn out between 60 to 70, 80, and 100,000 feet of film a day.

"Reckless Disorder 2": Cutting Rooms from Hell.

Editors' Note: The phrase "Reckless Disorder" inevitably called to mind several photographs from the Kevin Brownlow Collection. Although they have nothing in common with the foregoing evidence, which they post-date by several years, they are too good to omit, and so are reproduced below.

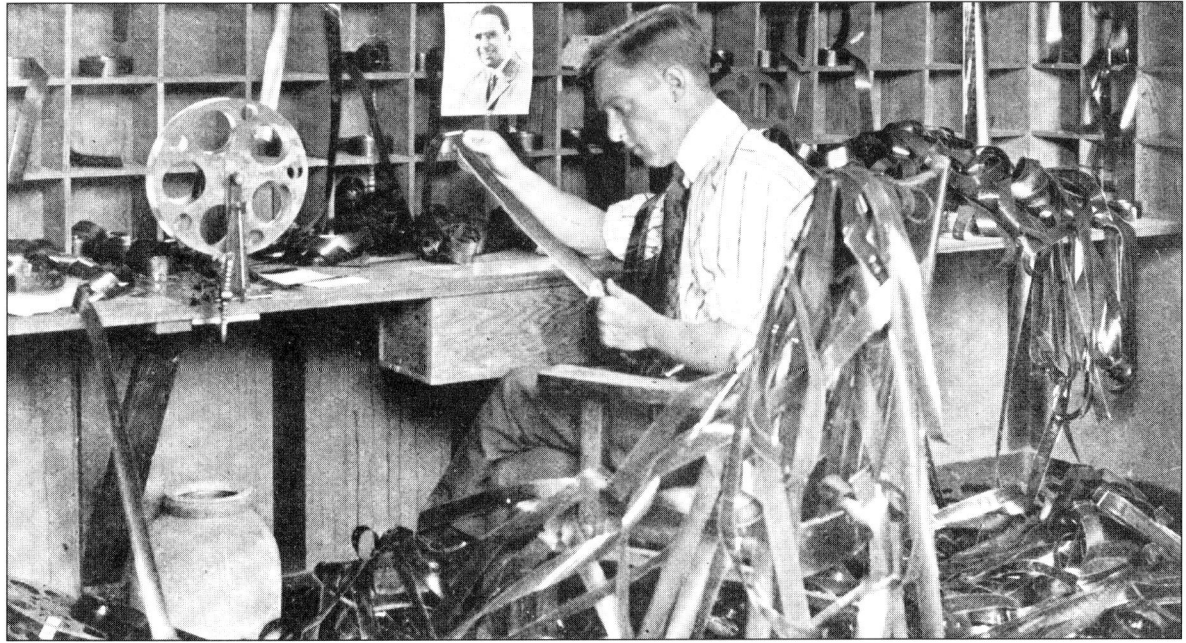

Editor William ("Billy") Shea in the cutting room, ca. 1920.

Kevin Brownlow Collection.

Erich von Stroheim in the cutting room.

Kevin Brownlow Collection.

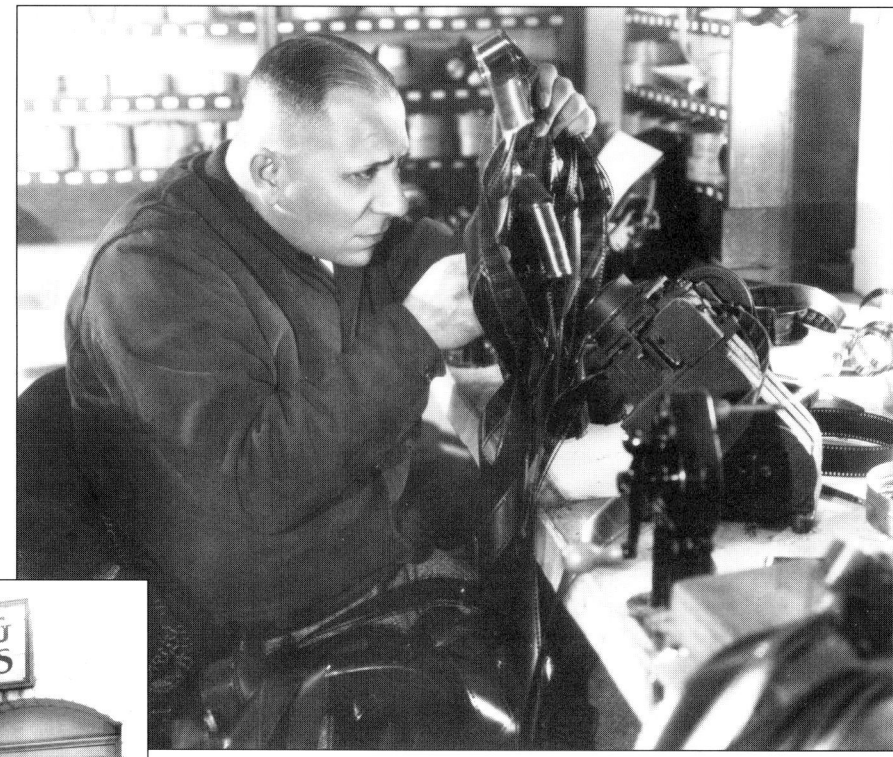

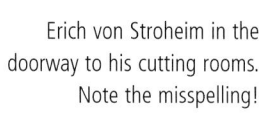

Erich von Stroheim in the doorway to his cutting rooms. Note the misspelling!

Kevin Brownlow Collection.

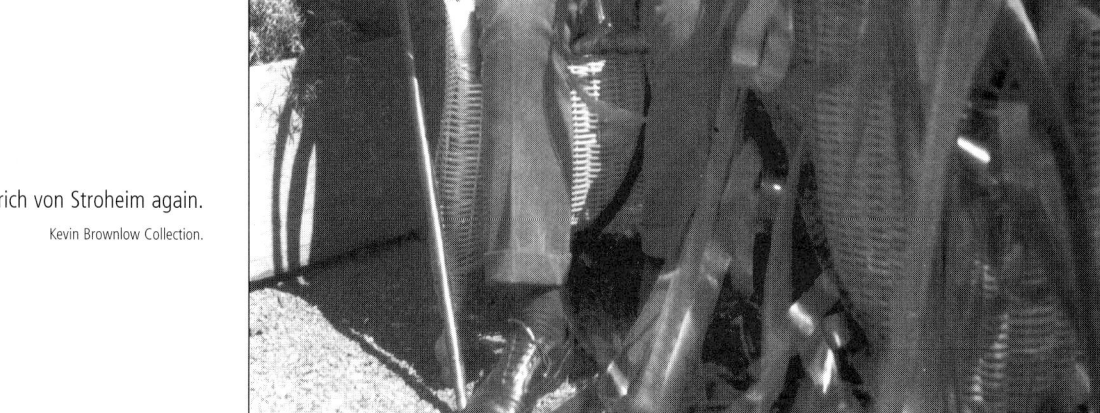

Erich von Stroheim again.

Kevin Brownlow Collection.

Charles Urban and Nitrate

The following paragraphs are based on material from Leslie Wood, The Miracle of the Movies *(London: Burke Publishing, 1947), pp. 253–255. (Submitted by Luke McKernan.[1])*

The American Charles Urban has an important role in the early history of British cinema, not least for his promotion of the pioneering "natural colour" system, Kinemacolor – the restoration of which is the subject of Nicola Mazzanti's contribution elsewhere in this volume.

In the words of one writer on cinema, "The curious thing about the big part he [Urban] played in developing and promoting colour films was that, according to technicians who worked with him, his technical knowledge of photography was small, and he was apt to send his co-workers into a panic by leaning over bins containing films which were being cut with a lighted cigar in his mouth quite oblivious to the fire risk."

Another story which confirms Urban's nonchalance in the presence of nitrate film is associated with his greatest Kinemacolor achievement – the filming of the "Delhi Durbar", the coronation of King George V as Emperor of India in 1911. Urban took a team of eight Kinemacolor cameramen to India to cover this event. To ward off the attentions of jealous competitors, he was given an armed guard to watch over his cameras and equipment when they were not in use, but to protect the precious film itself – both from the risk of sabotage and from the tropical heat – he was reported to have dug a pit in the ground below his tent, and gone to sleep each night on top of the exposed filmstock. Remembering that these were the rushes for what would open in London on 2 February 1912 as a two-and-a-half-hour spectacular (and that the Kinemacolor process consumed film twice as fast as regular black-and-white filming), it will be understood that this was a considerable quantity of nitrate!

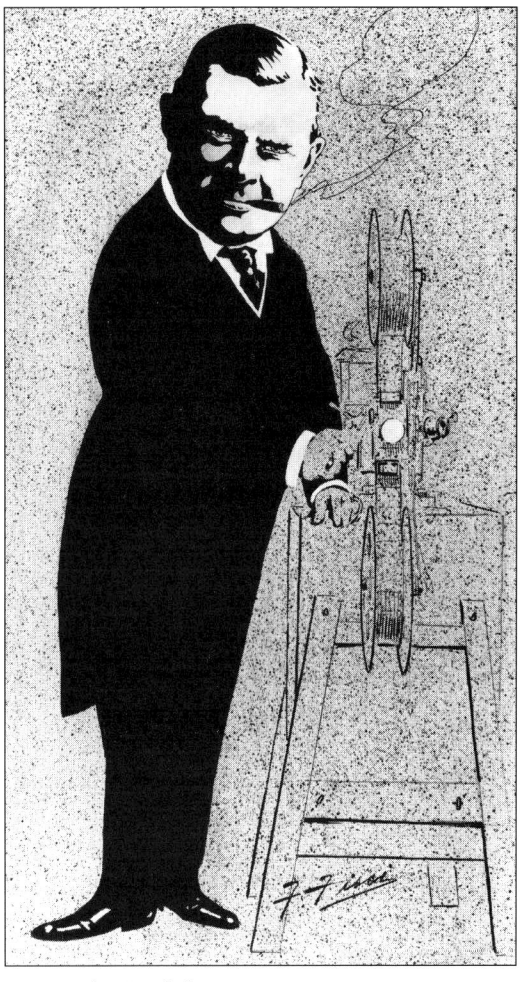

Charles Urban remains "quite oblivious to the fire risk" as he smokes while operating a projector in this undated caricature by F Fissi.

BFI Collections – Stills, Posters & Designs, London. 0-19781.

Notes

1. Luke McKernan is the editor of *A Yank in Britain: The Lost Memoirs of Charles Urban, Film Pioneer* (Hastings: The Projection Box, 1999).

"A Complete Loss"

Harry K McWilliams, interviewed by Ronald S Magliozzi

Harry K McWilliams, 1907–1999, was born the first of 5 children in Middlesboro, Kentucky, and raised in Knoxville, Tennessee. After his father's death, the family moved in 1923 to Denver, Colorado, where McWilliams' career in the motion picture business began when his friendship with the doorman of a neighbourhood movie theatre led to his becoming an usher and eventually the manager and advertising director of two cinemas in the city at the age of 18. He later worked as a press representative in film, radio, and television for Columbia Pictures, MGM, Al Jolson, Gene Autry, Major Bowes and the Amateur Hour, and the Cincinnati Opera, before retiring in 1975. His memoir *Drum Beater* was published in 1997.

The following excerpt is from an oral history interview recorded with Mr McWilliams (HMcW) by Ronald S Magliozzi (RM) at the Museum of Modern Art on 18 October 1993.

HMcW: One of the theatres I managed in Denver was the Aladdin. The theatre was built in the days of silent pictures. It had 1200 seats and . . . the owner was a druggist. He had a drugstore and two little theatres . . . He had the idea of building a first-run theatre in a neighborhood . . . up to that time first-runs were never in neighborhoods [in Denver]. He had a house, a car, and two little theatres . . . The Aladdin Theatre had a mosque on top, like they have in Arabia, so it was different. The product he had was Warners and Fox, I think,[1] which just wasn't that strong at that particular time. He had a 7-piece orchestra in the pit at the Aladdin, and . . . the other, in a nice neighborhood with 600 seats and a player organ, [was] the Blue Bird Theatre – I managed the two of them. He was about to go broke, and then came Vitaphone . . .

RM: Would you talk about your experience shuttling nitrate prints between the film exchanges and the theatres you managed? You mentioned being involved in a nitrate fire.

HMcW: Yes. I had to take my sister home from the movies one night around 1926 or early '27. We were in my Model T Ford coupe, and I started smelling something. I figured it was a battery cable, so I got out and opened up the back end. Boy! This flame shot up three or four feet in the air! The car was on fire. I got my sister out, and luckily we were only a few blocks from the fire station. The fire chief got there before the truck, and his driver took one of those little hand extinguishers, you know. The chief said, "You dumb son of a bitch!" They put 30 gallons of chemicals on that fire, all the chemicals they had in the truck on that fire, but [the car] was a complete loss.

The bad thing about it in a way was that the feature [in the trunk] that night was a hand-colored feature – this was before Technicolor . . . A normal print would have cost no more than a nickel a foot, and this one cost probably 50 cents a foot . . . and a feature was 6 or 7 reels, a pile of cans so high.

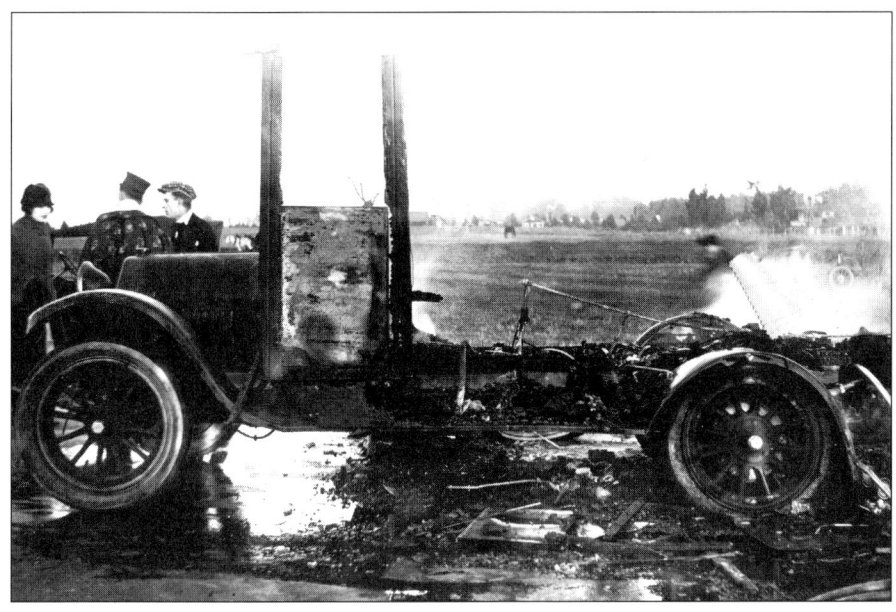

Another "complete loss" offers a dramatic example of the explosive dangers of transporting nitrate. According to the original caption, this truck was destroyed by nitrate fire "on location", ca. 1916.
Kevin Brownlow Collection.

RM: Do you have any thoughts on what caused the print to catch fire?

HMcW: I always thought – I don't think there was any question about it – our projectionist used to smoke in the booth in those days... We had a fireproof door between [the booth] and the hallway. He would open that fireproof door and stand there and smoke. Of course, this was the days before they had safety matches; you got matches out of a big box.

RM: He was aware he shouldn't smoke around the film?

HMcW: Of course he was aware of it. I think he obviously dropped a match that hadn't been lit in a can and then put the film in it, and in the car [the cans] jiggled. I'll never believe it was any different than that, but I have no proof.

RM: You don't think the film might have sparked on its own, moving around in the trunk?

HMcW: I don't know... of course the nitrate did burn... In those days the exchanges, the 26 exchanges around Denver I was telling you about, had to be separate buildings. They couldn't be in an office building like they are today. Today a film is as safe as paper, but in those days a film had to get special handling... They were in buildings with space around them like a house... they were carefully watched by the fire department; they had fireproof vaults.

RM: Was picking up and carrying this nitrate film back and forth a regular practice of yours?

HMcW: Yes, from two theatres. Sometimes I'd probably had 10 or more different films in the car... we had a comedy, a newsreel, maybe a travelogue, and a feature – that's four – and trailers for the next week. That's only for one theatre, and we had two theatres. Not only that, sometimes I'd have films for two programs in one theatre. You'd have a matinée for children on Saturday afternoon that would be

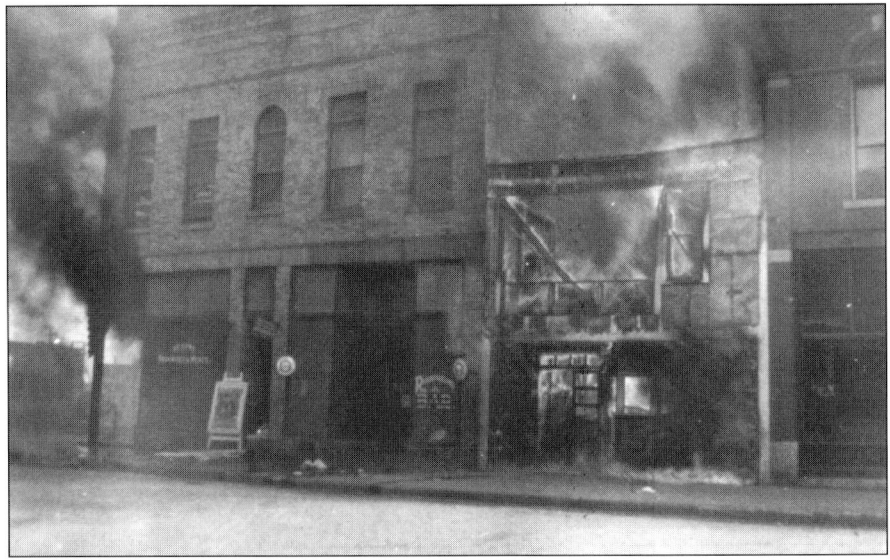

A postcard recording the scene of a nickelodeon fire somewhere in the USA, ca. 1914.

Special Collections, The Museum of Modern Art Department of Film and Video, New York.

completely different from what we'd show at night. I could have a serial or a Western, entirely different programs. I had loads [of nitrate] film in my car. And of course I had no insurance. The car was strictly my loss... I got 40 dollars from an advertising customer of mine whose son wanted a racer. So he bought the Model T Ford's engine and the frame... Why I had to buy the car was because part of the job of managing the theatres was getting and returning the films... The films that burned were for the Blue Bird.

Notes

1. McWilliams' scrapbook indicates that while Warners and Fox titles did predominate, MGM and Paramount titles were also regularly booked. – RM

Unseen Showmen and Unsung Heroes: Projectionists in the Nitrate Era in the United Kingdom

by Roger Smither

This paper is extensively based on material given to me directly by Ronald Grant, Nicholas Hiley, Bernard King, Ken Locke, Len Petts, and Ian Rintoul, and on interview transcripts supplied by Catherine Surowiec and Janet McBain. To all the above – and to the subjects of the interviews, David Angus, John Boll, Bob Douglas, Elizabeth Edmiston, David Gillespie, and Vess Hudson – my sincere thanks.

If one leaves aside for the moment the fear of spontaneous combustion, concern about the dangers posed by the extreme inflammability of nitrate film can, for the majority of those who work with it, at least be countered by the knowledge that an outside agent is still required to start a fire. If the cigarettes, the matches, the electrical spark, and other sources of heat are all kept safely at a distance, the risk can be minimised and effectively excluded. For one group of workers with nitrate, however, the work itself required bringing nitrate film into very close proximity with a significant heat source. As Robert A Mitchell graphically explained in his *Manual of Practical Projection:*

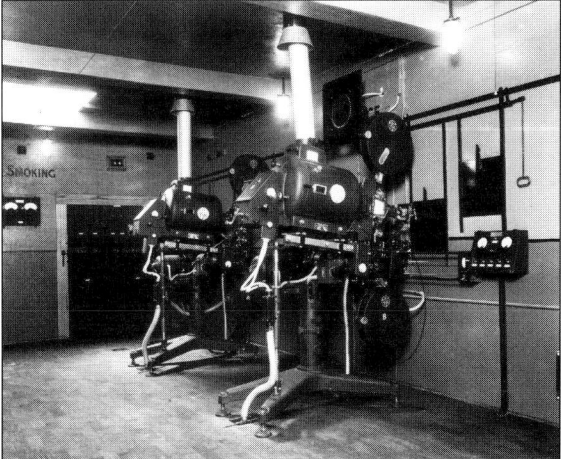

The projection box at the Kingstanding Odeon, Birmingham, ca. 1935. Note the metals shutters over the projection ports and other fire precautions.

BFI Collections – Stills, Posters & Designs, London.

> 'Still' film is never subjected to the severe conditions of heat and physical stress prevailing in motion-picture projection. Movie film is spared complete destruction only because it is drawn so rapidly through the blazing "spot" of concentrated arc light... The rather frightening combination of intense radiation and explosively inflammable nitrofilm was a necessary condition of theatre projection during the first half century of commercial motion pictures. (Eastman Kodak introduced satisfactory safety film in the late nineteen forties.) The projectionist, unseen showman and unsung hero, lived dangerously indeed before the advent of theatre-release safety stock! He faced most emergencies with a single predominating thought – film fire and its prevention. Human life depended upon his clear thinking and quick action.[1]

The same information was conveyed in a rather more direct way in a brusque set of instructions issued by the British Admiralty in 1943:

> Celluloid inflammable film will be ignited by the heat of the projector unless the film is kept moving through the projector. It should be noted that the heat from the illuminant will set fire to inflammable film if it stops in the "gate" for more than 1½ seconds.
>
> It should also be noted that film can be ignited by friction (e.g., from wooden "guides" on rewinders), and by electric sparks.

Damp or dirt will cause a film to stick in the projector, and a fire will result.

A fire caused by the film stopping in the projector will normally be dealt with effectively by the automatic fire extinguisher. It is possible, however, that the highly inflammable nature of the film may cause the fire to spread to the spool box. If this happens, the seat of the fire must be wrapped in an asbestos blanket and left for at least 10 minutes – on no account should the door of the spool box be opened before the expiry of this safety period. Celluloid fires in rewinding rooms are similarly dealt with.

The fumes of burning films are poisonous.[2]

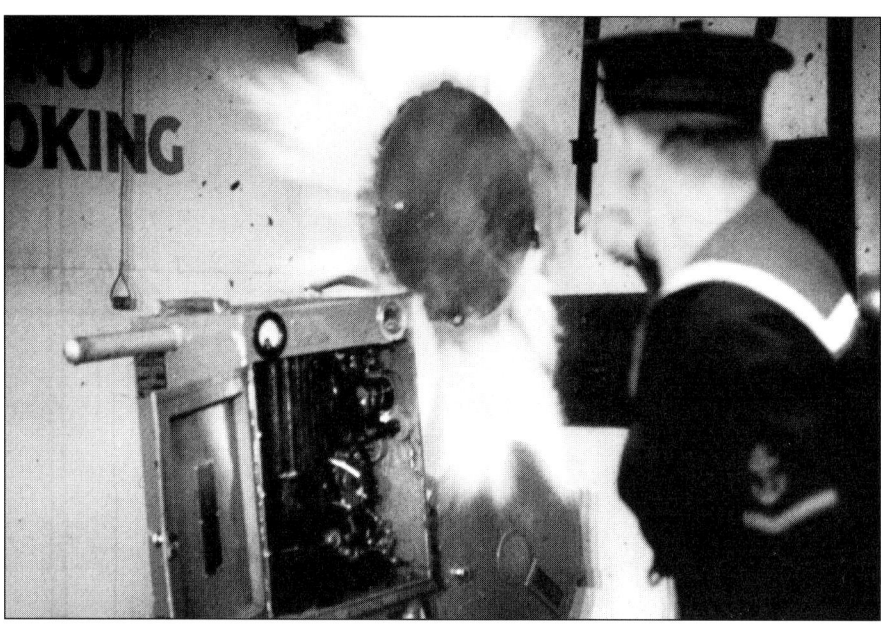

A Royal Navy projectionist fights a fire in a scene from the Admiralty training film *This Film Is Dangerous!*

Imperial War Museum, London. IWM FLM 3231.

In his interview with Scottish film archivist Janet McBain, projectionist David C Angus (DA) gave a graphic description of precisely the sort of accident at which Mitchell and the Admiralty hint:

DA: I had a fire in the Empire! Aye. A frightening damn thing it was. I had more respect for it afterwards, I can tell you. What happened was, it was a kiddies' matinée and we would run the feature . . . aye . . . and tied on the last reel of the feature – a trailer for a Western. Johnny Wilson was in the box with me. Now, they were front-shutter machines, and I had stopped, after the last reel, I stopped the machine and I went round to start the serial, but Johnny came in the door and he started the serial, so I came back round and – I remember this as though it happened yesterday – and I opened the two spool boxes. I started to undo . . . Rather than run through which was quite a biggish couple of trailers, I would take it out. And as I opened the gate, the film flipped back and touched the back of the gate, and it just went **Woomph!** into the top spool box, into the bottom. I slammed them both shut, but it was too late. There was flame coming out, so I shouted to Johnny: "Johnny! Fire!" So he came tearing round, got to me, so he went to the phone and called the manager, told him he's shutting down, and came back. By this time, I had the gas extinguisher going, and I seemed to have put the flame out, but there was still smoking, and the smoke was getting thick, thick and thicker, you know, and, well, I thought: "Och well, there is no more we can do." "Johnny!" – I looks round, and he was flat on the floor. Well, Johnny had succumbed to the fumes of this thing. So I dragged him by the heels out into what was the ladies' toilet, but he came round all right. But it must have been the fumes of the extinguisher on the film. But it just burned itself out, and we had a show running that night, and the projectors were cleaned and cleaned. Johnny came round; he was OK after awhile. We had coughs for a bit, for a couple of days.

The gate was so hot, you see, although the arc was off. The gate was so hot, and the film was – if I had run it through just a few frames onto cold film, it would have been all right, but the hot film touched the [hot gate] and just went **woomph**, and for a second, you know... and so I slammed the boxes shut, but too late. Burned out the reels completely.[3]

The intensity of heat generated by the lamps in early projectors was sometimes known to threaten damage to the projectors themselves. The heat could then also affect the working of the mechanism. Writing on "The Joys of Operating Twenty Years Ago", British film pioneer Will Day recalled both these problems for a trade journal in 1917:

I used to set up my apparatus in the centre of the hall, the lenses of that period being nearly all about $2^{1}/_{2}$ in. focus, and the illuminant limelight, from an oxy-hydrogen jet and a pair of gas bags. There was nothing to keep the more inquisitive persons in the audience from tampering with the apparatus, and the one thing that always used to worry me was not the fear of the loose film – which used to run into a canvas bag hung on the baseboard of the projector – firing; that never received a thought. It was the fact that I had to keep my lamp house from catching fire, and the smell of the burning mahogany was always a very necessary part of the entertainment, to overcome which I always kept handy a wet sponge, with which to put out the smouldering wood, and prevent it bursting into flame.

Although the lamp house was lined with Russian iron, it was always considered by the makers absolutely necessary to have the outfit made beautiful by coating it with highly-polished mahogany and brass mounts, and the necessary movement was imparted to the projector by a large grooved wheel mounted on the side of the lamp house and a half-inch rubber band running on to a small grooved pully on the projector. This application of the power to drive the machine was beautiful when everything was cold, and all went well until it got properly warmed up, when the belt would stretch with the heat, and the mechanism would refuse to revolve. Then the fun would commence, and you would be turning away at the handle, and the belt stretched by the heat simply running over the pulley, and the picture standing stationary on the sheet, until you took up the slack by getting a friend to hold a pencil or anything suitable for the purpose on the inside of the band.[4]

Writing in the same journal a week later, another correspondent recalled an episode from his own early days, when he had been asked by a local member of the aristocracy to lay on a picture show – using both a magic lantern and the new moving-picture technology – to entertain her tenants. On this occasion, the heat from the lamp caused the metalwork of the projector literally to fall apart:

The film had nearly run its course when I heard Crash!... Crash!... Crash!... Crash! Crash! Crash! I ran up to the machine and found that it was dropping in bits on to the baseboard. With the intense heat of the high-power jet, it had become unsoldered and was merely a skeleton of its former self. I immediately turned off the oxygen at the jet, and the lights were turned up. I explained the position, and I shall never forget the disappointment of that audience when they realised what had happened. Her ladyship was furious and threatened all kinds of punishment, legal and otherwise, although I offered to give the show again on some future occasion. We went on with the lantern exhibition, but it was a perfect fiasco.[5]

I am grateful to historian Dr Nicholas Hiley for pointing out both of these alarming reminiscences. To the modern reader, it seems extraordinary that nitrate film projection was routinely undertaken in such circumstances, with highly inflammable gases or ether (as fuel for the projector lamp) frequently present as well as the nitrate film itself, but the pioneer days were clearly ones where insouciance was a common characteristic. Here is another recollection from this period:

My father who died in 1915 went to London in the autumn of '96 in search of Novelties for "The Carnival" in Glasgow, alternatively called the Scottish Bellvue [sic].

He brought back two new things – samples of a new toffee for his children, as he said 'Like white lead paint with nuts in it' – it was French Nougat; and a machine that projected moving photographs on to a screen, like moving magic lantern slides. He bought it from Robt. W. Paul who was an electrical and scientific instrument maker, whose workshop was in Hatton Garden...

We fitted it up with a carbon arc lamp in an animal house for trial in the closed season (about December). The films varied from 30 to 60 feet. "The Skirt Dance", "The Blacksmith", and "The Rough Sea at Dover" all worked well but "The Highland Dancers" an endless film, having been taken at 30 pictures per second the then American speed, instead of the British 16 pictures per second, was just slow motion. My brother and I, as school boys, were allowed to take turns, and could not make them dance quickly enough. It was hard turning and made us perspire, and our arms ached...

We first showed pictures to the public at Christmas 1896 in a circus building in "The Carnival" Glasgow. The Screen was across the ring with the machine behind to help the illusion. Part of the show was the squirting of the screen with water to make it transparent. There were no titles, but a pianist and an announcer. There was no take up or automatic cut off. Two big nails sufficed for the spools for rewinding. The films ran into one half of one of those old fashioned luggage baskets that are held together with a strap carrier....

Next season, to save the trouble of wetting the screen, the projector was placed amongst the audience with a handrail round it; and on Queen Victoria's Jubilee day about May 1897 we had a fire, and a rush for the exits; but as the whole 6 films did not consist of more than about 250 feet, no harm was done. We borrowed films left over from the Christmas "Magic Cave" of Walter Wilson's drapery warehouse, and carried on.[6]

Another account from London at a slightly later period indicates a broadly similar attitude – "the show must go on", especially if the alternative might involve giving the customers their money back!

So popular did the show become that we divided our programme into halves. We would show half a dozen films, few of them more than a hundred feet or so in length, and then, when the performance was over, would tell our patrons that they could stop on and see a further selection on payment of another penny. One Saturday night we had just made this announcement and collected all the pennies when, on going to the back of the premises to start up the projector, I found the films were on fire! The authorities frowned on such shows as ours in those days, and I dared not go to the fire station next door. Instead, I rushed home – it was only a few hundred yards away – and, sprinting up the stairs three at a time, yelled out to my wife to give me a bath and a blanket. She thought I was crazy, but, realising the urgency of the appeal, she straightway snatched the blanket off our baby's crib and thrust his tin bath on to me. The next moment the Saturday night crowd in Bishopsgate was astonished to see "Mr. Miller of the Moving Pictures" tearing down the pavement with a blanket under his arm and a bath over his head. Though the fire was soon extinguished, we had collected the audience's pennies and, with our programme destroyed, I did not feel like refunding the money if it could be avoided, so, calling a hansom, I went as fast as the horse could take me to Charing Cross Road, where, in Cecil Court... I bought a fresh supply of films. When I returned I found the audience still quite content, enjoying an impromptu sing-song to the strains of the more popular airs of the barrel-organ.[7]

Of course, as other contributors to this volume have pointed out, in most countries of the world film projection came to be increasingly tightly regulated in the wake of tragedies like the Bazar de la Charité fire in Paris in 1897. By 1910, an operator in London was subject to both national legislation (the Cinematograph Act, 1909) and local regulation (London County Council Regulations Respecting the Use of Cinematograph Apparatus). Regulations required the segregation of the projector and its operator into a purpose-built fireproof booth, placed limits on the amount of film to be kept near the machinery, stipulated the number and experience of staff to be present when film was projected, demanded that certain kinds of fire-fighting equipment were to be available, and otherwise strove to contain the risk as much as possible. In addition to the statutory require-ments, private enterprise offered additional possibilities. Will Day, whom we have already encountered recalling his own days as a film pioneer, advertised in the British trade press in 1919 a device called the Kinekone – "a simple coned hood composed of sheet steel fitted to a length of piping which... is continued until free access is given to the open air. In the event of fire all smoke, flame and fumes are carried away, leaving the operator free to attend to the fire while the audience remains in ignorance of anything having occurred." The tag-line of the advertisement read: "Insure yourself against panic with a Kinekone."[8]

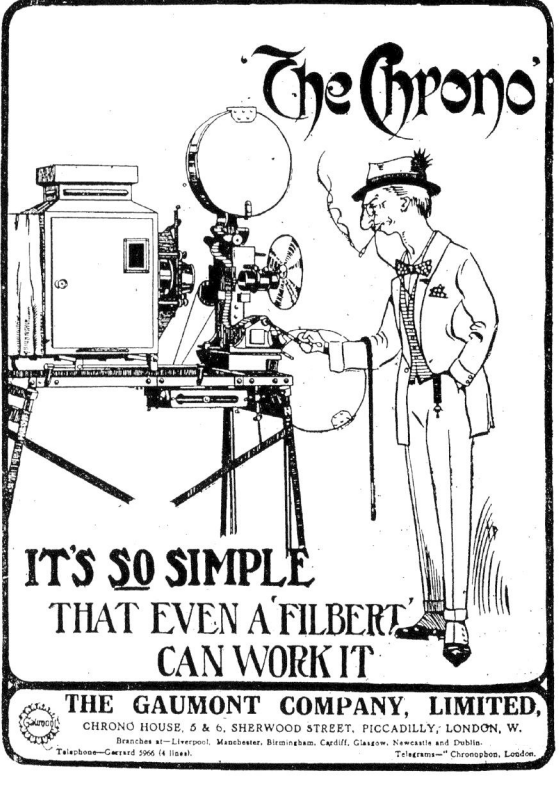

A poor role model (1): an advertisement from *The Bioscope* for an allegedly foolproof projector, 1915.

British Library, Colindale, London. 425.

The inventive Mr Day was not concerned only with the hazards of film projection in the products he offered to the trade. Another of his devices advertised in 1919 was the Clairal, which was claimed to be "A Modern Aladdin – New Films For Old – No More Rainy Pictures". It comprised an attachment which was claimed to give any projector capabilities which are identical to those that modern film processing laboratories offer as "wet gate" printing. Just before the film reaches the gate, it is treated with a fluid which softens the film base, effectively smoothing out or filling in some of the scratches that give the "rainy" effect which the advertisement mentions. According to Mr Day, "This fluid, apart from removing every sign of scratching, renders the film fireproof while passing through the gate, converts old and brittle stock into its original supple condition, and being PERFECTLY VOLATILE, leaves no trace of moisture either on the film or the machine." Sceptical readers were invited to come for a demonstration – "and bring the oldest film you can find". The Clairal, however, never seems to have become the standard element of projection equipment that its manufacturer's claims might lead one to expect.[9]

Recollections of old fire-fighting precautions were offered to industry professional Ken Locke:

> I remember a chat with an elderly "projy" who recalled a fire system in the 1920s consisting of a WC cistern, chain, and pipe running to the projector – in case of fire, flush! Pretty useless, I suspect, as sand buckets were far better to quench nitrate fires. They often also served as ashtrays (and emergency urinals) but must have wrecked any projector they were poured into![10]

A similar healthy scepticism about several of the official fire precautions imposed on British cinemas, as well as a sincere respect for the hazards of nitrate film, are both evident in the recollections of former projectionist turned audio-visual specialist Len Petts:

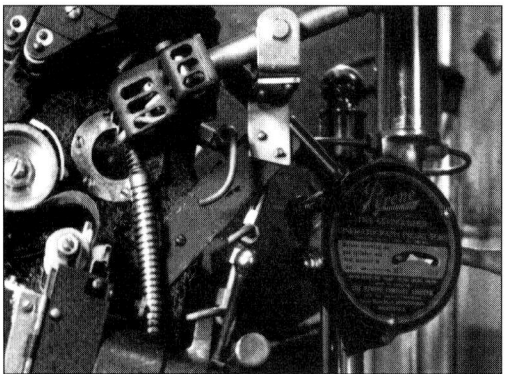

A close-up of an automatic Pyrene fire extinguisher rigged over the top loop and gate of a projector.

Bernard King.

> One of the first things that a newcomer to the projection game was that they were allowed to set fire to a small piece of nitrate film, just to give them an idea of what they were playing with. Believe me, setting fire to a foot (30 cms in new money) was impressive and made people aware of the danger they faced.
>
> I can't say I have heard of anybody being killed as a direct [result] of a nitrate fire, but we were if nothing else a pretty agile lot, and as far as nitrate fires were concerned, discretion was the better part of valour. There were, however, some brave souls. There was the Chief of a cinema who, on finding his top spool box alight, wrapped it in an asbestos fire blanket, unbolted it from the projector, and hurled it on to the flat roof, whereupon the spool box burst open and the film caught fire to the Tarmac roof...
>
> There are other tales where the operators, in a panic, threw sand over the projector with disastrous results. One thing that always amazed me, in the projection room there had to be two buckets of water and a bucket of sand; there was also a car-type extinguisher, using 'Pyrene' (carbon tetrachloride). I never could imagine any instance when you would use sand and water in a mechanical and electrical environment, and the Pyrene gave off toxic fumes. However, all was not lost as the sand buckets were usually full of dog ends from the smokers, and the Pyrene was empty because people used it to get stains off their clothes! The Fire Prevention Officers were wise to this and on their inspections would run their hands through the sand to detect the offending dog ends, only to find them clean as the operators roughly knew when the "Fire Chief" was due. There always seemed to be enough Pyrene left to satisfy them, although perhaps they were aware of the toxicity of the CTC, and let it go at that.
>
> The last nitrate print was issued in May 1952, much to the relief of us all, as we were sitting on dynamite, although we didn't realise or indeed worry about it. Of course the Home Office realised the danger of all this and as governments always do made legislation to protect themselves in case of

anything serious happening. Only 4,000 feet of film was to be in the projection room at any one time, and a projectionist on duty in the projection room at all times. In fact, in the circuit houses it was dismissal if you were caught not actually sitting by the machine whilst running the reel. There were always three projectionists on duty in the projection area or suite. The projection room was always in charge of a person over the age of 21, etc. The strange part of all this was that the person in charge did not have to have any qualifications. It seemed that if a person over 21 was around and said they were in charge, that seemed to be sufficient to satisfy any visiting local authority inspector (yes, they were involved too). The circuits, of course, would always have proper projectionists on duty. The smaller shows, however, were less caring.

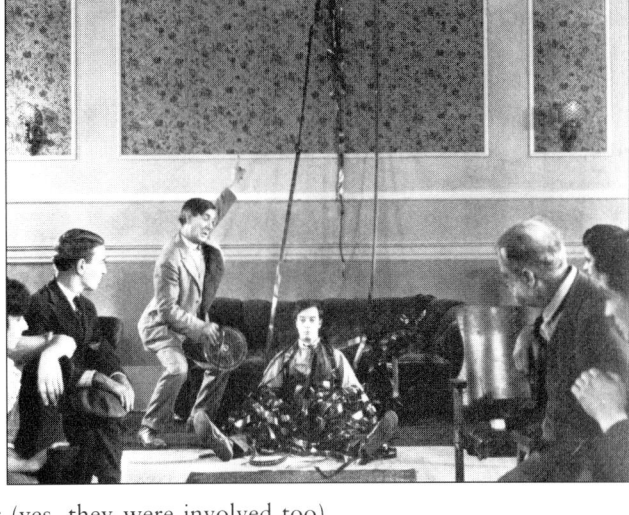

A poor role model (2): Buster Keaton in *Sherlock Jr.* (1924).

BFI Collections – Stills, Posters & Designs, London.

At the Central/Cannon Cinema, Folkestone during 1944 the film caught fire on the rewind bench just before the start of the film *Desert Song*. There were three of us on duty in what was a small projection room, and we had to run through the flames to get out as there was only one door. After this another door was put in the other end of the projection room, but the place was opened in 1912, and this particular box was in use from 1921, so one could say it was about time. This fire destroyed six films, including our two 'standby' films (for use if a film never arrived on the screening date). It also closed the cinema for two weeks, something the Germans couldn't do in spite of a shell one side of the building and a bomb [on] the other. The only film saved was the first two reels of the *Desert Song* which were on the projector waiting to be shown. The two films we were showing were on spools in the film cabinet, and the other four were in transit cases, which were metal cases lined with fireproof wood (still in use today). The films in the film cabinet on spools were hurled across the length of the rewind room, crashing against the opposite wall, by the force of the film being alight in the film cabinets and eventually forcing its way out of the spring-loaded doors on each compartment. If these had hit anybody they would have caused severe injury, but although there were ARP messengers, firemen and us taking it in turns to quell the blaze, nobody was hurt in any way.

I cannot really think of anything more on the subject of nitrate film. We just accepted it, and it is only looking back on it after 50 years that I shudder to think what could have happened, and indeed may have happened and got covered up.[11]

The wartime setting of Mr Petts's fire reminiscence, his account of the rather hit-and-miss approach of projectionists to the officially regulated precautions, and his rather cynical attitude to official inspections, all recall some of the trials and tribulations listed in a humorous eight-verse poem entitled "With the Manager's Compliments", by Charlie Kohn, Manager of the Granada cinema in Woolwich in June 1944, which is included in a very readable account of London's cinemas during the Second World War. Verse 7 reads:

> Then in walks the Fire Inspector -
>   If ever there's a bad time, he'll pick it –
> The exits are locked, the lavatory's blocked

> *And he's going to give you a ticket.*
> *Then up to the box in a panic,*
> *Where your second, an ex-cooking teacher,*
> *Has, just for a lark, fried some spam in the arc,*
> *And burnt up two reels of the feature.*[12]

A rather kinder explanation of the supposed function of the various safety measures, and some good general advice, was provided in a 1933 publication called *The Projectionist's Handbook* (I am grateful to former projectionist Bernard King of Hampton, Middlesex, for supplying this reference):

> FIRE is a nasty word – but the results, both direct and indirect, can be appalling. The authorities, quite rightly, have drawn up a list of regulations which should be hung up in every box, and which should be faithfully obeyed, both in the letter and in the spirit.
>
> Never start a show without a quick glance round to make sure that all fire-fighting equipment is in its place; that the water in the buckets has not fallen too low to be of any use, owing to evaporation; and that the sand in the sand buckets is loose and dry...
>
> Fire blankets are now available ready-made, and have displaced the old familiar wet woollen blanket, which was so difficult to keep soaked and often smelt horribly. The present-day asbestos blanket is either kept hanging flat against a wall, or else it is kept coiled up in a bright red tin canister. In this case it is wise to ease it in and out of the cylinder occasionally to make sure that it is free. Cases have occurred where a long period of disuse has resulted in the blanket rusting firmly in, so that when it was wanted urgently the sudden pull broke the tape and the blanket stopped in the canister.
>
> It seems a wiser plan to keep the blanket unfolded, thus saving valuable seconds in the rush when it has to be gathered and flung over burning film. (And if the film is on a machine, be sure to stop the machine first, otherwise the blanket will jam in the mechanism and much expensive damage will ensue.)
>
> Sand is for use on arcs in the wrong place – until you can switch off the supply feeding the point in trouble. Keep sand out of machines.
>
> Above all, because the indirect results of even a small fire are more serious than any question of money or damage to property, do all you can to deceive the audience into sitting still. If the show can be kept going – keep it going. If non-sync music only can be kept playing – keep it playing. Otherwise isolate the operating box by dropping the shutters, and put up the house lights.
>
> Whatever the circumstances, keep cool. Do the right things in the right order. It is not given to every man to be able to think quickly in an emergency, so here is a tip which one day may save you – and others – a whole lot of trouble. Every now and again, as you stand or sit at your machine – especially towards the end of the week when you are quite probably getting very bored with the whole show – just turn over in your mind what your first action should be in certain events. At that moment imagine the film catching fire in the gate! Imagine a spark from the arc dropping into the bottom spool box just as you had opened it to glance in! And so on. Think it all out before it ever happens. Practice in prompt action will pay better than prayers.[13]

Recruitment into the profession was generally on the basis of interest or experience, interview, and references. Former projectionist David Gillespie (DG) recalls in his interview with Catherine A Surowiec (CAS):

CAS: Did you have to take any kind of examination?

DG: No, I just went for an interview. I can't remember, it's so long ago now, but I was just asked, "Any experience?", and I said, "Well, I've got a toy one at home, but I've been going round cinemas and I know a little bit about it, and I am very interested." I always remember my headmaster writing a lovely testimonial… He said, "His one great passion is the cinema. He's determined to get in it, and as he can't get in as a film editor or in the studios, he'll go into projection. Although I've tried to dissuade him from taking this lowly job, I admire his courage and all that…"

But after a year and a half there, I went into the Army. After five and a half years I went back to the Gaumont, Richmond, for 4 years. Then I fell foul of a rather nasty manager… I remember him shouting out once, "You've got that record out of focus!" How do you get a record out of focus? I haven't yet worked it out to this day… [Later] I went to the Odeon, Hammersmith… The old chief there was a crafty one; the co-chief was bad-tempered, but a very clever man. He could change an arc while a 20-minute reel was running…[14]

Len Petts described earlier the value to a trainee projectionist of actually seeing what burning nitrate looked like. Another of the projectionists interviewed by Janet McBain (JMcB) had such a demonstration without the benefit of choice. As that comparatively rare creature, a woman projectionist, Elizabeth Edmiston (EE) was considered to have a lot to prove in the course of her training. One wonders whether male trainees would have received quite the same treatment. Mrs Edmiston was a projectionist at the Gaumont cinema, Edinburgh, beginning her career during the Second World War.

EE: Well, I wasn't in any part of the cinema business at all until the war. I happened to be just under the age for being called up, and I thought, "Well, I better get a job that lets me be in town," because I had a small daughter, you see. So, I had a great notion for this projection business, so I went to find out if there were any vacancies. And it happened to me at the New Vic, I [was] interviewed [by] the chief engineer, a Mr Mitchell, and he asked me a lot of questions. You know – did I mind getting my hands dirty? I said, "Oh no, not at all," so they took me on, and I was drafted to the Gaumont. That was in 1942, I think – I know I joined the union in '43. So I got all my training at the Odeon, or rather the New Vic as it was then. Of course it's a very different place now to what it was then, and in fact we worked very much harder, I think, than they have to work now, because everything is done for them, you know – the press of a button. But as I say, I started, and I had to go to school for a fortnight, classes you know, just to get the routine of it.

JMcB: Where was the school – was that in Napier College? I know they used to…

EE: No, no, no, that was for the apprentices, the boy apprentices went to the Napier College. We got it from Mr Mitchell up at the New Vic. He was the circuit engineer, you see, and he gave us all our training up there. Because I was very small, and they had to get a stool for me to stand on to put the spool up. It was alright at the Gaumont because it was on a lower level. And one thing that tickled them was that if he handed me a screwdriver to do something, you see, and I just looked at it and then I used it. Then he said, "Oh, I see you know how to use screwdriver," and it happened to be a ratchet one, you see, and he was amused that I would know how to use a screwdriver; however, I'm inclined to be that way. But oh, it was a very, very interesting job, and we were kept busy all the time. When I was ready I was sent back to the Gaumont. That's where I was to be stationed, you see.

JMcB: So you never had any great problems with the old nitrate films? I suppose you would be, everybody would be, very careful.

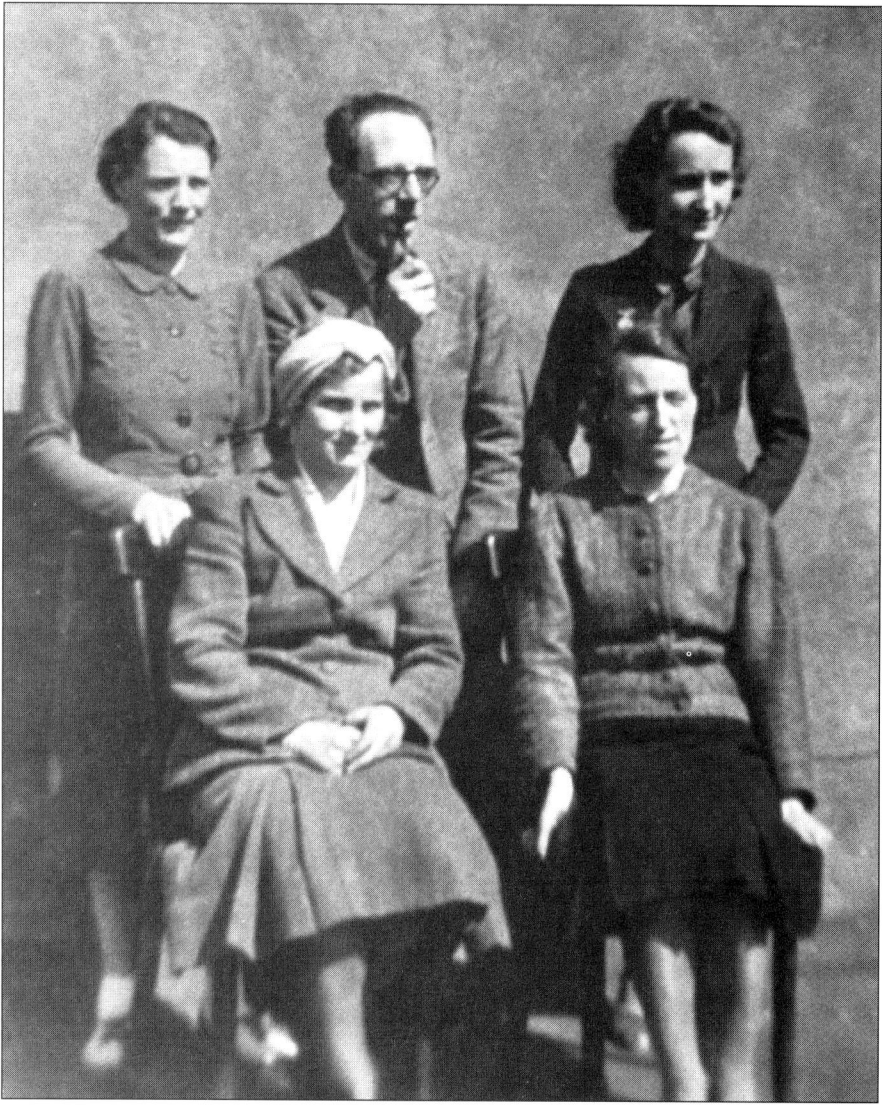

Norman Mitchell, chief engineer at the New Victoria, Edinburgh, with "Mr Mitchell's Humming Birds" – trainee women projectionists – ca. 1942. Elizabeth Edmiston front row left (wearing turban).

Scottish Screen Archive, Glasgow.

EE: Well, I did have a wee fire one morning. I was running something – it was the morning. I had been on a test actually, although I wasn't really. Mr Mitchell was there at the time, and all of a sudden the damn thing – smoke started coming out, and I pushed it off. And I discovered afterwards that he had done it deliberately, to see if I was watching what I was doing. It wasn't anything that would have been spoiled or anything, you know, but it was to see if I was paying attention to the machine. That was away at the very beginning, of course. Oh, we had some very good times.[15]

Bob Douglas (BD), another of Janet McBain's interviewees, recalled his own brushes with nitrate film fires, and the physical effects that even a non-lethal fire could have on the projectionist:

JMcB: How did you feel about nitrate film?

BD: It was very dangerous stuff.

JMcB: Did you ever have any nasty accidents with it?

BD: The biggest was the one reel, that was in the Wee King's in Sauchiehall Street. I was at my tea this night when the second operator... a join had broke and stuck in the gate, and he opened the top spool box and the whole reel went away. It was the fumes off the nitrate – it used to turn your skin yellow, because it happened once when I was down in the Gaumont film office. There was a small theatre where they run through some of the shows, and they were showing the latest newsreel and the evening news and the 'Pathétone Weekly'. And I was at the counter outside when I heard "Fire!", and we were all put into Sauchiehall Lane. And the operator was trapped in his box, and when he was brought out his skin had become yellow with the fumes off the nitrate – very dangerous stuff. They were glad when they went over to safety.[16]

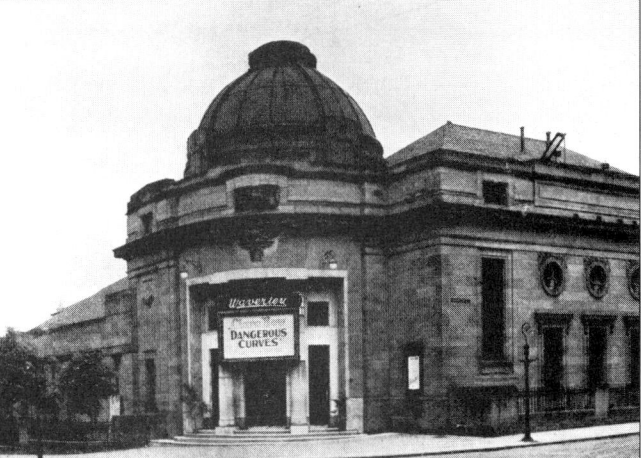

The exterior of the Waverley Picture House, Glasgow, where Bob Douglas was projectionist. The cinema is seen here at its opening in 1920.

Scottish Screen Archive, Glasgow.

Considering how serious the real thing might be, it should come as no great surprise to find that projectionists did not like having the appearance of projector fires sprung upon them. I am grateful to Sarah Davy, who found the following passage for me during her time at the National Film and Television Archive in London. Ivor Montagu, associate producer of several of Hitchcock's early "talkies", while discussing in his book *Film World* the theoretical value of a technique he calls "the dialectical change", incidentally describes one projectionist's anger over a hand-coloured fire sequence, which reflected only too accurately the potential danger of projected nitrate:

An identical 'leap' was attempted for the conclusion of the Alfred Hitchcock film [*The*] *Secret Agent*. The British agents (John Gielgud and Madeleine Carroll), having already brought about one murder – of the wrong man – wait anguished in their own compartment as their minion the Hairless Mexican (Peter Lorre) makes his way along the rattling, swaying train to kill the right one (Robert Young) in a distant carriage. The tension rises as the rushing train rattles and roars. Suddenly there is a train-crash, smashing all to glory and anticipating the killing.... We decided to heighten the climax by a change to colour, and we got Len Lye to hand-paint scarlet and yellow flames across the picture frames at the same time as we stuck sprocket holes from the side of a torn strip of film across them. The effect we wanted, and got, was to bring the fire resulting from the train-crash right into the audience. When we first ran the scene in the projection theatre, the projectionist stopped the film immediately and emerged from his box threatening to punch us on the nose. In the end cold feet prevailed and the public never saw the scene, which was removed from the copy only minutes before the trade show. Nevertheless, the whole experience left no doubt at all of the power of the dialectical change."[17]

Similar shocks to the system were still being administered to more experienced projectionists in the late 1980s – for example, by a cinema advertisement for Heineken beer, as discussed in this further extract from Janet McBain's interview with David Angus:

DA: It is a frightening thing to see – suddenly your film disappearing.

JMcB: You haven't seen... just recently, Heineken have brought out a cinema advert for lager, and they've used a burning frame...

DA: Yes. The operator went in a panic the first day they played that?

JMcB: I can imagine. It was very effective, though. I first saw it, and I was standing right at the side and I could see what was happening in the box. They should have put a wee notice in, I think, a wee note in the box for the operator.[18]

(The projectionist's folk memory of the really serious danger of fire in the gate may be fading, however. A similar effect was used in the cinema release of *Gremlins 2 – The New Batch* in 1990: half way through the film, an apparent fire in the projector signals that Gremlins have taken over the projection box, and the intervention of 'Hulk' Hogan from the audience is needed to get the show back under control. No specific steps were taken to warn projectionists of this sequence, and – at least in the United Kingdom – no complaints were received by the distributors.[19] In the video release of the film, the scene was replaced by one which simulated a VCR breakdown.)

Although projectionists were rightly concerned for themselves, their major concern – and that of those who regulated their activities – was, of course, the safety of the audience. Another item supplied by Dr Hiley is the official account of a fire on 5 November 1907 at the Carlton Theatre in Greenwich (in south-east London). The fire was once again started by the over-heating of stopped or slow-moving film, and an estimated 4,000 ft (1,220 m) were lost, but the main purpose of the report is to show how well certain safety precautions had worked to minimise the danger. For example, in this theatre the projection box was a self-contained iron enclosure, a theatre fireman had been on hand to start to tackle the fire as soon as it started, and there were no problems in evacuation. However, while management and the fire brigade took the matter very seriously, the audience (and the orchestra) seem to have reacted as if the fire were part of the entertainment. The report solemnly records: "The manager states that the members of the orchestra on becoming aware that something was amiss appropriately struck up the tune 'Oh dear! What can the matter be?' and that many of the occupants of the stalls instead of leaving as requested watched with interest the operation of extinguishing the fire."[20]

Many of the entries in the Calendar of film fires printed elsewhere in this volume, however, demonstrate only too clearly both that the curiosity of the Greenwich audience could have been tragically misplaced and that the more predictable reaction – fright – could frequently turn to panic that would be far more lethal than the fire itself. Another incident, reported in the trade press less than two years after the Greenwich fire, showed an artiste using her performance to quell the danger of panic when a fire broke out:

Singing in Front of the Flames.

Miss Madge Goodall, a clever and charming artiste, who [sic] vocal abilities have earned her a high place in her profession, recently proved that she was possessed of other sterling qualities as well, for while performing at the Royal Theatre, Hyde..., the films fired, flames shot up, followed by thick clouds of smoke, and a panic seemed imminent. Miss Goodall, however, with most praiseworthy courage, continued her song. She sang two choruses and then commenced to dance, and the people in the building, reassured by her coolness and splendid example, commenced to leave the place quietly and in orderly fashion. In three minutes the premises were cleared, but before that time Miss Goodall was practically enveloped in thick blinding smoke, in spite of which, however, she continued her performance until all danger to her audience was at an end.[21]

A manual such as *The Cinematograph Book*, written for people working with film, encouraged projectionists to react to fire with a business-like nonchalance, for which the real purpose was to prevent the risk of starting and spreading panic among the audience. The chapter entitled "What To Do If the Film Fires" in the 1919 edition offers the following simple instructions:

> Should the film fire in the gate of the projector, always remember that the first thing to do is to keep cool. Don't be in a hurry. Know exactly what you should do, then do it, deliberately and promptly, entirely without flurry. This is just where the difference comes in between a well-trained operator and a mere "handle-turner."
>
> First, switch on the auditorium lights with the left hand, and with the right hand pick up the wet blanket and beat out the flame... The switching on of the auditorium lights gives the pianist the cue to continue playing, and so keeps the attention of the audience while the operator looks after their interests, although they would and should know nothing about it. Having put out the flame, which should be a mere nothing in a properly-constructed and well-cared-for machine, switch off the arc, and see that the film trap is clear. Then proceed, without losing a second of time, to thread in the remaining film, just as if nothing had happened, and go on with the show exactly as before the accident."[22]

John Boll (JB), another of Janet McBain's interview subjects, describes a fire where exactly this procedure was followed, although his description shows that the safety precautions did not always work quite as the textbook specified, and the projectionist was not always left "as if nothing had happened". The cinema he is describing, where he started work in 1923, is the King's Cinema, Charing Cross, Glasgow, which had a projection box behind the screen, using back projection.

JB: I remember, as I say, the King's Cinema – back projection. We were just boys, you know. At that time, in the cinema, there was an awful lot of responsibility put on them. I was only about 16, 17. I was in the box myself this time, and we had a picture on. It was in pretty good condition – a new film, as a matter of fact. I think that this is what was wrong. At the time [a new film] generally got waxed, and it hadn't been waxed. And I was in the spool room bringing out the film to go into the next machine, when the one that was running caught fire. Of course, I put down the spool on the floor and I tackled this fire, and I broke the film and threw it down and – did it not fall on top of the spool, and the flame went **Whooooho** and... I don't know if you've ever seen celluloid burning? Well, this was a whole hundred feet, it went up like a blow lamp, you know, roaring... We had buckets with sand and water and that, and another bucket with a blanket, and it was – nobody had used it – it was pretty bad, when you lifted it up it fell away. However, I got it in the top of it. Oh, and the smoke – we started the picture, and even [with] a 30-foot throw, we couldn't get the picture through, you know. But I remember, I was working on this when the operator came in, Billy McIntyre, and between the two of us we got it out, but the whole film was away.

JMcB: Did you keep the programme going then?

JB: Oh, yes. It was a Saturday night, and fortunately that next spool, it could go on, you know. They did carry on...

JMcB: But surely the fumes and the smoke in the box...

JB: Och aye, well, that, as I say, we was coughing, and as soon as the blanket went on it with the smoke, you know it started smoking more, then there were no flames. But, as I say, the blanket was that rotten, and had been lying for years. You know, a blanket soaked in water for a year, and as soon as you lifted it up it had plenty of [holes], you know. And I remember meeting Johnny that night at the corner of Renfield Street and Gordon Street, and I was telling him about it, and he said, "Aye, I smell it off you". Oh, it was thick, you know, but I carried on the show that night.

JMcB: Despite the fact that you could hardly see the pictures through the smoke...

JB: That's right.

JMcB: ... and nobody in the audience clued up, and nobody panicked or anything like that?

JB: No, well, you see, there was no way you could see anything. They only saw the picture had gone off. You know, there were no flames showing or anything, and we were sort of isolated from the audience.

JMcB: You were lucky.

JB: Aye. Because if they had seen it... And in those days they had fire shutters, certainly – that wooden shutter that went down over all the windows – but it didn't really go to that length, you know. As I say, the flames had been put out, but the smoke was still belching out.[23]

The importance of the fire shutters in containing panic as well as fire also features in the recollections of Ian Rintoul, who worked as an apprentice projectionist in the late 1940s before going on to become a freelance film and video producer:

> ... If a piece of damaged film went through the projector and tore in the picture gate, the film ignited and the fire swept upwards towards the top loaded spool – only two feet away. My training had been, if the film ignited in this way, to risk burning your hands by quickly tearing the film above the gate, before the fire could travel. Nitrate fires were frightening to watch: experienced operators knew of the potential dangers – to the audience

below, and to the film projector, which could be almost totally destroyed by subjection to the intense heat from the burning of the film which had been giving so much pleasure to hundreds minutes before.

If a fire reached the top spool you had to think fast, the first priorities being to get the blazing reel pulled off the projector and thrown onto the concrete floor away from any equipment, and to pull a lever closing all the projection ports with metal shutters to prevent fire and smoke being seen by the audience – and sealing the projection room from the rest of the building. There might also be time to set off a fire extinguisher...[24]

Missing from such guides as *The Cinematograph Book* was any suggestion of a dress code for the projectionist, but many wore a cap while working – for reasons which the following extract from the published reminiscences of projectionist Geoffrey Carder will make clear:

> ... In fact, it was during one of Barrington's bouts of drowsiness one night that he had a film break in his projector – and I promptly learnt why the projectionist in those days invariably wore a cap! Startled into immediate action by a tongue of flame as the film ignited in the picture gate, my colleague snatched his tattered cap smartly from his blond head and snuffed out the flame as he closed down the projector. With a quick smile and a nod from the Chief, I opened up immediately on my projector. The show went on. What might well have been a disaster in any other similar circumstances, was averted by the skilful hands of this tired projectionist, and his dedication to his public ... I also remember, by the way, that the following day I too, acquired a suitable cap for myself.[25]

As cinemas became more sophisticated, the need for the projectionist to communicate a subtle warning to fellow staff members transcended what could simply be signalled to a pianist by turning the lights on and off. In his contribution to this book, David Cleveland has recalled the passing of a coded message such as "Mr Sand has arrived" and the use of a "fire record" – both practices which conform to the advice given in a 1937 guide for managers:

> Usually a form of general alarm in case of fire is decided upon. It is recommended that this alarm should be passed to the staff in various ways but at no time should the word FIRE be used. A password in case of fire is decided upon. It should be a phrase or name of a simple nature that may be displayed on the screen or passed by word of mouth without giving alarm to an unauthorised listener. The phrase may be incorporated in a specially prepared slide suitably marked and placed in a conspicuous position in the operating box. Explicit instructions are prominently displayed that this must only be exhibited on the manager's instructions. A suitable tune may also be arranged, to be played by the organist or on the non-sync if the manager gives instructions to that effect. The record of the tune should be treated in a similar manner to the slide. It should be in a specially sealed container away from other records and steps taken to ensure that no person may misunderstand its primary use.[26]

Bernard King, who supplied this reference, recalls that in 1946 in Kingston, Surrey, "the Odeon fire record was an orchestra – I think it was Harry Fryer who was the Gaumont/Odeon musical director – playing 'Three Blind Mice'. I never saw it used. It was a yellow-labelled, 10-inch, 78 rpm double-sided thing which was hung on a nail above the non-sync. I always wondered what would happen if, after waiting for years to use it, the hurried operator caught the head of the nail on the hole in the record and

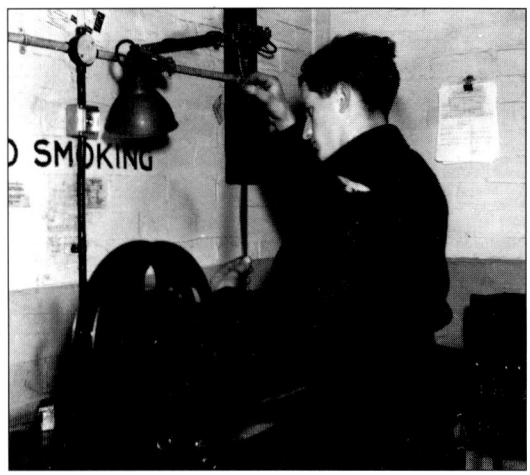

Bernard King with a Kalee rewinder in the rewind room of the cinema at RAF Hawarden, near Chester, ca. 1944.

Bernard King.

broke the bloody thing!"[27] No such accident befell Geoffrey Carder during the worst fire he encountered: remembering the important instruction "to keep the audience calm at all costs", he writes: "I staggered across to the non-sync and placed the nondescript 'fire' record into operation which unobtrusively advised the management to be prepared to clear the theatre".[28]

Of course the projectionist's life was not all fire and the fear of fire. We have already seen Elizabeth Edmiston's opinion that modern projectionists have it easy: "everything is done for them, you know – the press of a button." Here is another extract from her interview, in which she recalls the nitrate-era projectionist's care to see a job done to the best possible standard:

EE: I remember once – a newsreel – something happened in the winding room in the Gaumont, and the newsreel – the spool fell, and the whole spool was out on the floor. I have never seen anybody show such patience as George Morrison did getting that spool back – the film, getting it back, the whole length of the thing, carefully putting it back. I have never seen anybody, a man particularly, you know, working so carefully to get that back without getting it broken or damaged. That very seldom happened.[29]

A Chief Projectionist could be a person of many talents and interests. David Gillespie, whose own career as a projectionist was, like many others, foreshadowed by visits to the projection box of the local cinema while he was still a schoolboy, offers the following recollection:

DG: I always remember going in there [the little cinema at Notting Hill Gate] to the projection box: they were showing *Rosalie*, and the boy was doing all the work, and the Chief was upstairs, up some winding stairs. It was a tiny little projection room. Every now and then the Chief would go down, and he had a sort of enlargement of the carbons, and if the boy had let them drift – they were hand-fed arcs – if he let them drift, he'd give a great curse, which even Captain Bligh would had envied, down to the boy to get it working. And all the Chief was doing to pass the time was colourising a ["God Save the King"] trailer; I always remember that. He did it with an old paint brush. Do you remember those tiny little paints? You know, I'm going back to 1937, and I'm no good on art. He'd probably have a little poster-paint tin and that, and he'd sort of dab it in and put a drop of water.[30]

Another of the projectionists from whom we have already heard also recalls the degree of manual skill required of nitrate-era projectionists:

Joins in the film were made by hand – no splicers in these days. One end of the film was cut on the frame line and the other piece was cut one perforation over the frame line. This was licked on the emulsion side, and the emulsion scraped off. The overlap was coated with film cement, and the two pieces brought together to form a weld. The film cement was equal parts of amyl acetate and acetone, which was purchased at the chemist's shop, although commercial film cement was around. Film cement used to lose some of its "goodness" after a while, and to get a Sunday film with a join every 20 or 30 ft was quite common, the ends and beginnings of reels being the worst areas of course. Every join had to be checked and often remade, a time consuming process. (A 90 minute film is 8,100 feet.)[31]

The projectionist's responsibilities extended beyond checking a film before and after screening and nursing it through the projector. In the days of nitrate film and arc lamps, the procedure for change-over between reels to ensure safe but continuous projection could call for precision handling of the "dowsers". David Gillespie explains:

DG: Behind the projector, or the one we used in the first two cinemas I was at... There must have been one also at Hammersmith. These ones had a flattish piece, and I think it was this stuff that's asbestos, that wouldn't burn, or it was something that would stop the flame. The idea was this: when you took the change-over it was a dangerous time, because you've got the arc lit on the machine that's going to take over and continue the show. And you couldn't just start it up straightaway. You had this dot for starting up, and 12 seconds later the change-over dot. So you mustn't start it up and then shoot this dowser up straightaway... There was terrific heat from the arc lamp, especially on a summer's day; at the end of the day it might be enough then to catch the film, even though it was moving slowly. So you were always told to get it halfway, not quite up to speed, and then open it up. You pulled it up, *then* it released the beam, and let the beam go through, you see...[32]

Two projectionists and a supervisor at work in a British projection box in the 1930s.

BFI Collections – Stills, Posters & Designs, London. 267096.

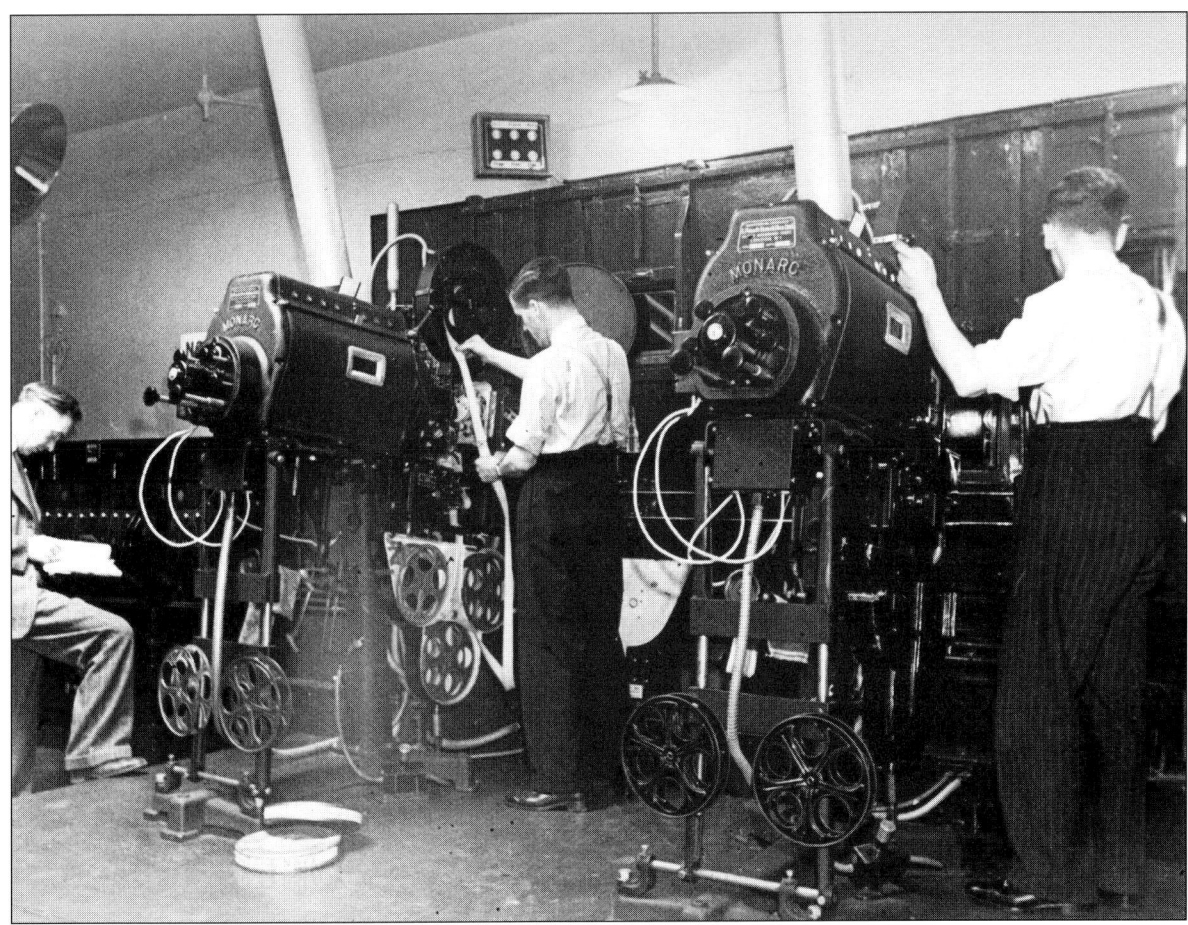

As Bernard King describes, procedures at "break of house" – the intermission between one programmed screening and the next – could offer their own combination of pressure and complexity:

> It was not unusual, even in the more staid and formal general release atmosphere of the Odeon, Kingston, for one operator to run the whole of the "break of house". At the end of the main feature, and programme, the screen tabs would be operated, the house lights brought up along with the presentational use of the colour floods on the old black-and-white end titles. To this we must add the starting of the non-sync interlude music to amuse the mob as they moved out after the big picture and another lot moved in. Some houses also used a few advertising slides... [Remember also] that under the Surrey County regulations the non-sync room was always sited separately to the projection room, i.e., alongside it with its own observation port. At the Kingston Odeon this entailed pushing open a heavy fire-resistant wood door fitted with an air pressure self-closing device... then similarly pulling open the non-sync room door to gain access to the twin non-sync turntables. (All projection suite doors opened outwards.) Having set up the "gram", the two self-closing doors were re-negotiated to get back to the aforesaid series of jobs in the "box" itself!
>
> This frantic activity goes on until it is reversed on receiving the signal – via the buzzer or house phone – from the front of house manager to start the show! Even if the single operator is now joined by another, just back from his or her meal break, one of them is still restricted to the incoming machine. If the first film on is the newsreel, it could be possible that it would be run as a 'single'. This was common practice during the war, as newsreels were frequently run on a shared basis with another 'house' nearby to save film stock. So we have only about seven minutes into the show before we get a change-over to a second feature, cartoon or a two-reel short. While the last two reels of the big picture still have to be rewound, one operator has seven minutes to carbon-up and lace-up during the single reel news which opened the show. Normally, on such a tight spell one operator would run the short reel and lace-up the next reel – leaving his machine with the newsreel running, while the other would be rewinding the last 2,000 feet of the main feature. Although the latter could be achieved if the break of house was long enough.
>
> To complicate matters at this busy time around the break of house, if the single-reel news is followed by trailers, a large number of houses would superimpose a 'MONDAY NEXT' or 'SUNDAY' etc. slide along the lower edge of the screen during the showing of the trailer. This would entail an operator leaving the projector to strike the low-intensity slide lantern arc and then, intermittently, open up the lens cover to project the wording.
>
> All this activity was not, I hasten to add, a frighteningly tense life-style. We knew what we were doing and it became routine.[33]

Another occasion for frenetic activity could be when distribution arrangements broke down, as is suggested in another reminiscence by David Gillespie, here recalling his days at the Walpole Cinema in Ealing:

DG: It was on the Odeon circuit; they had the Odeon at Northfields, which was the posh one, and the Walpole, Ealing... I had a year and a half there, until the War... We had to take the Paramount News between us, and share it with the Odeon, Northfields. The second week I was there, I think, was *Idiot's Delight*. Only one copy turned up, so it was an idiot's delight! Doormen, managers, assistant managers,

> projectionists – everyone was taking the reels up . . . But after about 3
> days they got another copy down . . .[34]

Ronald Grant, now Director of the Cinema Museum in Kennington, South London,
started his working life as a projectionist in Scotland just after the official end of
the nitrate era. His recollections show the way in which nitrate remained part of the
projectionist's life for several years after its theoretical demise – and also how
nitrate and its fires had literally left their mark on the villages where he worked:

> I entered the film business professionally in 1952, a year after safety was
> generally introduced, beginning a five-year apprenticeship as a 'cinema
> operator' (an abbreviation of 'cinematograph operator' I suppose). Looking
> back at the listing which I made – I listed the first thousand films I showed,
> noting copy numbers, film stock, etc. – about 50% were still nitrate copies.
> We checked the films meticulously after each screening. Each join had to be
> tested rigorously in case it was dry (no tape then) and each V-cut peered at
> for signs of tearing.
>
> I remember only one film fire which was really a non-event. There was
> always an operator by the machine, and on this occasion it was an old
> Technicolor film with badly strained perfs and it ripped in the gate and
> jammed. The frame immediately burned out, but as the Simplex projector
> gate was so enclosed it stifled the fire from progressing and there was only
> this one frame lost.
>
> On my evenings off as an operator in Aberdeen, I helped out free at a
> twice-a-week village hall show in a village named Culter. The community
> centre hall was all wooden with a wooden operating box lined with tin
> sheeting and asbestos. The back of the box was in the small hall and the front
> in the main hall, and it was entered by a wooden ladder. When I worked there
> about 1954, there was a brown mark on the tin floor where a reel which had
> caught fire had been grabbed from the top spoolbox and flung over near the
> door then been kicked out, where it fell into the small hall (I hope there
> wasn't a whist drive in progress!) where it burned a deep scar in the linoleum.
>
> Another village hall cinema operated by the same owner in the seaside
> town of Cullen (just along the coast from Pennan, where the *Local Hero*
> phonebox is) caught fire in the late '40s, maybe just after the war, and
> completely destroyed the Town Hall. The operator was quite badly burned,
> I think, and it is said to have been caused by throwing broken bits of film,
> scraps of leader, etc., through an open trap door in the ceiling of the box, so
> that when the film caught fire in the machine the flames went up across the
> ceiling and into the trapdoor and spread along the roof. Only the walls of
> the building survived.
>
> I went on holiday to an Aberdeenshire village called Alford about 1946-
> 48 and went to the Public Hall to watch a film, and remember four things:
> the right-hand edge of the picture went past the screen and shone on the wall
> behind; the wooden forms had no backs; there was a really exciting serial
> shown, the cliff-hanger of which I remembered in detail for over 40 years;
> and the film caught fire during the feature, and I remember turning round
> and seeing flames at the porthole. There was no panic. We sat patiently in
> the dark (after whistling and stamping our feet initially) and after a while the
> film started again at a bit that bore no relation to where it had reached –
> presumably a reel further on.
>
> The company who ran all these places, including the one in my home
> village where as an 11-year-old I helped the operator, was Glen Cinemas – a
> rival cinema circuit run from Aberdeen with local part-time staff who were
> not properly trained.[35]

It is, inevitably, stories of fire and the risk of fire that dominate the recollections of projectionists. Most who worked in that period have at least one nitrate fire story, as well as the ability to recall, usually in a humorous way, the projectionist's talent for coping with the worst when it happened and keeping the show on the screen. Here are two last extracts from the collection of interviews with projectionists recorded by Janet McBain of the Scottish Film and Television Archive, offering admirably phlegmatic – almost philosophical – reactions to the danger of fire.

The first speaker is Vess Hudson (VH), who was projectionist at and later owner of the Hillfoot Picture House, Alva, starting in 1931. The Hillfoot was on the main street of the village, with the projection box located above the front entrance, overlooking the road.

VH: It was during the summer. The film just broke in the gate and began to pile up, and of course the arc lamp was still on, and it just – **whoomph!** – went up like that, and then the flames went up into the top spool box which had the cartoon in it. I just opened the door and grabbed it – like that – and luckily the window was open – **whoof** – it went right out into the main street. Fortunately in those days there weren't as many cars about. It landed just on the edge of the pavement and burned out down there. Of course it didn't take long to burn out. But that was the best way to get rid of it – just chuck it oot the windae![36]

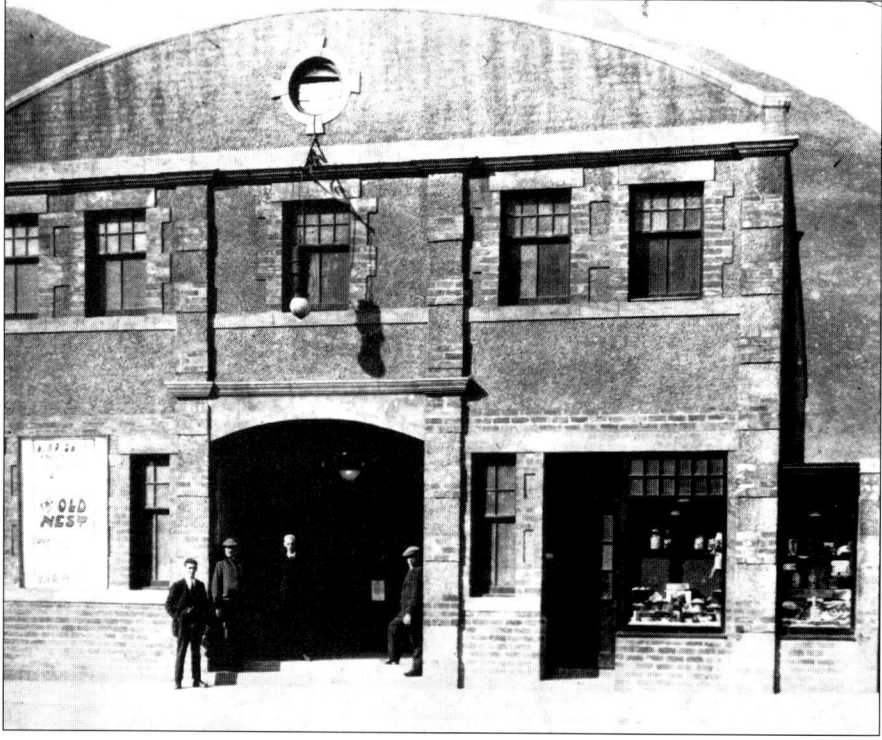

The exterior of the Hillfoot Picture House, Alva, in the early 1920s. The window of the projection box is directly above the main entrance.

Scottish Screen Archive, Glasgow.

David Angus was the first projectionist quoted in this chapter. It is fitting that he should have the last word.

DA: Well, and then – the danger: you're rewinding, you see, and you get a fair speed rewinding. Put the lights out in the rewind room and the sparks are flying everywhere, off your fingers, off the spool. So why worry? I mean, if it happens, it happens... You knew the dangers. There was an operator here, Willie Overbie, always wore his bonnet in the box. That was for putting out the fire, with his tartan bonnet you see – it was quite sensible. We had a fire plan in the cinema like everyone else. That was the only fire I ever had, though, apart from – you know: if there was a flicker, and you would be watching your film, and suddenly the centre disappeared, you know, burnt out, so you realised – shut off! Take the two loops and break them! You took your two loops, your top loop and your bottom loop, pulled them, and broke them, and that sealed the fire off, you know. This bit carried on into the box... And clean the gate, thread up again, and away you go.[37]

Notes

1. Robert A Mitchell, *Manual of Practical Projection* (New York: International Projectionist Publishing Co., 1956), pp. 31–32.

2. Inter-Services Training Committee, *Notes on the Use of the Cinema as an Aid to Training*, B.R. 873 (London: Admiralty, 1943), p. 9.

3. Interview with David C Angus, conducted on 11 May 1989 by Janet McBain, Scottish Film and Television Archive, Glasgow.

4. Will Day, "The Joys of Operating Twenty Years Ago", *Kinematograph and Lantern Weekly*, 1 March 1917, p. 12.

5. J B Wilkinson, "Early Experience with a Kinematograph Machine", *Kinematograph and Lantern Weekly*, 8 March 1917, p. 16.

6. Herbert J Green, letter to Henry Simpson, 8 January 1945; the letter is now held by the Scottish Film and Television Archive, Glasgow.

7. G Miller, interviewed in Leslie Wood, *The Romance of the Movies* (London: Heinemann, 1937), pp. 73–76.

8. Will Day Kinutilities advertisement, supplement to *The Cinema*, 27 March 1919, p.xxxi.

9. Will Day Kinutilities advertisement, supplement to *The Cinema*, 20 February 1919, p.xxxi.

10. Ken Locke, letter to Roger Smither, 5 December 1999. A "flushing" system is also mentioned (and illustrated) in David Cleveland's essay "Don't Try This at Home" elsewhere in this volume.

11. Len Petts, letter to Roger Smither, March 1993.

12. Quoted in Guy Morgan, *Red Roses Every Night – An Account of London Cinemas under Fire* (London: Quality Press, 1948), p. 57.

13. R Pitchford and F Coombs, *The Projectionist's Handbook* (London: Watkins-Pitchford Technical Publications, 1933), pp. 38–39.

14. Interview with David Gillespie, conducted in July 2000 by Catherine A Surowiec.

15. Interview with Elizabeth Edmiston, conducted on 20 November 1984 by Janet McBain, Scottish Film and Television Archive, Glasgow.

16. Interview with Bob Douglas, conducted on 21 March 1978 by Janet McBain, Scottish Film and Television Archive, Glasgow.

17. Ivor Montagu, *Film World* (Harmondsworth: Penguin Books, 1964), p. 124.

18. Interview with David C Angus, loc. cit.

19. Richard Huhndorf, Technical Manager, Warner Bros. Distributors Ltd., London, correspondence with Roger Smither, July 1998.

20. Report by S G Gamble of the London Fire Brigade for the Theatres and Music Halls Committee of the London County Council, 13 November 1907: Public Record Office, HO 4S/10376/161425, file 6.

21. *The Bioscope*, no.136 (20 May 1909), p. 9.

22. Bernard E Jones, ed., *The Cinematograph Book: A Complete Practical Guide to the Taking and Projecting of Cinematograph Pictures* (London: Cassell, Revised Edition, 1919; first published 1915), p. 70.

23. Interview with John Boll, conducted on 4 July 1983 by Janet McBain, Scottish Film and Television Archive, Glasgow.

24. Ian Rintoul, personal reminiscence sent to Roger Smither, 1998.

25. Geoffrey H Carder, *The Man in the Box: Memoirs of a Cinema Projectionist* (St Ives, Cornwall: United Writers, 1984), p. 25.

26. J H Hutchison, *The Complete Kinemanager* (London: Kinematograph Publications, 1937), p. 184.

27. Bernard King, letter to Roger Smither, 25 August 1998.

28. Geoffrey H Carder, op. cit., p. 50.

29. Interview with Elizabeth Edmiston, loc. cit.

30. Interview with David Gillespie, loc. cit.

31. Len Petts, loc. cit.

32. Interview with David Gillespie, loc. cit.

33. Bernard King, loc. cit.

34. Interview with David Gillespie, loc. cit.

35. Ronald Grant, letter to Roger Smither, April 1998.

36. Interview with Vess Hudson, conducted in December 1984 by Janet McBain, Scottish Film and Television Archive, Glasgow.

37. Interview with David C Angus, loc. cit.

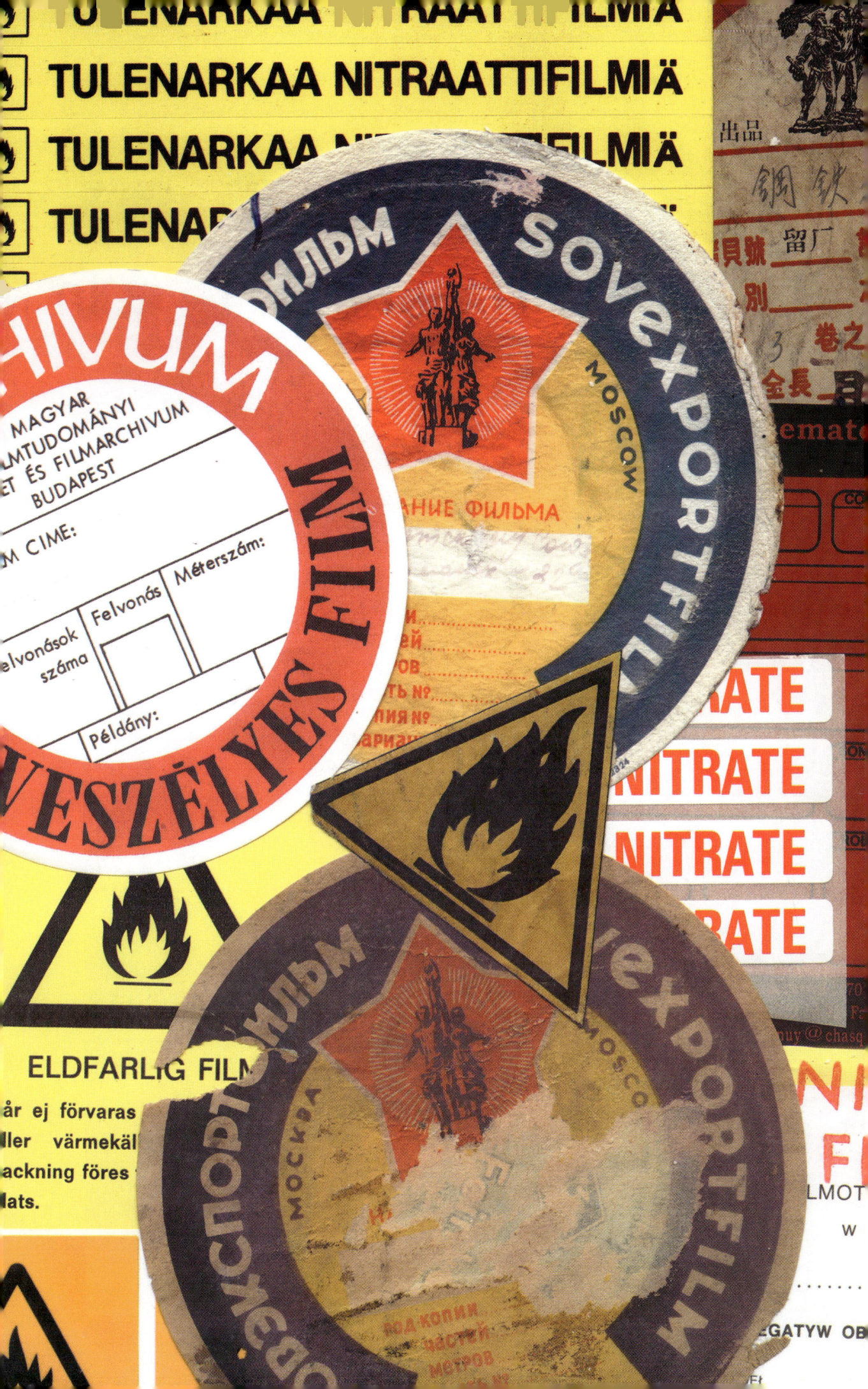

TULENARKAA NITRAATTIFILMIÄ

TULENARKAA NITRAATTIFILMIÄ

TULENAR... ...ILMIÄ

TULENAR...

ОРИЛЬМ

SOVEXPORTFILM

MOSCOW

ОПИСАНИЕ ФИЛЬМА

ARCHIVUM

MAGYAR
FILMTUDOMÁNYI
...ET ÉS FILMARCHIVUM
BUDAPEST

...M CIME:

...elvonások száma	Felvonás	Méterszám:

Példány:

VESZÉLYES FILM

NITRATE

NITRATE

...RATE

ОРИЛЬМ

MOSCO

...vexPORTFILM

МОСКВА

ELDFARLIG FILM

...år ej förvaras
...ller värmekäl...
...ackning föres...
...lats.

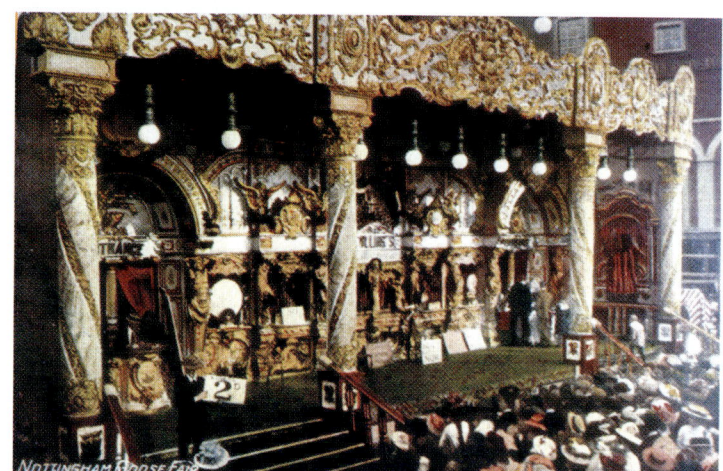

Hand-coloured close-up of
Pat Collins No 2 Wonderland Show,
Nottingham Goose Fair, 1908 –
see p.110.

© National Fairground Archive, Sheffield.

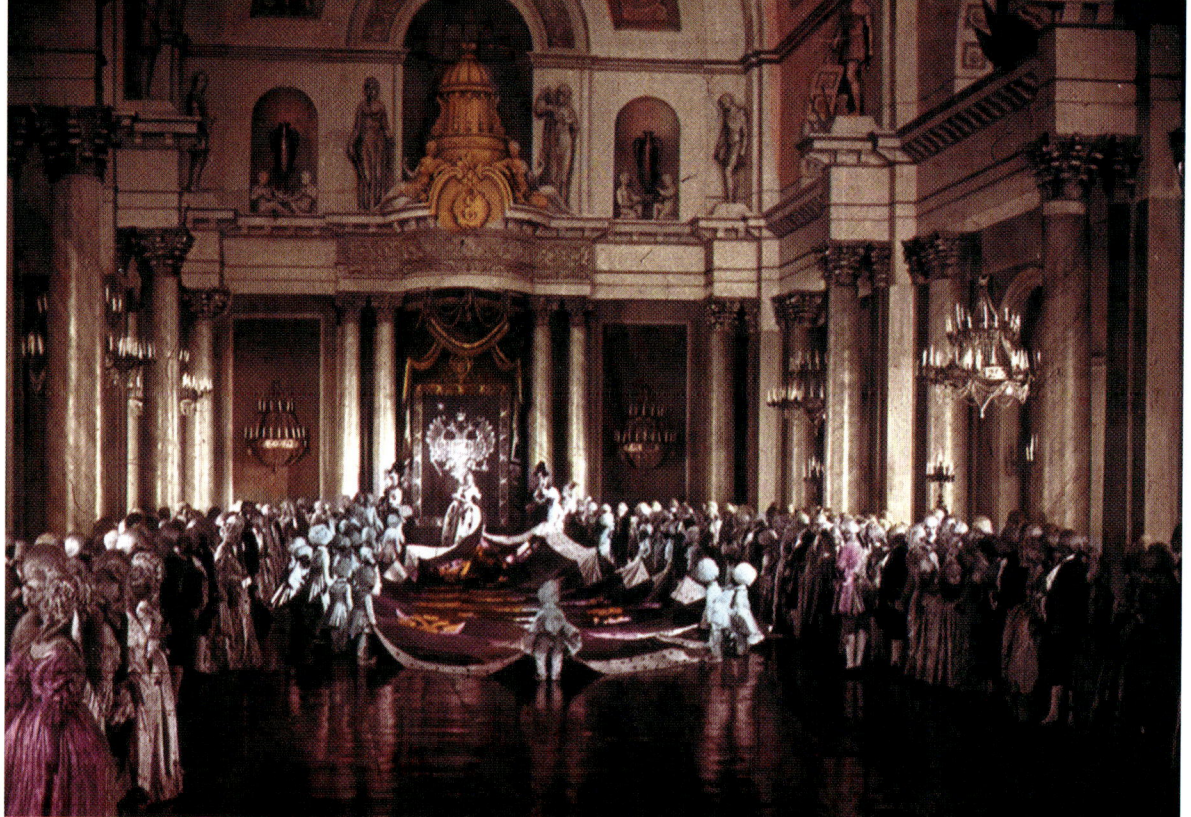

Stencil colour: a scene from
Casanova (1927) – see p.118.

Kevin Brownlow Collection.

Hand colouring: a scene from
Serpentine Dance (1897)
– see p.118.

Kevin Brownlow Collection.

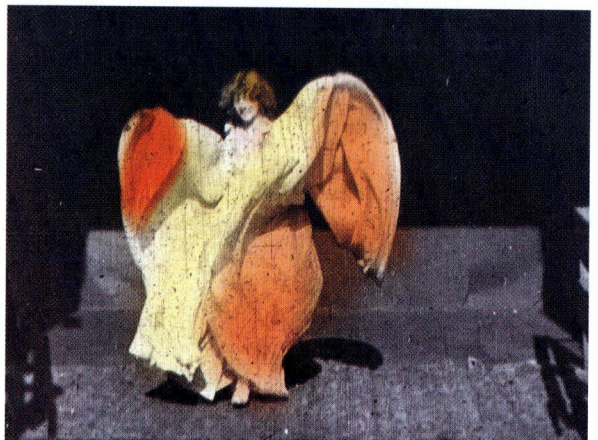

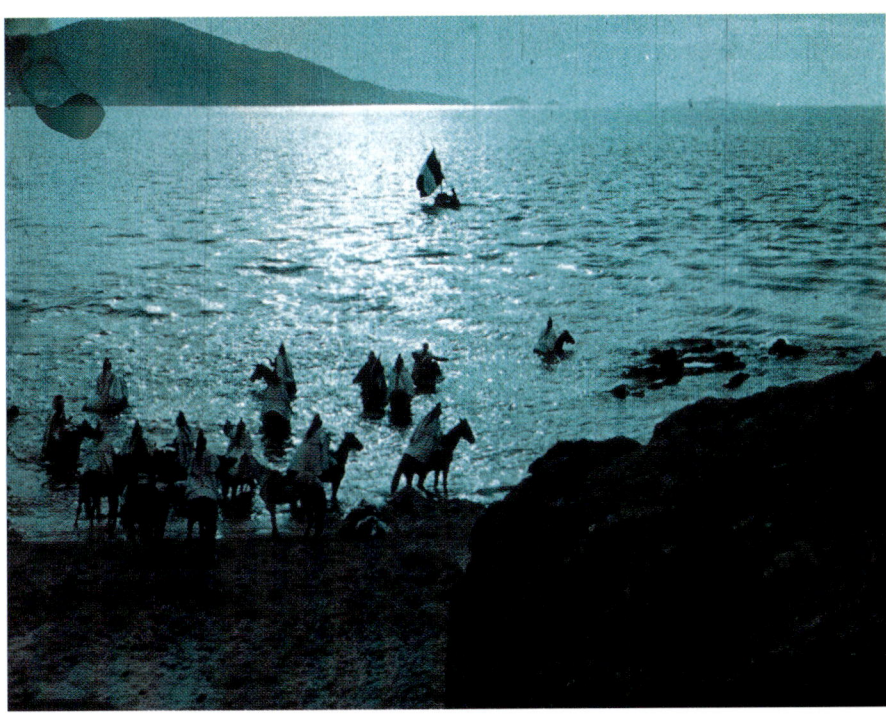

Cyan dyed film base:
a scene from *Napoléon*
(1927) – see p.120.

Kevin Brownlow Collection.

Two-colour Technicolor:
a scene from *Ben-Hur*
(1925) – see p.123.

Kevin Brownlow Collection.

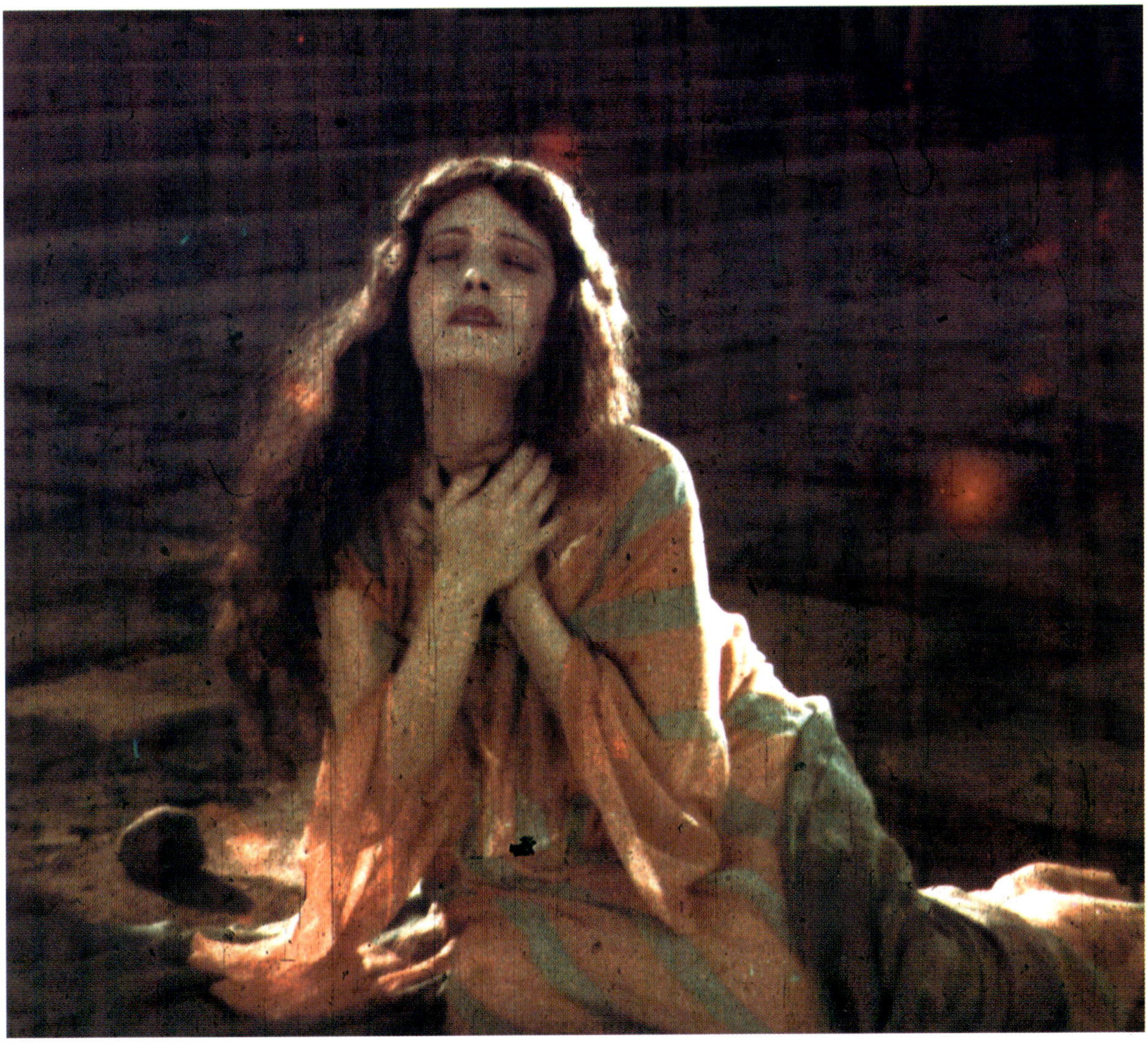

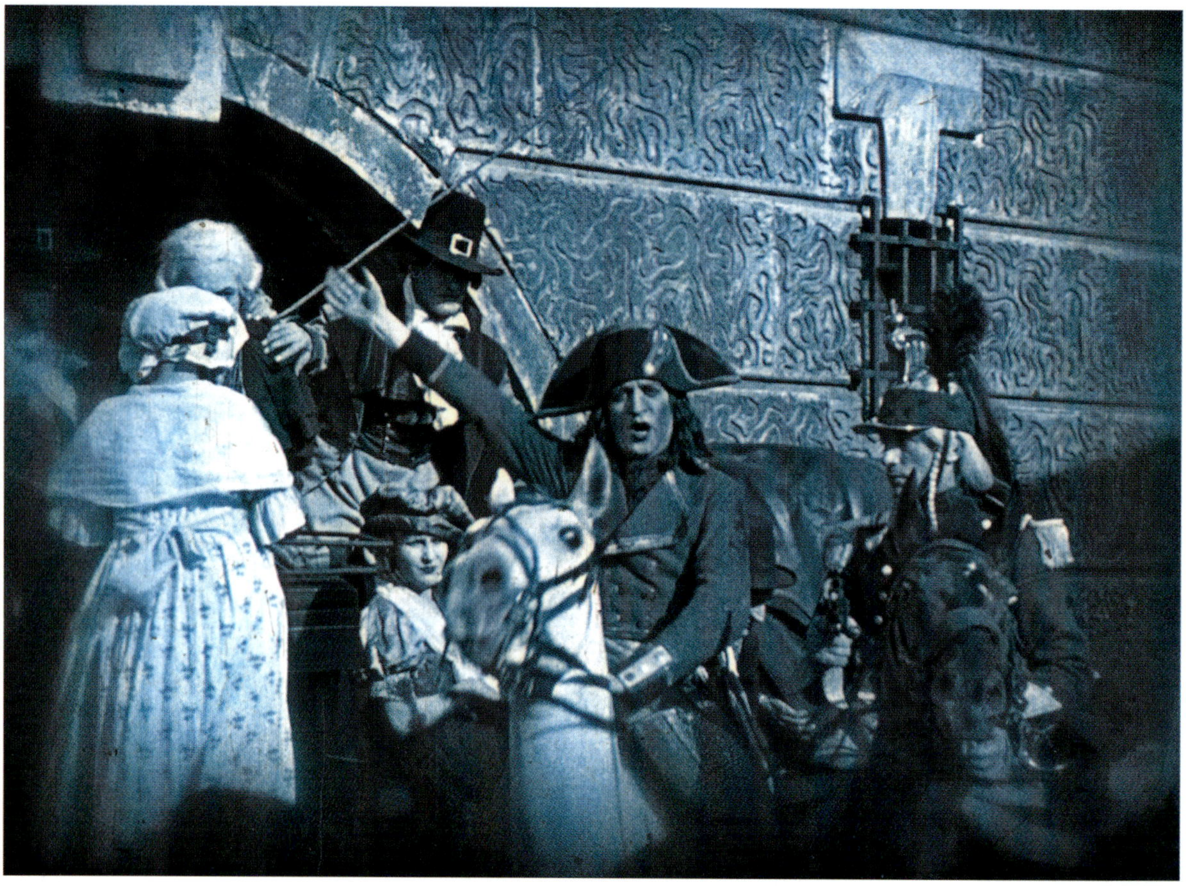

Blue chemical toning
(ferric-ferrocyanide):
a scene from *Napoléon*
(1927) – see p.119.

Kevin Brownlow Collection.

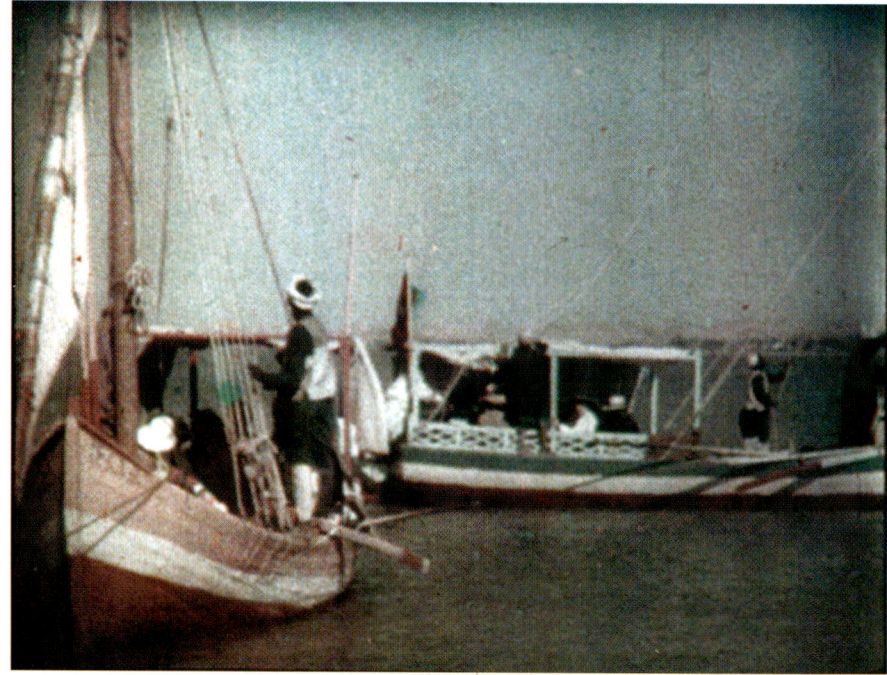

The combined colour
image recreated from a
pair of black-and-white
frames through the
Kinemacolor process –
see p.125.

L'Immagine Ritrovata, Bologna.

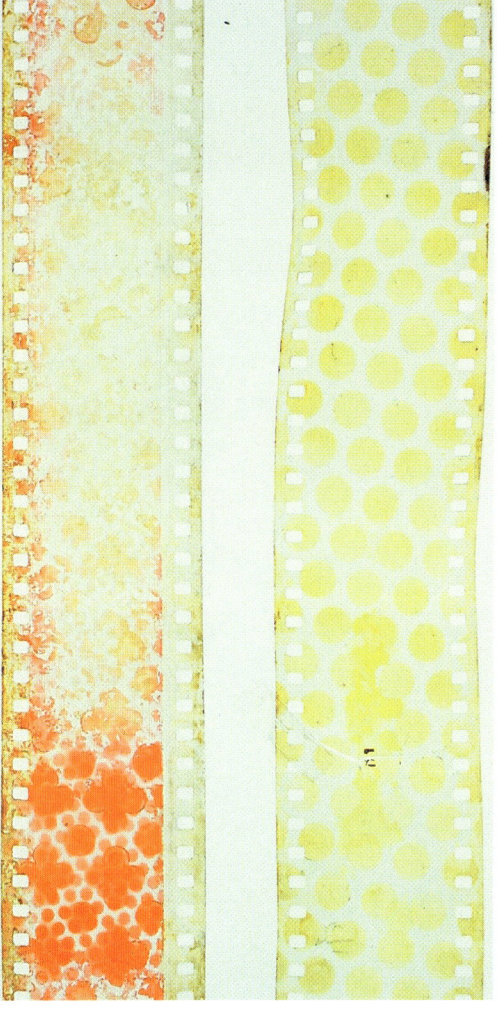

The original hand-painted
picture element for
A Colour Box (1935)
– see p.127.

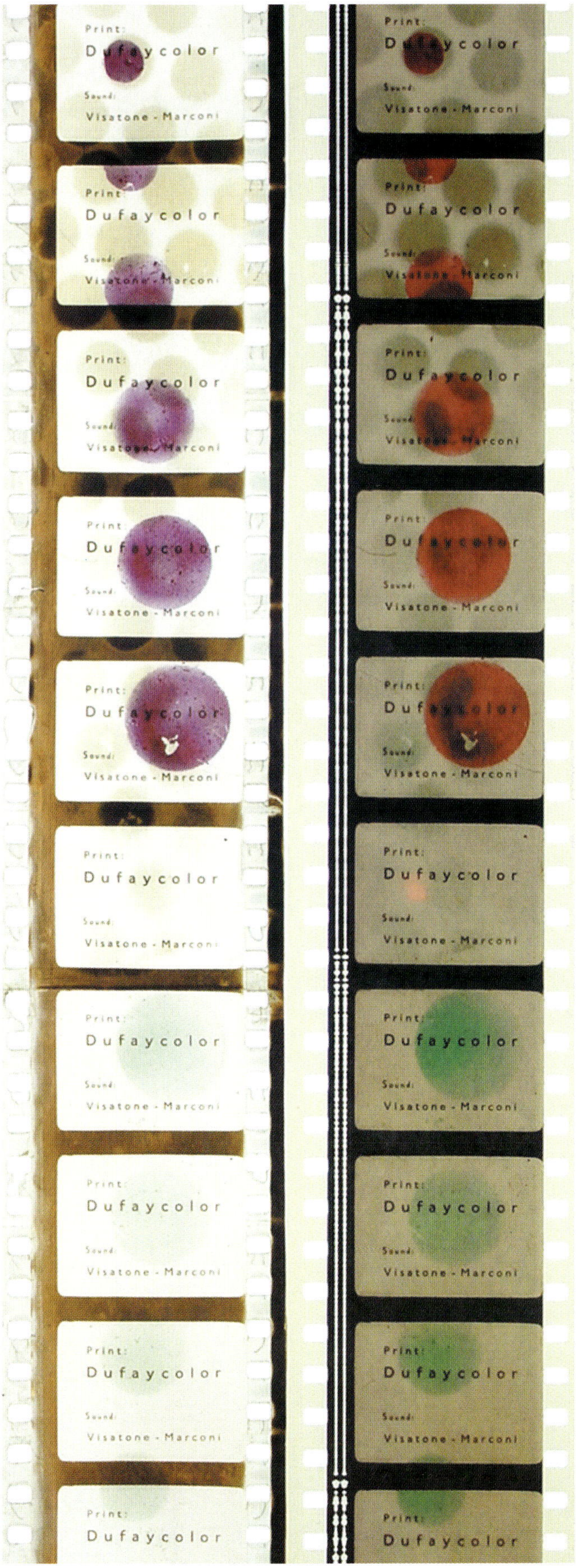

A comparison between a print replicating
the original Dufaycolor appearance of
A Colour Box (on the left) and the
"far more saturated and more intense"
colours of the new print generated from
the nitrate element found by the BFI –
see p.127.

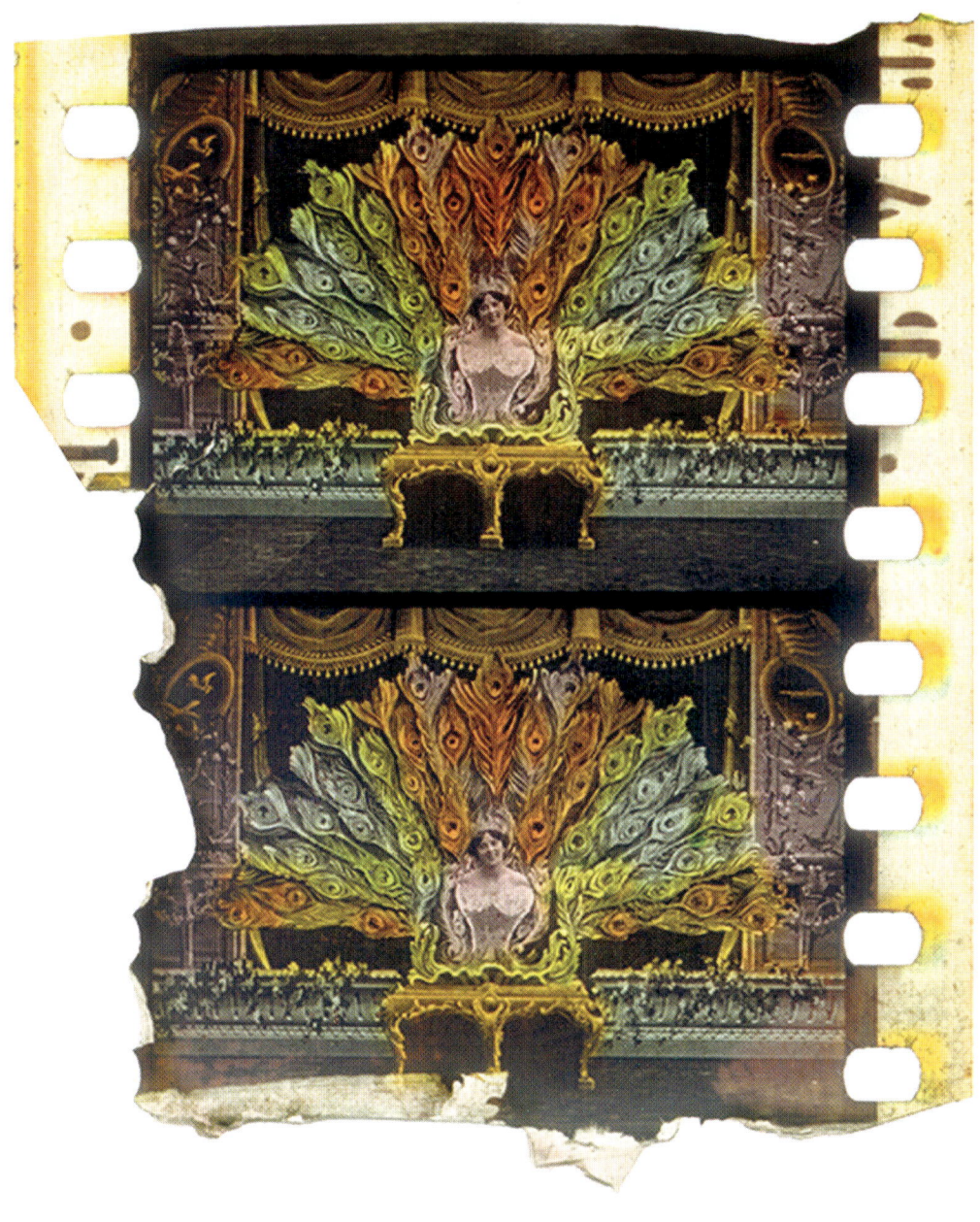

A fragment of the stencil-
coloured Pathé film
Fée aux pigeons (1906)
– see p.128.

Paolo Cherchi Usai.

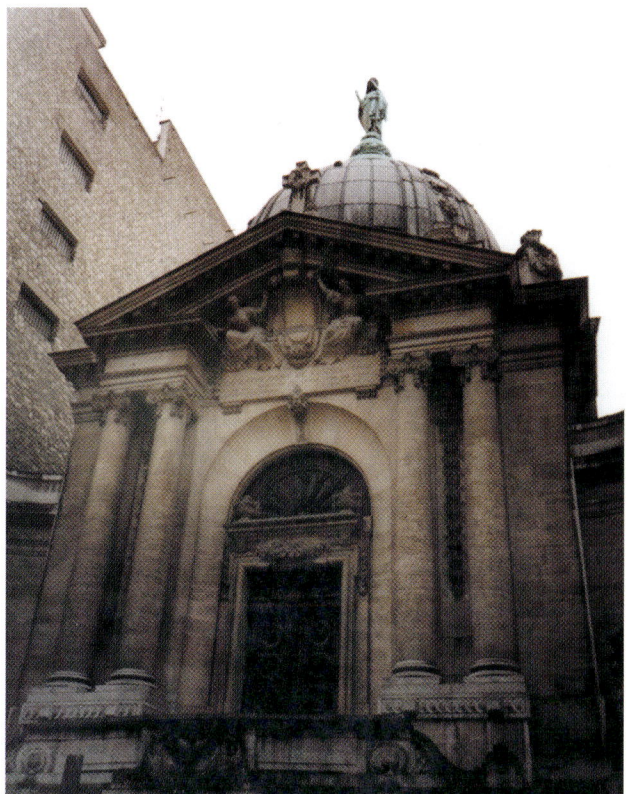

Notre Dame de Consolation –
the memorial chapel in rue Jean Goujon,
Paris, photographed in March 2001.
A sign at the foot of the stairs reads:
"Sur ces lieux, le 4 mai 1897 un terrible
incendie ravagea la vente de bienfaisance
organisée par l'œuvre philanthropique
du Bazar de la Charité. 127 personnes
périrent brûlées vives parmi lesquelles
la duchesse d'Alençon et 250 grièvement
blessées." – see p.166.

Roger Smither.

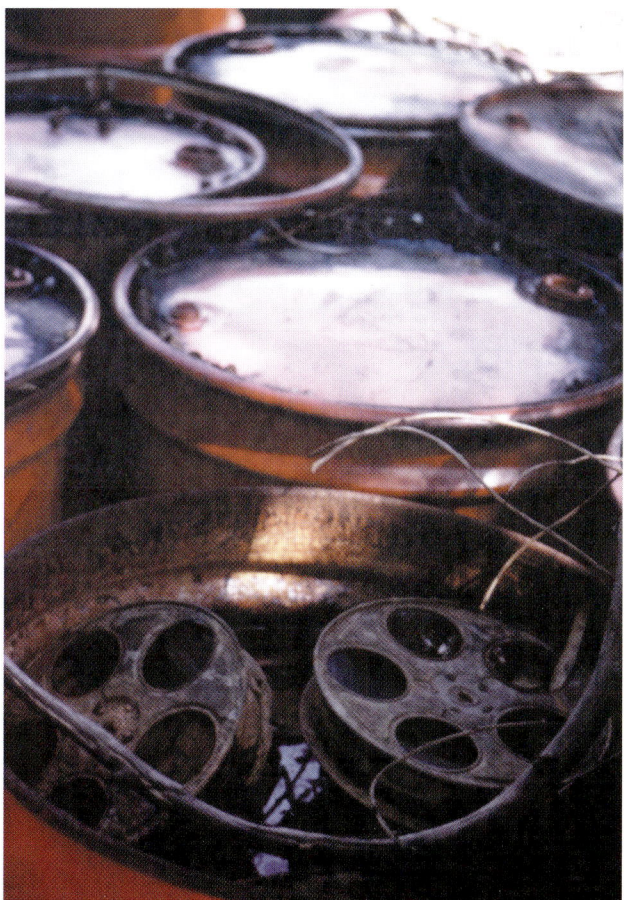

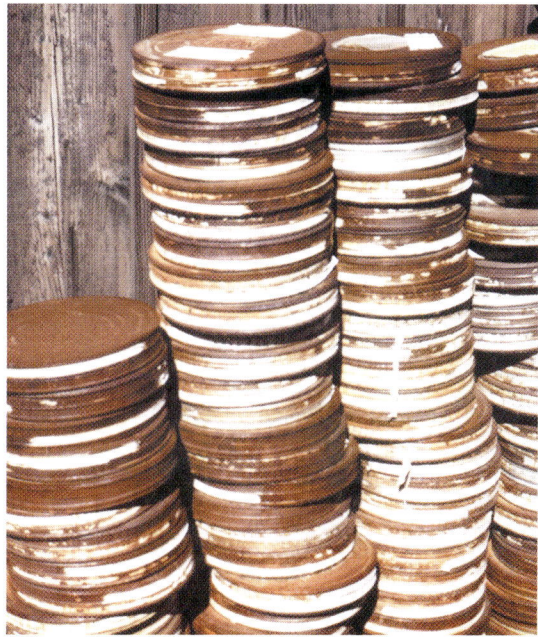

"One of the most horrifying sights…":
two views of Lot 3 at the MGM auction,
Culver City, 1970 – see p.179.

Kevin Brownlow Collection.

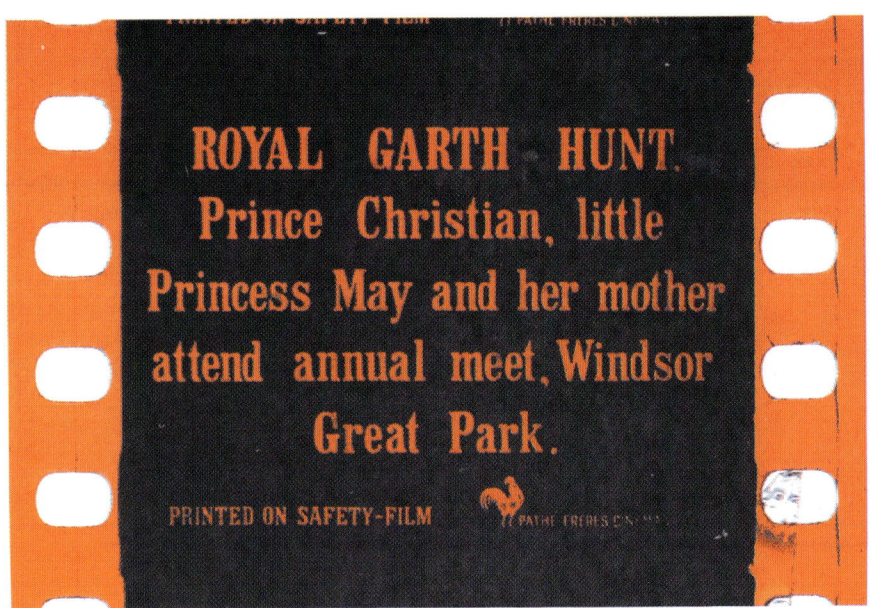

Pathé's *Animated Gazette* advertises its safety film credentials – see p.193.

East Anglian Film Archive, Norwich.

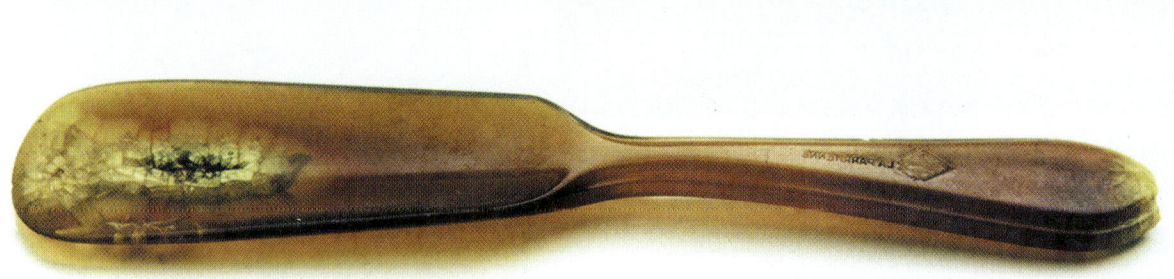

Decomposing domestic celluloid artefacts: a shoehorn from the USA (above – photographed by Ken Kirkwood) and a 1920s cellulose nitrate dressing table tray (right) – see p.199.

© Katz Collection.

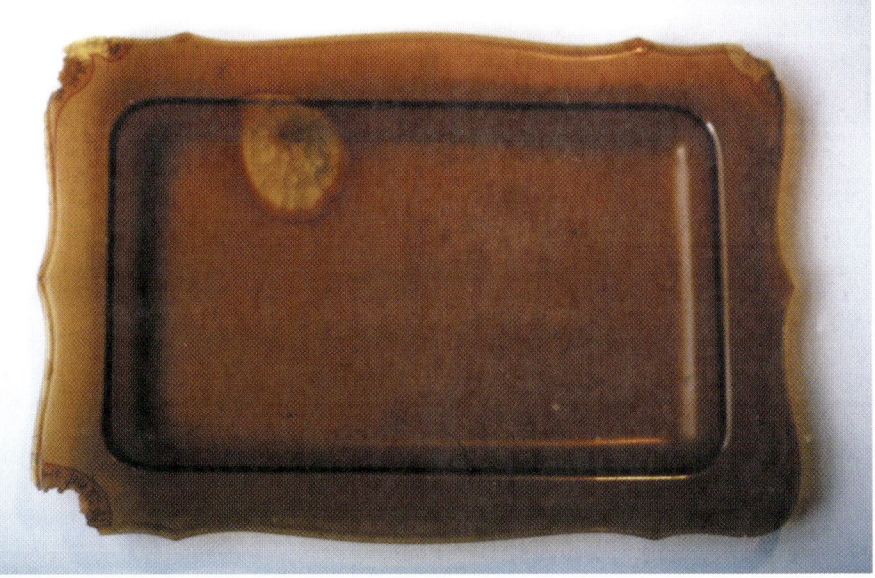

Flash Frame

by Clive Donner

8 a.m., on a crisp September morning. My first job since leaving school, and my first day at work as an assistant editor in the film cutting rooms. Sammy – film editor Sam Simmonds, known as "One-Snip Sim" – my tyrannical but benevolent boss, took me across the backlot of the studios, past the large tank where they had recently been shooting David Lean's first film, *In Which We Serve*, until we reached the wire netting that divided Korda's great Denham Studios from Denham Laboratories, where all the film shot in the studios was processed. Sam took me to a patch of bushes, and parted them to reveal a piece of strong wire netting that could be lifted. I ducked under, and followed him through into the grounds of the lab. We took a path and came finally to the back entrance of the plant. Sam stopped and faced me. He told me that never, ever was I to enter the building, front door or back, with a cigarette in my mouth, even unlit, nor should I ever be smoking when carrying or opening cans of film, or at any time handling the film indoors or out. Danger. Movie film stock was nitrate-based and highly flammable. This was a lesson to be heeded.

We entered the plant. A wave of warm air carrying a marvellous smell of chemicals engulfed me and whirled round in my head. I was dizzy. Intoxicated. I have never forgotten those smells; they were part of processing the film that was travelling at speed through the machinery carrying and developing the previous day's filming. We went into the room where the lab contact men brought in 12-inch clips of each shot of the previous day's filming. Gary, our contact man, was riffling through these strips, which showed the different densities at which the film might be printed, thus giving the director of photography the choice of exposure he preferred. The strips were put into slim brown envelopes, each envelope marked for the relevant production and cameraman.

Back in Sammy's cutting room every surface was kept free of dust. Only film that was being edited was allowed out of cans, no leftovers from other sequences were permitted, no pieces of blank "leader" film allowed to fall ignored into the bins where the work in hand hung on slim hooks. My first lesson: I had to learn how to join one piece of film to another. The studios had very up-to-date equipment, and the film joiners, state-of-the-art for then, would be regarded today as obsolete, antiquated, useless. The Bell and Howell film-joining machine was a heavy metal piece of equipment, bolted to the floor. I sat in front of it. There was a spool of film each side of me – on one side film clips, on the other side another spool waiting to take up the film splices I made from them. In front of me a mechanism, electrically warmed to soften the nitrate stock, locked and clamped the left-hand piece of film into position first, while the other piece, also locked and clamped, was miraculously raised into the air – a movement achieved by my pushing with my right leg a lever, which I had to manoeuvre so that it securely locked before I removed my leg. A mistake would result in a deafening crash, and the possibility of losing a finger.

The piece of film on the left-hand side had about a centimetre of film sticking out, resting on a solid plate. Manoeuvring my left leg brought down another piece of cast iron to hold the film securely, while with a thin scraper I removed the emulsion, leaving the raw stock. In front of me was something like an inkwell filled with acetate, and a soft hair brush, which, used very carefully – with not too much acetate, nor too little – bound the two pieces of film firmly together. With another smart kick by my leg, the right-hand piece of film was brought down to make a perfect and secure join. The nitrate film that ran through my fingers as I mastered this monstrous piece of machinery was safely held and secure – no cigarettes, thank you very much – but the possibilities for making a lousy join were legion. I laboured; I persevered. The film clips I was joining were leftover cuts from the last film that Sammy had edited – a Technicolor film called *The Great Mr Handel*, part of J Arthur Rank's desire to make films with a religious purpose. Although most of the utterings which accompanied my early blunders on the Bell and Howell were blasphemous, I finally had the monster successfully under my control.

When all the leftovers were joined up and packed into cans I staggered with them out to the vaults, which lay a short distance behind the cutting rooms. "No Smoking" signs were everywhere. All the films were nitrate-based. As I dumped the reels of film onto shelves, I could see all around me cans containing film history. Some films I had never heard of, some never seen, some were part of my film education: *The Scarlet Pimpernel, Sanders of the River, The Ghost Goes West, Things to Come, Elephant Boy, The Four Feathers, The Thief of Bagdad*, and most intriguing of all, Josef Von Sternberg's unfinished spectacular *I, Claudius*, with Charles Laughton. All and everything identified and held in place, but waiting to be seen again, a mausoleum of nitrate.

Danger lurked everywhere, and precautions were scrupulous. The camera assistants loaded the unexposed film in darkrooms or, when out of reach of a darkroom, by using a black "changing bag", into which unopened cans of unexposed film were zipped while the assistant pushed his arms into elasticated openings and by touch only unsealed a virgin can of film and then transposed the contents into a camera magazine waiting to be loaded. An inexperienced assistant cameraman carrying out this manoeuvre might be seen staring into space like a holy mystic when this crucial technique was carried out. Once the magazine was locked shut the changing bag was unzipped, and the magazine, securely lightproof, was passed to the camera for the next shots. Assistant cameramen might have a smoke when the task was done, but never while doing it, and in any case keeping a weather-eye open for any sources of flame indoors or out.

The projection room has always been vulnerable, because nitrate film is totally unprotected when it is taken out of its can and laced up on the film projector. Official safety instructions dusty with lack of anyone interested in reading them hung round the walls, and any projectionist with a brain in his head knew the risks that attended a lack of concentration. I only saw one projection room fire, in a small theatre at Pinewood Studios. In spite of all the proper precautions a piece of film had jammed in the projector gate during a screening. The heat from the lamp immediately set it on fire. The projectionist was, as he should be, standing by, and quickly reached up and broke the film unspooling from the upper reel, switched off the power, and scampered out of the projection room. Fire extinguishers quickly made the room safe.

But even in the safest environment accidents could happen. The film *The Blue Lagoon*, made in 1949 with Jean Simmons, was being edited at Pinewood. An experienced editor was using a Moviola, a machine on which the film ran through with a strong magnifier to make it easier to see the image. A clip at the side of the magnifier released the film in order to take it out or replace it with another. In this instance, the clip was released and the film was left hanging loosely. The editor turned away. It was a fine day, about noon; the sun was at its hottest, and shining into the cutting room. For a brief moment the angle focused the sun's rays onto the lens of the Moviola and then directly onto the strip of film loosely lying there. A chance in a billion. The magnification of the sun's rays immediately set fire to the film. Within seconds a blaze was started. The editor had the sense to run straight for the door, and got out. The spring hinge automatically closed the door, safely sealing and isolating what immediately became a blazing inferno inside. The sprinkler system and fire alarms were automatically set off. The editor was in shock, but stopped anybody trying to open the door. If they had opened it the blaze would have spread at once, and would have whipped along the corridor. People would have been in great danger. The editing block was evacuated. Chaos. The supervising editor was marching up and down shouting "Save the cutting copies!" – the only record of work that existed at that moment, and whose destruction could cost great expense, and loss of time in finishing films, as well as the massive detail of creative editing. Cans of film were thrown out of windows, doors, anywhere to get them safely away. The fire was left to burn itself out, with hoses playing on the door and windows. Eventually it did. When everything had cooled down from the outside, the door into the stricken cutting room looked quite normal. Very wet, but nothing else. When it was opened, the whole of the interior was black from the burned film, all of which was reduced to flakes. The inside of the door – strong, thick, hard teak – was burned through, so that only a few centimetres of it remained. Even though it was intact, had the heat not diminished in time that door, too, would have collapsed, and the fire would have been left free to run amok.

In 1951 nitrate as a base for film stock was replaced at last by non-flammable stock. For film editors and their assistants it was a revolution. Film was no longer joined to film using foot-operated joining machines, nor even the older, smaller hand-joiners. A new device was made, and two pieces of film placed in sprockets to hold them firm merely needed a piece of transparent sticky tape to make a join, in a fraction of the time it took with the old nitrate stock. Rather than hand an assistant a reel full of joins to be made, the editor, with a quick flick of the joining tape, did the job himself. No longer would nitrate joins come adrift in the projector at some important screening. Cigarettes began to be left on the workbench within a few inches of the film – not that it was allowed, because the nitrate-free stock still had some flammable quality. The only damage made to a reel of film was the eternal scratches that a workprint inevitably suffered. In the old nitrate days David Lean, himself an ex-editor, used to say that he liked to have a screening of a film with lots of black frames replacing the two frames that were always cut on the Bell and Howell. He said it made the producer think that a lot of hard work attempting alternatives had gone into an edited sequence. Assistants no longer sweated at joining piles of reels at the last minute in time for an important screening, followed by the dash to the projection room and then the anxious wait until the viewing had finished, and, fingers crossed, no joins had broken or become unstuck. Sitting in on those screenings and the discussions that followed them was where I listened and learned huge and valuable lessons about what could be achieved in the cutting rooms, and how a film could be changed, and sometimes turned from a disaster into a triumph.

There was excitement in the days of nitrate, apart from the danger of fire. The urgency to get hundreds of edited cuts made quickly, securely, without unwanted marks, and rushed to the projection room in time for a screening, brought with it a sense of excitement and satisfaction. Of having been a part of the complex making of a film, and in some way of having contributed entertainment and knowledge to audiences everywhere.

(August 2000)

Nitrate Portraits: A Photo Gallery

Editors' Note: It was and is inevitable that the cinema industry should use the tools of the trade – cameras, lights, Moviolas, props, director's chairs, and the like – as set-dressing in publicity shots of its stars and leading practitioners. Film itself is one of those tools, and we should not be surprised that film duly appears in a number of photographs, including those taken in the nitrate era. In fact, its presence in such stills helps once again to remind us that nitrate was just an everyday working material in the days before it acquired its demonic reputation. Having said that, it is still difficult for the modern viewer not to feel at least a faint frisson of retrospective apprehension on behalf of some of the subjects of these portraits. They were, after all, allowing themselves to be placed in close proximity to significant quantities of celluloid while a photographer worked round them with lights or flashgun…

Several such "nitrate portraits" were found or offered while this book was in preparation, some of which will be found illustrating other papers elsewhere in this book. On these pages, we offer a gallery of studio images which can be enjoyed on their own merits.

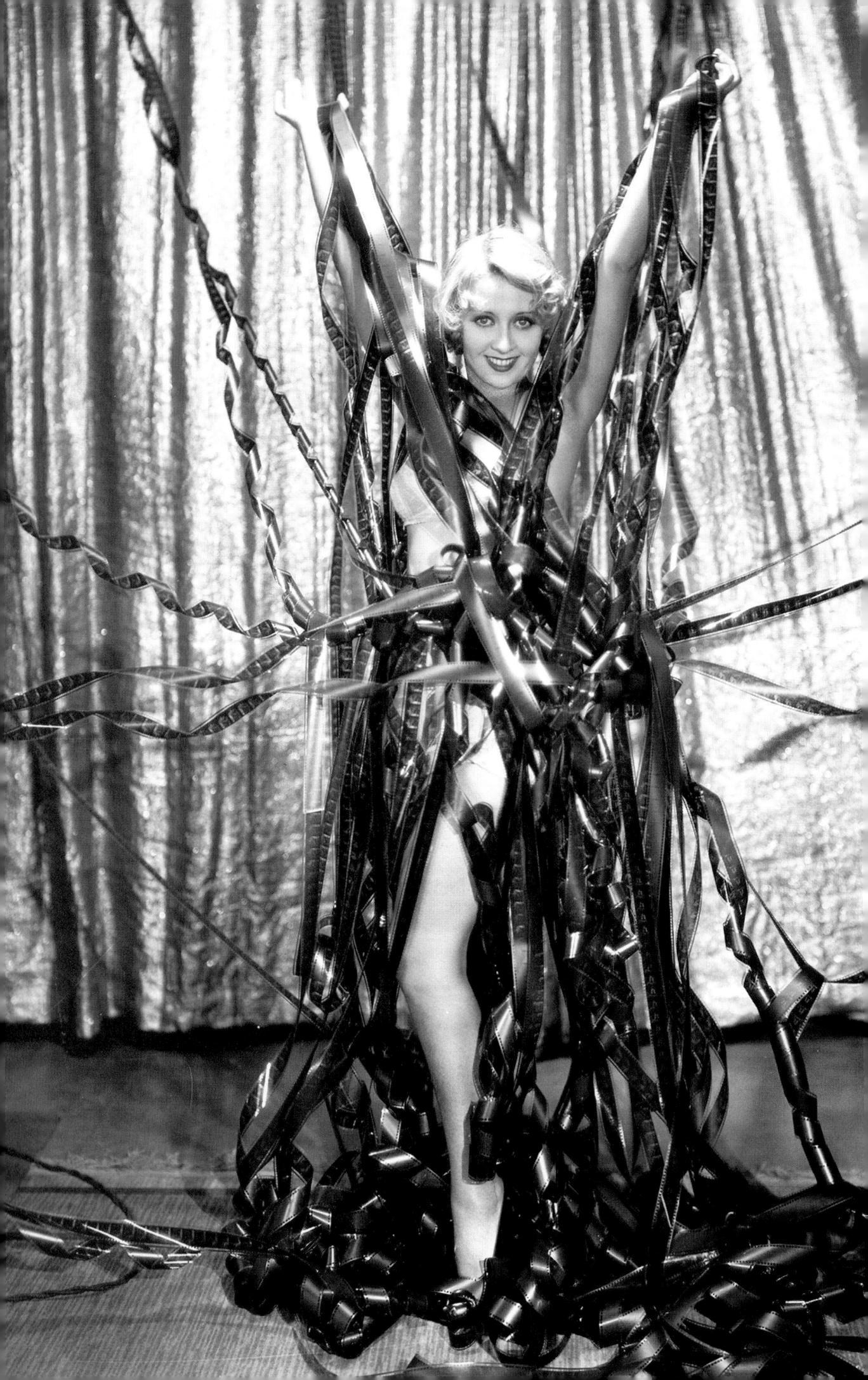

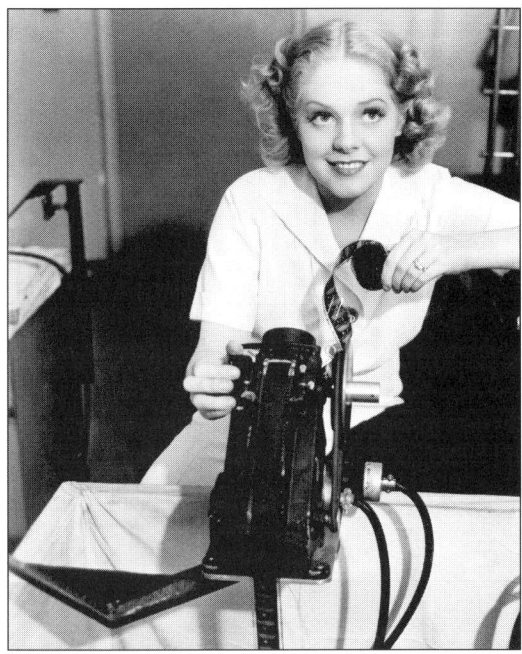

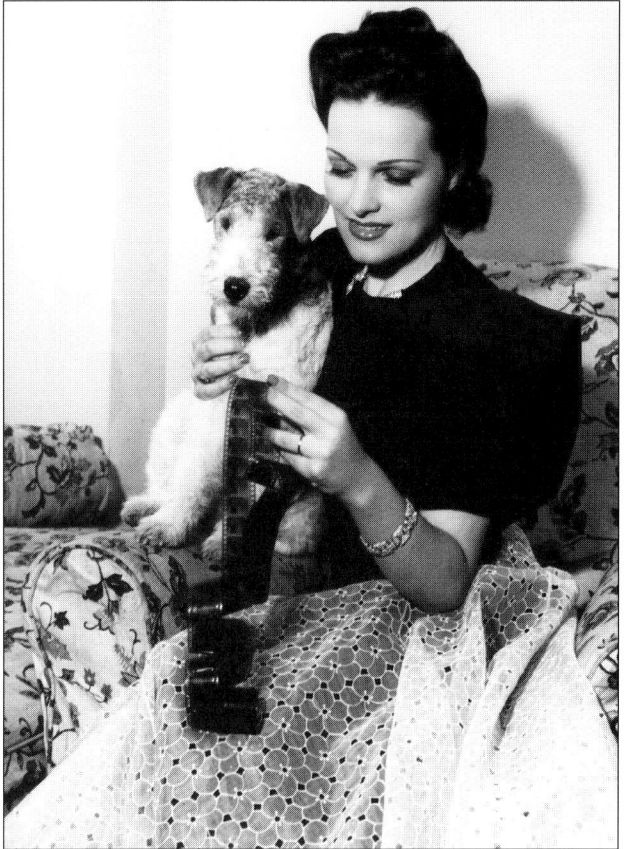

Linden Travers (with Chum, director Walter Forde's dog) in a publicity still for Inspector Hornleigh on Holiday (1939).

The Cinema Museum, London.

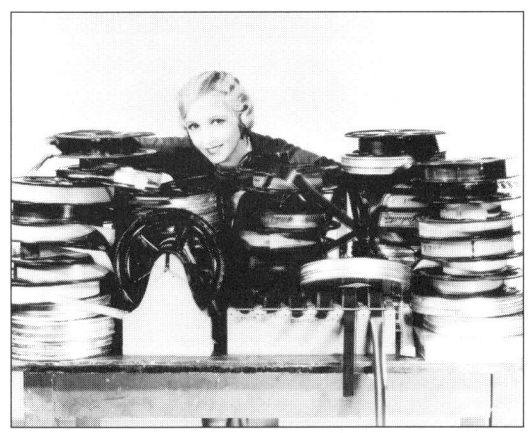

Twentieth Century-Fox's musical sweetheart, Alice Faye, plays editor for a studio photographer.

Photofest, New York.

Bessie Love posing – according to the original caption – "with 50,000 feet of film shot in her new MGM picture".

BFI Collections – Stills, Posters & Designs, London.

Jean Epstein – and a rather less cooperative dog.

BFI Collections – Stills, Posters & Designs, London. 194723.

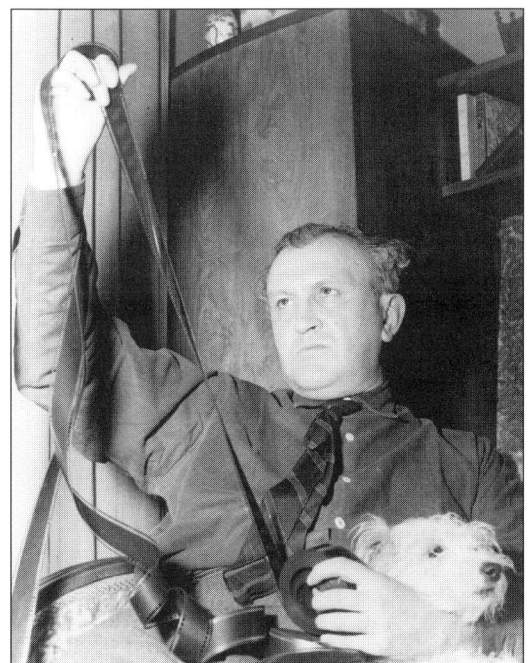

Joan Blondell, photographed by Bert Longworth for Warner Brothers and First National, in what must be the ultimate nitrate publicity portrait.

Photofest, New York.

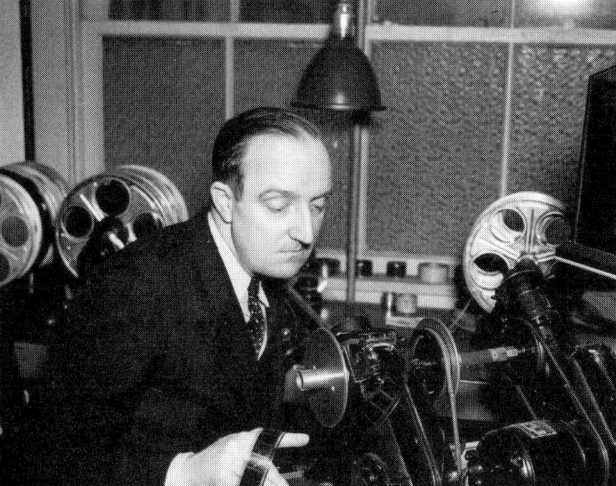

Editor Hal C. Kern in the
cutting room.

Photofest, New York.

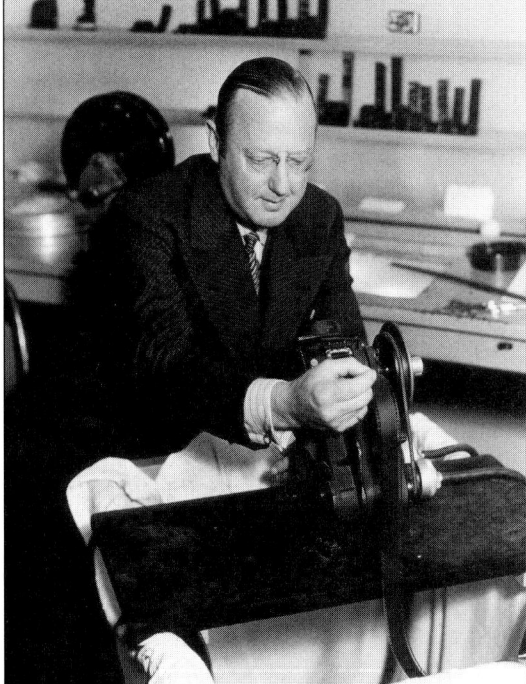

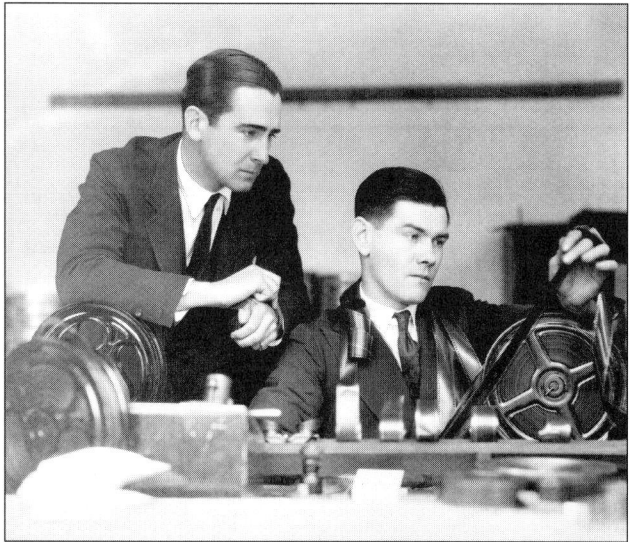

Producer Jesse Lasky
strikes a similar pose.

BFI Collections – Stills, Posters &
Designs, London. 155888.

Director Rex Ingram with
editor Grant Whytock. (Grant
Whytock's recollections of the
1916 Inceville fire are quoted
in the notes to "A Calendar of
Film Fires" elsewhere in this
volume.)

Kevin Brownlow Collection.

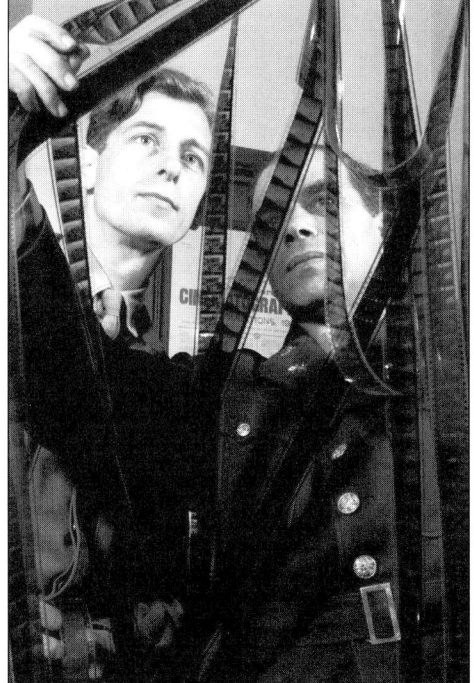

(Colonel) Frank Capra, right,
and (Captain) Roy Boulting in
a joint portrait photographed
to demonstrate their
collaboration on the official
Anglo-American documentary
Tunisian Victory (1944).

Imperial War Museum, London. D18377.

Anna May Wong with co-star Sessue Hayakawa in a portrait issued by Paramount to
publicise *Daughter of the Dragon* (1931).

Roger Smither.

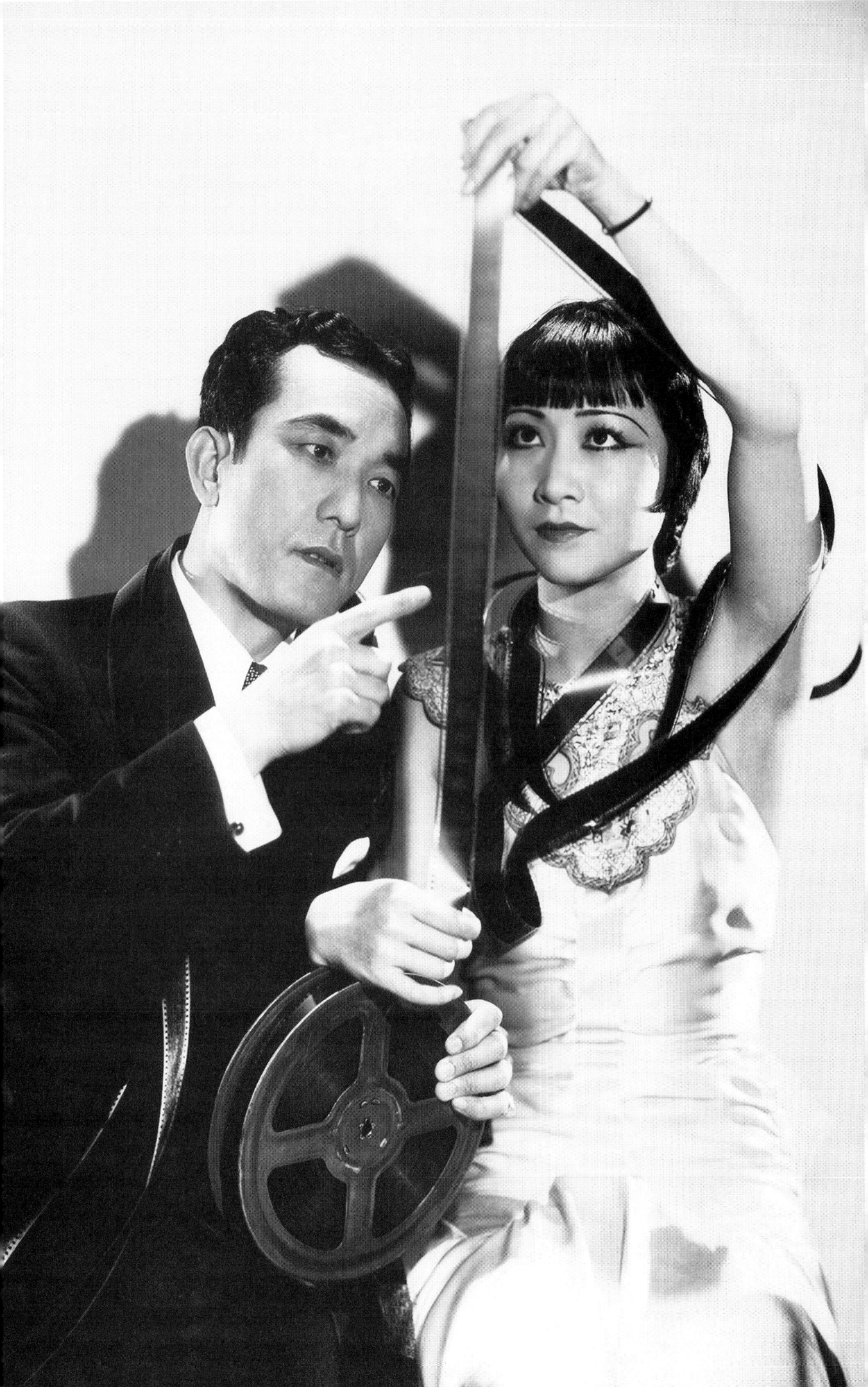

The William T Madigan Scrapbook

by Ronald S Magliozzi

The William T. Madigan scrapbook was acquired by the Museum of Modern Art Department of Film and Video in September 2000.

William T Madigan began his career in cinema exhibition at the age of 14 in Duluth, Minnesota. He joined "The Moving Picture Operators Union" in 1911, travelled the American Midwest with the road show presentation of *The Birth of a Nation*, and settled in Minneapolis in the 1920s, where he worked as a projectionist and manager of the United Theatre Equipment Corporation. In 1930 he was elected a vice-president of the International Alliance of Theatrical Stage Employees and Motion Picture Machine Operators of the United States and Canada.

The scrapbook contains 253 pages of press clippings and typewritten transcriptions, many of them unfortunately lacking precise attribution, dating from 1926 to 1932. It is assumed that the book was compiled by a secretary or other employee of the IATSE/MPMO and ended up with Madigan, although he may have compiled it himself.

Although it contains some other material, the main function of the scrapbook is to document the conflict between organized labor and theatre-owners during the transition to sound – a "war" that included theatre bombings, the employment of "scab" (strike-breaking non-union) projectionists, out-of-work musicians, and so forth. The struggle for control of exhibition practices at the time continued to include the issue of how safely nitrate was handled by operators – the scrapbook contains about 12 pages of material on cinema fires (not only in the USA). This material was collected as evidence of the very real dangers inherent in nitrate film, and to demonstrate the heroism and expertise of union operators, in contrast with the likely behavior of inexperienced scabs. In addition to newspaper stories, there are sworn affidavits from projectionists describing fires that happened (or that became more serious than they need have been) because management had not employed enough staff in the projection box.

One story, which typifies the argument represented in the scrapbook, is a transcription described as an item from the *Miami News* of Miami, Florida, dated 30 July 1931. It reads as follows:

FILM FIRE CAUSE OF NEAR PANIC AT CAPITOL THEATRE
"Ooh La La" Comedy Skit Explodes While Lone Operator Fights For Life

Here's a "Front Page" story that for some reason or other was overlooked or passed up [by] Monday's Miami daily newspapers, possibly by request.

During the running of the two-reel comedy film "Ooh La La" at the Capitol Theatre on N. Miami Ave., at 8:15 Sunday night while the Sunday night theatre crowd was at its peak, with many women and children in the audience, the film, reported to have been in bad condition, exploded after catching fire from a spark and a near panic resulted until K. H. Cram, a city fireman stationed at the theatre, assured the audience that the film booth was fire-proof. The main picture of the evening was a seven-reeler entitled "Their Mad Moment".

To add to the fear of the audience, the explosion of the reel was vividly pictured on the screen while flashes of the fire could be seen through the portholes which were not closed because two fire drops were in a machine shop for repairs. Then came the clang of the fire gong as equipment of the city fire department, called by fireman Cram, dashed up to the theatre entrance.

Meanwhile V. R. Kortright, the lone operator stationed in the booth under new working conditions recently established by a board of arbitration, when members of Operators' Local Union 316 and the theatre owners came to deadlock over wage scale and agreement, was having a fight for his life in the small booth while heroically fighting to put the fire out with fire extinguishers. Kortright's first thought was for the safety of the audience. Cut off by flames from one of the two fire extinguishers in the booth Kortright used the one nearest him then called to a reporter just ouside the door for another extinguisher and an usher was sent for a third as the fire seemed about to get beyond control. The fire was put out in about 20 minutes.

Until the decree handed down by the arbitration committee, after the theatre owners had announced their intention to rescind an existing agreement under special clause and had locked the union operator out of the booth, two operators had been employed in each shift as a safety factor and because of the amount of equipment needed for projection of the movie-talkie picture, so union operators were re-employed under the arbitration committee's decree.

Elsewhere in the scrapbook, an unidentified Minneapolis newspaper, following up an incident "last Friday night when a fire started from a motion picture machine operated by a strikebreaker at the Hennepin-Orpheum theatre", gives the union case in these words:

Motion picture machine experts, in explaining probable causes of the fire, are emphatic in stating that no greater fire menace can be created than that brought about by placing an inexperienced operator on a motion picture machine. These experts point out that the base of a film is composed of the same material as is used in high explosives – gun cotton, and it requires constant alertness on the part of the operator and a thorough knowledge of the mechanism of projection machinery to prevent disastrous fires. A good operator, they say, can tell by the sound of his machine if everything is all right. The moment he detects a strange sound he is able to locate the trouble and thus stop a fire before it starts.

With [three exceptions], all of the theatres in Minneapolis are operating, or trying to, with non-union stage employees, picture operators, musicians, scenic artists and bill posters.

Two examples will illustrate the scrapbook's coverage of self-sacrifice by projectionists. On the subject of Leonard Lee Hickson, a 27-year-old projectionist who died in a fire in Huntsville, Texas, on 1 January 1932, a columnist with the byline "The Spectator" wrote in the *Huntsville Item:*

The Spectator is at loss for words to express the sympathy of the citizenship of Huntsville and Walker county to the family and kinsmen of

Leonard Lee Hickson, who lost his life in the fire of the Dorothy Theatre last Friday afternoon, in saving the lives of the employees and patrons of the Theatre. He had plenty of time to leave the booth and save his life, but the duty to the patrons and the owner of the theatre was first in the mind and heart of young Hickson. He stayed with the job until the last, and went down fighting so that the show might go on, and the theatre saved from the flames.

The second extract, though wholly unattributed, recalls a similar act of self-sacrifice in May 1932:

St. Louis – William Gibson, 25-year-old Negro projectionist at the Palace theatre, sacrificed his life to protect his audience when film caught fire. About 120 men, women and children were in the theatre when a strip of the film broke and ignited. Gibson told his helper, Timothy Moman, also a Negro, to jump from the projection room to call aid, then proceeded to fight the fire alone. A few minutes later Gibson leaped from the booth with his clothing in flames, ignited when he tried to extricate a piece of the burning film from the projector. He was rushed to the City Hospital, where he died early the next morning. When smoke filled the theatre, a cry of "Fire!" caused part of the audience to run out, but the rest were quieted by Charles McCrow, Negro janitor, and all got out safely. The Palace Theatre is operated by Julius A. Sanowski. Damage is estimated at $1,000.

One last treat contained in the scrapbook is the following poetic effort. Details of its original publication are unknown, but it appears as a newspaper cutting believed to date from ca.1930-32, with the subtitle: "A twenty-two year old epic. — By Ernest Eade."

THE GUY AT THE CRANK

Did you ever go to a picture show,
    To sit in the dark and stare,
And wonder how in creation
    The pictures got up there?

It isn't the soft, slick manager
    Whom you have got to thank,
It's the half-baked, oily son-of-a-gun,
    Who cusses and twists the crank.

He goes to his little two-by-four,
    Iron-lined like a prison cell;
He starts to make the film chase through,
    And soon it's hotter than – well

You talk of the steamship stoker,
    And the heat of his fire's bank,
But the stoker's dream is like ice cream
    To the chump who turns the crank.

To the picture show is where you go
    To sit in the dark and stare;
You forget there's another world outside
    When you're snugly seated there;

You watch the actors play their parts;
        To you it is all a dream,
But it's very real to the guy at the wheel
        Of the picture show machine.

Interview with Enrique Blanco, January 2000

by Rosa Cardona Arnau and Jennifer Gallego Christensen

Translated by Dwight Porter

Enrique Blanco Pallarés, cameraman and founder of the Madrid Film Laboratories (and father of the speaker), during a shoot using a Parvo-Debrie camera.

Enrique Blanco Arroyo.

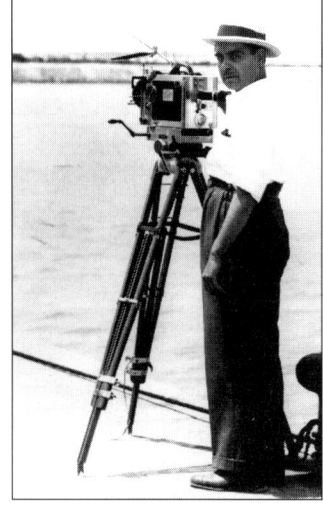

The surname Blanco is closely linked to the history of Spanish cinema from its beginnings until the mid-1970s. In 1910, Domingo Blanco and his son Enrique Blanco Pallarés – a professional photographer and cameraman – set up the first film production company in Madrid, and shortly afterwards founded the Madrid Film studios and laboratories, one of the most enduring enterprises in the Spanish film industry.

Enrique Blanco Arroyo (EB) represents the third generation of Blancos in the company, and has been a privileged witness to the development of Spanish cinema – the introduction of talkies, the replacement of nitrate-based film stock with the more stable acetate-based "safety" stock, and the launch of colour film. In the Madrid Film laboratories, Enrique Blanco has dedicated his life to cinema, in the crucial technical aspects that are so often ignored by historians. He is uniquely qualified to talk to us about the early years when nitrate film was the norm.

Q: Your father's first laboratory was located on Veronica street in central Madrid. Can you remember anything about it?

EB: I'm afraid I was born a bit too late for that. But I have the most vivid recollections of the laboratory on Carrera de San Francisco, which was set up in 1921. I can close my eyes and tell you every detail about the place.

Q: What was it like?

Bath processing preparation room of the Madrid Film laboratories at Number 4, San Francisco Street in 1923.

Enrique Blanco Arroyo.

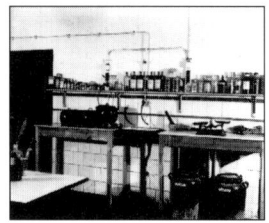

EB: I remember how the laboratories were arranged, the equipment that was there, and especially... the smell! If smells could be drawn, I could draw that one. It was strong, deep, and penetrating, the smell of film and acetone and I don't know what other chemicals. But it wasn't an unpleasant smell at all. To me, it was the smell of black-and-white, very characteristic of the days before colour film. I also remember the studio, the wooden models, the panels that were painted for the sets. In the laboratory, on the left, is where the negatives were developed. Here are some photographs...

See these planks set above the floor, to make it easier to clean? My father also installed special plumbing to keep the used developing fluid and especially the sodium hyposulphite from corroding the pipes. The only materials that were impervious to it were earthenware, slate, and lead, and many of the containers and vats were lined with mineral pitch.

Developing and coloured print room in San Francisco Street, 1923.

Enrique Blanco Arroyo.

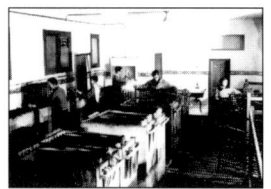

At first, to dry the film it was rolled around frames. When the weather permitted, these were taken to the roof terrace of the building and leaned against the wall. One could tell when the film was dry because it curled up in a certain way. We used frames that could hold 30 metres of film, with bezels to separate the film; this turned very slowly, drying a little more with each turn. As the workload increased, two independent drying drums were installed. In the far corner of the room, a developing tray, 50 x 60 cm, or 60 x 70 cm, was placed. Inside it was cotton soaked in alcohol, which would be set alight if help was needed to dry the film. Of course, care was taken to keep the flames from reaching the drying drums – just imagine!

Q: But it must have been dangerous to have fire nearby if the film was nitrate? Did you ever have any problems with this particular drying method?

EB: No, that never caused a fire. My father was a smoker, but he didn't smoke when he was handling film, but his concern was not with fire, but cleanliness. They were experienced, careful people.

Q: How was nitrate film stored at the Carrera de San Francisco laboratory?

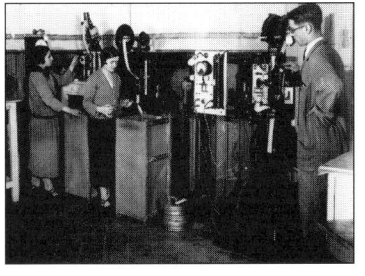

Madrid Film operators rolling the film processed on the modern drying drums, 1923.

Enrique Blanco Arroyo.

EB: It was kept in the basement, where the projection room was also located. Today it's safety film, but then it was all nitrate – there was no other kind. If you were born with colour film and safety film, you're not surprised to see cases of film all around and people smoking. But when I visit my old Madrid Film laboratory and I see people smoking, it scares me to death. Not only because of the risk of fire, which I've been through personally, but because of cleanliness. To me, smoking and film is a bad combination. But nowadays everybody smokes, so what are we going to do?

Q: Were any safety measures observed when handling nitrate film?

EB: None. Not during shooting, or in the laboratory, or when cutting. There was a rule, but it wasn't written down; you made it yourself, using common sense. The rule was: don't smoke around film. I've had some minor fires in the laboratory on Diego de León street. I've seen a Moviola catch fire when an editor set a roll of film alight. My father pulled out the burning roll with his hands. He flung it to the floor and kicked it down the hallway, and from there he kicked it down the stairs, where it finished burning. And then, without a word, my father sat down and invented the aluminium chassis to protect film in the Moviolas. But I've seen editors and other people smoking near film. It's one of those things you learn from experience. Sometimes from very sad experience.

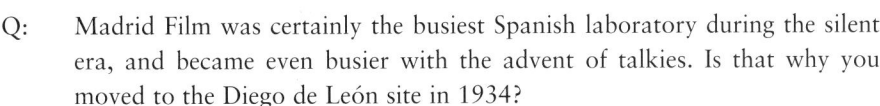

The Madrid Film printing room, containing various printing machines, perforators, and other equipment, 1923.

Enrique Blanco Arroyo.

Q: Madrid Film was certainly the busiest Spanish laboratory during the silent era, and became even busier with the advent of talkies. Is that why you moved to the Diego de León site in 1934?

EB: Yes, it was. Keep in mind that not only Madrid Film but all the laboratories and people involved in the industry had to keep changing with the times. When my father was working with silent film at the Carrera de San Francisco laboratories there were no continuous developing machines, and everything was done in two rooms. When he had to install the continuous developers he needed a larger laboratory. Remember that when these great changes were upon us, not just my father, but everyone in the business was facing the same dilemma: silent, or sound? Are talkies really going to work? Like they said in *Singin' in the Rain*, "Bah, this is just a gimmick!" Now we know that sound film would succeed. But in those days, nobody was at all sure. The old locales became too small, but who was going to say flatly "yes" or "no" to talkies?

Naturally, my father knew he had to keep moving forward, though he may well have thought that silent films were like a child that hadn't gone beyond early youth. Silent films were going to disappear. Anyway, he invested his money, and he got it right, while others didn't want to take the risk, and they fell by the wayside. My father's decision was right, and he made a lot of money.

Q: Were special facilities designed for storing nitrate film in the new laboratory?

EB: No. What we did was to keep buckets full of water in the storerooms, which we called the vaults, to raise the humidity and keep the film from curling excessively. But you couldn't raise the humidity too much, because the tin film canisters would start to get mouldy. A little moisture would get into the film, but not too much. After the fires in New York and elsewhere, people began building safety vaults. The most famous ones were in Moscow. But no, no special precautions were taken in storing film. And we were going to pay a high price for our ignorance – an ignorance that was forced upon us, as it happened.

Q: But weren't there municipal safety regulations and inspections for businesses using nitrate?

EB: Then there was nothing else besides nitrate. All we had to have were fire extinguishers, ventilation, and that sort of thing.

We knew the film was very inflammable, and we took what precautions we could to keep it from burning. We used high-quality stock, and we handled it with care. And we were very confident in ourselves and our work.

Speaking of the storage of nitrate film, I can tell you an interesting story, though I am sorry to have to tell it. It was in 1945, when the temperatures in New York were extremely high. It was the hottest and driest year of the century, and there were a lot of spontaneous fires. One film laboratory – I can't recall the name – was blown to smithereens. Everybody thought it had been sabotage. But then it was discovered that nitrate film decomposes over time, crumbling into dust. First, white spots appear, then the film breaks down, and – when the temperature is high and the air is dry – spontaneous combustion can occur. And that's what happened. The burning nitrate blew the canisters open, freeing the oxygen, and making an inextinguishable flame.

Q: But wasn't this known before 1945?

EB: Of course not. It was learned, tragically, in New York. And that's when the SMPTE [Society of Motion Picture and Television Engineers] published some guidelines to prevent such fires. Every two years each roll of film had to be inspected, and when white spots were found, a safety copy was made or the film was simply destroyed.

And here comes the second part of the story. It's a little complicated to explain, and very sad. One of the many things thing I cannot forgive [Spanish dictator Francisco] Franco and his regime for, was something that affected me very personally. My father, who was a Mason, had to go into temporary exile in Mexico to escape the repression of the times. It was then that I had to take over the laboratory for the first time. Fortunately, the Nazis lost the war, and my father came home, and tried to resume his old life – his prison sentence had been reduced from 30 years to just 12 years and a day, and he was free on bail. By 1945, things were looking up again. Now, my father was probably the only Spanish member of the SMPTE, at least before the war. But the government refused him the dollars to renew his annual subscription to the SMPTE journal. It was probably just a few dollars, I don't remember exactly how much. Consequently, when the story of the nitrate explosion in New York was published, he didn't see it. If my father had received the journal, he would certainly have checked all his negatives. Not so much to safeguard what is known today as the "national historical film heritage", but just to save his own work, the work of his whole life since 1910 – the bullfights, the King's public appearances – it was all there. So what happened, due to our ignorance, was that in 1950, on the first day of August, at a few minutes before 7 p.m., it all blew up in a gigantic explosion – I can show you the photographs. All because of a few lousy dollars! And that is how history is written in this poor, benighted country, and this is how it happened, never to be told. How Madrid Film disappeared, and with it Spain's film heritage. For a handful of dollars, denied to a man who deserved them.

Q: Issues of the SMPTE journal from those years are hard to find, at least in Spain. Do you still have your father's collection?

EB: Yes and no. I'd really rather not talk about this, but they're mostly gone. My father had the whole collection until the fire.

They can be found in the United States, where, as you know, they don't throw anything away, and, of course, at the Museum of the Moving Image in London. Do you know that museum? The first time I visited it and saw what they were doing there, I cried like a baby, because of the memories it brought back. There was a Fox Movietone sound truck, the same one I used to ride in to the soccer games and all over. It hadn't changed a bit since it reached Spain in 1929. MOMI is a fabulous museum.

Q: Tell us more about the fire in August 1950. Was there anybody there at the time?

EB: Yes, because we worked until 7 p.m.

Q: Were you there?

EB: Well, no. What saved me was that, as usual, I was chasing a woman. I had a date that evening, so I was going to have a shave with my new electric razor, the first model that appeared in Spain. But then I changed my mind and decided to go to the barbershop instead, which was very close by. I was sitting there when I heard a noise, and then I saw people running up and down the street, and noticed an awful smell. Somebody shouted, "The film place is on fire!" I ran out as fast as I could, and I saw that my building was on fire, and masonry was falling.

Q: Were the causes of the fire determined?

EB: Unfortunately, yes. It was spontaneous combustion.

Look at these photos. Here's what was left of the laboratory. In an old patio, which my father had closed off, all the old negatives were stored, at some distance from the laboratory itself. What happened was that the storeroom blew up, and part of the building collapsed in the blast. The Fox Movietone studios were on the same site, but they were undamaged.

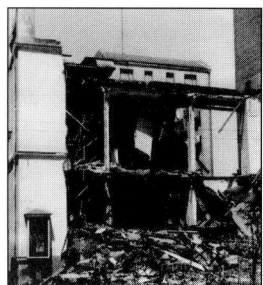

The state of the Madrid Film laboratories at Number 39, Diego de Léon Street after the fire of 1 August 1950.

Enrique Blanco Arroyo.

In these photos you can see the ruins of the building, the burnt machinery, and the blackened film canisters. And here is what remained of the storeroom, and all the film my father shot in his whole life. Some of the canisters melted, but others survived, full of ash... And that, my friends, is the story of nitrate film.

I'd rather not look at these any more. It still gives me a chill and a lump in the throat to think about that fire.

Q: Were there any other fires at Madrid Film or any of the other laboratories or studios in Madrid?

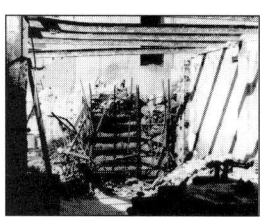

The remains of the film vaults where the fire of 1 August 1950 started.

Enrique Blanco Arroyo.

EB: Yes. There had already been a fire at the Riera laboratories, although that one was thought to have been started deliberately, to get rid of politically embarrassing film when NO-DO [producer of newsreels and propaganda for the Franco regime] was being set up. And after 1951 the Arroyo Rosales laboratories also burned.

Q: And what happened after the fire?

EB: We were ruined. Three months later I set up a temporary laboratory, and in three years we had completely rebuilt the Diego de León laboratory, in record time and on a shoestring. We worked day and night, laying bricks and plastering, using film projectors to illuminate the place when it was dark. We managed to rebuild some of the printing machines, but it wasn't easy to replace the damaged parts – we weren't allow to import them. I went to André Debrie in Paris and came back with my suitcases stuffed with contraband parts.

Q: Did you change the way you worked when you began to use safety film?

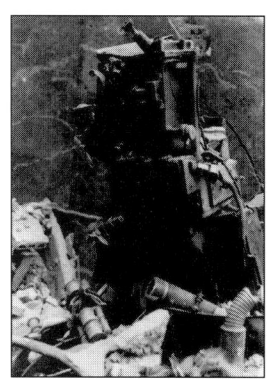

A MATIPO-Debrie printing machine after the fire of 1 August 1950. This and other printers were later wholly reconstructed by Enrique Blanco.

Enrique Blanco Arroyo.

EB: The danger of nitrate film has been magnified, I think, into some kind of psychosis. Obviously, if the cooling system in the copier failed while you were printing film the negative could catch fire. But I can't remember anything like that ever actually happening in our laboratories. The danger persisted even after we started using safety film, since all the laboratories still had collections of nitrate film. Later, Madrid Film built some storage vaults outside Madrid.

What did happen was that a lot of laboratories refused to make safety prints from nitrate negatives, and not only because of the danger, but also because the nitrate films were very old, shrunken, and in poor condition. It was a lot of work to copy them and it wasn't worth the money. Despite all this, I've done it – in the 1960s I made print number 108 or 112 of *La Verbena de la Paloma* (Benito Perojo, 1935), which is now regarded as a classic of Spanish cinema, and another one of *Morena Clara* (Florián Rey, 1936), because it kept coming back for commercial showings in Spanish theatres.

It was the new laboratories that didn't want to touch nitrate – I think some of them even charged a special price to make prints. But this was due to fear. Anyway, the work was exactly the same with acetate film. A special acetone glue was used – we called it acetone cement. That was the only difference.

Q: What are the differences between nitrate and triacetate film? Did the nitrate film have any special qualities? It is said that nitrate films had an amber hue, and that they were smoother, more transparent, and more luminous than triacetate-based films.

EB: Safety film had all the advantages. First, it was easier to ship, by mail or by rail. As far as special qualities of photographic reproduction go, nitrate film had none. Film is absolutely transparent. The quality of the image depends on the emulsion, not the film stock. There is a great misunderstanding in this regard. For instance, Gevaert and Du Pont made some positives in which the white wasn't pure white, but a slightly bluish white, and it had a fantastic projection quality, with intense blue-blacks, especially with the carbon lamps that were used at the time, American carbons that gave a yellowish light. If the projectionist wasn't any good there would be a dominant yellowish haze. So what happened with those films? Well, they compensated for the yellow projection light and the old and dirty screens. The real improvements have come in the resolution and the quality of the emulsions, and, above all, the quality of the negatives. I appreciate this more in black-and-white than in colour films, because I think it's still much harder to do good photography in black-and-white than in colour. In black-and-white it's much more difficult to get the nuances and the entire range of greys that you need. With colour, you can cheat and lie, but black-and-white really separates the men from the boys! American cinematographers have come here and said: "The way these Spanish guys make films is some kind of miracle!" We worked blindly, in the dark, and yet, look at the photography from those years, the black-and-white films made in the 1950s!

Not many countries can boast the kind of cinematographers we've had since the 1940s. The Spaniards that were trained by people from the silent era have turned out to be real geniuses. They learned their trade in the school of hardship and ignorance, and they fought every inch of the way. The same thing can be said about our directors' assistants and film editors.

You ask me whether you can notice any difference between nitrate and safety film. The difference I see is that the emulsions today are fresh and good. The emulsions, not the stock.

Q: Wasn't it hard to get film stock during the Franco dictatorship?

EB: Yes, and there's a very sad story dating from the time that everybody in the world had decided not to use nitrate stock. After our laboratories burned down I had to request film from the government office in charge of such things. The man there said, "Well, you're in luck, because a big shipment of film is arriving tomorrow from Kodak (Harrow) in England. Since it's nitrate, nobody wants it, so we got the government to buy it at a bargain price!" I said, "Don't you know my place burned down? And you're still buying nitrate film?" "Government orders," was the reply. So we picked up all the stock that Kodak couldn't sell – it was dumped on Spain. I mean hundreds of thousands of metres. Nobody had learned a thing from the fire.

But not everything about nitrate is tragic. I still have a letter that an Austrian sent to my father in the early 1930s, offering to buy any old nitrate films we had in the laboratory. He used them to make sausage casings! You know how film-makers will say, "I've just made my masterpiece, the film of the century"? Well, now you know the fate of these epoch-making films – they ended up in Austrian and German stomachs, as sausages. *Sic transit gloria mundi* – that's the story of nitrate film.

"Throw me out"

In a world which has seen such incidents as the 1925 Boston subway car fire, it is no surprise that the authorities in most countries imposed a strict ban on the carriage of nitrate film by public transport. Those in London were no exception – a fact which, incidentally, provides a small but crucial part in the plot of Alfred Hitchcock's 1936 film *Sabotage*. In his autobiography, *Useless If Delayed*, Movietone newsreel cameraman Paul Wyand recalled how one of his fellow cameramen in another British newsreel company used these regulations to circumvent an attempted economy drive on the part of his employers in the 1920s.

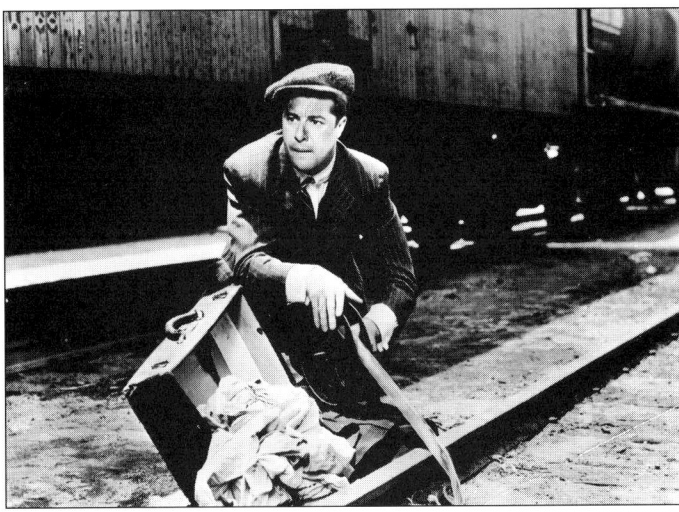

Different continent, different circumstances – but thrown out just the same: Don Ameche as Mike Connors rescuing a reel of film in *Hollywood Cavalcade* (1939).

Cinémathèque Suisse, Lausanne.

Newsreel staff, like other journalists in fact and fiction, relied on their expense accounts to help stretch their salaries, so it was not good news for the staff of the British newsreel company Topical Budget when management introduced a cost-cutting policy that required staff to travel by public transport rather than taxi. Wyand takes up the story:

> ... There is, of course, a law forbidding the transport of inflammable film by Underground, so a Topical Budget cameraman promptly lugged his gear to Piccadilly and said to the ticket collector: "Give me your name and number."
>
> "What the devil for?" asked the man.
>
> "You're permitting me to break the law. I have inflammable film here, and it's not allowed to be transported by tube." When the ticket collector hesitated the cameraman persisted: "Either give me your name and number or throw me out."
>
> The ticket collector willingly acceded to this last request, and the cameraman returned triumphant to his office. The order was rescinded, and thereafter (although there may have been cases of men travelling by Underground and charging for taxis) no one was specifically instructed to use this plebeian form of transport.[1]

Notes

1. Paul Wyand, *Useless If Delayed* (London: George G Harrap, 1959), pp. 27–28.

Early Days in New Zealand Government Film-making

by Lawrie Morton

The following paragraphs are extracted from a longer article, "The Formation of New Zealand's National Film Unit", which Lawrie Morton has written from notes dictated by his father, Cyril Morton, in 1985, about a year before he died. Cyril Morton was the producer of the New Zealand National Film Unit almost from its inception, until he retired in about 1965.

My real desire was to be making films . . . so in about 1923 I joined the Government Photography Office, which came under the Tourist and Publicity Department. There was already a staff of two, and I made a third member. There were two cine cameras, both hand-cranked. We were expected to photograph all the scenery over the whole of New Zealand, carrying a cine camera, its large, heavy, wooden tripod, all our film stock (in cans), and whatever else we needed. Sometimes we had to take a still camera as well, with its tripod and lenses, and a supply of glass-plate negatives. Frequently my equipment weighed as much as I did. We were to use public transport wherever possible. Taxis were not to be hired if cheaper transport was available.

After shooting the required scenes, we had to bring the film back and process and print it ourselves. We also had to cut and edit the film, make up and shoot the titles (they were silent films of course), process and print the title films and splice them into the main film. In other words, we were required to make complete films, ready for screening, of all the tourist attractions and facilities throughout New Zealand.

In 1926 Zane Grey visited New Zealand on a big-game fishing expedition, and I was assigned to him as his official photographer. I accompanied him on many of his deep-sea fishing expeditions, and photographed his activities in both still and cine.

Working conditions in the Government Photography Office were atrocious. The building in which we were housed was a corrugated iron shed originally built as a stables for horses. Inside, there were three rooms: a cine darkroom, a still darkroom, and a general workroom.

Cine film was processed by being wound, about 50 or 100 feet at a time (emulsion side out), on big wooden frames. The frames were lowered into wooden vats of developer, rinse, fixer, then washing water. The washing vat had no outlet plumbing – the water just poured over the edges and onto the floor. The room had not seen daylight for years and the floor was covered with a thick green slime. Very soon after I started, I took in my brace and bit, and bored holes in the floor to let the water out. All the time that cine film was being processed our feet were slopping wet. We had tried wearing gumboots, but the rubber slipped on the wet, slimy floor and it was dangerous. I tried to arrange for a set of duckboards to keep our feet up out of the water, but the Department refused to sanction the expenditure of the two pounds ten shillings I had been quoted by the Works Department . . .

The building had been condemned by the Health Department, but in typical fashion the Government had exempted itself from the regulations it applied to everyone else.

After some years of this (and one or two other temporary arrangements), A A P McKenzie came to our rescue and set up a place in the ABC Building in Lambton Quay. It must be remembered that film of the period had a base of cellulose nitrate and was extremely flammable. Trying to dry this film quickly by heating it over a gas ring or a film tin of burning methylated spirit meant that fires were fairly common, and a fire we had in the ABC Building disrupted all the other tenants and put their insurance premiums sky-high. A A P McKenzie again came to the rescue, and decided to set up a film studio in the suburbs. He arranged for the purchase of land at Miramar, and had a building constructed. We were combined with Filmcraft Ltd, a private company who did processing and printing for the Government under contract. The building was owned and operated by Filmcraft Ltd, with storage space for Government camera equipment and film stocks. This meant that the Government staff could better concentrate on the actual camera work, since they were relieved of the drudgery of processing and printing the film they shot.

We survived the slump of the 1930s by the skin of our teeth (the staff went from 40 to 4 overnight, but that's another story). Around 1936 the film studios were, like everyone else, starting to get back on their feet. As before, almost all the films made by the film studios were for screening overseas to help promote tourism in New Zealand.

"Occasional Mishaps"

Acknowledgement: This page comes from Walt Disney and Assorted Other Characters – An Unauthorized Account of the Early Years at Disney's, *by Jack Kinney* (*New York, Harmony Books, 1988*)

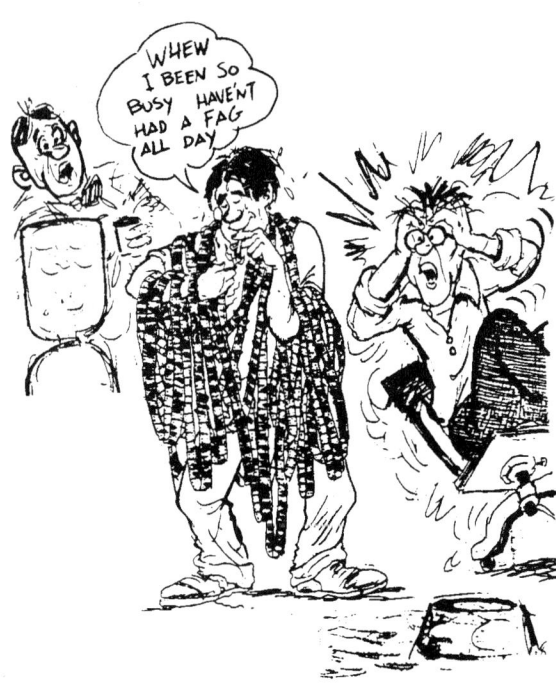

"Kinney"

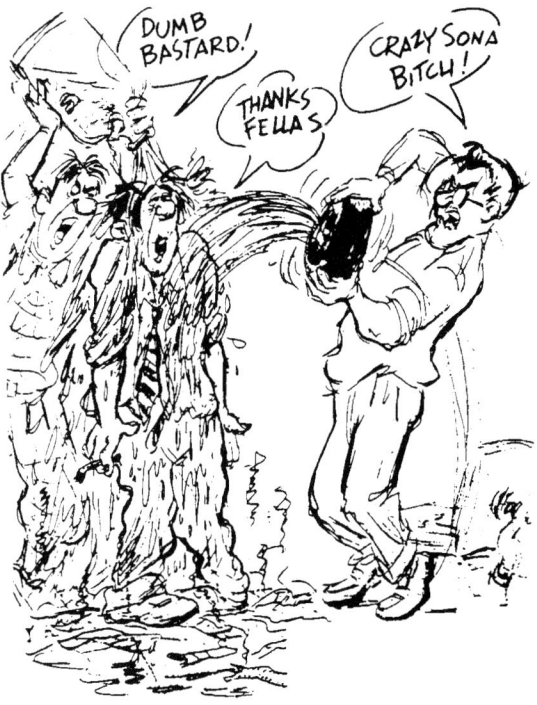

Production continued, in spite of occasional mishaps. One time one of the new guys almost blew us all up! He was working as a gofer, running errands and delivering the rough-test film to the animators all day long.

This particular day he was just loaded with the stuff—it was all over his shoulders, around his neck, the whole bit. Nitrate film was highly flammable—explosive, really—but he hadn't been around long enough to realize how dangerous it was. Just a spark did it.

As If It Was Yesterday

by Queenie Turner

Although I am writing about 66 years ago, I can remember as if it was yesterday! I first came into contact with nitrate film in 1934 – although as you know it was in use years before. I remember when I first started work in the Pathé Labs at 103 Wardour Street in London – I was 14 years old at the time, and the wage was all of 12s 6d (62.5p) per week! – the sergeant at the door took all the matches and lighters off the employees as they entered the building.

I thought it was wonderful to work in the film industry. Don't forget that there was no television in those days, and film was very much the "in" thing – I considered myself very lucky. Of course, I had to start at the bottom of the ladder. My first job was stripping old labels off film cans and putting on the new labels for the *Pathé Gazette* midweek or weekend editions.

Then I was promoted to the examination table, making double perforation joins on a brass joiner with a pin in the centre, on clear spacing. 1,000 feet of clear spacing was used for loading the developer and drying cabinets for the film. It may not have looked all that important, splicing spacer rather than "real" film with pictures on it, but if that spacing snapped or the joins came undone so the film stopped in the developer, then that whole batch would have been ruined by being over-developed.

Negative developing was done in the basement, where conditions were terrible – pitch dark: I don't know how Bill Sharp, Frank Fuller, and Frank Baker could stand working there. These three men are now Honorary Members of BECTU[1], and their names are on the Roll of Honour at Union Headquarters, and well deserved too.

I was then promoted to positive examining, where my boss was Mr Touze. We made one-perforation hand joins (with a scraper and straight edge). We always had to handle the film between our fingers and thumb, never touching the film, only the edges. Our work was subject to careful examination! We also handled sepia and lavender nitrate stock, long before colour film came along. We used hand-winders – never winding too fast, to avoid friction – and bins with white covers for scrap film, at the end of our tables, which had to be changed regularly. All waste film was collected every night and sent to the basement, to the silver recovery room, where it was put in a solution in huge white cone cloth bags, and the silver drained to the bottom of the bag. All negatives and fine grains (lavender stock) were wrapped in white tissue paper, and even positive films were put into vaults every night at an even temperature, although those were the days before air conditioning and central heating. I remember coke and ice being delivered – and plenty of fire drills!

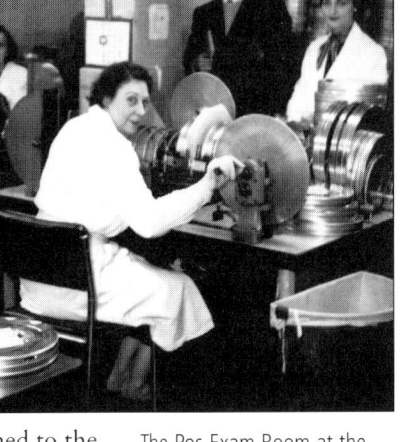

The Pos Exam Room at the Pathé Labs in Wardour Street, London. Queenie Turner standing, right.

Queenie Turner.

After a while, Mr Touze gave me a pay-rise of 2s 6d (12.5p), and I thought I was in clover. Although there were some features, the films we were working on were mainly the newsreel, *Pathé Gazette*, and the magazine *Pathé Pictorial*. The cameramen worked on the third floor of the building in those days – they had a tickertape machine up there, reporting the news. When a story came up, the Editor, Freddy Watts, used to send them out on assignments, trying of course to get there ahead of their rivals at Paramount and Movietone. Frank Bassill was one of the cameramen then, also Terry Ashwood, Jock Gemmel, Ben Vettrano, Oscar Bovill, and Bert Starmer. (Bert's brother Jim was the stoker, working down at the furnace with all that coke I just mentioned, together with another man called Bob Robinson.) Some of these cameramen, like Frank Bassill and Oscar Bovill, had filmed in France and Belgium during the First World War, and Oscar and others would pick up similar battle honours during the Second World War – and in due course I would find myself handling this wartime work of theirs when I joined the Imperial War Museum.

Down on the first and second floors, I used to see two or three men whispering in corners – that was really the start of the Union in Pathé, although Frank Fuller, Bill Sharp, and Frank Baker were already members. Our hours in those days were 8 a.m. to 6 p.m. Monday to Friday, and 8 a.m. to 12.30 p.m. on Saturday, with just a ten-minute tea break morning and afternoon (no canteen), and we had to take it in turns in the cloakrooms. Still, I felt quite well off, because you mustn't forget we were just coming out of a terrible depression, and lucky to have a job.

Those secret meetings continued to take place, and gradually members of the staff were being approached to join. The ACT (Association of Cinematograph Technicians[2]) offices were two little rooms over a barber's shop in Wardour Street opposite No. 111, where the present office now stands. I remember that George Elvin was the General Secretary, with his assistant, Bunny Garner, and Miss Pearson. I joined the Union when I was nearly 18: I was the first girl to join, but another joined soon after, then another, and so on. Messages were passed from mouth to mouth at first, and then we started our own meetings at Head Office. The Union soon grew.

Then I started on negative work. Every scene was numbered, and film cleaned by hand, I always remember, although we wore white coats and gloves at all times. No fluffy jumpers, for fear of getting a hair in the printer's gate!

The sequence of events for the processing of *Pathé Gazette*, and later of *Pathé News*, went like this. The cameramen would bring in their negatives to be developed and a fine grain print and cutting prints were made. The cutting prints then went up to the third floor for editing and the addition of the commentary – recorded at first by Roy de Groot and later by Bob Danvers Walker. The negative was cut and sent down to the labs for printing. First each scene was numbered, then it was sent to the grader, whose job was to allocate the correct light exposure for it. When the grader was finished, the neg worker had to put each light value on a large white card with the right size of holes punched in it. Meantime, the neg was being cleaned for printing. In the printing room, we had two large printers, which printed four prints at a time: these were our Quad Printers. The news was usually printed in two sections, section 1 on Quad 1, section 2 on the other Quad, hence the speed – because we had earlier made a fine grain copy, we always had a duping print at hand if anything went wrong. Sometimes in later years (not always) we had colour sections from Technicolor. If anything dramatic happened, such as the Aberfan disaster (1966) or the death of someone important, we would have to do a "special" to get the news out fast.

We selected special copies for West End cinemas, and kept stand-by copies too. I remember once the Empire in Leicester Square complained about a scratched copy and I was sent round to see the newsreel and find out if they were right. When I arrived, the newsreel had just finished, but the big film was about to come on. It was *Sergeant York*, so I could not resist sitting there and watching the whole programme. Gary Cooper was every girl's idol, just like Tom Cruise is today, so I really enjoyed my afternoon out!

War broke out in September 1939. Women were exempt from national service because we were in a reserved occupation, although the men were called up later. We had a bad time travelling between home and work and home again because of the blackout and the bombing. We had raids during daylight as well – one of our lady cleaners was killed in Brewer Street, just off Wardour Street.

I got married on 1 June 1941 – and I'll never forget it. We published the banns on 10 May, and then there was that terrible night raid when the Elephant and Castle was bombed. The church where we were to get married was gutted, and we ended up getting married in the church vestry with a wind-up gramophone playing the Wedding March. Most of my friends still managed to come, and we laugh about it now.

I left Pathé in 1942, because my son was born in November that year, but I went back in 1943, once he was started in a nursery. Then in 1948, the labs closed for renovation. The staff went to Elstree, but I did not go because of the journey. I got another job in Wardour Street, at Sydney Wakes – it was a nice little laboratory (which was later taken over by Reeds). I was put in charge of the negative cutting room.

In 1952, Pathé asked me to go back. Now they were working with safety film. It was completely new, and what a change! All new machinery – new tables and joiners, and a cleaning machine: no more cleaning by hand! All the departments were run by men, and there were lots of new faces among the staff. We had our own lockers and canteen, and if you needed anything, you got it! They asked me to go in the Pos Exam Room. I went willingly, because the man in charge was Bill Sharp. He was in poor health, so I was his assistant. Frank Fuller was made Progress Supervisor, and Frank Baker was in charge of all developing (all done in daylight now!), so it wasn't all new faces.

When Bill Sharp retired through ill health and moved to Sussex, the Manager asked me to take over. I was the only woman chargehand there, and remained so until Pathé closed in September 1967. After Pathé closed, I took on several other jobs, but could not settle in any of them until one of my ex-trainees rang me and asked me to go to Reeds Colour Labs back in Wardour Street. I went there and found several ex-Pathé staff members so I felt right at home with them.

In 1972 I had to leave to nurse my husband, and then he died in September 1973. I just did not feel like going out to work again. My father noticed how depressed I was getting, and showed me an advertisement from the Imperial War Museum: they were looking for an assistant film librarian. I went, and got the job, but I was not impressed at first – it was so different from lab work – but I stuck it because it was near home. Then Mr Coultass, the Head of the Film Department, asked me to take on the Film Librarian job. I met so many interesting people and made many friends with researchers from all over the world, and gave them advice, and really felt I was giving them a service. I stayed with the IWM until I retired in 1985 – they were indeed very happy years.

Nitrate film was clearly marked – NITRATE – on the edge of the perforation. I have found that heat buckles the film, and cold and damp cause it to deteriorate. My own theory is that you need to change cans regularly. If a reel of nitrate was left in a can for a length of time, the base of the can discoloured, causing deterioration. I still think that nitrate was far better in quality and definition. It had a certain bloom on the emulsion. I have a personal piece of lavender nitrate – about 20 ft. I have had it for almost 60 years. It has been kept in a brown paper bag in my sideboard drawer, and the condition is perfect. It is a piece of film that Pathé shot to explain the workings of a new system which the army introduced during the war to speed up the sending of letters to soldiers serving overseas. It used a kind of microfilm technology, and was called the airgraph. The cameraman used me as the "star" for one of the sequences he shot, so that is my personal nitrate souvenir.

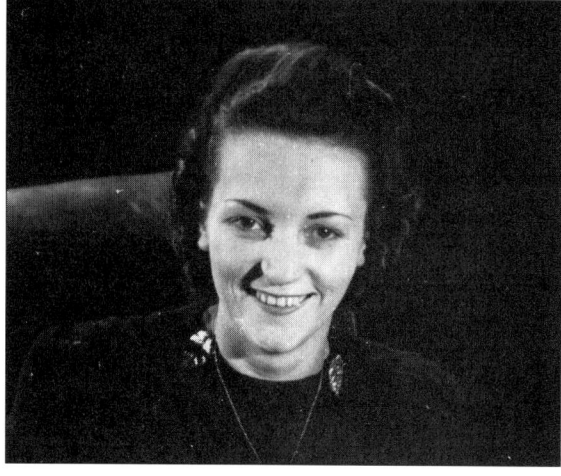

Queenie Turner in her starring role in the Pathé "airgraph" film.

Queenie Turner.

It was not the only time I went to the studio on the fifth floor at Pathé to do bit parts in short films and adverts – I did not get paid, but I had a good time. We used to get visitors to the studio as well. In 1937 or 1938, Joseph P Kennedy, the American Ambassador, came with his wife and a crowd of their children – I think it was eight – to see a 17.5mm newsreel. (Pathé started making a 17.5mm issue in about 1936 for screening on long-distance train journeys; the film had to be made by slitting 35mm in half.) I had to show the newsreel to the Kennedy family: little did I know that my audience contained a future President of the United States!

Notes

1. The Broadcasting Entertainment Cinematograph and Theatre Union, established in January 1991 by the amalgamation of the Association of Cinematograph Television and Allied Technicians (ACTT) and the Broadcasting and Entertainment Trades Alliance (BETA).

2. It added "Television" to its name to become ACTT in March 1956.

Safety Film: False Dawns

Editor's Note: Although several contributors to this book mention the early availability of "non-flam" filmstocks and their application particularly in the non-professional domain, no writer – with the conspicuous and welcome exception of Leo Enticknap in his essay concentrating on the final switch-over to safety film in Britain in the late 1940s – has provided a paper specifically on the issues relating to the replacement of nitrate by safety film. I did, however, receive from several correspondents a quantity of interesting source material relevant to this subject. Michelle Aubert and her colleagues at the Service des Archives du Film of the Centre National de la Cinématographie provided several items from the French trade press; Eva Orbanz and her colleagues at the (then) Stiftung Deutsche Kinemathek similarly offered a number of German items. British stories were supplied by Stephen Bottomore and Tony Fletcher, and some fascinating evidence on the practicalities of the switch to acetate in the late 1940s and early 1950s in the UK came from Ronald Grant of the Cinema Museum. US items were forwarded by David Pierce. In appreciation of the work of these contributors, and in recognition of the inherent interest of the material supplied, the following pages have been compiled to offer a brief overview which – while falling far short of the considered analysis which this topic clearly deserves – may perhaps help to inspire such a study in the future. (RS)

The following anonymous item was published in a French scientific journal within two weeks of the Bazar de la Charité disaster in May 1897:

> **Non-inflammable celluloid.** – The fire which has just caused such a terrible catastrophe in Paris makes sad publicity for the cinématographe and the materials on which its photographs are held. In fact, we gather from the preliminary results of the enquiry that the fire which started in the lamp of the cinématographe at the Bazar de la Charité immediately spread to the reel which is formed by the ribbons of celluloid in the machine; of course this celluloid caught fire and, flaring up, became a deadly torch. A well-known chemist and inventor, Mr Tommasi, has been researching ways to make these cinematographic strips non-inflammable, and has been able to demonstrate for us some samples which burn scarcely as fiercely as heavy-weight paper, while the normal strips blaze like gunpowder. Self-evidently the discovery is important and deserves to be announced, as it certainly has relevance to all products made of celluloid.[1]

It is not known what happened to M Tommasi's invention. Later, useful work seems to have been achieved in Britain, though it may be doubted that the process patented in 1904 by one George E Woodward for producing a non-inflammable material by "mixing the celluloid with liquefied fish glue" had much to do with it.[2] Possibly more relevant was a project with which former Edison associate W K-L Dickson was associated in 1907.[3] An article published in Germany in 1911 described in detail the work being done by "the Englishman Arino" to treat celluloid with various mineral salts to reduce its inflammability.[4] Early British experiments with cellulose-acetate were also mentioned in accounts of the discovery in Germany of "Cellit" or "Zellit", such as the following French report:

319

Cellit

Attempts were made a few years ago to replace celluloid, the dangers of which are only too well known, with another less inflammable substance, cellulose actetate. The experiments which were carried out with this new product in England did not go well, and celluloid remained master of the situation.

Today it seems that that position is in jeopardy, because celluloid has found, in a new product called "Cellit" a formidable rival. Cellit is basically a cellulose acetate produced industrially following a process invented by Dr Eichengrün.

Cellit will dissolve in acetone and still more easily in acetic ether. From it can be made blocks of all sizes, films, plates, etc. F P Liesegang has tried out this new material for the preparation of photographic films: it is able to pass all tests, and can be perforated, spooled, spliced, etc., without breaking. Moreover, while an equivalent piece of celluloid cannot stay exposed to the heat of the rays given off by an arc lamp without bursting into flames after a few seconds, a Cellit film remained for 10 minutes exposed to those same rays – without a tank of alum or any other kind of cooling device – and while the exposed portion did catch fire at the end of that time, it soon went out of its own accord. One may therefore consider that Cellit offers no danger in this regard, and it may be foreseen that this new material will soon find numerous applications in the photographic industry.[5]

German papers on "Raw Film" and "Uninflammable Film" written in 1922 and 1923 respectively also referred to Eichengrün's work in the development of Cellit, which, as they were by then able to note, failed to win the battle against the more established and more commercially determined American and French stock manufacturers. One of these pieces also mentioned experiments by a Berlin engineer named Werthen with the use of aluminium (which would obviously predicate a technology based on reflection) to replace the transparency of celluloid.[6]

In 1909, an international congress of film manufacturers convened in Paris in full knowledge – as *Ciné-Journal* put it – that Eastman Kodak was ready to launch a non-inflammable film which would certainly create a major disturbance in the film production and distribution market. *Ciné-Journal* went on to ask: "Ce film incombustible est-il d'une qualité qui ne puisse laisser place à aucune autre marque?" (Is this incombustible film of a quality equal to any other product?), and to point out the dangers of the spreading into Europe of American trust practices.[7] An article entitled "Non-Flam Film" in the editorial "Topics of the Week" section of the British trade journal *The Bioscope* on 21 January 1909 warned its readers (in a splendid flurry of metaphors) to expect to be compelled to adopt safety film if they did not embrace it voluntarily:

The trade must be prepared for remarkable developments in the non-flam film in the course of the next few weeks. At the present time there is undoubtedly a strong trend of opinion in favour of its adoption, and the fact that ten firms are now prepared to supply pictures on Lumière non-flam film is in itself an eloquent testimony to the favour with which this safeguard is regarded. There are still, as there always must be, some who lay behind and lose the opportunity, but they would be well advised to reconsider their position. There are ways of making a horse drink even if he does not want to, in spite of the old proverb, especially if the taking of water is necessary for his health, and it must be obvious to everyone that there is a strong current of activity under the apparently still waters of officialdom. In what way that current will make itself felt it would be inadvisable for us to say at present. It is possible to anticipate news so intelligently that the materialisation of that news is effectually prevented. We are not without hope, indeed, that it may prove ultimately unnecessary to publish the news at all, and that the voluntary adoption by all firms of the non-flam film may render any persuasive measures superlative [sic]. But the trade may rest assured that forces are at work whose power it would be foolish to underestimate, and that the mailed fist is prepared to strike, and strike hard, from a position which is as unexpected as it is impregnable.[8]

A month later, the same journal was reporting from the Paris Congress of Kinematograph Publishers that a minimum price of 4d per foot was agreed for ordinary film and 4$^{1}/_{2}$d per foot for non-flammable films "when they are delivered in Europe several months hence" – a price differential, whatever currency it was expressed in, of 12.5%.[9]

Material from the American *National Fire Protection Association Quarterly* includes one article which reported (in January 1910):

> At present about 50 per cent of the films handled in New England are of the N.I. (non-inflammable) kind. These first came into use in Boston last August. Since September all new films purchased have been N.I. films, and all future ones will be the same. The exchanges are required to return to the manufacturers each month a number of old films equal to the number of new ones purchased, so it is estimated that within nine months, or a year at most, practically all of the celluloid films will have been replaced by N.I. films, and as these concerns put out about 90 per cent of all [film] used in New England, we may look for a material reduction in the hazards of this business.[10]

There is ample evidence to show how closely – sometimes eagerly, sometimes nervously – such developments were watched by the trade. One company which embraced them wholeheartedly was the Artograph Company ("Film Specialists, Dealers and Exporters"), which published a multi-page advertisement in a British trade journal in 1911. One page offered three newspaper-style cartoons. In the first, an anxious lady and her daughter ask the box office attendant, "Are you showing those nasty things that flare up?" They receive the reassuring reply, "No, lady, we now show only non-flam films, not fireworks!" In the next, we see, lounging against a doorpost, a cinema fireman who, the caption tells us, has got the sack – "What for? Because the Governor has taken up them Non-Flam Films." The third cartoon is similar, as the Commissionaire brings a load of buckets, fire-extinguishers, and hoses out to the cart of a scrap metal dealer. On another page, a 6-panel comic strip tells the story of a showman who places his order with Artograph, "With the result: – no risk, no troubles, full house every time!"[11]

A speaker from the Eastman Kodak Company was later (in 1940) to offer the following recollection of what had happened next:

> In 1909, Eastman had developed cellulose acetate to a point where the Company felt it could be substituted for nitrocellulose in motion picture film. To give effect to this development, Mr. Eastman arranged a meeting with the leaders of the motion picture producing companies. Because the advantages of the new film were obvious to all, little argument was needed to reach an agreement whereby only cellulose-acetate film was to be supplied by the Company thereafter.
>
> Experience demonstrated, however, that acetate film was not as strong

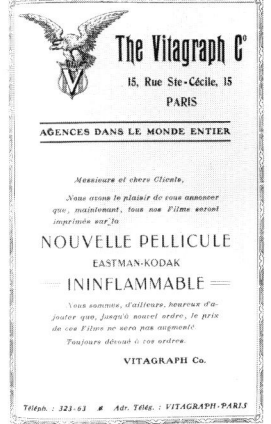

Vitagraph advertises in *Ciné-Journal* No.88 (30 April 1910) that all of its films will in future be printed on Kodak "ininflammable" stock, at no extra charge.

© Gaumont.

The ARTOGRAPH Co.

Central Film Exchange.
London Clearing House for films.

8 New Compton Street, Charing Cross Road, W.C. (Opposite Palace Theatre.)

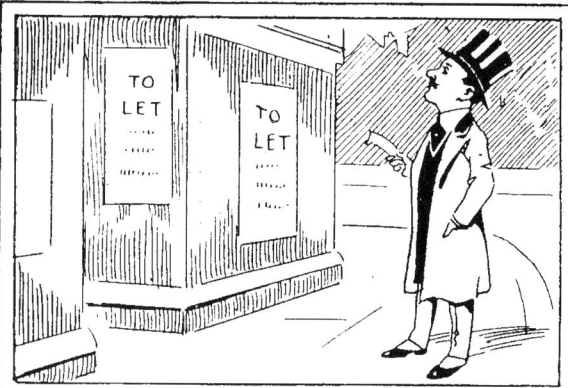

THE PROSPECTIVE SHOWMAN SELECTS HIS FUTURE PICTURE SHOW:

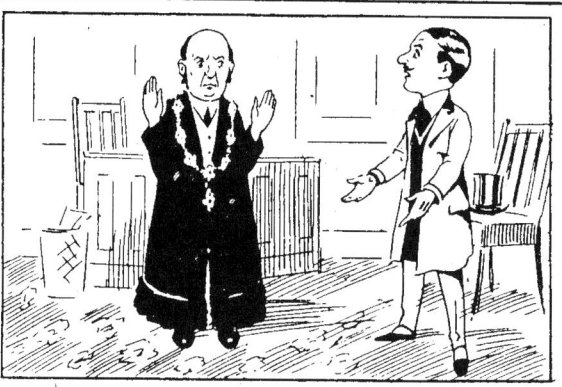

HE APPLIES FOR A LICENCE BUT APPEALS IN VAIN!

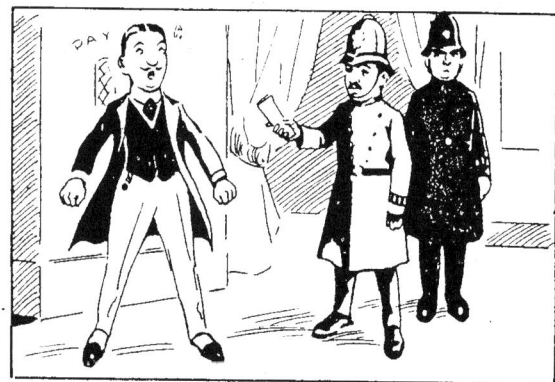

IN SPITE OF WHICH HE OPENS HIS SHOW BUT THE LAW STEPS IN!

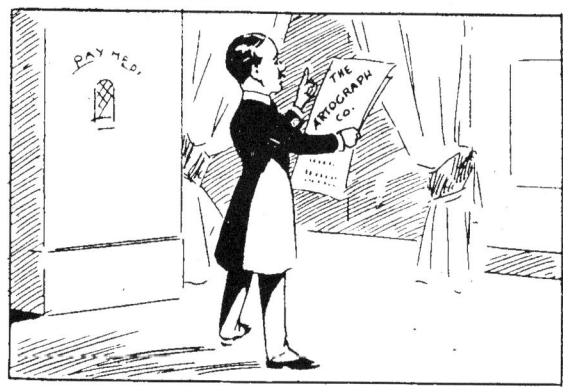

HA! WHAT'S THIS? ARTOGRAPH COMPANY. NON-FLAM FILMS, NO RISK. NO DANGER!

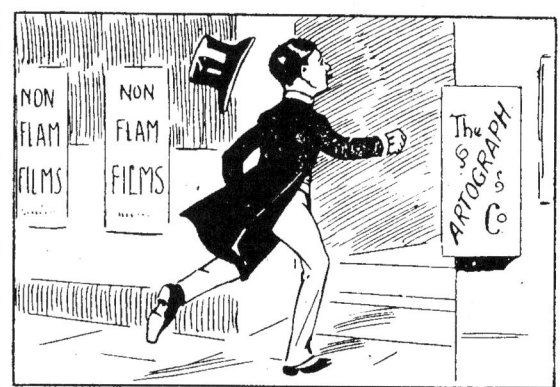

HE LOSES NO TIME IN PLACING HIS ORDER FOR REGULAR SERVICE OF NON FLAM FILMS

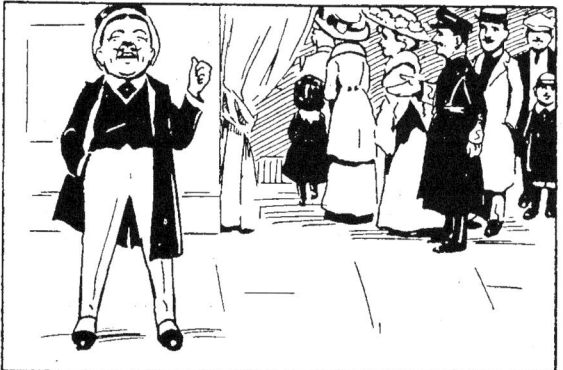

WITH THE RESULT:-NO RISK, NO TROUBLES, FULL HOUSE EVERY TIME!.

Film Dealers, Exporters and Buyers on Commission.

Telephones—664 and 834 CITY, 372 CENTRAL.　　　　Telegrams—"FILMOGRAPH, LONDON."

A British film exchange advertises "Non-Flam Films, No Risk, No Danger!" in a story with a happy ending, in *Kinematograph Weekly*, 30 March 1911.

mechanically as nitrocellulose film, and that it became brittle with use. Difficulty in the projection of the acetate film was experienced partly because of the inferior quality of the film but also because of the inferior projection equipment of that day and the rough handling to which the film was subjected.

Although some improvements ensued in film, in projection equipment, and in handling, the motion picture producers asked in 1911 to be released from their agreement to use only cellulose-acetate film. Thus, in less than two years, the Eastman first attempt to substitute slow-burning cellulose acetate film for nitrocellulose film came to an end. This attempt failed, not because of lack of coöperation [sic] on the part of the motion picture producers, but because of the failure of the cellulose-acetate film to perform satisfactorily under the conditions to which it was subjected.[12]

The American journal *Motography* in August 1911 reprinted an article from a French source which also noted the tendency of "denitrated" celluloid to shrink (and to shrink unevenly at that), and to become brittle, although it claimed that these problems were now being overcome.[13] When Mr H A Browne, chairman of the cinema supplies company Walturdaw, was interviewed for the British trade press in 1914 about non-flam film, among other subjects, he too provided a contemporary recital of these physical shortcomings:

> ... in the evidence I gave I stated that, so far, we had not yet been able to obtain a commercially satisfactory non-flam film. A vastly different thing from saying that there was no such thing as a non-flam film ... I mean that the film is not commercially satisfactory because it is brittle, joins badly, sometimes not at all, breaks frequently, does not wear well, and is, therefore, more expensive and sometimes dense.[14]

Another article, this time from *The American Architect* of July 1918, however, reported that:

> The use of these highly inflammable films has been prohibited in France since July 1, 1915. The very small extra cost of the nitro-cellulose film over that of the slow-burning kind [sic – although this appears to say the reverse of what is clearly intended] has as yet prevented the prohibition of their use in this country.[15]

Following another report of a French ban on nitrate – this time the ordinance of 10 April 1922, prohibiting the display of nitro-cellulose motion picture film in Paris after 1 January 1925 – the International Association of Fire Engineers (despite its title actually the organisation of American fire chiefs) was reported to have unanimously adopted the following resolution at their Convention in San Francisco on 17 August 1922:

Resolution on Inflammable Picture Film

WHEREAS: The nitro-cellulose motion picture film now in general use is of the nature of gun-cotton, and the handling, transportation and storage of the same is therefore a menace to life and property, and

WHEREAS: There is now commonly manufactured in America and in Europe a film of cellulose acetate or slow-burning material rendering the same safe and non-hazardous: it is therefore hereby unanimously

RESOLVED: By the International Association of Fire Engineers that in view of the availability of a safe film the present expensive burden of inspection, regulation and surveillance of motion picture displays placed by

Cinémagazine No.18 (5 May 1922) reminds its readers that a ban on the projection of "inflammable" film will come into effect at the start of 1925.

Archives du Film du Centre National de la Cinématographie, Bois d'Arcy.

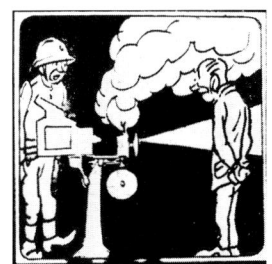

A partir du 1ᵉʳ janvier 1925 les directeurs de cinés ne pourront plus projeter de films inflammables.

the motion picture industry upon public fire and safety departments is unwarranted and indefensible and it is the moral duty of this industry to adopt at once in the production of all new pictures the exclusive use of the slow-burning film: and it is further

RESOLVED: That the International Association of Fire Engineers hereby calls upon the Federal, State and municipal governments to take proper steps to prohibit by law the use of the nitro-cellulose motion picture film on and after January 1, 1925.[16]

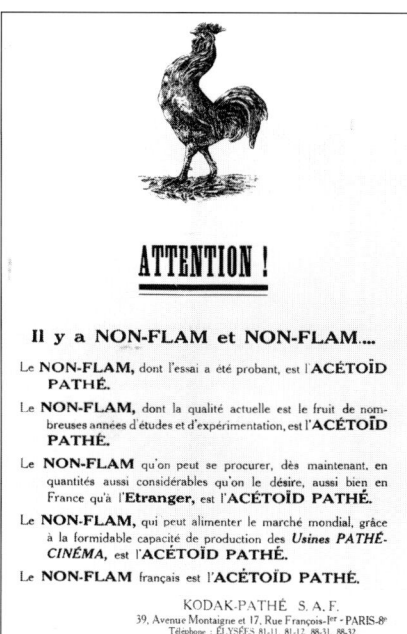

ATTENTION !

Il y a NON-FLAM et NON-FLAM....

Le **NON-FLAM**, dont l'essai a été probant, est l'**ACÉTOÏD PATHÉ**.

Le **NON-FLAM**, dont la qualité actuelle est le fruit de nombreuses années d'études et d'expérimentation, est l'**ACÉTOÏD PATHÉ**.

Le **NON-FLAM** qu'on peut se procurer, dès maintenant, en quantités aussi considérables qu'on le désire, aussi bien en France qu'à l'**Etranger**, est l'**ACÉTOÏD PATHÉ**.

Le **NON-FLAM**, qui peut alimenter le marché mondial, grâce à la formidable capacité de production des **Usines PATHÉ-CINÉMA**, est l'**ACÉTOÏD PATHÉ**.

Le **NON-FLAM** français est l'**ACÉTOÏD PATHÉ**.

KODAK-PATHÉ S. A. F.
39, Avenue Montaigne et 17, Rue François-Ier - PARIS-8e
Téléphone : ÉLYSÉES 81-11, 81-12, 88-31, 88-32

Kodak-Pathé aggressively trumpets the advantages of "Acétoïd Pathé" in *La Cinématographie Française* No.469 (29 October 1927).

Archives du Film du Centre National de la Cinématographie, Bois d'Arcy.

This renewed flurry of interest in the mid-1920s began when Pathé thought it had solved the technical problems associated with earlier forms of safety film, and initiated another campaign to have the use of "non-flam" film rendered mandatory. Such a requirement was indeed passed into French law, but the industry – on the one hand concerned by the traditional problems of price and durability, and on the other unwilling to concede an effective monopoly to a single film-stock manufacturer – managed repeatedly to have the deadline for its implementation postponed, until the whole question was seemingly forgotten among other more important issues in the 1930s. By this time, in any case, the increasingly rigorous regime of regulation in most countries, and rising standards in projection technology and cinema construction, created a safer environment for mass audiences in city-centre cinemas even if the films shown were still inflammable.

When safety film did come finally and irrevocably to replace nitrate film in the early 1950s, it required some changes to the working practices of projectionists – not least, the acquisition of new habits and new equipment for joining and repairing film. In Britain, its arrival coincided with a continuing period of post-war austerity and rationing, and early expressions of concern about the impact of television on cinema attendances. Ronald Grant has supplied a sequence of advertisements and announcements from the Cinematograph Exhibitors' Association *Film Report* from July 1949 onwards which illustrates this world, of which the following provide a brief selection:

(29 July 1949)   **Safety Film Release**

Members who have not ordered their splicing presses are requested to do so without delay... Delay in placing orders will result in delay in releasing the new safety base and it was hoped to release two million feet before the end of the year.

(7 October 1949)   **SAFETY FILM**

Members who have not yet placed their orders for the approved type of press are requested to do so without delay.... The devaluation of the pound will not materially affect the introduction of safety base and, in early 1951, no more nitrate base will be manufactured.

(21 July 1950)   **IMPORTANT NOTICE**

Warner Bros. Pictures Ltd. announce that all of their films the edges of which are marked on one side 'Nitrate' in black letters and on the other 'Safety' in white letters **are in fact on Nitrate Stock**. All such films are inflammable and highly dangerous if exposed to naked flame or intense heat.

Steps are being taken to remedy the unfortunate situation that has arisen and when the words 'safety film' have been deleted from all nitrate copies in circulation, an "all-clear" notice will be published.

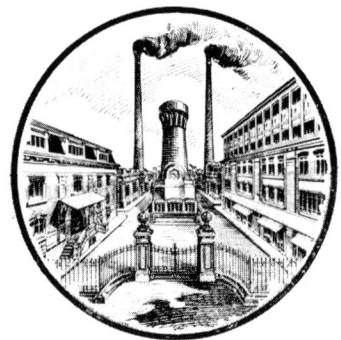

Pellicule Négative

PANCHROMATIQUE

Kodak

Seule, la négative **"PANCHRO"** donne à l'écran l'exacte reproduction visuelle des objets colorés.

Son emploi, de plus en plus répandu, est entièrement justifié par les résultats qui dépassent de beaucoup la qualité de ceux obtenus par les émulsions ordinaires.

Pellicule Positive

"NON FLAM"

Pathé

La Pellicule **"NON FLAM"** Pathé - émulsion positive - a toutes les qualités de la pellicule positive ordinaire.

Elle peut être utilisée partout sans le moindre danger, libérant ainsi l'industrie cinématographique des derniers risques qui entravaient encore son expansion.

Demandez les notices gratuites :
La Pellicule Panchromatique "Kodak"
Le Film "Non Flam Pathé"

Société **"Kodak-Pathé"** S. A. F.
39, Avenue Montaigne, PARIS (8ᵉ)
Téléph. : Élysées 81-11, 81-12, 88-31, 88-32.

Kodak-Pathé suggests that the best of both worlds can be had by combining Kodak's (nitrate) panchromatic negative stock with Pathé's "Non Flam" positive stock, in an advertisement printed in *Le Courier Cinématographique* No.18 (5 May 1928).

Archives du Film du Centre National de la Cinématographie, Bois d'Arcy.

(10 November 1950) **SAFETY FILM CEMENT**

Safety film cement can now be obtained through normal trade channels. Consequently the emergency stocks arranged in January last will not be replenished.

Finally, it is worth noting several items which underline that the switch to safety when it did arrive did not result in the instantaneous disappearance from commercial film circuits of nitrate film and the concerns it carried with it. A typically cryptic headline in *Variety* in March 1953 read: "...Complete Switch to Safety Film Still Way Off, Impeding Insurance Cut".[17] A notebook, in which Ronald Grant recorded the details of every title which he screened when he began work as a projectionist in Scotland in the early 1950s, shows that in 1953 more than a quarter of those titles – 37 out of 143 – were still on nitrate. Although the proportion had fallen off to less than 7% by 1956, that still meant that 8 out of 123 films screened that year were on nitrate.[18] As late as 2 July 1956, the British *Daily Film Renter* carried an interesting front-page story, "Analysis of Fires in Cinemas", which noted that 43 cinema fires had been reported in the previous year, of which the largest number, 12, were attributed to "carelessly discarded smoking materials", but 6 – "seldom serious" – were still due to (nitrate) film jamming in the projector.[19]

Spreading the word: an announcement from the UK Cinematograph Exhibitors' Association *Film Report* for 18 November 1949.

The Cinema Museum, London.

SAFETY FILM LECTURES

The following lectures dealing with the characteristics, handling and technique of joining the new safety film will be given during November:—

Tues.,	22.11.49	Capitol, Newport	...	...	10.45 a.m.
		Electric, Bournemouth		...	10.30 a.m.
Wed.,	23.11.49	Park Hall, Cardiff	...	...	10.45 a.m.
		Forum, Southampton		...	10.30 a.m.
Thurs.,	24.11.49	County, Pontypridd		...	11.00 a.m.
Fri.,	25.11.49	Albert Hall, Swansea	...	...	10.45 a.m.
Tues.,	29.11.49	Regal, Ferensway, Hull	...	...	10.30 a.m.
Wed.,	30.11.49	News Theatre, Upper Parliament Street, Nottingham	...	...	10.15 a.m.

Members are reminded that it is most desirable that all projectionists in the areas have the opportunity of attending.

Notes

1. «Le celluloïd ininflammable. – L'incendie qui vient de causer une si terrible catastrophe à Paris a fait une triste réclame au cinématographe et aux bandes sur lesquelles s'étendent ses photographies. En effet, si l'on s'en rapporte aux premiers résultats de l'enquête, le feu qui a pris dans la lampe du cinématographe du Bazar de la Charité s'est communiqué immédiatement au rouleau que forment les rubans de celluloïd dans l'appareil: naturellement ce celluloïd a pris feu, et, en jaillissant, a formé un brandon redoutable. Un inventeur et chimiste bien connu, M. Tommasi, a cherché à rendre ces bandes cinématographiques ininflammables, et il a pu nous en montrer des échantillons qui brûlent à peine comme un papier épais et chargé, alors que les bandes ordinaires s'enflamment comme de la poudre. On comprend que la découverte est importante et mérite d'être signalée, car elle s'appliquera certainement à tous les produits fabriqués en celluloïd.» *La Nature*, no.1251 (22 May 1897), pp. 398–399.

2. "Non-Inflammable Celluloid", *Optical Lantern and Cinematograph Journal* (February 1905), p. 80.

3. "Non-Inflammable Films", *Kinematograph and Lantern Weekly* (19 September 1907), p. 325.

4. "Englisches Verfahren zur Erzeugung von unentzündlichem Zelluloid", *Der Kinematograph – Düsseldorf*, no.238 (19 July 1911).

5. «La "CELLITE". On avait essayé, il y a quelques années, de remplacer le celluloïd, dont les dangers ne sont que trop connu, par une autre matière moins inflammable, l'acéto-cellulose. Les tentatives qui furent faites en Angleterre avec ce nouveau produit n'ont pas été heureuses et le celluloïd resta maître de la situation. Il semble, aujourd'hui, que la situation soit pour lui bien compromise, car il vient de trouver, dans un nouveau produit, la «cellite », un concurrent redoutable. La cellite n'est autre chose qu'une acéto-cellulose préparée industriellement suivant un procédé dû au Dr Eichengrün. La cellite se dissout dans l'acétone et plus facilement encore dans l'éther acétique. On peut en préparer des blocs de toutes dimensions, des pellicules, plaques, etc. Cette matière se laisse travailler avec la plus grand facilité. F. P. Liesegang a essayé cette nouvelle matière en vue de son application à la préparation des films cinématographiques: elle a pu résister à toutes les épreuves, se laissant perforer, dévider, coller, etc., sans se briser. D'autre part, tandis que la même section d'une pellicule en celluloïd ne peut rester exposée à la chaleur des rayons caloriques émis par la lampe à arc, sans s'enflammer au bout de quelques secondes, une pellicule en cellite a pu rester pendant 10 minutes, exposée à ces mêmes rayons, sans interposition d'une cuve à alun ou d'aucun système de refroidissement: au bout de ce temps, la portion exposée aux rayons caloriques prenait feu, mais pour s'éteindre bientôt d'elle-même. On peut donc considérer la cellite comme ne présentant aucun danger de ce côté, et il est à prévoir que cette nouvelle matière trouvera bientôt, dans l'industrie photographique, de nombreuses applications.» *Ciné-Journal*, no.4 (8 September 1908), p. 4.

6. Paul Knoche, "Der Rohfilm", in *Das Tage-Buch*, v.3, no.14 (8 April 1922), pp. 547–550, and "Homunculus" (pseud.), "Der unverbrennbare Film", *Reichsfilmblatt*, no.42 (20 October 1923), pp. 12–13.

7. *Ciné-Journal*, no.21 (7 January 1909).

8. "Topics of the Week – Non-Flam Film", *The Bioscope* (21 January 1909), p. 4.

9. "The Paris Congress", *The Bioscope* (18 February 1909), p. 5.

10. "The Moving Picture Business in Massachusetts", *National Fire Protection Association Quarterly*, v.3, no.2 (January 1910), pp. 282–283.

11. *Kinematograph and Lantern Weekly* (30 March 1911), pp. 43–47.

12. Albert F Sulzer, "The Epoch of Progress in Film Fire Prevention", *SMPE Journal* (April 1940), p. 401.

13. "How Non-Flam Film Is Made", *Motography*, v.VI, no.2 (August 1911), pp. 88–89, credited as "From Chimie Industrielle".

14. "Non-Flam. Mr. H.A. Browne interviewed by W. Gavazzi King", supplement to *The Cinema* (12 November 1914), p. 32.

15. "Film Exchange Regulations", *The American Architect*, v.CXIV, no.2221 (17 July 1918), pp. 88–94.

16. "The Inflammable Picture Film Prohibited in Paris after January 1, 1925", *National Fire Protection Association Quarterly*, v.16, no.2 (October 1922), pp. 109–110.

17. *Variety* (4 March 1953).

18. Information from Ronald Grant, Cinema Museum, London.

19. *Daily Film Renter*, no.7159 (2 July 1956).

Nitrate Nightmares

by Frank Worth

I must admit that I had never seen the First World War photograph of Geoffrey Malins carrying film before Roger Smither showed it to me, but it is true that I was, at least for a time, tempted to try something similar myself during the Second World War.

Serving as a junior officer in a Naval Film Unit as a combat cameraman covering combined operations against the Japanese in Burma and the Far East, I took part in several sea-borne assault landings on enemy-occupied beaches. While most of my cameraman colleagues favoured the smaller Bell and Howell Eyemo camera, which could be loaded only with 100 feet (30 metres) of film at a time, I personally preferred the Newman-Sinclair, the tried-and-tested warhorse of many pre-war newsreel cameramen. With the model I had, the distance of the subject did not have to be estimated – the lens could be focused through the viewfinder, and then shifted over to the filming position. It had the further definite advantage that it could be loaded with 200 feet (60 metres) of film at a time, giving, with its large clockwork motor, more than two minutes of continuous filming for each loading, and that it was comparatively easy to slip in a new pre-loaded magazine of film when you needed to change rolls. As will be told in *Worth's War*, a TV documentary series based on my wartime career which is currently in production, in order to make sure that I was as ready as I could be, before a landing I used to prepare five 200-ft magazines, and for the first few operations that I covered I used to go into battle with these five magazines strapped around my chest and back. Not only was this intended to keep the film as far as possible from the water as I waded ashore, but I also had the fond hope that the densely wound rolls of film and their aluminium containers would give me some protection against enemy fire.

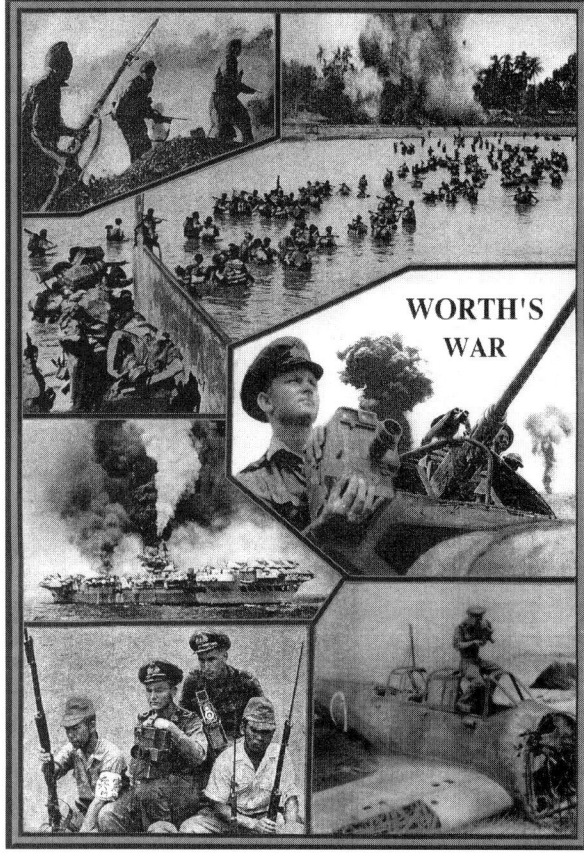

Front cover for the script of *Worth's War*, including several action shots of the author with his Newman-Sinclair camera.

© Frank Worth.

If any of the reels that I was so trustingly carrying had ever been hit by a bullet, I doubt I would have lived to tell the tale. The precise nature of the material that I was so carefully wearing into battle was tragically brought home to me one night at unit headquarters. Most of my colleagues were at the neighbouring American forces film unit, at the invitation of the renowned Hollywood director John Ford, then a US Navy Commander, who was showing one of his films there. I was unable to attend because I was duty officer that night, meaning that I was formally responsible for our base, even though it was virtually deserted. Usually at night it was a dull, uneventful task and a good opportunity for a quiet read, even a nap – but not a nightmare! Suddenly I became aware of dense smoke coming from the cutting room area, which should certainly have been empty at the time. Hurrying to the scene as the smoke turned to raging flames, I encountered the girlfriend of a colleague, Steve Heyne. She was burned and utterly distraught. Steve had recently returned with some sensational film from a mission with the Chindits, General Orde Wingate's special forces unit which was famous for its operations far behind the Japanese lines. It had been cut into the cutting copy of *Burma Victory*, the feature-length film which was being edited there by Roy Boulting, of the Boulting Brothers. I gathered that Steve was still in the cutting room.

Entrusting the girl to the care of some soldiers who had by now appeared on the scene, I entered the cutting room to look for my friend. On my hands and knees, because I had heard that this was the best way to try to keep out of the worst of the smoke, as visibility in the pitch black was virtually zero, I searched by touch all over the entire floor area of the room. Shouting Steve's name, I inhaled vast quantities of acrid nitrate smoke, but could find no trace of him. When the fire brigade arrived, they found that I was on the point of passing out from the effects of the fumes, and they had to pull me semi-conscious from the room. Apart from burn marks, my tropical rig – the high-buttoned formal evening Naval uniform of immaculate white – was now black, and totally ruined. But at least I was alive. They later found Steve Heyne's body in an alcove off the main cutting room, where there was a Moviola viewing machine. He had taken his girlfriend into the cutting room to show her some of the film he had just brought back, but it was never clear exactly what had happened: the fire brigade officers surmised that an electrical spark had started the fire. Many reels of rushes and the cutting copy of *Burma Victory* had been destroyed. Steve had covered countless enemy attacks on film, and survived, but not one by film itself – an enemy called nitrate! The experience brought home to me how dangerous a form of body armour nitrate film actually was, and from then on nitrate and I became a little less intimately entwined. I carried my spare film into combat in a more sensible, if less convenient, separate box.

At the end of the war I was posted to Japan itself, to film some of the after-effects of the conventional and atomic bombing, and some of the early stages of the Allied occupation. When I returned to what had been the central command post for service filming, in Calcutta, it was like visiting a ghost town – the place was almost completely deserted. In an empty room, I found a pile of film cans, many of them bearing labels that identified them as my work. Feeling that I might need some sort of evidence of my competence if I was to succeed in getting a job in the peacetime film industry, I packed them up carefully and brought them back to England with me. I never needed to produce them, however, as I worked to add editing and script-writing skills to my experience as a cameraman and so progress to work as a film director. For years the films lay undisturbed in a shed in my garden. Then one day a friend casually asked me whether I had forgotten that they were nitrate, and if I had ever calculated how far the shed was from the bed I slept in every night. He was right, of course. I contacted the British Film Institute, who sent somebody to collect the material – which actually turned out to be in very good condition. I asked for, and received, 16mm safety copies of some of the reels that meant the most to me. Some decades after the relationship had begun, nitrate film and I had arrived at an amicable separation.

Or so I thought... Recently, while trying to buy the rights of an old movie I had directed and co-written, I had forgotten how long ago it was, until I was told, "If we do a deal, the original neg and prints are yours – they're nitrate!" Were nitrate nightmares back to haunt me? Nitrate's hara-kiri complex, involving its own destruction, alarmed me less than its occasional kamikaze compulsion, its *burning* desire to propel those around it to premature cremation. Odd slogans began to occur to me, like "Night-rate calls may cost you less, but nitrate film may cost your life!" – and then the muse tapped me gently on the shoulder and whispered these cautionary lines:

Old nitrate never dies
It just lies in wait, to seal your fate.
When the time is right, it'll then ignite.
Its grisly plan, those flames to fan,
Its aim to try, to make you fry.
If no danger's dawning,
With this warning –
I bet'cha, it'll get'cha!

"You always treat the film with respect."

– Frank Holland (FH) Interviewed by Catherine A Surowiec (CAS) –
23 June 2000, London

CAS: When did you start working with the British Film Institute? Did you always work in the vaults?

FH: No. I joined the BFI in London in 1952, which was the same year the NFT opened. So I am as old as the NFT, in a sense. I've been with the BFI that length of time. But of course now I have been retired 10 years or more. But I didn't completely retire; I went back again to do research work in the Stills department.

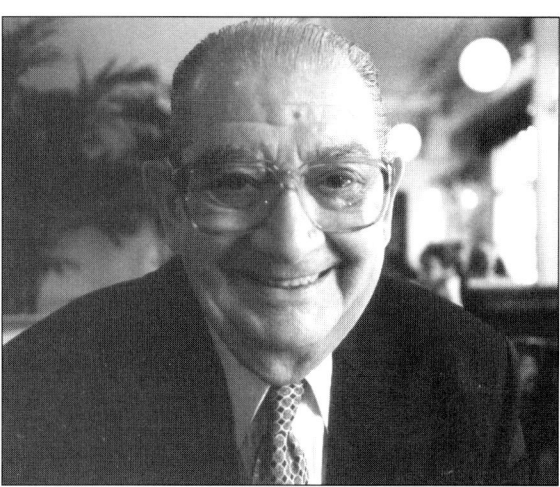

Frank Holland, photographed on 4 May 2001 on a return visit to the restaurant where this interview took place.

Kevin Brownlow Collection.

So I did work for 10 years in the BFI proper in London before I went to the vaults. Then in 1962 I got offered a job to go into preservation, which meant moving out of London, down to the preservation vaults, which were located outside London, in Aston Clinton in Buckinghamshire. Now, the reasons for the archive's being there... Prior to the War, the archive as such didn't consist of a large number of actual films. In fact, the story that I have heard – because I wasn't there at the time, we're talking about 1938-39. This was early on, when Harold Brown was [already] working for the BFI. By chance some films happened to be delivered in a carrier bag, which ended up in the Curator's office. They were films in tins. Now, nobody there had really seen actual film as a commodity, in tins. You knew about movies on the screen, but you didn't know them as actual material. Apart from that, they couldn't read the labels, because the cans were rusty. The films were actually identified by somebody looking at the image, or one of the images. Because they had no projection equipment in those days; it was a straightforward office. Somebody got a film book out of the library, and matched up a photograph from the book with the film. So the first cataloguing, you might say, was done in that way. It was primitive...

CAS: They were lucky that they matched.

FH: Well, they matched, and I think – I'm not certain, this would have to be confirmed with somebody like Harold Brown, because I think he was involved with it – that the film was *Queen Elizabeth*, with Sarah Bernhardt; you know, the French production.

So that was basically how it all started. Then came a problem, because somebody thought it would be a good idea, if they started as a British Film Institute, that we ought to ask for donations of films. Well, the donations were very slow at first, as I understand. However, it started to build up quickly. And there wasn't anywhere to keep these films other than under the desk of the librarian at the time.

Then came the advent of the War, and possibly in 1939 somebody made enquiries whether the material was nitrate. There was a government order that highly inflammable material ought to be moved out of the city, so that really started the BFI investigating where they could possibly go. And it was just by chance in a sense, that through, I think, a London agency, they found... in about October or November of that year, they found this property in Buckinghamshire, in Aston Clinton, a village. It consisted, I think, of a house, which had been a farmhouse, and some farm buildings, like cattle sheds. With a bit of ingenuity, these were turned into nitrate film vaults, with the usual adaptation of having escape vents in case of a fire. Each block was individually divided so that if something did happen, the ventilators at the top would open. Because as far as a nitrate fire is concerned, you cannot put it out. You can put foam on it, you can put water on it – we've tried experiments. You put a reel of nitrate film in a bucket of water and it will burn under the water, simply because it creates its own oxygen. So the best thing, in some respects, providing it's safe within an area, is to let the furnace go. You lose what's in there, but then that's part of the thing itself.

The other thing about it... is the examination of nitrate film. Providing this is done periodically, no matter how old your film is, it doesn't mean to say that because it's old it's going to deteriorate fast. We've had some film material that was made in the War – feature films, but made on inferior film stock, simply because the raw material wasn't available. So the danger period was sort of 1940 to 1945, when the film stock... when any film [that] was made was on nitrate was likely to deteriorate faster than [stock of] the 1930s. Which is something we also discovered, which a lot of archives are now aware of, because it's been written up.

It started with a very small staff. I think originally the British archive probably had something like four people: one senior preservation technician, who became the Preservation Officer; one junior; one secretary for the records; and one boy from school to wheel the films in and out of the vaults. Then it developed, obviously, as time went on and more money was gotten from the Government, which was a constant fight over the years anyway. But they started to expand. It expanded with negotiations with companies recognising the film archive as a place to deposit films... As the archive developed and went on, I think the most important thing was of course the expansion of the viewing materials. At one time there was a strict policy that we didn't show things in the archive, purely because there wasn't the money to make a second copy. And we were attacked many times, you know: "You have a copy. Why can't you show it?"...

I found that when I worked with the technical staff at Aston Clinton, in my regard, being Film Examiner, day in, and day out, winding through film, so many hundreds of feet, or maybe only 50 feet, or maybe 10,000 feet, that there is a certain monotony. The people get to know the material. They can tell by winding a film... The people we had who examined the film were mostly lady technicians, mostly from the local village, because it was within walking distance from home. So it had a kind of very countrified atmosphere about it. Everybody knew everybody. They all got on their bicycles at the end of the day, and cycled home, in between the cows being led in from the fields for milking. It was very rural.

So you could be winding through *Birth of a Nation*. You had to get your mind working. I always used to say to them, "You have a film in front of

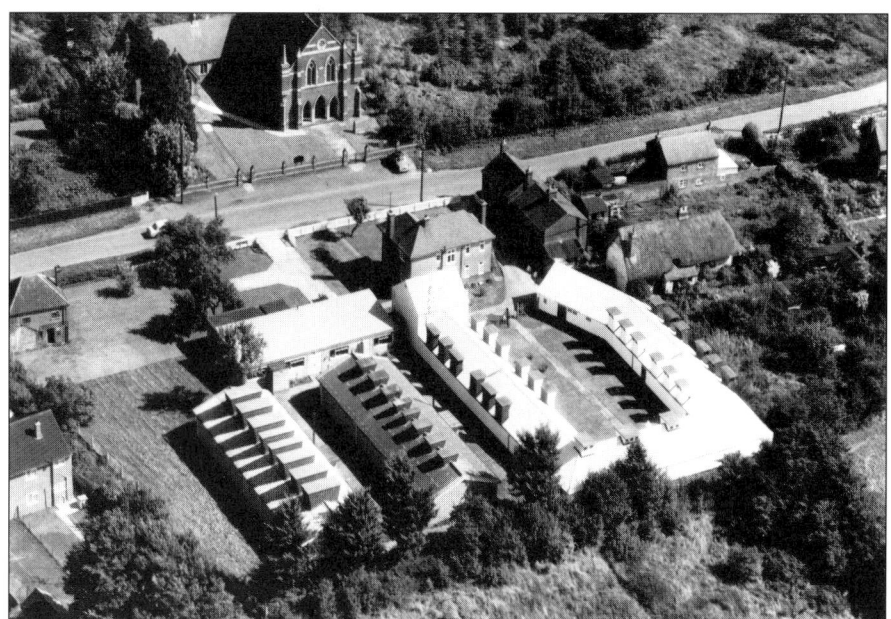

Aerial view of the National Film Archive's vaults in the village of Aston Clinton.
Frank Holland.

you. Do you know how old it is? Do you know who made it? Directed it? Do you know what it is? Do you know what the content is?" They would say, "No, no, no. I'm only looking for broken perforations." I'd say, "OK. But you're doing more than that. You could be winding through a piece of original negative. A particular director may have actually cut it, joined it, put it together, with the help of his editor. So the work is a bit more than just winding a piece of film from A to B. Right?" So what I used to get them to do, when we had visitors... They used to say to me, "Will you tell the visitors coming around what it is?" And I'd say, "No, *you* tell them." And in front of them there used to be a condition report. On the condition report it would have all the details about the film, with as much information as possible. So that when they were asked a question, they could say, "Yes, it was 1910. Yes, it was hand-coloured." So this gave them an incentive to be a bit more interested in what they were doing. It took me quite a while to get these people interested, because they didn't... They weren't film historians, but eventually they felt that what they were doing *was* important. And it was important.

CAS: When did they first start hiring these women from the village?

FH: I think they started it during the War. But again, money was very short, so it wasn't until after the War that expansion really started. When I went there, in 1962, which was another 10 years later, there would be something like 8 people there. By the time I'd left and retired, it had expanded. The film vaults had expanded, and there was talk about the development of another site. Because we had accumulated so much nitrate film, in what was regarded as a built-up area – which the village was becoming – we had to consider moving. Which is why in the 1960s and '70s they found a site in Warwickshire. We went to a place called Gaydon, which strangely enough used to hold ammunition and bombs for the RAF. So our nitrate material was moved into bunkers, special bunkers, and the nitrate film was transported daily. Now with the advent of the programme of transferring nitrate to safety, which is still going on, and is likely to go on even though people think it's coming to the end... Because there is always nitrate film in the world, although it's becoming more difficult to use it, which is understandable.

But in my opinion, nitrate film was never dangerous. It was in existence for a very long time. If you treated it with respect, like you would anything which had an explosive nature... It is really mistakes that were made outside the film itself that were cause for concern. But now, 90–100% of material is safety-based, as far as film is concerned.

CAS: But that has its own problems.

FH: Well, tape will have its own problems. So the development hasn't finished yet. I don't know whether they'll ever find anything, maybe electronically they'll find a preservation image. But it depends what you mean by permanency, and what you want to keep it for.

I can remember being interviewed for the job at the National Film Archive. I can't remember now who interviewed me, but he asked me if I was afraid of the dark. I said, "No". And he said, "Well, we've got a job in the vaults for you!"

CAS: Did you learn about the technical aspects of film on the job?

FH: Yes, the only training that one could get was practical training. When you arrived there, if you were a young technician or a young examiner, you would carry a notebook with you, and you would write down things, when your teacher, which in my case would be Harold Brown... He would point out negatives, fine grains, and he would teach us how to *look*. If the film wasn't marked, for instance, whether it was Nitrate or Safety, how would we know? There were certain things we were taught to look for. Sizes of perforations meant certain things. He could date film by looking at it, and by simply looking at its structure, the way it was photographed, framelines. It was incredible, the knowledge he had built up from practical experience. You know: certain films couldn't be between that date and that date, because Pathé didn't produce that kind of material. So he had all this kind of background information. I think he did a paper once for FIAF, on the identification of movies...

CAS: Yes, he talked about the different film stock, the edge codes, the perforations...

FH: Yes, well, all that was learned simply by observation and winding. And that information was passed on to every new technician who came in, so that they knew what they were looking for. And the longer you did it, the more expert you became. Visitors used to be absolutely amazed when we could dig out a piece of film, and show them something, on the bench. It might be Méliès, at the turn of the century, 1900/1905, like *A Trip to the Moon*. And they would say, "But it's in colour! All old films are black-and-white." We would say, "No." You're almost saying that silent films were silent and never had any music – they *did* have music. But history doesn't write itself that way. Only occasionally.

People used to say to me, "What do you do?" I'd say, "I'm in the film industry." "Oh, lucky for you! What part have you been in?" "I'm not part of the people who make the films. It's my job to keep them for the next 100 years, maybe 200 years. No, I'm in conservation and preservation." "Well, what do you do with all the old films?" I'd say, "We're there so that people can look back on it. You can go to the library – nowadays you've got a computer – and look things up in the *Encyclopaedia Britannica*. If you want to know what film was shown, or what happened, you can come to us. We have newsreels, we have documentaries, and we can do it, from 1895 up to date." And now we can do television. What's after television? We'll never lose *Coronation Street*...

But I would never have... You know, maybe at one stage, when I was in the Forces, I wanted to get into movies. I really didn't know what I wanted to do. But the technical side seemed to interest me, and it wasn't until I joined the BFI that I suddenly realised: Right, I'm not in movies, but I'm as close as I shall ever be to film. And so I became a student, studied it, learned the history of it, wrote it, lectured on it. And the thing that I found more interesting than anything else was the young people. I used go around the schools locally. The younger they were, if you showed them the earliest material, you'd got them. That was really good stuff; they would enjoy it. At first they would say, "Oh, no – old movies!" And I would say, "You hang onto your seats, we haven't finished yet!"

CAS: In the vaults, could you tell just by walking around if something was deteriorating?

FH: It would be possible if something *had* deteriorated; you could smell it. You see, it's got this process first, of becoming sticky; it sticks together. Now, I'm not sure whether the aroma would come after that, or when it had gone to the dangerous stage. The "dangerous stage" is when it's powder; that's when it can ignite from high temperatures or being near an open flame, something like that. But, yes, you could. But I haven't experienced a lot of it. I had 112, maybe 115 vaults, that I would have to go round. And I had an extra job. I lived there. I lived "above the shop", as they say. I had a house at the vaults, within the compound, and I would walk around at night, and make sure – now this is *important* – and make sure that every vault door was *closed*. Because of the specially constructed doors, if there were a fire, they would contain the fire. They were heavy-duty, made of oak, specially painted with a non-flammable material; "slow-burning", it was called. It wouldn't stop the actual fire itself, but what would be likely to happen because of the fierceness. And in each block, each cell, there would be nearly 400 to 500 cans, in each little cell.

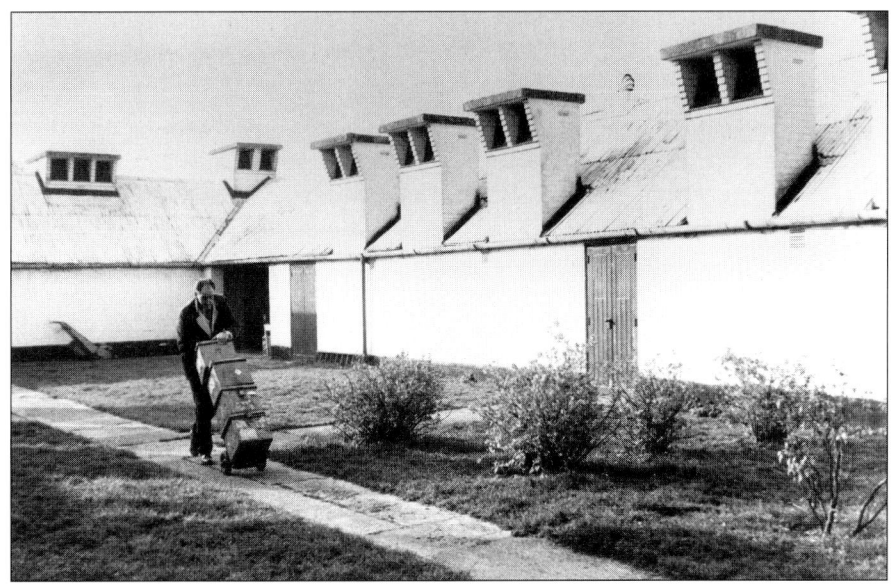

Moving film at Aston Clinton.

BFI Collections – Stills, Posters & Designs, London. 132141.

CAS: Were they kept on metal shelves?

FH: They would be metal shelves. And there was something else important: you never stand your film on *edge*. I know space is important, but you *always lay it flat*. Because if you laid it on its edge, the pressure at the bottom didn't allow the gases to escape where the pressure was. Even nowadays, putting film – safety film – on its end doesn't help the film; it will put it out of shape. Which is why even in the preservation vaults, in the safety area, they are all stored flat. Which is the way it should be. But if in the nitrate block there were actually a fire, because of the build-up prior to what you would call the flame itself, there would be an explosion, which would ignite. It would probably at that stage blow the door off; the fire would start. So we built a vent at the top of each, which was like a chimney, so that if it did explode, it would go up through the vents straight out into the sky. The doors would probably remain, but catch fire, because of the force. That was it. Once you put nitrate film in a tight container… That is the worst thing to do. You need to let it *breathe*. But in the 25 years there, we never had a nitrate fire. And I'm touching wood here.

I lived with it for years and years. I lived there over 25 years, handling nitrate. And it's *never* dangerous; *people* are dangerous. People do silly things. Which is the case in any situation where there's danger: the human factor is normally 95%. If you obey the rules and regulations, there is no reason… As I say, nitrate film has been handled and shown in cinemas for years and years. You take precautions, yes, as much safety as possible, isolate it, and make sure that… Having said that, our staff – or they were in the old days – were all shown what effect a nitrate fire could have. So that when you were initiated into the organisation, you'd be told, "You will be handling this material. This is what could happen. It *won't*, but you need to be aware that this *can* happen. And the rules and regulations are, *get out*." Ask any fireman, anywhere. You never fight a fire, you find the quickest way out. Phone the authorities, but *get out*. And it's the same with nitrate film.

CAS: So, as you say, there were all kinds of regulations and everyone knew them. Were there lots of directive signs, like "No Smoking"? Nobody was ever foolish enough to smoke around it?

FH: No, nobody.

CAS: If they had to smoke, would they have to go outside, and walk away?

FH: Yes, they would go out into the countryside, or they would go out of the building. Like they do now in the big office blocks; it's the same kind of situation. But we never found anybody that… You know, we made absolutely sure, certainly among the younger generation. The thing was, we didn't have many young trainees, and if we did, we made absolutely sure, you know, that [they knew] smoking was not allowed. Which was one of the reasons why we had to leave the area, because, as I said, with the area expanding as much as it did, as far as housing was concerned, the location became wrong for that kind of work, in that area. The Home Office came down, and that was when they decided that it was too dangerous. If something *really* happened, which may be not our fault, but if something *really* happened, we needed to be isolated – actually, the *material* needed to be isolated. The people remained where they were, and the material would be brought in, in smaller quantities. Which is one of the reasons why eventually we moved to the new storage at Berkhamsted, where the development is still going on and still expanding. But nitrate film goes there as well.

CAS: I was going to ask you about that. When they closed Aston Clinton... when was that, when did they actually move everything out of there?

FH: Oh, that must have been after I retired. I'm trying to think. In the late 1980s, or something or other. It's got to be there on the record.

You'll also find a lot of information in the archive stills... If you look through that file, you'll find some photographs. I've got an aerial photograph of Aston Clinton, quite early as well. You can distinguish the cattle sheds that were converted. This is what we used to get a lot of: "What are they over there?" "Well, they're the cattle sheds." "Why were they cattle sheds?" Because the cattle shed was open to put the cows in. Well, they bricked up both sides, and inside they built the individual walls of brick and mortar. And they were there for 30 years, and served a purpose. But like I say, we never had a problem, because everybody knew their job, everybody knew what could happen.

CAS: Were the vaults temperature-controlled?

FH: Temperature controlled, 55 degrees Fahrenheit. There were readings every day. Then in each vault there would be a reading for humidity, to make sure that the humidity was kept. There are pictures of people doing the humidity readings. Plus stills of the working rooms, plus technicians actually winding films. There's a picture file on Aston Clinton, a file on Berkhamsted as well, and there is another file about visits, because you had a lot of MPs and Governors coming down. So you've got pictures of visitors as well. I think there are some stills of David Lean visiting, and Michael Powell.

The real problem, neither was maintained. The British Film Institute never sold itself. They do a lot of enormously important work, and there is not enough said. It's a modest organisation. The people who work there believe in what they are doing, that what they are doing is worthwhile. What they needed was somebody beyond them, to actually shout out, and publicise, much much more than was ever done in the past. It was always cap in hand: "Do you mind if we have more money?" We should have been banging a table, we should have had a few MPs. We should have had a few Governors who *were* MPs...

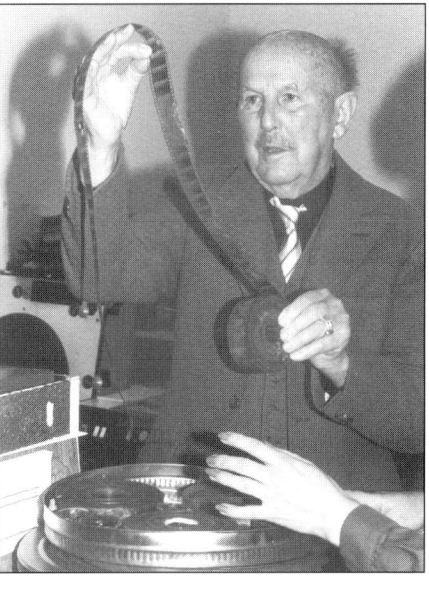

Michael Powell examines some deteriorating nitrate film at Berkhamsted. (See also Colour Section 2.)

BFI Collections – Stills, Posters & Designs, London. 227597.

But the people were quite content. The man who was really like the Godfather, if you like, of British film preservation, is Harold Brown. His service there is unique. He spent hours and hours, and days, and months, on films. He was only alive when his fingers were on a piece of celluloid. And he could use his ears. Because I, too, have suffered from remarks that he said, very kindly. He could *hear* if you were winding that film too fast. He'd say to me, "Excuse me, Frank, but you're winding the film too fast." And he wasn't even looking! Because if you go too fast you lose control, and if you happen to have a join in it, you could cut your fingers, you could break the film, or all sorts of things, and cause a lot of damage to the film.

CAS: Was there ever a film that caught fire on a rewind?

FH: When you run them too fast? No. You know, it gets impatient, to do 1,000 feet, 2,000 feet. There are a lot more motorised rewinds now. But as far as what you did in Harold Brown's section: You *always* treat the film with *respect*. So you *don't* go a hundred miles an hour. If so, you are more likely to destroy a piece of film. A piece of film which could be the only piece, which *could* be unique. It may not be, but it could be. And if you do something to it, and you've got to repair it, then you will be surprised the hours and hours the women work on repairing film, film which other people would have thrown in the bin. But their patience and dedication to put them back together, and in the end actually make it good enough to project – that was even harder. Some material, of course, was too far gone. In that case you had to print it on a very unique mechanical invention put together by Harold Brown, made of Meccano, which would print one frame at a time. I'm not so sure whether the machine went to the Museum [of the Moving Image – MoMI].

CAS: It's still at Berkhamsted, as a kind of a museum piece.

FH: It *is* a museum piece, priceless, made up of all sorts of things, clips, string... I used to have a moving picture of it actually working. And I always used to say, the best thing about this machine is it's not like a modern prototype, which constantly breaks down. Now, with this machine, made of Meccano, bits of string, knicker elastic – you could always get a bit of string, you could always get a bit of knicker elastic (we had plenty of women working there) – this machine would continue working through the night, one frame at a time. OK, a slow process, but if the thing that you had, that you were trying to reproduce, were the only copy held, well, it was worthwhile. That was the kind of dedication that this man gave. Incredible.

The other device that he developed there had to do with colour. It was always difficult to tell people that early films were in colour. Colour is not new. Colour has been in existence since movies started, in some form or another. Either it was hand-painted, or stencil-colouring. Or in the Twenties – yes, mostly in the 1920s – whole scenes would be coloured one colour: blue, or red. And sometimes, in the early black-and-white films, if you saw what might be two robbers going into a house – they would have a mask on, and they would have these bull's-eye lamps like policemen have, and they would be shining – but the film that you saw was black-and-white, and you would wonder why they were breaking into a house with lamps, in daylight. Because not realising when the film was shown, it was coloured blue, tinted, which gave the light effect. Light pink, if it were an inside ballroom scene. So colour was used in a dramatic sense.

Well, in order to put a film back to that colour, we used to do and record the colour guide. When you had the original, you would measure how long the blue, how long the red, how long the pink, how much black-and-white. This produced a colour chart. When you reproduced a black-and-white film, you cut your new print up, then you would mark it up. So you would join all the blue together, all the red together. Then, when it was dry, you would cut it back, and then you would have a tinted print. Many a time I've seen Mr Brown come our of the darkroom all colours of the rainbow. Because all the baths that they had, the blue, and the red... that was all constructed and put together by him. Such dedication, to get a film back as it was.

Yes, I enjoyed it all. I'm disappointed I'm too old to still do it. Although I'm not too old to talk about it!

CAS: You talked about the women inspecting the film. On what basis did they do that? I mean, who decided what they were going to inspect, and when?

FH: It came from two sources. One of the most important aspects was known as the artificial ageing test. Every so often, I think every 5 years, every nitrate film was tested. I think you'll find that this is all documented by FIAF. A portion of film is taken, punched, and then it is actually put aside for a certain period of time, and depending when the litmus paper turns colour, this would indicate how far off it was from going unstable. If the results were bad, then the report would go back to the technical staff: "This needs to be printed." But in between the technical decision would be a preservation policy decision, which was made in London. A list of the titles, the date of the film, would be presented to a committee in London, called the Preservation Committee. And they would say, "Yes, print," or "No, we can exchange with another archive," or "No, we're not interested." Or, "Do we have more than one copy?" Things like that.

So the material the women would work on, would be material which was showing signs of deterioration. Not going to deteriorate straightaway, but certainly within maybe another year it would really go. Now, that meant that you had to have a programme where all films in the archive, which were given a location number, were registered on a test sheet. So you get year 1, year 5, year 10... And so you work through your collection. You go through basically the steps I outlined.

The key to preservation of nitrate film is to wind it, to let it breathe, and to check it. But if you ignore it, or you leave it, or you don't open it... This is where it becomes difficult. If you've got 5,000 cans, or 100,000 reels, of nitrate, who's going to do the winding? You need people – that's your resources. You need that examination, regularly. And that's in fact what happened in the end. Because the deterioration of nitrate needs money – that's why we had the 25-year nitrate scheme. And it's still going on. Because certain items will certainly be lost. I'm talking like an old archivist!

CAS: As an old archivist, there's another thing I wanted to ask you about nitrate: What about the pictorial quality of it, compared to copies, safety copies? What do you think about that? Do you think there is something special about nitrate, the way it looks up on the screen?

FH: You say silent movies, and people think Keystone Kops – soot and whitewash. The quality of the early film was superb. It was always something the examiners were amazed at. Now, a lot of people think that early film was scratched, but it wasn't. We have to remember that you are probably winding film, right, that has gone through a machine maybe 100, 200, 300 times. Now, think back. If you are talking about the early cinema – let's say we're talking about the 1910-ish period, and earlier than that – films as we know them weren't any longer than maybe 500 feet. They were short items. The audience didn't sit that long; you didn't make features. When they started doing 4 reels, 3-reelers, and even Chaplin's were 2-reelers – I mean, all that early stuff was never very long. Because in those early days, the people who made the films, also sold them to people in the fairgrounds, the show grounds. Now, after showing it 100 times, or 200 times, it was worn out.

When things really developed, the major companies would have what they called an "insurance print", which was really a fine grain. From that fine grain you could make negatives. When you sent your negative to the laboratory in order to make 200 copies, or 500 copies, for release across the country, you would know that after a certain period of time that neg would wear out. So you take your insurance print, or your fine grain, go back to the lab to make a negative, then produce another 500 copies. So you never used the original; but you had to make this one fine grain to protect it. Because if that got lost – and in certain instances, *they* did get lost – if that fine grain was on nitrate stock, they would seal it. I know major companies with film vaults that have actually said, "But it can't have gone unstable; the cans were *sealed*." "But did you ever take it out?" "No, no. We don't use it." You see, it was never allowed to be used. You'd say, basically, "Why didn't you break the camera tape, and wind the fine grain?" "Well, there's nothing wrong with it." Yes, there is. If you leave it long enough, you're not going to find a fine grain, you're going to find a tin of sticky glue, or powder. Which is what happened a lot; that was the only thing that they found. Then they had to go back to a print which had been run in a cinema. Subsequently they made a neg from that, whatever the blemishes were.

CAS: If you found something that was decomposing, how would you dispose of it?

FH: Well, there was a procedure for this. You just didn't take it out and put a match to it. What you had to do was to tell your records. You declared on a report that it had gone unstable and it was sticky. On it, it would say: destroy; burn; save what you can. It may only be frames, but if it is the only thing in existence, then 3 or 4 frames for illustration purposes could be valuable, as a record, or for illustration. That decision would be made by the powers that be. You would send the report up for discussion. They would make the decision. If it came back marked to be disposed, then you would put it all together and get it sent away to people who destroyed it.

CAS: Where would you send it, and who would destroy it?

FH: Well, there were people who specialised in it. There are two things about this. Nitrate film can be melted down, disposed of, to get silver from it. There were people who did this … that was their job. So you made contact with these people [i.e., the film-strippers]. But they wouldn't come to you, unless you'd got 500 reels, or 1,000 reels. You know, the more you had … Which is what they got from the commercial companies. Well, the film archive was very, very little. We *never* had that amount. We wouldn't allow that amount, if you see what I mean. For us, it would really have to have been in a state where you couldn't do *anything*. In other words, if there wasn't an image, there wasn't even the sign of a film, it looked like Nescafé.

In certain circumstances, in order to show our staff, we would take it out into a field and demonstrate, and we would burn film. You know, in a bucket of water. We would set 2 or 3 cans on top of each other, heat the ground first, put the 3 cans on top, and watch. You would be surprised, even with 3 cans. And they weigh about 7 pounds each; 1,000 feet of film in a can would likely be about 7 pounds. And even with that weight, when the bottom one would start or would ignite, it would have kept the gases in. It would *lift* the other two, and then it would explode, and the flames would come out like a flame-thrower, all around that can, and *shoot* the top one off the pile! You see the explosive power. So you would treat it with *respect*.

You would only have to do one demonstration, and believe you me, you would have a lot of very careful people. Which is the lesson. And I found factual demonstrations were much more… I won't say interesting, but it made people *think*.

CAS: Instructional.

FH: It was very instructional: they'd go back, and they would wind much slower. And the young boys with their wheelbarrows of 24 four cans of nitrate wouldn't run like a Grand Prix; they would walk very slow. But yes, there was a procedure that we followed.

That could be quite a job, undoing a piece of film that was sticky and didn't smell very nice, and was brittle, and would break off. And invariably you would find, like I described, that a particular nitrate can had been stood on its end. So you would find three-quarters of the film had an image, but that last quarter, where it was resting, would be all sticky, and glue. So you took a knife, and you could cut it up; you could literally cut through it. Then you were left with these other little bits. You *could* put it back together again if possible. You could, but you had gaps where that was, with loose frames. But, you could, depending on the subject, the year, and all the other background of it.

So, what was important from preservation techniques, from my point of view? I was a film historian in interest first, not really a technician. I learned to be a technician, or respect the work the technicians do. But from a historical point of view, my interest is: what was it, who made it, who handled it, how long was it originally? So I used to spend a lot of my time doing research, myself, *about* the films. Because I found when you fed that information to the people who were working with it, it made what they were working on much more interesting. Otherwise it may as well be chocolate bars, you know. You had to get them interested. It certainly wasn't for the money they stayed! It's the same in all organisations.

Frank Holland (centre) with NFA Deputy Curator Clyde Jeavons and Shirley Pluckrose (Personal Assistant to CJ) outside the Aston Clinton vaults in the mid-1970s (possibly at the party marking the 40th anniversary of Harold Brown's joining the British Film Institute).

Clyde Jeavons.

CAS: When you lived at Aston Clinton, did you and your family ever think, anxiously, oh, we're living right near nitrate, or were you just…

FH: No. I never really thought of it as a danger to us. When I say "us" that's not true. To *me* it was never dangerous. I never had any doubt at all, living among the highly explosive. I can tell you something. It might be official, I don't know. When the Home Office came down and investigated… I wish I'd kept a particular article, because a young man came down from a magazine, I think it was *Amateur Cine World*, or something like that. He came down, and did an article on the archive, and he did an article on me there. Somehow he got some information that was issued by the Home Office explosive people, saying that when they came down to examine the whole of that site they got an Ordnance Survey map, and they put a pencil in the middle of the site and drew a perimeter circle, and said, "If this site went up, we would lose half the village." They did a kind of circle… it must have been half a mile. Now, I lived 200 yards away… In fact, I used to park

341

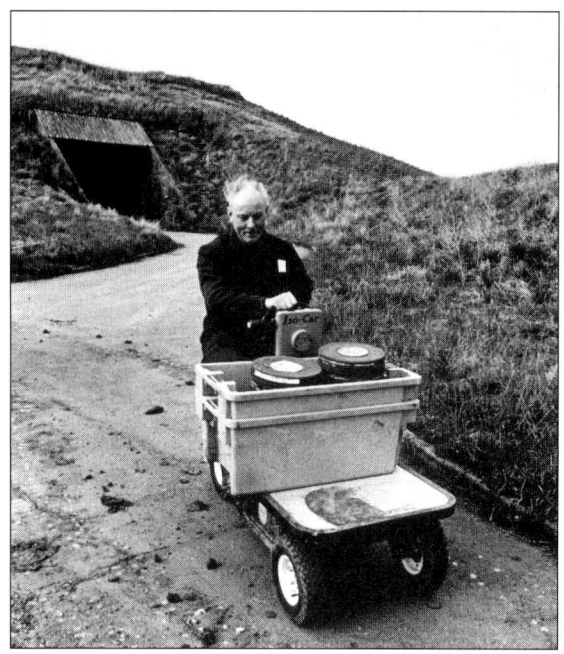

Moving film at the NFA's new nitrate store at Gaydon.

my car in a nitrate shed; we used to keep our coal there, in a nitrate shed. And strangely enough, it was only many, many years later, when we had a very, very hot summer, that the Fire Brigade actually came out, because the vault temperature reached a certain temperature. And they had to spray water onto the vaults to keep the temperature right.

That was unusual, though. Most of the time it wouldn't matter, because when you went into the vaults themselves, the vaults themselves were already within a field, with circulation of air above, between the roof. The vaults didn't go to the roof, they only went a certain height. So the circulation of air was all the way around. So you would have two lots of 24 vaults – 48 vaults, separated in two units of 24. When you would go in there, it was cooler, much, much cooler than outside. There was no air-conditioning.

CAS: Was there a generator, or a fan?

FH: No. Because the vaults were designed to keep the temperature and the circulation of air constant. The doors were always closed; you only went in to collect your film. The doors were always closed. And the ventilators had a hinge at the top. Now, that wasn't locked – that hinge was loose, so if anything happened it would blow open. So in a way, if there was air or a high wind... It used to scare my dog to death. At 12 o'clock at night I'd go around, and sometimes you'd hear the hinges rattling. But that was the only occasion.

So, this article written by this young man for this amateur magazine – I wished I'd kept it – caused a bit of trouble. Because when it reached the London area, they accused me of being interviewed. I said, "I wasn't interviewed. I spoke to him. I speak to everybody who is on an official visit. But the information he found out, I don't know where he got that information." I don't know how or where, but he was smart enough to get the information – but it didn't come from us, because we weren't even aware that those were the findings of the Home Office!

CAS: They didn't tell you?

FH: No. So with Home Office help, and a government grant, of course we found another government property, through the Air Ministry. At a disused airfield. Gaydon.

"35 was the real thing": A Film Collector Interviewed by Catherine A Surowiec.

This interview was conducted at the informant's home, in southern England, during the year 2000. For obvious reasons, the collector prefers to remain anonymous.

CAS: When did you get interested in film? Does that go back to childhood?

A: Yes. It's hard to remember ages, when you're 79. But I think it first happened when I was between 10 or 12. I went to a school in the evening, and people were showing off their hobbies and things ... One boy had a reel of film, and it was like the old song, "I took one look and then my heart stood still." I think once I saw that reel I was captured.

Then I was a bit crafty. I got my brother to buy a projector so that I could have a Hornby train ... Then when he started going around on his bike with Dad, I got hold of his projector and started to get bits of film. I suppose, again, I was between 10 and 12. And I started going to the cinema, of course.

CAS: Was that a 9.5 projector?

A: No, that was a 35mm projector, one of the little, what we now call "toy projectors", with a spool that would take about a quarter of a 1,000-foot reel, about 250 feet. It used an ordinary household lamp, this particular model, probably a 60 watt – might have been a 40, I can't remember. And you just turned a handle. You laced it up on a spool, pulled the gate open – it had a beater movement that would turn the film through as you turned the handle. It was marvellous. I've never forgotten it, and some of the bits of film I had with it.

CAS: Where would you get this film? Was it all nitrate?

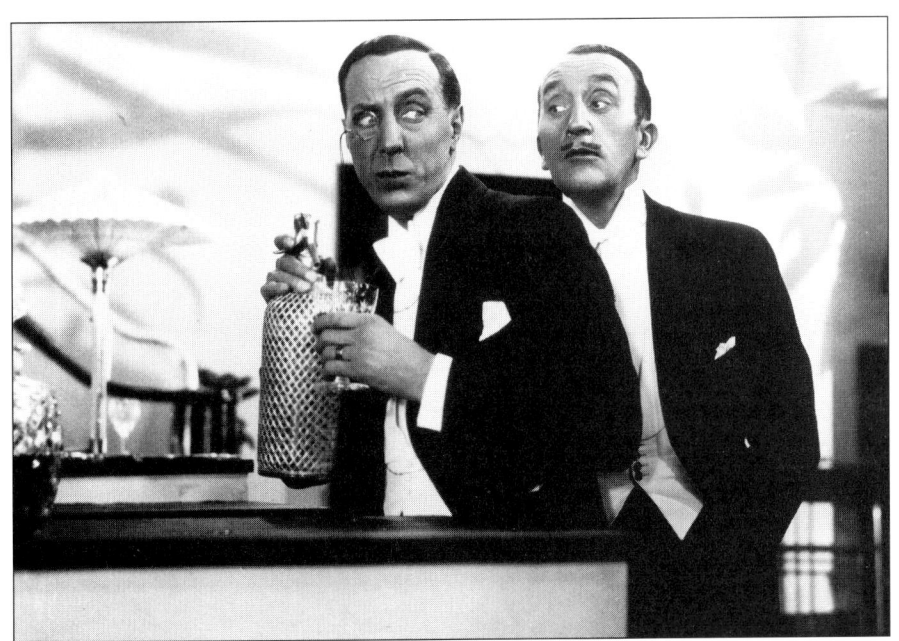

A scene from *Plunder* (1931).

343

A: Oh, everything then was nitrate, everything. You'd get the film... I remember we lived then in a flat, ... and there was a toy shop, just where there is a ... bank now on the corner, when you go into Chiswick [in west London]. There was a shop there, which dealt with trains, and all kinds of toys for children. I still remember the man smoking heavily, and opening the tins, and saying, "This one is half a crown, sir," and it was a bit of *Plunder*. But what these were, were toy shop films. I may still have somewhere one of the original cans. It had a sort of warning on it, about don't let it get near a naked light, and all that.

CAS: Yes, I wondered if you were told any cautions.

A: Well, that was the caution on the can. They would range from about sixpence to half a crown or 3 and 6, for the very big lumps, about 100, 200 feet.[1] The smaller ones were about 60, 100 feet. They just sold them openly in toy shops to children, to anybody. I think what happened, although I'm not certain, is that some children probably started a fire in a cellar. One firm I know used to lease out or sell acetylene lamps. Whether they had too strong a lamp or whatever, somehow the film caught fire, and they were killed or suffocated, or just injured, I don't really know; I'm just surmising. But there was a clamp-down then, and all the shops were told they couldn't sell them.

They were junked films. But they were good quality. It was stuff that was going to go to what they called the film-strippers, who recovered the silver from the nitrate. All they did was take a reel and just hack it up. Some of the girls sat there, I suppose, cutting 40 feet; they chopped it into a thing, and so it went...

CAS: So you think these originally would have come from the distributors?

A: I think some of them must have. I can remember trailers, and, as I say, this clip from *Plunder*, which must have come from Gaumont-British, or whoever was distributing the film. They probably thought, it's two or three years old, and I suppose they thought it had no more commercial life to it. It's had its Sunday show, it's got to be junked. The toyshop people obviously offered them more money for it, so they did it that way. But then they were finally told they couldn't get any more that way.

A scene from *La Merveilleuse Vie de Jeanne d'Arc* (1929).

BFI Collections – Stills, Posters & Designs, London. 183093.

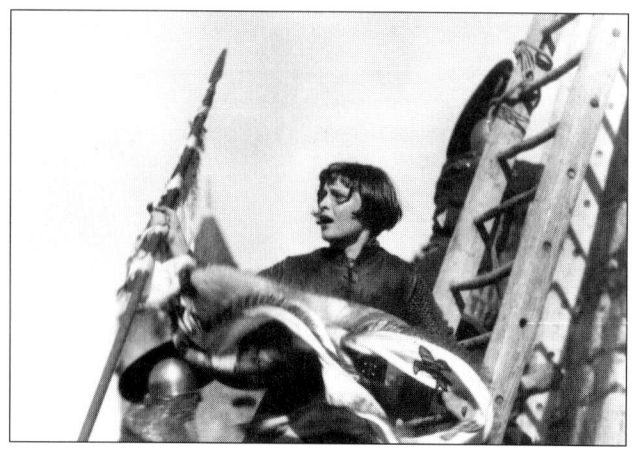

Chiswick had the toy [shop]. My second source was another shop... that used to get things in from Denham, junk and stuff. I'll always remember, I nearly got a Disney cartoon, and I was terribly excited about getting that. It was *The Old Mill*, a lovely early colour one. A copy did turn up later, but somebody else beat me to the post and got it. But I did get some wonderful stuff there, including an old reel of *St Joan the Maid*, the silent film – not the Dreyer one with Falconetti, but the other one, the French one. I forget the name of it now, but I've got it now on video.

CAS: The one with Simone Genevois? [*La Merveilleuse Vie de Jeanne d'Arc*, 1929]

A: Yes. It's a wonderful film. I had a reel of that, and curiously enough... This is not specifically about nitrate, but about trying to make it last. It had what they called metal sprockets. All the way along were stamped on it something like a metal sprocket, rather like those things you have through a Dymo machine for labelling. It was an invention that they'd obviously tried, and there was an odd reel of another feature with that. It was murderous to join, too, because you had to peel it up. And of course it would have worn the projector's sprockets. But the film would never have worn out, been torn and all that, because they were strong. So it was an interesting invention.

Later, I lost all my films, during the War. We lived in a flatlet, and I didn't think it was safe to store them there. In fact we did have a piece of shrapnel come in. A huge piece of paving-stone, four flights up, came through the top flat and right into our sitting-room, smashed one of these chairs to match-wood, and the table now in the kitchen got the end cut off from it. I decided, well before then, that I couldn't keep them there in the War. So I took them to a friend's garden in Chiswick, bought a coal bunker, and shoved them in there. When I came home from leave I found the whole lot were burnt, but not these metal sprockets, because they wouldn't burn, you see. The cans were charred, of course, and the transit cases, too, but all the film – whoosh, it had gone, every inch! So I started all over again, in 1946.

CAS: So his garden was hit?

A: I still to this day can't remember. I don't think his mother knew. He was in the International Brigade... His mother, who looked after the house and everything while he was away, said she didn't know. So I've never known if it was a bomb, or kids got a match and threw it in. I can't be sure, but I think a bomb was the most likely. But how it got into the lid I could never tell. So that was the end of that. And I started again in 1946, through Bert Langdon giving me addresses...

CAS: Ah, Bert Langdon. Now that's a name I've heard, because Kevin Brownlow used to know him in the early days...

A: I'll tell you about him. Yes, he was my chief, almost my first, mentor. I can't remember now who introduced me to him, but there was a circle of people, including a chap called Stan Smith, who had a projector in the cupboard. I met Bert, I think, through the *Exchange and Mart*, he was advertising in it. Anyway, I got in touch with him, and he wrote me letters. I've still got several of them, not all, because I'm a hoarder.

He used to have a Power's Cameragraph, which had a beautiful action... It was so beautifully made, it was like a clockspring. You could turn it, and it would take almost any rubbish-condition film through. A guy... called Sebastian brought him some stuff, about 40 feet with nothing at either side, hoping that would go through, but that was asking too much. But it was wonderfully good on awful old silent stuff. What he used to do was sit there, and he would have a take-up spool, an automatic mechanical one; he pushed a cardboard reel by hand. So with one hand he was turning, and at the same time he had two record players. He had 3,000 78s. He loved music-hall and musical comedy. And he would put these 78s on, which he'd chosen specially to blend with the film. He had some wonderful silents. He had *The Girl from State Street* [original American release title: *State Street Sadie*], a 1927 Warners gangster film. And he had Charlie Chaplin's *The Circus*. And *My Best Girl*, with Mary

Pickford. And *The Heart of Wetona*, with Norma Talmadge. He had some wonderful silent stuff. And, as I said, he had this way of doing it with all these records. He managed all these beautiful shows. Just pulled the curtains with a string, I think. He was a member of the Music Hall Society, and he knew W MacQueen-Pope, the theatre [historian]... Bert chiefly specialised. He had a wonderful collection of music-hall records... He loved musical comedy as well. He had all those old shows – you know, the old Columbias with the original artists in the shows. It was a wonderful collection...

CAS: When did he die? Do you remember? Was it a long time ago?

A: Sometime in the 1970s. He had a stroke. He had a lot of bad luck. He was carrying a film – I think it was *The Rat* or *The Return of the Rat* – to have it printed, and he left his jacket on the train, and lost £100, I think, and his holiday ticket, and then he lost this reel of film. I suppose all the worry gave him a stroke, and he never really... He managed to project a bit, but he kept banging his arm to try to get it up, but he never really recovered. The BFI... didn't give him much of a job. They knew about his expertise, but they just gave him a job as a packer down in the Lower Marsh... I mean, they should have given him a job in research, because he had marvellous knowledge...

What more can I tell you about Bert? The film collection went to a chap called Carl... I think some of the films have come on telly, because Bert had a very large collection of the ABs [Biographs], you know, the Griffith single-reelers and all that. He really liked them, and he had a good collection of them... I have one or two that have come my way, but as I say I haven't collected many silents...

CAS: Talking about collecting after the War: Once they started to phase out nitrate, did it become easier to collect it?

A: For a while, yes. But it became a sort of "dead man's shoes". After the War, I got in touch with Bert Langdon again, and he gave me the address of a man in Nottingham who had some films. I got a copy of one of my favourite films around, I can remember it 50 years after: *The Challenge*, a Luis Trenker mountaineering film. And the chap said, "This has not been through the hands of the amateurs." I still kept the original cans for years, but it's now doubled up in four parts. It's one of my favourites. And I've tried to keep the flare away from it, with another copy.

But going back to the ease of collecting nitrate after the War. One or two people in the Midlands helped me out with copies of films. The big one was... a man who lived in Leicester. Now, he was the sort of man who'd had all sorts of deals during the War... And we got to hear of his address, and started to write to him, and he would send us films. Roughly, a 7-reel film, which would run just about an hour and ten minutes, would cost about £13. That sounds an absolute giveaway now, but of course in those days it was rather a lot. So I got a few of the specials from him, but I waited, really, until he was giving up, some years later. And then all his collection was sold to someone down in South London, and I was buying them then at 7 and 6 a reel. I was buying a film like *Inquest*, a neat little British Boulting Brothers film, for about 50 shillings. I also managed to get all the trailers that he'd sent down with the residue of the stuff, which I rescued for my collection. Another chap in the Midlands had bought a lot trailers from him, but decided he wouldn't go ahead with the hobby, and he sold me those.

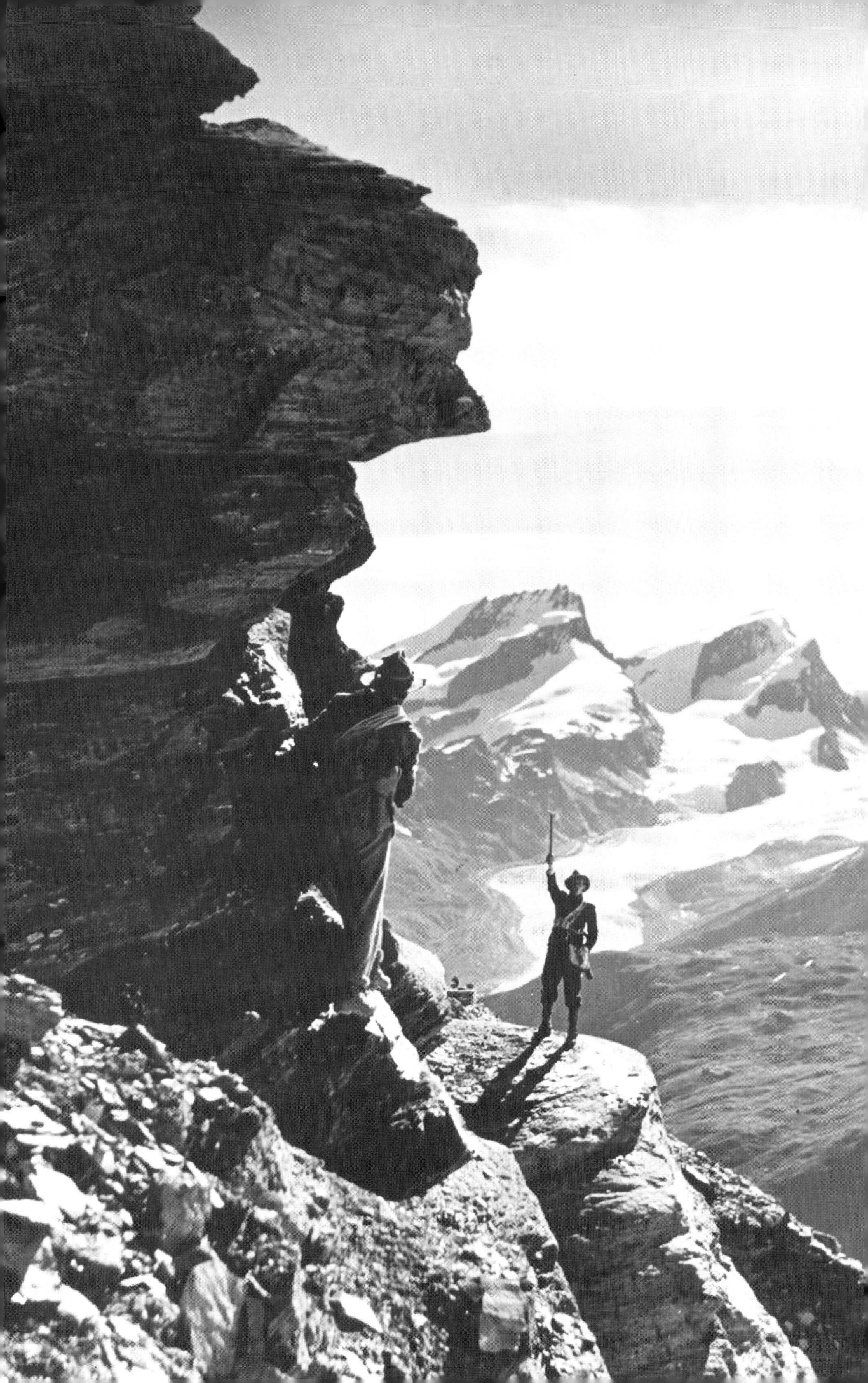

Well, it was a case of slowly becoming "dead man's shoes". You'd swap with collectors, and there were more collectors in those days, after the War, doing films, than there are now. Well, I mean the ones doing them now... The percentage is gradually becoming more and more safety films, and of course the only safety film you can easily get is tons and tons of modern stuff, which doesn't greatly interest me at all...

CAS: How were these films transported? If you went to a dealer, and bought some, how would you get them back home? Because I think legally they are not supposed to be taken on public transport.

A: That's true. And this is true with a film that we sent out to an archive, which was nitrate. A certain friend – I'd better not give his name even – delivered it, but I brought it back. It was only three little bits... Somehow I found out that Eastman Kodak was looking for a film I'd got, called *The Lottery Bride* [1930]. I'd got two copies, one a shortened version, black-and-white all through, the other the full version, with a Technicolor ending. And they said they hadn't got the Technicolor ending, and they'd like to see the credits of both copies. So I gave the copy to this brave man, who took it out. They kept it for 3 years... In the end, after pushing them, they brought back the original bits. I mean, the copies I had were ruined without them. I was arranging a swap of the film anyway; I'd promised it to someone, and I wanted to get rid of it. To my way of thinking it's one of the worst films ever made. I mean, even though you'd think with Friml music, and Jeanette [MacDonald] in it, and all the rest of it... But the Technicolor bit is interesting, of course, for its time. So in the end, in desperation, because it would have been so much, I took a chance and brought the three little bits back... when this chap brought them to Pordenone...

Normally I would never take nitrate on a plane. But you can send it; there are special planes that will take it, by certain freightage. They will take it under conditions on boats and that, but it's got to be known and done. The normal way, I suppose, of sending it, and the way in the cinemas, was always in transit cases. These were aluminium outside or corrugated steel, with a wooden sort of thing inside, and the cans then went into that. That was the normal way the transport men used to bring films to the cinemas, unlike now. You couldn't do then like you can do today, just carry them under your arms, a reel in a sort of plastic can. I mean, as it won't set fire, it's OK.

CAS: But it was clearly labelled that it was nitrate?

A: Well, not in the early... The film itself, usually said it on the sides. Not every one has got it, but practically every film, every foot along, it says "Nitrate film".

CAS: Yes, but would the transit boxes be labelled?

A: Well, yes, I imagine they would be. I've got some of them. I imagine they would have had... I know it said, "Cinematograph Film/Keep in a Cool Place"; I know it said that on them. But I don't remember that the boxes were always labelled. But the transport men had a key to the cinema in case it was closed. They could unlock it, open the gates, and put the new programme in and take the old programme away. And that was how it was done.

CAS: And was there a limitation as to how much footage you could have at one time on the premises?

A: Yes, I think it's all down in the *Kine Yearbook*. But I think, from memory, it was something like only 4,000 feet of film could be in the . . . 2,000 feet only could be kept in a rewind room. The film had to be kept in those bins, with a spring clip to clip on and close on it for safety. And you could only have one reel to work on in the rewind room, and two on the projectors. You'd have one running, and you would be threading up the other one. And as soon as the one running was finished it was brought to the rewind room, then wound back and put back into these steel things. So of course "No Smoking" was obviously the thing around that. But of course you couldn't help the bombs [during the War]. I mean, there were one or two cases – I never knew, and I didn't want to know, directly of them – when, you know, there was a direct hit, and the projectionist must have been blown up, with the films and that. But that didn't seem to happen very much. I mean, if it happened a lot, I suppose they would have had to close the cinemas.

       The Germans had safety film long before we did. Some of our early ones were very brittle, even in the 1950s you had to watch out because of them being brittle. I've got an old safety one called *Old Sussex* . . . I ran it once, and it snapped because it was so brittle. But I've got another one. It's a lovely film, called *How Talkies Talk*, which I've been told is a much better instructional film on that subject than even the American ones or other ones. It shows you an old projectionist, and they split the screen, and they show a lovely number, "You Ought to See Sally on Sunday". It's not actually a clip from the film . . . but it shows you the making of it. And that's safety. I imagine they intended it to be shown in schools. It's made by Gaumont-British Instructional. But there weren't many. I mean, $99^{1}/_{2}$% were nitrate, until the 50s.

CAS: Going back to the days when you were buying things for toy projectors. You were given those in little cans, in tins?

A: Yes, I think I have one. Before you came I was trying to look and see.

CAS: But were you told, as children, that these were dangerous, don't play with them . . . ?

A: I think it said it on the film. I'll let you look in there later, but I couldn't find one for sure. I think one or two have come to me and I've kept them, but I'm not certain.

CAS: Because you hear of children playing with them, and setting them alight, using them as fireworks . . .

A: Well, yes, they used to use them for making fireworks. I had an example of that, it reminded me, on the Isle of Wight. But I think these had something like "Keep Away from Naked Lights and Flames", or something like that. It wasn't terribly strong wording, I suppose; perhaps it just wasn't thought about. But I think that they had warnings. I'll try and find one and let you see one . . .

       Now, what happened, actually: when I was teaching on the Isle of Wight for a year, I went down to a bizarre sort of shop in Ryde, one of those sort of shops with all sorts of holiday stuff, flicker books, and everything else. So I went inside. In the window was a sign about some cinema film: "35mm, 4 feet a penny", or something like that. I went inside and saw the chap there... I started to go over to see him. And eventually he had some films he'd gotten from renters. He had a copy of a Balinese film, 1931, which I bought from him, and he had a film which I exchanged, *Dirigible*, the Columbia one, 10 reels. And he had an old heavy Italian Prevost projector. But, as I say, I think he was selling those little bits. He probably knew that children would take them away and strike a match and see how they fared. But I suppose that at 4 feet, unless it was put in the wrong place, it wouldn't do too much trouble.

Have you seen, by the way, the Italian film about the archive? It was shown last year in Pordenone, and at the Nitrate show at the NFT.

CAS: Oh, *The Suitcase of Dreams?* [*La Valigia dei Sogni*]

A: Yes.

CAS: Oh, that's a lovely film.

A: But, mind you, rather like *The Smallest Show on Earth*, there are a lot of technical faults. I mean, for instance, when the chap's robbing the archive, or taking the bits that have only got to be destroyed – it's not really robbing, but preserving them. But he just sort of rolls the reels down, and takes away 300 feet off it. In actual fact, unless he'd taken the whole film, he'd only have a clip, he wouldn't have the complete feature. So you would have thought they would have got that right. But, I mean, in *The Smallest Show on Earth*, there are quite a few errors. You see them sort of re-feeding projectors, and not loading them again, and all of this. You know, if you want to be carpy... But it's a lovely film.

You've seen the Italian one, I'm sure, *Cinema Paradiso*, the long version? The long version has all about what happens at the end. You know at the start he's booking to go away on a journey? Well, in the long version you see him go on the journey, and he meets the girl of his dreams, and they have a long chat in the car, talking. It's very, very useful and interesting, and it makes more sense of the ending. I think it's much better. But, mind you, the short one is very good, too. But the Director's Cut is worth seeing. You might still be able to get it; I've got a video of it ... but they didn't make many copies of the film, so it's doubtful if many will get out to amateurs, but you never know...

CAS: Speaking of collecting: I know we talked about this before, but I want us to get it down for the record. If you have a film, and it starts to go off, what do you do with it? What do you think is the best way to deal with it?

A: Well, as I said before, some of them may not go off in the same way. I've got one reel of an early Humphrey Bogart film, which curiously enough has never been shown, and it looked bad. I kept watching it, and opening it, and it doesn't seem to have gone. But most of them ... When you see what I call "the fatal flare". Have you seen examples of it?

CAS: What do you call "the fatal flare"?

A: Well, it goes in different ways. Sometimes you get it, it goes brown, and you get little gases bubbling up. Sometimes it goes all yellow. Sometimes it burns a hole through; it's so strong it will burn a hole right through the can. It's brutal stuff. I could show you some. We burnt some of the worst stuff when we were burning the leaves. But I can show you some of them out in that shed, if you want to see them, or a few not so bad, which I've moved to the terrible bedroom; when they're there, you know...

When it starts to go, there is only one thing you can do. You can slow the progress by cutting out ... every bit of a flare, and joining it up. I'll tell you an example. Years ago, I got a print of *Queen Victoria*, which is *Sixty Glorious Years* and *Victoria the Great*. They made more footage out of it by putting the two together. Now the black-and-white is going badly on the ends of two reels, but the Technicolor doesn't seem to have changed. That's the thing about it. But in the black-and-white, there is one bit where they are dancing on the ballroom floor, and now it has a stuttering sound, because there is a splice every 4 inches. Because that's all you can do. Cut bits out. And also leave it in the air. You can't really have everything in the air, even if you're the only one in the house, but that's about the best. And the other thing is, especially if it's a film that nobody else has got, or you haven't got, is to get it onto video, which, again, may not last forever. Not even we last forever.

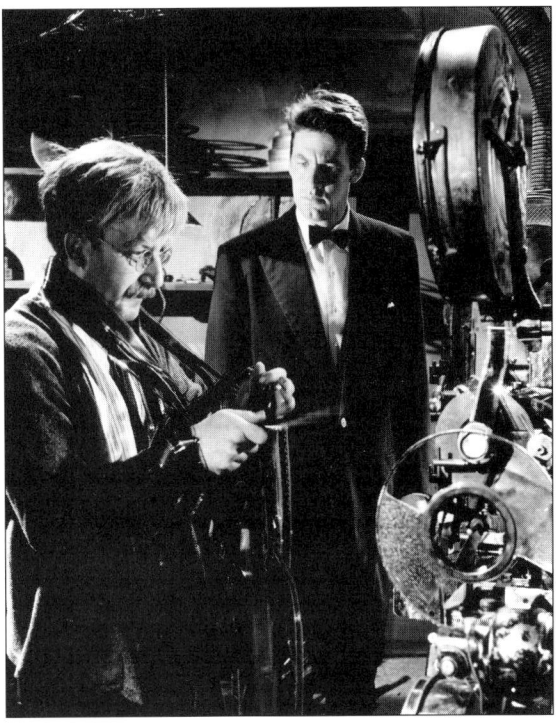

A scene from *The Smallest Show on Earth* (1957).

BFI Collections – Stills, Posters & Designs, London. 183093.

But that's all you can do, you see. Some are worse than others... *Quartet*, for instance. I had a trailer that went. The whole film went very quickly. It was on a cheap Ilford stock, made about 1948.

[Bert once told us that] "Rank called up. J Arthur wants to see a print of *The Wicked Lady*, in his projection booth," at wherever he lived. So Bert went up to Highgate, or Highbury, I think, where they were stored. And he said, every print had gone sticky; great mushrooms growing out of them. But, of course, they managed to find a negative, and print one for His Lord and Master.

I've got a print, and it hasn't yet gone, but you never know. I've got a nice film – which I've got a good trailer for, and I've got it on video – *The Stars Look Down*. That's starting to go. Another one is *The Prisoner of Zenda*, both copies. One copy was a throw-out copy; it had a fault, the sound on one reel goes bad. It's sad when it's something that's...

I [had] a lovely Betty Boop cartoon... The black-and-white was going, and now it's just a solid lump; I've just burnt it. Once they go, you almost have to break them like coconut ice sort of thing. There is a great mass of white stuff, and you can only peel off the rims, and then keep slicing.

I remember this chap down at Deal [in Kent] who died.... He kept begging me to repair his copy of *Intermezzo*, but I said, "I'm sorry; every 4 inches there is a flare, and then another flare. It would be a mess to look at and to go through." Of course, we didn't have video then. I don't how long I can keep mine. I've only shown it once, this other copy that's come in; one reel was completely gone out of the eight.

CAS: Are there certain periods of film stock that you think are more apt to go than others?

A: I think it depends on a matter of factors, rather like doctors looking at... If the film was well washed, and that. For instance, I met a chap who was giving a lecture on Broncho Billy, G M Anderson, the cowboy star of the early movies. And I said, "I've got one with all the credits, the original certificate, but the end is slightly missing." And he said, "Well, we are using a clip of that, but I would love to see it." And he came over and saw it. That's about 1911, and that's still OK. It just depends on the washing, and the rest of it.

CAS: I know I've heard that British films during the War used a cheaper stock.

A: Well, this is true of the ones like just after the War, like *The Wicked Lady* – what was it, about 1946? I haven't got very many of the Harold French films, but you may be interested in seeing this one since you're interested in him. It's not a full sequel [to *Quiet Wedding*], but it's the same sort of story, *Quiet Weekend*. With Derek Far... That's a nice film. The critics said of it, "Trouble is, it's too quiet and nothing much happened." But I loved Barbara White in it, I think she is superb. And in the Quinlan book you'll find that practically every film that French directed, Quinlan gives him a nice pat on the back. I think he was probably a better director... One film he made was a lovely, lovely film, *Dear Octopus*. According to what I've heard, Margaret Lockwood, although she's dead now, wouldn't allow it to be on telly, or her people who come after her. Well, it almost made me cry out, I was so *moved* by that film. Beautifully acted, a wonderful story. I'd love to get that on video. But if it's never shown, what can you do? I've got enough, really. There is always one more around the corner...

CAS: Going back to the physical condition of that trailer, the best thing is for it to get some air, and to use it?

A: Yes, those are the two things. And the cutting out. Those are the three good things. But, of course, the trouble is, how, with so much, can you? I think you have to be ruthless. I remember going down to help a friend... He had loads of newsreels ... and I went through them... I remember once I had some mute junk on the floor, and he came in and said, "Oh, what you did is dreadful." I said, "Well, it's a matter of time. This is junk stuff. You'll never want to show it, you'll never probably have time." I said, "I've just got it down as mute, you know, to see it go through. There is nothing particular on it, but I just brought it down, just to check there is nothing on the end of the reel." You have to. I mean, you don't want to, you want to help, to save everything, but...

CAS: Do you try to inspect them every once in a while, or is this when you happen to take them out to use them?

A: Well it's the Forth Bridge job really. If you saw what I have here...

CAS: No, don't worry!

A: But if you saw it, if you want me to show you, I've got approximately about

250 features, and a good proportion, I'm sorry to say... I keep them because I like them, because of what the contents are. I've got good nitrates, and bad nitrates. I can show you the "hospital". In the "hospital", when they get to the danger stage, I don't... Hopefully, touch wood, they won't go.

Well, the answer to that is, I would like to, but at 79, with 3,500 videos... Two and a half thousand or so 78s; all those LPs; I don't know how many, 600 or 700 cassettes; not to mention open-reel tapes... I used to have a rewinder in the kitchen; it's now in the den at the minute, but I used to wind there. I got help to clear the den table, which isn't very good now, but it gradually gets worse. But it is a nightmarish job... So I try with the stuff I show, and I'm always grateful for the ones I've worked on, because some of those that have been worked on, I go through them, as I said, before I show them, and then I write on every lead, checked, and the date checked. But it's all the four-devil word T-I-M-E.

CAS: Do you find that taking these precautions of cutting out the bits – does that prolong their life?

A: Well, it has done. I had a film made all round near Ely Cathedral. It was a 4-reel documentary. And the archive from down there ... came over, and I let them borrow my print, and they managed to juggle it around. Now that print had been saved from being very bad, because ... I cut out every bad frame... I wouldn't like to say, but it may have gone now. They sent me a very nice video of it...

[Someone] once said to me, "Oh, I don't really like to see video; I like to see *film*." I mean, I'd like to own a place as large as ten Buckingham Palaces, to have all my videos on film! ... I don't like 16 [mm] much, although I've got some 16. I've got stuff on 16 that I don't think I would ever get on 35, and haven't got on video, and so I keep it. But I don't like it. Used to call that "bootlace", and 8mm "shoelace"; but 35 was the real thing!

CAS: Another thing I was going to ask: When do you get to the point when you look at something and say, "I really just have to destroy this." When does it get to that point?

A: Well... When it's a solid lump. When it's like those that are all out there. They are all going to be collected, hopefully, next week by [someone who] ... can get the silver out.

You get to the point where the ones in the upstairs bedroom, the "hospital" – if you want to come and have a look now – I've told you all my secrets, you might as well have the lot, and come up and see them. Some of them, it's just one reel. This *Underneath the Arches*, 3 reels seem to be OK. But you can never be certain, with one that's gone, without running it right through. Because even though the outside looks OK, when you get to the point and you've got these great gouges and stuff, you know; they are a solid mass...

CAS: After that, once they are gone, or going, what precaution do you take? Do you take them out of the house?

A: Well, they go into this outside shed, which used to be an outside toilet. It's now just a shed for them really, because the toilet is gone. And I just put them in there.

CAS: Do you ever try to bury them, or...?

A: Well, no. I burn a few, like we did one Friday, with the leaves. No, the only way is to... I mean, I'm lucky that [someone] can take them; otherwise, well, I'd have to slowly burn a bit at each time, and it would be a long job. But when they are in a solid lump, they don't burn nearly as brutally. Have you ever seen a short film called *This Film Is Dangerous?*

CAS: Yes.

A: Well, they show it burning, and they say you can never put it out.

CAS: Yes. They try all different ways. They throw a blanket over it, foam, everything, and it just keeps going. It may be stifled for a little while, but you can see the smoke coming through, because it makes its own oxygen.

A: It's terrible stuff.

CAS: This guy who comes to pick the films up, is he able to take them to a place where...?

A: Well, he said he had a fire with the last lot he had from me, so it's amazing that he's still coming; but I don't suppose it did much harm. You see, what was done... This was the whole thing in the cinemas years ago, and in some of those early *Kine Yearbooks* they mention them. Film-strippers, as they were called, they'll spare your old celluloid. They had to sign a contract with the film companies that they wouldn't sell or give them to anyone, that they would definitely do that. So the idea was, when the film renters decided it was junk, you know, had no commercial value, then, right, junk it. A lorry would come along, take it to the film-strippers' depot, and then they'd do whatever chemical process they needed to take the silver back from the film. That's why they sparkled so, and the prints looked so good, because of the silver in it.

CAS: Yes, I think nitrate has a certain visual quality which is really unique, because of the silver content. It really has a lot to do with it; it really looks luminous.

A: Well, Kevin told them, this should be saved. Again, it's all the storage and that. I think David Meeker said in one of his talks, "You know these renters realise there's no money in them; they hadn't bothered to check them, and that..." Have you seen that wonderful interview with Kevin Brownlow and Liam O'Leary? Oh, that's wonderful... I've got it on video. It's in two parts. First of all, Kevin talks about a phone call. He had to tell a lie to his headmaster that his grandmother was ill or something. It was a phone call [from Liam O'Leary] to say that the maker of *Napoléon* [Abel Gance] was in town, and Kevin could interview him. So Kevin sneaked off to interview him. Liam talks about going up to get film from the renters for the BFI. All the other people would do it with kid gloves, and wouldn't bother. We met this chap, Oliver Bell. I met him years ago, but the one after him – I forget his name now, but he had white gloves on when he looked at film... Even Penelope Houston, or someone, said, "Aren't you ever going to show any films? Have they been put away for the next thousand years or so?" Because he would only have perfect prints, and all the rest of it.

But dear old Liam, he went down to the renters. He told a wonderful story on the tape, how he came in and said, "I'm from the British Film Institute." He was told, "Oh yes, I suppose I can see you for 10 minutes, I suppose. You know, you realise you're wasting time from my work. These girls are not here to find films for you. They are here to help get these films distributed." Old Liam said, "I'll wait around until you're ready, sir," and sort of kowtowed a bit. And the chap said, "Where's the list, where's the list? Have that, have that, have that, have that, have that." But, I mean, the BFI wouldn't have got it. I mean, they were so long-nosed, and too proud, or whatever it is. In the early days, they were only after films like Grierson's *Drifters* and all that: "Oh, we don't want *feature* films, you know."

I was a bit cocky like that. When I came out of the War I went down to Pinewood to see a guy called Terry Trench. I was a bit nosey and airish. I wanted to be a film editor. "Well, I think we can give you a job as a tea boy, and then get you into documentaries, and after a while, if you are good, you might be editing some documentaries for 5 or 10 years, and then perhaps get to features." "Oh," I said, "I wanted to get onto features right away, not waste 10 years." I must admit I wasn't very keen, because of the travel.

Then I tried once again. I was teaching in a school on the Isle of Wight, and ... a very nice fellow came down to see his son. He worked for ITV. He came here and saw some of my films, and he said, "Stick to it as a hobby. It's a rat race; I don't know if you would be very happy with it." So I took his advice ...

Years ago, I found out through the Meccano magazine an advertisement for Filmways company, 57 Station Road, Leystonstone. And I hobbled up by the old early train, the old second-class carriage train to Liverpool Street. One day I made a mistake, and I went Shepherd's Bush Underground station, carrying a can of film. And the booking clerk said, "You can't take that on this train, sir." So I hurriedly rushed away and got a bus, and put it in my big pocket. I can't remember now, but anyway that was the start of the story ...

An awfully nice man was there, though. He had two huge Alsatian dogs, rushing around in cages in case you tried to take anything. But I always remember the beautiful copies of newsreels, Pathé newsreels of the First World War, they had. What they'd obviously done was found somewhere where they could buy up a lot of stuff. They had marvellous lists of old features. And the Chaplins were always double the price of everything else. I couldn't afford too many things, but I remember buying a film called *His Honour Redeemed*, with Lou Tellegen and Sessue Hayakawa and his wife in it. I always remember the wonderful intertitle Tellegen said: "If you harm one hair of this lady's head, England will visit you with a punishment more terrible than you can conceive." And I think that's about the most fabulous intertitle in a silent film that I've ever seen in all these years! It was a ragged film, and I worked away, patching it. At first I tried patching it with cotton, but of course I soon learned that that wouldn't wind through. We had no tape then; I can't remember how I did the patches, but I know I did work some AV cuts and did all I could to save it. But of course the flames got it.

The English title of the other one was *An Ancient Evil* ... It was the most beautiful copy. It had "Transatlantic Film Company", the words for the old Universal Company, on it, and it was the most beautiful print, tinted. I've always remembered all the scenes at the end. I never thought I would see it again, but a few years ago in Pordenone they showed *Shoes*, in a very bad copy from Czechoslovakia: I believe they've found some more tinted footage, but how much I don't know. But it's a superb film. She [Lois Weber] must have had a bit of a fixation with shoes, though, because a friend of mine [who] sends me tapes from Ireland, sent me one of hers. And it's all about how people who work in shoe factories get more money than university people. I don't know what it's called, but I've got it in my collection if I can find it.

CAS: *The Blot.*

A: Yes, that's it, I think, *The Blot*, yes. I went up to see what they had at the NFT of hers because I was very interested in that.

CAS: So your print has gone?

A: Of that? Totally. I mean, that went in the War, in 1946; just went, blown up completely. No hope.

CAS: Oh, one of those films you left?

A: In the coal bin in Chiswick.

As I say, you didn't see in the kitchen, but there is an edge off that kitchen table, and one of these chairs was smashed to match-wood. It was a landmine; it hit, and it brought up a piece of paving-stone ... right through the roof, three flights above, right through the flat above (lucky they weren't there), right into our sitting-room, and smashed the chair to match-wood, and I think dug a hole in the carpet. I can't remember all the details now.

CAS: Was it at night?

A: It was a night raid; an air raid at night.

CAS: Luckily you weren't sitting at the table ...

A: We were down in the basement, and we heard the crash, a terrific crash. It was about five flights down ...

CAS: ... Did you ever hear of [any collector] who had an accident?

A: I've heard of [some] who had. Not anyone terribly close to me. There was a chap ... somewhere out near South London [who] had an accident. He had a film, and it had gone on the floor. And there had been a soldering iron alight, and it had hit on that. He lost the reel, but he didn't lose anything else.

CAS: That was lucky.

A: Very lucky! And I have heard of other ones, other people who have had fires at home, and that ...

CAS: I guess it's usually caused by film jamming in the gate?

A: Well, a friend once said to me, "Take up all the film. Don't have all those bits of film lying around." [Another friend] told me, "Get anything away from the electric switches, just in case there's a kickback." It may be one in a thousand, but once it's started . . .

[A friend of mine] in Ireland lost all his nitrate and pretty well blew up the whole house. He had everything out of cans, and I think his wife or someone went in and switched on an electric clothes drier. What happened I don't quite know. Probably they left it on, or it wasn't switched off properly. Somehow or other it caught the open film, and blew the whole thing. It took 6 hours for the firemen to put the lighted bit out, and it melted the top of he fire engine . . . It was lucky it didn't break his windows, because his house was only about 40 yards away from the barn . . . He has now rebuilt [the house], just the bottom, because it was beautifully built stone. And it stood up, after it was all over.

They were lucky. That was the most frightening one I know of. I've heard of one or two, and they are frightening. On the other hand, people say if you store petrol in the house it's just as bad. And they say of electricity, it's a good servant, but a dangerous master. So one hopes. I'm glad I'm getting old, so there won't be too much longer to worry. But for people who just come in and sit in the seats here, and sort of get the old fun . . . they don't know how lucky they are. But I don't talk much about it to the neighbours . . .

This little film I had out ready, by Michael Powell. It's called *The Love Test*. It's about the laboratories.

CAS: Yes, that's right. There's a wonderful opening in a lab.

A: Yes, there's a few bits on that at the start. But I've got other bits on films, where they say... I've got a bit where they do show, it may be *This Film Is Dangerous*, where they show and tell you all the horror stories. But all those I wouldn't show to my neighbours . . . I play it down to them. I just tell them, "Oh, well. They self-destruct. You just have to get rid of them."

Notes

1. These references are to Britain's old pre-decimal currency, in which the pound was subdivided into 20 shillings and the shilling into 12 pence. 3 and 6 (also written 3/6 or 3s. 6d.) meant three shillings and sixpence, 17.5p after decimalisation; "half a crown" was 2 and 6, two shillings and sixpence, 12.5p.

The Common Hazards of Fire Insurance

The following paragraphs are taken from the section "Hazardous Goods" (pp.45-51) in a book with the above title, written by W G Kubler Ridley, of the Legal Insurance Company, and published in London by Sir Isaac Pitman and Sons, Ltd, in 1924 (second edition). The extracts are reprinted here with the kind permission of Pearson Education Ltd, successors to Sir Isaac Pitman and Sons. (Submitted by colleagues at the New Zealand Film Archive.)

Editor's Note: The alternating emphasis between film and non-film hazards reflects the original sequence of the book, and is in itself a useful reminder that the cinema trade in this period was not the only consumer of celluloid. I have not been able to trace the exact date and location of the fire in Newcastle referred to towards the end of these extracts. (RS)

Celluloid.   Celluloid is prepared by treating gun cotton or collodion wool with camphor, after which it is pressed and rolled, the manufacture of course being a most dangerous process. It is thus easy to understand why it is such a dangerous substance, and although it is not readily explosive it is one of the most inflammable articles in general use. The burning point of celluloid is 180° F., which is not such a very great heat, and it decomposes and flashes at 282° F., and the same result ensues when it is placed in contact with flame or incandescent bodies. All celluloid articles, whether in store in shops or in use, must be sheltered from the rays of the sun or from radiant heat. Celluloid was formerly known as xylonite, and the two are identical, and it would be difficult to name all the articles which are now made of celluloid. It takes the place of horn for combs and similar articles; it takes the place of bone and ivory for knife handles, paper cutters, piano keys, and a thousand and one similar articles. It is used as a substitute for glass; it is used for pictures and advertisements, photographic films and cinematograph films, artificial amber, varnishes, zapon lacquer, even for waterproofing textiles, and also as a leather substitute such as pegamoid. A terrible fire occurred in London a few years ago, when several girls lost their lives. They were working on celluloid articles, and cutting and printing on celluloid. The dust and refuse cuttings would be most inflammable, and without doubt spread the fire with alarming rapidity.

The fire was caused by the use of sealing wax at a naked light for packeting Christmas cards, and it is easy to understand the danger of doing this with such an inflammable substance about.

Shop fires have been known which almost without doubt have originated from the rays of the sun being concentrated upon some celluloid article, and a case is known where a little girl who wore a celluloid comb in her hair was sitting in front of a fire reading, when the comb suddenly took fire and she was severely burned...

The trade in cinematograph films requires separate consideration, for the following reasons. Whilst the composition of cinematograph films does not differ from that of an ordinary photographic film, it presents a much larger surface than any other celluloid article. The exigencies of the trade require the concentration of great quantities of film at various exchange centres once or twice weekly. The operations involved are of a different order, and are conducted under conditions different from those involved in other celluloid industries.

Several fires which have occurred were of an alarming nature and endangered neighbouring tenants as well as causing great difficulty to the brigade. In three of them the flames spread to the other side of the road. There can be no doubt that if a large quantity of film becomes involved in a fire, a very serious conflagration is liable to result, and it is necessary that steps should be taken to prevent this eventuality. The danger is greatly reduced if the reserve stock is stored in a fire-resisting chamber. On an examination of the premises after the serious fire which occurred in Shaftesbury Avenue, it was found that the film stored in the fire-resisting chamber was untouched.

Accidents due to the ignition of celluloid combs in the hair have been recorded from time to time. With a view to ascertaining the conditions under which such accidents may occur, experiments have been conducted with combs purchased at various centres in London and the provinces. In one series of experiments the comb was partly inserted in a small pad of cotton wool and the exposed portion placed in contact with an electric lamp. In every case, decomposition ensued after about three or four minutes' contact with the bulb of the lamp, but in no instance did actual inflammation occur. The decomposition was very rapid, and was accompanied by much charring of the cotton wool, a large gap being burned in the place where the comb had been inserted. In several cases the wool was found to be glowing after the decomposition of the celluloid, and upon being lightly blown upon, burst into flame. In a brisk draught, therefore, ignition would probably have occurred.

In another series of experiments, combs, inserted in cotton wool as before, were exposed in front of a gas stove. The temperature at the position selected for the comb was about 165° C. (329° F.). Decomposition ensued in almost every case in from one to two minutes, the results being similar to those in the experiments with electric lamps. The naked hand could be held for about 15 seconds without discomfort in the place in which the celluloid was heated, and when the hand was lightly covered with cotton wool or hair, the heat of the stove was scarcely felt in the time taken for the celluloid to decompose...

We might also mention a very serious fire at Newcastle, which resulted in the death of at least ten persons. The building was very lofty, and though well constructed and having floors of ferro-concrete, there appears to have been an open hoist through all floors, and the basement was occupied by a firm of film renters.

The fire may or may not have started in the film renters' premises, but the result was that the fire leaped up the open hoist, probably fiercely fed by the films, and giving out suffocating fumes in addition to the fierce heat, cut off the escape of a large number of persons who were driven to the upper floors.

There are several points of interest to mark here—
1. The hazard of an open hoist in a building otherwise well constructed.
2. The fierceness and rapidity of a film fire.
3. Overpowering fumes given off by burning celluloid...

So much attention has been given to celluloid because it has come into such general use as to form a very common hazard, and it should be thoroughly understood by everybody that, in reality, celluloid is a very dangerous article of common use.

Mort du Film

Editors' Note: We acknowledge with gratitude the help given by Michelle Aubert and her colleagues at the Archives du Film du CNC in providing the source material for this item. The translations are our own.

The French trade press appears on several occasions to have printed depressingly matter-of-fact views of what became of a film at the end of its useful life, several of them with the title "Mort du Film". Here is the first, which did not have that title but takes the same tone, from an issue of *Ciné-Journal* in May 1908:

Use of Old Films
The first step is to remove the layer of gelatin which is stuck to the celluloid.

The easiest method is to plunge the film into hot water. If the layer resists this procedure, one must use a solution of ammonium fluoride, made very slightly acid. The gelatin will come away much more easily than with the use of hydrochloric acid.

After this step, the celluloid can be used:

1st. As an artificial light source.
Celluloid, burning quickly, can be used instead of magnesium powder. The light it produces, being less actinic because it is yellowish, gives more agreeable pictures when orthochromatic plates are used.
To ensure rapid burning, the celluloid must be finely shredded.

2nd. Manufacture of a varnish.
This varnish is inexpensive, easy to apply, very transparent, and completely waterproof.
Mix: 500 cc of amyl acetate, 500 cc of acetone, and 15 grams of celluloid.[1]

Broadly speaking, the same sort of fate was still described as waiting for film almost two decades later, in the following determinedly cheerful account from 1924:

The Death of the Film
- Let's turn to the end of the film.
- Here we are: two years have passed; the film is senile. It is turning yellow, opaque, it is full of scratches and blemishes; it "rains" badly in a fine hall – or indeed in full sunshine (which results from scratches in the gelatin). At last it is condemned!
- What is done with it?
- Two things: either it is left to deteriorate slowly until it is decided to commit it to the flames together with several of its fellows; or, if its celluloid is worth the effort, the film is immersed in hot water and left in a steam-bath until the gelatinous emulsion which carries the pictures comes off of its own accord. Then the celluloid, restored to its raw material, is sent to be recast.
- It is recast?
- Oh, yes. Our celluloid factories work over it, and after a while the film re-emerges clear and perfect. Our laboratories re-coat it with fresh emulsion, and there it is – ready to be exposed again and embark on a

The manufacture of new film – one of the uses of recycled celluloid, according to the French film *L'Age du Plastique* (1943).

Archives du Film du Centre National de la Cinématographie, Bois d'Arcy.

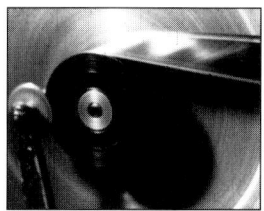

- new career!
- For two years!
- Just so – assuming that it comes out well! [This is a poor equivalent for the original French pun, as the same phrase is used in French to mean both "turn out well" and "be well shot". – *Translators' note*.]
- So, in summary: this film, born in a moment – perhaps an inspired moment – of great art, ends its days in a sorry state!
- Like everything to do with art, sir, it enjoys but a passing glory, and its fame leaves it ... with its emulsion!
- In a hot bath?
- In a Turkish bath!
- It is dead indeed! [The original here offers another pun, this time completely untranslatable: "maure", as in "un bain maure" (a Turkish bath), is a homophone for "mort" (dead). – *Translators' note*.]
- Peace to its ashes.[2]

The same title – *Mort du Film* – was also picked up by a series of articles published by Maurice Bessy in the pages of *Cinémonde* during 1933. The first of these articles was quite encouraging. In the issue for 27 April, Bessy told the story of the discovery by Jean Mauclaire of an important cache of films – including numerous works by Méliès, many of them stencil-coloured – in the dairy of the Château at Geufosse, and of Mauclaire's subsequent efforts to save other films. Mauclaire's efforts foreshadowed the creation of the Cinémathèque Française, and their story has been told elsewhere[3], although their appearance in this context is interesting.

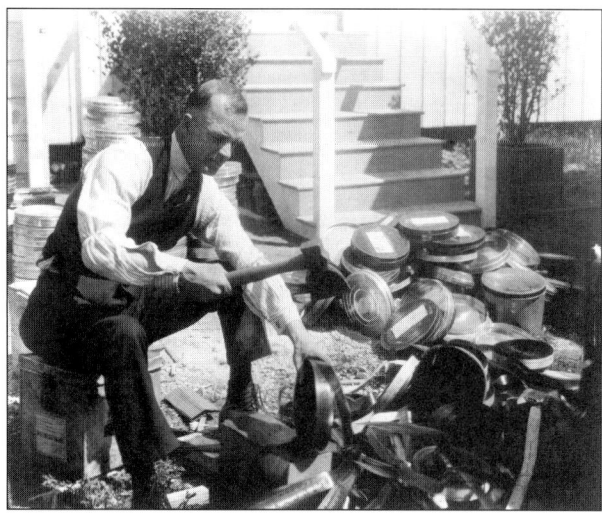

Prints of obsolete films "rendered unusable by [an] axe blow" – in this case, at the Fairbanks Studio in 1922.

Kevin Brownlow Collection.

The second of Bessy's articles (in issue no.237, 4 May 1933) spoke of the cinematheques "where films avoid death, but only to endure a slow agony". This gloomy introduction gave way to a rather more upbeat commentary, which noted the recent founding of the Cinémathèque Nationale at the Trocadéro, and recorded the words of congratulation with which film pioneer Louis Lumière had greeted its creation. Bessy concluded by noting that it was a cause for regret that such a "museum of film" had not been created earlier. He was not to know that this was only a false dawn: the Cinémathèque Nationale achieved nothing of note, and the creation of the Cinémathèque Française was still some three years away.

Two weeks later, on 18 May 1933, Bessy shifted to a more downbeat tone when he wrote of the wholesale shipment of old films to the colonies, where they would be exploited to death. A week after that (issue no.240, 25 May 1933), he concluded his depressing survey, following a brief mention of the last traces of the tradition of the travelling showman with a look at the work of the film recycler:

> ...He has just taken a delivery: in tons the film piles up, rendered unusable by the axe-blow that has been inflicted on it, guarantee of certain death. The murder has been committed, but the body will not be made to disappear – *it will be used*. So appears on the scene, in spite of the aesthetes, the triumph of the cinema-industry: cinema-for-money, sworn enemy of cinema-as-art, of cinema-of-ideas. Rather than immortality, those whose profession is to make a living by film or through film prefer profit. The meagre corpse of film must be stripped.

To begin with, a first picking-over, with the goal of sifting out of this interesting-smelling heap the gloves, the scissors, the scrapers, the tools, the rubber bags, which all habitually lurk in this jumble.

Next, a bath of soda, which will separate the gelatin from its support. And don't imagine that the dark mud that results from this process will be thrown away: a suitable chemical process will facilitate the recovery of silver salts in sufficient quantity soon to make possible the casting of ingots of pure silver!

And the support? That will be cut up, chopped up into flakes; and from here on we enter the realm of surprises...

Your nail polish, mademoiselle, which allows you to show your pretty little hands with the nails pink, red, pearlised, or whatever? Perhaps Ramon Novarro is lurking there still? And how many nitro-cellulose varnishes! How many glues and glazes!...

...It is not only for the manufacture of chemical products that it is bought to be turned into powder for delivery to laboratories.

But, above all, let us say it again, polish, enormous quantities of polish. Just think that a kilo of film will sell for about 6 francs, and that about 50 litres of polish can be made from it![4]

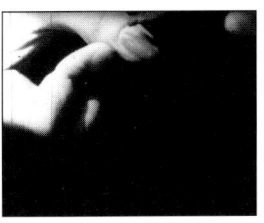

Nail varnish – another of the uses of recycled celluloid in *L'Age du Plastique* (1943).

Archives du Film du Centre National de la Cinématographie, Bois d'Arcy.

Notes

1. «**Utilisation des vieilles Pellicules**

   La première opération consiste à enlever la couche de gélatine qui adhère au celluloïd.

   Le moyen le plus simple, c'est de plonger la pellicule dans l'eau chaude. Si la couche résiste à cette action, il faut employer une solution de fluorure d'ammonium, très légèrement acidulée. La gélatine se détache beaucoup plus facilement que par l'emploi de l'acide chlorhydrique.

   Cette opération terminée on peut employer le celluloïd:

   1°. Comme lumière artificielle.

   Le celluloïd, brûlant rapidement, peut remplacer les poudres magnésiques. La lumière produite, moins actinique parce-qu'elle est jaunâtre, fournit des images plus harmonieuses en employant des plaques orthochromatiques.

   Pour que l'inflammation se produise rapidement, if faut découper le celluloïd en copeaux fins;

   2°. Fabrication d'un vernis.

   Ce vernis est peu coûteux, facile à étendre, très transparent et tout à fait imperméable.

   Mélanger: acétate d'amyle, 500 cc ; acétone, 500 cc ; celluloïd, 15 grammes.»

   Ciné-Journal, no.6 (22 May 1908), p. 5.

2. «**La Mort du Film**
   – Arrivons à la fin du film.
   – Nous y sommes. Voici deux ans révolus: le film est sénile. Il devient jaune, opaque, il est plein de bavures, d'éraflures; il pleut lamentablement dans un riche salon ou, encore, en plein soleil... (ce qui provient de traces d'éraillement sur la gélatine). Enfin il est condamné!
   – Qu'en fait-on?
   – Deux choses: ou on le laisse se décomposer lentement jusqu'à ce qu'on se décide à y mettre le feu en compagnie de plusieurs de ses congénères; ou, si le celluloïd en vaut la peine, on trempe le film dans l'eau chaude et on le laisse dans une étuve jusqu'à ce que s'en aille d'elle-même l'émulsion gélatineuse où étaient imprimées les images. Alors, le celluloïd, revenu à sa matière initiale, est envoyé à la refonte.
   – On le refond?
   – Mais oui. Nos usines de celluloïd le retravaillent et ce film redevient quelque temps après limpide et immaculé. Nos laboratoires le recouvrent d'émulsion vierge et le voilà redevenu apte à être de nouveau impressionné et à refaire une nouvelle carrière!
   – De deux ans?

–   Hélas! Encore faudra-t-il qu'il ait bien «tourné»!
–   En somme, ce film, né dans une manifestation – parfois enthousiaste! – de grand art, finit lamentablement sa vie!
–   Comme tout ce qui touche à l'art, Monsieur, il n'a qu'une gloire éphémère et sa célébrité le quitte … avec son émulsion!
–   Dans un bain chaud?
–   Das un bain … maure!
–   Il est bien mort!
–   Paix à ses cendres.»

Jacques Faure, *Mon Ciné Almanach*, 1924: «La naissance, la vie et la mort d'un film. 3ème partie: la mort du film».

3.   See, for example, Raymond Borde, *Les Cinémathèques* (Lausanne: Editions L'Age d'Homme, 1984), pp. 50–51.

4.   «… Il vient de faire une livraison: par tonnes, le film s'amoncelle, rendu inutilisable par le coup de hache dont on l'a gratifié, assurance d'une mort certaine. Le meurtre est accompli, mais on ne fera pas disparaître le cadavre: *on va l'utiliser*. Et alors apparaît, en dépit des esthètes, le triomphe du cinéma-industrie: du cinéma-argent, cet ennemi par vendetta du cinéma-art, du cinéma-idée. A l'immortalité, ceux qui font profession de vivre du film et par le film, préfèrent le bénéfice. Il faut détrousser ce mince corps de pellicule.

Et d'abord, un premier crochetage, afin de débarrasser cet amas aux odeurs piquantes, des gants, ciseaux, grattoirs, peignes, attaches de caoutchouc qui prennent l'habitude de se dissimuler dans ce désordre.

Puis un bain de soude qui décollera la gélatine du support. Et ne croyez pas qu'on va jeter la boue noirâtre qui en résulte: un traitement chimique approprié permettra de récupérer des sels d'argent en quantité suffisante pour donner naissance bientôt à des lingots d'argent pur!

Le support? On va le couper, le hacher en paillettes; dès lors, nous pénétrons dans le domaine de la surprise…

… Votre vernis à ongles, mademoiselle, qui vous permet d'exhiber de jolies menottes aux ongles roses, rouges, nacrés ou autres? Peut-être Ramon Novarro s'y dissimule-t-il encore? Et combien de vernis nitro-cellulosiques! combien de colles et d'enduits! …

… Il n'est pas jusqu'aux fabriques de produits chimiques qui n'en achètent pour le réduire en poudre livrée aux laboratoires.

Mais, avant tout, répétons-le, des vernis, des quantités énormes de vernis. Songez en effet que le kilo de film se vend près de six francs, et qu'il permet le fabrication de cinquante litres environ de vernis! …»

Maurice M Bessy, "Mort du Film", *Cinémonde*, no.240 (25 May 1933).

Nitrate Memories from TK2

by Christine Whittaker

It is said that when the BBC's new Deputy Director General, John Birt, was first shown around Lime Grove Studios in 1987, his determination to make radical changes in the Corporation was strengthened – he knew as soon as he saw the labyrinthine corridors, stone staircases, and clanking lifts that his vision for the streamlined, management-led BBC could not work as long as the 50-year-old former film studios remained the beloved home of the flagship News and Current Affairs Department. Lime Grove Studios was bought from J Arthur Rank in the late 1940s, and adapted by the BBC to produce television programmes such as *Tonight, That Was the Week that Was, Panorama*, and even *Muffin the Mule*, but it retained the infrastructure of the film studios, with its projection rooms, rows of dressing rooms, and film vaults. It also housed the only authorised nitrate vault and telecine channel in the BBC – the legendary TK2.

My memories of TK2 are from the early 1980s. By then it was no longer used for BBC nitrate film – that had all been transferred to safety stock – but it was frequently used by researchers like myself, who were working on archive-based programmes, to copy films from outside sources on to tape, at that stage usually onto 1-inch tape. Before then we had had to make dupe negs and prints of chosen sections, but the possibility of film-to-tape transfers changed our whole way of working. We were now able to copy longer sections, giving much more scope in the cutting room. In fact, complete films would frequently be copied, as it was not advisable to stop and start too much when handling fragile nitrate film. And of course there was an awful lot of nitrate film around in the early 1980s – most of the pre-1952 newsreel film was still on nitrate stock, as was much of the National Film Archive collection, as well as the industrial films that lay forgotten in company vaults. We loved to find those.

So TK2 was very popular; in fact historical documentary series were queuing up to book its facilities. It had its disadvantages. It was, as far as I remember, on the first floor of Lime Grove, in C Block, and could be reached on foot by those in the know, who could negotiate the lonely corridors behind Reception. The nitrate vault, on the other hand, was on the fifth floor in another block, and that involved either climbing dark and steep stone staircases or risking the infamous and temperamental lift, in which an Ambassador from the Far East once got stuck during a live transmission of *Panorama*. The trouble was that you had to make this journey frequently during your transfer, because you were only allowed up to 5 cans of nitrate film in the telecine channel at the same time. You could not cheat on this, because there had to be a fireman present in TK2 during a nitrate transfer: GLC regulations.

The firemen would frequently act not only as anti-combustion agents but also as film critics, and sometimes complained when they found the films particularly boring. I would find myself apologising when I produced yet another can containing nothing more exciting than a filmed description of a certain industrial process. I never found a fireman, however, who offered to help me with the rewinding of the film. This was a strenuous and time-consuming job, as nitrate film had to be wound onto special enclosed spools, by hand of course, and back onto 35mm film cores to go back in to the can, before you could trudge up those stone stairs to return them to the vault, and collect another 5 cans. The bookings would always last several hours, as in TK 2 you could not speed through the film – you could not risk that with nitrate, and anyway the telecine machinery was not that sophisticated. It did give you some leeway with film speed, which could be adapted to silent film; this was very useful in the days before digital editing. TK2, being the only nitrate machine in the BBC, was very over-subscribed, and somehow I always managed to get my bookings at the weekend, in the evening, or during the holidays. I remember one particular Christmas Eve when I did not leave TK2 until 11 p.m. – no drinks with the fireman though, not on nitrate duty!

Lime Grove was somehow an appropriate place to view nitrate film – we felt we were carrying on the tradition of the film studios. A film editor friend told me that when he was a young trainee and the cutting room got very boring, he and his colleagues used to set fire to a small section of nitrate and chuck it out of the upstairs window, just for the hell of it. In the 1980s we took a lot of precautions, and followed all the rules. One thing still puzzles me though. Obviously, the many cans of nitrate film had to be transported from their place of origin to Shepherd's Bush, and this was done by van or taxi. I know that some of the journeys were carried out by special vans provided with fireproof boxes. But I do remember seeing ordinary London cabs turning up. Did they know what they were carrying? No fireman accompanied those loads. Oh, well – happy days.

Luminous Impressions

A selection of accounts of restoration projects involving nitrate films.

Al-Dahaia – An Egyptian Case History in the Restoration of Nitrate Film

by Magdi Abdel Rahman

Egypt held its first film performance a few months after the world's first projection in 1895. Since then, the country has been a pioneer of cinema in Africa and in the Middle East, yet despite this long history, Egypt is still unable to allocate a building for a National Film Archive to preserve its film heritage in accordance with scientific principles. In accordance with Decree No. 34 of 1975, the National Archive of Egyptian Film (NAEF) has a collection of legal deposit material comprising approximately 2,000 feature films and 1,500 documentary films, but these are held only as release prints. All the negatives of these films are scattered in many places, although most of them – including all those that survive from the period before 1952, which are certainly on nitrate film stock – are retained in the huge main store of the country's only laboratory.

Unfortunately this repository, like the other locations used for film storage, does not provide proper conditions for preservation. Film is placed constantly at risk by the absence of temperature and humidity controls and even of adequate ventilation, and those who enter the vaults can quickly detect the classic symptoms of film deterioration. Film that is still in good condition can easily be preserved almost indefinitely if the appropriate conditions are provided: we must hope that those conditions will be made available to us before too long.

Meanwhile, we would like to draw attention to the problem of film preservation in Egypt, with a tribute to our country's film heritage through the case history of our continuing work on the restoration of the film *Al-Dahaia* (The Victims), which was made in 1932 and released in 1933.

Al-Dahaia is the earliest film negative found in Egypt from the nitrate era – earlier prints survive, but not negatives. It is also in its own right a very significant film in the history of the Egyptian film industry. It was produced, directed, and acted by Bahiga Hafez, one of the early women pioneers in the Egyptian film industry, who had the courage to risk everything in order to produce films, and who helped to set that industry on its feet at this early stage. Her contributions are now receiving increasing attention in the Egyptian film community.

The Cultural Development Fund supports the efforts of the NAEF to complete the restoration and preservation of *Al-Dahaia*. The background information on Bahiga Hafez and *Al-Dahaia*, and the technical report on the restoration procedures which follows, are offered to show the reader the long journey which such a project represents.

Bahiga Hafez

Bahiga Hafez was one of the first generation of Egyptian women to receive an education. She was born on 4 August 1908, in Alexandria, just over a decade before the women of Egypt took to the streets in the nationalist demonstrations of 16

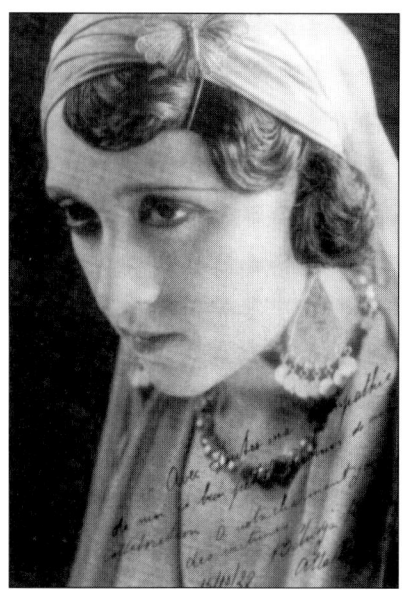

Bahiga Hafez.
Egyptian Film Centre, Giza.

March 1919 to claim a right to political and public life. Her father was a former employee in the Sultanate's civil service. Her maternal grandfather was the well-known Muhammad Sayyed Pasha, who was also the maternal grandfather of the political leader Ismail Sidqi Pasha.

Bahiga went to foreign schools and grew up surrounded by the arts, as her father was a patron of musicians. She married very young, but the marriage did not last. She then went to study music in France, where she received a music diploma in 1930. She taught music after the death of her father.[1]

Although Bahiga came from a liberal family, her participation in cinema was not acceptable to them. When director Muhammad Karim asked her to participate in *Zainab*, after meeting her at a party, her family objected to her decision to act. She went ahead and acted in the film, however, and also wrote a musical score for it, which was played on records during the screening.

The legendary Youssef Wahbe chose her to act opposite him in the talking film *Awlad al-Ozawat* (The Rich People), again directed by Muhammad Karim. While they were shooting the talking scenes in Paris, conflicts developed between the three of them which led to her dismissal from the film. On her return to Egypt she filed a lawsuit against Youssef Wahbe for unfair dismissal – the first such lawsuit between an actress and a producer in the history of the Egyptian film industry.

Feeling that she also had to become a producer in order to have decision-making power, she founded Fanar (Pharos) Films with her husband at the time, Mahmoud Hamdi. She then embarked on producing her first film, the originally silent *Al-Dahaia*, in 1932. In 1934, she produced the talking *El-Etiham* (The Accusation).

After the founding of Studio Misr in 1935, with its ability to finance large production, Bahiga Hafez was determined not to be upstaged. She decided to produce the lavish historical film, *Leila Bint al-Sahra* (Leila, Daughter of the Desert), which told of the abduction and rape of a desert girl by the Khosros of Iran. The film was banned for political reasons, in order not to damage relations between Egypt and Iran. As the film languished without release, Bahiga lost a lot of money. The ban was not lifted until 1944, when the political situation had changed somewhat. She then re-cut the film and released it as *Leila al-Badaouia* (Leila the Bedouin).

As a result of these losses, Bahiga took a 10-year respite from producing, which ended in 1947 when she produced *Zahrat al-Souk* (The Flower of the Market). When this film failed, Bahiga withdrew from producing, but maintained her contacts in the Egyptian film industry through supporting her artistic salon as a meeting-place for artists and writers. She is credited with giving luminaries of the Egyptian film industry, such as the editor Kamal Abou Sefi, their first break in the industry. In 1966, Salah Abou Sefi insisted on paying tribute to her by giving her a small role as a princess in *Al-Qahira Thalatin* (Cairo 30), in order to put her in the public eye once more.

This daughter of aristocrats, who spoke three languages fluently, composed many musical scores, and helped found the Egyptian film industry against tremendous odds, risking all she had in the process, died alone in her apartment on 13 September 1983, in poor physical and financial health. Her phone and her electricity had been cut off because the bills had not been paid. She died of old age and heart failure, and was found by her doorman two days later, sitting at a table in her living room with the remains of an unfinished meal.

In *Al-Dahaia* we have a record of the unique and diverse talents of Bahiga Hafez as a producer, director, actress, music scorer, wardrobe designer, and film editor.[2]

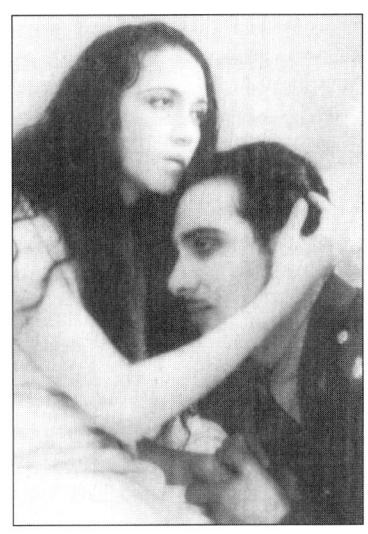

Bahiga Hafez and Attalah Michael.

Egyptian Film Centre, Giza.

AL-DAHAIA [The Victims] (Pharos Film, Egypt, 1932).
CREDITS

Producer	Bahiga Hafez
Director (silent version)	Ibrahim Lama
Director (sound version)	Bahiga Hafez
Sound Engineer	Ladislas Szabo
Music Composer	Bahiga Hafez

CAST
Bahiga Hafez
Zaki Rsotem
Attalah Michael
Abdel Salam Nabolsi
Leila Murad

First Projection (silent version): 28 November 1932
First Projection (sound version): 25 February 1935

Al-Dahaia has to be seen as part of the effort of the early women pioneers of the Egyptian screen to tell stories dealing with the victimisation of women. Of course, these women film-makers did not have the feminist consciousness that is more widespread now, and as they came mostly from well-to-do families they did not tell stories about women of the underclass. Nonetheless, what we see in their films are early attempts to reflect the plight of women on the screen truthfully. In *Al-Dahaia*, Bahiga Hafez treated the social issue of the marriage of a younger girl before her older sister. She also resisted the demand for a happy ending, insisting on an unhappy ending, with the death of her heroine.

The film combines colloquial Arabic with classical Arabic, in an attempt to appeal to a regional Arab market which at that time did not understand Egyptian dialect. The film's use of flashbacks is creative, and there is beautiful camerawork in the use of silhouette, and in many of the exteriors, especially the sea sequences. The locations are very well chosen, but the acting suffers from being melodramatic and theatrical at times. The most outstanding scene of the film is the one when Bahiga Hafez performs and sings one of her musical compositions after her husband has stolen her jewellery. This scene is very delicate, with powerful, understated acting from Bahiga Hafez, expressing her sorrow. The score she composed for the film is very expressive, although the soundtrack is rough, as the mixing of that time was primitive.

The Status of the Negative before Restoration

It is commonly believed that the only difference between the silent version of the feature film *Al-Dahaia* and the one with dialogue was the addition of a soundtrack. This is not true, however.

The first silent projection of *Al-Dahaia* was on 28 November 1932. Bahiga Hafez, the producer, had intended to make it with sound, and she shot it at 24 frames per second. Because of the lack of sound equipment in Egypt, most early Egyptian sound films, or sound sequences, were shot in Paris. We know that there was film equipment in Egypt which recorded at sound speed of 24 frames per second, instead of the silent 16 frames per second. For financial reasons, Bahiga was unable to go to Europe for the sound recording, and so *Al-Dahaia* was projected silent.

Ladislas Szabo, a Hungarian engineer living in Egypt at the time, succeeded in founding a synchronisation laboratory in 1934. He encouraged Bahiga to produce her first sound film *El-Etiham* (The Accusation), and then persuaded her to make a soundtrack for her first production, *Al-Dahaia*.

The silent version of *Al-Dahaia* had intertitles to explain the action. Bahiga, who was sophisticated in film, realised that her silent scenes would not be good enough if a soundtrack was simply added to them. She shot a number of additional new scenes, which she directed herself; in addition to the dialogue scenes, there were others, such as songs and dances, which were then cut into the silent version. The evidence for this conclusion includes the following:

1. The credits of the film were shot on panchromatic Kodak film, and included the names of people involved only in the sound portion of the film, such as Leila Murad, etc. These credits would not have been present in the silent version.

2. All the silent scenes, such as the ship sailing at the beginning of the film, or the meeting between Bahiga and the gang members on the steps of the palace, etc., were shot on Kodak nitrate stock with edge markings which indicate manufacture in 1932. The dialogue scenes were shot on panchromatic nitrate Kodak film with edge markings appropriate to 1934.[3] There are also a few dialogue scenes shot on Agfa Pankine stock.

3. There are some scenes which were shot in the aspect ratio appropriate to silent film frame proportions, with the image covering the full width between the sprockets, rather than the aspect ratio of the talking-film frame. In fact, the film alternates between these two framings.

The status of the negative before restoration can be summarised as follows:

1. The film comprised 10 reels of image and 10 of optical sound, measuring in total 2,950 metres.

2. About 11 or 12 scattered shots had suffered excessive development and had crease stains, but most of the rest were in good condition. No yellowish tinge, the characteristic indicator of the first stages of nitrate deterioration, was observed.[4]

3. All the reels had many black 'slugs'[5] from 2 or 3 frames to about 15 frames.

4. There was much perforation damage or edge damage, which had been repaired badly.

5. There were 2 or 3 breaks, where footage was missing.

6. Some shots had 2 or more grading or timing notches, as a result of adjusting the printing exposure several times during the printing of that scene; some notches had been closed by badly-made celluloid patches.

7. As a whole, the film was in a brittle, slightly curled condition, and on examination most of the splices came apart.

8. The optical sound reels were recorded on Ferrania film. Sound was recorded using the variable-density system, and the reels were severely faded (a known problem with variable-density recording, which explains why it was usually replaced with variable-area recording).

9. About 150 metres of the optical sound of reel 6 had decomposed completely.

10. There were no synchronisation marks on image or sound reels, either because of lack of leader, or because they had been erased.

A Stage-by-stage Report on the Restoration to date

1. The negative cutter, Mrs Leila Fahmy, first carefully repaired all the perforation damage and breaks. She also put on new leader and replaced the rusting cans.

2. The film was graded on colour master with the FCC (Frame Counting Cuing) system to avoid the haphazard notches.

3. The negative was treated in an ultrasonic cleaning machine, to reduce its brittleness before it went to the printing room.

4. In order to strike a synchronised combined print, a positive copy was made on a Bell & Howell CL continuous printer with wet gate. The result displayed two symptoms

   a) The copy suffered greatly from the phenomenon of optical slippage because of shrinkage of the negative due to its age. (Motion-picture film is susceptible both to age-related shrinkage and to change of size with varying relative humidity and temperature. The former, which is caused largely by the loss of solvent or plasticiser from the base film stock, is permanent, while the latter is reversible. For good performance in making new prints, dimensional change in negatives must be restricted to a narrow range. Because of the history of the material from which we were working, shrinkage had frequently gone beyond the 'acceptable' level.[6])

   b) In addition to the fading already noted, the variable-density soundtrack was characterised by the high noise levels associated with bad recording, and background noises. On some reels it was necessary to re-adjust the sync marks, while others suffered from original bad dubbing.

5. In order to try to remedy the defective sound, the track only was printed on both sides of the film, from which a transfer was made to magnetic tape. This recording went through many cycles of noise reduction procedures, until we got the best possible results.[7] The editor, Ahmed Daoud, found the exact sync marks for each reel, in addition to doing his best whenever possible to improve the errors in the original dubbing. The magnetic tapes were then transferred to optical stock with variable-area.

6. Mrs Leila Fahmy checked the picture reels against the new optical soundtrack, put in the exact sync marks, and removed the slugs.

7. The main problem was still not solved, however, for we do not have the facility to change the sprocket dimensions in our continuous printer. We tried to print the film on our Bell & Howell Seiki step-printer, which works at 6 frames per second, but the difficulty was again the high percentage of shrinkage. The gate of the Seiki printer has infinitely variable stroke, which solved half the problem, but unfortunately it does not have the equivalent facility for width adjustment, and our negative has also suffered shrinkage in width.[8]

8. Until we can obtain another gate for the Seiki printer, modified to give infinitely variable adjustments to both stroke and width, we have put to one side the idea of printing a master interpositive on Kodak 5366, to be used in turn to generate a new dupe negative on Kodak 5234. For the time being, we intend to make a second positive print on the continuous printer, with many repetitions to avoid the optical slippage as much as possible.

Notes

1. M A Shousha, Rowad wa Raedat *Al-Cinema Al Masriya* (Male and Female Pioneers of Egyptian Cinema) (Cairo: 1977), p. 25 (in Arabic).

2. H Osman, *Tariekh Al-Cinema Al-Arabia* (History of Arab Cinema) (Cairo:1968), p. 138f (in Arabic).

3. Harold Brown, *Physical Characteristics of Early Films as Aids to Identification* (Brussels: FIAF, 1990), p. 17.

4. P L Gordon, ed., *The Book of Film Care* (Rochester, NY: Eastman Kodak Company, 1968), p. 68f.

5. "Slugs" are pieces of leader, etc., inserted to replace missing or damaged footage.

6. C R Fordyce, et al., "Shrinkage Behaviour of Motion Picture Film", in *Journal of the SMPTE*, v.64 (1955), pp. 62–66.

7. E Koppe, "Aspekte der Restaurierung von Lichten", in *Miteilungen aus dem Bundesarchiv*, 1 (1995), 3 Jahrgang, pp. 54–58, 65f.
   Also, Henning Schou, *Preservation of Moving Images and Sound* (Brussels: FIAF, 1989), pp. 50–51.

8. C L Gregory, "Printer for Old and Shrunken Film. Report of the Committee on Preservation of Film", in *Journal of the SMPTE*, v.35 (December 1959), p. 9.
   Also, "Survey of Printing Machines; FIAF Technical Commission Project No.10" (Brussels: FIAF, 1994). Point 412 covers the adjustment of the distance between the pins to accommodate shrinkage in the width of the film.

Helen Gardner's *A Sister to Carmen*: A Granddaughter's Restoration

by Dorin Schumacher

In October 1996, while doing research for my book on Helen Gardner, the United States' first film star-producer, I crossed the Atlantic to view her films in British and European archives. Gardner is important as a pioneering producer, actress, and early woman director, as well as a scenarist, film editor, and costume designer. She was also the grandmother I never knew. My trip would lead to my restoration of one of her films, and a deeper understanding of her art.

Gardner achieved stardom as Becky Sharp in Vitagraph's *Vanity Fair* (1911). In early 1912, she announced her company, "The Helen Gardner Picture Players", declaring as its purpose to make feature films. Hers was probably the first US company established solely to make feature films, and the first formed around a single star.[1]

Helen Gardner set out to make history, and she did. Her first production, *Cleopatra* (1912), is considered one of the first full-length feature films made in the United States, and the first by a woman.[2] Her roles in this and her other productions led to her being called the screen's first vamp, a type later exploited by Theda Bara.

For scenarist and director, she hired Charles L Gaskill, with whom she had worked at Vitagraph. (She took Gaskill as a lover but never as a husband. Gardner and my grandfather, Duncan Pell, were married in 1902 and never divorced.) She established her studio in Tappan, New York, and made 10 feature films before closing her company in 1914.

At the Cinema Museum in London I found a nitrate positive of Gardner's third production, *A Sister to Carmen* (1913). Ronald Grant, one of the Museum's directors, had acquired it in 1992 from Mr Marshall of Ripley, Derbyshire, whose father had opened the Ripley Hippodrome in 1913. Mr Marshall had found *A Sister to Carmen* in a garden shed on his property.

On a Steenbeck at Kevin Brownlow and David Gill's studio, we watched the 1,449-meter (4,754- ft) feature film; it was this print's first screening in perhaps 80 years. Gill found Gardner "very daring for her time, playing a very strong woman, doing a dance that was daring for the time, playing a Spaniard/gypsy type and earth woman, knocking men around, playing a man, and playing the vamp."

With the encouragement of Martin Humphries, the other director of the Cinema Museum, I applied for a restoration grant from the New York Women in Film and Television Women's Film Preservation Fund, and in 1997 was awarded $8,500. In my ignorance, I thought this would cover my costs.

The restoration plunged me into a world of unfamiliar terms and unfamiliar issues. Working with Haghefilm in the Netherlands added international complexities. Just to view the answer print, I had to rent a special lens, find a specialized projector,

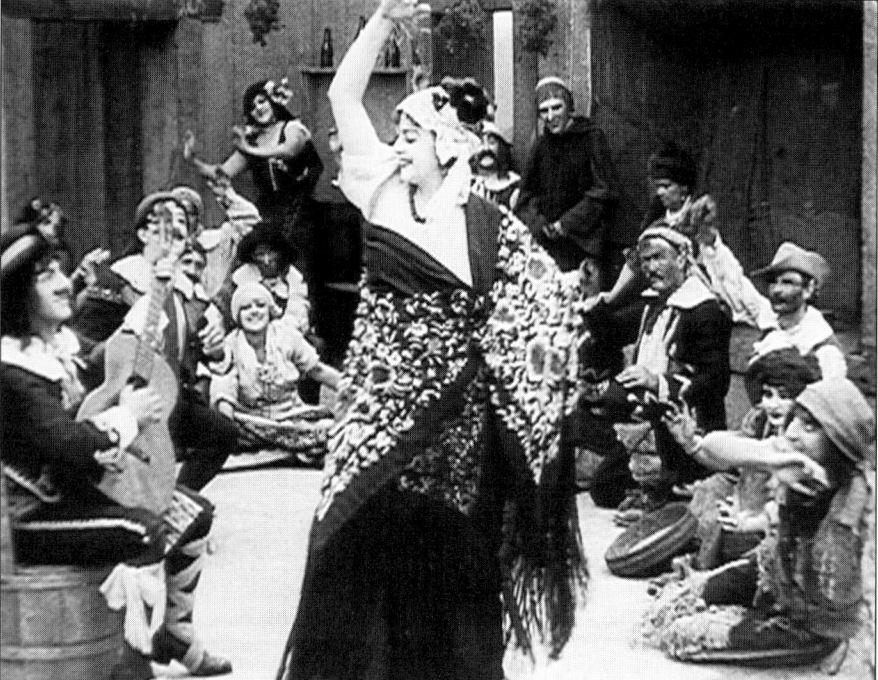

Helen Gardner in *A Sister to Carmen* (1913).

Restoration still, © 2001 Dorin Schumacher.

hire a projectionist, and find a place to show it in the closest big city, 400 miles away. The costs kept mounting. I was Pauline facing overwhelming restoration Perils.

But on 27 May 1999, as I watched the brilliant answer print and saw my beautiful grandmother in *A Sister to Carmen* on the big screen, I knew it had all been worth it.

I now saw that The Helen Gardner Picture Players did more than produce some of the earliest feature films. Gardner's company provided a rare opportunity in the early years of the 20th century for a convention-defying woman to express her spirit and her vision through art. A production company so strongly centered on one woman, on her acting, her abilities, her interests, her desires, and her self-image, was bound to produce films that were strongly autobiographical. Helen Gardner's *A Sister to Carmen* is about a woman's identity – her sensuality, her feelings, her moods, her body, her outer expressions of her inner world, her daring attempts, first as a female and then disguised as a male, to manipulate and dominate men and the external (male) world, and her ultimate punishment for this.

On 14 October 1999, the restored *A Sister to Carmen* had its international premiere at the festival Le Giornate del Cinema Muto, in Sacile, Italy, and I felt privileged to share with the silent film world Helen Gardner's prophetic creation.

Notes

1. Roy Liebman, *Silent Film Performers: An Annotated Bibliography...* (Jefferson, NC: McFarland & Co., 1996); Ralph Sessions, *The Movies in Rockland County: Adolph Zukor and the Silent Era* (New City, NY: Historical Society of Rockland County, 1982); Evelyn Mack Truitt, *Who Was Who on Screen* (New York/London: R R Bowker Co., 1983; 3rd edition); and Edward Wagenknecht, *The Movies in the Age of Innocence*, (Norman, OK: University of Oklahoma Press, 1962).

2. Steven Higgins, personal communication, October 1999.

Fragile History

by Cushla Vula and Kurt Otzen

The earliest surviving moving images shot in New Zealand total just 50 feet (15 metres) of film. These precious frames show the second contingent of troops sent from New Zealand to participate in the Boer War in South Africa in early 1900. The film was deposited at the New Zealand Film Archive, in response to publicity for the "Last Film Search" (described elsewhere in this volume), by Havell Stephen-Smith, and originated from the collection of his relative Enos Silvanus Pegler, an Auckland still photographer.

Dr Chris Pugsley and other military historians confirmed the occasion, and identified the specific contingent from the buttons on their uniforms. After further research, it was established that the troop was parading at Newtown Park in Wellington on 13 or 14 January 1900. It was authenticated by Wellington film historian Clive Sowry as one of the films produced by showman Alfred Whitehouse, New Zealand's first film-maker, and taken by Whitehouse to the United Kingdom in 1900. The cameraman was W H Bartlett.

When deposited, the film was a small, tightly wound piece of nitrate. During accessioning we realised that the contents demanded a closer look – the shape of the hats led us to believe it could be early NZ army footage. The film was so brittle that examining it was not possible without causing a great deal of perforation damage. (*Illustration A*) Even with extreme care, each time it was handled new breaks would appear.

Despite this, we decided to take a series of frame enlargements. These were sent to Chris Pugsley. After a preliminary examination of the frames with the National Archive's film historian Clive Sowry, a probable date and contents were established. Chris circulated our frame enlargements to other military historians and militaria experts. A general agreement was returned, and the title *The Departure of the Second Contingent for the Boer War* was given, with a date of 1900.

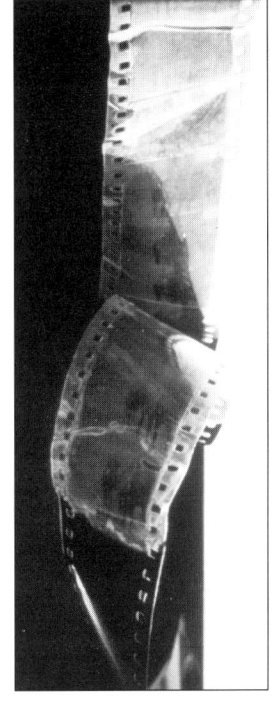

(A) The extremely brittle film as it appeared on first examination.

New Zealand Film Archive, Wellington.

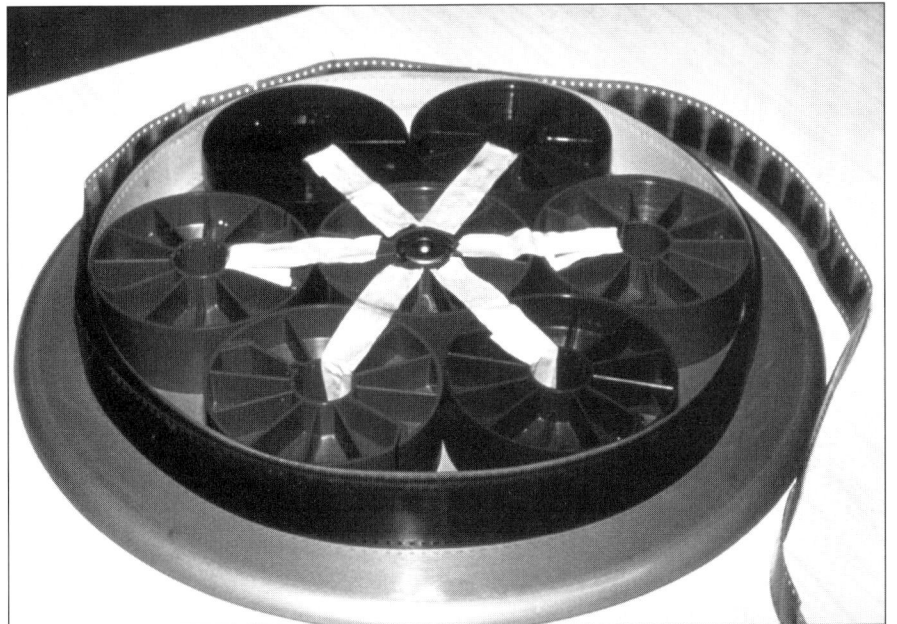

(B) The specially constructed core used to condition the film.

New Zealand Film Archive, Wellington.

After consultation with Geoff Rogers at The Film Unit, where we send our films for preservation copying, we agreed that even with modifications to the printer to allow for excess shrinkage and curl, the Unit would not be able to print it. They were also not equipped for wet-gate printing, which the image quality needed. This meant that we possibly had the earliest surviving piece of New Zealand film in our hands – but might not be able to preserve it. We decided to repair the film, and the following exhaustive and exhausting steps were taken. Repair of the 33 seconds of film was to take a total of 160 hours.

To ease the handling difficulty described earlier, we taped each piece together and wound it round a specially constructed core, which we suspended over a fuming agent of Glycerol and hot water. (*Illustration B*) We replaced the fuming agent daily, until the film had relaxed sufficiently to enable us to start repair work.

(C) Emulsion separating from the base.

New Zealand Film Archive, Wellington.

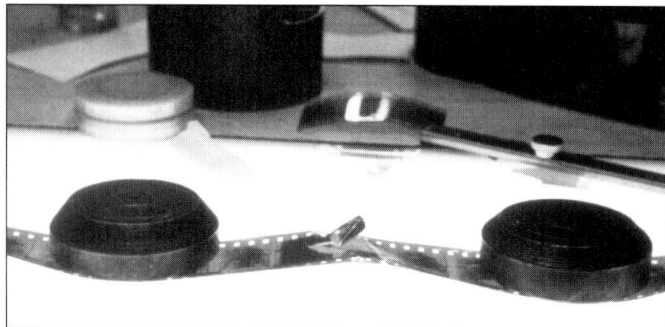

Because of the persistent springy brittleness, we were unable to use traditional repair techniques, and resorted to rather less-preferred methods, involving large amounts of clear 3M perforated repair tape. In many instances, as the film uncurled the emulsion separated from the base. (*Illustration C*) We reattached it using nitrate cement, and secured it with tape, ensuring that the tape cuts corresponded with the framelines.

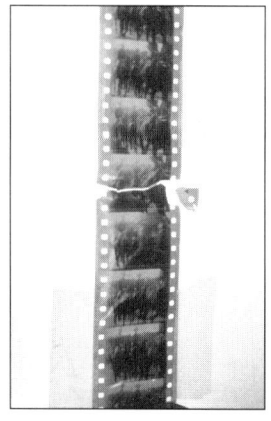

The many breaks in the film had left us with a lot of small chips. These were matched like a jigsaw puzzle and secured as before. (*Illustration D*) The edge curl made it necessary to secure the edges of the film with masking tape as repairs were made. The emulsion had flaked off some frames where breaks had occurred, and to prevent further flaking we taped over the entire area. Edge damage was repaired with tape and new perforation holes cut, as the shrinkage – 2.2% – precluded using pre-cut perforation tape.

(D) Breaks in the film.

New Zealand Film Archive, Wellington.

Where we were unsure of continuity, black frames were inserted to indicate possible missing frames. This was to allow for future additions, or editing after printing. The film was stored on the big core during the entire repair period, and eventually, by the time the repair was finished, looked more relaxed and printable.

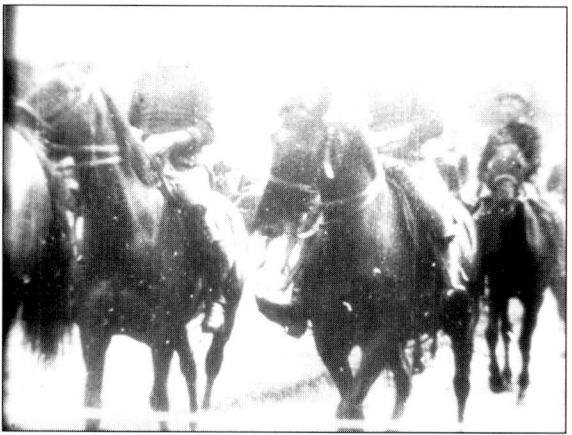

(E) At last, a viewable print of the earliest surviving moving images shot in New Zealand: the second contingent of troops leaving to fight in the Boer War in South Africa, January 1900.

New Zealand Film Archive, Wellington.

During 1994 Cushla attended the FIAF Congress in Bologna, Italy, where she visited the Immagine Ritrovata laboratory and arranged for them to try and print the film for us. The laboratory produced a contact dupe negative, and then successfully wet-gate printed a dupe negative from which they struck two prints. (*Illustration E*) The original nitrate sent to them was returned to us with the new print material. Apart from a small amount of new damage to two frames, we felt the film repair techniques we used were justified.

The Guano Deposit

by Janet McBain

I first met Jenny Gilbertson in about 1980. She was a self-taught film-maker based in the remote Shetland Islands. We discussed the making of the story documentary *The Rugged Island* (UK, 1933), shot and edited on her island home. The film was shot on 35mm, with a hand-held Eyemo camera. Once shooting was complete and she had received the rushes from the laboratory, editing of the 6,000 feet of camera negative was done by Jenny herself, using an old hand-cranked Butcher's Empire Cinematograph, a set of rewind handles, and a splicer, in the only space available to her – her own living room.

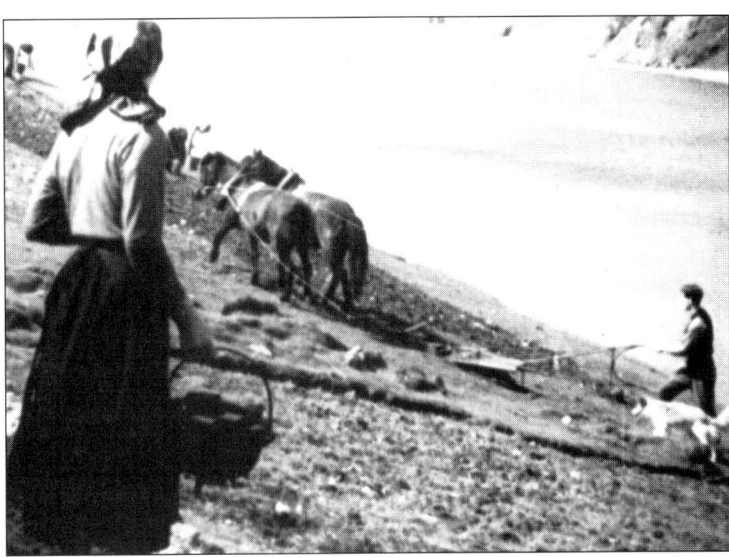

A still from *The Rugged Island* (1933).

Scottish Screen Archive, Glasgow.

She spent hours festooned in nitrate film in front of a glowing open peat fire. She knew the film was inflammable and dangerous, and when it was completed and had been handed over for distribution she had to find somewhere safe to store the negative and unused footage. She used the safest place she could find. The materials were put into cans and stored in the hen house on the glebe lands next to the family croft – the minister was happy to oblige with the storage facility. The collection stayed there until 1979, when a TV documentary crew interviewing Jenny about her life in film retrieved the cans and brought them down to the Scottish Film Archive, covered in chicken droppings, but still containing viable nitrate stock. It was tempting for us, a relatively young archive, to acquire the collection as the "guano deposit".[1]

Reference

1. For an account of the Archive's plans for the restoration of this film and further information on the career of Jenny Gilbertson see: Janet McBain, "Scottish Film and Television Archive preservation project: *The Rugged Island* (1933)", *Journal of Film Preservation*, no. 57 (FIAF, December 1998), pp. 39–40.

The *Man Haters* Project

by Nancy Turner

Editors' Note: unless otherwise indicated, the following text comprises direct quotations from the complete account given in the 44-page booklet "Having Fun With It": The Man Haters *Project, by Nancy Turner, published in 1996 by Friends of Alexander M Bracken Library, Ball State University, Muncie, Indiana.*

The headline in the *Muncie Evening Press* for 19 October 1915 read "Who Will Be Ruth?" With these words, the Press and the Majestic Theater began a search for a young woman to play the lead role in a motion picture. The picture would be made in Muncie, Indiana, with a local cast using Muncie streets, homes, buildings, and locations for background.

The "Who Will Be Ruth?" contest was scheduled to start on October 20 and run through November 2. Contestants were required to reside within 5 miles of the Muncie city limits. Anyone who had previous professional, dramatic, or screen experience was ineligible. The woman receiving the most votes by November 2 would play "Ruth", and the next 9 young women in the vote standings would be offered other parts in the movie. There would also be parts for 3 young men, but there was no contest held to select them. Production of the movie was scheduled to start the day after the contest closed on Tuesday, November 2. As the completed film was first shown in a Monday matinee on November 15, the producers had less than 2 weeks to complete their work.

Wednesday, November 3rd's *Press* stated "Miss Dora Grim is to be 'Ruth'" as she "came from behind in the last day's balloting and when the tickets were all counted, she led the list [of 21 contestants] with 4,434 votes to her credit." The contest was over, the winners announced, and the work of making the movie began.

Action in the film's plot took place over one week. With the unusual title of *The Man Haters*, the film's story followed the adventures of a group of young women

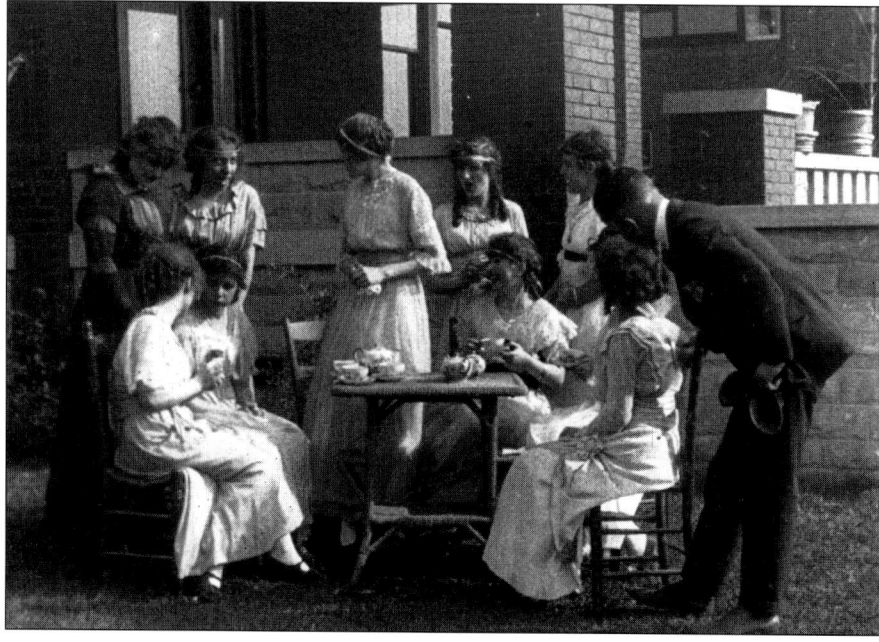

The Man Haters: Ruth ignores Henry at the Club tea party.

"Manhaters" Collection, Archives and Special Collections, Ball State University.

who decide to form a club devoted to the idea that "man is an animal". Ruth, the heroine, is the president of the club. Henry, the hero, sees her and is infatuated. He asks his sister, Alice, also a member of the club, to introduce him. At first, Alice refuses but soon takes pity on her brother. When the women gather for a tea party, Alice sends a message to Henry telling him to make an appearance at the party. However, when he does Ruth ignores him, much to Henry's angry dismay. He and his sister quarrel and Henry attempts to meet Ruth on his own, visiting her as she sits on the front steps of her home. Again he is rebuffed. The next day, when several of the club members stop to chat outside a local bank, Henry escorts Ruth away from her friends. The two sit down on a bench to get acquainted, and Ruth's haughty manner soon melts. The next scene shows Ruth slipping out of an upstairs window, climbing down a ladder and then rushing to meet Henry, who is waiting in the street beside his Stutz Bearcat. After embracing, the two young people speed off to a tryst in a park where their love scene is secretly observed by one of the club women. Shocked as she observes the young couple kissing, the club member immediately rushes off to alert the others to Ruth's defection. Henry and Ruth race away as the members give chase. Henry tells Ruth they are going to the courthouse to be married. The ceremony is performed on the courthouse steps by the mayor himself. As the young couple walk back to their car, they are confronted by the agitated club members. The final scene shows Ruth and Henry sharing a kiss after Ruth declares she still "hates men, except for one".

The newspaper review of the film on November 18 complimented the actors on their performances, especially considering the fact that, as the newspaper pointed out, the "cast is without special training".

The producer of *The Man Haters* was Basil McHenry, a circus and theatrical man whose company operated out of Akron, Ohio. McHenry evidently recognized the financial potential of motion pictures and sought to play a part in popularizing the new medium. It was not an unusual path for the early movie-makers to have followed. Ads in the trade journals for the time offered to provide all of the equipment necessary to begin producing movies with the cost of the equipment paid from "future profits". McHenry was 47 years old when he produced *The Man Haters*. Very much the entrepreneur, he made a similar movie in Anderson, Indiana, during the same month, using the same contest gimmick and substituting an Anderson cast and scenes from the Anderson area. The copy of the Anderson version, also called *The Man Haters*, survives but is still privately owned. Besides ventures into movie-making, McHenry continued to tour the country as an agent with such film classics as *Les Miserables*, *Tarzan of the Apes*, and *The Four Horsemen*.

How do we know so much about a film made over 80 years ago? For the answer it is necessary to explain how the film became the property of Ball State University and how *The Man Haters* Project began.

For over 2 years, Bill Kirtley, owner of Muncie Volkswagen/Audi, and Bill Barnett, director of business services at the Ball State University Libraries, discussed a film that had belonged to Bill Kirtley's grandmother, Dora Grim Vlaskamp. Relying on his memory of the film, which he hadn't seen in years, Bill Kirtley was fairly certain that it contained some footage of antique cars. He also thought that the action had been filmed in Muncie and contained local scenes. At first, Bill Barnett wondered if the movie might have been a home movie made by the Ball family. At Barnett's urging, the two men began searching for the film in the greasy confines of the Volkswagen garage, where Kirtley remembered it was stored. They finally located a canister which contained a 16mm safety copy of the original film. With Kirtley's permission, Barnett had it converted to videotape so he might view the contents. Although the film had no title frame, Bill Barnett quickly realized that this was a professional motion picture production. Meanwhile, Bill Kirtley had located the original 35mm positive nitrate copy of the film, stored on a closet shelf at the home of his sister, Jenny Leach. Jenny's husband, Tim, is a local fireman and probably was unaware that this volatile film stock had been resting for many years in their home. Kirtley turned the nitrate copy over to Barnett, who took it to Ron Partain, director of Photo Services at Ball State, to see if he could make still photos of the movie's major scenes. With some difficulty, Ron painstakingly printed 25 8x10 photos from the volatile nitrate positive. These prints later proved invaluable when it came to identifying cast members and researching local settings.

Questioning Bill Kirtley further, Bill Barnett discovered that the film was the result of a city-wide contest won by Kirtley's grandmother when she was a teenager. Surmising that such a contest would probably get newspaper coverage, Barnett, himself a history buff, began a long search of local newspapers. Once he had determined the movie's origin and done some preliminary research on the young women involved in the contest, Barnett turned the movie over to the University Libraries Archives and Special Collections staff.

It was a cold Sunday afternoon in January 1994 when Bill Barnett called me at home and asked me whether I knew of any early film footage featuring Muncie. I answered that the Archives did have a copy of a local film made in Muncie in 1936, but nothing earlier. I must admit that I was somewhat sceptical of the film's value, thinking that it would be so faded that it would not be viewable. However, I assured Bill that if, indeed, the film had been made in 1915, it would have a value simply because it still existed and that the Archives would be happy to accept it as a donation. In early February, the Kirtley and Leach families agreed to donate both the 16mm and the 35mm version of the film to the University Libraries, and that is when I got my first glimpse of *The Man Haters*. As soon as I saw it, I knew that we had a gem.

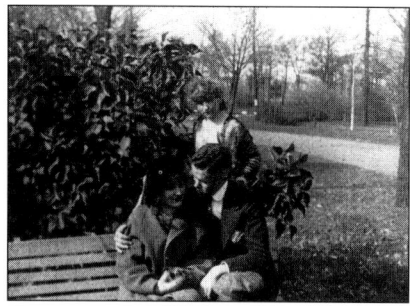

The Man Haters: a member of the Club spies Ruth and Henry in the park.

"Manhaters" Collection, Archives and Special Collections, Ball State University.

I was curious about its path from the producers to the Volkswagen garage, and Susie Vlaskamp Cooke, one of Dora Grim's 3 daughters, gave me the explanation. She said that her mother loved to reminisce about the time when she had starred in a real movie and talked in later life about wanting to see it again. Hoping to surprise her on her birthday, Dora's husband, Arnold, and Susie searched for the film and finally located a copy in the possession of the projectionist at the old Rivoli theater. Whoever it was had the good sense to keep the film wrapped in camphor to preserve it. He was willing to sell it, so Arnold purchased the film and presented it to Dora for her birthday. Soon afterwards, Arnold sent the original nitrate film away to be copied onto 16mm safety film. From time to time, on special occasions, the family would bring out the film and show it.

After Arnold passed away the film was shown less and less. It got passed around in the family, granddaughter Jenny Leach said, stored under beds and in closets; generally just shoved out of the way. Dora's sister Susie said that the family always believed that the State Archives had the original print of the film, but a check with Archives personnel proved fruitless.

The film would have simply lived in storage in Archives and Special Collections if it hadn't been for Michael Wood, Dean of University Libraries. When he viewed *The Man Haters*, Dean Wood recognized its possibilities as an entertainment for the annual Friends of Bracken Library dinner, scheduled for the following April. His idea was to create a video production using the film as a centerpiece and include all of the information we could uncover concerning the discovery of the film, its producers, cast members, and what the city of Muncie was like during this pre-World War I era. He asked me to be in charge of the video production. I remember that when we first talked about the project, his words were: "Have fun with this one!" Prophetic words, indeed.

The dean also suggested that I investigate the possibilities of obtaining an Indiana Humanities Council grant to finance the project. With encouragement from my supervisor and help from the Office of Academic Research, I applied for and received a $3,000 IHC Mini-Grant.

Meanwhile, Nyal Williams (music librarian, Bracken Library), seeking a way to slow down the 16mm to determine the tempo of the musical accompaniment, asked me if we might review the 35mm nitrate version to compare the two for clarity. We unwound the 35mm film manually, and were both surprised and pleased to find that it had the original title frame and included footage evidently lost in the 16mm version. Since the 35mm version was more complete, we decided to use it as our master, even though it was nitrate.

With financial support from the Friends of the Library, I made arrangements to ship the 35mm film to WRS, a film laboratory in Pittsburgh, which would transfer the nitrate film to 16mm safety film and also to broadcast-quality videotape. When the original and the 2 new copies of *The Man Haters* returned to Muncie, technical planning of the video production began.

Bill Barnett, Nyal Williams, Bill Spurgeon (retired editor of Muncie Newspapers and a respected local historian), Bruce Kirkham (executive secretary of the Friends of the Library), Alan Gordon (of WIPB, Ball State's video production unit), and myself met on 30 January 1995 to discuss plans.

Nyal Williams suggested that we slow the action on the video, saying that the slower speed would allow viewers to see the faces of the cast more clearly. We compromised on the amount of reduction.

Nyal had asked Kevin Purrone, in Ball State's School of Music, to provide musical interpretation for the film. Kevin's improvisations centered around several pieces indigenous to the time period. He watched the video through a couple of times to familiarize himself with the script, and then, on the day of the taping, he simply sat down at the piano and played an accompaniment to the action as it unfolded. The result is very satisfying.

With an introduction explaining the contest and how the library acquired the film, and the music tape completed, the small production crew began to feel somewhat smug that we were going to finish in plenty of time for the April 11 deadline. With its new slower speed and Ed's introductory remarks, the whole video ran about 24 minutes. I was disappointed to think that we weren't going to include anything about the cast members, but bowed to professional opinion that if the tape were any longer, we would lose our audience's interest. I turned the tape over to the dean for his final approval in mid-March.

When Dean Wood saw the tape, he said that he liked what we had done, but that it was his understanding that we would include information about the cast members. Knowing that he was stating out loud only what I was thinking, I went back to my office and back to the drawing-board. On April 7, we finished the production and I could report to the dean that, indeed, we did have a research segment that told something about the scenes and the cast. The video was completed at last. Why, we even had 4 days to spare before the Friends Dinner. With our track record, we could have redone the whole thing in that time.

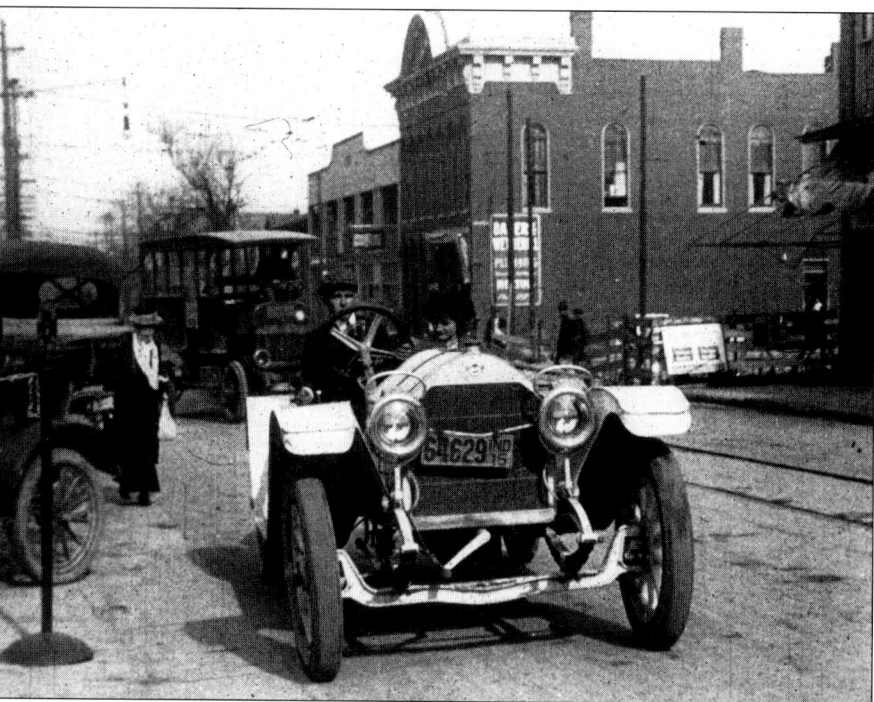

The Man Haters: Ruth and Henry drive to the courthouse to be married.

"Manhaters" Collection, Archives and Special Collections, Ball State University.

The Man Haters proved to be a big hit at the Friends dinner and at programs before numerous groups since that April evening. *The Man Haters* Project is finished, but Dean Wood was right. We who had a part in the project did "have fun with it". The work that went into researching and producing the video was well worth the effort. It is particularly rewarding to know that through our efforts the 13 young people who appeared in the cast will live on, forever young and full of life, as they were in *The Man Haters*.

A Melody Lost in 1939...

by Sakari Toiviainen

Nyrki Tapiovaara (1911–1940), a great talent in the Finnish cinema, made only five films before his death in the Winter War, at the age of 28. Many of his films were unfortunate either in production or reception, but the most unlucky was his most ambitious film, *Herra Lahtinen lähtee lipettiin* (Mr Lahtinen Takes French Leave; 1939).

In 1937, Tapiovaara had made his debut with an excellent adaptation of *Juha*, the classic novel by Juhani Aho, the same story which Finnish-born Mauritz Stiller had directed as *Johan*, a silent classic of the Swedish cinema, in 1921. In his second film, *Varastettu kuolema* (Stolen Death; 1938), Tapiovaara, in the framework of a thriller, indulged himself in experimental fervour in the style of the Soviet masters and the French avant-garde. In his next project, Tapiovaara was going to invest the entire knowledge of his art and its means: he felt that *Melodien der blev vaek* (The Lost Melody), a play by a Dane, Kjeld Abell, was the perfect work for his ideas and ideology. The subject was close to his personal concerns at the time. Tapiovaara had seen the play in the Swedish Theatre of Helsinki and written an enthusiastic review of the performance. He adapted the play into a film scenario with Ralf Parland, and offered it to cinematographer-producer Erik Blomberg, who accepted it as the first production of his newly-founded company Eloseppo.

Shooting of *The Lost Melody* began in autumn 1938 and was finished in early summer 1939. Meanwhile, Tapiovaara directed a successful light comedy, *Kaksi Vihtoria* (Two Victors), which was to secure the financial situation of the new company. Tapiovaara's *Melodien der blev vaek* was premiered at the beginning of September 1939, retitled as *Herra Lahtinen lähtee lipettiin*: the distributor did not believe in the film and wanted a more commercial title. The change did not help – the film played at two cinemas for one week and then disappeared. In part this was caused by a surfeit of Finnish premieres at that time – seven new Finnish films opened in five weeks – under which *Herra Lahtinen* was smothered. However, people also had weightier matters than cinema on their minds: Nazi Germany had attacked Poland at the beginning of September and conquered the country in two weeks. The clouds of another World War were beginning to threaten, and became real enough for Finland shortly thereafter, when the Winter War against the Soviet Union broke out at the end of November.

Tapiovaara met his death in the Winter War, and the prints of *Herra Lahtinen* gathered dust on the shelves of the distributor – Erik Blomberg paying the heavy debts caused by the production. The negatives of the film were destroyed during the war of 1941–1944, when a film store in an attic was emptied during the bombardments. Even if Tapiovaara was highly regarded after the war, nobody seemed to be interested in *Herra Lahtinen*, or else the film was thought to have vanished. The positives of *Herra Lahtinen* were destroyed on 27 July 1959, in a fire at Adams Filmi. In principle, the nitrate prints should have been deposited in the Finnish Film Archive, which was founded in 1957, but because of the lack of storage space they had been left in the attic of Adams Filmi.

When the Finnish Film Archive started its project of "Saving the Finnish Nitrate Films" in 1972, *Herra Lahtinen* – or "The Melody Case" – was one of the most

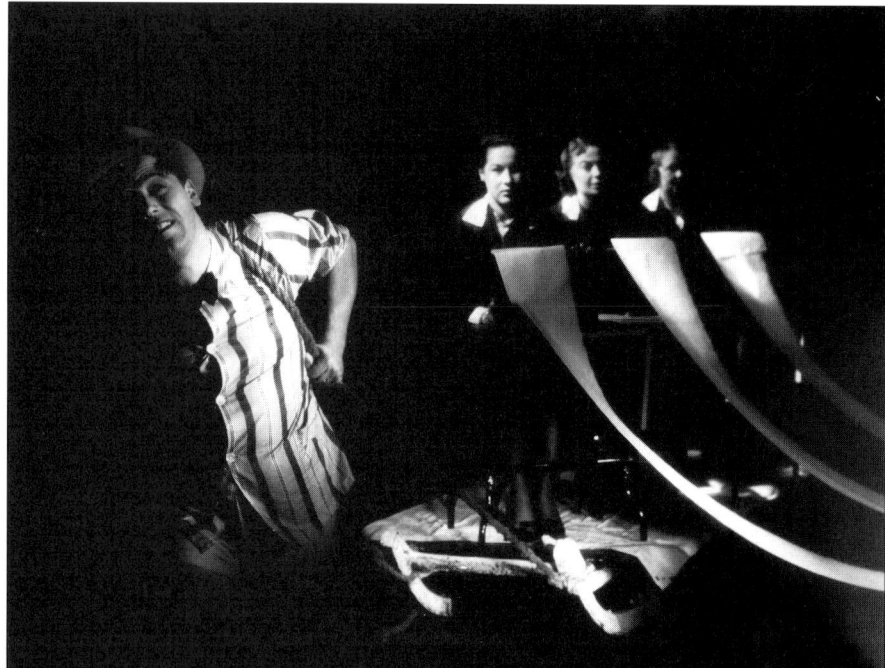

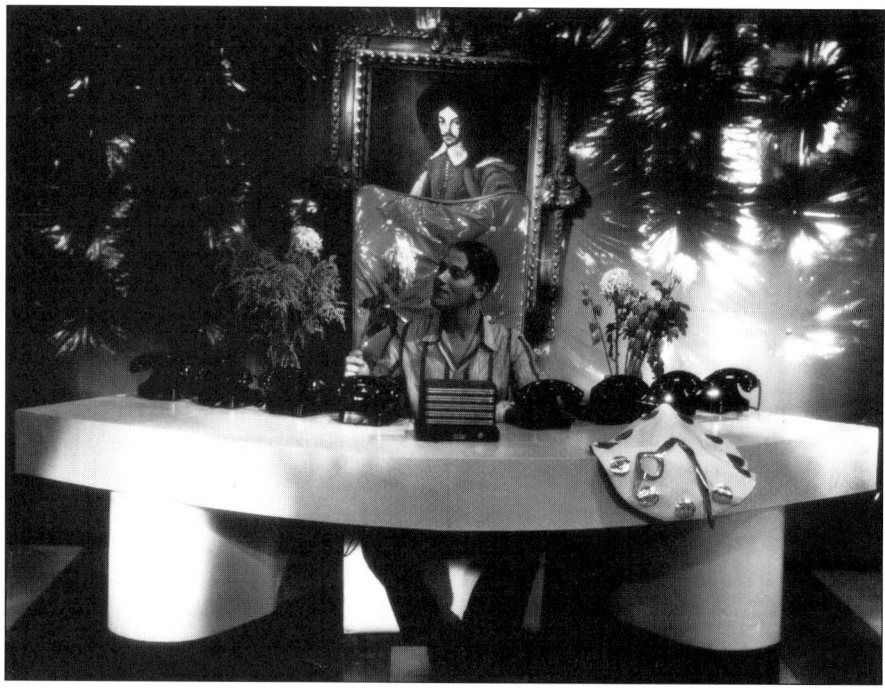

Daydreams and nightmares:
stills from *Herra Lahtinen
Lähte Lipettiin* (1939).
Suomen Elokuva-Arkisto, Helsinki.

urgent objects of the search. The leader of the project, film researcher Lauri Tykkyläinen, had studied the life and works of Tapiovaara in his film school diploma work. He had interviewed many friends and collaborators, and heard that a print of *Herra Lahtinen* had been delivered to a trade union after the war, to be used as entertainment during courses in the countryside. Tykkyläinen quickly found out that a print had indeed been given to the Union of Shop Workers – a veteran trade unionist from northern Savo knew that the film had been screened and then sent back to Helsinki; he remembered that he had taken the print to the railway station himself, but then it had disappeared. Another source told Tykkyläinen that an old nitrate film box with a label reading "Melody" had been stored in the cellar of the Union Course Centre in Hattula, southern Häme. However, this box proved not to contain Tapiovaara's *Melody* but a copy of *Morgondagens melodi* (Melody of Tomorrow), a Swedish film from 1942 directed by Ragnar Frisk. This was another film which had seemed to have shared the same fate as *Herra Lahtinen* –

all the negatives had been destroyed and all the prints were thought to be lost. The Film Archive in Stockholm was therefore very happy with the discovery, especially when the Finnish Film Archive was at the same time able to send another rare Swedish print that had also turned up – the silent film *Lev livet leende* (Live Your Life Smiling; 1921), directed by Pauline Brunius. In exchange, the Finnish Film Archive received from Sweden a print of *Isoviha* (Time of Great Hatred), a Finnish film by Kalle Kaarna, which was also thought to be lost. But there was still no trace of *Herra Lahtinen.*

At this point in the search, Tykkyläinen thought that all possible measures to find *Herra Lahtinen* had been taken, but then in 1975 an inventory of an old nitrate store at the Finnish Film Archive revealed a pile of rusty film cans from which the labels had been lost because of humidity. Examining the material – which consisted of scattered fragments of film and sound negatives – more closely, Tykkyläinen soon realised that he had found what was left of *Herra Lahtinen* after the attic of the Metropol film theatre was emptied in spring 1944 because of the danger from bombardment and fires. The original material was technically in surprisingly good condition, but it turned out that it comprised only a little more than half the original length of *Herra Lahtinen* – 43 minutes (including 12 without sound), compared to its original total length of 76 minutes. As a guide to the restoration, Tykkyläinen had the copy of the scenario which Tapiovaara himself had used. He was able to arrange the material according to this, and to prepare it for printing with the assistance of the conservators of the Finnish Film Archive.

Thus, *Herra Lahtinen lähtee lipettiin* has been preserved only as a torso; *The Lost Melody* has become a broken, unfinished symphony. Even on the basis of this torso, however, one can conclude that the film is the most ambitious and courageous that Tapiovaara ever undertook, an experimental, visionary work utilising many styles and many dimensions of reality. In those sequences that are preserved, one can see an abundance of elements and genres: drama and comedy, satire, musical, and fairy tale, the realist narration overlapping with dreams, nightmares, stream of consciousness, parallel presence of different "mind screens", experimental use of montage and sound, "pure cinema" with a surrealist flavour. Visions of this kind, combinations of this kind, jumps from everyday reality to poetry and fairy tale, from laughter to serious social commitment, from operetta to *Dreigroschenoper*, were not conventional in the Finnish cinema of the 1930s – or in the cinema of any other country. We still have reason to recognise *The Lost Melody* of Nyrki Tapiovaara as the lost masterpiece of Finnish cinema. And Lauri Tykkyläinen still hopes and dreams that one day he will find a complete print of the film in some forgotten storage depot in the countryside...

The Cobra's Hoard

by Suresh Chabria

I joined the NFAI in 1992, beginning a stint that was to last for six eventful years. Shaped by the twin enthusiasms of cinephilia and the mystique of the cinema's silent and nitrate years, I naturally prioritised India's silent film heritage and renewed the search for silent and early sound nitrate-base films. The former came under the spotlight initially at the Pordenone Silent Film Festival (1994), where the first-ever Indian silent film retrospective was presented. This was followed by the screening of several silent classics with live musical accompaniment during the Cinema Centenary celebrations in India. But the latter objective – the renewed search for nitrate films – required more patience and luck. One was basically following leads provided by veteran film enthusiasts and cine-club organisers who had been assisting the archive over the years. As usual, much of the "information" was myth based on youthful memories and nostalgia; or, in many cases, the copies had simply decomposed.

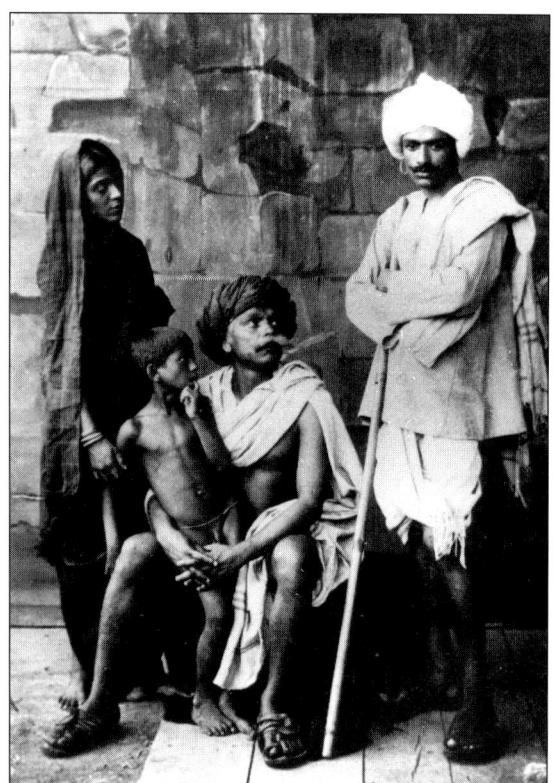

A still from *Savkari Pash* (1925).

National Film Archive of India, Pune.

Fortunately, there was one promising lead. A business family in Kolhapur named Vankudre was known to possess a large amount of nitrate material by the famed pioneer Baburao Painter (1890-1954). Kolhapur is a town some 200 kilometers from Pune, where many film pioneers of western India had begun their careers. One of the reasons for this was a remarkable patron: the then Raja of Kolhapur. Legend has it that not only did the Raja extend the services of his staff and his stables of elephants and horses for film shoots, but he would also grace the sets in person with his retinue, and even offer script suggestions – which, in most cases, had to be immediately carried out. To this day, Kolhapur bears traces of the fading legacy of his benevolent rule. As one drives through winding lanes, crumbling *wadas* or traditional mansions are pointed out as once having housed famous film ateliers or studios. And on a monumental pedestal at a shaded intersection close to Painter's house-cum-museum stands a camera, a replica of the one he put together in 1918 with his disciple V G Damle.

Baburao Painter produced and directed numerous mythological and historical films in the 1920s and 1930s. Various histories of Indian cinema acknowledge Painter's multi-faceted career as a scenic backdrop painter, an avid technical innovator, and as the prime mover of what is often referred to as the Kolhapur school of film-making. He influenced another well-known pioneer, Balji Pendharkar, and all the founders of the Prabhat Film Company – one of the most important institutions of Indian film history. Particularly talked about is his 1925 film *Savkari Pash* (also known as "Indian Shylock"), which was said to be a path-breaking realistic film that tackled contemporary social issues while the bulk of Indian production was mythological and fantasy-oriented.

However, all that was known to have survived of Painter's work were a few stills from his silent films and copies of three of his sound films. Thus, the works on which his legend firmly rested, the films produced in the 1920s by his Maharastra Film Company, were considered lost – unless the Kolhapur connection should amount to anything. My predecessor, P K Nair, had tried to explore this possibility, but for various reasons the negotiations had failed.

It was in the hope that some of the films of this period might still be found that I got in touch with Pune-based film critic and enthusiast S Kinikar and A V Damle. The latter had been chiefly responsible for safeguarding the legacy of the Prabhat Film Company, which had been co-founded by his father in Kolhapur in Painter's heyday, before the studios were moved to Pune in 1933. With their help, contact was once again established with the Vankudre family.

The Vankudres had the material, for a very good reason. In the early 1930s their grandfather, Dhandiram Gopal Vankudre, a dealer of utensils for household use, had attempted to diversify the traditional family business by launching a film distribution company, that was to be followed by setting up a film production firm. Even as the early sound films had begun to appear on Indian screens, he bought up the distribution rights and existing prints of Painter's silent films for re-issue, at the same time initiating steps to produce talkies under his own banner, Samrat Cinetone.

It was during the monsoon that we set out, reasoning that the cool cloudy weather would be the most favourable for returning safely with the nitrate material. As it happened, that year we had had an excellent monsoon, and the roads and adjoining fields were flooded for miles. Eventually, after several detours, we pulled up, damp with rain and anxiety, at a shop front to the welcoming sight of gleaming stainless steel and metal buckets, pots, pans, ladles, and tumblers. We had arrived, but not quite. The four Vankudre brothers, the third generation, were cordial to A V Damle and me, offering us hot sweet tea and agreeing on a solitary point – that this material must be got rid of soon. They then took us to the material itself. They led us towards the back of the shop, towards a wooden staircase below which sat a row of black painted tin trunks.

As I approached someone shouted, "Wait!" "No, it has left," an old shop-hand interjected, "I saw it returning to its hole this morning." A sigh of relief went up, and the mystery was soon explained. A cobra had apparently taken up residence among the trunks, and it could occasionally be seen slithering over them before returning to its hole beneath the stairway. On this day it had slid away. This much is fact. The myth follows.

Folk myth has it that the cobra guards treasures, ready to strike any intruder, but gently acceding to the surrender of its hoard when the true claimant comes along, suitably full of veneration and hope.

In this case it was, undoubtedly, the spirit of film archiving. All present were suitably impressed, even, I presume, the generous cobra, for it had long guarded the trunks, preventing the most recent brood of grandchildren from pulling out strips of film to burn as fire-sparklers, as had been the case with the earlier generation – as one of the Vankudre brothers recalled, the trunks had once been a source of fireworks for their entertainment.

How had D G Vankudre, producer and founder of Samrat Cinetone, allowed this to occur? What had happened to his enthusiasm for cinema, that he later disowned it virulently? His faith in the commercial viability of the re-issued Painter silents seems to have been, shall we say, somewhat misplaced. The commercial failure of his very first talkie venture, a mythological feature called *Nagananda* (1935) – about the legendary foes, snakes and eagles – had sealed his distaste for motion pictures. Taken together, these adventures had constituted a great financial loss for this small merchant-cum-businessman. One of his sons informed us that after this financial disaster he got his entire family together and made them all swear that they would never again have anything to do with the movie business. So disappointed was the patriarch that the customary visits to the local cinema hall or the several studio and location shootings going on in Kolhapur was strictly forbidden. Films were a taboo for the Vankudres until the passing-away of the disillusioned head of the family.

After some negotiations about compensation and the mode of payment, we loaded all the trunks into a van and had them carefully driven back to Pune through the flooded landscape.

Was Painter's *Savkari Pash* in that hoard? One will never know. Most of the material was decomposed, and the assorted material included a number of unidentifiable reels. The footage that could be salvaged by painstaking frame-by-frame printing by K P R Nair, the archive's printing consultant, was badly damaged and scratched. However, almost 4,000 feet of *Muraliwala* (1927), Painter's version of Phalke's *Kalia Mardan* (1919), could be salvaged, along with fragments of three of his other silents: *Maya Bazaar* (1925), *Bhakta Prahlad* (1926), and *Sati Savitri* (1927). As I began to study the salvaged reels, they revealed a distinct and different elaboration of the mythological genre as compared to the work of the more famous D G Phalke. Painter's mythological films were more anecdotal, and delved into the philosophical underpinnings of the stories through the intertitles – thus anticipating the narrative style of this genre in the sound period. As a bonus, good copies of both the Hindi and Marathi versions of *Nagananda* were found.

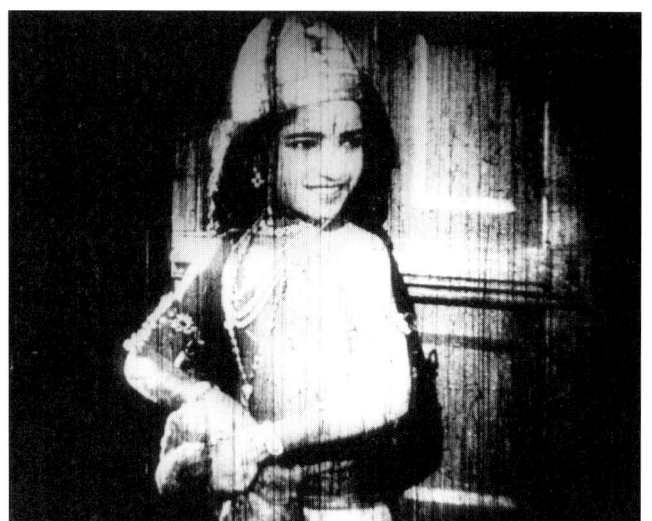

A still from *Muraliwala* (1927).
National Film Archive of India, Pune.

While the salvaged fragments awaited further restoration, and proper public presentation during the Cinema Centenary celebrations, one reel from *Muraliwala* was screened at the archive theatre. In the auditorium was a special invitee – Lalji Gokhale, who had acted as a 9-year-old Sri Krishna in the film. In the reel he briefly appeared in his avatar as Sri Krishna, floating down from the heavens, playing the flute. A senior tabla player today, it was a moving experience for the invited audience to see the child and the man reunited after nearly 70 years. Against all odds, cinema had once again vouchsafed us a rare treat of crossing the barriers of time and space, past and present.

When Time Ran Out...

Looking back at a number of "Nitrate Can't Wait" and "Last Film Search" campaigns from around the world. Note that France's "Nitrate Plan" is recalled in Michelle Aubert's paper in "The Last Nitrate Picture Show".

24 Years to Safety

by Clyde Jeavons

The mid-1970s to the late 1980s was a period of unprecedented hope, promise, even achievement, for the cause of nitrate film rescue and preservation in the United Kingdom. Yet the starting point was a crisis.

On the afternoon of 2 June 1974, a catastrophic explosion at a chemical plant at Flixborough on England's north-east coast killed 29 of the people who worked there and wrecked a hundred or so stone-built houses nearby. The findings of the inevitable public inquiry led a year later to new regulations, which effectively forbade the housing of hazardous materials in built-up areas. Nitrate film was included in this category, and the National Film Archive was given one year to find a new storage site for its own nitrate collection, kept at its preservation centre in the small but closely-populated village of Aston Clinton in Buckinghamshire. (Ironically, the Archive had moved there at the beginning of World War II because of the threat of enemy attack.) If the Archive failed to move, the films were to be destroyed. In fact, it took two years and a stay of execution to secure the necessary funding and re-locate the collection – this time, with compounded irony, at a remote ex-nuclear munitions store near the village of Gaydon in the British midlands, where the Archive took over the existing bunkers and began a programme of new building in 1977.

To some extent, the Archive itself added to the general level of anxiety. Concerned about the lethal properties of nitrate, the NFA in 1976 prompted an official experiment in which a specially-constructed nitrate vault filled with a ton of junk film was ignited in the middle of Ministry of Defence land on Potton Island in the Thames Estuary. A fire should be containable, even at Aston Clinton – the design of the vaults was meant to see to that – but what of the toxic gases emitted? How far would they spread? How rapidly would any toxicity disperse? I remember we stood behind glass in a concrete building on Potton Island several hundred metres away from the controlled conflagration – rather as if observing an atom bomb test – and watched not only a spectacular, explosive fire, but also a huge, dense cloud of poisonous fumes drift slowly across the landscape. One of the cameras used to record the test melted before our eyes... New recommendations on nitrate film storage, including the paper *Handling, Preservation and Storage of Nitrate Film*, published by FIAF's own Preservation Commission in 1986, began to cite the Potton Island test as indicating a need for a protective zone up to 300 metres wide between nitrate stores and inhabited buildings.

Film companies and laboratories were, of course, included in the government's new safety directives. After years of indifference, the cinema industry's eyes started turning with interest to the National Film Archive – now, at its Gaydon site, one of the few repositories considered fit to store nitrate. The Archive prepared itself for an influx of homeless film materials from the various commercial film organisations still anxious to have them available, and indeed, the reels began to roll in. One company, however, seemed to have panicked. Rank Film Distributors at Denham had dumped its entire nitrate holdings onto its car-park: up to 50,000 cans of film piled willy-nilly into an alfresco heap! There may have been some method in this madness. Rank were the main distributors and storekeepers for many of the major US and British film companies, such as Universal, MGM, and British Lion, as well as numerous smaller fry, and this could have been seen as a timely opportunity to be rid of a mass of celluloid now considered largely redundant and little-used.

Horrified, the NFA moved fast to save the threatened car-park collection, the film cans already visibly rusting. Systematic overtures to the various film owners, big and small, were received mostly with relief and gratitude that the Archive was willing to take over long-term storage of their nitrate collections, albeit on a selective basis, and existing deposit agreements were invoked or new ones drawn up. With one strange exception: MGM. The Archive had a perfectly airtight standing agreement with MGM to acquire prints and dupe negatives in the UK which were no longer active, but suddenly the US Chief Executive decided that the MGM nitrate held at Rank should be destroyed and not passed to the NFA. When we asked why, we were told rather puzzlingly that it was because MGM did not want to put these films at risk of piracy (in a national archive?!), and, in any case, they had all the titles adequately covered and preserved back in their own stores in Los Angeles. MGM was adamant. All arguments failed – even the one that pointed out to MGM that, while they were claiming on one telephone that they had all their films safely preserved back in LA, other MGM personnel were telephoning the world's film archives seeking MGM's missing titles which they needed to put into their musical compilation *That's Entertainment!* The press got wind of the story, accused MGM of "cultural vandalism", and corporate and archival horns became locked.

Enter one of the anonymous heroes of film archiving. Anonymous for obvious reasons. We shall call him Reg. Reg was a print manager at Rank. His politics, attitude, and lifestyle were somewhat dubious (he claimed to keep a gun in his car), but they included a natural rebelliousness against authority which turned out to be useful. With a little wooing, Reg was converted to the Archive cause, and, without putting a foot wrong, found ways to hinder and obfuscate the declared fate of MGM's nitrate long enough for tempers to cool and diplomatic negotiations to take place. And, as they often do in the movie world, boardroom changes took place at MGM, and the new regime had no problem with the sensible idea of valuable duplicate film materials finding a home with a responsible institution which had served them well in the past.

David Francis, Curator of the National Film Archive, makes a presentation to mark the 40th anniversary of Harold Brown's joining the staff of the BFI; Deputy Curator Clyde Jeavons waits with a second gift. Aston Clinton, 1975.

Clyde Jeavons.

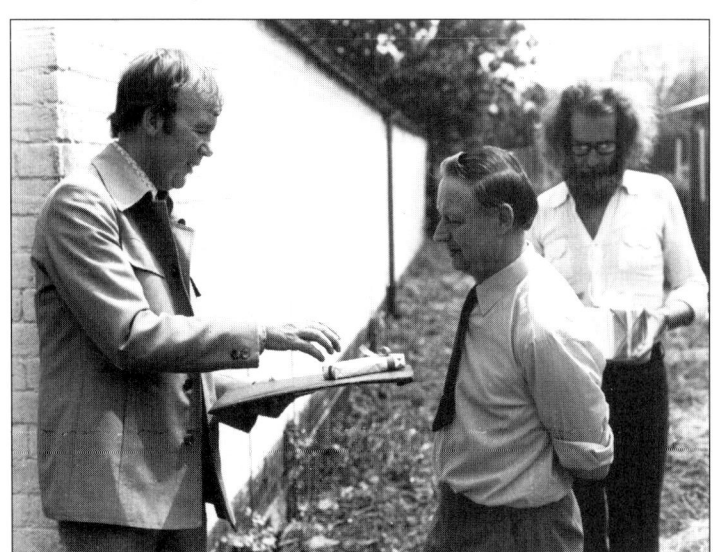

The MGM incident aside, the upshot for the NFA of the great nitrate throw-out and the partisan vigilance of Reg was a mountain of the stuff needing re-housing in preservation conditions – another spur for the expansion of its custom-built vaults at Gaydon in the Warwickshire countryside. The Archive now found itself with an accumulated 140 million feet of nitrate film in its collection, and Curator David Francis could see that the figures did not add up. The thinking then was that nitrate had an average life of 50 years before it would destabilise and decay. That meant that most of it would not last beyond the year 2000 – an evocative date, and one which David was able to quote convincingly in proposing to the government, in 1976, his rescue plan: the 24-Year Nitrate Duping Scheme. The idea was perfectly simple – to copy the Archive's nitrate at the rate of 5 million feet a year (instead of the few thousand feet it could currently afford), so that, by 2000, most of it would be saved by being duplicated onto acetate stock.

It is a sign of more buoyant and enlightened times that the government bought this proposal, and the funding of the National Film Archive became radically transformed so that, for a number of years, previously unimagined targets for copying threatened nitrate film were achieved – never the 5 million feet originally foreseen, but often 3 million and above. This rate of turnover – plus the need to optimise costs and maintain duplicating standards – necessitated the purchase of Hendersons, a commercial black-and-white laboratory. The modest price included a bonus: 30,000 reels of Warner Bros films. Eventually, as completion of the NFA's purpose-built J Paul Getty Conservation Centre in Berkhamsted, with its own in-built lab, approached in 1986, Hendersons was sold again at a healthy profit.

In time, of course, recession and competition for diminishing funds within the BFI ate into the Archive's idealistic equation for copying nitrate to a deadline, and by 1990, the 24-year scheme had become unsustainable, despite another campaign to keep its spirit alive (Nitrate 2000 – described elsewhere in this book).

Curiously, this was not the tragedy it might have seemed, for two connected reasons. One was that the scheme, because it had been rigorously and correctly carried out, had eliminated all the backlog of visibly and predictably unstable nitrate film to a point that considerably less than 5 million feet needed urgent attention each year; and the second was that it had become clear that good storage conditions were prolonging the life of the Archive's nitrate, so that a more relaxed (but not complacent!) view could be taken of the copying imperative for at least another decade or so.

Just as well, really, now that archives face the new and unquantified threat to their safety film collections from the "vinegar syndrome". Nevertheless, time has been bought for nitrate in the UK, thanks to curatorial foresight and good policy-making at the right time. But, as an ex-conservation manager at the National Film and Television Archive was fond of saying, beware the upward curve lurking in every graph...

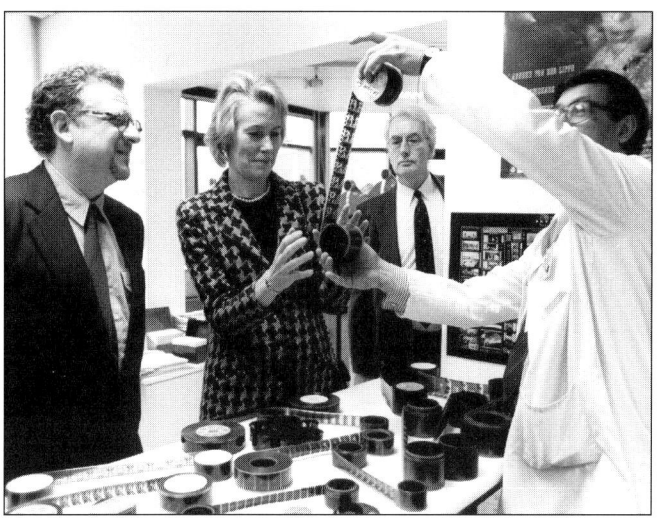

Virginia Bottomley, Secretary of State for National Heritage, visits the National Film and Television Archive's J Paul Getty Conservation Centre at Berkhamsted in the mid-1990s. Kevin Patton, Head of the Technical Inspection Department, shows her the display of early non-standard gauges and other curiosities; looking on are Jeremy Thomas (left – Chair of BFI Governors) and Clyde Jeavons (Curator, NFTVA).

Clyde Jeavons.

The Last Film Search

by Ray Edmondson

Sometime in 1979, the Chairman of the Council of the National Library of Australia, Kenneth Myer, was seeking a way to boost the work of the National Film Archive. He suggested that I devise a worthwhile, sponsorable project which he could recommend for support by a particular foundation with which he had contacts.

An organised and very public national search for nitrate film seemed to me the logical project. While the Archive had for 20 years or more pursued various approaches in searching for lost material, they had been low-key, intermittent, and – for reasons of expense – had involved only limited fieldwork. Outside the collector network and the incidental discoveries which came our way, which I have described in another article in this volume, I believed there was more material in private hands – in old, closed picture theatres, attics, barns, and garages, and elsewhere – that we would never turn up unless we had the means to add a new dimension to the task.

Furthermore, at the time it was received wisdom within FIAF that the world's remaining nitrate film holdings would have pretty well disintegrated by year 2000 (we now know better, of course). We were therefore running out of time. Added to that, the survival rate of Australian silent films was poor – less than 5% of the estimated output was known to exist in archive collections. Sound films of the 1930s and 40s fared better, but there were still major gaps. Finally, there was the sheer size of Australia: a big country with plenty of out-of-the-way places where films might have been left and forgotten. A non-current film programme ending up in an outback country hall at the end of its circuit could easily stay there, because it wasn't worth the distributor's while to chase it up.

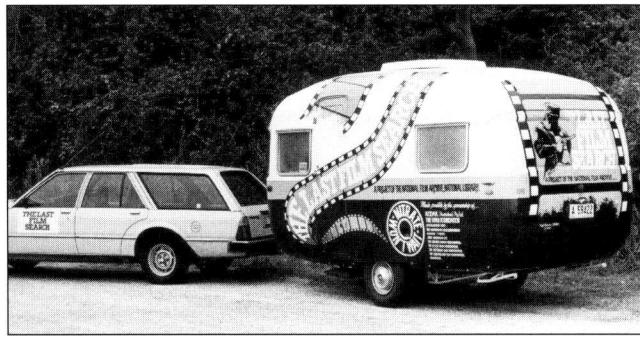

The Last Film Search caravan on its travels.

ScreenSound Australia, Canberra.

How would the task be conducted? A field officer would travel the country, with car and caravan, on a literal treasure hunt. He would have a back-up person at the Canberra archive "base". His arrival in each locality would be pre-publicised through the local radio, TV, and newspaper and his contact details made known. On arrival, he would be interviewed by the media, respond to enquiries, and would proactively search likely locations (such as closed-up theatres) or seek out promising individuals. The Canberra back-up person would follow up on the contacts made once the field officer moved on.

As a working name, I first called the proposed project "Operation Nitrate". Further reflection brought to mind the Peter Bogdanovich film *The Last Picture Show*, an alternative lifestyle book with the striking title *The Last Whole Earth Catalog*, and an article I'd written some years earlier called "The Last Newsreel". So it seemed to me that "The Last Film Search" combined a proper sense of apocalyptic urgency with accurate description. As a slogan, "Nitrate won't wait" – borrowed from "Nitrate can't wait", used by a Canadian colleague – seemed simple, direct, and apt.

In the event, the project proved to be outside the parameters of Ken Myer's intended foundation (later they bankrolled an entirely different project for us), so my deputy, Mike Lynskey, and I went looking for corporate sponsors. Kodak and the Utah Foundation led the final consortium, which collectively provided the required A$100,000-plus. While corporate sponsorship for cultural institutions is common today, it was not so in 1980: it was a new experience for the National Library, and none of us were sure how to handle it!

The Last Film Search was formally launched in October 1981, with film director Peter Weir doing the honours. It immediately gained a media profile, enhanced the following March when former Prime Minister Gough Whitlam launched an associated book, *Australia's Lost Films* (which I had written in conjunction with film historian Andrew Pike). In my favourite press clipping from the Search, the national newspaper *The Australian* did a front-page story on 26 March 1982, headlined (not entirely accurately), "Archivist in Race against Silver Nitrate Time Bomb: Raider of the Lost Art Scours the Countryside for Old Film". The "raider" was field officer Michael Cordell, and as he travelled the backblocks in his brightly-painted caravan he became, for a while, a media phenomenon. For its first year and beyond, the Search garnered immense free publicity in the press, and on television news and chat shows. It ultimately yielded two one-hour television documentaries. My impression was that most Australians came to hear about the Search, picked up the slogan, and understood its basic message. Once a taxi driver in Sydney, who did not know where I worked, regaled me with great enthusiasm about the project – and, as everyone knows, taxi drivers are the best barometer of public opinion!

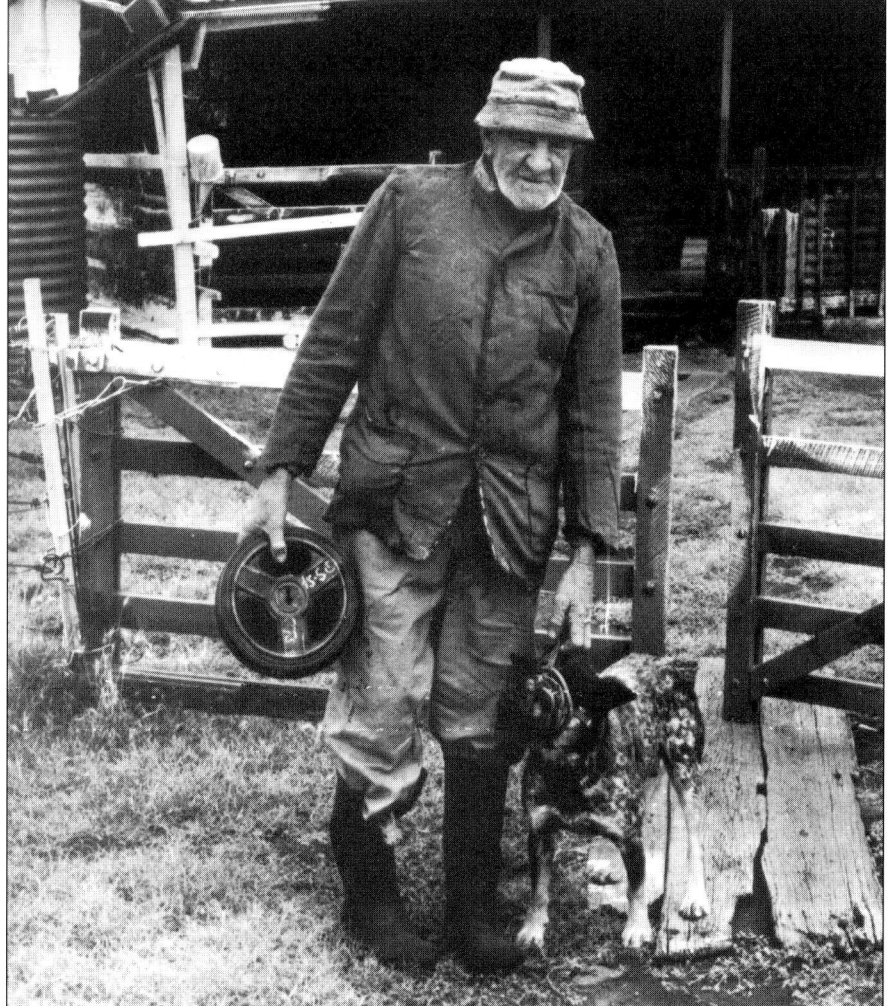

"Blue" Walsh, a collector in the rural backblocks encountered during the Last Film Search.

ScreenSound Australia, Canberra.

Throughout, we did not spend a penny on paid advertising, though we did produce what is now called "collateral" – a project logo, information brochures, "Nitrate won't wait" badges, Last Film Search stationery, wall posters, and even T-shirts – and we distributed these judiciously. Under the sponsorship arrangement, we had access to Kodak's public relations and design department, and their people created the "look" of the Search. At the outset, the relative prominence of each sponsor's name and logo in publicity had been agreed; all of these, in turn, were subsidiary to the project name itself.

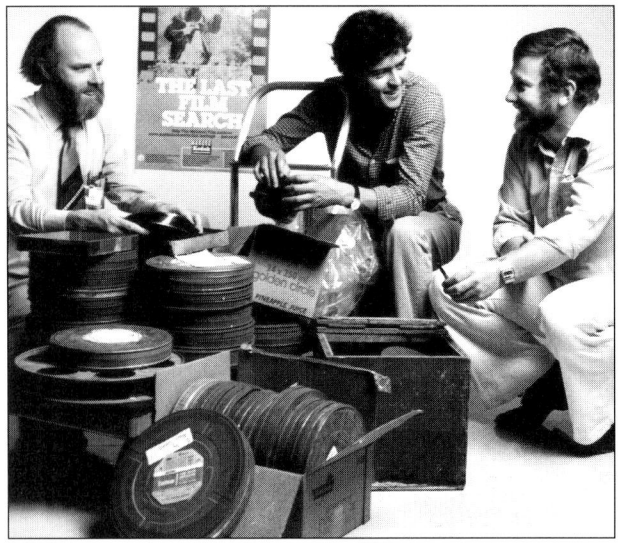

Last Film Search field officer Michael Cordell (centre), dubbed the "Raider of the Lost Art" by a national newspaper, poses with some of the material gathered on one of his tours, flanked by Ray Edmondson (left) and Mike Lynskey.

ScreenSound Australia, Canberra.

The Search officially ran for 5 years, though its most active phase, when it generated the most publicity, was the first 18 months. It turned up over a million feet of nitrate film (plus a lot of acetate), it served its sponsors very well, and it permanently lifted public awareness of the loss and vulnerability of our film heritage. "Nitrate won't wait" is a simple message, and it hit home, publicly and politically. I believe it hastened the day when, in 1984, the National Film and Sound Archive was separated from the National Library to become an autonomous institution, and ultimately achieved adequate funding and means for preserving its nitrate collection. By any measure, the project was a signal success, and to my delight other archives have since used it as an effective model.

I have often asked myself *why* it was so successful, for its public impact was well beyond any of our expectations. I think it was a combination of many things: the name and the slogan, the romantic appeal of a national treasure hunt, the simplicity of the message, the fact that the results were showable on television, and the sentiment Australians have for their film heritage. These insights were all *post-facto*: at the time our strategy (if that's what it was) arose more from intuition than analysis. Perhaps intuition – the conviction that the material was there, and this was the way to find it – was the most important ingredient of all!

Remembering the United Kingdom's Nitrate Project 2000

by Jerry Kuehl

Nitrate Project 2000 was born in April 1986, when Roy Lockett of the ACTT circulated a "private and confidential" letter inviting a number of sympathetic individuals "to discuss the idea of a broad-based campaign to preserve the unique and invaluable film stock in the Pathé and Movietone libraries." The ACTT was the Association of Cinematograph, Television and Allied Technicians, the British motion picture industry's principal trade union (since reconstituted as BECTU – the Broadcasting, Entertainment, Cinematograph and Theatre Union), and in launching their initiative the ACTT was acting on a resolution passed at their annual conference in 1984. At the meeting that resulted from Lockett's letter, however, the ACTT representatives explained that it would not wish, or be able, to take the lead in any campaign – in the high summer of Thatcherism, trade union involvement was no way to persuade the Government to look favourably on any issue. Nonetheless, the Union would of course continue to speak on the issue (indeed its delegate, Jack Amos, would make a stirring speech which won the unanimous support of the 1986 Trades Union Congress for a motion on the subject[1]), and its behind-the-scenes role as facilitator and host for the campaign remained invaluable.

Responding to the ACTT's lead and accepting its hospitality, those of us who were brought into the campaign included members of a number of communities, including film archives, newsreel libraries, laboratories, broadcasters, and historians. An organising committee was recruited through a kind of old boys' – and girls' – network. The issue that we were to address was the fate of nitrate film held in collections outside the UK's publicly-funded archives. The principle of preservation had been accepted (even if the resources remained inadequate) where the National Film Archive, the Imperial War Museum, and the Scottish Film Archive were concerned, but there remained substantial and important collections of nitrate film in other hands, such as those of the two private newsreel libraries named in the ACTT letter. The goal would be to raise public awareness of the threat to these collections, and if possible to open the tap for some public funding to address the problem. Those in the campaign knew we were sailing into stormy waters. No government cares to offer public money to commercial enterprises which have neglected to care for their own assets. This was especially true of the Conservative ministry of the mid-1980s.

The Committee realised it needed to work simultaneously to convince public opinion and the Government on three issues. In the first place, the campaign needed acceptance for the idea that all kinds of film merited preservation, and not only the recognised classics of cinema art that were already protected in the archives. Next, we needed to explain the nature of the "Nitrate Problem" in a way that would compel attention. Finally, the campaign would need to answer the "taxi owner" question: if the State does not bail out taxi owners who fail to maintain their vehicles, why should it come to the rescue of short-sighted owners who let their stocks of moving images deteriorate to the point where they are of no use to anyone?

The Committee began serious work immediately. It acknowledged from the start that it would have to demonstrate precision in estimating the size of the task, responsibility in the way nitrate material was handled by those who held it (for example, recognition in the commercial library sector of the archive principle that original material should not be put at risk by commercial usage), and a credible structure to justify the expenditure of public funds. We spent a year getting this structure in place, then presented it to the public in a 4-page manifesto, which was extensively circulated to a mailing list of hoped-for supporters in May 1987.

The back page of our manifesto carried a listing of "organisations with significant holdings of nitrate material", which included, in addition to the Scottish Film Archive, the North West Film Archive, the Yorkshire Film Archive, and the newsreel libraries originally named by the ACTT, the London Transport Museum, the National Motor Museum, the Sikorski Museum, Cannon Screen Entertainment, the Austin Rover Car Company, the Ray Hooley-Ruston Collection, and London Film Productions. The list was then expanded by careful tabulation of the quantities of material requiring preservation, which at the time ranged from 2,000 ft at the Yorkshire Film Archive to 4.6 million ft at Pathé, and came in total to 12.2 million ft – nearly 4 million metres. The table also noted the costs of carrying out laboratory work to an appropriate level to ensure preservation and access, which were estimated at about £14.5 million.

The two middle pages of the manifesto provided the Committee's answers to the three questions noted earlier. In dealing with the first issue – the value of preserving non-art film – the Committee faced its easiest task: public opinion was simply challenged to deny the case, in the knowledge that such denial was unlikely to come from those who constituted an appreciative audience for a regular diet of archive-based documentary television. In presenting the "Nitrate Problem" the campaign lapsed into the lurid but effective prose that characterised "Nitrate Can't Wait" campaigns at that time, even if archivists blush to recall it 15 years later. "The 'Nitrate Problem' is simple," stated Nitrate Project 2000. "All nitrate film is dangerous to store and use, and it is self-destructive. It is not 'at risk' in some abstract sense. Even as these words are being read, nitrate-based images are self-destructing in British film libraries and private collections." The document then moved on to the big question: why should public money be spent on private collections?

It answered its own question with two simple statements of principle. The first was to maintain that government did indeed have a responsibility, as the films at risk were national assets – a parallel was drawn with the assertion that the British Library spent public money to buy books from private publishers, from which the text moved on quickly, before the reader could reflect on how many questions that statement begged. The real defence on this subject was mounted by explanation of the careful structure that it was proposed should be set up to spend the money the project demanded. "The scheme will be operated through institutions already concerned with the preservation of Britain's heritage, and will be administered by individuals with a proven commitment to the aims of the project," read one assertion. Another said: "The material will be made accessible to all," while acknowledging that commercial libraries would continue to charge for the use of material to which they owned the copyright.

Following circulation of the leaflet, expressions of support flowed in, together with occasional expressions of concern along the anticipated lines (ACTT involvement and benefit to commercial companies). There were also financial contributions, and the Committee decided to use the resulting modest resources on two profile-raising

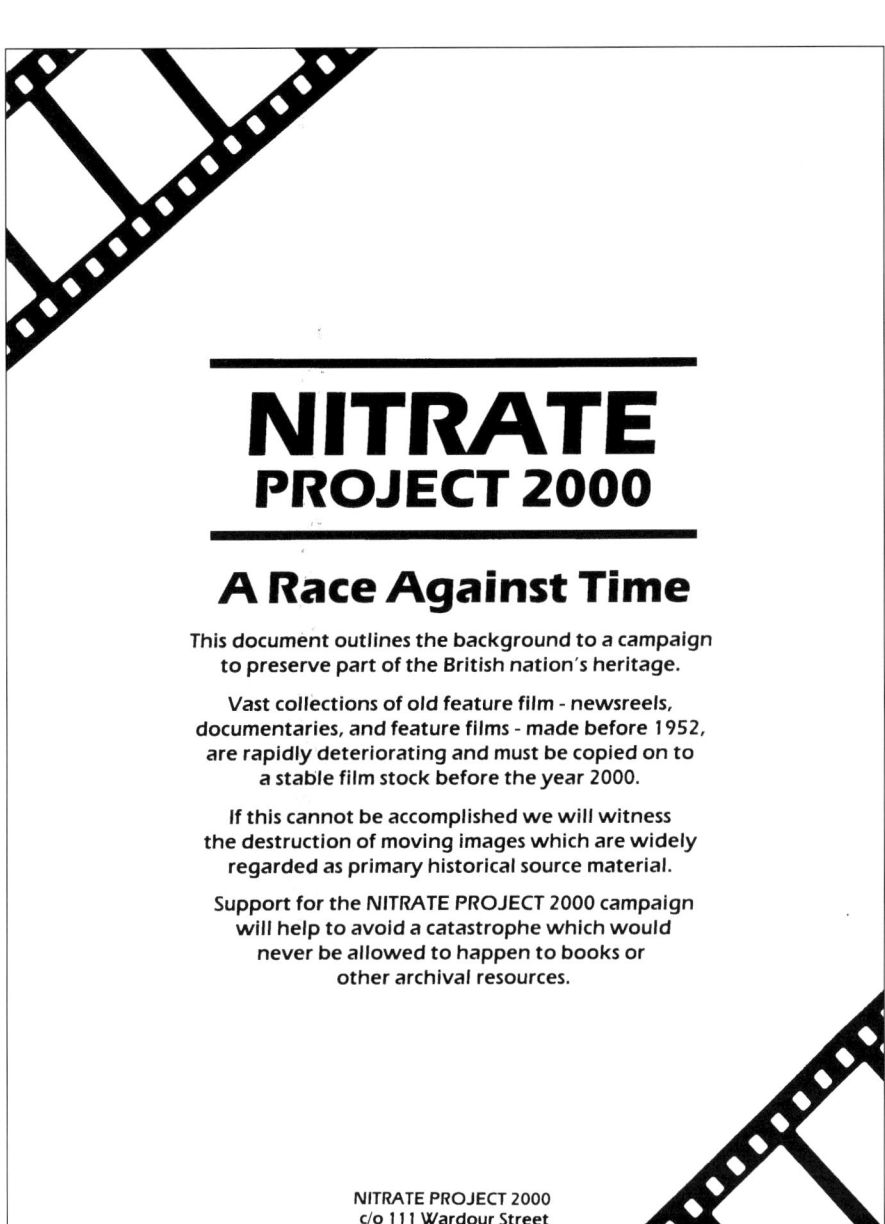

NITRATE
PROJECT 2000

A Race Against Time

This document outlines the background to a campaign
to preserve part of the British nation's heritage.

Vast collections of old feature film - newsreels,
documentaries, and feature films - made before 1952,
are rapidly deteriorating and must be copied on to
a stable film stock before the year 2000.

If this cannot be accomplished we will witness
the destruction of moving images which are widely
regarded as primary historical source material.

Support for the NITRATE PROJECT 2000 campaign
will help to avoid a catastrophe which would
never be allowed to happen to books or
other archival resources.

NITRATE PROJECT 2000
c/o 111 Wardour Street
London W1V 4AY
Tel: 01-437 8506

The front of the manifesto
circulated in May 1987.

Imperial War Museum, London.

events for October 1987: a press conference at the National Film Theatre on 14
October, and a gala launch at BAFTA (the British Academy of Film and Television
Arts) the following evening. Speakers for this event included cinema veterans, such
as Bob Danvers Walker, the veteran Pathé newsreel commentator, who made what
would sadly prove to be his last public appearance at this event. There were also
current practitioners, critics, historians, and committee members. The media paid
attention.

Although it had to compete for headlines with a more literally ground-shaking
event – hurricane-force winds left a broad trail of serious damage across south-
eastern England in the early hours of the following morning – the BAFTA launch
was an unquestioned success. It proved a difficult act to follow, however. The
Committee had gone about as far as it could with its existing rather *ad hoc*
composition. To make real progress, the project would need professional full-time
leadership, clarity about its legal standing (the involvement of commercial
companies made the possibility of charitable status dubious), serious financial

resources, agreement about the interests and intentions of the various participants in the project if such resources were forthcoming, and unambiguous government support. It also had to decide whether to keep its focus on nitrate, or widen its horizons to include other problems in moving-image preservation.

This list offered an insuperable range of problems, and although the Committee continued to meet for another couple of years, it had no further achievement to match the profile of the October 1987 launch. It met for the last time in September 1990. Among its last formal acts was to transfer its balance of £1,500 to the University of East Anglia to help in the setting-up of the world's first degree-level course in film archiving.

We did not succeed in our principal stated aim, which was to persuade the central government to fund the project, but, to be perfectly honest, we had never expected to do that. What we *did* do was to raise consciousness about nitrate film. It is at least arguable that without the ground-breaking work of the Nitrate 2000 committee, a range of projects – from Pathé's commitment to digitise the entirety of their library, to the £14 million National Heritage Lottery Fund grant to the National Film and Television Archive's preservation and access work – would never have happened. There is an irony to it all, however. The Committee's strategy for the safeguarding of this endangered heritage was to transfer nitrate at risk to acetate film, and we now know that acetate film is at much at risk as nitrate.

Notes

1. Here is part of his speech: "… The emulsion becomes sticky and without warning welds together into a frothing mass which malignantly eats through film cans, so that what is left of our visual history is a vile smelling bubbling mass. And that is the end of it – all the efforts and expertise of the workers in our industry gone forever. … If I came to this Congress and reported that all paintings before 1951, because of the pigment used, would gradually but inevitably decompose, there would be outrage. If I told this Congress that books, because of the paper used up until 1951, would become dangerous pulp, then we would take immediate action. But when it comes to our visual history … nothing seems to be done. … I should point out, Brothers and Sisters, that this is our history. The Royals and their ilk are saved for posterity because such film is economically viable, but working-class history of the 20th Century – the Suffragettes, hunger marchers, International Brigades; the terrible suffering here and abroad in two World Wars, the Cold War, Korea – all these major events are disappearing. Of course some of these world-shattering moments have been transferred to safety film, but what about our sports and leisure activities and of course the newsreels concerning the Trade Union and Labour movement? … This is not a motion by a small union based on parochial ideas of nostalgia, but one that concerns all member unions. It is your history, your background and indeed your future that is disappearing. I ask you to support. Thank you."

Seven Years on the Road – The New Zealand Film Archive's Last Film Search, 1992–1999

by Jane Paul and Diane Pivac

Late in 1999, the New Zealand Film Archive completed its Last Film Search project. The 7-year hunt for New Zealand's film history scoured New Zealand for early films, from Kaitaia in the far north to Stewart Island in the south. Thirteen regional searches were undertaken in New Zealand, and one "across the ditch" in Australia. The need to locate and preserve nitrate film was the central theme of the publicity – nitrate, with its connotations of instability, fragility, and volatile nature, offered the most potent symbols for the urgency of preservation – and nitrate film was indeed discovered, but so too was acetate of all gauges, ranging from professional films to amateur productions and home movies. In 7 years the LFS collected 8,000 films. During the period of the LFS, however, the total Film Archive collection grew from 8,000 film titles in 1992 to 37,000 film titles in 2000. Much of the direct deposit of Archive material during these years was a result of the awareness produced by LFS tours.

Logo of the New Zealand Last Film Search.

New Zealand Film Archive, Wellington.

Our inspiration for embarking on our own Last Film Search came from Australia's National Film and Sound Archive, described by Ray Edmondson elsewhere in this book. With hindsight, however, the NFSA told us they were aware of gaps in their planning which had caused some problems and strained their relationship with a few film collectors. They thought their search would have been improved with dedicated project staff, clearer documentation procedures, and more resources to deal with the material brought in. In light of this friendly warning, we took a very cautious approach, involving a region-by-region search, even though New Zealand is only a fraction of Australia's size. Jane Paul devised a plan for a trial search in the Wairarapa region during an Archives Management Course, which drew both on the Australian experience and on the New Zealand National Library historic records search of the Wairarapa in 1990.[1]

The Bank of New Zealand, the Archive's major sponsor, accepted this outline, and the pilot search took place in April 1992. Based on strong local networks, it achieved excellent publicity, including local radio station involvement (with a car painted with LFS slogans following us around with a loudhailer), while national television recorded us climbing around in the eaves of a derelict theatre hunting unsuccessfully for nitrate. We launched the search with two film screenings at the local theatre in Masterton, and the next day the Film Archive's acquisition officer Bill Asher and Jane set themselves up in the local bank. People brought in films, or often the team would go and see them. Two nitrate collections were received, one from an auction house and one from the estate of a film collector, though most deposits were 16mm and 8mm. In total 150 films were received from 40 depositors. It was a useful exercise for us to gauge the amount of film in a small rural community, with one main service town and a handful of smaller towns scattered over a 70-km radius.

After the pilot, the Bank of New Zealand agreed to continue to sponsor a series of regional searches over the next 7 years at a rate of 2 searches a year. A typical search period was 3 weeks, although areas such as Auckland (the largest NZ city) required 6 weeks, as did the Australian search. The project depended on the sponsorship of the BNZ, which covered costs associated with publicity, film screenings, acquisition, and some preservation costs. As well as financial sponsorship, which was generous by New Zealand standards, the project also received regional and local support through bank staff involvement throughout New Zealand.

Three strategies were pivotal to the success of the Last Film Search:
- the Film Archive's policy on deposit of films, and its willingness to be flexible in allowing short-term loan of film collections as an alternative to donation.[2]
- the making of video copies for depositors within an agreed timeframe.[3]
- the holding of screenings in each main town to launch each regional search, followed within a year by a return screening of a selection of films received.

People thus received a circular message: free public screenings, deposit (and gathering of vital data from depositors), videos returned, and finally – with associated publicity – a presentation of a selection of local films received, with due mention of their provenance.

The success of each project relied on extensive community networking. The 6-week pre-search period was crucial in meeting representatives from local archival, museum, and historical groups. Service clubs and collectors' groups were networked. Local Runanga – Maori tribal trust boards – were also invited to speak at our film screenings. This was important to explain our aims to the wider community and build up goodwill. It also helped us form a picture both of "lost" films made in the area, and of significant community events that might have been recorded on film.

Leaflet announcing a typical community screening for the Last Film Search.
New Zealand Film Archive, Wellington.

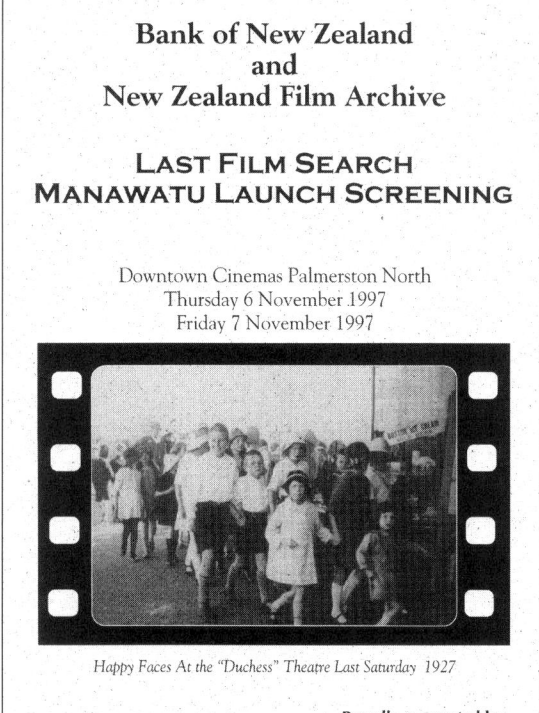

Bank of New Zealand
and
New Zealand Film Archive

**LAST FILM SEARCH
MANAWATU LAUNCH SCREENING**

Downtown Cinemas Palmerston North
Thursday 6 November 1997
Friday 7 November 1997

Happy Faces At the "Duchess" Theatre Last Saturday 1927

THe FILM ARCHIVE

Proudly supported by
Bank of New Zealand

Liaison with the sponsor was also fundamental. For a large corporation, with a network of branches throughout New Zealand and a broad customer base, the searches represented an ideal sponsorship opportunity, and the Bank valued this community-based cultural/arts project, which held equal appeal to cities, towns, and rural areas. It played an integral part in the processes of the search: its name was prominent on all publicity materials, including the van. Local Bank staff were fully briefed in-house by Film Archive staff on the project's aims, and their local knowledge benefited the planning of each regional search. This local contact was particularly important both before we arrived in the district and after initial publicity. Bank tellers often knew which people were collectors or had theatre connections and could identify customers who had long ties with the district and who might have made amateur films, besides which of course they also helped with the one-to-one spreading of the film search message. Staff participated in publicity campaigns, organised vintage car parades, sausage sizzles, and displays of projectors and cameras in branches. Bank branches were primary information bases. These bases were normally managed by three Film Archive staff, the "Last Film Search team", answering enquiries, ringing people who had films or might know who did, following up leads and playing detective. Meanwhile, the branch's own staff passed on messages, filled out forms, and on occasion received and receipted films.

We carted around in our van a portable accessioning table, complete with film viewers and winders, magnifying glasses, a laptop computer with database to check duplication of titles, spools, cans, bags, labels, receipt books, brochures, and posters (including a New Zealand "lost film list" of features and community comedies). We had a portable display and videos of local material to play in the Bank branches. People arrived with films, plastic bags full, and we would gather information, receive films, and physically examine them. We were able to view most 16mm in this way, although large collections of small-gauge films and all the nitrate would be sent back to the Film Archive for appraisal (understandably, the Bank was not keen to have nitrate on its premises). Sometimes we linked up with the BNZ's own activities, in some cases using their marquees at Agricultural & Pastoral Shows as our base.[4] Bank staff were also involved in screenings – the local bank manager as speaker, and staff in period dress handing out programmes and jaffas. In each main centre of the search an opportunity was provided to host a free public screening, and an invitation screening for Bank clients and Archive guests.

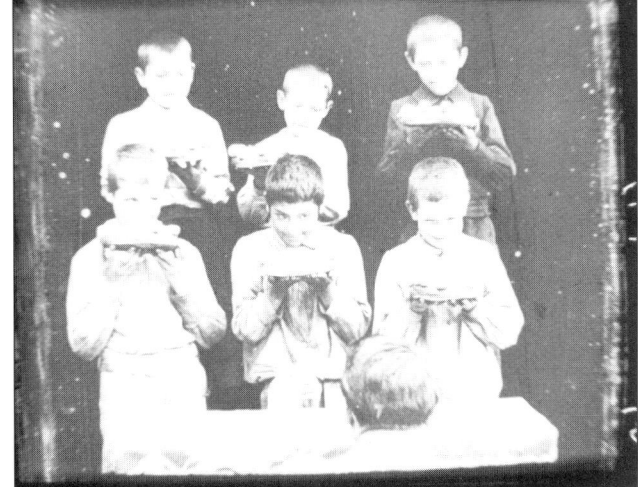

A scene from *Concours de Gourmand*, a French Pathé film of ca. 1905, recovered as part of the Alan Roberts Collection.

Alan Roberts Collection, New Zealand Film Archive, Wellington.

The project recovered a huge range of films recording essential aspects of New Zealand's social history. The film stock was mainly 16mm, followed by 8mm, 9.5mm, and 35mm (both acetate and nitrate). Although nitrate only accounted for 8% of all LFS deposits, it was still a significant quantity. Predictably, many of the nitrate films were received from film collectors. Many of these men (they are almost exclusively male) had links to the NZ theatre industry – theatre managers or projectionists who had taken prints home. It would be naïve to imagine that we have all the nitrate from these people, but we have received many deposits, and made links that are likely to lead to further deposits in due course.

Commonly, film collectors held foreign films – features which we collected only if they were deposited with no strings attached. New Zealand nitrate is relatively scarce, as the country had only a small film industry in the nitrate era. However, very early foreign films with New Zealand connection were more actively sought, with the hope of having this possibly rare film preserved overseas.

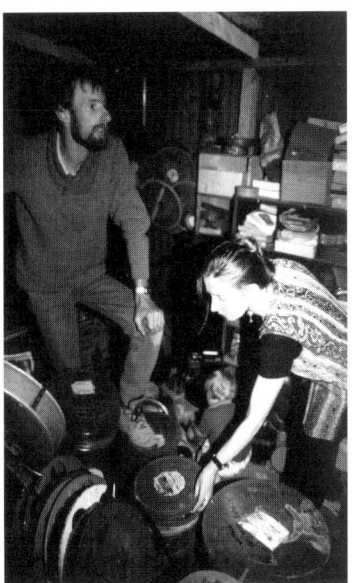

Jane Paul (LFS Co-ordinator) inspecting the Murtagh collection.

New Zealand Film Archive, Wellington.

Nitrate films were produced during the LFS from drawers, wardrobes, attics, sheds, chicken coops, basements, under porches and beds, and even stored under a tarpaulin sheltered by a macrocarpa tree. It is possible that many of these films would have been deposited without a nationwide search project – there is, for example, an active collector group in New Zealand, the Film Buffs, who keep in close contact with the Film Archive – but without doubt some collectors found attractive the possibility of film screenings containing copies of their material and the associated excitement, publicity, and community recognition. This was true of the macrocarpa tree deposit – the nitrate collection received from Alan Roberts during the Hawkes Bay search. Alan's rare European films had been tantalisingly drip-fed to the Archive over a period of 10 years, but it was not until 1993 that he deposited the entire collection, which (with the exception of one film with significant local content, *Fiji and the South Sea Islands*, already preserved by The New Zealand Film Archive) has now been preserved by Cinémathèque Royale in Belgium.[5] It is hoped to make similar arrangements for the preservation by a US film archive of Jack Murtagh's foreign nitrate collection, the other big deposit of nitrate received during the Last Film Search.

Surprising finds were made not only from collectors, but also from people who somehow had a connection with a film-maker, or film subject. These included a number of contest films – beauty, swimsuit, and baby contests from the silent period. Sometimes only a section that related to themselves or a relative survived – possibly an offcut, an indication of who was not regarded as beautiful in 1928! Local "topicals" from Thames, Te Hoe, Carterton, Whanganui, Wellington, and Nelson were also deposited. Other finds included early actuality films, newsreels, documentaries, travelogues, and shorts, as well as promotional films and advertising.

Several New Zealand "community comedies" were deposited during film searches – *Daughter of Dunedin, Daughter of Invercargill*, and *Mary of Marton*. These are examples of a genre that originated in the USA in the mid-1920s, but which New Zealand film-makers made, too: around 24 are thought to have been made, though only 5 survive. The film-maker would arrive in a community, recruit a large unpaid local cast, including schoolchildren and local fire brigades, and shoot a film using a stock script, with a simple plot line (revolving around a lovely schoolteacher and her two suitors, for example), which could be set amid the town's recognisable beauty spots, and which featured car chases, intrigue, and near-misses with trains. Quickly made and hurriedly processed, the films would do good business with the same audience that had supplied their cast. Community comedies were always very popular, and offered a method of survival for early film-makers, who would move on and repeat the formula in the next town.[6]

LFS publicity led directly or indirectly to the deposits of a number of "firsts", including:

- The earliest New Zealand film, showing the second contingent of troops in Wellington before their departure for the Boer War in 1900. (Its restoration is described in the article "Fragile History", elsewhere in this volume.)
- The earliest international rugby test footage so far located, showing the "Original" All Blacks playing England at Crystal Palace, London, on 2 December 1905. The origins of this film – which was received from Mr and Mrs Batchelor of Christchurch – are unknown: the donors think the late Ernest Batchelor may have picked it up at the local rubbish tip. After his death, the film was kept for many years in his son's garage. Conservation Manager Cushla Vula

A frame enlargement from the film of the "original" All Blacks playing against England in London in 1905.

New Zealand Film Archive, Wellington.

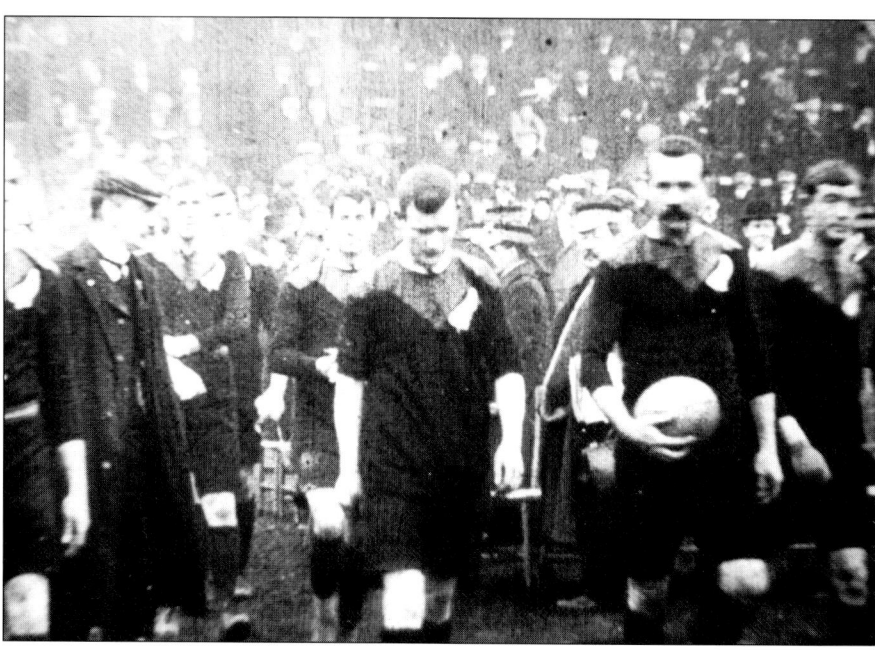

was able to identify the film's age from the small perforations; subsequently the date and location of the event were identified for us by local rugby historians. Apart from being a little brittle and shrunken, the film was in good condition and was repaired and copied. The 250 ft (80 metres) of film include good shots of both teams, the famous All Black *haka*, and a minute or so of the game. What does not appear is even one of the three winning All Black tries, which for us suggests the cameraman was an Englishman!

- The earliest home movie in the FA collection, made in 1910 by Wellington still photographer Lesley Hinge.
- The earliest known film of an international rugby league game in Australia or New Zealand – a match between Auckland and England at Auckland Domain on 25 July 1914. This film was received from an Auckland film collector, Roger Stewart, who was given it by his father.
- The earliest NZ sound-on-film tests, made by Ted Coubray in about 1928, were found in a shed in Papakura and deposited during the Waikato LFS. A section of the early feature film, *Rewi's Last Stand* (made by pioneer New Zealand film-maker Rudall Hayward in 1925) was also deposited during the Waikato search.

The LFS in Australia (1999) was an interesting extension of the project. The expectation of significant amounts of New Zealand film being held in Australia was derived from my earlier (1995) ANZAC Fellowship research, which uncovered significant New Zealand material largely within newsreel collections at ScreenSound Australia, or the National Film and Sound Archive, as it was then known. These included film of the funeral of New Zealand Premier Richard John Seddon (1906) in SSA's Corrick collection, a newsreel showing the return of the Pioneer Maori Battalions to Auckland in 1919, and a previously unidentified nitrate film of the World Sculling Contest on Whanganui River in 1909, which features New Zealand competitors Dick Arnst and William Webb.

The Last Film Search team (Jamie Lean and Jane Paul) continued the research into the SSA's own collection while also contacting other large film-collecting institutions and film collectors, and targeting New Zealanders in Australia as likely sources of historic New Zealand films. The LFS in Australia was hosted by SSA in their branches in Melbourne and Sydney, while in Brisbane we were based at the Queensland State Library. Important nitrate footage was found at SSA and from a Sydney film collector. Altogether, nearly a hundred films were repatriated from Australia, including significant private collections made by New Zealanders now living "across the ditch". Most deposits from SSA were, however, Beta copies of Australian-produced newsreel items showing New Zealand or New Zealanders. *Australian Gazette* and later *Cinesound Review* and *Movietone* newsreels provided a feast of New Zealand items, ranging from historic footage of the funeral of King Mahuta (1938) and the Napier Earthquake (1931) to the idiosyncratic "World's Biggest Egg-Laying Contest" (ca. 1930).

This Australian research was followed by a Winston Churchill Fellowship award in late 1999 to research New Zealand items in film archives and film libraries in United Kingdom and USA. This also resulted in the discovery of a large number of significant New Zealand items. Copies of some of these films have now been repatriated, and more are to follow. These research projects have greatly added to New Zealand documentation on film, particularly pre-1940.

The LFS was an acquisition project of unprecedented scope and breadth in New Zealand. It meant the Film Archive had to adapt many new processes very quickly to keep up with acquisition, accessioning, preservation, and depositor and project requirements, and it is a credit to the staff that they met these demands and continued to do so for 7 years. The extraordinary range and quantity of films that have been collected is now accessible for public screenings, school programmes, and research projects. In most cases the Archive was able to copy the films received, although in a small number either vinegar syndrome or nitrate decomposition was too advanced. The Search also benefited the Film Archive by ra~ing its public profile, strengthening its relationship with the Film Buff organisati~ ~, and helping to create a strong local network of community support. This was ~strated a few years ago when a construction worker stopped his bulldozer wh~ ~he unearthed some old cans of film, and brought them into the Archive. Anot~ ~of the many spin-offs of the project was the connection made with people wh~ ~oduced films, starred in films, or ran theatres. This has enlarged our picture o~ ~ ~Zealand film history.

The LFS screening programmes were very popular, and the Bank of New Zealand in 2000 extended the sponsorship to a Travelling Film Show – free public screenings, including the best LFS finds replayed in the regions. In the 8 months of the Travelling Film Show, 103 shows were screened to 23,000 people. Crowds filled halls, cinemas, and even a tent in the Chatham Islands, to watch the specially-tailored local programmes with piano accompaniment. The response to the images has been poignant, continually reinforcing the message of the LFS project: to find, preserve, and take the films back to the communities they came from.

Notes

1. The aim of the National Library's search, however, was to document the whereabouts of collections rather than to acquire them.

2. The depositor always retains ownership of the material. Loan for copying was, however, a popular option for film collectors.

3. Videos were returned between 3 months and 1 year, at an average cost of NZ$30. Roughly half of depositors took up this option.

4. New Zealand has a tradition of A&P Shows – agricultural fairs held annually in most rural areas.

5. See Jonathan Dennis's introduction to *Under the Macrocarpas: Treasures of Early European Cinema – The Alan Roberts Collection* (Wellington: New Zealand Film Archive, April 1996).

6. *Editors' Note*: An article about an American example of such a film, *The Man Haters*, is featured elsewhere in this volume.

Tradition Is…the Preservation of the Nitrate Film Heritage in Austria

by Ernst Kieninger

Just as in other countries, the year 2000 has been seen by the Filmarchiv Austria as a kind of magical watershed in matters relating to the safeguarding of the national film heritage. The pessimistic predictions of the 1970s and 1980s, when we believed in the irretrievable decay of any film material not preserved by the turn of the century, have been replaced by a cautious and sometimes even euphoric optimism. All the efforts which we mobilised in 1996 concentrated on the Archive's leading project, to safeguard the endangered stock of nitrate film, under the banner *Preservation of the Film Heritage*.

In the mid-1990s the situation was not particularly encouraging. Low levels of financial support meant that up to that time only 35% of the overall stock of 12,000 nitrate reels kept in our Laxenburg stores (20 kms south of Vienna) had been reprinted. Moreover, it had to be faced that large parts of our national film production were missing.

The first priorities were to raise people's awareness and to try to convince the authorities responsible for cultural affairs of the necessity to preserve the audiovisual documents which bear witness to Austrian history in the 20th century. In both cases it was important to emphasise that the matter is one of common interest, not one which is limited to the private pleasures of a small group of film fans.

Our strategy was to work simultaneously in two directions: the actual safeguarding of films, and the public preparation of the subject to secure the necessary financial means.

The first task was to search for the lost nitrate films. The success rate for film stocks already preserved was quite modest when compared to the totals of our national film production. A preservation ratio of no more than 5% of silent film production and less than 30% of sound film production before 1938 made the Austrian film archive rank far below the European average. Many reasons can be found why the nitrate films only survived by chance in our country. Two of the most important were that there had never been any obligation for legal deposit (dépôt légal), and that nitrate films were destroyed at the end of their distribution, the same as everywhere else.

In 1967 a safety film law was passed in Austria, together with a decree on nitrate film. From then on it was forbidden to keep nitrate films on domestic property, especially on the top floors. Many private collectors and some public institutions got rid of their "hot property" almost in panic.

The nitrate vault which was built at Laxenburg by the Austrian Film Archive in 1972 then became a central place for the deposit of unwanted films. Unfortunately, the Archive had a serious fire disaster in the early years of nitrate film preservation. In the summer of 1974 a reel of nitrate film caught fire, causing several thousand reels to be completely destroyed.

In the 1980s, the journalist and historian Hugo Portisch presented a big series on Austrian national television recalling Austria's history from the fall of the Habsburg Empire up to the recent past. The 30 episodes of that television series were composed mainly of material from our film collection, and in this way treasures from our nitrate film stock were introduced to the public for the first time, in a way that made a deep impression. Referring to our endangered nitrate film heritage, Hugo Portisch invented the slogan "the audiovisual memory of the nation", and emphasised the importance of its needing to be preserved from now on. The Film Archive received a lot of attention following that popular TV series. Nonetheless, the financial means for film preservation remained modest.

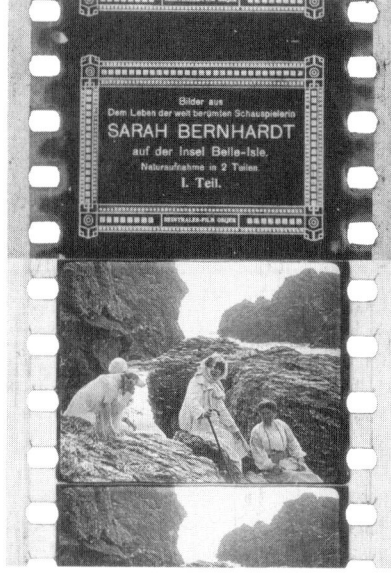

In the early 1980s, the Film Archive started the restoration of important Austrian film classics in a systematic way. Particular attention was paid to silent films. The research work dedicated to this subject intensified the connections with foreign film archives organised through FIAF. In the Nederlands Filmmuseum, Amsterdam, the long-lost Austrian silent film *Die Stadt ohne Juden* (City without Jews; 1924) starring the popular comedian Hans Moser in an early role, was discovered, while in the Cinemateca Brasileira, São Paulo, were found both *Die Ahnfrau* (The Ancestress; 1919), a silent film of the Austrian pioneer production company Wiener Kunstfilm, and *Der Märtyrer seines Herzens* (The Life of Beethoven; 1918), the first film biography of the composer. An outstandingly spectacular example of a restoration case came with *Sodom und Gomorrha* (Sodom and Gomorrha; 1922), the most expensive Austrian movie of all time. Nitrate footage of this screen epic made by Mihály Kertész (Michael Curtiz) was found at Gosfilmofond, Moscow, at the former Staatliches Filmarchiv der DDR in Berlin, at Magyar Filmintézet, Budapest, at Národní Filmový Archiv, Prague, and at the Cineteca del Comune di Bologna.

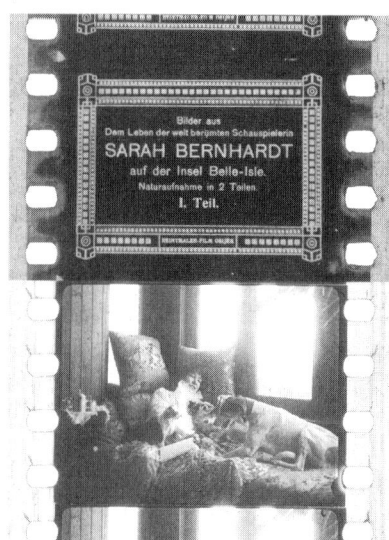

Within the remit of our main nitrate film project, *The Preservation of the Film Heritage*, the search for films was expanded to all lost feature films shot before World War II. More Austrian movies were found to have survived than we had dared suspect or hope. We have to be very grateful to all our fellow FIAF archives, who also care for the films of smaller countries in addition to their own national preservation programs. The Filmarchiv Austria now is at work to update the Austrian Filmography, which will be the basis for national film research in the future.

Besides the films discovered via deliberate searches, it sometimes happens that films find their way into the film archive by chance. The history of nitrate film in Austria is therefore a history of odd and sometimes remarkable discoveries. From time to time anonymous tin boxes still turn up somewhere in our country containing genuine rarities and even material unique on a worldwide scale.

Frame enlargements from the film *Scenes from the Life of the World Famous Actress Sarah Bernhardt on the Island of Belle Isle* (ca. 1910). (See also Colour Section 2.)

Filmarchiv Austria, Vienna.

How often can one find an unsuspected work of art in the cellar of a condemned building? In 1995, employees of our archive saved a whole nitrate film collection from such a house, including the silent film classic *Varieté* (1925), a key work in the aesthetic tradition of sober realism. A few hours later, and the builders would have buried a manifesto for a new perception in cinema, the use of the free-moving camera by Austrian cinematographer Karl Freund, here demonstrated more strikingly than in any other material. This turned out to be a print made from the film artist's original negative, including many previously unknown takes. The Filmarchiv Austria has started the restoration of this unique material with international co-operation. In the same condemned building were found the long-missing screen tests for *Der blaue Engel* (The Blue Angel; 1930), starring Marlene Dietrich, as well as near-complete nitrate prints of Leni Riefenstahl's 2-part *Olympia* (1938). Altogether, we managed to save 3 cubic metres of film material from partially-disintegrating cardboard boxes; after a thorough cleaning they were put into proper storage.

Odd stories of film discoveries recur again and again. In the cellar of a Viennese building films of Sarah Bernhardt and Georges Meliès lay dormant, to mention only two highlights from the complete stock of a distributor from the years between 1910 and 1920 which we uncovered in 1998. Ignaz Reinthaler was a distributor and the owner of a cinema in the Croatian town of Osijek, which belonged to the Austro-Hungarian monarchy at that time. From there he obviously provided the Balkan regions with films from Pathé Frères, Gaumont, Messter, Sascha Film, or Wiener Kunstfilm. By some unbelievable luck this collection of more than 70 films from that period found its way to Austria despite the turmoil of World War I. After Ignaz Reinthaler's death the nitrate films were left in the cellar of a Viennese house, where they remained until their discovery by the Filmarchiv Austria. It is worth noting that the films were packed in their original boxes, partly retaining the actual order in which they had been programmed. The main restoration problem in this case is the high degree of mycosis caused by the humid rooms in which the films had been stored for decades.

In 1985 another attractive discovery took place, on the top floor of a workshop used to print labels for wreaths. The film cans, sprinkled with gold dust from the label inscriptions, were found at the bottom of a chest containing printing colours. They appeared to be the forgotten store of the owner of a travelling showman. The films were covered with labels carrying inscriptions like "Last Greetings" and "In eternal memory". During the closing-down sale of that print shop we succeeded in saving this unique treasure of the early Austrian cinema at the very last minute, because some of the films had already been thrown into the trashcan. This collection included partly-hand-coloured nitrate film prints of almost 70 titles from Pathé Frères, in excellent condition. They have been now preserved.

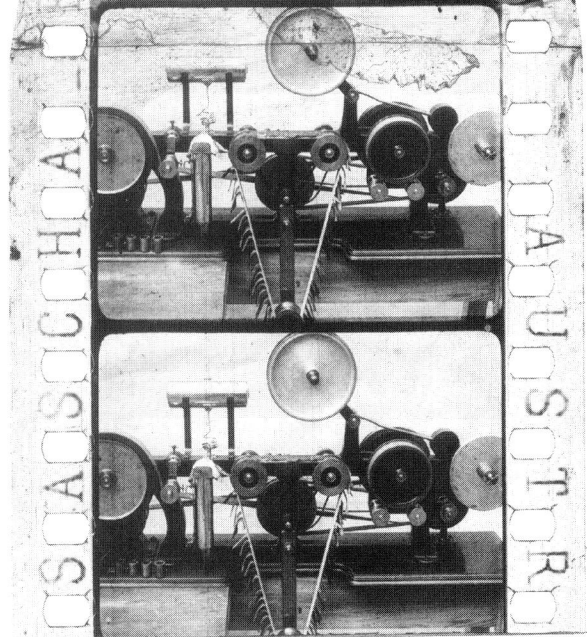

Frame enlargement from the film *Ideale Filmerzeugung* (The Ideal Way of Film Production; 1916).
Filmarchiv Austria, Vienna.

It is amazing how these discoveries reveal the fragile basis for the survival of the film medium. The very fact of the technical possibility for virtually unlimited reproduction which is characteristic of the medium is what also nearly leads to its vanishing. Being a mass-produced article, the single screening print, the central tool of the cinema, is thought to be of no value after exploitation. Even today many prints are dropped at the rubbish tip. This helps explain the fact that not one single useful print is left today of many important films, whether they were trivial box-office hits or classics of film art, even though they were distributed worldwide in hundreds of copies. Does the incidental way that films are passed on – which often culminates in absurdities – reveal the low level of cultural validity still granted them by society at large?

After years of consistent endeavour to preserve the nitrate film heritage in Austria we can offer the following conclusions:

1. The remains of the Austrian film heritage are more extensive than was thought until quite recently. The scope of that heritage extends beyond the concerns defined by a traditional perception of film history based on established codes and value systems. One has to take into account discoveries outside official lists of wanted materials, and respond to the numerous fragments and the various artefacts that are passed on by chance. By extension from this point of view, we can see that the overall archival task needs to be defined as not only meaning the preservation of the national film production but also the collection and preservation of the pioneer era of the whole new media system which is in progress at this moment, through its various manifestations, such as TV or the Internet.

2. The general conditions for the preservation of our film heritage have to be improved significantly. On the threshold of a new age, important parts of this heritage are still endangered by decay. One main reason for this is the problem of inadequate storage. Films of all kinds of genres – mainstream features as well as anonymous moving images, mainstream commercial cinema history beside small private stories, landmarks of film art alongside documents of everyday culture shot quite by chance – all representing the most important form of culture of the 20th century, are currently being stored by the Filmarchiv Austria, already in containers and other places not properly adapted for storage, because of lack of money and storeroom capacities. In addition to this, a large amount of features and documentaries discovered at home and abroad are waiting to be stored at our archive. Austria has to be aware of its responsibility towards its international partner archives, who have cared for and stored our material for so long. The time has come to finish the long debates, and build new storage facilities.

Film is an extremely fragile and vulnerable material. Improper storage leads to decay, especially where nitrate film is concerned. In the end, only powder and dust remain from the moving images that make our world immortal. But: **Tradition is the passing on of the fire, and not the worship of the ashes.**

This aphorism, first uttered by Gustav Mahler, is used as the title of a new trailer for the Filmarchiv Austria, made by Gustav Deutsch.[1] It pleads for the preservation of our nitrate film heritage by using the tools of the medium. The film-maker treated and edited pieces of decayed nitrate film belonging to the Reinthaler collection. The last flickering of an anonymously burning fire, the devastated frames transformed by slow-motion and doubling effects, symbolise the leading subject of our work, made visible via the artistic treatment of these film fragments.

Fire, which represents the immanent signature of nitrate film, also describes the passion which is necessary for the race against time to readapt for the screen the old nitrate material stored for decades in rusty tin boxes. It is by no means a matter of invoking a romantic view of past cinema eras – the point is to intensify awareness of how this past could function nowadays. Habits of reception have changed today. Even if the best goal is still an original style of presentation, this is no longer universally effective, especially where silent film is concerned. Illusion has to be replaced by information, which means that a highly transparent description of the ways in which historic film can be treated and made ready for screening is required. At last year's Vienna International Film Festival, Viennale '99, the Filmarchiv Austria introduced to the public for the first time the results of its project *The Preservation of the Film Heritage*.

During the spring of the year 2000, the Filmarchiv Austria started a new style of presentation: within the monthly screening schedule, full-length programmes of compiled fragments ("Bits and Pieces") as well as restored Austrian features and documentaries will be shown in the best quality available, accompanied by detailed information. The intention is to establish a form of cinema archaeology applied to the screen. It should provide insights into our film heritage, to expose a universe of moving images hardly uncovered so far. It is also a matter of public relations, to cope with one of the most striking cultural challenges of the years to come.

What has to be decided is this: whether to lose the documents of the most important cultural revolution of the 20th century, or to pass on these documents into the new Millennium in the best way still possible. The route forward has been figured out. The subjects are defined. Now the moment has come to act without delay. What we need for that challenge is the well-proved co-operation with our FIAF partners, and the full aid of the authorities responsible for cultural affairs in Austria. "Nitrate won't wait" has been the watchword of many archives, and so now we proclaim: "**Tradition is... the preservation of the film heritage.**"

Notes

1. „Tradition ist die Weitergabe des Feuers und nicht die Anbetung der Asche." (Although Mahler's aphorism is quoted in various forms in the original German, this is the most common rendition.) A description of the trailer is included in the Filmography elsewhere in this volume.

Nitrate Film Repatriation – a diplomatic experience

by Ann Baylis

It is not often that we hear stories of reciprocal generosity, hard work, enthusiasm and commitment on a grand scale. It is my great pleasure to have been a part of one such episode, and to be able now to tell the tale of the repatriation of nitrate films to be preserved and made accessible once again in their countries of origin.

This exchange of treasures happened during the five-year period 1989 – 1994, between countries that lie at the opposite ends of the world, and it came about through the hard work and determination of the staff in a number of organisations. The largest single exchange of film treasures took place between the Australian National Film and Sound Archive (NFSA) and the American Film Institute (AFI) acting on behalf of a number of American archives, with other significant exchanges taking place between the NFSA and the national film archives of Canada, France, Germany, New Zealand and the United Kingdom.

In a number of stages over many years, NFSA staff selected, sorted, rewound and packed over 5,000 cans of nitrate film for efficient and safe transport. We negotiated with curators, shipping companies and customs departments in many locations, and then arranged to have the films shipped to various archives around the World. Finally, archivists at their destinations identified the films, added them to their inventories and integrated them into their own stores. As they did so, some unexpected treasures were rediscovered, including a number of unique early French films, the first Canadian regional film – a Vancouver travelogue from 1907 – and two lost Harold Lloyd films. Since then, the work has continued with smaller consignments of nitrate films repatriated as they are identified.

There was sadness within the NFSA as these films were packed, and a reluctance to lose such a large part of the Australian heritage. We generally recognised, however, that, if the films were to be copied and accessible within a reasonable time, then they had to be repatriated for attention in their country of origin. The first nitrate film repatriations in 1989–90 came about as a result of finding that much of the material had begun to deteriorate. The later and larger repatriations in 1994, however, were of material that did not require immediate attention. They were entered into in a spirit of genuine desire to see the best outcomes for the early heritage of other countries. In return, the NFSA wished to be given copies of selected non-Australian films that form part of the Australian film heritage.

Prior to the repatriation exchanges, Australia had already been the grateful recipient of early films of Australian relevance. Films from the established archives in other countries helped to fill the gaps for the fledgling National Film Archive of Australia. They included the 1896 Lumière footage of scenes in Melbourne shot by Marius Sestier, which were sent by the Cinémathèque Française in the 1970s; prints of Frank Hurley films from the NFA in London; and copies of early films that featured Australian film stars from the American archives.

As Jane Paul has acknowledged elsewhere in this book that the New Zealand Film Archive's 'Last Film Search' was based on a precedent set by the National Film and

Sound Archive in Canberra, it gives me pleasure to acknowledge in turn that the idea of large scale repatriation of nitrate films to their countries of origin was hatched between Jonathan Dennis, the Founding Director of the New Zealand Film Archive, and Eileen Bowser, then Curator of the Film Department of the Museum of Modern Art (MOMA) in New York. Eileen and Jonathan came to an agreement that American films in New Zealand would be freighted to New York at the expense of the American archives, and that copies of 50% of the films would be returned to the NZFA. This repatriation happened in 1988.

A modified version of this idea was negotiated between Ann Baylis of the NFSA and Susan Dalton of the American Film Institute, on behalf of the North American film archives. Eileen Bowser was a keen supporter of this proposal. The first repatriation of American films from Australia happened in 1989, to be followed later by further, larger batches. The responsibility for preservation, storage, and copying of these films was to be shared among a number of American archives, such as UCLA, MOMA, George Eastman House and the Library of Congress. The films were freighted by the AFI to the Library of Congress facility, then catalogued and distributed to the participating archives. It was an absolute pleasure to collaborate with Susan Dalton, who managed the whole project for the AFI with professionalism, enthusiasm and sheer hard work, and for whom nothing was too much trouble. The scale of the task confronting her and the range of material involved were described in an AFI press release:

> Dalton describes the 1600 films as ranging from pre-1900 through the 1950s and including all types and genres of film. Many are apparently the only existing copies. Among the earliest "lost" films are AN INDIAN SUNBEAM (1912), with Broncho Billy Anderson, the world's first cowboy film star; AMONG THE MOURNERS, a 1914 Keystone comedy starting Charley Chase; and BRINGIN' HOME THE BACON (1924), one of the earliest features starting Jean Arthur.

This repatriation also included two lost Harold Lloyd films *Once Every Ten Minutes* and *Peculiar Patients' Pranks* (both 1915). The feature film *Alias Jimmy Valentine* (1915), directed by Maurice Tourneur, was also repatriated, as was the trailer of *The Patriot* (a silent film, not the Mel Gibson title of 2000!).

Where Canada was concerned, the earliest regional film, *Vancouver* (1907) and *A Canadian Winter Carnival* (1905) were found in the repatriated treasures. As the Canadian archivist Bill O'Farrell wrote to me:

> while the Vancouver item was the subject of great interest, I doubt anyone has suggested the following. Those 3 copies represent the earliest emulsion we have yet collected for the national collection – of images shot in Canada. We have a few dozen cans of Edison and Lumiere, but the Vancouver item was an especially stunning canuck addition to the holdings.

There has been a long tradition within FIAF of supporting archives to acquire prints of their own country's heritage and the Australian archive has been the beneficiary of this tradition. The latest of these reciprocal gifts is the American version of the classic Australian silent feature, *The Sentimental Bloke* (directed by Raymond Longford, 1919), which came from the George Eastman House Film archive in the late 1990s in circumstances described by my colleague Ray Edmondson elsewhere in this book. The following paragraphs list only a few of the films of Australian importance that have had a significant impact for us.

- The Centre Nationale du Cinématographie (CNC) at Bois D'Arcy has developed the equipment necessary to print original Lumière films onto modern 35mm film stock (which uses a different perforation format), and Mme Michele Aubert, the Conservateur of the CNC's film archive, organised the transfer of a number of Australian Lumière films so that she was then able to send both duplicating negatives and prints to Canberra in late 1988 as a gift for Australia's Bicentennial. The Australian Lumière films had been shot in Sydney and in Queensland in 1899 by the first Government-employed cinematographer, Fred C Wills. These films have recently been the subject of much celebration in Queensland, where their centenary was observed with a recreated screening of the original footage in Brisbane in November 1999.

- In the Australian National Film Archive's early years, prints were acquired of the Antarctic films shot by the Australian cinematographer, Frank Hurley. These prints were acquired from the British Film Institute's National Film and Television Archive, and included *Pearls and Savages* and *Endurance*. As part of the 1994 repatriation agreement, the BFI/NFTVA has agreed to provide prints of the restored versions of the Frank Hurley films in their possession. The first of these was supplied in 1999, when a beautiful print of the restored version, tinted and toned, of Hurley's film *South* was sent to the NFSA. This film has been screened in both Australia and New Zealand, to much acclaim and acknowledgment of the restoration skills of the NFTVA.

Conclusion

The many staff within the National Film and Sound Archive of Australia who worked so hard on all the stages of the various repatriation consignments deserve a huge vote of thanks from the film archiving community. My thanks and appreciation go to the various curators in the different archives who contributed with passion and enthusiasm to the successful repatriation of their country's nitrate films. Thanks are especially due to Susan Dalton whose organisational skills and expertise in identification of early films benefited us all.

Saving Egyptian Film Classics

by Sayed Badreya

Unlike the majority of the campaigns described in this section, which have effectively run their course, I want to bring to your attention a project which has only recently gotten under way.

In October 2000 I travelled to Cairo to study and garner support for my efforts to preserve Egyptian film classics. Before I visited the Egyptian Film Company, which stores the negatives and positives of nearly all surviving Egyptian film, I knew about the fires at Studio Misr in the 1950s and 1980, which were reported to have destroyed a lot of nitrate negatives. However, that was nothing compared to what I was about to find happening to beloved Egyptian classics in the Company's so-called storage facilities...

When I arrived in Giza, on the outskirts of Cairo, at the office of the director in charge of storage, I was impressed with how grand his office was, and how cool the air-conditioning was keeping it. My hopes rose that the storage facility was doing its job. Then the staff took me back to the warehouse where the movies of my childhood heroes and idols were stored. A decaying wooden door with an old rusted lock separated the non-nitrate films from the nitrate.

I was in a nitrate film slaughterhouse. It was 4 ft x 12 ft of rusted nitrate film cans, being cooled by a creaky overhead fan and a broken glass window through which blew in the smog and dust of Cairo. I held in my hands the rusted and decomposed reels of the films I had grown up with. Even worse were the films that had dissolved into something resembling a pale powder as they rotted in rusted cans. Stunned, I asked the technician why these films were being kept in the same room with films still in salvageable condition. He shrugged and said, "It's part of the inventory."

Some of these films could still be saved, if they could be removed from the nitrate slaughterhouse. Without the reminder of another tragic fire, however, the majority of Egyptians are unaware of what is happening to their film heritage. These infected films were slowly fading, taking with them much of Egypt's modern history. With the help of the international community, we can get the Egyptian government the help it needs to save these films.

Egyptian films are representations of this great culture, and are an extension to the work of the ancient Egyptians, who used drawing and painting to represent the social life of their time. It is estimated that 50% of Egypt's movies are already lost. Half of the surviving old Egyptian films are owned by private-sector concerns such as cable companies and satellite stations based in the Gulf countries. The rest are still owned by the Egyptian government. Unfortunately, because of the lack of financial support and the lack of understanding of film preservation at the ministerial level, the Egyptian government does not have a film preservation centre. Our friends at the Egyptian Film Center/National Film Archive (Al-Archive Al-Kawmy Lil-Film) in Giza are obliged to relinquish control of their nitrate films to the store of their neighbours, the Film Company just described.

Over the last hundred years, Egypt has been documented by a nation of film-makers – professional and amateur alike – working in every corner of the country. These film-makers have recorded our traditions, captured the events of the day, and expressed our ambitions. Their work is the collective memory of the 20th century. Film, however, is fragile. As it ages, it decays. Film needs ongoing care and attention if it is to continue to tell our story.

Over the years hundreds of films burned in fires at the Studio Misr, where movie negatives were stored until the 1980s. As a result, Egyptian cinema lost several very important movies. Half the films of Nagib Elryhany, the most famous Egyptian actor of the 1940s and the 1950s, have turned to powder. The first movie of the most famous Egyptian actress, Shadia, *Azhar w ashwak*, is gone. A movie called *Last Malaka*, representing the work of the most famous Egyptian musician of his generation, Aboud Elwahab, is lost. Also lost is *Elmontkam*, the second movie directed by the godfather of Egyptian films, Salah Abu Saif. The list goes on. It is estimated that there are around 400 films for which there is no longer any information.

Historically, Egypt has produced the most popular cinema in the Middle East. Our project to make a campaigning documentary, *Saving Egyptian Film Classics*, has two goals. First, it aims to bring home to the existing audience for Egyptian films the harsh consequences of neglecting films in storage rooms without preservation, and to expose the misguided movement that opposes film preservation, believing celluloid is dead, and which is consequently destroying and selling old Egyptian films. Second, although Egyptian films are generally unheard-of in the United States and elsewhere in the Western world, it is our hope that our production will also help build a greater interest in the films themselves, and thus a truer appreciation of their value. Since we began working on this project, we have found supporters in both the United States and the Middle East. They helped us with this film, which we hope will inform the public and other film-makers about the importance of preserving films – which is, after all, a universal message. Whether Egyptian, American, Indian, or Chinese, films are in danger. It is our universal language that is being threatened.

We plan to tell the story through archive footage, our own reportage, and provocative interviews with film-makers, critics, and film-lovers, both in Egypt and overseas. The crew travelled to Egypt to search for missing films and visit the storage facilities, where we found – as already described – that the facilities are unfortunately in a terrible state. In Egypt, the crew interviewed Professor Dr Mohamed Kamel el Kalyoubi, the President of the Egyptian Film Center; Mustafa Darwesh and Samair Faraid, film critics and historians; Nabila Abaad, the Egyptian actress; Madeah Ysseri, actress and Member of Parliament; Sawfat Ghattas, producer and studio head; and Ahmed Al Hadary, film historian.

Through conferences and other events, the film-makers launched a media campaign to expose the danger of losing this treasure. This caused a media outcry and public debate. There are many other important figures who expressed their concern about the deterioration of old Egyptian films. The film-makers did not have the time or the resources to interview them.

In the United States, the film crew attended a "press day" on the topic of film preservation, in which the UCLA Film and Television Archive preservation staff presented a number of examples of their work. They took the opportunity to interview Roger Mayer, President and Chief Executive of the Turner Entertainment Company, and Chairman of the National Film Preservation Foundation (NFPF). Others interviewed were Robert Gitt, Preservation Officer at the UCLA Film Television Archive; Robert Rosen, Dean of the School of Theater, Film and

Television at UCLA; Arthur Hiller, Director of the Academy of Motion Picture Arts and Sciences; Michael Pogorzelski, Director of the Academy Film Archive; and Ken Wlaschin, Director for Creative Affairs and Vice Chairman of the National Center for Film and Video Preservation at the American Film Institute (AFI).

In the care of Paul Stambauchtake, Vice-President, Imaging Group, and Robert Dennis, Director of Marketing, the film crew had an intensive tour of the preservation and storage facility at Consolidated Film Industries (CFI), and heard about the company's history and commitment to the preservation community in the USA and its willingness to extend that commitment to the Egyptian preservation movement. The crew also met other preservation and storage experts, including Milton Shefter, President of Miljoy Enterprises; David Cipes, Operations Manager of Cine-Tech; Rick Utlay, Vice-President of Pro-Tek Vaults; Dave Reynolds, Laboratory Manager and UCLA Film and Television Archive Consultant; Michael Friend, leader in the preservationists' movement (who is a consultant for "Saving Egyptian Film Classics"); and Malcolm Clarke, director of the Oscar-winning documentary *You Don't Have to Die* (1988).

The film crew shot preservation segments at the UCLA and Academy Film Archive facilities, the Consolidated Film Industries (CFI) and Cine-Tech laboratories, and the state-of-the-art PRO-TEK storage facility. We were grateful to receive a commitment from the Academy Film Archive at the Center for Motion Picture Studies to help the movement by preserving an Egyptian film for the first time: Michael Pogorzelski, the Director, has scheduled to start the preservation in the beginning of the year 2001.

The film-makers would like to thank the Farrelly brothers, who have called our work "a noble project", for their financial and moral support. We believe that by making our film we can raise the awareness of the danger that faces old Egyptian films. Our goal is geared towards opening a preservation centre in Egypt and bringing Egyptian students to learn the craft in the USA. We have made a 10-minute demo tape for review, which we screened at the AMIA Conference in Los Angeles in November 2000, but we still need financial support, as well as film equipment and preservation equipment to help in the struggle to save these great national treasures.

419

The Cost of Nitrate

Fire and nitrate film.

"Calamity Howlers":
An Introduction

by Roger Smither and Catherine A Surowiec

Ask the man in the street what he knows about nitrate film, and the answer – if he knows anything at all – will be: "It burns." In the collective sub-conscious, and unfortunately in the minds of planning departments and fire officers, the very idea of nitrate film is linked indissolubly to the concept of disaster. Such notorious incidents as those at the Bazar de la Charité in Paris, at Drumcollogher in Ireland, at the Laurier Palace Cinema in Montréal, or at the Glen Cinema in Paisley, Scotland, are internationally well known, and practically every country has its own tragedy to add to this sad register. Added to the sense of human loss, there is an awareness of damage to property – represented most publicly in a number of fires at film studios, factories, and processing plants – and of lost film heritage resulting from fires in the film stores of production and distribution companies and in archives. Nitrate burns, and nitrate is demonised as a result.

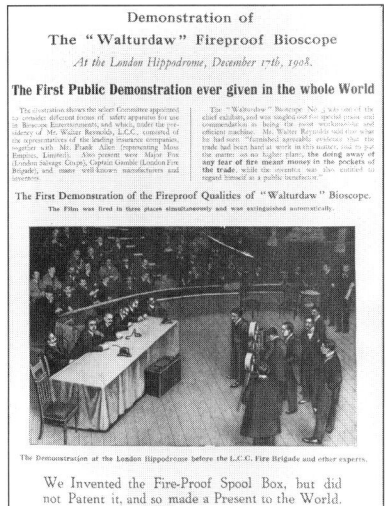

Demonstration of the Walturdaw "fireproof" projector to a panel of fire experts, insurance companies, etc., in London in 1908. The advertising copy reads: "The film was fired in three places and was extinguished automatically ... We Invented the Fire-Proof Spool Box, but did not Patent it, and so made a Present to the World."

The Cinema Museum, London.

No book on nitrate can ignore the fact of its inflammability, or deny that there has been an occasionally terrible price to pay for that fact. As this book turns its own attention specifically to the subject of losses caused by nitrate fires, its editors hesitate in the knowledge that what we are about to do will inevitably feed the flames (pun intended) of exactly this prejudice. We therefore ask the reader's indulgence for a few minutes, as we try to establish a sense of perspective on this topic.

Nitrate film is inflammable, but so are many other substances on which civilised human behaviour has at times been thought to depend. The desire for light after dark, for domestic warmth, and for hot meals – not to mention the craving for fashionable appearance or the occasional indulgence in a nicotine habit – have all brought combustible products into much closer and more regular proximity to many more people than nitrate film managed to do, even in the heyday of its hundred years of history. Whether those products are or were matches, candles, cigarettes, oil lamps, coal fires, gas cookers, or any number of electric domestic appliances, they have caused far more fires than nitrate film ever has – and continue to do so without causing palpitations to planners. Cars, trucks, and buses throng our streets, each equipped with its own little reservoir of highly combustible fuel, but society shows no wish to exclude them. These hazards, of course, are familiar, and it is well known what familiarity breeds. But nitrate film was familiar once, as well. One speaker in 1936 said of motion picture exchanges in the United States and Canada: "They handle about 30,000 miles of film daily."[1]

Consider the situation in Britain. The British film industry operated out of the heart of Soho throughout the nitrate era, but did not trigger a second fire of London. Until the late 1940s there were about 5,000 cinemas in Britain, in almost all of which at least two features played each week. At a conservative estimate, it may therefore be calculated that at any given time in this period over 80,000 reels of nitrate film were in active use – either being projected or in transit – somewhere in the country, yet relative to the amount of nitrate in circulation serious accidents

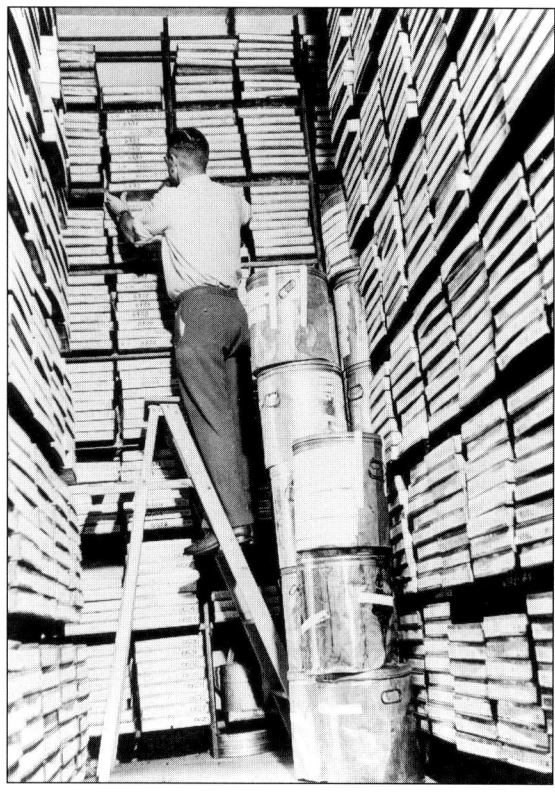

A publicity photograph from the MGM studios. The original caption reads: "A man of many troubles is a film editor, who must keep track of hundreds of bits of film which he assembles into the finished picture...". It makes no mention of the fire risk.

BFI Collections – Stills, Posters & Designs, London. 159744

were few. In 1922, the *Daily Mail* newspaper noted quite casually that the Imperial War Museum's film collection – "seven hundred thousand feet of films, weighing about two tons" – was "stored in protected vaults in the basement of the War Office", and it was only moved from this location in the heart of Whitehall in the late 1930s. The point of these observations is not that people were complacent about nitrate, but that they recognised it as a necessary part of contemporary civilisation – like the gas in the cooker or the petrol in the tank. It needed to be treated with respect, but not with paranoia.

Where city-centre celluloid fires did break out, they were not always caused by film. A harrowing report in the American *National Fire Protection Association Quarterly* for January 1910 entitled "The Serious Hazard of Nitro-Cellulose" does indeed include a film fire at the Ferguson Building in Pittsburgh which is noted below, but it is principally concerned with "the burning to death of ten people in the Brooklyn comb factory, and three days after, the death of two and the injury of many in a similar fire in West 31st Street, Manhattan" – events which it notes as "horrible holocausts".[2]

We should also remember that celluloid was not the only risk involved in the film trade. The tale of three fires in the early days of the industry's conversion to sound is instructive. The fire on 16 January 1929 that destroyed the new sound studio which was being built for the Paramount-Famous-Lasky Corporation in Hollywood, resulting in a loss estimated at $500,000, was apparently due to a construction accident and was not in any sense a film fire.[3] Similarly, although there were 369 reels of film in the building when fire broke out in the Pathé Sound Studio in New York less than a year later, on 10 December 1929, only 11 reels burned, and it was categorically reported that they made no contribution to the spread of the fire and certainly were not responsible for the 10 deaths, which included those of 4 chorus girls. On that occasion, the fire started in the velvet drop curtain on the studio stage set, and was attributed either to a cigarette or to a lighting or other electrical accident.[4] On the other side of the Atlantic, when fire destroyed the Gainsborough Studios in Islington, London, a month later, on 18 January 1930, the cause was the overheating of paraffin wax needed for part of the sound recording equipment, and again had nothing to do with film at all.[5] Non-film hazards could also kill in cinemas as well – a distressing story from the suburb of Tacubaya in Mexico in April 1924 told of a fire starting when an electric cable became loosened from the ceiling and fell on the audience; apparently several people were electrocuted as they tried to leave the auditorium when they encountered the same wire "hanging neck high in the main aisle".[6] A short circuit and poor construction, rather than nitrate film, were also to blame for a 1947 fire in the Reuil district of Paris in which almost 90 people died,[7] while the explosion of "an oil reservoir of the heating system", rather than nitrate film, led to 39 deaths when "the screen burst into flames" at a cinema in Sclessin, near Liège in Belgium, in 1955.[8]

Another necessary observation even about disasters that did involve nitrate is that it was not always nitrate that made them disastrous. Many of the incidents that are included in the following pages are ones in which the involvement of nitrate film is almost incidental – in several of them, the tragic death tolls result from panic and from human negligence or incompetence, and not from burns or smoke inhalation.

Of course, it will be pointed out correctly that awareness of past cinema fires meant that a cry of "fire" in a crowded cinema was more likely to generate panic, so that the fear of nitrate has helped to generate its own justification, a kind of self-fulfilling prophecy. From a number of known cases where deaths resulted from just such false alarms, 3 sad examples will suffice. In 1910, 4 children died in an incident in Deptford in London when panic ensued after some loud bangs were heard and taken to be explosions (they were later attributed to children outside the cinema throwing stones into the blades of a ventilator fan).[9] In 1911, at Canonsburg, Pennsylvania, a false cry of "Fire!" when a fuse blew in a projector causing "a sharp report from the machine, followed by a dense cloud of smoke" led to a panic-stricken rush for a narrow staircase where those trying to escape crashed into others waiting for admission to the auditorium: 26 people died in the crush.[10] One year later, in 1912, 44 people died at the Circo del Ensanche in Bilbao after a woman's scream during a pause in projection started a frightened stampede down a precipitate escape route that became known only too accurately as "the staircase of death".[11]

Finally, it must be recalled that not all disasters – not even all disasters related to places of entertainment – took place in premises associated with nitrate film, although the urge to blame nitrate sometimes led to a false attribution. This phenomenon may be strikingly seen in the case of the 1908 fire at Boyertown, Pennsylvania, which involved a lantern show and some amateur theatricals, and had nothing to do with moving pictures at all – a fact which does not prevent Boyertown appearing in several lists of cinematograph disasters. It may be macabre or tasteless to make such comparisons, but it remains undeniably true that of the 4 notorious cinema tragedies named earlier – Paris (125 dead), Drumcollogher (48), Montréal (77), and Paisley (70) – only the Bazar de la Charité fire killed more people than died in the disaster at Calumet, Michigan, in December 1913. On that occasion, 56 children and 24 adults died when panic broke out at a false cry of "Fire!" as the children of striking miners lined up in the Italian Hall to receive Christmas presents from Santa Claus. In fact, the total death toll from these 4 infamous cinema disasters amounts to little more than half that of the single disaster that struck the Iroquois Theatre in Chicago on 30 December 1903. The Iroquois was a newly opened "legitimate" theatre, and it was a live musical comedy – *Mr Bluebeard*, starring popular comedian Eddie Foy – that was in the course of a matinée performance when a stage light ignited some painted scenery. The fire

In this slide from a French cinema, patrons are requested not to smoke – but out of chivalry, and a concern for the quality of projection, not for safety reasons.

Archives du Film du Centre National de la Cinématographie, Bois d'Arcy.

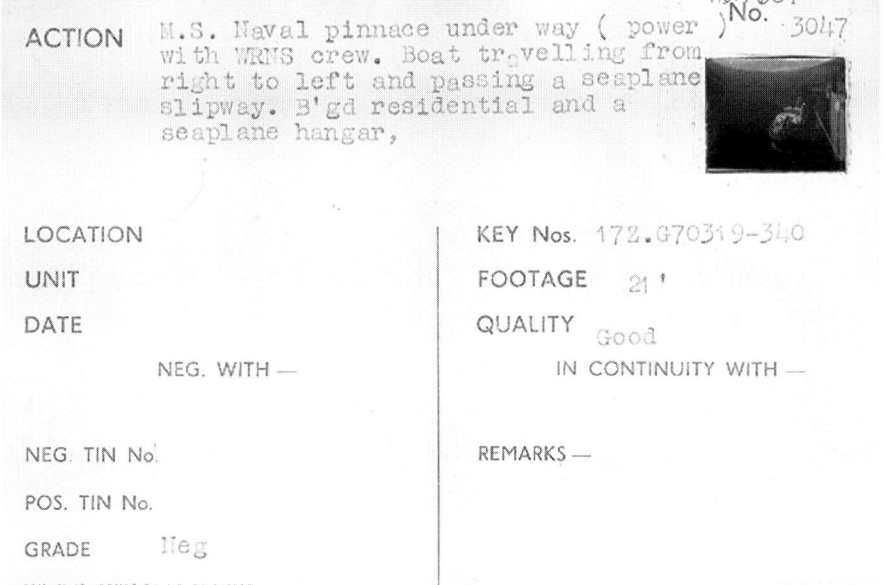

This index card is dangerous? Most of the official film collections transferred to the Imperial War Museum after the Second World War came with their original finding aids. Films from the Admiralty arrived with a large file of these cards: in each one, a single frame from the shot described was stuck behind the window in the top right-hand corner of the card. In most cases, of course, the stock was nitrate.

Imperial War Museum, London.

spread into the auditorium because of an inadequate safety curtain and poorly trained and equipped stagehands. The fire, the resulting panic, and blocked emergency exits resulted in the loss of over 600 lives, mainly those of women and children. The story of the Iroquois is told to explain the need for careful management, proper precautions, and thorough inspection, not to demonise the art of theatre. Is it ignorance, or artistic, social, or cultural prejudice that means that cinema fires have historically been treated differently?

The arguments rehearsed here are not, of course, new ones. The cinema industry has been complaining of unfair or irrational treatment since its earliest days. In September 1910, a film trade journal in Chicago published a table listing the official causes of fires in that city the previous year, in order to point out that not one of the more than 7,000 fires reported was attributed to film. Apart from its premature announcement of the widespread adoption of safety film, the list provides an interesting window into Chicago life 90 years ago, as well as serving to make the same point to today's reader.

THE CAUSES OF FIRES

In spite of the general adoption of noninflammable films, we hear nearly as much as ever of the fire danger of the picture theater and the film exchange. There were 7,075 fires in Chicago in 1909. The following table gives the causes of those fires and the number of fires due to each cause:

Ashes and hot coals	87
Blown down and ignited	16
Bonfires and burning rubbish	399
Candles and torches, carelessness with	81
Carelessness, not otherwise specified	36
Children playing with fire and matches	82
Chimney fires	435
Christmas trees	18
Cigar stubs and tobacco pipes	81
Defective flues	60
Dry-room overheated	5
Electric wires and lights	231
Engines and boilers, stationary	32
Explosions, alcohol, benzine and naphtha	8
Explosions, chemicals	9
Explosions, dust	3
Explosions, gas	27
Explosions, gasoline and kerosene	74
Explosions, lamps and lanterns	69
Explosions, oil	8
Explosions, oil and gasoline stoves	111
Explosions, water-backs	2
Fireworks	27
Forge, coals from	1
Friction	28
Fumigating	24
Furnaces, heating	156
Furnaces, foundries, etc.	2
Gas jets	99
Gas pipes, leak in	50
Hot iron and molten metals	3

Ignition, alcohol, benzine and naphtha 10

Ignition, chemicals 6

Ignition, gas 35

Ignition, gasoline and kerosene..126

Ignition, grease, oil and meats 79

Ignition, paints and varnish 9

Ignition, tar, rosin and wax 63

Incendiarism, known 60

Incendiarism, supposed...133

Lamp and lantern accidents 48

Lighting 56

Matches, carelessness with..454

Matches, rats and mice with 17

Mischievous children, etc...62

Open fire places and grates..34

Overheated and defective kiln 1

Overheated and defective ovens..25

Plumbers' and tinners' furnaces 1

Prairie fires 94

Rekindlings 24

Salamanders...9

Smokehouses, overheated 6

Sparks, chimney, etc. 240

Sparks, locomotive..109

Sparks, river craft 3

Spontaneous combustion 131

Steam-pipes...56

Stoves and ranges..285

Stove-pipes..29

Tailor's goose 2

Thawing water pipes..156

Thawing gas pipes 18

Tramps..5

Unknown 2,225

Total 7,075

There is no reference whatever to picture theaters or to motion picture films. It will be noted that they are not represented under "explosions" – that favorite expression of the theater fire reporter; neither are they mentioned under "ignition". The conclusion grows upon us that there were no film fires in Chicago in 1909.

In the amount of motion picture film it uses, Chicago is the second biggest city in the world. Isn't it about time the calamity howlers ceased crying the danger of picture-theater fires?[12]

Notes

1. Henry Anderson, "Fire Safety in the Motion Picture Industry", *National Fire Protection Association Quarterly*, v.30, no.1 (July 1936), p. 23.

2. "The Serious Hazard of Nitro-Cellulose", *National Fire Protection Association Quarterly*, v.3, no.3 (January 1910), pp. 279–281.

3. Henry Anderson, "Paramount Studio Fire", *National Fire Protection Association Quarterly*, v.22, no.4 (April 1929), pp. 438–441.

4. "The Pathé Studio Fire", *National Fire Protection Association Quarterly*, v.23, no.3 (January

1930), pp. 220–226.

5. Michael Balcon, *Michael Balcon Presents... A Lifetime of Films* (London: Hutchinson, 1969), pp. 45–48.

6. *New York Times* (2 April 1924), p. 1, col.4.

7. *New York Times* (31 August 1947), p. 1, col.2; (1 September 1947), p. 21, col.4; and (2 September 1947), p. 7, col.5.

8. *New York Times* (4 April 1955), p. 11, col.4.

9. Terry Staples, *All Pals Together: The Story of Children's Cinema* (Edinburgh University Press, 1997), p. 19.

10. *New York Times* (27 August 1911), p. 1, col.7, and (28 August 1911), p. 3, col.3.

11. See the essay "Fires in the Spanish Cinema" by Jorge Martín Neira elsewhere in this volume.

12. From *The Nickelodeon*, v.IV, no.5 (1 September 1910), p. 120. We are grateful to Ron Magliozzi of the Museum of Modern Art for bringing this to our attention.

A Calendar of Film Fires

Editors' Note: This is in no sense a comprehensive catalogue of all film fires. It is rather a chronological listing combining those fires which form part of the established history and folklore of cinema with a number of others that have come or have been brought to our attention while this book was in preparation. Of the latter group we have included those that seemed to us to be of particular interest, either because they reflected some particularly unfortunate cause for a fire, or because they revealed the truly worldwide reach of such tragedies. We have, however, limited ourselves to stories that we have been able to confirm with at least one specific published reference, so that in addition to stories of which we are obviously completely unaware we acknowledge the omission of several of which we are only partially aware. For example, was there a true story behind a rather dubiously humorous article on the editorial page of the New York Times *for 31 August 1906 concerning "a moving picture show with a gasoline attachment which blew up as soon as the concern was arranged" which was alleged to have been "intended for the entertainment of the Dowager Empress" in China? What were the details of the apparently recent "Lisbon conflagration" associated with the 1911 fire at Bologoie, Russia, in one British trade press report? Was nitrate involved in the fire at a silver recovery plant in Bayonne in France mentioned as having occurred "a few years ago" in an article written in Germany in 1929? We were not able to answer these or several similar questions, so such incidents are not included in our "Calendar". We do hope, however, that the publication of a partial list will help to promote further study and research in this field.*

Several people have helped with information for this section. One source which we are particularly pleased to acknowledge is the listing "Incendis causats pel nitrat" compiled by the Filmoteca de la Generalitat Valenciana as part of the publication Protecció i Conservació de l'Obra Cinematogràfica *(Oficina Catalana del Cinema, 1988) and later used in a travelling exhibition – La Imagen Rescatada – which circulated in South America in 1993. Information on many US fires was supplied by David Pierce. Others who have provided advice or information used in the following pages are: Michelle Aubert, Lenny Borger, Kevin Brownlow, Paolo Cherchi Usai, Gabrielle Claes, David Cleveland, Carlos Roberto de Souza, Tony Fletcher, Manuel Gonzalez Casanova, Barbara Heinrich-Polte, Yoshiro Irie, Bernard King, Reto Kromer, Sam Kula, Fred Lake, David Lemieux, Vigdis Lian, Martin Loiperdinger, Janet McBain, Ron Magliozzi, Jorge Martín Neira, Bill Murphy, Hassan Muthalib, Sunniva O'Flynn, Hisashi Okajima, Fernando Osorio, Gillie Potter, Brian Pritchard, Maite Rodon, Jan Slodowski, Ned Thanhouser, Sakari Toiviainen, Angela Tong, and Inmaculada Trull.*

1896   **10 June – Acres Kineopticon, Piccadilly Circus, London, UK.**
A fire, attributed by inventor Birt Acres to the carelessness of an assistant in Acres's absence, brought to an end the short commercial life of the Acres Kineopticon, an exhibition of projected moving pictures which had opened on 21 March offering subjects including Acres's famous film of the 1895 Derby. The Kineopticon was unusual, compared to other contemporary public moving picture shows, in that the films were the sole attraction – they were not interspersed with other acts. While it is possible that this is the earliest recorded fire involving projected moving pictures, it is, therefore, almost certain that it represents the first time a dedicated moving picture theatre was closed by fire.

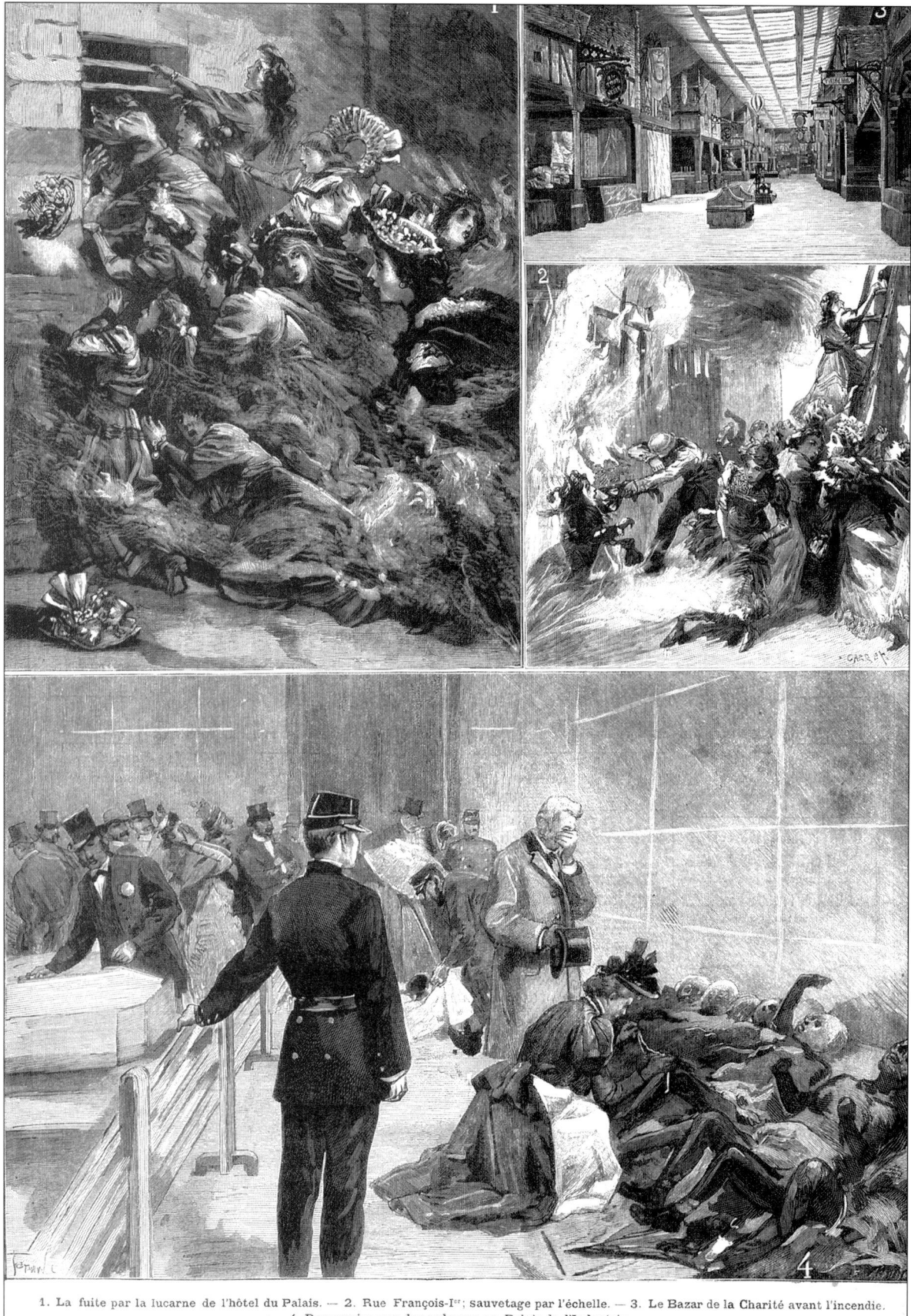

1. La fuite par la lucarne de l'hôtel du Palais. — 2. Rue François-Iᵉʳ; sauvetage par l'échelle. — 3. Le Bazar de la Charité avant l'incendie. 4. Reconnaissance des cadavres au Palais de l'Industrie.

Coverage of the Bazar de la Charité fire from an illustrated supplement to *Le Petit Journal* published on 16 May 1897. On this page, a view of the Bazar before the fire (top right), two scenes of attempted escape by the victims, and the identification of the bodies.

David Robinson.

References: John Barnes, *The Beginnings of the Cinema in England* (Newton Abbot: David & Charles, 1976), pp.66–70.

1896   **16 August – Edison Pavilion, Treptower Park, Berlin, Germany.**
A fire due to an electrical short-circuit in a back-room broke out in the pavilion of Ludwig Stollwerck's Deutsch-Oesterreichische Edison-Kinetoscop-Gesellschaft at an industrial fair in Berlin, used to demonstrate the Lumière Cinématographe as well as various Edison kinetoscopes and phonographs. The public was safely evacuated, and the projectionists had time to rescue the apparatus (though they suffered some burns in the process), but the pavilion itself – designed by architect Bruno Schmitz – was completely burned out, with (uninsured) damage estimated at 6,000 Marks. This is thought to be the earliest fire involving a Lumière Cinématographe, even though the machine itself was not the cause.

References: Martin Loiperdinger, *Film & Schockolade: Stollwercks Geschäfte mit lebenden Bildern* (Frankfurt am Main/Basel: Stroemfeld, 1999), pp.172–173.

1897   **4 May – Bazar de la Charité Fair, Paris, France.**
Fire broke out during a cinematograph screening in a temporary building on the rue Jean Goujon, killing some 125 people, the majority of them women and children from the upper classes of French society. Although the fire started in the screening area, it was not initially the film that caught fire – rather, it appears that when the projector light went out, one of the operators struck a match to help his colleague see what he was doing while trying to refill the lamp with ether. The flames spread rapidly from the burning fuel to the decorative drapes (and of course also to the films being projected) and from there to the tarred planks of which the building was constructed, and the building was completely gutted within minutes of the fire starting.

References: H Mark Gosser, *"The Bazar de la Charité Fire: The Reality, the Aftermath, the Telling"*, in *Film History* v.10, no.1 (1998), pp.70–89.

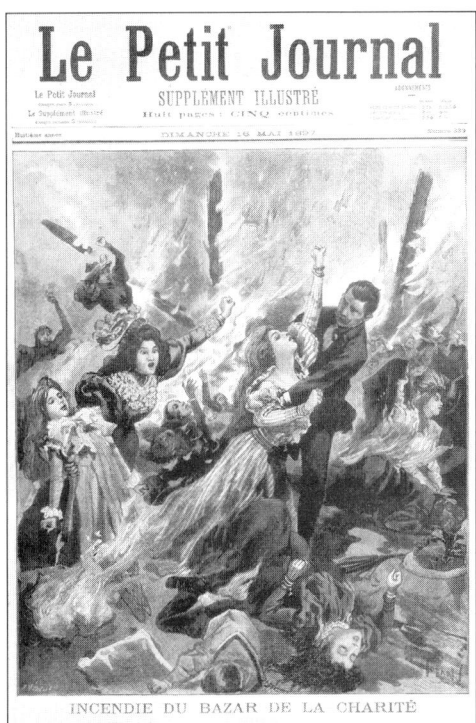

The front cover of the illustrated supplement published on 16 May 1897 by *Le Petit Journal* to report on the Bazar de la Charité fire. (See also Colour Section 2.)
David Robinson.

1898   **4 July – Market Place, Bilston, Stafford, UK.**
A travelling bioscope show was destroyed by a fire which the proprietor, "Captain" Payne, attributed to the panic-stricken reaction of the audience to a "trifling" incident. One of the gas pipes feeding the lamp came loose, and someone shouted "Fire!". Although Payne tried to calm the 200 spectators, in their rush to the exits they knocked over the projection apparatus, a film caught fire, and the flames spread to consume both the apparatus and the tent. After the incident, Payne said he had never had a fire or accident in more than 25 years as a showman, and blamed this one on the person who shouted. Newspaper pressure following this, the Bazar de la Charité tragedy, and other more local incidents (e.g., one at the Tivoli Music Hall in London on 17 October 1898, when a curtain fell onto the arc lamp of a projector as it was being prepared for a show), led to the issuing of the first regulation of film shows by the London County Council (8 November 1898).

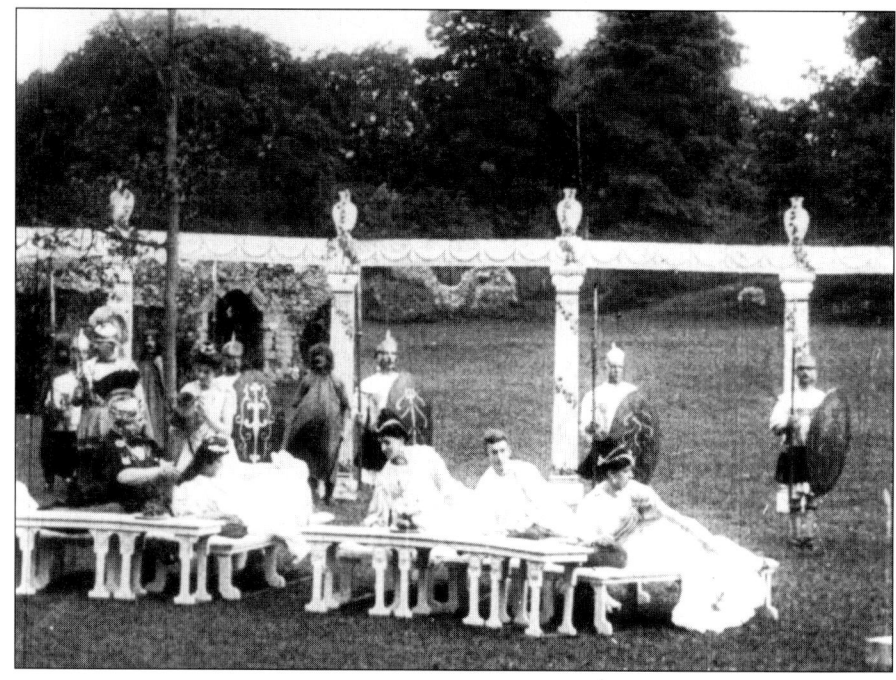

A scene from the Gaumont film of the 1907 Bury St Edmund's Pageant – the attraction that brought 700 people to Newmarket Town Hall on the night of the fire.

East Anglian Film Archive, Norwich.

References: John Barnes, *Pioneers of the British Film* (London: Bishopsgate Press, 1983), pp. 72–73, 80–82, 88, 90–91.

1898   8 August – Salão de Novidades Paris no Rio, Rio de Janeiro, Brazil.
A fire started as operators were cleaning the projectors between shows in Brazil's first motion picture theatre, and spread rapidly to consume the whole building. Also destroyed, shortly before their advertised first public screening, were the first images filmed in Brazil, shot just over a month previously.

References: Carlos Roberto de Souza, *"Inconfidência Archiveira"* (in this volume).

1907   7 September – Town Hall, Newmarket, Suffolk, UK.
The connections from the gas cylinders feeding the projector lamp were dislodged when an intermission was announced and there was movement towards the main exit by some of the 700 people crowded into the town hall to watch Gaumont "local topicals" of recent festivities in nearby Bury St Edmunds. Although the resulting film fire was quickly dealt with, there were serious injuries and at least one death from burns, and some further injuries in the panic-stricken rush to evacuate the hall.

References: "Extraordinary Incident at a Cinematograph Exhibition – Woman Burned to Death", *East Anglian Daily Times*, 8 September 1907.

1907   22 November – Hepworth Film Studios, Walton-on-Thames, UK.
One of the first recorded studio fires started in the perforating room, possibly caused by human error: Hepworth himself suggested a dropped match. The fire killed the operator who was working there at the time and caused extensive damage to the structure of the building and to the equipment used for perforating and developing film.

References: Cecil M Hepworth, *Came the Dawn: Memories of a*

Film Pioneer (London: Phoenix House, 1951), pp.86–89.

"A Disastrous Fire at Hepworths", *Dial Stone: The News Sheet of the Walton and Weybridge Local History Society*, no.143 (January 1994), pp.198–199, quoting *Surrey Herald*, 30 November 1907.

1908   **13 January – Rhoads Opera House, Boyertown, Pennsylvania, USA.**
The Boyertown fire is noted here because it was at the time widely cited as a precedent by campaigners anxious to tighten up the regulations governing "nickelodeons" (for example, in a *New York Herald* headline "Boyertown Tragedy Emphasizes Danger in Moving Picture Shows of New York") and has therefore come to be thought of as a cinema disaster itself. As has already been pointed out, however, the known circumstances do not appear to justify the attachment to film of any blame at all for the deaths of some 167 persons at Boyertown.

The tragic sequence of events started when the audience was frightened by a "sharp report and hissing" as a gas connection on a projector came undone. The projector is, however, variously described as "lantern show apparatus" and as a "stereopticon", rather than as a moving picture machine, and in any case the operator quickly dealt with the problem and was praised for his efforts to quell the panic. The real disaster appears to have been caused when a number of the members of the cast of an amateur dramatic production, hearing the commotion caused by the first incident, came from behind the curtain on the stage to try to help their families. Their action overturned one or more of the kerosene footlights, starting the real blaze which triggered the fatal panic in the overcrowded building.

References: *New York Herald*, 18 January and 20 January 1908.

1908   **23 August – Teatro Principal de Gracia, Barcelona, Spain.**
This fire, together with another the same year at the Palacio de las Arenas, also in Barcelona, are listed among "some cinemas and theatres that were destroyed in spectacular fires but without causing death or injury" in the article by Jorge Martín Neira.

References: Jorge Martín Neira, "Fires in the Spanish Cinema" (in this volume).
La Vanguardia (Barcelona), 24 August 908, p.3.

1909   **January – Ferguson Building, Pittsburgh, Pennsylvania, USA.**
An employee in a film exchange entered the "specially constructed vault" with an extension lamp and somehow set fire to a reel of film. He threw the burning reel out and shut the vault door, but other films in the nearby workroom then caught fire, wrecking the building and causing some fifty injuries, including ten fatalities.

References: David Pierce, "The Legion of the Condemned", reprinted in this volume, previously published in *Film History*, v.9, no.1 (1997), pp.5–22.
See also *Proceedings of a Board* ...listed under the 1927 Cleveland fire, below.

1909   **February 14 – Flores Theatre, Acapulco, Mexico.**
During a gala in honour of the Governor of the state of Guerrero, attended by over 1,000 people, a blaze said to have started when a film caught fire in the projector spread rapidly to the theatre's furnishings and wooden structure, ultimately causing the roof to collapse. The panic-stricken crowd blocked the inadequate exit doors, and over 250 deaths were reported.

References: *Ciné-Journal*, 18 February 1909.
New York Times, 16 February, p.1, and 17 February 1909, p.4.

1910   **UK.**
A fire started when a film can short-circuited the terminals of a battery as one of British film producer Cecil Hepworth's staff was carrying a set of Vivaphone equipment (an early synchronised sound system) by passenger train for delivery to a customer. There were no serious casualties or damage, but the fire provides an interesting precedent for both the contexts of other train fires (see 1914 and 1925) and the cause of the Paisley disaster in 1929.

References: Cecil M Hepworth, *Came the Dawn: Memories of a Film Pioneer* (London: Phoenix House, 1951), p.99.

1910   **8 February – Municipal Theatre at Trujillo, Peru.**
50 persons were reported killed in a panic following a fire which "started among the apparatus used in connection with a moving picture show".

Reference: *New York Times*, 24 February 1910, p.1.

1910   **9 June – Eclair Factory, Epinay-sur-Seine, France.**
The Union des Grands Éditeurs de Films staged a public burning of a large quantity of obsolete distribution copies in the first of a planned series of deliberate acts of self-styled "commercial purification".

References: "Un Autodafé Sensationnel" (in this volume).

1911   **6 March – Bologoie, Russia.**
An early *New York Times* report stated that "nearly 100 persons, many of them children", were burned or crushed to death in the fire and panic after "a moving picture machine in a small theatre at Bologoie, in the southern part of Novgorod Province, exploded". The same report placed this fire in the context of other cinematograph disasters, incidentally naming the 1908 Boyertown fire (see above) as "one of the worst of such accidents in the United States".

A later story in the British trade press (apart from containing the imprecise reference to the "Lisbon conflagration" noted earlier) said that a Mr Landmann of the Nordisk Film Company had established that the fire started when the amateur operator – an actor from a Moscow theatre – accidentally knocked over and broke a bottle of ether near the limelight light source for the projector. According to the same source, "The alarm was at once given, but the audience had been told that a railway collision was to be shown, and thinking that the cry of 'fire' was part of the effects, did not budge until too late to make their escape and in the panic which ensued, 183 out of 245 who were in the place, lost their lives."

References: *New York Times*, 7 March 1911, p.8.
                Kinematograph and Lantern Weekly, 16 March 1911, p.1325.

1912   **28 May – Cine La Luz in Villareal de los Infantes, Castellón, Spain.**
        Seventy people died and more than 200 were injured when a film broke in the projector, leading to a serious fire in a structure built entirely of wood and canvas and equipped with only one small emergency exit.

        References: Jorge Martín Neira, "Fires in the Spanish Cinema" (in this volume).

1912   **22 December – Baraque Cinema, Menin, Belgium.**
        A projection fire during an afternoon performance – although completely contained within the strengthened projection box and quickly brought under control – provoked a panic-stricken rush for the exits, in which 13 people were killed and several more injured.

        References: *Ciné-Journal*, 28 December 1912.

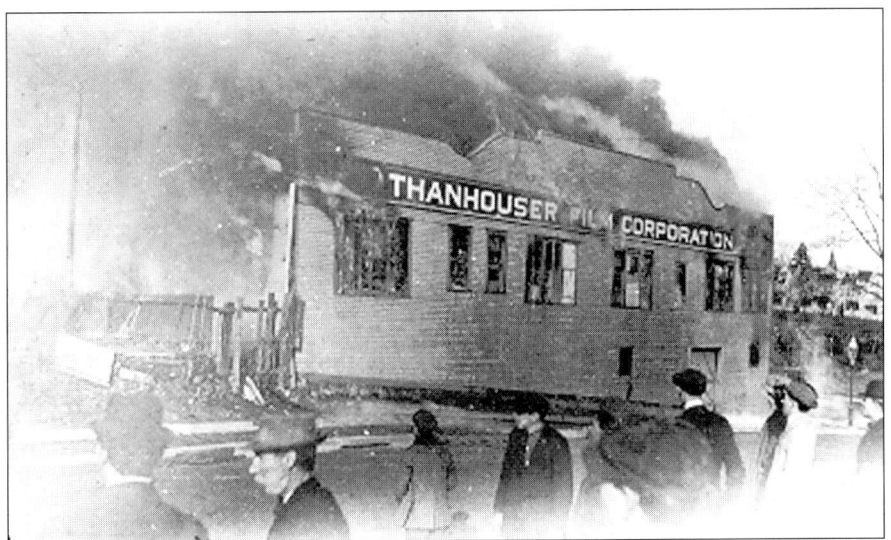

Photograph taken early in the afternoon of 13 January 1913, showing the Thanhouser Film Corporation studio ablaze (from the Thanhouser family archive, courtesy of Pego Paar).

Thanhouser Company Film Preservation, Inc.

1913   **26 January – Thanhouser Corporation, New Rochelle, NY, USA.**
        A fire, believed to have started with a short-circuit or friction spark igniting a reel of film in the perforating room, destroyed the Corporation's entire factory and studio complex (a building formerly used as a skating rink) in less than an hour. Two adjoining houses were destroyed, and others damaged, and the total cost of the fire was estimated at over $75,000. Also lost – in spite of efforts by staff to save them – were negatives of some of the studio's films, including *The Star of Bethlehem*. While the company was building new studios, it produced a filmed re-enactment of the event entitled *When the Studio Burned*, released on 4 February (see Filmography).

        References: Q David Bowers, *Thanhouser Films: An Encyclopedia and History* (Thanhouser Company Film Presevation Inc., Portland OR, 1997), [CD-ROM], pages "When the Studio Burned", etc.

1913   **10 March – Vervins, France.**
10 people were killed and a further 45 seriously hurt (out of an audience of 120, most of them children) in a panic caused by a projector explosion in "a small upstairs theatre", although the fire itself was reportedly "rapidly extinguished by the fire brigade".

Reference: *New York Times*, 11 March 1913, p.4.

1914   **13 June – Lubinville Studio, Philadelphia, Pennsylvania, USA.**
Fire completely destroyed all the film in store at Lubin's studio complex in Philadelphia – a loss valued at over $500,000. Although the fire was officially blamed on the effects of sunlight through a frosted glass skylight in one of the 5 vaults, suspicion also attached to an employee known as a heavy smoker. Irretrievable losses included not only a number of feature films (such as Romaine Fielding's *The Golden God*) but also all of Lubin's collection of historic actuality film, dating back to his earliest involvement in film-making.

[Lubin had a narrow escape less than a year later at his new studio in Betzwood, when an unexplained fire broke out in a film shipping room, shortly after 100,000 feet of film had been packed and shipped; on this occasion, damage was limited to $5,000.]

References: Joseph P Eckhardt, *The King of the Movies: Film Pioneer Siegmund Lubin* (London: Associated University Presses, 1998), pp.181–184, 204–205.

1914   **24 November – Chicago, Illinois, USA.**
Two people died and 38 were seriously injured when 4 reels of film, casually wrapped in paper, caught fire in the smoking car of a suburban train into which they had been carried by a man who was delivering them for a screening at a club. The company which had supplied the films was held culpable for failing to follow Federal regulations for the safe packing of films: "The film company saved a few cents; the public paid with valuable lives."

References: B W Dunn, "Moving Picture Films in Smoking Car", *B.E Special Bulletin No. 1* (New York: Bureau of Explosives, 1914).

1914   **9 December – Edison Factory, West Orange, New Jersey, USA.**
Most of the buildings comprising inventor and manufacturer Thomas A Edison's New Jersey plant were destroyed in a fire which was reported as starting "with a tremendous explosion in the film finishing building" (although a film trade journal categorically denied that this was a "Film Fire", claiming that on the contrary the source was the varnishing department of the phonograph building). At least one employee lost his life, and damage was estimated at around $5 million. The one significant building saved from the fire was Edison's Experimental Laboratory. Edison immediately undertook to rebuild the plant, saying, "I am 67, but I'm not too old to make a fresh start."

References: *New York Times*, 10 December, pp.1 and 5, and 11 December 1914, p.9.
"Great Edison Plant Burned", *Moving Picture World*, 19 December 1914.

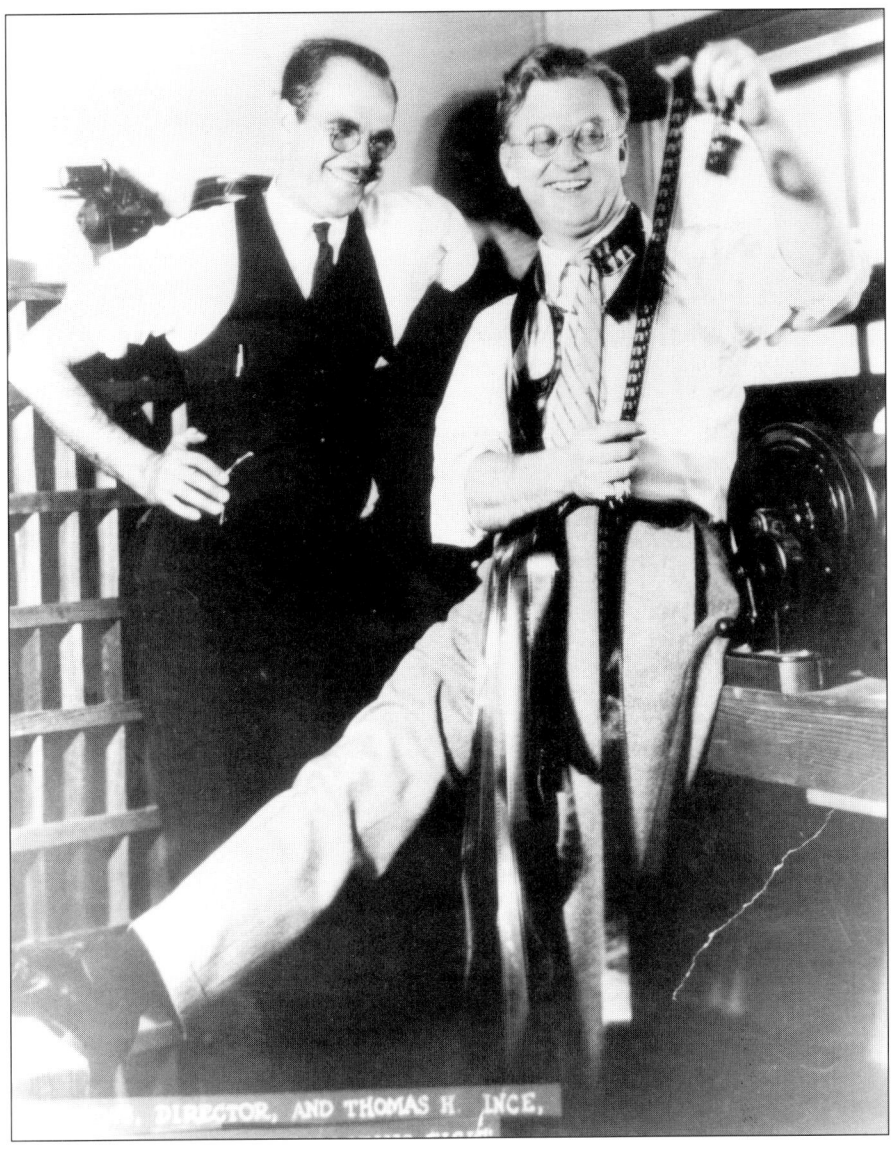

Apparently not traumatised by the 1916 fire: producer Thomas H Ince getting close to nitrate film with director Del Andrews in a photograph taken to publicise *The Galloping Fish* (1924).

BFI Collections – Stills, Posters & Designs, London. 100002.

1915 **26 July – Pyke's Cambridge Circus Cinematograph Theatre, London, UK.**

A fire broke out in the basement where an employee was soldering a tin-lined box used to send waste film (of which up to a ton at a time would be accumulated there) to France. The employee died in the flames, the theatre was extensively damaged, and Pyke was bankrupted and subsequently found guilty of manslaughter.

References: Allen Eyles and Keith Skone, *London's West End Cinemas* (Sutton: Keystone Publications, 1991), p.29.

1916 **January – Inceville, Santa Monica, California, USA.**

Producer Thomas H Ince was himself among those injured in escaping from a fire which started in the cutting rooms of the Inceville studio complex.[1] In addition to the cutting room and 60,000 feet or so of printed positive film, the fire destroyed some of the administrative offices and the "scenario bureau", where 300 scripts, including 35 ready for production, were reported lost. Ince's determination to rise above this and other setbacks inspired a poem by Richard Willis with the refrain "You can't stop Ince!".

References: "Inceville Suffers From Fire – Production Already Resumed", *Motography*, 29 January 1916, pp.227–228.

1917   **20 October – Filmfabrik Karl Geyer, Berlin, Germany.**
A fire of unexplained origin broke out in the underground vault of Germany's leading independent film processing company: initially contained by the safe-like structure of the vault, the fire burst out with explosive force, and caused severe damage to the rest of the plant. Reported losses included up to 170 irreplaceable negatives, for new films awaiting release.

References: Martin Koerber, "'Fire!' The 1917 Nitrate Fire in Berlin, and Its Consequences" (in this volume).

1919   **1 June – Valence-sur-Rhone, France.**
Fire broke out in the projection box during a performance in a large cinema. Although the fire itself was quickly brought under control, the ensuing panic caused the loss of at least 80 lives in the rush for the exits (some reports speak of 120), the majority of them those of women and children.

References: *New York Times*, 2 June 1919, p.17.
"Le Film Ininflammable", *Les Cahiers de la Cinémathèque*, Autumn 1981, p.126.

1919   **20 June – Mayaguez, Puerto Rico.**
A fire of unspecified origin destroyed a motion picture theatre, with heavy loss of life including many children. Reports spoke of 60 bodies recovered from the ruins, with many more seriously injured.

References: *New York Times*, 21 June, p.10, and 22 June 1919, p.4.

1922   **11 November – Cinéma-Palace, Montreux, Switzerland.**
Fire broke out in the basement of the cinema, which was used as a store for some 300 reels of film; a few minutes after the fire brigade started to put water on the fire, there was a "formidable explosion" in the basement. Although damage on this occasion was limited to property damage, concern as to whether it was the action of the fire-fighters that led to the explosion prompted a thorough study of the nature and processes of nitrate fires by a local expert, which explored among other things the different characteristics of "combustion without flame" (*deflagration*) and "combustion with flame", and exonerated the officers.

References: R Mellet, "Combustibilité des films cinématographiques et explosion du Cinéma-Palace de Montreux", *Bulletin de la Société Vaudoise des Sciences Naturelles*, v.55, no.212 (1923), pp.101–122.

1924   **21 September – Smyrna [Izmir], Turkey.**
More than 100 deaths were reportedly caused in a "disastrous kinema fire" which was "due to the igniting of the film". Among the dead was a sister-in-law of the Turkish prime minister, Ismet Pasha.

References: *Manchester Guardian*, 22 September 1924, p.7.

1925   **3 January – Boston, Massachusetts, USA.**
A burlap bag filled with film scraps placed against a heater under a seat burst into flames in a crowded subway car: of the more than 50 passengers suffering burns, 27 required hospital treatment. The scrap film was being carried by a 70-year-old employee of a firm which used it to produce cement for the manufacture of brushes. The president of the brush company indicated that he had been buying scrap film for over 3 years, and denied any knowledge that it held any special risk or that its carriage was controlled by law.

References: "Film Fire in Boston Subway", *National Fire Protection Association Quarterly* v.18, no.3 (January 1925), pp.223-225.

1926   **5 September – Dromcollogher, Ireland.**
A fire broke out during a screening in a poorly equipped upstairs room being used for a travelling cinema performance, causing the deaths of 48 victims.

References: Sunniva O'Flynn, "The Drumcollogher Disaster" (in this volume).

1927   **9 January – Laurier Palace Cinema, Montréal, Canada.**
During the evacuation of the audience of children and teenagers following a minor fire in the projection box, panic broke out in one blocked exit. 77 children aged from 4 to 18 died of suffocation and crush injuries. The fire led to new regulations under which children under 16 were banned from cinemas in the province of Québec – a ban that lasted for 40 years.

References: Dan Lanken, *Montreal Movie Palaces: Great Theatres of the Golden Era 1884–1938* (Waterloo, Ontario: Penumbra Press, 1993), pp.44–46.
The Globe (Toronto), 10 January 1927, p.1.

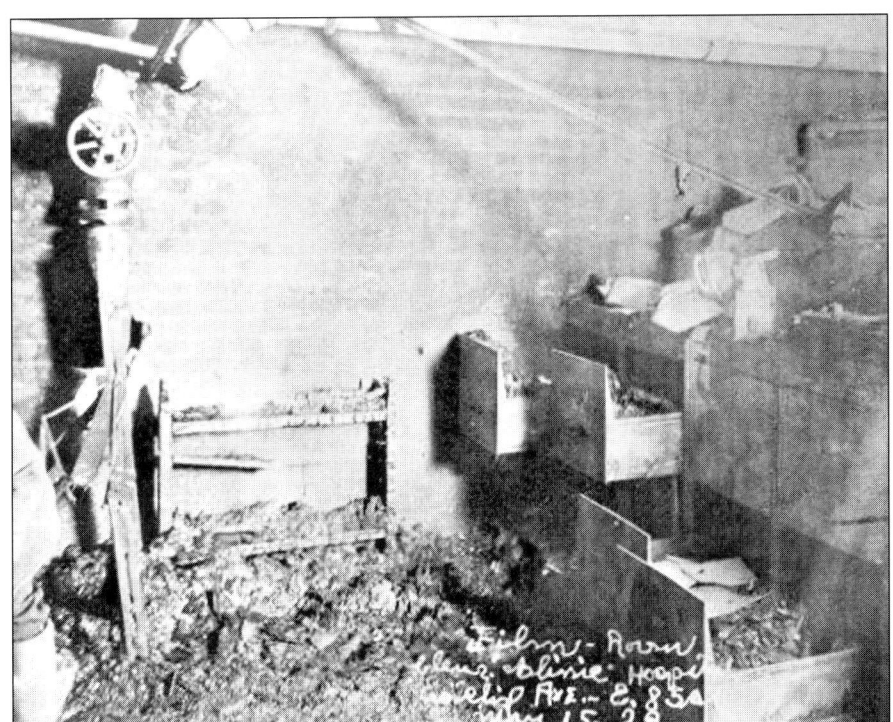

A photograph of the film room at the Cleveland Clinic after the 1927 fire included in the published proceedings of the investigative board of the Chemical Warfare Service.

Imperial War Museum, London.

1927   **15 May – Cleveland Clinic, Cleveland, Ohio, USA.**
A hospital basement was used to store 8,500 pounds (nearly 4,000 kilograms) of X-ray photographs made on nitrate film. A fire broke out while repairs were being made to a steam pipe in the store, which caused 125 deaths, mainly from the inhalation of toxic fumes given off in the fire and spread throughout the building by way of the elevator shaft and the network of risers used to carry the hospital heating system. The official report noted that although "practically noninflammable film" was available for X-ray photography, it had not yet become popular – partly because it was less easy to handle (a tendency to roll made it difficult to file), and partly for reasons of cost. The same report noted 6 other fires of a similar nature, including one (on March 17, 1928 at the Union Memorial Hospital in Albany, NY) said to have resulted in 8 deaths.

References: Lt. Col. Walter C Baker C.W.S., commanding Edgewood Arsenal Maryland, *Proceedings of a Board of the Chemical Warfare Service appointed for the purpose of investigating conditions incident to The Disaster at the Cleveland Hospital Clinic, Cleveland, Ohio on May 15, 1929* (Washington, DC: US Government Printing Office, 1929).

1927   **23 October – Tammerfors, Finland.**
A fire started in the projection box of a motion picture theatre and the operator warned the spectators to flee. Panic broke out when they found the exits blocked by lines of people waiting for the next performance. 21 men and women were either burned to death or suffocated, and a number more were seriously injured.

References: Associated Press report, dated 24 October, cited in several un-sourced US newspaper cuttings included in the William T Madigan Scrapbook (see article by Ronald S Magliozzi in this volume).

1928   **14 March – on board the *SS Duilo*, Atlantic Ocean.**
Film jamming in the projector gate started a fire which then spread to the other reels in the wooden projection box used for film shows in the music salon below the liner's bridge. The fire was brought under control with difficulty owing to some inadequacies in the fire-fighting equipment, and injuries were restricted to burns suffered by one of the operators. Although the incident passed without serious casualties, the risk to 2,000 passengers and crew was thought to have been severe.

References: "A Film Fire at Sea – A letter from Mr. Jac. R. Manheimer", *National Fire Protection Association Quarterly* v.21, no.4 (April 1928), pp.337-338.

1929   **22 October – British Talking Pictures Studios, Wembley, UK.**
A fire, of unknown origin, gutted two sound stages at the Wembley Studios with "a considerable loss of unexposed negative".

There is a persistent story that this fire delayed completion of the film *Dark Red Roses* and so prevented it from being Britain's first "talkie", allowing that honour to pass instead to Hitchcock's *Blackmail*. This claim, however, fails to stand up for two compelling reasons: one is that the report quoted below states categorically that "firemen were able to save all prints and the negative of the company's latest picture, 'Dark Red Roses'", and the other is that *Blackmail* was shown to the trade in June 1929, three months before this fire.

References: *Today's Cinema*, v.33, no.1313 (22 October 1929), p.1.

1929   24 October – Consolidated Film Industries, Hollywood, USA.
A fire, described as "one of the most disastrous fires of recent years", broke out in the Hollywood laboratories "where the negatives of 75 per cent. of the leading companies are stored awaiting presentation and release". Probably started by friction or static electricity, the fire started on a polishing machine in the positive assembly room shortly after midnight. The low death toll (one developer lost his life) was attributed to the fact that the building was comparatively empty; at the same time, the rapid spread of the fire and the large amount of equipment damage was thought to be due to the very large amounts of film which were in the working areas rather than in the vaults even during the night shift.

References: *Today's Cinema*, v.33, no.1316 (25 October 1929), p.1. "Consolidated Film Laboratory Fire", *National Fire Protection Association Quarterly* v.23, no.3 (January 1930), pp.243–251.

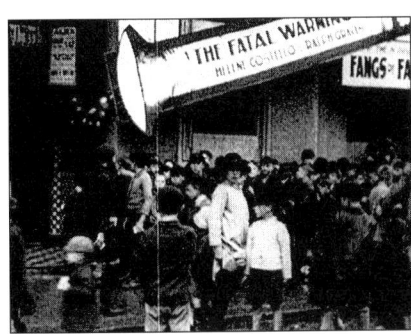 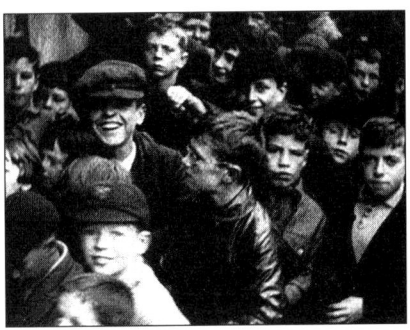

Children filmed for a local topical entitled *Paisley Children's Happy Hunting Ground* (1929), queuing outside the New Alex, another Paisley cinema, to see its first talkie show on 29 August. The Scottish Screen Archive has been able to identify victims and survivors of the Glen Cinema disaster among the children captured on this film, which gives the title of the (silent) serial in the placard over their heads an ominous tone. For example, the boy in the centre of the right-hand frame looking left, wearing glasses, is Hugh Blew, one of the fatalities.

Scottish Screen Archive, Glasgow.

1929   31 December – Glen Cinema, Paisley, Scotland, UK.
Working in the rewind room during a matinee attended by some 700 children, an assistant placed a can of film on top of a wet-cell battery, causing a short-circuit between the terminals. This was the apparent cause of a fire which, in itself, was not particularly serious, but the assistant then left the burning can in a passage while he went to look for the manager to open an exterior door so that he could throw the can outside. During this delay, smoke and panic spread through the auditorium and the audience rushed to escape. One of the emergency exits was obstructed, and 70 children died while some 30 or 40 more were injured in the resulting crush. Eighteen years after the Paisley tragedy, the author of a popular work on British cinema could still note: "quite recently I heard a careless visitor to a cutting room who had a cigarette between his lips adjured with: 'Would you mind dropping that and putting your foot on it, sir – remember Paisley.'"

References: Major T H Crozier, HM Chief Inspector of Explosives, *Report to the Right Honourable the Secretary of State for Scotland on the Circumstances attending the Loss of Life at the Glen Cinema, Paisley, on the 31st December, 1929* (London: HMSO, 1930).

Leslie Wood, *The Romance of the Movies* (London: Burke Publishing, 1947), p.116.

1930   **10 March – Japanese Navy Station, Shinkai [Chinhae], Korea.**
104 people – 102 children and 2 adults – died and over 100 were injured when "a film burst into flames, setting fire to the building" at a base for the Japanese occupation forces in Korea during a film show held as part of the celebrations of the 25th anniversary of the Japanese victory over the Russians at the Battle of Mukden. The victims were members of the families of Japanese naval personnel stationed there.

References: *The Times* (London), 11 March, p.15, and 12 March 1930, p.13.

1932   **27 February – "Royal Cinema, Rustchuk" (now Rule), Bulgaria.**
Fifteen people were burned ("several … reported to be dying") when fire broke out at a performance for children. "For some reason as yet unexplained, two school boys acted as operators" and, when the film caught fire in the projector, "instead of observing prescribed safety measures, [they] took flight", whereupon the flames spread to the gallery provoking "a terrible panic". The crush at the exit was made worse by mothers who had been waiting outside trying to force their way into the building to look for their children.

References: *New York Times*, 29 February 1932, p.13.

1932   **29 March – Star Film Company, Zagreb, Jugoslavia.**
Five or 6 people died and 40 were severely injured when an apartment house occupied by 4 families was destroyed in a fire which started in the adjacent premises of the Star Film Company. When some film caught fire while being processed in the laboratory, the employees fled without sounding the alarm, and the fire spread to the hundred or more rolls of film which the company had in store. The resulting blaze blew out the walls and floor of the second storey and collapsed the wall of a coffee-house; people trapped in the upper floors had to jump into a sheet held by firemen.

References: Un-sourced US newspaper cutting included in the William T Madigan Scrapbook (see article by Ronald S Magliozzi in this volume).
The Times (London), 31 March 1932. p.13.

1932   **13 July – Esmerelda Theatre, Talcahuano, Chile.**
A projector fire broke out in the Esmeralda Theatre at the Talcahuano naval base during an afternoon film show attended by about 300 children, and someone at the rear of the auditorium shouted "Fire!". During the ensuing panic, although the fire was confined to the projection box, 21 children were killed and 50 or more injured by suffocation, trampling, or other injuries.

References: "Nitrocellulose Film Fires", *National Fire Protection Association Quarterly*, v.26, no.1 (July 1932), p.108.
New York Times, 14 July 1932, p.13.

1934   **4 December – Warner Brothers Studio, Burbank, California, USA.**
A massive fire burned more than a third of the 40-acre backlot, taking

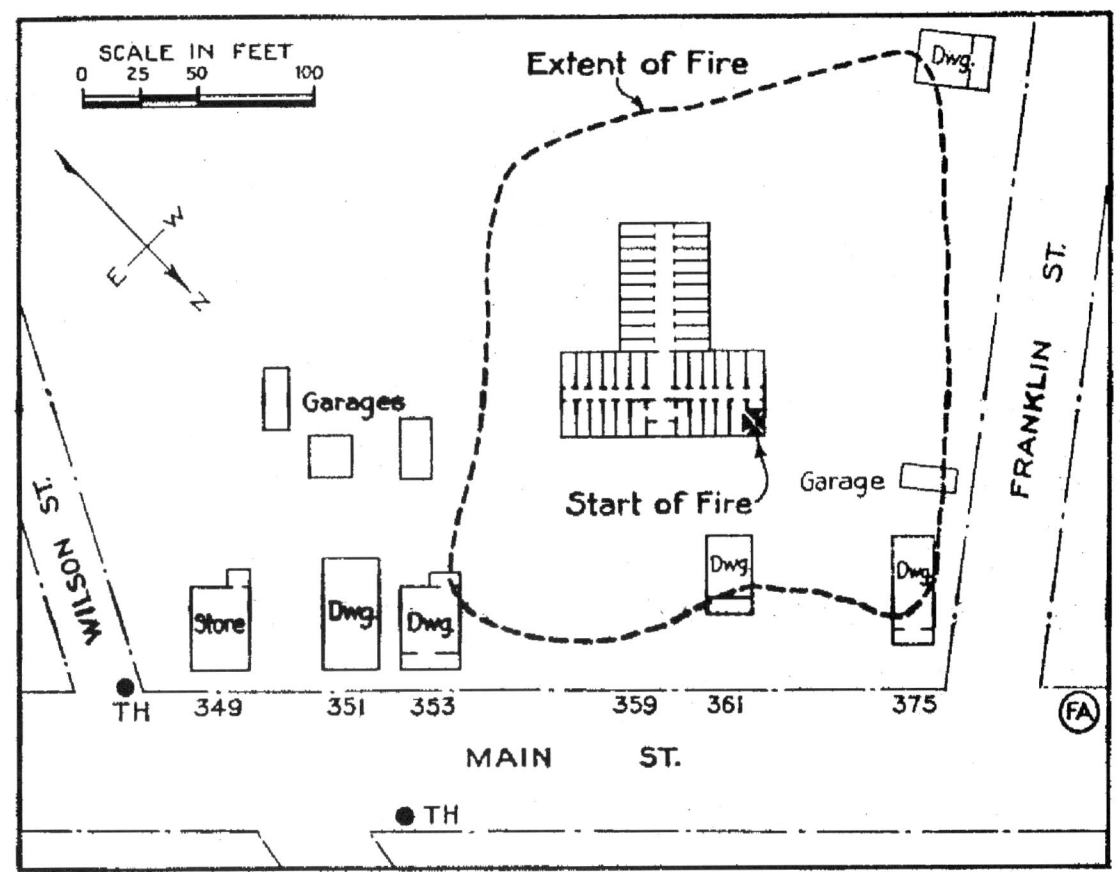

The fire area. Flame shooting from the film storage building caused the ignition of frame dwellings over one hundred feet distant.

with it 6 film vaults reportedly containing "many valuable and irreplaceable films of the Vitagraph era", as well as a large quantity of stock shots of foreign scenes.

References: David Pierce, "The Legion of the Condemned", reprinted in this volume, previously published in *Film History*, v.9, no.1 (1997), pp.5-22.

Diagram showing the extent of the 1937 Fox Film Corporation film store fire at Little Ferry, New Jersey, from the *National Fire Protection Association Quarterly* report. The boy who died lived at 353 Main Street.

David Pierce.

1936   **9 February – British & Dominion Studios, Elstree, UK.**
A fire, of unknown origin, broke out in the early morning and effectively destroyed the premises of British & Dominion – "about five acres of studio buildings" – as well as two of the nine adjacent British International Pictures stages. B&D employees managed to rescue the completed films and camera equipment, and some power and recording equipment was also saved. A principal effect of the fire was to hasten the separation of Herbert Wilcox and B&D from Elstree – they did not rebuild there, but instead became part of a new studio consortium at Pinewood. The early months of 1936 were a bad time for studio fires in Britain; on 17 March, fire destroyed one of the barely-completed stages at the new studios which Alexander Korda was building at Denham.

References: *Today's Cinema*, v.46, no.3230 (10 February 1936), p.1, and no.3231 (11 February 1936), pp.1,3,6.
The Times, 10 February 1936, p.12.
The Cinema News, v.46, no.3262 (18 March 1936), p.1.

1937 **9 July – Fox Film Corporation, Little Ferry, New Jersey, USA.**

A serious fire broke out in a purpose-built Fox Film Corporation film store located in a residential district. "The building was used exclusively for the storage of old motion picture film. Some of the film was as much as 25 years old and none was less than five years old." The fire, which was apparently caused by spontaneous combustion at the end of a long period of consistently hot weather, spread to all the 46 self-contained cells in the 2-year-old structure and destroyed all of the 40,000 cans of film in the store, severely damaging the building itself. (The roof, a reinforced 4-inch concrete slab, was noted after the fire to be "badly bulged" or "bowed" at several points.) Damage was also caused to some nearby frame houses, and one local resident later died of injuries caused by the fire.

References: "Fox Film Storage Fire – Report by Schedule Rating Office of N.J.", *National Fire Protection Association Quarterly*, v.31, no.2 (October 1937), pp.136–142.

1939 **20 March – Brunot Laboratories, Saint-Cloud, France.**

Four people were killed trying to save the life of a colleague when a fire attributed to a short-circuit destroyed a large part of a modern printing and processing laboratory. Also lost were 6 films recently completed or awaiting completion, among them *Quartier Latin* (directed by Pierre Colombier), and *Le Plancher des Vaches* (directed by Pierre Ducis and starring Betty Stockfeld). Note, however, that another of the films listed as lost – *Campement 13* – has subsequently been restored from other elements by the Archives of the Centre National de la Cinématographie.

References: G-R Rol, "A propos d'un incendie", *Cinéma-Spectacles*, no.969 (31 March 1939).
Claude Bernier, "Des films que vous ne verrez pas", *Ciné-Miroir*, no.734 (28 April 1939).

1941 **22 September – Stockholm, Sweden.**

A fire consumed virtually all the negatives of Swedish silent cinema, including all but one of the films made by Victor Sjöström before 1916 (two were later found in other countries) and almost the entire oeuvre of Mauritz Stiller. Out of 43 films Stiller produced in Sweden, only two survived in almost complete and original prints. Speaking to Sam Kula, Einar Lauritzen described the 1941 fire as the equivalent, in terms of Swedish film history, of the total loss of the Museum of Modern Art collection at the time Iris Barry retired.

References: Gosta Werner, ed., *Svensk Filmforskning* (Stockholm: P A Norstedt & Soners, 1982).

1943 **5 August – Harold Lloyd Residence, Beverly Hills, California, USA.**

An explosion in the private vault at Harold Lloyd's Benedict Canyon Drive estate destroyed original master material on the star's early comedies. Lloyd, who placed a value of $2 million on the loss, was himself rescued by his wife, Mildred Davis Lloyd, as he collapsed in the vault doorway. Seven firemen and a Lloyd employee were taken to hospital, affected by gas as the fire spread to chlorinating equipment connected to the swimming pool.

References: "Harold Lloyd Saved from Fire by Wife" (AP Report), in *New York Times*, 6 August 1943.

1945   **16 August – Cinematiraje Riera, Madrid, Spain.**
Two people died, and 650,000 metres of film were lost, in a huge fire at the Cinematiraje Riera workshops. The material destroyed included all the films that had been produced by both camps during the Civil War, which had been collected by the National Department of Cinematography in the aftermath of the conflict. Among the feature films also lost irrevocably was the still-unreleased *Nuestra Natacha*, by Benito Perojo.

References: Jorge Martín Neira, "Fires in the Spanish Cinema" (in this volume).

1947   **24 June – Ministère de l'Instruction Publique, Brussels, Belgium.**
The Ministry of Education suffered a major disaster following a nitrate film fire which started in the basement store and was then carried throughout the 7-storey building by way of the lift shafts. Trapped on the upper floors, some staff tried to jump to the roof of a neighbouring building and a few fell to their deaths. The total casualty list was later confirmed as 18 dead and 34 injured, and subsequent legal proceedings drew attention to the failure of building standards and handling procedures in the Ministry to conform to controls imposed – by government legislation – on the film industry itself.

References: *Ciné-Journal*, 28 June 1947, p.1.
La Cinégraphie Belge, 4 February 1950, pp.1–2.

1948   **22 September – Hong Kong.**
A massive fire, which burned down the whole 9-building warehouse complex of the Wing On department store in Central, Hong Kong Island, causing the deaths of 119 people and damage estimated at HK$30 million, is attributed to the illegal storage of nitro-cellulose film scraps in the warehouse.

References: Angela Tong, "Nitrate Tales – Hong Kong's Vanishing Film Heritage?" (in this volume).

1949   **June – New York/New Jersey area, USA.**
A spate of film fires – at least 4 in a 10-day period – in the Greater New York area prompted an official enquiry by officers of the US Army Signal Corps to discover whether any government film had been lost, and whether any lessons could be learned about the prevention of such fires. The officers visited the locations of the fires[2] and their report concluded that a combination of deteriorating film, poor storage conditions, and a prolonged period of high summer temperatures was to blame for the fires, and noted the immediate recommendation that "every can of film in the possession of the National Archives, either accessioned or courtesy storage, be immediately inspected for deterioration and that the affected part be destroyed".

References: James W Cummings to Mr Wayne C Grover, Archivist of the United States, 13 July 1949, "Report on Film Fires in the New York Area, June 1949" (in the US National Archives).

1951   Misr Studios, Cairo, Egypt.
A fire started after one of the studio porters dropped a cigarette end or other burning material into some waste near the film store and failed to notice what happened next. From this small beginning, the blaze ultimately spread, in spite of the efforts of the studio fire-fighters, to the laboratories, the editing suites, the projection rooms, and other parts of the complex. The losses, which included a large number of prints and negatives, are described as "enormous".

Refererence: Ahmed al-Hadari, "Les Studios Misr", in Magda Wassef, ed., *Egypte: 100 ans de cinéma* (Paris: Editions Plume, 1995), pp.96-97.

1953   19 July – Malayan Film Unit Library, Kuala Lumpur, Malaya.
Fire destroyed the building in which the Film Unit's negatives were stored, causing damage estimated at $150,000. Beyond the financial damage, press coverage noted the loss of "films of historic interest to Malaya, and which would have been of ever-growing interest as the years went by" and commented: "Although it is easy to be wise after the event it seems a pity that films ... should not have been at least duplicated and copies stored in separate places as a safeguard against loss".

Refererence: *Malay Mail*, 20 and 21 July 1953.

1954   4 December – Atlantic-Filmverleih GmbH., Munich, German Federal Republic.
A fire in the vaults of a distribution company resulted in the loss of some 200 copies of German and foreign films, valued at about 150,000 DM. The fire started when a dispatcher lit a cigarette between 2 storerooms, and the burning match-head fell into a box of off-cuts.

References: *Der neue Film* (Wiesbaden), 13 December 1954.

1955   11 May – Wielopole Skrzyńskie, Poland
Fire broke out in an overcrowded wooden building being used for a travelling cinema performance; 58 people lost their lives.

References: Jan Slodowski, "Poland's Worst Nitrate Film Disaster" (in this volume).

1957   28 January – Cinemateca Brasileira, São Paulo, Brazil.
Fire broke out late at night in the Cinemateca's rooms on the 13th floor of the Museu de Arte Moderna. It was brought under control after 2 hours, but by then the archive had lost important collections of stills, posters, and documentation – and perhaps 500,000 metres of film, including unique copies of important Brazilian documentaries.

References: Carlos Roberto de Souza, *"Inconfidência Archiveira"* (in this volume)

1959   July 10 – Cinémathèque Française, Paris, France.
Fire broke out among films stored under a glass roof in a courtyard at the Cinémathèque's headquarters in the rue de Courcelles. The cause of the fire, the extent of the loss, and the identity of the material

destroyed all remain the subject of debate to this day, although it is generally believed that the fire was started by spontaneous combustion and accepted that a substantial quantity of film was lost, including material on loan from Warsaw and elsewhere, as well as some of the Cinémathèque's own unique treasures. The atmosphere of suspicion and controversy surrounding the fire contributed to the breach between the Director of the Cinémathèque, Henri Langlois, and FIAF which developed later the same year.

References: Richard Roud, *A Passion for Films: Henri Langlois and the Cinémathèque Française* (New York: Viking Press, 1983).
Glenn Myrent and Georges P Langlois (translated from the French by Lisa Nesselson), *Henri Langlois: First Citizen of Cinema* (New York: Twayne Publishers, 1995).
Roger Smither, "Henri Langlois and Nitrate, Before and After 1959" (in this volume).

1959   **July 27 – Adams Filmi, Helsinki, Finland.**
A fire at the premises of Adams Filmi destroyed, among other material, the surviving nitrate prints of *Herra Lahtinen lähtee lipettiin* (Mr. Lahtinen Takes French Leave, 1939), by Finnish film-maker Nyrki Tapiovaara.

References: Sakari Toiviainen, "A Melody Lost in 1939 . . ." (in this volume).

1960   **July 24 –Yokohama Cinema Developing Laboratory, Japan.**
A fire, apparently caused by the spontaneous combustion of nitrate film, burned the entire film storage area, a 38-square-metre mortared frame bungalow. As well as 400 reels of raw film stock, a substantial quantity of processed film was also lost, one report speaking of "2,200 cans of deposited original negatives." Although rumour includes Yasujiro Ozu's *Tokyo Story* among the films lost, there is no proof for this story.

References: Hisashi Okajima and Yoshiro Irie, "Kyoto Tales and Tokyo Stories" (in this volume).

1961   **April 17 – Munich, German Federal Republic**
Fire broke out in a Second World War bunker in the Feldmoching district used by a film valuation company named Rohwert to store approximately 40 tons of material, mainly comprising old features and newsreels. The initial explosion – apparently caused when an ultraviolet light blew up – injured 3 women employees, one of whom subsequently died, and 10 firemen were injured in a further small explosion the next day. Although the fire service filled the whole lower level of the bunker with water, the fire repeatedly broke out again, and was not declared finally extinguished until 6 days after it started.

References: *Frankfurter Nachtausgabe*, 20 April 1961.
General-Anzeiger (Bonn), 24 April 1961.

1967   **July 23 – National Film Board Archives in 'Beaconsfield', Canada.**
Fire broke out in a temporary store (actually at Kirkland, though conventionally known as Beaconsfield) in Québec province, used by the

National Film Board of Canada to store nitrate film. For want of better premises, the Board was obliged to store its film in a building – little more than a corrugated tin roof, supported on wooden posts – which was far from suited to the purpose. The fire started in an area of the building near an electrical junction and fire boxes, though the exact cause was never established. The loss, reckoned as "millions of feet", and including much irreplaceable material, extended beyond films produced by the Board itself, as the NFB had become the unofficial repository for many agencies, such as the Canadian Film Institute and the Canadian Armed Services, which did not wish to store potentially dangerous film on their own premises.

References: Bill Galloway, "The 'Beaconsfield' Story", and Jack Ponting, "Catch as Cats Can", *Perforations* (March-April 1982), pp.14-18

1969   **February – Cinemateca Brasileira, São Paulo, Brazil.**
Fire broke out in one of the small lodges in the Ibirapuera Park, where the Cinemateca had been obliged to keep its films since the 1957 fire. Total loss was estimated at 350 films.

References: Carlos Roberto de Souza, *"Inconfidência Archiveira"* (in this volume)

1972   **July 20 – Prague Film Library, Czechoslovakia**
A fire, caused by spontaneous combustion during a period of extreme summer heat, started in one cell in a non-air conditioned vault used for the storage of both nitrate and acetate film. Automatic sprinklers and the prompt attention of the fire service prevented the fire spreading to other cells, but extensive work on film salvaged from the vault was required to make good the effects of damage resulting from the interaction of water and the corrosive fumes given off by the fire. Of 600 reels stored in the cell, 200 nitrate reels were completely destroyed. While the majority of these were duplicates, the losses did include some 50 reels of unique newsreel and actuality material relating to Czechoslovak history in the 1920s, 1930s, and 1940s.

References: Vladimir Opela, "Fire in the Prague Film Library", *FIAF Bulletin* no.V (December 1973), pp.6–7.

1974   **August 19 – Austrian Film Archives' Building, Laxenburg.**
In the early morning following the hottest day in 20 years, fire – apparently caused by spontaneous combustion – broke out in one chamber of the preliminary storeroom for nitrate film. Laxenburg had been called on to house considerably more nitrate than would fit into the 8 proper air-conditioned vaults, and use of the unconditioned "preliminary store" was the only option available. Although there was some damage to a garage and other adjacent buildings, the fire was restricted to the preliminary store. By immediate action, the fire was kept from the second chamber, but it had spread to the roof of the building. Firemen displayed considerable courage in rescuing about 4,000 reels of nitrate from beneath the heated roof and carrying it to safety in the anteroom of the proper nitrate store. Fewer than 150 reels of film were reported completely lost in the fire.

References: "Vienna", *FIAF Bulletin* no.VII (December 1974), pp.11–12.

1977   February 7 – Filmoteca de la UNAM, Mexico.
A fire with curious characteristics – the damage was much less than would have been expected – occurred in one of the Filmoteca's nitrate storage vaults. The curator had his suspicions about the reasons for this discrepancy, which are now published for the first time.

References: Manuel Gonzalez Casanova, "Fire in the UNAM Film Archive" (in this volume)

1977   August 29 – National Archives, Suitland, Maryland, USA.
An outbreak of fire at the Federal Records Center, Suitland was attributed to spontaneous combustion of dangerously decomposed nitrate in a store with a malfunctioning air-conditioning system in a period of hot and humid weather. Although the fire destroyed a quantity of *March of Time* out-takes, it did not spread beyond the vault where it started – behaviour which would later be specifically contrasted with the course of the December 1978 fire (see below).

1978   May 29 – George Eastman House, Rochester, NY, USA.
A weekend fire destroyed 3 outbuildings, one of them used as a nitrate film store to contain some of the estimated 15% of the collection which could not be accommodated in the purpose-built air-conditioned vaults of the Henry A Strong Archives Building (opened 1952). Reports disagree about whether the fire started in the film store and spread to an adjoining wooden structure used to store 12 travelling photograph exhibitions, or moved in the opposite direction. Some 3,195 reels of nitrate film (representing 516 titles of all types – shorts, features, and cartoons) were reported lost in the fire, the majority of them having already been copied to safety stock. Although flames from the fire reached the Strong building, the films inside were not affected

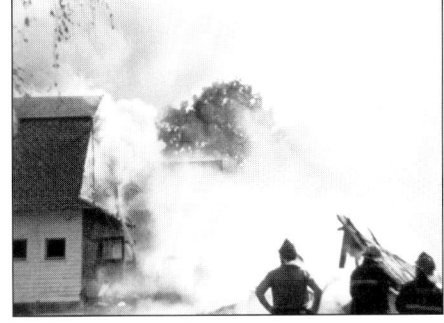
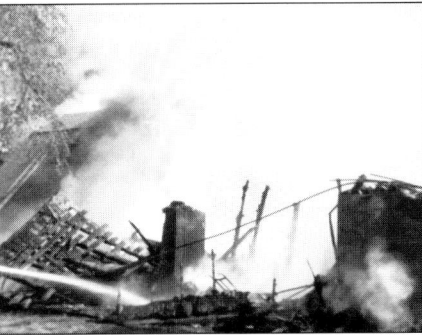

The 1978 fire at George Eastman House.
(See also Colour Section 2.)
George Eastman House, Rochester, NY.

References: "Report of Damage from May 29, 1978 Eastman House Fire", *FIAF Bulletin* no.XV, December 1978, pp.30-31.
A Collective Endeavour – The First Fifty Years of George Eastman House, (Rochester, NY: George Eastman House, 1999), p.82.

1978   December 7 – National Archives, Suitland, Maryland, USA.
A very large collection of unique Universal Newsreel out-takes, estimated at over 12.5 million feet, was lost when a second fire broke out at Suitland (see August 1977, above). The fire also destroyed some 600,000 feet of other nitrate film, which had been copied. It is generally accepted that the origin of the fire was linked to the presence of workmen with electric power tools in the vaults on that day; and that the protection supposedly offered to the film by its separation into small vaults was fatally compromised by well-intentioned but inappropriate actions – for example, opening doors to check that no staff were trapped, or breaking

open vents – on the part of those attempting to fight it.

References: *National Archives and Records Service Film-Vault Fire at Suitland, MD. – Hearings before a Subcommittee of the Committee on Government Operations, House of Representatives, Ninety-Sixth Congress, First Session, June 19 and 21, 1979* (Washington DC: US Government Printing Office, 1979).
W H Utterback, Jr, "An Opinion on the Nitrate Film Fire Suitland, Maryland 7 December 1978", *Journal of the University Film Association*, v.32, no.3 (Summer 1980), pp.3–16.

1980   July 29 – Aladdin Cinema, Kristiansand, Norway.
On a hot summer's day, fire started during an afternoon screening: of the 60 members of the audience, 10 were injured, 2 seriously. The cause was eventually confirmed as being the combustion of some nitrate film kept by the cinema director, who claimed to be unaware of regulations concerning the storage of such materials.

Reference: Vigdis Lian, "The Last Nitrate Fire in a Commercial Cinema?" (in this volume).

1980   August 3 – Cinémathèque Française, Le Pontel, Villiers Saint-Frédéric, France.
Fire, attributed either to a short-circuit following a storm or to spontaneous combustion, broke out during a hot summer at one of the Cinémathèque's film stores near Paris. The building (described as "a hangar of very light construction") was not designed for nitrate storage and had neither shelves nor air-conditioning. The loss in films was estimated at 7,000 films – perhaps some 50,000 reels – but as there was no inventory, the figure is impossible to substantiate. Thirteen neighbouring buildings were significantly damaged. As was the case with the 1959 fire, the Le Pontel incident gave rise both to legend (there were rumours of scores, even hundreds, more secret stores of nitrate film deposited by Langlois around the country) and controversy – why, it was asked, had the Cinémathèque withdrawn its films to such inadequate storage when space was available for them in the Centre National de la Cinématographie's new purpose-built vaults at Bois d'Arcy? Following the fire, 20,000 reels of nitrate – the balance of the Cinémathèque's holdings – were transferred to the CNC.

Reference: Raymond Borde, "After the Fire at the Cinémathèque Française", *FIAF Bulletin* no.XX (March 1981), pp.31–33.

1982   March 24 – The Cineteca Nacional, Mexico.
A fire that burned for 14 hours completely destroyed the building of the Cineteca Nacional, opened in 1974. First reports of the incident concerned dense smoke coming from all 4 of the film vaults in the building (although only one was at the time in use for nitrate film), but its climax came at 6:45 p.m. with the eruption of fire from behind the screen while the audience in the Fernando de Fuentes theatre was being evacuated. Although rumours placed the toll higher, official reports spoke of 5 deaths (including that of a senior Fire Officer).

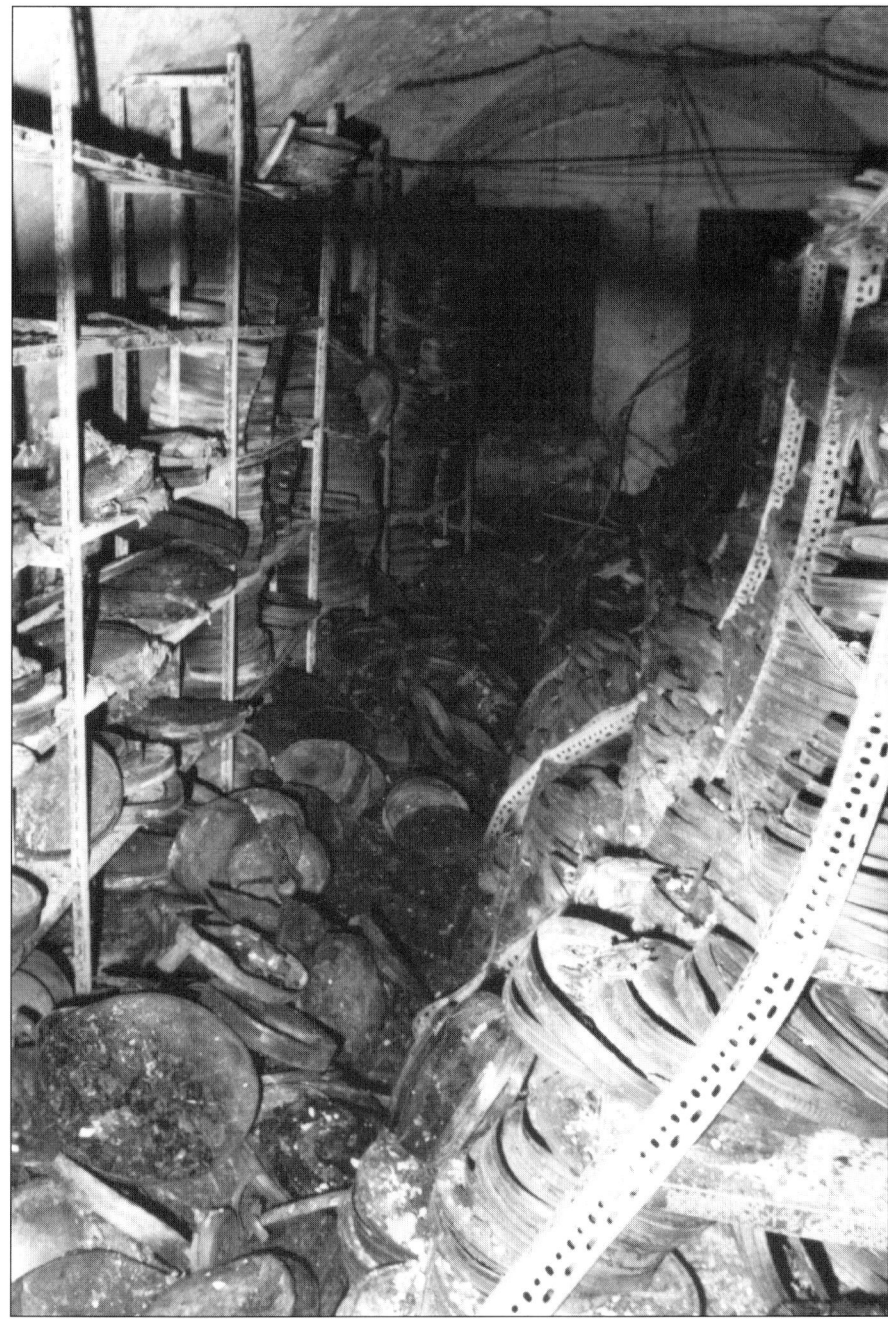

The scene after the 1988 fire in one of the Bundesarchiv's nitrate vaults in the Ehrenbreitstein Fortress, Koblenz.

Bundesarchiv-Filmarchiv, Berlin.

References: Fernando Osorio, "The Case of the Cineteca Nacional Fire" (in this volume).

Ing. Carlos de Navia Osorio and Juan Aymes Coucke, "Report on Fire and Explosions to the Representative of the Federal Public Ministry, Mexico, D.F., April 13, 1982", translation printed as Appendix 14 in the Minutes of *FIAF Congress XXXVIII, Oaxtepec, June 1982* (Brussels: FIAF, 1982).

1982   November 6 – Cinemateca Brasileira, São Paulo, Brazil.
Fire again broke out in one of the small lodges in the Ibirapuera Park, where lack of government support and continuing financial problems meant little had changed since 1969. 1,600 reels were burned, including some irreplaceable actuality material, although some of the lost nitrate had previously been copied to safety film.

References: Carlos Roberto de Souza, "Inconfidência Archiveira"
(in this volume).

1984   **September 3 – Film Center, National Museum of Modern Art, Tokyo, Japan.**
A fire, attributed either to a breakdown in the cooling system or to a short-circuit, started in a store on the fifth floor used for foreign feature films. Of some 450 films in this collection, 320 were totally and 32 partly destroyed; there was also damage to the rest of the floor and to an adjoining auditorium, but no personal injuries.

References: "Rare Foreign Movies Lost in Flames at Film Center Fire" and "Cause of Film Fire Probed by Officials", in *Asahi Evening News*, September 1984, reproduced in *FIAF Bulletin* no.XXVIII (December 1984), p.36.

1985   **September 27 – Service des Archives du Film, Centre National de la Cinématographie, Bois d'Arcy, France.**
Fire broke out in one of the 181 cells in the Archive's nitrate storage vaults, destroying 1,086 reels of film, mainly comprising foreign shorts of the 1940s, many of them received from the Cinémathèque Française in 1980 already in poor condition. Not more than 50 titles were considered to have been unique copies, and Curator Frantz Schmitt said that "no major cinematographic work" was lost. The cause of the fire was thought likely to have been a short-circuit, but thanks to the prompt intervention of the fire services and the intrinsic strengths of the vaults' design, the fire did not spread beyond the cell where it started.

References: *Le Monde*, 1 October 1985.

1988   **January 26 – Bundesarchiv, Koblenz, German Federal Republic.**
A fire, probably caused by an electric fault, burned out one cell of the Bundesarchiv's nitrate vaults in the Ehrenbreitstein Fortress. 1,900 reels of film were lost, but 85% of this material had previously been copied to safety stock; the uncopied material comprised German documentaries of the 1930s. Following the fire, the Archive reduced its nitrate holdings by offering to FIAF partners, returning to donors, or destroying approximately 30 tons of film.

References: *Frankfurter Rundschau*, 27 January 1988.
Rhein-Zeitung, 28 January 1988

1993   **July 4 – Hendersons Laboratories, South Norwood, London, UK.**
A serious fire, the cause of which has never been found, broke out at 9:00 p.m. on a Sunday evening in the vaults of Hendersons, a purpose-built film laboratory dating from the 1920s used by many archives for preservation printing. Starting in the right- hand of 3 ground-floor vaults, the fire spread rapidly to the left-hand vault, but missed out the one in the middle. Flames from the vent on top of the vaults set fire to the wood-enclosed water tank on the roof, and a third-floor cleaning room and the negative preparation room on the second floor were set alight by burning cans which were thrown through the windows by the force of the blaze. A fireball spread throughout the building, and much damage was caused; many rolls of nitrate film were destroyed, as well as safety material.

References: Brian Pritchard, e-mail message to Roger Smither, 5
                January 2001.

Notes

1. Grant Whytock, one of those in the cutting room when the fire started, gave the following
    account of the event in an interview recorded by Kevin Brownlow in 1977: *"Well, it was
    wintertime, and later on they found somebody had put a penny behind one of the fuses
    downstairs. We had a small heater on a shelf up above the bench box where 'Dell' Andrews
    was working, and I was standing there looking at him when this – something – I see something
    drop into it, which was lead or something that had melted, and smoke came up. Not having
    any fear of film go up because I'd never seen it burn, he said, "Get me a fire extinguisher". So
    I rushed over and got him a fire extinguisher, and came back, and he said, "Get me another
    one." And I didn't get back with the second one; the thing exploded all over the room – we
    had probably a million feet of film exposed in the room, nitrate. The windows were out, and
    we all rushed to the door at the same time – the door opened in – and I think there were eleven
    or twelve of us, trying to get out of the door. Well, I was a small one, and Cyril Gardiner was
    a small fellow, so the big fellows crowded around back of us and saved us from being burned
    too badly. So when we finally got the door open, I went down – I jumped the whole flight of
    stairs, which didn't hurt me at all. But my blue shirt had been scorched to a yellow, you know,
    the heat was so strong, and still I wasn't... They all went to the hospital, but Cyril and I. And
    of course one of them died later from the [fumes]; it had gotten into his lungs. ... A
    projectionist, one of the young projectionists, named Arthur Sist."*

2. Fires were reported at Bonded Film Storage Co., 146th Street/Seventh Avenue, New York City,
    and at Woodbridge, Ogdensburg, and Boundbrook (all New Jersey). During their investigation,
    the officers learned that the temperature had been around 98° F (36.5° C) for the previous 30
    days, and that there had been 2 smaller fires at Ogdensburg in the 2 weeks before the big fire
    on 26 June, which destroyed 4 buildings and 11 vaults (each containing up to 1,344 cans of
    film).

"Un Autodafé Sensationnel"

Editors' Note: We acknowledge with gratitude the help given by Michelle Aubert and her colleagues at the Archives du Film du CNC and by Robert Daudelin of the Cinémathèque Québécoise in providing the source materials for this item. The translations are our own.

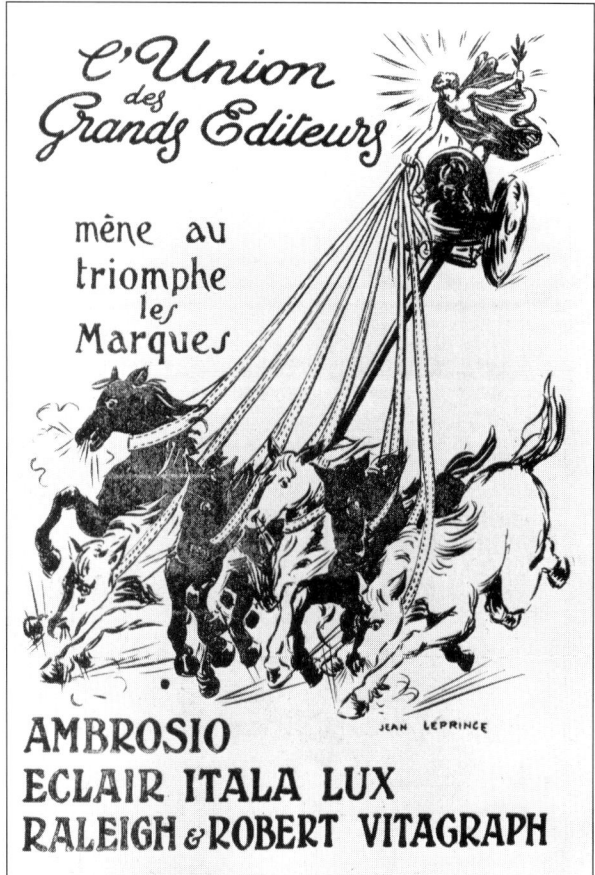

A press advertisement for the Union des Grands Editeurs, August 1910.

© Gaumont.

These three words promise something lurid: the phrase "auto-da-fé" (literally: "act of faith", from the Portuguese) was originally used for the ceremony at which the Inquisition handed down its verdict on those who had appeared before it, but has subsequently been almost universally, if not strictly correctly, associated with the actual execution of its sentences, and especially with the public burning of heretics. A story with just this headline appeared in the *Ciné-Journal* of 28 May 1910. It explained the concrete steps which L'Union des Grands Éditeurs de Films (the Union of Major Film Producers) – a grouping which brought together the famous brand names Ambrosio, Éclair, Itala, Lux, Raleigh & Robert, and Vitagraph – planned to take to improve the market in films:

Convinced that one of the main reasons for the current cinema crisis is the persistence in the market of old, used films, not worthy of a decent screening, the Union has decided gradually to eliminate these bad products. Does it not actually do the cause of theatrical presentation a grave disservice to offer the public films which will give them a poor impression of production in general, destroy their taste for an entertainment that is still quite profitable, drive them from the halls, and ruin the proprietors?

The interest of the renters, bound up with that of the public and the producers, is to purge all these worn-out films bit by bit from the market.

What other method to use than incineration? The Union is resolved: it will stage, on 9 June next, a public burning of films which it has rented for some months and which now seem to it to be no longer fit to be offered to the public. So that nobody should doubt the sacrifice that it is making, and in order to convince the sceptics, the Union invites cinema professionals to attend this voluntary conflagration.

The friends of cinema will therefore assemble on 9 June, at 3 o'clock, at Epinay-sur-Seine in the factories of the Éclair Company. The next public burning will take place at the premises of another of the companies belonging to the Union.

Thus will be achieved the work of commercial purification which has been made necessary by the faults committed in the film trade thus far.

People wishing to attend the operation are asked to apply for a ticket from the Union of Major Producers at 17 Rue du Faubourg-Montmartre.[1]

The following week, the same journal carried a response from correspondent Georges Dureau, which spoke of a response made up of a mixture of "stupefaction and regret":

> To begin with, the great majority of dealers, projectionists, renters, and manufacturers have what I might call an innate respect for film. This is easy to understand. You need only the simplest understanding of the worker's psychology to appreciate that someone who creates, transforms, or puts to use any kind of material does not look on its destruction without regret. The carpenter never burns his wood, even when it he thinks it unusable. The artisan becomes attached to the material he works: it is one of his noblest attributes. There is more. Any product, even as waste, retains some market value. Is there no worse waste than to destroy it? Through the small proceeds of resale one may write off overheads...

> Meanwhile, the reasons which have guided the directors of the Union in their decision are blindingly obvious... There are too many films on the market. This is a fact. There are too many producers, and each of them generally produces too much... This destruction is a clear-out: in the general state of congestion, it will give the market a bit of fresh air and clear the ground.

An earlier press advertisement for the Union des Grands Editeurs – "the only organisation which burns used-up films" – in July 1910.

© Gaumont.

> This necessary sacrifice recalls that demanded in a city under siege, when, in order to save the city, it is decided to get rid of the useless mouths and expel the old people. You will tell me that they are not consigned to the flames – but that is out of a respect for humanity which celluloid (even exposed celluloid) does not receive.[2]

The fire went ahead, and was described in the issue of 11 June, in an account which loses something in translation, as it contains several puns for which there are no English equivalents:

> Those condemned were brought to the scene, having been taken from their cells/cans [the French word "boîte" has both meanings] shortly before, and the scheme worked through thousands of metres, across the wild grass, between a few necessary sheets of metal. We saw – and not without some sadness – the passing of certain brave souls who had certainly made their living but whose death would make it easier for others to make theirs. Ambrosio, Éclair, Itala, Lux, Raleigh & Robert, and Vitagraph each passed in their turn. The confused state of affairs in their art was being sorted out, and the director of the Union, executor/executioner in these matters, threw the first brand.

> A few tears flowed. They were immediately dried by a powerful flash – I was going to say a lightning bolt (Éclair) – which burst out. It was terrible and brief.[3]

Subsequent issues of *Ciné-Journal* carried advertisements which pictured the Union as the divine charioteer holding the celluloid reins of the six proud member steeds, and reminded readers that it was the only organisation that burned used-up films – not a claim calculated to endear it to film archivists in a later age!

Notes

1. «Persuadée qu'une des causes principales de la crise cinématographique est la persistance sur le marché de films vieillis, usés, indignes d'une projection honnête, l'*Union des Grands Editeurs* a décidé d'anéantir progressivement ces mauvaises oeuvres. N'est-ce pas, en effet, porter un grave préjudice à la cinématographie théâtrale que de servir au public des films qui lui donnent une triste opinion de la production générale, le dégoûtent d'un plaisir pourtant lucratif, l'éloignent des salles de spectacle et ruinent les exploitants?

   L'intérêt des loueurs, lié à celui du public et des fabricants, c'est de purger peu à peu le marché de tous les films vieillis.

   Quel autre moyen employer en dehors de l'incinération? L'*Union* s'y est résolue. Elle fera, le 9 juin prochain, un autodafé des films qu'elle a loués depuis quelques mois et qui lui paraissent désormais indignes d'être offerts au public. Pour qu'on ne doute point du sacrifice qu'elle s'impose et que les sceptiques soient convaincus, elle prie les cinématographistes d'assister à cet incendie volontaire.

   Les amis du cinématographe se réuniront donc le 9 juin, à trois heures, à Epinay-sur-Seine, dans les usines de la Société *Éclair*. Le prochain autodafé aura lieu au siège d'une des Sociétés adhérentes à l'*Union*.

   Ainsi s'accomplira l'oeuvre d'hygiène commerciale que nécessitent les fautes commises jusqu'à ce jour dans le commerce du film.

   Les personnes qui désirent assister à l'opération sont priées de demander une carte à "L'Union des Grands Editeurs", 17 rue du Faubourg-Montmartre.» *Ciné-Journal*, no.92 (28 May 1910), p. 4.

2. «Tout d'abord, la grosse majorité des exploitants, des opérateurs, des loueurs, des fabricants ont, ce que je pourrais appeler le respect inné du film. Cela se conçoit aisément. Pour peu qu'on ait deux doigts de psychologie ouvrière, on devine bien que l'homme qui crée, transforme, met en oeuvre une matière quelconque ne se résigne pas, sans regret, à la détruire. Le menuisier ne brûle jamais le bois qu'il possède, même lorsqu'il lui paraît être inutilisable. L'artisan s'attache à la matière oeuvrée: c'est une de ses plus hautes noblesses. Il y a plus. Tout produit, même à l'état de déchet, conserve une valeur marchande. N'est-ce pas pire gaspillage que de le détruire? Avec les petits bénéfices de la revente, on amortit ses frais généraux....

   Et pourtant, les raisons qui ont guidé les directeurs de l'Union dans leur determination, sont de celles qui paraissent d'une clarté éblouissante....

   Il y a trop de films sur le marché. Voilà le fait. Les éditeurs qui les produisent sont trop nombreux et chacun d'eux en produit trop généralement....

   Cette destruction est une épuration. Dans l'encombrement général, elle va donner un peu d'air au marché et déblayer le terrain.

   Ce sacrifice nécessaire est un peu semblable à celui que s'imposent les assiégés, lorsque pour sauver la ville, ils se débarrassent des bouches inutiles et éloignent les anciens. On me dira qu'ils ne les brûlent pas. Mais c'est par respect humain que ne mérite pas le celluloïd, même imprimé.» *Ciné-Journal*, no.93 (4 June 1910), p. 3.

3. «... On apporta les condamnés qu'on avait extraits de leur ... boîte quelques instants avant et leur théorie se développa sur des milliers de mètres, à travers les herbes folles, entre quelques plaques de tôle nécessaires. Nous vîmes passer – et non sans quelque tristesse – de vaillants sujets qui avaient certes gagné leur vie, mais dont la mort fera mieux gagner la vie des autres. Ambrosio, Éclair, Itala, Lux, Raleigh & Robert et Vitagraph passèrent à tour de rôle. On débrouilla leur art épars confusément et le directeur de l'Union, exécuteur de ces œuvres, jeta le premier tison.

   Quelques larmes avaient coulé. Elles furent immédiatement séchées par une formidable lueur – j'allais dire par l'Éclair – qui surgit. Ce fut terrible et bref.» *Ciné-Journal*, no.94 (11 June 1910).

"Fire!" The 1917 Nitrate Fire in Berlin, and Its Consequences

by Martin Koerber

"A big fire, of a size hitherto unknown in the history of our industry, raged through the Filmfabrik Karl Geyer GmbH on Wednesday afternoon," reported the trade journal *Lichtbildbühne* on October 20, 1917. "The damage is believed to amount to more than one million Marks, besides which the loss of artistic work is tremendous, because quite a number of new negatives perished. The exact number of burnt negatives is not yet established; there is talk of 170, some of which belong to this year's season. In those cases where there is no good positive from which dupe negatives can be struck, the fire will have a great impact on the economic aspects of this year's market."[1]

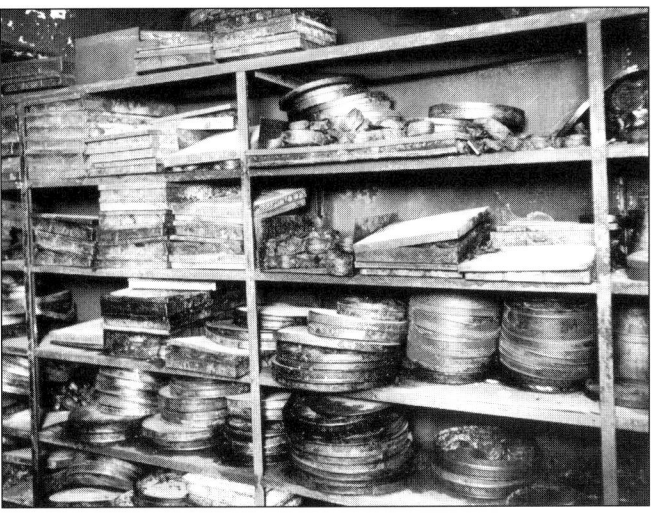

The interior of the old vault at Filmfabrik Karl Geyer after the 1917 fire.

Filmmuseum Berlin – Deutsche Kinemathek.

Geyer's laboratory in the Neukölln district of Berlin had been established in 1911. It was one of the first companies in Germany to service the film industry and specialise in the developing and printing of films while remaining independent from a filmmaking company. To this day Geyer-Werke is one of the leading labs in Germany, and it can still be found at the location that was almost wiped out by a big blast of fire in the autumn of 1917. Smaller fires were, of course, not unheard of in the many studios and small laboratories scattered around the city of Berlin, mainly in the so-called "film district" around Friedrichstrasse. Legend has it that most directors used to edit their films while enjoying a good cigar, bluntly ignoring the "No Smoking" signs displayed everywhere, or stacking up loose ends of rushes so high that they would catch fire from open light bulbs dangling from the ceiling. However, a blast like the one at Geyer's did not just destroy a few reels of rushes, but was a major blow to the industry. Almost every leading company, including Decla, May-Film GmbH, PAGU, and Richard-Oswald-Film, lost a number of films, and this time what went up in smoke were irreplaceable original negatives. No titles of films are given in the articles covering the disaster, except for one PAGU film: it seems that Paul Wegener's *Der Yoghi* was lost forever that day, for all we know one of the masterpieces of early German cinema, according to secondary sources.

What happened? That afternoon Geyer's establishment became in a way a victim of the current police rules for the storage of celluloid. These stated that film vaults had to be (preferably) underground, and that film had to be stored in metal cases on non-flammable metal shelving. Geyer's vault had been constructed to fulfil these requirements. It was situated under the floor of the courtyard of the building, and had been built like a bank safe, with brick walls reinforced by iron bars, accessible only through a heavy steel door with double locks. The room was 4 by 4 metres, 2.80 metres high, and there was a ventilation shaft of 20 by 20 centimetres, which played a fateful role in the disaster. Approximately 1,000 reels of film were stored in the vault. As is so often the case, exactly how the films caught fire was never quite established. There were no open electric outlets or contacts in the room, illumination was provided by a lamp with double glazing which could only be switched on and off from the outside, and the wiring was laid under the plaster in the walls and ceiling. Thus a short circuit or any electric sparks can be ruled out, even though the article in *Lichtbildbühne* reported that "only a short circuit" could have caused the disaster, as self-ignition "can be seen as completely impossible from our experience".

Contrary to this statement, investigations by the police and by Karl Geyer himself both came to the conclusion that some negatives had ignited themselves (curiously enough, in a statement written as late as 1953, Geyer wrote that "presumably French films" had ignited, as if anybody would have been able to determine this after the content of the entire vault had been reduced to a mass of dented cans smothered with black ashes).[2] Whatever the nationality of the fatal film can which acted as a trigger for the incineration of the rest of its companions, the fact is that due to the metal cases and the metal shelving, the high temperatures from the first ignited film spread around the room very easily. Thus all the film was reduced to nitrate gas within minutes. The high pressure of the (so far) flameless self-destruction of the film made the gas stream out through the ventilation shaft with a tremendous noise. Only seconds later a blast cracked one of the underground walls of the vault and a huge ball of fire shot up over the courtyard, smashing in all the windows of the five-floor building and immediately setting on fire all film on the developing racks, drying drums, or rewind benches in the various departments. "The workers, most of them women, panicked, as everyone knew that more film was kept everywhere in the building. Many of them took to the windows, even on the upper floors, and only by shouting at them energetically was Herr Geyer able to prevent most of them from jumping. Even so, some female employees threw themselves down and unfortunately some of them were badly hurt by the fall."[3] Meanwhile, the alarm had been answered by the local fire brigade, who did what they could to extinguish the fire in the laboratory, and rescued those who had fled to the roof of the building. When the destroyed vault was inspected later, it was found that the strong steel door had not opened, but the ceiling forming the floor of the courtyard, built to withstand 1,500 kg per square metre, had been raised 10 centimetres through the pressure of the gas, and was no longer resting on the walls of the vault.

A view of the burnt-out Geyer laboratories.

Filmmuseum Berlin – Deutsche Kinemathek.

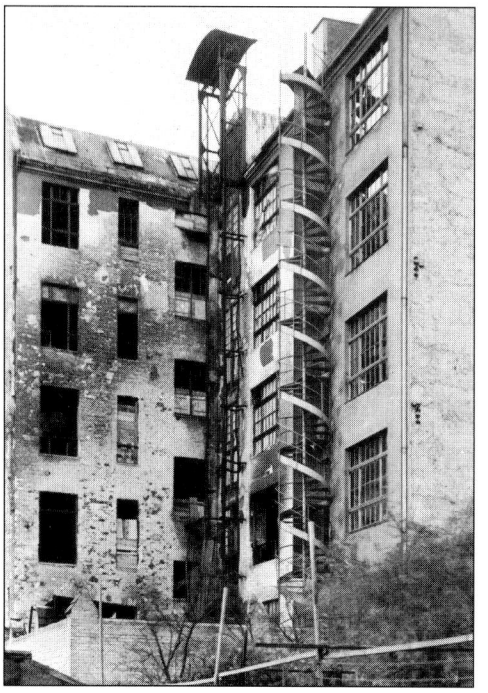

The fire at the Geyer lab was widely reported, and quickly Karl Geyer, who was running a small factory for printing and developing devices as a sideline, seized the opportunity to develop new products to offer to the film industry. A few months after the disaster, tests were under way to study film fires, and it was found that metal cases in combination with metal shelving definitely had a devastating effect once a fire was started. Even film boxes made from cardboard proved to be better than film cans on metal shelves. In 1918 Geyer patented fireproof cabinets for storing film, designed in strong wood and manufactured by his brother Alfred Geyer, who ran a carpenter's shop in Ilmenau in Thuringia. Geyer started to advocate a completely different strategy to store celluloid, and soon he was heeded by the authorities. The laws on nitrate storage were changed following his findings and suggestions: henceforth film was no longer stored underground, but on the roof, and the rooms were divided into little well-ventilated cabinets with walls made either from "fire-resisting" wood or asbestos. The rebuilt Geyer laboratory was one of the first establishments in Berlin to boast such a "Film-Tresor" on its upper floor. Several such facilities were built around town, and in fact the design of some of the later ones was quite luxurious, resembling the treasure chambers of the bigger banks, with marble floors and ornamented doors with fine wooden inlays.

In a way it seems ironic and unfair that Geyer's company was the victim of a disaster like a nitrate fire, since Karl Geyer himself had been advocating safety film as early as 1913. As soon as non-inflammable "Cellit-Film" produced by Bayer tried to cut into the market, Geyer made tests, with good results. Apparently the film industry greeted the new product with great reluctance, and Geyer tried to help by having the following statement published in *Lichtbildbühne*: "...I have developed and printed a large order of Cellit-Film within the last six months, to the utmost satisfaction of my clients. This material is presenting some small problems at first, but these can be overcome easily if one is not prejudiced. It is my experience that the results achieved with this type of film are equal to the celluloid film currently available. The general prejudice against Cellit-Film is not explicable to me, as I am of the opinion that any modern film factory should be able to work with this material without difficulty. Not only theatres, but also servicing factories, should see the advantage in the use of non-inflammable film, as work becomes significantly less dangerous, and one also enjoys the benefit of less strict policing of the fire laws."[4]

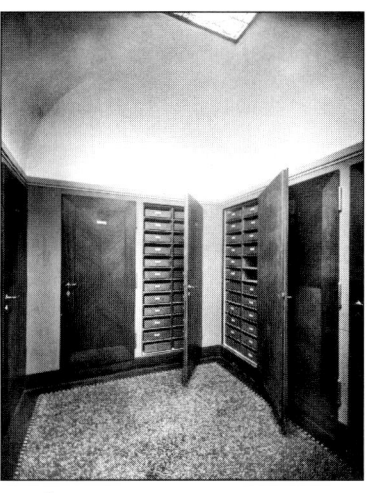

The new "Film-Tresor" with fireproof walls and vented cabinets for each reel of film.

Filmmuseum Berlin – Deutsche Kinemathek.

Another aspect discussed in film circles after the fire was the problem of proper insurance for films stored by customers at laboratories. At the time of the fire Geyer was insured for 300,000 Marks, well under what the films in his vault were worth by all estimates. But what were they worth? Luckily some companies storing films at Geyer's such as Decla had their own insurance to cover the loss, but in general the laboratory obviously was found to be responsible. The lawyer Georg Wolfssohn discussed the Geyer case in a two-part article in *Lichtbildbühne*.[5] He came to the conclusion that in the case of a brand-new negative which had cost 50,000 Marks to be made, this sum had to be reimbursed, plus the profit that the film would have made had it not been destroyed. In the case of an older negative, Wolfssohn concluded the lab would have to pay much less, since the old film already had been exploited and was thought to be of little value once its commercial run was over. However, if the loss of the material was not caused by any wrongdoing of the laboratory, and especially if the vaults were maintained according to current laws, the lab's reponsibility was still further limited, and would amount only to the material replacement value of the burnt film. "Considering the fact that the majority of production companies have insured their negatives themselves, one can conclude that they have been saved from great losses. We are happy to see that the Geyer laboratories, who surely do most of the copying in our industry, have already gone back to work, and thus are enabling production companies to fulfil their obligations towards the theatres soon."[6]

Notes

1. *Lichtbildbühne* No. 42, 20 October 1917, p. 26.

2. This later statement, as well as the technical details of the vault and a description of the event, can be found in *Chronik der Karl Geyer-Filmfabrik, volume 1 (1911–1921)*, now held at the Stiftung Deutsche Kinemathek, Berlin.

3. ibid.

4. *Lichtbildbühne* No. 21, 24 May 1913, p. 36. Geyer's statement appeared with similar praise of Cellit-Film, mainly from exhibitors.

5. *Lichtbildbühne* No. 42, 20 October 1917, and No. 43, 27 October 1917.

6. ibid.

The Drumcollogher Disaster

by Sunniva O'Flynn

Ireland in 1926 was enjoying a period of calm after many years of political and military turmoil which had resulted finally in the establishment of the Irish Free State in 1922. Drumcollogher, on the Cork/Limerick border in the south-west of Ireland, was a small market town where monthly cattle and sheep fairs brought in farmers from surrounding farmlands to meet and do their business. Those who lived in the village were butchers and shopkeepers, publicans and teachers, carpenters, maids, and labourers. On the night of 5 September 1926, the villagers prepared for a new and welcome diversion – the opening of the Drumcollogher cinema. Between 150 and 200 people were to attend and become participants in a tragedy in which 48 members of the community would perish in a fire caused by carelessness, breach of public safety regulations, and mishandling of nitrate film.

By 1926 cinema was well established as an extremely popular form of entertainment in Ireland.

> The 'pictures' may claim to have brought real solace to a weary world. Today, the clientele of the picture house is larger than that of any other form of entertainment, dramatic, musical or sporting, and the influence of the pictures for good or ill on the human mind is immeasurable.
> – *Irish Times*, 13 March 1924

Films had been shown and made in Ireland since the late 1890s, with the first purpose-built cinema opening under the management of James Joyce in Dublin in 1909. The terms of the British Cinematograph Act of 1909 had been superseded by the Censorship of Films Act of 1923, which operated throughout the Free State. While the Act removed from county and city councils the power they had enjoyed under British legislation with regard to censoring of films, it allowed them continued responsibility for licensing of exhibitors and implementation of by-laws covering the means of exhibition, construction of premises, fire regulations, and so on. In Dublin, for example, by 1926 relevant Corporation by-laws included the following:

> ...no building capable of containing 1,000 persons or upwards shall be allowed to be built unless sufficient access can be obtained to it from at least two streets or thoroughfares.

> The staircases and floors of the passages lobbies and corridors and landings of such house, room or place of public resort shall be of fire resisting materials and so placed that they shall be easy of access from every part of the building.

> Cinema projectors must be enclosed within a metal case fitted with sliding doors to prevent spread of fire should one occur.

In rural areas the responsibility for the implementation of the clauses of the Act lay with county councils and the recently appointed Civic Guard (Garda Síochána). However, in the mid-1920s there were still many rural towns and villages, sometimes served by travelling showmen, where there were not yet any purpose-built cinemas.

Drumcollogher was one such village – until William Forde, the local taxi proprietor, bought a secondhand film projector in Cork with the intention of establishing a twice-weekly film schedule for the village. The venue was the upper floor of Patrick Brennan's hardware shop, which was occasionally used as the town hall. Films were to come from Cork after they had been screened there, being – possibly unofficially – detoured for a single showing in Drumcollogher before they were returned to the Dublin distributor.

On the fateful night of Sunday 5 September 1926, between 150 and 200 people queued up for the first screening in the hall. They were to see Cecil B De Mille's biblical epic *The Ten Commandments* (1923), a title that was guaranteed to bring in people of all ages and from all corners of Drumcollogher and neighbouring villages.[1] They climbed the narrow wooden stairway and entered the upper room. Rows of wooden "forms" were set out for seating in the main part of the hall. A small room, often used as a dressing room for amateur dramatics, was partitioned at one end. Blackout curtains at the end of room concealed sets of iron bars on the windows. Electricity was provided by an external generator, which alternately powered the lighting in the hall and the projector.

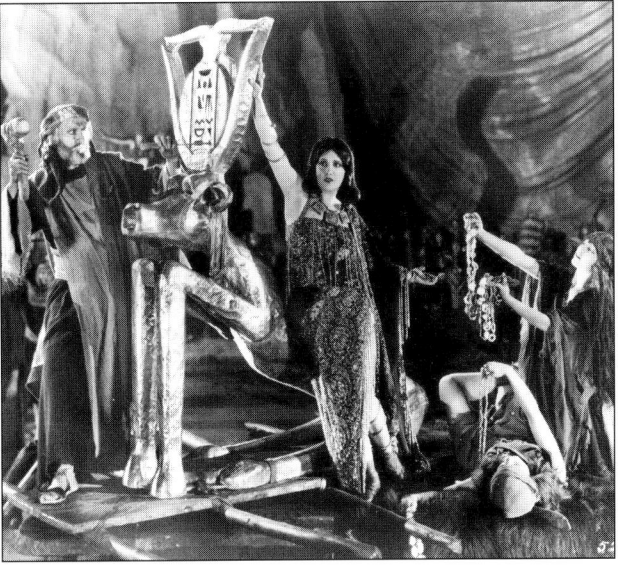

A scene from *The Ten Commandments* (1923), the film reported to have been the attraction that drew the crowds to the upper floor of the hardware shop.

BFI Collections – Stills, Posters & Designs, London. 159374.

William Forde's account of events recorded at the inquest the following Monday was reported in the *Irish Independent* (6 September 1926): "The projecting machine was in the centre of the hall, about 15 feet from the door. It was totally unprotected. The films were on a table about 10 feet away on the side and they were also unprotected. There was a candle burning on one end of the table. There was no fire extinguishing apparatus in the hall."

The projectionist was Patrick Christopher Downing, of 42 MacCurtain Street in Cork; he had been brought by Forde from Cork with *The Ten Commandments* in a portmanteau. At the inquest, Downing stated: "When I came down here I did not want to start the thing at all. I did not like the place, but Mr Forde said he would like to start the first performance that night." He agreed that he should have carried and stored the films in metal cases when they were not being used in the projector. "I was working the machine when I looked around and saw a glare on the table. I immediately cut off the current from the machine and this automatically lit up the hall. I ran over and just as I got to the table I clapped my hands on the burning films.... unfortunately someone came along and hit the burning film with a cap and the flame went on to the other films."

The speed with which the highly inflammable nitrate reels ignited was terrifying. Within minutes the entire building was ablaze. Panic ensued as those people at the end of the hall nearest the exit tried to escape on the narrow stairway, which soon became jammed. Others, trapped by the fire at the far end of the hall, entered the dressing room and desperately tried to bend the iron bars which covered the windows. One survivor, John Gleeson, the local parish clerk, described his escape: "Everything happened so quickly that it seemed as if it were but three minutes before the whole hall was in a blaze. I thought of the windows and rushed to the one near to the screen. I knew that there were iron bars on the window but that they would not be hard to remove. I worked frantically at them while my wife stood by my side.[2] The heat and the smell were terrible. I got none of the flames. It was the terrible heat that singed us all. I could feel the skin crisping on my hands and face and there was terrible pain. I saw my wife lying on her face and hands near the window. I lifted her up, got out through the window and pulled her out to safety."[3]

Attempts to quench the fire with water from a nearby stream were useless against the blazing inferno. Eventually the stairway collapsed, the roof caved in, and the upper floor fell into the hardware store below, catapulting the victims into the furnace beneath their feet.

As dawn broke, the full horror of the catastrophe emerged. Forty-eight people – almost a tenth of the population of Drumcollogher – had perished in the fire. The youngest victim was 6-year-old Tom Barret, who died with his sister Mollie (8) and his mother Mary (40). Entire families were lost. Jeremiah Buckley, the local schoolteacher, his brother Thomas, his sister-in-law Katie Wall, his wife Ellen, their daughter Bridget, and their maid Nora Kirwan, all perished in the fire. Many tales of great heroism were told. William R Ahearne (31) rescued his young wife from the fire, but perished with his mother-in-law, Mrs Mary O'Callaghan, when he returned to save her. A son of Mr Pat Vaughan saved several lives by breaking the bars on the window at the back of the building, but tragically failed to save the life of his young cousin Violet Irwin (18) when she was wrenched from his grasp by the force of the crowd.

By Tuesday, permission had been secured from the Bishop of Limerick to bury 47 of the victims together in a mass grave in the village churchyard. The grave was dug by 20 or 30 of the grieving villagers. The funeral mass was attended by thousands. President Cosgrave motored from Dublin for the funeral, with the following statement: "It is a great shock to the heart of the nation and I cannot express how deeply I deplore the appalling loss of life. It may be some comfort to those in distress or who have suffered the loss of someone near and dear to them that the sympathy of the nation and of the whole world is being extended to them at this hour." Messages of sympathy poured into the little village from King George V, the Governor-General, the Governor of Northern Ireland, the Dublin Consul of the Netherlands, the Jewish Community in the Free State, the Synods of the Methodist Church, and the Chancellor of the German Consulate General.

The Bishop of Limerick, the Most Reverend Dr Keane, who had known Drumcollogher since boyhood, spoke at the graveside: "If you were to pick out of this parish those whom you regarded as the most upright conscientious Catholics, you would have picked out the names published in the Press today of those who fell victims. They attempted to save their friends."

Less measured were the words of Most Reverend Dr Fogarty, Bishop of Killaloe, who in a letter to the Very Reverend Canon Begley, Parish Priest of Drumcollogher, said: "This wretched Cinema craze was bound to end in a disaster sooner or later; but this one is appalling, and how sad that it should fall on your village."

In the days following the fire, President Cosgrave inaugurated a disaster fund to solicit aid for those suffering loss in Drumcollogher and to centralise the many generous subscriptions already made. Donations came in from individuals and from businesses and other institutions such as Guinness, An Garda Síochána, Dockrell and Co., the British and Irish Steam Packet Company, Mr Fitzpatrick of the Remington Typewriter Co., New York, and Independent Newspapers.

Several fundraising concerts were arranged. On 8 September, Will Rogers, the world-famous American entertainer, travelling around Europe on a goodwill tour, offered President Cosgrave his services in a benefit concert at the La Scala Theatre in Dublin. The theatre was lent by proprietors McConnell and Reddin, and all proceeds went to the Drumcollogher Disaster Relief Fund.

In the wake of the disaster, attention focused on the legislation which had allowed such a tragedy to occur. Clearly what by-laws were in existence had been breached. In its editorial of Wednesday 8 September, the *Independent* called for an examination of fire-training provisions for the Civic Guards. However, on Friday a response by General Eoin O Duffy, Chief Commissioner of the Garda Síochána, said that all recruits passing through the Depot undertook a course in fire-fighting. The course, however, was not of much assistance in places where there was no extinguishing apparatus, although naturally the Gardai always did their best.

At a meeting of Cork County Council on Thursday 9 September, a motion was unanimously passed that all unlicensed cinemas under their jurisdiction be closed and not re-opened or issued with a licence until the County Surveyor had reported on their suitability. Other county councils followed suit.

When the British Home Office published new Safety Requirements for Places of Public Entertainment in 1934, it explained that recommendations were based on experience of disasters at home and abroad. The Drumcollogher fire was one of 9 fires highlighted.

Tragically, almost 55 years later, the Drumcollogher Disaster was recalled when, at a St Valentine's Dance on 13 February 1981, 48 young people lost their lives in a fire in the Stardust Ballroom in Dublin. The public enquiry following the fire showed that, just as at Drumcollogher, numerous fire and public safety regulations had been breached, although this time obviously no nitrate film was involved.

Today in Drumcollogher a memorial Celtic cross inscribed with the names of those who died stands by the mass grave in the churchyard, and a memorial library stands on the site of the cinema.

[With thanks to John O'Leary, Archivist, and Declan McLoughlin, Co-ordinator of the Limerick Film Archive Projects.]

The memorial to the Drumcollogher disaster, photographed in 2000. Behind the wall, the plinth of the cross carries the names and dates of birth of the 48 victims. Photograph by John Power.

Film Institute of Ireland, Dublin.

Notes

1. While no contemporaneous newspapers identify the film screened, Anthony Slide's *The Cinema and Ireland* (Jefferson, NC: McFarland & Co., 1988) and the *Limerick Leader* of 19 November 1983 both cite De Mille's *The Ten Commandments*. Some reports do, however, suggest that the film to be shown in Drumcollogher that night was *The White Outlaw* (USA, 1925), a Universal Western starring Jack Hoxie.

2. Dan O'Callaghan, retired principal of Drumcollogher National School, said that this small partitioned room at the end of the hall had been used as a venue for local IRA meetings during the Troubles. To guard against a surprise raid by the British forces during such meetings, the bars in the windows had been sawn through in the middle. This would have helped any of the "boys" present to escape immediately if there was a sudden raid by the Black and Tans. Luckily for those who escaped through these windows on the night of the fire, Gleeson, being in the local IRA, had been the person responsible for originally cutting through the bars many years before.

3. *Irish Independent* (8 September 1926).

Inconfidência Archiveira: Nitrate Fires in Brazilian Film History

by Carlos Roberto de Souza

If it were not for the political police of dictator Getulio Vargas, the Brazilian film archive could have been among the world's oldest. The group of people who would form the nucleus of the Cinemateca Brasileira had actually already come together at the foundation of the Clube de Cinema de São Paulo in 1940. They were students of the Faculty of Philosophy of the Universidade de São Paulo (the first Brazilian university), and in fact used to meet for film projections and discussions at the house of Paulo Emilio Salles Gomes even before the official creation of the Cinema Club. The club lasted for several screenings of film classics, which were always followed by discussions with special guests, such as Giuseppe Ungaretti and Roger Bastide. The police forced the closure of the club in 1941, however, after it was accused of leftist tendencies, and its members had to resume their meetings at Paulo Emilio's house.

A second Cinema Club was created in São Paulo in 1946, following the end of Vargas's dictatorship. Ironically, it started its film screenings at the American Consulate. Almeida Salles – a young film critic – was its first President. Paulo Emilio was by then living in Paris, where he worked as a correspondent. In 1948 he was elected to a seat on the FIAF Executive Committee, representing the Filmoteca de São Paulo (as the Cinema Club had by then been renamed). In 1951 he was elected Vice-President of FIAF. He worked closely with Henri Langlois, and by this time was writing a study – which would be recognised as a classic – on the French film-maker Jean Vigo. His contacts with film archives in London, Paris, and New York enabled the Filmoteca to begin its collection of film classics.

Among the several cultural institutions created in São Paulo at the end of the 1940s – thanks to the economic strength of the industrial bourgeoisie resulting from World War II – was a Museum of Modern Art. In 1949, the former Cinema Club accepted an invitation to become the Filmoteca do Museu de Arte Moderna. The public activities of the new Filmoteca began on 10 March 1949, with a screening of Carl Dreyer's *La Passion de Jeanne d'Arc*.

An interest in old Brazilian films (rather than simply in the field of recognised "world classics") started at the future Cinemateca Brasileira, thanks to a young member of the staff called Caio Scheiby. He began collecting all kind of films as well as documentation relating to the history of Brazilian Cinema. Together with some veteran producers and young critics interested in the subject, he organised the 1st Retrospective of Brazilian Cinema, in 1952. The screening of Brazilian silent films was an attempt to alert both the public and the government to the importance of preserving the nation's film heritage. One of the most important historical consequences of this event was the rediscovery of Humberto Mauro, who – together with his film *Ganga Bruta*, made in 1930-33 – was soon to be chosen as a symbol of Brazilian cinema by the young people who came to constitute the Cinema Novo movement.

Many events were planned for the commemoration of the 4th Centenary of the city of São Paulo in 1954. The city's treasury was in excellent condition, and its industries were flourishing – there was even money for arts and culture. Schools and a big new stadium were built, a large park was open, and squares were renovated. The city put on a new dress, and among the events which took place was the 1st Brazilian International Film Festival, organised by the Museu de Arte Moderna and its Filmoteca. Paulo Emilio returned from Europe to stay, assumed the direction of the Filmoteca, and prepared the cultural manifestations of the Festival. As well as Hollywood stars, important film-makers were invited for special tributes, including Erich von Stroheim, Abel Gance, and Alberto Cavalcanti. André Bazin, Jean Painlevé, and Henri Storck also came. Ernest Lindgren, Henri Langlois, and Gianni Comencini, among others, were present for a meeting of the FIAF Executive Committee. The 2nd Retrospective of Brazilian Cinema was presented, with an extensive programme of silent and sound films, and a wonderful catalogue gathering together all the information that researchers had so far collected about the history of cinema in Brazil. It seemed that good times had started for the activities of the Filmoteca.

By 1955, the film collection was stored on the 13th floor of the Museum building, in the middle of the city. On the same floor were the library, the collections of posters, stills, and objects (magic lanterns, old cameras, etc.), and the Secretariat. The film theatre was on the 2nd floor.

In 1956 Paulo Emilio began to write a weekly column for an important newspaper. As well as publishing essays on different aspects of the cinematographic art, he analysed the history of film preservation in Brazil, wrote about FIAF activities, and pointed out the lack of serious support given to the Cinemateca Brasileira – however much its importance as a cultural agency was accepted.[1]

The consequences of the lack of material support for the work of the Cinemateca Brasileira would soon be dramatically demonstrated. At about 11 p.m. on 28 January 1957, flames were seen on the 13th floor of the Museum building. The firemen came immediately – two brigades – and fought the fire from the front and side of the building. The fire had started in the rooms of the Filmoteca, and quickly spread to the whole floor. After two hours the flames were extinguished, but the 12th and 13th floors were completely destroyed. All the documentation was lost, including the inventory of the holdings of the archive, so we can only infer what was destroyed from the data given in the press and from the recollections of witnesses.

The 1957 fire at the Cinemateca Brasileira in São Paulo.

Cinemateca Brasileira, São Paulo.

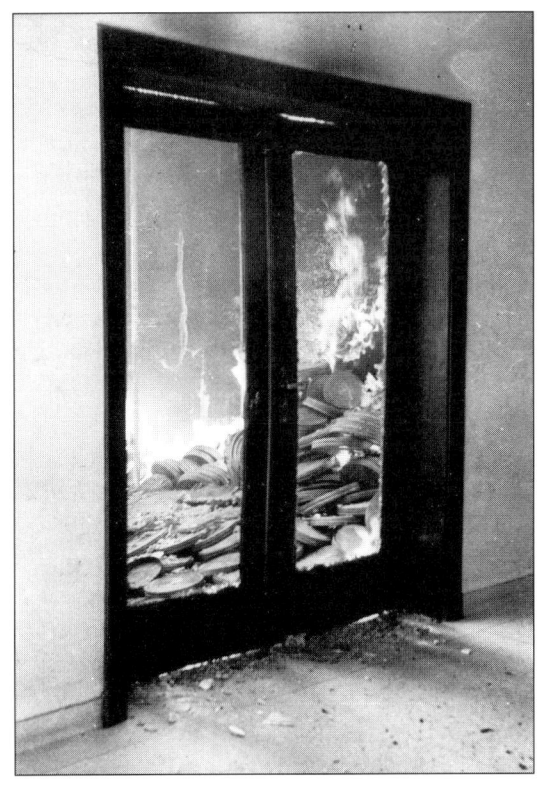

The library was completely lost, including extensive collections of the journals *Cinearte, A Scena Muda, Sight and Sound*, and *Bianco e Nero*; around 5,000 stills; all the documentation gathered on Brazilian Cinema; the collection of screenplays (including some originals donated by von Stroheim when he visited São Paulo); the entire collection of film posters; all the old objects such as magic lanterns and optical toys, and the first film camera handmade in Brazil by the pioneer photographer Antonio Medeiros.

The film collection was – before the fire – estimated to be some 2 million metres. Two-thirds of the films were not in the building at the time of the fire, so the archive must have lost at least 500,000 metres of material. The papers spoke of 150 to 200 titles, including both Brazilian and foreign films, and mentioned prints of *La Passion de Jeanne d'Arc, Sunrise, Caligari*, the first film with Greta Garbo, silent German and Russian films, and films by René Clair, Fritz Lang, G W Pabst, and Jean Vigo. Several of these films had certainly come from FIAF archives in Europe and the United States, but the papers made explicit references to some Lubitsch films that had been found in Catanduva (a small town in the hinterland of São Paulo) that were apparently unique on a worldwide scale. This story is credible, because years later researchers from the Cinemateca Brasileira found in the same town some other unique nitrate prints, which were sent to their countries of origin (primarily Germany and Italy) in the 1980s for restoration.

Unfortunately, it is quite certain that all the Brazilian material lost was unique. The material destroyed included documentaries dating from the second decade of the century up to the 1940s (films from the first ten years of Brazilian cinema had probably already disappeared before then, in circumstances to be described later), including films about the revolutions of 1924, 1930, and 1932. The most tragic loss was certainly a complete collection of documentaries by Anibal Requião, filmed in the period 1909/12 in the neighbouring State of Paraná. This fact would always be recalled from then on, whenever somebody wished to say something offensive about the Cinemateca Brasileira. Paulo Emilio wrote a few months later: "It was as if the Cinemateca Brasileira had striven to gather films that were deteriorating and slowly disappearing in different parts of the country, just to destroy them together, once and for all."

The fire provoked an enormous brouhaha. All around the country, politicians, intellectuals, and artists wrote and spoke about the Cinemateca Brasileira and how important it was for Brazil to have and preserve its cinematographic heritage. But nothing was effectively done. The governments of the City, the State, and the Union promised emergency funds, but these never reached the archive.

Afraid of another fire, the directorate of the Museu de Arte Moderna asked the Cinemateca's staff to vacate the building in 12 hours, with all their belongings. The archive was provisionally sheltered in the building of the Bienal de São Paulo, and the film collection piled up in 6 lodges at the gates of the Ibirapuera Park (constructed for the 4th Centenary of São Paulo). While attempts were made to raise funds to build the Cinemateca a proper home, its directors started campaigning for the reconstruction of the collections. The press reported the donation of magazines, books, and films. The National Film Board of Canada made a solemn donation of prints of some of its productions, including a complete series of Norman McLaren's films. The British Film Institute gave a collection of classic British documentaries. American and Japanese film distributors gave the archive large quantities of stills and posters from new releases. In telephone conversations with Paulo Emilio, Henri Langlois and Ernest Lindgren offered FIAF's assistance in replacing the film classics lost in the fire. Langlois wrote in a cable: "We are sure the Brazilian authorities will understand the urgency of helping you in order to avoid forever a new catastrophe."

In 1958 the Cinemateca moved again, to different "provisional" accommodation: a big warehouse near one of the back gates of the Ibirapuera Park. The archive would occupy this site for the next 30 years. The country was entering a difficult period: from that time onwards inflation was to be a permanent economic companion to the whole population. Promises of financial help for the Cinemateca Brasileira did not lead to a happy ending. In 1962 a foolish political quarrel in the Chamber of Deputies in Brasilia obstructed the approval of an agreement with the Federal Government that could have saved the archive. Struggling against the stagnation, Paulo Emilio obtained a motion at the FIAF General Assembly in Belgrade stating that FIAF trusted "in the Brazilian authorities and hopes they will do their best to help the work of the Cinemateca Brasileira, today the most important centre of cinematographic culture in Latin America."

Although he never stopped campaigning, Paulo Emilio seemed at this time to be getting tired when he asked: "After all, is not the idea of a film archive in Brazil quite premature, when we are so underdeveloped in everything?" In 1964, to prevent the coming to power of a socialist government, the Army mounted a coup d'état. Paulo Emilio, who had ancient links with the Communist Party, slowly withdrew from the archive, in order to avoid adding political problems to its economic ones.

For the next 10 years the Cinemateca Brasileira sunk into a kind of lethargy, from which it was eventually shaken by dramatic incidents. One of these came in February 1969 – another fire, this time in one of the little lodges where films were stacked. The newspapers reported some bangs, a little smoke, and an explosion. When the firemen arrived two hours later, they found only burned rolls of film. The total loss was estimated at 350 films; there was no inventory, so it is impossible to know how important the losses were. Again the authorities promised this and that, but nothing was done. It seems as though the archive was so weak that it did not even have the strength to react to so tragic an event.

When my generation came into the archive, in 1975, the Cinemateca Brasileira was a spectre – piles of films and papers, lots of dust and dirt. Everything had to be started from scratch: compiling an inventory, rationalising the collections, raising funds to hire staff, and so on. This is another story, but it is important to underline that we have also had our own baptism of fire. It was early on a Saturday morning – 6 November 1982 – when an old keeper who lived at the archive's premises called me on the phone: "One of the nitrate vaults is burning!" The "vaults" were six little isolated rooms where we kept the nitrate reels. When I arrived at the Ibirapuera Park, less than 15 minutes later, the firemen were already there, but nothing could be done, except to pull down the fire-damaged walls and water the scorched trees. In the notice we sent to the press we explained the lack of proper conditions in the vaults and stated that, although part of the 1,600 lost reels had already been transferred to safety stock, one irreplaceable loss was a collection recording the work of the First Brazilian Commission of Frontier Settlement of the Ministry of Foreign Affairs.

The authorities again promised support. A National Programme for Film Restoration was created, ministers and secretaries signed protocols, and so on – and the archive received only a little part of the promised funds. But this is quite common in our history. If the Cinemateca Brasileira had received all the money that the press has reported was on its way to the institution over the years, it would probably be one of the richest archives in the whole world. We would have wonderful vaults for the whole film collection, and certainly the 3,600 reels still on nitrate would have been copied to safety a long, long time ago...

In case it should be thought from the previous pages that nitrate film fires have damaged Brazil's film history only since the creation of the Cinemateca Brasileira, let me observe sadly that such is not the case. Nitrate fires have marked the history of Brazilian cinema since its beginnings. Some examples will illustrate this.

The first moving image shows in Brazil took place in 1896, and for years newspapers reported the pilgrimage of foreign showmen to present the new invention/entertainment to audiences in the most important towns of our vast country. Rio de Janeiro, then Brazil's capital, was the first city to boast a theatre dedicated to moving images: it opened in July 1897 and was called the "Salão de Novidades Paris no Rio" (The Paris-in-Rio Hall of Novelties). The Paris no Rio shows included mechanical puppets, vaudeville sketches, and optical inventions just arrived from Europe, such as the Cinématographe Lumière. The moving images were hugely successful, and Alfonso Segreto, the youngest of the Italian brothers who owned the theatre, made frequent journeys to Paris in order to renew the stock of short films. On one of these trips he brought back with him a Lumière camera, and before he disembarked he filmed fortresses and warships stationed in Guanabara Bay on 18 June 1898.

These images, along with others shot during a visit by the President of Brazil to the cruiser *Benjamin Constant*, were certainly intended to be shown at the Paris no Rio theatre. The Segretos had publicised a special screening of national moving pictures, but on 8 August 1898 a violent fire destroyed the whole building in which the theatre was located. The smartest street in town was quite narrow, and the neighbouring buildings were threatened. It was 3:30 p.m., and one of the afternoon showings had just finished. The workers were cleaning the motor of the projecting machine when the electric wires exploded. The flames caught the satin that covered the walls, the chairs, and the wooden ceiling, and in less than 3 hours the whole 3-storey building was reduced to ashes. On the second floor were stored films and machinery – both photographic and cinematographic – while the families of two of the Segreto brothers lived on the third floor. Everybody was saved, but that was the end of what are considered to be the first moving images shot in Brazil

The Segretos were rich – they earned a lot of money both through a newsstand business and with their theatres – and one of the brothers, Paschoal, was soon to be popularly known as Rio de Janeiro's "Minister of Entertainment". Their contribution as cinema producers decreased, however, as film entered new narrative trends; it seems they never produced a fiction film.

The first Brazilian comedy appeared in 1908, and marked the opening of a period of great success for national films. It is important to note that the major producers of the period were also the owners of the most popular film theatres.

Among the different genres of short films then produced, particularly noteworthy are the *filmes cantantes* (singing films). In 1909, when they first appeared, they were just arias from well-known operas or operettas, with the additional appeal that, as the film was projected, a singer stood behind the screen and tried to synchronise his or her voice to the image on the screen. The genre triumphed, and soon the films became bigger and bigger. Whole operas were screened, with whole companies singing behind the screen. Not only foreign works were covered in this way: yearly revues satirising national events were specially written for the screen, and were sensationally successful.

The most popular of these works, *Paz e Amor* (Peace and Love), was released in 1910. The film dealt lightheartedly with social and political events (the new President had promised "to govern with love and peace"), and closed with an apotheosis on board the warship *Minas Gerais*, jewel of the Brazilian Navy, built in a shipyard in Newcastle, England. *Paz e Amor* opened at the end of April, and was about to reach its 400th show when on 7 July a fire completely destroyed the Cinematographe Rio Branco, then the smartest film theatre in Rio de Janeiro and the only one that was screening the picture. The fire began in the film storage room and the firemen could not stop the blaze. Some of them were injured, and there was a suspicion that the fire could have been started on purpose. Fortunately the printing materials were kept safely elsewhere, and a new print of *Paz e Amor* was in exhibition in another theatre less than a fortnight after the fire. The film was shown in several parts of the country, but it does not survive today – it is presumed lost in other fires, in other stores.

Although national films were successful, no permanent Brazilian film industry was born from them. Brazil was then an agricultural country, with only rudimentary industries. Cinema was of course a flourishing enterprise in the developed countries; films from Europe and United States were gladly welcomed by Brazilian audiences and came to dominate the cinema market. It was so much cheaper for the owners of film theatres to buy or rent prints of foreign films that they gave up the idea of producing their own. Films were made only by a few cinematographers, who filmed newsreels or documentaries on commission from tradesmen, farmers, politicians, and so on.

One of these cinematographers was the Italian, Gilberto Rossi. Having arrived in Brazil in the second decade of the 20th century, Rossi tried hard to make fiction films, but was disappointed at the lack of understanding shown by the people to whom he explained his ideas. The alternative was to make documentary films. Sponsored by the government of the State of São Paulo, Rossi produced the longest series of Brazilian newsreels of the silent era, the *Rossi Actualidades*. The newspapers report over 200 editions of the series, from 1921 to 1931, covering a wide range of subjects. Rossi had his own laboratory next to the film vaults. His son Ludovico worked with him, and it was he who one day forgot a cigarette at the lab. Everything went up in flames: machinery and films. When the firemen tried to save the Rossi house, there was no water in the hose-pipes. At present the Cinemateca Brasileira has only a fragment of one edition of the *Rossi Actualidades* – one 60-metre reel from 10 years of production.

Just as disastrous for Brazil's film heritage was the fire that destroyed the stock of the Botelho brothers. Alberto and Paulino Botelho started as photographers, working for newspapers and magazines. In 1907 they were attracted by moving images, and became the most proficient photographers of Brazilian cinema for over 30 years. The Botelhos acted as correspondents for Pathé, and tried to establish their own newsreel series, but most importantly they made documentaries all over the country.

It was a hot Sunday afternoon in March 1929, in Rio de Janeiro. After lunch, Paulino Botelho and his wife went out to visit some relatives in a neighbouring town. Paulino's house was also his photographic studio, and he kept some quantities of magnesium in it. In the backyard there was a large storage vault for films. It was there that the fire began, at about 4 o'clock in the afternoon. The neighbours heard some bangs, attributed to the magnesium, and in a few minutes the film vault was completely engulfed by flames. The firemen came immediately, but there was no water! With the help of a pump, some was brought from nearby. The firemen isolated the house from the neighbouring ones and tried to extinguish the flames. People came from all around, attracted by the clouds of smoke, which gave the impression of an even bigger fire. In quite a short time, however, everything was destroyed. Even the pets – a little dog and two cats – were dead. When the firemen went to pull down the burned walls they stopped, surprised: although its frame was destroyed and the glass broken, a picture of Saint Teresa of the Sacred Child was hanging on a wall, untouched by the fire. "It's a miracle!" exclaimed one of the firemen.

Unaware of the event, Paulino and his wife returned home at half-past nine. He stopped the car and was astonished by the vision: everything was destroyed, except the picture of Saint Teresa. And nothing was insured.

A few years later it was the turn of Alberto Botelho. It was March again, in the hot summer of 1932. Alberto had built two sheds to store films in his backyard, separated from the house. A fire began in one of them during the night, and in a few minutes 200,000 metres of nitrate film were destroyed. The newspapers reported titles from as far back as 1907, and commented on the importance of the documents lost.

During the sound era, many other fires continued the destruction of Brazil's film heritage. To mention just two more cases:

The first concerns Raul Roulien. Born in Rio de Janeiro, he performed a solo show as a child star and toured in Argentina, Uruguay, Chile, and Peru before his family returned to Brazil. Singer, actor, dancer, composer, and writer, Roulien was attracted to Hollywood at the beginning of the 1930s. For some time he had no luck, professionally or personally. A car driven by the young John Huston (who swears in his autobiography that he was not drunk on this occasion) killed his first wife. Then Roulien was hired by Fox, and appeared in several films which were made both with English dialogue and in Spanish, for the Latin-American market – films such as *Delicious*, with Janet Gaynor, in which he sang the title song, composed by George Gershwin, and the musical *Flying Down to Rio*, nominally starring Dolores Del Rio but which is more famous as the first teaming of Fred Astaire and Ginger Rogers. In 1937, riding the crest of popular acclaim, he returned to Brazil and directed two feature films, which were well received by the public. After that, Fate turned against him again. His next two films were destroyed by fires before their release, and Roulien began a new career, writing radio soap operas for about 20 years.

Carmen Santos, actress and producer, is our last story. Portuguese-born, she started very young, making movies as a star in Rio de Janeiro, but the man with whom she lived did not permit the films to be released. She was obstinate, however. In 1929 she co-produced and starred in the fourth feature film of Humberto Mauro, Brazil's most important film-maker until the Cinema Novo movement. During the 1930s

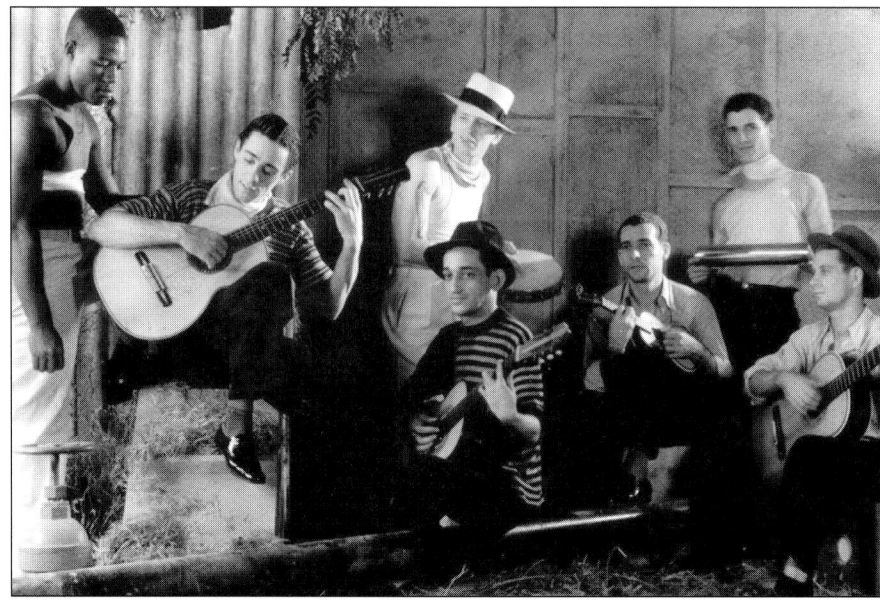

A scene from *Favela dos meus amores* (1935).
Cinemateca Brasileira, São Paulo.

she produced two other films by Mauro: *Favela dos meus amores* (Favela of My Loves) and *Cidade mulher* (Womanly City). These films – especially the former – were extraordinarily popular and were acclaimed by the critics. *Favela* was almost entirely shot in a real slum, showing the people's life in almost-documentary fashion, and the most famous samba composers contributed songs that became classics of Brazilian popular music. After that, Carmen Santos spent 10 years writing, starring in, and directing the film that was to be her greatest contribution to the history of Brazilian cinema: *Inconfidência mineira*, based on the true story of a rebellion against Portuguese oppression in Brazil at the end of the 18th century. Released in 1948, the film was a failure. Tired and ill, Carmen Santos died a few years later. Humberto Mauro told me in an interview that he asked Carmen's son for permission to pick up what was still left of his own pictures, as well as a copy of her film, from the storage vaults of the producer. Permission was granted, but he did nothing about it for some time. The delay was disastrous, because a sudden fire completely destroyed the vaults, and all the works that had been produced by Carmen Santos were lost.

Far from being an exhaustive survey, the above examples have been picked almost at random to show the numerous losses of important historical materials and works of art of Brazilian cinema due to nitrate fires.

Notes

1. For some time the name "Cinemateca Brasileira" was used in parallel with that of the "Filmoteca of the Museum of Modern Art". The Cinemateca was instituted as a separate organisation in December 1956.

Poland's Worst Nitrate Film Disaster

by Jan Slodowski

The most tragic accident in Poland connected with a fire caused by using nitrate film occurred on 11 May 1955, in Wielopole Skrzyńskie. A travelling cinema, of a type that was very popular in Poland in the 1950s, organised an evening projection of the film *Sprawa do zalatwienia* (Matter to Be Settled; 1953), directed by Jan Rybkowski and Jan Fethke. The performance took place in a wooden building, in a small clubroom suitable for no more than 100 people. There was such great interest in the film, however, that more than 200 people came to see it. At the end of the performance the nitrate film caught fire. Flames spread rapidly, and the whole clubroom was immediately engulfed. Panic broke out. The source of the fire was near the only door in the building, so people tried to get away through the windows. Some of them did not manage to do so. It did not take long before the burning roof fell in on top of all those who remained in the building. All the fire brigades from the surrounding area joined in the rescue attempts. They managed to stop the fire in the burning building and to prevent it from spreading to other nearby houses, but the wooden building where the projection had taken place was totally burned out. Fifty-eight people died.

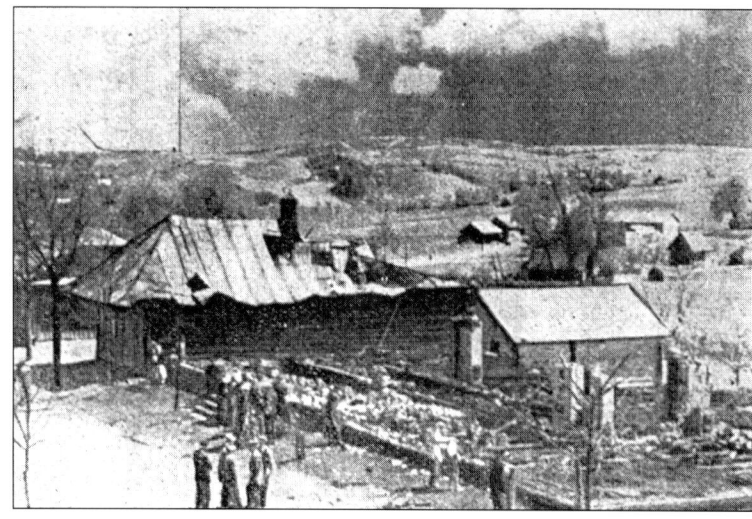

The scene after the 1955 fire at Wielopole Skrzyńskie.
Filmoteka Narodowa, Warsaw.

A Government board was called upon to investigate the cause of the fire. They decided that cinema personnel had seriously violated several of the rules of fire safety: (1) the performance took place in an overcrowded room, where there were no fire extinguishers or other fire-fighting equipment; (2) the projection apparatus was located by the only door in the building, meaning that once fire broke out, evacuation through the door was impossible; (3) the smoking of cigarettes was allowed during the performance; and (4) the rolls of nitrate film were wrapped in paper, not contained in a proper metal transit case. Four employees of the cinema were arrested and charged with causing the fire in which 58 people lost their lives. The court sentenced them to several years' imprisonment.

After the tragic accident in Wielopole Skrzyńskie, Polish fire safety rules were radically strengthened, and all copies of films on nitrate stock were withdrawn from public use.

Fires in the Spanish Cinema

by Jorge Martín Neira

Translated by Dwight Porter

In Spain, the dangers inherent in the use of nitrate film were evident from the earliest times. The new invention had still been seen in very few Spanish cities when, in August 1896, a fire completely destroyed the Edison Pavilion at the Berlin Trade Fair, where the newest scientific inventions were being displayed. This pavilion was normally full of spectators avid to see the movies projected inside, and on this day more than 200 people managed to escape the conflagration unscathed.

During the days of itinerant cinema projections, mostly at annual town fairs or festivals, many small fires were reported by local chroniclers. The most serious occurred in Oviedo on the night of 21 September 1906. The fire, which broke out shortly after a screening, spread to other stands until the entire fair was destroyed. Whole pavilions also burned down in Murcia, Santiago de Compostela, Badajoz, and Valencia. After 1905, there were fires in downtown movie theatres and other places where films were shown. Often the fires were brought under control inside the projection room, and the projectionists themselves were the only ones to suffer injuries. But sometimes even minor fires had terrible consequences, as was the case at Barcelona's Sala Olympia theatre on 3 April 1906, when one person died and several others were injured while fleeing the flames. Some cinemas and theatres that were destroyed in spectacular fires but without causing death or injury were the Palacio de las Arenas and the Teatro Principal de Gracia in Barcelona (both in 1908), the Reina Victoria in Madrid (also 1908), the Rosalía de Castro in Vigo, and the Cinematógrafo Escudero in Cadiz (1910), followed by the Chantecler (December 31, 1911) and the Noviciado (1912) in Madrid. In all these incidents, burning movie film appears to have sparked the fires, although short circuits and projector faults were blamed for some.

Tragedy struck on 28 May 1912, in the town of Villarreal de los Infantes, in Castellón, when fire broke out in the La Luz cinema, which was built entirely of wood and canvas, and had only one small emergency exit. Seventy people died and more than 200 were injured. The film being shown was called *Little Moritz, Reporter-Photographer*, and the fire began when the film broke in the fourth reel. A Gaumont cameraman, Francisco Puigvert, was sent to film the scenes of grief when the caravan of 70 coffins filed through the town, but his filmed report does not survive.

A fortnight later, on 13 June 1912, the 70 spectators in an Algeciras cinema were saved almost miraculously when the cinema burned down completely. They managed to escape unharmed through the establishment's only door, located under the projection room. Later in that same year, however, on 24 November 1912, another great disaster took place in Bilbao at the Circo del Ensanche theatre, which specialised in films for children. In this case there was no actual fire, but a false alarm caused panic and 44 people, mostly children, perished in the ensuing stampede. It happened on a cold Sunday afternoon, with the cinema full to capacity. A feature called *¿Quién se lleva un millón?* (Who's taken a million?) was being shown, and during the last reel there was a brief interruption. A woman screamed, spectators in the upper tiers became alarmed, and the audience bolted towards the only staircase, which was very steep and rather narrow. This was to become known as "the staircase of death", because a great number of children were trampled to death there. The newspapers referred to the event as the "Bilbao holocaust". According to a witness's account, the fact that the movie was in colour may have played a part in the tragedy, since during the interruption the image on the screen was of a reddish hue, and anyone looking back towards the projection room would have "perceived a red glow, like that of a fire".

As early as 1897, after the fire in the Bazar de la Charité in Paris, the Civil Governor of the province of Zaragoza set safety regulations for public entertainments, predating by more than a decade the first national safety legislation, which was contained in the Royal Decree of 15 February 1908. However, in all recorded incidents the safety rules were not observed: cinemas were filled beyond their capacity, there were no emergency exits, flammable building materials were used, or the projection room was not separate from the audience. Following the disasters of 1912, the authorities became more strict, inspecting and closing cinemas *en masse*, and on 19 October 1913 the more thorough *Reglamento de Policía de Espectáculos* was proclaimed. This practically did away with the itinerant cinemas and shaped the public entertainments of the future.

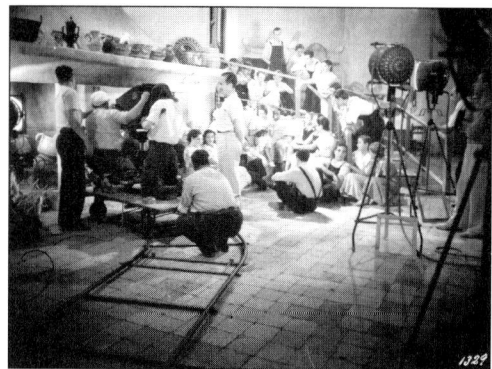

Shooting of a scene for *Nuestra Natacha* (1936) by Benito Perojo. This film was never released, and all the materials for it were lost in the fire at the Cinematiraje Riera laboratories in Madrid in 1945.

Filmoteca Española, Madrid.

Even so, the second decade of the century saw new fires, though the loss of human life was much reduced – there were no fatalities in the burning of the Variedades cinema in Orense or the Arriaga theatre in Bilbao (1914), or the Pabellón Lino in La Coruña (1920). On 19 November 1918, however, 21 children and one soldier died in a stampede following another false alarm at the La Paz cinema in Castellón. Worse than any cinema fire to date was the one that consumed the Novedades theatre in Madrid, when a curtain was set alight during a performance of a *zarzuela* (Spanish light opera) on 23 September 1928.

The first fire to damage Spain's stock of films occurred in Barcelona on 18 June 1918, when Hispano Films' Barcelona warehouse, laboratory, and studios were destroyed, with the consequent loss of an important collection of films stored in the basements. Hispano Films, founded in 1906 by the pioneers Albert Marro and Ricardo de Baños, led the golden age of Barcelona cinema. This fire is blamed for the loss of the *Campaña del Rif* series of newsreels about the Morocco War (1909), as well as the negatives of numerous feature films made before 1914, such as

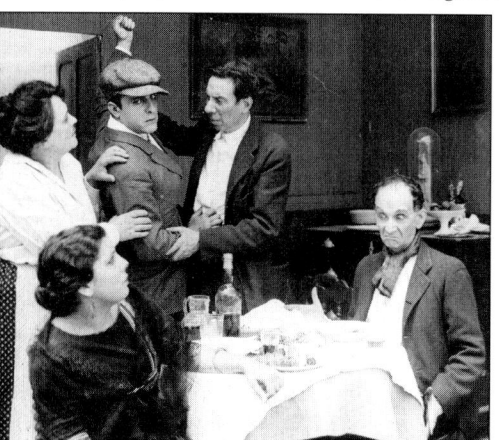

A scene from *Alma de Dios* (1923) by Manuel Noriega. Following the fire at the Madrid Film laboratories in 1950, just 23 minutes of this film survive (preserved at the Zaragoza Film Archive).

Filmoteca Española, Madrid.

Locura de Amor, Don Pedro el Cruel, Carmen o La Hija del Bandido, and *La Fuerza del Destino,* and the serials made by Albert Marro shortly thereafter, including the celebrated *Los Misterios de Barcelona,* which Jean Mitry hailed as one of the best in its genre. The fire began on a film set, and it spread through the corridors to the laboratory, where it caused a powerful explosion. While rescuing his partner, Capsir, Albert Marro suffered serious facial burns. This accident marked a turning point in Spanish cinema, with Barcelona losing its hegemony as the country's film capital, to be replaced by Madrid.

From 1939 until 1950, a series of fires in major Madrid laboratories destroyed a large proportion of Spanish films made in the nitrate era. Almost all the negatives of the films made in the 1920s were lost. Most of the films of this era that have survived are worn copies that had been distributed around the

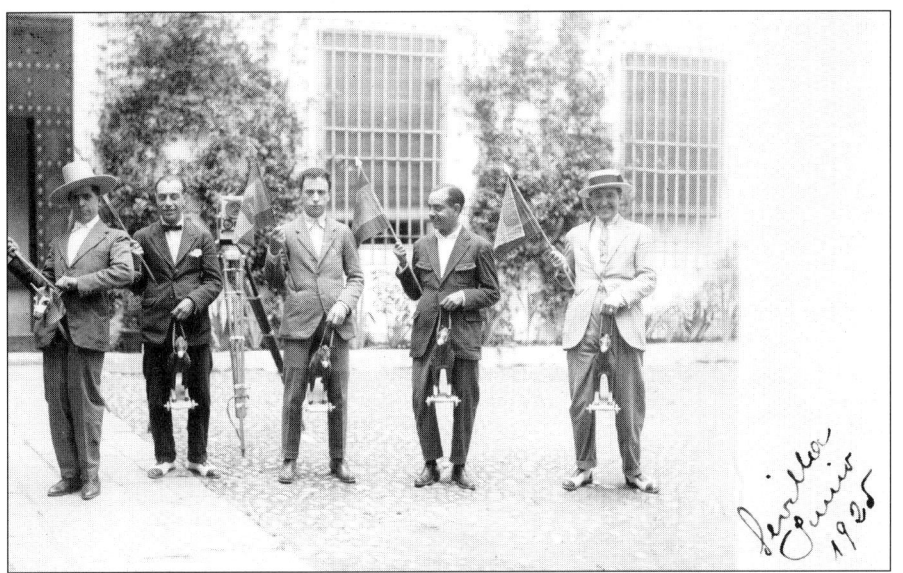

A break during the shooting of *Currito de la Cruz* (1925) by Alejandro Pérez Lugím and Fernando Delgado – another of the victims of the 1950 fire. From left to right, Domingo del Morral, Gregorio Cruzada, Jesús Tordesillas (actors), Enrique Blanco (cinematographer), Julio Rodriguez (actor).

Filmoteca Española, Madrid.

world.

On 16 August 1945, there was a huge fire in the Cinematiraje Riera workshops in Madrid. It was the third outbreak of fire on this site, and by far the most serious. About 650,000 metres of film were destroyed, including all the films that had been produced by both camps during the Civil War, which had been collected by the National Department of Cinematography in the aftermath of the conflict. Also destroyed were the negatives of the first 33 NO-DO newsreels, and another 16 reels made between numbers 36 and 418. Among the feature films irrevocably lost were *Nuestra Natacha*, by Benito Perojo; it had not yet been released, so no other copies existed.

Five years later, on 1 August 1950, the Madrid Film laboratories burned down. This catastrophe was caused by the combustion of raw stock material stored in a room, and began with the explosion of celluloid canisters. Seventeen people were injured, some very severely, and the storeroom was completely destroyed. These laboratories had been founded by one of the pioneers of Madrid cinema, Enrique Blanco, the sponsor of the first producer and laboratory to appear in Madrid (Iberia Cines and Madrid Cines, in 1910). Working in partnership with Alberto Arroyo since 1912, he made documentaries such as *Las Inundaciones del Barrio de Triana*, and *Asesinato y Entierro de Canalejas*, which included a reconstruction of the assassination of the Spanish premier. In 1921 Blanco founded Madrid Film, the heir to the previous laboratory; it lasted until the 1950 fire, and still survives today,

On the set of *Agustina de Arágon* (1950) by Juan de Orduña – one of the survivors of the 1950 fire.

Filmoteca Española, Madrid.

under different owners.[1] During the 1920s Madrid Film had processed three-quarters of Madrid's production (*Flor de España, Alma de Dios, Currito de la Cruz, Viva Madrid que es mi pueblo, Al dos de Mayo, Al Hollywood madrileño*, etc.), which gives us some idea of the gravity of the losses. In the moments following the fire there were fears for the survival of some films in the editing stage, such as *Balarrasa, Agustina de Aragón*, and *Sangre en Castilla*, but all in fact did survive.

Despite the efforts of Spain's Filmoteca Nacional, founded in 1953, and the introduction of "safety" film in same decade, it

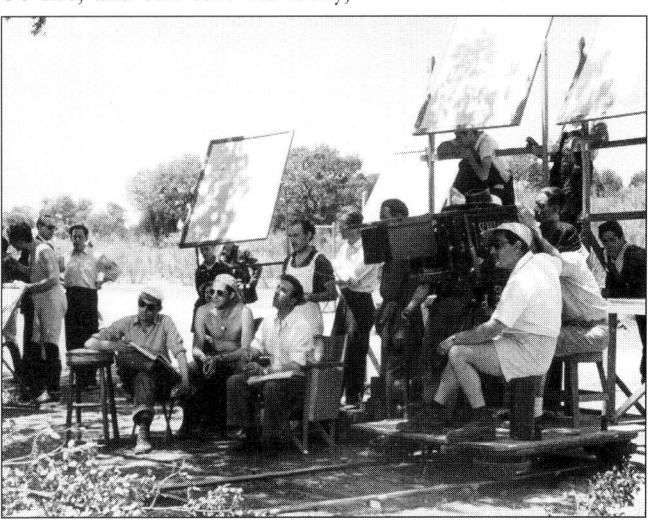

was impossible to avoid the destruction of many nitrate films which laboratories chose not to preserve. However, on 4 July 1959 one more major important archive, that of Laboratorios Arroyo, went up in flames. The fire, which levelled the building on Madrid's Paseo de Rosales, was blamed on the hot summer night itself. The high ambient temperature caused some film cans to explode, demolishing the room where they were kept. This set off another explosion in the storeroom, leading to a fire. In addition to the archive, 200 copies of films intended for projection in Madrid cinemas were destroyed. Alberto Arroyo, a pioneering film-maker with his partner Enrique Blanco, had founded his own laboratories in 1926, and his collection probably dated back much further, since in 1920 he took possession of all the materials collected by Francisco Oliver, who in his turn had processed much of the work of Patria Films, the company founded by the Perojo brothers in 1915. (Arroyo and Oliver had photographed Jacinto Benavente's *Los Intereses Creados*, of which no trace remains.) The losses extended to the negatives of movies from made in the 1940s and 1950s, as well as much uncut documentary material.

Fires would continue to plague Spanish cinema long after nitrate film had fallen into disuse. On 28 April 1962, the Estudios Orphea in Barcelona, the oldest in Spain and the first to possess sound equipment, burned to the ground.

Notes

1. Enrique Blanco's son's account of this fire was given to Rosa Cardona Arnau and Jennifer Gallego Christensen in a January 2000 interview, which is published elsewhere in this volume. It is also mentioned in the personal reminiscence of Spanish film veteran Tedi Villalba.

A Subconsciously Intended Burnt Offering?

by Tedi Villalba

Translated by Dwight Porter

Tedi Villalba Rodríguez belongs to a family of well-known art directors and producers. He is the grandson of Tadeo Villalba Monasterio (Valencia 1886–1956), and the son of Tadeo (Tedi) Villalba Ruíz (Valencia 1909–Madrid 1969), the renowned and innovative set decorator, who founded the production companies Valencia Films and Cooperativa del Cinema de Madrid. His brother José Villalba is a cinematographer, and his son, Tadeo Villalba Ruíz, also works in film production. Tedi Villalba began his film career collaborating with his elders in the art direction field, and later became a producer. He is at present the General Manager of the Spanish Academy for Cinematographic Arts and Sciences, as well as of the Madrid Cinema School (ECAM). When invited by colleagues at the Filmoteca Española to set down some reminiscences for this book, he wrote the following:

> Throughout a long professional career, I have been involved in all kinds of events. The importance of the visual impact of some of them was such as to fix them indelibly in my memory. One of these was the death of Tyrone Power during the shooting of a movie. Another was the destruction of the temple in *King of Kings*, during a windstorm. I also remember how Samuel Bronston's empire collapsed in a single morning, and the dignity with which Fernando Rey faced the final curtain. But the three episodes that have marked me the most all involved fire.

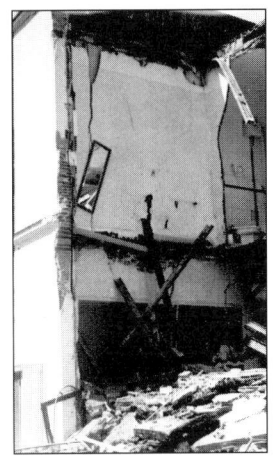

The Madrid Film laboratories at Number 39, Diego de Léon Street after the fire of 1 August 1950. Photograph taken by Enrique Blanco Arroyo days after the fire.

Enrique Blanco Arroyo.

> On Tuesday, 1 August 1950, at around 7 p.m., there was a huge explosion at Laboratorios Madrid Film. The news was broadcast by nearby Radio Intercontinental, and it quickly spread. My father, who had just returned home after work, received a telephone call. Minutes later, on Diego de León street, next to the broadcasting studios, he and I viewed the Dantean scene as the firemen, between tongues of flame and thick, black, foul, toxic smoke, had to face what seemed an endless series of explosions. Inexplicably, and to the firemen's despair, the water from their hoses seemed to make the fire burn even more strongly. Then a young teenager, I clutched my father's hand tightly as we witnessed the tragedy.

> The hours went by, and, now soaked by the rain and the water from the fire-hoses, we and a growing crowd of horrified film professionals watched helplessly as a large part of Spain's film heritage disappeared forever. Among this legacy were all the negatives of my father's films. That day changed our lives forever.

> Years later, fires at Sevilla Films and in the studios of my father and grandfather in Madrid's Puerta del Sol destroyed all the work they had done in the entire lives. Destiny decided that the artistic work of the Villalbas, long linked to the burning pageant of the Valencia *fallas*, was to be consumed by the flames, perhaps as a subconsciously intended burnt offering.

Dutch Flames and Flickers

by Ivo Blom

Fire and fire brigades have fascinated Dutch audiences from the earliest years. One of the first Dutch film productions was the so-called *Brandweer-film* (Fire-Brigade Film), a local production shot by Alex van Dijck in 1897 at the Agneta Park in Delft. The film was produced by the Koninklijke Nederlandse Gist- en Spiritusfabriek, and the factory's own fire brigade provided the cast. The managing director, the enlightened industrialist J C van Marken, was keen on novelty, and had purchased the first film camera in Holland when visiting Léon Gaumont in Paris.[1]

Counting both non-fiction and fiction titles, hundreds if not thousands of Dutch and foreign films about fires were shown to Dutch audiences, as the holdings of the Dutch film archives show today. Fires function as sensational ingredients in newsreels, or as spectacular climaxes in fiction films such as *Padre* (Itala, 1912). Often the scenes are tinted in flaming reds. They record the destruction of factories, hotels, and rows of houses by the irresistible flames. Or they show the results of conflagrations, such as the twisted ironwork of the Brussels exhibition of 1910 (Alberts Frères, 1910) or the collapse of the smoking ruins of the Palais d'Eté in Zandvoort (Pathé, 1921).

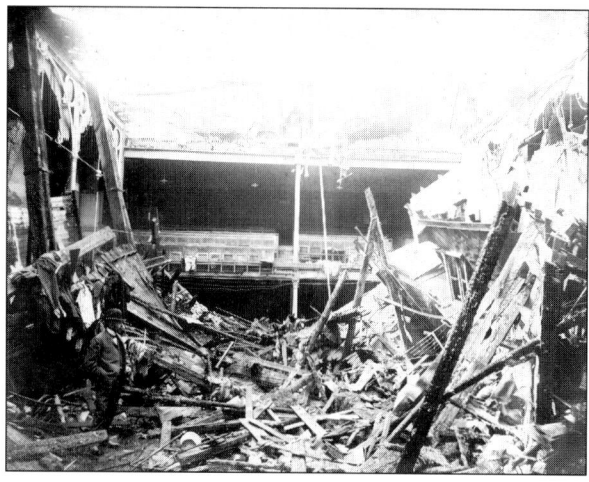

The remains of the Flora Theatre after the fire of 1929.

Nederlands Filmmuseum, Amsterdam.

Fire did not only serve as a spectacular topic for the movies – it reflected a daily threat as well. It was a regular visitor to the Dutch film world, although never causing the heavy casualties associated with the French Bazar de la Charité disaster or fires in other countries. One of the best vaudeville theatres of Amsterdam was the Flora Theatre, which started showing films in 1896.[2] It was twice destroyed by fire, the first time in 1902 and the second in 1929. The Flora was owned by Anton Nöggerath, Senior, who produced short comedies in a small studio on the roof of the theatre. In the fire of 29 August 1902, the Flora burned down "and with it burned the historically valuable films, the cameras and equipment to a value of 50,000 guilders," as Nöggerath's son Anton Junior remarked.[3] In 1929, the temperature was so low that the water from the fire brigade's hoses froze, transforming the ruin into an ice palace and giving aesthetically pleasing shots to the Polygoon Film Company when it shot the smoking ruins.[4] After this, the theatre was never rebuilt. Only in the 1950s did an ordinary cinema, also called the Flora, fill the gap in the street. The multifunctional Paleis voor Volksvlijt, the Dutch Crystal Palace, was also used for film shows, occasionally in the 1900s and more regularly in the early 1910s. Like the Flora, it was almost entirely destroyed in 1929.[5] Again, Polygoon was present to shoot the burning and collapsing building.

People were well aware of the inflammability of nitrate film, as is shown by a copy of a German film held in the Nederlands Filmmuseum. In *Ein neuer Apparat zur Verhütung von Kinobränden* (1912?), a new type of projector is shown which has covers that close automatically when a reel of nitrate film catches fire. Audiences must also have laughed at the British comedy *Picture Palace Piecans* (Vaudefilms, 1914) – which is also in the Filmmuseum collection – a story about two tramps who buy a run-down cinema. Along with typical jokes like dropping the film and pestering kids at the entrance, the two new owners are seen smoking in the booth and putting a candle in the projector.

All these cinematic warnings, both fictional and non-fictional, did not prevent accidents from happening. Often it was just the films that would be burned, but occasionally the scale of the misfortune would be bigger. The film stock of the most popular and prestigious Dutch travelling cinema owners, the Mullens Brothers, also known as Alberts Frères, was consumed by fire in 1906, when they were at the fair at Bruges in Belgium.[6] With the rise both of permanent cinemas and of local distributors, more nitrate film came into circulation. Not every exhibitor and projectionist in the "newfangled" cinemas was sufficiently experienced to prevent accidents from happening. Several films from Jean Desmet's rental business were thus lost in the flames: a copy of *Den hvide Slavehandel* (The White Slave Trade; Nordisk, 1910), a copy of the Pathé *Passion-film* (1907), one reel of the two-reeler *L'Assommoir* by Pathé, and one reel of *Kaiserin Elisabeth* (Indra-Gross Films, 1920). The burning of the reel from *L'Assommoir* and the copy of *Den hvide Slavenhandel* are particularly to be regretted. The Cinémathèque Française owns only a fragmentary copy of *L'Assommoir*, and – to the best of my knowledge – the copy of *Den hvide Slavehandel* in the Danish archive lacks colour, while all of Desmet's copies were exhibition copies and therefore mostly tinted and/or toned. The Danish film burned in 1911 at the Villa Nova cinema in Tilburg.[7] Apparently the owner did not learn his lesson – one year later, in February 1912, the Villa Nova burned to the ground because of a film that caught fire.[8]

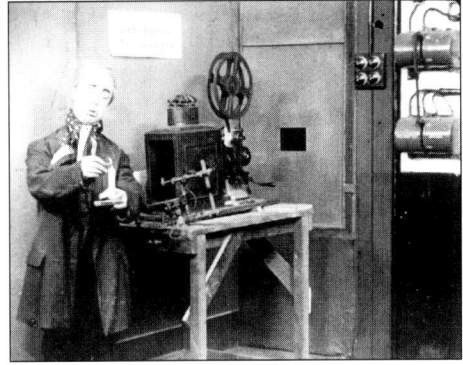

A scene from *Picture Palace Piecans* (1914).

Nederlands Filmmuseum, Amsterdam.

Incidents such as these caused the city of Amsterdam to design new fire regulations for cinemas, which became law on 1 May 1913. Among other things, these required that only projectionists with a diploma could operate in a cinema, and that two operators had to be present in every booth.[9] Other cities adopted the Amsterdam regulations. Separate booths became common. At the same time, exhibitors and distributors started to offer fire extinguishers for cinemas. This did not stop the fires in the Dutch film world, however.

In the 1920s, several accidents happened, sometimes with drastic consequences. On 18 March 1922, the Victoria Theatre in Amsterdam went up in flames. The theatre, which had only opened in November 1920, was the pride of its owner, G H van Royen, who possessed a large Amsterdam-based chain of cinemas. The Victoria contained 900 seats, which was quite large for Dutch cinemas at the time. The cause of the fire was probably a cigar or cigarette thrown away on the balcony, which was built entirely of wood and was where the fire started. The popular Dutch production *De Jantjes* (The Jack-Tars; Hollandia, 1922) had premiered in the Victoria on 17 March, the night before the cinema burned down. The copy was saved, but was mutilated. It subsequently ran for 5 weeks in another of Van Royen's cinemas, the Witte Bioscoop. The lecturer probably had to use his imagination to fill in the gaps.[10]

Two years later, on 17 July 1924, the film world was shocked by the fire in Haarlem at the Dutch Film Company, which had taken over the studio and other buildings of the Hollandia company when the latter went bankrupt in 1923. The top floors burned down, but the studio remained. One of the company's cameramen filmed the fire. Most of the material was saved, but the negative of *Cirque Hollandais* (1924) by Theo Frenkel, Senior – then in the editing phase – was lost. The whole film had to be shot again, but the artists only received half-pay for this.[11]

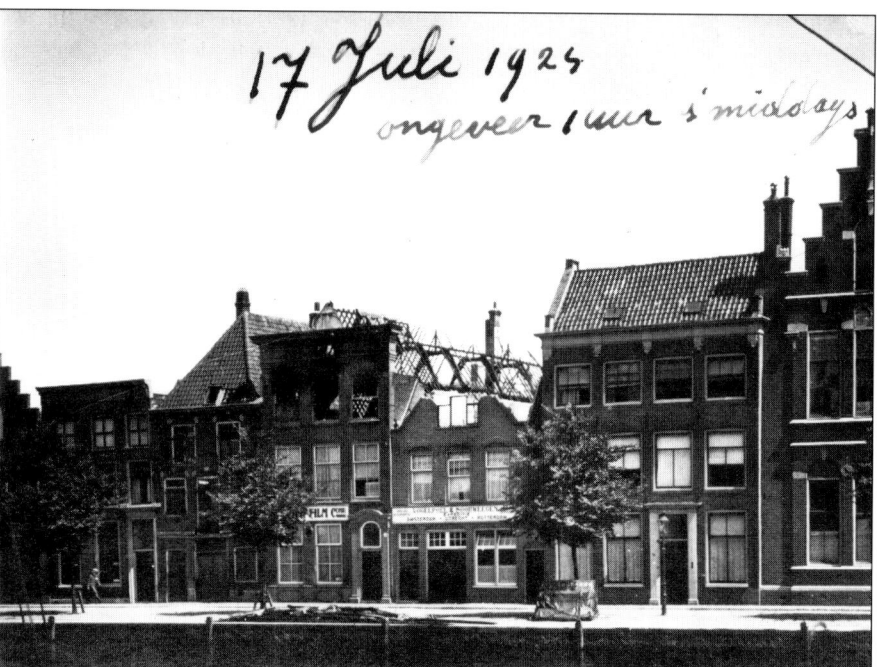

The premises of the Dutch
Film Company in Haarlem
after the fire of 1924.

Nederlands Filmmuseum, Amsterdam.

Three years later, in 1927, two major accidents happened. One was the fire in the
laboratory of Willy Mullens in The Hague on 12 December. Film historian Bert
Hogenkamp cynically states: "Mullens himself was in Brussels at the time of the
fire. One could say this was a blessing in disguise, as he would have confronted the
dilemma of filming the fire or participating in the work of extinguishing it. A
cameraman from the competing Orion company managed to take some shots of the
last extinguishing work."[12] Because of all the nitrate material, the fire brigade had
a hard time putting out the fire. Some of Mullens's material from his recent trip to
the Dutch Indies was lost. Luckily he had stored away most of his negatives in the
fireproof safe of the Algemeen Rijksarchief, the national archive in The Hague.

The other disaster of 1927 was the fire in the Emelka distribution office in
Amsterdam, on 27 February. The Dutch film company Polygoon took shots of the
ruins. As it burned, the whole building on the Herengracht exploded. Mrs Debs-
Justet, daughter of the Dutch Pathé agent Louis Justet, recalls how she went out to
see the fire and arrived just in time to see the whole building collapsing.[13] The fire
and the explosion eventually caused the city of Amsterdam to ban all nitrate film
from the inner city. This did not bother Jean Desmet though, who kept all his films
in the attic of his Cinema Parisien, until a fire in 1938 destroyed part of the attic
where his publicity materials and archive were stored. By sheer good luck, the
Cinema Parisien escaped the fate of the Emelka building. Had the flames reached
the place where the films were stored, then the whole cinema would probably have
blown up, and we would not nowadays be able to speak of the Desmet Collection.[14]

Even the fire at the Parisien was not the last Dutch cinema fire, although nitrate
usually had little to do with later ones. Several formerly outstanding cinemas
burned down after the Second World War, in particular those that had ceased to
function as cinemas. The most recent example was the Roxy discotheque, formerly
a cinema built in 1912 by Jean Desmet, Elias De Hoop, and David Hamburger. In
1999, after the death of one of the founders of the discotheque, a memorial
firework spread through the ventilation system and set the building ablaze. Only
the façade remains today.[15] However, the largest single destruction of Dutch
cinemas by fire occurred in Rotterdam at the outbreak of World War II. All the city-

centre cinemas, including Abraham Tuschinski's luxurious Grand Theatre, were swept away by the German bombardment of 14 May 1940. It was the biggest fire in the Netherlands in the 20th century.[16]

Notes

1. Geoffrey Donaldson, *Of Joy and Sorrow: A Filmography of Dutch Silent Fiction* (Amsterdam: Stichting Nederlands Filmmuseum, 1997), p. 51. As far as is known, the "Fire-Brigade Film" is the second Dutch film production.

2. For the Flora and the Nöggeraths Senior and Junior, see Ivo Blom, "Chapters from the Life of a Camera Operator. The Recollections of Anton Nöggerath – Filming News and Non-fiction", in *Film History*, no.11 (1999), pp. 262–281.

3. F A Nöggerath, *Ons Bioscopisch bedrijf voorheen en thans* (1911; reprinted 1975).

4. The theatre was then in the possession of Jean Desmet, who had just taken it over and wanted to transform it into a multifunctional building, including a theatre, a cinema, a skating rink, and a wintergarden café-restaurant. The project was never realised. Ivo Blom, *Pionierswerk: Jean Desmet en de vroege Nederlandse filmhandel en bioscoopexploitatie 1907–1916* (Amsterdam: University of Amsterdam, 2000; PhD thesis), pp. 292–293. An English-language edition of this thesis will be published in 2001 by the Amsterdam University Press.

5. Only a gallery remained until the 1960s. J C Polak – van 't Kruys, *Het Paleis voor Volksvlijt* (Amsterdam: Stadsuitgeverij, 1991).

6. Guido Convents, "Motion Picture Exhibitors on Belgian Fairgrounds", in *Film History*, no.6 (1994), p. 245.

7. Blom, op. cit. (2000), pp. 128–129, 229, 286, 301.

8. *Nieuws van de Dag* (8 February 1912).

9. *De Kinematograaf* (7 March 1913).

10. Donaldson, op. cit., p. 1922; Interview with Mrs B van Royen-Fontaine, 4 October 1994.

11. Ruud Bishoff, *Hollywood in Holland: De geschiedenis van de Filmfabriek Hollandia 1912–1923* (Amsterdam: Thoth, 1988), p. 110.

12. Bert Hogenkamp, *De Nederlandse documentaire film 1920–1940* (Amsterdam: Van Gennep, 1988), p. 21.

13. Interview with Mrs L Debs-Justet, 15 December 1995; *Algemeen Handelsblad* (27 February 1927).

14. Blom, op. cit. (2000), pp. 299–301.

15. *De Volkskrant* (22 June 1999); Het Parool (2 June 1999).

16. Actually, the fire caused by the bombs destroyed more than the bombs themselves. Henk Berg, *Over stalles en parket: Rotterdam en het witte doek. Een populair-historisch overzicht van de Rotterdamse en Schiedamse bioscopen 1896–1906* (Rotterdam: Ad. Donker, 1996).

Kyoto Tales and Tokyo Stories: Incidents in Japanese Film History

by Hisashi Okajima and Yoshiro Irie

Translated by Ayako Saito

We feel a great deal of hesitation in discussing the relationship between nitrate films and Japanese film history since such studies are hard to find, and, even then, they are often anecdotal and lacking in historical accuracy. Although nitrate films have caused a considerable number of fires at studios, laboratories, vaults, and theatres, there has been little study of the history or location of nitrate prints. Thus, the history of nitrate films will also reveal the sad fact that this valuable aspect of Japanese film heritage has long been neglected.

Of course, history is full of little tales. A veteran technician who worked for a film laboratory for over 40 years told us very recently that in the old days NG cuts were used for starting fires at employee picnics! He also said that since nitrate film could easily be melted and made flexible by using film cement, children used to make swords, airplanes, and model ships from discarded nitrate footage. These kinds of stories may seem trivial, and even rather amusing, but there are more sombre stories.

The most problematic fact is that hardly any 35mm nitrate film has survived in Japan. This is mainly due to the common practice among production companies of discarding the original negatives after transfer onto safety master positives (sometimes, not even onto a 35mm safety print, but only onto a 16mm print). What is worse, original negatives were often lost, for reasons that were both avoidable and unavoidable, before studios made master positives.

At any rate, we would like to note that most of the titles produced during the nitrate era that are presently available for screening are not made from the original negatives.

Instead of outlining the overall history of nitrate films, we would like to focus on the stories of how two Japanese masterpieces, Akira Kurosawa's *Rashomon* (1950) and Yasujiro Ozu's *Tokyo Story* (1953), were involved in nitrate fire accidents.

1. The case of *Rashomon*

Rashomon is one of the two films made for Daiei by Kurosawa, who had made films mainly for Toho. *Shizukanaru Ketto* (1949) was a Daiei Tokyo production, and *Rashomon* (1950) a Daiei Kyoto production.

The production of *Rashomon*, a historically world-renowned film, was fraught with trouble and difficulty. The shooting of the film ended on 14 August 1950; however, during postsynchronization, the final stage of postproduction, the film was affected by two fires. The following is a summary of how these accidents occurred, based on both the record kept by Daiei and the description by the film's script-girl, Ms Teruyo Nogami.

Rashomon's release date had already been decided by Daiei before the completion of the film: the premiere screening was scheduled for 25 August 1950 at the Teikoku Theater in Tokyo, with the national release on the 26th and thereafter. These dates were imperative, and Kurosawa and his crews had been working on postsynchronization for several straight days and nights, a practice not unusual in the Japanese film industry of the day.

At about 6:00 p.m. on 21 August 1950, the first fire broke out – it was believed to have been caused by an electric short-circuit – at the second soundstage of Daiei Kyoto. In the editing room nearby was a great deal of nitrate footage from films currently in production, including *Rashomon*. "Negatives! Negatives!" cried Kurosawa. Firemen rushed in, and, with the help of other people, they moved every negative from the room. However, when they checked the negatives, they found out that a piece of sound negative was missing. It was of a famous line delivered by the character Tajomaru (Toshiro Mifune): "I've never seen a woman of such impetuous temper."

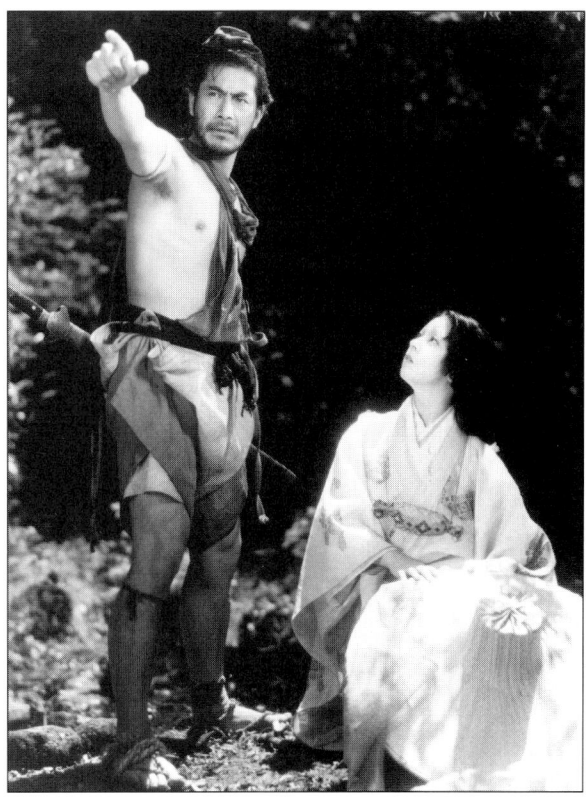

A scene from *Rashomon* (1950).

BFI Collections – Stills, Posters & Designs, London. 182296.

Mifune was immediately summoned from Tokyo, a journey of 8 hours by the fastest express train. But the sound-mixing machine created another huge problem: during the fire, it had been flung out of the mixing room next to the soundstage and had been shattered. Because of the schedule they had no choice but to resume the postsynchronization the following day, 22 August, but with an old type of sound recorder used on location, rather than with the broken mixer (although one account does say that they fixed the broken machine that night and used it).

However, during the second test, a nitrate positive film for transferring the soundtrack became stuck in the projector and burst into flames. Absolutely panicked by this second fire, they were forced to move the films out of the projection room again, and buckets of water were thrown in relays into the room. Toxic gas was generated, and a number of the staff were overcome and taken for medical treatment. About 30 people are said to have fallen ill. However, the final deadline was still imperative, the staff was still eager, and the postsynchronization was begun again. The sound recording was done live, and even a single mistake would have caused the redoing of an entire take. Imagine the difficulty and tension involved in recording the famous bolero scene, which continues for 10 minutes! Musical composer Fumio Hayasaka was present with Kurosawa during the entire postsynchronization work.

It was indeed a miracle that postproduction was completed by the morning of 23 August (some say it was actually the 24th when the film was completed). Assistant director Tokuzo Tanaka carried the just-completed film by train to Tokyo. The Daiei executives previewed it, and it went into release according to schedule. Masaichi Nagata, then president of Daiei, said at the preview, "Well, I don't understand it very well, but it looks like a high art kind of picture."

Unfortunately, none of the original nitrate negatives of *Rashomon* have survived.

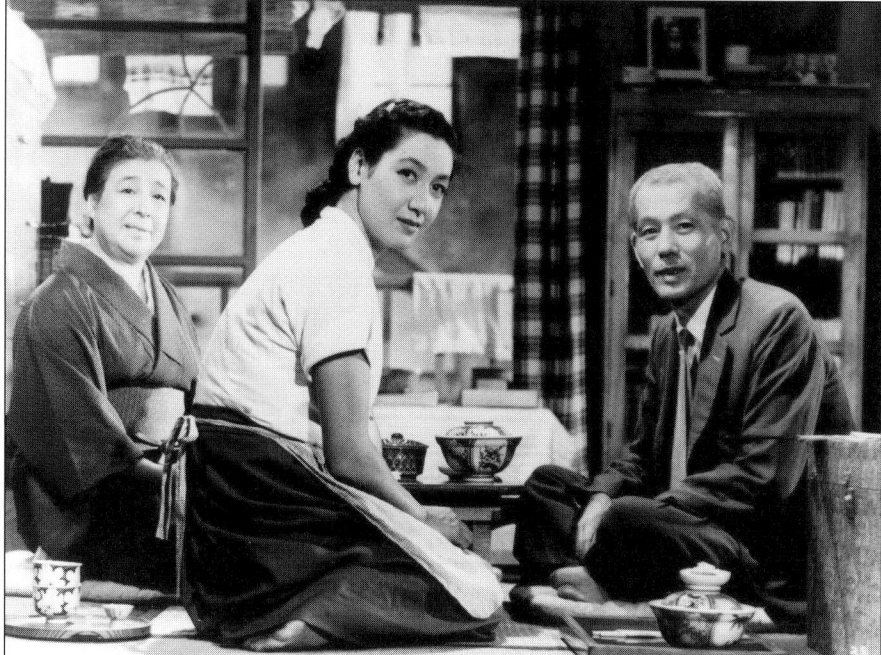

A scene from *Tokyo Story* (1953).

BFI Collections – Stills, Posters & Designs, London. 88314.

2. The case of *Tokyo Story*

All the original negatives of Yasujiro Ozu's masterpiece, *Tokyo Story* (1953), then thought to be the director's last black-and-white film,[1] were tragically lost, and therefore the quality of the viewing print turned out to be extremely disappointing, especially to the film-maker and his staff. Yuharu Atsuta, the film's cameraman, who strove to express the subtle vicissitudes of spring and early summer by maximizing lighting effects, spoke of his disappointment in a later interview. For example, in indoor scenes set on a hot summer's day, Atsuta managed to sharpen the contrast between the indoor darkness and the brightness outside by using the lowest exposure of light possible on the characters' faces. However, the extant print is overexposed throughout; the subtlety of the original photography has been lost.

It is not clear when the original negatives were lost. One version says that they were lost in 1953 before the release, and another version that they were lost in 1960.

I. *The 1953 version*

In the Japanese film industry, studios customarily made the viewing print directly from the original negatives. According to Atsuta, in the early 1950s Shochiku used to prepare about 30 viewing prints for the national release of a film. Because of the busy schedule at the Ofuna studio's developing laboratory, the printing of the original negatives of *Tokyo Story* was contracted to the Yokohama Cinema Developing Laboratory, where a fire occurred and destroyed the negatives before the film's release. Therefore, it is said that the extant print was made out of one print among the 5 or 6 prints which remained at the studio.

II. *The 1960 version*

The Yokohama Cinema Developing Laboratory (the present Yokohama DIA), whose predecessor was Yokohama Cinema Shokai, was the pioneering production company of culture films founded in 1923. The most well-known fire that the Laboratory suffered, however, actually occurred on 24 July 1960. According to a contemporary newspaper account, the spontaneous combustion of nitrate films caused the fire, which burned the entire film storage area, a 38-square-metre mortared frame bungalow. Although no itemized list of the lost films exists, 400 reels of raw film stock and over 1,000 reels of feature films are said to have been lost in the blaze. However, there is no proof that *Tokyo Story* was lost that day. A history of the laboratory reports the number of the lost films as "2,200 cans of deposited original negatives", and explains that this fire accelerated the transfer of nitrate films onto safety stock, the construction of separate film storage facilities, and the installation of air-conditioning facilities within the storage. The accident demonstrates the slowness of the Japanese film industry's conversion from nitrate materials to safety, and indicates how these disastrous experiences led to the movement away from nitrate film.

III. Other versions

David Robinson has stated that he saw *Tokyo Story* as a new release before 1956, and that the original negatives of the film were destroyed in 1956. There are other stories about the origin of the existing print. One report says that the existing print is a dubbed version of one of the prints exported to Poland before the fire. Another version states that it is an enlarged reproduction of a 16mm print left at Shochiku's international section for export to Portugal. Additionally, it is documented that this 16mm print was reduced and printed directly from the original 35mm negative, and sent to Poland as planned.

All these facts and theories emerged and were examined in the 1980s, with the reappraisal of Ozu.

References

A. Rashomon

1. Anon., "Fire and *Rashomon*", in Hideo Matsuyama, ed., *Daiei Today and Yesterday: 1942–1951* (Tokyo: Daiei Motion Picture Company, Ltd., 1951).

2. Nogami, Teruyo, "*Rashomon* this and that (5)", in *Kinema Club Bulletin* (25 April 1995), pp. 6–7.

B. Tokyo Story

1. Atsuta, Yuharu, and Shigehiko Hasumi, *Yasujiro Ozu Story* (Tokyo: Chikuma Shobo, 1989).

2. Kitagaki, Yoshinori, "Discovered Original Trailer of *Tokyo Story*", Cinetique, no.2 (1995).

3. Sakamura, Ken, and Shigehiko Hasumi, *From Behind the Camera: A New Look at the World of Director Ozu – Based on Private Materials of the Late Yuharu Atsuta* (Tokyo: The University Museum, University of Tokyo, 1998).

4. Yokocine DIA, *As a Bearer of Image Culture: A History of Yokocine* (Yokohama: Yokocine DIA, 1995).

Notes

1 In point of fact, however, Ozu did go on to make two more black-and-white pictures after *Tokyo Story*, before his first colour film, *Higanbana*, in 1958.

Fire in the UNAM Film Archive

by Manuel González Casanova

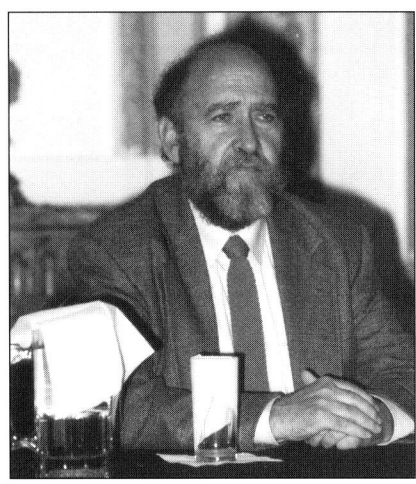

Manuel González Casanova.
Filmoteca de la UNAM, Mexico.

It was in February, 1977. I remember it was a Monday morning when I got the message that one of the secure vaults where the nitrate films were stored had burst into flames.

Let's retrace our steps a bit. At that time the UNAM Film Archive already had two secure vaults, which contained all their nitrate film material. They had been built according to a design of my own, a very simple one, as the Film Archive could not afford much technological equipment. The design was based on advice passed on to me verbally by Edmundo Gavilondo, owner in the 1920s of a distributing company called La Imperial Cinematografica. He told me that at one point he had in his care over 200,000 reels of nitrate film, without ever having suffered the slightest accident. He used to say that a tank of domestic gas was more dangerous than any nitrate film.

The vaults were built inside Ciudad Universitaria, the university campus, in a secluded area near the offices then used by Radio Universidad. As I say, they were very simple, each consisting in essence of one room inside another. The inner room, if I remember correctly, measured about 4 by 4 metres, and there was room for a passage between the inner room and the outer wall about a metre wide. The idea being that the vaults be cool and airy, 8 windows were installed in the upper part of the outer wall, 4 in the inner wall, placed in such a way as to facilitate draughts of air. The outer windows measured 75 cm high by 1 metre wide; the inner ones were slightly larger and were permanently open, protected only by metal blinds. The roof simply rested on top of the walls, allowing for it to lift up in the event of an explosion.

Attached to the first vault was a small, sparsely furnished room, where one employee in the mornings, another in the afternoons, checked the nitrate reels every day. There was never any trouble. All the material was perfectly preserved, having recently been submitted to a process of cleaning and protection in a commercial laboratory.

At that time, all the material was collected inside the first vault. Francisco Gaytán, in charge of the Film Archive's Restoration and Conservation Department, had recently returned from a course organised by FIAF. He was very enthusiastic about what he had learned, and we managed to collect the necessary resources to be able to apply the techniques he had acquired in one of the vaults. So the second vault was emptied in order to install a commercial cooling system, and all the nitrate material was concentrated in the first storage room.

That first Monday of February in 1977, the day of the fire, the employee told me that he arrived early that morning as usual, and opened the outer door of the vault to go into the annex room. As he opened the door he heard what sounded like something falling over inside the vault where the films were stored. He opened the inner door, looked inside, saw nothing out of the ordinary, went over to his work-table, and forgot about the noise he had heard. A short while later, he began to smell something. When he looked towards the vault he saw dense smoke coming from the inner door. Following instructions he ran outside, to put as much distance as possible between himself and the fire. We all know that when nitrate begins burning there is nothing else to be done, as the blaze is impossible to extinguish. To help stop the fire from spreading he called the University fire brigade.

A few minutes after he had left the installation there was a loud explosion in the first vault, and a cloud of black smoke rose towards the sky. The explosion was not as bad as it might have been, however, considering the large amount of film stored inside the vault. The tiles did not fall off the roof and the gases escaped through one of the outer windows, somewhat deforming the metal blind. That was all.

That was what made me think the fire might have been caused intentionally, with the idea of covering up a theft. Somebody, I cannot say who, as there is no real evidence, but certainly somebody able to enter the university grounds at the weekends and take the films, had left the vault almost empty, leaving behind a mechanism which was activated on opening the door, provoking the fire which destroyed what little was left behind. In that case what the employee saw when he glanced inside were just empty tins.

With this suspicion on my mind, I asked the Attorney General of the UNAM, at that time my dear friend Diego Valades, to have an inspection carried out, which would either confirm my hypothesis or find it unwarranted. Not just one but two inspections were made: one by the Chemistry Faculty of the University itself, another commissioned by the Federal Department of Justice. (Remember, University property is also the property of the nation.) Both inspections resulted in the same verdict: at the time of the fire only about 10% of the material that should have been there was in fact stored inside the vault.

When I was given the results of the inspections, I was also told by a high university official that it would be most prudent on my part to keep the news to myself. I was not at liberty to talk.

FIAF was, of course, informed of the accident, but we avoided all mention of a possible theft. Shortly afterwards, at a FIAF meeting, I was approached by Mr Herbert Volkmann, Head of the FIAF Preservation Commission and well-known expert in film preservation, who was concerned about the characteristics of the explosion and the opinion expressed at the time by Francisco Gaytán (as mentioned, responsible for the preservation of film materials belonging to the UNAM Film Archive) – an opinion which I think he still holds, disagreeing with my suspicion of a theft and that the fire had been started deliberately. Mr Volkmann asked me how many reels of film should have been in the vault. I told him (at the time I had the statistics fresh in my mind, although now, 20 years later, I do not recall the exact quantity), and he scribbled quickly on a paper napkin. He answered me more or less as follows – I quote from memory: "I think you are right. If the vault really had contained that quantity of materials, the explosion would not only have blown the tiles off the roof but would have destroyed at least the inner walls."

I can make no further comment; there is no evidence. The only possible proof would be the appearance somewhere of one of the missing films. But I doubt that will ever happen – later events have led me to believe the material is lost forever. The only good thing, in all this sad story, is that most of the lost material had already been copied onto acetate for its preservation in the UNAM Film Archive. Some of the copies, however, might not be as good as one would wish, since for lack of resources many were copied onto positive material treated as negative, this being more economical. The commercial laboratory we used at the time assured us that the copies made in that way would be adequate, and we did not then have enough experience to judge. Really, the only material which was not copied were films which had been colored by hand, of which there were about 35 short films and two copies of *Cyrano de Bergerac* by Augusto Genina, none of which had been copied onto acetate because of the cost of the color processing. Nor had we copied (to avoid trouble with the laboratory) some pornographic material which the Film Archive had been receiving, among which were a few rather primitive short films. Of all the rest, I do not recall anything that was not backed up by a copy kept elsewhere.

(October 1999)

The Last Nitrate Fire in a Commercial Cinema?

by Vigdis Lian

On 29 July 1980, a hot summer's day, during the first showing at the Aladdin Cinema in Kristiansand, a violent explosion occurred in the cinema's administrative building, which lay between the cinema theatre and the street. A huge fire broke out. Sixty people were sitting in the cinema theatre. Ten were taken to hospital, 8 of whom were discharged the same evening. One of the two who were seriously injured was a 16-year-old boy. His skull fractured in two places, he remembered little of what had happened: "I remember going to town to go to the cinema. And I must have bought a ticket because my parents found the ticket in my pocket afterwards...."

There was speculation as to the cause of the fire. It was a fact that nitrate film was stored in the Aladdin Cinema, but there was also a (dubious) theory that an explosive device had been placed in the building (Kristiansand is a relatively peaceful, medium-sized town in southern Norway).

The cinema director initially doubted that there had been an explosion in the fireproof vault. He claimed that only the remains of rolls of film were stored in the vault, and, moreover, the vault had not been damaged in the explosion.

The nitrate film theory was eventually confirmed. However, the cinema director strongly insisted that he was unaware of the regulations concerning the storage of nitrate film, created by the Ministry of Justice in 1954. (It was not until 1968 that a ban was introduced on using or producing films on highly inflammable material such as nitrate stock.)

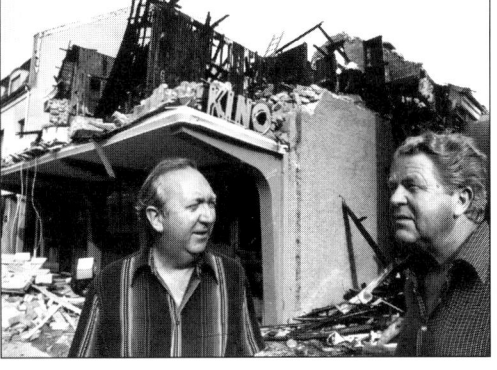

The aftermath of the fire at the Aladdin cinema in 1980.

Fedrelandsvennen, Kristiansand.

It had never occurred to the cinema director that the film could be explosive. Considering that other things were known to be stored in the vault, which was opened several times a week, it has to be said that for a long time the cinema management was more lucky than wise.

When the shock had died down, some positive things did arise from the whole situation.

The police received confirmation that the town's emergency plans worked very well!

In addition, an unwanted building was disposed of, albeit in a very dramatic way.

The cinema management immediately began planning a new cinema on the site of the fire – a cinema building that the town wanted badly, with several theatres and the ability to meet the future with greater flexibility in terms of cinema repertoire.

The fire also acted as a warning to all those who had nitrate film in their attics and cellars. The Norwegian Film Institute issued an alert, and other inflammable films were delivered to the Institute's depot. These films are currently safely stored in the National Library's storage halls in the mountainside in Mo i Rana.

Not Guilty: Nitrate Film an Innocent Witness at Two of the 20th Century's Great Fire Disasters

by Roger Smither

In the course of researching this book, two episodes came to my attention in which nitrate film – that well-known focus for fire-related paranoia – proved not to have been in any way responsible for major fire disasters in the 20th century. Although the news that something did not happen would typically be seen by journalists as something for which it is hardly worth holding the front page, there is another proverb, which says that "No news is good news." Perhaps, to conclude this particular section of this particular book, it may be worth telling these two stories precisely for their no news/good news content.

1. Nitrate Film Survives the Dresden Fire Storm[1]

The destruction of the beautiful baroque city of Dresden in Germany by a massive air raid on the night of 13/14 February 1945 is universally recognised as one of the major cultural tragedies of the Second World War. The question of how far (if at all) the raid was strategically justified remains controversial to this day, and many

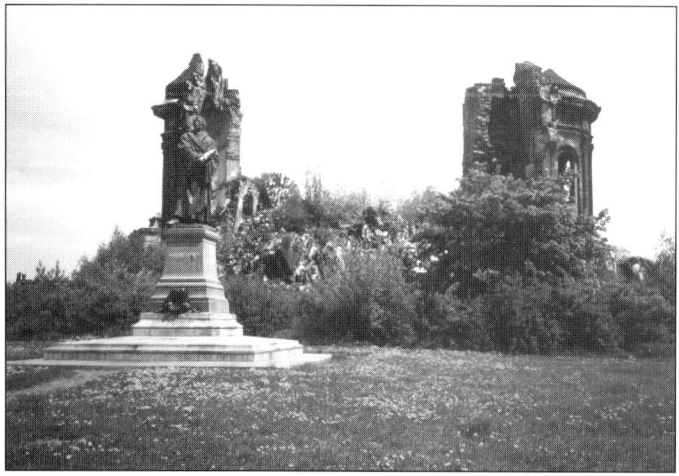

have argued that the raid constituted a serious war crime. For almost 50 years after the war, the ruins of the Frauenkirche – one of the most beautiful of Dresden's buildings, and therefore one of the most poignant victims of the raid – were left untouched by the government of what was then the German Democratic Republic, as a monument and memorial to the events of February 1945. A campaign for the reconstruction of the Frauenkirche was launched following the unification of Germany, and the painstaking process is now well under way.

The ruins of the Frauenkirche, Dresden, photographed in 1987.
Roger Smither.

The Frauenkirche survived the initial RAF raid, and was still standing on the morning of 14 February 1945. What caused the church to collapse was the fact that, after a further raid on 14 February in which incendiary bombs were largely used, a fierce firestorm broke out in the area around the church. According to eyewitnesses, the church itself was not set on fire during the raid, but the fire spread from surrounding buildings through blown-out windows to the church interior. There it burned so fiercely that the columns supporting the Frauenkirche's celebrated bell-shaped dome were fatally weakened. The church collapsed into rubble on the morning of 15 February.

Stored behind asbestos-lined doors in the north crypt below the Frauenkirche were over 700 reels of nitrate film belonging to the Reichsluftfahrtministerium – the German air ministry. The films were divided between two vaults, one containing 413 and the other 300 reels. Remarkably, however, the presence of this significant quantity of nitrate film does not seem to have been a factor in the church's collapse, and more than half of it – the film in the larger store – did not burn at all. In the other vault, all but 10 reels burned, but apparently did so only after the dome had already fallen. When the reconstruction work uncovered the surviving reels, they were handed over to the Bundesarchiv, where they were found to consist mainly of Luftwaffe training films, with some unexposed film stock. Of all the places where nitrate film has unexpectedly survived, buried beneath the rubble of the symbol of one of the world's most notorious firestorms must surely count among the strangest.

2. A New Take on the *Hindenburg* Disaster

The following two paragraphs are quoted, with the author's kind permission, from Professor Raymond Fielding's definitive history of the *The March of Time*, the American news-and-opinion film series of the 1930s and 1940s:[2]

> In time, the flood of film which poured into the Lexington Avenue headquarters [of *The March of Time*] from around the world mounted to almost alarming proportions. Because of the flammable nature of nitrate, exposed negative could not be sent through the regular mail. Instead, it was shipped by domestic air freight express, automobile, bus, or Railway express – the fastest available under the circumstances. Footage from Dick de Rochemont's headquarters in Europe arrived by boat during the middle 1930's, this being the only way to transport freight across the Atlantic in the days before regularly scheduled, trans-Atlantic air flight was introduced.

> Beginning on July 1, 1936, Dick de Rochemont began shipping his flammable negatives to New York on board the German zeppelin *Hindenburg*, thereby saving a day or two in transit time. Lifting power for this beautiful, lighter-than-air ship was provided by hydrogen, a gas that was even more explosive than the *March of Time* negatives in its hold. In some circles, the *Hindenburg* came to be called "the flying crematorium". When it finally exploded, at Lakehurst, New Jersey, on May 6, 1937, it carried 5701 feet of the *March of Time's* nitrate negative which had been shot for a story about the British "Defense of the Realm Act."

An extraordinary "rider" to this story is that recent research has suggested that although the nitrate film in the *Hindenburg's* hold was entirely innocent of causing the tragedy that took the lives of 36 of the 97 people on board that night, it might have been cellulose nitrate – in another form – rather than the hydrogen that lifted the airship that was partly responsible for bringing it down. A retired NASA scientist called Addison Bain has in recent years made a study of the *Hindenburg* crash, starting from the observation that the pictorial records and eyewitness accounts of the manner in which the fire developed and the way it looked did not suggest a fire in the hydrogen gas-bags, but in the actual skin of the zeppelin itself. By analysing fragments of the skin that had been retained as souvenirs since the crash, Bain has accumulated evidence that suggests that the fabric was treated with a cellulose acetate or nitrate doping compound, to which had been added flaked or powdered aluminium, to make the surface reflective of sunlight. In fact, as Bain points out, aluminium powder is used in rocket fuel, so the whole of the *Hindenburg* was effectively painted with a highly volatile chemical compound.[3] His alternative explanation of the tragedy at Lakehurst serves to remind film archivists – and others – that dangerous celluloid products other than film were in widespread use at the same time, while they reflect that the *March of Time* reels that the *Hindenburg* carried were victims, not villains, in this particular story.

Notes

1. The information for this section is derived from "Der letzte Trümmerberg Dresdens sagt aus", by Wolfram Jäger and Dieter Rosenkranz, in *Verbrannt bis zur Unkenntlichkeit: die Zerstörung Dresdens 1945* (Altenburg: DZA Verlag, 1994). The assistance of Dr Claus Fischer of the Gesellschaft zur Förderung des Wiederaufbaus der Frauenkirche Dresden is gratefully acknowledged.

2. Raymond Fielding, *The March of Time, 1935–1951* (New York: Oxford University Press, 1978), p. 216.

3. "What Really Downed the *Hindenburg*", an article by Mariette Dichristina for the journal *Popular Science*, copied into the US *Congressional Record* (Senate, 6 October 1998, p.S11631); "Hydrogen Exonerated in Hindenburg Disaster", an article by Jacquelyn Cochran Bokow, posted on the National Hydrogen Association website at www.ttcorp.com/nha/advocate/ad22zepp.htm.

Fiery Tails

In addition to the accounts of major fire tragedies listed in the previous section, "The Cost of Nitrate", contributors to this book also offered – and the editor's own researches discovered – a number of additional, less traumatic stories relating to fires and other aspects of the wilful destruction of celluloid or the self-destructive nature of nitrate film. Although, to be sure, such material always has its serious side, these stories seemed to be appropriate ingredients for a rather more light-hearted and anecdotal section.

Fiery Tails

by Roger Smither

Editor's Note: The title for this section was suggested by John Reed of the Wales Film and Television Archive. My sincere thanks to him, and to all those who contributed the stories used below. (RS)

I. Going Up in Smoke

Following up what seemed like a promising lead in 1994, I asked the managing director of a British manufacturer and importer of fireworks about the use of nitrocellulose in pyrotechnics. His reply was that "Nitrocellulose has a use in fireworks but it is very small indeed and highly specialised". However, he also included the following personal reminiscence: "My memory of the old film was an accidental use we found as children during the war, when we used it to make smoke bombs! A small roll of film wrapped in paper would burn quite happily to produce volumes of smoke which had a most characteristic smell since I assume that it contained camphor in those days. What the [Health and Safety Executive] would have to say about that and the production of oxides of nitrogen is another matter. However we have survived it because we burnt every bit of film we could get our hands on at that time!"[1]

The same unwelcome habit was also recalled by one of the projectionists interviewed by Scottish archivist Janet McBain:

A. We used to take odd cuttings of it, you know, and roll it up tight, put it in cardboard or brown paper, pull the end out, the centre out, and make a smoke bomb.

Q. Aye, I've heard of that before. How many feature films have disappeared because of wee boys making smoke bombs![2]

In fact, as readers will discover, confessions to "nitrate bombs" and similar activities occur in a number of the personal reminiscences included in this book. Several respected archivists, film trade veterans, and historians confess in these pages to having a small element of nitro-pyromania buried in their own pasts. Here is one such story from Madeline Matz of the Motion Picture, Broadcasting and Recorded Sound Division of the Library of Congress:

As a lonesome only child, I spent a lot of time going to the movies – every night in the summer, and every Saturday and Sunday in the winter. When I wasn't in the theatres, I and my friends prowled around the backs of theatres (my favorite was The Bridge in Baltimore, Maryland). We'd go through their trash cans. Sometimes the "movie people" threw stuff out – rusty stuff, old posters, and sometimes treasured reels with film left on them ... which is really what we were after. Once found, we would run to a huge empty lot and roll the reel out so that the film stretched across the entire field. We would light the end of the film and watch it burn lickety-split across the field, leaving blackish scorch marks and puffs of yucky smoke all the way. Then, thrilled with our devilish pyrotechnics, we'd run like heck. A great time we had at the "movies". There were lots of scorch marks fanning across that empty lot. As a film archivist, I look back on these days and cringe a little to think how many parts of films, or probably trailers, I destroyed.

Perhaps it was my guilty conscience that drew me to film preservation as a profession.[3]

The urge can even surface in adulthood, as is recalled in this account by Clyde Jeavons, former Curator of the National Film and Television Archive at the British Film Institute:

Taking time off from the Jerusalem Film Festival, my wife Orly Yadin and I were wandering around the (modern) city centre of Jerusalem in 1997, looking for her father's old school, and came across what was once Jerusalem's most resplendent art deco picture house – the Edison. Needless to say, curiosity and nostalgia – plus ease of entry through the smashed glass doors – drew us into this sadly now derelict and almost completely gutted movie palace. A few bits of torn and mangled fabric and furnishings were all that was left to see apart from a large expanse of bare, concrete terracing covered with streamers of celluloid: unravelled 35mm film. No archivist can resist picking up a piece of film and studying the frames, as did I. Mostly, it seemed to be colour feature film of recent vintage, damaged and worthless. But what got into me next is hard to explain....

Just to prove a point to myself, I suppose – just to satisfy myself that even a ruined old picture palace shut down in the 1990s couldn't possibly still harbour nitrate stock – I started to put random fragments of film into the flame of a lighter. Nothing happened with the first few bits – they just fizzled and melted – and then suddenly a piece flared into life and a flame hurtled down the lengthy strip I had been holding and raced across the film-strewn floor like one of those gunpowder trails which are a cliché of old action movies. Thankfully, this specimen of rogue nitrate quickly, if spectacularly, burnt itself out without setting anything else alight – but not before panic-fuelled visions of a new holocaust in Jerusalem had flashed across both our minds. Feeling slightly stupid, guilty and ashamed, we fled the scene – unobserved, I think – and later told the Cinémathèque that we suspected the abandoned Edison might still contain (we weren't certain, but you can never be too sure with old cinemas) some left-over bits of nitrate film and perhaps, for safety's sake, the authorities should be warned....

Orly, by the way, means something like "my light" in Hebrew, and after it was first invented – for the daughter of Yigael Yadin, a hero of Israel – it was adopted as, among other things, a name for cinemas. How (with hindsight) very appropriate![4]

Occasionally, however, the propensity of nitrate to burn was used for a more altruistic purpose – even in very unusual circumstances. Don Swift, a former film cataloguer at the National Film and Television Archive in London, found the following in an account of the 1922 Everest Expedition. John Noel, the expedition photographer and cinematographer, accompanied George Finch and Geoffrey Bruce to the North Col, from where Finch and Bruce launched an unsuccessful oxygen-assisted attempt on the summit, reaching the then-record height of 27,300 ft (8,320 m). Noel was left waiting for their return at Camp 4, pitched at 22,967 ft. In his account of the expedition, Noel writes the following: "At the lower camp I had been experiencing grave anxiety for the two men. They were a day and night beyond their schedule time, and in the evening I burned at intervals out in the open all my spare unexposed motion-picture film. This made brilliant illumination, and I hoped by it to signal to the men on the mountain that we were hanging on to this camp. Happily they rejoined me in safety and we all descended to Snowfield Camp below."[5] Don Swift adds: "I would imagine that, at 23,000 ft (7,010 metres), this is the highest recorded nitrate film fire...."

II. Lethal Weapon 35?

In the US cinema industry during the Second World War, as film historian Thomas Doherty notes, "officials loved to point out that the chemical ingredients of film – nitric acid, sulphuric acid, methyl alcohol, and cotton liners – were the same as for making smokeless gunpowder."[6] The point such officials were making was of course generally a metaphorical one, intended to emphasise the importance of their work to the national war effort, but the close chemical relationship between nitrate film and explosives has contributed a number of distinctly practical elements to the history and mythology of nitrate. Here are a few examples.

In the World War before the one that Doherty covers, the British cinema trade press took notice of a promising business opportunity for contemporary film distributors, which now seems calculated to offer a retrospective nightmare for film archivists. Published in June 1918, the story ran as follows:

> The fact that celluloid film contains several ingredients useful in the manufacture of munitions has led to quite a rapid rise in the price of "junk" of recent months, and the very keen fraternity of small dealers have earned a nice profit in transferring this material in bulk to certain firms engaged in the output of war material. There must be still a vast amount of film stored away in all parts of the countries, and renters appear to have here an ideal opportunity of clearing their shelves at a profit.[7]

In smaller "theatres" than those offered by world wars, participants were allegedly capable of taking matters (and materials) into their own hands. The following story derives from the famously lawless "Northwest Frontier" territory on the fringes of the British Empire in India – the area now constituting the border between Afghanistan and Pakistan and extending into other former areas of imperial ambition in modern Iran and Iraq. It was found in a book entitled *Pistols, Revolvers and Ammunition* by Michel H Josserand and Jan Stevenson, and I am grateful to David Penn – former member of FIAF's Cataloguing Commission, now Keeper of the Department of Exhibits and Firearms at the Imperial War Museum, London – for supplying the reference.

> The belligerent tribes of the Khyber Pass area of India and also those of the Kurdish region of Iran and Iraq, who were in a chronic state of rebellion against the British or whatever hapless authority chanced to hold sway at the moment, used to raid the local cinemas periodically and cart off all the movie film on hand, which they would later shred up for gunpowder. It worked fine, and put British patrols in the tragi-comic predicament of being decimated by an early edition of *Beau Geste* or *The Great Train Robbery*. Movie film, by the way, is no longer made of nitrocellulose.[8]

Despite the almost irresistible charm of this story, it must be noted that Dr Henning Schou – former Deputy Curator and Head of Conservation of Britain's National Film and Television Archive, and long-standing Head of FIAF's Technical Commission – has expressed serious doubts, on grounds of chemistry, that shredded nitrate film would actually make a good working substitute for gunpowder in the *jizail* or musket of the average frontier *badmash*. Here perhaps is an opportunity for an interesting practical experiment…

The possibilities for recycling film for munitions, described earlier as a likely source of nightmares for film archivists, are reported to have offered actual nightmares to the world's most famous film archivist when war broke out again two decades later. The biography of Henri Langlois by Glenn Myrent and Georges Langlois testifies to the mounting concern of the founder of the Cinémathèque Française as the approach of war in the late 1930s again gave such proposals currency. After the 1940 *Blitzkrieg* brought German occupation to France, and with it the knowledge that the resulting munitions would be in enemy hands, then, as the biographers note:

> Henri's torment could only grow: The Germans were making the rounds of all the film labs, confiscating everything on hand in order to salvage the cellulose and silver salts lurking in the prints and negatives. Langlois was haunted by the idea that these precious lengths of film would be transformed into incendiary bombs. In the wake of the Luftwaffe's bloody raid on Coventry, in November 1940, Langlois's sleep was long disturbed by the same vivid nightmare: As a city went up in flames, from the billowing smoke emerged the ghostly forms of characters from English films.[9]

On the opposite side of the world, similar "rounds" were being made by another occupying power. The circumstances surrounding the loss and possible rediscovery of the silent Korean classic *Arirang* (described elsewhere in this volume) are directly linked to reports that the Japanese authorities rounded up nitrate film for re-use in munitions factories.

Losses of nitrate film at the hands of soldiers were not always because of the usefulness of the component materials for munitions. Was it only the British Army that discovered the usefulness of burning nitrate film to help boil the water for making tea? The practice is affectionately recalled by film-maker Richard Leacock in his contribution at the start of this book.

After the end of the Second World War, bored conscripts found themselves guarding obscure outposts of mighty armed forces that were rapidly demobilising. These locations included depots for the storage of resources which were at least temporarily without any obvious purpose – including service film libraries. A bored guard will look for ways to pass the time, and an exploration of whatever it is that he is guarding is a good place to start. Although the people involved have in each case expressed an understandable preference for anonymity in telling their story, two remarkably similar accounts from two quite different countries derive from this period. In the first, the depot to be guarded was at the top of a hill, and the storyteller and his friends discovered the fun that could be had from setting reels of film on fire and then sending them rolling down the hill into the valley below. In the second country, without a hill to help them, the culprit and his comrades are supposed to have been more inventive. Here, they allegedly passed their time by drilling little holes in the cans containing reels of nitrate film. The cans were then placed on a plank of wood, propped up at one end to form a kind of ramp. When ignited, a can would take off like a rocket – and bets could be placed on whose can would travel furthest. It is not known how much film, or which titles, bounced down hills or took off from ramps in this way. Film is of course a well-known cure for boredom, but the cure is not always so potentially costly to film heritage.

Whatever the connotations of "film as a weapon" elsewhere in this section, the phrase is most often used by those who have in mind the power of film to inform or inspire a population at war – an effect which is frequently achieved by showing film of the war itself, filmed of course by the combat cameraman. It takes a special kind of mentality to go into battle armed with a camera not a gun, and with a mind concentrating on framing, exposure, and the shape of the story rather than the progress of the mission. In the days of 35mm nitrate film, the cameraman had in addition to contend with the problems that each hundred feet (30 metres) of film carried into battle would give him barely one minute's worth of film – and that the film itself was a dangerous comrade in arms.

In spite of the danger, a British First World War kinematographer called Geoffrey Malins included in his memoir *How I Filmed the War* a photograph showing "How I carried my film in the early days of the war in Belgium and the Vosges Mountains" which is remarkably (though probably deliberately) casual – especially when one notices the cigarette held in his right hand. Elsewhere in this volume, Frank Worth recalls how he was briefly tempted to try something similar as a combat cameraman during the Second World War.

In case it should be thought that interest in possible military uses for nitrate film must have finished at the end of the nitrate era, it is worth noting that one of the most unusual proposals for disposing of nitrate ever made to the US Library of Congress came during the Vietnam War. It was at the time that American tactics included attempts to "defoliate" the forests in order to deprive the North Vietnamese of their jungle cover. According to Paul Spehr, former Assistant Chief at the Library's Motion Picture, Broadcasting and Recorded Sound Division, a representative of the US Air Force asked staff of the Division whether it would be practical to use reels of nitrate film for this purpose. The notion was that the film would be strung out from planes flying low over the jungle, then ignited to fall on the trees, causing the jungle to burn and so exposing the enemy. Spehr adds that he does not think that this proposal ever got any farther than the mind of some over-enthusiastic and under-experienced planner – it certainly was not taken seriously in the Library, where the USAF was simply told that the Library did not get rid of enough nitrate to make it worth considering. He notes, in closing: "We never heard from them again."[10]

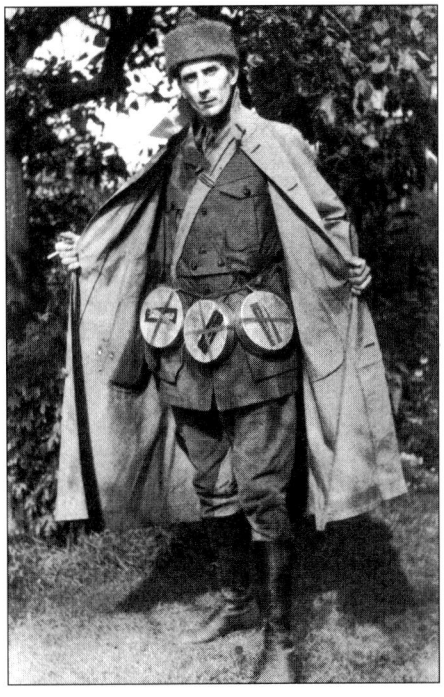

Geoffrey Malins, British Official Kinematographer during the First World War, shows "How I carried my film" in an illustration from his memoirs.

Imperial War Museum, London. HU 64117

III. Nitrate Special Effects

In his autobiography *The Celluloid Mistress*, British playwright, screenwriter, actor, and would-be director Rodney Ackland repeats a story told to him by Hungarian émigré Alexander Esway, who characterised it as "the saddest of all stories in the history of the cinema". It concerns a haulage contractor who was persuaded to underwrite the production of a film by a small studio in Germany. Anxious to keep track of his investment, he moved into an office at the studio, and followed proceedings with interest. The last scene to be shot was the film's climax, and required a house to be burned down. When the match was first applied, the result was anything but impressive, and the contractor had a moment of inspiration. Recalling that the office he was occupying was full of old celluloid, he suggested that it should be brought to the set and used to generate a better blaze. A team of willing boys fetched down can after can of film, and this time a highly satisfactory blaze was achieved. When the time came to edit this fine sequence into the rest of the film, however, there was no film to which it could be added: the over-enthusiastic boys had fetched down from the novice producer's office every scrap of film they could find – including all the materials so far shot for the film he was helping to produce! "So the contractor retired from the film business and went back to hauling," Esway said. "It was very, very sad."[11]

Although Esway's story has the suspiciously polished elegance of the classic urban legend, the certainty that nitrate would burn, and would make a lot of smoke while it did so, has made it a suitable material – in some people's eyes – for special effects throughout the history of cinema. Some other, possibly more reliable examples have been provided by contributors to this book.

Dr Stephan Michael Schröder, a scholar in Scandinavian studies at the Humboldt University in Berlin, points out that the use of burning nitrate to help generate special effects was recommended in one of the first comprehensive books about the film business in the world, written by Danish director Urban Gad. Gad's book *Filmen, dens Midler og Maal* ("The Film, Its Means and Aims") was published in 1919, and had already been translated into German by 1920. In the context of problems a director may face when taking pictures outside the studio, Gad wrote:

> Flame effects are mostly achieved with the help of old films, which are always available; they give beautiful flames, though they also generate intense heat and are difficult to control; sometimes one can help the effect with bright luminant chemicals. [...] Torches of film which are suddenly plunged into water are said to generate marvellous smoke effects, although with poisonous vapour.[12]

Dr Schröder adds, "Let us just hope he is talking about waste film and not about older films!"

There are several stories from the world of professional film production to confirm the existence of this practice, which was of course an intrinsically dangerous one. I am grateful to film historian Tony Fletcher for pointing out this story in the British trade press describing an effect that nearly went disastrously wrong, and which pre-dates Gad's book by four years:

ACTORS IN FLAMES.

Three men in flames and a boatload of others capsized in a mad effort to escape an explosion were some of the unexpected and unrehearsed incidents of a film-taking enterprise at Burnham-on-Crouch last week.

The Burlingham Standard Films stock company went down to this watering-place to burn a yacht, which was to be the climax of a sensational exclusive Crook picture produced under the direction of Mr. Ernest G. Batley.

Martin Valmour and his *fiancée*, Miss Merry, were placed aft on the yacht, and told not to jump into the sea until the cameras were going. Several hundred feet of film cut-outs were thrown into the yacht's cabin to feed the flames, and three petrol tanks hermetically sealed were to explode when heated by the flames.

"Throw in the fuses," shouted Batley, "and get out of the picture." Something went wrong, for the fire did not start, and cautiously in a yawl Batley and his assistants swung back alongside of the yacht to see what was the matter.

Bang! Bang!! And there was a roar of flames on all sides! Pandemonium reigned! "Get out of the picture," shouted the camera men. "Wait a minute! We're on fire!" yelled Batley. Choking with the flames, Valmour and the girl, their clothes burning, leaped into the sea. Batley, Jimmy Russell, and Jack Mullins, who can't swim, splashing with burning petrol, were on fire.

"Pull away for God's sake!"

In the effort to get as far as possible from the flames the three men working the explosion all got on the far side of the yawl, which took water and then turned over. Fortunately, the accident cleared the picture, and the camera men began turning, and caught the big explosion when the deck went into the air, and the sails fell in pieces like an infernal rain of fire.

"I suppose the firm will buy me another overcoat," said Batley, when the excitement was over.

"How about my hair and burned neck?" said Mullins.

Fortunately, Spring has come, and neither is needed.[13]

Ken Locke, one of the correspondents who contacted me while this book was in preparation, also recalls the destruction of an old film in the cause of a film production – in his case, a decidedly amateur one. His account is also interesting for the explanation it gives of where the film came from.

> Tightly rolled and partly sealed, nitrate gives off voluminous smoke if ignited by a cigarette. I tried this when a group of us were making an 8mm 'horror-monster' B&W home movie epic in 1953. I was 14 at the time, growing up in Queensland Australia, and almost asphyxiated my cast of friends. We were fans of the old Universal films, and our 'monster' was to escape from the laboratory in an explosion and emerge outside through the smoke. My parents were not amused to find a wall of the house covered in black smuts, and I was made aware that nitrate did not have to brightly blaze to be a serious hazard to health.
>
> As for where the film had come from, I had befriended the local cinema's projectionist, and he gave me an old 1-reel short whose 'standby' days were over – a join every few feet! Most of the suburban projectionists in Brisbane had amassed a little collection for standby use – a 'classic' feature (our local had *Little Lord Fauntleroy* from 1936), a colour cartoon, and a 'general interest' 1-reel short. The delivery system was far from perfect, and once or twice a year they got a showing when something failed to turn up. Well into the late 1950s stacks of these old nitrate items could be found in most cinema projection booths.[14]

One of the most famous stories linked to the use of old nitrate to ensure spectacular fires in new films concerns the greatest example of Australian silent film production, the 1927 Australasian Films epic, *For the Term of His Natural Life*. This story also has a legend attached. Both aspects are retold here, in the words of Ray Edmondson of the National Film and Sound Archive, Canberra:

> *Midnight. Moored in a backwater of Sydney Harbour, the derelict old sailing ship rides the gentle swell as the moonlight reflects shimmering patterns off the swirling water onto the aged timbers of the hull. A lifetime plying the seven seas, but tomorrow the end will come. In the open ocean, sad but spectacular, it will go down in a literal blaze of glory, its fiery end captured by the movie camera. The thousands of reels of nitrate film it now holds will leave nothing to chance when the torch is applied.*
>
> *Faintly through the gloom comes the plash of oars. A large rowing boat heaves to alongside. Ropes are silently thrown and made fast. Two figures climb up over the gunwales and drop down into the hold. Torches flicker and flash as they begin to sort through the mountain of film cans, stowing their selections in hessian bags. They return on deck and lower the bags to their companion in the rowing boat, then go back below to continue their quest. Finally they clamber back down to their craft of the night, now overloaded with just a few inches of freeboard, and disappear back into the darkness. In a matter of minutes, the film cans will be transferred into a waiting van, and the excursion to the hulk will be repeated. Only the approaching dawn will end the adventure, for secrecy is of the essence.*
>
> *The cameras will get their spectacle, even if the ship burns a little less*

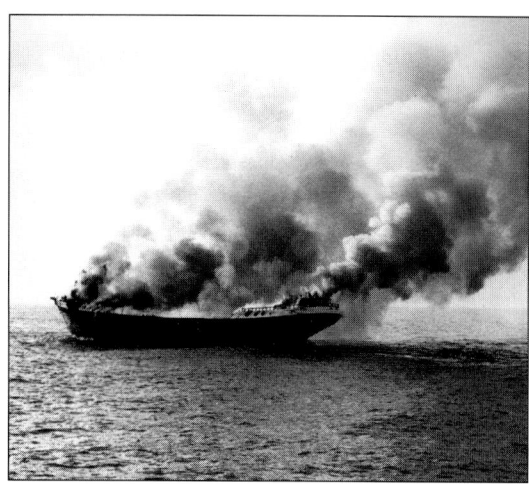

The nitrate-fuelled fire at sea from *For the Term of His Natural Life* (1927).

ScreenSound Australia, Canberra.

fiercely for the lightening of its load. A circle of film collectors will rejoice in the spoils of the odyssey. What they have saved may well have a longer life than ever did the ship in which they rested.

A spectacular scene in the 1927 Australasian Films epic, *For the Term of His Natural Life*, involves a blazing ship discovered at sea. To create the scene, the producers obtained an old hulk and filled it with discarded nitrate film. Towed out to sea, the ship was torched and the resulting scene was highly effective. The real thing – no studio models here!

There is, of course, no record of what films were actually destroyed in the blaze, but it is a reasonable surmise that a significant slice of the first 30 years of Australian cinema perished with finality. Even in 1927, Australasian Films was a venerable company: it, and its predecessors, had for two decades produced the country's main weekly newsreel, and a large percentage of its feature films and documentaries. The company was a distributor too, so the fuel was probably not confined to its own, or even to Australian productions. The scene is a record of film history going up in smoke!

The "midnight raid" on the hulk is one of the insistent, apocryphal stories that circulate among collectors. There is no direct evidence that it ever occurred: on the other hand, it is highly plausible. In the circumstances, such a treasure trove would be too tempting to ignore: and since collectors often had links with people working in the industry, it's likely the news got around quickly. Quite possibly there was more than one boat descending on the night's pickings!

The practice was not confined to Australia. After the introduction of sound, Carl Laemmle Junior is reputed to have been quite happy to allow the use of prints and negatives of old silent films to ensure a better bonfire in the production of *Splashing Thru* (1927), an episode of *The Collegians*, a popular series of featurettes at Universal. *Splashing Thru* concerned the winning of a swimming marathon by the home team at Calford (the college in the series), after which all the students celebrate by dancing around a big bonfire, in a "Calford Pajamaree". "It made a lovely blaze," it has been said, "but oh! The years of cinematic history that went up in the blaze!"[15]

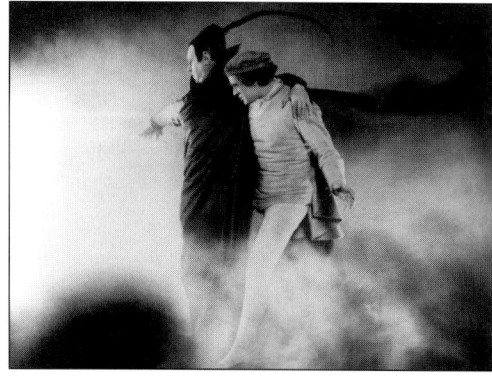

A scene from F W Murnau's *Faust* (1926).

BFI Collections – Stills, Posters & Designs, London. 88860.

Burning film was not only good to ensure a good blaze – as Gad had noted, you could get marvellous smoke effects from burning celluloid as well. German film historian Martin Koerber has long been aware of a piece of nitrate folklore attached to the filming of Murnau's *Faust*. Supposedly, the mist effects for the famous "flight on Mephisto's cloak" scene had been obtained by burning nitrate film. In an echo of the legend told to Rodney Ackland, the "mythologised" version of this story even told how the smoke-maker once made a mistake, and burnt the entire stock of film shot so far that day to produce the smoke for the last take....

Koerber was initially cautious about how far to believe this story, observing, "It is, however, possible that this good nitrate story is nothing but legend, given the poisonous character of nitrate smoke. Imagine this in a working environment." For the purposes of this book, he took it upon himself to try to find some evidence on whether nitrate film had even been burnt to create special effects for *Faust* or any other film shot in the Ufa studio. For a long time, the quest was unsuccessful – none

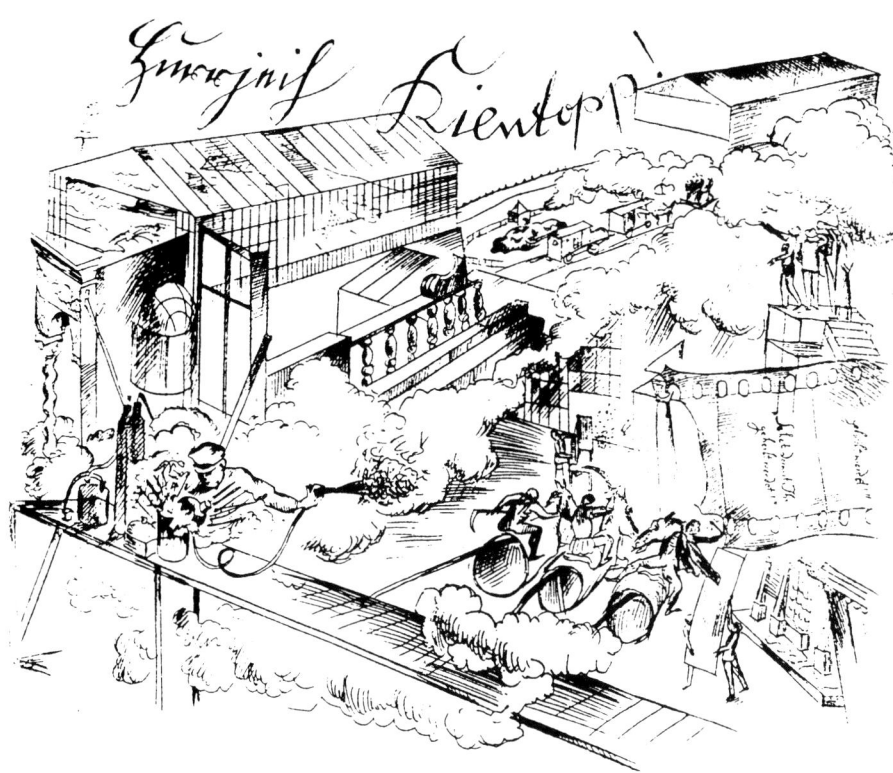

Arno Richter's greeting card design showing – among other scenes at Tempelhof during the making of *Faust* – the use of burning nitrate film for smoke effects.

Filmmuseum Berlin – Deutsche Kinemathek.

of the serious accounts about the making of *Faust* said anything about such a practice, and neither did the reminiscences of those involved. Then, in April 1993, Koerber struck gold – he found a design for a New Year's card, produced in December 1925 by Arno Richter and reproduced here. (Richter would later become a famous film designer in his own right, but in 1925 was a disciple of Robert Herlth, the designer for *Faust*, among many other films.)

The text across the top of the card is hard to decipher, but it appears to say "*Hurrjeif Kientopp!*", which is most probably a representation of a dialect or slang expression meaning something like "Hurrah for the Movies." The design for the greeting card was accompanied in the file by an explanatory text, which is translated below – note the third paragraph:

Arno Richter: Greeting Card for New Year 1926.

This New Year card originated in December 1925, at the time when the film of *Faust* was being shot, and under the influence of this activity.

In the background are the stages at Tempelhof (which can still be seen today, but with sound stages built where the earlier glass stages stood), in the middle of which is the decorative duck pond. The film of Faust was shot in the stages to the left (Stage 2, and the adjacent Stage 1), while *Varieté* was being shot at the same time in the group of studios to the right.

To the right we see Murnau, standing on a pedestal and dressed in a decidedly old-fashioned style in an over-long coat, while the short figure of Carl Hoffmann peeps through the camera and a second prop-man or stage-hand holds up a film can nailed to the end of a stick. In the can film is being burnt to create smoke, which is here symbolically enveloping the whole scene.

On the street by the duck pond are travelling horse-drawn wagons carrying props and sets.

In the left foreground, the prop-man Meyer characteristically stands on a platform contriving more smoke, with the help of various bottles, chemicals, and oxygen – the activity that earned him the general nickname of 'Smokey Meyer'.

In the centre foreground, three of the Horsemen of the Apocalypse – from left to right, Death, War, and Pestilence. Behind them, inside Stage 1, the piano player typically on hand during the shooting of silent films, unleashing a hurricane of music. Among the tunes he played most often were "Laugh, Bajazzo!" or the motif from Schubert's "Unfinished Symphony", which was well suited to the scene where Mephisto appears.

On the fragment of film to the right can be read the words "Behold, that you may be healed" in the authentic script designed for *Tartüffe*.[16]

Koerber observes: "It is interesting that Richter notes the different ways of creating smoke (burning film, oxygen, etc.), obviously in order to create smoke in different colours, or rather different photogenic qualities – thick or transparent, dark or white, moving faster or slower, etc. If one watches the film, it is indeed striking how many different kinds of smoke and clouds are presented. Herlth notes two more ways in his memoirs of the shooting: "Dampf" (which probably means steam from boiling water under pressure) used to create the mythical sunbeam-like imagery around the angel in the prologue of the film, and a thick, dark smoke made by blowing paint particles from underneath the big "Mephisto over the village" model to symbolise pestilence (incidentally almost asphyxiating the actor Emil Jannings in the process). What effect did they use nitrate smoke for?"

Nitrate's role in generating special effects for films was not always intentional. There is a story, told by both the DeMille brothers in their autobiographies, about how a nitrate fire forced itself back into a Hollywood script from which it had been reluctantly excluded.[17]

The script was one adapted by brother William from the Rupert Hughes novel *We Can't Have Everything*. It told the story of an ambitious young screen actress, whose prospects are ruined when the studio burns down with her break-through film unfinished. At the time, in 1918, the California-based production wing of the Lasky company was under strict instruction from the New York-based financial wing to keep costs down. As "fire stuff" was expensive to achieve, William pointed out to Cecil that there was a simple way to please New York and save on expensive special effects in the new picture – the heroine's career would be just as effectively blighted if the studio went bankrupt as by a catastrophic fire. The director was not particularly enthusiastic, as the dramatic possibilities of financial failure did not exactly live up to those of a spectacular blaze, but the arguments of budget carried the day, and production began with a script along the lines that William had proposed. Some weeks into production, however, on a day when Cecil was out filming on location, a real fire broke out at the studio, apparently caused by a short-circuit in the colour laboratory setting fire to a rack of film. While the studio's own fire-fighting crew struggled to contain the blaze, and outside fire brigades arrived to help, somebody had the bright idea to call out some camera crews as well, and film as much material from as many angles as possible. According to William, this idea was all his: the fire was over, some 3,000 feet of film was in the can, and the script had been rewritten to accommodate the new material by the time his brother returned from Griffith Park. In his own account, however, "C.B." claims that his crew returned in time to join in the filming, and in fact had time to stage some acted scenes among the real fire-fighting, to the bemusement of the firemen, who had never seen the victims of a fire quite so happy about it. Either way, a very realistic studio fire was after all able to be included in the finished film – although, with half the studio burned down and damage estimated at over $100,000, the fears of the finance office in New York could indeed be seen to have been justified: "fire stuff" truly was very expensive. At least it was also effective – reviewing the film, the *New York Times* noted: "The scene of a burning moving picture studio, for example – which is said to have been made possible by the opportune fire at the Lasky Studio in California – is remarkable, both for the staged confusion of the studio people and the many entertaining scenes concerned with the making of a movie...."[18]

A further note by William de Mille suggests that *We Can't Have Everything* was not the only film made that year in which the Lasky Studio fire featured: he claims that two rival companies were on the street outside within 20 minutes of the fire breaking out, using the fire as a background to their own improvised comedy one-reelers, and notes wryly: "Professional courtesy has never risen to greater heights."

Another story about the deliberate use of nitrate film to help guarantee a spectacular climax takes us back to Australia, to another contribution suggested by Ray Edmondson, and to the filming of Ken G Hall's 1933 production *The Squatter's Daughter*, which starred Jocelyn Howarth (later known in Hollywood as Constance Worth). The film-makers had permission from a landowner to burn off up to 300 acres of bush to create the desired fire, but the weather, in one of the wettest winters in memory, was definitely against them, and on location in Australia they had no access to some of the special effects equipment that would have solved the problem in a Hollywood studio.

The first requirement was to achieve a travelling shot showing the Jocelyn Howarth character behind a wall of fire as she ran looking for her handicapped brother. The crew built a 100-foot bank of dried scrub timber. On one side was veteran cameraman Frank Hurley, with his camera on dolly tracks and the camera enclosed in a kapok blimp, out of a concern – wildly misplaced, as events would shortly show – that there should be no extraneous camera noise to spoil the scene. On the other was the female lead, some fire-fighter extras, and the sound man. To make sure that the complicated set-up should not be wasted, the prop man helpfully laced some old nitrate film through the scrub. When the director

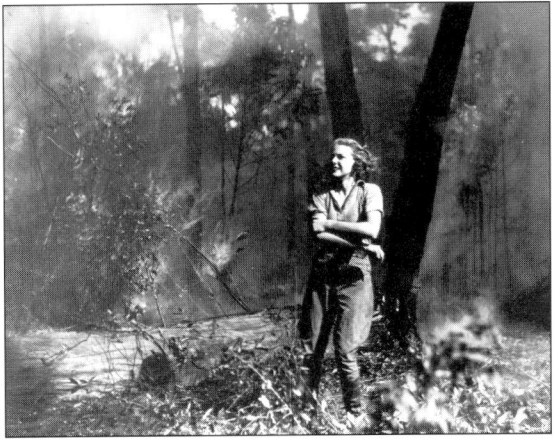

The nitrate-fuelled bush fire from *The Squatter's Daughter* (1933).

ScreenSound Australia, Canberra.

called "Action", three of the extras plunged kerosene torches into the bank. The camera and the actress started to move, and – as Hall himself described it – "the scrub exploded with a terrifying roar.... The actors took off and didn't stop for half a mile, the camera ran off the tracks and overturned, the blimp caught fire, Hurley's hair singed and I lost a fine set of eyebrows."[19]

The finale of the film required another dramatic scene – as the bush fire rages on, the principals rush for sanctuary to a waterhole, only to find the villain there ahead of them, and armed. With his cameras looking across the water, the director wanted to film the effect of a massive, out-of-control fire sweeping towards the audience. On the other side of the pool stood a 40-foot-high patch of woodland, but after the wet winter it was unlikely to burn convincingly without some human intervention. Once again, that intervention took the form of thousands of feet of old nitrate film wrapped around the tree trunks and threaded through the brush, as well as engine oil and diesel acquired from garages. As before the effect was terrifying – in Hall's words again: "The cameras rolled, the fires were lit on cue in the background and immediately the scene became an incredible inferno of flame sweeping towards us at frightening speed. Although there was a pool between us and the fire, it looked certain to engulf us all. Lookers-on behind the cameras took off for the hills like a herd of startled antelope.... It made a knockout of a scene in the film."[20]

The closing of the 'nitrate era' did not put an end to this practice. In this extract from an interview conducted for the journal *American Film*, and reprinted here by kind permission of the American Film Institute, director Richard Brooks and his wife Jean Simmons recall the staging of the famous tent fire scene in the 1960 production of *Elmer Gantry*:

Question: What were the problems?

Brooks: For example, we needed extra money to do the interior fire sequence. Now, budgets are made up by people who look at a piece of paper and say, "Well, this ought to take this number of hours to make." But you can't shoot a budget. You can only shoot a scene. I looked at all the films I could find dealing with fires, trying to learn. How do you make a fire? How do you shoot a fire scene? I found out something interesting. No pictures had been made up till then – 1959 – with mass scene interior fires. Everything was from outside. Either it was an outside fire or the camera was outside. In *Rebecca*, as I remember, a woman ran by the window and that was that, but the camera was outside. I couldn't find out how the hell you make a fire and how you shoot a fire sequence. And how do you shoot 900 people in a riot? That was the major point. Here was a lady who thought that if she could cure someone of deafness, she could also say, "Don't be frightened of the fire because the Lord is here." Well, if there's a fire people don't want to hear about the Lord; they want to get the hell out of the building.

Question: Where did you get those people?

Brooks: I'd say about 750 of them were *not* from the Screen Extras Guild. We used to bus them in from Ventura and from Orange County. They had been to tent revival meetings, they knew the songs, and I wanted these faces. As a matter of fact, Jean's stand-in one day came out in a pair of slacks, and some of the women came up and said, "Not in a place like this. She can't wear trousers in the tabernacle." They really believed that they were in a tabernacle. All you had to do was to turn them loose to sing the songs, and they were marvelous.

The budget for the fire was for six days. Thank God Burt Lancaster was one of the stars. He went to United Artists and said, "Brooks says he can't do it in six days." They said, "How long would it take?" "He doesn't know." They said, "How much money do you think it's going to take?" "It might take an extra $200,000." They said, "$200,000 for a fire?" "Yes, maybe more." They said, "Well, will you and he take it out of your fees?" We agreed to do that, so they advanced the money. It took us five to six weeks to shoot that fire.

Question: In one place?

Brooks: We shot it on three different locations. We shot partly on the stage, where we had to have forty Los Angeles firemen and the sprinklers and everything else. We shot partly on the backlot and partly out at the Santa Monica pier. Furthermore, we had to stop and start the fire over and over again. It was supposed to be a flash fire. Somebody throws a cigar or something into an oil can and all the bunting and all of the banners – God is Love and We'll be Saved – were supposed to go "Whoosh!" and the fire was on.

We had a thousand people and two cameras and Jean Simmons out there in a white robe. I said, "Roll 'em. Action." Everybody started acting. The cameras were going. No fire. Nothing. Which, of course, didn't leave me pacified. When they scraped me off the ceiling I said, "What's going on here? Where's the fire?" The special effects guy came around and said, "I don't know. I pressed the button." I said, "That's not very good that you don't know because that could be dangerous. Do you know what you're doing?" Somebody said, "Oh yes, he's been around a long time." That's scary right away. When somebody says, "Let me see the dailies – I've been in the business twenty-five years," be wary. My father drove for twenty-seven years and was a lousy driver till he died.

We got ready again. With great trepidation I said, "Action." Everyone started to act, we rolled, and nothing happened. The special effects man came around again and said, "I talked to the firemen. They soaked the bunting and the drapes and all the paper. They can't burn." I went to a fireman and said, "Did you do that?" He said, "Yes, we have to do that. Suppose the building burns down?" I said, "Let it burn! The studio would love to see it burn down. It's insured." He said, "Well, we're paid to see that there are no fires, not by the studio but by the insurance company." I said, "Let's call a halt for a while. Miss Simmons, go to your dressing room. Mr. Lancaster, go eat."

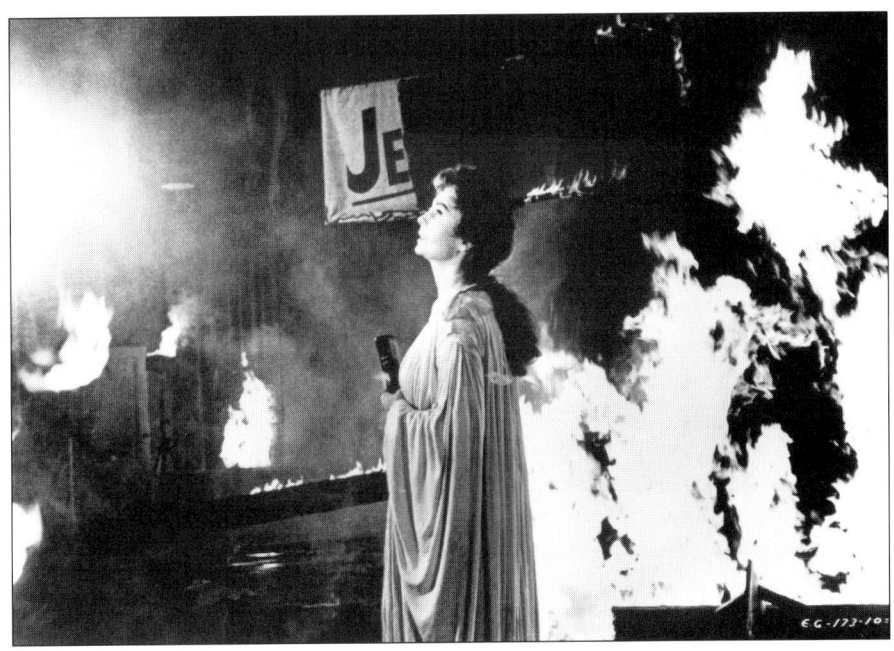

The nitrate-fuelled tent fire scene from *Elmer Gantry* (1960).

BFI Collections – Stills, Posters & Designs, London. 88860.

I called one of the firemen and said, "Let's go for a walk." We went for a walk. I said, "How do you start a fire?" He said, "I'm a fireman. How the hell would I know how to start a fire?" I said, "You're a fireman because you like fires. So how do you do it?" He said, "Only one way. You get yourself some old nitrate film and lay it in that stuff there. That'll go." So we went to Columbia and bought fifty or sixty cans of film. They went down into the vault where all the rats are. Then we laid the film along the streamers, everywhere. After lunch we called out Miss Simmons, Mr. Lancaster, 900 people. She came on stage, and everybody was ready. The cameras started going, the button was hit, and that fire went "Whoosh!" across the room. She heard that "Whoosh!" and she left the stage.

Simmons:	Well, there was an explosion. I thought something had gone wrong.
Brooks:	No, something went right.
Simmons:	I not only left the stage, I left the state.
Brooks:	I must say, it was really terrific. The stunt people were marvelous, and those trusting souls – I don't know why they trusted us. It's about four-and-a-half minutes of film on the screen. It was worth it.[21]

IV. Film Fire of the Vanities

One of the suggestions for this book which there was not enough time to take up was the idea of a collection of all the occasions on which film actors – or directors and other participants in the art of cinema, although the sentiment is most often voiced by actors – have expressed the wish that some or all of their work could be obliterated by fire. Typical of such expressions is the following, attributed to Mary Pickford: "I am adding a codicil to my will. It says that when I go, my films go with me. They are to be destroyed. I am buying all my old films for this purpose. I would rather be a beautiful illusion in the minds of people than a horrible example on celluloid. I pleased my own generation. That is all that matters."[22] Sterling Hayden said something similar: "If I had the dough, I'd buy up the negative of every film I ever made ... and start one hell of a fire."[23]

It was not always necessarily the films that might conveniently have perished in the flames. Award-winning British director of photography Freddie Young recalled his annoyance on the occasion of one studio fire, when his assistant carefully rescued the cameras – Young had been hoping for some new ones![24] Destruction was not always the occasion for humour, however: one of the sadder stories in film history is that of film pioneer Georges Méliès destroying all the copies of his films still in his possession when he was driven into bankruptcy in 1925.[25]

In an advertisement in *Kinematograph Weekly*, 2 March 1911, the Globe Film Company apologises to would-be exhibitors of *Henry VIII* (1911) that the film is already fully booked for its intentionally restricted distribution life.

British Library, Colindale, London. LD 94.

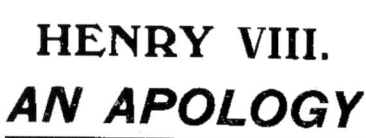

Although such a collection of quotations has not been prepared, I did receive many items which touched on the desirability or otherwise of a long life for particular pieces of film, or for film as a whole, that were much too good to ignore. One of them appeared to indicate that the syndrome of actors wishing to eradicate all traces of a performance had a history stretching back at least to 1911.

Described by critic and historian Geoff Brown as "the landmark film" in the process by which the so-called legitimate theatre "allowed early cinema to bask in the reflected glory of respected cultural traditions", Will Barker's film of Shakespeare's *Henry VIII* (1911) was based on a production and performance by the legendary British actor/manager Sir Herbert Beerbohm Tree. What was special about this film was, in the words of the same writer, "the unprecedented ballyhoo" that surrounded it. In addition to the high-profile casting, and a running-time and rental charge that were both greater than usual, the ballyhoo also included an unusual publicity gimmick, in the shape of an announcement that the film would literally only be available for a limited period. Six weeks after its release, there was a public burning of all prints at Barker's Ealing studio, on 13 April 1911.[26]

Unusual though the idea of such an emphatic writing-off of a potential asset may be, however, it is noteworthy that an entirely different explanation for this particular bonfire is offered in a second source. According to the memoirs of veteran film producer Low Warren, it was Tree himself who insisted on it. Warren describes Tree as being initially amused but happy at his appearance on celluloid. At first, Sir Herbert is quoted as saying, "In playing before the camera I found that an entirely different method is required, as different as sculpture is from painting. Still, I was greatly interested and pleased to see the result. In fact, looking at what was on the film, I thought I was quite passable – thanks to the operator." However, Warren continues, Tree came to be "rather unmercifully chaffed by his friends about his movie experiments", and approached the film-maker to ask that the film be withdrawn, as he was "not anxious that his art should be perpetuated in celluloid". According to Warren, it was this request that led to the collection and incineration of all copies of *Henry VIII*.[27]

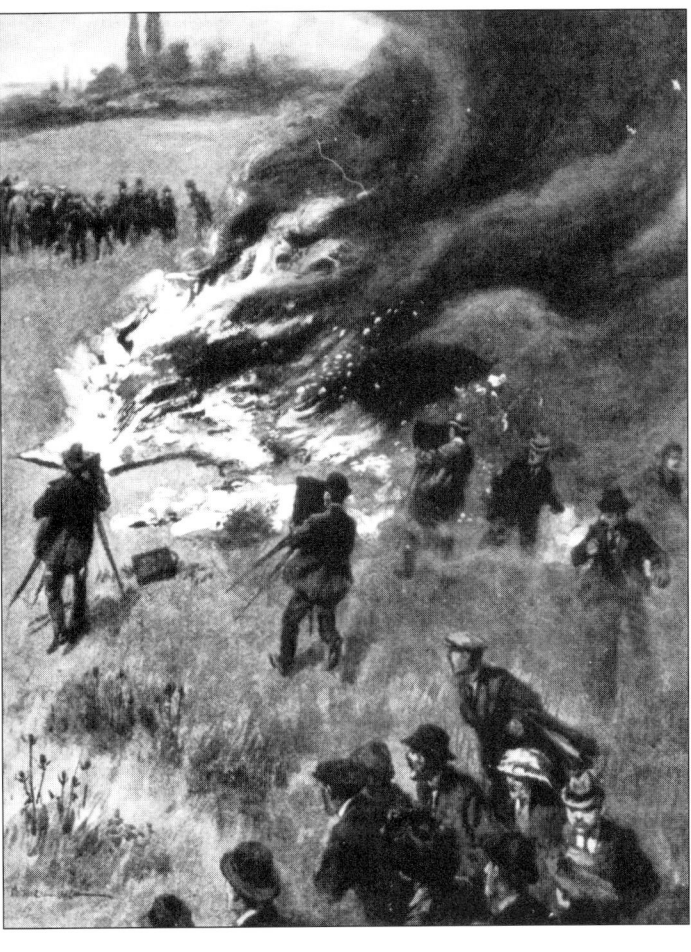

An episode during the deliberate destruction of *Henry VIII* on 13 April 1911. According to the original caption: "Suddenly the wind caught the flaming mass and blew it across the grass. The crowd fled, but the Cinema men who were there to record the unique event, caught up their machines and ran backwards, "turning" ceaselessly even in that moment of danger."

Stephen Bottomore.

Stephen Bottomore's contributions to this book contain a number of examples of opinions directly contrary to those here attributed to Tree. As he notes, expressions of concern about the permanence or otherwise of the filmed record were common from an early date. Michael Friend, then Director of the Academy Film Archive, found the following paragraphs in a press kit offering cinema managers text which they might seek to have inserted into their local newspapers to increase interest in the release of *Lost Horizon* (1937):

> Most recent distinguished man of letters to thrust aloft the cinema's torch, is James Hilton, author of such novels as "Goodbye, Mr. Chips" and "Lost Horizon", which Columbia has made into its most pretentious [sic] film. Directed by the famed Frank Capra, the picture, showing .... at the .... Theatre, stars Ronald Colman.
>
> But Hilton is not thinking solely of the picture that has been made from his novel when he advances the opinion that the screen should be seriously numbered among the arts, and that it is in desperate need of a method of preserving its masterpieces.
>
> "Literature is fortunate in having the printed page, which, in some instances, has been preserved in the original edition for hundreds of years," says the young British author. "And when books have worn out it has been possible to print new editions. Thus the works of literature can be preserved indefinitely.

"Paintings are a little less durable, although masterpieces can be retained for many generations.

"Masterpieces of sculpture," Hilton further points out, "have lasted for thousands of years. Daily we hear of expeditions unearthing some great work of sculptors who lived ages ago.

"But the motion picture art is at a great disadvantage. I am told that because of chemical reactions, motion picture negative holds the picture images only twenty-five years at the most. Then the pictures fade and it is impossible to make new prints. This is a pity. Some great pictures have been made and greater ones will be made as this important art develops. These should in some way be preserved for posterity. It is definitely the duty of chemical engineers to evolve some process that will make the artistic achievements of this great industry more lasting."[28]

The assumption that "chemical engineers" should or could solve the problem of film deterioration is of course an echo of earlier demands also noted by Stephen Bottomore. A similar concern that scientists should direct their attention to the question of film permanence could apparently distract even those who might be expected to have other, less uplifting matters on their minds. According to the memoirs of Leni Riefenstahl, Adolf Hitler found time to muse on the subject in 1940. "It would be fantastic," she quotes him as saying, "if today we could see films from the past, films about Frederick the Great, Napoleon, and great historic events." Referring to the problem of the transience of celluloid, she recalls that he then asked her to do something for him: "Please contact the Kaiser Wilhelm Institute in Berlin and discuss the problem with outstanding scientists and scholars. I could imagine a film stock made of the finest metal, which would not be altered by time or weather and could hold out for centuries. Just imagine what would happen if, a thousand years from now, people could see what we have experienced in this era."[29]

Misplaced confidence in the longevity of the celluloid record is evident in the following anecdote offered by Janet McBain of the Scottish Film and Television Archive:

> In 1936 and again in 1937, Gaumont-British News presented special commemorative copies of their newsreels of the Funeral of King George V and the Coronation of King George VI to every Royal Burgh in Scotland (there are about 10 of them). Each set of newsreels was soldered into a special shiny can with a commemorative plaque on the centre of the lid, and was accompanied with a deed of gift which trumpeted that this was a gift in perpetuity, to the citizens of X Burgh, and that the cans were not to be opened until 2036. One such can of decomposing nitrate, stored in the Manuscript room of the Burgh archives, was found wrapped in brown paper with the pencilled instructions "Not to be opened for 100 years!"

This very practice led a participant in the discussion following a paper given by National Film Library Curator Ernest Lindgren to the British Society for International Bibliography in December 1943 to provide possibly the most hurtful description of archive film ever offered. A Mr R A Fairthorne wished to say that: "The distribution of newsreels of the Coronation to local authorities was a good example of cashing in on popular misconception of technical advances. Only a perpetual charge on the ratepayers could keep them in condition." However, he prefaced this entirely accurate comment with the following pithy dismissal: "Motion picture records, as Mr Lindgren has shown, are white elephants bedridden in perpetuity." Mr Lindgren, there can be no doubt, had never intended to "show" any such thing![30]

Another kind of misunderstanding of the value of the film can in preserving its contents is evident in a story told by Yvette Hackett of the National Archives of Canada, concerning a man who wished to donate a reel of nitrate to the collection:

> When he was told to put it in a can to ship it, he arranged to have it sealed into a food can at a local cannery. His accompanying letter informed the archivist that all he needed was a can opener to get at the film. It turned out to be a particularly valuable piece of Canadian footage, from *Universal Animated Weekly*, Issue 6, Volume 4. It showed the aftermath of the 1916 fire which destroyed Ottawa's original Parliament Buildings, including the ruins, firemen and spectators.

Returning to the subject of the destruction of unloved performances, the Marx Brothers are another set of celebrities reported to have wished to burn some of their own work. According to Jesse Lasky's autobiography the Brothers were so "disgusted" at Paramount's 1929 attempt to film their Broadway hit *The Cocoanuts* (and especially at the sound quality) that they wanted to buy back the negative and destroy it. Paramount stood firm, and the film turned a handsome profit – in part, Lasky suggests, because audiences came back for second or third viewings, to try to work out what it was about.[31]

Sometimes a pretence of destruction could be a useful ruse. Terry Ramsaye, in his massive history of early cinema, *A Million and One Nights*, tells such a story about the American minstrel comedian Lew Dockstader, whose act involved him wearing "blackface" make-up while he commented on the passing world from the basket of a pretend balloon. In 1904, Dockstader had the idea of filming a gag in which President Theodore Roosevelt would apparently come to his assistance after he had fallen from his balloon over Washington, and persuaded Edwin S Porter (maker of *The Great Train Robbery*) to undertake the project. A convincing stand-in for the President was found, and the scene was filmed in front of a deserted Capitol in the early hours of one morning. The filming, however, aroused the curious interest of a watchman, so the secret was out.

There were important reasons why the episode should seem deeply suspicious to Roosevelt and his supporters. The President had recently and very controversially had lunch with the African-American activist Booker T Washington, and his political opponents were busily playing the race card in their campaigns. The filming of a replica Roosevelt picking up a replica black man and driving off with him in a carriage strongly suggested the making of a piece of hostile propaganda. The affair was considered at Cabinet level, and the decision was taken to suppress the film. A Secret Service man was sent to the Edison Studio in New York to demand the negative. Porter persuaded Dockstader that the messenger could be palmed off with a reel of unexposed negative. The comedian was reluctant, but the director went ahead anyway, correctly guessing that the Secret Service man would pull the film from the can to check it, and could then be told he had ruined the unprocessed negative.

"One evening shortly after that," writes Terry Ramsaye, "down in Washington, there was another meeting of the cabinet at the White House. Theodore Roosevelt and his confrères repaired to a sheltered place on the lawn and there was a lurid brief bonfire as they watched the film burn." The original negative survived – but Dockstader did not dare use it in his act, and Porter kept it. Ramsaye says Dockstader later had the chance to explain to Roosevelt the real purpose of the film – and to tell the President that he had burned a blank. However, in concluding the anecdote, he notes: "But Fate had its way. The historic roll of film was stored in a chest of Porter's archives in his office at the Famous Players studios when they burned some ten years later. They might just as well have given the film to Roosevelt."[32]

Almost half a century later, a case of *lèse-majesté* in the United Kingdom had a more straightforward ending. In about 1950, an opportunistic BBC cameraman followed a car containing the infant Prince Charles to some park or other and snatched some minutes of film showing the heir to the British throne playing on the grass with his nanny. His superiors at the BBC did not dare to transmit this film without first seeking authorisation from Buckingham Palace. Not only did the Palace refuse permission, but it demanded that the negatives be brought to the Palace by those responsible and burned in the grounds. The BBC complied.[33]

It is tempting to claim that the Palace had a taste for this form of censorship – two years later, during the preparations for the coronation of Queen Elizabeth II, journalist Guy Eden of the *Sunday Despatch* reported on 26 October 1952 on the elaborate precautions that were being planned to censor film of the Coronation ceremony the following year. On the day, he explained, the film shot by the newsreel cameramen "will be lifted from the cameras by executives of the film companies and put at once into sealed canisters. These will be taken by car direct from Westminster Abbey to Buckingham Palace". In a private room, a single projectionist would then show the uncut film to the Archbishop of Canterbury, the Lord Chamberlain, and the Earl Marshal, and any section to which they took exception was to be "cut out on the spot and burnt at once".[34] The media in the year 2001 are less obliging in the matter of control of Royal stories.

Another example of censorship by fire was the subject of a story in *Variety* of 7 April 1916, found by novelist and biographer Simon Louvish, and written up by him for the journal *Sight and Sound*. This described how D W Griffith was obliged by pressure from the Jewish anti-defamation society B'nai B'rith to re-shoot a sequence from the film that was to be released as *Intolerance*, then known by the working title *The Mother and the Law*. Griffith had shot the episode dealing with the crucifixion of Christ using orthodox Jewish extras in the role of executioners as well as cheering mob. B'nai B'rith was understandably alarmed at, as Louvish puts it, "the news that America's most famous film director, who had already inflamed racial tensions with the pro-Ku Klux Klan *The Birth of a Nation*, had shot a sequence which illustrated the Christian world's worst assumptions about the Jewish people as Christ killers." They first attempted to persuade Griffith to drop the sequence, pointing out (with what *Variety* rather superciliously referred to as "so-called indisputable proofs") that crucifixion was a Roman, not a Jewish method of execution. Griffith initially rejected their request, but when it returned in the form of a 48-hour ultimatum with destruction of the filmed sequence the only way of avoiding a concerted national campaign of boycott and other financial or political pressure, he changed his mind. The *Variety* piece concludes: "Confronted with such formidable antagonism, Griffith burned the negative of the scene in the presence of the committee and has retaken it, showing Roman soldiers nailing Christ to the cross."[35]

V. Nitrate Auteur

The disruption of the production of a film by fire was of course by no means confined to episodes of censorship. A number of more or less well-known stories where the flammability or other physical characteristics of nitrate affected the timing – or even the very completion – of a film-making project suggested the title for this section. One well-known example is that of the Famous Players-Mary

Pickford Company film, *The Foundling* – a drama of a father's rediscovery of the daughter he had earlier abandoned that recalls (with appropriate gender changes) some of the story lines of *Oliver Twist*. Originally scheduled for release on 6 September 1915, a first version of *The Foundling*, directed by Allan Dwan and starring Frank Mills, Harry Ham, Gertrude Norman, and others had been not only completed but even reviewed by trade papers in August when it was destroyed in a studio fire. A new version was hastily shot, this time under the direction of John O'Brien, and with a new cast in which actors such as Edward Martindale and Maggie Weston replaced the original line-up. The re-shot film was released in January 1916, only four months behind the original schedule. *The American Film Institute Catalog* notes incidentally that The Foundling is the only film copyrighted in the name of the Famous Players-Mary Pickford Co.

A similar story relating to a 1924 studio fire in the Netherlands is told by Ivo Blom in his contribution elsewhere in this book: on this occasion, the whole of Theo Frenkel senior's *Cirque Hollandais* had to be shot again.

Among the most decisive interventions of "nitrate auteur" was a fire that took place at the St Margaret's Studios, Twickenham, in June 1918, described 19 years later by one of those affected as "one of the most disastrous fires in the history of the business".[36] The casualties included two major pieces of British film propaganda then in production. One was generally known at the time and subsequently simply as "The National Film", although the title intended for its release was to have been either *Victory and Peace* or *The Invasion of Britain*. "The National Film" was a project for a major feature film sponsored by the National War Aims Committee, a body set up by the Government in Britain to rekindle enthusiasm for the defeat of Germany among a population wearied by 3 years of inconclusive and costly fighting. By showing the imagined horrors of a German invasion of the British Isles, the film would remind Britain and the world of the evil nature of German militarism and the vital need to defeat it. Popular novelist and playwright Hall Caine was asked to write the scenario. Successful Irish-born director Herbert Brenon was brought from Hollywood to realise the project, accompanied by American cameraman J Roy Hunt and editor James McKay. A cast including several stars of the British stage of the standing of Ellen Terry, Matheson Lang, Marie Lohr, and others were joined by huge numbers of extras supplied both by the city of Chester, where the action was set, and by the British Army (whose men represented both British and German troops). Caine claimed literary help from Thomas Hardy and Rudyard Kipling and the preparation of a special musical score supposedly involving both Sir Edward Elgar and Sir Alexander Mackenzie. The budget was correspondingly epic. The first results of all this work were lost in the fire.

The second victim of the Twickenham fire was an equally epic filmed life of the British naval hero Lord Nelson, directed by Maurice Elvey and produced by Low Warren and Jack Sallmayer. Although the impetus for this film came from the industry rather than from the government, the Nelson project also received lavish official support. Help received from the Admiralty included access to naval experts and documents, the use of a large number of sailors as extras, the services of England's oldest living Admiral, who introduced the story in a filmed prologue, and permission to film on board HMS *Victory* itself. According to Warren, it was the day that the producers were expecting to view a first print of the finished film that they instead received a telephone call to tell them that the works had been completely burned out and all the negatives destroyed. Warren writes: "In an hour – the fire hardly lasted longer – we had lost over £20,000. Practically every negative we possessed was at St. Margaret's and, as we soon discovered, they were almost entirely uncovered by insurance, owing to a misunderstanding. Worst of all, our beautiful 'Nelson' picture was gone."[37]

The fire was not the end of the road for either *The Life of Lord Nelson* or "The National Film". Where *Nelson* was concerned, the commercial, artistic, and naval contributors rallied round and the film was re-shot in "a little over six weeks". It went on to open to considerable commercial success. The other major victim of the fire suffered a more cruel fate. "The National Film" was also re-shot, possibly on an even more lavish scale than before, certainly on a somewhat slower timescale than the "Nelson" film – stories describing location shooting in Chester found their way into the trade and national press in September 1918. The time-scale was to be the film's undoing. It was finished in the first weeks of November 1918 – just as the war ended. With Germany defeated, the film had lost the reason for its existence. It was never screened for an audience, and an economy-conscious government soon decided it was not even worth the cost of storage. The film which had been made, lost to an accident, and re-made, was lost again – this time deliberately junked. Only a fragment survives in the National Film and Television Archive.[38]

Another studio fire which affected the completion of at least two films was that at the Popular Players Studio on West 53rd Street, New York City, on 3 January 1917. The report in the *New York Herald* of the following day (found for the editors by Ron Magliozzi of the Museum of Modern Art) failed to treat the disaster entirely seriously. The headline read "Disastrous Fire in a Film Studio Gives Public 'Close Up' of Emotional Acting", and the story made light of the behaviour – and the costumes – of some of the participants and the spectators. One passage read: "Some of the young women who dashed out of the burning building wore Roman drapery, but a great many of them apparently had been deciding what to put on just as the heat struck the building. Citizens who would normally run immediately to turn in an alarm did nothing of the sort and for a time the fire had hard work obtaining recognition as such." Later, the reporter noted: "Emotional actresses running along the side of the building encountered an iron gate which could be readily opened. Each in turn, however, halted to shake the gate frantically, beat upon it and cry out and their work was, in the main, very effective. It was not until the last character had made an exit into some nearby house that the matter of a fire was taken up seriously." The tone of the report was emphasised by an accompanying cartoon, in which a number of young women appeal for rescue from the windows of the burning building, one of them calling, "Oh save me! No not you – the one with the curly hair!", while another, already on the pavement, clutches a passing fireman, saying, "Oh fireman save me! You look so big and strong and brave 'n' everything!" Meanwhile, on the other side of the picture, a workman draws on a cigarette, musing, "I suppose by rights I should save the hero too – aw, wot d'ell – I've saved everything of importance".

In spite of the flippant tone of the coverage, the report does note that the fire disrupted progress on a new drama, *The Waiting Soul*, and destroyed another, *To the Death*, which had already been completed. (*The American Film Institute Catalog* records that the former was released in April 1917, while a remake of the latter appeared from Metro Pictures in August.) It also records that Olga Petrova, the star of both pictures, lost personal property valued at $25,000 in the fire.

Sometimes fire has been invoked deliberately by a film-maker. When Kevin Brownlow discussed with Abel Gance the troubled history of his epic masterpiece *Napoléon* (1927), the French maestro said of one of his film's most famous technical innovations: "I burned the triptychs from this film. Not the final panoramic one – that I couldn't find. But the others – I threw the negative into the fire. I was profoundly depressed. I felt the industry had no place for me. How long ago? It feels like a century." The image is a profoundly sad one, though it is worth adding Kevin Brownlow's own comment on this statement: "No film maker would throw film into a fire, unless he wanted to start a larger one, so I held out hope that the missing triptychs still existed."[39] (The restoration of *Napoléon* on which Brownlow worked so long was screened by the British Film Institute as the unforgettable prelude to the FIAF Congress in London in June 2000, which also featured the symposium *The Last Nitrate Picture Show*.)

Possibly the best known case of a film-maker claiming to have used the incinerator as the ultimate editing tool is the case of Frank Capra's shortening of *Lost Horizon* (1937). According to his autobiography, Capra was left in a state of shock for two days by the first preview audience's unsympathetic reaction to the film. On the third morning, he rushed back to the cutting room and simply told editor Gene Havlick to remove the main title from the start of reel 1 and put it at the start of reel 3, making no other change but the cutting of some 20 minutes. It did the trick: at a new preview, the audience was spellbound. "But before I celebrated," Capra wrote, "I had a chore to do. I ran up to the cutting rooms, took those blasted first two reels in my hot little hands, ran to the ever-burning big black incinerator – and threw them into the fire. Being nitrate film, they flamed up with a whoosh that lit up the night sky."[40]

Good though the story is, since Capra's death history has not been kind to this particular piece of myth-making. According to Capra biographer Joseph McBride, the story of the simple remedy (cutting the first two reels) "covered up what in fact was a massive overhauling job, of which shortening the opening was but a single, though crucial, part." When interviewed by McBride, co-editor Gene Milford expressed polite doubt that anyone would casually throw two reels of nitrate film into an incinerator – and, more prosaically, "Whatever the director might have wanted to do, Milford said, 'The negative would have been in the vault. And I had the first two reels [of positive print from the preview version] sitting in one of the cabinets in my cutting room for a long time, thinking they might reinstate it.'"[41]

The incendiary intervention of the "nitrate auteur" was, of course, frequently not deliberate. One famous case is that of Carl Dreyer's 1928 masterpiece *La Passion de Jeanne d'Arc*, the original negative of which was destroyed by fire in Germany shortly after its release. Dreyer assembled a substitute negative from takes that had originally been rejected, but even that was later reported to have been lost in a fire at the French laboratory where it was being stored, combining with censorship and distributors' cuts to contribute to the film's long history of distribution in inferior versions.[42] The story of the recovery of an original print of Dreyer's film is told in Ib Monty's contribution to this book. Several of the fires listed in "The Cost of Nitrate" section in this volume are reported to have involved the loss of master negatives, or of cutting copies, and so to have resulted, in the words of one *Ciné-Miroir* headline of 1939, in "Des films que vous ne verrez pas" – films you will not be seeing.

Although a studio fire might not be deliberate, it could sometimes be convenient. Another case of a cutting-room fire threatening the completion of a feature film was that of *The Third Man* (1949). Carol Reed's biographer simply notes that "despite a fire in the cutting room which damaged some footage, Reed brought the film in on time in March 1949."[43] Exactly what lay behind such remarks is recalled in a letter from Martin McLean, one of those involved in "picking up the pieces":

> Just out of H.M. Forces 1948 and back to my old job as sound assistant in a sound studio in Wardour Street, one of our picture editors asked me if I'd like some extra money. The job was working nights at Shepperton Studios

assembling seven reels of "THE THIRD MAN" lost in a cutting room fire. I would work on a sequence printed from the negative trying to match a frame of the sequence from the many takes reprinted. Not an easy job when 4,000 slates were taken and usually 3 or 4 takes on that slate number. After about three hours I was then taken off assembling, and given sequences from other editors who had managed to match takes with scenes. I was the only one on the shift who could use the "BELL & HOWELL" hot foot splicer. Sir Carol Reed would come along about 4AM and view in the theatre the night's work – the editor OSSIE HOFFENRICHTER [sic] would then take over on day shift and carry on with the final edit.[44]

Although the fire and the extra work it caused are established facts, a recent study of *The Third Man* by Charles Drazin has pointed out that the fire was undeniably convenient for Alexander Korda, the British producer. It is not so much the fire that arouses Drazin's suspicion as the use to which it was put – it provided Korda with an alibi for deferring a screening for his American partner, David O Selznick. Selznick had the contractual right to demand changes to anything he disliked about the film. However, the film had already been scheduled for screening at Cannes. If Selznick's first sight of the film could be delayed, he would not be able to demand too many changes, as the resulting delays could endanger the Cannes entry. Drazin points out that there were two copies of the rough cut – Reed had been using the second one when working on the music with Anton Karas – so it would have been possible for Selznick to see something in spite of the fire, if his partners had so wished.[45]

Allegations of suspicious convenience have also been levelled – though this time less credibly – at another celebrated intervention by the "nitrate auteur". This was the loss to fire of Robert Flaherty's first attempt in 1916 to make something coherent of the footage he had shot over the previous three years in the Canadian Far North. Flaherty himself gave this account in a 1950 interview:

> Some time after this expedition returned to civilization – we were away for a year and a half – I took up the matter of the film I had shot. I was getting it together in Toronto to ship to New York when carelessly, amateur that I was, I dropped a cigarette off the table in the little room where the film happened to be.[46]

Another writer takes up the story: "There was a burst of flame. Flaherty was thrown across the room, burned deep by the blast, scorched as though he had stepped into the roaring vortex of a giant blow-torch. He struggled out of the room and ran to the street in a frenzy of pain, clothes afire. Weeks later, he recovered in the hospital."[47] (The story is also recalled by Richard Leacock in his contribution to this book.)

Again, the disaster had its convenient side. Flaherty reported that the whole negative – variously estimated as 25,000 or 30,000 feet of film (though the figure has climbed to 70,000 in the interview quoted!) – had been destroyed. A work print survived, but at that time it was impossible, or at least it suited Flaherty's purpose to say it was impossible, to make a duplicate negative from it. The truth was that, although his "work in progress" had been enthusiastically received on several occasions, Flaherty was himself less than satisfied with it, considering it lacking in story, structure, and commitment to the people he had filmed. He determined to return among the Inuit people to make a film that would focus on the way of a life of a single Inuit man and his family. The result of the re-make would, of course, be *Nanook of the North* (1922). The convenience of the fire, in this sense, has generated at least one attempt at a more conspiratorial interpretation, in a recent interview with film-maker D A Pennebaker:

There is a story about how the first version of the film was destroyed. People say that something fell off a building and set it on fire while he was in a cab. I think what happened was that he took a look at it, said, this is terrible, and decided to go back and try and do it again. At this stage, Flaherty had never made a film before in his life. He was nearly 40, he was an explorer, not a film-maker. When he got it wrong, he needed a good reason to get his sponsor Révillon Frères to put up more money for him to do it again. So he invented that story.[48]

The general consensus, however, is that Flaherty's fire was real enough, and much too serious to have been risked as a mere fund-raising device. There is a certain irony in *Nanook* falling victim to a nitrate fire in Toronto since, according to an account which Flaherty gave in 1926, describing the circumstances of the making both of *Nanook* and of his then-current production *Moana*, the environment in northern Canada had been much more obviously unsafe than the cutting room. Flaherty related how the film shot in Canada had been processed and printed in situ. The improvised darkroom/laboratory was a converted "clerk's dwelling" near Cape Dufferin, where the processed film was dried on a home-made drying reel of 1,600 foot capacity. This was turned by hand – the hands belonging to Nanook himself and another local known as "Harry Lauder" – in front of a coal-burning box stove, the drying sometimes needing a whole night. Meanwhile, wrote Flaherty, "I slept in my sleeping bag just beyond cremation range".[49]

It may be noted in passing that a nitrate print of *Nanook of the North* appears in another context, playing a talismanic role at a dangerous time in the life of another great figure in the film archive world – Jacques Ledoux, who was curator of the Cinémathèque Royale de Belgique in Brussels from 1948 until his death in 1988. At the start of the Second World War, the teenage Ledoux was already a confirmed cinephile, active in the creation of a film club called Camera Obscura. Under the German occupation, in 1942, he was rounded up with other Jews for transport to a concentration camp, but managed to jump from the train. He then decided to hide out in the countryside until the end of the war. According to the volume compiled in tribute to Jacques Ledoux by Anne Head:

> He found refuge with different families, worked as a farmhand, was assistant to a baker and spent a while at the Benedictine abbey of Maredsous. It was probably there that he interested himself in Christian philosophy and he claimed it was there that he found a print of Flaherty's *Nanook of the North*. Apparently oblivious to the dangers of nitrate film, he carried this film around with him until the end of the war and his return to Brussels. Ledoux told me in 1988 that "the print I gave to the Cinémathèque was used by Mrs. Flaherty when she restored the film in the 1970s".
>
> … The Cinémathèque, which found itself after the war with neither films nor staff, was in fact housed in Henri Storck's home. Ledoux, who had known him before the war at a screening or a meeting of the Belgian Cinémathèque, went to see him and offered him the print of *Nanook of the North*. Storck recalls that he suggested to André Thirifays "that this young man may be of some use to the Cinémathèque".[50]

Sylvia Katz's essay elsewhere in this volume has looked at the impact that the physical characteristics of celluloid can have on artistic endeavour in fields other than film. Here is a story on the cross-over line, from a London evening newspaper of 1949:

> Sixty original cartoons by David Hand, painted on celluloid, were today ordered to be taken from the foyer of the Cameo News Theatre in Charing Cross-road [sic], because of the risk of fire. An L.C.C. inspector on a routine visit made the order when he was told they could not be encased in glass.
>
> David Hand, one of Disney's early cartoonists, is over here building up British cartoons.[51]

Finally, in case it should be thought that it was always through fire that "nitrate auteur" might intervene in a film-maker's career, or that only the recognised deities of the film-making pantheon might be so afflicted, I am grateful to my colleague John Kerr of the Imperial War Museum Film and Video Archive for bringing to my attention one of the contributions to a composite biography of Edward D Wood, Jr. Wood is of course famous – or infamous – as the director of such celebrated low-budget films as *Plan 9 from Outer Space*, and as the man who gave Bela Lugosi his last screen appearances. According to John Andrews, after Lugosi's death, Wood had a collection of unused footage of the actor, which he planned to use in a new project. "But," Andrews continues, "he shot it on nitrate. One morning he opened up the can – all this priceless footage, and it had gone to dust. All the poison, the vapors, hit him, and he threw up immediately. So that's what happened to his *Ghouls of the Moon project*."[52]

VI. Frighted with False Fire

Given the fearful power of the image of nitrate film fire, it is no surprise that suggestions or threats of fire have sometimes been used for more or less dubious purposes. A comparatively innocent example was quoted by Jay Leyda in his history of compilation film, *Films Beget Films:* a New Jersey film collector whom Leyda calls Johnnie (actually John E) Allen had told the British publication *Radio Times* a story which began when he heard of a sale by the US Customs authorities of some unclaimed Russian films. Arriving at the sale, he found he was surrounded by network representatives, whose spending power would, he just knew, be much greater than his own. He took a look inside some of the film cans just the same. "As I did so, out shot red dust – the sign the old nitrate film has gone to pieces and is dangerously inflammable. 'Put out your cigarettes,' they yelled. And then they all went away, thinking it was no good. So I bought the lot – 200 cans – for a price that it's not fair to those big boys to mention."[53]

Rather less innocent is the practice described by Tom Dewe Matthews in his history of film censorship in Britain. Control of the risk of nitrate film fires underpinned the right of British local authorities to control film exhibition in the areas under their jurisdiction, although in doing so it depended on what an editorial in a liberal newspaper referred to as "roundabout means never contemplated by Parliament when the 1909 Act was passed".[54] When left-wing film clubs started showing non-nitrate 16mm prints, this opportunity for low-level censorship was lost. Here is his description of how it could be reasserted:

> The police would usually prevent workers' film society performances through the use of safety regulations; failing that, they would interrupt them to conduct on the spot "inflammability tests". Because a cinema was threatened with the withdrawal of its licence if it showed film on inflammable stock, local authorities would often demand that propagandist films prove their resistance to fire. This culminated in a notorious incident at the Manchester Labour Hall in August 1933 when the police raided a showing of the pro-revolutionary American documentary *The Road to Hell* (1931). The secretary of the society passed a burning match under a strip cut

from this film, but the police were not satisfied. They insisted that the whole reel be laid on an open fire for at least half an hour. When this order was carried out the film still did not burst into flames; however, it had become too distorted to pass through the projector.[55]

A less malicious example of the deliberate invocation of fire hazard was reported in *Variety* in February 1954. A demonstration of the safety of the new acetate film which had since the start of the decade been introduced to replace nitrate was arranged by the Eastman Kodak Company in Rochester. The hope was to overcome the "cautious reservations" of municipal authorities about just how safe the material really was, and so lead to an easing of regulation and a lowering of insurance premiums. Overall, the programme seems to have been a success, but one cannot help wondering whether one of the showier aspects of the demonstration could possibly be replicated: "In one test … nitrate and acetate film were interwoven and ignited. While the nitrate film was burned to ashes … the acetate film was good enough to reprint."[56]

A strange example of what might be termed the propagandist use of the idea of nitrate fires within the film archive movement is to be found in the pages of *Seductive Cinema*, an intensely personal book, part memoir and part reflection on "the Art of Silent Film", by James Card, the founding curator of the film archive at George Eastman House in Rochester, New York. Not content with the assertion that "Disastrous nitrate fires have happened to every major film archive handling old 35mm film" – a claim that several archives would vehemently dispute, even if they would do so with their crossed fingers touching wood – Card goes on to allege, twice, that "in a carefully concealed series of fires in [the Museum of Modern Art's] vaults, a tragic number of irreplaceable films were lost".[57] Current and former staff at the Museum have no knowledge of any such fire – let alone fires in the plural – and one can only wonder what could be the author's purpose in making such a claim. Perhaps as a lifelong critic of MoMA (as his book frequently demonstrates) and a major supporter of Henri Langlois, James Card was trying to besmirch the reputation of the former while simultaneously suggesting that the latter had done nothing particularly unusual or reprehensible in creating the circumstances for the Cinémathèque Française's disastrous fires of 1959 and 1980.

VII. You Talkin' to Me?

Because film archivists spend so much of their time thinking about nitrate, they can sometimes forget that the word is not so familiar to other audiences. Here are three stories which illustrate such misunderstandings.

When the Imperial War Museum's film archive activities were discussed in the House of Lords in 1993, *Hansard*, the supposedly infallible official record of proceedings in the British Parliament, at one point transcribed a speech as referring to "bids for additional funding for the conservation of the night freight film stocks".[58] The phrase somehow suggests something a little dishonest, possibly calling to mind a paraphrase of Rudyard Kipling's poem about smugglers – "Watch the wall, my darling, while the Archivists go by!"

Still in the United Kingdom, a few years earlier, when Jack Amos was preparing to address the Trades Union Congress on the subject of film preservation in 1986 (as described in Jerry Kuehl's essay on the British *Nitrate Project 2000* elsewhere in this book), he recalls that his nerves before making this, his first speech to a full TUC session, were not helped by the amount of teasing he received from colleagues who – pretending to misunderstand the word "nitrate" as "night rate" – asked him why a Congress of trade unionists should be expected to vote in support of overtime![59]

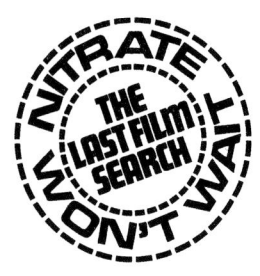

The logo for the Australian Last Film Search campaign, which featured on badges like the one worn by Bob Rosen in the accompanying anecdote.

ScreenSound Australia, Canberra.

Perhaps the most puzzling story of mistaken identity, however, is the following experience described by Robert Rosen of the UCLA Film and Television Archive: some sort of communication gap is apparent, even if the exact nature of the misunderstanding is not quite clear. He recalls visiting a store soon after a major film preservation campaign was launched, wearing the campaign's brightly coloured badge, which read NITRATE WON'T WAIT. The cashier read the badge, looked at him sympathetically, and then said, "Yes, I know: my brother was hooked on it." Bob is still uncertain just what substance the cashier had in mind – a new meaning for the concept of "film addict", perhaps?[60]

VIII. A Hard Act to Swallow

In addition to the loss of nitrate to deterioration and to fire – accidental and deliberate – several of the contributors to this book have noted other reasons for destruction. The value of silver recovered from the salts in the emulsion is one such: it has even found a poetic echo. The celebrated story that Irving Thalberg sold off the "missing reels" of Von Stroheim's *Greed* to recover 43 cents' worth of silver per reel is quoted in the admonitory poem "Orson Welles, Are You Listening" by William David Sherman, which the reader will find in the anthology *The Faber Book of Movie Verse*, edited by Philip French and Ken Wlaschin.[61]

Elsewhere in this volume, *This Film Is Dangerous*, Professor Sami Sekeroglu describes rescuing a precious film that was about to be turned into film cement. Until the quite recent past guitar picks were made from old film, and P K Nair notes the recycling of celluloid into "bangles, ladies' handbags, wallets, and such utilitarian items", while Stephen Bottomore recalls the transition of celluloid into the shine on people's footwear, and the theme of varnish is taken up emphatically in the section "Mort du Film". Among the several reports on nitrate fires found by David Pierce in the pages of the *US National Fire Protection Association Quarterly* was one in 1925 when fire broke out in a factory where cotton-felt was impregnated with a solution derived from nitro-cellulose film scrap "to be used in manufacturing shoe counters and box toes".[62]

A specific link between an important film and another article of clothing was mentioned in the material submitted for this book by Jane Paul and Diane Pivac of the New Zealand Film Archive:

> *Carbine's Heritage* (1927), a drama of the turf, was the only feature made by Ted Coubray, one of New Zealand's few pioneer film-makers. The film opened successfully in three Queen Street cinemas. Session times were staggered, so the only print could be cycled between venues. The film is now lost. Sadly, the nitrate negative was melted down during the war to make belts. As Ted once remarked: "Someone now wears it around their waist!"[63]

Of all the sad fates described as befalling nitrate film, however, the one that strained the editor's credulity the furthest was the thought of nitrate being recycled for human consumption – and yet such stories arrived from two separate sources. The first is to be found among more of the pages from the *National Fire Protection Association Quarterly* sent to the editors by David Pierce. This particular story dates from 1925, and *NFPAQ* itself attributes it to the *Times-Picayune* of New Orleans. It deserves repeating, although it is told in language that unfortunately reflects the casual racism of the time it was written.

A New Film Fancy

It cannot be said that all movie films leave a pleasant taste in the mouth, or are all of them safe for the public!

After such an introduction one might fear we were about to complain about the artistic or moral worth of some recent Hollywood production. Not at all! We have said movie film and we mean movie film, not moving pictures. It happened in Mexico and the inventive genius who overreached himself was a Japanese – all of which may sound confused. It really is very simple.

A Jap dwelling in the Mexican state of Campeche thought to "buck" the chewing gum magnates by putting in a small gum factory of his own. Mexico, as you know, is a large producer of chicle, the basic gum of the everlasting chew. But the price of that resin, due to the enormous gum-hunger of American flappers, was too high for profit under the somewhat crude manufacturing methods of the Nipponese innovator. The Jap, however, had business relations with a local film exchange at a town that appears to have been at the end of the circuit. When films had gone every place else imaginable and had been cut and repaired and worn and discolored to the limit, they halted at Campeche as their final resting place – they weren't even worth paying freight on to another stop.

However, the experimental Jap found that by cutting up and boiling the defunct films, it was possible to obtain a pulp that would, when mixed with a small amount of chicle, give a fair imitation of the famous wiggly product.

All was well with the Jap's world until the other day, in a thoughtless moment, the manufacturer lit his pipe and placed the match end upon a shipment of his home-brew chiclets.

It will be remembered that movie film is a close cousin to nitroglycerine. At last accounts not a trace had been found of either the Jap or his plant. It is therefore too late now to ascertain whether or not the nature of the scenes depicted on the film affected the taste of the gum. We have seen some photoplays that have seemed strong enough to do so.[64]

While the above carries many of the characteristics of the classic urban legend, and should perhaps be dismissed as such, the second instance of edible nitrate offers more serious credentials: it is the reference to the sale of nitrate film for use in sausage skins which is contained in the interview with Enrique Blanco that appears elsewhere in this volume. One can only hope the sausages were intended for boiling, not for frying or grilling!

Notes

1. R Lancaster, letter to Roger Smither, 30 June 1994. (The Rev R Lancaster is Managing Director of Kimbolton Fireworks in Huntingdon.)

2. Interview with David Angus, conducted on 11 May 1989 by Janet McBain, Scottish Film and Television Archive, Glasgow.

3. Madeline F Matz, undated letter to Catherine A Surowiec.

4. Clyde Jeavons, letter to Roger Smither, May 1998.

5. Captain J B L Noel, *Through Tibet to Everest* (London: Edward Arnold, 1927), pp. 190–191.

6. Thomas Doherty, *Projections of War: Hollywood, American Culture, and World War II* (New York: Columbia University Press, 1993), p. 86.

7. *The Kinematograph and Lantern Weekly* (13 June 1918), p. 50.

8. Michel H Josserand and Jan Stevenson, *Pistols, Revolvers and Ammunition* (New York: Crown Publishers, 1972), p. 9.

9. Glenn Myrent and Georges P Langlois, *Henri Langlois: First Citizen of Cinema* (New York: Twayne Publishers, 1995), p. 73.

10. Paul Spehr, e-mail to Roger Smither, 12 April 2000.

11. Rodney Ackland and Elspeth Grant, *The Celluloid Mistress* (London: Allan Wingate, 1954), p. 42.

12. Urban Gad, *Filmen, dens Midler og Maal* (Copenhagen and Kristiania: Gyldendal, 1919), p. 42; extract translated into English with the assistance of Dr Schröder.

13. *The Cinema* (22 April 1915), p.xix.

14. Ken Locke, letters to Roger Smither, 25 October and 5 December 1999.

15. Information from Kevin Brownlow (conversation with Catherine A Surowiec); quotation from DeWitt Bodeen, "Laura La Plante", *Films in Review*, v.XXXI, no.8 (October 1980), pp. 449–450.

16. Reference Xerokopi 4.5 – 80/10–0 FAUST-0 in the archive of the Stiftung Deutsche Kinemathek; submitted by Martin Koerber, Berlin.

17. William C. deMille, *Hollywood Saga* (New York: Dutton, 1939), pp. 140–144; *The Autobiography of Cecil B. DeMille*, edited by Donald Hayne (London: W H Allen, 1960), pp. 197–198.

18. *New York Times*, 15 July 1918.

19. Quotations from Ken G Hall, *Australian Film: The Inside Story* (Sydney: Summit Books, 1980).

20. Ibid.

21. Extract from *American Film*, v.III, no.1 (October 1977), pp. 40–42; reprinted by kind permission of the American Film Institute.

22. Ruth Biery, "As Mary Faces Forty", *Photoplay*, v.39, no.6 (May 1931), p. 67; quoted by David Pierce in his paper "Beggars of Life (Why Some American Silent Films Survive)", delivered at the Symposium "The Last Nitrate Picture Show" at the London FIAF Congress, June 2000.

23. Leslie Halliwell, *Filmgoer's Book of 'Quotes'* (London: Mayflower/Granada, 1978, augmented edition), p. 227.

24. Author's telephone conversation with Mrs Freddie Young, 1998.

25. Iris Barry, "Georges Méliès, Magician and Film Pioneer", in Mary Lea Bandy, ed., *Rediscovering French Film* (New York: The Museum of Modern Art, 1983), p. 43.

26. Geoff Brown, "'Sister of the Stage': British Film and British Theatre", in Charles Barr, ed., *All Our Yesterdays: 90 Years of British Cinema* (London: BFI Publishing, 1986), pp. 145–146.

27. Low Warren, *The Film Game* (London: T. Werner Laurie, 1937), pp. 60–61.

28. Press kit for *Lost Horizon* (1937), in the Margaret Herrick Library of the Academy of Motion Picture Arts and Sciences.

29. *The Sieve of Time: The Memoirs of Leni Riefenstahl* (London: Quartet, 1992), p. 271.

30. Ernest Lindgren, "The Permanent Preservation of Cinematograph Film", *Proceedings of the British Society for International Bibliography*, v.5, part 5 (1943), pp. 97–104; Mr Fairthorne's comment, p. 101.

31. Jesse Lasky, *I Blow My Own Horn* (London:Victor Gollancz, 1957), p. 228.

32. Terry Ramsaye, *A Million and One Nights* (New York: Touchstone/Simon & Schuster, 1986 reprint edition; originally published by Simon & Schuster in 1926), pp. 437–439.

33. Paul Ferris, *Sir Huge: The Life of Huw Wheldon* (London: Michael Joseph, 1990), p. 258.

34. Quoted in James Ballantyne, ed., *Researcher's Guide to British Newsreels Vol. III* (London: British Universities Film and Video Council, 1993), p. 18. Dr Nicholas Hiley points out that Guy Eden's account makes no mention of the fact that the film would have to be developed and printed at some point between Westminster Abbey and Buckingham Palace!

35. Simon Louvish, "Burning Crosses", *Sight and Sound*, v.10, no.9 (September 2000), pp. 12–13.

36. Low Warren, op.cit., p. 105.

37. Low Warren, op.cit., p. 123.

38. Nicholas Reeves, *Official British Film Propaganda during the First World War* (London: Croom Helm, 1986), pp. 125–130.

39. Kevin Brownlow, *Napoleon: Abel Gance's Classic Film* (London: Jonathan Cape, 1983), p. 182.

40. Frank Capra, *The Name Above the Title* (New York: Macmillan, 1971), pp. 200–201.

41. Joseph McBride, *Frank Capra: The Catastrophe of Success* (London: Faber & Faber, 1992), pp. 361–363.

42. Gary Morris, "Denounced, Cut, and Burned – but Triumphant: Dreyer's *Passion of Joan of Arc* on DVD", in *Bright Lights*, no.27 (January 2000), http://www.brightlightsfilm.com/27/joanofarc.html.

43. Nicholas Wapshott, *The Man Between: A Biography of Carol Reed* (London: Chatto & Windus, 1990), p. 232.

44. Martin McLean, letter to Roger Smither, July 1993. The correct spelling of the editor's name is Hafenrichter.

45. Charles Drazin, *In Search of The Third Man* (London: Methuen, 1999), pp. 110–111.

46. Quoted in Kevin Macdonald and Mark Cousins, eds., *Imagining Reality: The Faber Book of the Documentary* (London: Faber & Faber, 1996), p. 37; there attributed to Roger Manvell, ed., *The Cinema*, 1950 (London: Penguin, 1950).

47. Kevin Brownlow, *The War, the West and the Wilderness* (London: Secker & Warburg, 1979), p. 475, quoting Terry Ramsaye in *Photoplay* (March 1928), p. 125.

48. Geoffrey Macnab, "Looking Back: D. A. Pennebaker on the Artistry and Technique of Flaherty, Powell and Godard", *Sight and Sound*, v.7, no.4 (April 1997), p. 61.

49. Robert J Flaherty, "The Handling of Motion Picture Film Under Various Climatic Conditions", originally in *Transactions of the Society of Motion Picture Engineers, no.26* (Meeting of May 3–6, 1926), pp. 85–93, accessed from David Pierce's *Silent Film Bookshelf* website, http://www.cinemaweb.com/silentfilm/bookshelf/23_smp_6.htm.

50. Anne Head, *A True Love for Cinema: Jacques Ledoux, 1921–1988* (The Hague: Universitaire Pers Rotterdam, 1988), p. 8. Storck and Thirifays were two of the three founding members of the Cinémathèque de Belgique in 1938. The Cinémathèque became "Royale" in 1962.

51. "'Danger' in Cinema", *Evening News* (London), 10 March 1949.

52. Rudolph Grey, *Nightmare of Ecstasy: The Life and Art of Edward D. Wood, Jr.* (London: Faber & Faber, 1995), p. 126.

53. Jay Leyda, *Films Beget Films: Compilation Films from Propaganda to Drama* (London: Allen & Unwin, 1964), p. 104, quoting the *Radio Times* (4 January 1962), p. 31.

54. *Manchester Guardian* (23 November 1939).

55. Tom Dewe Mathews, *Censored: The Story of Film Censorship in Britain* (London: Chatto & Windus, 1994), pp. 44–45.

56. "Dramatic Demonstration at Eastman Plant of Acetate Film's Safety", *Variety* (24 February 1954).

57. James Card, *Seductive Cinema: The Art of Silent Film* (New York: Alfred A Knopf, 1994), p. 103 (and p. 108).

58. *Hansard*, v.545, no.131 (Wednesday, 28 April 1993), col.429.

59. Jack Amos, telephone conversation with Roger Smither, July 2000.

60. Bob Rosen, conversation with Roger Smither at the Prague FIAF Congress, 1998.

61. Philip French and Ken Wlaschin, eds., *The Faber Book of Movie Verse* (London: Faber & Faber, 1993).

62. "A Nitro-Cellulose Process Fire", *National Fire Protection Association Quarterly*, v.19, no.3 (January 1926); contributed by David Pierce. The fire cost three lives.

63. Diane Pivac, correspondence with Roger Smither, August 1999.

64. *National Fire Protection Association Quarterly*, v.19 no.2 (October 1925), p. 129; contributed by David Pierce.

Speaking of Nitrate...

An anthology of archivists' anecdotes.

Nitrate Pussy

Editors' Note: This contribution arrived anonymously from America's West Coast.

As an ardent film student in the mid-1970s, I sought out literally every venue for "old" movies offered by the City of Angels. One should remember that, before the mass commodification of "classic" cinema via small format video, learning about film history presented challenges which severely tested one's resolve, which literally defined the boundaries of one's cinephile curiosity. Meeting these challenges and satisfying this curiosity chiefly meant visiting the local repertory theatres, the art houses, and some downtown cinemas which used to run quintuple bills for a dollar. The extremely modest price of admission at such fine establishments as the Cameo, Optic, and Broadway, and the (once historic) Million Dollar Movie, proved a felicitous and democratic inducement for drug addicts in need of shelter, weary prostitutes in need of a rest, and, of course, film students on limited budgets.

During this time, I heard a rumour about a large collection of films held by an only slightly more reputable institution, the University. Although the campus appeared to be a safer, more sanitised venue, the road to the nascent film archive presented a similarly difficult set of logistical, political, and bureaucratic challenges. When I finally arrived in the office of this now much-respected cultural institution, it only seemed marginally safer than those downtown theatres. The term "office" should be used cautiously here. The room was jam-packed with 35mm film cans stacked in no particular order, from the floor to almost the ceiling. Most of the films in the "office" were nitrate prints of classic Hollywood titles.

Sitting on a dishevelled couch with feet spread over a small coffee table – the table itself was propped up by film cans – the then-curator of this new collection waxed poetic about Fellini, Kubrick, and Sam Fuller. I was only just a little alarmed that the curator blissfully chain-smoked, even though surrounded by nitrate film from the floor to the rafters, to either side of the couch, and literally under his feet! I tried to convince myself that a hypothetical nitrate fire certainly couldn't be as serious as the very real dangers I often faced in those downtown theatres.

I just knew that I had found archival heaven. All I need do was impress the curator with my passionate commitment to cinema art, and I would certainly be allowed entrance to the hallowed ground. I would certainly be granted viewing access to its forbidden treasures. My approach was quite simple. I would express my concern over the potential fire hazard, thus demonstrating both my knowledge of archival matters and my dedication to these precious objects:

> "Isn't this that n-i-t-r-i-t-e stuff? Do they really let you smoke around it?"

The guardian's scornful response plainly told me that my career in the film archive craft was still a long way away:

> "Oh boy, that's really just what we need around here. Another nitrate pussy."

For several years afterwards, his remark made me wonder if I ever really had the right stuff to become an archivist. I never found a satisfying answer to this question. But when the downtown theatres began to close, all my doubts vanished. "Nitrate pussy" or not, to discover new/old films, I simply had to make a home in that office both dangerous and full of promise.

Gosfilmofond Silhouettes:
Nitrate in the Russian Manner

by Vladimir Antropov and Valerij Bosenko

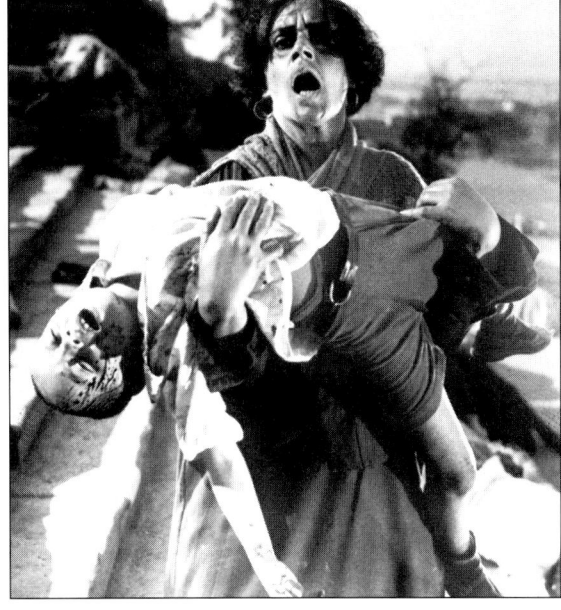

Bronenosets Potemkin
(Battleship Potemkin, 1925).

BFI Collections – Stills, Posters & Designs,
London.

The expiring 20th century has decreed silver nitrate, the creation of the last century, the perpetual keeper of the era's images. Like all the world's film archives, Gosfilmofond recognises this. Each negative has its own history and destiny, and deserves a separate story, but here we have time to tell only a couple of them.

1. *Potemkin* and *Que Viva Mexico!*

Our first stories are related to the name of the great Sergei Eisenstein.

The negative of *Battleship Potemkin*, the film recognised in Brussels in 1958 as "the best film of all times and peoples", was sent by Soviet distributors to Germany in 1926. Goebbels later demanded that German film-makers create their own *Battleship Potemkin*, and he had the negative handy to show them.

In 1930 fascist and Soviet censors acted virtually simultaneously. In German versions of *Potemkin*, several shots of a character that was politically unwelcome to the Nazis were cut from the negative. In the USSR, the opening intertitle was changed in the remaining prints of the film: as a result of a political purge, the original opening, which had quoted Trotsky, was changed to an appropriate quotation from Lenin.

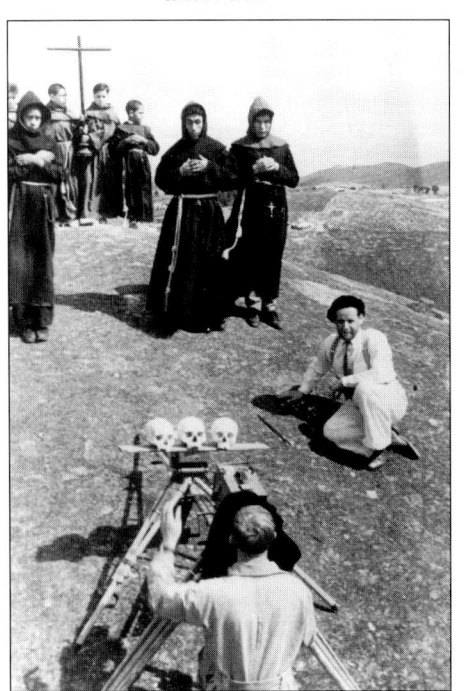

Sergei Eisenstein setting up a shot for *Que Viva Mexico!* with cameraman Eduard Tissé.

BFI Collections – Stills, Posters & Designs,
London. 112707.

After Eisenstein's death in 1948 the epoch of the film's reconstruction began, which lasted about half a century. During that time the negative was finally returned from Germany and stored with Gosfilmofond. Since then, every restoration has added to the original something which had previously been lost. At present Gosfilmofond, together with a number of European film archives, is commencing a restoration of the author's original integral version. Along with previously cut shots, the Trotsky quotation, recently found in the film's documentation, will be reinstated.

The fate of the negative of Eisenstein's unfinished Mexican film, *Que Viva Mexico!*, is no less dramatic, and perhaps even more so. Owned and handled by the family of Upton Sinclair and his American associates, the film passed from one hand to another, but was never returned to its original director during his lifetime. Part of the negative perished in a fire in Hollywood; the remaining part was bought by historian Marie Seton for her own edited version of the film. It was not until after World War II that the negative was finally deposited with an archive, the Museum of Modern Art in New York.

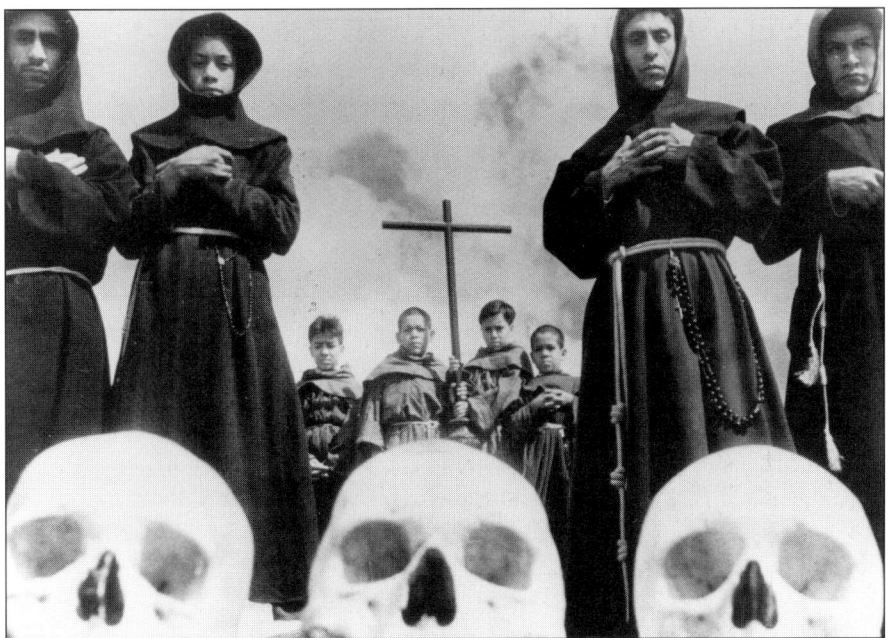

The scene resulting from the previous set-up.

BFI Collections – Stills, Posters & Designs, London. 112225.

Years later, after long archival negotiations, the remaining 1,666 cans of negative finally crossed the Atlantic and returned to its director's homeland. During the 1970s the negative was carefully checked and scientifically analysed and attributed. The result of this work is a complete card-catalogue of all existing 10,000 shots of the unfinished *Que Viva Mexico!*

2. A Suppressed Film by Dovzhenko

In 1958 several cans of nitrate film with the intriguing title *Farewell America!* were transferred in conditions of the strictest confidence to Gosfilmofond. The covering documents said that this was an unfinished film by director Alexander Dovzhenko. His widow, Julia Solntzeva, once a beautiful actress of the Soviet silent cinema and later a director, strictly forbade us to do anything with the material. Forty years passed before we were finally able to undertake the first attempt to reconstruct the film. In 1998, to mark the 90th anniversary of Russian cinema, Gosfilmofond, together with the Mosfilm Studios, released their reconstructed version of this unfinished film by the great director.

Alexander Dovzhenko started working on the film in 1949. That year a small book entitled *The Truth about American Diplomats* appeared in bookstores. Written by a woman, a former employee of the American Embassy in Moscow, it apparently was inspired by state security bodies of the USSR.

It was strongly recommended that Dovzhenko make a film of this "work of art". This recommendation came from the highest government authorities, so the director could not refuse. He rewrote the script many times, trying to squeeze something from the material. Censors, security bodies, officials from the Ministry of Foreign Affairs, all constantly interfered in his work. At last, in 1950, the director started shooting, but he had shot less than half of the film when he arrived on the set one day and found that the electricity was cut off. Without any explanation he was told that the shooting was stopped. The rumour was that the order was given by Stalin himself.

All the material that had been shot was hidden somewhere, and there was never any record anywhere that Dovzhenko had ever shot such a film. It was even said that the film was destroyed. Only years later, after the director had died, his widow Julia Solntzeva, then a director, found what material survived at the Mosfilm Studios, and passed it to Gosfilmofond.

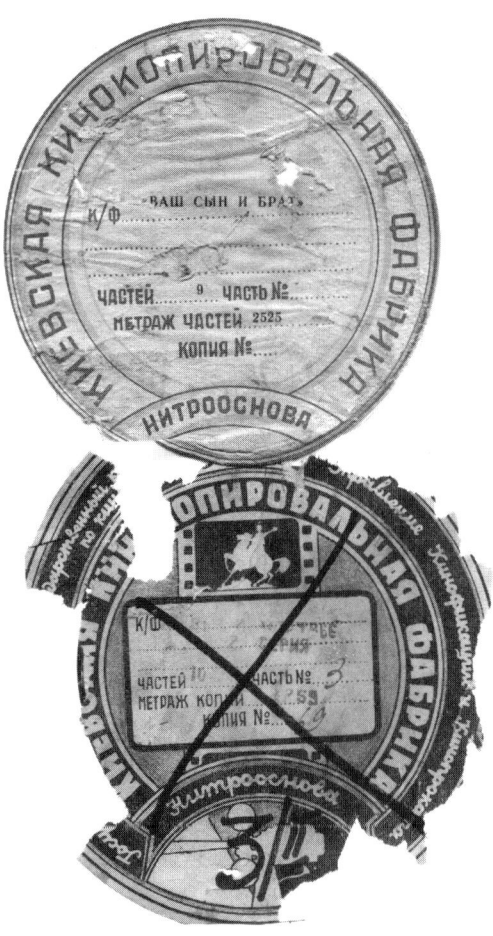

A distributor's label for the Soviet film *Vash Syn i Brat* (Your Son and Brother) still offers a nitrate warning, although the date – 1965 – suggests this precaution is unnecessary.

Israel Film Archive / Jerusalem Cinematheque.

3. A Discovery in a Garden

It was the early Spring of 1971. The eminent Soviet military leader and World War II hero Marshal Vasilij Tchuikov was working at his country house near Moscow, when his spade suddenly struck something solid. The Marshal carefully removed the soil with his hands and found one metal can, then another. When he opened them he was a little disappointed, as there were no jewels. In the cans he found reels of cinema film. Although useless to him, Tchuikov did not cast away his find, and within several days the film safely reached Gosfilmofond.

What the earth had kept turned out to be an old Russian film, *Umer Bednjaga v Voennoi Bol'nitze* (Died a Miser in a Military Hospital), made in 1916 and long considered a lost film. Unfortunately the film was incomplete and in poor condition. Gosfilmofond's experienced specialists did their best to save it, as every metre of preserved old film is a real treasure for the history of cinema.

The unearthed film was based on a folksong composed to the verses of, as he was described in the film's titles, the "August poet Konstantin Romanov", a famous Russian poet who wrote under the *nom de plume* "KP/KR". Romanov was a member of the Russian imperial family, and Tchaikovsky was among the Russian composers who were inspired by his verses. The film was shot by Alexander Levitzki, a great cameraman of early Russian cinema.

The Game of Freeze Out: A Celebration of Nitrate Vaults

by Mary Lea Bandy

This is a story about some clever little nitrate vaults and how they got their names. Once upon a time in the United States, almost every cultural, educational, hospital, and governmental structure was named in honor of its donor(s), or of a public figure recently or long previously accorded status among the historically distinguished. Thus we have a national library building, sports stadium, space launch station, expressway, and movie studio commemorating the accomplishments of, respectively, Thomas Jefferson, Roberto Clemente, John F Kennedy, Dwight David Eisenhower, and the Warner Bros. The greatest number of sites, whether natural features, man-made constructions, or movie studios, refer to the glorious explorations of Christopher Columbus than to any other national hero.

With regard to cinema's icons, studios realized added value by naming individual buildings on the lot, such as the Louis B Mayer Building and the Cary Grant Theater at the MGM Studios. After the Sony corporation acquired Columbia Pictures, and MGM relocated, Sony moved onto the former MGM lot. Mr Mayer's headquarters were renamed the Sony Building; the Cary Grant Theater could retain its original name thanks to Mr Grant's collaborations with George Cukor, Leo McCarey, and Howard Hawks during the Harry Cohn administration at Columbia. Generally, however, cinematic naming opportunities have taken advantage of the multi-faceted careers of major figures such as Thomas Alva Edison and Will Rogers, Frank Sinatra and Bob Hope. George Eastman is often in our thoughts, but where is there a shrine to D W Griffith? Pickfair, tragically, has been demolished. Fortunately, we can visit the Dorothy and Lillian Gish Theater in Bowling Green, Ohio. We also may choose to bypass mundane LAX to arrive at John Wayne Airport in Orange County on our pilgrimage to Hollywood Boulevard, where we can spot many names, and pause outside Mann's Grauman's Chinese Theater to marvel at the tiny shoe sizes of our favorite stars.

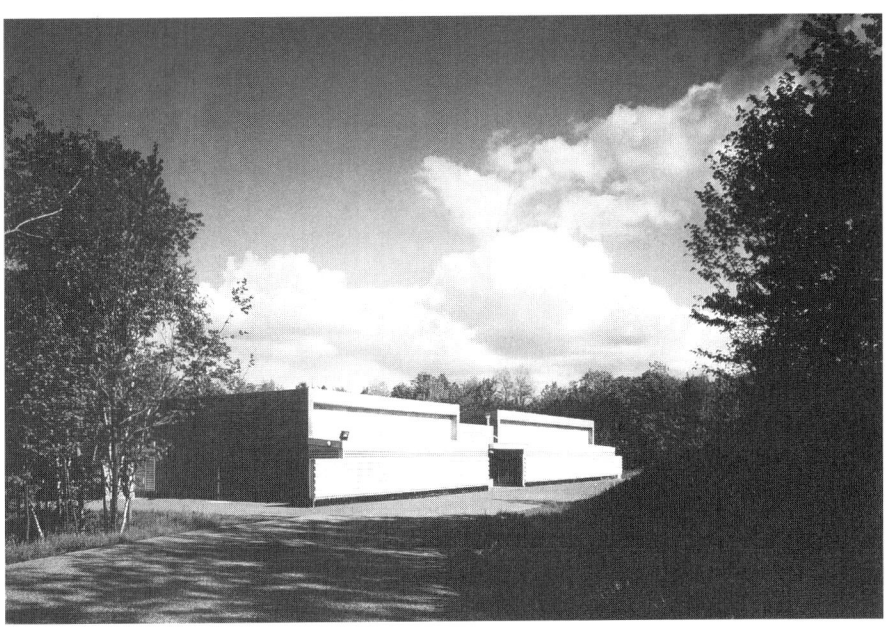

An exterior view of Building #2 (the nitrate vaults) at The Museum of Modern Art's Celeste Bartos Center for Film Preservation in Hamlin, Pennsylvania.

The Museum of Modern Art, New York.

531

The US Postal Service picked up the slack on Griffith with a fine stamp, and has gone on to issue first-class portraits of Marilyn Monroe, Elvis Presley, Humphrey Bogart, and Alfred Hitchcock. There will be a major campaign for Miss Lillian beginning on the 10th aniversary of her death, in 2003, when the rules deem her career eligible for the postal board's consideration.

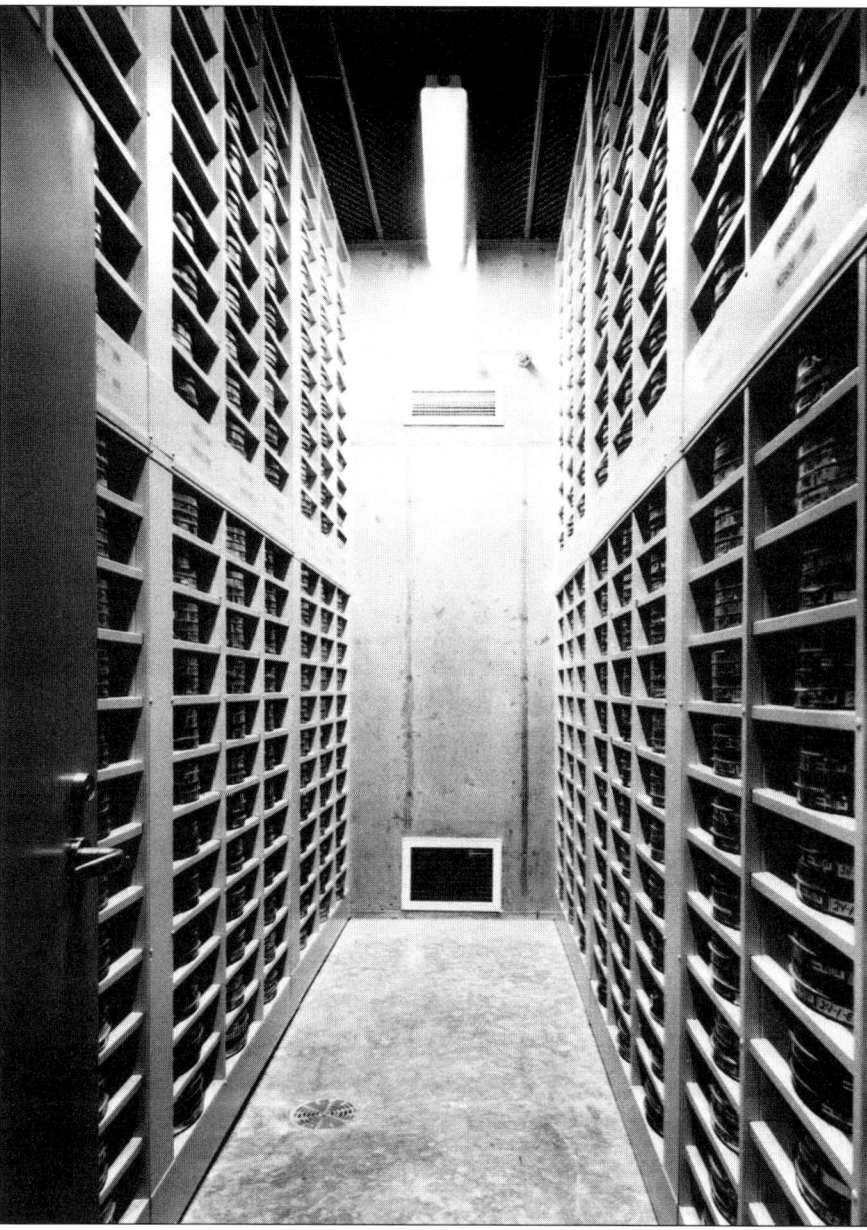

Interior of typical nitrate vault in Building #2 of the Celeste Bartos Center.
The Museum of Modern Art, New York.

These efforts, while addressing the importance of honoring various pioneers and artists of the motion picture, haven't properly done the job in celebrating the bright luminous flower that earned many of them their place in history. MoMA's Department of Film and Media has taken modest steps to correct this neglect. Traditionally, MoMA gratefully acknowledges its extraordinary Trustees, as at the Celeste Bartos Center for Film Preservation in Hamlin, Pennsylvania. Inside the Bartos Center, we have dedicated each "dedicated space" (i.e., every room or vault assigned for specific use) to the glories of nitrate by naming it after a nitrate film, and not just any nitrate title. This naming opportunity emerged during the hectic weeks of the relocation of MoMA's moving image materials during the dreadful winter of 1996, a bitterly cold and stormy March-April when snow and ice stalled deliveries, upset schedules, and frustrated our early return to the cosy warmth of midtown Manhattan. It was, however, a climate entirely supportive of the transfer of some 18,000 cans of nitrate, safely and smoothly packed, delivered, unpacked, labeled, and shelved in fire-retardant units inside temperature and humidity-controlled vaults built precisely to NFPA40 Code.

The idea to name the vaults came about one gray snowy day, after we exchanged pleasantries and exclamations upon opening cans of Biograph negatives and looked at stunning black-and-white images on remarkably sharp nitrate stock. What a thrill it was! And so a footnote to MoMA's Biograph preservation program was devised. The Biograph nitrate materials were acquired by the 4-year-old MoMA Film Library in 1939, when some 1,000 titles were "salvaged from the mouldering Biograph studio" in the Bronx. We would celebrate the survival of these nitrate negatives by titling each room and vault with, here and there, a title that made reference to function or contents, and we would include the titles of films featuring our favorite Biograph actresses.

The American Mutoscope and Biograph Company, which had begun production in 1896, struggled with the Edison Company in the fiercely competitive early years of production. One-reel dramas and comedies were dispatched to theatres from the New York studios in Manhattan and the Bronx as well as from its Los Angeles studio. In 1909 its name was abbreviated to the Biograph Company, and production continued until the studio closed in 1916. D W Griffith joined Biograph in 1908, directing or supervising up to three one-reelers a week through 1913. Three of his starring actresses, Mary Pickford, Blanche Sweet, and Lillian Gish, were supportive of the film archives at MoMA, the Library of Congress, and George Eastman House. At Lillian Gish's instigation, Griffith donated to MoMA 19 of his features and his production records. Mary Pickford hosted a reception for MoMA at Pickfair in 1935, at which Iris Barry pitched the idea of a museum film collection to a receptive audience of Hollywood's top film-makers. Blanche Sweet and Lillian Gish, both dearly loved for many years by all at MoMA, often introduced screenings of their films in our theatres, and prior to her death at 99, in 1993, Miss Gish established the Lillian Gish Trust to include support for the restoration of the Biograph Collection.

The Bartos Center comprises two buildings. The Main Building houses non-nitrate films, videos, posters, stills, rare books, manuscripts, and documents in 16 large vaults, as well as conditioning, inspection, and cataloguing rooms, receiving and shipping, offices, conference room and staff lounge. Building No. 2 stores nitrate films in 34 vaults. We decided no space was too insignificant to merit a title or two. Labels were designed using the Biograph Company logo AB as the background of the labels in the Main Building, and the Biograph eagle for the background of the nitrate vault labels. As an aid to the local Fire Department, each vault carries a number preceded by a letter indicating its floor, A (upper) or B (lower) in the Main Building, and N in Building No. 2. What follows is the complete list of each Biograph film title and its dedicated space.

MAIN BUILDING

Title	Dedicated Space
The Goddess of Sagebrush Gulch	Conference Room
All on Account of the Milk	Staff Lounge
Those Awful Hats	Coat Closet
A Mix-Up in Raincoats	Coat Closet
As the Bells Rang Out!	Main Entrance
The Way of Man	Gents
Just Like a Woman	Ladies
A Blot in the 'Scutcheon	Maintenance
The Plumber's Picnic	Maintenance
In the Aisles of the Wild	Office of Vault Manager (an avid fisherman)
Fools of Fate	Office of Building Manager and Assistant
If They Only Knew	Main Work Room
The Camera Fiend No. 1	Inspection
The Recreation of an Heiress	Cataloguing
The Adventures of Dollie	Receiving & Shipping
The Open Gate	Delivery Entrance
Caught by Wireless	Cleaning/Electrical
Just Kids	Unisex Bathroom
The Musketeers of Pig Alley	Conditioning Vault A01, Main Entrance
At the Crossroads of Life	Conditioning Vault A01, North Entrance
The Road to Yesterday	Conditioning Vault A01, South Entrance
The Power of the Camera	Vault A02
A Troublesome Satchel	Vault A03
Won Through a Medium	Vault A04
And Her Name Was Maude	Vault A05
The Battle at Elderbush Gulch	Vault A06
Betrayed by a Handprint	Vault A07
In a Hempen Bag	Vault A08
Dyed but Not Dead	Vault A09
He's a Lawyer	Vault A10
What Is the Use of Repining?	Vault A11
A Dash Through the Clouds	Vault A12
Through His Wife's Picture	Vault A13
A Misappropriated Turkey	Vault A14
A String of Pearls	Vault A15
Not So Bad As It Seemed	Vault A16
A Delivery Package	Vault A17
At the Road's End	Main Floor Stairwell
A Corner in Wheat	Main Floor Elevator
The Rise and Fall of McDoo	Lower Level Elevator
The Lonedale Operator	Elevator Maintenance
Their One Good Suit	Vault B01
The Painted Lady	Vault B02
Out from the Shadow	Vault B03
Bobby's Kodak	Vault B04
The Trail of Books	Paper Materials, Vault B05, North Entrance
Yale Laundry	Paper Materials, Vault B05, South Entrance
The Game of Freeze Out	Mechanical Room, North Entrance
Through the Breakers	Mechanical Room, South Entrance

BUILDING No. 2

Title	Dedicated Space
The Lady and the Mouse	Inspection
His New Lid	Maintenance
One-Round O'Brien	Mechanical Room
His Trust	East Corridor, Entrance
His Trust Fulfilled	West Corridor, Entrance
Mr. Bragg, a Fugitive	Vault B01
When Kings Were the Law	Vault B02
A Foul and Fearful Plot	Vault B03
A Smoked Husband	Vault B04
The Sweat-Box	Vault B05
The Feud and the Turkey	Vault B06
The Trimmers Trimmed	Vault B07
An Unseen Enemy	Vault B08
A Knot in the Plot	Vault B09
Nursing a Viper	Vault B10
Ashes of Inspiration	Vault B11
Over Silent Paths	Vault B12
The Dancing Girl of Butte	Vault B13
A Salutary Lesson	Vault B14
Chocolate Dynamite	Vault B15
The Influence of the Unknown	Vault B16
Never Again	Vault B17
The Deadly Cheroot	Vault B18
"Got a Match?"	Vault B19
The Tragedy of a Dress Suit	Vault B20
A Beast at Bay	Vault B21
Judith of Bethulia	Vault B22
A Child's Impulse	Vault B23
The Mothering Heart	Vault B24
What Drink Did	Vault B25
One Is Business; the Other Crime	Vault B26
The Lonely Villa	Vault B27
Won by a Fish	Vault B28
In the Days of '49	Vault B29
Oh, What a Boob!	Vault B30
The Mender of Nets	Vault B31
The Dream of the Race-Track Fiend	Vault B32
Oil and Water	Vault B33
Professional Jealousy	Vault B34

Vault Farce

by Kevin Brownlow

Author's Note: This is an extract from an unpublished manuscript about Chaplin, written in 1989 and revised especially for this volume. Some of the material whose discovery is described in this text was later featured in the 1983 series The Unknown Chaplin, *made for Thames Television by Kevin Brownlow and David Gill.*

The greatest archival discovery I was ever involved in occurred by accident. David Gill and I were hard at work on a series about the American silent film for Thames Television (*Hollywood*, first broadcast in 1980). We were engrossed in trying to write the script for the comedy episode when David threw down his pen and said it was impossible to plan unless we had some idea of what Chaplin material we could use. The Chaplin rights were controlled by one of the most implacable and unhelpful men in the business, and he made it plain there was no hope. Our rivals, the BBC, had the rights for several more years. We had written to Chaplin, who was then still alive, but had had no reply. David Robinson, Chaplin's future biographer, offered a ray of hope; he advised us to try Chaplin's business manager, Rachel Ford. This we did, and one day she telephoned us and invited us down to the vaults at Denham Laboratories. She said she had authorisation to find for us "a snippet". I did not know how "a snippet" was going to save our comedy episode. When we entered the vault, I was initially disappointed; the cans were all brand-new and marked with the familiar titles. Suddenly, my eye fell on something unfamiliar. It turned out there was a small pile of films which had never been released. Miss Ford allowed us to see them – and to our astonishment we saw the opening to *City Lights*, cut before the 1931 premiere.

We got our "snippet" – plus a few other morsels. But we knew we had to do something with this material ... one day.

And then David mentioned the find to Raymond Rohauer.

I knew Rohauer to be unscrupulous, and had banned the *Hollywood* team from having anything to do with him. David pointed out that he had much to offer, and he was no worse than the people who ran other film collections – and there was no answer to that. David used to have dinner with him once a month. Rohauer wouldn't talk to me because I was a collector, and therefore tainted. David was clean. At one of these meetings David mentioned the Chaplin find, and Rohauer reacted as if shot. "How many cans?", he asked. David estimated 30-40.

"Is that all? I've got more than that."

"More than that of what?"

"Chaplin material that hasn't been seen before."

"Why didn't you tell us?"

And Rohauer came out with his favourite line: "You didn't ask."

He explained he had rescued the rushes to the Mutual comedies when, in 1952, Chaplin had been barred from returning to the US and much of his footage had been consigned to the incinerator.

There was only one problem. Miss Ford had spent most of her years with Chaplin suing Raymond Rohauer. How would we persuade Miss Ford to co-operate on the same programme? "The legal documents fill cupboards," she told us, when we tentatively suggested the idea. "I would never allow the two names to appear together without a v. between them."

Rohauer revealed to David that most of the film had been squirreled away, with the connivance of Henri Langlois, in vaults in various parts of France.

Rohauer admitted that he also had a lot of other material, apart from the Chaplin footage, stored in vaults in France. He suggested bringing it all over. "Then you'll have the Chaplin material here, wouldn't you?"

"Yes," thought David. "We'd also have a lot of stuff we weren't interested in." But any means were justified by the ends.

Now Rohauer wanted David to arrange trips to Paris for him. We all nodded sagely. "He's just stringing you along for free flights to France."

"Maybe," said David. "We've got to take the risk."

Rohauer's Channel-hopping went on for four months. Things we all hoped would happen didn't. The person he was to meet wasn't there, or was sick, or the car broke down. Alibis that fitted our scenario of suspicion.

But David was more than tenacious – he was relentless. Long after ordinary mortals would have given up in disgust he continued to meet Rohauer, to accept his excuses, to advance him money, and to put up with his midnight telephone calls. Above all, he treated him like a friend, and I'm sure it was this quality that kept Rohauer going. For the experience must have been humiliating – knowing the material was there, but being sabotaged by those who were supposed to be safeguarding it. On one occasion, when we all thought we were on the brink of D-Day, David hired a van to meet Rohauer near Lyons. The van got hopelessly lost, Rohauer had to leave for Paris, and the van's owner, Freight Bond, billed us for three times the agreed amount!

One morning, David and editor Trevor Waite set off at the crack of dawn to meet a vehicle coming off the boat at Newhaven. I was frustrated to be left out of this adventure, but Rohauer's instructions were clear; at almost every meeting, he had raised the matter of the *Sunday Times* article, which he was convinced I had written under John Baxter's name.[1]

When the boat docked, the vehicle was delayed by customs. David and Trevor sat for four hours. "My apprehension and distrust were at their height," said David. "And then I met the driver. He had one eye, which never really looked at you. He was a parody of Robert Newton as Long John Silver. 'You should have been with me the last few days,' he chortled. 'I've seen things. I've been to garages and barns and chateaux. I don't know what you'll make of it all. They're all rusty cans. Hundreds of 'em. Look at my hands. Can't get it off.'"

He warned David not to try to rush the customs, otherwise they would make trouble. As it happened, the customs were within their rights to make a fuss on this occasion – because the truck contained enough nitrate to blow the customs sheds out of Newhaven harbour. Highly inflammable in its normal state, nitrate becomes more dangerous as it decomposes. And one could safely assume a lot of this material was in an unstable condition!

"Ours was the last van to go through," said David. "The back was unlocked and wound up and there was pile upon pile of cans, of varying degrees of rust, spreading to the far back of this enormous van. They had started about ten high, but had been knocked about en route. The van was a mosaic of ancient film cans. The customs man groaned. 'Jesus Christ,' he said. 'What are we going to do with all this?' He looked at the list and then clambered up and tried to identify the titles. He wasn't going to release us until he had identified every title on his inventory. The idea of nitrate hadn't occurred to him."

"We negotiated that if he could find ten titles on the list, that would be enough. He was clearly beginning to lose interest. A crowd had gathered round the van, saying, 'Blue movies then, is it?' We found those ten titles, he ticked off his list with relief, and cleared us through. But we still had this problem with the one-eyed driver. Was he going to disappear with the precious cans? He was. 'My instructions are that Mr Rohauer will meet us at the vaults tomorrow. So I'll take the van to the yard – it's a lockup, so it'll be all right.'"

"I thought, 'That's a good one. Should we follow him?' But I said, 'Fine. Here's the address of the vaults.'"

"To avoid another night of tension, I rang Rohauer and he confirmed the story. In fact, looking back, everything was absolutely straight and aboveboard – as far as it could be in such a cloak-and-dagger operation. All the little hitches had been genuine hitches."

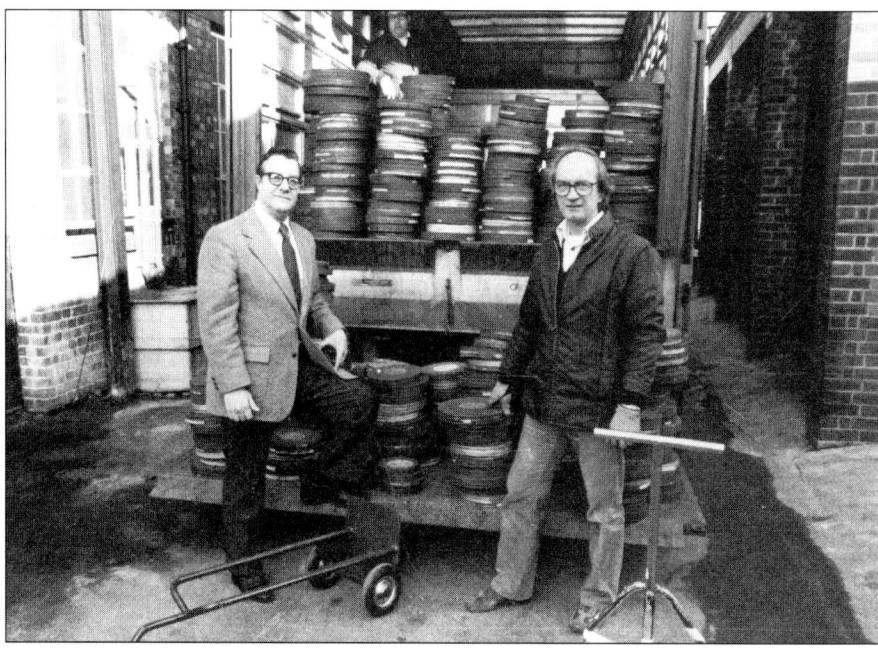

The "souvenir photograph" of Raymond Rohauer (on left) and David Gill with the van-load of Chaplin material.

Kevin Brownlow Collection.

It was a miserably cold February morning when the huge vehicle drove up to the vaults at Perivale, to be met by David, Trevor, and Raymond Rohauer. An assistant from Thames, Malcolm Newnam, had been press-ganged into helping, too. David got him to take a souvenir photograph of them all, lined up in front of the cans, frozen but proud.

"Only then did it really begin to hit me," said David. "We were sorting out the cans and we had decided that all the Chaplins would go in one vault, and all the rest into another. There were piles and piles of cans – 30, 40, 50 cans just labelled *The Immigrant* … 20, 30, 40 cans *Behind the Screen* … 30, 40, 50, 60 cans *The Cure*. And then: 'Oh, we've only got six cans of *The Vagabond*.' Tragic! We were soon in the kind of state where anything less than 30 or 40 cans for one title was a major disappointment."

"I thought to myself, wait till Kevin hears about this! He had said, 'look inside the cans,' and that was the next thing. They were very rusty, of course, and it was hard to get them open with freezing hands. But it was amazing – it was all nitrate negative – not positive, but negative, most of it in perfect condition, just as it had come out of the camera 64 years ago. I think Raymond was as surprised, and relieved, as we were. Some of it had gone – there was practically nothing of *Easy Street* or *The Vagabond*. But most of it was as good as the day it was born."

"A lot of the film was not Chaplin. Raymond was able to say: 'That is – that's not.'"

"Then there was the enormous task of organising it all. How do you go about collating it? How can there be 50 cans of *The Immigrant*? What could be in those cans? Our next task was to view the material."

David arranged with Colour Film Services – a nearby laboratory – to hire us some space at their Perivale plant, and we shipped in our Steenbeck. This viewing machine, made in Germany, was fitted with special smaller sprockets to enable it to accept ancient shrunken nitrate.

On the morning of 12 February 1981, a Nova hire car picked me up and drove me to the Mayfair Hotel, where I met Raymond Rohauer. For two people who had been at each others' throats for so many years, we survived the journey to Perivale in surprisingly agreeable spirits.

When we reached the laboratory, we discovered that no one had heard of us, and no one was expecting us. There was no sign of David or Trevor, so Raymond began to have the uneasy feeling we had come to the wrong place. I fired "Thames Television" at everyone in sight, but there was no glimmer of recognition from anyone.

It is strange how often this happens; you make arrangements for an important event, and somehow you imagine the people at the other end of the phone are infected with the same degree of enthusiasm. It is deflating – and, I suppose, salutary – to discover that they have no interest either in your project or in you.

Raymond and I sat in the canteen sipping tea, waiting for David and Trevor. It was such a red-letter day, I could not imagine them wanting to miss a minute of it. But they were quite incredibly late, due to severe traffic jams. Rohauer and I discussed the Chaplin material, how he found it and whether the story could ever be told.

Our viewing area was a bleak corner, at the end of a corridor of offices. The Steenbeck had been trundled in, and connected up, and all seemed ready.

Eventually, David and Trevor turned up, with assistant editor Malcolm Newnam, who brought in a pile of cans. We eagerly clustered around the machine as Trevor laced it up and very gently eased the Steenbeck forward. The first can we chose because it was marked "Camera test" – was this the Lita Grey screen test which

Rohauer had promised? It was in perfect condition, but it was not Lita Grey – it was Georgia Hale doing the final scene for *City Lights*. The film appeared on the ground-glass viewing screen, and although we all knew it was a negative, we somehow expected a positive image to leap before our eyes. It was bewildering to see black where there should be whites, and white where there should be blacks. Watching negative requires an adjustment of the eyes.

Before we were able to achieve this, a smell hit our nostrils – a powerful and alarming smell.

This is a stage in the decomposition of nitrate, which is a complex mixture. We could hear the first section coming – a sticky sound, as though we were slowly unwinding a roll of Sellotape.

Just as the picture began to make sense to our untrained eyes, and we began to thrill to the first proof of our discovery, unsightly blobs appeared, like the evidence of migraine. The picture was soon bombarded by these blobs, to the accompaniment of the violent sticky noise, until it was overwhelmed, and the only visible evidence were dancing shapes, the sort of thing Norman McLaren used to do in his cartoons.

The spacing inserted between the takes seemed mainly responsible – it was probably cheap stock, which deteriorated before the rest, but took some of it with it. One could also see evidence of an interaction between the metal can and the celluloid. On a badly decomposed shot the film would jam in the gate and a pile of brown dust spread everywhere. But what amazed us was how little decomposition had taken place, and how smoothly the 65-year-old negative went through.

Notes

1. This was an exposé by John Baxter, published under the title "The Silent Empire of Raymond Rohauer" in the *Sunday Times* (London) on 19 January 1975, which Rohauer was convinced I had written, and for which he never forgave me.

The Legend of the Earth Vault

by Paolo Cherchi Usai

Sometime in 1972, film curator James Card took a decision that was destined to become a legend in the world of moving image archives. A total of 3,045 reels of nitrate film, amounting to 2,588,250 feet of flammable stock, were buried in the garden of George Eastman House as an extreme measure in response to the lack of storage space in the Henry A Strong Archives, the museum's repository for the most venerable portion of its motion picture collections. I first heard of the episode when I was hired in 1989 as Assistant Curator at GEH, and it did not take much to realise it was all true. Even today, the area in which the films were buried appears as a slight bump in an otherwise even surface, where the grass is greener than elsewhere. The term "Earth Vault" (as it was called at the time) was commonly used by staff members to indicate the place where hundreds of inaccessible films were held. Cataloguing cards make mention of this strangely evocative term in the upper right corner designated for the location code. There is even an inventory list of the holdings, typewritten with flawless precision and religiously kept in the Motion Picture Department files.

When interviewed a few years later by Penelope Houston for her book *Keepers of the Frame*, I had no hesitation in telling her the whole story. There was no reason to keep it as a secret. It was history, after all. Yet her introduction to the book describes the episode without mentioning the place or names, nor the date of that amazing occurrence.[1] I think she did not believe me. It must have seemed so outlandish to her that its perversely romantic undertones were the invention of a demented storyteller; if so, then it would be better to keep it as such – the archivist's ultimate nightmare.

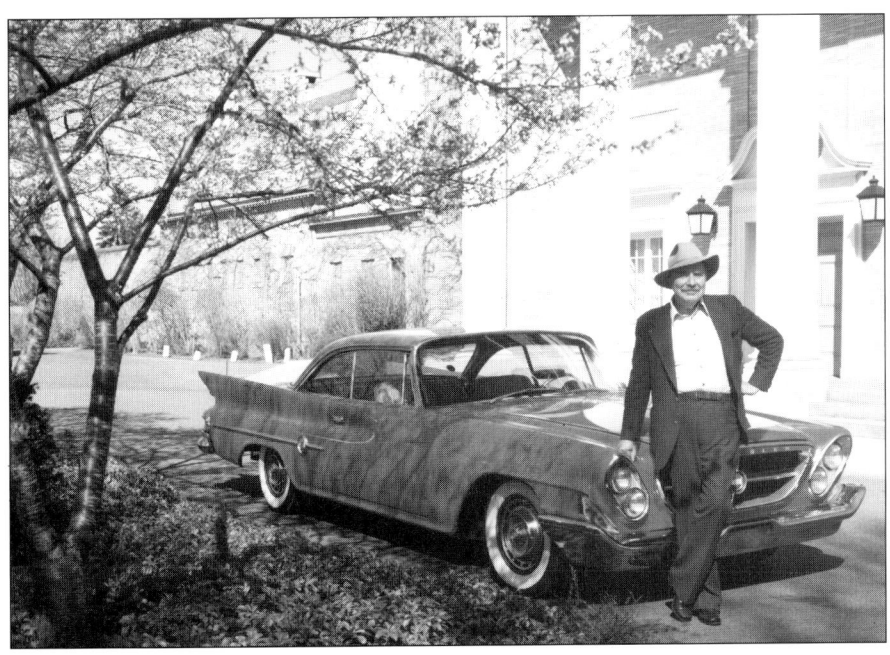

James Card, founding film curator of George Eastman House, in front of the museum's Dryden Theatre, ca. 1965.

George Eastman House, Rochester, NY.

Yet the facts are there: the papers, the cards, that bump on the lawn. There's even an official 1982 annual report, describing the event as a matter of course. When the gardeners helped to open the massive grave of images on celluloid several years later (of course there was nothing left but tiny shreds of metal containers), the revelation made the headlines of the local newspapers. It was not so much the loss of a portion of film heritage that mattered to them, as the environmental issue: a "team of experts" visited the site, then concluded that there was no potential harm to humans. Nitrate film is a great fertilizer. Even museum docents talk about it to the tourists in search of spicy anecdotes: "That's where George Eastman shot himself... That's where explosive movies were hidden." Visitors seem unimpressed, presumably because they do not know much about cold storage, or because of the seemingly unfathomable motives surrounding a resolution so inherently bizarre in its nature, so incomprehensible by today's standards. They, too, probably do not believe the tour guides.

James Card has sadly died in the interval between my writing this article and its publication. But at the time of writing he was still alive. He was, however, at age 87, confined to a wheelchair in a hospital near Rochester, still suffering from the consequences of a stroke he had several years earlier. He could express himself only with extreme difficulty, and I was not going to ask him the reasons behind the facts. Why should I? Jim was struggling for his life, and the films were gone, and nothing would bring them back.

The facts are known. Fortunately for us, the first thing we know is that most of the reels had been duplicated before the burial, or are held by other institutions. We know that Card had received most of the films from Metro-Goldwyn-Mayer. We know he tried to put them in storage with Kodak when it became apparent that there was no room in the vaults. We know that Kodak rejected them, thus forcing Card to find another repository for them within 24 hours. We know that he made his decision without the knowledge of the museum's director, Van Deren Coke. We also have a key witness. Seymour Neusbaum, the now-retired head of security and maintenance who helped Card to create the nitrate enclave under two feet of soil, is still around, and can give you all the details of the ceremony – the size of the excavated area; the plastic bags wrapped around each can, in the assumption they would protect the reels under the ground; the curator's assurance that such a procedure was meant to be temporary; snippets of nitrate film coming to the surface together with the growing grass: culture and nature being periodically trimmed by the lawnmower.

Details such as these deserve no further scrutiny. If there is a mystery worth solving, then it is the persistence of the gossip according to which Card implemented his plan after a suggestion from the Cinémathèque Française's guru Henri Langlois. Langlois is said to have reassured his colleague about the safety of the plan in unequivocal terms. According to long-term GEH employees, Langlois told Card that "There's nothing better than Nature". No evidence, however, has so far been found to support the use of the quotation marks. There are hundreds of folders and thousands of carbon-copy letters in the Department's files under the Card heading. They are not inventoried, and no one has ever dared look through them. Who knows? Maybe those words were never written. Maybe they were pronounced over the phone, or in a casual conversation at a FIAF conference. Maybe they were never said. Maybe it was Card himself who made up the whole thing, very much in accord with his brilliantly elusive personality, his strategic yet consuming love for convoluted stratagems and misleading innuendos.

Years after listening to these mysterious relics of a lost oral tradition of film archiving, I told the late Alain Marchand (who knew Henri Langlois well, and worked with him for several years) about everything I had heard concerning the Card-Langlois conspiracy over the Earth Vault. Marchand vehemently denied the allegations, and almost looked offended by what he must have taken as a tactless *jeu d'esprit.* "Henri would never have said that. Who told you such a thing?" he would argue, as if I were trying to blemish the image of a fondly remembered hero. Alain could not care less about the actual goal of my inquiry – just trying to understand. I must have been young and reckless, still under the illusion that truth will come out of a simple question, and prevail over ignorance as easily as dust is blown away from the cover of a book.

So, for the last time: who knows what was in Card's mind when those cans were slowly disappearing under the fresh soil? He was then a lover of cinema, wasn't he? He saved countless treasures of the moving image, didn't he? So why did he do that? I eventually gave up asking all these questions when I started to feel like the unworthy censor of a past which never belonged to me and which I have no right to judge. Some day, what I thought were my own sound curatorial decisions will be perceived to be just as inexplicable as those made by Card himself. Thirty years from now, someone may look at my own past and wonder how "something like that" could have happened. I shall not be there to apologise to posterity. Even if I were, it would probably be too difficult to explain. There were reasons for Card. I am sure I will have had plenty of reasons, too. Then and now, there is the same anxiety in the effort to save moving images, with very much the same ambitions, the same limitations, the same mistakes each generation inherits from its predecessors, the same determination not to repeat them. That is how we have built our sense of history.

Notes

1. Penelope Houston, *Keepers of the Frame* (London: BFI Publishing, 1994).

Waiting for *Arirang*

by Hong-taek Chung

Among Korean cineastes, the most sought-after "lost" film in their national cinematography is *Arirang*, made in 1926, at the height of the silent film era, by director Na Woon-Kyu. This legendary Korean film tells the story of Youngjin, a philosophy student who is driven crazy by the attempted rape of his sister and kills her attacker with a sickle. As he is arrested and sent to jail, the villagers bid him farewell by singing "Arirang", a traditional Korean folksong. The film accurately reflected both the racial and class discrimination rife in the Japanese-occupied Korea of the 1920s, with a cast of social types including landowners, tenant farmers, secret police, intellectuals, women ridiculed for their class and poverty, etc. *Arirang* is hailed as a production that placed Korean cinema on a level with artistic film production anywhere else in the world at that period. However, this classic film has not been seen in its native country for several generations.

A tantalising glimpse: reproduction of a newsprint still from the lost film *Arirang* (1926).
Korean Film Archive, Seoul.

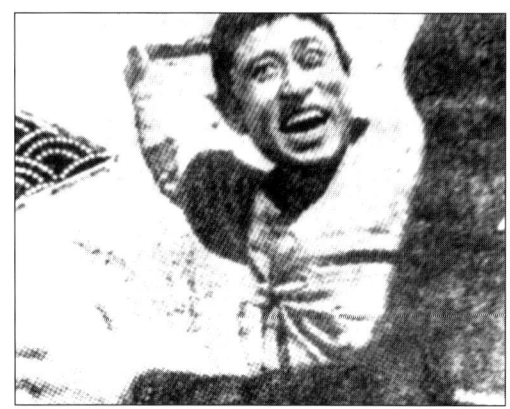

In the late 1980s and 1990s, therefore, considerable interest was naturally aroused in the Korean press by reports that a copy of *Arirang* was in the possession of a Japanese collector called Mr Abe Yoshishige. According to Mr Abe, the print was one of more than 60 films which he had inherited from his father, Dr Abe Dey. The family maintained that Dr Abe had worked as a doctor for the Japanese colonial administration in Korea, and that he had been given the films as tokens of gratitude from former patients. Others suggested, however, that the Abe family had been employed as chemical engineers during the Pacific War, and that it would be more plausible to suppose that the prints had originally been among the film material requisitioned by the Japanese Imperial Army for re-use in the manufacture of munitions during World War II. It is known that a very large number of British and American film prints were rounded up for this purpose in 1940, and it seemed inevitable that prints from Korea and Manchuria would have suffered the same fate.

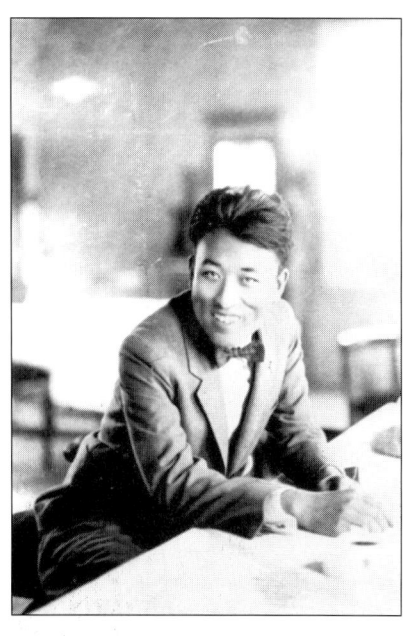

Na Woon-Kyu, director of *Arirang*.
Korean Film Archive, Seoul.

Since the existence of the print was first reported in 1985, a number of Korean individuals and pressure groups have been lobbying Mr Abe for the return of *Arirang*. One such campaign had the goal of making the film available for a screening in 1996 at the Pusan International Film Festival or elsewhere, on the 70th anniversary of its premiere and coinciding with worldwide celebrations of the centenary of cinema. Regrettably, all these efforts have so far come to nothing. Mr Abe has on occasion suggested that he would be willing to restore the print – once even suggesting that he would send copies simultaneously to Seoul and to Pyongyang – but at other times he has been wholly dismissive of such appeals, and his comments have occasionally seemed to suggest that he holds regrettably dismissive views of Korea and its people. In one report, he is alleged to have said that "he didn't collect and preserve *Arirang* just so he can hand it back to Korea," and that he could not understand "why Korea holds so strong a grudge against Japan, when Japan doesn't hold any grudge against the USA even though Japan lost the war to them". On another occasion, he is reported to have said: "Na Woon-Kyu may be a national hero in Korea but is a traitor to Japan."

Of course, through all this period, no certain information has emerged about exactly what material is held by Mr Abe, or what condition it is in.

More recently, it has been urged in Korea that the issue should be taken up between the Korean and Japanese governments. Meanwhile, Mr Abe has reportedly said that he would not return the film "unless it is the wish of the Emperor", but he has also said that "he would give the print when Korea is united" and that "he would send the print with the Emperor's visit to Korea during the 2002 World Cup Games". Perhaps there is room for hope that the story will still have a happy ending.[1]

Notes

1. Information and quotations for this article were derived from the following journalistic sources: "Regaining Our Lost Cinema", by Ahn Jung-Sook, in *Hankyorye Daily* (30 August 1995); "*Arirang* Still under the Japanese Occupation", by Kim So-Hee, in *Cine 21 Weekly* (19 September 1995); "The Movement to Regain *Arirang* Becomes a Quest for the Return of a 'National Cultural Treasure'", in *Chosunilbo* (1 October 1997).

Eternal Hope

by Carlos Roberto de Souza

During the second half of the 1970s (when I had been at the archive for just 2 or 3 years), I received a phone call. It was from an address near our premises. A family had recently moved to a house, and the former occupants had left a dozen film cans in the garage, with no labels or identification. What could they be?

My hopes rose. On occasions such as these I always hope I'll find one of the Brazilian classics lost along the path of our film history (Humberto Mauro's musicals, or some silent features known only by a title and newspaper advertisements). In less than half an hour I was at the door of the old man who had called me. He explained that the former occupant of the house was a lawyer, and that the film cans had been given to him as a kind of payment for one of his cases. When the lawyer moved, he left the cans, telling the old man that he was not interested in them, and thought they could be thrown away. But the old man had been informed by someone of the existence of a film archive, and decided to call us. Thank heaven! We took the cans, and I immediately examined them at a winding table. It was a nitrate copy of a sound feature film made in São Paulo in 1940 (the only feature film made in the city during a period of more than 10 years), ironically titled *Eterna Esperança* (Eternal Hope).

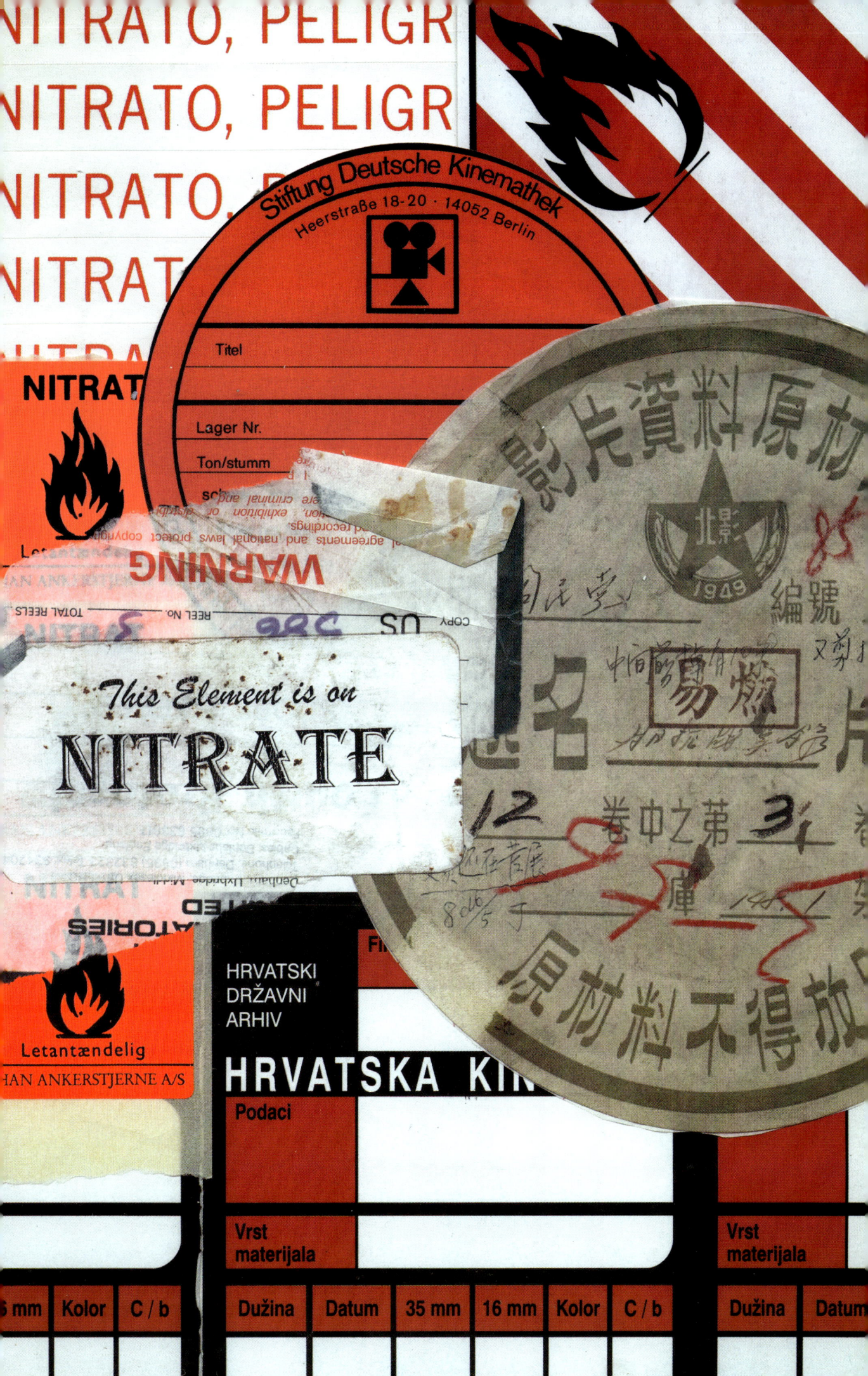

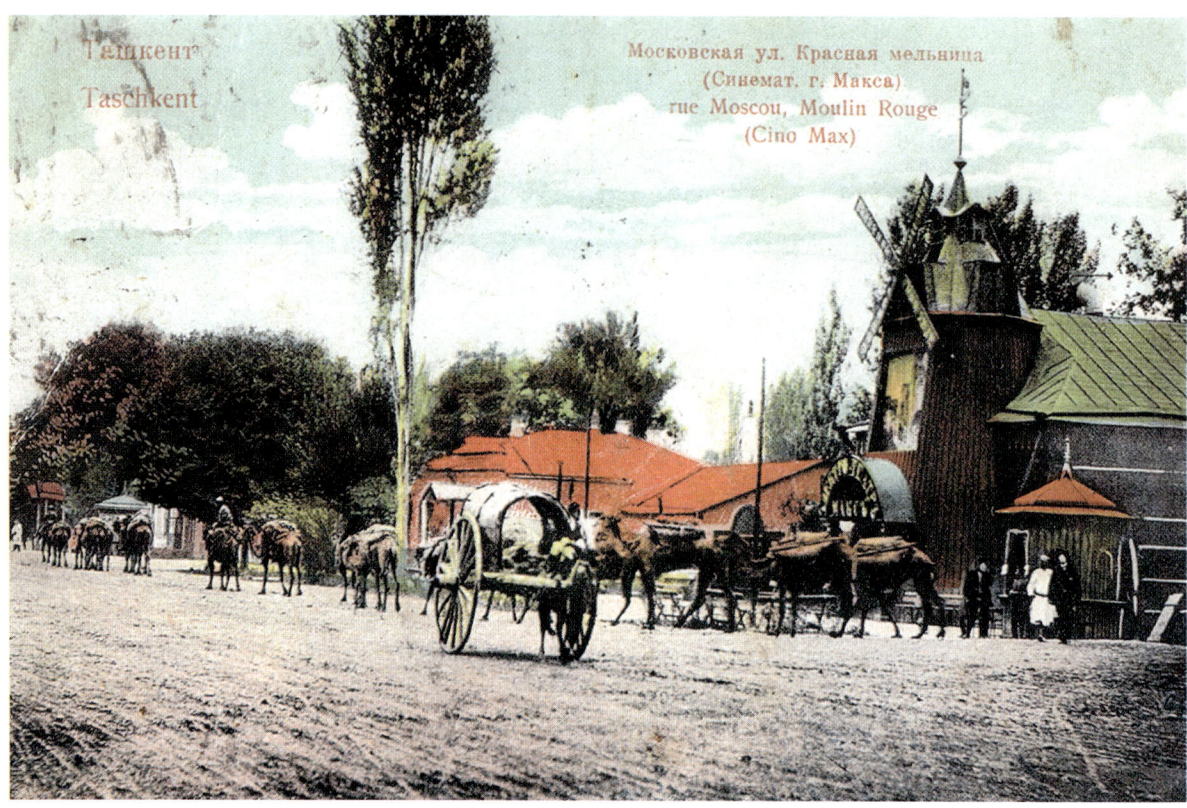

The Moulin-Rouge Electro-Theatre in Tashkent – see p.226.

David Robinson.

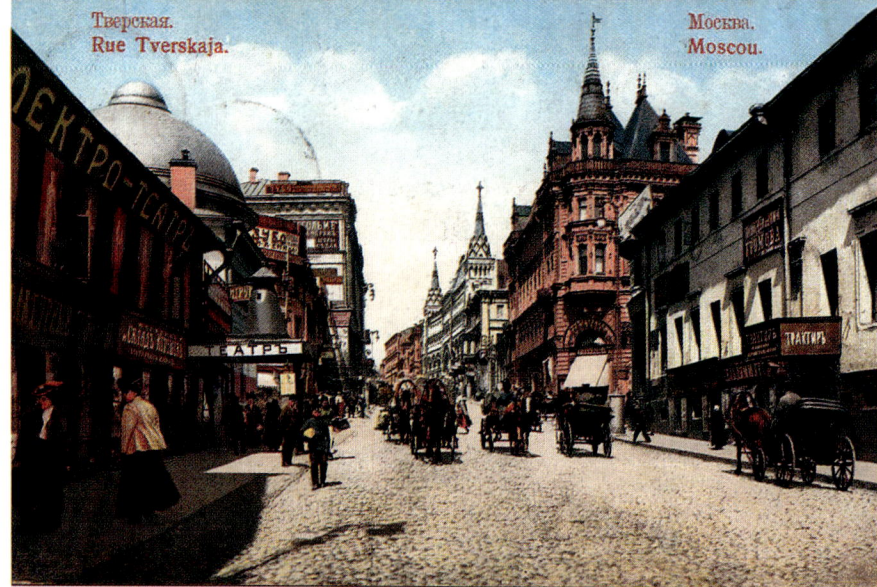

The "Moulin"(?) on Tverskaia Street, Moscow – see p.226.

David Robinson.

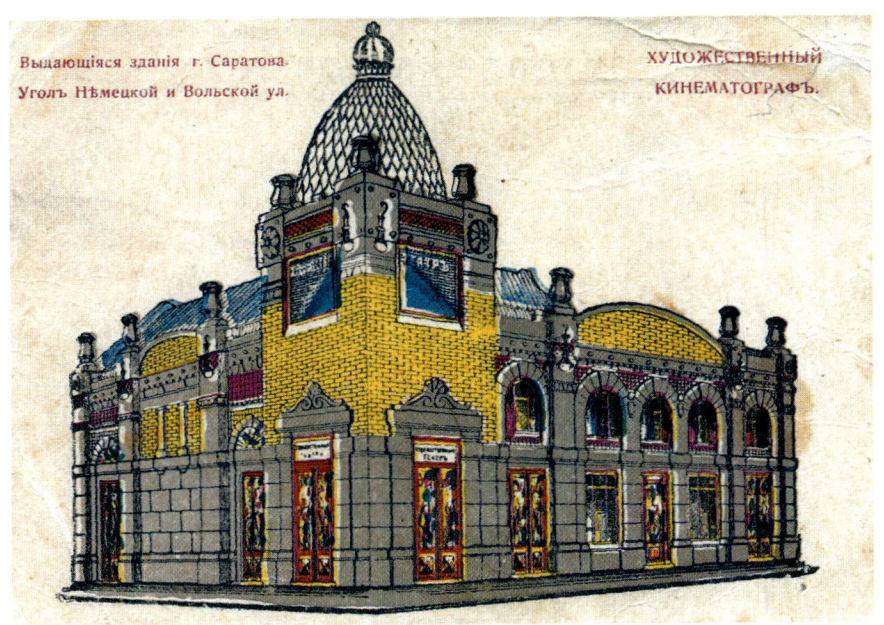

The "Art Kinematograph" in Saratov – see p.227.

David Robinson.

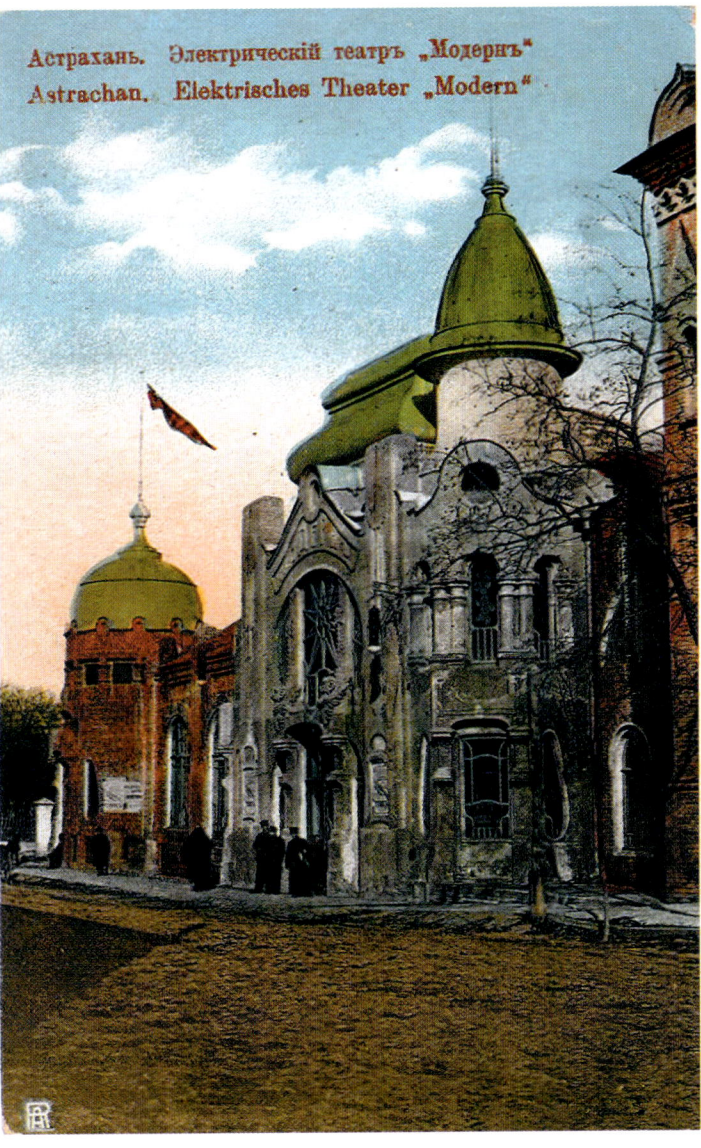

The "Modern" Electric Theatre, Astrakhan – see p.227.

David Robinson.

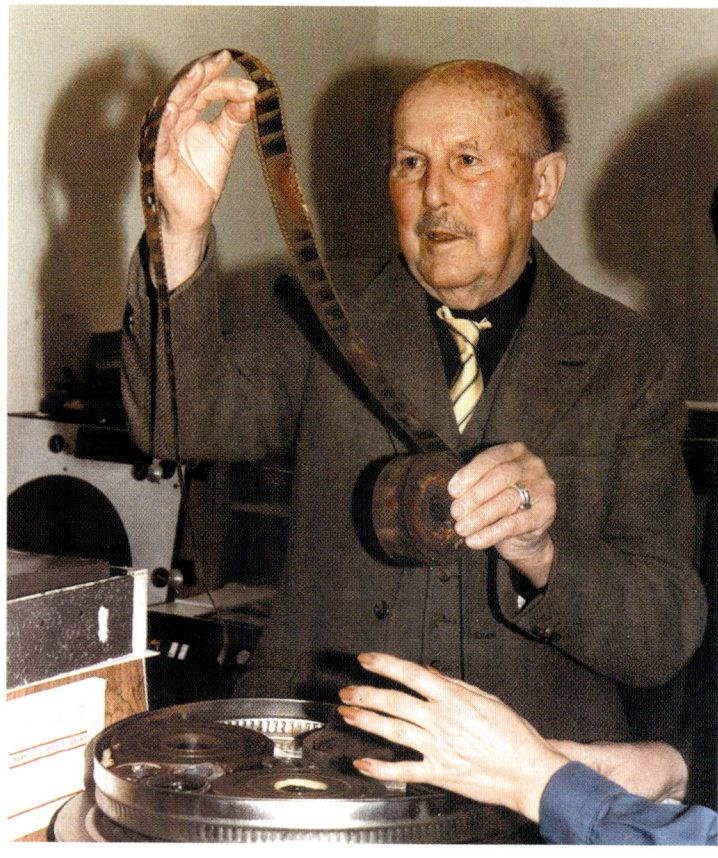

Michael Powell examines some deteriorating nitrate film at the National Film Archive, Berkhamsted – see p.337.

BFI Collections – Stills, Posters & Designs, London. 227597.

Frame enlargements from the film *Scenes from the Life of the World Famous Actress Sarah Bernhardt on the Island of Belle Isle* (ca. 1910) – see p.410.

Filmarchiv Austria, Vienna.

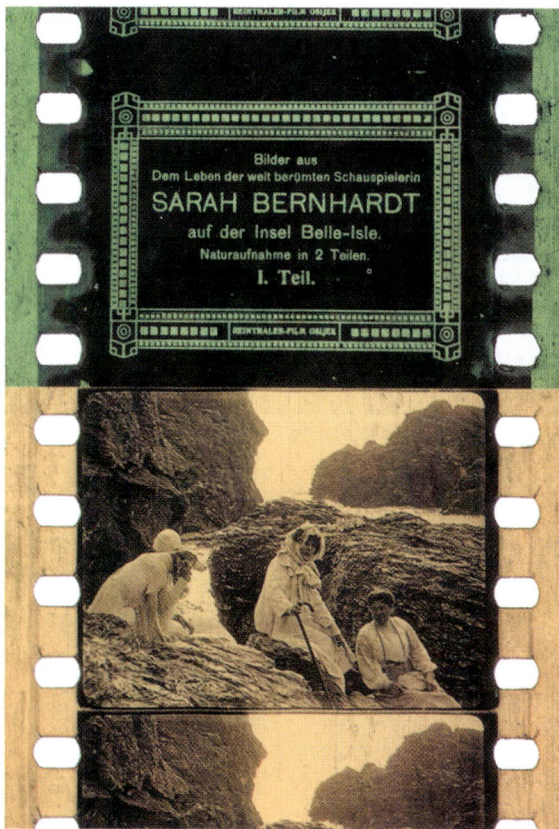

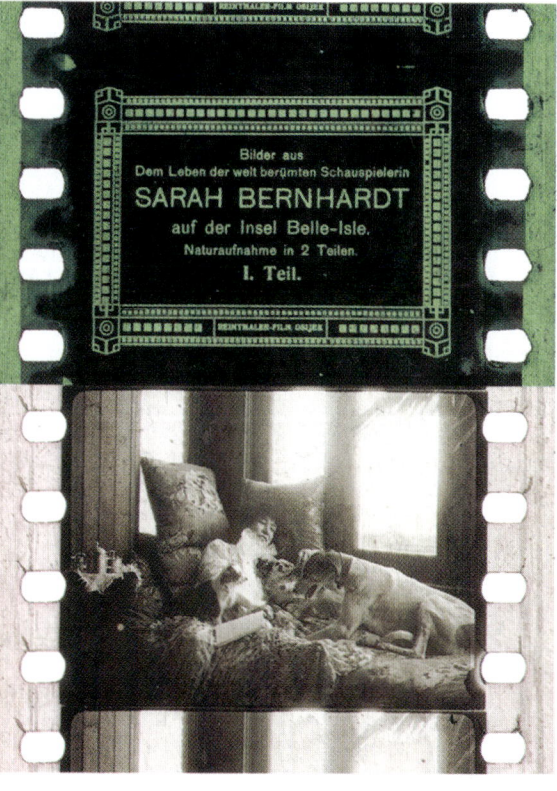

The front cover of an illustrated supplement published on 16 May 1897 by *Le Petit Journal* to report on the Bazar de la Charité fire – see p.431.

David Robinson.

Le Petit Journal

SUPPLÉMENT ILLUSTRÉ
Huit pages : CINQ centimes

Le Petit Journal
CHAQUE JOUR 5 CENTIMES
Le Supplément illustré
CHAQUE SEMAINE 5 CENTIMES

ABONNEMENTS

	SIX MOIS	UN AN
SEINE ET SEINE-ET-OISE	2 fr.	3 fr. 50
DÉPARTEMENTS	2 fr.	4 fr.
ÉTRANGER	250	5 fr.

huitième année   DIMANCHE 16 MAI 1897   Numéro 339

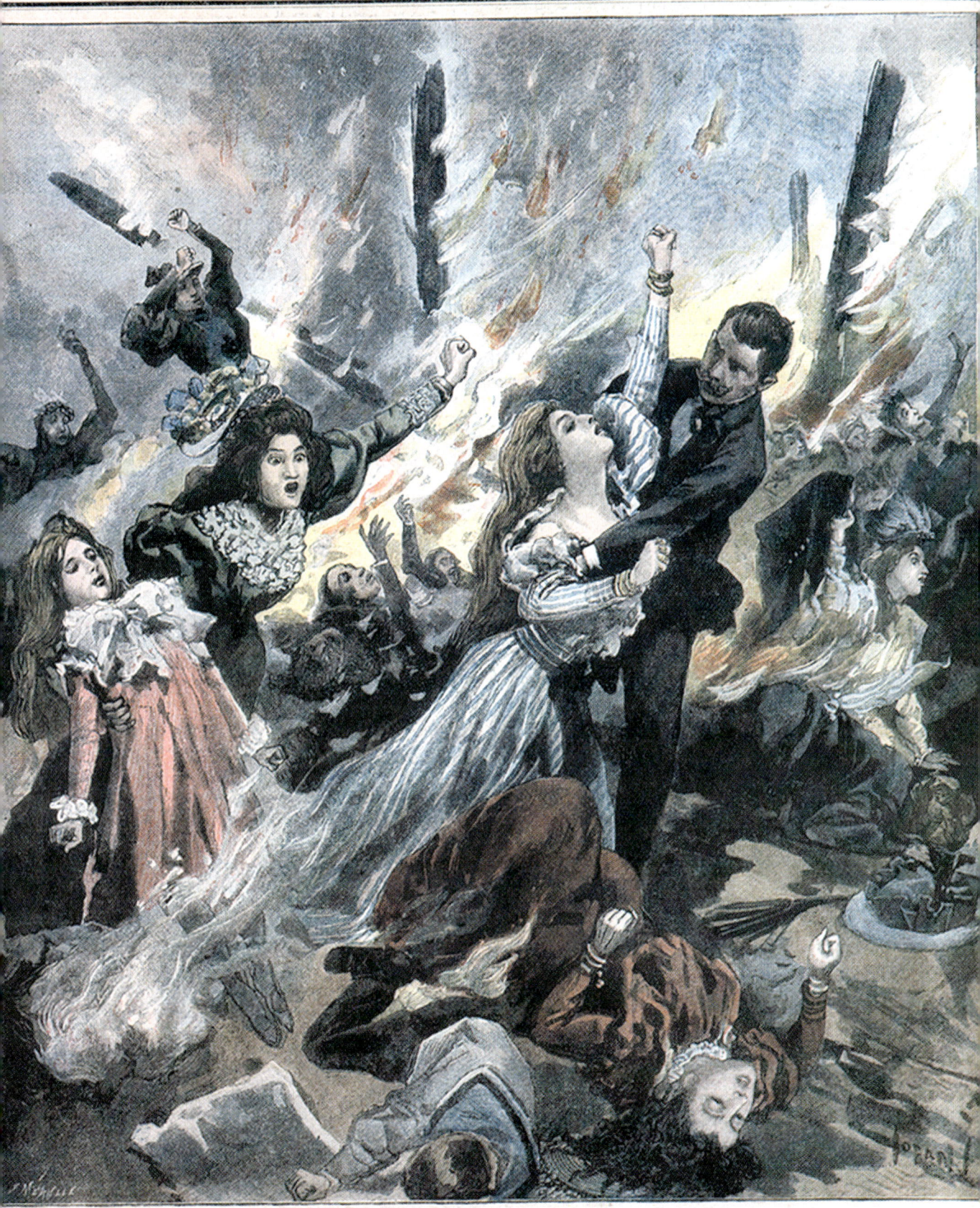

INCENDIE DU BAZAR DE LA CHARITÉ

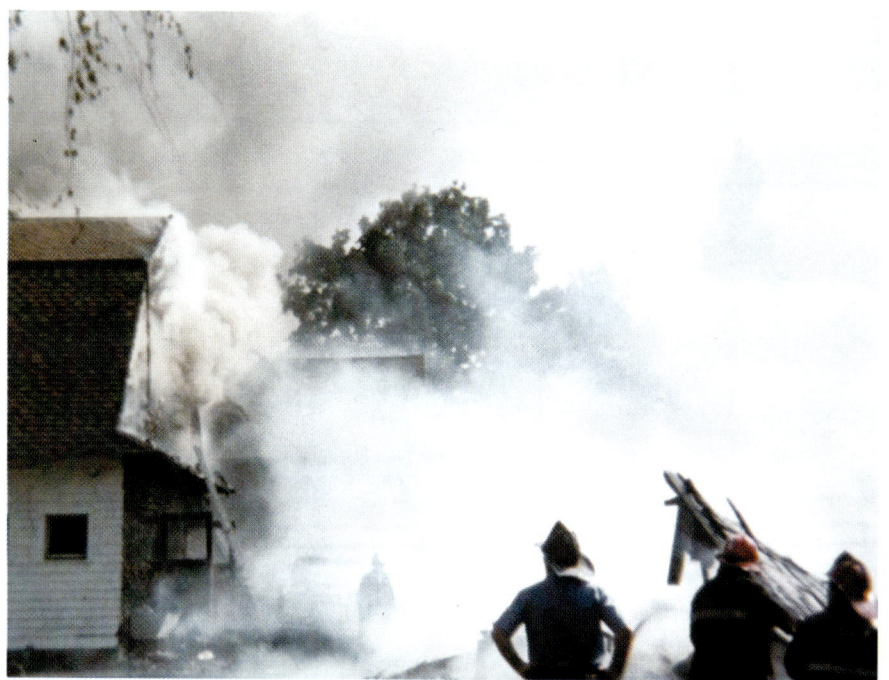

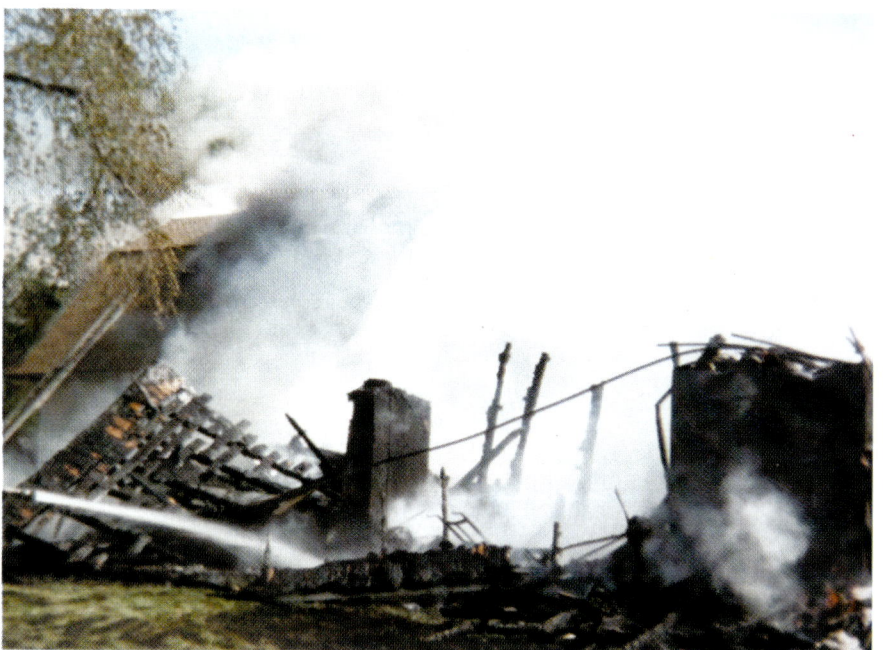

**The 1978 fire at
George Eastman House
– see p.449.**

George Eastman House, Rochester, NY.

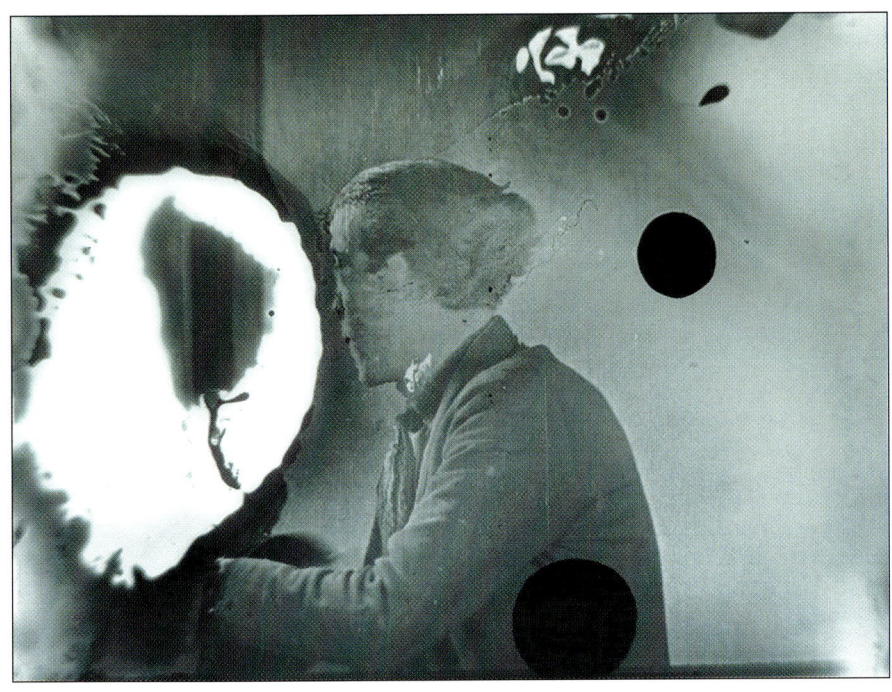

Le Voyeur: number 4
in the published version
of *Moires*
(Paris, Filigranes/Galerie
Michel Chomette: 1998)
– see p.604.

Éric Rondepierre.

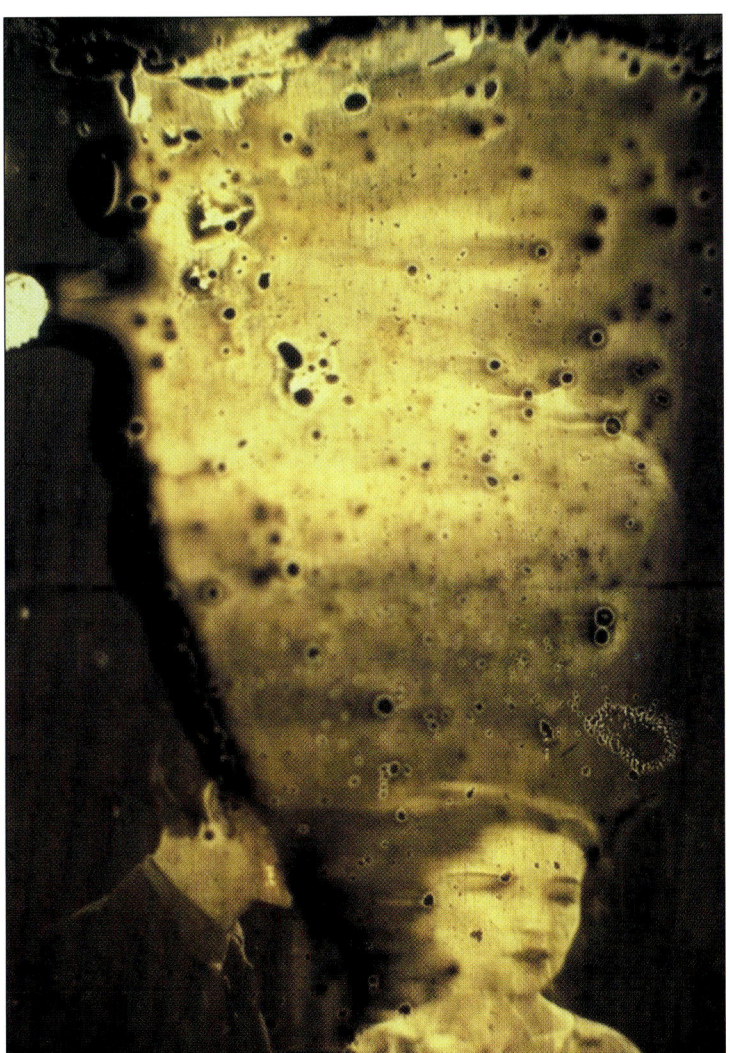

Couple, passant: number 18
in the published version of *Moires*
(Paris, Filigranes/Galerie Michel
Chomette: 1998) – see p.606.

Éric Rondepierre.

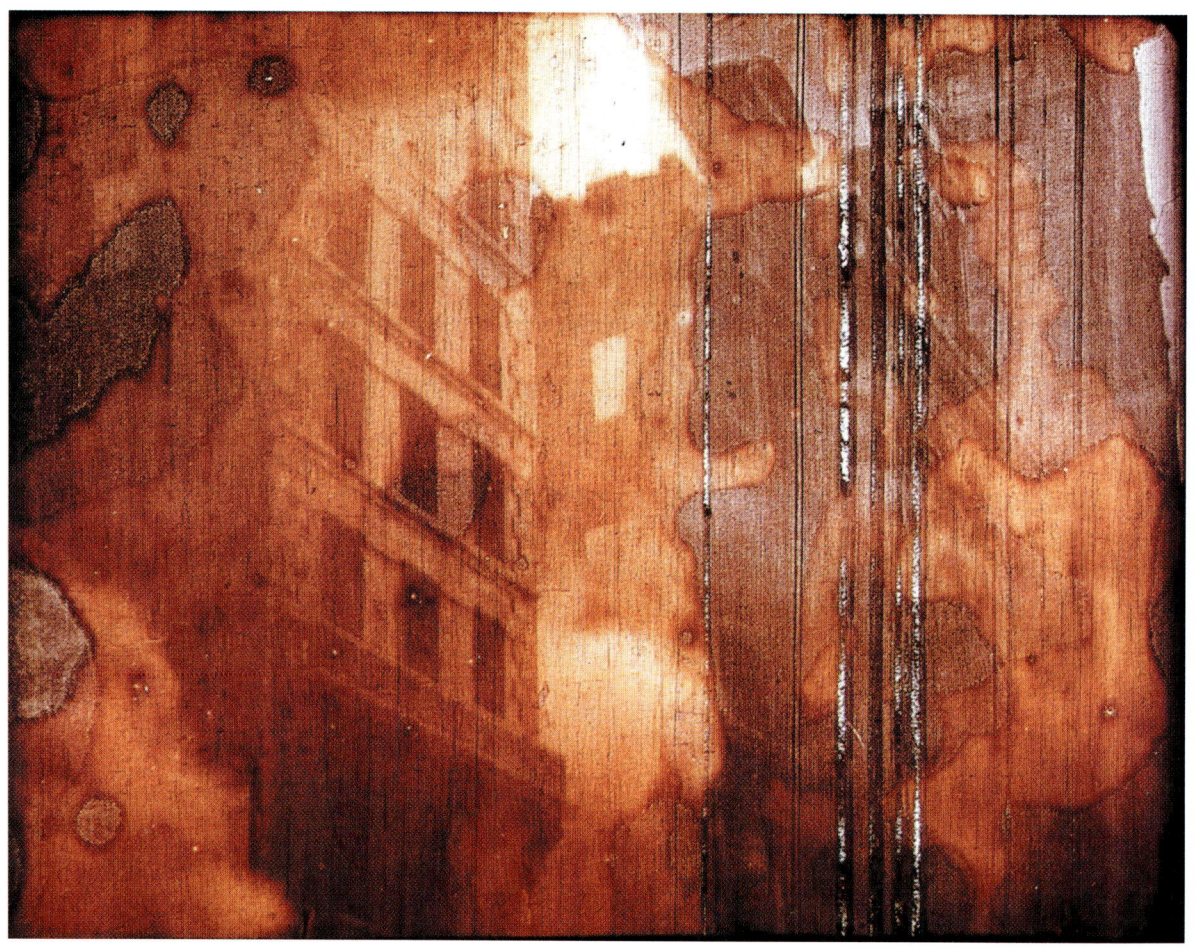

The triple threat of fire,
damage and deterioration
in a single image:
Tradition ist ... (1999)
– see pp.412 and 656.

Filmarchiv Austria, Vienna.

Local Topicals in the North West Film Archive

by Maryann Gomes

The North West Film Archive (NWFA) in Manchester – the professionally-recognised home for the North West of England's filmed heritage – originated from a research project which sought to save films about local people's lives before they were lost forever through chemical deterioration, neglect or destruction. While the mission of the NWFA is to care for all the region's moving images, there has always been a special concern to find footage that illustrates and illuminates the lives of working people. This is reflected in our adoption of a 1934 image of local "Kinematographer and Producer" Gerry Somers as our logo. Readers of this book will note with interest the cigarette that Mr Somers smokes as he turns the handle of his camera! This same commitment is also the reason why, within the urgent search for nitrate films, a particular emphasis was placed on attracting local topicals.

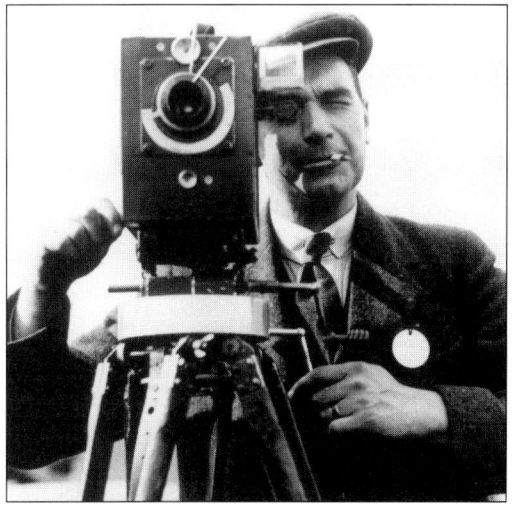

Local "Kinematographer and Producer" Gerry Somers – the 1934 image adopted as the logo of the NWFA.

North West Film Archive, Manchester.

Essentially, local topicals are a form of the newsreel genre, though they have a distinctly different character from the national and international productions made by the major companies such as Pathé, Gaumont, Universal News, and Movietone which recorded the key players and events of Britain's political, social, and economic life during the first half of the 20th century. Local topicals reflect cinema's modest origins, at the turn of the last century, in fairgrounds and music halls, which were heavily patronised by working people.

Independent cinemas needed to attract audiences, and, in the face of mounting competition during the 1910s and 1920s, the marketing ploy of filming local events was hit upon as an enticement to win paying customers. The idea was simple but effective. Arrange for a cameraman to record a local event. Ensure that the lens was pointed at as many faces of the participants/spectators as possible (sometimes at the expense of recording what was actually taking place on the day!). Advertise the film with the inducement "Come and See Yourself on the Screen". Wait for admission ticket sales to soar.

Local topicals were mainly filmed during the silent period of cinema (up to 1929), with production continuing until World War II. These films are always "exclusives" – only one print was made, which was then screened over several nights in the same week to maximise its earning potential with audiences. Local topicals were normally programmed between the official newsreel and the feature film. While the owner or manager of a particular cinema (sometimes the same person, in smaller family-run businesses) would typically instigate the film, it is often difficult to ascertain who actually shot it. Occasionally, cameramen who worked for the national newsreel companies would be employed (probably in an unofficial freelance capacity), or local film production companies commissioned. Owner/managers also hired cameras and filmed events themselves, or delegated this responsibility to the projectionist.

The NWFA collection includes more than 130 local topical films, which represents about 11% of our collection of professional material. These films often survived thanks to the concern of cinema staff, who took them home when their workplace was demolished or converted. I sometimes refer to these films as the "collective camera of working people". The cinema provided an animated version of family albums that went far beyond the scope of still photography in its range of subject matter and its celebration of community spirit. The actuality footage that makes up local topicals is, to a large extent, unrehearsed and uncut. Those who are filmed are also the intended target customers.

One outstanding collection of local topical material is the one known to us as the Empire Cinema Milnrow Collection.

In 1913, Ernest Greenwood opened a cinema in Milnrow to serve this and the nearby town of Newhey. The textile industry was the dominant employer in Lancashire during the 19th and early 20th centuries. At the time, no fewer than 14 cotton manufacturers were in operation in the Milnrow area.[1] Mill towns, with their dense populations of working people, were fertile grounds for the mass entertainment medium of cinema. Following easily from the popular (but seasonal) attraction of touring fairs, where early films were presented by itinerant showmen at the turn of the last century, the introduction of the Cinematograph Act in 1909 heralded an era of purpose-built cinemas, logically located where there was a good paying audience.

That Greenwood's contribution to the recording of working people's lives has survived is largely due to a chance telephone call that I received in 1983. While I was working on my own at the North West Film Archive, an appointment that I had made was rescheduled at the last minute. I was, therefore, very fortunately in the office, when I was asked if I was willing to accept a rubbish bag full of rusty old film cans that had been left at the headquarters of a local television company. My contact, suspecting that the films were on nitrate-based stock, which, due to its inflammability, would invalidate the company's insurance policy if brought into the building, had dumped the consignment in the car-park, until he could speak to either myself (to remove it immediately) or the fire service (to incinerate it). I managed to get there first, and must admit that once I had the first film reel on the manual inspection bench back at my office I had little idea of how significant a find this collection would prove to be. The 35mm cans were very rusty, with no identification evident, and prising the lids open proved difficult. The first reel was large and dirty, and the initial feet consisted of colour stock that was clearly part of a feature film. I started to regret the time that I had spent in rushing over to collect this material, but my hopes very soon revived when the stock changed to early black-and-white footage, and I began to see the first signs that this was indeed a prized local topical film.

While the reel was in very poor condition, and was already suffering from chemical deterioration, the opening title – *Milnrow and Newhey Gazette* – was followed by scenes of people outside a building (which later proved to be the Empire Cinema, Milnrow, and its staff), a street procession, and, most precious of all, sequences showing textile workers both working inside various mills, leaving work, and setting off for an outing. The reel ended with a shot of children outside the cinema, presumably gathered for the start of the Saturday matinee. While the Archive already held coverage of the textile industry, the earliest title was made in 1919. This was film that could be dated to 1913, and therefore was the only known pre-World War I coverage.

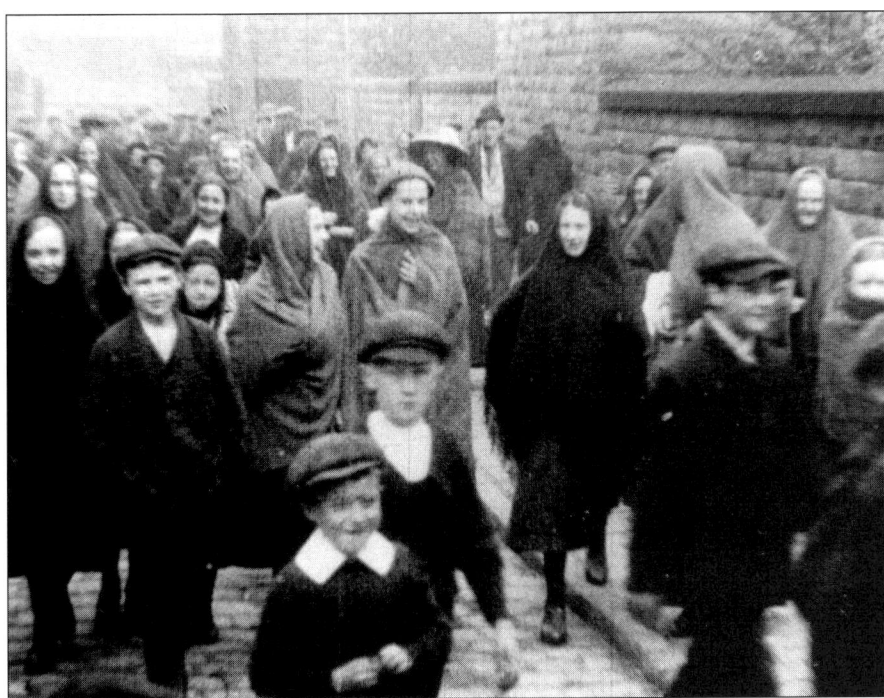

A scene from *Workpeople Leaving William Clegg's Mill, Milnrow* (1913).

North West Film Archive, Manchester.

Original title sequences could be dated to 1913, while new, bolder titles had a 1935 stockmark. I suspected that several original reels of local topical films had been edited and compiled in the mid-1930s, so that the material could be shown again to an audience of a later generation. This view was confirmed when I managed to track down the family of Ernest Greenwood, who told me about his early days as a cinema owner and how he had commissioned films of local events to show to his neighbourhood audience before and during World War I. Four generations of the Greenwood family visited the Archive for a special screening of this collection, which provided valuable information on its provenance and content. The family have been very supportive of the Archive's efforts to both preserve and promote access to this material which has proved to be among the most popular of our holdings.

The four other titles cover activities in Milnrow and Newhey, and allow us to see aspects of how this community worked and played between 1913 and 1917. One reel features a shot of the cinema exterior, which has a large billboard placed in front exhorting people to "Come and See Yourself". This film also shows the local chemist shop, and it is possible (though this has not been proved) that its owner was responsible for the making of these films, a practice not unknown in early cinema days. Of particular poignancy is a film entitled *Milnrow and Newhey Roll of Honour* (1917), for which Ernest Greenwood asked his (by now predominantly female) audience to bring in photographs of their husbands, sons, fathers, and brothers who had died during the Great War. This moving record, which consists entirely of studio portraits copied onto film, shows us 125 men sacrificed from that community alone by the third year of the war – though even this was only a proportion of the real loss. The impact of the film on its initial screening is still recalled today by older residents. It has now been copied for inclusion in the Film and Video Archive of the Imperial War Museum in London.

A recent (March 2000) example shows that the acquisition of local topicals is sometimes an extremely challenging technical problem. The story began when the Archivist at Lancashire County Record Office contacted us to discuss 2 reels of film that had been discovered within a collection of papers and photographs belonging to Mrs Patricia Callander, a local resident. In order to perform its specialist role in

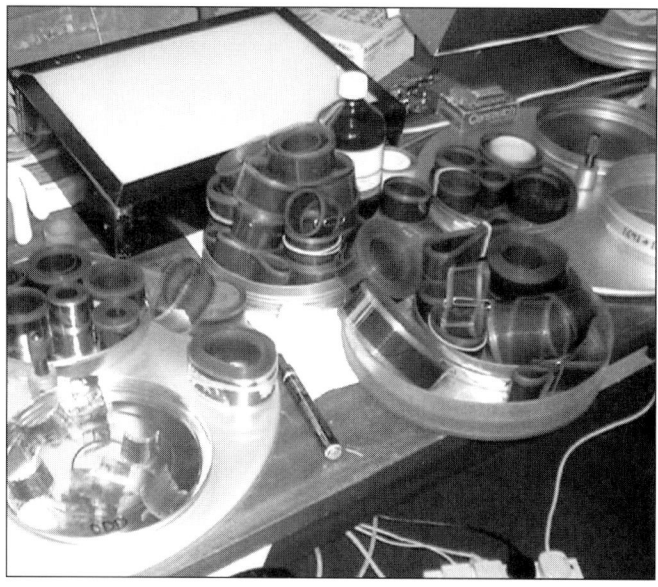

The problem confronting Technical Officer Mark Bodner when Mrs Callandar's film cans were opened.

North West Film Archive, Manchester.

the region, the NWFA naturally works closely with colleagues in the North West of England's mainstream custodial sector. A strong network of professional contacts ensures that material is delivered into our care so that we can take responsibility for its long-term survival and provide access opportunities. On each occasion, agreement to acquire the films – if appropriate to our collection – and to preserve them, if necessary by copying unstable material, is negotiated in advance, as the investment of NWFA resources must be carefully judged. Suspecting that Mrs Callander's reels were on nitrate-based stock, the NWFA arranged for the films to be inspected at the archive by our Technical Officer, Mark Bodner.

Both reels of film proved to be on nitrate stock, and the work of technical inspection and content assessment was prioritised in line with the NWFA's policy on nitrate. The first reel, which consisted of 1920s footage of local processions and celebrations, was fairly straightforward to handle. The second reel, however, presented a very real challenge. This 727-ft reel had been cut up with scissors into over 50 short film sections, each between 6 and 30 ft (2–10 metres) long, possibly with the intention of making stills. Mark identified that this reel contained three separate news items (shot in Chorley in 1913, 1922, and 1924), and had to extract the relevant footage, reassemble this into coherent, correctly ordered sequences (using a lightbox and Agfalupe), and then painstakingly join the strips into a secure, smooth reel for copying. Work was further complicated by the fact that there were different degrees of shrinkage among the sequences, which meant that the splice box could not be used and joins had to be made by hand.

The footage related to three separate events – a 1920s football match, a local celebration, and additional coverage of a royal visit to Lancashire in 1913 that complemented the NWFA's existing holdings. These films have now been copied for us at the National Film and Television Archive's J Paul Getty Conservation Centre, and the NWFA has new 35mm master negatives of each title which are stored within our vault suite. While we were pleased to have saved this material, we are also disappointed that, at some stage, the original local topicals had been chopped up and sections lost or destroyed. This is not the first time that we have come across this practice, which makes the work of rescuing uniquely surviving local professional films even more demanding.

Notes

1. Information from Clegg's *Commercial Directory of Rochdale*, 1913.

Three Nitrate Stories

by Jan-Christopher Horak

I. Two Collections

In 1991, when I was Senior Curator of the Film Department at George Eastman House, I got a call one day from a gentleman who lived in Elmira, New York, about 60 miles south of Rochester, asking me whether I was interested in some old film. Being used to receiving several such calls a week from individuals who happen to find an 8mm Chaplin film in their closet, I was not necessarily interested, but then the gentleman said the films were about 2 inches wide and had no sound. That could only mean 35mm silents, so I made a date to drive down to look at the collection. When I got to Elmira a few weeks later, I found a modest cottage in a street of equally neat little houses and gardens. The gentleman and his wife invited me in, and proceeded to tell me that the films had belonged to his brother-in-law, who had been slightly "cracked." The said party had been vaguely involved at the extreme fringes of some sort of show business, and for years he had schlepped around this "trash," along with a hand-cranked, portable projector. He would screen the films without an audience, for his own enjoyment. Since the man in question had passed away several years before, the films and projector had been sitting in the basement, but now my contact was himself retiring and moving to Florida, which meant the stuff had to go. I got the distinct feeling that Mr Elmira had not gotten along well with his wife's brother. Only then did he take me into the basement, where the nitrate cans were neatly stacked up against the oil-burning furnace. I told the gentleman that he was lucky he hadn't blown himself, his wife, his dog, and his house to Kingdom Come. Back in Rochester, we were able to identify almost all of the 90-some reels, finding many unique, tinted prints by such today-unknown, low-budget companies as Tiffany, Aywon, and Powers.

That such collectors were not unique to the United States became clear to me several years later, when I was Director of the Munich Filmmuseum. In 1996 I was contacted by the German film director Michael Verhoeven, whose production assistant had pulled two 35mm projectors out of the basement of an abandoned cottage in the centre of Munich. He told me there was also a sizable collection of films there. When we went to take a look, we found a little cinema with 10 theatre chairs, an electric generator, and a projection booth. The house had apparently belonged to an electrical engineer who worked as a city inspector. With his generator he was able to screen films, even in the midst of the War, when electricity was rationed. Unfortunately, the basement was very damp, so that all the acetate films stored there were totally eaten away by mould. Not one of them could be saved. However, in a little shed behind the cottage, we found a cache of over 50 nitrate films, mostly produced by local Bavarian companies that had long since ceased to exist. Like the Elmira films, there was virtually no decomposition, and they have now been preserved.

II. One Vault

My second nitrate story goes back to my earliest days as a film archivist. In September 1975, I joined the staff of George Eastman House as a postgraduate intern. My very first task was to inventory the nitrate collections with the son of the then-Director of Eastman House, Robert Doherty. The museum's first computer database was being put into place against the wishes of James Card, who regarded the film collection as *his* property, and harbored a deep mistrust of any documentation which might impinge on what he considered his private affair. The nitrate vaults were located at that time at the back end of the property, and had been built 25 years earlier in the standard manner, with asbestos shelves to segregate each individual 1,000-ft can of film. Needless to say, I had little notion of either the dangers of asbestos or nitrate fumes. We two students only noticed that we would get light-headed after several hours in the vaults.

Being novices, we assumed that whatever information was on the can was relevant to what was inside the can. This was of course a mistake, as I realized years later, when my staff actually began looking inside the cans. However, there was another problem, because Mr Card went into the vaults afterwards and switched films around, just in case someone would want to find a film without his permission.

To make matters worse, a few months later, Metro-Goldwyn-Mayer called the Film Department and told us that they would be dumping several hundred nitrate Technicolor negatives into the Pacific Ocean, if Eastman House did not take them. The collection included *Gone With the Wind*, *The Wizard of Oz*, *Meet Me in St. Louis*, and all the great MGM musicals, as well as lots of Technicolor cartoons by Chuck Jones. Since these separation negatives (YCM) constituted three times as much film as a more "modern" colour negative, they were thought to be too costly to store. Metro had generated composite fine grain masters, which were housed in their vaults in the bottom of a mine in Kansas, and they were confident that they would *never* need the nitrates again. Jim Card said he would take the material, so a week later a very large truck arrived at 2 o'clock in the morning. The boxes were unloaded, and – against all fire regulations – stacked floor to ceiling in the narrow hallways of the nitrate vaults, making any access virtually impossible. Ten years later, Turner Entertainment, which had bought the MGM catalogue, began requesting the YCMs, in particular *Gone With the Wind*, because the interpositives had proven to be unusable due to extreme color fading. I learned then that saving nitrate was more important than following the letter of the law.

III. No Fire

Having had a lot of exposure to nitrate film, I was never very paranoid about handling it. We now know that nitrate will last decades longer than we once supposed. Certainly, I knew of the dangers of nitrate fires, but felt that as long as you didn't smoke around it, nitrate was perfectly safe to handle, to look at on a flatbed editing table, even to project. Both in Rochester and later in Munich, we screened nitrate with some regularity. However, I once did have a serious scare.

One of my first programs at Eastman House was a season in the fall of 1984, dedicated to classic titles from the collections, including a well-known French film that had always been popular with local audiences. We had a full house that night in the Dryden Theatre, and the projection of our pristine nitrate print began without incident. However, in the middle of the screening, the film suddenly slowed down and stopped in the gate, the image melting away. Fearing the worst, I jumped up from my seat, rushed out of the cinema, and collided head-on with a wooden stand, used to collect ticket stubs, putting a deep gash into my shin. Bleeding and in extreme pain, I limped upstairs to the projection booth, only to find the projectionist happily rewinding a reel with no sign of fire. I had not previously seen Marcel Carné's *Les Visiteurs du soir* (1942), so I couldn't know that the film has a scene in which the devil's emissaries cast a spell over the medieval castle, stopping the passage of time so that they can do their dirty work – it was the action, not the film that was stopping. I still have the scar on my leg.

It Happened One Nitrate: Acquisition Memories from the National Film and Television Archive

by Clyde Jeavons

1. Great Expectations (or: Oliver with a New Twist)

On 9 April 1973, when I was Head of Acquisitions at what was then the National Film Archive, I reported the following to *BFI News*, the British Film Institute's Staff Newsletter:

The Mystery of Doughty Street

In the basement of Dickens House in Doughty Street, London WC1, there is a small, immensely solid vault with a large iron door rusted firmly in place. Behind this, we believe, there may be several old films adapted from Dickens's novels and presented to the Dickens Fellowship (which runs Dickens House) over the years.

The films, if indeed there are any in the vault, will be nitrate and therefore hazardous (hence the Dickens Fellowship's anxiety to have them removed from their premises) and could include the following: the version of OLIVER TWIST with Jackie Coogan made in 1923, as well as several '30s and '40s adaptations, including THE OLD CURIOSITY SHOP, GREAT EXPECTATIONS, NICHOLAS NICKLEBY and SCROOGE. There may also be earlier silent material.

So far, all efforts to open the door of the vault have proved unsuccessful. It is constructed of heavy iron and has rusted seamlessly to its surrounding frame. Harold Brown, Chief Preservation Officer of the Archive, has, however, managed to drill some tiny holes in one of the panels, sufficient to establish that there are film cans inside the vault – though what they contain may be another story. The Archive intends to make further attempts to open the door now that it knows there is a potential cache of films behind it.

The Dickens Fellowship is an organisation devoted to the memory, works and relics of Charles Dickens. It administers Dickens House in Doughty Street, where the Victorian novelist lived for a while and which is run as a small museum. The films which the Archive believes are stored in the basement are copies presented to the Fellowship over the years by film-makers who have been allowed access to Dickens House and the Fellowship's research material.

*With luck, we will have more and better news to report in the next issue of **BFI News**.*

Sadly, I seem to have failed to follow up this tantalising beginning, as there is no further mention of the story in BFI News. The memory has faded somewhat, but perhaps it is because the conclusion was disappointing. I recall that Harold and I did persevere with the vault door, and that we invited television and radio reporters to cover the Tutankhamun-like moment of breakthrough. I seem to remember that we took an acetylene torch to the stubborn iron door – but that can't be true, can it? Surely I, and even less so Harold, would never have been so reckless as to invade a nitrate vault with a naked flame? But somehow we got in (the freelance radio reporter dropping and breaking his tape recorder at the vital moment) and pulled out some rusty cans of film…

Too late, alas. Most of the expected titles were no longer there. The one that remained – the Jackie Coogan *Oliver Twist* – had already decayed beyond salvation, and there was an unidentified reel in similar condition, which might have been a news item of some celebrity or dignitary visiting Dickens House. A bleak moment.

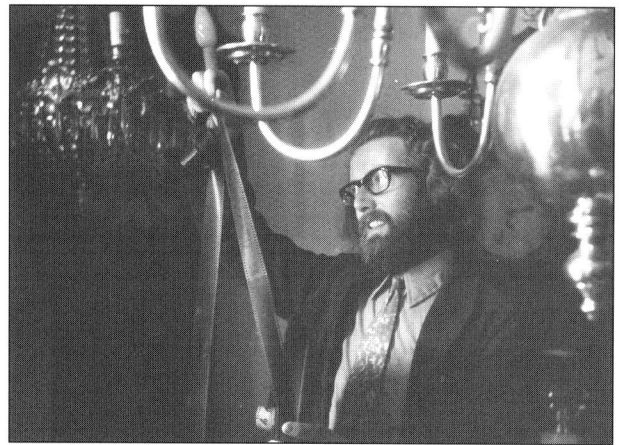

Clyde Jeavons inspecting a potential acquisition in the early 1970s.

Clyde Jeavons

2. Smoking in bed

There was a time in my acquisitions career at the National Film Archive when all private collectors seemed to be called Edwards. There was always at least one Edwards Collection listed on my desk.

One day, one of these Edwardses turned up at my office and declared himself to be a film collector, with an impressive and desirable stash of historic newsfilm items which he kept under his bed. He was a very nice, gentlemanly old man, who was only telling me this because he had promised his daughter, with whom he lived in suburban Essex, that he would at least seek advice about the films under his bed. She had heard that they might be a fire hazard and was anxious about their domestic safety. He had no intention of giving the films to the Archive – at least, not yet – but nevertheless supplied me with a neat, detailed inventory.

My advice, of course, was to put the films in a safe place – such as the NFA – but he agreed only to think about it. I was, not for the first or last time in dealing with private collectors, pessimistic about reaching any agreement, and Mr Edwards went home.

Two days later, Mr Edwards's daughter telephoned me in some alarm. She said that she had found her father's mattress smouldering one morning and had put it out on the front steps. She presumed he had been smoking in bed. As far as she was concerned, that was it – either the films went or he did! I collected the films immediately. But I still wonder about the coincidence of the burning mattress and Mr Edwards's visit – and the fact that all the time he was in my office Mr Edwards had politely declined each and every offer of a cigarette which I (at that time a heavy smoker) had made to him…

3. Sunken Treasure: The 'Lusitania' yields an archaeological curiosity

In the winter of 1982/83, the following account appeared on page 4 of the new issue of *Sight and Sound* (v.52, no.1):

> Film archivists get used to finding films in unlikely places. A few years ago the National Film Archive was handed a couple of reels of silent Hollywood nude-starlet footage dug up, alongside a First World War hand grenade, from a Hampstead garden. More recently, major discoveries have been made in locations as diverse as the Yukon permafrost of Dawson City and a Jesuit abbey in Switzerland. Film archiving often seems closely akin to archaeology.

Even the longest-serving practitioners of the craft, however, expressed surprise when, last September, divers carrying out salvage work on the liner 'Lusitania' (sunk by a German torpedo ten miles off the coast of Ireland on 7 May 1915) brought to the surface a reel of film. What it in fact looked like was a large lump of sodden coal, but once some of the silt had been cleared away, the celluloid was plain to see, complete with an intact image and a few surviving perforations. BBC's *Newsnight* – on site to cover the 'Lusitania' salvage story, partly to ascertain whether or not the liner was carrying munitions, which it apparently was – realised it had a bonus scoop on its hands and called in Laurie Ward, then the BBC's technical advisor at Kay's Laboratories and a well-known wizard at restoring damaged film.

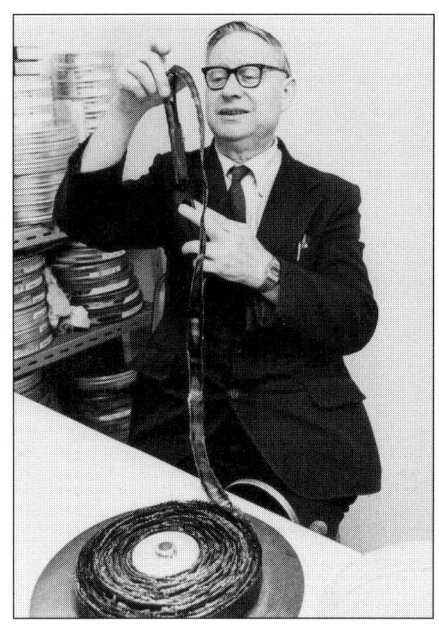

Harold Brown inspects the reel of film recovered from the wreck of the *Lusitania*.

BFI Collections – Stills, Posters & Designs, London.

Laurie Ward succeeded in recovering a portion of the eroded reel, sufficient to reveal a number of complete images and, by good fortune, the film's title, *The Carpet from Bagdad*, an American five-reeler produced by the Selig company in 1915. A missing masterpiece? Luckily no, say the silent cinema experts (despite a hype review in the British *Bioscope* of 9 December 1915, which called it 'a difficult production to submit to the ordinary process of criticism, for it is less of a film drama than a series of gorgeous tableaux, fascinating, almost bewildering, in their vivid orientalism, their crowded animated scenes of native lives and customs'), for there is no chance of the surviving footage being put back into projectable form. Further work at the National Film Archive has led to the recovery of a few more image-bearing feet, but they will remain an archaeological curiosity, preserved as a freakish footnote to a larger piece of history.

Why *The Carpet from Bagdad* was travelling on the 'Lusitania' is a minor mystery. There was, oddly enough, a cinema on the liner – perhaps it was the in-cruise movie? More likely, it was being brought to Britain for preview purposes, since the film was not registered for copyright in the USA until a week after the sinking, and was not shown in the UK until the end of the year. It is known that at least three cinema executives were travelling on the ship – an American, Charles Frohman, of the Famous Players Film Company, who died, and two Britons, E. Hounsell and Edward Barry, who escaped.

The film archiving world now awaits with bated breath the source of the next movie discovery. Perhaps Prince Charles, as patron of the BFI, should make a closer inspection of the 'Mary Rose'?

Almost 20 years later, the rescued reel of *The Carpet from Bagdad* still survives as a "museum piece" in the collection of unusual film gauges and other celluloid oddities at the National Film and Television Archive's J Paul Getty Conservation Centre in Berkhamsted – testimony to the longevity of at least certain examples of nitrate film, even when exposed to the most trying or traumatic of circumstances.

The Sad Story of *Abi va Rabi*

by Fereydoun Khameneipour

The first Iranian fiction feature, *Abi va Rabi* (Abi and Rabi), received its premiere in Tehran on 2 January 1931. It was directed by Avaness Ohanian (1900-1961), an Armenian-Iranian who started his film-making career in Russia, where his surname was styled "Oganiantz". It was a silent slapstick comedy in black-and-white, depicting the adventures of two men, one short and fat, the other tall and lean, modelled upon the "Pat and Patachon" characters played by the popular Danish comedy team of Harald Madsen and Carl Schenstrom in the 1920s and 1930s, in films such as *1000 Wörte Deutsch* (1,000 Words of German; 1930).

Abi va Rabi was one of a handful of early Iranian features on nitrate, and unfortunately no copy of it survives today. The only existing nitrate print was completely destroyed by fire during a screening at the Cinema Mayak in 1932. The film was lost forever. Ironically, the owner of the Cinema Mayak, Grisha Sakvarlidzeh, was one of three investors in the film's production.

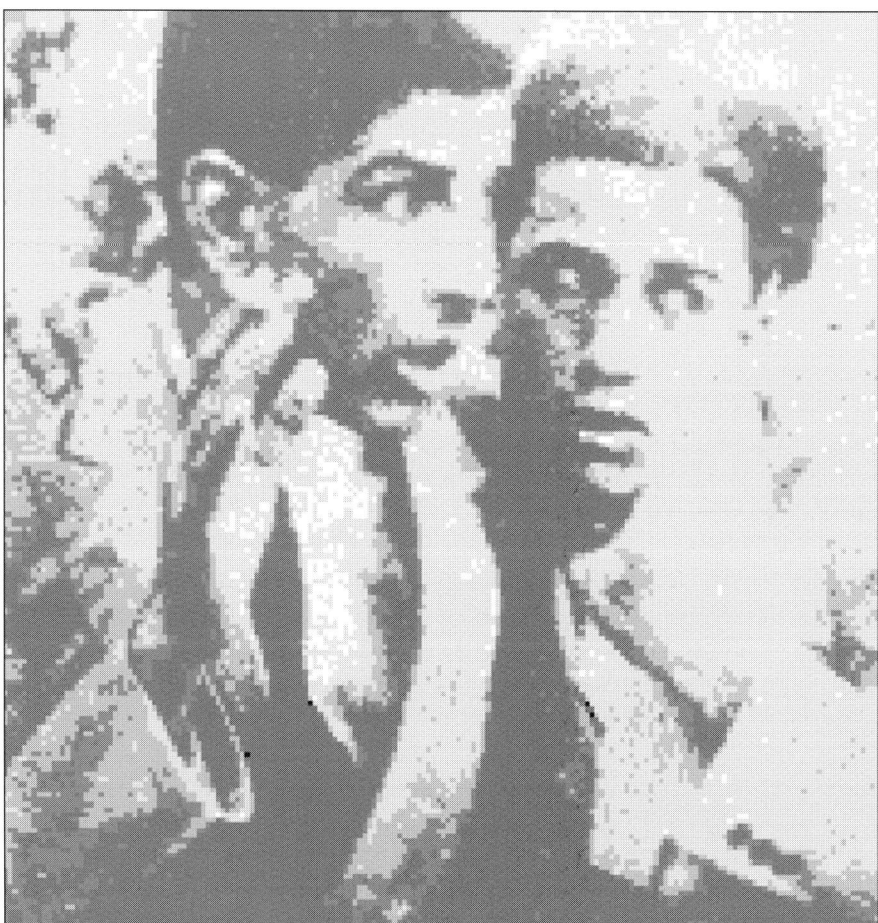

Lost forever: reproduction of a newsprint still from the lost film *Abi va Rabi* (1931).

National Film Archive of Iran (Film-Khane-ye Melli-e Iran), Tehran.

Fires and Feedbags: Nitrate Stories from the Steven Spielberg Jewish Film Archive

by Marilyn Koolik and Hillel Tryster

Just like all other FIAF members, the Steven Spielberg Jewish Film Archive in Jerusalem was confronted with the problems of nitrate preservation from its inception. An additional problem in our country has been the lack of laboratory facilities. This has meant that all nitrate requiring preservation had to be shipped to laboratories abroad. Aside from the headaches of nitrate shipment with all the safety regulations involved, imagine the difficulties doing this from a country as security conscious with its air freight as Israel! But over the years we have managed, and, as of today, the Spielberg Archive has no nitrate prints in its vaults. Before we begin to tell the nitrate stories of our own experience, we would like to recall a few nitrate anecdotes from the more distant past.

First, a reminder that nitrate film has not always been treated with the care and respect that the world now bestows on it:

> …The local climatic conditions, that guaranteed an entire season free of rain, made the development of the open-air summer cinemas a natural one…. While it was virtually a certainty that rain would not disrupt the screenings, winds could not always be prevented and the screen of Haifa's Carmel was once blown away. A lot more could have been blown away had luck run out for the owners of the Colosseum; they were also in the benzine business and stored their stock under the cinema in close proximity to the highly inflammable reels of nitrate film.[1]

If anybody needed reminding of the dangers, however, there were occasions like the following. In late September 1928 there was a large fire at the AFIFA film plant in Berlin. Joseph Gal-Ezer, of the Palestine Foundation Fund, was then in the early stages of re-editing his film *Springtime in Palestine*, together with UFA editor Willi Prager. Prager, who was simultaneously working to complete a film record of the Amsterdam Olympic Games, was only free to work with Gal-Ezer between 5 p.m. and midnight every day. The following firsthand account of the fire, translated from the original German, was contained in a letter written by Gal-Ezer to his colleague Hans Kohn in Jerusalem:

> It was in the evening, the day before yesterday, half an hour after I had begun to work with our director. (Dr. Mechner had not yet appeared.) Suddenly the splicer who helps us in the work storms in and screams, "Afifa's burning," then she has an attack of hysteria. The building is shaken by an explosion, and already from the main building (we work in the building next door) comes a mighty darting flame in front of our window. Herr Regisseur [Director] Prager, who had the negative of the big film of the Olympic Games spread out on a worktable, while our work positive lay on the second table, was like a madman. I thought immediately of our negative that was housed somewhere in the main building. But this was already engulfed in smoke and flame and so, as the only one with presence of mind in our room,

I had to bring our director and our assistant to safety. As the way to the main gate was covered in clouds of smoke, we ran in the other direction, climbed over a wire entanglement, and found ourselves in safety by the Spree canal.

Then we could observe the progress of the fire and the fire brigade working on its extinguishing. The fire brigade had immediately cordoned off the burning main building, but it took nearly an hour till it was fully isolated, and during this time the adjacent buildings were in the gravest danger. Our director was most agitated, and finally I could not hold him anymore and he ran back into our workroom. I didn't want to let him go alone, so I had to go with him. Our workroom was untouched inside by the fire. I helped the director load his negative onto a metal trolley; we threw in two reels of our film as well and then rolled the trolley downwards to the Spree. I would have liked to have found out something about our negative, but it was naturally impossible. I went back with a heavy heart, and only on the next day did I learn that our negative, with a number of other negatives, had happily been transported out of the burning building by an official of "Afifa" and deposited at the "Geyer" film plant. We will be able to get it from there in two to three days. As for our workprint, I saved two whole reels myself; three reels which we had already removed were collected by our assistant the morning after the fire, and presumably not much of them is missing. Approximately 200 metres of positive apparently got lost in the tumult.[2]

Not all nitrate stories result in such narrow escapes and (relatively) happy endings. Only the last five minutes of Helmar Lerski's film *Adamah* (1948) survive today, in the form of an extremely poor quality 16mm dupe print. This situation arose as the result of an extraordinary chain of unfortunate events. The film was shot in 1947 at the Ben Shemen Youth Village in Palestine, and post-production was carried out in Hollywood in late 1947 and early 1948 under the supervision of Dr Siegfried Lehmann, founder and Director of the Youth Village. Almost as soon as the 8-reel feature had been completed, Hadassah, the Women's Zionist Organization of America, began to work on its own version of the film. Hadassah was entitled to do this by virtue of an earlier agreement involving finances, but Dr Lehmann insisted that no changes be made to the original negative of *Adamah*. Hadassah's version, entitled *Tomorrow's a Wonderful Day*, was ready by mid-year. It was 3 reels shorter than Adamah, and contained a radical reorganization of the remaining footage, as well as a largely new soundtrack. 16mm prints of *Tomorrow's a Wonderful Day* were struck almost immediately, replacing a still-unfilled order for reduction prints of *Adamah*. In 1960, all known materials relating to the original version of *Adamah* were destroyed when they ignited in storage at the Ben Shemen Youth Village. The film cans had apparently been sealed, causing chemical emissions from the nitrate stock to build up under pressure, though it has also recently been claimed that children playing with matches began the blaze, which also destroyed the Youth Village's dining room. A long search for surviving prints elsewhere finally turned up one at the offices of the Jewish National Fund in Paris. This was brought to Israel, where the first thought was to strike a reduction print for preservation purposes. The laboratory chosen was Tel Aviv's National-Film, which copied the last 5 minutes onto 16mm as a test. The quality was so poor that the project was given up, and the

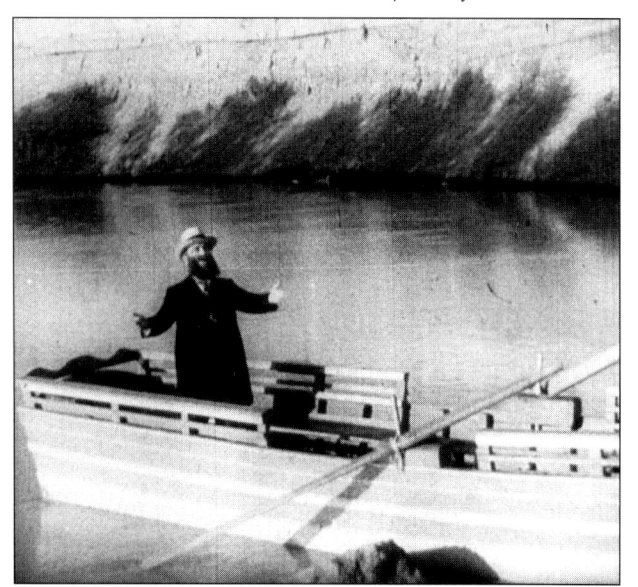

Yossele Rosenblatt in *My People's Dream* (1933).

Steven Spielberg Jewish Film Archive, Jerusalem.

sole full print was stored at the laboratory. A few years later a fire broke out in the bank above the National-Film laboratory, and the damage done by the water used to extinguish the conflagration was so great that this last known print of *Adamah* was destroyed.

In 1972 the Hebrew University provided temporary quarters for the film archive it had established 4 years previously. This archive "facility", if it could be called such, was located in 4 small rooms in the basement of one of the oldest buildings on the campus – a building that was opened in the 1920s. Over the years, as the film collection grew, more and more nitrate material was acquired, and in the mid-1980s it became a significant problem with the recognition of the dangers involved. Letters were written to the various University authorities trying to make them aware of the safety problem in their midst. These letters went round and round the University bureaucracy, which simply didn't know how to cope with the fact that there was a basement full of "bombs" smack in the middle of the campus. The solution came only in the late 1980s with the donation of a significant contribution from Mr Moses Rothman of London, when all of the nitrate was sent off to Hendersons Laboratories in London for transfer to safety.

Before the problem was solved, however, one particular incident took place that is worth recalling. In the mid-1980s it was decided, as a stopgap measure, to telecine all of the nitrate films in the collection of the Spielberg Archive – just in case! The films were taken in small shipments to Jerusalem Capital Studios, a local production and post-production house, which was doing the telecine work. Ultimately, over 400 cans of nitrate were stored in a small "broom closet" next to the telecine machine. Also, next to the telecine room was a small television studio where programmes, mostly interviews, were recorded. On one occasion the interviewee was Yitzhak Rabin. As is customary, his security guards did a preliminary check of the facilities and discovered the small "broom closet" of potentially explosive films. Needless to say, for safety reasons every single one of the 400 nitrate cans had to be moved to another part of the building (and later back again) so that the half-hour interview could take place.

Not many nitrate films have been newly acquired by the Steven Spielberg Jewish Film Archive in the last 20 years, but interesting preservation histories accompany some of those that have. Baruch Zvi Rechtman, former proprietor of Jerusalem's National cinema, possessed Hebrew and Yiddish prints of one of Palestine's earliest sound films, *My People's Dream* (1933), which he had purchased from one of the film's producers, Jerusalem Mayor Daniel Auster. The film featured legendary cantor Yossele Rosenblatt, who had died during the production. Rechtman kept the film under his bed, apparently believing it to have magical powers. The Spielberg (then Rad) Archive acquired the film from Rechtman and preserved the reels, but several years later, after Rechtman's death, was approached by his granddaughter, who had further reels of the same title to offer. It transpired that Rechtman had taken the request to acquire "the Yossele Rosenblatt film" very literally and had parted only with the sequences featuring the star, cutting up both prints in the process. The acquisition of the remainder helped to clear up several puzzles regarding the film's continuity.

The widow of Israeli film-maker Ze'ev Havatzelet had also kept his films under her bed for about 30 years following her husband's death in a tractor accident, though in this case, unfortunately, the nitrate in the collection was beyond salvation. Beds begin to seem commonplace nitrate storage facilities when compared with the survival history of *Work and Ceremony in Palestine* (1926). This was a privately produced film subsequently acquired, adapted, and distributed by the Jewish

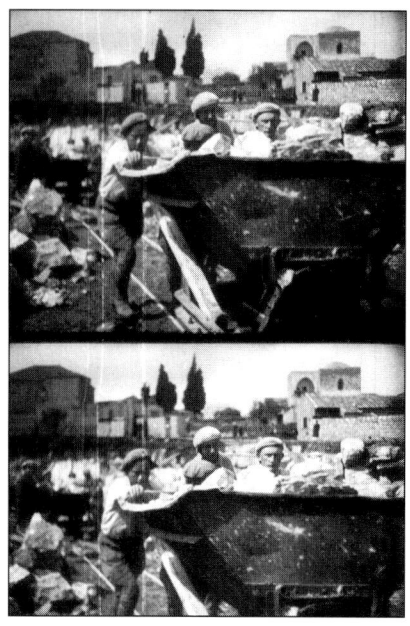

A scene from *Work and Ceremony in Palestine* (1926).

National Fund. Written sources indicated that a total of 10 prints had been struck, none of which were known to be extant until early 1993, when Gerard Yunes, a Tunisian-born resident of France, arrived at the Spielberg Archive with 4 reels of nitrate film. Following their preservation, 3 of these reels could be seen to match written descriptions of 3 of the 1926 film's 4 reels. The fourth reel contained footage that had originally appeared in the 1923 film *Palestine Awakening*. Only a few fragments of the latter were known to exist till then, and the material in the new reel both duplicated and complemented them. Mr Yunes related that his father, Clement Yunes, had saved the reels at the time of the German occupation of Tunisia during World War II. Because of their Zionist content he did not dare simply to keep them at home, and at various times during the occupation he kept them hidden in a horse's feedbag, and buried in the ground. Following the unrest of the late 1950s that accompanied Tunisia's struggle for independence from France, the family emigrated, taking the film with them as a treasured possession, finally repatriating it to Israel, at the request of Mr Yunes Sr, several decades later.

In 1992, Henriette Bodenheimer, the daughter of Max Bodenheimer, one of the most prominent early Zionist leaders, died in Jerusalem. Among the possessions that then passed into the hands of the Central Zionist Archives were a number of small reels of 35mm film. As a matter of course, these were passed on to the Spielberg Archive. While hopes that these might contain rare historical footage relevant to Zionist history were disappointed, some of the films were a delightful surprise. Along with some Dutch newsreel footage of the funeral of King Albert of Belgium were 3 reels of breathtakingly beautiful early stencil-coloured material. Two of these showed a landscape with peasants, while the third was a scientific film, bearing the scratch title "Insects Imitateux". This last, demonstrating the camouflage abilities of various insects, had clearly belonged to Henriette's brother, Shimon "Fritz" Bodenheimer, who had been a noted zoologist, specializing in entomology. Because of evidence that all the films had originated in Dutch laboratories, they were repatriated to the Nederlands Filmmuseum.

Notes

1. Hillel Tryster, *Israel Before Israel: Silent Cinema in the Holy Land* (Jerusalem: Steven Spielberg Jewish Film Archive, 1995), pp. 186–187.

2. Quoted, ibid., pp. 121–122.

Budapest Experiences[1]

by Márton Kurutz

1. Uncle Weiser

Once upon a time, there lived in Budapest an old chimney sweep who fell in love with the silent cinema and stayed faithful to it even after the birth of sound film. This passion was so great that he arranged a cinema in the flat where he lived, and regularly screened his favourite silents to his family and neighbours. When the war broke out, he dug a hole in the courtyard, wrapped the films professionally, and laid them carefully in their new shelter. Sadly, the courtyard took a direct hit, and all the films, which were of course themselves explosive, were destroyed. Ironically, the only reels that survived were the few which he had forgotten to put in the hole, and had kept in his flat. These were the ones that Uncle Weiser, as he was called, later brought personally to the Hungarian Film Archive.

2. Mór Jókai – Out of the Shadows

A few years ago, I was walking in the flea-market with one of my friends. We were talking about some old films which we knew about only through some faded stills and posters when an elderly gentleman came up to me: "I have quite a few old films, and I don't know what to do with them. I'd be very grateful if you could help me." I gladly took the opportunity to give him the address of the Hungarian Film Archive.

A couple of days later, the gentleman visited the Archive and told us that these reels of film had been given to him in the 1960s by a friend who used to screen them in cafés on a hand-cranked projector back in the 1920s. He directed the Archive's car to his plot in the village of Pécel, where he had a shabby wooden shack. On that hot summer day we were afraid that all those old nitrate reels would blow up in our hands... After about half an hour of careful exploration, we managed to rescue about 50 cans from the shelves in the shed. Back in the Archive, it took days to open them, one after the other – but what a thrill! On the Moviola I could see, among other fragments, a Hungarian film of 1916 with the title *By the Time We Get Old*. This often scratched and incomplete print starred some great names of the Hungarian stage – Oszkár Beregi, Zoltán Szerémy, Erzsi Mátrai, Lili Poór, Sacy von Blondel, and many others from the turn-of-the-century theatre scene.

Since then, the first film adaptation of Mór Jókai's brilliant novel has been restored, and lives in the Archive among the many other Hungarian treasures. These reels, which were believed to be lost but have – thank God – been found again, prove once more that Jókai transcends his era not only on the page but also on the screen.

Notes

1. These stories are translated from articles that originally appeared in issues 28 and 29 of the journal *Szám*, in 1994.

How State Production Targets Helped Save Nitrate

by Natasha Lako

A total of 164 kilometres of nitrate was transferred to acetate by the Albanian Film Archive between 1970 and 1990. This is a great amount for such a small country, one of the poorest in Europe.

I was nominated as the archive's director during the terrible time of the country's collapse in 1997, when the AFA won its independence from the previous state production company, where I had worked as a screenwriter. When I started my new job I found that 164 km of film had already been transferred, and started to wonder about it because of the tremendous cost involved. Faced with an array of various difficulties regarding our archive, I asked a lot of older people how such a terrifically expensive transfer to safety had been achieved. My film studio colleagues told me how the film had been transferred at the end of a fiscal year during which it had been impossible to realise some new pictures. The central economy's footage targets had to be met, and the "Shqiperia e re" studio was thus obliged to transfer the nitrate to acetate. It was imperative to achieve 100% production as far as total annual footage was concerned. Everyone was forced to work until the last minute; they were told, "Hurry, and be happy." The year's "production" was all from nitrate!

The 164 km comprised 52 features, 19 documentaries produced by other countries (including Britain), and 15 documentaries from Eastern Europe. The AFA is now co-operating with the Cineteca del Comune di Bologna to copy 60 reels.

Fortune on Our Side!

by Vigdis Lian

When the Norwegian Film Institute opened the Filmmuseum in March 1998, the National Museum of Photography contributed to the collections – together with other artefacts – a certain camera. When the camera was examined, we found inside it a couple of metres of processed nitrate film. This turned out to be a film showing a British plane landing at what is now our new main airport, Gardemoen. We could date the film to 1919, and were able to identify among the persons seen Director Meisterlin with his wife posing in front of the plane; the pilot, Captain Stewart; and a parachute expert named Faulder. We even knew that the film was produced by AS Cinema, Tivoli. Unfortunately, the material was in very bad condition, and there was no way of restoring it.

And this leads us to the interesting part of the story. The camera had been kept for who knows how many years, in a wooden house, a villa that continued to serve as a museum up till 1999,[1] situated in a peaceful neighbourhood in a small Norwegian city, Horten. The museum has had regular visits by groups of pupils from the neighbouring cities, and is was of course a tourist attraction in summertime (this is the sunny part of Norway), being well known to a wide audience for its fine collections.

We were given the camera on a visit to the museum, and happily brought it back by private car to put in the cellar at the Institute – all the time knowing nothing about its little secret, until a week or so later when we started examining it. And we are quite certain that the donor knew nothing about it either. With vivid memories of the fire in Kristiansand in 1980 (described elsewhere in this volume as "The Last Nitrate Fire in a Commercial Cinema?"), we must say that fortune was on all our sides.

Notes

1. The museum in Horten is currently closed, waiting for new, modern buildings, though this has no direct connection to this little story!

Henri's Magic

by Tom Luddy

In the fall of 1976, Henri Langlois came to visit me at the Pacific Film Archive. Although he did not look well, of course I could not know that this was to be our last meeting – his enthusiasm was as infectious as it had ever been, and he still had his talent for making extraordinary discoveries.

He noticed a pile of film cans that had been standing around for some time, waiting for my attention: I had looked at a couple of reels, and decided they were nothing special – from what I could see, it was just a consignment of newsreel, training and educational films of no particular interest. Henri was astonished that I had not looked at them all properly. How did I know there was not something extraordinary included among them?

He grabbed a can at random, opened it, took out the film reel and – looking just like the stereotype archivist – held up the first few frames to the light. "But this is Francesca Bertini in *La Tosca!*" he yelled. "I've been looking for this film for 20 years!"

"You must be joking," I replied. "You can't come just come in here, pick up a film at random and tell me that it's *La Tosca* from 1919 with Francesca Bertini. Things don't happen like that"

He assured me that it was so, and showed me the blue-tinted nitrate film, where a woman stood on a rooftop with a domed church behind her. "You see", he said, "that's Bertini in the finale, with Saint Peter's behind her."

We checked the film and rushed it to the projection room, and sure enough, it was the sixth reel of *La Tosca*. Of course, we looked through the rest of the films to see what other treasures might be included. Henri was convinced that one particular film from the 1920s had to be a significant film by an important director.

One of the actors in the film that had attracted his interest was clearly Tully Marshall, whom we recognised from some of Erich von Stroheim's films. We looked down the list of titles in Marshall's filmography. Henri picked out one and said, "There you are – *The Village Blacksmith*." He had no reason for this conclusion beyond his own conviction that it just had to be true, but when we looked over a synopsis for *The Village Blacksmith*, it matched the film we had been looking at. I could not believe it. Henri Langlois had simply arrived in Berkeley and pulled an early work by John Ford out of a pile of neglected nitrate – and that was not the only find: there had also been the reel from *La Tosca* and other important material.

It was magic, and I am sure it was special Langlois magic. Anyone other than Henri would have looked at those films and there would have been nothing to find. But for Henri, the films were there.

Thinking of Henri and his special feeling for film, I also remember one screening at PFA where he presented a group of Lumière films on safety film, films he transferred from excellent condition nitrate prints...

There was what appeared to be some kind of terrible water damage on the films: all kinds of blotches and other disfigurements. Henri explained that it is not true that nitrate disintegrates but safety film does not: it is quite the contrary, as these prints revealed. Nitrate may burn, and some nitrate films choose to die by disintegration, but basically well-stored nitrate does *not* disintegrate, while the opposite is true of acetate film.

At this point Linwood Dunn stood up and challenged Langlois: he was the man who did the effects for *King Kong* and was in town for another PFA show. He said he was the person who personally supervised the transfer to safety film of *Gone With the Wind*, and he went on and on, stating that Langlois did not know what he was talking about.

Henri then smiled, threw up his arms, and said: "There, you see – it's bad enough that these technical film specialists know nothing about the art of cinema, they don't even know anything about their own area of expertise!"

So I guess Henri was one of the first to note the vinegar syndrome...

A Sobering Lesson

by Janet McBain

On 14 July 1982, the Scottish Film Archive (as it then was) had an alarming experience, which was described in an internal report submitted to the Scottish Film Council immediately afterwards:[1]

Report on Nitrate Accident: Wednesday 14/7/1982

The Scottish Film Archive acquired a collection of nitrate film found in the Regent Cinema, Renfield Street, [Glasgow], during demolition, a few days prior to the accident.

On inspection, one reel was found to be badly decomposed – the emulsion on the film stock had dried and crumbled into dust. That can was immediately set aside for disposal. Another six reels, in a perfectly stable condition (i.e., with no signs of decomposition) were viewed, not selected for preservation, and were added to the material for disposal.

The decomposed reel was discovered on Tuesday afternoon. The Archive's Technical Officer Alan Crossan left the premises on Wednesday afternoon for the District Council Disposal Works at Dawsholm (material for disposal has to be delivered between 1:00 p.m. and 3:00 p.m.).

Going west along Great Western Road, 500 yards past Byres Road, he heard a "boom". Instinctively he braked, switched off the engine, and flung himself out of the van. The force of the explosion, which was initially contained within a lead-lined transit case, burned the interior of the van. The remaining six stable reels in a separate transit case did not ignite. The transit cases were not damaged. The Fire Brigade arrived 4-5 minutes later and were persuaded to let the remaining fire burn itself out. The police took Alan and the remaining film to Dawsholm before returning to Dowanhill.

The explosion was caused by a single reel of badly decomposed film and may have been due to a combination of factors – the heat inside the van and the jolting and shaking of the powdered remains.

Looking back on this incident after more than a decade, it is possible to suggest, with the wisdom of hindsight, that we should perhaps have resisted the temptation to agitate the powder any more than necessary. The decomposed reel was of sufficiently awful appearances that we took the unusual step of photographing it before scooping the dust back into the can. It was only a few hours later that the can was in transit.

At the time we got a fright, myself and our premises manager more so than the technical officer who was involved. He was not unduly disturbed – in fact, he regarded it as a bit of an adventure having to restrain a heroic civilian who rushed into the road to help, followed by the fire officers whose chemical sheets advised them to "douse with water". Eventually they were persuaded to let the fire burn itself out, and then they gingerly opened the back doors of the van with long-handled poles.

The incident had its amusing aspects. The police brought the technical officer back to the premises, whereupon his colleagues immediately assumed he had been arrested! Some hours later the charred remains of the mini-van were towed up the drive, much to the speechless, almost comic, distress of the premises manager, who supervised his vehicle with a fierce protectionism, and could be guaranteed to belabour any member of staff who so much as put a scratch on the paintwork.

It was a sobering lesson, however, and in the ensuing weeks we revised and tightened up our handling procedures. I am thankful that the footage that was lost was material we had already rejected, and that (tempting fate) we have never had such a fire in our stores on our premises. We fully intend never to do so.

Notes

1. This account is compiled from information sent to the editor in a letter from Janet McBain in September 1993.

She Needed to Get Rid of Them...

by Mona Nagai

One summer day in 1993 the Pacific Film Archive received a call from a man who wondered if we might be interested in "old Japanese films" which an elderly family friend was cutting up and burning in her fireplace – not for fuel, but because she needed to get rid of the films. Yes, we were interested.

When a PFA projectionist and I went to investigate, we met a vivacious woman of 82 who prepared lunch for us and told us how she had acquired the nitrate films she was conscientiously trying to dispose of. Starting in the 1930s, she and her husband had travelled to Japanese-American community centres and churches in northern California, showing Japanese films and occasionally hosting Japanese entertainers and movie stars. From town to town they hauled 35mm projectors as well as feature films, shorts, and newsreels. Most films were returned to the distributors (whom she believed had ties to the yakuza), but her husband had purchased two prints, and these along with a few stray reels ended up in the family's garage.

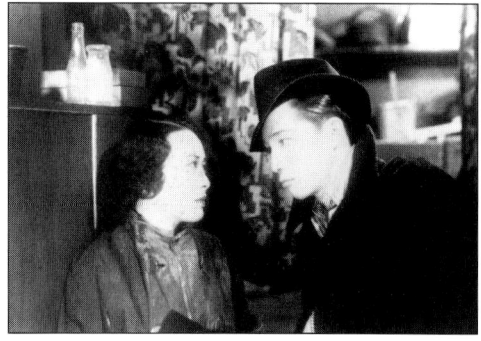

A scene from *Hodo no sasayaki* (1936).

Pacific Film Archive, Berkeley.

Somehow the property had survived the World War II years, when she and her husband were sent to a relocation camp. Now, over 20 years after her husband's death and the end of their business, she felt it was time to clear away these artefacts of their profession. Knowing that nitrate films were not to be put into the trashcan, and not knowing anyone who wanted the films, she took out her scissors and opened a canister to begin the challenging task of hazardous materials disposal.

Fortunately she had not progressed as far as the two feature films, which we later learned were extremely rare. Thanks to funding from colleagues at the National Film Center's archive in Tokyo, the Pacific Film Archive was able to preserve both films. The first treasure was *Chi-kyodai* (Foster Sisters), a 1932 silent melodrama by a well-known director, Hotei Nomura. Except for some loss of footage from nitrate decomposition in reels 5 and 6, the print was in excellent condition, and it provides a rare record of several stars of early Japanese cinema. (A 16mm master positive was subsequently discovered in the Shochiku studio vaults.) The other find was a nitrate print of a 1936 jazz and tap dance musical, *Hodo no sasayaki* (Whispering Sidewalks), directed by Denmei Suzuki, a matinee idol, and photographed by Sadao Yamanaka, a great director. Believed lost for many years, this musical melodrama stars Betty Inada, a second-generation Japanese-American who had a successful career as a singer and dancer in Japan.

Our encounter with these nitrate prints led us into a fascinating area of film exhibition history as well as the history of jazz in Japan.

How We Salvaged *Kalia Mardan*

by P K Nair[1]

The following article by the Assistant Curator of the National Film Archive of India (Poona) gives a thrilling account of how an old film was rescued from complete extinction, in order to be given a new life, preserved for posterity. It shows the pressing need for all those who have the interests of cinema at heart to send to the National Archive whatever old film material they may have, as in the case of this 50-year-old Phalke film. But it must be done before it is too late.

Ever since we got the first reel of *Raja Harischandra* (1913), we have been looking for the remaining reels, as well as other films of Dadasaheb Phalke, for preservation in the National Film Archive of India. The fact that we could not locate at least one complete work of the film pioneer, who made more than 50 films during his lifetime, has long been a matter of great concern to all of us.

And so, when Mr Nadgaonkar of Prabhat Chitra Mandal told us one day that the whole of *Kalia Mardan*, the Phalke film made in 1919, was available in Nasik, we were naturally thrilled. We immediately set our network rolling. Mr Raim Gabale telephoned and confirmed that Mr Neelkanth Phalke, one Phalke's sons, was willing to hand over to the Archive some Phalke material he had. I wrote to Mr Neelkanth. There was no immediate response. Several days later, Mr Neelkanth's brother Mr Prabhakar (who lives at Nasik) called on us at the Archive office. Later I realised that the purpose of his visit was to learn about the Archive and what we proposed to do with the film. I explained to him the scope and function of the Archive, and how we were attempting to perpetuate the memory of Dadasaheb. I also explained to him the danger of keeping inflammable nitrate material, and the immediate need to transfer it to a safety base to ensure its long-term preservation. Once convinced, he confirmed that he did have a few reels of *Kalia Mardan*. He promised to hand over the material to the Archive during his next trip to Poona.

A still from *Kalia Mardan* (1919).

National Film Archive of India, Pune.

Soon afterwards I contacted Mr R Washikar, a mutual friend, who had arranged my meeting with Mr Neelkanth Phalke. It was the second Sunday of the New Year, 1970. We first spent some time discussing our strategy, along with Mr S Nadgaonkar and Mr L G Soneji of Prabhat Chitra Mandal, who also joined us for the discussions. We set out for Dombivili, and reached Mr Neelkanth's place in the afternoon.

I was introduced to Mr Neelkanth, and immediately noticed the son's striking facial resemblance to his illustrious father. An enlarged photograph of Dadasaheb adorned the small drawing room. After the preliminary introductions, Mr Neelkanth brought out two rusted tins and placed them before me. I examined the tins one by one. They contained a number of bit pieces of positive nitrate film, surprisingly in fairly good condition. Two bits were tinted blue. On closer examination, I noticed the bit contained the last sequence of *Raja Harischandra*. I was thrilled at the possibility of having the complete *Raja Harischandra*. We had obtained one reel (the first part) earlier. But alas! The reel we got from Mr Neelkanth was the last portion (the fourth part) – the middle reels (parts number 2 and 3) still to be located. What we have now are the first and fourth parts. I am confident that the remaining reels may also turn up sometime in the near future from somewhere. The bits also contained negatives of a short actuality, *Sinhasta Mela*, made by Dadasaheb in the early 1920s. The title of each bit was neatly written in Marathi on the leaders. The light suggestions for printing were also noted on the leader, along with the titles. Mr Neelkanth told me his father used to write a few numbers on each film roll, which he later found were instructions for printing.

Mr Neelkanth confirmed that the whole of *Kalia Mardan* was available with his brother at Nasik, and advised that we go to Nasik immediately and collect the material before it was too late. He also gave me a letter addressed to his brother, instructing him to hand over the material to the Archive.

Bidding goodbye to Mr Neelkanth and his family, we set out for Nasik that same day. We waited at Kalyan for the Nasik train. We were thinking what a historic day it would be if we could manage to acquire a whole film by Phalke, which could be shown during the Phalke Centenary celebrations being planned by the Maharashtra Government. Leaving our two friends from Prabhat Chitra Mandal, Mr Washikar and I boarded the Nasik train at about 8 p.m. We reached Nasik Road Station round about midnight. It was chilly and the streets were deserted. We managed to reach the residence of our friend Dr Berde, who was expecting us. Dr Berde confirmed that he had discussed the matter with Mr Prabhakar, and that we were to meet him the next morning. Dr Berde understood the significance of our mission, and extended all hospitality; we spent the night at his home.

Early the next morning we went to Mr Phalke's house, the same house, I was told, where Dadasaheb spent his later years. I could see the insignia of a camera at the entrance of the building. The house was modest, and rather old. The sands of time had left their imprints on the wall. Mr Prabhakar had taken out all the reels of *Kalia Mardan* by the time we reached there. One look at the tins and I could see they had not been taken out for a considerably long period. We had a difficult time opening some of the tins, the lids were so jammed. A strong nitrate smell was emanating from each tin. I noticed that some of the bits had started decomposing. In fact, a couple were already reduced to yellow pulp, and there was no alternative but to discard them there and then, lest they create problems for the transport of the remaining reels to Poona. Mr Prabhakar was very particular about having a list of the contents of the reels copied for his records.

We were in a hurry to catch the earliest transport back to Poona, so we could not spend more time with Mr Prabhakar. I was keen to check whether he had more material than had been shown to us. He later confirmed that those were all the tins he had.

The newspaper taxi which used to ply between Poona and Nasik for the dispatch of the daily Marathi newspapers *Sakal* and *Kesari* was very convenient for our return transportation. Dr Berde's car was put at our disposal to bring the material from Phalke's place to the taxi-stand. We started from Nasik at about 10:30 a.m. The journey was long and tedious. I was constantly looking back, always conscious of the archival reels kept behind us, and every time the car bumped my heart took a jump. The transport of nitrate film was indeed risky, but we had to go through with it, as there was no other alternative, and it was in the national interest to salvage a Phalke film of 1919. We reached Poona by evening, deposited the tins in the Archive nitrate vault, and gave a sigh of relief.

It is true that we did physically bring the material to the Archive. But that was only one small part of the job. In fact, the real trial, and the much more arduous work, awaited us in our attempt to copy the material onto safety film in a presentable form which could be shown to audiences everywhere.

Notes

1. This article first appeared as pp. 66–67 in the *Phalke Centenary Souvenir*, edited by Firoze Rangoonwala, published by the Phalke Centenary Celebration Committee (Chairman: Shri M D Chaudhari) in Bombay on 30 April 1970. It is reprinted here by permission of the author.

Role Models

by Dinu-Ioan Nicula

In 1994, as a student at the Film Academy, I became an employee of the National Film Archive in Bucharest. At that time the word "nitrate" meant for me only a page from the technical history of the cinema, or, alternatively, a humid and mysterious warehouse, which at the beginning of the century had been one of the prisons around our capital. An atmosphere of indifference seemed to surround the Archive's collection of nitrate, and of course as a mere newcomer I could only accept what I found.

A year went by, and in the autumn of 1995, Gian Luca Farinelli and Vittorio Martinelli came to us, for research in the framework of the "Search for Lost Films", part of the LUMIERE Project. In recognition of my interest in silent film, whose existence is synonymous with the nitrate, and also because of my good knowledge of the Italian language, I was appointed to work with the two experts.

Suddenly, working with them revealed to me not only what "nitrate" really is, but first and above all the meaning of the archivist's passion. Sitting at a rewinding table, taking reel after reel, some of them gluey as mud, others fossilised hard as stone, Farinelli and Martinelli were trying to discover the secret values of forgotten films. In this way appeared a beautiful collection of frames, tinted and toned, from films whose existence was forgotten in Romania. One surprise was the discovery of a marvellous documentary – *India, a Country of Dreams* – while another was an old film featuring the Italian comic Atoff. How many more moments of delight were spent in the three days when I was at the side of the two great Italian researchers, presenting to them some of the principal dishes of Romanian silent film?

Gian Luca Farinelli and Vittorio Martinelli left our country, to continue their pilgrimage dedicated to the value of the world's film archives, and for us things returned to how they had been before. From somewhere far away, however, I always felt their friendship, and their example was decisive last year, when nitrate came back to the attention of the National Film Archive with the full awareness of the urgency that, to ensure its conservation, we must make good what has been forgotten or neglected for years upon years.

Les miracles ont lieu non seulement une fois

by Vladimir Opela

Every year, the Národni Filmový Archiv receives prints on nitrate film stock. For the most part they come in as single films, or as small specialised collections. The first large collection – some 100 films from the 1910s and 1920s – was donated soon after the founding of the NFA by Mr Bouda, the proprietor of a travelling cinema. The second big collection came to the NFA under rather unusual circumstances.

In 1966 we received a call from a small Czech village, from someone saying they had found some films at their chicken farm. I immediately set out to investigate. To my great surprise, I unearthed from under a layer of chicken droppings about half a metre thick around 80 tinted feature films from the 1920s, largely Westerns starring Tom Mix, Buck Jones, and so on. They were the collection of another travelling cinema proprietor, Mr Pisvejc, who had died some years before. Only one of the films – *The Red Dance* (1928), directed by Raoul Walsh, and starring Dolores Del Rio – was too deteriorated to be saved. What we had found were the films that had been programmed in Mr Pisvejc's cinema. We knew that in his collection there had also been documentary films, but all our further searching proved unsuccessful. We failed to find any of them, and had to conclude that they were lost.

Then, on September 23rd, 1998, Mrs Kotrbova handed over to us 96 boxes of film which she had found in the loft of her country house. They turned out to be the missing documentary films from Mr Pisvejc's collection!

It may take time – 32 years, in this case – but fortune does sometimes smile on the archivist.

"I am opening the 2nd gathering year of the 4th Quarter of the Parliament! ...": A Nitrate Memory

by Professor Sami Sekeroglu

It was 1975. We had decided to go to the flea market with a friend of mine who taught at the same University with me. He had a Peugeot car. It was quite old. He had covered the worn-out seats with a black and red checked cloth. It was a large piece of cloth, almost covering the inside of the whole car.

We were both interested in antiquities. The flea market was far from where we were, on the west side of the city. I used to visit it whenever I got a chance. I had once seen a 35mm camera from the early years of cinema, but could not buy it, as I could not afford it. This visit, we wandered around for a long time, but did not find anything.

There was a big grocery store where we parked our car. The grocer had arranged the fruits and vegetables so nicely that they almost looked like a picture. It attracted my attention because I had studied painting. "Look," I said to my friend, "if this guy were trained he could have been a very good painter." "Never mind," answered my friend. "Let's buy some fruit and spoil the painting…"

While my friend was busy with the fruit my eyes caught sight of a 10-to-12-year-old boy who was working industriously. There were many 35mm film cans by his side. He was scrubbing off the film emulsion, cutting the films into very small pieces, and pushing them into a bottle. I watched him carefully. I understood what he was trying to do, but tried to seem uninterested. It was obvious that the films were of nitrate stock, and that there was acetone in the bottle. He was dissolving the pieces in the bottle and producing film adhesive.

I asked him, as if I were not aware of what he was doing: "What are you up to?"

"I am dissolving these films in acetone to make film adhesive," he replied. "I make it up in small bottles and sell them."

I glanced at the labels on the cans. They were handwritten, and illegible. I picked one up for a closer look. "Oh my God!" I was sweating all over. The film was *Attatürk's 4th Quarter Speech*. This was exactly what was written on the can.

I was very excited, but I was trying not to show my excitement to the boy. I was worried that my friend would notice the films after his shopping was over, and that he would spoil everything by showing his excitement. I threw the can from where I stood. It rolled a little bit. Then I bent down and put it back in its place.

I got closer to my friend and said, "There are some very important films. Don't show any sign of excitement; don't talk. Please don't say anything." He was astonished, but played along. "Weigh these, young man," he said to the boy, handing over the fruit, "and tell us what we owe."

I looked at the films while they were busy. "Give these films to me," I said to the boy. "I have a small nephew, he can play with them."

The boy answered, "No. I can make at least 550 liras out of these films."

We started to bargain. The boy was pleased with the deal. He understood that he would be freed from his wearisome task, and still make more money than he was hoping to earn. I bought the films for 250 liras.

The boy then said they had many more films, and took us to the warehouse. There were many more. "Wait here," he said. "I will call my father."

In the meantime, I had thrown 20 or 30 cans under the seatcover of my friend's car. I was satisfied. The boy came back with his father. His father understood that we were interested in the films, and kept raising difficulties. I was afraid he would demand the films I already had back. I said, "OK. Let it go." We got back into the car and left.

A scene from *Attatürk's 4th Quarter Speech* (1934) – the original sequence filmed with insufficient light in the Parliament chamber.

Sinema-TV Enstitüsü, Istanbul.

The films we got were *Attatürk's 4th Quarter Speech* as well as an original print of Visconti's *Senso* and a dupe negative of *Rocco and His Brothers*.

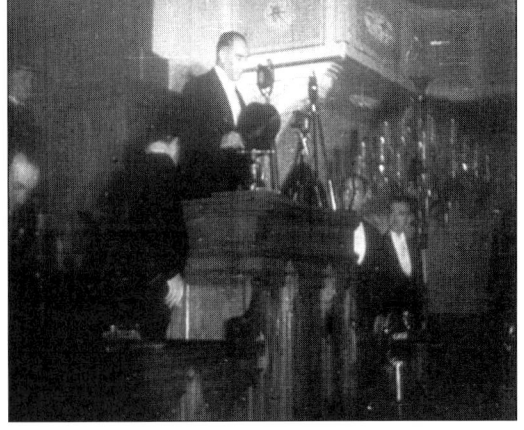

I knew all about the film of *Attatürk's 4th Quarter Speech*. I had conducted an interview with Cezmi Ar, the cameraman who took the film, and he had told me the whole story – but he had also told me that the film was lost in a fire.

Cezmi Ar was one of the first cameramen of early films in Turkey. He was the cameraman on almost all the films of Muhsin Ertugrul, one of the first Turkish theatre and film directors. This was what he had told me:

> I was summoned urgently one day. "Come to the Parliament. You are going to shoot Attatürk's speech. Make your preparations. Nothing should be missing." I mounted my camera, but the light was not strong enough in the chamber. "The light is insufficient here – it is not possible to shoot film, there will be no images," I said. But the answer I got was "Shoot."...

A scene from *Attatürk's 4th Quarter Speech* (1934) – the repeat reading specially arranged for the camera in front of a black curtain.

Sinema-TV Enstitüsü, Istanbul.

> The result was not good. The images were weak. Everyone was worried. Baransel Pacha said sadly, "I will inform him." He came back smiling. "It is not important," he [Attatürk] had said. "Prepare a suitable place. I will come and make the speech again, then you can shoot."

> Everyone was satisfied. I shot the speech again in front of a black curtain in a room.

> You could see that he took this very seriously. Afet Inan and Salih Bey entered the room while we were shooting. He got nervous and said, "We are shooting a film here, as you see. Go to the Parliament...," he said angrily.

[The year was 1934. Baransel Pacha was a General, Afet Inan a female Turkish historian, and Salih Bey was Attatürk's aide-de-camp.]

The film consisted of 3 reels: a 35mm nitrate combined sound print, a

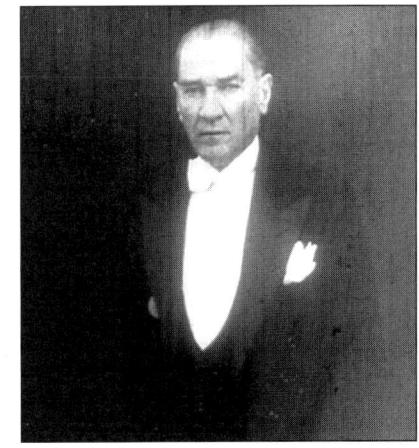

separate optical soundtrack, and the original camera negative. The negative was shot full frame – when projected, a print made from it would be cut at the sides and at the top and bottom. Later I made a new print reduced to sound aperture.

Fifteen years went by. Some films arrived from the archives of the Army Photo Film Centre. A small package was among them. It was an untitled sound print. The images were weak, but you could make out Attatürk speaking at the Parliament: "I am opening the 2nd gathering year of the 4th Quarter of the Parliament...," he was saying, and people were applauding. This was the beginning of the film Cezmi Ar had told me about. It was the beginning of the film I had bought at the grocery store – the version shot in the Parliament with insufficient light. It started with the same words of Attatürk: "I am opening the 2nd gathering year of the 4th Quarter of the Parliament..."

I united the two pieces of film, but left the opening words of both versions, because it could be seen that the setting had changed: *"I am opening the 2nd gathering year of the 4th Quarter of the Parliament! ..."*

Northern Lights: Father Hubbard's Alaskan Bonfires

by Francine Lastufka Taylor

Father Bernard Hubbard (1888–1962) was a Jesuit priest. Not only was he a priest, but he was quite an adventurer as well. He was called the "Glacier Priest", but this nickname did not come about because of his exploits in Alaska – he had already earned it climbing in the Himalayas some time before he came to Alaska. He was a missionary, and he used his talents to help raise money for the Catholic missions. He was an interesting character in that he managed (as Jesuits have traditionally done) to keep his vows but also to engage in a very full sectarian life following his passions and interests. His talents as cinematographer and photographer in particular were very professional. He shot on 35mm, and his footage and programmes released as Pathé films were seen by millions throughout the country in movie houses from the 1930s through to the late 1950s.

When Father Hubbard came to Alaska, it is not clear to me exactly how large his parish was. I know he travelled among the Inupaq Eskimos from Nome, down along the coast, skipping over to Diomede Island and roaming as far south as Katmai National Park and into the interior on the Yukon River, visiting with Athabaskan Indians and Alutiiq people. It is clear, though, that the village of (Ukivok) King Island became a special interest of his. (Ukivok, incidentally, means "kayak", not "king".) In the years between 1937 and 1939, he decided to stay there. It is hard to say whether this was a result of the Islanders' spiritual needs or because he wanted to more thoroughly document their life, culture, and traditions. My suspicions favour the latter. I think, because the islanders were separated from the mainland of Alaska by 40 miles of often rough weather and churning seas, he felt they were possibly more innocent and less corrupted by western culture. In true colonial, paternalistic fashion, he wanted to keep them that way, innocent "children of God".

Among the fruits of his stay there is the King Island Hubbard Collection of film and photographs. The master materials belong to, and were initially housed at, the University of Santa Clara, his home-base Catholic college, which dictated his missionary efforts. Around 1990, long after Hubbard had died, one of the King Island elders, Paul Tiulana, an old friend of mine who resided in Anchorage, came to me, concerned about this collection. It seemed that the archivist – Julia O'Keefe – recognised that the collection was historically very valuable, and that the storage area where it resided was totally inadequate. She had initiated an effort to find money either to properly store and archive the materials, or to find a more suitable institution that could house them.

The Alaska Moving Image Preservation Association was then in its first year of existence, and we did not have a temperature/humidity controlled vault. Since we were coming from a production background, not an archival background, moreover, our knowledge of preservation was yet to be learned. The decision was made by Santa Clara to send the collection to the Smithsonian, with the provision that we should have Beta-SP and VHS distribution dubs made for our archive, in effect repatriating the collection back to Alaska. This was duly done.

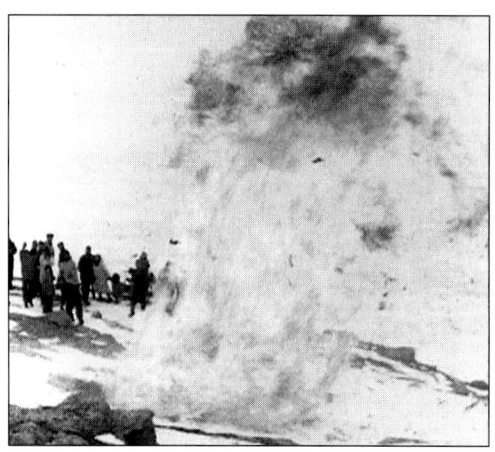

One of Father Hubbard's nitrate-fuelled bonfires on King Island.

If you look through the 25 hours of moving-image materials that Father Hubbard filmed on King Island, you will occasionally see spectacular bonfires celebrating different events at special times. I asked Paul what they were using, because the bonfires almost looked like fireworks spurting upwards from the ground. He chuckled and told me that they were pieces of nitrate film. At first I assumed that he meant scraps of undeveloped nitrate from the film that Father Hubbard was shooting. Paul said no – it was portions of Hollywood feature films. Hubbard would bring the films with him from Hollywood to King Island to entertain the villagers. He was something of a celebrity, and had great connections in Hollywood so he was able to get the latest films. However, in some instances he would decide that certain scenes were inappropriate for these innocent "children of God" to see, so he would snip off the offending scenes and re-splice the film before showing them.

Paul was around 13 years old at the time, always curious and very precocious. He didn't go into any detail on what the cut scenes were because I suspect the good Father made especially certain that young, curious eyes were denied these titillating spectacles. We both giggled, agreeing that they had to do with sex. I would assume they might have been love scenes, but the good Father's concerns were probably also about indecency in the matter of clothing. If you think back to the uncensored years of the 1930s before the Legion of Decency (organised by the Catholic Church) was established, you will remember those clingy satin body-hugging gowns with low v-neck bodices and no bras, and probably get the picture. Female bodies have always been a problem for the Church.

There is an irony in viewing one of the bonfires. It is in celebration of the successful dragging of the statue of Christ the King to its position above the village. There is no flat land on King Island. The village is unique in that the houses are all on stilts sticking off the side of a steep slope, in a way inviting comparison with a bird rookery. It was a tremendous effort to haul the statue, which was larger than life, up to its resting place on the very highest point of the island. We have footage showing almost the entire village pushing and pulling the crate that contained it (which looks something like a casket) up the steep side of the island. After the religious dedication ceremonies were over, they had a bonfire. I smile when I think of those scantily-clad women and kissing scenes dissolving into sparks dancing above the saintly statue of Christ the King that night.

When I would ask Paul, who has since died, about what it was like living on King Island, he would say it was "just like heaven", but the village is now abandoned. The statue of Christ the King has these days lost his crown, but the rest of him is still perched high over the village, standing guard over this tiny piece of heaven on earth, and watching for the occasional return of the King Islanders. These days, they visit only during the walrus-hunting season, or during the height of the berry season in the fall, or in the spring when the fresh young greens are popping up out of the ground that is perhaps still fertilised by the ash of Father Hubbard's bonfires.

Nitrate Tales – Hong Kong's Vanishing Film Heritage?

by Angela Tong

It is difficult today in Hong Kong to come across anything relating to nitrate film, since our pre-war film history is mostly caught up in decay and changes as studios close down and people pass on. The content and technology of cinema have also undergone dramatic evolutions. For the new generation, knowledge of nitrate film is a dead-end, since it is not a medium that is used today. We have been lucky to find one or two persons able to provide oral testimony about the history of nitrate film, and it is our pleasure to share their stories.

Delivering Film Inside an Ice Bag

Mr Wong Ming (born 1928) is the managing director of a film processing laboratory. He joined the film industry in the 1940s and was a famous cinematographer in the 1950s and 60s. From his testimony, we know that when a crew went on location shooting, film was packed inside ice bags, and the process of loading the camera had to be done under the shade of a tree or in shadowy places in order to avoid the risk of spontaneous combustion from the heat.

Processing Film for Extra Income

There has long been a practice in Hong Kong's darkrooms whereby the fixing solution is saved rather than thrown away, and the used solution is sold to "chemical traders" who extract silver from the solution. Currently, after each 10,000 feet of black-and-white film is processed, about 250 grams of silver can be extracted. According to current prices of silver, every 60 grams fetch only HK$40. The processing of one feature film today yields just over HK$100; thus the "silver value" is considered slight. In the old days, however, the "silver value" was far greater, and was, in fact, the main source of income for most lab technicians. At that time the amount of nitrate film was twice as great as other types of film, and the price of silver was around HK$200 per 60 grams. In other words, an average feature film could yield over HK$1,000 in silver value. All technicians, from master down to apprentice, benefited from the practice of extracting silver from film. Little wonder that veterans recall those days with relish, and why more copies of nitrate films did not survive.

The Projectionist's Dilemma

Kwok Wah has worked as a projectionist for over 30 years. He is 73 this year. To Kwok Wah, projecting nitrate film was a particularly taxing experience because of its highly inflammable nature. During projection, if the light from the carbon lamp should ignite the nitrate film, the repercussions would be too horrendous to contemplate. Therefore, if there was even the slightest hint of a fire, safety procedures were implemented right away. The projector had to be switched off, and the power cut off immediately. Otherwise, not only would the feature film not be saved, but the whole cinema was in danger of being burnt down.

Nitrate Film Raising Hell

On 22 September 1948, a great fire burned down the warehouse of the Wing On department store in Central, Hong Kong Island. The cause of the fire was believed to be nitrate film. The fire burned for 32 hours before it was extinguished, necessitating the mobilisation of the whole of Hong Kong Island's fire-fighting force. The whole warehouse complex, comprising nine 5-storey blocks, was completely destroyed. Damage was estimated to cost HK$30 million dollars, and the fire claimed the lives of 119 persons. The report following the inquiry stated that the fire was caused by nitro-cellulose film scraps, resulting from the illegal storage of some 30 metric tons of photographic film in the warehouse.

Preserving Nitrate Film

Hong Kong's climate is subtropical, and its humidity levels are on average over 70%. Such a climate is not suited to preserving film. Lacking the necessary resources and conditions to preserve film, many of our feature films made on nitrate stock have not survived. The Hong Kong Film Archive has managed to secure over 10 copies of nitrate films from the early days, including a few classics from the 1940s and 50s starring Zhou Xuan, a famous songstress of the period. Apart from the collections of a few film veterans in Hong Kong, the archive's collection has been built up by the preservation of some early Hong Kong films from the World Theatre in San Francisco. The more congenial climate in San Francisco, plus the attitude that film should be preserved and cared for, have undoubtedly prolonged the lives of some of our film classics. As for Hong Kong, apart from about 10 or so extant nitrate films, our nitrate tales to be passed on to future generations mainly consist of the recollections of our film industry veterans.

Nitrate Film in the Slovenian Film Archive

by Lojz Tršan

The Slovenian Film Archive was founded within the Slovenenian National Archives in the year 1968, with the agreement of Triglav Film, the only Slovenenian film company. The collection of the Film Archive now comprises 450 titles – some 480,000 metres of film. All have been copied onto acetate stock.

After Liberation, Triglav Film had taken possession of most of the Slovenenian films shot in the decade before 1945. As a business organisation, Triglav Film had no commercial interest in the storage of the film material and therefore made no serious arrangements for its preservation. A considerable part of the material has consequently been more or less damaged.

Triglav Film had tried to solve its storage problem by building a temporary storehouse to be used until they could find a better alternative. This storehouse was situated in Trnovo, in a swampy district near Ljubljana. The ground beneath the storehouse was waterlogged, and due to inadequate heating and poor damp-proofing in its construction, the survival of the films was put at risk. Many of them, especially those on the lower shelves, were affected by damp, and mould attacked either the emulsion or the base. The storehouse also suffered huge variations in temperature – Triglav Film's records show that the temperature in the storehouse could rise alarmingly in summer, and fall to –15° C in winter.

Ivan Nemanic, the first Head of Slovenian Film Archive, remembers conditions at Trnovo:

> My memory goes back to the beginning of the 1970s, when I used to call regularly on the Triglav Film film stores in Trnovo. As I approached, I looked at the building in which this first film company in post-Second World War Slovenia was located. Its provisional look seemed to confirm that it could only house films temporarily – its thin brick wall and tin roof were hardly a sufficient protection for films. The temperature in the building varied according to the seasons. During the winter, it was so cold that one had to button up one's fur coat, while in the summer, the temperature climbed to 28°C. The cans on the lower shelves were covered with a greenish coating of mildew. How could Slovenian films survive in such conditions? I knew that the older, pre-war films of which Triglav Film had taken custody and the entire post-war production of the company were all sharing the same fate.
>
> The working conditions of the archivist were fairly primitive. Her working space was an office and a warehouse at the same time. There were heaps of boxes full of inflammable films stacked on wooden shelves. Somewhere nearby, an old electric stove was placed in winter to provide some heat for the room. The archivist used to view the films on a simple rewinding bench, using a magnifying glass to view individual frames.

Of course all 35mm films from before 1953 were shot on inflammable nitrate stock, and it was recommended to build special secure vaults for these films. Until this could be achieved, the Archive suggested that it might be possible to store its older inflammable films in the former chapel of the Mala Loka castle near Trebnje. This idea has not been realized, and there has as yet been no other prospect for the building of new vaults. Meanwhile, for strict safety reasons, the Archive was not able to accept nitrate at its storehouse in Ljubljana.

Because of all this, Triglav Film made an agreement with the Jugoslovenska Kinoteka to store its original film material shot on inflammable stock, its nitrate prints, and part of its safety material in Belgrade. The first consignment was sent there in February 1968, and the remainder had followed it to Belgrade by 1974.

The Archive meanwhile decided on a programme to rescue Slovenia's film heritage and to copy all inflammable films on safety acetate film. Since 1968, the first year of activity by the Slovenian Film Archive, Triglav Film has transferred the films produced between the two wars, those made during the war, and part of the film material produced in the post-war period (mostly newsreels produced before 1950) – 56 films in total.

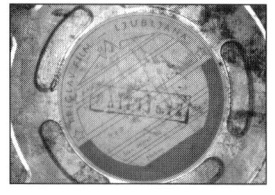

In 1971 the production company Viba Film delivered to the Archives part of its holding of sound films and all the original materials of feature films and short films shot between 1955 and 1965 (12 feature films and 131 short films). The company had decided to clear its own vaults of all films older than five years, and those considered to be without market value.

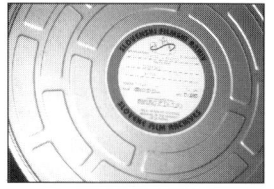

By 1972, the Archive had copied 44 older films on nitrate film stock and also some new films, altogether 18,500 meters. The copying process was undertaken in Viba Film's laboratory in Ljubljana. Finance problems presented huge difficulties – the fact that 15 copied film prints had to be left in the laboratory reveals the extent of the Archive's problems.

Slovenian nitrate film – an old can still carrying the Triglav label, and a new can with our own label.

Slovenski Filmski Arhiv, Ljubljana.

Ivan Nemanic takes up the story again:

> When Triglav Film merged with Viba Film, the nitrate films were put into large parcels, catalogued and sent to the Jugoslovenska Kinoteka in Belgrade. They were then stored in the warehouse for inflammable film, where they stayed until 1991. When Slovenia showed the first aspirations to independence, I was informed by the Jugoslovenska Kinoteka that Slovenian films would not be stored any longer in Belgrade if Slovenia were to insist on her secession. I began to look actively for an appropriate storage site for inflammable films within Slovenia.
>
> Before independence, I had seen a television broadcast about the underground premises of the Home Office in Gotenica. The idea occurred to me that the nitrate films at the Jugoslovanska Kinoteka could be stored there. In June 1991, those films were transported to Gotenica on a refrigerated lorry. This is the way that the original nitrate films were saved.

As Mr Nemanic indicates, in co-operation with the Jugoslovenska Kinoteka in Belgrade, the Archives of the Republic of Slovenia managed to recover all its nitrate films just a few days before the attainment of independence and the outbreak of war in Slovenia in 1991. (These were the films that Triglav Film had earlier transferred to Belgrade.) However, Slovenia still had no adequate storehouse for inflammable and explosive nitrate films, and the Archive could not ensure special storage conditions for film with these characteristics. It therefore reached an agreement with the Home Office for the storage of both the inflammable and acetate films in the air-conditioned underground rooms of a training centre in Gotenica near Kocevje. The majority of our archival film collection, including all nitrate material, is now stored there.

Two Important Nitrate Deposits

by Inmaculada Trull

Translated by James Smither

1. After the Flood

The Valencia flood of 1983 may not have been either the most spectacular, or the most costly in terms of lives, but it is remembered by the Cots family because it allowed the discovery and the partial recovery of the only known copy of *El Monje de Portacoeli* (The Monk of Portacoeli), the sole film by cinéaste Ramon Orrico Vidal, made in 1926. When the water level subsided and access to the basement was possible, the Cots beheld the grim sight of hundreds of metal cans, corroded with rust, almost forgotten for the last 60 years. The family then decided that this was the moment to move them to a safe place and try to save what could still be rescued, and they contacted the Filmoteca de la Generalitat Valenciana.

Like Moses in his floating basket, many of the cans had miraculously preserved their contents from the effects of the floodwaters. Millions of cubic metres of water, which had broken their banks, devastated fields of produce, and flooded entire towns, showed respect to the unique cinematic legacy of Ramon Orrico, a good proportion of the rolls of nitrate lovingly numbered by the hand of their own creator.[1]

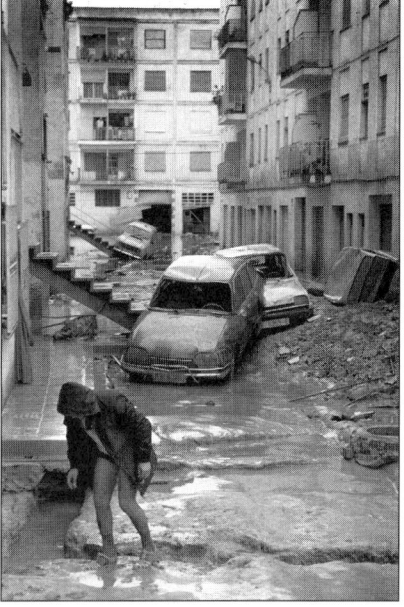

The aftermath of the 1983 flood in Valencia.

Jesús Ciscar, *El Pais.*

2. Memory of a Sad Honeymoon

In March 1992, a young woman deposited in the archive of the Filmoteca de la Generalitat Valenciana 7 metal cans containing as many rolls of nitrate film. She explained that the owner was her aunt, Maria Elena Rodriguez Bauza, and that she herself (her name is Silvia) – being conscious of the danger posed by keeping such material in the house and aware of the rescue work carried out by the Filmoteca – thought that perhaps we might be able to derive something worthwhile from the images. She also told us that her aunt was very elderly, and that she would dearly love to surprise her by showing her a copy of the film on video, provided that the condition of the materials would allow it. I can perfectly recall the moment when we opened the cans: those reels of nitrate appeared defiant, impeccable, with no trace of decomposition, odourless, their perforations intact – just as if they had been sleeping for 60 years, peacefully, expectant...

As moving as watching the images was the story behind them. Maria Elena and her husband Rafael had embarked on their honeymoon to the Matto Grosso in 1934 – a scientific expedition, into the deepest Amazonian forest. Emotionally and practically committed naturalists, forerunners of the ecology movement, they devoted almost 2 years to the collection and classification of animal and plant species, and to the study of the local ethnic communities. They carried with them a 35mm camera, and made a filmed record of their journey, but the documentary was never completed. Rafael was ill when he returned to Spain, and died 4 years later. Maria Elena, widowed at 27, put away those reels of nitrate that contained the last pictures of her husband, posing happily among the indigenous people. It took her

583

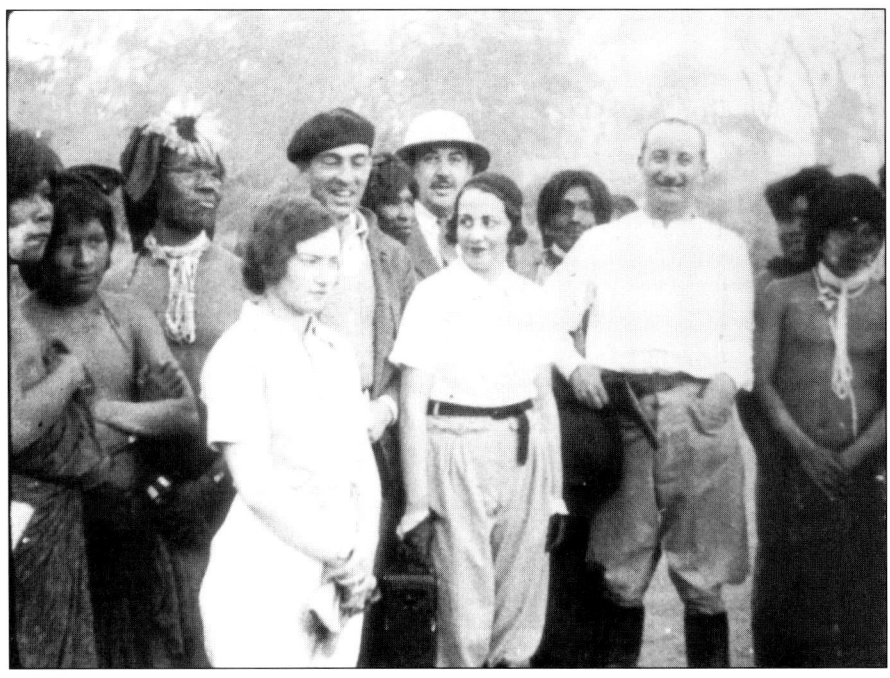

Maria Elena Rodriguez Bauza (centre) with her husband Rafael in a posed group in the Matto Grosso, 1934.

Instituto Valenciano de Cinematografia
(La Filmoteca), Valencia.

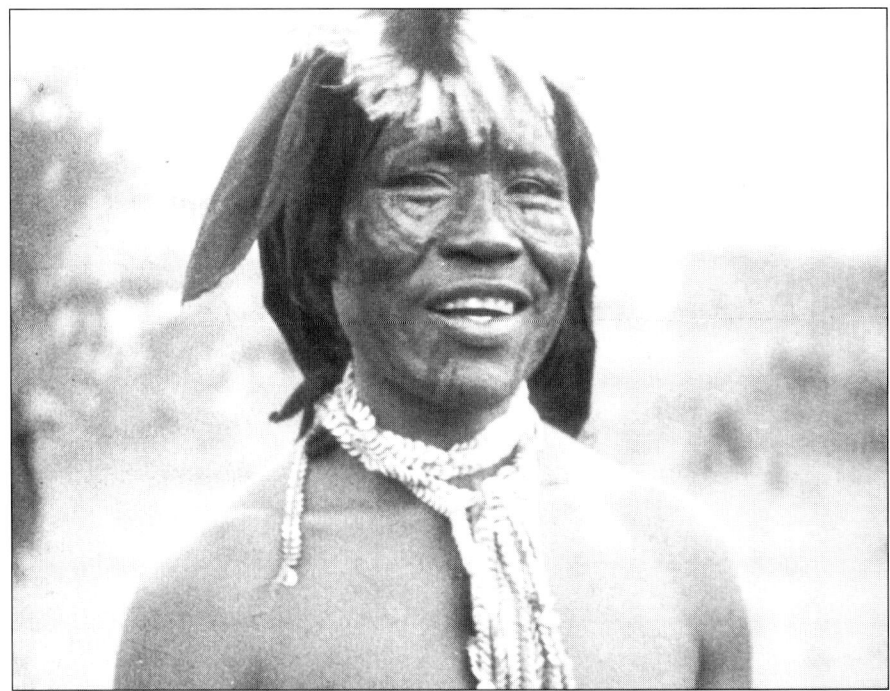

Another picture from Maria Elena Rodriguez Bauza's unusual honeymoon film.

Instituto Valenciano de Cinematografia
(La Filmoteca), Valencia.

niece, 60 years later, to rescue from certain death those fragments that showed not only the life of her family but also the geography and history of South America – fragments on nitrate, which had valiantly survived hostile conditions on both sides of the Atlantic Ocean.[2]

Notes

1. Information supplied by the Cots family, owners and donors of *El Monje dePortacoeli*.

2. Information supplied by Silvia Garay, owner and donor of her aunt's film.

Some Good Advice
(And Some Rather Less So)

by David Walsh

When the Imperial War Museum in London unprecedentedly set out to include the films of the recently-concluded First World War among the materials which it collected, the materials made available to it offered cause for serious concern. Some negatives were showing "considerable signs of wear, whilst others were slightly discoloured" (these were films which could have been no more than 4 years old). In 1920, therefore, Edward Foxen Cooper, the "Government Cinematograph Adviser" whose responsibilities included care of this prototype archive, sought professional advice from Kodak and others about what would be necessary to ensure the long-term survival of a film collection.

The reply which he received from Kodak is possibly the first formal advice ever offered by a film manufacturer on the problems of preservation. Although conservators today would strongly disagree with the advice on moisture levels, and might question the notion of wood and rubber as suitably inert storage media, the "Report" would still constitute a useful set of guiding principles and instructions for anyone confronted with a need to preserve a collection of nitrate film. Here it is, in its entirety.

Report by Messrs. Kodak, on the preservation of Cinematograph Films.

We do not think that anybody has sufficient experience in the keeping of motion picture film to be able to state what will happen to film kept for fifty years; films [are] often kept for long periods without showing any visible change and it is quite possible that film might be usable in fifty years' time. At the same time, films usually shrink with keeping so that they cannot be projected, and it may even be difficult to print them, while there is always a danger of the film becoming brittle with age.

The time which will elapse before any difficulty is encountered will depend very much on the circumstances under which the film was prepared and has been kept. Any failure to wash the film completely or to fix it in clean hypo will greatly accelerate change, the change being least in a perfectly clean film in which, in addition to the base, there is present only clean silver and gelatine. All film which is to be kept for a long time should, after the ordinary fixing bath, be given another bath in fresh hypo and should then be washed very thoroughly indeed, being given a final rinsing in distilled water before drying.

The conditions of keeping the film will also have a great influence. We do not think that anything would be gained by keeping the film in a vacuum; indeed, it is not impossible that change might be accelerated by diminished pressure, but the film should be kept cool and not too dry, the lower the temperature the better, provided the film is not actually frozen, and the film would probably keep best under the conditions prevailing in an ordinary refrigerator containing ice so that the air is moist to the extent of the vapour pressure of water a degree or two above the freezing point. If this is not convenient another suggestion would be an underground vault arranged so that it keeps cool in summer, and well ventilated.

The film should be spooled on wooden spools, not on metal, without paper wrapping, and should be contained in sealed tin, or better, fibre or hard rubber boxes. The film should then be carefully examined annually by rewinding so that any alteration can be detected and the film copied.

It does not necessarily follow, however, that even with these precautions, film fifty years old can be run through a motor picture machine, but film of this age even if shrunk could probably be printed upon a slow speed printer arranged not to produce any strain upon the film and the freshly printed film could then be run.

Film stock is composed chiefly of nitre cotton and this substance, while apparently stable, is subject to very slow change. The rate of change at normal temperature is so slow that no effect would result if it continued for many years at this rate, but under certain circumstances the rate may increase so that decomposition may set in. Once decomposition has started no treatment will stop it, and copying is the only remedy.

Nitrate's inflammability and its process of chemical deterioration may be the most famous causes for concern in preservation terms, but film – whether acetate or nitrate – is also liable to shrinkage as it ages and dries out, and of course beyond a certain point a shrunken film can no longer pass without risk of serious damage through most standard forms of projector, printer, or other film-handling equipment.

In 1921, having obtained government funding for this purpose, Foxen Cooper began to act on the advice he had received from Kodak. The measures which he adopted included not only such standard precautions as refixing and rewashing the original films, but also the preparation of what were probably the world's first "archive protection masters" – duplicate "soft print" copies of endangered films, printed from the original negatives onto Eastman Rochester No. 1 Positive stock for the specific purpose of preservation rather than exploitation. In all, over the following 2 years, some 80,000 ft (ca. 25,000 metres) of new master positives would be printed as the result of this programme.

Inspired by the importance of the responsibility placed on his shoulders, Mr J W Smith, the General Manager of the Williamson Film Printing Company to which the work had been entrusted, came up with a novel suggestion. Given that these masters were for long-term storage, he proposed that the separation of the perforations of the new stock should be some 4% greater than the standard "to allow for shrinkage in years to come". Fortunately, his suggestion was tactfully turned down: the typical nitrate film of this vintage has now (after about 80 years) reached a shrinkage of around 2%, meaning that, printed to his proposed specification, Mr Smith's masters would still be a good 2% *over* pitch!

The "Tenacity" of Nitrate Film

by George R Willeman

Several years ago, we received a number of original Biograph negatives of some Mary Pickford shorts. As it is my job to do preliminary examinations on new nitrate material, I was very excited at the prospect of working with such old and rare material. When I opened the first can, however, my heart sank. The reel was a crusty brown mass of deterioration. I was about ready to consign it to the deep when I noticed that some parts did not seem as bad as others. I decided to dig into the reel to see if I could save anything.

What I found was amazing. It seems that in the 1920s an enterprising gentleman named Nathan Hirsch got hold of Miss Pickford's old Biographs and decided to reissue them. To tart them up a bit, he created a new set of titles, very long and florid, which often expanded the one-reel films into two-reel films! This is what I found when I began taking apart that reel: Hirsch's 1922 titles were completely rotted – they could not even be unrolled, and I had to cut them off the reel. Sandwiched between the rotten titles, however, was the original 1911 era Biograph negative – *and it was unaffected by the rotting film!* Even where the Biograph film was right up against the 1922 Kodak stock, there was no sign of deterioration! I was, to say the least, truly amazed. I believe that once the bad material was removed, we had a complete Biograph negative, sans titles, but that is the way they did their negatives anyway. I found this same phenomenon on several other Pickford Biographs, and the only explanation I can find is that in 1911, film was still somewhat of a "cottage industry" and more care was taken in the making of that film stock. Well, whatever they did, these negatives are now pushing 90 years old and are still in excellent condition!

Nitrate Muse

A sampling of original works inspired by the theme of nitrate film.

Captain Nitrate – A Superhero for the Centenary of Cinema

by Borislav Stanojevic

Borislav Stanojevic is currently the Head Librarian of Jugoslovenska Kinoteka's Library. He was born on 23 April 1953, and raised in Belgrade, Serbia, Yugoslavia. He has diplomas from the Academy of Dramatic Arts (Film and TV Production) in Belgrade and the Music Academy (Theory & Composition) in Bucarest, Romania. Since 1981, he has worked as a composer, screenwriter, and producer in a wide range of creative and professional venues for theatre, video, TV, and film. For a time he was a Professor of Film and TV production, and from 1988-1996 he was an archive researcher of film music, animation, and avant-garde films in Yugoslav Film Archives. (Like any sane Taurean, he proudly boasts of his pretty woman, teenage daughter, and other quite disparate masterpieces.)

As part of its response to the worldwide commemoration of the Centenary of Cinema in the mid-1990s, the Jugoslovenska Kinoteka published in 1996 *Usamljenost super-heroja: Kapetan Nitrat* (Loneliness of a Superhero: Captain Nitrate), written by Kinoteka employee Borislav Stanojevic and illustrated by Russian-educated artist Sinisa Radovic. Also known as *The Nitrate Sting*, it was intended to be the first volume a series of graphic novels featuring the superhero Captain Nitrate, which would open up a new popular format for the exploration of some of the issues of film preservation. The second volume, *War Games*, was published in 1999, the artist this time being Macedonian cartoonist and illustrator Aleksander Sotirovski.

As Radoslav Zelenovic, Director of the Kinoteka, explained in 1996:

> The project's overall goal is summarised by FIAF's own, "to promote film culture", but even more to draw closer attention to the cause of film preservation and the noble philosophy of film archiving, film ark-ives being a module for saving our visual heritage for the future. The author of this project, himself an archives researcher employed by the Jugoslovenska Kinoteka, felt that the cause of film archiving, although a worthy and inspiring idea, tends to circulate in an academic, somewhat hermetic "Ivory Tower" manner, mainly between the archives themselves and those organisations and individuals that are already professionally inclined to be sympathetic. The cause of archiving – "to preserve, to show, or to promote film" or however it is expressed – must seek to inspire as broad a range of public support and interest as possible. There is a broad potential public – from 7 to 77 years old – that we archivists continue to neglect.

> There is a whole generation, basically mythologically oriented (as in every millenarian age) that is easily accessible through the informational channel of a medium with contemporary mythic appeal – the comic book. There is little or no need to emphasise that comic books are becoming a successful art form and educational tool, and have been acknowledged as such in recent decades. Much serious research would confirm that the public for comics is

a large one, and is substantially the same as those whose primary moving-image awareness comes from channels other than classic cinema (such as TV or video, computer games, etc.).

To these multitudes, *Captain Nitrate* wishes to convey, in a Méliès-like or Gilliam-esque manner, mythologically disguised truths about the detective work that is film archiving, the truly superhuman work of preserving film, and so on. Captain Nitrate and 'Troll Remote (a kind of Don Quixote and Sancho Panza for our times) are conceived as semi-grotesque guides and mediators through the aesthetically as well as mythologically linked worlds of celluloid and electromagnetic moving pictures.

In addition to the publication of the graphic novels themselves, the project offers additional content. Thus, the first volume includes an essay on the superhero phenomenon, and the second continues the analysis. Volume 2 also provides an elaborate background scenario, placing the story of Captain Nitrate in the context of a quasi-real world of superpower domination and global machinations. In this world, state interference with film and television has progressed to a point where the comic strip offers the only valid outlet for a documentary message.

Captain Nitrate – The First Two Chapters
Usamljenost super-heroja: Kapetan Nitrat (Loneliness of a Superhero: Captain Nitrate)/*Kapetan Nitrat 1: Nitratna Zavera* (Captain Nitrate 1: The Nitrate Sting)
Script: Borislav Stanojevic; Illustrations: Sinisa Radovic
(Belgrade: Dedalus, 1996; published in Serbian, with an English summary)

The action takes place in Slavigrad, capital city of the small central European state of South Beovia.

Ace, a plainclothes police agent, presses the remote control to set off an explosion in the house of Vatroslav Vostok, an employee of the state film archive. Entering the ruins, Ace is confronted by two strange characters: Captain Nitrate and 'Troll Remote. Ignoring 'Troll's warning, Ace fires a shot at Captain Nitrate, but is burned up as a laser-like ray is emitted by the "wound". The police and television attribute the explosion to Vostok's unauthorised private experiments on nitrate film, and imply terrorist connections. DD, a film director and critic and friend of Vostok's, claims on TV that on the contrary the explosion was a political assassination, forming part of a worldwide conspiracy regarding nitrate film. He is immediately arrested. Captain Nitrate, watching from a rooftop, and DD in the police van, recall the events that led up to this situation.

DD watches as Vostok conducts alchemistic experiments to develop a process to remove the inflammability from nitrate film, while agents of a sinister international alliance compete to lay explosives in the basement with a view to destroying his workshop at home. The alliance is making propaganda that nitrate represents a kind of plague and is responsible for the majority of the world's ills. The resulting panic is used to justify the gathering of all surviving nitrate film into central depots – allegedly for copying and to protect the public, but in reality to be used to create an ultimate source of energy that will assist their ambitions for global or even galactic domination. FIAF – the International Federation of Film Archives – is bribed and bullied into submission, but an illegal militant wing calling itself IFAF (the International Front of Avenging Film) remains active.

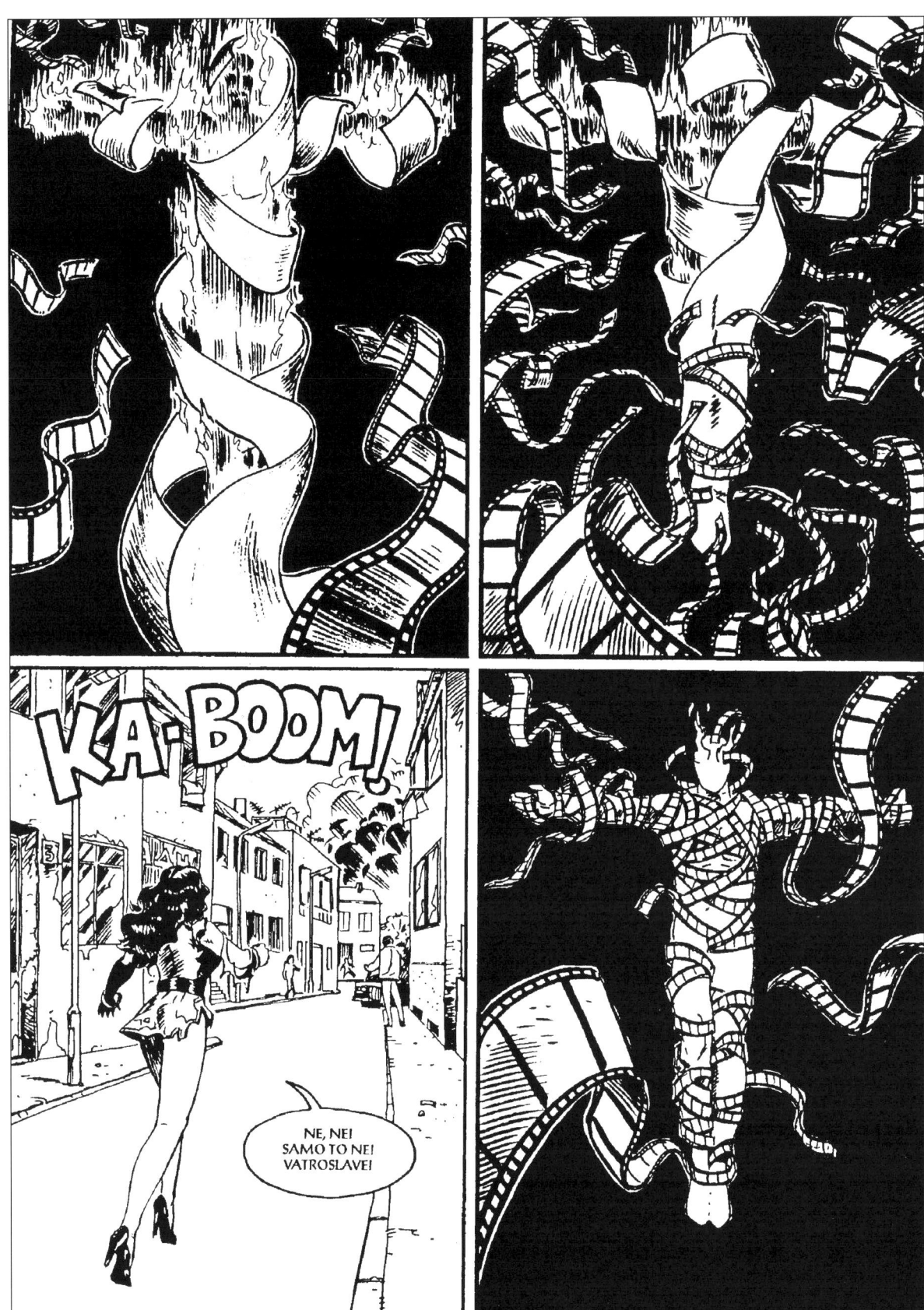

A panel from *Usamljenost super-heroja* (Belgrade: Dedalus, 1996): the explosive birth of Captain Nitrate.

Borislav Stanojevic.

In his dreams, Vostok encounters 'Troll Remote, a herald from the world of electronic moving images, who explains the reality of the nitrate sting, and Vostok's future role as superhero; he also meets the Jonglars – a troupe of grotesque atomic angels who watch over his work and assist it at the molecular level – and the gods of moving pictures (an array of luminaries from Aristotle and Archimedes to Edison and the Lumières). The Gods are too busy disputing the question of which of them is entitled to claim primacy in inventing film to take much interest, but the Lumières finally confirm that Vostok will become Captain Nitrate. 'Troll Remote – and a kind of satanic incarnation of Georges Méliès – subsequently appear in the real world as well, as Vostok's destiny catches up with him.

When he awakes, Vostok discovers that his experiments have produced a semi-sentient substance called Aaanirezis (Auto-Adhesive Asbestoid Nitro-Resistant Substance) which envelops him and confers protection and other powers on him. Refusing an order to give up his experiments and to write a letter condemning IFAF, Vostok is fired from his job at the archive. 'Troll Remote helps him to discover that his superpowers are not to be treated lightly, and that he is not yet in full control of them. He ignores the warnings of The Bomb, a highly seductive female police agent who has fallen in love with him, and returns home to continue his experiments. The house is destroyed in a huge explosion. Aaanirezis protects Vostok. His transformation into Captain Nitrate is complete, and his mission begins: Nitrate can't wait.

Captain Nitrate 2 – War Games

Written by Borislav Stanojevic; Illustrated by Aleksander Sotirovski
Translated into English by Anica Stanojevic
([Macedonia]: Data Pons, 1999; published in English)

The story continues from Volume 1. Outside Slavigrad, Captain Nitrate is not happy in his new incarnation. 'Troll Remote asks him how strong his commitment to nitrate ever was if it cannot survive the transformation, and points out that in any case there is no time to waste – a large military convoy carrying nitrate is on the road, and may be about to be hijacked. While the Captain is struggling to master the skill of flying, the hijacking does indeed take place: the convoy is taken over – and almost all of its escort wiped out – by the agents of the monster Filmfungus, who claims the cargo in the name of IFAF. Filmfungus's agents leave alive one driver from the convoy, who is able to answer correctly two questions on film history. Falling back to earth, Captain Nitrate is engaged by a patrolling flight of jet fighters, whose leader discovers (like Ace in Volume 1) that it is not a good idea to shoot at the Captain. 'Troll Remote extricates the Captain from the fight.

Back in town, The Bomb is threatened with dismissal for her indiscipline in the earlier episode, but her irresistible charms ensure that she is kept on the force, and given the task of finding and infiltrating the IFAF organisation in Slavigrad.

Captain Nitrate and 'Troll Remote follow the hijacked convoy to a disused factory, where they confront Filmfungus. It transpires that he too is a former researcher, who had turned himself into a living cure for the fungus that can eat away at old film. Now, embittered that the world has ordered the wholesale destruction of all nitrate film anyway, he plans an apocalyptic explosion of the hijacked load, taking as much as possible of the army, the media, etc., with him. The two super-characters fight. Filmfungus is the stronger, but Captain Nitrate first ties him up in strips of film and subsequently destroys the conditions for fungal growth by careful application of heating.

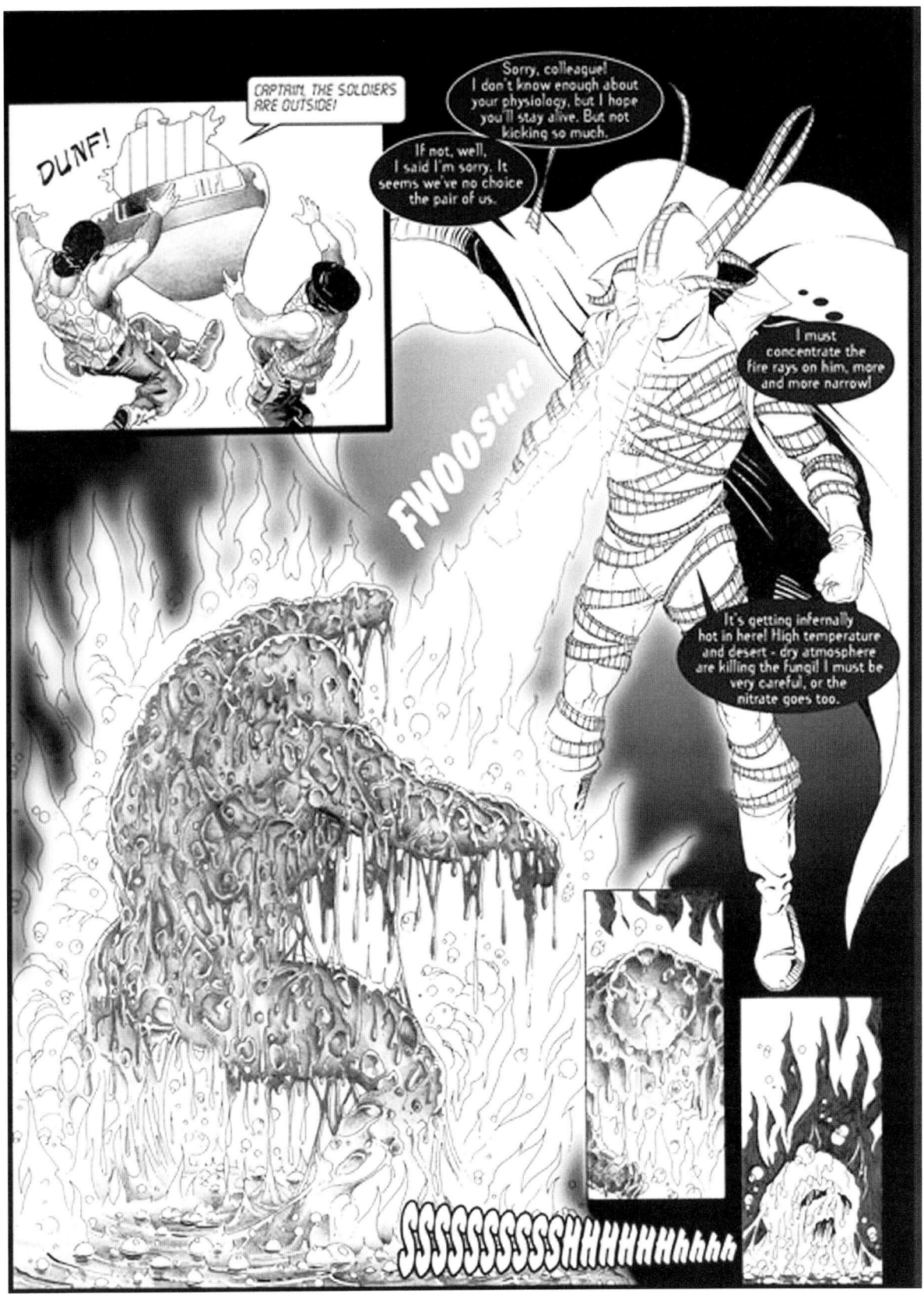

A panel from *Captain Nitrate 2 – War Games* ([Macedonia]: Data Pons, 1999): the confrontation between Captain Nitrate and the monster Filmfungus.

Borislav Stanojevic.

Captain Nitrate orders the IFAF agents to save the hijacked load, and 'Troll Remote to try to infiltrate the military control and communications system, while he himself distracts the armed forces – although he has still not mastered the art of flying. Inside the Army HQ computer, 'Troll Remote is attacked by the system's anti-virus defences; seeking to escape through cyberspace, he is next challenged by the Cybernet-Weaver and its own antibodies. He is losing the fight until the Jonglars intervene and save him. He is now able to take over the system.

Captain Nitrate saves the lives of a helicopter crew, but after he has returned them to their colleagues, their commander still opens fire on him. Angered at this betrayal, the Captain almost launches his own attack, but relents at the last minute. The taken-over computer orders the soldiers to attack each other. While the battle rages outside, Captain Nitrate, reunited with 'Troll, constructs an Aaanirezis-powered spacecraft to launch the salvaged nitrate film into sanctuary in Earth-orbit.

On Earth, The Bomb continues to try to uncover exactly what happened at Vostok's house. Captain Nitrate again rages dangerously at the loss of his original identity, but 'Troll shows him that Aaanirezis can give him back his former outward appearance. Exhilarated, the Captain sets off to return to his original life.

An Appeal

In 1996, the Kinoteka invited international collaboration in the further publication and development of the *Captain Nitrate* project. The invitation remains open. Any national moving-image archive or publisher who is interested in responding is encouraged to add to the existing Captain Nitrate saga its own national episode, developing its own film archival context, problems, and cinema history, and introducing its own graphic and/or textual material, created by its own artists and writers. In this way, Captain Nitrate will become both a universal national and international publication – and hero.

Footage – a poem

by Mario Petrucci

Mario Petrucci is a physicist, ecologist, freelance writer, teacher and poet. His first full-length collection, Shrapnel and Sheets *(Headland), was published in 1996 to wide acclaim, including a Poetry Book Society Recommendation. In 1998 he received a London Arts 'New Writers' award, and he is a Fellow of the Royal Literary Fund. During 1999 he was Poet in Residence at the Imperial War Museum in London, supported through the Poetry Society's* Poetry Places *scheme. He developed a variety of educational resources relating to war and poetry for the Museum (including* "Search and Create", *a uniquely-styled Poetry Hunt) and wrote a number of new poems inspired by his explorations of its collections, one of which is published for the first time here, by generous permission of the author. He is currently the Museum's Literacy Consultant, creating innovative activities and* "synaesthetic" *educational captions at the Cabinet War Rooms and IWM-North.*

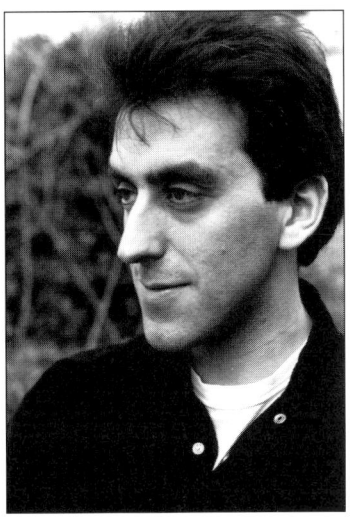

Mario Petrucci.
Imperial War Museum, London.

FOOTAGE

Trenchcoats bedraggled
limb-fluent behind
the flickering hair

the mad zag of a scratch.
Mist of time, literally.
Watching

That quenched hour
of afternoon waiting
for you, when people walk

like the dead, I pace
for you, I watch
like the dead

Children.   Stood like stock
on grass, innocent as cows
in Red Square.   But they know

the camera's eye, are still
for it, shy to it.   Time
has brought blood to celluloid –

blushes these scarecrow men
who gap-tooth into camera
who waltz to silence

Yesterday.   Bracket fungus.
Palace balconies scalloped
with gold.   Today

collapsed by frost
into curd.   Like walking wounded
I walk you to the car

A man wrenches back
Falls to death in four frames
He does not fall

continuously, but as he falls
finds four selves for company
Always the same

Side-on, a woman, facing camera
places a finger in the black wound
of her limewashed hearth

Woman.   Trying to climb back
into you, into you, but only
finger, tongue, prick at a time

The large part of conflict –
standing, the drag
at the cigarette, pacing

the sudden dash of eyes
through smoke, just four frames
to fall in

For whom do I watch?
Ghost-blur on the screen
that flicks a leg, a hand?

A pony.   Shock across pelt
as the thorn of shrapnel
is tweezered from shag

You push back
a boy, complete, formed right
to the thumbnail

Pat on the back.   Cigar.
I don't smoke.   All breath
is smoke

Men, leap into frame
swim across frame, a river
of shaggled men, walking

A press of men, dull slug
of flesh, slow ripple
of defeat

Co-ordinate animal, grey-slick
of muscle, each man a scale
of the snake surging

past old nests
that once were houses, walking,
lifting hats, smiling

for the lens, men without
teeth smiling, nursing
a bundle the size of a fist

A bundle brought in
for display   the crushed face
squeezes out its cry

who squeezes out
my cry when I've got it
so good?

Commandant walks in
and the hand at the lathe
is half a frame too keen

their grin at His arrival
half a face too soon
into camera   *Hello*

they stride me into smoke,
up to the bar, clear the old
stout bottles, part the stench

Stout bottles! cannons
like stout bottles
that poff into men

a black crawl of men
staggered across unbroken snow
like a thaw

You bend to the water
so I can scrub your back
You gasp into heat like a thaw

rock with my pressure as I
pace you, keep eyes on the bundle
that frets by the tub

A man lathers
another man's back.   Two horses
stumble in mud.

A cow, pick-axed
through the white locks
of its forehead.   Twice.

The image plants the germ
but is not the germ.
It is innocence

violate.   I must watch
the men, the snake
because they show it

here in the afternoon while I
wait, in this quenched hour
that the fungus melts in

till the smoke you stumble
out of, your gasp at the child
you lift from the tub

This woman, your body,
this child yet to come
to manhood –

will we smile at camera
at the cannon, at the cannon
that is a stout bottle, will he

Then the counting
of legs, ranks of ankles
faces covered, chests

sunk into mud
the ranks of legs, a horse
rearing, flaring, smells

death.   Boys eager
with the shovel
to stand with the men

in this canal
that is a grave
the next corpse

flops into
casual as a father
rolling from his couch

I see the foam
brown with your rust
the tub

that is a canal
of rust
sunk in snow

I can see
This, see this, yet
do not act

and the boys with shovels
look into camera
with each carcass that

rolls to final sleep
Their eyes say – *do you see,*
do you, you eye

of long memory?   Do you
see that?   But they
and I

do not act

Éric Rondepierre –
A Fascination with Decomposition

Edited and translated by Catherine A Surowiec

Editor's Note: The work of Éric Rondepierre, and his book Moires, *were first brought to the attention of the editors of this book by Gabrielle Claes of the Cinémathèque Royale/Koninklijk Filmarchief, Brussels, and by Michelle Aubert and the staff of the CNC, Bois d'Arcy. A review of* Moires *by Philippe Azoury, which had appeared in* Cinémathèque *(1999), no.15, pp.142–145, was provided, and this led us to the published folio itself.*

Additional insights into Rondepierre's work and its background came to our attention when Sonia Dermience, then on the FIAF staff in Brussels, told us about a detailed, illuminating study, Eric Rondepierre. Un art de la décomposition, *by Thierry Lenain, Professor of Aesthetics at the Université libre de Bruxelles, published in 1999 in Brussels by La Lettre volée. The following brief introduction owes a great deal to Professor Lenain's work. We would also like to thank Madeline Matz of the Library of Congress for information regarding Rondepierre's research there. (CAS)*

There is a whole aesthetic about the art of ruins, decay, and destruction, and the ephemeral qualities intrinsic in the properties of some artistic media. In this context, the physical characteristics of nitrate possess a certain fascination for artists. Primary among them is the work of Éric Rondepierre, a French artist born in Orleans in 1950, who can be said to be the first artist to work with images of decomposing nitrate. After studies at the Sorbonne and the Ecole des Beaux-Arts, and a period as an actor/dancer in avant-garde troupes, he wrote a theoretical thesis on the work of Marguerite Duras, and turned to the exploration of the nature of cinematic images in his work. In 1988 he began producing a series of images from videocassettes, pausing the images frame by frame, isolating and photographing blank black screens with subtitled dialogue. This resulted in a 1993 exhibit entitled "Excédents", in which he explored "le noir sous-titré" (subtitled blackness). In 1990 he began a second series of works, "Annonces", using the same method of *stoppage* (a term used by Marcel Duchamp, originating from a word for "patching" or "mending" in the vocabulary of cobblers and tailors), this time photographing paused video images of coming-attraction trailers and credit sequences, incorporating fragments of lettering. These images, from films ranging from the 1930s to the 1960s, were the basis of exhibitions in 1992 and 1993.

After these intriguing shows, in 1993 Rondepierre received a travel grant from the French foreign ministry to research in American film archives. This time he was unsure of what he was looking for. His first stop was the Museum of Modern Art in New York, where he spent several weeks looking at 16mm study prints, trying to gain his bearings in the world of archival research. Prior to this he had always worked at home from videos, and found his images by the pure accident of *stoppage*, producing his photogrammes simply by experimental manipulation. Now he encountered the films themselves, approached via requesting specific titles from printed catalogues, dealing with staff and viewing restrictions, and he had to devise a photographic set-up with a Steenbeck viewer. His next port of call was the Library of Congress. Here the detective story continued, although he was still without a goal. He felt, he later said, like a blind man, feeling his way towards an unknown destination. He was going through some old acetate trailers when purely by chance Madeline Matz brought him something completely new: preservation copies of early films showing the effects of nitrate deterioration. Here was his epiphany: the discovery of decomposition. At last he found what he had been seeking. By the time he reached his third and final archive, George Eastman House, he was able to request original nitrate prints, sometimes only fragments, displaying signs of deterioration, and was able to photograph them directly, frame by frame. He would know right away when he found exactly the right frame: "C'est ça."

These photogrammes, of images corrupted by chemical instability in various ways, completely by chance, metamorphosing into haunting, striking effects, their original features sometimes mutilated or almost totally obliterated, took hold of his imagination, creating their own universe, a mysterious, sometimes nightmarish, surrealistic other-world, full of its own meanings, open to interpretation. Upon his return to France, Rondepierre formulated his own "Précis de décomposition" (published in *Recherches Poïétiques*, I, Winter 1994), where the image plays with its own destruction, a form of "aberration" described as "aléatoire", in other words an accidental product of the interplay of art and nature. Back in his studio, Rondepierre spread out the images and started selecting the strongest ones for exhibition purposes. Three sub-ensembles grew out of this, "Masques", "Scènes", and "Cartons". The images of "Masques" were centred around the human figure; "Scènes" explored the relation of one or more figures to their spatial surroundings; while "Cartons" presented a selection of corrupted intertitles from silent films. Around 20 images from the first two groups formed the basis of a show, "Précis de décomposition", at the Galerie Michèle Chomette in Paris in March-May 1995, the year of the Centenary of Cinema. A further selection from all three groups travelled to the Museum of Modern Art in New York later that year, where it was exhibited in the photography galleries, again under the title "Précis de décomposition".

This theme evolved into his next exhibition, "Moires", a new series of decomposed photogrammes, all in colour, which was displayed at the Galerie Michèle Chomette in March-April 1998, as well as a related book of texts and photos. Published by Filigranes/Galerie Michel Chomette, Paris, in 1998, *Moires* consists of an unbound folio of fiches featuring 23 frame stills of nitrate images in various stages of decomposition, accompanied by 22 Proustian fictional texts. Rondepierre acts as a combination of narrator, artist, and protagonist, as well as spectator and voyeur, weaving a mixture of intimate journal, memoir, travel narrative, and work of fiction, with fragments of reflections, notes, and descriptions, inspired by, interpreting, or deconstructing the images and our perception of them. "Moires" translates literally as "watered silks", fabrics whose appearance changes with the position of the spectator; the verb "moirer" means to cloud or water a ribbon, drawing a parallel with the blurring and distortion of the nitrate images selected by the artist. Confounding and blurring points of view, space, time, and identity, *Moires* is a complex experience in the art of interpretation and seeing, whose images invite us to consider them in their singular autonomy as well as in the more or less oblique relation that they establish with the text.

A new series of Éric Rondepierre's photogrammes of decomposing nitrate images, "Les Trente Étreintes", was projected in slide/diapositive form during the 2001 Cinema Ritrovato in Bologna, as part of a series of programmes of avant-garde films and films about film.

Excerpts from Moires

The following translated extracts seek to give the English language reader a flavour – they can do no more – of the texts written to accompany the images in the published version of Moires. *The passages chosen are some of those in which the artist addresses most directly his feelings about the materials on which he worked and the circumstances in which he encountered them. The translations are my own, with apologies to the original. (CAS)*

3. La Lecture/[Reading/Perusal] (excerpt)

A film archive is a world apart. In order to understand it, one must go through its card indexes, its ribbons of film, its rows of shelves, set in motion its apparatus and machines, go along its corridors, its cities, take trains, planes, and automobiles, inhabit its dwellings, supervised or not, wait for delays, knock at the right door, be on the lookout. Certain archivists are on guard, ever watchful; one must meet them, talk with them. Advances, reticence, much patience, time. At the start there is never anything, then little by little tongues start to loosen, the fear of fires recedes ("we have only just received..."). Sometimes nothing; one is never sure. One has to show things, discuss, make oneself understood. In general two syllables suffice to interfere with all communication: "ni-trate". Pardon? Nitrate: everyone commonly calls by this name the support on nitrocellulose base used until the middle of the 1950s, and forbidden after that. Nitrate films that have escaped destruction by decomposition or fire (very few) are often unable to be viewed or projected. This is a characteristic which differentiates them from acetate films, which themselves can also be very damaged. These problems do not interest the world at large, except for some rarefied historians, researchers, and professionals. From Tokyo to Moscow, New York to Mexico, Paris to London and Brussels, the attitudes, the solutions, change and evolve. But everywhere there is the same secretive, more or less paranoid atmosphere, the same subterranean struggle against death and decomposition, the same mania, compulsive and doubtless legitimate....

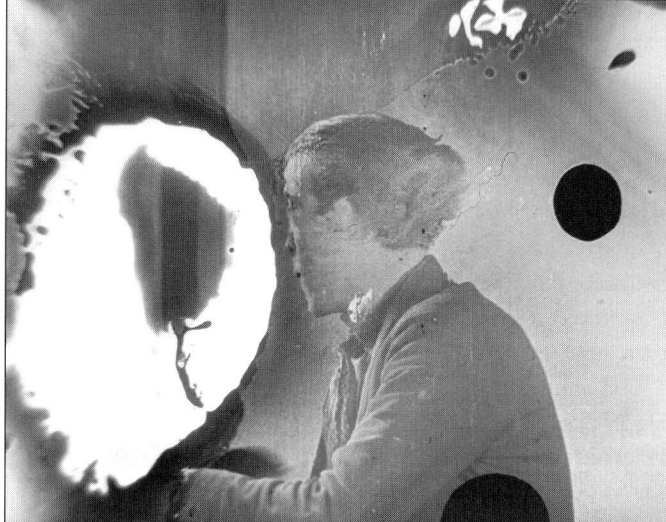

Le Voyeur: number 4 in the published version of *Moires* (Paris, Filigranes/Galerie Michel Chomette: 1998). (See also Colour Section 2.)

Éric Rondepierre.

4. Le Voyeur [The Voyeur] (excerpt)

Everything is a party to chance, as in an inert logic, despite the interest provoked in me by this sort of knowledge made of supernatural determinism, most often by indifference. From all this immortal death subject to caution ... I had a devastating vision of destruction....

6. La Table [The Table/The Editing Table] (excerpt)

Little by little, the difference diminishes between my feeling for her and the object of the research into which I hurl myself. I emerge from my dullness, and each day I start to investigate a quantity of elementary phenomena. I discover the cold rooms where thousands of round metal cans stagnate.... At the same time I study her body and the archive building, the idea of pleasure and that of revelation.... A simple direct contact, the closest to the object I can manage, is enough for me. I leave the editing room in order to work directly with the footage counter over the rollers. My white-gloved hands turn yellow, rose, then black. To each ancient image corresponds an amazingly high number of impressions. This convulsed or reversed face, this languished pose, belongs to the history of one of our nights; this whiteness comes from the daylight shining on her skin – the very idea of a territory begins to disappear. Some shots no longer have any perforation for several metres; others no longer have any image. Time has erased the marks that once made an impression. Sometimes the film stops by itself, and literally crumbles into dust (I can brush up the residue it produces) between two shots. I do not even try to re-splice it (indeed I have been forbidden to do so). So I wind on the two pieces of film, overlap them as if nothing happened, and continue the slow pace on the winder, one hand on the reel, the other on the handle. When I detect a threatened section, I pull down the section of film between the reels, flatten it against the little luminous rectangle below, lean over, and begin my in(tro)spection. This can be either with the apparatus when I detect an interesting section (I sometimes then include two or three consecutive images in the same frame, vertically), or with the footage counter (which I mask with black adhesive to the exact dimensions of the frame). Each photogramme becomes a tableau vivant, a scene from our life. And in this bewitching proximity, where I devote myself to conserving the steadiness of the visible image, I am no longer aware of the photograph, and I am soon led to take more from it. Thus begins a story to the interior; in which my knowledge of Alice superimposes itself on that of the images, of the city, of my own solitude, where the idea of love is determinedly absent....

10. 02314R (excerpt)

... I have always been interested in what I do not understand.... Thus it was with the fragmentary film that I'm beginning to discover, entitled "02314R" in the catalogue.

In general, many films are coloured. Films change colour, sometimes within shots and even sometimes within frames; some of this must have been achieved by stencils, by zones. Add to this all the toning mixed with tinting, and the effects due to deterioration, and one has an idea that silent films (contrary to the accepted notion) were almost never black-and-white (and furthermore, as one knows, were not silent).

This one is difficult to date. The only reference point is the intertitles (when there are any), because of the language. There are also some reels with optical sound, if this is to be believed.

On the curled-up cards inside the reels: year, country, title, director, format, original or copy, positive or negative, length or number of reels, language of subtitles if there are any, a brief note on the condition of the print or the reels....

Those which bear no title, no author, no production company, no credits, nothing, have to make do with a 5-digit number and a letter.

The most troubling thing about "02314R": one doesn't know where it starts, or where it ends. All you have are a certain number of reels bearing this numeral, and you have to try to make do....

Don't leave the lamp in the viewer switched on very long. The heat from it risks igniting the nitrate. Slide a piece of thick chamois between the ribbon of film and the machine to avoid any risk.... Take some photos, and then extinguish the light, draw the film forward, remove it from its notches, and re-thread it in the slide duplicator, hunch over, sometimes on the floor on all fours, regulate the bellows, adjust them slowly, until you get the right framing, light it, take the picture. This, once a minute, once an hour, once a day, or not at all. Today I took this photo. Why?

When I reflect upon what I've seen, the number of images, it frightens me. Besides, can one quantify this in images? How does one measure viewing, the trajectory covered by seeing? By kilometres of film? By hours of viewing time? What is the right speed? (And all viewing is this speed.) By the number of reels? But each reel is not identical, its contents may vary entirely.

The first of two images used in *Les Heures:* number 5 in the published version of *Moires* (Paris, Filigranes/Galerie Michel Chomette: 1998).

Éric Rondepierre.

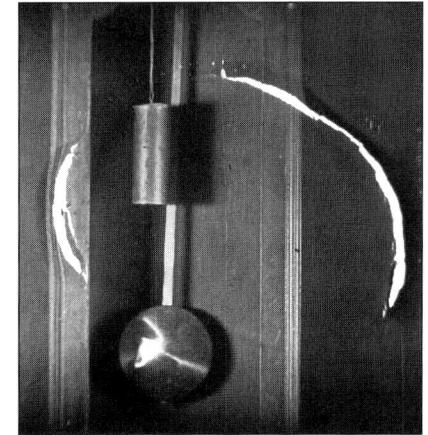

12. Le Feu, la Glace [Fire, Ice] (excerpt)

An aesthetic fragment, a piece of sociology, a shred of physiology, of morality, of the imaginary, openings cut in the wall of absent sound....

It is not a question of any old image, but of film images: objects, landscapes, people, all are represented, all are activated by rapport with an eye which mounts a chronology, a space, without respite....

In retrospect, I am amazed by the way in which some people saw my last series. There was much talk of film in the process of burning, of the effects of burning... The persistence of this misconception can only be the fruit of a subjective illusion, even though, truly, the decomposition of films arises rather from the conjunction of the actions of humidity and storage temperature (this was already the case with my series "Annonces"). Doubtless, the effects of this corrosion, these manifest signs on the image, often become associated with burns, irradiations of fire, explosions, disintegration. An equivalent description could be that of Hiroshima. This is a matter of impression above everything else, a chaos, a mélange of impressions, a confusion of signs (even if, happily, it all passes for us at one remove). It is as if two

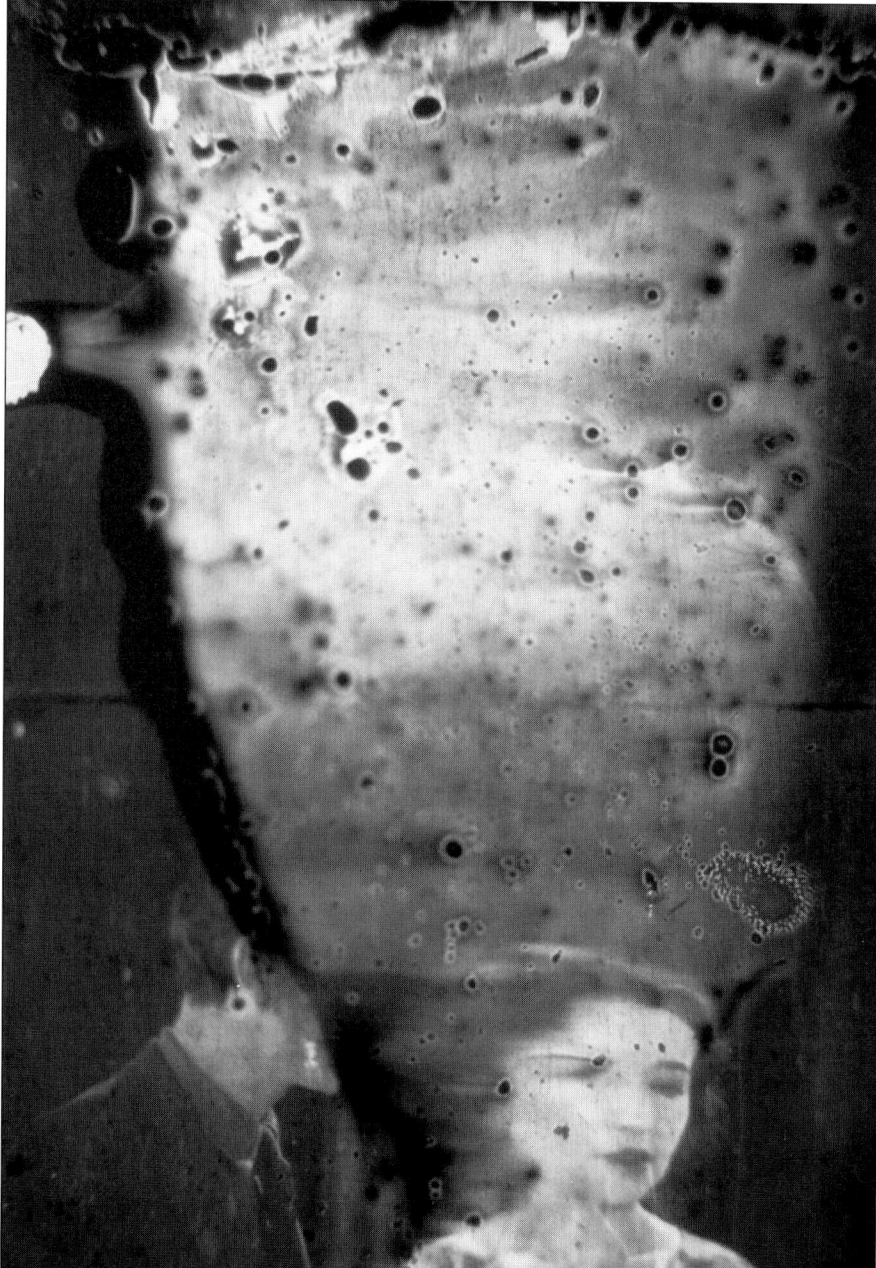

Couple, passant: number 18 in the published version of *Moires* (Paris, Filigranes/Galerie Michel Chomette: 1998). (See also Colour Section 2.)

Éric Rondepierre.

contiguous images (not necessarily consecutive: they can be on top of one another in the roll or reel, for example) exchange their impressions. Thus, sometimes the effect of montage, of perfect collage: an encounter that would not displease the Surrealists. It is really a question of a convulsion of signs, as if the image were distorted in front of us, in a sort of excessively rapid spasm, which one sees in arrested, contracted movement, in a sort of dull flash. One, two, three: sun!

18. Couple, passant [Couple, Passing] (excerpt)

As for procedure, the concrete activity of research in an archive, of the archive itself, this white vein where beats the pulse of youth immemorial, it would be improper to fix its autonomous character. Historians tell us about the extreme slowness, the impression of infinite reckoning, always different, the small forward steps by which are attached the miniscule elements of decision, the long solitary waiting, institutional experience, mediatrix, lost in the anonymous spheres of implicit laws unless in the strong presence of a rigid system where the fragile edifice of research nevertheless yields under the repeated blows of chance, of accident. Let us pass over the enormous quantity of documents handled and gone through, useless or relevant documents, unexpected fragments, contradictory pieces, etc. ...Orchestrated secondarily by the fiction of a play becoming empty, the reel starts to make its effect.... With this proximity of the clue vibrating under the fingers of the researcher: the letter, the police report, the text found, torn, manipulated by the hands, and a corpse which blinds us; this film projected in the white light of the apparatus, marked (I see the reference marks on the leader, the marks of the reel changes), watched in a public space, the actors have inscribed their shadow upon it, the film tells us that they have loaned their bodies, if not perhaps their souls, to this play.... Then, one fine day, it all disappears. Forgotten, not written down, not archived. Another fine day, almost a century later: a woman is crouched, short of breath, she caresses a metal can, then slowly the image emerges between her fingers; she examines it, sniffs it. The scent of horse-dung and nitrate form a curious amalgam of intoxicating fragrances, while a slender string of mangled grasshoppers blocks the openings. In accordance with the law one calls an official to be part of the findings, the reels are forwarded and become the property of an institution of the State. The facts: no one ever sees these films. They remain, thus, in a certain fashion, "private", inaccessible. Someone passes, cautiously denouncing the layers of intervention which imprison the invisible film, but this criticism achieves nothing: financial reasons, questions of priority, of time and space, of the global ethic of conservation, of subjective tastes, of located cultural deeds, etc. And then, this prehistory interests no one; besides, people do not even suspect its existence. As I was saying: someone passes. A century or so later, the museum opens its doors to him, he views the films at random, takes photos, fixes once and for all time the traces of a journey. Here, above all the thousands of incidents distributed by chance, these routes become the images of their trajectory by the simple fact of isolating them. Thus is born the illusion of crossing the layer of the image in order to accede to the real, where bodies and faces – sense, matter, and form – are thrown back into play in the brutal impatience of an encounter, an arrest. Breaking open its veneer, little islets of the living Present or the Past and Memory regain strength in the porosity of a substance programmed to die.... The historian becomes a detective: he makes the facts speak. But the facts do not exist, it is always a question of their relation(ship), of the recitation of facts, whose function is to deny the temporal distance which separates us from them. Historians write scenarios based on recitals of facts; they fill in the holes and restore a coherent face to that which does not have a face. Foucault talks about the fiction at the interior of Truth. I could talk about the truth at the interior of Fiction....

Preservation – a short story

by Sarah St Vincent Welch[1]

Sarah St Vincent Welch, writer of short stories, novels, and poetry, worked in film preservation at the National Film and Sound Archive in Canberra (now ScreenSound Australia) for 10 years. She was constantly inspired by the beauty and history of its nitrate film collection and the Art Deco building that housed the growing institution, and the experience was the basis of her story "Preservation". Her stories have been published in various literary magazines and anthologies in Australia. Her first novel, Islands in Lakes, Lakes in Islands *won the Jessie Litchfield Award in 1995 in manuscript. She also won the inaugural Marion Eldridge Award in 1998 for the proposal for her second novel,* The City Beautiful.

Preservation

Max couldn't believe he had found her; she was almost perfect for him. Although Charlotte did have some strange ideas. As they held hands in the foyer, she described their work as the preservation of a past centred on war, propaganda, and pain. The death masks of scientists looked down on them from their dedicatory plaques set high on the wall. She looked down at their hands, and asked where such simple moments as these were recorded? How were they less important? He didn't know what to say. He felt the moment had been spoilt.

Some mornings they would share a smoke on the roof before starting work. They passed the cigarette carefully between them, standing there shivering amongst the bare cement and stained pipes. Max knew this building: its history and soul. Charlotte had only been there a couple of months, and nearly every day he found another oddity of the building to point out to her. This didn't seem to bore her like it did some other people. She loved old things too, collected antique clothes and furniture, and her house was full of bric-a-brac. Max secretly thought that Charlotte wasn't particularly discerning in what she collected. She was too sentimental. But she seemed to love the building almost as much as he did, and he felt that was a bond between them. They fantasised about living there. The marble foyer would be their bedroom: they would fill it with lilies, drape it with shot silk, and lie in a huge circular bed beneath the skylight.

A wealthy scientist had commissioned the Institute of Anatomy in the 1920s. Now it was the National Film and Sound Archive. The architect had embellished its surface with eccentric flourishes of Australiana. It was unique. A giant platypus swam suspended in the skylight over the foyer. Plaster koala heads set into the white courtyard watched busloads of tourists, pensioners, and schoolchildren finding their way to the exhibition hall. Max always entered through the front doors so he could enjoy the building's elegant line and peculiar details before he started work in the basement. As he approached the building it appeared to him to have a face. The curve of sandstone stairs was a mouth with shining brass rails leading into it, the long windows like eyes shaded with blinds.

Max felt his connection to this place helped him survive in the modern landscape; it provided him with a gateway to the beauty of the past. When the old Institute building was chosen to house the Archive, Max immediately volunteered for work.

Shortly afterwards he was offered a paid job in the Film Preservation section. One of his first tasks was to pack away the remaining bottles of specimens. The foetuses pressed their faces against the glass like homunculi. Max dropped a bottle, and its contents slithered over the floor. He put it in the garbage and didn't tell anyone. He watched as Phar Lap's giant racehorse heart was carefully sealed in a box to be sent to Melbourne. Visitors sometimes left disappointed, still expecting to see that icon of grey flesh enlivened only by clever display and lighting.

He did not like these remnants of the past. He wanted to make history solid, everlasting. Flesh could never really be preserved. He preferred the permanence of a building protected by heritage laws, and the reality of the images he restored. In the films there were real people and places exactly as they had once looked. He wanted to capture them forever, before they started to decay. A film's life could only be extended by hundreds of years. Max was certain that new technologies would fulfil his desire for the film collection's eternity, just as Charlotte had fulfilled another of his desires. He thought of their fantasy bed, and the real one they shared.

Max worked in the basement, which was the only area large enough to fit the equipment and people. He was now used to being underground, and even had an affection for the dank surroundings. As he turned off the lights at night he remembered that vivisection had been performed here. When Max headed for the door at the end of the hall in the darkness he often heard the scuttle of rats.

The basement was an enclave of white coats which marked their wearers as lesser beings in the hierarchy and which hid their identities, except from each other. They had the peculiar nonchalance of the obscure specialist, enthralled by the identification of old film, researching its content, repairing its edges, and piecing it back together.

Max looked at his watch. Charlotte was very late today. She had left some films on her bench overnight. That was very careless of her. He decided to put the films in the fire safety cupboard in case a supervisor walked past. The nitrate base of the films was highly flammable and very unstable. Once a film was alight there was no way of putting it out. It would burn underwater, even underground. The nitrous gases it emitted were deadly. It was a cardinal sin to leave a film out overnight in the Archive, exposed to any stray electrical spark.

Max could hear the steady, comforting sound of a film being rewound by hand. The films had to be wound slowly and evenly so that they could breathe and shift with any changing environmental conditions. To Max all the processes in their makeshift laboratory had become sacred. He knew what each fellow worker was doing just by the sound: the scraping of scalpels cleaning the dirty splices and the crackling of decomposing film sticking to itself as it was carefully unwound. He could hear the hand wind was coming to an end, and then the flapping of the last piece of film as the wind was finished. Max turned to watch George carefully place his film in a plastic can. George must have sensed him watching.

"Where's our Charlotte?"

" I don't know. I don't think she's rung in."

"Big night out probably."

Max thought that if this was the case he would have liked to have known about it. She was meant to ring him last night. He suspected George had said it to irritate him.

George checked the computer screen for the time.

"Morning tea."

Charlotte's cup was unused. It was deeply stained and sat among the dregs. He decided to wash it for her. Taking tea outside was part of official policy. No one could eat or drink near any part of the collection. The fading images were so precious, there could be no risk of damaging them.

The Director had told the staff that they were preserving the memories of Australians. George said it was the history of the rich as he sucked a jube over the bench. "Don't worry, I'm not going to spit on the film," he'd say, grinning while holding the half-sucked jube between his teeth. Max hated George sometimes. The slightest speck could trigger the growth of mould on the film, eat into the history. And the decomposing film could also invade the body, through a cut, through the mouth or eyes. It was dangerous.

Max spotted Charlotte straightaway. A bit rough joining in a break before you've even started work, he thought. That's not like Charley.

Charlotte was wandering around and seemed distracted. She walked straight past him and then stood on the edge of a group of people. Her hair was different, she was wearing it in soft rolls around her head, covered with a fine net. She seemed to have some new old clothes, more tailored than her usual style, though her shirt was hanging out a bit. She kept looking around.

"Hi, Charley. Your hair looks nice."

He lifted a hand to touch her hair. She jerked her head away. She jumped back and moved quickly behind a group of people.

He watched her. She was behaving very strangely. She kept looking around, and if anyone came near she retreated a few steps. She stared at the road, and the cars driving past. Maybe she was expecting somebody. George must have observed their little scene.

"Having a tiff, are we?"

"Mind your own business, George."

Max looked at his watch, and decided that morning tea was over. He was very conscious of Charlotte's empty bench. What was she doing? The rest drifted back to work, and the slow whirr of the winding film began again.

He couldn't stand it, she really should have started work. What was wrong with her? What had he done?

Charlotte ran in. She stopped and looked around. The door slamming behind her reverberated through the basement. Everyone stopped work and looked. Her hair was loose, and she was panting. She looked behind out into the hall, turned back, and straightened her coat. She forced a quick smile.

"Hi."

Charlotte strode to her bench. She thought for a moment, checked the table next to her, then under the bench.

"Where are my films?" She said this softly.

"Where are my films?" She said it a little louder. She ran her hands over the empty bench. "I left them here."

Max approached her, buttoning and unbuttoning the top of his white coat.

"I put them away for you, Charley. In the cupboard."

She ran to the fire cupboard and heaved open the door and searched the shelves. She lifted up each film and read the label, then crashed it back down onto the metal shelves.

"It's not here. What have you done with it, Max? George? George, if you've hidden it I'll kill you, I mean it."

George started to giggle. He loved a diversion.

"Stop it, George. She can't find her film. I put all the ones on your bench in here, Charley."

"We'll find it eventually. Bound to turn up in the next couple of years." George was always helpful.

"Don't say that. It's not funny." She almost yelled at him.

"What's it called? Can you remember its number?"

"It's something like *Wodonga Disaster, circa 1940...*"

She paused, and said softly and slowly: "*Servicemen and Women Killed in Collision.*"

She looked at Max. "And I can't remember its number."

"We should go through this lot again before looking anywhere else. You know how easy it is to miss them."

As they went through the cans he realised she was very upset. She was still breathing heavily. Her hands were shaking. Everyone started to look through the stacks of films on other benches. Charlotte was as white as her coat.

"I think I'd better do a bit of research in the computer. Come with me, Max."

She gripped his arm hard, increasing the pressure as she pushed him through the door in front of her. She took him to the small computer room where the can labels were printed. She shut the door and wedged a chair under the handle.

"What the hell do you think you're doing?"

"You're not going to believe me. You're going to say I'm mad."

"Just tell me. What is it? Why didn't you talk to me at morning tea?"

"Morning tea?"

"Come on. You walked straight past me."

"I never saw you. I was running and running. And then the door was in front of me and I saw you all on the other side and so I pushed through. I've been here all night. Somewhere here, I think."

Max was confused. "Did you get locked in?"

"In a sense. I know you're not going to believe me. But I've got to tell someone, though you'd be the last to believe this sort of thing. And I need you to help me find my film." Charlotte paced the room.

"You say you saw me, Max? That must mean that she was here, and I was there. My God, what did she think had happened?"

"I don't understand."

"Max, I got sucked into a film and I only just got out. I don't know how it happened. That's just what I think."

Every few moments the printer produced a new can label. They hung down in a long line.

"Sucked in?"

"Remember? Yesterday. I think it was yesterday. Remember when Patricia called me over to her bench?"

Max remembered. Charlotte and Patricia had been laughing over a film. He and George went over to have a look. George bent over the frame with a magnifying loop.

"What are you doing in there, Charley?" He pinched Charlotte's leg.

"It's bizarre isn't it? She really looks like Charley."

Max examined the frame. The scene was of a group of women dressed in overalls, their arms around each other. Behind them was a large building. The next frame was an intertitle which read – OUR GIRLS IN THE FORCES.

The light shining through the film showed up fine scratches, cracks in the emulsion, and a swirl of projector oil over the image. These blemishes did not hide the special quality of the images. No modern film or photograph had it. It was this quality, and the innocence of the subjects exposed to the camera's eye, that caused their dedication to these reflections of the past. The women in the film smiled at each other and out to the camera and the people in the basement. They could have been from any time, except for their Forties' hairstyles, and that the film was in black and white. In the middle of the group was a woman who looked just like Charley, right down to the freckles. Everybody laughed. Patricia gave Charley the film to work on, with a warning.

"Don't laugh too much. This one doesn't end too well. The next intertitle says something about 'tragedy'."

Max tore the labels off the printer and began sorting them. He put them in piles, preparing to distribute them in the lab.

"Yes, I remember. Patricia gave you her film to work on."

"Yes, the one with the woman that looked like me in it. I did everything as usual, examined it, filled out the tech sheet, put the info in the computer, then went to the outside vault to get my next film. The vault door shut behind me. The light went out. I nearly died of fright. I thought someone else was in there, that they were playing a trick on me. The light came on, and the vault was full of people! Then it got really bright, it was daytime, and it wasn't the vault at all, we were in a bus. A woman pulled me down beside her, and kept patting my arm. She seemed to know me. They were all dressed in uniform. They were soldiers, men and women. They began to sing, wartime songs. I thought I was going mad. Or someone had slipped me something. Then I remembered the film, and how it ended, and I realised. They were real people. I could smell it, feel it all. They knew me, I was one of them. We were heading towards the train, and no one knew except me. I ran down the front to the driver, he wouldn't stop, so I grabbed the wheel. He slammed on the brake, and the door flew open and I fell out. Everyone was screaming. I ran. I could still hear screaming. I was running into darkness, like a train tunnel. I kept falling."

She lifted her skirt and her knees were scabbed over. She held out her palms and the skin was raw.

"I saw a light, and a door, and it was our lab, and you were all there. I knew I had to find that film, and do something with it, I don't know what. If I'd stayed there, I know I would have died with them. Smashed into the train. So many people were killed, Max. Did you see that film?"

Max just sat. He had done his coat up and undone it so many times that two of the buttons had come off. He had forgotten about sorting the labels and they lay in his lap. He thought that she'd gone mad. Maybe not completely mad, but just hallucinating a bit. Maybe it was the effects of the gas from the decomposing film. Maybe she had been locked in the bunker overnight, and was traumatised from that.

Charlotte had started working at the computer, searching through the titles. Max leaned over to read the lists of titles too.

"*Wodonga Disaster*, are you sure that's what you called it?"

"Positive. Hang on, I'll try searching on 'level crossing collision'." She waited, placing her hands on either side of the screen, as if she could will the information out of it.

"It's not here. I know I put it in the computer because it generated a label for it. I picked it up on the way to the bunker."

"Charlotte, this is crazy. You must have got locked in the bunker or something and dreamed this. Let me take you home."

He tried to hold her. The stiff starched cotton of their white coats rubbed together. She pushed him away.

"It did happen. I've got to find that film."

"You can't blame me for finding this a bit difficult. You're right though, about looking for the film. I shouldn't have moved it in the first place. I'm willing to try a can-by-can search."

Charlotte hugged him. At least he would help her. The compacter was just outside the computer room. They pulled it open and started the search. There were shelves and shelves of neatly stacked cans of film. They had to drag a stack towards them, and then lift each can to read the title on the front. It would have been easier if they had the number to look for on the side of the can. They worked steadily. Charlotte was very quick. She was down the end of the aisle before Max started on his second shelf. Max read the titles methodically to himself. *You Can't See 'round Corners, The Restless and the Damned, Devil's Playground, A Current Affair: Milperra Massacre, Picnic at Hanging Rock, Beyond Reason...*

Max's back was aching. Why would anyone put nitrate films here in the viewing collection? It would be a big mistake. He shouldn't have suggested looking here. He wished he hadn't moved Charlotte's films. He knew he had put them in the cupboard. Someone else must have done something with them then. He felt guilty, as if it were his fault.

Charlotte had moved on to the next bay. He realised it was too big a job just to humour her. Someone would notice them mucking around. He called her. She didn't answer. Then he heard footsteps. He listened and then followed their direction. He ran, and as he got to the end of the compacter he saw Charlotte on the other side, and she was running too, out into the hall. He stopped and turned back to see who was chasing her and could see no one. She was running from him.

Halfway up the hall she paused, holding onto the shelving to stop falling. Max felt a tremor run through the floor beneath him. She ran to the end of the hall and looked back at him, and then around, trying to see where to go.

This wasn't Charley. It was the other woman, the one from the film, the one he had seen outside that morning. He yelled, "Stop! I'm not going to hurt you!" She ran up the old stairs. They led to the foyer. He might catch up to her there.

Max pushed open the glass doors and ran straight into a group of men and fell at their feet. He stared at the mosaic tiles beneath him and then looked up into the men's faces. One leaned over him. He had a thin ribbon tied around his winged collar. His face was framed by the platypus skylight above them. Blue light fell in through its perspex geometry. The man's eyes were so dark that there seemed to be no difference between iris and pupil. As Max looked into those eyes he heard a high voice singing an aria. He realised the foyer was filled with people milling about. There were women in long dresses. A man was filming with a huge old camera. A rat ran over Max's leg. Max held onto the man leaning over him, who pulled him up. The man's face was as still as a mask. Then it split with an obscene smile.

"Welcome to the official opening of the Institute of Anatomy. Conserve your energy, my lad. Preserve your dignity. Smile for the camera, if you please."

The lens leered over the man's shoulder. Max saw over the man's other shoulder a luxurious bed, strewn with exotic flowers. There seemed to be someone in it. Max pushed the man away. He ran back to the stairs, back to the hall. He thought he was running towards the lab, but the light was wavering, and he couldn't find the lab door. He was going mad. He and Charley had both gone stark staring mad.

The next day George and Patricia were examining a film. They bent over the bench, peering at a single frame through a magnifying loop.

"You're right. It's happened again! Look at this."

Everyone stopped work and peered at the frame too.

"Max, come over here and look! You're a bit quiet this morning. Come on! This is good! Is that a new haircut mate? A bit short, eh?"

He ran his fingers through the stubble on his head. The frame they showed him was of a train station filled with diggers in their turned-up hats. They were boarding a train, going off to war. The image had shifted, and was swirling and bubbling at the edges with decomposition. This was one of the last frames with some area of image left. There was a young soldier in the middle, with his arm around a woman. The decomposition had almost completely obscured her. But the soldier's face could still be seen. It was Max.

Notes

1. "Preservation" was first published in Jenny Millea and Katrina Iffland, eds., *Pressing the Flesh: Stories by ACT region writers* (O'Connor, ACT : Top Drawer Press, 1997). It is reprinted here by kind permission of the author.

Hermit – a poem

by Tony Bicât

Tony Bicât is a writer/director and lyricist. He was the co-founder with David Hare of the influential 1970s theatre company Portable Theatre. His films include Skinflicker *and* Dinosaur *(both 1973). He has written and directed over twenty films for television, including* Christmas Present *(1985),* The Laughter of God *(1990; US:* Married to Murder*), and* An Exchange of Fire *(1993). His book* Creative Screenwriting *is to be published in August 2002 by The Crowood Press (Ramsbury, Wiltshire). His latest stage play,* A Buyer's Market, *opens at the Bush Theatre in London in April 2002, and he has a feature film,* The Film Monk, *whose origins lie in the poem below, in development with Kestrel Films.*

HERMIT

High over Ladbroke Grove he sits
Living on crackers and boiled water
His senses stripped and sanded like his floor
To a single, perfect, bleached-white beam of light.

His cell is all projector
The throw cut by a cunning prism
Shows him singers crooning, show-girls dancing
Leaping in the very lens that Murnau used for Nosferatu.

The walls are racked with relics
From country auctions and from Wardour skips
Kodak, Ilford, and in a silver fridge
Enough nitrate stock to blow the building down.

In this cold room gauges as strange
As trans-Siberian trains will play.
(The videos are just an aide-memoire
There is no real presence in the VCR.)

In the dark years he kept the faith
Renouncing flesh, fame, fortune, family
To cry the gospel of a dying art
But now this prophet pays to visit their museums.

"How dare you call this suffering
Save when with bleeding hands and broken feet
My eyes weeping from their blasphemy
I stumble from the high street ABC?

"Warmth rises from the flat below.
My life is rich. Each night I eat
A masterpiece. I am in bliss
'Till my devotions cool like the white bulb in the grey dawn."

Tony Bicât '97

Two Cartoons

by Roy Boyd

Roy Boyd is an art director, graphic designer and cartoonist. His cartoons have appeared in a number of British publications (The Sun, The Weekly News, The Herald, etc.) as well as greeting cards (Hallmark UK) and a variety of promotional and advertising materials. He is the regular cartoonist for Scottish Screen's newsletter, Roughcuts, and PSYBT's (The Prince's Scottish Youth Business Trust) Review.

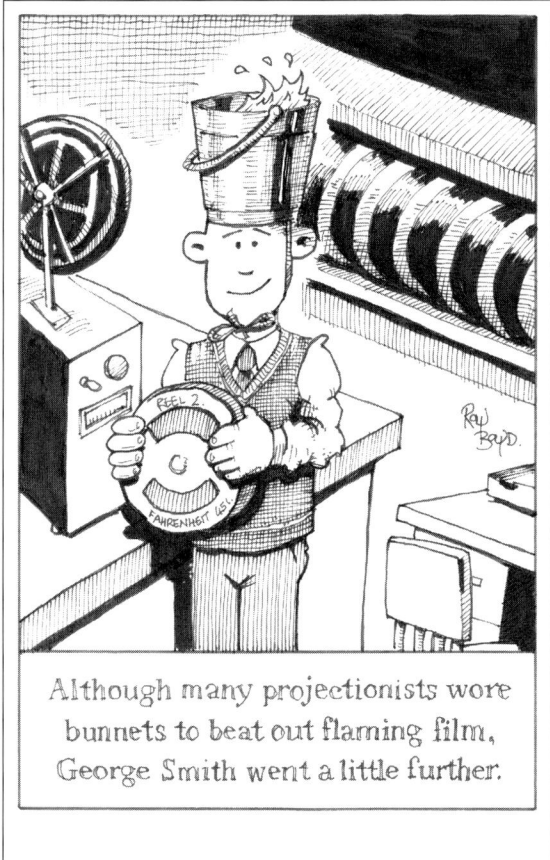

Although many projectionists wore bunnets to beat out flaming film, George Smith went a little further.

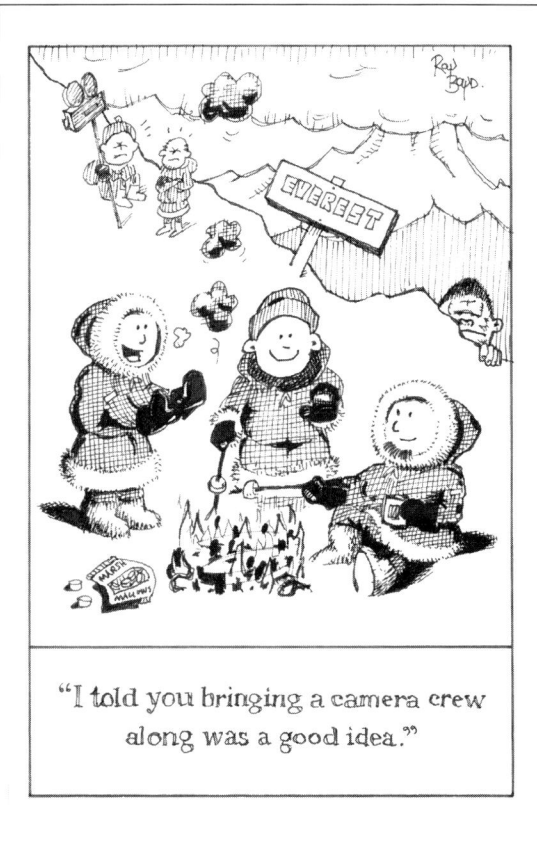

"I told you bringing a camera crew along was a good idea."

The two cartoons printed here were specially drawn for this book, and were inspired by anecdotes included in the sections "Unseen Showmen and Unsung Heroes" and "Fiery Tails – Going Up in Smoke".

Bibliography & Filmography

Suggestions for further reading and viewing on the subject of this book. They do not claim to be comprehensive or definitive, and include only the relatively small number of titles previously known to the editors, and those additional titles which were brought to our attention by the contributors whose help is gratefully acknowledged. There has been no systematic process of research to identify additional materials, although one hopes that this preliminary listing will inspire more research into this territory in the future. Additional limitations are noted in the introductions to specific sections.

Nitrate Bibliography

1. Fiction

The properties of nitrate film or celluloid occasionally make significant, if usually destructive, contributions to the plot developments of novels and short stories. The following examples are known to the editors, or have been suggested to them by the people named at the end of each entry.

Adams, by René Clair (Paris: Grasset, 1926) – see *Star Turn*

"Djævlebesættelse" [Demonic Possession], by Thomas Krag
Included in *Tubal den Fredløse: Natskygger fra en Verdensby* [Tubal the Outcast: Nightshades from a Metropolis] published by Gyldendal, Copenhagen and Kristiania, 1908.
At an annual fair, a strange man who claims to be the descendant of an old French aristocratic family tells the narrator the story of his life – in the established tradition of the fantasy genre, the question of whether his story is true or he is simply drunk or crazy remains unresolved. His father had lost all his money in a speculative venture, and he was therefore obliged to earn his own keep. By chance, he discovered one day that his hatred for particular people brought harm on them: an employer had an accident on the stairway; a woman who rejected him became a morphine addict. As high society no longer wanted to have anything to do with him, he took his revenge by using his mental powers to cause the famous fire in the Bazar de la Charité on 4 May 1897. This telepathic fire-raising is presented in the form of a vision.
Note: The Norwegian Thomas Krag (1868-1913) wrote several film scripts, starting in 1909, and that same year was the first person who tried to convince a reluctant Asta Nielsen that her future lay in silent film.
(submitted by Dr Stephan Michael Schröder, Humboldt University, Berlin)

The Doll's House, by Rumer Godden

Originally published by Michael Joseph, London, 1947, and sometimes known as *Tottie, The Story of a Doll's House.* (The edition consulted is that published by Puffin Books, New York, 1976.)
This story by a celebrated children's author takes place in the "austerity" years in England immediately after the Second World War. A family of four dolls yearn for a proper home. At the very moment their dreams come true in the form of a fully refurbished Victorian doll's house, their happiness is blighted by the arrival of Marchpane, a restored Victorian doll who conspires to take over the house. When Marchpane places the child-doll Apple in danger from a lit candle, Birdie, the celluloid mother-doll, sacrifices herself to save him.
(submitted by Linda Smither, London)

"Expedition to Earth", by Arthur C Clarke

Originally published as "History Lesson" in *Startling Stories,* v.19, no.2 (May 1949), then included as the title story in the anthology *Expedition to Earth,* first published by Ballantine, New York, 1953. (The edition consulted is that published by Pan Books, London, 1966.)
This science-fiction short story depends for its punch line on a life expectancy for a reel of celluloid that might be considered optimistic even in deep-freeze conditions.

(In fairness, however, it must be noted that, although the story was written in the nitrate era, the author does not specify whether the reel is a nitrate original or a later copy print.) In the distant future, before they are crushed beneath the returning glaciers of a final ice age, the last remnants of the human race bury their sacred relics in a cairn on a mountaintop. Thousands of years later, an exploratory ship from Venus discovers the cairn. Among its contents is "a flat metal container holding a great length of transparent plastic material, perforated at the edges and wound tightly into a spool". Scientists work out its purpose and function, and are excited to be able to screen to Venus's intellectual elite "a record of life as it was on the Third Planet at the height of its civilization", although they warn their audience that it "seems to have been very violent and energetic, and much that you will see is quite baffling". Because they have not managed to decipher the language of Earth, they do not understand the meaning of the closing lettering: "A Walt Disney Production".
Note: The anthology *Expedition to Earth* also contains "The Sentinel" – the short story, itself first published in 1951, from which the film *2001: A Space Odyssey* (1968) was later derived.
(submitted by Roger Smither, Imperial War Museum Film and Video Archive, London)

The Face on the Cutting Room Floor, by Cameron McCabe [Ernst Julius Bornemann]

Originally published by Victor Gollancz, London, 1937. (The edition consulted is that published by Penguin Books, London, 1986.)
This idiosyncratic murder mystery has been acclaimed as a masterpiece by some readers and reviled as unreadable by others. It was written in English by a German émigré screenwriter, and is set in a film studio. In chapter 14, a nitrate fire is started deliberately as a distraction.
(submitted by John Kerr, Imperial War Museum Film and Video Archive, London)

Flicker, by Theodore Roszack

Published by Bantam Books, New York, 1992.
The narrator in this novel is a cineaste on the trail of Max Castle, a lost auteur of horror films, and his story takes the reader on a unique exploration of film history and theory. Ultimately, he discovers "The Orphans", linear descendants of the heretical medieval Cathar sect, who are secretly seeking to use the content and technology of the movies to advance their vision of the apocalypse. (The Orphans are ineffectually opposed by Occulus Dei, an organisation of militant Catholics repudiated by the Vatican – one crazed OD member has previously tried to assassinate Henri Langlois.) In an early episode, the funeral of a film collector turns out to have been arranged so that he is cremated on a pyre of his nitrate treasures. To silence the narrator, the Orphans finally abduct him to a desert island, where he finds Castle himself, endlessly re-editing films that nobody will ever see.
(submitted by Frank Stark, New Zealand Film Archive, Wellington)

"History Lesson", by Arthur C Clarke – see "Expedition to Earth"

Marion's Wall, by Jack Finney

Originally published by Simon & Schuster, New York, 1973. (The edition consulted is that included in *Three By Finney*, a Fireside Book edition published by Simon & Schuster, 1987.)

Nick, the narrator, and his wife Jan discover while redecorating their apartment in San Francisco a graffito by Marion Marsh, an actress of the 1920s who had died before she was able to develop her career in Hollywood. Marion tries to reclaim her flapper-era life and her career by taking possession of Jan's body, but is disillusioned at the directions taken by the modern studios; her friend Rudolph Valentino makes occasional similar incursions into Nick's body. Through Marion, Nick establishes contact with Ted Bollinghurst, a rich old collector, whose vaults contain every lost treasure in film history (including, inevitably, the complete 42-reel Greed). In his mansion's private theatre, Ted screens for "Marion" and Nick the film that should have made her breakthrough. A fire breaks out. Nick rescues Jan, but Ted and the ghost of Marion remain watching the film as theatre, collection, and mansion burn around them.

Note: Anthony Slide points out that *Marion's Wall* was the basis for the 1985 Orion film called *Maxie* (alternate title: *Free Spirit*), directed by Paul Aaron and starring Glenn Close as Jan/Maxie – "Maxie" being the character known as Marion in the novel. As the film dispenses with the Bollinghurst fire episode entirely, however, it lacks sufficient nitrate relevance for inclusion in this book's filmography.

(submitted by Roger Smither, Imperial War Museum Film and Video Archive, London)

Merle, by Anne-Marie Garat

Published by Seuil, Paris, 1996.

The title character is a woman film editor who becomes involved in a film project by a Brazilian director. At the beginning of the novel she travels to Bois d'Arcy to join the director in watching an old nitrate film at the vaults. A major portion of Chapter 1, entitled "Bois d'Arcy", is about the vaults, with lingering descriptions of nitrate and decomposition. It compares the explosive physical qualities of old film stock with the effects film can have on the minds and memories of those who watch it.

(submitted by Michelle Aubert and the staff of the CNC, Bois d'Arcy, and Catherine Surowiec, London)

"Nitrate", by Christopher Burns

Included in the anthology *Shorts: New Writing from Granta Books*, published by Granta Books, London, 1998.

In a moribund marriage, a renowned film archivist from an anonymous British "institute" feels only technical curiosity as his tax-adviser wife starts an affair with a potential business partner. Instead, he gives his care and attention to the painstaking restoration of an early pornographic film. (The story does not make film archivists out to be very nice people, but then the descriptions of film restoration techniques are not particularly accurate either.)

(submitted by Jane Alvey, East Anglian Film Archive, Norwich)

"Preview of Death", by Cornell Woolrich – see "Screen Test"

Reel Murder, by Marian Babson

Originally published by Collins, London, 1986. (The edition consulted is that published by Bantam, New York, in 1988.)

Evangeline Sinclair, ageing Hollywood star, travels to London with her former co-star, sidekick, and companion Trixie Dolan. The occasion is a retrospective of Evangeline's films at a theatre in the "Cinema City" complex built by Beauregard

Sylvester, one of her one-time leading men. While staying in classic detective-story London (permanent fog and implausible geography), the ladies are given an apartment in a house belonging to Sylvester, where the other tenants include his grandson and a mixed ménage of struggling actors, musicians, etc. A number of murders take place, with some awkward cinematic overtones... Although not really essential to the plot, the author includes some well-meaning but not entirely accurate references to the problems of nitrate film restoration and preservation.
(submitted by Roger Smither, Imperial War Museum Film and Video Archive, London)

"Screen Test", by Cornell Woolrich

A re-written version of a story originally published as "Preview of Death" in the 15 November 1934 issue of *Dime Detective*, included in the anthology *Nightmare*, published by Dell, New York, 1964.
The narrator, a novice police detective, is instructed against his will to protect a Hollywood star who has been receiving death threats. He has hardly started the assignment when the star dies, apparently in a horrible studio accident: while she is filming a scene from a Civil War drama, the celluloid stiffening of her period costume catches fire. By studying the rushes of the incident, our hero proves that the death was no accident, and finds out the method used – and the culprit.
(submitted by Michael Friend, Academy Film Archive, Beverly Hills, who also researched the earlier history of this short story)

The Shattered Helmet, by Franklin W Dixon

Published by Grosset & Dunlap, New York, 1973.
One of the "Hardy Boys Mystery Stories" series. The plot revolves around an ancient Greek helmet, loaned many years ago as a prop for a silent movie and subsequently lost. In the course of the action, the Boys track down a copy of the film and the bad guys start a nitrate fire to try to destroy it.
(submitted by Yvette Hackett, National Archives of Canada, Ottawa)

Smokescreen, by Elsie McCutcheon

Published by Dent, London, 1986.
In 1907, 11-year-old Chrissie Gallant, the elder sister of Harry and Chip, struggles to support the family's independence in a small East Anglian town after their father leaves home to look for work. She is taken on as "Fenbury Fred", juvenile lead in a film being made by Frank Sheringham, the ambitious rival to the town's "fleapit" cinema proprietor Albert Gold, and becomes the go-between in an illicit liaison between Sheringham's daughter Vicky and Sidney Greenaway – not realising that Greenaway works for Gold. The rivalry between the two cinema owners reaches a climax when Gold undercuts the première of Sheringham's film by staging a gala of his own, during which a fire breaks out. In its aftermath, Chrissie learns several lessons about friendship and family values.
Note: The climactic fire is based on the real-life tragedy in Newmarket Town Hall on 7 September 1907. See also the entry for *Smokescreen,* a BBC children's television series based on this book, in the Filmography.
(submitted by David Cleveland, East Anglian Film Archive, Norwich)

Somewhere in England, by Reg Gadney

Published by Heinemann, London, 1971.
Possibly the only thriller so far written to feature a film cataloguer as hero. The plot

revolves around a piece of film which would reveal the identity of a Nazi war criminal now living in Britain, and which is therefore sought by the secret services of many countries, and by the ODESSA organisation. Action includes a double murder in a film store in the Imperial War Museum, and reaches its climax on the roof of Waterloo Station. One passage describes an explosion/fire in a nitrate film vault.
(submitted by Roger Smither, Imperial War Museum Film and Video Archive, London)

Star Turn: A Novel of the Films, by René Clair

Originally published as *Adams* by Grasset, Paris, 1926. This edition, translated from the French by John Marks, was published by Chatto & Windus, London, 1936.

In the author's own words, printed in the preface to the English edition:

"Star Turn – *either by chance or by predestination – is a story laid in a cinematographic setting with which the author at that time was but imperfectly acquainted. His aim was to present this background in a flippant and fantastic light. He imagined that the crazy outlines of his picture bore only the most distant relation to reality. Experience has shown him that, in the weirdest of all worlds, sense and insanity are interchangeable terms.*

Star Turn *tells the story of the world's greatest film star, Cecil Adams, who is driven mad by his own greatness. Adams has brought certain dramatis personae to life on the screen. By degrees these characters invade the personality of their creator, whose real existence eventually becomes absorbed in their imaginary lives."*

For the purposes of this anthology, the most striking paragraphs are those with which the book closes, relating how the negatives of all of Adams' films are destroyed in a warehouse fire.
(submitted by Philip French, film critic of The Observer, London)

Tottie, The Story of a Doll's House, by Rumer Godden – see *The Doll's House.*

2. Poetry

Several poems refer to the transience of nitrate. Vachel Lindsay's "Mae Marsh, Motion Picture Actress" likens old films to papyrus from Ancient Egypt, crumbling to dust, while Martin Bell's "To Celebrate Eddie Cantor" conjures up the Goldwyn Girls of 1933 as they "fade beyond nostalgia", thanks to brittle, crackling celluloid. "Orson Welles, Are You Listening", by William David Sherman, bemoans how Welles' talents were employed in unworthy films for "lesser men" to finance his own film projects, and, invoking Von Stroheim, recalls how Irving Thalberg burned 14 reels of *Greed* "to extract 43 cents of silver per reel".

The full texts of these poems can be consulted in *The Faber Book of Movie Verse*, edited by Philip French and Ken Wlaschin (London: Faber and Faber, 1993). Vachel Lindsay's poem about Mae Marsh can also be found in Lindsay's *Collected Poems*, first published by Macmillan in 1925. Lindsay, who published one of the first books on film aesthetics, *The Art of the Moving Picture*, as early as 1915, also wrote poems about Mary Pickford, Blanche Sweet, and John Bunny, none of which alas contains imagery relevant to our purposes. One suspects, and hopes, that in the vast realm of 20th-century poetry there must surely be other references to nitrate and its properties and consequences, but unfortunately they have eluded our net for this publication.

3. Non-Fiction

The editors offer their regrets for three different types of omission that are particularly evident in this section.

(1) As was explained in the Introduction, most of the content of this volume comprises material offered voluntarily by contributors, not the fruits of systematic research. Applied to bibliography, this approach has meant, no doubt, that several books that deserve inclusion are not listed because nobody has suggested them. There is a definite under-representation of works published in languages other than English.

(2) To save space, the editors' goal in compiling this bibliography has been to supplement the references available elsewhere in these pages, rather than to replicate them. The majority of the books, and virtually all the articles, which authors have cited to authenticate individual anecdotes, arguments, or points of fact, are not mentioned here: the conscientious reader may track them down through the footnotes and references provided at the end of the papers concerned. This bibliography confines itself to books which are considered to have general relevance to the topics indicated – a category which does include several that are also mentioned in footnotes – and to articles and technical manuals which have (for the most part) not been cited in any of the papers.

(3) A further consequence of the two preceding types of omission is our decision not to attempt to compile a listing of works of national or international cinema history in the nitrate era. After much deliberation, we concluded that such a list would never be comprehensive, and would have hugely extended this bibliography, while to make it selective, even within the ground rules established above, would have been invidious. With reluctance, therefore, the editors have decided to dispense with such a section altogether, even though this means that we are regretfully unable to mention a number of outstanding works, including several by some of our own contributors.

3A. The History and Science of Plastics, and especially of Celluloid

Books, Monographs, Dissertations, and Reports

Agronoff, J, ed., *Modern Plastics Encyclopedia*, v.59 (New York: McGraw-Hill, 1982)

Celluloid Committee, *Report of the Departmental Committee on Celluloid* (London: HMSO, 1913)

Friedel, Robert, *Pioneer Plastic: The Making and Selling of Celluloid* (Madison: University of Wisconsin Press, 1983)

Kaufman, Morris, *The First Century of Plastics: Celluloid and Its Sequel* (London: Plastics Institute, 1963)

Kroschwitz, J I, ed., *Encyclopedia of Polymer Science and Engineering. Vol.3: Cellular Materials to Composites* (New York: John Wiley & Sons, 1985, 2nd edition). [Especially pp.139–157: "Celluose Esters, Inorganic: Cellulose Nitrate"]

Morgan, John, *Conservation of Plastics – An Introduction* (London: Plastics Historical Society/The Conservation Unit, Museums & Galleries Commission, 1991)

Mossman, S T I, and P J T Morris, eds., *The Development of Plastics* (Cambridge: Royal Society of Chemistry, 1994)

"PLASTES", *Plastics in Industry* (London: Chapman & Hall Ltd, 1942, 2nd edition, revised; 1st edition 1940)

Quye, Anita, and Colin Williamson, eds., *Plastics Collecting and Conserving* (Edinburgh: NMS Publishing Ltd, 1999)

Selwitz, Charles, *Cellulose Nitrate in Conservation* (*Research in Conservation*) (Los Angeles: Getty Conservation Institute, 1988)

Articles

Hager, Michael, "The History of Nitrate Film", *Image*, v.2, no.4 (December 1983), pp.2–9

"How Non-Flam Film Is Made", *Motography* (Chicago), v.VI, no.2 (August 1911), pp.88–89. [Translation of an article originally from *Chimie Industrielle*]

3B. "Lost Films", the Need for Preservation, and the History of Film Archives and Film Archivists

Books, Monographs, Dissertations, and Reports

Borde, Raymond, *Les Cinémathèques* (Lausanne: Editions L'Age d'Homme, 1984)

Borde, Raymond, and Freddy Buache, *La Crise des Cinémathèques ... et du monde* (Lausanne: Editions L'Age d'Homme, 1997)

Butler, Ivan, *"To encourage the art of the film": The Story of the British Film Institute* (London: Robert Hale & Co., 1971)

Card, James, *Seductive Cinema. The Art of Silent Film* (New York: Alfred A Knopf, 1994)

Carey, Gary, *Lost Films* (New York: The Museum of Modern Art, 1970)

Eyles, Allen, and David Meeker, eds., *Missing Believed Lost. The Great British Film Search* (London: BFI Publishing, 1992)

FIAF, *50 ans d'Archives du Film, 1938–1988* (Brussels: FIAF, 1988)

George Eastman House, *A Collective Endeavor: The First Fifty Years of George Eastman House* (Rochester, NY: George Eastman House, 1999)

Head, Anne, *A True Love for Cinema: Jacques Ledoux, 1921–1988* (The Hague: Universitaire Pers Rotterdam, 1988)

Houston, Penelope, *Keepers of the Frame. The Film Archives* (London: BFI Publishing, 1994)

Koszarski, Richard, ed., *The Rivals of D W Griffith. Alternate Auteurs 1913–1918* (Minneapolis: Walker Art Center, 1976) [Includes section on "Lost Films", pp.49–55]

McGreevey, Tom, and Joanne L Yeck, *Our Movie Heritage* (New Brunswick, NJ: Rutgers University Press, 1997)

Matuszewski, Boleslaw, *Une nouvelle source de l'histoire* (Paris, 1898, and several subsequent reprints). [For details see footnote 3, "The sparkling surface of the sea of history...", by Stephen Bottomore, in this volume]

Myrent, Glenn, and Georges P Langlois, translated by Lisa Nesselson, *Henri Langlois: First Citizen of Cinema* (New York: Twayne Publishers, 1995)

Renzi, Renzo, et al., *Sperduti nel buio. Il cinema muto italiano e il suo tempo (1905–1930)* (Bologna: Cappelli, 1991)

Roud, Richard, *A Passion for Films: Henri Langlois and the Cinémathèque Française* (New York: Viking Press, 1983)

Shales, Tom, et al., *The American Film Heritage: Impressions from the American Film Institute Archives* (Washington, DC: Acropolis Books, 1972)

Slide, Anthony, *Nitrate Won't Wait. A History of Film Preservation in the United States* (Jefferson, NC: McFarland & Co., 1992)

Surowiec, Catherine A, ed., *The LUMIERE Project. The European Film Archives at the Crossroads* (Lisbon: Projecto Lumiere, 1996)

Thompson, Frank, *Lost Films: Important Movies That Disappeared* (New York: Carol Publishing Group/Citadel Press, 1996)

Toffetti, Sergio, ed., *Le Dragon et l'Alouette* (Turin: Museo Nazionale del Cinema, 1992)

Articles and Specialist Periodicals

Bandy, Mary Lea, "Nothing Sacred: 'Jock Whitney Snares Antiques for Museum'. The Founding of the Museum of Modern Art Film Library", in *The Museum of Modern Art at Mid-Century: Continuity and Change* (*Studies in Modern Art 5*) (New York: The Museum of Modern Art, 1995), pp.74–103

Barry, Iris, "The Film Library and How It Grew", *Film Quarterly*, v.XXII, no.4 (Summer 1969), pp.19–27

"Filmes Portugueses Recuperados", *Cinema Novo*, no.18 (July–August 1981), pp.19–20

Gerard, Lilian, "The Study and Preservation of Films at the Museum of Modern Art", *Film Comment*, v.5, no.3 (Fall 1969), pp.13–14

Ingalls, Zoë, "Notes from Academe: At UCLA, a Movie Medic Practices Triage to Save Classic Films", *Chronicle of Higher Education*, 15 October 1995, p.B2

Jeavons, Clyde, "The Bernard Happé Memorial Lecture 1999: Film Preservation – Why Bother?", *Image Technology/Journal of the BKSTS, The Moving Image Society*. Transcript published in 3 instalments: Part 1: v.82, no.2 (March 2000), pp.6-9; Part 2: v.82, no.3 (April 2000), pp.16-19; Part 3: v.82, no.4 (May 2000), pp.16-19

Jeavons, Clyde, "Nitrate", *Sight and Sound*, v.47, no.1 (Winter 1977/78), pp.40–41

Jones, G William, "Nitrate Film: Dissolving Images of the Past", *Conservation Administration News*, no.31 (October 1987), pp.1–31

Journal of Film Preservation (Brussels: FIAF), 1993- .

Karr, Lawrence F, "Film Preservation: Why Nitrate Won't Wait", *I.A.T.S.E. Official Bulletin*, no.477 (Summer 1972), pp.18–21

Koszarski, Richard, "Lost Films from the National Film Collection", *Film Quarterly*, v.XXIII, no.2 (Winter 1969-1970), pp.31–37

Kula, Sam, "Film Archives at the Centenary of Film", *Archivaria*, no.40 (Fall 1995), pp.210–225

Lindgren, Ernest, "The Importance of Film Archives", in Roger Manvell, ed., *The Penguin Film Review No. 5* (London: Penguin Books, 1948), pp.50–51

Nason, Richard W, "Emergency Operation. Campaign to Save Desiccating Movie Classics Begun by Film Library", *The New York Times* (9 October 1955)

Pearson, Harry, "HP Interviews Ron Haver. The Head of the Film Department at the Los Angeles Museum of Art Discusses the Preservation of Our Film Heritage", *The Perfect Vision*, v.4, no.13 (Spring 1992), pp.31–43

Ponting, Jack, "The Involvement of the NFB in the Acquisition, Storage, and Preservation of Motion Picture Film", *SMPTE Journal*, v.91, no.4 (April 1982), pp.382–383. [About fire at the National Film Board of Canada's vaults at "Beaconsfield" (Kirkland), near Ottawa]

Rosen, Robert, "The First One Hundred Years", introduction in programme booklet for UCLA Film and Television Archive's Fifth Annual Festival of Preservation (9 April–8 May 1993), p.2

Smither, Roger, and David Walsh, "Unknown Pioneer: Edward Foxen Cooper and the Imperial War Museum Film Archive, 1919–1934", *Film History*, v.12, no.2 (2000), pp.187–203

Spotnitz, Frank, "Riddle of the Archives", *American Film*, v.15, no.7 (April 1990), pp.44-46

Variety (New York), 1 June 1988, pp.33–62: "50th Year Perspective: FIAF Film Archives/FIAF – At 50". [Special section, with collection of articles and tributes]

Weinberg, Herman G, "The Legion of Lost Films" – Part One, *Sight and Sound*, v.31, no.4 (Autumn 1962), pp.172–176; Part Two, *Sight and Sound*, v.32, no.1 (Winter 1962-63), pp.42–45; plus correspondence in subsequent issues

Weinberg, Herman G, "Lost Ones", *Film Comment*, v.5, no.3 (Fall 1969), pp.6–12, 15

Young, Colin, "An American Film Institute: A Proposal", *Film Quarterly*, v.14, no.4 (Summer 1961), pp.37–50

3C. The Theory and Practice of Film Preservation

Books, Monographs, Dissertations, and Reports

Aubert, Michelle, and Richard Billeaud, eds., *Archiver et communiquer l'image et le son: Les enjeux du 3ème millénaire/Image and Sound Archiving and Access: The Challenges of the Third Millennium* (Bois d'Arcy: Centre National de la Cinématographie, 2000) [Proceedings of the Joint Technical Symposium, Paris, 20–22 January 2000; bilingual publication, with a CD-ROM]

[Billington, James H], The Librarian of Congress, *Film Preservation 1993: A Study of the Current State of American Film Preservation* (Washington, DC: Library of Congress, 1993)

Bowser, Eileen, and John Kuiper, eds., *A Handbook for Film Archives* (Brussels: FIAF, 1980). [Plus new edition, New York: Garland Publishing, 1991]

Brown, Harold G, *Physical Characteristics of Early Films as Aids to Identification* (Brussels: FIAF, 1980). [Written for the FIAF Preservation Commission]

Cherchi Usai, Paolo, *Burning Passions. An Introduction to the Study of Silent Cinema* (London: BFI Publishing, 1994)

Cherchi Usai, Paolo, *The Death of Cinema. History, Cultural Memory and the Digital Dark Age* (London: BFI Publishing, 2001)

Cherchi Usai, Paolo, *Silent Cinema: An Introduction* (London: BFI Publishing, 2000). [Revised and expanded edition of the author's 1994 book *Burning Passions*]

Comencini, Luisa, and Matteo Pavesi, eds., *Restauro, conservazione e distruzione dei film* (Milan: Editrice Il Castoro/Quaderni Fondazione Cineteca Italiana, 2001)

Eastman Kodak Company, *Safe Handling, Storage, and Destruction of Nitrate-Based Motion Picture Films* (Kodak Publication no.H-182, 1995)

Farinelli, Gian Luca, and Nicola Mazzanti, eds., *Il Cinema Ritrovato. Teoria e metodologia del restauro cinematografico* (Bologna: Grafis Edizioni, 1994)

FIAF, *Handling, Storage and Transport of Cellulose Nitrate Film* (Brussels: FIAF, 1992). [Guidelines produced with the help of the FIAF Preservation Commission]

FIAF, *Preservation and Restoration of Moving Images and Sound* (Brussels: FIAF, 1986). [A report by the FIAF Preservation Commission]

FIAF, *Technical Manual of the FIAF Preservation Commission* (Brussels: FIAF, 1993)

Films en péril/Films in Gevaar/Films in Distress (Brussels: Cinémathèque Royale, 1989). [Trilingual booklet; main essay: "La décade de la preservation/La génération de la restauration/The Preservation Decade/The Restoration Decade", by Lenny Borger]

Galloway, Christopher, *"Too Late For Nitrate? The Future of Nitrate Film in the 1990s"* (Norwich: University of East Anglia, 1996; unpublished MA dissertation)

Gamma Group, The, eds., *L'Utilizzo delle nuove tecnologie nel restauro cinematografico: Problemi tecnici e etici/The Use of New Technologies Applied to Film Restoration: Technical and Ethical Problems* (The Gamma Group/Caleidoscopio, 1996). [Trilingual publication, in Italian, French, and English]

Giacci, Vittorio, et al., *Via col tempo. L'immagine del restauro* (Rome: Centro Sperimentale di Cinematografia/Gremese Editore, 1994)

Gordon, P L, ed., *The Book of Film Care* (Rochester, NY: Eastman Kodak Company, 1968)

Hertogs, Daan, and Nico de Klerk, eds., *'Disorderly Order'. Colours in Silent Film. The 1995 Amsterdam Workshop* (Amsterdam: Stichting Nederlands Filmmuseum, 1996) [Especially pp.71–82, Session 6: "On Colour Preservation"]

International Standard ISO 10356, *Cinematography – Storage and Handling of Nitrate-Base Motion-Picture Films* (Geneva: International Standards Organisation, 1996)

Païni, Dominique, *Conserver, montrer* (Paris: Yellow Now, 1992)

Read, Paul, and Mark-Paul Meyer, eds., *Restoration of Motion Picture Film* (Oxford: Butterworth-Heinemann, 2000)

Reid, William Scott, *A Multi-Component Study of the Administration and Preservation of Nitrate Negatives* (Vancouver: University of British Columbia, 1991; unpublished Master's thesis)

The Rescue of Living History. Report on the Needs of The National Film Archive by a Committee of the Governors of The British Film Institute (London: BFI, 1969). [12–page pamphlet; especially p.6: Part 7, "The Nitrate Film Problem"]

Schou, Henning, for the FIAF Preservation Commission, *Preservation of Moving Images and Sound* (Brussels: FIAF, 1989)

Technologisch Laboratorium RVO-TVO for the Stichting Nederlands Filmmuseum, *Onderzoek naar de veilige opslag van cellulose-nitraatfilms/Investigation into the safe storage of cellulose nitrate films/etc.* [4 languages] (Rijswijk, 20 December 1968)

Tutti i colori del mondo. Il Colore nei mass media tra 1900 e 1930/All the Colours of the World. Colours in Early Mass Media 1900–1930 (Reggio Emilia: Edizioni Diabasis, 1998). [Bilingual publication; anthology, promoted by The Gamma Group, Cineteca del Comune di Bologna, and Istituto Beni Culturali – Soprintendenza Beni Librari Regione Emilia-Romagna]

Vivié, Jean, and Louis Didiée, "Technical Problems Arising in the Preservation of Cine Films". [Draft report prepared for submission to the Technical Commission of the International Film and Television Council at its meeting on 17 October 1961]

Volkmann, Herbert, *Film Preservation. A Report of the Preservation Committee of the International Federation of Film Archives [FIAF]* (English version, published London: National Film Archive/British Film Institute, 1965). [Originally published in German by the Staatliches Filmarchiv der DDR, Berlin, German Democratic Republic, in 1963; a French version was also published, by the Cinémathèque Royale de Belgique, Brussels]

Volkmann, Herbert, with Henning Schou, eds., *Preservation and Restoration of Moving Images and Sound* (Brussels: FIAF, 1986)

Articles

Brown, Harold G, "Problems of Storing Film for Archive Purposes", *British Kinematography*, v.20, no.5 (May 1952), pp.150–162

Cherchi Usai, Paolo, "The Color of Nitrate", *Image*, v.34, nos.1–2 (Spring/Summer 1991), pp.29–38

Daily, Jess, "The Care and Handling of Hazardous Nitrate Film at UCLA's Unique Projection Facilities", *SMPTE Journal*, v.99, no.6 (June 1990), pp.453–456

"Film Conservation Methods – A Symposium", *Journal of the Society of Motion Picture Engineers*, v.41 (November 1943). [A collection of papers reporting on procedures followed at eight US film studios: Universal, Republic, RKO, Columbia, Paramount, Goldwyn, Disney, and Warner Bros.]

Lindgren, Ernest, "The Permanent Preservation of Cinematograph Film", *Proceedings of the British Society of International Bibliography*, v.5 (1943), pp.97–104

Lindgren, Ernest, "Preservation of Cinematograph Film in the National Film Archive", *Journal of the SMPTE*, v.78 (October 1969)

Mitchell, Robert A, "Common Sense: Best Film Preservative", *International Projectionist*, v.37, no.5 (May 1962), pp.4–6

Zavada, Roland J, "Standards – It's History: 'Managing' the Moving Image – From an Engineering Point of View", *Image Technology* (July/August 1998), pp.14–17

3D. The Technology and Practice of Cinema in the Nitrate Era

Books
Coe, Brian, *The History of Movie Photography* (London: Ash & Grant, 1981)

Fielding, Raymond, ed., *A Technological History of Motion Pictures and Television. An Anthology from the Pages of The Journal of the Society of Motion Picture and Television Engineers* (Berkeley/Los Angeles: University of California Press, 1967)

Lescaboura, Austin, *Behind the Motion Picture Screen* (New York: Munn and Co., 1919; reprint edition, Benjamin Blom, 1969)

Talbot, Frederick A, *Moving Pictures. How They Are Made and Worked* (London: William Heinemann/Philadelphia: J B Lippincott, 1912)

Talbot, Frederick A, *Practical Cinematography and Its Applications* (London: William Heinemann, 1913)

Projection, Technical, and Insurance Manuals
Bennett, Colin N, *A Guide to Kinematography (Projection Section). For Managers, Manager Operators and Operators of Kinema Theatres* (London: Sir Isaac Pitman & Sons, 1923)

Bennett, Colin N, *The Guide to Kinematography; for camera men, operators, and all who "want to know"* (London: E T Heron, 1917)

Bomback, R H, compiler, *Cine Data Book* (London: The Fountain Press, 1950)

Cameron, James R, *Motion Picture Projection* (Manhattan Beach, NY: Cameron Publishing Co., 1928, 4th edition, Tenth Year)

Cameron, James R, *Motion Picture Projection: An Elementary Text Book* (New York: Theatre Supply Co., 1921, 1st ed.; New York: Technical Book Co., 1922, 3rd ed.)

Cameron, James R, Aaron Nadell, and John F Rider, *Motion Picture Projection and Sound Pictures* (Woodmont, Connectitcut: Cameron Publishing Co., 1933)

Cricks, R Howard, ed. by Alex J Martin, *The Complete Projectionist. A Textbook for All Who Handle Sound and Pictures in the Kinema* (London: Kinematograph Publications Ltd, 1933, 1st ed.) [2nd, revised ed., 1937; 3rd ed., with supplementary chapters, ed. by James Benson, 1943]

Cricks, R Howard, *The Complete Projectionist. A Textbook for All Who Handle Sound and Pictures in the Kinema* (London: Odhams Press, 1949)

Filmos [R Aylmer], *Vade-Mecum de l'Opérateur et de l'Exploitant Cinématographiste* (Paris: P Leymarie, n.d., 3rd edition)

Filmos [R Aylmer], revised and updated by G Lechesne, *Le Vade-Mecum de l'Opérateur Projectionniste. Traité pratique de projection muette et sonore. Tome II: Partie Pratique* (Paris: Nouvelles Editions Film et Technique, 1948, 5th edition)

Hodges, E S, *Electricity and Fire Risk* (London: Sir Isaac Pitman & Sons, 1935) [Especially Chapter 13, "Theatres and Cinemas"]

Hulfish, D S, *Cyclopedia of Motion-Picture Work* (American Technical Society, 1911), 2 vols.

Hutchison, J H, *The Complete Kinemanager* (London: Kinematograph Publications, 1937)

Ibbetson, W S, *The Kinema Operator's Handbook. Theory and Practice* (London: E & F N Spon, Ltd, 1921)

Johnson, R V, *Motion Picture Theatre Electrical Equipment and Projection* (London: Crosby Lockwood, 1927; enlarged, 2nd ed., London: The Technical Press Ltd, 1927)

Jones, Bernard E, ed., *The Cinematograph Book: A Complete Practical Guide to the Taking and Projecting of Cinematograph Pictures* (London: Cassell & Co., revised edition, 1919; first published 1915)

Knopp, Leslie, *The Cinematograph Regulations 1955* (London: The Cinema Press, 1955)

Linse, Hugo, *Der Lichtspiel vorführer. Hilfsbuch für Ausbildung und Praxis, besonders zur Vorbereitung auf die Prüfung* (Stuttgart: Franck'sche Verlagshandlung, 1949)

Mannino-Patanè, Gaetano, *L'Operatore cinematografico. Proiezione – acustica* (Milan: Editore Ulrico Hoepli, 1949) [3rd edition, completely revised, of *Il Cine sonoro*, 1943, 1945]

Mather and Platt Ltd, *Research Department, Fires of Reels of Motion Picture Film Stored in Tins in Vaults: an account of tests carried out at Park Works, Manchester, from the Beginning of August 1932 up to date, at the request of the Home Office* [Unpublished typescript, 5 December 1932, originally marked "Confidential", North West Film Archive, Manchester, UK]

Meinel, Dr. Walter, *Hilfsbuch für die Prüfung des Filmvorführers in Frage und Antwort* (Halle: Verlag Wilhelm Knapp, 1949)

Mitchell, Robert A, *Manual of Practical Projection* (New York: International Projectionist Publishing Co., 1956)

The Modern Bioscope Operator (London: Ganes, Ltd, 1913, 3rd edition) [First edition published 1910]

Nadell, Aaron, ed., *F H Richardson's Bluebook of Projection* (New York/Chicago/Hollywood: Quigley Publishing Co., 1942, 7th edition; 1953, 8th edition)

Pitchford, R, and F Coombs, *The Projectionist's Handbook. A Complete Guide to Cinema Operating* (London: Watkins-Pitchford Technical Publications, 1933)

Richardson, F H, ed., *Richardson's Handbook of Projection, for Theatre Managers and Motion Picture Projectionists* (New York: Chalmers Publishing Co., 1923, 4th edition)

Richardson, F H, ed., *Richardson's Handbook of Projection. The Blue Book of Projection* (New York: Chalmers Publishing Co., 1927, 5th edition, in 2 volumes)

Ridley, W G Kubler, *The Common Hazards of Fire Insurance* (London: Isaac Pitman & Sons, 1924, 2nd edition)

Rosenberg, E, *Electrical Engineering: An Elementary Textbook* (Harper & Bros., 1903)

Röwer, Karl, *Die Technik für Filmvorführer* (Halle: Verlag Wilhelm Knapp, 1953)

Rutenberg, Joachim, and Hermann Strödecke, *Handbuch des Filmvorführers* (Berlin-Wilmersdorf: Franke & Co./Film Kurier, 1941)

Schrott, Dr. Paul, *Leitfaden zur Vorführung von Lauf- und Tonbildern, für Vorführer und Theaterbesitzer* (Vienna/Berlin: Verlag von Julius Springer, 1930)

Sloane, T O'Conor, *Motion Picture Projection* (New York: Falk Publishing Co., 1922)

Williamson, J J, *Common Features of Fire Hazard: A Textbook on Common Hazards and General Fire Hazards of Industry* (London: Isaac Pitman & Sons, 1935); Chapter 12: "Celluloid".

Articles and Specialist Periodicals

1895 (Paris: Association française de recherche sur l'histoire du cinema), 1984–.

Anderson, H, "Fire Prevention in the Motion Picture Industry", *Journal of the*

Society of Motion Picture Engineers, v.27 (December 1936), pp.662–676

[Anon.], "Film und Feuersgefahr" and "Die Aufbewahrung der Negative", both in *Internationale Lehrfilmschau*, v.1, no.1 (Rome: Internationales Institut für Lehrfilmwesen, July 1929), pp.77–81

Calhoun, J M, "Old Nitrate Films Are Dangerous!", *International Projectionist*, v.37, no.5 (May 1962), pp.8–9, 17–18

Cinegrafie (Cineteca del Comune di Bologna), 1989– .

Film History, 1987– .

Fletcher, Tony, "Serial Publication of LCC Records Project", *Living Pictures. The Journal of the Popular and Projected Image Before 1914*, issue 2 (Autumn 2001). [Records of fires in London, 1896–1900]

Griffithiana (Gemona, Italy: Cineteca del Friuli), 1978– .

Nitrate dossier and bibliography, compiled by Michelle Aubert, Pierrette Lemoigne, and Jean-Jacques Meusy. [Unpublished dossier, submitted to the editors of this publication by Michelle Aubert of the Archives du Film du CNC, Bois d'Arcy, 1999]

Olivier, M E, "Pour conserver le film positif", *Cinémagazine*, no.30 (27 July 1923), pp.122–123. [Note: Written solely in terms of film handling – celluloid deterioration and film fires are not mentioned.]

3E. Restoration Festival Programmes and Catalogues

Publications of regular specialist festivals featuring archival treasures from the nitrate era:

Il Cinema Ritrovato, Bologna, 1986– .

CinéMémoire, Paris, 1991– .

Le Giornate del Cinema Muto, Pordenone, 1982–1998; Sacile, 1999– .

UCLA Film and Television Archive, Annual Festival of Preservation, 1988– .

Nitrate Filmography

As was the case with the companion bibliography, this filmography includes only the relatively small number of titles previously known to the editors, and those additional titles which were brought to our attention by the contributors whose help is acknowledged after each entry.

Although efforts have been made to ensure that those films which are included are identified as accurately as possible, there are inevitably some instances where original titles could not be traced, so that some entries have had to be listed under supplied titles, while with several others production information is incomplete or of necessity conjectural.

The production credits which are included use the following conventional abbreviations:

d	= director
asst. d	= assistant director
p	= producer/production company
exec. p	= executive producer
assoc. p	= associate producer
ed	= editor
ph	= photography
sc	= scenario/screenplay
rel	= released
tx	= transmitted/broadcast
b/w	= black and white

Elements of technical description generally refer to the format in which the title was originally released, and do not necessarily reflect the material, format, or length available today. In fact, inclusion in this filmography conveys no guarantee that the item mentioned is currently available at all, although we have tried to indicate cases of known incompleteness.

1. Fiction

A small number of feature films, shorts, and serials have been listed, in the majority of which the properties of nitrate film or celluloid play a greater or lesser part in determining the course of the action.

CALICHE SANGRIENTO (Chile, 1969)
English-language title: **BLOODY NITRATE**
35mm, colour; sound. Spanish dialogue. (124 mins.)
d/sc: Helvio Soto
p: Icla Films
ph: Silvio Caiozzi
Principal cast: Hector Duvauchelle (captain), Jaime Vadell (lieutenant), Jorge Yanez, Jorge Guerra
This fiction feature is not about cinematic nitrate per se, but is thought to deserve a place in this Filmography if only for its title, and the fact that nitrate ore is the spur of the action. Set during the War of the Pacific in 1879, fought over the control of the nitrate fields, this action adventure tells the story of a small group of Chilean

soldiers crossing the Atacama Desert in northern Chile, who encounter hardships in the form of nature and the enemy; the survivors eventually meet their deaths at the hands of Peruvian forces. A controversial closing title (suppressed by censors at the time) informed audiences that 25,000 Chilean, Peruvian, and Bolivian soldiers died so that foreign economic interests could take possession of the nitrate fields.

Note: "Caliche" is the Latin American Spanish word for the mineral-bearing gravel or rock of the sodium nitrate deposits in Chile and Peru. The cinematic resonance of the Chilean nitrate industry is noted in Michael Chanan's reflections on the "Nitrate Railways" photograph, printed elsewhere in this volume.

(submitted by Catherine Surowiec, London; description from the original *Variety* review, 5 November 1969)

CAPTAIN CELLULOID VS. THE FILM PIRATES (USA, 1969)

b/w; silent (English titles & intertitles), with music soundtrack. (4 chapters, total 56 mins.)

d: Louis McMahon

p: Louis McMahon, Adventure Pictures

sc: Robert Miller, Louis McMahon, and Alan G Barbour, based on an idea by William K Everson

Principal cast: Robert Clayton, Doris Burnell, Alan G Barbour, Barney Noto, John Cullen, Jean Barbour, Al Kilgore, Grant Willis, William K Everson

Chapters: 1. The Master Duper Strikes; 2. Nitrate Fury; 3. Satan's Coffin; 4. Unmasked

An affectionate pastiche of the cinema serial, complete with masked heroes and villains, plentiful chases, fisticuffs, and three full-blown cliffhangers. When the lost negative of the uncut version of Greed *is found, the Association of Film Distributors donates it to the Film Museum in Rochester. En route, it is intercepted and copied by the Master Duper – a sinister master criminal whose aim is to have a dupe negative of every motion picture classic and "make a fortune selling prints to film societies and private collectors all over the world". The next time the Master Duper's gang attempt an interception, they are thwarted by Captain Celluloid but manage to escape. The Master Duper offers a print of* Greed *to D W Hart, the head of the Classic Film Society. Captain Celluloid interrupts the transaction at a secret film store on an old barge, and in the ensuing fight a gunshot sets off a nitrate fire from which the Captain barely escapes. Eventually Captain Celluloid follows the Master Duper to his lair for a final showdown.*

(submitted by Roger Smither, Imperial War Museum Film and Video Archive, London)

CINEMA PARADISO – see NUOVO CINEMA PARADISO

FORGOTTEN SILVER (New Zealand, 1995)

Colour; sound. English dialogue. (52 mins.)

d/sc: Peter Jackson and Costa Botes

p: Sue Rogers, WingNut Films, in association with the New Zealand Film Commission and New Zealand On Air

Narrator: Jeffrey Thomas

Cast: Peter Jackson, Costa Botes, Marguerite Hurst, Hannah McKenzie, Leonard Maltin, Jonathan Morris, Sam Neill, Lindsay Shelton, Harvey Weinstein

Clever, convincing hoax documentary about a fictitious, "forgotten" New Zealand director, Colin McKenzie, touted as a cinema pioneer and unsung legend responsible for many innovations, with re-enactments, copious footage with digitally-enhanced signs of nitrate decomposition, and supporting interviews with historians and critics. In the film, McKenzie's life work is rediscovered when a trunk containing cans of decomposing nitrate is discovered in a garden shed. Made to

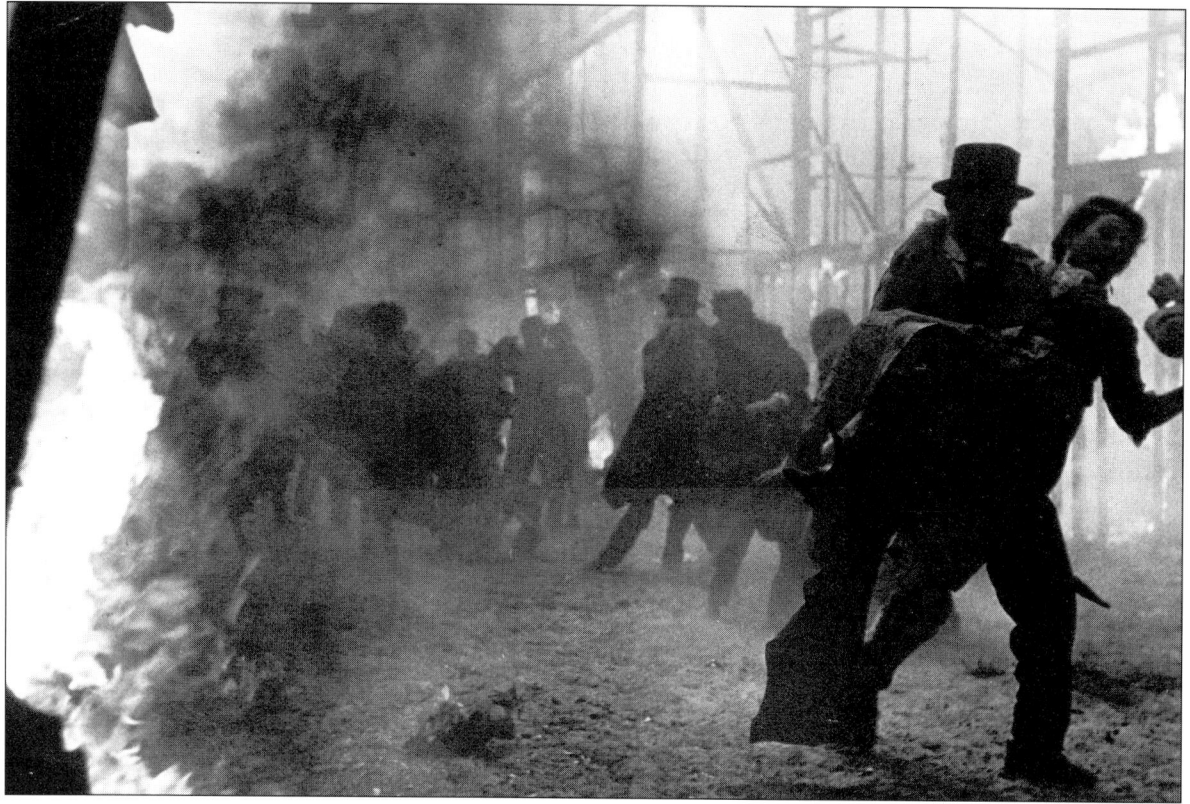

The Bazar de la Charité fire,
re-enacted in *La Kermesse
Rouge* (1947).

celebrate the centenary of cinema, this lavishly produced film provoked complaints from viewers, who were completely taken in when it aired on New Zealand television that year.

(submitted by Frank Stark, New Zealand Film Archive, Wellington, and Roger Smither and John Kerr, Imperial War Museum Film and Video Archive, London)

La KERMESSE ROUGE (France, 1947)
translated title: **RED FAIRGROUND/The SCARLET BAZAAR**
35mm, b/w; sound. French dialogue. (86 mins.)
d/sc: Paul Mesnier
p: Jacques Panhaleux, UTC
Principal cast: Albert Préjean, Andrée Servilanges, Germaine Kerjean, Jean Tissier
Fiction feature. Period melodrama detailing the ill-fated romance and marriage of two artists of differing social classes, which has as its climax a recreation of the disastrous fire at the Bazar de la Charité in 1897, in which the wife meets her death.
(submitted by Roger Smither, Imperial War Museum Film and Video Archive, London)

The LOVE TEST (GB, 1935)
35mm, b/w; sound. English dialogue. (63 mins.)
d: Michael Powell
p: Fox-British Pictures
sc: Selwyn Jepson; based on a story by Jack Celestin
ph: Arthur Crabtree
Principal cast: Judy Gunn (Mary), Louis Hayward (John), David Hutcheson (Thompson), Googie Withers (Minnie), Morris Harvey, Aubrey Dexter, Jack Knight, Gilbert Davis, Eve Turner, Bernard Miles
Fiction feature. Romantic comedy in which research scientists are trying to meet a deadline to produce a formula for non-flammable celluloid. One of the team, Thompson, an ambitious young man out for promotion, is not pleased when Mary,

a solemn young woman, is awarded the appointment, and stirs up resentments among the men in the lab. He persuades John, who is already in love with Mary, to distract her from her work. When the pair actually do fall in love, however, Thompson tells Mary that John is out for her job. Only John, jilted by the outraged Mary, continues to seek the key to the formula.

(submitted by NFTVA cataloguing staff, British Film Institute, London)

MYEST KINEMATOGRAFICHYESKOVO OPERATORA (Russia, 1911)

translated title: The **CAMERAMAN'S REVENGE**

35mm, b/w, tinted. Print viewed with rhyming British English intertitles. (285 metres/11 mins. @ 22 fps)

d: Ladislas Starevitch

p: Khanzhonkov

The most famous of Starevitch's pioneering stop-motion animation films, this amusing, meticulously detailed, and sophisticated short presents a dramatic parody of intrigue, adultery, and revenge among the insect world. Mr Beetle's affair with a dragonfly cabaret star is documented by a grasshopper cameraman. When Mr Beetle takes his wife to the pictures, the screening turns out to be the film of his adultery, complete with a compromising scene shot through a keyhole at the Hotel d'Amour, and all hell breaks loose. Chased by his umbrella-wielding wife, Mr Beetle attacks the cameraman in the projection booth, starting a nitrate fire which destroys the evidence.

Note: The British print, with rhyming intertitles, presents the story as being that of Bill and Sal, a beetle brother and sister who are each trying to hide their secret marriages, as the will of their late, unhappily married father leaves his fortune to the one who marries last.

(submitted by Robert Daudelin, Cinémathèque Québécoise, Montréal, Sterling Hedgpeth, Oakland, CA, and Catherine Surowiec, London)

NITRATO D'ARGENTO/NITRATE D'ARGENT (Italy/France, 1996)

translated title: **SILVER NITRATE**; also known as: **NITRATE BASE**

Colour and b/w; sound. Italian, French, and English dialogue. (88 mins.)

d: Marco Ferreri

sc: Marco Ferreri, Gianni Romoli, David Maria Putorti

p: Audifilm (Rome), Salomé (Paris)

Principal cast: Iaia Forte, Lucianna De Falco, Sabrina La Leggia, Marc Berman, Christelle Legroux

Despite its title, this fiction feature, made to celebrate the Centenary of Cinema, is not about nitrate per se, nor is nitrate mentioned; it earns a place in this Filmography for its title alone. The director mixes staged sequences about filmgoing with historical footage and numerous film clips, in the process examining the effect movies have had on 100 years of filmgoers. Shot mainly in Hungary, with dialogue in various languages.

(submitted by Enrica Serrani, Cineteca del Comune di Bologna, and Catherine Surowiec, London)

NUOVO CINEMA PARADISO (Italy/France, 1988)

also known as: **CINEMA PARADISO**

Colour; sound. Italian dialogue. (155 mins., but widely first released in a 123-min. version)

d/sc: Giuseppe Tornatore

p: Franco Cristaldi

Principal cast: Philippe Noiret, Salvatore Cascio, Jacques Perrin

Fiction feature, set in a small Italian town in the years after World War II, about a boy who loves movies and makes friends with the local projectionist. In an early

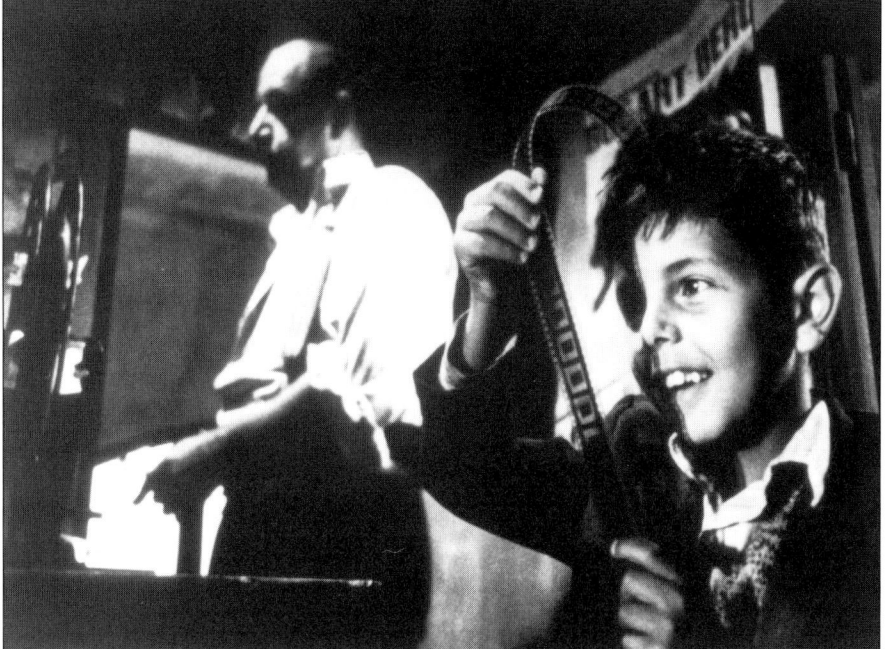

Toto exploring the forbidden pleasures of film in Alfredo's projection box: *Nuovo Cinema Paradiso* (1988).

BFI Collections – Stills, Posters & Designs, London. 282234.

scene, Toto's collection of film fragments cut from show-prints at the insistence of the parish priest catches fire and places the family home at risk. In a later climactic scene, after projectionist Alfredo redirects the beam of the projector to share the film experience with the whole population of the town in the piazza, a nitrate fire breaks out in the projection box and Alfredo is blinded. The film won a Special Jury Prize at Cannes, and an Oscar for Best Foreign Film.

(submitted by Roger Smither, Imperial War Museum Film and Video Archive, London)

PICTURE PALACE PIECANS (GB, 1914)
35mm, b/w; silent. (595 ft.)
d: W P Kellino
p: Vaudefilms
Cast: Sam T Poluski, Will Poluski, Hanvair & Lee
Fiction short. Comedy about two tramps, Flick and Flock, who buy a rundown cinema. Nothing works, and the two are pestered by young kids at the ticket booth. They smoke in the projection box, and put a candle in the projector. The last intertitle says: "Now the cinema is lost and we have to perform ourselves."

Film scholar Ivo Blom surmises that the film was probably used as an insert in a variety show, and seems to have been intended as a satire on all the non-professionals trying to start a career as cinema exhibitors. The term "piecan" is an old British expression once used to label somebody a fool or rogue.
Note: The copy held by the Nederlands Film Museum has the Dutch title *Moderne Bioscoop te Koop*, which translates literally as "Modern Cinema for Sale".
(submitted by Ivo Blom, Amsterdam)

PRAGUE (GB/France, 1991)
35mm, colour; sound. English dialogue. (89 mins.)
d/sc: Ian Sellar
p: Christopher Young, Claudie Ossard, Christopher Young Films (London)/ Constellation-UGC-Hachette Première (Paris), in association with BBC Films, British Screen, Canal +, and the Scottish Film Production Fund
Principal cast: Alan Cumming, Sandrine Bonnaire, Bruno Ganz
Fiction feature. Alexander Novak arrives from Scotland to search in the National

Film Archive in Prague for a wartime newsreel which he believes will explain part of his mother's life history. The film proves difficult to find, and Alexander becomes attracted to the assistant archivist Elena. Elena finds the film and (incredibly) entrusts the unique reel of nitrate to Alexander. A serio-comic chain of events leads to the film's accidental destruction by fire, but all is not lost, as Elena is able to describe to Alexander what it showed.

(submitted by Janet McBain, Scottish Screen Archive, Glasgow)

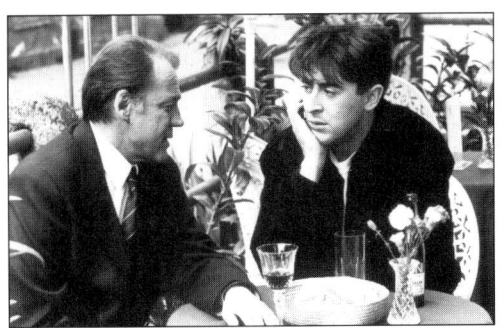

Alexander (Alan Cumming) with archive head Josef (Bruno Ganz) in *Prague* (1991).

BFI Collections – Stills, Posters & Designs, London.

RAMBLIN' 'ROUND HOLLYWOOD (USA, 1955)

35mm, b/w; sound. English dialogue and narration. (10 mins.)
d: Ralph Staub
p: Columbia Pictures
series: "Screen Snapshots"
ed: Harold White
Cast: Ralph Staub, Ken Murray, Pamela Murray

Columbia "Screen Snapshots" series producer Ralph Staub chats by the pool with Ken Murray, harking back to the Hollywood of yesteryear, and Murray's famous home movies. He reminds Murray of an old "Screen Snapshot" in which he appeared 15 years previously, which follows in flashback. Ken Murray enters a dusty film vault, where even the telephone has cobwebs. He places his trademark cigar on a nearby film can, where it continues to burn while he proceeds to run film through a moviola, showing us a number of clips and stars from the silent period, accompanied by Murray's often flippant running commentary. By the end of his "ramble 'round old Hollywood", strips of film from the moviola are everywhere; cut to the cigar, now a stub, which finally ignites the film and causes an explosion which rocks the vault. Murray emerges from the door of the vault, his face blackened to look like a blackface minstrel comic. Murray and Staub chuckle about this footage, and continue their present-day chat, during which Murray introduces his little daughter Pamela. Staub leaves Murray studying his latest script by the swimming pool.

(submitted by Anthony Slide, Los Angeles)

SABOTAGE (GB, 1936)

35mm, b/w; sound. English dialogue. (76 mins.)
d: Alfred Hitchcock
p: Michael Balcon, assoc. p: Ivor Montagu, Gaumont-British Picture Corporation
sc: Charles Bennett (from the novel *The Secret Agent*, by Joseph Conrad)
Principal cast: Oscar Homolka, Sylvia Sidney, John Loder, Desmond Tester, William Dewhurst

Fiction feature. The plot, based somewhat loosely on Conrad, concerns Verloc, an anarchist who runs a cinema as a cover for his activities. Verloc's gang plans a bomb outrage in central London. Verloc knows he is being watched by the police, so he sends Stevie, the innocent schoolboy brother of his wife Winnie, to take some cans of film, together with another package in which the time-bomb is concealed, to a left-luggage office in Piccadilly Circus. Because of the rules prohibiting the carriage of nitrate film on public transport, the boy has to walk, getting caught up in the crowds watching the Lord Mayor's Show, suspensefully taking up more and more time. Eventually a friendly bus conductor lets him ride,

Stevie (Desmond Tester) delayed on his errand with the film cans and the fateful parcel: *Sabotage* (1936).

BFI Collections – Stills, Posters & Designs, London. 132578.

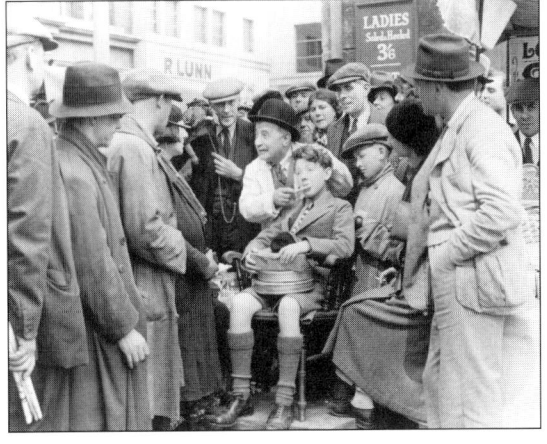

and at the correct time the bomb explodes with the boy still on the bus. The rest of the film is concerned with the fallout from this action: Verloc's wife kills him, but her crime is conveniently covered up by another explosion, and she goes off with policeman Ted.
(submitted by Luke McKernan, NFTVA, British Film Institute, London)

SCIUSCIÀ (Italy, 1946)
English-language release title: **SHOESHINE**
b/w; sound. Italian dialogue. (95 mins.)
d: Vittorio De Sica
p: Paolo William Tamburella, for Alfa Cinematografica
script and story: Cesare Zavattini, Sergeio Amidei, Adolfo Franci, Cesare Giulio Viola
Principal cast: Franco Interlenghi, Rinaldo Smordoni, Aniello Mele, Bruno Ortensi
One of the most famous neo-realist feature films of post-war Italy, starring non-professionals. Two friends, poor but honest shoeshine boys living on the streets of Nazi-occupied Rome, get involved in the black market and end up in prison as hardened juvenile criminals. One key sequence features a nitrate fire that starts during a projection in the prison courtyard, allowing one of the protagonists to escape. A moving indictment of the prison system, the film won a special Oscar in 1947.
(submitted by Clyde Jeavons, London)

The SIMPSONS: The DAY THE VIOLENCE DIED [episode 3F16] (USA, 1996)
The SIMPSONS: The TROUBLE WITH TRILLIONS [episode 5F14] (USA, 1998)
Colour; sound. English dialogue. (22 mins. per episode)
series creators: Matt Groening, James L. Brooks
p: Twentieth Century Fox
This cult animated television series is noted, among many other characteristics, for the number of film references which are included in each episode, demonstrating a high level of cinema awareness (and wit) on the part of its creators. The most direct nitrate allusion brought to the attention of this publication is in the first of the two episodes cited below.

(1) The Day the Violence Died
d: Wesley Archer
exec. p: Bill Oakes and Josh Weinstein
sc: John Swartzwelder
In this episode, Bart Simpson discovers, reduced to poverty and homelessness, Chester J Lampwick (voiced by Kirk Douglas). Lampwick is the true originator of Itchy and Scratchy, the cat-and-mouse "stars" of a hugely successful – and violent – cartoon series, which has earned a fortune for the Myers family, who stole the idea from him. As evidence of his claim, Lampwick has an original 1919 print of Itchy's very first appearance, as Itchy the Lucky Mouse in: Manhattan Madness. *Bart screens the film on an old projector at his school, but just after the end credits roll, the film is lost in a projector fire. In the subsequent court case,* Steamboat Itchy, *the 1928 film which the Myers family claim as the original appearance of Itchy, is also screened.*

(2) The Trouble with Trillions
d: Swinton Scott
exec. p: Mike Scully
sc: Ian Maxtone-Graham
In this episode, Homer Simpson is pressured into helping the IRS and FBI in their case against his boss, multi-millionaire C Montgomery Burns, who is believed to

have absconded with a trillion-dollar note that he was supposed to deliver fifty years earlier to war-torn Europe. An awareness of archival issues (if not quite a direct nitrate allusion) is indicated when the Mission: Impossible-*style briefing message assembled from 1945 newsreel footage announces, "This film will self-destruct if not properly stored."*

(The first title in this section was submitted by Ray Edmondson, of ScreenSound Australia, Canberra, and Sterling Hedgpeth, Oakland, CA, and the second by Sophie Smither, London; the section was compiled with the help of Steve Bryant of the NFTVA, British Film Institute, London, and John Kerr of the Imperial War Museum Film and Video Archive, London.)

SMOKESCREEN (GB, 1994)

Colour; sound. English dialogue. (6 episodes, total 180 mins.)
d: Giancarlo Gemin
sc: James Andrew Hall
p: Jill Green, Red Rooster, for BBC TV
Principal cast: Sally Walsh, Michael Sanderson, Sam Townend, Joan Sims, Timothy West, Kate Hardie, Peter Guiness, Paula Wilcox, Sean Murray, Anita Dobson, David Cleveland

BBC children's series in six 30-minute episodes, based on the novel by Elsie McCutcheon (see Bibliography). For the purposes of the television adaptation, the action is relocated to the north of England, and the characters of Gold and Sheringham, and the rivalry between them, are more developed. The climactic fire is caused not by an accident with the projector but by Gold's cigar butt, and Chrissie heroically rescues Gold from the fire (although, as she is in "Fenbury Fred" costume at the time, she is not recognised as the hero).

(submitted by David Cleveland, East Anglian Film Archive, Norwich; production details courtesy of Sue Malden, BBC Resources, London)

La VALIGIA DEI SOGNI (Italy, 1953)

translated title: SUITCASE OF DREAMS/The PORTMANTEAU OF DREAMS
35mm, b/w; sound. Italian dialogue. (96 mins.)
d: Luigi Comencini
asst. d: Gianni Comencini
sc: Giuseppe Bannati, Luigi Comencini, Ettore M Margadonna
p: Mario Villa, Produzione Cinematografica Mambretti
Archive material selected by Gianni Comencini, with the collaboration of, and in consultation with, the Cineteca Italiana, Archivio Storico del Film, and the Cineteca Nazionale
Principal cast: Umberto Melnati, Mariapia Casilio, Roberto Risso, Ludmilla Dudarova

Fiction feature. The gentlemanly ex-actor Omeri is a passionate collector of early films, which he shows in educational institutions and at social occasions. One evening, at a society occasion, his enthusiasm causes ridicule among the younger members of his audience. A former star of silent films, now married to an influential film producer, Elena Makowska is upset by the uncouth reaction. She sends her son to Omeri to try to buy up his films. When Omeri refuses to sell, the son approaches Mariannina, Omeri's assistant, offering her a film role in return for the films. While searching in Omeri's vaults, Mariannina carelessly sets fire to the entire collection. Omeri is threatened with prosecution for illegal storage of dangerous materials, but the timely intervention of the film producer ensures his release. The friendship between producer and collector grows, and Omeri is eventually made director of a film museum financed by the producer.

Note: Shown as part of the season "The Last Nitrate Picture Show" at the National Film Theatre, London, in conjunction with the 2000 FIAF Congress.

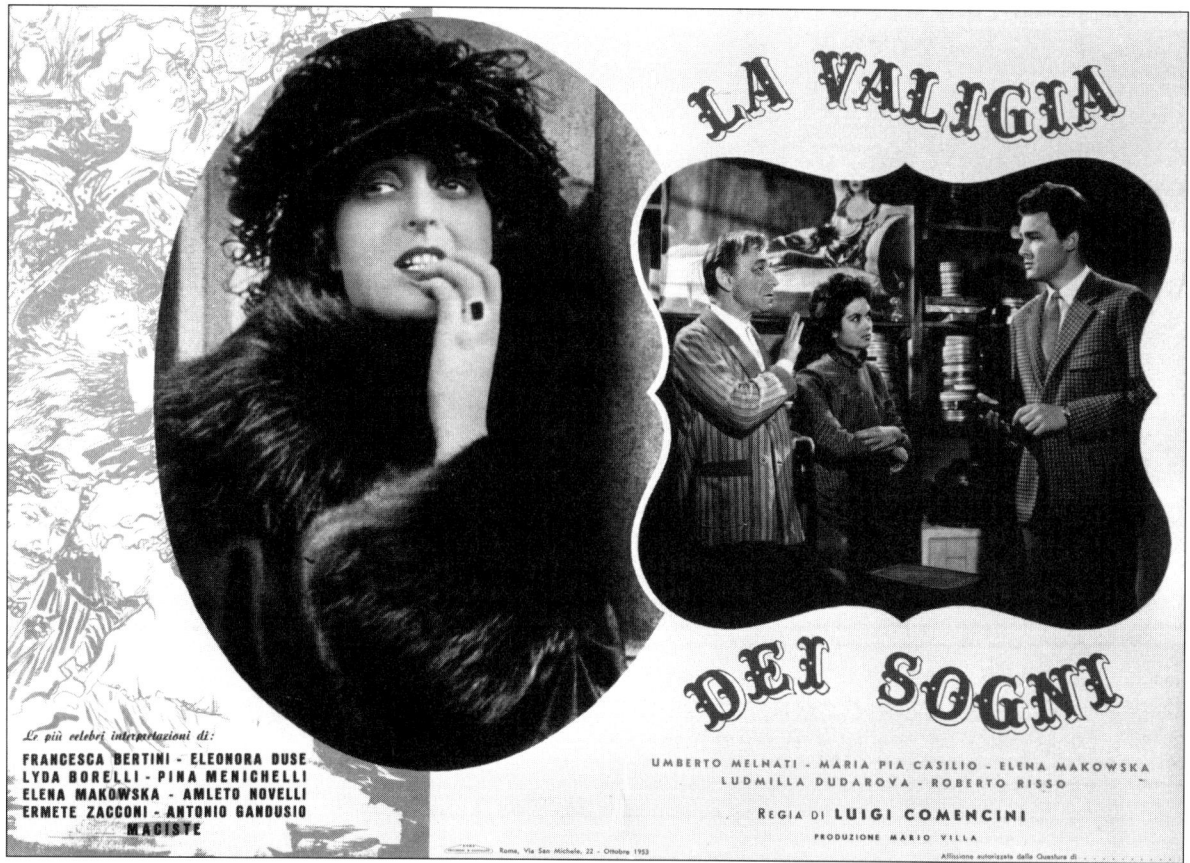

A lobby card for *La Valigia dei Sogni* (1953).

Fondazione Cineteca Italiana, Milan.

(submitted by Luisa Comencini, Fondazione Cineteca Italiana, Archivio Storico del Film, Milan)

WHEN THE STUDIO BURNED (USA, 1913)
working title: **A THANHOUSER HEROINE**
35mm, b/w; silent. English intertitles. (1 reel)
d: Lawrence Marston
sc: Lloyd F Lonergan
p: Thanhouser
Principal cast (as themselves): Marguerite Snow, Helen Badgley, Marie Eline, James Cruze
Fiction short. While represented in some contemporary press coverage as an actual record of the Thanhouser Studio fire of 13 January 1913, the film is actually a dramatised re-enactment, which, while including some elements of what really happened (for example, the efforts by employees to rescue the company's negatives), also takes considerable liberties with the truth. Most notably, it features a scene in which Helen Badgley, the "Thanhouser Kidlet" (so called to distinguish her from the "Thanhouser Kid", 7–year–old child star Marie Eline), is rescued by leading lady Marguerite Snow, even though in reality the latter was away from the studio at the time of the actual fire.
(submitted by Catherine Surowiec, London; compiled with the help of Ned Thanhouser, Portland, OR)

2. Creative responses to Nitrate Film
A small but important sub-genre of films have made the material nature of archival film – including its liability to damage and deterioration – an important part of the visual experience which the auteur seeks to share with the audience.

ARCH'ANGE (France, 1997)
translated title: **ARCHANGEL**
16mm, b/w and colour; silent and sound. French titles and voiceover dialogue. (33 mins.)
d/p: Laure Saint-Rose
Avant-garde 16mm film about different aspects and qualities of film, including segments on archive work and decomposition. Begun in 1995, it combines old, found material with material from the CNC archive and newly-shot footage. The closing credits describe the film as a collage, and thank the staff at Bois d'Arcy. Filmmaker's quote: "Because film is a corpse riddled with holes, saturated with loss, always on the brink of breakage, as if torn from ephemeral nitrate."
(submitted by Michelle Aubert and the staff of the CNC, Bois d'Arcy, and Catherine Surowiec, London)

LYRISCH NITRAAT (Netherlands, 1990)
translated title: **LYRICAL NITRATE**
35mm, colour; sound. Dutch intertitles. (50 mins.)
d/sc: Peter Delpeut
p: Suzanne van Voorst, YUCA Film
A compilation of film fragments dating from the years 1905–1915, constructed like a musical composition, using feature and documentary footage from the collection of Jean Desmet, the first Dutch film collector, which is currently being preserved by the Nederlands Filmmmuseum.
(submitted by Roger Smither, Imperial War Museum Film and Video Archive, London; compiled with help from the filmmaker, Peter Delpeut)

NITRATE KISSES (USA, 1992)
16mm, b/w; sound. English dialogue. (67 mins.)
d/p/ph/ed: Barbara Hammer
Experimental feature documentary exploring eroded emulsions and images for lost vestiges of the forbidden and invisible history of lesbian and gay culture, put in context by the contemporary sexual activities of four gay and lesbian couples. Archival outtakes from the first gay film in the US, Lot in Sodom *(1933), by James Sibley Watson and Melville Webber, and footage from German narrative and documentary films of the 1930s are interwoven in this multi-faceted construction. Filmmaker Barbara Hammer worked with Sibley's original nitrate outtakes at the George Eastman House archive, as well as rolls of segments of 35mm nitrate prints collected by a German projectionist over the years. She later recalled: "These scenes were from newsreels, documentaries, feature narratives and cartoons of the Thirties German cinema. They were heavily scratched, but I liked these marks as they signified age."*
(submitted by Roger Smither, Imperial War Museum Film and Video Archive, London; compiled with help from the filmmaker, Barbara Hammer)

3. Contemporary documentaries about film production and film handling in the nitrate era

L'AGE DU PLASTIQUE (France, 1942)
translated title: The **AGE OF PLASTIC**
b/w; sound. French narration. (13 mins.)
d: Paul de Roubaix
p: Je Vois Tout
ph: G A Turenne
Technical documentary presenting the fabrication and uses of several of the most

common plastic materials, beginning with celluloid – first as an inexpensive imitation of tortoise shell, ivory, etc., and then as motion-picture film – before proceeding to cellulose and its products galalith (milk casein) and bakelite.
(submitted by Michelle Aubert and the staff of the CNC, Bois d'Arcy)

Une CITÉ FRANÇAISE DU CINÉMA (France, 1929)
translated title: **A FRENCH CINEMA CITY**
35mm, b/w; silent. French titles and intertitles. (200 metres/11 mins. @ 18 fps)
d: Pierre Chenal
p: Pathé-Natan
Documentary short depicting a day at the Pathé-Natan studios. Activities shown include developing, printing, and drying kilometres of film; the colouring of films by the stencil method (showing a roomful of women doing "colori au pochoir" and how a stencil is created); and editors at work. Gauges are briefly discussed, ranging from 35mm to 9.5mm "Pathé Baby" for home use.
Note: Extract shown at the 2000 FIAF Nitrate Symposium. Footage from this film was incorporated into the 1988 Cinémathèque Française restoration of Pierre Chenal's film *Paris-Cinéma* (1929) (also in this Filmography).
(submitted by Michelle Aubert and the staff of the CNC, Bois d'Arcy)

FILM DE SÛRETÉ À BASE D'ACÉTATE DE CELLULOSE (France, 1922)
translated title: **SAFETY FILM WITH ACETATE CELLULOSE BASE**
35mm, b/w; silent. French intertitles. (6 mins.)
Director and Producer unknown
Dramatised documentary short presenting the case for safety film vs. inflammable nitrate.
(submitted by Michelle Aubert and the staff of the CNC, Bois d'Arcy)

IDEALE FILMERZEUGUNG (Austria, 1914)
translated title: **The IDEAL WAY OF FILM PRODUCTION**
35mm, b/w, tinted; silent. German intertitles. (406 ft./7 mins. @16 fps)
p: Sascha-Film
Trickfilm. Several examples of technical apparatus – a perforator, camera, printer, splicer, and cleaning machine – are shown at work, animated via stop-motion pixillation.
Note: Shown at the 2000 FIAF Nitrate Symposium.
(submitted by Dr Nikolaus Wostry, Filmarchiv Austria, Vienna)

JURNAL DE ACTUALITATI ONC-UFA N° 5/1942
(1942, Romania/Germany)
translated title: **NEWSREEL JOURNAL ONC-UFA No.5/1942**
b/w; sound. (length of story: 103 metres)
p: Oficiul National al Cinematografie [National Office of Cinematography], Romania, and UFA, Germany
The second story in this issue of the newsreel shows King Mihai of Romania visiting the ONC's laboratories and film archive.
(submitted by Dinu-Ioan Nicula, Arhiva Nationala de Filme – Cinemateca Romana, Bucharest)

Ein NEUER APPARAT ZUR VERHÜTUNG VON KINOBRANDEN (Germany, ca.1912?)
translated title: **A NEW MACHINE FOR THE PREVENTION OF CINEMA FIRES**
35mm, b/w; silent. German intertitles. (67 metres)
Director and Producer unknown

The film shows a new way to prevent cinema fires by introducing a projector with automatically closing lids. When a reel is set on fire, the lids close and suffocate the fire. The film can be cleaned afterwards. Management and patrons no longer run any risk.
(submitted by Ivo Blom, Amsterdam)

PARIS-CINEMA (France, 1929)
alternate title: Les **COULISSES DU CINEMA** [Cinema Behind the Scenes]
35mm, b/w; silent. French titles and intertitles. (30 mins.)
d: Pierre Chenal
asst. d: Jean Mitry
Documentary about filmmaking, in three main sections. The first deals with technical equipment and developments, including the manufacture of raw film stock at the Kodak-Pathé factory at Vincennes, processing, printing, tinting, and women editing and assembling film. The second section deals with animators at work, including André Rigal, Alain Saint-Organ and his animator M. Bizot, and Ladislas Starevitch and his puppets and miniature studio at Fontenay-sous-Bois, where each 2-reel film takes 10–12 months of painstaking work. The third section deals with filmmaking, with scenes at the Billancourt, Joinville, and Pathé-Natan studios. Director Alberto Cavalcanti films scenes for Le Capitaine Fracasse. *Augusto Genina shoots night scenes for* Quartier Latin *at the Gare de Lyon with his star Carmen Boni.*
Note: The print was restored in 1988 by the Cinémathèque Française, according to the director's instructions, integrating fragments from Chenal's 1929 documentary about the Pathé-Natan studio, *Une Cité française du cinema* (also in this Filmography).
(submitted by Catherine Surowiec, London)

PATHÉ PICTORIAL NO. 434: HISTORIC FILM (GB, 1963)
35mm, colour; sound. English narration. (length of entire cinemagazine: 955 ft./11 mins.)
p: Associated British-Pathé
Cinemagazine containing an item about the work of the National Film Archive, London. Note: The material held by the archive consists of mute outtakes only. Formerly entitled "(The National Film Archive's Work)".
(submitted by Elaine Burrows and NFTVA cataloguing staff, British Film Institute, London)

The ROMANCE OF CELLULOID (USA, 1937)
35mm, b/w; sound. English narration and dialogue. (10 mins.)
p: Metro-Goldwyn-Mayer
Documentary short. The first part of the film shows the making of nitrate film stock for motion pictures, before the film develops into a promotional for MGM.
Note: Shown as part of the season "The Last Nitrate Picture Show" at the National Film Theatre, London, in conjunction with the 2000 FIAF Congress.
(submitted by Paolo Cherchi-Usai, George Eastman House, Rochester, NY)

SPECCHIO DELL'UNIVERSO (Italy, ca. 1940)
translated title: **MIRROR OF THE UNIVERSE**
b/w; sound. Italian narration and titles. (12 mins.)
d: Umberto Rossi
Documentary short. A brief survey of the history of photography, including a section which shows the manufacture of nitrate film stock at the Ferrania plant in Italy.
(submitted by Paolo Cherchi-Usai, George Eastman House, Rochester, NY)

THIS FILM IS DANGEROUS! (GB, 1948)
35mm, b/w; sound. English dialogue and narration. (19 mins.)
d/ed: Ronald Haines
p: British Documentary Films, for the British Admiralty

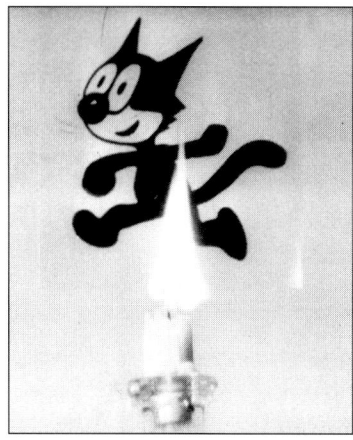

An illustration of the saying "as much chance as a celluloid cat in Hades": *This Film Is Dangerous!* (1948).

Imperial War Museum, London. IWM FLM 3228.

A Royal Navy instructional film on the dangers of nitrate film fire, consisting mainly of demonstrations, in each of which a reel of film is ignited and the resulting fire attacked with a different kind of fire-fighting equipment. In virtually all cases, the film continues to smoulder and decompose, emitting dangerous fumes: only a concentrated attack with a gas/water extinguisher within 10 seconds of the outbreak of fire is shown to be effective. Projector, projection booth, and rewind-room equipment, procedures and safety precautions, and classic errors are examined to show that almost all fires are the result of carelessness, and almost all damage the result of incorrect methods of attack.
Note: Shown at the 2000 FIAF Nitrate Symposium.
(submitted by Roger Smither, Imperial War Museum Film and Video Archive, London)

L'USINE DE VINCENNES DE LA SOCIÉTÉ PATHÉ-KODAK (France, date unknown)
translated title: The **VINCENNES PATHÉ-KODAK FACTORY**
35mm, b/w. (length/running time unknown)
p: unknown [Pathé?]
Dramatised documentary short. Inside the Pathé-Kodak factory, carbon is handled with the aid of a caterpillar hoist. Film manufacture involves intense refrigeration, and the workers who operate these machines wear masks to protect them against ammonia. Nitrocellulose, the primary raw material in the manufacture of film, is always kept in zinc cases, under controlled humidity, and is stored in a special location far from the main buildings. All areas devoted to film manufacture have emergency escape stairs. Film is manufactured in great quantities, under quality control. Security measures are strictly observed. In case of fire, personnel must evacuate the premises and immediate precautions must be taken to limit any danger, until firemen arrive and order is re-established.
(submitted by Michelle Aubert and the staff of the CNC, Bois d'Arcy)

VANITY FAIR PICTORIALS, NO. 13: SECRETS OF A WORLD INDUSTRY – THE MAKING OF CINEMATOGRAPH FILM (GB, 1922)
35mm, b/w; silent. English intertitles (480 ft./8 mins. @ 16 fps)
p: Walturdaw Company
Cinemagazine story about the manufacture of film, showing perforation, developing, printing negative and positive images, drying on revolving drums and racks, examination, splicing at an editing bench, cleaning, measuring, packing into cans, and labelling, ending with the display of a finished strip of film.
Note: Shown at the 2000 FIAF Nitrate Symposium.
(submitted by Elaine Burrows, NFTVA, British Film Institute, London)

4. Documentaries about film history and the role of archives

This section, and the following one on archival test films, exemplify most fully the shortcomings which were noted in the general introduction to this Filmography, and the undoubted scope for further research and expansion in the future. We are certain that many more archives around the world beyond those that are represented here must have examples of news or documentary coverage of their activities, or will have produced their own promotional films and trailers, or training and test material. This situation has admittedly arisen from the fact that we never specifically asked for such films, and the only archives that have supplied them are therefore those which placed a certain interpretation on the general request which we did make for filmographic nominations. We can only apologise to any institution which feels it should be included in these sections but finds that it is not.

The AUSTRALIAN IMAGE (Australia, 1988)
Video, colour and b/w; sound. English narration and dialogue. (12 parts; 24 mins. each)
d: Christina Hunniford
series concept: Ray Edmondson, Nick Hildyard
script executive: Graham Shirley
p: Nick Hildyard, Ray Edmondson
exec. p: Christina Hunniford
p: Australian Capital Television, Canberra
Presenter: Bill Hunter
Produced in co-operation with the National Film & Sound Archive
12-part television documentary series dealing with various aspects of the history of Australian film, television, radio, and recorded sound, in which Part 1, Lost and Found, *deals with the importance of collecting and preserving the nation's heritage of the moving image and recorded sound, and tells how much has already vanished. Several of the nitrate-related incidents and examples explored in Ray Edmondson's paper "Wizards of Oz" (elsewhere in this volume) are also covered in this series.*
(submitted by Ray Edmondson, ScreenSound Australia, Canberra)

CES FILMS QUI NE VEULENT PAS MOURIR (France, 1988)
translated title: **THESE FILMS WHICH WOULD NOT DIE**
Video, colour; sound. French narration. (2 films, total 120 mins.)
d: Jacques Mény
p: FR3/Droits INA
Narrator: Michel Piccoli

Part 1: **L'Age des Cinémathèques** (The Age of Cinematheques)
(60 mins.)
tx: 12 May 1988, FRANCE 3.
Documentary exploring what is being done by the Archives du Film, the Cinémathèque Française, the British Film Institute, and the world's other cinematheques and specialist institutions to save our film heritage, and the preservation and restoration issues surrounding the fragility of the film medium itself and its chemical decay. Showing examples of films saved throughout Europe, this documentary also examines the work of pioneer film curators and collectors like Henri Langlois, through interviews with Jean Rouch, film director and president of the Cinémathèque Française, and Anna-Lena Wibom, a past president of FIAF.

Part 2: **Le Temps des Restaurations** (The Time of Restorations)
(60 mins.)
tx: 16 May 1988, FRANCE 3.
*Part 2 of this documentary deals with the range of intensive research and work involved in film restoration. Includes interviews with a number of practitioners about their projects: Kevin Brownlow (*Napoléon*), Enno Patalas (*Metropolis*), Renée Lichtig (*Casanova*), Jacques Champreux (*Les Vampires*), Henri Colpi (*L'Hirondelle et la mésange*), and Jean Dréville (*L'Inhumaine*). A segment on colour film restoration is illustrated by a Technicolor restoration project at the UCLA film archive. The programme concludes by discussing when, where, and how restored films can be shown.*
(submitted by Michelle Aubert and the staff of the CNC, Bois d'Arcy)

CINÉTRÉSORS... À LA RECHERCHE DES FILMS PERDUS (France, 1989)
translated title: **CINEMA TREASURES... IN SEARCH OF LOST FILMS**
Colour; sound. French dialogue, narration, and titles. (60 mins.)
d: Gilles Nadeau, Jean Douchet
p: Georges Benayoun, Paul Rozenberg, Institut du Monde Arabe
ed: Laurence Bidou
Presenter: Martine Jouando
Interviewees include: Freddy Buache, Raymond Borde, Bernard Martinand, Vincent
Pinel, Frantz Schmitt, Fred Junck, Enno Patalas, Renée Lichtig, Bernard Chardère,
Michelle Aubert, Jonas Mekas
French television programme devoted to European film archives, archivists, and
their work, with interviews and clips from over 40 films.
(submitted by NFTVA cataloguing staff, British Film Institute, London)

CITIZEN LANGLOIS (France, 1994)
35mm, colour and b/w; sound. French dialogue and narration. (65 mins.)
d/sc: Edgardo Cozarinsky
p: Serge Lalou, Dominique Païni, Les Films d'Ici
ph: Jacques Bouquin
ed: Martine Bouquin
Interviewees: Lotte Eisner, Marie Epstein
Vintage interviews: Henri Langlois, Georges Franju, François Truffaut, Eric Rohmer
Narrator: Niels Arestrup
Documentary about French archivist Henri Langlois (1914–1977), presenting a
kaleidoscopic portrait of this still-controversial figure, exploring the legend via film
clips, photos, interviews, and anecdotes.
Note: The film also includes excerpts from a vintage French documentary about
recycling films, showing how they are used to produce varnish and patent leather.
(submitted by Catherine Surowiec, London)

COMMENT ON SAUVE UN FILM (France, 1996)
translated title: **HOW TO SAVE A FILM**
Colour; sound. French narration. (3 mins.)
d: Philippe Truffaut
p: Centre National de la Cinématographie
voice: Claude Chabrol
Animation short about film preservation, made to promote the French Nitrate Plan.
Shown at the 2000 FIAF Nitrate Symposium.
(submitted by Michelle Aubert and the staff of the CNC, Bois d'Arcy)

DUE DOLLARI AL CHILO (Italy, 2000)
translated title: **TWO DOLLARS PER KILO**
35mm, colour and b/w; sound. Italian narration and dialogue, English subtitles. (15
mins.)
d: Paolo Lipari
sc: Matteo Pavesi; based on an idea by Gianni Comencini and Matteo Pavesi
p: Fondazione Cineteca Italiana
Opening narration: Gianni Comencini
Interviewees: Tony Patellani (Kodak Company, European Branch), Mario Perugini
(Presidente LACIM s.r.l. Milano, Stabilimento di Millesimo, Savona)
Archive material from Archivio Film Fondazione Cineteca Italiana, Milan
Documentary short. A startling and often heart-rending visit (for cinephiles) to the
disposal plants for films, where films die, and the value of creativity, art, and
dreams is reduced to "two dollars a kilo" – 40 dollars for a film, for two hours of
cinema that may have moved and entertained us, or changed our lives. Taking as its

starting point Luigi Comencini's 1949 short Il museo dei sogni *(also in this Filmography),* Due dollari al chilo *intercuts footage from the 1949 film with new footage of current film disposal plants and the recycling processes to which films are submitted today, underlining the fact that our cinematic memory is still at risk. As Gianni Comencini states in conclusion: "Movies are written on water. They are fragile, just like our lives."*

Note: Premiered at the 2000 Giornate del Cinema Muto.

(submitted by Catherine Surowiec, London; compiled with the help of Luisa Comencini, Fondazione Cineteca Italiana, Archivio Storico del Film, Milan)

ELECTRIC THEATRE (Luxembourg, 2000)

b/w and colour; sound. Luxembourgish dialogue and narration, with some French dialogue. (30 mins.)

d/sc: Andy Bausch

p: Andy Bausch, Rattlesnake Pictures

ph: Klaus Peter Weber

ed: Pia Dumont, Amin Jaber

Principal cast: Thierry van Weverke, Jean-Paul Raths, Frank Sasonoff, Joseph Gudenburg

Narrator: Camille Felgen

Interviewees: Lolo Maroldt, Catherine Seil, Laure Koster

Documentary about the beginnings of the cinema in Luxembourg, covering the period 1896–1914, combining interviews, film extracts, photos, and graphics with fictional re-enactments. These scenes include the pioneers at work making their movies, explaining the principles of moving images, and the public running to church and talking about films as "the devil's work". A scene in a steel miners' pub in 1911 features the drunken owner of a movie theatre telling how his theatre burned down, thanks to the inattention of a drowsy projectionist; his account is combined with shots of a reel of nitrate film going up in flames.

(submitted by Claude Bertemes, Cinémathèque Municipale de Luxembourg; additional information from the filmmaker, Andy Bausch)

The FILM THAT WAS LOST (USA, 1942)

35mm, b/w; sound. English narration and titles. (10 mins.)

p: MGM; no. 36 of the series "John Nesbitt's Passing Parade"

d: Sammy Lee

sc: Doane Hoag

Documentary short about the film preservation work of the Museum of Modern Art in New York, largely made up of archive footage, exclusively actuality, including shots of Queen Victoria, William Jennings Bryan, and Rasputin. It stresses the importance of salvaging filmed records of the living past, stating that the archive came into existence just in time to prevent much historic material of the cinema's first 30 years from becoming "film that was lost".

(submitted by Ron Magliozzi, Museum of Modern Art Film & Video Archive, New York)

FORGOTTEN TREASURE (USA, 1943)

35mm, b/w; sound. English narration and dialogue. (10 mins.)

p: MGM; no. 43 of the series "John Nesbitt's Passing Parade"

d: Sammy Lee

sc: Doane Hoag

Dramatised documentary short about the Museum of Modern Art's programme to preserve historic film. "Nesbitt explains how vital it is for us to save the film we have, and speculates about future generations learning from this film. We see a group of students sitting in a theatre watching World War Two footage, labelled on the titles as

a textbook might be. One kid turns to his friend, marvelling at how students used to use books to learn history. 'How primitive!' his friend replies." (Leonard Maltin, The Great Movie Shorts, *New York: Bonanza Books, 1972, p.176)*
(submitted by Ron Magliozzi, Museum of Modern Art Film & Video Archive, New York, and Catherine Surowiec, London)

HERE AND NOW (series): (The NATIONAL FILM ARCHIVE) (GB, 1963)
35mm, b/w; sound. English narration and dialogue. (250 ft./9 mins)
d: Jim Pople
p: Michael Ingrams, Rediffusion
Interviewer: Huw Thomas
Cast: Ernest Lindgren, Harold Brown, Frank Holland
tx: 2 January 1963, Associated-Rediffusion
Television magazine programme segment. Huw Thomas interviews Ernest Lindgren, Curator of the National Film Archive, about its preservation work.
Note: The U-matic format viewing material currently held by the archive appears to include only the film inserts, not the whole programme.
(submitted by NFTVA cataloguing staff, British Film Institute, London)

Las IMAGENES PERDIDAS (Spain, 1989)
translated title: **LOST IMAGES**
Subtitle: **Cuando el cine español no sabia hablar...** [When Spanish Cinema could not speak...]
Colour; sound. Spanish and Catalan dialogue, Spanish intertitles and subtitles. (55 mins.)
d: Outi Saarinen, Vicente Romero
p: Vicente Romero, TV España (TVE)
sc: Vicente Romero
ed: Alfredo de Frutos
Interviewees: Albert Gasset I Nicolau, Ramon de Baños, Aurora Redondo, Vicente Romero, Joan Francesc de Lasca, Miguel Nicolau, José Gines, Juan Marine, Agustin Macasoli
Made for the TV España series "TV Documentos: Equipo de Investigacion", in collaboration with the Filmoteca Española, Filmoteca de la Generalitat de Valencia, and the Filmoteca de la Generalitat de Catalunya
Spanish television documentary about Spain's silent film heritage, giving an overview of Spanish film history, and touching on pertinent issues such as censorship; how the government was slow to recognise the importance of supporting film production, protection, and conservation; and the role played by private film collectors in rescuing films. Spain's silent film losses are cited as a staggering 90%, and a daunting task faces the Madrid, Valencia, and Barcelona archives to rescue what little is left. Featuring scenes showing disintegrating nitrate film, extracts from a number of Spanish silent films, ranging from 1896 to 1930 – including some glimpses of all that now exists of some titles – and interviews with cameramen and an actress from the silent era, as well as a collector, film historians, and archivists.
(submitted by Lynne Wake, Photoplay Productions, London)

IMAGES EN PÉRIL (France, 1968)
translated title: **IMAGES IN DANGER**
35mm, b/w; sound. French narration. (375 ft./4 mins.)
p: Pathé-Journal
Documentary about the work of the Centre National de la Cinématographie at Bois d'Arcy near Paris and the National Film Archive, London.
(submitted by NFTVA cataloguing staff, British Film Institute, London)

KEEPERS OF THE FRAME (USA, 1999)
Colour; English dialogue. (70 mins.)
d: Mark McLaughlin
p: Randy Gitsch, Mount Pilot Productions
Featuring: Alan Alda, Roddy McDowall, Debbie Reynolds, Stan Brakhage, Jean Picker Firstenberg, Leonard Maltin, Bob Gitt, and others
Documentary on the fragility of film history and the work of film archives to preserve what remains, moving beyond the more familiar territory of feature films lost or at risk to look also at newsreels, ethnographic records, experimental or avant-garde films, home movies, and other materials outside the mainstream of cinema, and considering a range of technical issues as well as the well-known problems of nitrate film.
(submitted by Catherine Surowiec, London)

LONDON LINE NO. 396 (GB, 1972)
16mm, b/w; sound. (263 ft.)
p: Granville Television Studios
sponsor: Central Office of Information
Television magazine series. Includes an item on the National Film Archive in London.
Note: The archive holds only the NFA item. The British-made COI series *London Line* is thought to have been for overseas distribution only.
(submitted by NFTVA cataloguing staff, British Film Institute, London)

The LONG VIEW (GB, 1958)
35mm, b/w and colour; sound. (30 mins.)
d: Richard Evans
p: Victor Poole, BBC
tx: 23 September 1958
Television documentary. Documentary filmmaker and producer Basil Wright tells the story of 25 years of the British Film Institute, illustrated with film excerpts and interviews.
Note: The material held by the archive consists of four minutes of film sequences only, showing film preservation at the NFA vaults at Aston Clinton; testing nitrate film for deterioration; and repairing and printing fragile film. "The Long View" was later the title of a book about film by Basil Wright published in 1974.
(submitted by Elaine Burrows and NFTVA cataloguing staff, British Film Institute, London)

MAGYAR VILÁGHIRADÓ 583 (Hungary, 1935)
translated title: **HUNGARIAN WORLD NEWS No. 583**
story title: Filmraktár – faépületben [Film storage in a wooden building]
b/w; sound. Hungarian titles and narration. (length of story: 32 metres/2 mins.)
p: Magyar Világhiradó
The first story in this issue of the newsreel shows the deliberate burning of 1,000 pounds of celluloid (supervised by the fire brigade in the city of Györ) to demonstrate the greater safety of an earth-reinforced wooden storage building compared to conventional brick construction.
Note: Shown at the 2000 FIAF Nitrate Symposium as an untitled and unidentified film fragment held by Britain's National Film and Television Archive; identified by colleagues from the Magyar Nemzeti Filmarchivum, where the complete newsreel is held.
(submitted by Ildikó Berkes, Magyar Nemzeti Filmarchivum, Budapest)

The MARCH OF TIME, v.5, issue 12: THE MOVIES MARCH ON! (USA, 1939)
35mm, b/w; sound. English narration. (18 mins.)
p: March of Time, Inc.
rel: July 1939
"... produced in association with the Museum of Modern Art, ... an entertaining and affectionate portrait of Hollywood's film industry, in which the medium's remarkable 40–year history was traced from silent shorts to musical comedy features." – Raymond Fielding, The March of Time, 1935–1951 *(New York: Oxford University Press, 1978, pp.240–241)*
Note: The MoMA catalogue entry notes that the film shows Iris Barry at work, and the Museum building.
(submitted by Ron Magliozzi, Museum of Modern Art Film & Video Archive, New York)

MÉMOIRE DU CINÉMA (France, 1996)
translated title: The MEMORY OF CINEMA
Video, colour; sound. French narration. (2 parts, total 137 mins.)
d: Jacques Mény
p: On Line Productions/La Sept – Arte
Narrators: Thomas Cousseau, Jacques Mény
Featuring: Michelle Aubert, Mary Lea Bandy, Ann Baylis, Freddy Buache, Paolo Cherchi-Usai, Gabrielle Claes, José Manuel Costa, Jean-Louis Cot, Ray Edmondson, Gian-Luca Farinelli, Anton Giménez, Clyde Jeavons, Gaston Kaboré, Wolfgang Klaue, Janine Langlois-Glandier, Eric Le Roy, Fédérico Mayor, Madeleine Malthête-Méliès, Vladimir Malyshev, Martine Offroy, Eva Orbanz, Robert Rosen, Martin Scorsese, Iván Trujillo Bolio
tx: 2 April 1996, ARTETV

Part 1 : À la recherche des films perdus (In Search of Lost Films) (1995) 75 mins.
From Mexico to Australia (where more than 150 pre-1914 French shorts were discovered), with many stops around the world, this documentary tells the story of films lost through destruction, recycling of their material, or censorship. A recent success story which is examined is the case of the films of Méliès and Lumière, as well as the research and work accomplished to save them.

Part 2 : La Mémoire retrouvée (Memory Rediscovered) (1996) 62 mins.
To avoid the loss of today's films, to establish international co-operation among archives around the world, from Europe to Africa to the United States, to rediscover the film heritage of each country – this is the mission of professional archivists. Legal deposit for films can help stop future losses. Should film archives preserve all films, including amateur films? How can filmmakers and producers help to save our film heritage? Curators, producers, and filmmakers like Martin Scorsese discuss these questions, while film extracts from unknown and rare classics provide a living picture of the memory of cinema.
(submitted by Michelle Aubert and the staff of the CNC, Bois d'Arcy)

1001 FILMS (Belgium, 1989)
35mm, colour; sound. (8 mins.)
d: André Delvaux
p: Cinémathèque Royale de Belgique
Film made for the 50th anniversary of the Cinémathèque Royale de Belgique, during European Cinema and Television Year, and dedicated to archivist Jacques Ledoux. Images include hand- and stencil-coloured film on a winding machine; vaults with cans of film; the opening of a can of film, revealing powder; a montage of shots, sequences, and frames of film. The soundtrack consists of music, and the

sound of brittle, sticky film on a rewind machine.
2001 Bologna Cinema Ritrovato festival programme note: "A reflection on the life and death of films, on the deterioration of films, and on the possibility of their resurrection. From the niches in archive hallways, figures that would otherwise have been lost forever seem to come back to life."
(submitted by Catherine Surowiec, London)

Il MUSEO DEI SOGNI (Italy, 1949)
translated title: **MUSEUM OF DREAMS**
35mm, b/w; sound. Italian titles and narration. (13 mins.)
d: Luigi Comencini
p: Gigi Martello, Cortimetraggi
Narrator: Piero Gallinari
Archive material from the Cineteca Italiana, Archivio Storico del Film, Milan
Documentary short about the origins of the Cineteca Italiana. A forerunner of Comencini's 1953 feature, La Valigia dei sogni, *this eloquent plea, made before the advent of safety film, calls upon us to preserve the glories of cinema history for future generations before they are lost forever. A major section of the film concentrates on the processes involved in the destruction of film by sending it to the film strippers for recycling. Rescue is on its way: in 1935 cinema-lover Marco Ferrari begins to collect films, and the cans soon multiply, coming from all kinds of sources. As the film is made, the Cineteca Italiana's new headquarters in Milan houses one of the richest collections in the world, devoted to the collection and conservation of film and related material. But still the guillotine keeps executing film, and many films have already disappeared forever. All that remains today of the silent Italian masterpiece* Sperduti nel buio *is its photo album, whose pages are lovingly turned.*
Note: Extracts from this film play a key role in Paolo Lipari's 2000 documentary short *Due Dollari al Chilo* (also in this Filmography).
(submitted by Luisa Comencini, Fondazione Cineteca Italiana, Archivio Storico del Film, Milan)

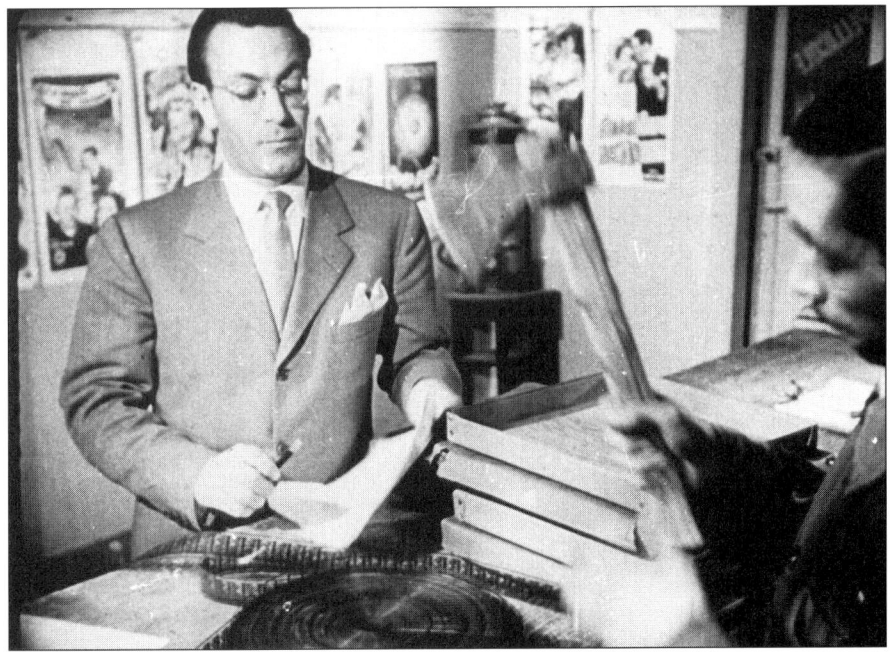

The inspector makes sure a film is thoroughly mutilated before it is disposed of: *Il Museo dei Sogni* (1949).
Fondazione Cineteca Italiana, Milan.

NITRATO (Brazil, 1974)
translated title: **NITRATE**
35mm, b/w; sound. Portuguese narration. (525 metres/19 mins.)

d: Alain Fresnot

p: Cinemateca Brasileira, Cinemateca do Museu de Arte Moderna do Rio de Janeiro, Filmes da Matriz

Documentary relating the dramatic situation of the Cinemateca Brasileira, via interviews (including one with Paulo Emilio Salles Gomes, the Cinemateca's founder), photos, and film extracts. The archive's invaluable film collection and documents have been threatened for decades by a combination of ominous storage conditions (especially the poor premises at Ibirapuera Park) and government neglect. The film also includes remembrances of the fires that have destroyed parts of the nitrate collection.

(submitted by Carlos Roberto de Souza, Cinemateca Brasileira, São Paulo)

OUR INFLAMMABLE FILM HERITAGE (Netherlands/Italy, 1994)

Colour; sound. English narration. (23 mins.)

d/sc: Mark-Paul Meyer

p: Ecipar, Italy

Instructional documentary filmed at the Nederlands Filmmuseum and Haghefilm laboratory, featuring archive films preserved and restored by the NFM. The film uses the case history of the early Lubitsch film Meyer aus Berlin *(1918) to illustrate archive work, from identification and cataloguing to nitrate conservation and preservation onto safety film. Includes a segment on nitrate film deterioration and handling.*

(submitted by Catherine Surowiec, London)

The RACE TO SAVE 100 YEARS (USA, 1997)

Subtitle: **Preserving Film, the Art of Our Century**

Colour and b/w; sound. English narration. (56 mins.)

d: Scott Benson

sc: John DeGroot, May Adair Kaiser

exec. p: James Gentilcore, Richard P. May, Roger L. Mayer, Patrick Murphy

p: May Adair Kaiser, Warner Bros./Turner Entertainment Co.

Narrator: Peter Brooks

Interviewees: Mary Lea Bandy, Martin Scorsese, Kevin Brownlow, David Gill, Richard P May, Roger L Mayer, Robert Gitt, Ned Price, Dr James H Billington, Robert Rosen

Lively, absorbing documentary about film preservation and restoration, intended to make the general public aware of the work and efforts of a range of archive professionals in the race against time to save our film heritage by charting approaches and considering a range of technical and historical issues. Presents the AFI's 10 Most Wanted Films, and discusses the National Film Preservation Board, which selects 25 films annually to join the National Film Registry. Ends with a plea for resources to support the work of film archives and the importance of a working "partnership for preservation" between industry and archives.

Includes segments on nitrate deterioration and losses, and the "Vinegar Syndrome" now facing acetate safety film. Contains many film clips, including footage from the British training film about nitrate, This Film Is Dangerous! *(1949) (also in this Filmography).*

(submitted by Kevin Brownlow and Lynne Wake, Photoplay Productions, London)

SAFE AND SOUND (GB, 1996)

Colour; sound. English narration. (6 mins.)

d/p: Orly Yadin

p: Halo Productions for the British Film Institute.

sc: Clyde Jeavons

Narrator: Kevin Brownlow

A short publicity video, derived from the 1996 revised version of The Work of a Film Archive *(also in this Filmography).*
(submitted by NFTVA cataloguing staff, British Film Institute, London, and Clyde Jeavons, London)

SAUVER LES FILMS. UNE MÉMOIRE POUR DEMAIN
(France, 1991)
translated title: **SAVING FILMS. A MEMORY FOR TOMORROW**
Colour; sound. French dialogue and naration. (33 mins.)
d: Jacques Mény
p: SODAPERAGA/CNC/Ministère de la Culture et de la Communication
Narrator: Nicolas Fournier
Documentary, made for the French educational television series "Outil pedagogique – Bac A3". Films are fragile, and for almost 60 years were printed on a base generally assumed to be condemned to perish into dust or smoke before the end of the century. Their survival has long depended on their market value; many were destroyed as soon as they were deemed of no further public interest or profit. Cinematheques were born during the 1930s to fight against the disappearance of silent cinema: there are now more than 100 national archives worldwide. They work to conserve and restore films from the past menaced by chemical decomposition, as well as protecting recent films so that they may be passed on to future generations. Long negligent or distrustful, public authorities and producers are now participating in the collective battle to safeguard our cinema heritage.
(submitted by Michelle Aubert and the staff of the CNC, Bois d'Arcy)

SCREENSOUND AUSTRALIA (Australia, 1999, revised 2001)
Video, colour and b/w; sound. English dialogue. (15 mins.)
d: Michael James Rowland
p: Thea Carone
ed: Anne Ker
Interviewees: Wendy Harmer, John Singleton, David Stratton, Mary Kostakidis, Deborah Mailman, Betty Churcher, Tim Fischer, Greig Pickhaver, Molly Meldrum, Gillian Armstrong, Phillip Adams, Grahame Bond, Chris Masters, Graham Richardson, Peter McGauran, Bruce Beresford, Peter Sculthorpe, Bill Collins, Magda Szubanski, Charles Perkins
Revised version of a short promotional documentary for ScreenSound Australia, the National Screen and Sound Archive (the original having been made specifically for screening at the opening of the archive's new building on 21 June 1999). A number of interviewees testify to the role that film, television, radio, and recorded sound have played in their lives, and praise the work and goals of the institution in seeking and preserving as much as possible of this heritage. The second part of the film consists of a chronological montage of a variety of images and sounds from Australian media history, ranging from historical events to popular culture, and includes some footage from the nitrate era bearing the marks of deterioration. It concludes with a montage of scenes and faces.
(submitted by Ray Edmondson and Meg Labrum, ScreenSound Australia, Canberra)

THIS WEEK IN BRITAIN, NO. 701: DON'T SHOOT THE PIANIST (GB, 1972)
16mm, b/w; sound. English narration. (182 ft./5 mins.)
sponsor: Central Office of Information
Documentary short about the work of the preservation department of the National Film Archive at Aston Clinton, Buckinghamshire.
(submitted by NFTVA cataloguing staff, British Film Institute, London)

TRADITION IST DIE WEITERGABE DES FEUERS UND NICHT DIE ANBETUNG DER ASCHE (Austria, 1999)
translated title: **TRADITION IS THE PASSING ON OF THE FIRE, AND NOT THE WORSHIP OF THE ASHES**
35mm, colour; sound. (1 min.)
d: Gustav Deutsch
p: Filmarchiv Austria
Trailer made for the Filmarchiv Austria's nitrate preservation initiative, "Preservation of the Film Heritage" (discussed in Ernst Kieninger's article, elsewhere in this volume), using decayed nitrate film from the archive's Ignaz Reinthaler collection. Tinted footage of an unidentified building on fire dramatically displays scratches and the effects of nitrate decomposition.
Director's note: "Found footage – on nitrocellulose – is the material. Fire – which threatens this material – is the motif. A quote – from Gustav Mahler – is the message. The soundtrack – by Christian Fennesz – is the bridge."
(submitted by Catherine Surowiec, London)

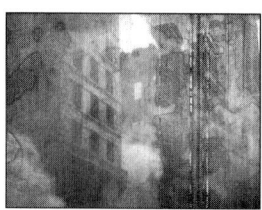

The triple threat of fire, damage and deterioration in a single image: *Tradition ist...* (1999).
(See also Colour Section 2.)
Filmarchiv Austria, Vienna.

20th CENTURY TREASURE TROVE (GB, 1981)
Colour and b/w; sound. English narration. (70 mins.)
d: Elizabeth Sussex
p: BBC TV; series: "The Lively Arts"
ph: Colin Waldeck
ed: Ray Frawley, Dave King
tx: 15 February 1981
Documentary about the aims and work of the National Film Archive, illustrated with numerous extracts from films, and including interviews with David Francis, Curator, Harold Brown, Preservation Officer, and Frank Holland, Vaults Manager.
Note: Robert Vas first conceived this project in the early 1960s, and went into production with Elizabeth Sussex as his researcher in 1976. The difficult circumstances under which she came to complete it after his death in 1978 were described in her article "The Film that Nearly Never Was", *Sight and Sound*, v.50, no.1 (Winter 1980/81), pp.58–60.
Extracts shown at the 2000 FIAF Nitrate Symposium.
(submitted by Clyde Jeavons, London)

The WORK OF A FILM ARCHIVE (GB, 1992)
Colour; sound. English narration. (30 mins.)
d: Orly Yadin
p: Flashback Television for the National Film Archive
sc: Clyde Jeavons
Narrator: Clyde Jeavons
Video using the activities of the National Film Archive at its John Paul Getty Conservation Centre in Berkhamsted, at its nitrate vaults near Gaydon, and at the British Film Institute's headquarters building in London to demonstrate the range of responsibilities of a film archive. Commissioned for use as a training film on the occasion of the FIAF Summer School hosted by the NFA at Berkhamsted in 1992.
(submitted by NFTVA cataloguing staff, British Film Institute, London, and Clyde Jeavons, London)

The WORK OF A FILM ARCHIVE [revised version] (GB, 1996)
Colour; sound. English narration. (19 mins.)
d/p: Orly Yadin
p: Halo Productions for the National Film and Television Archive
sc: Clyde Jeavons
ph: Simon Priestman, Tim Jones

Narrator: Kevin Brownlow
A revised and updated version of the 1992 training film described in the previous entry; updates include the NFA's change of name, to become the National Film and Television Archive. Commissioned on the occasion of the second FIAF Summer School at Berkhamsted in 1996.
Note: A shortened version, *Safe and Sound* (6 mins.) (also in this Filmography), was simultaneously produced for use by the BFI Press Office.
(submitted by NFTVA cataloguing staff, British Film Institute, London, and Clyde Jeavons, London)

5. Archival test films

Det BRINNER I HOLLYWOOD (Sweden, 1986)
translated title: **BURNING IN HOLLYWOOD**
Colour; sound. Swedish narration. (12 mins.)
p: Svenska Filminstitutet
ph: Lisa Hagstrand
ed: Barbro Lidell
Archive staff speaking on camera: Inga Adolfsson, Rikard Gramfors, Rolf Lindfors, Barbro Lidell
A record of the 1986 destruction by fire of a large consignment of deteriorated nitrate film from the Film Archive of the Swedish Film Institute on open ground at Rotebro – the last action of this kind before a new environmental law prohibiting such disposal came into force. Various members of the film archive staff explain what they are doing, and take the opportunity to comment on the amount of Swedish nitrate-era film that is still considered "lost", and on the types of damage and deterioration now threatening non-nitrate film. Though not a film of a test fire per se, it includes an interview with a fireman and some contemporary footage recalling a 1971 exercise in which 10 tons of nitrate film were burned as a fire-fighting drill. On that occasion, the fire brigade underestimated the safety margin appropriate to such a large nitrate fire, and there was damage to some fire engines and to a caretaker's house, though human casualties were fortunately limited to a couple of cases of shock among a TV crew.
Note on the title: The area of Rotebro surrounding the film laboratory used by the Swedish Film Institute is known as Hollywood, and the laboratory, now called Rotebro Filmservice AB, formerly traded as Hollywood Film Laboratorium.
Note: Copies of a film of the 1971 exercise are separately held in some archives, for example in Britain's National Film and Television Archive, where it has the allocated title *Swedish Fire Engine*. Extracts from this print were shown on video at the 2000 FIAF Nitrate Symposium.
(submitted by Henry Jones, Cinemateket, Svenska Filminstitutet, Stockholm)

IMPERIAL WAR MUSEUM NITRATE TEST 2000 (GB, 2000)
Video, colour; sound. [Natural sound only – no commentary.] (47 mins.)
p: BRE Cardington and Imperial War Museum Film and Video Archive
A record of the deliberate burning of 500 reels (1 ton) of nitrate film on 1 August 2000 to test the design of new vaults to be built for the IWMFVA near Duxford, Cambridgeshire. The successful trial was conducted on the Museum's behalf at the Building Research Establishment (BRE) at Cardington, Bedfordshire. In addition to material showing the removal of the film from the Archive's old vaults at Hayes, Middlesex, the layout of the test site, and coverage of the fire itself from the viewing area, the record also includes material from the "sacrificial" camera placed inside the vault to record the early stages of the fire.
(submitted by Roger Smither, Imperial War Museum Film and Video Archive, London)

R A R D E EXPERIMENTS (GB, 1975–76)
also known as: **(POTTON ISLAND)**
16mm, colour; silent. (2243 ft./37 mins.)
A series of short silent actuality films recording twelve nitrate test fires (six each of two types) conducted on Potton Island in the Thames Estuary on behalf of the British Film Institute. The tests were carried out by the Royal Armament Research and Development Establishment (RARDE), which in addition to its service work was used to help with official civilian tests on explosives and dangerous chemicals. These tests are discussed more fully in Clyde Jeavons's essay "24 Years to Safety", in this volume.
Note: Extract shown at the 2000 FIAF Nitrate Symposium.
(submitted by NFTVA cataloguing staff, British Film Institute, London)

(STICKY – SPECIMEN FILM) (GB, 1955)
35mm, b/w; silent. (122 ft./1 min.)
Nitrate film stock, seen before and after deterioration.
(submitted by NFTVA cataloguing staff, British Film Institute, London)

(SWEDISH FIRE ENGINE) (Sweden, 1971) – for information, see note for **Det BRINNER I HOLLYWOOD** (also in this section of the Filmography)

Das **VERHALTEN VON BRENNENDEN NITROFILM GEGENÜBER LÖSCHMITTELN** (Austria, 1976)
translated title: **BEHAVIOUR OF BURNING NITRO-CELLULOSE FILM AGAINST EXTINGUISHING TREATMENTS**
16mm, colour; silent. German intertitles. (633 ft./19 mins.)
p: Bundesstaatlichen Hauptstelle für Lichtbild und Bildungsfilm
A record of tests conducted on behalf of the Österreichisches Filmarchiv following a nitrate fire in 1974. The film shows attempts made by helmeted firemen to extinguish burning nitrate film using a variety of extinguishing agents (explained in the intertitle before each sequence), including water, sand, and foam, none successfully. One fireman appears to be injured when his extinguisher runs out.
Note: Copies of this film are held in the Museum of Modern Art Film & Video Archive and a number of other archives, acquired for instructional purposes after it was screened at the 1976 FIAF Congress in Mexico. Extracts from the print held by Britain's National Film and Television Archive were shown at the 2000 FIAF Nitrate Symposium.
(submitted by Jon Gartenberg, New York, and Catherine Surowiec, London; with additional details from Peter Williamson, Museum of Modern Art Film & Video Archive, New York, and Dr Nikolaus Wostry, Filmarchiv Austria, Vienna)

Afterwords

A variety of material was produced outside the framework of the main effort to compile this volume which the editors still wished to include.

The Appendix offers the results of some studies published by FIAF in the mid–1990s as part of its preparations for the Centenary of Cinema. Although now dated, these statistics represent the last systematic attempt known to the editors to make this kind of quantitative analysis, and remain instructive in spite of their age.

The two "Stop Press" items are contributions that were considered "too good to leave out", in spite of their last-minute arrival.

The remaining item is a piece of self-indulgence by the editor. We hope you'll sing along!

Appendix: Some Nitrate Statistics

The following information is based on previous FIAF publications, as indicated.

Size of Film Collection in 1995

The *Etude Internationale des Archives de la FIAF 1995/FIAF Statistical Survey 1995*, compiled and edited by Michelle Aubert with technical assistance from Daniel Toussaint, was published by FIAF with help from the Centre National de la Cinématographie, Paris, as part of the materials prepared for FIAF's "Centenary of Cinema" Los Angeles Congress, 1995.

According to the 1995 FIAF Survey, 32 archives had unfinished nitrate copying programmes.

The same survey also concluded that the total collection of films archived worldwide, of all gauges and all types (nitrate, acetate, and polyester), amounted to 6,891 million feet [2,102 million metres]. Within that total, the worldwide collection of nitrate film still awaiting copying or restoration amounted to 546.6 million feet [167.8 million metres].

The table below indicates how these totals break down according to geographical regions.

Continent	Total Footage [metres] (x 1,000,000)		Number of Archives with Nitrate	Nitrate Footage [metres] still to copy/restore (x 1,000,000)	
Africa	3.3	[1]	0	0	[0]
Latin America	492	[150]	6	3.3	[1]
North America	1,344	[410]	3	108	[33]
Asia	688	[210]	4	8	[2.5]
Europe	4,262	[1,300]	16	426	[130]
Middle East	46	[14]	0	0	[0]
Oceania	56	[17]	2	4.3	[1.3]
Total	6891.3	[2,102]	32	546.6	[167.8]

Graph 1 (reproduced from the 1995 Survey) offers a pictorial representation of the same data.

Note that none of these figures take into account any nitrate which may be in any collections outside the FIAF membership, which may be largely undocumented, and obviously offers a field for further research.

Projections based on the annual rate of nitrate copying declared in 1995 would suggest that an estimated further quantity of 150 million feet [45 million metres] of nitrate should have been copied by the year 2000, leaving a revised total of some 400 million feet [130 million metres] of nitrate still to be copied and restored.

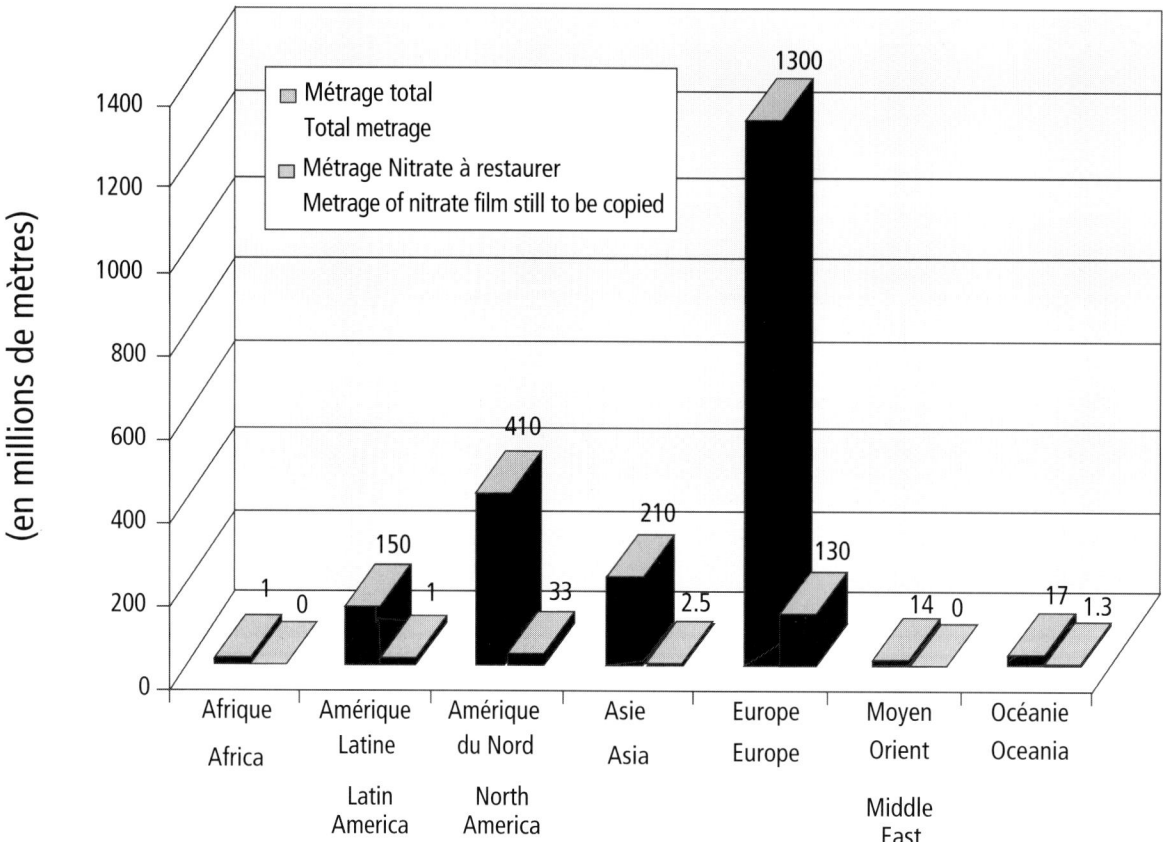

Nitrate Programming and Access:

In April 1994 the FIAF Commission on Programming and Access issued the results of a survey carried out in 1992 under the supervision of Catherine Gauthier of the Filmoteca Española, Madrid. According to this survey, the following 28 member archives had technical facilities for viewing nitrate (those marked with an asterisk indicated some sort of control or limitation on nitrate access):

Amsterdam
Bangkok
Beijing
Beograd
Berkeley*
Bois d'Arcy*
Bologna
Bruxelles*
Budapest
Helsinki*
Kobenhavn*

La Paz
London IWM*
London NFTVA
Los Angeles UCLA
Madrid*
Montevideo SODRE
Moskva
München*
Oslo
Paris CF*
Praha

Rochester*
São Paulo*
Torino*
Warszawa
Washington AFI (via LOC and other US archives)
Wien FM.

Stop Press

Stop Press (1) Danger on Meals by Janet McBain

Editors' Note: The following story came to light well after several "final deadlines" for this book had expired, but is so perfect that space simply had to be found for it.

Despite a massive public campaign to save it, the Salon – one of Scotland's earliest purpose-built cinemas (1913) – was closed in the 1990s, and turned into a restaurant. The new owners retained the cinematic theme: they kept the screen, on which were screened "al fresco" movies as patrons enjoyed their meals, and a number of props were placed around the interior – cameras, projectors, film posters, and so on.

The premises were sold again in February 2001 to a nightclub owner, and on the day before the restaurant closed its doors for the last time the former engineer of the Salon went to dine there for old times' sake, together with the manager of another neighbouring cinema. Midway through the following morning, the Scottish Screen Archive received a telephone call to say that Danny (the retired engineer, and an old friend of the Archive) had spotted five reels of film among the objects on display, and in wandering over between courses for a closer look had recognised them right away as nitrate stock. He and his dinner companion had rescued them, and put them into the office of the modern cinema along the road.

Suitably armed with some polythene bags and a couple of FIAF Congress bags (they do have their uses), a team from the Archive called in an hour later to be presented with several 2,000–ft reels of 35mm tinted stock on large rusty spools. They had been used on the old stage area in the smokers' section of the restaurant – nitrate film stock lying open and draped around the "set" for several years!

On inspection, the contents, which had fortunately evaded cigarette smokers' best attempts at incineration, proved to include several issues of the silent British newsreel *Topical Budget* – including several items posted as "missing believed lost"!

Stop Press (2) The Manufactum Catalogue

Editors' Note: Manufactum, a well-known company in Germany, Austria, and Switzerland, which defines its mission as "to hold on to quality standards in the face of a massively growing industrial production," launched its first British catalogue in the autumn of 2001. When we received a copy, one item in particular demanded our attention. We are grateful to Manufactum for permission to reprint it.[1]

Celluloid.

Together with rubber, ebonite, viscose, vulcanised fibre and galalith, celluloid belongs to a group of "chemical products" still made with raw materials of a natural origin, like rayon, caoutchouc, casein. Sadly, though, most manufacturers have stopped using these materials. Celluloid, made of cotton fibres and camphor, enjoyed its heyday at the beginning of the century, when this elastic, almost unbreakable and infinitely mouldable material became a substitute for such costly natural products as amber, tortoiseshell, ivory and horn. It was used to make combs, dolls, fountain pens and containers. Today celluloid has itself become a "costly" material, since it has been almost completely ousted by much cheaper petrochemical substitutes.

Combs – celluloid and hand-sawn.

A set of three "proper" celluloid combs from what is to our knowledge the last German comb maker who processes this material.

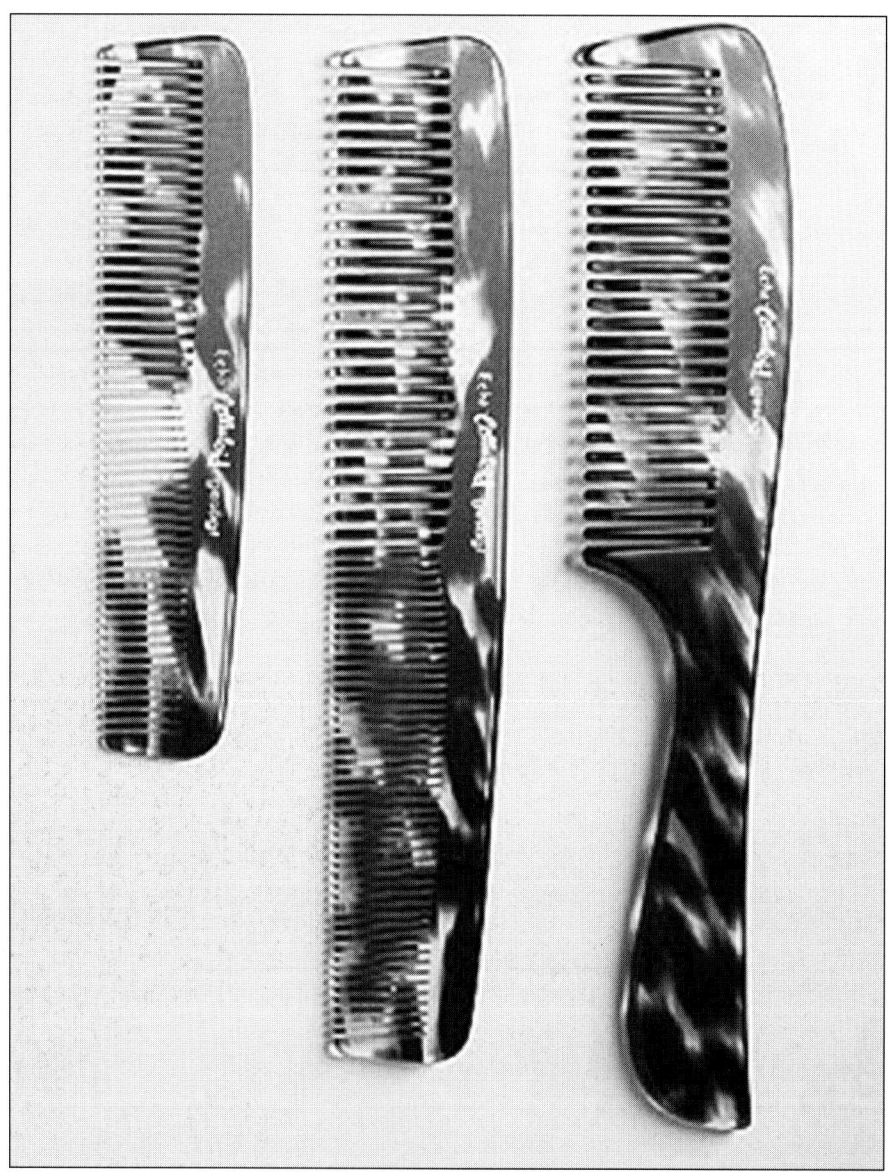

SET OF CELLULOID COMBS

1 comb with handle (19.5 cm), 1 ladies' comb (18 cm), 1 pocket comb (12 cm).
Order no. **22818**   **£8.50**

Notes

1. *Catalogue No. 1.*, Manufactum Ltd (Ground Floor, 6–12 Triangle Road, London E8 3RP), 2001, p. 92. The full catalogue may be consulted on line as well, at www.manufactum.com. We are also grateful to Manufactum for the information that the German company which makes the combs is named Hohrmann Celluloidwaren, in Bad Salzuslen.

"I don't know…": A Cadence Call for Trainee Film Archivists

by Roger Smither

The history or folklore of FIAF relates that at one time the Federation had its own anthem, although details of both tune and words have proved elusive. During my time as a member of the Executive Committee, various colleagues have entertained themselves and each other during dinner breaks at EC meetings by trying to suggest, usually in a mood of extreme flippancy, what might make a good FIAF song for the modern era. One example of some relevance to this book was to be sung to the tune of "The Lumberjack Song" from *Monty Python's Flying Circus*, and began, as I recall, "I'm an archivist and I can't wait/Half of my films are on nitrate…"

The verses printed below are my own contribution to this particular game. They are written in the style of one of the better known "cadence calls" sung in training by US service personnel both in real life and in numerous films. Cadence calls – also known as "Jody calls" or simply as "Jodies" – are songs sung to keep time and maintain the pace when marching or running, and derive from the tradition of "work calls" sung to ensure concerted or rhythmic effort in any collaborative piece of work. The songs require a caller, who is or represents the leader or commander, and who sets the pace by singing a line. The rest of the gang or squad then sing the line (or a variant of it) back to the caller, in unison and in the same tempo.[1]

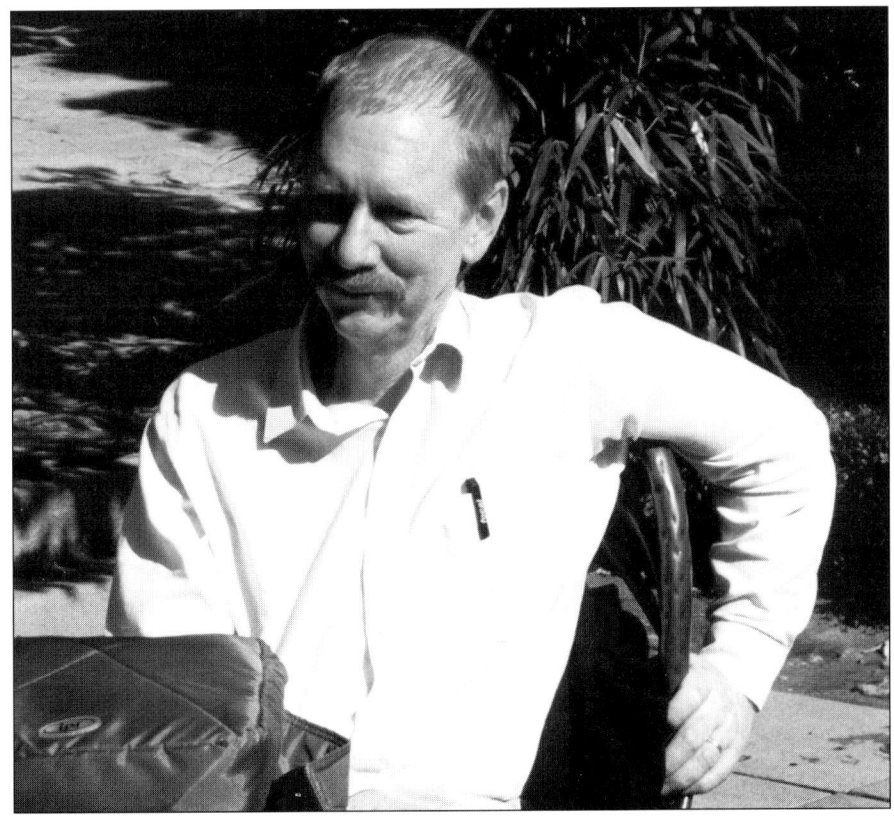

Roger Smither takes time out from a FIAF Executive Committee Meeting.

A Cadence Call for Trainee Film Archivists

I don't know but I've heard tell
Nitrate film will burn like Hell.
If you don't fry, then you'll choke
'Cause it gives off toxic smoke.

I don't know but I've been told
Acetate stinks as it gets old.
Vinegar syndrome, real bad scene,
Film won't go through the machine.

I don't know but I would bet
Videotape is the worst yet:
Lousy picture, it's all lines,
Standards changing all the time.

I don't know so please relate
Why digital is all that great.
Where's the master for my vaults
When my film's just ones and noughts?

I don't know but I've heard shout
Archives have their work cut out.
Archivists need friends and cheer
Someone buy us all a beer.

Readers who do not recognise the form or know the tune for this particular example can discover a polite version sung by Louis Gossett Jr (as Sergeant Foley) with Richard Gere and the other cadets in Taylor Hackford's *An Officer and a Gentleman* (1982), and a rather more bawdy set of words sung by R Lee Ermey (as Sergeant Hartman) with Matthew Modine and the other trainees in Stanley Kubrick's *Full Metal Jacket* (1987). A suitably adapted variant even makes its way into one of the unconventional English lessons given by Robin Williams (as Mr Keating) to his pupils in Peter Weir's *Dead Poets' Society* (1989).

The FIAF 'Jody' still awaits public performance. There were plans to close the 2000 London FIAF Congress by persuading those attending to sing it, and a volunteer had been found to act as caller. Regrettably, time ran out before the attempt could be made. I am exercising an editor's privilege in making its first publication my final contribution to this book.

Notes

1. Collections of cadence calls and information on the form can be found at several websites, such as http://users.erols.com/loriryan/cadence.html.

Index

The index to this book is provided in three sections – the General Index is followed by an Index of Personal Names, and an Index of Film Titles. To save space in what is already an over-long part of the book, the number of cross-references has been kept to a minimum in all three sections. The most noticeable impact of this policy is in the Index of Film Titles. In accordance with FIAF principles, films are where possible indexed only by their original titles (i.e. *Bronenosets Potemkin* rather than *Battleship Potemkin*). The only significant departure from this practice has been films which were helpfully named in English translation by the authors who referred to them in their articles: except where the original title is well-known, the editors have not been able to undertake the necessary research to identify them properly, and this small number of films is thus technically misidentified.

INDEX OF PERSONAL NAMES

INDEX OF FILM TITLES